MACROECONOMICS

The McGraw-Hill Economics Series

SURVEY OF ECONOMICS

Brue, McConnell, and Flynn
Essentials of Economics
Fourth Edition

Mandel
M: Economics—The Basics
Fourth Edition

Schiller and Gebhardt
Essentials of Economics
Eleventh Edition

PRINCIPLES OF ECONOMICS

Asarta and Butters
Connect Master: Economics
Second Edition

Colander
Economics, Microeconomics, and Macroeconomics
Eleventh Edition

Frank, Bernanke, Antonovics, and Heffetz
Principles of Economics, Principles of Microeconomics, Principles of Macroeconomics
Seventh Edition

Frank, Bernanke, Antonovics, and Heffetz
Streamlined Editions: Principles of Economics, Principles of Microeconomics, Principles of Macroeconomics
Third Edition

Karlan and Morduch
Economics, Microeconomics, Macroeconomics
Third Edition

McConnell, Brue, and Flynn
Economics, Microeconomics, Macroeconomics
Twenty-Second Edition

Samuelson and Nordhaus
Economics, Microeconomics, and Macroeconomics
Nineteenth Edition

Schiller and Gebhardt
The Economy Today, The Micro Economy Today, and The Macro Economy Today
Fifteenth Edition

Slavin
Economics, Microeconomics, and Macroeconomics
Twelfth Edition

ECONOMICS OF SOCIAL ISSUES

Guell
Issues in Economics Today
Ninth Edition

Register and Grimes
Economics of Social Issues
Twenty-First Edition

ECONOMETRICS AND DATA ANALYTICS

Hilmer and Hilmer
Practical Econometrics
First Edition

Prince
Predictive Analytics for Business Strategy
First Edition

MANAGERIAL ECONOMICS

Baye and Prince
Managerial Economics and Business Strategy
Ninth Edition

Brickley, Smith, and Zimmerman
Managerial Economics and Organizational Architecture
Sixth Edition

Thomas and Maurice
Managerial Economics
Thirteenth Edition

INTERMEDIATE ECONOMICS

Bernheim and Whinston
Microeconomics
Second Edition

Dornbusch, Fischer, and Startz
Macroeconomics
Thirteenth Edition

Frank
Microeconomics and Behavior
Ninth Edition

ADVANCED ECONOMICS

Romer
Advanced Macroeconomics
Fifth Edition

MONEY AND BANKING

Cecchetti and Schoenholtz
Money, Banking, and Financial Markets
Sixth Edition

URBAN ECONOMICS

O'Sullivan
Urban Economics
Ninth Edition

LABOR ECONOMICS

Borjas
Labor Economics
Eighth Edition

McConnell, Brue, and Macpherson
Contemporary Labor Economics
Eleventh Edition

PUBLIC FINANCE

Rosen and Gayer
Public Finance
Tenth Edition

ENVIRONMENTAL ECONOMICS

Field and Field
Environmental Economics: An Introduction
Seventh Edition

INTERNATIONAL ECONOMICS

Appleyard and Field
International Economics
Ninth Edition

Pugel
International Economics
Seventeenth Edition

MACROECONOMICS
Improve Your World
THIRD EDITION

Dean Karlan
Northwestern University and Innovations for Poverty Action

Jonathan Morduch
New York University

McGraw Hill

MACROECONOMICS: IMPROVE YOUR WORLD, THIRD EDITION

Published by McGraw-Hill Education, 2 Penn Plaza, New York, NY 10121. Copyright © 2021 by McGraw-Hill Education. All rights reserved. Printed in the United States of America. Previous editions © 2018 and 2014. No part of this publication may be reproduced or distributed in any form or by any means, or stored in a database or retrieval system, without the prior written consent of McGraw-Hill Education, including, but not limited to, in any network or other electronic storage or transmission, or broadcast for distance learning.

Some ancillaries, including electronic and print components, may not be available to customers outside the United States.

This book is printed on acid-free paper.

1 2 3 4 5 6 7 8 9 LWI 24 23 22 21 20

ISBN 978-1-260-52116-0 (bound edition)
MHID 1-260-52116-8 (bound edition)
ISBN 978-1-260-52098-9 (loose-leaf edition)
MHID 1-260-52098-6 (loose-leaf edition)

Portfolio Director: *Anke Weekes*
Senior Product Developer: *Christina Kouvelis*
Marketing Manager: *Bobby Pearson*
Senior Project Manager, Core Content: *Kathryn D. Wright*
Senior Project Manager, Assessment Content: *Keri Johnson*
Project Manager, Media Content: *Karen Jozefowicz*
Senior Buyer: *Laura Fuller*
Senior Designer: *Matt Diamond*
Content Licensing Specialist: *Lorraine Buczek*
Cover Image: *©Sashkin/Shutterstock*
Compositor: *SPi Global*

All credits appearing on page or at the end of the book are considered to be an extension of the copyright page.

Library of Congress Cataloging-in-Publication Data

Names: Karlan, Dean S., author. | Morduch, Jonathan, author.
Title: Macroeconomics / Dean Karlan, Northwestern University and Innovations for
　Poverty Action, Jonathan Morduch, New York University.
Description: Third Edition. | New York, NY : McGraw-Hill Education, [2020]
Identifiers: LCCN 2019033349 | ISBN 9781260521160 (hardcover)
Subjects: LCSH: Macroeconomics.
Classification: LCC HB172.5 .K374 2020 | DDC 339—dc23
LC record available at https://lccn.loc.gov/2019033349

The Internet addresses listed in the text were accurate at the time of publication. The inclusion of a website does not indicate an endorsement by the authors or McGraw-Hill Education, and McGraw-Hill Education does not guarantee the accuracy of the information presented at these sites.

mheducation.com/highered

dedication

We dedicate this book to our families.

—Dean and Jonathan

about the authors

Dean Karlan

©Dean Karlan

Dean Karlan is the Frederic Esser Nemmers Distinguished Professor of Economics and Finance at the Kellogg School of Management at Northwestern University and President and Founder of Innovations for Poverty Action (IPA). Dean started IPA in 2002 with two aims: to help learn what works and what does not in the fight against poverty and other social problems around the world, and then to implement successful ideas at scale. IPA has worked in over 50 countries, with 1,000 employees around the world. Dean's personal research focuses on using field experiments to learn more about the effectiveness of financial services for low-income households, with a focus on using behavioral economics approaches to improve financial products and services as well as build sustainable sources of income. His research includes related areas, such as charitable fund-raising, voting, health, and education. Dean is also cofounder of stickK.com, a start-up that helps people use commitment contracts to achieve personal goals, such as losing weight or completing a problem set on time, and in 2015 he cofounded ImpactMatters, an organization that produces ratings of charities based on impact estimates. Dean is a Sloan Foundation Research Fellow, a Guggenheim Fellow, and an Executive Committee member of the Board of the MIT Jameel Poverty Action Lab. In 2007 he was awarded a Presidential Early Career Award for Scientists and Engineers. He is coeditor of the *Journal of Development Economics*. He holds a BA from University of Virginia, an MPP and MBA from University of Chicago, and a PhD in Economics from MIT. He has coauthored *The Goldilocks Challenge* (2018), *Failing in the Field* (2016), and *More Than Good Intentions: Improving the Ways the World's Poor Borrow, Save, Farm, Learn, and Stay Healthy* (2011).

Jonathan Morduch

©Jonathan Morduch

Jonathan Morduch is Professor of Public Policy and Economics at New York University's Wagner Graduate School of Public Service. Jonathan focuses on innovations that expand the frontiers of finance and how financial markets shape economic growth and inequality. Jonathan has lived and worked in Asia, but his newest book, *The Financial Diaries: How American Families Cope in a World of Uncertainty* (written with Rachel Schneider and published by Princeton University Press, 2017), follows families in California, Mississippi, Ohio, Kentucky, and New York as they cope with economic ups and downs over a year. The new work jumps off from ideas in *Portfolios of the Poor: How the World's Poor Live on $2 a Day* (Princeton University Press, 2009), which Jonathan coauthored and which describes how families in Bangladesh, India, and South Africa devise ways to make it through a year living on $2 a day or less. Jonathan's research on financial markets is collected in *The Economics of Microfinance* and *Banking the World,* both published by MIT Press. At NYU, Jonathan is executive director of the Financial Access Initiative, a center that supports research on extending access to finance in low-income communities. Jonathan's ideas have also shaped policy through work with the United Nations, World Bank, and other international organizations. In 2009, the Free University of Brussels awarded Jonathan an honorary doctorate to recognize his work on microfinance. He holds a BA from Brown and a PhD from Harvard, both in Economics.

Karlan and **Morduch** first met in 2001 and have been friends and colleagues ever since. Before writing this text, they collaborated on research on financial institutions. Together, they've written about new directions in financial access for the middle class and poor, and in Peru they set up a laboratory to study incentives in financial contracts for loans to women to start small enterprises. In 2006, together with Sendhil Mullainathan, they started the Financial Access Initiative, a center dedicated to expanding knowledge about financial solutions for the 40 percent of the world's adults who lack access to banks. This text reflects their shared passion for using economics as a tool to improve one's own life and to promote better business and public policies in the broader world.

brief contents

Thinking Like an Economist

Part 1 The Power of Economics 1
1. Economics and Life 3
2. Specialization and Exchange 25

Part 2 Supply and Demand 47
3. Markets 49
4. Elasticity 79
5. Efficiency 103
6. Government Intervention 129

Macroeconomics: Thinking Like a Macroeconomist

Part 3 The Data of Macroeconomics 163
7. Measuring GDP 165
8. The Cost of Living 197

Part 4 Labor Markets and Economic Growth 223
9. Unemployment and the Labor Market 225
10. Economic Growth 249

Part 5 The Economy in the Short and Long Run 273
11. Aggregate Expenditure 275
12. Aggregate Demand and Aggregate Supply 299
13. Fiscal Policy 333

Part 6 The Financial System and Institutions 357
14. The Basics of Finance 359
15. Money and the Monetary System 395
16. Inflation 427
17. Financial Crisis 459

Part 7 International Policy Issues 483
18. Open-Market Macroeconomics 485
19. Development Economics 523

improve your world

The field and practice of economics has changed a lot. Most textbooks haven't. This one is different.

Economics is now much more empirical, even compared to 15 years ago. The incredible data and computing power available today have transformed research on economic inequality, mobility, health care, trade, the environment, media, finance, macro mechanisms, and—well, you name it. Almost every part of economics is being reshaped by new evidence. Topics often not thought of as "economics," such as love, happiness, sports, and social networks, are now regularly analyzed through economic frameworks.

We've found that **incorporating new research and evidence makes teaching and learning easier, not harder,** by connecting to what students see in everyday life. The new economics of inequality, for example, shows students that the field is not single-mindedly concerned with overall growth of an economy but also with whether and why some are left out of that growth (and what to do about it). Similarly, new work on international trade shows that economists are deeply engaged by who's winning and who's losing as markets expand. Increasingly, **economic research is also leading to new, practical ideas to improve lives.**

In our own work, for example, we show how financial innovations inspired by behavioral economics can help people save and invest more effectively, and we've worked these insights into the text where appropriate.

Another transformation in economics is happening as the field attracts **new voices.** Younger economists have taken a broad view of economics. They come from a wider variety of backgrounds, and they are more likely to be women, compared to scholars a generation ago. This edition brings their voices more fully into the intro course.

- In Chapter 4, we describe an experiment by Pascaline Dupas and Jessica Cohen that shows how elasticities shape policies to prevent communicable disease.
- In Chapter 35, we describe Gita Gopinath's work on why it matters that the dollar is the leading "international currency."

The work of these economists has inspired us, and we hope that examples of their work will help students find new connections—and maybe even some new role models—in economics.

Throughout the text, we have worked hard to **inspire students.** Students' impressions of economics sometimes are right: The field can be dry and technical—and thus often harder to learn. But it doesn't have to be that way.

We've aimed at a casual tone, imagining that we're having a conversation with students, with **down-to-earth situations and personal examples that resonate with student readers.** For example:

- How understanding price elasticity can help you spend less money on plane tickets.
- Whether the cost of college is worth it. (Spoiler: It probably is.)

Teachers know the value of a good story, one that connects economic principles to ideas and issues in the world. In our text, **we weave real stories into the presentation**—at the start of every chapter and as recurring examples and in boxes throughout the chapters. For example, Chapter 2 uses the cell phone market to illustrate supply and demand, and Chapter 4 uses the price of a latte to demonstrate elasticity. **We employ economic tools as a way of explaining real people and their decisions.**

We then layer policy implications into the discussion of economic ideas and principles. For example, in Chapter 1, the idea of opportunity cost is first framed as a personal example of whether to spend the evening having dinner with friends. We next broaden the idea to the opportunity cost of an unpaid internship, and later in the chapter broaden the idea still further with a box that asks students to compare the cost of an iPad to charitable giving as a way to think about opportunity costs in a global context.

Our goal in this third edition is to help close the gap between economics in the classroom and the economic world that students see around them. **Our aim is not just to bring students up to date, but to demonstrate the idea that "Economics can improve your world."**

Who are we? Why did we write this text?

Macroeconomics draws on our own experiences as academic economists, teachers, and policy advisors. We are based at large research universities and often work with and advise nonprofit organizations, governments, international agencies, donors, and private firms. Much of our research involves figuring out **how to improve the way real markets function.** Working with partners in the United States and on six continents, we are involved in testing new economic ideas. *Macroeconomics* draws on the spirit of that work, as well as similar research, taking students through the process of engaging with real problems, using analytical tools to devise solutions, and ultimately showing what works and why.

One of the best parts of writing this text, promoting its first edition, and revising for the second and third editions has been the opportunity to spend time with instructors across the country. We've been inspired by their creativity and passion and have learned from their pedagogical ideas. One of the questions we often ask fellow instructors is why they originally became interested in economics. A common response—one we share—is an attraction to the logic and power of economics as a social science. We also often hear instructors describe something slightly different: the way that economics appealed to them as **a tool for making sense of life's complexities,** whether in business, politics, or daily life. We wrote this text to give instructors a way to share with their students both of those ways that economics matters.

We also are grateful to the many adopters and near-adopters of the first two editions who provided many helpful suggestions for ways to make the third edition an even better resource for instructors and students. As you'll see in the list of chapter-by-chapter changes that starts on page xxiii, we've worked hard to fulfill your expectations and meet that goal.

We hope to inspire students to continue their studies in economics, and we promise this text will give them something useful to take away even if they choose other areas of study.

Finally, we hope that, in ways small and large, the tools they learn in these pages and this course will help them to think critically about their environment, to live better lives, and to make an impact on their world. Our underlying motive throughout has been to demonstrate—through stories, examples, research, and policy discussions—**the good that economics can do to "improve your world."**

Dean Karlan
Northwestern University

Jonathan Morduch
New York University

inspire student learning

Karlan/Morduch connects with students—from its consistent data-driven and impact-based approach to a wide variety of examples and case studies, demonstrating how questions can be used to address real issues. By **teaching the** *right questions to ask,* the text provides students with a method for working through decisions they'll face as consumers, employees, entrepreneurs, and voters. Here are the four questions:

- **Question 1:** *What are the wants and constraints of those involved?* This question introduces the concept of *scarcity.* It asks students to think critically about the preferences and resources driving decision making in a given situation. It links into discussions of utility functions, budget constraints, strategic behavior, and new ideas that expand our thinking about rationality and behavioral economics.
- **Question 2:** *What are the trade-offs?* This question focuses on *opportunity cost.* It asks students to understand trade-offs in any decision, including factors that might go beyond the immediate financial costs and benefits. Consideration of trade-offs takes us to discussions of marginal decision making, sunk costs, nonmonetary costs, and discounting.
- **Question 3:** *How will others respond?* This question asks students to focus on *incentives,* both their incentives and the incentives of others. Students consider how individual choices aggregate in both expected and unexpected ways, and what happens when incentives change. The question links into understanding supply and demand, elasticity, competition, taxation, game theory, and monetary and fiscal policy.
- **Question 4:** *Are resources being allocated in the best way possible?* This question relates to *efficiency.* It asks students to start from an assumption that markets work to provide desired goods and services, and then to think carefully about why something that seems like a good idea isn't already being done. We encourage students to revisit their answers to the previous three questions, to see whether they missed something about the trade-offs, incentives, or other forces at work, or are looking at a genuine market failure. When we consider allocations, we also ask who's winning and who's losing through economic changes. This fourth question links topics such as public goods, externalities, information gaps, monopoly, arbitrage, and how the economy operates in the long run versus the short run.

Engaging pedagogical features

Compelling examples and stories open each chapter and are woven throughout the narrative. These include such examples as eBay, gifts of ugly holiday sweaters, how to curb littering, the cost of prescription medicines, why diamonds are expensive, the music-recording industry, why MLB pitchers are paid more than farm workers, why politicians haven't enacted a carbon tax, how a jar of peanut butter relates to the size of the U.S. economy, the Great Recession and the housing bubble, cigarette money in World War II, and the iPhone as an import. Through these stories, we introduce to students issues that consumers, voters, businesspeople, and family members face in their lives.

Additionally, the following **features add interesting real-world details:**

- **Economics in Action** boxes, originally titled Real Life, describe a short case or policy question, findings from history or academic studies, and anecdotes from the field.

> **When education pays off**
> **Economics in Action**
>
> *Economics in Action boxes show how the concept you're reading about relates to the real world. Often these boxes present interesting ideas or describe situations in which people used an economic idea to solve business or policy questions.*
>
> Why go to college? Well, of course, you learn a lot of important things and can make amazing friends. Also—not to be too crass about it—a college diploma will generally lead to bigger paychecks. On average, completing college roughly doubles lifetime earnings compared to earnings without a degree. In fact, the earnings advantage from having more education has grown bigger

xiii

> **Does ice cream cause polio?**
> From Another Angle
>
> *From Another Angle boxes show you a completely different way of looking at an economic concept. We find that a little bit of weirdness goes a long way in helping us to remember things.*
>
> Polio is a disease that once crippled or killed thousands of children in the United States every year. Before the cause of polio was known, doctors noticed that polio infections seemed to be more common in children who had been eating lots of ice cream. Observing this *correlation* led...

> **The opportunity cost of a life**
> What Do You Think?
>
> *What Do You Think? present questions that require you to combine facts and economic analysis with values and moral reasoning. There can be many "correct" answers, depending on your values and goals.*
>
> The philosopher Peter Singer writes that opportunity costs can be a matter of life or death. Imagine you are a salesperson, and on your way to a meeting on a hot summer day, you drive by a lake. Suddenly, you notice that a child who has been swimming in the lake is drowning. No one else is in sight.
>
> You have a choice. If you stop the car and jump into the lake to save the child, you will be late...

> **Finding a travel bargain**
> Econ and YOU
>
> *Econ and YOU boxes show tips, strategies, and other ways that economics can inform choices—big and small—in your own life.*
>
> Are you fantasizing about traveling someplace warm for spring break? Taking a trip to see family or friends? If you've looked at airline prices, you'll know that some tickets can be really expensive and some much cheaper—even on the same routes. Why?

- **From Another Angle** boxes show a different way of looking at an economic concept—a different way of thinking about a situation, a humorous story, or sometimes just an unusual application of a standard idea.
- **What Do You Think?** boxes offer a longer case study, with implications for public policy and student-related issues. They present relevant data or historical evidence and ask students to employ both economic analysis and normative arguments to defend a position. We leave the student with open-ended questions, which professors can assign as homework or use for classroom discussion. Many of these boxes are current ideas: the $15 minimum wage, who should be able to buy assault rifles, payday lending, preventive health care, immigration, the estate tax, affirmative action in college admission, and more.
- **Econ and YOU** boxes are **new to this edition** and have been created to show students how they might apply economics in their personal decisions. Topics included in this new boxed feature include personal finance, raising a family, unpaid internships, among others. We weave these every day scenarios with economic principles to help students develop economic intuition.

In this edition, we've added numerous new stories across the four categories of boxed examples, and we've updated many more with fresh data. Throughout, our approach is to offer a **positive outlook** that can be achieved through the application of economic principles to real-world problems.

Our voice throughout the text is casual and (we think, and hope!) fun to read. We've tried to include examples, products, issues, and problems that students will find of interest. In addition, where terminology or ideas are potentially confusing, we've built in two additional features to help clarify:

> **⚠ CAUTION: COMMON MISTAKE**
>
> You may notice that these five factors include price-related issues such as the price of related goods and expectations about future prices. So why do we refer to them as *nonprice determinants*? We do so in order to differentiate them from the effect of the *current price* of the good demand for that good.

> **TAKE NOTE...** ✎
>
> - Remember that the elasticity of *demand* is calculated by dividing a positive number by a negative number, or by dividing a negative number by a positive number, so the answer is always negative.
> - The elasticity of *supply*, on the other hand, is calculated by dividing either a positive number by a positive number...

- **Caution: Common Mistake** and **Take Note**—offer in-depth explanations of a concept or use of terminology. These boxes call attention to common misunderstandings or provide further explanation of tricky concepts. Students appreciate that rather than smoothing over confusing ideas and language, we offer the support they need to understand economic language and reasoning on a deeper level.

Throughout this text, every chapter contains built-in review tools and study devices for student use:

- **Test Yourself questions tied to learning objectives** appear at the end of each major section and prompt students to make sure they understand the topics covered before moving on.
- **Conclusions** at the end of each chapter sum up the overall lessons learned and look ahead to how the topic just presented will be used in other chapters.
- **Key Terms** provide a convenient list of the economic terminology introduced and defined in the chapter.
- **Summaries** give a deeper synopsis of what each learning objective covered.

Also located at the end of each chapter and smoothly integrated with the chapter text, are questions and problems for each learning objective:

- **Review Questions** guide students through review and application of the concepts covered in the chapter. These range from straightforward questions about theories or formulas to more open-ended narrative questions.
- High-quality **Problems and Applications** problem sets provide quantitative homework opportunities.

Both sets of content, plus **additional Extra Practice Questions,** are **fully integrated with Connect®**, enabling online assignments and grading.

Unique coverage

Macroeconomics presents the *core principles* of economics but also seeks to present some of the **new ideas that are expanding the basics of economic theory**. The sequence of chapters follows a fairly traditional route through the core principles. The text proceeds step-by-step from the personal to the public, allowing students to build toward an understanding of aggregate decisions on a solid foundation of individual decision making.

Macroeconomics offers several stand-alone chapters focused on new ideas that are expanding economic theory, which can add nuance and depth to the core principles curriculum.

In addition, because students need reinforcement with the math requirements of the course, *Macroeconomics* contains seven unique math appendixes that explain math topics important to understanding economics. **McGraw-Hill Connect®** also offers a math preparedness assignment for those needing a refresher.

digital solutions

The Karlan and Morduch product was built "from the ground up" with the expectation of *complete digital integration* of the text and related hands-on learning materials. All content in the chapter and online is tagged to the chapter learning objectives. Further, this text comes with a robust line-up of learning and teaching products, built for simple and reliable usability. See below for the highlights of our digital offer within **McGraw-Hill Connect®**.

McGraw-Hill Connect

SmartBook adaptive reading, assignable end-of-chapter exercises, additional problem sets, interactive graphing practice, assignable video resources, math remediation, and more! See pages xx–xxi for more information.

Instructor resources

All supplements accompany this text in a completely seamless integration. The following ancillaries are available for quick download and convenient access via the instructor resource site available through McGraw-Hill Connect. Instructor resources are password protected for security.

- **Test bank**: Thousands of quality static and new algorithmic questions have been thoroughly accuracy checked and are tagged with the corresponding learning objective, level of difficulty, economic concept, AACSB learning category, and Bloom's Taxonomy objective for easy filtering.
- **PowerPoint presentations**: Each presentation covers crucial information and supplies animated figures that are identical to those in the book. The presentations also contain sample exercises, instructor notes, and more.
- **Instructor guide**: This resource provides a wealth of resources to help organize and enrich the course. Elements include: learning objectives, chapter outline, beyond the lecture, and clicker questions.
- **Solutions manual**: Answers to all end-of-chapter review questions and problems have been separated for the instructor guide for quick access.

Your book, your way

McGraw-Hill Create™ enables you to select and arrange the combination of traditional and unique chapters and appendixes that will be perfect for *your* course, at an affordable price for *your* students. Visit www.mheducation.com/highered/learning-solutions/create.html for more information.

Assurance of learning ready

Many educational institutions today are focused on the notion of *assurance of learning,* an important element of some accreditation standards. Karlan and Morduch's *Macroeconomics* is designed specifically to support your assurance of learning initiatives with a simple, yet powerful solution. Each test bank question for *Macroeconomics* maps to a specific chapter learning outcome/objective listed in the text. You can use our test bank software or Connect to easily query for learning outcomes/objectives that directly relate to the learning objectives for your course. You can then use the reporting features to aggregate student results in similar fashion, making the collection and presentation of assurance of learning data simple and easy.

AACSB statement

McGraw-Hill Education is a proud corporate member of AACSB International. Understanding the importance and value of AACSB accreditation, Karlan and Morduch's *Macroeconomics* recognizes the curricula guidelines detailed in the AACSB standards for business accreditation by connecting selected questions in the text and the test bank to the general knowledge and skill guidelines in the AACSB standards.

The statements contained in *Macroeconomics* are provided only as a guide for the users of this textbook. The AACSB leaves content coverage and assessment within the purview of individual schools, the mission of the school, and the faculty. While *Macroeconomics* and the teaching package make no claim of any specific AACSB qualification or evaluation, we have within *Macroeconomics* labeled selected questions according to the general knowledge and skills areas.

McGraw-Hill customer care contact information

At McGraw-Hill, we understand that getting the most from new technology can be challenging. That's why our services don't stop after you purchase our products. You can reach our Product Specialists 24 hours a day to get product training online. Or you can search our knowledge bank of Frequently Asked Questions on our support website. For Customer Support, call **800-331-5094,** or visit www.mheducation.com/highered/contact.html. One of our Technical Support Analysts will be able to assist you in a timely fashion.

Connect Economics

McGraw Hill

As a learning science company, we create interactive learning content that supports higher order thinking skills. Read below to learn how each of our market-leading Connect assets take students higher and drives a deeper level of content understanding. Elevate your Economics course!

SmartBook 2.0

SmartBook 2.0 makes study time as productive and efficient as possible. Students move between reading and practice modes to learn the content within the chapter. As they progress, the adaptive engine identifies knowledge gaps and offers up content to reinforce areas of weakness.

Videos

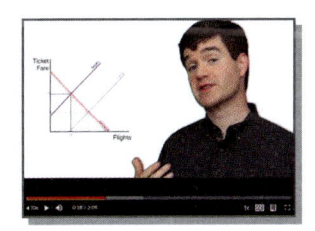

Tutorial videos provide engaging explanations to help students grasp challenging concepts. Application videos bring economics to life with relevant, real world examples. All videos include closed captioning for accessibility and are assignable with assessment questions for improved retention.

Interactive Graphs

Interactive Graphs provide visual displays of real data and economic concepts for students to manipulate. All graphs are accompanied by assignable assessment questions and feedback to guide students through the experience of learning to read and interpret graphs and data.

Math Preparedness

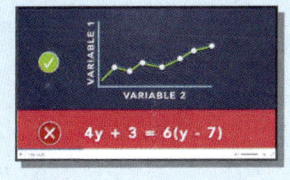

Math Preparedness assignments help students refresh important prerequisite topics necessary to be successful in economics. Tutorial videos are included to help illustrate math concepts to students visually.

Graphing Exercises

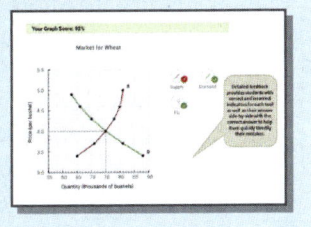

Graphing tools within Connect provide opportunities for students to draw, interact with, manipulate, and analyze graphs in their online auto-graded assignments. The Connect graphing tool is easy to use and helps students apply and practice important economic ideas.

Homework Problems

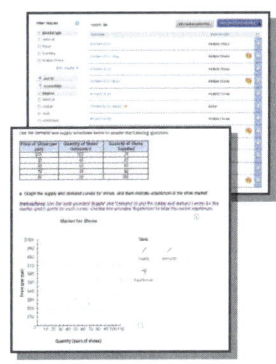

End-of-chapter homework problems reinforce chapter content through a variety of question types including questions that make use of the graphing tool. Problems with algorithmic variations and auto-grading are also available.

For more information, please visit **www.mheducation.com/highered/economics**

McGraw Hill connect

FOR INSTRUCTORS

You're in the driver's seat.

Want to build your own course? No problem. Prefer to use our turnkey, prebuilt course? Easy. Want to make changes throughout the semester? Sure. And you'll save time with Connect's auto-grading too.

65%
Less Time Grading

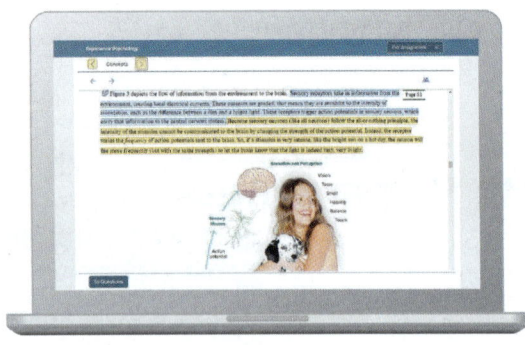

They'll thank you for it.

Adaptive study resources like SmartBook® 2.0 help your students be better prepared in less time. You can transform your class time from dull definitions to dynamic debates. Find out more about the powerful personalized learning experience available in SmartBook 2.0 at **www.mheducation.com/highered/connect/smartbook**

Laptop: McGraw-Hill; Woman/dog: George Doyle/Getty Images

Make it simple, make it affordable.

Connect makes it easy with seamless integration using any of the major Learning Management Systems—Blackboard®, Canvas, and D2L, among others—to let you organize your course in one convenient location. Give your students access to digital materials at a discount with our inclusive access program. Ask your McGraw-Hill representative for more information.

Padlock: Jobalou/Getty Images

Solutions for your challenges.

A product isn't a solution. Real solutions are affordable, reliable, and come with training and ongoing support when you need it and how you want it. Our Customer Experience Group can also help you troubleshoot tech problems—although Connect's 99% uptime means you might not need to call them. See for yourself at **status.mheducation.com**

Checkmark: Jobalou/Getty Images

FOR STUDENTS

Effective, efficient studying.

Connect helps you be more productive with your study time and get better grades using tools like SmartBook 2.0, which highlights key concepts and creates a personalized study plan. Connect sets you up for success, so you walk into class with confidence and walk out with better grades.

Study anytime, anywhere.

Download the free ReadAnywhere app and access your online eBook or SmartBook 2.0 assignments when it's convenient, even if you're offline. And since the app automatically syncs with your eBook and SmartBook 2.0 assignments in Connect, all of your work is available every time you open it. Find out more at
www.mheducation.com/readanywhere

"I really liked this app—it made it easy to study when you don't have your textbook in front of you."

- Jordan Cunningham, Eastern Washington University

No surprises.

The Connect Calendar and Reports tools keep you on track with the work you need to get done and your assignment scores. Life gets busy; Connect tools help you keep learning through it all.

Calendar: owattaphotos/Getty Images

Learning for everyone.

McGraw-Hill works directly with Accessibility Services Departments and faculty to meet the learning needs of all students. Please contact your Accessibility Services office and ask them to email accessibility@mheducation.com, or visit
www.mheducation.com/about/accessibility
for more information.

Top: Jenner Images/Getty Images, Left: Hero Images/Getty Images, Right: Hero Images/Getty Images

detailed content changes

We've made numerous changes to the third edition of this text, prompted by users, reviewers, and developing ideas in economics. This section provides a detailed list of changes.

In all chapters

In all chapters, the authors have made the following changes:

- Updated real-world data in text, figures, and tables.
- Added a **new category of boxed insert, "Econ and YOU,"** that offers examples of economics at play in personal decisions large and small. Topics include personal finance, raising a family, and unpaid internships, among others.
- Added new boxes (see details in the chapter lists below).
- Freshened existing boxes either by updating or by substituting new box topics for old ones, as detailed below. In addition, we've retitled the "Real Life" boxes as "Economics in Action."
- Reformatted long discussions into smaller bites of content, to further sharpen the text's already-strong readability and student interest.
- Added more female names and examples throughout. Added more non-Western names in end-of-chapter materials.
- Added photos in some boxes, for greater student interest.

The following list does not repeat these text-wide changes but, rather, details specific changes made to each chapter.

Chapter 1: Economics and Life

- Changed the fourth economist's question from "Why isn't someone already doing it?" to "Are resources being allocated in the best way possible?" to clarify the idea of efficiency. Revised the associated text section on efficiency, with discussion of the practical implications of efficiency.
- Clarified the opportunity cost example—changed from going on a road trip to having dinner with friends. Added example of unpaid internship.
- Added "Marginal decision making" subheading.
- New Figure 1-1 (showing total revenue generated by bowling alleys correlated with per capita consumption of sour cream) illustrates the need to differentiate between correlation and causation.
- Replaced the box about Malthus's model with a new Economics in Action box, titled *When education pays off,* about Goldin & Katz's model explaining gains from education.

Chapter 2: Specialization and Exchange

- Slightly revised and shortened the From Another Angle box about Babe Ruth as an example of absolute and comparative advantage.
- Replaced Bill Gates as a text example of specialization with Stacy Brown-Philpot, CEO of TaskRabbit.
- Replaced the Economics in Action *Is self-sufficiency a virtue?* box with a new box *Winners and losers;* the new box describes the closing of an Ohio factory as a way to show how

international trade results in some winners and some losers (suggesting that getting the benefits of trade can depend on compensating those who lose out from trade).
- Moved from online-only into the print product the Economics in Action box *Comparative advantage: The good, the bad, and the ugly* that discusses whether a country's loss of comparative advantage at producing a particular good is something to worry about.

Appendix A: Math Essentials: Understanding Graphs and Slopes

- Revised Figures A-1 and A-3 with new data.
- Replaced Figure A-2 with data showing market share for domestic and imported vehicle types.

Chapter 3: Markets

- Replaced the Real Life *The Prius shortage of 2003* box with a new Economics in Action box, *The great Elmo shortage*.
- Revised the Economics in Action *Give a man a fish* box to clarify the findings of economist Robert Jensen's research on how cell phones changed the market for fish in Kerala, India.

Chapter 4: Elasticity

- Revised the Economics in Action *Does charging for bednets decrease malaria?* box, to clarify and better highlight the work of Jessica Cohen and Pascaline Dupas on the price elasticity of demand for bednets in Kenya.
- Updated the What Do You Think? *Should entrance fees at national parks be raised?* box to include the 2017 proposal to increase fees in national parks.
- Removed the Where Can It Take You? *Pricing analyst* box and replaced it with a new Econ and YOU *Finding a travel bargain* box that discusses how understanding price elasticity can help when you buy airline tickets.

Chapter 5: Efficiency

- In the "Willingness to sell and the supply curve" subsection, revised the example (and related figures) by changing Seller #1 from a comic book collector to a college student wanting money to see a favorite band.
- Changed the Real Life *Haggling and bluffing* box to an Econ and YOU *It pays to negotiate* box that discusses salary negotiations as a common version of price negotiation. The new box references recent research by Marianne Bertrand; Hannah Riley Bowles, Linda Babcock, and Lei Lai; Andres Leibbrandt and John List; and Ellen Pao on gender differences in negotiation.

Chapter 6: Government Intervention

- Revised the What Do You Think? *Put a cap on payday lending?* box (including questions) to make it more personal (a broken-down car).
- Revised the data in the "Buyers pay more" example in Figure 6-10.
- Removed the Where Can It Take You? *Public economics* box and replaced it with a new Econ and YOU *Out of sight, out of mind* box that looks at research by Raj Chetty, Adam Looney, and Kory Kroft to test whether grocery-store shoppers "forget" about sales tax when they look at price tags.
- Replaced the What Do You Think? *Farm subsidies* box with a new *Fight for $15* box that looks at the debate and economic research about a $15 federal minimum wage.

Chapter 7: Measuring GDP

- Changed the numbers in the text example used to explain the value-added approach to clarify the value added at each step of production.
- Expanded the text discussion of NBER's definition of recession.
- Moved the discussion of well-being before data challenges (home production, the underground economy, and environmental degradation), and revised LO 7.7 to reflect that transposition.
- Retitled the From Another Angle *Valuing homemakers* box as *Not everything that counts can be counted* and expanded the discussion to highlight cases of production that are not counted in GDP.
- Shortened the From Another Angle *The politics of Green GDP* box (by removing focus on French efforts) and retitled it as *Green GDP*.

Chapter 8: The Cost of Living

- Under the "Cost of Living" heading, added a discussion reviewing the concept of *real value* of goods and services and differentiating real value from *nominal price changes.*
- Added a new paragraph (at the end of "Changes over time: Substitution and innovation" subsection) using the price of an iMac computer as an example of hedonic quality adjustment.
- Revised the What Do You Think? *COLAs for better or worse* box to Economics in Action *Poverty and the minimum wage*. The revised box focuses on the federal poverty line and the real value of the minimum wage over time, using as its "hook" a story about Senator Elizabeth Warren's family in 1961.
- Moved from online-only into the print product Real Life *Counting the poor, give or take 400 million* box, now retitled Economics in Action *What can you buy for $1.90?*

Chapter 9: Unemployment and the Labor Market

- Revised LO 9.6 to focus on unemployment insurance.
- Revised the From Another Angle *Immigration's effects on the labor market* box with a paragraph that expands economists' debate whether immigrant workers directly compete with native workers.
- Added a new Economics in Action *Employment guaranteed* box about economic arguments for and against a federally guaranteed $15-an-hour job, including research by economists Stephanie Kelton, Darrick Hamilton, and William Darity.
- Deleted the Real Life *Unemployment and developing countries* box.
- Repurposed the What Do You Think? *Youth employees on trial* box as Econ and YOU *Are internships experience or exploitation?*, focused on the economics and ethics of internships.

Chapter 10: Economic Growth

- Moved the Real Life *Green revolutions in Asia and Africa* box from the "Growth and Public Policy" section to the earlier subsection "Accounting for growth." Retitled Economics in Action *Feeding the world,* the box discusses why the Green Revolution has not been as successful in Africa as in Asia, including research by economists Esther Duflo and Micheal Kramer.
- Revised the discussion of investment funds from within a country to include corporation profits as a source of domestic savings.
- Added the new subhead "Public policy" under which "Education and health," new "Infrastructure and industrial policy" discussion, and "Technological development" appear. The revised LO 10.7 covers this revised content.

- Moved from online-only into the print product the Economics in Action *Planning for growth* box about the idea that governments can effectively plan growth by "picking winners."
- Retitled the What Do You Think? *Should poor countries be as earth-friendly as rich ones?* box to *Is it okay to pollute one's way to progress?*

Chapter 11: Aggregate Expenditure

- Revised all relevant chapter figures to show PAE touching the *y*-axis.
- Revised and transposed LOs 11.5 and 11.6.
- Revised the CO feature story to make it more general (and removed quotations from the Bill O'Reilly book).
- In the "Components of Aggregate Expenditure" section, removed the "Autonomous expenditure and simplifying assumptions" subsection and the related LO (old LO 11.5).
- Moved the discussion of autonomous expenditure (and the related LO 11.5, now LO 11.6) into the "Aggregate Expenditure Equilibrium and the Keynesian Cross" section.
- Heavily revised the "Aggregate Expenditure Equilibrium and the Keynesian Cross" section, focused on planned aggregate expenditure. To improve student understanding, the section now starts by looking at PAE in a closed, private economy and then moves to an open economy.
- Added new Figures 11.2 (the investment schedule) and 11.3 (consumption and GDP).
- Expanded the text discussion of the significance of Keynes's insights about how economies can get stuck and introduced the term *Keynesian cross* (as an italicized term).
- Added new Table 11.5 with data showing values of GDP and its components against aggregate expenditure for a hypothetical country, enabling students to practice aggregate expenditure calculations.
- Added new Figure 11.6 (disequilibrium in the Keynesian cross), which captures the results of new Table 11.5 graphically.
- Near the end of the chapter, added an explicit discussion of government intervention to put the Keynesian model to powerful use.

Chapter 12: Aggregate Demand and Aggregate Supply

- In all relevant figures in the chapter, changed the label on the *x*-axis to read "Output, or GDP, Y," for clarity.
- Revised the "Tying It All Together" heading to "Building a Model of the Economy."
- Added a new subheading "Why does the aggregate demand curve slope downward?" and expanded that section to elaborate on the *real-balances effect,* the *interest-rate effect,* and the *exchange-rate effect.*
- Transposed Figures 12-1 and 12-2.
- Expanded the paragraph discussing debate among economists about the strength of the negative relationships among the components of aggregate expenditure and the price level. The discussion now includes mention of *autonomous spending* (introduced in Chapter 11).
- Revised the discussion of confidence in the economy to better highlight the factors that affect consumption and investment decisions.
- Revised the "Multiplier and shifts in aggregate demand" subheading to "Stimulus spending or tax cut?"
- Added as new key terms *long-run aggregate supply (LRAS) curve* and *short-run aggregate supply (SRAS) curve.*

- In the subsection on "Long-run aggregate supply," added a new subheading "The business cycle."
- In the subsection on "Effects of a shift in aggregate demand," add the subheadings "Increases in aggregate demand" and "Decreases in aggregate demand" for smaller bites of content.

Chapter 13: Fiscal Policy

- In the "Fiscal Policy" section, added new text that further describes what fiscal policy is and introduces the idea of automatic stabilizers.
- Revised the "Expansionary or contractionary" subhead to "Fiscal Policy and aggregate demand," and under that heading added new subheads "Effects on aggregate demand" and "Expansionary or contractionary policy."
- In the "Real-world challenges" subsection, added *crowding out* as a key term.
- Replaced the Real Life *A timeline of the 2009 stimulus plan* box with a new Economics in Action *A check in the mail, or more in your paycheck?* box that looks at the effectiveness of two different ways of delivering tax-cut stimulus through research by Claudia Sahm, Matthew Shapiro, and Joel Slemrod.
- Updated the discussion of the budget deficit with a projection about an increase in the deficit as a result of the 2017 tax cut.
- Moved from online-only into the print product the Economics in Action *And the projection is. . .* box, retitled *From surplus to deficit.* The revised box succinctly chronicles how wars, tax cuts, and a recession caused the U.S. to go from a budget surplus in 2001 to its current deficit.
- Deleted the paragraph that discussed TIPs.
- Deleted Figure 13-7 (foreign holders of U.S. debt) and moved that information into a short text discussion.

Chapter 14: The Basics of Finance

- Added subheads "Adverse selection" and "Moral hazard" to break the text discussion of information asymmetries in financial markets into smaller bites and highlight those terms.
- In the section "Major players in the financial system," added the subheadings "Commercial banks," "Investment banks," "Mutual funds," "Pension funds," and "Life insurance policies" for smaller chunking and greater clarity.
- Repurposed the Real Life *The incredible index fund* box into the new Econ and YOU category and moved it closer to the mutual funds discussion.
- Repurposed the What Do You Think? *Are speculators a good influence on markets?* box to the From Another Angle category and removed the discussion questions at the end of the box.
- Deleted the text reference to inflation-linked bonds.
- Revised the definition of standard deviation.
- In the section "Predicting returns: The efficient market hypothesis," added the subheadings "Fundamental analysis," "Technical analysis," and "Efficient-market hypothesis" for smaller content bites and greater clarity.
- In the efficient-market hypothesis discussion, added data about the percentage of managed funds that have beat the market average over time.
- Moved from online-only into the print product the Economics in Action *Behavioral finance and the efficient market hypothesis* box and retitled it *Behavioral finance.* The revised box addresses questions that behavioral finance asks about the validity of the efficient-market hypothesis.
- In the "National Accounts Approach to Finance" section, added new Equation 14-5 to show the formula for national savings (and renumbered subsequent formulas).

Chapter 15: Money and the Monetary System

- In the "What Is Money?" section, added a new What Do You Think? *No card, no service?* box that addresses the arguments for and against a cashless—though not moneyless—economy, particularly focusing on how going cashless may affect the poorest members of society.
- Added a discussion of the resource cost of commodity-backed money.
- Slightly expanded the discussion of the money multiplier, for greater clarity.
- Updated and shortened the From Another Angle *Is bitcoin the currency of the future?* box.
- Added *zero lower bound* as a key term.
- In the discussion of the liquidity-preference model, expanded the discussion of interest rates as a determinant of money demand. The revised text example replaces the discussion of government bonds with interest rates on CDs.

Chapter 16: Inflation

- In the "Measuring inflation" discussion, added the formula for how to compute the inflation rate, first introduced in Chapter 8, to remind students.
- Slightly revised the wording of the definition of *core inflation*.
- Revised the discussion of the quantity theory of money, to work through the intuition more carefully, and added new Equation 16-3 as part of that revised discussion.
- Replaced four maps in Figure 16-4 with one graph.
- Retitled the Economics in Action *Inflating away the debt* box as *Just print money!*
- Slightly shortened and simplified the text discussion of the Phillips curve.
- Added a brief mention, with an italicized term, of *stagflation* in the 1970s, moved from Chapter 16 in the previous edition.

Chapter 17: Financial Crisis

- Shortened the From Another Angle *Do investors rationally inflate bubbles?* box and retitled it *Timing is everything*.
- Added a new paragraph about the effects of declining house prices during the housing bubble.
- Revised Figure 17-4 to show total debt service as a percent of income for U.S. consumers; demonstrates the effect of low interest rates on debt service.
- Retitled the Economics in Action *Japan's lost decade* box as *The walking dead*.

Chapter 18: Open-Market Macroeconomics

- Added a new discussion (text plus new Figure 18-4) showing U.S. exports and imports of services.
- Under the "Foreign investment" heading, added new subheads "Foreign direct investment," "Foreign portfolio investment," and "Net capital flow" for smaller chunks and better student understanding.
- Added an equation that shows total expenditure in an economy and reworked the intuition surrounding the balance of payments calculation, for greater clarity.
- Deleted the Real Life *Iceland and the banking crisis* box.
- In the "Exchange Rates" section, added a new Economics in Action box *The almighty dollar* that features research by Gita Gopinath that discusses the predominance of the U.S. dollar, describes costs for other countries, and explores possible alternative currencies.
- Under the subheading "Another example: A rising interest rate," expanded the explanation of the effects of tighter U.S. monetary policy.

- Under the subheading "Is the Chinese currency undervalued?" revised the text discussion about China's floating *renminbi* and the effect on trade balances.
- Moved from online only into the print product the From Another Angle box *Cooling down hot money* about the possible application of a small tax to all foreign-capital transactions (e.g., the Tobin tax or the Spahn tax).

Chapter 19: Development Economics

- In the chapter-opening introduction, added a short paragraph about the authors' interest in development economics.
- Revised the What Do You Think? *Utility versus capabilities* box to focus less on utility and more on capability (work of Amartya Sen).
- Revised the From Another Angle *Trillion-dollar bills on the sidewalk?* box, retitled as *Is immigration the answer?*
- Updated (and shortened) the What Do You Think? *Should the U.S. give more in foreign aid?* box.
- Updated the discussion of the U.N. Millennium Development Goals—now known as Sustainable Development Goals.
- Replaced the From Another Angle *In Zambia, did the Steelers win Super Bowl XLV?* box with a new Econ and YOU *Buy a shoe, give a shoe* box about TOMS (shoes) goods-in-kind giving program.
- Added a new From Another Angle *Cash, no strings attached* box about GiveDirectly, an organization built around the idea that the best way to give aid is to give cash.

Guide to Data Sources

- Made updates to sources and revised accompanying questions, for currency.

acknowledgments

Many people helped us create this text. It's said that "it takes a village," but it often felt like we had the benefit of an entire town.

We thank Meredith Startz, Ted Barnett, and Andrew Wright for the foundational work they contributed to the first edition, which still shines through in this edition. Thanks, too, to Victor Matheson (College of the Holy Cross), Diana Beck (New York University), Amanda Freeman (Kansas State University), and John Kane (SUNY–Oswego) for their contributions to and thoughts about early drafts of chapters.

An energetic group of collaborators helped us shape second-edition content in ways that are relevant and engaging for a student audience: David "Dukes" Love (Williams College) steered us through the writing of the macro chapters, helping us revamp our treatment of the aggregate expenditure model and how it leads into the aggregate demand and aggregate supply model. Erin Moody (University of Maryland) applied her extensive classroom experience as an essential contributor throughout the micro chapters, ensuring that we addressed the many suggestions we received from users and reviewers of our text since the first edition published. Our IPA team of researchers, Radhika Lokur and Noor Sethi, brought a recent-student perspective to the text and helped us update many of our examples and figures with the most current data.

Many other talented individuals have contributed to previous editions. We thank John Neri and Murat Doral for providing detailed feedback on all the macro chapters of the text. We appreciate Jodi Begg's help in providing a base to work from for Chapter 11, "Aggregate Expenditure." We thank Chiuping Chen, Ashley Hodgson, Michael Machiorlatti, and Germain Pichop for reviewing said chapter in its draft stages to ensure we were on the right track.

We thank Peggy Dalton (Frostburg State University) and Erin Moody (University of Maryland) for their many and varied contributions to end-of-chapter and test bank content, both in the text and in Connect. We are very appreciative of the extensive work done by Katrina Babb (Indiana State University) and Susan Bell (Seminole State College) in accuracy-checking this content. In addition, we thank Greg Gilpin (Montana State University) for authoring the PowerPoint Presentation and Russell Kellogg (University of Colorado Denver) for authoring the LearnSmart content.

Ted Barnett played an essential role in this edition, helping us introduce new material and new ways of describing economic ideas. We are grateful for his creativity and knowledge of pedagogy and economics. He also made improvements to the test bank content. We thank Dick Startz for sharing his insights about new approaches in macroeconomics and for his feedback. Fatima Khan led the efforts to update the data and figures throughout the text.

We also want to share our appreciation to the following people at McGraw-Hill for the hard work they put into creating the product you see before you: Anke Weekes, Portfolio Director, helped us communicate the overarching vision and promoted our revision. Bobby Pearson, Marketing Manager, guided us in visiting schools and working with the sales team. Ann Torbert, Content Developer, has been an exemplary editor, improving the exposition on each page and keeping attention on both the big picture and key details. We feel lucky to have had her partnership on all three editions. Christina Kouvelis, Senior Product Developer, managed innumerable and indispensable details—reviews, manuscript, and the many aspects of the digital products and overall package. Kathryn Wright, Senior Core Content Project Manager, helped turn our manuscript into the finished, polished product you see before you. Keri Johnson, Senior Assessment Content Project Manager, skillfully guided the digital plan. Thanks, too, to Douglas Ruby, Senior Director of Digital Content, for his careful shepherding of the digital materials that accompany the text.

Thank You!

Creating the third edition of a book is a daunting task. We wanted to do everything we could to improve upon the previous editions, and we couldn't have done this without professors who told us honestly what they thought we could do better. To everyone who helped shape this edition, we thank you for sharing your insights and recommendations.

Symposia

Luca Bossi
University of Pennsylvania

Regina Cassady
Valencia College

June Charles
North Lake College

Monica Cherry
St. John Fisher College and State University of New York at Buffalo

George Chikhladze
University of Missouri-Columbia

Patrick Crowley
Texas A&M University-Corpus Christi

Attila Cseh
Valdosta State University

Susan Doty
University of Texas at Tyler

Irene Foster
George Washington University

Don Holley
Boise State University

Ricot Jean
Valencia College

Sarah Jenyk
Youngstown State University

Stephanie Jozefowicz
Indiana University of Pennsylvania

Nkongolo Kalala
Bluegrass Community and Technical College

Carrie Kerekes
Florida Gulf Coast University

Brandon Koford
Weber State University

Soloman Kone
City University of New York

W. J. Lane
University of New Orleans

Jose Lopez-Calleja
Miami Dade College

Erika Martinez
University of South Florida-Tampa

Geri Mason
Seattle Pacific University

ABM Nasir
North Carolina Central University

Eric Nielsen
Saint Louis Community College

Rich Numrich
College of Southern Nevada

Michael Polcen
Northern Virginia Community College

Martin Sabo
Community College of Denver

Latisha Settlage
University of Arkansas-Fort Smith

Mark Showalter
Brigham Young University

Warren Smith
Palm Beach State College

Kay Strong
Baldwin Wallace University

Ryan Umbeck
Ivy Tech Community College

Ross vanWassenhove
University of Houston

Terry Von Ende
Texas Tech University

Jennifer Wissink
Cornell University

Focus Groups

Siddiq Abdullah
University of Massachusetts-Boston

Seemi Ahmad
Dutchess Community College

Nurul Aman
University of Massachusetts-Boston

Aimee Chin
University of Houston

Can Erbil
Boston College

Varun Gupta
Wharton County Junior College

Moon Han
North Shore Community College

Hilaire Jean-Gilles
Bunker Hill Community College

Jennifer Lehman
Wharton County Junior College

Mikko Manner,
Dutchess Community College

Nara Mijid
Central Connecticut State University

Shahruz Mohtadi
Suffolk University

Victor Moussoki
Lone Star College

Kevin Nguyen
Lone Star College

Jan Palmer
Ohio University

Julia Paxton
Ohio University

Tracy Regan
Boston College

Christina Robinson
Central Connecticut State University

Rosemary Rossiter
Ohio University

Sara Saderion
Houston Community College

Reviews

Steve Abid
Grand Rapids Community College

Eric Abrams
McKendree University

Richard Ugunzi Agesa
Marshall University

Seemi Ahmad
Dutchess Community College

Jason A. Aimone
Baylor University

Donald L. Alexander
Western Michigan University

Ricky Ascher
Broward College and Palm Beach State College

Shannon Aucoin
University of Louisiana at Lafayette

Gyanendra Baral
Oklahoma City Community College

Klaus Becker
Texas Tech University

Pedro Bento
West Virginia University

Jennifer Bossard
Doane College

Kristen Broady
Fort Valley State University

Gregory Brock
Georgia Southern University

Giuliana Andreopoulos Campanelli
William Paterson University

Paul Chambers
University of Central Missouri

Sewin Chan
New York University

Joni Charles
Texas State University

Chiuping Chen
American River College

Tom Creahan
Morehead State University

Nicholas Dadzie
Bowling Green State University

Can Dogan
North American University

Brandon Dupont
Western Washington University

Matthew J. Easton
Pueblo Community College

Jennifer Elias
Radford University

Linda K. English
Baylor University

Irene R. Foster
George Washington University

Alka Gandhi
Northern Virginia Community College

Soma Ghosh
Albright College

Gregory Gilpin
Montana State University

Lisa Workman Gloege
Grand Rapids Community College

Cynthia Harter
Eastern Kentucky University

Darcy Hartman
Ohio State University

Ashley Hodgson
St. Olaf College

Don Holley
Boise State University

Yuri Hupka
Oklahoma State University

Harvey James
University of Missouri

Sarah Jenyk
Youngstown State University

Allison Kaminaga
Bryant University

Mina Kamouie
Ohio University

Russell Kellogg
University of Colorado Denver

Melissa Knox
University of Washington

Benjamin Kwitek
Pueblo Community College

Greg Lindeblom
Broward College

Michael Machiorlatti
Oklahoma City Community College

Rita Madarassy
Santa Clara University

Edouard Mafoua
State University of New York at Canton

C. Lucy Malakar
Lorain County Community College

Geri Mason
Seattle Pacific University

Katherine McClain
University of Georgia

Bruce McClung
Texas State University

Robin McCutcheon
Marshall University

Tia M. McDonald
Ohio University

William McLean
Oklahoma State University

Jennifer Meredith
Seattle Pacific University

John Min
Northern Virginia Community College

Sam Mirmirani
Bryant University

Ida A. Mirzaie
Ohio State University

Franklin G. Mixon Jr.
Columbus State University

Erin Moody
University of Maryland

Barbara Moore
University of Central Florida

Christopher Mushrush
Illinois State University

Charles Myrick
Oklahoma City Community College

Camille Nelson
Oregon State University

Per Norander
University of North Carolina-Charlotte

Ronald Oertel
Western Washington University

Constantin Ogloblin
Georgia Southern University

Alex Olbrecht
Ramapo College of New Jersey

Beau Olen
Oregon State University

Tomi Ovaska
Youngstown State University

Jan Palmer
Ohio University

Julia Paxton
Ohio University

James Peyton
Highline College

Germain Pichop
Oklahoma City Community College

Brennan Platt
Brigham Young University

Elizabeth Porter
University of North Carolina-Asheville

Mathew Price
Oklahoma City Community College

Christina Robinson
Central Connecticut State University

Matthew Roelofs
Western Washington University

Randall R. Rojas
University of California-Los Angeles

John Rykowski
Kalamazoo Valley Community College

Robert M. Schwab
University of Maryland

Gasper Sekelj
Clarkson University

James K. Self
Indiana University

Michael Scott
Pueblo Community College

Mark Showalter
Brigham Young University

Kevin Stanley
Highline College

Steve Trost
Virginia Polytechnic Institute and State University

Ross S. vanWassenhove
University of Houston

Allison Witman
University of North Carolina-Wilimington

Acknowledgments

In addition, we continue to be grateful to the first-edition contributors, who over the course of several years of development attended focus groups or symposia or provided content reviews. Thanks to the following, whose insights, recommendations, and feedback helped immeasurably as the project took shape.

Mark Abajian
San Diego Mesa College

Tom Adamson
Midland University

Richard Agesa
Marshall University

Rashid Al-Hmoud
Texas Tech University

Frank Albritton
Seminole State College-Sanford

Terence Alexander
Iowa State University

Clifford Althoff
Joliet Junior College

Diane Anstine
North Central College

Michael Applegate
Oklahoma State University-Stillwater Campus

Ali Ataiifar
Delaware County Community College

Roberto Ayala
California State Polytechnic University-Pomona

Jim Barbour
Elon University

Gary Benson
Southwest Community College

Laura Jean Bhadra
Northern Virginia Community College-Manassas

Prasun Bhattacharjee
East Tennessee State University-Johnson City

Radha Bhattacharya
California State University-Fullerton

Michael Bonnal
University of Tennessee-Chattanooga

Camelia Bouzerdan
Middlesex Community College

Dale Bremmer
Rose-Hulman Institute of Technology

Anne Bresnock
University of California-Los Angeles

Bruce Brown
California State Polytechnic University-Pomona

Ken Brown
University of Northern Iowa

Laura Bucila
Texas Christian University

Andrew Cassey
Washington State University

Kalyan Chakraborty
Emporia State University

Catherine Chambers
University of Central Missouri

Britton Chapman
State College of Florida-Manatee

Sanjukta Chaudhuri
University of Wisconsin-Eau Claire

Chiuping Chen
American River College

Ron Cheung
Oberlin College

Young Back Choi
Saint John's University

Dmitriy Chulkov
Indiana University-Kokomo

Cindy Clement
University of Maryland-College Park

Howard Cochran
Belmont University

Jim Cox
Georgia Perimeter College

Matt Critcher
University of Arkansas Community College-Batesville

Chifeng Dai
Southern Illinois University-Carbondale

Thomas Davidson
Principia College

Rafael Donoso
Lone Star College-North Harris

Floyd Duncan
Virginia Military Institute

David Eaton
Murray State University

Eric Eide
Brigham Young University-Provo

Marwan El Nasser
State University of New York-Fredonia

Harry Ellis
University of North Texas

Maxwell Eseonu
Virginia State University

Brent Evans
Mississippi State University

Russell Evans
Oklahoma State University

Fidelis Ezeala-Harrison
Jackson State University

Chris Fant
Spartanburg Community College

Michael Fenick
Broward College

Abdollah Ferdowsi
Ferris State University

Tawni Ferrarini
Northern Michigan University

Herbert Flaig
Milwaukee Area Technical College

Irene Foster
George Washington University

Joseph Franklin
Newberry College

Shelby Frost
Georgia State University

Fran Lara Garib
San Jacinto College

Deborah Gaspard
Southeast Community College

Karen Gebhardt
Colorado State University

Juan Alejandro Gelves
Midwestern State University

Kirk Gifford
Brigham Young University-Idaho

Otis Gilley
Louisiana Technical University

Gregory Gilpin
Montana State University-Bozeman

Bill (Wayne) Goffe
State University of New York-Oswego

Michael Gootzeit
University of Memphis

George Greenlee
St. Petersburg College

Galina Hale
Federal Reserve Bank of San Francisco

Oskar Harmon
University of Connecticut-Stamford

David Hedrick
Central Washington University-Ellensburg

Dennis Heiner
College of Southern Idaho

Andrew Helms
Washington College

David Hickman
Frederick Community College

Ashley Hodgson
Saint Olaf College

Vanessa Holmes
Pennsylvania State University-Scranton

Scott Houser
Colorado School of Mines

Gregrey Hunter
California Polytechnic University-Pomona

Kyle Hurst
University of Colorado-Denver

Jonathan Ikoba
Scott Community College

Onur Ince
Appalachian State University

Dennis Jansen
Texas A&M University

Shuyi Jiang
Emmanuel College

Barbara Heroy John
University of Dayton

James Johnson
University of Arkansas Community College-Batesville

Mahbubul Kabir
Lyon College

Ahmad Kader
University of Nevada-Las Vegas

John Kane
State University of New York-Oswego

Tsvetanka Karagyozova
Lawrence University

Joel Kazy
State Fair Community College

Daniel Kuester
Kansas State University

Gary Langer
Roosevelt University

Daniel Lawson
Oakland Community College

Richard Le
Cosumnes River College

Jim Lee
Texas A&M University-Corpus Christi

Willis Lewis
Winthrop University

Qing Li
College of the Mainland

Tin-Chun Lin
Indiana University Northwest-Gary

Delwin Long
San Jacinto College

Katie Lotz
Lake Land College

Karla Lynch
North Central Texas College

Arindam Mandal
Siena College

Daniel Marburger
Arkansas State University-Jonesboro

Geri Mason
Seattle Pacific University

Victor Matheson
College of the Holy Cross

Bryan McCannon
Saint Bonaventure University

Michael McIlhon
Century Community and Technical College

Hannah McKinney
Kalamazoo College

Al Mickens
State University of New York-Old Westbury

Nara Mijid
Central Connecticut State University

Martin Milkman
Murray State University

Douglas Miller
University of Missouri-Columbia

Gregory Miller
Wallace Community College-Selma

Edward Millner
Virginia Commonwealth University

Mitch Mitchell
Bladen Community College

Daniel Morvey
Piedmont Technical College

Rebecca Moryl
Emmanuel College

Tina Mosleh
Ohlone College

Thaddaeus Mounkurai
Daytona State College-Daytona Beach

Chris Mushrush
Illinois State University

Muhammad Mustafa
South Carolina State University

Tony Mutsune
Iowa Wesleyan College

Max Grunbaum Nagiel
Daytona State College-Daytona Beach

John Nordstrom
College of Western Idaho

Emlyn Norman
Texas Southern University

Christian Nsiah
Black Hills State University

Jan Ojdana
University of Cincinnati

Ronald O'Neal
Camden County College

Serkan Ozbeklik
Claremont McKenna College

Debashis Pal
University of Cincinnati-Cincinnati

Robert Pennington
University of Central Florida-Orlando

Andrew Perumal
University of Massachusetts-Boston

Steven Peterson
University of Idaho

Brennan Platt
Brigham Young University

Sanela Porca
University of South Carolina-Aiken

Gregory Pratt
Mesa Community College

William Prosser
Cayuga Community College

Gregory Randolph
Southern New Hampshire University

Mitchell Redlo
Monroe Community College

Timothy Reynolds
Alvin Community College

Michael Rolleigh
Williams College

Amanda Ross
West Virginia University-Morgantown

Jason Rudbeck
University of Georgia

Michael Ryan
Gainesville State College

Robert Rycroft
University of Mary Washington

Michael Salemi
University of North Carolina-Chapel Hill

Gregory Saltzman
Albion College

Ravi Samitamana
Daytona State College

Saied Sarkarat
West Virginia University-Parkersburg

Naveen Sarna
Northern Virginia Community College-Alexandria

Jesse Schwartz
Kennesaw State University

Abdelkhalik Shabayek
Lane College

Mark Showalter
Brigham Young University

Cheri Sides
Lane College

Megan Silbert
Salem College

Sovathana Sokhom
Loyola Marymount University

Souren Soumbatiants
Franklin University

Marilyn Spencer
Texas A&M University-Corpus Christi

Brad Stamm
Cornerstone University

Karl Strauss
Saint Bonaventure University

Chuck Stull
Kalamazoo College

Abdulhamid Sukar
Cameron University

Albert Sumell
Youngstown State University

Philip Isak Szmedra
Georgia Southwestern State University

Christine Tarasevich
Del Mar College

Noreen Templin
Butler Community College

Darryl Thorne
Valencia College East

Kiril Tochkov
Texas Christian University

Demetri Tsanacas
Ferrum College

George Tvelia
Suffolk County Community College

Nora Underwood
University of Central Florida

Jose Vazquez
University of Illinois-Champaign

Marieta Velikova
Belmont University

Jeffery Vicek
Parkland College

Jennifer Vincent
Champlain College

Terry von Ende
Texas Tech University

Craig Walker
Oklahoma Baptist University

Jennifer Ward-Batts
Wayne State University

Tarteashia Williams
Valencia College-West Campus

Melissa Wiseman
Houston Baptist University

Jim Wollscheid
University of Arkansas-Fort Smith

Jeff Woods
University of Indianapolis

Ranita Wyatt
Pasco-Hernando Community College-West Campus

Suthathip Yaisawarng
Union College

Jim Yates
Darton College

Daehyun Yoo
Elon University

Ceren Ertan Yoruk
Sage College of Albany

Chuck Zalonka
Oklahoma State University-Oklahoma City

Finally, thanks to the following instructors, and their students, who class-tested chapters of the first edition before publication. Their engagement with the content and their feedback from the "test drive" made this a better product.

Richard Agesa
Marshall University

Anne Bresnock
University of California-Los Angeles

Chiuping Chen
American River College

John Kane
State University of New York-Oswego

Jim Lee
Texas A&M University-Corpus Christi

Martin Milkman
Murray State University

Kolleen Rask
College of the Holy Cross

Jesse Schwartz
Kennesaw State University

Jennifer Vincent
Champlain College

detailed contents

Part 1
The Power of Economics 1

Chapter 1
Economics and Life 3

Making an Impact with Small Loans 3

The Basic Insights of Economics 4
- *Scarcity 5*
- *Opportunity cost and marginal decision making 6*
- *Incentives 9*
- *Efficiency 10*

An Economist's Problem-Solving Toolbox 12
- *Correlation and causation 13*
- *Models 15*
- *Positive and normative analysis 17*

Conclusion 19

Chapter 2
Specialization and Exchange 25

The Origins of a T-Shirt 25

Production Possibilities 27
- *Drawing the production possibilities frontier 27*
- *Choosing among production possibilities 30*
- *Shifting the production possibilities frontier 31*

Absolute and Comparative Advantage 33
- *Absolute advantage 33*
- *Comparative advantage 33*

Why Trade? 35
- *Specialization 35*
- *Gains from trade 37*
- *Comparative advantage over time 40*

Conclusion 42

APPENDIX A Math Essentials: Understanding Graphs and Slope 46A

Creating a Graph 46A
- *Graphs of one variable 46A*
- *Graphs of two variables 46C*

Slope 46F
- *Calculating slope 46G*
- *The direction of a slope 46H*
- *The steepness of a slope 46I*

Part 2
Supply and Demand 47

Chapter 3
Markets 49

Mobiles Go Global 49

Markets 50
- *What is a market? 50*
- *What is a competitive market? 50*

Demand 52
- *The demand curve 53*
- *Determinants of demand 53*
- *Shifts in the demand curve 57*

Supply 59
- *The supply curve 60*
- *Determinants of supply 60*
- *Shifts in the supply curve 62*

Market Equilibrium 63
- *Reaching equilibrium 64*
- *Changes in equilibrium 66*

Conclusion 72

APPENDIX B Math Essentials: Working with Linear Equations 78A

Interpreting the Equation of a Line 78A
- *Turning a graph into an equation 78B*
- *Turning an equation into a graph 78B*
- *Equations with x and y reversed 78D*

Shifts and Pivots 78E

Solving for Equilibrium 78H

Chapter 4
Elasticity 79

Coffee Becomes Chic 79

What Is Elasticity? 80

Price Elasticity of Demand 81
- *Calculating price elasticity of demand 81*
- *Determinants of price elasticity of demand 84*
- *Using price elasticity of demand 85*

Price Elasticity of Supply 92
- *Calculating price elasticity of supply 92*
- *Determinants of price elasticity of supply 93*

xxxvii

Other Elasticities 94
   Cross-price elasticity of demand 94
   Income elasticity of demand 95
Conclusion 98

APPENDIX C Math Essentials: Calculating Percentage Change, Slope, and Elasticity 102A
Percentage Change 102A
Slope and Elasticity 102B
   X over Y, or Y over X? 102D
   Elasticity changes along lines with constant slope 102D

Chapter 5
Efficiency 103

A Broken Laser Pointer Starts an Internet Revolution 103

Willingness to Pay and Sell 104
   Willingness to pay and the demand curve 105
   Willingness to sell and the supply curve 107
Measuring Surplus 109
   Consumer surplus 110
   Producer surplus 112
   Total surplus 113
Using Surplus to Compare Alternatives 115
   Market equilibrium and efficiency 115
   Changing the distribution of total surplus 117
   Deadweight loss 118
   Missing markets 119
Conclusion 121

APPENDIX D Math Essentials: The Area under a Linear Curve 128A
The Area under a Linear Curve 128A

Chapter 6
Government Intervention 129

Feeding the World, One Price Control at a Time 129

Why Intervene? 130
   Three reasons to intervene 130
   Four real-world interventions 131
Price Controls 132
   Price ceilings 132
   Price floors 136
Taxes and Subsidies 139
   Taxes 140
   Subsidies 146

Evaluating Government Interventions 150
   How big is the effect of a tax or subsidy? 151
   Short-run versus long-run impact 153
Conclusion 156

Part 3
The Data of Macroeconomics 163

Chapter 7
Measuring GDP 165

It's More than Counting Peanuts 165

Valuing an Economy 166
   Unpacking the definition of GDP 167
   Production equals expenditure equals income 169
Approaches to Measuring GDP 170
   The expenditure approach 170
   The income approach 173
   The "value-added" approach 175
Using GDP to Compare Economies 176
   Real versus nominal GDP 176
   The GDP deflator 178
   Using GDP to assess economic health 179
Limitations of GDP Measures 183
   GDP vs. well-being 184
   Data challenges 185
Conclusion 189

Chapter 8
The Cost of Living 197

Thank You for Not Smoking 197

The Cost of Living 198
Measuring Price Changes over Time 199
   The market basket 200
   Consumer Price Index (CPI) 201
   The challenges in measuring price changes 202
Using Price Indexes 205
   The inflation rate 205
   Deflating nominal variables 207
   Adjusting for inflation: Indexing 209
Accounting for Price Differences across Places 212
   Purchasing power parity 212
   Purchasing power indexes 213
   PPP-adjustment 214
Conclusion 216

Part 4
Labor Markets and Economic Growth 223

Chapter 9
Unemployment and the Labor Market 225

What Does It Mean to Be Unemployed? 225

Defining and Measuring Unemployment 226
- *Measuring unemployment 227*
- *Beyond the unemployment rate 231*
- *Where do the data come from? 232*

Equilibrium in the Labor Market 232

Categories of Unemployment 235
- *Natural rate of unemployment 235*
- *Cyclical unemployment 236*

Public Policies and Other Influences on Unemployment 238
- *Factors that may stop wage rates from falling 239*
- *Unemployment insurance 243*
- *Other factors 243*

Conclusion 244

Chapter 10
Economic Growth 249

Why Economic Growth Matters 249

Economic Growth through the Ages 250
- *History of world growth 250*
- *Compounding and the rule of 70 252*

Determinants of Productivity 254
- *Productivity drives growth 254*
- *Components of productivity 255*
- *Rates versus levels 257*
- *Accounting for growth 258*
- *Convergence 260*

Growth and Public Policy 261
- *Investment and savings 262*
- *Public policy 263*
- *The juggling act 266*

Conclusion 268

Part 5
The Economy in the Short and Long Run 273

Chapter 11
Aggregate Expenditure 275

The Big Crash 275

The Components of Aggregate Expenditure 276
- *Consumption (C) 277*
- *Investment (I) 279*
- *Government spending (G) 280*
- *Net exports (NX) 281*
- *A summary of the determinants of aggregate expenditure 283*

Aggregate Expenditure Equilibrium and the Keynesian Equilibrium 283
- *Actual versus planned aggregate expenditure 283*
- *Keynesian equilibrium 286*
- *Output gaps 289*
- *The multiplier effect 290*

Conclusion 293

APPENDIX E Math Essentials: Algebra and Aggregate Expenditure 298A

Using Algebra to Find Equilibrium Aggregate Expenditure 298A
- *Using algebra to derive the expenditure multiplier 298B*

Chapter 12
Aggregate Demand and Aggregate Supply 299

"Pop!" Goes the Bubble 299

Building a Model of the Economy 300

Aggregate Demand 301
- *The aggregate demand curve 301*
- *Shifting the aggregate demand curve 303*
- *Stimulus spending or tax cut? 306*

Aggregate Supply 309
- *The difference between short-run and long-run aggregate supply 309*
- *Shifts in the short-run aggregate supply curve 313*
- *Shifts in the long-run aggregate supply curve 313*

Economic Fluctuations 316
- *Effects of a shift in aggregate demand 316*
- *Effects of a shift in aggregate supply 319*
- *Comparing demand and supply shocks 321*

The Role of Public Policy 324
- *Government spending to counter negative demand shocks 325*
- *Government spending to counter negative supply shocks 326*

Conclusion 327

Chapter 13
Fiscal Policy 333

From Housing Bubble to Great Recession 333

Fiscal Policy 334
- *Fiscal policy and aggregate demand 334*
- *Policy response to short-run economic fluctuations 335*

Real-world challenges 338
Policy tools—discretionary and automatic 341
Limits of fiscal policy: The money must come from somewhere 342

The Government Budget 344
Revenue and spending 344
The U.S. budget deficit 344

The Public Debt 346
Size of the debt 347
How does the government go into debt? 348
Is government debt good or bad? 349

Conclusion 350

Part 6
The Financial System and Institutions 357

Chapter 14
The Basics of Finance 359

Henry Lehman and His Brothers 359

The Role of Financial Markets 360
What is a financial market? 361
Information asymmetries and financial markets 361
Functions of banks and financial markets 362

The Market for Loanable Funds: A Simplified Financial Market 364
Savings, investment, and the price of loanable funds 364
Changes in the supply and demand for loanable funds 366
A price for every borrower: A more realistic look at interest rates 370

The Modern Financial System 371
Functions of the financial system 372
Major financial assets 373
Major players in the financial system 375

Valuing Assets 379
The trade-off between risk and return 379
Predicting returns: The efficient-market hypothesis 381
Bubbles 383

A National Accounts Approach to Finance 384
The savings-investment identity 384
Private savings, public savings, and capital flows 385

Conclusion 387

Chapter 15
Money and the Monetary System 395

Cigarette Money 395

What Is Money? 396
Functions of money 396
What makes for good money? 397
Commodity-backed money versus fiat money 400

Banks and the Money-Creation Process 401
"Creating" money 401
Measuring money 406

Managing the Money Supply: The Federal Reserve 408
The role of the central bank 408
How does the Federal Reserve work? 410
Tools of monetary policy 411

The Economic Effects of Monetary Policy 414
Interest rates and monetary policy: The liquidity-preference model 414
Interest rates and the economy 416

Conclusion 420

Chapter 16
Inflation 427

A Land of Opportunity . . . and Inflation 427

Changing Price Levels 428
Measuring inflation 428
The neutrality of money 430
The classical theory of inflation 430
The quantity theory of money 432
Other causes of changing price levels 434

Why Do We Care about Changing Price Levels? 436
Inflation 436
Deflation 439
Controlling inflation, or not: Disinflation and hyperinflation 441
Why a little inflation is good 443

Inflation and Monetary Policy 444
The competing goals of the dual mandate 444
Inflation and unemployment 446

Conclusion 452

Chapter 17
Financial Crisis 459

A Financial Storm 459

The Origins of Financial Crises 460
- Irrational expectations 460
- Leverage 462
- Two famous historical financial crises 463

The Great Recession: A Financial-Crisis Case Study 465
- Subprime lending 465
- The creation of the housing bubble 466
- Effects of the housing bubble collapse 469
- The immediate response to the crisis 472
- Stimulus at the zero lower bound 476

Conclusion 477

Part 7
International Policy Issues 483

Chapter 18
Open-Market Macroeconomics 485

From Factory to Figures 485

International Flows of Goods and Capital 486
- Imports and exports 486
- Foreign investment 489
- Balance of payments 491

International Capital Flows 493
- Determinants of international capital flows 493
- Effects of foreign investment 494
- Can a country save too much? 496

Exchange Rates 498
- The foreign-exchange market 498
- A model of the exchange-rate market 502
- Exchange-rate regimes 505
- Macroeconomic policy and exchange rates 509
- The real exchange rate 511

Global Financial Crises 512
- The role of the IMF 512
- Debt crises 513
- Exchange-rate crises 513

Conclusion 516

Chapter 19
Development Economics 523

Poverty amid Plenty 523

Development and Capabilities 524
- The capabilities approach 524
- Economic growth and economic development 526

The Basics of Development Economics 526
- Human capital 527
- Institutions and good governance 529
- Investment 530
- Trade 531
- Migration 532

What Can Aid Do? 534
- Perspectives on foreign aid 535
- Impact investing 541
- How do we know what works? 541

Conclusion 545

Guide to Data Sources GU-1
Glossary GL-1
Indexes IN-1

feature boxes

ECONOMICS IN ACTION
When education pays off 17
Specialization sauce 37
Winners and losers 39
Comparative advantage: The good, the bad, and the ugly 41
Can instant noodle sales predict a recession? 56
The great Elmo shortage 66
Give a man a fish 71
Does charging for bednets decrease malaria? 87
The unintended consequences of biofuel subsidies 150
Can money buy you happiness? 185
The costs of living in New York City vs. Iowa City 199
Poverty and the minimum wage 210
What can you buy for $1.90? 215
Employment guaranteed 240
What a difference 50 years makes: The story of Korea and Ghana 253
Feeding the world 259
Planning for growth 264
The wealthy hand-to-mouth 278
The great multiplier debate 292
The Kobe earthquake and aggregate supply 324
A check in the mail, or more in your paycheck? 340
Spending your stimulus check 343
From surplus to deficit 345
Behavioral finance 383
Banking with a cell phone 399
Bank runs and the banking holiday 405
Where's George? 435
Just print money! 440
A *real* plan—with fake currency 442
Too big to fail? 474
The walking dead 476
The almighty dollar 499
Dollarization: When not in the U.S. . . . 506

FROM ANOTHER ANGLE
Does ice cream cause polio? 14
Babe Ruth, star pitcher 34
How much would you pay to keep the Internet from disappearing? 110
Not everything that counts can be counted 186
Green GDP 188
The wealthiest American? 209
Immigration's effects on the labor market 238
Save . . . no, spend! 307
Are speculators a good influence on markets? 378
Savings glut? 386
Is bitcoin the currency of the future? 409
Timing is everything 461
Cooling down hot money 515
Is immigration the answer? 533
Cash, no strings attached 544

ECON AND YOU
Finding a travel bargain 97
It pays to negotiate 108
Out of sight, out of mind 152
Are internships experience or exploitation? 243
The incredible index fund 377
Buy a shoe, give a shoe 539

WHAT DO YOU THINK?
The opportunity cost of a life 7
The cost of college cash 18
Should entrance fees at national parks be raised? 91
Kidneys for sale 120
Put a cap on payday lending? 135
Fight for $15 154
Is it okay to pollute one's way to progress? 266
No card, no service? 398
Are sweatshops good or bad? 490
Utility versus capabilities 525
Should the United States give more in foreign aid? 536

xliii

The Power of Economics

PART ONE

The two chapters in Part 1 will introduce you to . . .

the tools and intuition essential to the study of economics. Chapter 1, "Economics and Life," presents four questions that introduce the fundamental concepts of economic problem solving. We also describe how economists think about data and analyze policies: You'll see that we typically separate how one *wants* the world to look ("normative" analysis) from how the world *actually* works ("positive" analysis).

Chapter 2, "Specialization and Exchange," presents the ideas of absolute and comparative advantage, to explain how people (and countries) can most effectively use their resources and talents. Should you hire a plumber or fix the pipes yourself? Should you become a pop star or an economist? We develop these ideas to show how trade can make everyone better off, on both a personal and a national level.

This is just a start. Throughout the book, we'll use these tools to gain a deeper understanding of how people interact and manage their resources, which in turn gives insight into tough problems of all sorts. Economic ideas weave a common thread through many subjects, from the purely economic to political, environmental, and cultural issues, as well as personal decisions encountered in everyday life. Economics is much more than just the study of money, and we hope you'll find that what you learn here will shed light far beyond your economics classes.

Economics and Life

Chapter 1

Making an Impact with Small Loans

On the morning of October 13, 2006, Bangladeshi economist Muhammad Yunus received an unexpected telephone call from Oslo, Norway. Later that day, the Nobel committee announced that Yunus and the Grameen Bank, which he founded in 1976, would share the 2006 Nobel Peace Prize. Past recipients of the Nobel Peace Prize include Mother Teresa, who spent over 50 years ministering to beggars and lepers; Martin Luther King Jr., who used peaceful protest to oppose racial segregation; and the Dalai Lama, an exiled Tibetan Buddhist leader who symbolizes the struggle for religious and cultural tolerance. What were an economist and his bank doing in such company?

Grameen is not a typical bank. Yes, it makes loans and offers savings accounts, charging customers for its services, just like other banks. But it serves some of the poorest people in the poorest villages in one of the poorest countries in the world. It makes loans so small that it's hard for people in wealthy countries to imagine what good they can do: The first group of loans Yunus made totaled only $27. Before Grameen came along, other banks had been unwilling to work in these poor communities. They believed it wasn't worth bothering to lend such small amounts; many believed the poor could not be counted on to repay their loans.

©lev radin/Shutterstock

Yunus disagreed. He was convinced that even small loans would allow poor villagers to expand their small businesses—maybe buying a sewing machine or a cow to produce milk for the local market—and earn more money. Or perhaps a villager wouldn't expand a small business but would instead use the money to pay for a health emergency or to buy food when faced with hunger. Regardless of the way the loans were used, villagers' lives would be more comfortable and secure, and their children would have a better future. Yunus claimed that they would be able to repay the loans and that his new bank would earn a profit.

Muhammad Yunus was trained as an economist. He earned a PhD at Vanderbilt University in Nashville and then taught in Tennessee before becoming a professor in Bangladesh. When a devastating famine struck Bangladesh, Yunus became disillusioned with teaching. What did abstract equations and stylized graphs have to do with the suffering he saw around him?

Ultimately, Yunus realized that economic thinking holds the key to solving hard problems that truly matter. The genius of Grameen Bank is that it is neither a traditional charity nor a traditional bank. Instead, it is a business that harnesses basic economic insights to make the world a better place.

LEARNING OBJECTIVES

LO 1.1 Explain the economic concept of scarcity.

LO 1.2 Explain the economic concepts of opportunity cost and marginal decision making.

LO 1.3 Explain the economic concept of incentives.

LO 1.4 Explain the economic concept of efficiency.

LO 1.5 Distinguish between correlation and causation.

LO 1.6 List the characteristics of a good economic model.

LO 1.7 Distinguish between positive and normative analysis.

In this book, we'll introduce you to the tools economists are using to tackle some of the world's biggest challenges, from health care reform, to climate change, to lifting people out of poverty. Of course, these tools are not just for taking on causes worthy of Nobel Prizes. Economics can also help you become a savvier consumer, successfully launch a new cell phone app, or simply make smarter decisions about how to spend your time and money. Throughout this book, we promise we'll ask you not just to memorize theories, but also to apply the ideas you read about to the everyday decisions you face in your own life. Text discussions will spotlight such decisions as will boxed inserts such as those titled "Econ and YOU."

The Basic Insights of Economics

When people think of economics, they often think of the stock market, the unemployment rate, or media reports saying things like "the Federal Reserve has raised its target for the federal funds rate." Although economics does include these topics, its reach is much broader.

Economics is the study of how people manage resources. Decisions about how to allocate resources can be made by individuals, but also by groups of people in families, firms, governments, and other organizations. In economics, *resources* are not just physical things like cash and gold mines. They are also intangible things, such as time, ideas, technology, job experience, and even personal relationships.

Traditionally, economics has been divided into two broad fields: microeconomics and macroeconomics. **Microeconomics** is the study of how individuals and firms manage resources. **Macroeconomics** is the study of the economy as a whole, and how policy-makers manage the growth and behavior of the overall economy. Microeconomics and macroeconomics are highly related and interdependent; we need both to fully understand how economies work.

Economics starts with the idea that people compare the choices available to them and purposefully behave in the way that will best achieve their goals. As human beings, we have ambitions and we make plans to realize them. We strategize. We marshal our resources. When people make choices to achieve their goals in the most effective way possible given the resources they have, economists say they are exhibiting **rational behavior**. The assumption that people behave rationally isn't perfect. As we'll see later in the text, people can sometimes be short-sighted or swayed merely by the way choices are presented. Nevertheless, the assumption of rational behavior helps to explain a lot about the world.

economics
the study of how people, individually and collectively, manage resources

microeconomics
the study of how individuals and firms manage resources

macroeconomics
the study of the economy as a whole, and how policy-makers manage the growth and behavior of the overall economy

People use economics every day, from Wall Street to Walmart, from state capitol buildings to Bangladeshi villages. They apply economic ideas to everything from shoe shopping to baseball, from running a hospital to running for political office. What ties these topics together is a common approach to problem solving. Economists tend to approach problems by asking four questions:

1. What are the wants and constraints of those involved?
2. What are the trade-offs?
3. How will others respond?
4. Are resources being allocated in the best way possible?

rational behavior making choices to achieve goals in the most effective way possible

Underneath these questions are some important economics concepts, which we will begin to explore in this chapter. The questions and the underlying concepts are based on just a few common-sense assumptions about how people behave, yet they offer a surprising amount of insight into tough problems of all sorts. They are so important to economic problem solving that they will come up again and again in this text. In this chapter we'll take a bird's-eye view of economics, focusing on the fundamental concepts and skimming over the details. Later in the text, we'll return to each question in more depth.

Scarcity

Question 1: What are the wants and constraints of those involved?

For the most part, people make decisions that are aimed at getting the things they want. Of course, you can't always get what you want. People want a lot of things, but they are *constrained* by limited resources. Economists define **scarcity** as the condition of wanting more than we can get with available resources.

LO 1.1 Explain the economic concept of scarcity.

scarcity the condition of wanting more than we can get with available resources

Scarcity is a fact of life. You have only so much time and only so much money. You can arrange your resources in a lot of different ways—studying or watching TV, buying a car, or traveling to Las Vegas—but at any given time, you have a fixed range of possibilities. Scarcity also describes the world on a collective level: As a society, we can produce only so many things, and we have to decide how those things are divided among many people.

On the other hand, some things are not restricted by resources. Consider, for example, knowledge. The total quantity of available knowledge does not diminish as more and more people acquire it. Similarly, sunlight and air can also be considered nonscarce goods. In economic terms, however, it is safe to say that most goods are considered to be scarce.

The first question to ask in untangling a complex economic problem is, "What are the wants and constraints of those involved?" Given both rational behavior and scarcity, we can expect people to try to get what they want but to be constrained by the limited resources available to them. Suppose you *want* to spend as much time as possible this summer taking road trips around the country. You are *constrained* by the available time (three months of summer vacation) and by the amount of money you have available to pay for gas, food, and places to stay. Behaving rationally, you might choose to work double shifts for two months to earn enough to spend one month on the road. Since you are now *constrained* by having only one month to travel, you'll have to prioritize your time, activities, and expenses.

Now put yourself in Muhammad Yunus's shoes, back in 1976. He sees extremely poor but entrepreneurial Bangladeshi villagers and thinks they could improve their lives with access to loans. Why aren't banks providing financial services for these people? We can apply the first of the economists' questions to start to untangle this puzzle: *What are the wants and constraints of those involved?* In this case, those involved are traditional Bangladeshi banks and poor Bangladeshi villagers.

Let's look at both:

- The banks *want* to make profits by lending money to people who will pay them back with interest. The banks are *constrained* by having limited funds available to lend and needing to pay employees and branch expenses. We can therefore expect banks to prioritize making large loans to customers they believe are likely to pay them back. Before 1976, that meant wealthier, urban Bangladeshis, not the very poor in remote rural villages.

- The villagers *want* the chance to increase their incomes. They have energy and business ideas but are *constrained* in their ability to borrow money because banks believe they are too poor to repay loans.

Analyzing the wants and constraints of those involved gives us some valuable information about why poor Bangladeshis didn't have access to loans. Banks *wanted* to earn profits and managed their *constrained* funds to prioritize those they thought would be profitable customers. Bangladeshi villagers *wanted* to increase their incomes but couldn't follow up on business opportunities due to *constrained* start-up money.

That's good information, but we haven't yet come up with the solution that Dr. Yunus was looking for. To take the next step in solving the puzzle, we turn to another question economists often ask.

Opportunity cost and marginal decision making

Question 2: What are the trade-offs?

LO 1.2 Explain the economic concepts of opportunity cost and marginal decision making.

Every decision in life involves weighing the *trade-off* between costs and benefits. We look at our options and decide whether it is worth giving up one in order to get the other. We choose to do things only when we think the benefits will be greater than the costs. The potential *benefit* of taking an action is often easy to see: Having dinner with friends would be fun. Taking a loan from a bank would help pay emergency expenses that occur. The *costs* of a decision, on the other hand, are not always clear.

You might think it *is* clear—that the cost of a meal with friends is simply the amount of money you spend on dinner. But something is missing from that way of thinking. The true cost of something is not just the amount you have to pay for it. Rather, the cost also includes the *opportunity you must now give up for something that you might have enjoyed otherwise*. Suppose, if you hadn't gone out for dinner, your second choice would have been to spend that night watching a newly released movie. The true cost of going out for dinner includes passing up the enjoyment you would have had at the movie. Behaving rationally, you should go out to dinner only if it will be more valuable to you than the best alternative use for your time and money. This is a matter of personal preference. Because people have different alternatives and place different values on things like a dinner or a movie, they will make different decisions.

opportunity cost
the value to you of what you have to give up in order to get something; the value you could have gained by choosing the next-best alternative

Opportunity costs Economists call this true cost of your choice the **opportunity cost**. It is equal to the value to you of what you have to give up in order to get something. Put another way, opportunity cost is the value you could have gained by choosing your next-best alternative—the "opportunity" you have to pass up in order to take your first choice.

Let's return to the dinner. Say you're going with a friend and her plan B would have been staying home to catch up on homework. The opportunity cost of her dinner is different from yours. For her, the opportunity cost is the satisfaction she would have had from finally catching up on her work. If she's behaving rationally, she will join you for dinner only if she believes it will be more valuable than staying home with her assignments.

Opportunity cost helps us think more clearly about trade-offs. If someone asked you how much your dinner cost and you responded by adding up the cost of your appetizer, main course, and a drink, you would be failing to capture some of the most important and interesting aspects of the trade-offs you made. Opportunity cost helps us to see why, for example, a self-employed consultant and a factory worker earning the same amount of money may face truly different trade-offs when they dream about taking the same vacation for the same price. The self-employed consultant likely forgoes earning income in order to take the time off for a vacation. The factory worker likely gets paid vacation days. The opportunity cost for the consultant includes the value of what he or she would buy with the money earned by working instead of taking the vacation. The opportunity cost for the factory worker includes the benefit she would get from taking a different vacation. Thus the opportunity cost of a vacation for the consultant is much higher than it is for the factory worker. That difference makes it more expensive for the consultant to take a vacation than the factory worker.

Economists often express opportunity cost as a dollar value. Suppose you're offered a part-time job that pays $100 a week for four months (or $1,600 in total). Alternatively, you have the chance to take an internship for four months that offers useful career-related experience but no pay. Your time is tight, so you have to choose between the offers.

What are the opportunity costs of the choices? The opportunity cost of the unpaid internship is the $1,600 that you would have earned if you had instead chosen the paid job. The opportunity cost of the paid job is a bit trickier. It's what you would give up by not taking the internship. Part of the value of the internship is that you expect the experience to contribute to your career. It may be hard to put an exact number on the expected value to your career, but you may be able to predict whether the expected contribution of the internship is bigger or smaller than $1,600. The internship would be appealing if the expected gain to your career substantially exceeds $1,600. Otherwise, the paid job could make more financial sense.

Of course, we're simplifying a lot here. You might need the money now, rather than at a later date—which would push you toward the paid job. Also, you may be looking for gains that are not purely financial—like having interesting experiences and meeting new people. Either way, thinking about opportunity costs is a critical part of making good decisions of all kinds.

Once you start to think about opportunity costs, you see them everywhere. For an application of opportunity cost to a serious moral question, read the What Do You Think? box "The opportunity cost of a life."

The opportunity cost of a life
What Do You Think?

What Do You Think? boxes present questions that require you to combine facts and economic analysis with values and moral reasoning. There can be many "correct" answers, depending on your values and goals.

The philosopher Peter Singer writes that opportunity costs can be a matter of life or death. Imagine you are a salesperson, and on your way to a meeting on a hot summer day, you drive by a lake. Suddenly, you notice that a child who has been swimming in the lake is drowning. No one else is in sight.

You have a choice. If you stop the car and dive into the lake to save the child, you will be late for your meeting, miss out on making a sale, and lose $1,500. The *opportunity cost* of saving the child's life is $1,500.

Alternatively, if you continue on to your meeting, you earn the $1,500, but you lose the opportunity to dive into the lake and save the child's life. The *opportunity cost* of going to the meeting is one child's life.

What would you do? Most people don't hesitate. They immediately say they would stop the car, dive into the lake, and save the drowning child. After all, a child's life is worth more than $1,500.

(continued)

Now suppose you're thinking about spending $1,500 on a new MacBook. That $1,500 could instead have been used for some charitable purpose, such as immunizing a group of children in another country against yellow fever. Suppose that for every $1,500 donated, an average of one child's life ends up being saved. What is the opportunity cost of buying a MacBook? According to Peter Singer, it is the same as the opportunity cost of going straight to the meeting: a child's life.

These two situations are not exactly the same, of course, but why does the first choice (jump in the lake) seem so obvious to most people, while the second seems much less obvious?

WHAT DO YOU THINK?

1. In what ways do the two situations presented by Singer—the sales meeting and the drowning child versus the MacBook and the unvaccinated child—differ?
2. Singer argues that even something like buying a MacBook is a surprisingly serious moral decision. Do you agree? What sort of opportunity costs do you typically consider when making such a decision?
3. What might be missing from Singer's analysis of the trade-offs people face when making a decision about how to spend money?

Marginal decision making Another important principle for understanding trade-offs is the idea that rational people make decisions *at the margin*. **Marginal decision making** describes the idea that rational people compare the *additional* benefits of a choice against the *additional* costs, without considering related benefits and costs of past choices.

For example, suppose an amusement park has a $20 admission price and charges $2 per ride. If you are standing outside the park, the cost of the first ride is $22: You will have to pay the admission price and buy a ticket for the ride. Once you are inside the park, the *marginal* cost of each additional ride is $2. When deciding whether to go on the roller coaster a second or third time, you should compare only the benefit or enjoyment you will get from one more ride to the opportunity cost of that additional ride.

This may sound obvious, but in practice, many people don't make decisions on the margin. Suppose you get into the amusement park and start to feel sick shortly thereafter. If doing something else with your $2 and your time would bring you more enjoyment than another roller coaster ride while feeling sick, the rational thing to do would be to leave. The relevant trade-off is between the *additional* benefits that going on another ride would bring versus the additional costs. You cannot get back the $20 admission fee or any of the other money you've already spent on rides.

Economists call a cost that has already been incurred and cannot be recovered a **sunk cost**. Sunk costs should not have any bearing on your *marginal* decision about what to do next. But many people feel the need to go on a few more rides to psychologically justify the $20 admission.

Trade-offs play a crucial role in businesses' decisions about what goods and services to produce. Let's return to the example that started this chapter and apply the idea to a bank in Bangladesh: *What are the trade-offs involved in making a small loan?*

- For traditional banks, the opportunity cost of making small loans to the poor was the money that the bank could have earned by making loans to wealthier clients instead.
- For poor borrowers, the opportunity cost of borrowing was whatever else they would have done with the time they spent traveling to the bank and with the money they would pay in fees and interest on the loan. The benefit, of course, was whatever the loan would enable them to do that they could not have done otherwise, such as starting a small business or buying food or livestock.

Based on this analysis of trade-offs, we can see why traditional banks made few loans to poor Bangladeshis. Banks perceived the poor to be risky clients. The opportunity cost of making small

---

marginal decision making
comparison of additional benefits of a choice against the additional costs it would bring, without considering related benefits and costs of past choices

sunk cost
a cost that has already been incurred and cannot be recovered or refunded

loans to the poor seemed to outweigh the benefits—unless the banks charged very high fees. From the perspective of poor rural villagers, high fees meant that the opportunity cost of borrowing was higher than the benefits; they chose not to borrow under the terms offered by banks.

Notice that the answer to this question built off the answer to the first: We had to know the wants and constraints of each party before we could assess the trade-offs they faced. Now that we understand the motivations and the trade-offs that led to the situation Dr. Yunus observed, we can turn to a third question he might have asked himself when considering what would happen when he founded the Grameen Bank.

Incentives

Question 3: How will others respond?

You're in the mood for pizza, so you decide to go to a favorite neighborhood restaurant that has a short menu: pizza and spaghetti. When you get there, you discover that the prices have changed. Both used to cost $15, which made your decision relatively easy: which food were you in the mood for that night? Tonight you discover that pizza now costs $50, instead of $15.

LO 1.3 Explain the economic concept of incentives.

What will you do? You could leave, but you're already here, are hungry, and feel committed to stay. Unless you can easily afford $50 for a pizza or you just really hate spaghetti, you'll order spaghetti. We're sure that you can think of ways to spend $35 that are worth more to you than your preference for pizza over spaghetti. But what if the prices had changed less drastically—say, $18 for pizza? That might be a tougher call.

As the trade-offs change, so will the choices people make. When the restaurant owner considers how much to charge for each dish, she must consider *how others will respond* to changing prices. If she knows the pizza is popular, she might be tempted to try charging more to boost her profits. But as she increases the price, fewer diners will decide to order it.

If a trade-off faced by a lot of people changes, even by a small amount, the combined change in behavior by everyone involved can add up to a big shift. Asking "How will others respond?" to a trade-off that affects a lot of people gives us a complete picture of how a particular decision affects the world. The collective reaction to a changing trade-off is a central idea in economics; it will come up in almost every chapter of this book. You'll see it in questions such as

- What happens when prices change?
- What happens when the government implements a new policy?
- What happens when a company introduces a new product?

Answering any of these questions requires us to consider a large-scale reaction, rather than the behavior of just one person, company, or policy-maker.

In answering this question about trade-offs, economists commonly make two assumptions. The first is that people respond to incentives. An **incentive** is something that causes people to behave in a certain way by changing the trade-offs they face. Incentives can be positive or negative:

incentive something that causes people to behave in a certain way by changing the trade-offs they face

- A *positive* incentive (sometimes just called an *incentive*) makes people *more likely* to do something. For example, lowering the price of spaghetti creates a positive incentive for people to order it because it lowers the opportunity cost: When you pay less for spaghetti, you give up fewer other things you could have spent the money on.
- A *negative* incentive (sometimes called a *disincentive*) makes them *less likely* to do it. Charging people more for pizza is a negative incentive to buy pizza because they now have to give up more alternative purchases.

The second assumption economists make about trade-offs is that nothing happens in a vacuum. That is, you can't change just one thing in the world without eliciting a response from others. If you change your behavior—even if only in a small way—that action will change the incentives of the people around you, causing them to change their behavior in response. If you invent a new product, competitors will copy it. If you raise prices, consumers will buy less. If you tax a good or service, people will produce less of it.

Asking *how others will respond* can help prevent bad decisions by predicting the undesirable side effects of a change in prices or policies. The question can also be used to design changes that elicit positive responses. When Muhammad Yunus was setting up Grameen Bank, he had to think carefully about the incentives that both rural villagers and traditional banks faced; he considered how those incentives could be changed without incurring negative side effects.

One reason banks saw rural villagers as risky customers is that they were too poor to have collateral to offer the bank. *Collateral* is a possession, like a house or a car, pledged by a borrower to a lender. If the borrower cannot repay the loan, the lender keeps the collateral. The threat of losing the collateral increases the cost of choosing to not repay the loan; collateral gives the borrower a positive incentive to repay. When traditional banks thought about lending to poor Bangladeshis, they believed that without the threat of losing collateral, the villagers would be unlikely to repay their loans.

Yunus needed to think up a different way of creating a positive incentive for poor customers to repay their loans. His best-known solution was to require borrowers to apply for loans in five-person groups. Every person in the group would have a stake in the success of the other members. If one person didn't repay a loan, no one else in the group could borrow from the bank again.

Yunus's idea, called *group responsibility*, was simple but hugely significant. Yunus concluded that borrowers would have a strong incentive to repay their loans: They wouldn't want to ruin relationships with other members of the group—their fellow villagers, with whom they live every day and rely on for mutual support in hard times. This incentive, in turn, changed the trade-off faced by banks; they responded by being more willing to lend to the poor. By asking himself how villagers would respond to the new kind of loan and how banks in turn would respond to the villagers' response, Yunus was able to predict that his idea could be the key to spreading banking services to the poor.

Dr. Yunus's predictions proved to be correct. Seeing that poor villagers nearly always repaid their loans under Grameen's system gave other banks confidence that small borrowers could be reliable customers. Banks offering microloans, savings accounts, and other services to the very poor have spread around the world. As a result of Yunus's creativity and thoughtfulness about incentives, the poor have better access to financial services, and banks earn money from providing them. Today, other ideas have proved even more effective in providing the right incentives for small borrowers, continuing in the tradition of experimentation and innovation pioneered by Yunus and Grameen Bank.

Throughout this book, you will see many examples of how the power of incentives can be harnessed to accomplish everything from increasing a company's profits to protecting the environment. But before we get carried away with brilliant economic innovations, we have to ask ourselves one more question, the final test for any ideas that come out of our problem-solving process.

Efficiency

Question 4: *Are resources being allocated in the best way possible?*

LO 1.4 Explain the economic concept of efficiency.

efficiency
use of resources to ensure that people get what they most want and need given the available resources

Once you've considered needs, incentives, and trade-offs, it's natural to ask whether resources are being used in the best way possible. Of course, there are many ways to define "in the best way possible."

One way is to ask whether outcomes are fair or ethical. Of course, people debate what's fair or ethical, and we'll stop regularly to consider the fairness of economic outcomes too (especially in "What do you think?" boxes).

Here, we focus on a separate concept: efficiency. It's one of the building blocks of economic thinking, and it has a specific meaning that differs from the everyday usage of the word. For economists, **efficiency** is not just about maximizing productivity, it is also about ensuring that people get what they most want and need given the available resources.

Efficiency doesn't mean that outcomes are necessarily fair or ethical, but it reflects an important idea about economic outcomes. As described later in the text, when the economy is efficient, there is no way to reorganize things to make anyone better off *without someone else becoming worse off*.

A *resource* is anything that can be used to make something of value, from natural resources (such as water and trees) to human resources (such as talents and knowledge). When the economy is efficient, resources are being used to create the greatest *total* economic value to society. (We'll take a broad view for now: Something is *valuable* if someone wants it.)

Practical implications of efficiency Let's turn to a practical implication. There are millions of businesses in the world, each trying to make a profit. When consumers want a good or service, businesses have incentives to earn money by providing it. When you think you see a big, unexploited opportunity—a new product, policy, technology, or business model that could change the world or earn you millions of dollars—stop for a moment. Ask yourself: If it's such a great idea, *why isn't someone doing it?*

One possible answer is simply that nobody has thought of it before. That's possible. Perhaps you *have* seen an efficient way to allocate resources in a way that produces economic value for society. But if *you* have seen the opportunity, doesn't it seem likely that at least one of the billions of other smart, rational people in the world will have seen it too?

This leads to our final claim: *Under normal circumstances, individuals and firms will act to provide the things people want.* If a genuine profit-making opportunity exists, someone will take advantage of it, and usually sooner rather than later.

Don't get us wrong: We're not saying there is never an opportunity to do something new in the world. Great new ideas happen all the time—they drive progress. But there's a strong possibility that other people have already thought about the idea, and if they chose not to take advantage of it, that's a hint that you might be missing something. In that case, the first thing to do is backtrack to the first three economists' questions:

- Have you misjudged people's wants and constraints?
- Have you miscalculated the trade-offs they face?
- Have you misunderstood how people will respond to incentives?

If you think back through those questions and still think you're on to something, here are some more possibilities to consider. We said that *under normal circumstances*, the economy is operating efficiently and individuals or firms provide the things people want. What are some ways in which circumstances might not be normal?

- *Innovation:* Innovation is the explanation you're hoping is correct. Maybe your idea has not been used yet because it is too new. If you have come up with a truly new idea, whether it is new technology or a new business model, people cannot have taken advantage of it yet because it didn't exist before.
- *Market failure:* Market failures are an important cause of inefficiency. Sometimes people and firms fail to take advantage of opportunities because something prevents them from capturing the benefits of the opportunity or imposes additional costs on them. For instance, maybe your great new idea won't work because it would be impossible to prevent others from quickly copying it. Or perhaps your great new idea won't work because a few big companies already have the market for it sewn up. Economists call such situations *market failures*. We will discuss market failures in much greater depth later in the text.
- *Intervention:* If a powerful force—often the government—intervenes in the economy, transactions cannot take place the way they normally would. We'll see later in the text that many government economic policies intentionally or unintentionally interfere with people's ability to take advantage of profit-making opportunities.

- *Unprofitable idea:* Maybe your idea won't produce a profit. Individuals and governments have goals other than profit, of course—for example, creating great art or promoting social justice. But if your idea doesn't also generate a profit, then it is less surprising that no one has taken advantage of it.

When Muhammad Yunus asked himself the question, "Why isn't someone already lending to the poor?" he first identified a market failure involving lack of collateral. Understanding the market-failure problem enabled him to come up with the idea of group responsibility to fix it. But then he had to ask himself, "Why aren't other banks already using the group responsibility idea?"

Maybe there was another market failure Yunus hadn't spotted. Maybe some government policy prevented it. Maybe traditional banks had considered it and decided it still wouldn't generate a profit. Yunus wasn't primarily interested in making a profit, of course—he was interested in helping the poor. But if microloans weren't going to earn a profit for the banks even with group responsibility, then that would explain why no one was already doing it.

Fortunately, none of those answers were correct. This was a case in which the answer to *why isn't someone already doing it?* was that the idea was *genuinely new*. Grameen Bank was able to help very poor people in Bangladesh by lending them money, while making enough profit to expand and serve more customers. Today, over 20 million people in Bangladesh can get small loans from Grameen Bank and other organizations. Around the world, over 200 million low-income customers enjoy the same opportunity. Sometimes, something that seems like a great new idea really *is* exactly that.

✓ TEST YOURSELF

In every chapter of this book you will find a few Test Yourself quizzes. These questions test your understanding of the concepts presented in the preceding section. If you have trouble answering any of the questions, go back and review the section. Don't move forward until you understand these ideas.

- ☐ How do constraints affect decision making? **[LO 1.1]**
- ☐ What do opportunity costs represent? **[LO 1.2]**
- ☐ What is the name for something that changes the trade-offs that people face when making a decision? **[LO 1.3]**
- ☐ Give four reasons that might explain why a product isn't already in the market. **[LO 1.4]**

An Economist's Problem-Solving Toolbox

The four questions we've just discussed are some of the fundamental insights of economics. Using them to understand how the world *might* work is only half the battle. Understanding when and how to apply them is the other half. In this second part of this chapter, we will describe some tools economists use to apply these insights to real situations.

Accurately spotting the fundamental economic concepts at work in the world is sometimes less obvious than you might think. Throughout history, people have observed the world around them and drawn conclusions that have proved hilariously—or sometimes tragically—wrong. We now know that the sun doesn't revolve around the earth. Droughts are not caused by witches giving people the evil eye. Yet, intelligent people once believed these things. It's human nature to draw meaning from the patterns we observe around us, but our conclusions are not always correct.

Economic analysis requires us to combine theory with observations and to subject both to tough scrutiny before drawing conclusions. In this section we will see how to put together theories and facts to determine what causes what. We will also distinguish between the way things *are* and the way we think they *should be*. You can apply these tools to all sorts of situations, from personal life choices to business decisions and policy analysis.

Correlation and causation

A die-hard sports fan may wear a particular jersey while watching his or her team win the NBA finals or Super Bowl, and then forever insist that jersey is lucky. This is an exaggerated example of a common human tendency: When we see that two events occur together, we tend to assume that one causes the other. Economists, however, try to be particularly careful about what causes what.

To differentiate between two variables that move together and two variables that have a cause-and-effect relationship, we use two different terms. For the instance in which two variables have a consistent relationship, we say there is a **correlation** between them. Correlation can be positive or negative:

- If both variables tend to move in the same direction, we say they are *positively correlated*. For example, wearing raincoats is positively correlated with rain.
- When two variables move in opposite directions, we say they are *negatively correlated*. High temperatures are negatively correlated with people wearing down jackets.

If there is no consistent relationship between two variables, we say they are *uncorrelated*.

Correlation differs from causation. **Causation** means that one variable causes the other. As the preceding examples show, causation and correlation often go together. Weather and clothing are often correlated because weather *causes* people to make certain choices about the clothing they wear.

Correlation and causation do not *always* go together in a straightforward way, as Figure 1-1 humorously shows. Correlation and causation can be confused in three major ways: coincidence, omitted variables, and reverse causation.

Coincidence Does the result of the Super Bowl predict the performance of the stock market? A few years ago, some people thought it might. The Super Bowl pits the top team from the American Football Conference against the top team from the National Football Conference. For a long time, when a team from the AFC won, the stock market had a bad year; when a team from the NFC won, the stock market had a great year. In fact, this pattern held true nearly 80 percent of the time between 1967 and 2017.

Would it have been a good idea to base your investment strategy on the results of the Super Bowl? We think not. There is no plausible cause-and-effect relationship here. Stock market outcomes happened to be *correlated with* Super Bowl outcomes for a number of years, but there is no

LO 1.5 Distinguish between correlation and causation.

correlation a consistently observed relationship between two variables

causation a relationship between two events in which one brings about the other

---

FIGURE 1-1

Total revenue generated by bowling alleys correlates with per capita consumption of sour cream The graph shows the relationship between X and Y. Obviously, there's no connection between X and Y, but if you took these data at face value, you might think otherwise.

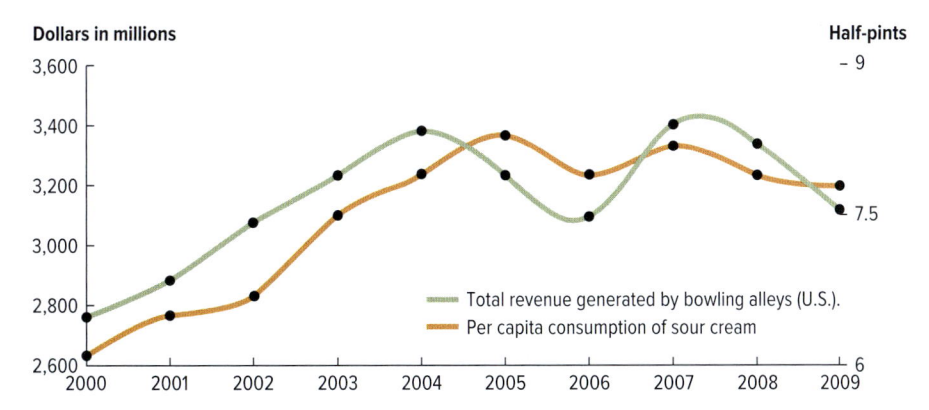

Source: www.tylervigen.com/view_correlation?id=28797

Omitted variables Consider the following statement: There is a positive correlation between the presence of firefighters and people with serious burn injuries. Does this statement mean that firefighters cause burn injuries? Of course not. We know that firefighters are not burning people; they're trying to save them. Instead, there must be some common underlying variable behind both observed outcomes—fires, in this case.

Sometimes, two events that are correlated occur together because both are caused by the same underlying factor. Each has a causal relationship with a third factor, but not with each other. The underlying factor is called an *omitted variable*—despite the fact that it is an important part of the cause-and-effect story, it has been left out of the analysis. The From Another Angle box "Does ice cream cause polio?" tells the story of an omitted variable that convinced some doctors to mistakenly campaign against a staple of summer fun: ice cream.

Does ice cream cause polio?
From Another Angle

From Another Angle boxes show you a completely different way of looking at an economic concept. We find that a little bit of weirdness goes a long way in helping us to remember things.

Polio is a disease that once crippled or killed thousands of children in the United States every year. Before the cause of polio was known, doctors noticed that polio infections seemed to be more common in children who had been eating lots of ice cream. Observing this *correlation* led some people to assume that there was a *causal* relationship between the two. Some doctors recommended that kids stop eating ice cream, and many fearful parents understandably took their advice.

We now know that ice cream is safe. Polio is caused by a virus that spreads from one person to another. The virus is transmitted through contaminated food and water—for example, dirty swimming pools or water fountains. It has nothing to do with ice cream.

The ice cream confusion was caused by an *omitted variable*: warm weather. In warm weather, children are more likely to use swimming pools and water fountains. And in warm weather, children are also more likely to eat ice cream. Polio was therefore *correlated* with eating ice cream, but it certainly wasn't *caused* by it.

Happily, in 1952 a scientist named Jonas Salk developed a vaccine that made polio a rare disease. One unintended benefit was that doctors, and parents, stopped telling kids to stay away from ice cream.

Source: Steve Lohr, "For Today's Graduate, Just One Word: Statistics," *New York Times,* August 5, 2009.

Reverse causation A third common source of confusion between correlation and causation is *reverse causation:* Did A cause B, or did B cause A? When two events always happen together, it can be hard to say which caused the other.

Let's return to the correlation between rain and raincoats. If we knew nothing about rain, we might observe that it often appears together with raincoats; we might conclude that wearing a raincoat (A) causes rain (B). In this case, we all know that the causation goes the other way, but observation alone does not tell us that.

Looking at the timing of two correlated events can sometimes provide clues. Often, if A happens before B, it hints that A causes B rather than vice versa. But grabbing a raincoat as you leave home in the morning frequently happens *before* it rains in the afternoon. The timing notwithstanding, taking your raincoat with you in the morning clearly does not *cause* rain later in the day. In this case, your *anticipation* of B causes A to happen.

An important lesson for economists and noneconomists alike is never to take observations at face value. Always make sure you can explain *why* two events are related. To do so, you need another tool in the economist's toolbox: a model.

Models

A **model** is a simplified representation of a complicated situation. In economics, models show how people, firms, and governments make decisions about managing resources and how their decisions interact. An economic model can represent a situation as basic as how people decide what car to buy or as complex as what causes a global recession.

Because models simplify complex problems, they allow us to focus our attention on the most important parts. Models rarely include every detail of a given situation, but that is a good thing. If we had to describe the entire world with perfect accuracy before solving a problem, we'd be so overwhelmed with details that we'd never get the answer. By carefully simplifying the situation to its essentials, we can get useful answers that are *approximately* right.

One of the most basic models of the economy is the **circular flow model**. The economy involves billions of transactions every day, and the circular flow model helps show how all of those transactions work together. The model slashes through complexity to show important patterns. Figure 1-2 shows the circular flow of economic transactions in a graphic format called the *circular flow diagram*.

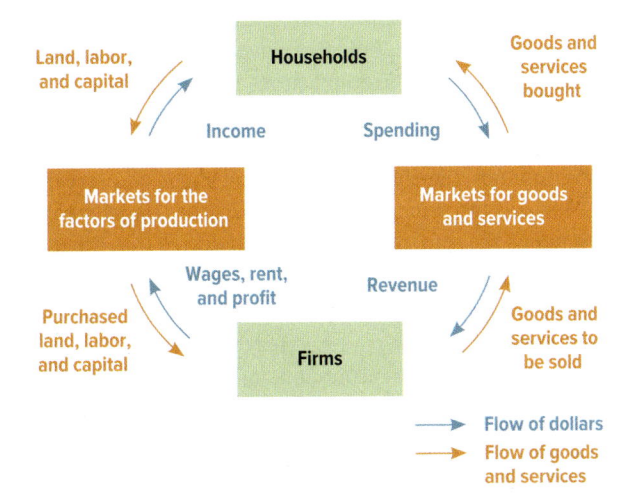

The first simplification of the circular flow model is to narrow our focus to the two most important types of actors in the economy, households and firms:

- *Households* are vital in two ways. First, they supply land and labor to firms and invest capital in firms. (Land, labor, and capital are called the *factors of production*.) Second, they buy the goods and services that firms produce.
- *Firms* too are vital but do the opposite of households: They buy or rent the land, labor, and capital supplied by households, and they produce and sell goods and services.

The circular flow model shows that firms and households are tightly connected through both production and consumption.

LO 1.6 List the characteristics of a good economic model.

model
a simplified representation of the important parts of a complicated situation

circular flow model
a simplified representation of how the economy's transactions work together

FIGURE 1-2
Circular flow diagram

In another helpful simplification, the circular flow model narrows the focus to two markets that connect households and firms:

- The *market for goods and services* is exactly what it sounds: It reflects all of the activity involved in the buying and selling of goods and services. In this market, households spend their wages from labor and their income from land and capital, and firms earn revenue from selling their goods and services.
- The second market is the *market for the factors of production*. Here, households supply land, labor, and capital, and firms hire and purchase or rent these inputs.

The model puts all of this together. The transactions we have described are part of two loops:

- One is a loop of inputs and outputs as they travel throughout the economy. The *inputs* are the land, labor, and capital firms use to produce goods. The *outputs* are the goods and services that firms produce using the factors of production.
- Another loop represents the flow of dollars. Households buy goods and services using the money they get from firms for using their factors of production. Firms get revenues from selling these goods and services—and, in turn, firms can then use the money to buy or rent factors of production.

You might be a little dizzy at this point, with everything spinning in loops. To help straighten things out, let's follow $5 from your wallet as it flows through the economy. You could spend this $5 in any number of ways. As you're walking down the street, you see a box of donuts sitting in the window of your local bakery. You head in and give the baker your $5, a transaction in the market for goods. The money represents revenue for the baker and spending by you. The donuts are an output of the bakery.

The story of your $5 is not over, though. In order to make more donuts, the baker puts that $5 toward buying inputs in the market for the factors of production. This might include paying rent for the bakery or paying wages for an assistant. The baker's spending represents income for the households that provide the labor in the bakery or rent out the space. Once the baker pays wages or rent with that $5, it has made it through a cycle in the circular flow.

As the circular flow model shows, an economic model approximates what happens in the real economy. Later in the text, we'll discuss other models that focus on specific questions—like how much gasoline prices will go up when the government raises taxes or how fast the economy is likely to grow in the next decade.

The best models lead us to clearer answers about complicated questions. What makes a good economic model? We have already said that good models can leave out details that are not crucial, and they focus on the important aspects of a situation. To be useful, a model *should* also do three things:

1. *A good model predicts cause and effect.* The circular flow model gives a useful description of the basics of the economy. Often, though, we want to go further. Many times we want a model not only to describe economic connections but also to predict how things will happen in the future. To do that, we have to get cause and effect right. If your model says that A causes B, you should be able to explain why. In the "Markets" chapter we'll learn about a central model in economics that shows that for most goods and services, the quantity people want to buy goes down as the price goes up. Why? As the cost of an item rises, but the benefit of owning it remains the same, more people will decide that the trade-off is not worth it.

2. *A good model states its assumptions clearly.* Although models are usually too simple to fit the real world perfectly, it's important that they be clear about their simplifying assumptions. Doing so helps us to know when the model will predict real events accurately and when it will not. For example, we said earlier that economists often assume that people behave rationally. We know that isn't always true, but we accept it as an assumption because it is *approximately* accurate in many situations. As long as we are clear that we are making this assumption, we will know that the model may not be accurate when people fail to behave rationally.

3. *A good model describes the real world accurately.* If a model does not describe what actually happens in the real world, something about the model is wrong. We've admitted that models are not perfectly accurate because they are intentionally simpler than the real world. But if a model predicts things that are not usually or approximately true, it is not useful. How do we tell if a model is realistic? Economists test their models by observing what happens in the real world and collecting data, which they use to verify or reject the model. In the Economics in Action box "When education pays off," take a look at a model that explains the returns that people experience when investing in a college education.

When education pays off
Economics in Action

Economics in Action boxes show how the concept you're reading about relates to the real world. Often these boxes present interesting ideas or describe situations in which people used an economic idea to solve business or policy questions.

Why go to college? Well, of course, you learn a lot of important things and can make amazing friends. Also—not to be too crass about it—a college diploma will generally lead to bigger paychecks. On average, completing college roughly doubles lifetime earnings compared to earnings without a degree. In fact, the earnings advantage from having more education has grown bigger over time.

What drives those gains to education? To answer that question, Claudia Goldin and Lawrence Katz, economists at Harvard University, pieced together a century of data on wages in the United States. Two models helped them explain the patterns over time.

The first model predicts that education boosts earnings because it allows workers to take advantage of technical innovations that increase productivity. The greater the pace of technical innovation, the bigger will be the wage gains from education. Goldin and Katz's data showed a century-long steady increase in technology (starting well before the latest mobile phones, office technologies, and self-driving cars), which helped sustain wage growth for educated workers.

But Goldin and Katz argue that the story doesn't end there. Their second model focuses on the number of people getting educated. The second model predicts that when opportunities created by new technology increase much faster than education rates, there's more competition for educated workers. To attract workers, firms offer higher wages, and wages grow even faster than predicted by the education rate alone.

So, why are the gains to education continuing at a high rate, and even growing over time? It turns out that college *completion rates* have been slowing in the United States in recent decades. Students are starting school, but many are leaving before getting degrees. Overall, nearly a third of students who started college in 2011 had not finished or were no longer enrolled six years later. One consequence is a bigger *relative gain* for those who ultimately do get diplomas—and a wider gap in earnings between those who finish college and those who don't.

Sources: Brad Hershbein and Melissa Kearney, "Major Decisions: What Graduates Earn Over Their Lifetimes," *Hamilton Project*, September 2014; Claudia Goldin and Lawrence F. Katz, "The Future of Inequality: The Other Reason Education Matters So Much," *Milken Institute Review*, Third Quarter, 2009.

Positive and normative analysis

Economics is a field of study in which people frequently confuse facts with judgments that are based on beliefs. Think about the following example:

- *Statement #1:* Income taxes reduce the number of hours that people want to work.
- *Statement #2:* Income taxes should be reduced or abolished.

LO 1.7 Distinguish between positive and normative analysis.

positive statement
a factual claim about how the world actually works

normative statement
a claim about how the world should be

A famous quote makes this point nicely: "Everyone has a right to their own opinion, but not to their own facts." If you search the internet for this quote, you'll see that it has been attributed to many people.
Source: Karen Glasbergen, used with permission.

Many people have trouble separating these two statements. Some feel that the second statement flows logically from the first. Others disagree with the second statement, so they assume the first can't possibly be true.

If you read carefully, however, you'll see that the first sentence is a statement about cause and effect. Thus, it can be proved true or false by data and evidence. A statement that makes a factual claim about how the world *actually* works is called a **positive statement**.

The second sentence, on the other hand, cannot be proved true or false. Instead, it indicates what *should be* done—but only if we share certain goals, understandings, and moral beliefs. A statement that makes a claim about how the world *should be* is called a **normative statement**.

To see how important the distinction between positive and normative statements can be, consider two claims that a physicist might make:

- *Positive statement:* A nuclear weapon with the explosive power of 10 kilotons of TNT will have a fallout radius of up to six miles.
- *Normative statement:* The United States was right to use nuclear weapons in World War II.

Although people could disagree about both of these statements, the first is a question of scientific fact; the second depends heavily on a person's ethical and political beliefs. The first statement may inform your opinion of the second, but you can still agree with one and not the other.

Earlier in this chapter, we introduced a feature called "What Do You Think?" that asks for your opinion about an important policy or life decision. From this point forward, you can use your understanding of the differences between normative and positive analysis to untangle the questions asked in these boxes and combine the two kinds of analysis to arrive at a conclusion. Begin trying your hand at this with the What Do You Think? box "The cost of college cash."

Throughout this text, remember that *you don't have to buy into a particular moral or political outlook in order for economics to be useful to you.* Our goal is to provide you with a toolbox of economic concepts that you can use

"You're certainly entitled to your opinion."

The cost of college cash
What Do You Think?

In 2014–2015, the average yearly cost of a college education ranged from $16,188 at public universities to $37,424 at private universities. Students have a number of options for paying the bill. They can take out federal loans, private loans, or a combination of the two to defer payments until later, or they can use savings or earnings to foot the bill.

Students who qualify for federal loans enjoy benefits such as limits on the interest rate they can be charged or the total payments they can be expected to make. They also have the possibility of loan forgiveness if they enter certain fields after graduation.

Lending to students is a controversial topic. Some people argue for more controls on private lending institutions, such as interest-rate caps and greater protection for students who default. They reason that lending programs should support students who would not otherwise be able to afford college. Furthermore, they argue, graduating with a lot of debt discourages students from going into lower-paid public service jobs.

Other people maintain that the existing lending system is fine. Getting a college degree, they argue, increases a person's future earning power so much that graduates should be able to handle the debt, even at high interest rates. They worry that overregulation will discourage private lenders from offering student loans, defeating the purpose of giving students better access to financial assistance.

WHAT DO YOU THINK?

Use the four basic questions economists ask to break down the problem. Remember that your answer can draw on both positive analysis (what *will* happen if a certain policy is followed) and normative analysis (what *should* be done, given your values and goals). You should be able to say which parts of your answers fall into each category.

1. What motivations and constraints apply to students who are considering different schools and loan options? What motivations and constraints apply to private lenders?
2. What opportunity costs do students face when deciding how to pay for college? Should they avoid loans by skipping college altogether or by working their way through college?
3. How would prospective students respond to government limits on the interest rate on student loans? How would private banks that offer student loans respond?
4. Why do you think the federal government has not yet implemented interest-rate caps on private student loans? Do you anticipate any unintended side-effects of that policy?
5. Consider your arguments in response to questions 1 through 4. Which parts were based on normative statements and which on positive statements?

Sources: "Trends in college pricing," *National Center for Education Statistics,* http://nces.ed.gov/fastfacts/display.asp?id=76; "How much student debt is too much?" http://roomfordebate.blogs.nytimes.com/2009/06/14/how-much-student-debt-is-too-much/?scp=1&sq=student%20loans&st=cse.

to engage in positive analysis. We will also highlight important decisions you may face that will require you to engage in normative thinking, informed by economic analysis. You will find that economics can help you to make better decisions and identify the most effective policies, regardless of your goals and beliefs.

✓ TEST YOURSELF

- ☐ What does it mean when two variables are positively correlated? **[LO 1.5]**
- ☐ What are the characteristics of a good economic model? **[LO 1.6]**
- ☐ What is the difference between a positive statement and a normative statement? **[LO 1.7]**

Conclusion

Economists approach problems differently from many other people. A basic principle of human behavior underlies economics—the idea that people typically make choices to achieve their goals in the most effective way possible, subject to the constraints they face.

In this chapter we have introduced the basic concepts economists use, as well as four questions they ask to break down problems. Throughout this book, you will see these concepts and questions over and over again:

1. Scarcity: *What are the wants and constraints of those involved?*
2. Opportunity cost: *What are the trade-offs?*
3. Incentives: *How will others respond?*
4. Efficiency: *Are resources being allocated in the best way possible?*

In later chapters, as we progress to more complicated problems, try using these four questions to break down problems into manageable pieces. Then you can tackle those smaller pieces using the four fundamental concepts presented in this chapter.

Key Terms

economics, p. 4
microeconomics, p. 4
macroeconomics, p. 4
rational behavior, p. 4
scarcity, p. 5
opportunity cost, p. 6
marginal decision making, p. 8
sunk costs, p. 8
incentive, p. 9
efficiency, p. 10
correlation, p. 13
causation, p. 13
model, p. 15
circular flow model, p. 15
positive statement, p. 18
normative statement, p. 18

Summary

LO 1.1 Explain the economic concept of scarcity.

Economists usually assume that people behave rationally and live within a condition of scarcity. Answering the question *What are the wants and constraints of those involved?* tells you what to expect from each player in the situation you are analyzing. Given rational behavior and scarcity, you can expect people to work to get what they want (their motivations) using the limited resources at their disposal (their constraints).

LO 1.2 Explain the economic concepts of opportunity cost and marginal decision making.

Trade-offs arise when you must give up something to get something else. Answering *What are the trade-offs?* will tell you about the costs and benefits associated with a decision. The full cost of doing something is its *opportunity cost*—the value to you of what you have to give up in order to get something, or the value you could have gained by choosing the next-best alternative.

Economists assume that rational people make decisions "at the margin," by comparing any additional benefits of a choice to the extra costs it brings. If people are behaving rationally when they face trade-offs, they will always choose to do something if the marginal benefit is greater than the opportunity cost. They will never do it if the opportunity cost is greater than the marginal benefit.

LO 1.3 Explain the economic concept of incentives.

The collective reaction to changing trade-offs is a central idea in economics. Asking *How will others respond?* will give you a complete picture of how a particular decision affects the world. You can assume that any action will bring a response because people react to changes in their incentives.

LO 1.4 Explain the economic concept of efficiency.

In economics, efficiency is the use of resources to ensure that people get what they most want and need given the available resources. Under normal circumstances, markets are efficient.

So, when you see what seems to be unexploited opportunity, you should ask: If it's such a great idea, *why isn't someone already doing it?* Markets usually allocate resources efficiently. When they don't, other explanations might be in play: a market failure may have occurred; government may have intervened in the economy; there may be goals other than profit involved; or there may be a genuine opportunity for innovation.

LO 1.5 Distinguish between correlation and causation.

When there is a consistently observed relationship between two variables, we say they are *correlated*. This is different from a *causal* relationship, in which one variable brings about the other. Three common ways in which correlation and causation are confused are coincidence, omitted variables, and reverse causation.

LO 1.6 List the characteristics of a good economic model.

A model is a simplified representation of the important parts of a complicated situation. In economics, models usually show how people, firms, and governments make decisions about managing resources and how their decisions interact. The *circular flow model* is a representation of how the transactions of households and firms flow through the economy.

A good economic model should predict cause and effect, describe the world accurately, and state its assumptions clearly. Economists test their models by observing what happens in the world and collecting data that can be used to support or reject their models.

LO 1.7 Distinguish between positive and normative analysis.

A statement that makes a factual claim about how the world actually works is called a *positive* statement. A statement that makes a claim about how the world should be is called a *normative* statement. Economics is a field in which people frequently confuse positive statements with normative statements. You do not have to adopt a particular moral or political point of view to use economic concepts and models.

Review Questions

1. Suppose you are shopping for new clothes to wear to job interviews, but you're on a tight budget. In this situation, what are your wants and constraints? What does it mean to behave rationally in the face of scarcity? **[LO 1.1]**

2. You are a student with a demanding schedule of classes. You also work part time and your supervisor allows you to determine your schedule. In this situation, what is your scarce resource? How do you decide how many hours to work? **[LO 1.1]**

3. Think about the definition of scarcity that you learned in this chapter. Name three ways that you confront scarcity in your own life. **[LO 1.1]**

4. When shopping for your interview clothes, what are some trade-offs you face? What is the opportunity cost of buying new clothes? What are the benefits? How do you balance the two? **[LO 1.2]**

5. You have an 8:30 class this morning, but you are feeling extremely tired. How do you decide whether to get some extra sleep or go to class? **[LO 1.2]**

6. It's Friday night. You already have a ticket to a concert, which cost you $30. A friend invites you to go out for a game of paintball instead. Admission would cost you $25, and you think you'd get $25 worth of enjoyment out of it. Your concert ticket is nonrefundable. What is your opportunity cost (in dollars) of playing paintball? **[LO 1.2]**

7. Suppose you have two job offers and are considering the trade-offs between them. Job A pays $45,000 per year; it includes health insurance and two weeks of paid vacation. Job B pays $30,000 per year; it includes four weeks of paid vacation but no health insurance. **[LO 1.2]**
   a. List the benefits of Job A and the benefits of Job B.
   b. List the opportunity cost of Job A and the opportunity cost of Job B.

8. Your former neighbors gave you their lawnmower when they moved. You are thinking of using this gift to mow lawns in your neighborhood this summer for extra cash. As you think about what to charge your neighbors and whether this idea is worth your effort, what opportunity costs do you need to consider? **[LO 1.2]**

9. Think of a few examples of incentives in your daily life. How do you respond to those incentives? **[LO 1.3]**

10. You supervise a team of salespeople. Your employees already receive a company discount. Suggest a positive incentive and a negative incentive you could use to improve their productivity. **[LO 1.3]**

11. Your boss decides to pair workers in teams and offer bonuses to the most productive team. Why might your boss offer team bonuses instead of individual bonuses? **[LO 1.3]**

12. Think of a public policy—a local or national law, tax, or public service—that offers an incentive for a particular behavior. Explain what the incentive is, who is offering it, and what they are trying to encourage or discourage. Does the incentive work? **[LO 1.3]**

13. Why do individuals or firms usually provide the goods and services people want? **[LO 1.4]**

14. You may have seen TV advertisements for products or programs that claim to teach a sure-fire way to make millions on the stock market. Apply the *Why isn't someone already doing it?* test to this situation. Do you believe the ads? Why or why not? **[LO 1.4]**

15. Describe an innovation in technology, business, or culture that had a major economic impact in your lifetime. **[LO 1.4]**

16. Why do people confuse correlation with causation? **[LO 1.5]**

17. Name two things that are positively correlated and two things that are negatively correlated. **[LO 1.5]**

18. Why is it important for a good economic model to predict cause and effect? **[LO 1.6]**

19. Why is it important for a good economic model to make clear assumptions? **[LO 1.6]**

20. What is the difference between disagreeing about a positive statement and disagreeing about a normative statement? **[LO 1.7]**

21. Would a good economic model be more likely to address a positive statement or a normative statement? Why? **[LO 1.7]**

22. Write a positive statement and a normative statement about your favorite hobby. **[LO 1.7]**

Problems and Applications

1. Think about how and why goods and resources are scarce. Goods and resources can be scarce for reasons that are inherent to their nature at all times, that are temporary or seasonal, or that are artificially created. Separate the goods listed below into two groups; indicate which (if any) are artificially scarce (AS) and which (if any) are inherently scarce (IS). **[LO 1.1]**
   a. Air of any quality _____
   b. Land _____
   c. Patented goods _____
   d. Original Picasso paintings _____

2. You are looking for a new apartment in Manhattan. Your income is $4,000 per month, and you know that you should not spend more than 25 percent of your income on rent. You have come across the listings for one-bedroom apartments shown in Table 1P-1. You are indifferent about location, and transportation costs are the same to each neighborhood. [LO 1.1]

TABLE 1P-1

Location	Monthly Rent
Chelsea	$1,200
Battery Park	2,200
Delancey	950
Midtown	1,500

   a. Which apartments fall within your budget?
   b. Suppose that you adhere to the 25 percent guideline but also receive a $1,000 cost-of-living supplement because you are living and working in Manhattan. Which apartments fall within your budget now?

3. Suppose the price of a sweater is $26. Jaylen's benefit from purchasing each additional sweater is given in Table 1P-2. He gets the most benefit from the first sweater and less benefit from each additional sweater. If Jaylen is behaving rationally, how many sweaters will he purchase? [LO 1.2]

TABLE 1P-2

	Marginal benefit ($)
1st sweater	60
2nd sweater	45
3rd sweater	40
4th sweater	33
5th sweater	22
6th sweater	18

4. Sweaters sell for $15 at the crafts fair. Allie knits sweaters; her marginal costs are given in Table 1P-3. Allie's costs increase with each additional sweater. If Allie is behaving rationally, how many sweaters will she sell? [LO 1.2]

TABLE 1P-3

	Marginal cost ($)
1st sweater	5
2nd sweater	8
3rd sweater	12
4th sweater	18
5th sweater	25
6th sweater	32

5. Last year, you estimated you would earn $5 million in sales revenues from developing a new product. So far, you have spent $3 million developing the product, but it is not yet complete. Meanwhile, this year you have new sales projections that show expected revenues from the new product will actually be only $4 million. How much should you be willing to spend to complete the product development? [LO 1.2]
   a. $0.
   b. Up to $1 million.
   c. Up to $4 million.
   d. Whatever it takes.

6. Consider the following examples. For each one, say whether the incentive is positive or negative. [LO 1.3]
   a. Bosses who offer time-and-a-half for working on national holidays.
   b. Mandatory minimum sentencing for drug offenses.
   c. Fines for littering.
   d. Parents who offer their children extra allowance money for good grades.

7. Consider the events that change prices as described in Table 1P-4. For each one, say whether the opportunity cost of consuming the affected good increases or decreases. [LO 1.3]

TABLE 1P-4

		Affected good
a.	A local movie theater offers a student discount.	Movie tickets
b.	A tax on soft drinks passes in your state.	Soft drinks
c.	Subsidies on corn are cut in half.	Corn subsidies
d.	Your student health center begins offering flu shots for free.	Flu shots

8. Your best friend has an idea for a drive-through bar. Indicate the best explanation for why others have not taken advantage of her idea: true innovation, market failure, government intervention, or unprofitability. [LO 1.4]

9. Your best friend has an idea for a long-distance car service to drive people across the country. Indicate the best explanation for why others have not taken advantage of her idea: true innovation, market failure, intervention, or unprofitability. [LO 1.4]

10. Determine whether each of the following questionable statements is best explained by coincidence, an omitted variable, or reverse causation. [LO 1.5]
    a. In cities that have more police, crime rates are higher.
    b. Many retired people live in states where everyone uses air conditioning during the summer.
    c. More people come down with the flu during the Winter Olympics than during the Summer Olympics.
    d. For the last five years, Punxsutawney Phil has seen his shadow on Groundhog Day, and spring has come late.

11. For each of the pairs below, determine whether they are positively correlated, negatively correlated, or uncorrelated. [LO 1.5]
    a. Time spent studying and test scores.
    b. Vaccination and illness.
    c. Soft drink preference and music preference.
    d. Income and education.

12. Each statement below is part of an economic model. Indicate whether the statement is a prediction of cause and effect or an assumption. [LO 1.6]
    a. People behave rationally.
    b. If the price of a good falls, people will consume more of that good.
    c. Mass starvation will occur as population outgrows the food supply.
    d. Firms want to maximize profits.

13. From the list below, select the characteristics that describe a good economic model. [LO 1.6]
    a. Includes every detail of a given situation.
    b. Predicts that A causes B.
    c. Makes approximately accurate assumptions.
    d. Fits the real world perfectly.
    e. Predicts things that are usually true.

14. Determine whether each of the following statements is positive or normative. (Remember that a positive statement isn't necessarily *correct;* it just makes a factual claim rather than a moral judgment.) [LO 1.7]
    a. People who pay their bills on time are less likely than others to get into debt.
    b. Hard work is a virtue.
    c. Everyone should pay his or her bills on time.
    d. China has a bigger population than any other country in the world.
    e. China's One-Child Policy (which limits families to one child each) helped to spur the country's rapid economic growth.
    f. Lower taxes are good for the country.

15. You just received your midterm exam results and your professor wrote the following note: "You received a 70 on this exam, the average score. If you want to improve your grade, you should study more." Evaluate your professor's note. [LO 1.7]
    a. Is the first sentence positive or normative?
    b. Is the second sentence positive or normative?

Chapter 2

Specialization and Exchange

The Origins of a T-Shirt

How can we get the most out of available resources? It's one of the most basic economic questions. (Remember the efficiency question in Chapter 1.) Factory managers ask it when looking for ways to increase production. National leaders ask it as they design economic policy. Activists ask it when they look for ways to reduce poverty or conserve the environment. And, in a different way, it's a question we all ask ourselves when thinking about what to do in life and how to make sure that we're taking full advantage of our talents.

To get a handle on this question, we start by thinking about resources at the highest level: the logic of international trade and the specialization of production between countries. By the end of the chapter, we hope that you'll see how the same ideas apply to decisions at any scale, right down to whether it makes more sense to fix your own computer or pay a specialist to do it for you.

We'll start with what seems to be a simple question: Where did your T-shirt come from? Look at the tag. We're betting it was made in a place you've never been to, and maybe never thought of visiting. Bangladesh? Honduras? Malaysia? Sri Lanka?

That "made in" label tells only part of the story. Chances are that your shirt's history spans other parts of the globe. Consider a standard T-shirt: The cotton might have been grown in Mali and then shipped to Pakistan, where it was spun into yarn. The yarn might have been sent to Bangladesh, where it was woven into cloth, cut into pieces, and assembled into a shirt. That shirt might then have traveled all the way to the United States, where it was shipped to a store near you. A couple of

©igor kisselev/Alamy

years from now, when you are cleaning out your closet, you may donate the shirt to a charity, which may ship it to a second-hand clothing vendor in Mali—right back where your shirt's travels began.

Of course, this is not only the story of shirts. It is remarkably similar to the story of shoes, computers, phones, and cars, among many other manufactured goods. Today, the products and services most of us take for granted come to us through an incredibly complex global network of farms, mines, factories, traders, and stores. Why is the production of even a simple T-shirt spread across the world? Why is the cotton grown in Mali and the sewing done in Bangladesh, rather than vice versa? Why isn't the whole shirt made in the United States, so that it doesn't have to travel so far to reach you?

LEARNING OBJECTIVES

LO 2.1 Construct a production possibilities graph, and describe what causes shifts in production possibilities curves.

LO 2.2 Define absolute and comparative advantage.

LO 2.3 Explain why people specialize.

LO 2.4 Explain how the gains from trade follow from comparative advantage.

This chapter addresses fundamental economic questions about who produces which goods and why. The fact that millions of people and firms around the globe coordinate their activities to provide consumers with the right combination of goods and services seems like magic.

This feat of coordination doesn't happen by chance, nor does a superplanner tell everyone where to go and what to do. Instead, the global production line is a natural outcome of people everywhere acting in their own self-interest to improve their own lives. Economists call this coordination mechanism the *invisible hand*, an idea that was first suggested by the eighteenth-century economic thinker Adam Smith.

To get some insight into the *who* and *why* of production, consider how the story of shirts has changed over the last few centuries. For most of the 1800s, Americans wore shirts made in the United States. Today, however, most shirts are made in Bangladesh, China, and other countries where factory wages are low. Have American workers become worse at making shirts over the last two centuries? Definitely not. In fact, as we'll see in this chapter, it doesn't even mean that Bangladeshi workers are better than American workers at making shirts. Instead, each good tends to be produced by the country, company, or person with the lowest opportunity cost for producing that good.

Countries and firms *specialize* in making goods for which they have the lowest opportunity cost. They then trade with one another to get the combination of goods they want to consume. Although the resulting *gains from trade* can be shared such that everyone ends up better off, finding the right policies to help workers and industries affected by trade can be difficult in practice.

The concepts in this chapter apply not just to the wealth of nations and international trade. They also illuminate the daily choices most people face: Who should cook which dishes at Thanksgiving dinner? Should you hire a plumber or fix the pipes yourself? Should you become a rock star or an economist? The concepts these questions raise can be subtle and are sometimes misunderstood. We hope this chapter will provide insights that will help you become a better resource manager in all areas of your life.

Production Possibilities

In Chapter 1, "Economics and Life," we talked about economic models. Good models help us understand complex situations through simplifying assumptions that allow us to zero in on the important aspects. The story of why Bangladesh now produces shirts for Americans that Americans themselves were producing 200 years ago is a complex one, as you'd expect. But by simplifying it into a model, we can reach useful insights.

Let's assume the United States and Bangladesh produce only two things—shirts and, say, bushels of wheat. (In reality, of course, they produce many things, but we're trying not to get bogged down in details right now.) The model uses "wheat" to stand in for "stuff other than shirts," allowing us to focus on what we're really interested in—shirts.

Using this model we'll perform a thought experiment about production using a tool called the *production possibilities frontier*. This tool is used in other contexts as well, many of which have no connection to international trade. Here we use it to show what has changed over the last couple of centuries to explain why Americans now buy shirts from Bangladesh.

LO 2.1 Construct a production possibilities graph, and describe what causes shifts in production possibilities curves.

Drawing the production possibilities frontier

Let's step back in time to the United States in 1800. In our simple model, there are 2 million American workers, and they have two choices of where to work: shirt factories or wheat farms. In shirt factories, each worker produces 1 shirt per day. On wheat farms, each worker produces 2 bushels of wheat per day.

What would happen if everyone worked on a wheat farm? The United States would produce 4 million bushels of wheat per day (2 bushels of wheat per worker × 2 million workers). This is one "production possibility." Alternatively, what would happen if everyone went to work in a shirt factory? The United States would produce 2 million shirts per day (1 shirt per worker × 2 million workers). Those production possibilities are represented as entries A and E (the top and bottom rows) in panel A of Figure 2-1.

Of course, the United States wouldn't want just shirts or just wheat—and there is no reason that all workers have to produce the same thing. There are many different combinations of shirts and wheat that American workers could produce. Some of these are shown as rows B, C, and D in panel A of Figure 2-1. For example, if one-quarter of the workers go to the shirt factory, they can make 500,000 (0.5 million) shirts (1 shirt per worker × 500,000 workers); the remaining workers can produce 3 million bushels of wheat (2 bushels per worker × 1.5 million workers). This production possibility is represented by row B. Or maybe 1 million workers would make shirts (1 million shirts) and 1 million would produce wheat (2 million bushels). That's row C.

For a graphic look at the production possibilities, we can plot them as points on a graph, as shown in panel B of Figure 2-1. If we fill in enough points, we create the solid green line shown in Figure 2-2. This is the **production possibilities frontier (PPF)**. It is a line or curve that shows all the possible combinations of outputs that can be produced using all available resources. In this case, the frontier plots all combinations of shirts and wheat that can be produced using all available workers in the United States. Points inside the frontier (such as point T) are achievable but don't make full use of all available resources.

The production possibilities frontier helps us answer the first of the economists' questions discussed in Chapter 1, "Economics and Life": *What are the wants and constraints of those involved?* People in the United States *want* to consume shirts and wheat (and other things, of course; remember, we're simplifying). The production possibilities frontier gives us a way to represent the *constraints* on production. The United States cannot produce combinations of shirts

production possibilities frontier (PPF) a line or curve that shows all the possible combinations of two outputs that can be produced using all available resources

FIGURE 2-1
Possible production combinations

(A)

Production possibilities	Bushels of wheat (millions)	Shirts (millions)
A	4	0
B	3	0.5
C	2	1.0
D	1	1.5
E	0	2.0

(B)

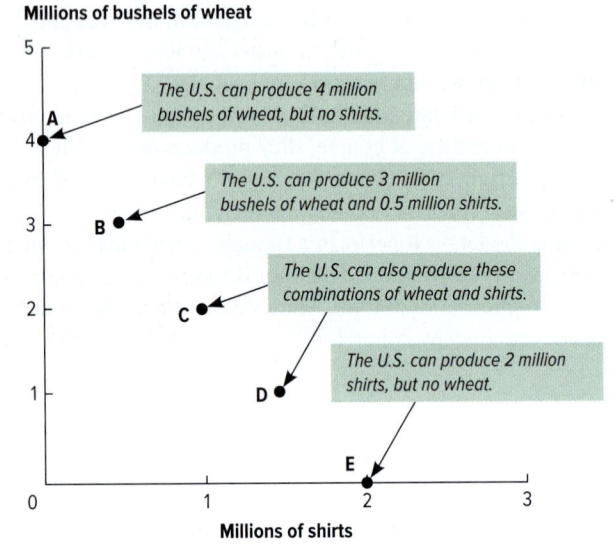

The U.S. can produce 4 million bushels of wheat, but no shirts. (A)

The U.S. can produce 3 million bushels of wheat and 0.5 million shirts. (B)

The U.S. can also produce these combinations of wheat and shirts. (C)

The U.S. can produce 2 million shirts, but no wheat. (E)

The United States can produce the maximum number of shirts or the maximum amount of wheat by devoting all its resources to one good or the other. But by allocating some resources to the production of each good, the United States can also produce many different combinations of wheat and shirts.

FIGURE 2-2
Production possibilities frontier

Attainable points require 2 million or fewer workers.

Unattainable points can't be reached because there aren't enough workers.

Production possibilities frontier (PPF)

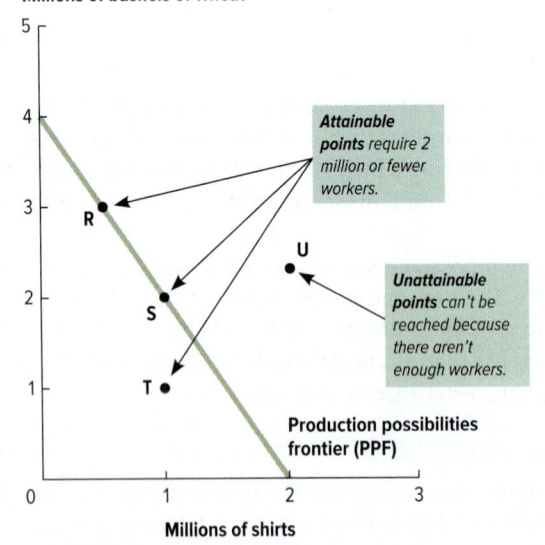

Points on or below the production possibilities frontier, such as R, S, and T, represent combinations of goods that the United States can produce with available resources. Points outside the frontier, such as U, are unattainable because there aren't enough resources.

and wheat that lie outside the frontier—such as point U in Figure 2-2. There just aren't enough workers or hours in the day to produce at point U, no matter how workers are allocated between shirts and wheat.

The production possibilities frontier also addresses the second economists' question: *What are the trade-offs?* Each worker can make *either* 1 shirt *or* 2 bushels of wheat per day. In other words, there is a trade-off between the quantity of wheat produced and the quantity of shirts produced. If we want an extra shirt, one worker has to stop producing bushels of wheat for a day. Therefore, the opportunity cost of 1 shirt is 2 bushels of wheat. Each bushel of wheat takes one worker half a day, so the opportunity cost of a bushel of wheat is half a shirt.

This opportunity cost is represented graphically by the *slope* of the production possibilities frontier. Moving up the frontier means getting more wheat at the cost of fewer shirts. Moving down the frontier means less wheat and more shirts. Looking at Figure 2-2, you'll notice that the slope of the line is −2. This is the same as saying that the opportunity cost of 1 shirt is always 2 bushels of wheat.

For a refresher on calculating and interpreting slopes, see Appendix A, "Math Essentials: Understanding Graphs and Slope," which follows this chapter.

Production possibilities frontiers when opportunity costs differ   So far, we've made the assumption that all workers are able to make the same amount of each good. In reality, some workers will probably be nimble-fingered and great at making shirts; others will be more naturally gifted at farming. What happens if we adjust our simple model to reflect this reality?

Let's start off with all workers producing wheat and nobody making shirts. If we reallocate the workers who are best at making shirts, we can get a lot of shirts without giving up too much wheat. In other words, the opportunity cost of making the first few shirts is quite low.

Now imagine almost all workers are making shirts, so that only the best farmers are left producing wheat. If we reallocate most of the remaining workers to shirt making, we give up a lot of wheat to get only a few extra shirts. The opportunity cost of getting those last few shirts is very high.

We can add a little more nuance to the model, to include land and machinery as resources also needed for production. We would find that the same pattern holds: As more of each resource is allocated to production, the opportunity cost of producing an additional unit of a good typically increases. This happens because we expect producers to always produce as efficiently as they can, which means, all else equal, using the resources with the lowest opportunity cost.

Let's start with everyone producing wheat. With wheat production pushed to the maximum, some farmers probably have to work on land that isn't well-suited to producing wheat. It could be that the land is swampy, or the soil has been overfarmed and depleted of nutrients. When farmers who had been working on this poor land switch over to making shirts, the economy will lose only a little wheat and gain many shirts in return. In contrast, if only a small amount of wheat is being grown using only the best, most fertile land, reallocating the last few farmers will cause a relatively large decrease in wheat production for each additional shirt.

Returning to the simplest model where workers are the only input to production, we can translate this increasing opportunity cost into the production possibilities frontier. Doing so, we get a curve that bows out (a concave curve) instead of a straight line, as shown in Figure 2-3. Panel A shows what happens if we have just three types of workers:

- For every bushel of wheat, some can make 1 shirt; they're the workers between points C_1 and C_2.
- For every bushel of wheat, some can make only $\frac{1}{2}$ of a shirt (between points C_2 and C_3).
- For every bushel of wheat, some can make only $\frac{1}{4}$ of a shirt (between points C_3 and C_4).

In other words, as we go down the curve, we move from those who are better at making shirts to those who are better at producing wheat. As we do so, the opportunity cost of making shirts in terms of producing wheat increases. As that happens, the slope of the curve gets steeper (−1 between C_1 and C_2, −2 between C_2 and C_3, and −4 between C_3 and C_4).

FIGURE 2-3
Bowed-out (concave) production possibilities frontier

(A) Constructing the PPF

Millions of bushels of wheat

1. Giving up 1 million bushels of wheat results in a gain of 1 million shirts. Slope = −1
2. Giving up 1 million bushels of wheat gains only 1/2 million shirts. Slope = −2
3. Giving up 1 million bushels of wheat gains only 1/4 million shirts. Slope = −4

Millions of T-shirts

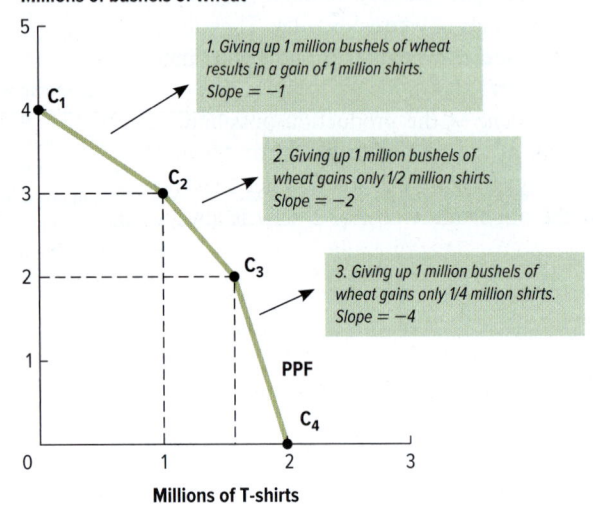

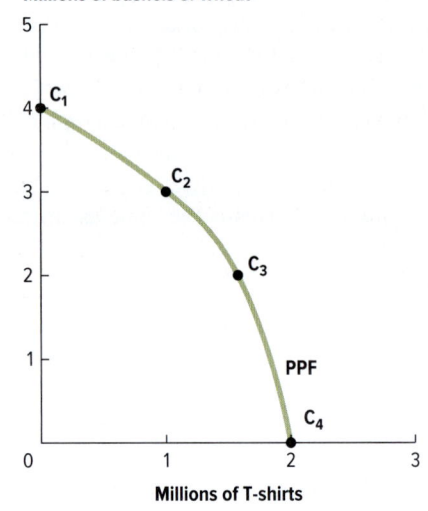

At point C₁, all workers produce wheat, and switching the best sewers to making shirts will result in a big gain in the quantity of shirts. As more and better farmers switch to making shirts, however, the gain in shirts produced decreases relative to the loss in the quantity of wheat. As a result the slope of the PPF is steeper from C₂ to C₃, and again from C₃ to C₄.

(B) The PPF

Millions of bushels of wheat

Millions of T-shirts

In reality, each worker has slightly different skills and therefore a slightly different opportunity cost of making shirts in terms of wheat. As a result, we get a smoothly curved production possibilities frontier.

In reality there aren't just three types of workers—each of the 2 million workers will have slightly different skills. The many possibilities will result in a curve that looks smooth, as in panel B of Figure 2-3. At each point of the curved production possibilities frontier, the slope represents the opportunity cost of getting more wheat or more shirts, based on the skills of the next worker who could switch.

Choosing among production possibilities

What can the production possibilities frontier tell us about what combination of goods an economy will choose to produce? Earlier, we noted that economies can produce at points inside the frontier, as well as points on it. However, choosing a production point *inside* the frontier means a country could get more wheat, more shirts, or both, just by using all available workers. For instance, in Figure 2-4, the United States can get more wheat without giving up any shirts, by moving from point B₁ to point B₂. It can do the same by moving from point B₂ to B₃.

But once at the frontier, the United States will have to give up some of one good to get more of the other. Points like B₃ that lie *on* the frontier are called **efficient** because they squeeze the most output possible from all available resources. Points *within* (inside) the frontier are *inefficient* because they do not use all available resources.

In the real world, economies aren't always efficient. A variety of problems can cause some workers to be unemployed or other resources to be left idle. We'll return to these issues in detail in future chapters. For now, we'll assume that production is always efficient. People and firms usually try to squeeze as much value as they can out of the resources available to them, so efficiency is a reasonable starting assumption.

efficient points combinations of production possibilities that squeeze the most output possible from all available resources

FIGURE 2-4
Choosing an efficient production combination

Millions of bushels of wheat

1. Producing at B₁ requires only 1.5 million workers...

2. ...so the U.S. can produce more wheat without giving up any shirts by moving toward the frontier.

Millions of T-shirts

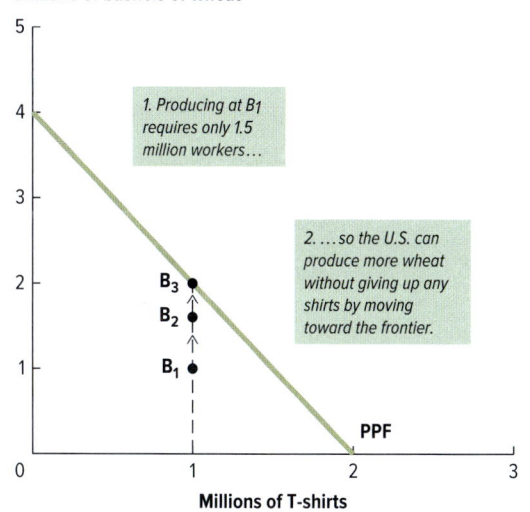

The United States needs only 1.5 million workers to reach point B₁. If the country employs more workers, it can reach point B₂ and get more wheat without giving up any shirts. The country can keep employing more workers until it reaches point B₃ (or any other point on the frontier) and there are no more workers left. Once the frontier is reached, getting more of one good requires giving up some of the other.

FIGURE 2-5
Choosing between efficient combinations

Millions of bushels of wheat

1. On the frontier producing more shirts...

2. ...means producing less wheat.

Millions of T-shirts

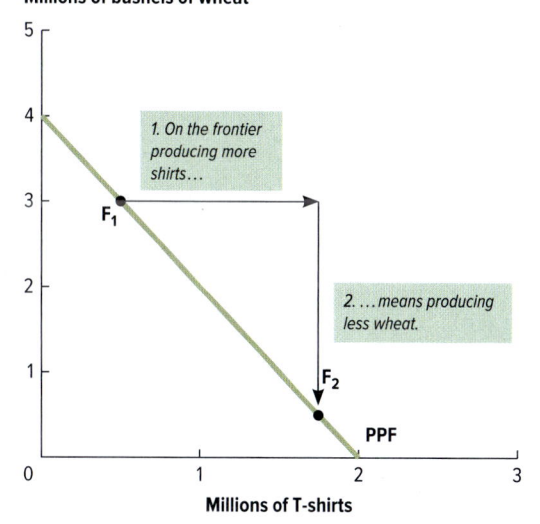

At all points on the production possibilities frontier, the United States employs the entire workforce. Because the country uses all its resources fully at each point, choosing between points on the frontier is a matter of preference when there is no trade with other countries. The United States may choose to produce more wheat and fewer shirts (point F_1) or more shirts and less wheat (point F_2), depending on what its consumers want.

Based on the assumption of efficiency, we can predict that an economy will choose to produce at a point *on* the frontier rather than inside it. What the production possibilities frontier cannot tell us is *which* point on the frontier that will be. Will it be F_1 in Figure 2-5, for example? Or will the United States choose to move down the curve to F_2, producing more shirts at the expense of less wheat? We can't say whether point F_1 or F_2 is better without knowing more about the situation. If the U.S. economy is completely self-sufficient, the decision depends on what combination of shirts and wheat people in the United States want to consume. If trade with other countries is possible, it also depends on consumers and production possibilities in those countries, as we'll see later in the chapter.

Shifting the production possibilities frontier

Thus far, we've built a simple model that tells us what combinations of T-shirts and wheat the United States could produce in 1800. However, a lot of things have changed since 1800, including incredible improvements in technology that improve production possibilities. The production possibilities frontier is a useful tool for illustrating this change and understanding how it affects the constraints and trade-offs the country faces. Two main factors drive the change in U.S. production possibilities: the number of workers and changes in technology.

First, there are more workers. The U.S. population now is about 60 times larger than it was in 1800. Having more workers means more people available to produce shirts and wheat. Graphically, we can represent this change by shifting the entire frontier outward. Panel A of Figure 2-6 shows what happens to the frontier when the U.S. population doubles, with each worker still able to produce 1 shirt or 2 bushels of wheat per day.

FIGURE 2-6
Shifting the production possibilities frontier

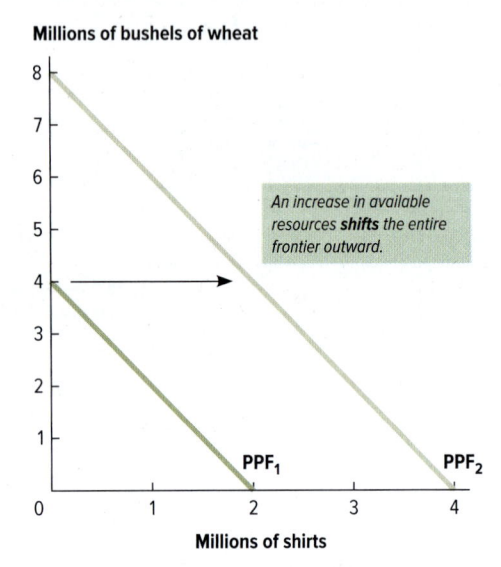

(A) Change in resources: Population growth

Millions of bushels of wheat

An increase in available resources shifts the entire frontier outward.

PPF₁ ... PPF₂

Millions of shirts

Production possibilities expand when resources increase. If the working population grows, the country can make more of everything by producing at the same rate as before. *This causes the frontier to shift outward.* If the population doubled, so would the maximum possible quantities of shirts and wheat.

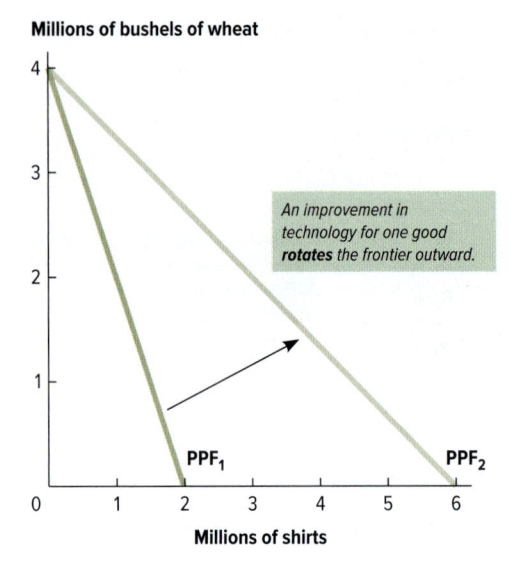

(B) Change in technology: Invention of the power loom

Millions of bushels of wheat

An improvement in technology for one good rotates the frontier outward.

PPF₁ ... PPF₂

Millions of shirts

Production possibilities expand when technology improves. If the textile industry adopts the power loom, workers can make more shirts in the same amount of time. *This causes the frontier to rotate outward.* The rate of wheat production remains constant while the rate of shirt production increases, so the slope of the frontier changes.

The real magic of expanded productive capacity lies in the incredible technological advances that have taken place. In 1810, a businessman from Boston named Francis Cabot Lowell traveled to England to learn about British textile factories and to copy their superior technology. He brought back the power loom, which enabled workers to weave much more cotton fabric every day than they could before.[1]

We can model this change in technology through the production possibilities frontier by changing the rate of shirt production from 1 to 3 shirts per day, as shown in panel B of Figure 2-6. As the rate of shirt production increases, while the rate of wheat production remains the same, the shape of the curve changes. In this case, it pivots outward along the *x*-axis: This pivot indicates that for any given number of workers assigned to shirt-making, more shirts are produced than before. At every point except one (where all workers are producing wheat), the country can produce more with the same number of workers, thanks to improved technology.

For a refresher about shifts and pivots in graphs, see Appendix B, "Math Essentials: Working with Linear Equations," which follows Chapter 3, "Markets."

✓ TEST YOURSELF

- ☐ Could a person or country ever produce a combination of goods that lies outside the production possibilities frontier? Why or why not? **[LO 2.1]**
- ☐ Would an increase in productivity as a result of a new technology shift a production possibilities frontier inward or outward? **[LO 2.1]**

Absolute and Comparative Advantage

The United States used to be the world's biggest clothing manufacturer. In the 1800s, it had the technology and scale to be a leader in producing cotton shirts. Since then, the U.S. population has grown larger, and manufacturing technology has improved even more. So, why do less than 5 percent of global clothing exports come from the United States?[2]

Up to now, we have worked with a very simple model of production to highlight the key trade-offs faced by individual producers. If there is no trade between countries, then the United States can consume only those goods that it produces on its own. In the real world, however, goods are made all over the world. If Americans want to buy more shirts than the United States produces, they can get them from somewhere else. Under these conditions, how can we predict which countries will produce which goods?

Understanding how resources are allocated among multiple producers is a step toward understanding why big firms work with specialized suppliers. It also helps explain why a wealthy, productive country like the United States trades with much poorer, less-productive countries. In this section we will see that trade actually increases total production, which can benefit everyone involved. To see why, let's turn to the question of why many T-shirts sold in the United States today are made in Bangladesh.

Absolute advantage

Suppose that taking into account all the improvements in shirt-making and wheat-growing technology since 1800, an American worker can now make 50 shirts or grow 200 bushels of wheat per day.[3] A Bangladeshi worker, in comparison, can produce 25 shirts or 50 bushels of wheat. (Why the differences? Perhaps U.S. workers use faster cloth-cutting technology, or maybe because U.S. farmers use fertilizers, pesticides, and irrigation systems that farmers in Bangladesh don't.) In other words, given the same number of workers, the United States can produce twice as many shirts or four times as much wheat as Bangladesh.

If a producer can generate more output than others with a given amount of resources, that producer has an **absolute advantage**. In our simplified model, the United States has an absolute advantage over Bangladesh at producing both shirts and wheat because it can make more of both products than Bangladesh can per worker.

LO 2.2 Define absolute and comparative advantage.

absolute advantage the ability to produce more of a good or service than others can with a given amount of resources

Comparative advantage

Absolute advantage is not the end of the story, though. If it were, the United States would still be producing the world's shirts. The problem is that for every T-shirt the United States produces, it uses resources that could otherwise be spent growing wheat. Of course, the same could be said of Bangladesh. But in our model of T-shirt and wheat production, the opportunity cost of making 1 shirt in the United States is 4 bushels of wheat (200 bushels ÷ 50 shirts = 4 bushels per shirt). The opportunity cost of making 1 shirt in Bangladesh is only 2 bushels of wheat (50 bushels ÷ 25 shirts = 2 bushels per shirt). The United States has to give up more to make a shirt than Bangladesh does.

When a producer can make a good at a lower opportunity cost than other producers, we say it has a **comparative advantage** at producing that good. In our model, Bangladesh has a comparative advantage over the United States at shirt-making: Its opportunity cost of producing a shirt is only 2 bushels of wheat, compared to 4 bushels of wheat for the United States.

The United States, on the other hand, has a comparative advantage over Bangladesh at producing wheat: Each time the United States produces a bushel of wheat, it gives up the opportunity to produce one-quarter of a shirt (50 shirts ÷ 200 bushels = $\frac{1}{4}$ shirt per bushel). For Bangladesh, however, the opportunity cost of producing a bushel of wheat is larger: it's one-half of a shirt (25 shirts ÷ 50 bushels = $\frac{1}{2}$ shirt per bushel). The United States has a lower opportunity cost for producing wheat than Bangladesh ($\frac{1}{4}$ shirt is less than $\frac{1}{2}$ shirt). Therefore, we say the United States has a comparative advantage over Bangladesh at wheat production.

comparative advantage the ability to produce a good or service at a lower opportunity cost than others

A country can have a comparative advantage without having an absolute advantage. In our scenario, the United States has an absolute advantage over Bangladesh at producing both shirts and wheat, but it has a bigger advantage at producing wheat than at making shirts. It can make four times as much wheat per worker as Bangladesh (200 versus 50 bushels) but only twice as many shirts per worker (50 versus 25). It's better at both—but it's "more better," so to speak, at producing wheat. (We know that "more better" is not good grammar, but it nicely expresses the idea.) Likewise, Bangladesh has a comparative advantage at the good it is "less worse" at (producing shirts), even though it does not have an absolute advantage at either compared to the United States.

You may have noticed that for each country, the opportunity cost of growing wheat is the *inverse* of the opportunity cost of producing shirts. (For the United States, $\frac{1}{4}$ is the inverse of 4; for Bangladesh, $\frac{1}{2}$ is the inverse of 2.) Mathematically, this means that it is impossible for one country to have a comparative advantage at producing both goods. Each producer's opportunity cost depends on its *relative* ability at producing different goods. Logic tells us that you can't be better at A than at B and also better at B than at A. (And mathematically, if X is bigger than Y, then $\frac{1}{X}$ will be smaller than $\frac{1}{Y}$.) The United States can't be better at producing wheat than shirts relative to Bangladesh and at the same time be better at producing shirts than wheat relative to Bangladesh. As a result, no producer has a comparative advantage at everything, and each producer has a comparative advantage at something.

We can check this international trade scenario against an example closer to home. When your family makes Thanksgiving dinner, does the best cook make everything? If you have a small family, maybe one person *can* make the whole dinner. But if your family is anything like our families, you will need several cooks. Grandma is by far the most experienced cook, yet the potato peeling always gets outsourced to the kids. Is that because the grandchildren are better potato peelers than Grandma? We think that's probably not the case. Grandma has an absolute advantage at everything having to do with Thanksgiving dinner. Still, the kids may have a *comparative* advantage at potato peeling, which frees up Grandma to make those tricky pie crusts.

We can find applications of comparative advantage everywhere in life. Sports is no exception. Look at the From Another Angle box "Babe Ruth, star pitcher" for another example.

Babe Ruth, star pitcher
From Another Angle

Babe Ruth had an absolute advantage at both pitching and hitting, but his comparative advantage at hitting made him one of the best hitters of all time.
Source: Library of Congress Prints & Photographs Division [LC-DIG-npcc-02009]

New York Yankees manager Miller Huggins faced a tough choice. It was 1920, and his baseball team had acquired the baseball legend Babe Ruth. Everyone knew that Babe Ruth was an amazing hitter. In 1920 he hit 54 home runs. That year, only one other baseball *team* collectively hit as many home runs as Ruth *alone* did.

But Babe Ruth was also an amazing pitcher. In 1918 he had set a record for the most consecutive scoreless innings pitched in the World Series—a record that was not broken until 1961. He could easily have become one of the best pitchers of his generation.

Huggins had to determine the right role for Babe Ruth. The problem was that Babe Ruth was both the best pitcher *and* the best hitter on the team. From a practical point of view, Ruth couldn't do both (pitching takes too much energy).

What does a manager do when one player has an absolute advantage at multiple positions? One answer is to turn to comparative advantage.

Although Ruth had an *absolute* advantage at both pitching and hitting, he had a *comparative* advantage as a hitter. The opportunity cost of having Ruth pitch was the number of games the Yankees would win by having him bat instead. Huggins decided the opportunity cost of Ruth's pitching was higher than the opportunity cost of his batting. The team would do relatively better when Ruth was hitting. Huggins' decision worked out well: Babe Ruth is now known as one of the greatest hitters of all time.

Source: 2016 Family of Babe Ruth and Babe Ruth League c/o *Luminary Group LLC.*

✓ TEST YOURSELF

- ☐ What does it mean to have an absolute advantage at producing a good? **[LO 2.2]**
- ☐ What does it mean to have a comparative advantage at producing a good? **[LO 2.2]**
- ☐ Can more than one producer have an absolute advantage at producing the same good? Why or why not? **[LO 2.2]**

Why Trade?

The United States is perfectly capable of producing its own shirts and its own wheat. In fact, in our simple model, it has an absolute advantage at producing both goods. So, why buy shirts from Bangladesh? We are about to see that both countries are actually able to consume more when they specialize in producing the good for which they have a comparative advantage and then trade with one another.

Specialization

If you lived 200 years ago, your everyday life would have been full of tasks that probably never even cross your mind today. You might have milked a cow, hauled water from a well, split wood, cured meat, mended a hole in a sock, and repaired a roof.

LO 2.3 Explain why people specialize.

Contrast that with life today. Almost everything we use comes from someone who specializes in providing a particular good or service. We bet you don't churn the butter you put on your toast. You probably wouldn't begin to know how to construct the parts in your smartphone. We are guessing you don't usually sew your own clothes or grow your own wheat. In today's world, all of us are dependent on one another for the things we need on a daily basis.

In our model, when the United States and Bangladesh work in isolation, each produces some shirts and some wheat—each in the combinations that its consumers prefer. Suppose the United States has 150 million workers and Bangladesh has 80 million. As before,

- each U.S. worker can make 50 shirts or 200 bushels of wheat and
- each Bangladeshi worker can make 25 shirts or 50 bushels of wheat.

Now, suppose these production combinations occur:

- Based on U.S. consumers' preferences, U.S. workers are split so that they produce 1 billion shirts and 26 billion bushels of wheat.
- In Bangladesh, workers are allocated to produce 0.5 billion shirts and 3 billion bushels of wheat.

TABLE 2-1

Production with and without specialization

When Bangladesh and the United States each specializes in the production of one good, the two countries can produce an extra 0.5 billion T-shirts and 1 billion bushels of wheat using the same number of workers and the same technology.

	Country	Wheat (billions of bushels)	T-shirts (billions)
Without specialization	United States	26	1
	Bangladesh	3	0.5
	Total	29	1.5
With specialization	United States	30	0
	Bangladesh	0	2
	Total	30	2

Even though Bangladesh's productivity per worker is lower, it has a large number of workers and so is able to produce a large total quantity of goods. (The quantities of shirts and wheat are unrealistically large because we are assuming they are the only goods being produced. In reality, of course, countries produce many different goods, but this simplifying assumption helps us to zero in on a real-world truth.)

We have seen that if the United States and Bangladesh are self-sufficient (each producing what its people want to consume), then together the two countries can make 1.5 billion T-shirts and 29 billion bushels of wheat, as shown at the top of Table 2-1 ("without specialization"). What would happen if, instead, Bangladesh put all its resources into making shirts and the United States put all its resources into producing wheat?

If each country focuses on producing the good for which it has a comparative advantage, total production increases. Focusing in this way is called **specialization**. It's the practice of spending all of your resources producing a particular good. When each country specializes in making a particular good according to its comparative advantage, total production possibilities are greater than if each produced the exact combination of goods its own consumers want.

The bottom section of Table 2-1 ("with specialization") shows us:

United States

200 bushels per worker × 150 million workers = 30 billion bushels

Bangladesh

25 shirts per worker × 80 million workers = 2 billion shirts

By specializing, the two countries together can produce 1 billion bushels of wheat more than before, *plus* 0.5 billion more shirts. Specialization increases total production, using the same number of workers and the same technology.

This rule applies to all sorts of goods and services. It explains why dentists hire roofers to fix a roof leak and why roofers hire dentists to fill a cavity. See the Economics in Action box "Specialization sauce" for an example of the power of specialization in a setting you are probably somewhat familiar with—McDonald's.

specialization spending all of your time producing a particular good

Specialization sauce
Economics in Action

Pizza Hut, Wendy's, and other fast-food chains serve food that's pretty fast and pretty cheap. On any given day, about one-third of U.S. kids and teens eat fast food. But fast food didn't always exist. Fast food as we know it was created in 1948 by Dick and Mac McDonald, the founders of McDonald's. The McDonald brothers were inspired by the way workers specialized on particular tasks when making cars on factory assembly lines. The McDonalds decided to use the same idea when running a restaurant. Instead of assigning employees to general food preparation, they split each order into parts, dividing the steps required to prepare a meal. One employee became the grilling specialist; another added mustard and ketchup. A different employee operated the potato fryer, and yet another mixed the milkshakes.

Specialization resulted in efficiency that created the fast-food business.
©WR Publishing/Alamy

Any single employee could almost certainly learn how to grill a burger, add condiments, make fries, *and* mix a milkshake. And in each restaurant, one particularly skilled employee may well have been the fastest at every step in making a meal.

Even so, specialization was far more efficient when employing a team of workers. By assigning only one specific task to each worker, the founders of McDonald's revolutionized the speed and quantity of food preparation. Harnessing the power of specialization allowed them to grill more burgers, fry more potatoes, and feed more hungry customers.

Source: Eric Schlosser, *Fast Food Nation* (Boston: Houghton Mifflin, 2002), pp. 19–20.

Gains from trade

When countries specialize in producing the goods for which they have a comparative advantage, total production increases. The problem with specialization is that each producer ends up with only one good—in our model, wheat in the United States, T-shirts in Bangladesh. If Americans want to wear T-shirts and Bangladeshis want to enjoy wheat, they must trade.

Suppose that Bangladesh and the United States agree to trade 3.5 billion bushels of wheat for 1.5 billion T-shirts. As a result, each country ends up with an additional 0.5 billion bushels of wheat, and the United States also has 0.5 billion more shirts than before. The improvement in outcomes that occurs when specialized producers exchange goods and services is called the **gains from trade**.

Figure 2-7 shows how the gains from trade affect a country's consumption. Before the trade, it was impossible for the United States and Bangladesh to consume any combination of goods outside their production possibilities frontiers. After the trade between the two specialized producers, each country's consumption increases to a point that was previously unachievable. If Bangladesh consumes the same amount of shirts as before and trades the remaining, both countries are able to consume 0.5 billion bushels more wheat after opening up to trade.

In Figure 2-7, the gains from the U.S.–Bangladesh trade are distributed equally: 0.5 billion bushels more wheat for the United States and 0.5 billion bushels more wheat for Bangladesh. In reality, the distribution can vary. The gains do not have to be equal for the trading arrangement to benefit everyone. If Bangladesh takes an extra 0.25 billion bushels of wheat and the United States an extra 0.75 billion (or vice versa), both countries will still be better off than if they worked alone.

Overall, there is room for trade as long as two things occur: (1) the two countries differ in their opportunity costs to produce a good and (2) they set a favorable trading price. A favorable trading

LO 2.4 Explain how the gains from trade follow from comparative advantage.

gains from trade the improvement in outcomes that occurs when producers specialize and exchange goods and services

FIGURE 2-7
Specialization and gains from trade

(A) United States' gains from trade

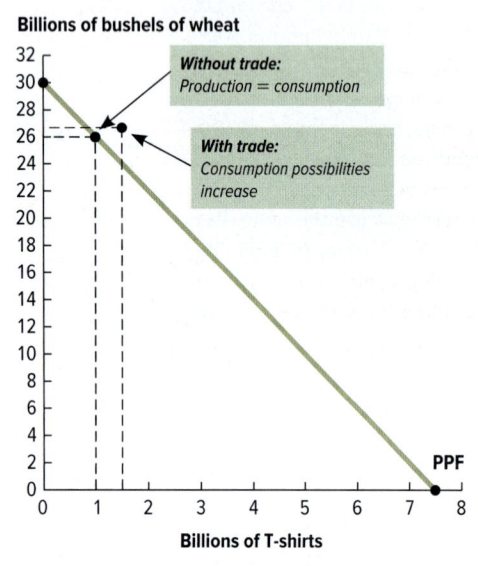

Billions of bushels of wheat (y-axis, 0 to 32)
Billions of T-shirts (x-axis, 0 to 8)

- Without trade: Production = consumption
- With trade: Consumption possibilities increase
- PPF

If a country does not specialize and trade, its production and consumption are both limited to points along its production possibilities frontier. By specializing and achieving gains from trading, the United States gains 0.5 million T-shirts and 0.5 billion bushels of wheat.

(B) Bangladesh's gains from trade

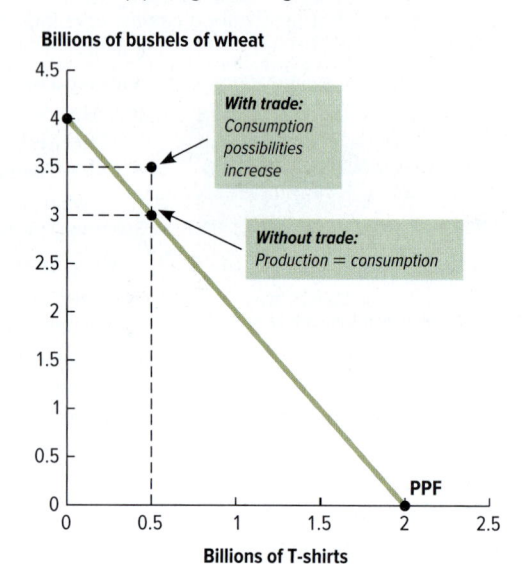

Billions of bushels of wheat (y-axis, 0 to 4.5)
Billions of T-shirts (x-axis, 0 to 2.5)

- With trade: Consumption possibilities increase
- Without trade: Production = consumption
- PPF

By opening up to trade, Bangladesh also gains 0.5 billion bushels of wheat compared to what it could produce on its production possibilities frontier.

---

price needs to benefit both parties. If T-shirts from Bangladesh are too expensive, the United States will refuse to buy them. Similarly, if U.S. wheat is too expensive, Bangladesh will not buy it. If the United States agrees to trade 3.5 billion bushels of wheat for 1.5 billion T-shirts, it must be because the United States values 3.5 billion bushels of wheat less than 1.5 billion T-shirts.

To see how much each country values a good, we must look at its opportunity costs. Recall that the opportunity cost of 1 T-shirt for Bangladesh is 2 bushels of wheat. In other words, the value of 1 T-shirt for Bangladesh is at least 2 bushels of wheat. If the United States offered to trade 1 bushel of wheat in exchange for 1 T-shirt, Bangladesh would refuse such a trade; Bangladesh could simply produce the wheat itself. Bangladesh needs to receive at least 2 bushels of wheat in exchange for 1 T-shirt.

To see how many bushels of wheat the United States is willing to give up in exchange for 1 T-shirt, we can look at the United States' opportunity cost. The opportunity cost of 1 T-shirt for the United States is 4 bushels of wheat. Thus, the United States will only trade up to 4 bushels of wheat in exchange for 1 T-shirt. More than 4 bushels of wheat would be worth more than 1 T-shirt. If Bangladesh tries to charge a price greater than the United States' opportunity cost, the United States will choose to make the T-shirts itself. In order for trade to benefit both countries, the trade price of 1 T-shirt must be at least 2 bushels of wheat but less than 4 bushels of wheat.

In general, two countries will benefit from a trade price that falls between their opportunity costs. In our example, the price at which Bangladesh and the United States are willing to trade T-shirts must fall between Bangladesh's opportunity cost for producing T-shirts and the

United States' opportunity cost for producing T-shirts. If Bangladesh is the country that has specialized in T-shirts, it cannot charge a price greater than the United States' opportunity cost. If it does, the United States will simply make the T-shirts itself. Conversely, Bangladesh must receive a price that covers its opportunity costs for making T-shirts or it will not be willing to trade.

What's true about countries is also true about individuals who specialize (and then pay for what they need). For example, consider Stacy Brown-Philpot, the chief executive officer of TaskRabbit. The company's business is all about creating gains from specialization and trade by running a global online marketplace that connects freelance workers to people needing jobs done. The same principles of specialization and trade guide Stacy Brown-Philpot in her own work. She hires many managers to help run TaskRabbit, but she is likely a better manager than most of them (after all, she very successfully ran TaskRabbit's day-to-day operations before becoming chief executive). Let's say Brown-Philpot can resolve a key operational issue in an hour, but for every hour she's distracted from leading TaskRabbit, the company's profits go down by $1,000. The less-experienced manager earns only $50 an hour, so even if he takes two to three times to resolve the problem, it's still worth it for Brown-Philpot to hire him and spend her own time keeping up TaskRabbit's productivity. Brown-Philpot may have an absolute advantage at managing day-to-day problems, but the opportunity cost in lost profits means the less-experienced manager has a comparative advantage. (Brown-Philpot's comparative advantage is at developing the business strategy for TaskRabbit.) Here, everyone can end up better off if they specialize in their jobs.

In spite of the gains from specializing and trading, not everyone considers this an obvious choice in every circumstance. We've seen that international trade can bring gains to countries, and specialization in jobs can bring gains to individuals. But it's not true that all citizens necessarily gain from international trade. In the example above, T-shirt businesses (and their employees) in the United States lose from international trade. Their well-being depends on their ability to shift into other, similar jobs and lines of business. They might also get help from the government. It may be hard to find similar jobs, however, and government help is not guaranteed. Thus, in practice, international trade policy can be controversial despite its many advantages. For some examples, see the Economics in Action box "Winners and losers."

Winners and losers
Economics in Action

Trade can bring big gains to economies, but that doesn't mean that everyone wins.

Tracy Warner knows that first-hand. She worked at the Maytag factory in Galesburg, Illinois, until 2004, when Maytag shut down the plant and shifted jobs to other countries where wages are lower. The refrigerator factory had employed 1,600 workers in Galesburg, and Warner was earning $37,000 a year. After the factory closed, she found a job as a teacher's assistant and worked nights as a janitor, taking home about $21,000 a year in total.

Other people in town had more positive benefits from trade:

- One of Warner's neighbors saw his paychecks triple. He's a foreman at the railroad, and increased trade keeps the trains busy, giving him ample opportunities to work overtime.
- The owner of the local appliance store happily reported a boom in sales of inexpensive high-quality televisions, thanks to trade with Asia.
- Customers of the local appliance store spent a lot less money on televisions and used that extra money to buy better food, go to more movies, and get more presents for their children.

The exact trade-offs created by trade—gains together with losses—are now being recognized thanks to data analysis and rigorous economic research. On the downside, the increase in

(continued)

imports from China was responsible for about one-quarter of the decline in manufacturing jobs in the United States between 1990 and 2007. On the upside, researchers estimate that access to cheaper goods has increased the purchasing power of middle-income Americans by 37 percent.

The U.S. government offers a patchwork of programs and benefits to help workers who have lost their jobs. Workers who can prove their jobs were lost to foreign competition can get an extra six months of unemployment insurance and enroll in job training programs. Workers over 50 years old can earn wage insurance worth up to $12,000 over two years.

These government programs help workers cope with job losses, but they require that workers be flexible. When Tracy Warner lost her job, she was able to use training money from the federal government to complete her degree in communications. However, she couldn't find a job in Galesburg that used her new credentials and had to find low-wage work.

A big question about trade, then, is not just whether it's good for the economy overall. (Most often it is.) The question is also about whether those who suffer initially can then adjust to the new economy.

Sources: Binyamim Appelbaum, "Towns Decline Illustrates Perils of Trade Deals," *New York Times*, May 18, 2015, p. A1; David Autor, David Dorn, and Gordon Hanson, "The China Syndrome: Local Labor Market Effects of Import Competition in the United States," *American Economic Review* 2013, 103(6): 2121–2168; Pablo D. Fajgelbaum and Amit K. Khandelwal, "Measuring the Unequal Gains to Trade," *Quarterly Journal of Economics* 131, no. 3 (August 1, 2016), pp. 1113–1180, https://doi.org/10.1093/qje/qjw01.

Comparative advantage over time

Our simplified model of production possibilities and trade helps us to understand why Americans now buy shirts from other countries. But we noted at the beginning of the chapter that this wasn't always the case: 200 years ago, the United States was selling shirts to the rest of the world. To understand this change, we can apply our model to shifts in comparative advantage over time. These shifts have caused significant changes in different countries' economies and trade patterns.

When the Industrial Revolution began, Great Britain led the world in clothing manufacturing. In the nineteenth century, the United States snatched the comparative advantage through a combination of new technology (which led to higher productivity) and cheap labor (which led to lower production costs). Gradually, the comparative advantage in clothing shifted away from the United States to other countries. Clothing manufacturing moved from country to country, searching for ever-lower costs:

- By the 1930s, 40 percent of the world's cotton goods were made in Japan, where workers from the countryside were willing to work long hours for low wages.
- In the mid-1970s, clothing manufacturing moved to Hong Kong, Taiwan, and Korea, where wages were even lower than those in Japan.
- The textile industry then moved to China in the early 1990s, when millions of young women left their farms to work for wages as much as 90 percent lower than those in Hong Kong. Similar changes happened in Bangladesh.

There's an upside to the progressive relocation of this industry and its jobs: Eventually high-wage jobs replaced low-wage jobs, and these countries experienced considerable economic growth.

Losing a comparative advantage in clothing production sounds like a bad thing at first. But as we know from our model, you can't lose comparative advantage in one thing without gaining it in another. Changes in clothing manufacturing were driven by workers in each country getting more skilled at industries that paid better than making clothes—such as making cars, or programming computers, or providing financial services. This meant the opportunity cost of making clothes increased. The comparative advantage in clothing production shifted to countries where the workers lacked skills in better-paying industries and so were willing to work in textile factories for lower wages.

Most historians would agree that it wasn't a sign of failure when countries lost their comparative advantage in clothing production—it was a sign of success. Former textile producers like Great Britain, the United States, Japan, Korea, and Hong Kong are all much wealthier now than they were when they were centers of clothing manufacturing.

However, these changes probably didn't look or feel like success at the time, especially for workers in textile factories who saw their jobs disappearing overseas. This same tension is arising today in other industries as companies "outsource" tasks that can be done more cheaply in other countries.

The Economics in Action box "Comparative advantage: The good, the bad, and the ugly" considers whether a country's loss of comparative advantage at producing a particular good is something to worry about.

Comparative advantage: The good, the bad, and the ugly
Economics in Action

You may have noticed that when you call the customer service line for many large companies, you are likely to end up speaking with someone in India or the Philippines. Thirty years ago, that was not the case—call centers for American customers were almost all located in the United States.

The United States has not become "worse" at running call centers. In fact, it may still have an absolute advantage at it. Over time, though, technology has improved the quality and lowered the cost of international phone calls. At the same time, higher education and fluency in English have become more common in other countries. As a result, the comparative advantage at running call centers has shifted, and many U.S. companies find it more profitable to move them offshore.

When jobs move overseas, people worry that the country is sliding down a slippery slope of economic decline. They ask, "Is something wrong with our schools? Have our companies lost their competitive edge?" Sometimes people mistakenly refer to this phenomenon as the United States "losing its comparative advantage." Based on what you have learned in this chapter, you know that cannot be the case. Everyone has a comparative advantage at something. If the United States no longer has a comparative advantage at running call centers, its comparative advantage has shifted to some other industry.

There are valid reasons to be concerned about shifts in comparative advantage. One is the disruptive effects on people who were employed in the industry that is in decline. They may find they do not have the right skills to find new jobs in industries that are growing. Retraining is often possible, but not always easy.

Comparative advantage has no moral compass. Sometimes high productivity in an industry is driven by factors we feel proud of, like hard work, innovative technology, or savvy business practices. At other times, it is driven by things of which we are now ashamed. The success of nineteenth-century cotton growers in the American South owed as much to the huge pool of cheap labor provided by the evil of slavery as it did to inventions like the cotton gin.

For a more recent example, consider the differences in regulations between wealthy and poor countries today. Factories in developing nations can often produce at lower cost than those in industrialized ones. In part, this advantage is due to the fact that they do not have to pay minimum wages, provide a safe workplace, or clean up the pollution they cause. Is that fair? That normative question is up for debate. Comparative advantage is not a matter of morals; it is simply a matter of fact.

✓ TEST YOURSELF

☐ Why do people or countries specialize? **[LO 2.3]**
☐ How do two countries benefit from trading with each other? **[LO 2.4]**
☐ Is it possible to not have a comparative advantage at anything? Why or why not? **[LO 2.4]**

Conclusion

Specialization and trade can make everyone better off. It is not surprising, then, that in an economy driven by individuals seeking to make a profit or improve their communities, people specialize so as to exploit their comparative advantages. That principle is as true for countries, like the United States and Bangladesh, as it is for individuals picking their careers.

No government intervention is required to coordinate production. The great economic thinker Adam Smith suggested the term *invisible hand* to describe this coordinating mechanism:

> It is not from the benevolence of the butcher, the brewer, or the baker that we expect our dinner, but from their regard to their [self-interest]. . . . he intends only his own gain, and he is in this, as in many other cases, led by an invisible hand to promote an end which was no part of his intention.[4]

The functioning of the invisible hand depends on a lot of other assumptions, such as free competition and full information. Later in the text we will discuss these assumptions, and will note when they work and when they do not.

Most people take for granted the prevalence of specialization and trade in their everyday lives. Few stop to think about the benefits and where they come from. In this chapter we tried to dig down to the bottom of the assumptions people make and expose the logic behind the gains from trade. We also noted the costs from trade. Even when a country, as a whole, gains from trade, some workers and businesses may lose out as they face more competition. As we proceed—especially when we return to topics like international trade and government intervention in the markets—try to remember the winners and losers, together with the possibility of broad gains when people interact with one another in economic exchanges.

Key Terms

production possibilities frontier (PPF), p. 27
efficient points, p. 30
absolute advantage, p. 33
comparative advantage, p. 33
specialization, p. 36
gains from trade, p. 37

Summary

LO 2.1 Construct a production possibilities graph, and describe what causes shifts in production possibilities curves.

A production possibilities graph shows all the combinations of two goods that a person or an economy can produce with a given amount of time, resources, and technology. The production possibilities frontier is a line on that graph that shows all the maximum attainable combinations of goods. Producers of goods and services are not likely to choose a combination of goods inside the production possibilities frontier because they could achieve a higher production level with the same amount of resources. They cannot choose points outside the frontier, which would require more than the available resources. The choice between combinations on the production possibilities frontier is a matter of preference.

Shifts in the production possibilities frontier can be caused by changes in technology, as well as changes in population and other resources. Increases in technological capabilities and population will shift the PPF outward; decreases in these factors will shift the PPF inward.

LO 2.2 Define absolute and comparative advantage.

Producers have an absolute advantage at making a good when they can produce more output than others with a given amount of resources. If you put two people or countries to work making the same good, the person or country that is more productive has an absolute advantage.

People or countries have a comparative advantage when they are better at producing one good than they are at producing other goods, relative to other producers. Everyone has a comparative advantage at something, whether or not they have an absolute advantage at anything.

LO 2.3 Explain why people specialize.

Specialization means spending all or much of your time producing a particular good. Production is highest when people or countries specialize in producing the good for which they have a comparative advantage. Specialization increases total production, using the same number of workers and the same technology.

LO 2.4 Explain how the gains from trade follow from comparative advantage.

The increase in total production that occurs from specialization and exchange is called the gains from trade. With specialization and trade, two parties can increase production and consumption, and each ends up better off.

Shifts in comparative advantage over time have caused significant changes in different countries' economies and trade patterns. These changes signal general economic success, although they can be painful for the individual workers and industries involved. Even when a country as a whole gains from trade, some workers and businesses may lose out as they face more competition.

Review Questions

1. You've been put in charge of a bake sale for a local charity, at which you are planning to sell cookies and cupcakes. What would a production possibilities graph of this situation show? **[LO 2.1]**

2. You manage two employees at a pet salon. Your employees perform two tasks, giving flea baths and grooming animals. If you constructed a single production possibilities frontier for flea baths and grooming that combined both of your employees' work efforts, would you expect the production possibilities frontier to be linear (a straight line)? Explain why or why not. **[LO 2.1]**

3. You and another volunteer are in charge of a bake sale for a local charity, at which you are planning to sell cookies and cupcakes. **[LO 2.2]**
    a. What would it mean for one of you to have an absolute advantage at baking cookies or cupcakes? Could one of you have an absolute advantage at baking both items?
    b. What would it mean for you or the other volunteer to have a comparative advantage at baking cookies or cupcakes? Could one of you have a comparative advantage at baking both items?

4. You and another volunteer are in charge of a bake sale for a local charity, at which you are planning to sell cookies and cupcakes. Suppose you have a comparative advantage at baking cookies, and the other volunteer has a comparative advantage at baking cupcakes. Make a proposal to the volunteer about how to split up the baking. Explain how you can both gain from specializing, and why. **[LO 2.3]**

5. At the flower shop, where you manage two employees, your employees perform two tasks: caring for the displays of cut flowers and making flower arrangements to fill customer orders. Explain how you would approach organizing your employees and assigning them tasks. **[LO 2.3]**

6. Suppose two countries produce the same two goods and have identical production possibilities frontiers. Do you expect these countries to trade? Explain why or why not. **[LO 2.4]**

7. Brazil is the largest coffee producer in the world, and coffee is one of Brazil's major export goods. Suppose that in 20 years, Brazil no longer produces much coffee and imports most of its coffee instead. Explain why Brazil might change its trade pattern over time. **[LO 2.4]**

Problems and Applications

1. Your friend Sam owns a catering business and has been asked to prepare appetizers for a university reception during homecoming weekend. She has an unlimited amount of ingredients but only six hours to prepare them. Sam can make 300 mini-sandwiches or 150 servings of melon slices topped with smoked salmon and a dab of sauce per hour. **[LO 2.1]**
    a. Draw Sam's production possibilities frontier.
    b. Now suppose that the university decides to postpone the reception until after the big game, so

Sam has an extra four hours to prepare. Redraw her production possibilities frontier to show the impact of this increase in resources.

   c. Now, in addition to the extra time to prepare, suppose Sam's friend Chris helps by preparing the melon slices. Sam can now make 300 mini-sandwiches or 300 melon appetizers per hour. Redraw Sam's production possibilities frontier to show the impact of increased productivity in making melon appetizers.

2. Your friend Sam has been asked to prepare appetizers for the university reception. She has an unlimited amount of ingredients and six hours in which to prepare them. Sam can make 400 mini-sandwiches or 200 servings of melon slices topped with smoked salmon and a dab of sauce per hour. **[LO 2.1]**

   a. What is Sam's opportunity cost of making one mini-sandwich?
   b. What is Sam's opportunity cost of making one melon appetizer?
   c. Suppose the reception has been postponed, so Sam has an extra four hours to prepare. What is the opportunity cost of making one mini-sandwich now?
   d. Suppose the reception has been postponed, so Sam has an extra four hours to prepare. What is the opportunity cost of making one melon appetizer now?
   e. Suppose Sam's friend Chris helps by preparing the melon slices, increasing Sam's productivity to 400 mini-sandwiches or 400 melon appetizers per hour. What is the opportunity cost of making one mini-sandwich now?
   f. Suppose Sam's friend Chris helps by preparing the melon slices, increasing Sam's productivity to 400 mini-sandwiches or 400 melon appetizers per hour. What is the opportunity cost of making one melon appetizer now?

3. Suppose that Canada produces two goods: lumber and fish. It has 18 million workers, each of whom can cut 10 feet of lumber or catch 20 fish each day. **[LO 2.1]**

   a. What is the maximum amount of lumber Canada could produce in a day?
   b. What is the maximum amount of fish it could produce in a day?
   c. Draw Canada's production possibilities frontier.
   d. Use your graph to determine how many fish can be caught if 60 million feet of lumber are cut.

4. The graph in Figure 2P-1 shows Tanya's weekly production possibilities frontier for doing homework (writing papers and doing problem sets). **[LO 2.1]**

FIGURE 2P-1

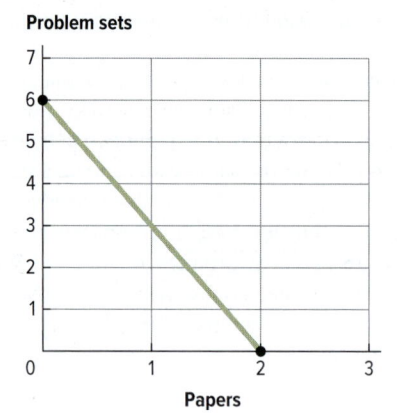

   a. What is the slope of the production possibilities frontier?
   b. What is the opportunity cost of doing one problem set?
   c. What is the opportunity cost of writing one paper?

5. Use the production possibilities frontier in Figure 2P-2 to answer the following questions. **[LO 2.1]**

FIGURE 2P-2

   a. What is the slope of the PPF between point A and point B?
   b. What is the slope of the PPF between point B and point C?
   c. Is the opportunity cost of producing hammers higher between points A and B or between points B and C?
   d. Is the opportunity cost of producing screwdrivers higher between points A and B or between points B and C?

6. For each point on the PPF in Figure 2P-3, note whether the point is attainable and efficient, attainable and inefficient, or unattainable. **[LO 2.1]**

FIGURE 2P-3

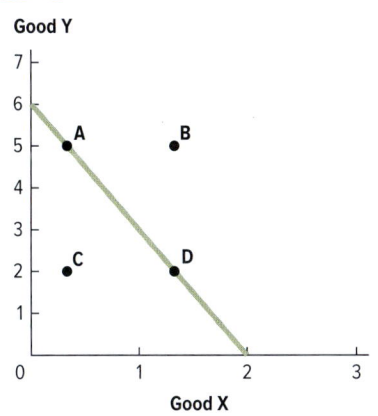

TABLE 2P-1

	Red Cross	WIC
Food packages	300	200
First-aid kits	50	20

9. Suppose that three volunteers are preparing cookies and cupcakes for a bake sale. Diana can make 26 cookies or 19 cupcakes per hour; Andy can make 24 cookies or 18 cupcakes; and Sam can make 9 cookies or 13 cupcakes. **[LO 2.2]**

    a. Who has the absolute advantage at making cookies?

    b. Who has the absolute advantage at making cupcakes?

10. Paula and Carlo are coworkers. Their production possibilities frontiers for counseling clients and writing memos are given in Figure 2P-5. **[LO 2.2]**

FIGURE 2P-5

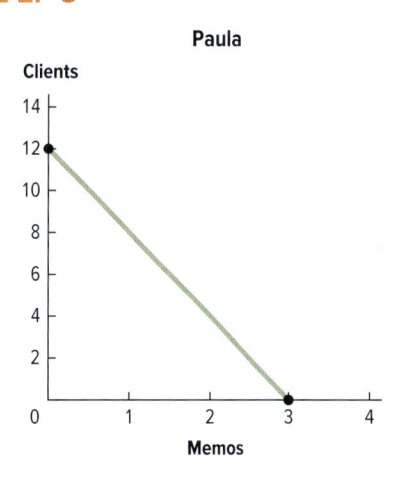

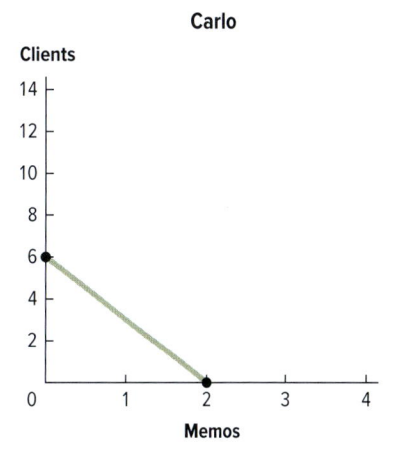

7. For each point on the PPF in Figure 2P-4, note whether the point is attainable and efficient, attainable and inefficient, or unattainable. **[LO 2.1]**

FIGURE 2P-4

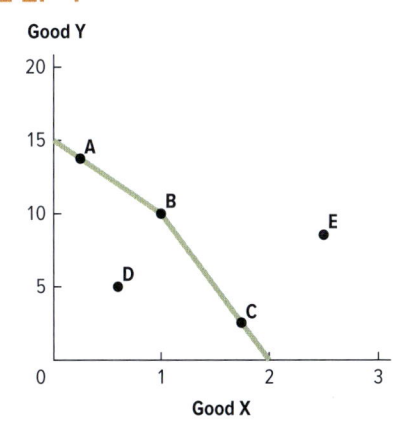

8. The Red Cross and the WIC (Women, Infants, and Children) program both provide emergency food packages and first-aid kits to New York City homeless shelters. Table 2P-1 shows their weekly production possibilities in providing emergency goods to NYC homeless shelters. NYC homeless shelters need a total of 20 first-aid kits per week. Currently, they get 10 kits from the Red Cross and 10 kits from WIC. With their remaining resources, how many food packages can each organization provide to NYC homeless shelters? **[LO 2.1]**

a. Which worker has an absolute advantage in counseling clients?

b. Which worker has a comparative advantage in counseling clients?

c. Which worker has an absolute advantage in writing memos?

d. Which worker has a comparative advantage in writing memos?

11. Two students are assigned to work together on a project that requires both writing and an oral presentation. Steve can write 1 page or prepare 4 minutes of a presentation each day. Anna can write 3 pages or prepare 2 minutes of a presentation each day. [LO 2.2]

    a. Who has a comparative advantage at writing?

    b. Suppose that Steve goes to a writing tutor and learns some tricks that enable him to write 4 pages each day. Now who has a comparative advantage at writing?

12. Suppose that the manager of a restaurant has two new employees, Rahul and Henriette, and is trying to decide which one to assign to which task. Rahul can chop 20 pounds of vegetables or wash 100 dishes per hour. Henriette can chop 30 pounds of vegetables or wash 120 dishes. [LO 2.3]

    a. Who should be assigned to chop vegetables?

    b. Who should be assigned to wash dishes?

13. The Dominican Republic and Nicaragua both produce coffee and rum. The Dominican Republic can produce 20,000 tons of coffee per year or 10,000 barrels of rum. Nicaragua can produce 30,000 tons of coffee per year or 5,000 barrels of rum. [LO 2.3]

    a. Suppose the Dominican Republic and Nicaragua sign a trade agreement in which each country would specialize in the production of either coffee or rum. Which country should specialize in producing coffee? Which country should specialize in producing rum?

    b. What are the minimum and maximum prices at which these countries will trade coffee?

14. Eleanor and her little brother Josh are responsible for two chores on their family's farm, gathering eggs and collecting milk. Eleanor can gather 9 dozen eggs or collect 3 gallons of milk per week. Josh can gather 2 dozen eggs or collect 2 gallons of milk per week. [LO 2.3]

    a. The family wants 2 gallons of milk per week and as many eggs as the siblings can gather. Currently, Eleanor and Josh collect one gallon of milk each and as many eggs as they can. How many dozens of eggs does the family have per week?

    b. If the siblings were to specialize, which should collect the milk?

    c. If the siblings were to specialize, how many dozens of eggs would the family have per week?

15. Suppose Russia and Sweden each produces only paper and cars. Russia can produce 8 tons of paper or 4 million cars each year. Sweden can produce 25 tons of paper or 5 million cars each year. [LO 2.4]

    a. Draw the production possibilities frontier for each country.

    b. Both countries want 2 million cars each year and as much paper as they can produce along with 2 million cars. Find this point on each production possibilities frontier and label it "A."

    c. Suppose the countries specialize. Which country will produce cars?

    d. Once they specialize, suppose they work out a trade of 2 million cars for 6 tons of paper. Find the new *consumption* point for each country and label it "B."

16. Maya and Max are neighbors. They both grow lettuce and tomatoes in their gardens. Maya can grow 45 heads of lettuce or 9 pounds of tomatoes this summer. Max can grow 42 heads of lettuce or 6 pounds of tomatoes this summer. If Maya and Max specialize and trade, the price of tomatoes (in terms of lettuce) would be as follows: 1 pound of tomatoes would cost between _____ and _____ pounds of lettuce. [LO 2.4]

Endnotes

1. http://www.encyclopedia.com/topic/Francis_Cabot_Lowell.aspx
2. http://www.economist.com/news/leaders/21646204-asias-dominance-manufacturing-will-endure-will-make-development-harder-others-made
3. http://www.agclassroom.org/gan/timeline/farm_tech.htm
4. Adam Smith, *An Inquiry into the Nature and Causes of the Wealth of Nations*, 1776.

Appendix A

Math Essentials: Understanding Graphs and Slope

Graphing is an essential component of economics. We touched on graphs in Chapter 2, "Specialization and Exchange," and we'll only see more graphs from here on out in the course. In order to truly understand the concepts of economics, you'll need to understand the basics of graphing. In this appendix, we'll discuss how to create and interpret different types of graphs.

Creating a Graph

A graph is one way to visually represent data. In this text, we use graphs to describe and interpret economic relationships. For example, we use a graph called a production possibilities frontier to explore opportunity costs and trade-offs in production. We use graphs of average, variable, and marginal costs to explore production decisions facing a firm. And—the favorite of economists everywhere—we use graphs to show supply and demand and the resulting relationship between price and quantity.

Graphs of one variable

Graphs of a single variable come in three main forms: the bar chart, the pie chart, and the line graph. In school, you've probably made all three and plastered them on science-fair posters and presentations or used them in reports. These graphs are versatile; they can be used to present all sorts of information. Throughout economics, and in this text, you'll come across these graphs frequently.

Probably the most common single-variable graph is the *bar graph*, an example of which is shown in Figure A-1. The bar graph shows the size or frequency of a variable using bars—hence the name. The size of the bar on the *y*-axis shows the value of the variable, while the *x*-axis contains the categories of the variables. In Figure A-1, for example, the bar graph shows the number of monthly average users (in billions) of the top five

LEARNING OBJECTIVES

LO A.1 Create four quadrants using *x*- and *y*-axes and plot points on a graph.

LO A.2 Use data to calculate slope.

LO A.3 Interpret what the direction and steepness of slope indicate about a line.

LO A.1 Create four quadrants using *x*- and *y*-axes and plot points on a graph.

46A

FIGURE A-1
Top five social networking websites

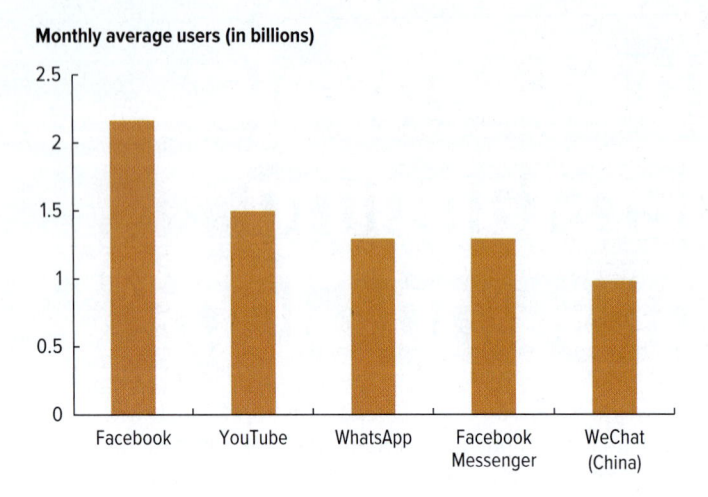

Monthly average users (in billions)

Site	Users
Facebook	~2.2
YouTube	~1.5
WhatsApp	~1.3
Facebook Messenger	~1.3
WeChat (China)	~1.0

Source: "Most famous social network sites worldwide as of January 2018, ranked by number of active users (in millions)," *Statista*, https://www.statista.com/statistics/272014/global-social-networks-ranked-by-number-of-users/, accessed March 18, 2018.

major social media platforms as of January 2018. Since the bars stack up next to each other, a bar graph makes it clear exactly where each news site stands in comparison to the others. As you can see, the larger bars for Facebook and YouTube mean that these sites get more visits than WhatsApp.

In general, bar graphs are versatile. You can show the distribution of letter grades in a class or the average monthly high and low temperatures in your city. Any time the size of a variable is important, you are generally going to want to use a bar graph.

Pie graphs (or *pie charts*) are generally used to show how much of certain components make up a whole. Pie graphs are usually a circle, cut into wedges that represent how much each makes up of the whole. Figure A-2 shows the market share of domestic and imported vehicle types (as of March 2018). The wedges show that trucks make up a much larger share of the market than cars, that domestic truck producers hold a much larger share of truck sales than car sales, and that imported cars have a larger market share than domestic-made cars.

The most common use of pie graphs is for budgeting. You'll often see government and business income and expenses broken down in a pie graph. Also, come election time, you'll see pie graphs all over the news media, representing the percentage of votes in an election each candidate receives.

A final type of graph is called a *line* (or *time-series*) *graph*. This type of graph is helpful when you are trying to emphasize the trend of a single variable. In economics, the most common usage of line graphs is to show the value of a variable over time. Inflation rates, GDP, and government debt over decades are all prime candidates to be presented on a line graph.

Figure A-3 shows the GDP growth rate in Mexico since 1960 on a time-series graph. Presenting the data this way makes it clear that Mexico's GDP growth was strong during the 1960s and 70s (anything above 4 percent growth is very good), dipped below zero in 2009, and rose into positive territory in 2010 and beyond.

Ultimately, single-variable graphs can take us only so far. In order to get at some of the most fundamental issues of economics, we need to be able to plot the values of two variables (such as price and quantity) simultaneously.

Math Essentials: Understanding Graphs and Slope   Appendix A

FIGURE A-2
Market share of domestic and imported vehicle types

This pie graph shows the market share of different types of vehicles in the U.S. market—the larger the wedge, the larger the market share. As the chart shows, trucks make up a much larger share of the market than cars. However, domestic producers hold a much larger share of truck sales than car sales.

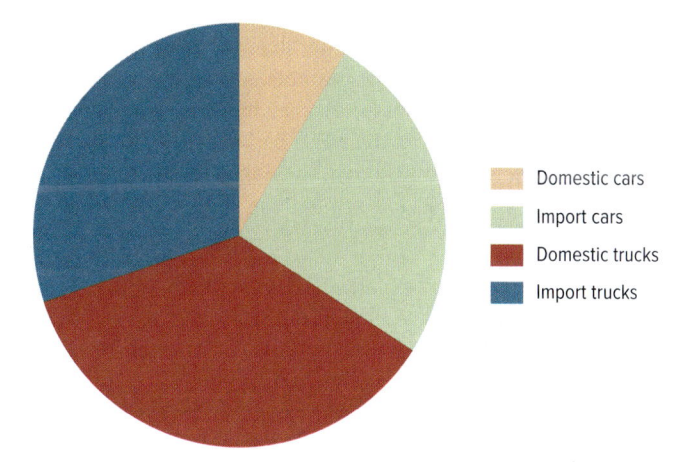

- Domestic cars
- Import cars
- Domestic trucks
- Import trucks

Source: *WSJ* Markets Data Center, www.wsj.com/mdc/public/page/2_3022-autosales.html.

FIGURE A-3
GDP growth in Mexico

A line graph commonly shows a variable over a range of time. This allows the trend in the variable to be clear. In this case, you can see that GDP growth in Mexico has been highly variable, but overall, GDP growth was higher on average before 1980.

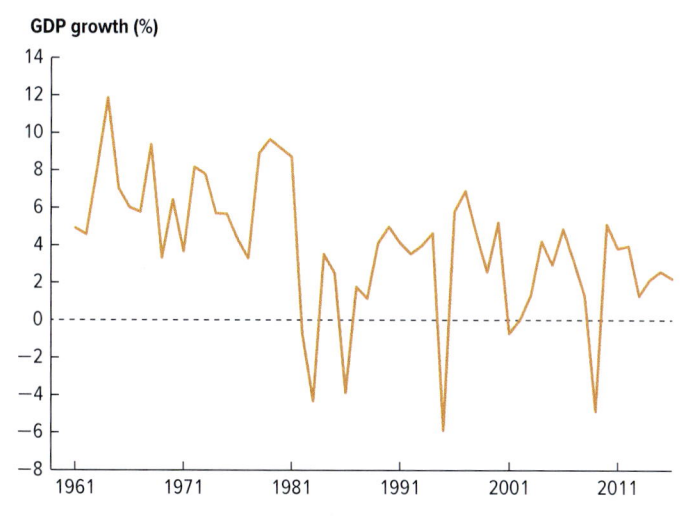

Source: World Bank World Development Indicators.

Graphs of two variables

In order to present two or more variables on a graph, we need something called the *Cartesian coordinate system*. With only two dimensions, this graphing system consists of two axes: the *x* (horizontal) axis and the *y* (vertical) axis. We can give these axes other names, depending on what economic variables we want to represent, such as price and quantity, or inputs and outputs.

In some cases, it doesn't matter which variable we put on each axis. At other times, logic or convention will determine the axes. There are two common conventions in economics that it will be useful for you to remember:

1. **Price on the *y*-axis, quantity on the *x*-axis:** When we graph the relationship between price and quantity in economics, price is always on the *y*-axis and quantity is always on the *x*-axis.
2. **The *x*-axis "causes" the *y*-axis:** In general, when the values of one variable are dependent on the values of the other variable, we put the "dependent" variable on the *y*-axis and the "independent" variable on the *x*-axis. For example, if we were exploring the relationship between test scores and the number of hours a student spends studying, we would place hours on the *x*-axis and test scores on the *y*-axis because hours spent studying affect scores, generally not vice versa. Sometimes, though, the opposite is true. In economics, we often say that price (always the *y*-axis variable) causes the quantity demanded of a good (the *x*-axis variable).

The point where the two axes intersect is called the *origin*. Points to the right of the origin have *x*-coordinates with positive values; points to the left of the origin have *x*-coordinates with negative values. Similarly, points above the origin have *y*-coordinates with positive values and points below the origin have *y*-coordinates with negative values.

To specify a particular point, indicate the *x*- and *y*-coordinates in an ordered pair. Indicate the *x*-coordinate first, and then the *y*-coordinate: (x,y). The intersection of the two axes creates four quadrants, as shown in Figure A-4.

Quadrant I: (x,y) The *x*- and *y*- coordinates are both positive.

Quadrant II: $(-x,y)$ The *x*-coordinate is negative and the *y*-coordinate is positive.

Quadrant III: $(-x,-y)$ The *x*- and *y*-coordinates are both negative.

Quadrant IV: $(x,-y)$ The *x*-coordinate is positive and the *y*-coordinate is negative.

Origin: $(0,0)$ The *x*- and *y*-coordinates are both zero at the origin.

FIGURE A-4

The four quadrants

The Cartesian coordinate system is a way to plot values of two variables simultaneously. Different quadrants reflect whether the values of *x* and *y* are positive or negative.

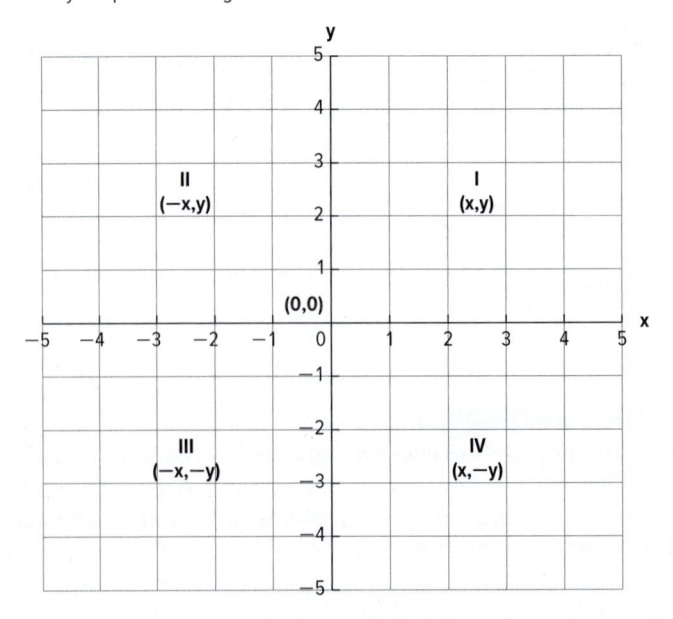

FIGURE A-5
Plotting points on a graph

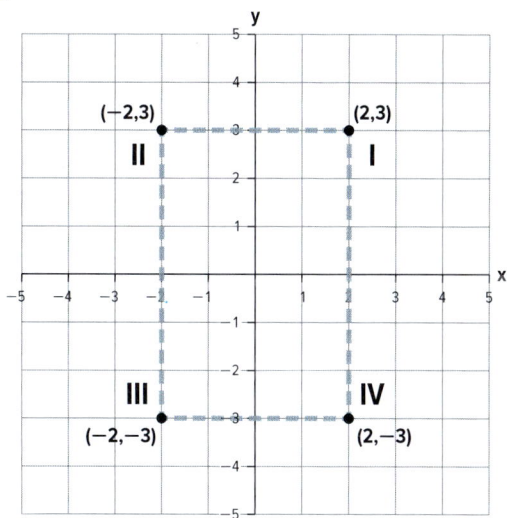

Each set of ordered pairs corresponds to a place on the Cartesian coordinate system.

Figure A-5 shows the following points plotted on a graph.

Quadrant I: (2,3)

Quadrant II: (−2,3)

Quadrant III: (−2,−3)

Quadrant IV: (2,−3)

In economics, we often isolate quadrant I when graphing. This is because there are many economic variables for which negative values do not make sense. For example, one important graph we use in economics is the relationship between the price of a good and the quantity of that good demanded or supplied. Since it doesn't make sense to consider negative prices and quantities, we show only quadrant I when graphing supply and demand.

Figure A-6 shows a line in quadrant I that represents the relationship between the price of hot dogs at the ballpark and the quantity of hot dogs that a family wants to buy. Price is on the y-axis and the quantity of hot dogs the family demands is on the x-axis. For instance, one coordinate pair on this line is (3,2), meaning that if the price of hot dogs is $2, the family will want to buy 3 of them.

We could extend this demand curve in ways that make sense graphically but that don't represent logical price-quantity combinations in the real world. For instance, if we extend the demand curve into quadrant II, we have points such as (−2,7). If we extend the demand curve into quadrant IV, we have points such as (6,−1). However, it doesn't make sense to talk about someone demanding negative 2 hot dogs, nor does it make sense to think about a price of negative $1.

Remember that we are not just graphing arbitrary points. Rather, we are illustrating a real relationship between variables that has meaning in the real world. Both (−2,7) and (6,−1) are points that are consistent with the equation for this demand curve, but neither point makes sense to include in our analysis. For graphing this price-quantity relationship, we would limit our graph to quadrant I.

However, some variables you will study (such as revenue) may have negative values that make sense. When this is the case, graphs will show multiple quadrants.

FIGURE A-6
Thinking about the logic behind graphs

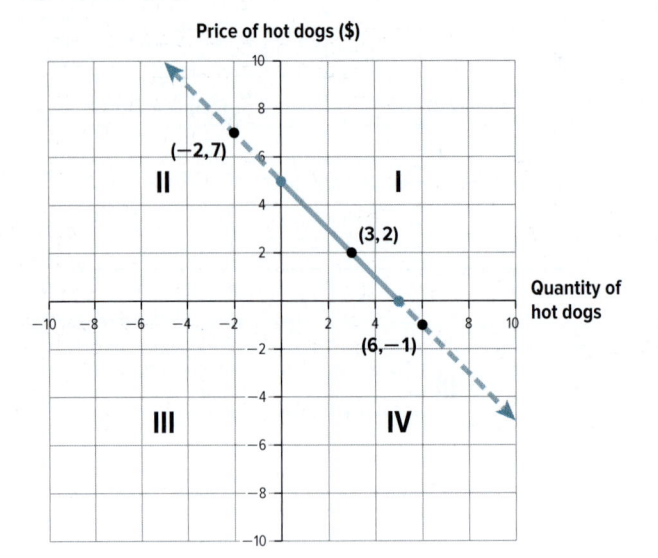

Plotting points in the four quadrants on a graph gives a line.

Slope

Both the table and the graph in Figure A-7 represent a particular relationship between two variables, x and y. For every x, there is a corresponding y. When we plot the points in the table, we see that there is a consistent relationship between the value of x and the value of y. In this case, we can see at a glance that whenever the x value increases by 1, the y value increases by 0.5. We can describe this relationship as the *slope* of the line.

FIGURE A-7
The slope of a line

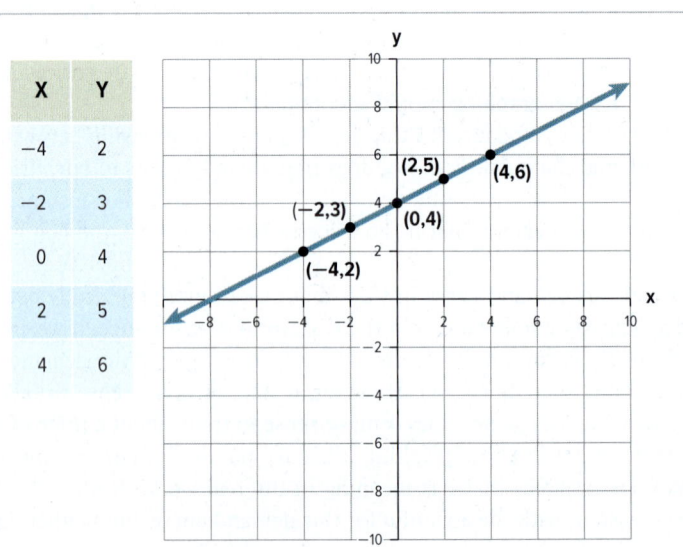

X	Y
−4	2
−2	3
0	4
2	5
4	6

Slope refers to the shape of the line and is determined by the change in y and x.

Slope is a ratio of vertical distance (change in y) to horizontal distance (change in x). We begin to calculate slope by labeling one point along the line Point 1, which we denote (x_1, y_1), and another point along the line Point 2, which we denote (x_2, y_2). We can then calculate the horizontal distance by subtracting x_1 from x_2. We calculate vertical distance by subtracting y_1 from y_2.

slope
the ratio of vertical distance (change in y) to horizontal distance (change in x)

EQUATION A-1
$$\text{Horizontal distance} = \Delta x = (x_2 - x_1)$$
$$\text{Vertical distance} = \Delta y = (y_2 - y_1)$$

The vertical distance is sometimes referred to as the **rise**, while the horizontal distance is known as the **run**. "Rise over run" is an easy way to remember how to calculate slope.

rise
vertical distance; calculated as the change in y

EQUATION A-2
$$\text{Slope} = \frac{\text{Rise}}{\text{Run}} = \frac{\Delta y}{\Delta x} = \frac{(y_2 - y_1)}{(x_2 - x_1)}$$

run
horizontal distance; calculated as the change in x

When the relationship between x and y is linear (which means that it forms a straight line), the slope is constant. That is, for each one-unit change in the x-variable, the corresponding y-variable always changes by the same amount. Therefore, we can use any two points to calculate the slope of the line—it doesn't matter which ones we pick because the slope is the same everywhere on the line.

Slope gives us important information about the relationship between our two variables. As you'll see, slope tells us something about both the direction of the relationship between two variables (whether they move in the same direction) and the magnitude of the relationship (how much y changes in response to a change in x).

Calculating slope

In Figure A-8, the rise, or vertical distance between point (2,3) and point (4,5), is 5 minus 3, which equals 2. The run, or horizontal distance, is 4 minus 2, which equals 2. Therefore, the slope of the line in Figure A-8 is calculated as:

LO A.2 Use data to calculate slope.

$$\text{Slope} = \frac{(y_2 - y_1)}{(x_2 - x_1)} = \frac{(5 - 3)}{(4 - 2)} = \frac{2}{2} = 1$$

Let's return to Figure A-7 and apply this same calculation. Because the relationship between x and y is linear, we can use any two points to calculate the slope. Let's pick the point (2,5) to be point 1, which we call (x_1, y_1). Then, pick the point (4,6) to be point 2, which we call (x_2, y_2).

$$\frac{(y_2 - y_1)}{(x_2 - x_1)} = \frac{(6 - 5)}{(4 - 2)} = \frac{1}{2} = 0.5$$

Note that it doesn't matter which point we pick as point 1 and which as point 2. We could have chosen 5 as y_2 and 6 as y_1 rather than vice versa. All that matters is that y_1 is from the same ordered pair as x_1 and y_2 from the same pair as x_2. To prove that this is true, let's calculate slope again using (2,5) as point 2. The slope still comes out to 0.5:

$$\frac{(y_2 - y_1)}{(x_2 - x_1)} = \frac{(5 - 6)}{(2 - 4)} = \frac{(-1)}{(-2)} = \frac{1}{2} = 0.5$$

Use two different points from the table in Figure A-7 to calculate slope again. Try using the points (−4,2) and (0,4). Do you get 0.5 as your answer?

FIGURE A-8
Calculating slope

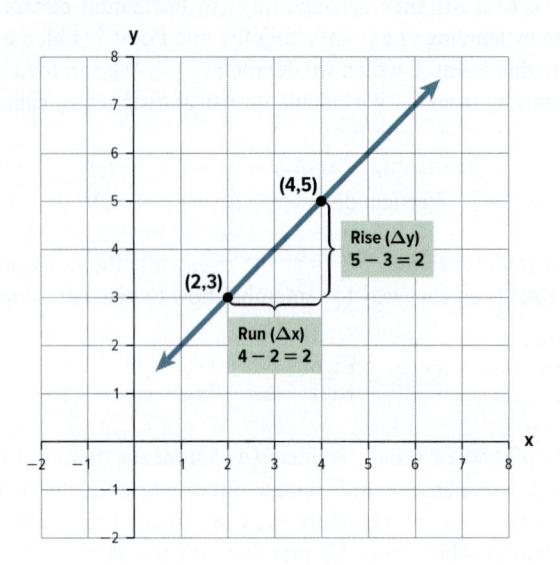

You can calculate the slope by dividing the change in the *y* value over the change in *x*—the rise over the run.

The direction of a slope

LO A.3 Interpret what the direction and steepness of slope indicate about a line.

The direction of a slope tells us something meaningful about the relationship between the two variables we are representing. For instance, when children get older, they grow taller. If we represented this relationship in a graph, we would see an upward-sloping line, telling us that height increases as age increases, rather than decreasing. Of course, it is common knowledge that children get taller, not shorter, as they get older. But if we were looking at a graph of a relationship we did not already understand, the slope of the line would show us at a glance how the two variables relate to one another.

To see how we can learn from the direction of a slope and how to calculate it, look at the graphs in panels A and B of Figure A-9.

In panel A, we can see that when *x* increases from 1 to 2, *y* also increases, from 2 to 4. If we move the other direction down the line, we see that when *x* decreases from 2 to 1, *y* also decreases, from 4 to 2. In other words, *x* and *y* move in the same direction. Therefore, *x* and *y* are said to have a *positive relationship*. Not surprisingly, this means that the slope of the line is a positive number:

$$\text{Slope} = \frac{\Delta y}{\Delta x} = \frac{2}{1} = 2$$

When the slope of a line is positive, we know that *y* increases as *x* increases, and *y* decreases as *x* decreases. If a line leans upward, then its slope is positive.

Now, turn to the graph in panel B. In this case, when *x* increases from 1 to 2, *y* decreases from 4 to 2. Reading from the other direction, when *x* decreases from 2 to 1, *y* increases from 2 to 4. Therefore, *x* and *y* move in opposite directions and are said to have a *negative relationship*. The slope of the line is a negative number:

$$\text{Slope} = \frac{\Delta y}{\Delta x} = \frac{-2}{1} = -2$$

FIGURE A-9
The direction of a slope

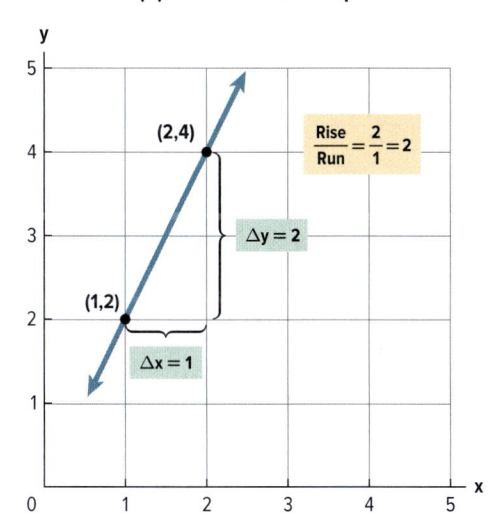

(A) Positive relationship

$\frac{\text{Rise}}{\text{Run}} = \frac{2}{1} = 2$

Points: (1,2), (2,4); $\Delta y = 2$, $\Delta x = 1$

If a line slopes upward, its slope is positive; y increases as x increases, or y decreases as x decreases.

(B) Negative relationship

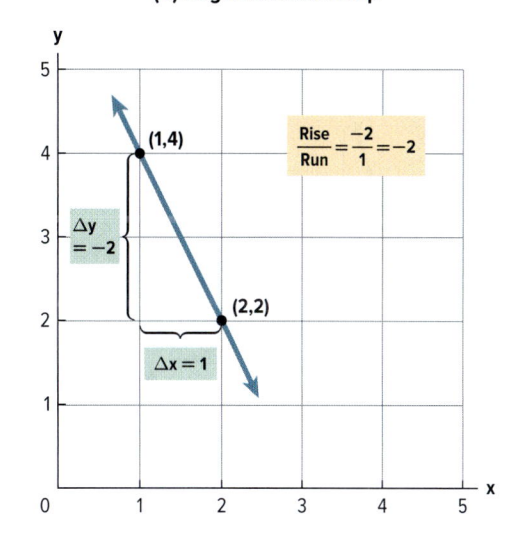

$\frac{\text{Rise}}{\text{Run}} = \frac{-2}{1} = -2$

Points: (1,4), (2,2); $\Delta y = -2$, $\Delta x = 1$

If a line slopes downward, its slope is negative: y decreases as x increases, or y increases as x decreases.

When the slope of a line is negative, we know that y decreases as x increases, and y increases as x decreases. If a line leans downward, then its slope is negative.

In Chapter 3, "Markets," you will see applications of these positive and negative relationships between the variables price and quantity. Here's a preview:

- You will see a positive relationship between price and quantity when you encounter a *supply curve*. You will learn the meaning of that positive relationship: As the price of a good increases, suppliers are willing to supply a larger quantity to markets. Supply curves, therefore, are upward-sloping.
- You will see a negative relationship between price and quantity when you encounter a *demand curve*. You will learn the meaning of that negative relationship: As the price of a good increases, consumers are willing to purchase a smaller quantity. Demand curves are downward-sloping.

From these examples, you can see that two variables (such as price and quantity) may have more than one relationship with each other, depending on whose choices they represent and under what circumstances.

The steepness of a slope

In addition to the *direction* of the relationship between variables, the *steepness* of the slope also gives us important information. It tells us how much y changes for a given change in x.

In both panels of Figure A-10, the relationship between x and y is positive (upward-sloping), and the distance between the x values, Δx, is the same. However, the change in y that results from a one-unit change in x is greater in panel A than it is in panel B. In other words, the slope is *steeper* in panel A and *flatter* in panel B.

FIGURE A-10
The steepness of a slope

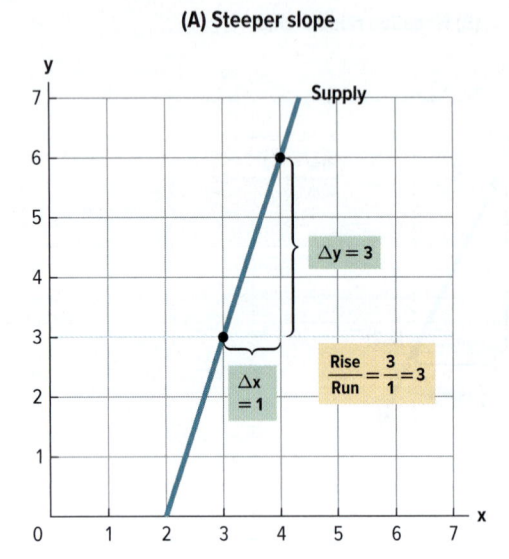

(A) Steeper slope

(B) Flatter slope

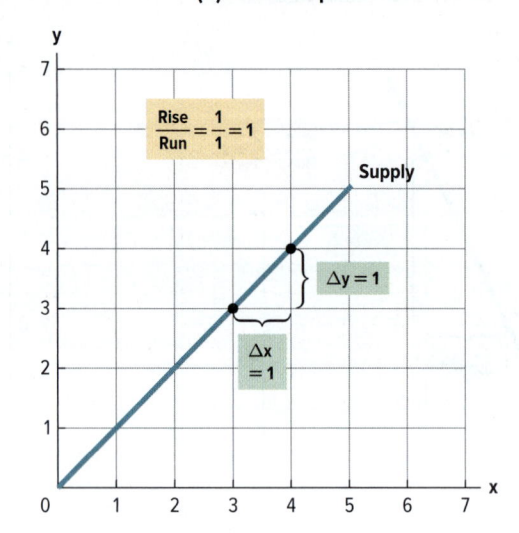

The larger the number representing slope is, the steeper the curve will be. The slope in panel A is steeper than the slope in panel B.

The closer the slope is to zero, the flatter the curve will be. The slope in panel B is flatter than the slope in panel A.

Numerically, the closer the number representing the slope is to zero, the flatter the curve will be. Remember that both positive and negative numbers can be close to zero. So, a slope of −1 is equally steep as a slope of 1, although one slopes downward and the other upward. Correspondingly, a line with a slope of −5 is steeper than a line with a slope of −1 or one with a slope of 1.

In general, slope is used to describe how much y changes in response to a one-unit change in x. In economics, we are sometimes interested in how much x changes in response to a one-unit change in y. For example, in Chapter 4, "Elasticity," you will see how quantity (on the x-axis) responds to a change in price (on the y-axis).

Key Terms
slope, p. 46G
rise, p. 46G
run, p. 46G

Problems and Applications

1. Create four quadrants using x- and y-axes. Use your graph to plot the following points. **[LO A.1]**
   a. (1,4)
   b. (−2,1)
   c. (−3,−3)
   d. (3,−2)

2. Create four quadrants using x- and y-axes. Use your graph to plot the following points. **[LO A.1]**
   a. (0,4)
   b. (0,−2)
   c. (1,0)
   d. (−3,0)

Math Essentials: Understanding Graphs and Slope ■ Appendix A   46K

3. Use the curve labeled "Demand" in Figure AP-1 to create a table (schedule) that shows Price in one column and Quantity in another. What is the slope of the curve labeled "Demand"? **[LO A.2]**

FIGURE AP-1

Price ($) vs Quantity graph showing a Demand curve from (0, 40) to (80, 0).

4. Use the curve labeled "Demand" in Figure AP-2 to create a table (schedule) that shows Price in one column and Quantity in another. What is the slope of the curve labeled "Demand"? **[LO A.2]**

FIGURE AP-2

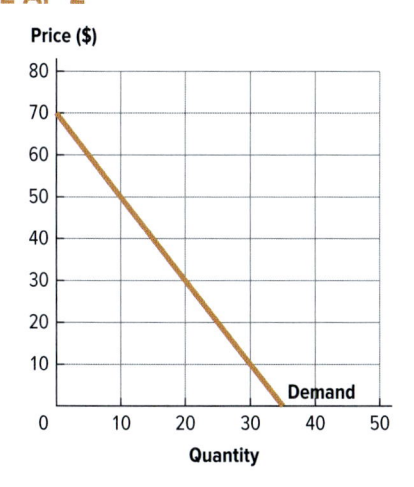

Price ($) vs Quantity graph showing a Demand curve from (0, 70) to (35, 0).

5. Use the information about price and quantity in Table AP-1 to create a graph, with Price on the y-axis and Quantity on the x-axis. Label the resulting curve "Demand." What is the slope of that curve? **[LO A.2]**

TABLE AP-1

Price ($)	Quantity
0	120
2	100
4	80
6	60
8	40
10	20
12	0

6. Use the information about price and quantity in Table AP-2 to create a graph, with Price on the y-axis and Quantity on the x-axis. Label the resulting curve "Demand." What is the slope of that curve? **[LO A.2]**

TABLE AP-2

Price ($)	Quantity
0	5
5	4
10	3
15	2
20	1
25	0

7. Use the curve labeled "Supply" in Figure AP-3 to create a table (schedule) that shows Price in one column and Quantity in another. What is the slope of the curve labeled "Supply"? [LO A.2]

FIGURE AP-3

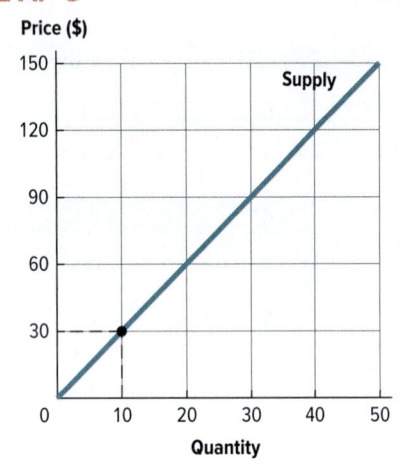

Price ($) vs Quantity, Supply curve from (0,0) through (10,30), (20,60), (30,90), (40,120), (50,150).

8. Use the curve labeled "Supply" in Figure AP-4 to create a table (schedule) that shows Price in one column and Quantity in another. What is the slope of the curve labeled "Supply"? [LO A.2]

FIGURE AP-4

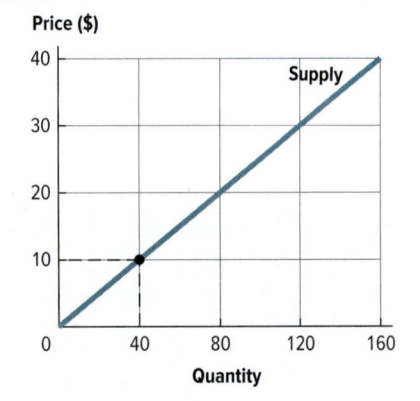

Price ($) vs Quantity, Supply curve from (0,0) through (40,10), (80,20), (120,30), (160,40).

9. Use the information about price and quantity in Table AP-3 to create a graph, with Price on the y-axis and Quantity on the x-axis. Label the resulting curve "Supply." What is the slope of that curve? [LO A.2]

TABLE AP-3

Price ($)	Quantity
0	0
25	5
50	10
75	15
100	20
125	25

10. Use the information about price and quantity in Table AP-4 to create a graph, with Price on the y-axis and Quantity on the x-axis. Label the resulting curve "Supply." What is the slope of that curve? [LO A.2]

TABLE AP-4

Price ($)	Quantity
0	0
2	8
4	16
6	24
8	32
10	40
12	48

11. What is the direction of slope indicated by the following examples? [LO A.3]

   a. As the price of rice increases, consumers want less of it.
   b. As the temperature increases, the amount of people who use the town pool also increases.
   c. As farmers use more fertilizer, their output of tomatoes increases.

12. Rank the following equations by the steepness of their slope from lowest to highest. [LO A.3]

   a. $y = -3x + 9$
   b. $y = 4x + 2$
   c. $y = -0.5x + 4$

Supply and Demand

PART TWO

The four chapters in Part 2 will introduce you to . . .

the basics of markets, which form the baseline for most economic analysis. Chapter 3, "Markets," introduces supply and demand. Any time we go into the store and decide to buy something, we act on our demand for that good. On the other side, the store figured out that it made sense for them to supply that good to us. The interaction between the forces of demand and supply determines the price we pay and how much gets bought and sold.

Chapters 4, 5, and 6 ("Elasticity," "Efficiency," and "Government Intervention") will use demand and supply to answer a variety of questions: Why do people rush to the store when Apple slashes the price of an iPhone? Why would the government ever want to set limits on prices in the market?

Together with Part 1, the chapters in this part introduce the basic concepts of economic problem solving. To start, we've stripped down these ideas to their simplest form. These same concepts will return throughout the text, and we will build on them as we turn to different problems.

Markets

Chapter 3

Mobiles Go Global

For many people, a cell phone is on the list of things never to leave the house without, right up there with a wallet and keys. For better or worse, cell phones have become a fixture of everyday life.

It's hard to believe that as recently as the late 1990s, cell phones were a luxury that only a third of Americans enjoyed. Before that, in the 1980s, they were big, heavy devices, seldom bought for personal use at all. In less than a quarter of a century, this expensive sci-fi technology became a relatively cheap, universal convenience. Today 95 percent of Americans own a cellphone. In fact, around two-thirds of the world's 7.4 billion people have a cell phone subscription.[1] For instance, 44 percent of Africa's 1.2 billion citizens now have service.[2] This phenomenal growth makes it easier to keep up with friends and family. It also connects small-town merchants to businesses in distant cities, opening up new economic possibilities.

©WAYHOME studio/Shutterstock

How does a product move from expensive to cheap, from rare to commonplace, so quickly? The answer partly lies in the relationship between supply and demand. This chapter shows how the forces of supply and demand interact to determine the quantities and prices of goods that are bought and sold in competitive markets.

The basic story of how a new product takes hold is a familiar one. In the beginning, cell phones were expensive and rare. Over time, the technology improved, the price dropped, the product caught on, and sales took off. Throughout this process of change, markets allow for ongoing communication between buyers and producers, using prices as a signal. The up-and-down movement of prices ensures that the quantity of a product that is available stays in balance with the quantity consumers want to buy.

To explain the leap in usage that cell phones have made over time, however, we need to go further than just price signals. Outside forces that influence supply and demand, such as changes in technology, fashion trends, and economic ups and downs, have driven that transformation. Markets have the remarkable ability to adjust to these changes without falling out of balance.

LEARNING OBJECTIVES

LO 3.1 Identify the defining characteristics of a competitive market.

LO 3.2 Draw a demand curve, and describe the external factors that determine demand.

LO 3.3 Distinguish between a shift in and a movement along the demand curve.

LO 3.4 Draw a supply curve and describe the external factors that determine supply.

LO 3.5 Distinguish between a shift in and a movement along the supply curve.

LO 3.6 Explain how supply and demand interact to drive markets to equilibrium.

LO 3.7 Evaluate the effect of changes in supply and demand on the equilibrium price and quantity.

In this chapter, we'll step into the shoes of consumers and producers to examine the trade-offs they face. We'll see that the issues that drive supply and demand in the cell phone industry are not unique. In fact, the functioning of markets, as summarized in the theory of supply and demand, is the bedrock of almost everything in this text. Mastering this theory will help you to solve all kinds of problems, from what price to sell your product for as a businessperson, to how to find the cheapest gasoline, to the causes of holiday toy shortages.

Markets

In Chapter 2, "Specialization and Exchange," we discussed the power of the "invisible hand" to coordinate complex economic interactions. The key feature of an economy organized by the invisible hand is that private individuals, rather than a centralized planning authority, make the decisions. Such an economy is often referred to as a **market economy**.

What is a market?

What do we mean by a *market?* The word might make you think of a physical location where buyers and sellers come together face-to-face—like a farmers' market or a mall. But people do not have to be physically near each other to make an exchange. For example, think of online retailers like Amazon.com or of fruit that is grown in South America but sold all over the world. The term **market** actually refers to the buyers and sellers who trade a particular good or service, not to a physical location.

Which buyers and sellers are included in the market depends on the context. The manager of a clothing store at your local mall might think about the market for T-shirts in terms of people who live locally and the other places they could buy T-shirts, like competing stores, garage sales, or online retailers. The CEO of a major clothing brand, on the other hand, might include garment factories in Bangladesh and the fashion preferences of customers living all over the world in her idea of a market. Which boundaries are relevant depends on the scope of trades that are being made.

market economy
an economy in which private individuals, rather than a centralized planning authority, make the decisions

market
buyers and sellers who trade a particular good or service

LO 3.1 Identify the defining characteristics of a competitive market.

What is a competitive market?

Making simplifying assumptions can help us zero in on important ideas. In this chapter, we will make a big simplifying assumption—that markets are *competitive*. A **competitive market** is one in which fully informed, price-taking buyers and sellers easily trade a standardized good or service. Let's unpack this multipart definition: Imagine you're driving up to an intersection where there is a gas station on each corner. This scenario demonstrates the four defining characteristics of a perfectly competitive market.

First, we bet you'd find that a gallon of gas costs almost the same in each station at the intersection. Why? Recall the third economists' question from Chapter 1, "Economics and Life": If one station tries to raise its price, *how will others respond?* Assuming the stations are offering standardized gallons of gas, customers should be indifferent between buying from one station or another at a given price. If one raises its price, all the drivers will simply go to a cheaper station instead. The gas station that raised prices will end up losing customers. For this reason, no individual seller has the power to change the market price. In economic terminology, a buyer or seller who cannot affect the market price is called a **price taker**.

The drivers going by are also price takers. If you try to negotiate a discount at one of the gas stations before filling your tank, you won't get far—the owner would rather wait and sell to other customers who will pay more. The price is the price; your choice is to take it or leave it. In competitive markets, both buyers and sellers are price takers.

Second, the gas sold by each station is the same—your car will run equally well regardless of *which* brand you buy. This means that the gas being sold is a **standardized good**—a good or service for which any two units of it have the same features and are interchangeable. In a competitive market, the good being bought and sold is standardized.

Third, the price at each gas station is prominently displayed on a big sign. As you drive by, you can immediately see how much a gallon of each type of gas costs at each station. In a competitive market, you have *full information* about the price and features of the good being bought and sold.

Finally, it's easy for you to choose any of the four gas stations at the intersection. The stations are very near each other, and you don't have to have special equipment to fill up your tank or pay an entrance fee to get into the station. In competitive markets, there are no **transaction costs**—the costs incurred by buyer and seller in agreeing to and executing a sale of goods or services. Thus, in competitive markets, you don't have to pay anything for the privilege of buying or selling in the market. You can easily do business in this four-station market for gasoline.

By thinking about the gas stations at a single intersection, you have learned the four characteristics of perfectly competitive markets. Table 3-1 summarizes the four characteristics of a perfectly competitive market: price-taking participants, a standardized good, full information, and no transaction costs.

In reality, few markets are truly *perfectly* competitive. Even gas stations at the same intersection might not be: Maybe one can charge a few cents more per gallon because it uses gas with less ethanol or offers regular customers an attractive loyalty scheme or has a Dunkin' Donuts to entice hungry drivers. In future chapters, we'll spend a lot of time thinking about the different ways that markets in the real world are structured and why it matters when they fall short of perfect competition.

The market for cell phones is not perfectly competitive either. Cell phones are not standardized goods—some models look cooler, or have better cameras, or have access to different apps or calling plans. You're unlikely to be completely indifferent between two different cell phones at the same price, as you are between two gallons of gas. Furthermore, the fact that there are a limited number of service providers means that sellers aren't always price takers. If only one network has

competitive market
a market in which fully informed, price-taking buyers and sellers easily trade a standardized good or service

price taker
a buyer or seller who cannot affect the market price. In a perfectly competitive market, firms are price takers as a consequence of many sellers selling standardized goods

standardized good
a good for which any two units have the same features and are interchangeable

transaction costs
the costs incurred by buyer and seller in agreeing to and executing a sale of goods or services

Characteristic	Description
Participants are price takers	Neither buyers nor sellers have the power to affect the market price.
Standardized good	Any two units of the good have the same features and are interchangeable.
Full information	Market participants know everything about the price and features of the good.
No transaction costs	There is no cost to participate in exchanges in the market.

TABLE 3-1

Four characteristics of perfectly competitive markets

good coverage in your area or has an exclusive deal with a popular type of phone, it can get away with charging a premium.

So, why do we *assume* perfect competition if markets in the real world are rarely perfectly competitive? The answer is that the simple model of competitive markets we will develop in this chapter leads us to useful insights, even in markets that aren't perfectly competitive. Taking the time now to make sure you understand perfect competition, inside and out, will better prepare you to understand why it matters when markets aren't perfectly competitive. As we go through this chapter, we'll note some ways in which the real cell phone market departs from perfect competition. By the end of the chapter, we hope you'll agree that the simple model of perfect competition tells us a lot, if not everything, about how the real cell phone market works.

✓ TEST YOURSELF

☐ What is a market? What are the characteristics of a competitive market? **[LO 3.1]**

☐ Why are participants in competitive markets called *price takers*? **[LO 3.1]**

Demand

Demand describes how much of something people are willing and able to buy under certain circumstances. Suppose someone approached you and asked if you would like a new cell phone. What would you answer? You might think, "Sure," but as a savvy person, you would probably first ask, "For how much?" Whether you want something (or how much of it you want) depends on how much you have to pay for it.

These days most people in the United States have cell phones, but that hasn't been the case for very long. Let's assume for the sake of our model that cell phones are standardized—one model, with given features and calling plans. Now, put yourself in the position of a consumer in the mid-1990s (maybe a relative of yours, for example). You face purchasing decisions at different prices:

- Maybe you've seen cell phones advertised at $499 and think it's not worth it to you.
- As the price goes down over time to $399, and $299, you're still not tempted to buy it.
- At $199, you start to consider it.
- Then, the first time you see a cell phone advertised for less than $125, you decide to buy.

Different people bought their first cell phone at different prices: At any given time, with any given price, some people in the population are willing and able to buy a phone and others aren't. If we add up all of these individual choices, we get overall *market demand*. The amount of a particular good that buyers in a market will purchase at a given price during a specified period is called the **quantity demanded**. For almost all goods, the lower the price goes, the higher the quantity demanded.

quantity demanded the amount of a particular good that buyers will purchase at a given price during a specified period

law of demand a fundamental characteristic of demand that states that, all else equal, quantity demanded rises as price falls

This inverse relationship between price and quantity demanded is so important that economists refer to it as the **law of demand**. The first requirement for the law of demand is the idea sometimes known as *ceteris paribus*, the Latin term for "all other things being the same." In other words, the law of demand says that, when all else is held equal (when all other factors remain the same), quantity demanded rises as price falls.

Economists frequently rely on the idea of *ceteris paribus* to isolate the expected effect of a single change in the economy. For example, suppose you want to predict what would happen next year to cell phone sales if cell phone prices go down. The law of demand tells us that if cell phone prices go down, *holding all else equal*, quantity demanded will go up.

But what if the economy is not doing well next year and consumers hold back on buying new cell phones? In this instance, we *cannot* say in general that "if cell phone prices go down, quantity demanded will go up" because not everything else has been held the same. Instead, the negative impact of the weak economy may offset the positive impact of the reduction in price. We need to be more specific. So, it is critical to "hold all else equal" in order to make clear statements about what we can predict.

The law of demand isn't a made-up law that economists have imposed on markets. Rather, it holds true because it describes the underlying reality of individual people's decisions. The key is to think about the *trade-offs* that people face when making the decision to buy.

What happens when the price of something falls? First, the benefit that you get from purchasing it remains the same because the item itself is unchanged. But the opportunity cost has fallen: When the price goes down, you don't have to give up as many other purchases in order to get the item. When benefits stay the same and opportunity cost goes down, this trade-off suddenly starts to look a lot better. When the trade-off between costs and benefits tips toward benefits, more people will want to buy the good.

Of course, falling prices will not have been the only consideration in people's decisions to buy their first cell phone. Some might have decided to buy one when they got a pay raise at work. Others might have bought one at the point when most of their friends owned one. Incomes, expectations, and tastes all play a role; economists call these factors *nonprice determinants* of demand. We'll discuss their potential effects later in this chapter. First, let's focus on the relationship between price and quantity demanded.

The demand curve

The law of demand says that the quantity of cell phones demanded will be different at every price level. For this reason, it is often useful to represent demand as a table, called a **demand schedule**. A demand schedule shows the quantities of a particular good or service that consumers are willing and able to purchase (demand) at various prices. Panel A of Figure 3-1 shows a hypothetical annual demand schedule for cell phones in the United States. (Remember, we're assuming that cell phones are a standardized good. This isn't quite right, but the basic principle holds true: When cell phone prices are lower, you're more likely to buy a new one.) The demand schedule assumes that factors other than price remain the same.

Panel B of Figure 3-1 shows another way to represent demand, by drawing each price-quantity combination from the demand schedule as a point on a graph. That graph, called a **demand curve**, visually displays the demand schedule. That is, it is a graph that shows the quantities of a particular good or service that consumers will demand at various prices. The demand curve also represents consumers' *willingness to buy:* It shows the highest amount consumers will pay for any given quantity.

On the demand curve, quantity goes on the *x*-axis (the horizontal axis) and price on the *y*-axis (the vertical axis). The result is a downward-sloping line that reflects the inverse relationship between price and quantity. The demand curve in Figure 3-1 represents exactly the same information as the demand schedule.

Determinants of demand

The demand curve represents the relationship between price and quantity demanded *with everything else held constant*. If everything else is *not* held constant—that is, if one of the nonprice factors that determines demand changes—the curve will shift.

The downward-sloping demand curve reflects the trade-offs that people face between (1) the benefit they expect to receive from a good and (2) the opportunity cost they face for buying it. Therefore, any factor that changes this balance at a given price will change people's willingness to buy, and thus their purchasing decisions.

The nonprice determinants of demand can be divided into five major categories:

- Consumer preferences.
- The prices of related goods.
- Income of the consumers.
- Expectations of future prices.
- The number of buyers in the market.

LO 3.2 Draw a demand curve, and describe the external factors that determine demand.

demand schedule
a table that shows the quantities of a particular good or service that consumers are willing and able to purchase (demand) at various prices

demand curve
a graph that shows the quantities of a particular good or service that consumers will demand at various prices

Since demand curves and other material in this chapter make extensive use of lines and linear equations, you may want to review those concepts in Appendix B, "Math Essentials: Working with Linear Equations," which follows this chapter.

FIGURE 3-1
Demand schedule and the demand curve

(A) Demand schedule

Cell phones (millions)	Price ($)
30	180
60	160
90	140
120	120
150	100
180	80
210	60
240	40
270	20

This demand schedule shows the quantity of cell phones demanded each year at various prices. As prices decrease, consumers want to purchase more cell phones.

(B) Demand curve

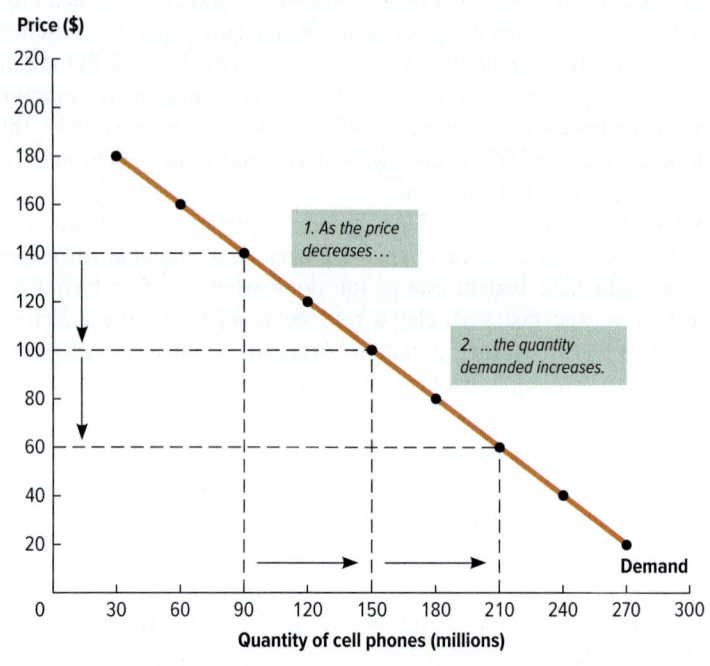

1. As the price decreases…
2. …the quantity demanded increases.

This demand curve is a graphic representation of the demand schedule for cell phones in the United States. Each entry in the demand schedule is plotted on this curve.

Table 3-2 summarizes the impact of each factor on demand. Each of these nonprice determinants affects either the benefits or the opportunity cost of buying a good, even if the price of the good itself remains the same.

> ### ⚠ CAUTION: COMMON MISTAKE
>
> You may notice that these five factors include price-related issues such as the price of related goods and expectations about future prices. So why do we refer to them as *nonprice determinants*? We do so in order to differentiate them from the effect of the *current price* of the good on demand for that good.

Consumer preferences Consumer preferences are the personal likes and dislikes that make buyers more or less inclined to purchase a good. We don't need to know *why* people like what they like or to agree with their preferences; we just need to know that these likes and dislikes influence their purchases. At any given price, some consumers will get more enjoyment (i.e., benefits) out of a cell phone than do others. That enjoyment may be based simply on how much they like talking to friends, or whether they use their phones for work, or any number of other personal preferences.

TABLE 3-2
Determinants of demand

Determinant	Examples of an increase in demand	Examples of a decrease in demand
Consumer preferences	A "Buy American" ad campaign appeals to national pride, increasing the demand for U.S.-made sneakers.	An outbreak of *E. coli* decreases the demand for spinach.
Prices of related goods	A decrease in the price of hot dogs increases the demand for relish, a complementary good.	A decrease in taxi fares decreases the demand for subway rides, a substitute good.
Incomes	An economic downturn lowers incomes, increasing the demand for ground beef, an inferior good.	An economic downturn lowers incomes, decreasing the demand for steak, a normal good.
Expectations	A hurricane destroys part of the world papaya crop, causing expectations that prices will rise and increasing the current demand for papayas.	An announcement that a new smartphone soon will be released decreases the demand for the current model.
Number of buyers	An increase in life expectancy increases the demand for nursing homes and medical care.	A falling birthrate decreases the demand for diapers.

Some consumer preferences are fairly constant across time, such as those that arise from personality traits or cultural attitudes and beliefs. For example, a recluse may have little desire for a cell phone; an on-the-go executive may find a cell phone (or two) to be essential. Other preferences will change over time, in response to external events or fads. For instance, it's more useful to own a cell phone when all your friends already have one. And more people may demand cell phones after a national disaster, knowing they want to be able to reach their families in emergencies.

Prices of related goods Another factor that affects the demand for a particular good is the prices of related goods. There are two kinds of related goods: substitutes and complements.

We say that goods are **substitutes** when they serve similar-enough purposes that a consumer might purchase one in place of the other—for example, rice and pasta. If the price of rice doubles while the price of pasta stays the same, demand for pasta will increase. That's because the *opportunity cost* of pasta has decreased: You can buy less rice for the same amount of money, so you give up less potential rice when you buy pasta. If the two goods are quite similar, we call them *close substitutes*. Similar fishes, such as salmon and trout, might be considered close substitutes.

For many Americans deciding whether to buy their first cell phone, the nearest substitute would have been a landline phone. Cell phones and landlines are not very close substitutes: You can use them for the same purposes at home or the office, but only one of them can go for a walk with you. Still, if the price of U.S. landline phone service had suddenly skyrocketed, we can be sure that change would have increased the demand for cell phones.

In fact, the very high cost of landline phone services in many developing countries is one reason why cell phones spread very quickly. In the United States, almost every household had a landline phone before it had a cell phone. In many poor countries, landlines are so expensive that very few people can afford one. That's why cell phones are often called a *leapfrog technology:* People go straight from no phone to cell phone, hopping over an entire stage of older technology.

Related goods that are consumed together, so that purchasing one will make a consumer more likely to purchase the other, are called **complements**. Peanut butter and jelly, cereal and milk, cars and gasoline are all complements. If the price of one of the two goods increases, demand for the other will likely decrease. Why? As consumers purchase less of the first good, they will want less

substitutes
goods that serve a similar-enough purpose that a consumer might purchase one in place of the other

complements
goods that are consumed together, so that purchasing one will make consumers more likely to purchase the other

of the other to go with it. Conversely, if the price of one of the two goods declines, demand for the other will likely increase. For example, when the prices of new cell phones fall, consumers will be more likely to buy new accessories to go with them.

Incomes Not surprisingly, the amount of income people earn affects their demand for goods and services: The bigger your paycheck, the more money you can afford to spend on the things you want. The smaller your paycheck, the more you have to cut back.

Most goods are **normal goods**, meaning that an increase in income causes an increase in demand. Likewise, for normal goods, a decrease in income causes a decrease in demand. For most people, cell phones are a normal good. If someone cannot currently afford a cell phone, she's more likely to buy one when her income rises. If someone already has a cell phone, she's more likely to upgrade to a newer, fancier cell phone when her income rises.

For some goods, called **inferior goods**, the opposite relationship holds: As income increases, demand decreases. Typically, people replace inferior goods with more expensive and appealing substitutes when their incomes rise. For many people, inexpensive grocery items like instant noodles, some canned foods, and generic store brands might be inferior goods. When their incomes rise, people replace these goods with fresher, more expensive ingredients. Decreases in income occur for many people during economic downturns; thus, the demand for inferior goods reflects the overall health of the economy. For an example, see the Economics in Action box "Can instant noodle sales predict a recession?"

normal goods
goods for which demand increases as income increases

inferior goods
goods for which demand decreases as income increases

Can instant noodle sales predict a recession?
Economics in Action

If you were to open a typical college student's kitchen cupboard, what would you find? Many students rely on a decidedly unglamorous food item: ramen instant noodles. Packed with cheap calories, this tasty snack is famously inexpensive.

Ramen noodles are an example of an inferior good. When people's budgets are tight (as are those of most students), these noodles sell well. When incomes rise, ramen sales drop and more expensive foods replace them.

In Thailand, ramen noodles have even been used as an indicator of overall economic health. The Mama Noodles Index tracks sales of a popular brand of instant ramen noodles. Because the demand for inferior goods increases when incomes go down, an increase in ramen sales could signal a downturn in incomes and an oncoming recession. In fact, observers of the Thai economy say that the Mama Noodles Index does a pretty good job of reflecting changing economic conditions.

Even the demand for inferior goods may decrease during severe economic downturns, however. Although the Mama Noodles Index has risen as expected when the Thai economy falters, the index unexpectedly dropped 15 percent during the deep recession of early 2009.

So are instant noodles an inferior good or a normal good? In Thailand, the answer may depend on who you are or how severely your income has dropped. For the middle class, who choose between ramen and more expensive

When budgets are tight, ramen noodles tend to sell well. When incomes rise, ramen sales tend to drop.
©Alexander Alexeev/123RF

foods, ramen may indeed be an inferior good. For the poor, whose choice more likely is whether or not they will get enough to eat, ramen may be a normal good. When their incomes rise, they may buy more ramen; when their incomes fall, even noodles may be a luxury.

Sources: "Using their noodles," *Associated Press,* September 5, 2005, www.theage.com.au/news/world/using-their-noodles/2005/09/04/1125772407287.html.; Kwanchai Rungfapaisarn, "Downturn bites into instant-noodle market as customers tighten belts," *The Nation,* March 20, 2009, www.nationmultimedia.com/business/Downturn-bites-into-instant-noodle-market-as-custo-30098402.html.

Expectations Changes in consumers' expectations about the future—especially future prices—can also affect demand. If consumers expect prices to fall in the future, they may postpone a purchase until a later date, causing current demand to decrease. If you think cell phones will go on sale in a few months, you might put off your purchase until then. Or you might delay upgrading your smartphone in the hope that when the next model releases, the current model will drop in price. When prices are expected to drop in the future, demand decreases.

Conversely, if consumers expect prices to rise in the future, they may wish to purchase a good immediately to avoid a higher price. This reasoning often occurs in speculative markets, like the stock market or sometimes the housing market. Buyers purchase stock or a house expecting prices to rise, so they can sell at a profit. In these markets, then, demand increases when prices are low and are expected to rise.

Number of buyers The demand curve represents the demand of a particular number of potential buyers. In general, an increase in the number of potential buyers in a market will increase demand. A decrease in the number of buyers will decrease it. Major population shifts, like an increase in immigration or a drop in the birthrate, can create nationwide changes in demand. As the number of teenagers and college students increases, the demand for cell phones increases too.

Shifts in the demand curve

What happens to the demand curve when one of the five nonprice determinants of demand changes? The entire demand curve shifts, either to the right or to the left. The shift is horizontal rather than vertical because nonprice determinants affect the quantity demanded at *each* price. When the quantity demanded at a given price is now higher, the point on the curve corresponding to that price is now further right. When the quantity demanded at a given price is lower, the point on the curve corresponding to that price is now further left.

Consider what happens, for example, when the economy is growing and people's incomes are rising. Let's assume the price of cell phones does not change ("all else held equal"). But with rising incomes, more people will choose to buy a new cell phone at any given price, causing quantity demanded to be higher at every possible price. Panel A of Figure 3-2 shows the resulting shift of the demand curve to the right, from D_A to D_B. In contrast, if the economy falls into a recession and people begin pinching pennies, quantity demanded will decrease at every price, and the curve will shift to the left, from D_A to D_C.

It is important to distinguish between these *shifts* in demand, which move the entire curve, and *movements along* a given demand curve. Remember this key point: *Shifts in the demand curve are caused by changes in the nonprice determinants of demand.* A recession, for example, would lower incomes and move the whole demand curve left. When we say "demand decreases," this is what we are talking about.

In contrast, suppose that the price of phones increases but everything else stays the same—that is, there is no change in the nonprice determinants of demand. Because the demand curve describes the quantity consumers will demand at any possible price, not just the current market price, we don't have to shift the curve to figure out what happens when the price goes up. Instead,

LO 3.3 Distinguish between a shift in and a movement along the demand curve.

FIGURE 3-2

Shifts in the demand curve versus movement along the demand curve

(A) Shifts in the demand curve

When demand decreases, the demand curve shifts to the left. When demand increases, the demand curve shifts to the right.

Curves shown: D_B, D_A, D_C

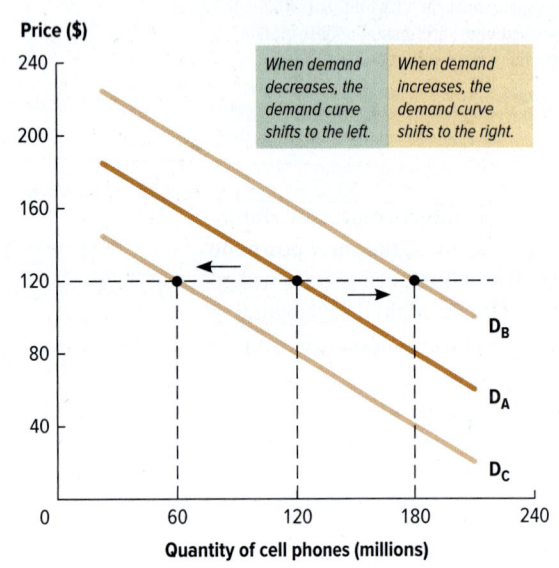

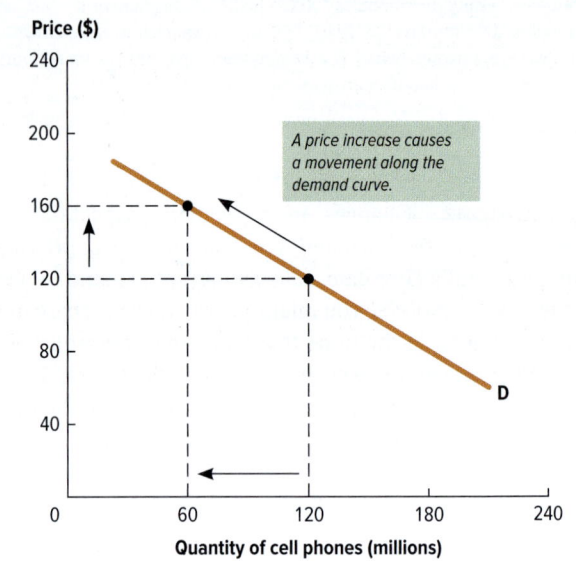

Changes in external factors cause the entire demand curve to shift. The shift from D_A to D_B represents an increase in demand, meaning that consumers want to buy more cell phones at each price. The shift from D_A to D_C represents a decrease in demand, meaning that consumers want to buy fewer cell phones at each price.

(B) Movement along the demand curve

A price increase causes a movement along the demand curve.

A price change causes a movement along the demand curve, but the curve itself remains constant.

---

we simply look at a different point on the curve to describe what is actually happening in the market right now.

To find the quantity that consumers will want to purchase at this new price, we move along the existing demand curve from the old price to the new one. If, for instance, the price of cell phones increases, we find the new quantity demanded by moving up along the demand curve to the new price point, as shown in panel B of Figure 3-2. The price change does not shift the curve itself because the curve already describes what consumers will do at any price.

To summarize, panel A of Figure 3-2 shows a *shift in demand* as the result of a change in the nonprice determinants; panel B shows a *movement along the demand curve* as the result of a change in price.

Economists use very specific terminology to distinguish between a shift in the demand curve and movement along the demand curve:

- We say that a change in one of the nonprice determinants of demand causes an "increase in demand" or "decrease in demand"—that is, a *shift* of the entire demand curve.
- To distinguish this from *movement along* the demand curve, we say that a change in price causes an "increase in the quantity demanded" or "decrease in the quantity demanded."

Just keep in mind that a "change in demand" is different from a "change in the quantity demanded." Observing this seemingly small difference in terminology prevents a great deal of confusion.

Understanding the effects of changes in both price and the nonprice determinants of demand is a key tool for businesspeople and policy-makers. Suppose you are in charge of an industry group whose members want to spur demand for cell phones. One idea might be to start an advertising campaign to increase the real or perceived benefits of owning a cell phone. If you understand the determinants of demand, you know that the advertising campaign would change consumer preferences. In other words, a successful advertising campaign would shift the demand curve for cell phones to the right. Similarly, if you are a congressional representative who is considering a tax cut to stimulate the economy, you know that a tax cut increases consumers' disposable incomes, increasing the demand for all normal goods. In other words, you are hoping that the resulting increase in incomes will shift the demand curve for cell phones to the right.

✓ TEST YOURSELF

- ☐ What are the five nonprice determinants of demand? **[LO 3.2]**
- ☐ What is the difference between a change in demand and a change in quantity demanded? **[LO 3.3]**

Supply

We've discussed the factors that determine how many phones consumers want to buy at a given price. But are cell phone producers necessarily willing to sell that many? The concept of *supply* describes how much of a good or service producers will offer for sale under given circumstances. The **quantity supplied** is the amount of a particular good or service that producers will offer for sale at a given price during a specified period.

As with demand, we can find overall *market supply* by adding up the individual decisions of each producer. Imagine you own a factory that can produce cell phones or other consumer electronics. You face production decisions at different prices:

- If the price of cell phones is $110, you might decide there's good money to be made and use your entire factory space to produce cell phones.
- If the price is only $80, you might produce some cell phones but decide it will be more profitable to devote part of your factory to producing laptop computers.
- If the cell phone price drops to $55, you might decide you'd make more money by producing only laptops.

Each producer will have a different price point at which it decides it's worthwhile to supply cell phones. This rule—all else held equal, quantity supplied increases as price increases—is called the **law of supply**.

(In reality, it's costly to switch a factory from making cell phones to laptops or other goods. However, the simple version illustrates a basic truth: The higher the price of a good, the more of that good producers will want to supply. Similarly, the lower the price of a good, the less of that good producers will want to supply.)

As with demand, supply varies with price because the decision to produce a good is about the *trade-off* between the benefit the producer will receive from selling the good and the opportunity cost of the time and resources that go into producing it. When the market price goes up and all other factors remain constant, the benefit of production increases relative to the opportunity cost, and the trade-off involved in production makes it more favorable to produce more.

For instance, if the price of phones goes up and the prices of raw materials stay the same, existing phone producers may open new factories, and new companies may start looking to enter the cell phone market. The same holds true across other industries. If air travelers seem willing to pay higher prices, airlines will increase the frequency of flights, add new routes, and buy new planes so they can carry more passengers. When prices drop, they cut back their flight schedules and cancel their orders for new planes.

quantity supplied
the amount of a particular good or service that producers will offer for sale at a given price during a specified period

law of supply
a fundamental characteristic of supply that states that, all else equal, quantity supplied rises as price rises

The supply curve

Like demand, supply can be represented as a table or a graph. A **supply schedule** is a table that shows the quantities of a particular good or service that producers will supply at various prices. Panel A of Figure 3-3 shows a hypothetical supply schedule for U.S. cell phone providers.

A **supply curve** is a graph of the information in the supply schedule. Just as the demand curve showed consumers' willingness to buy, so the supply curve shows producers' *willingness to sell*: It shows the minimum price producers must receive to supply any given quantity. Panel B of Figure 3-3 shows the supply curve of U.S. cell phone providers—visually representing the supply schedule.

Determinants of supply

The law of supply describes how the quantity that producers are willing to supply changes as price changes. But what determines the quantity supplied at any given price? As with demand, a number of *nonprice factors* determine the opportunity cost of production and therefore producers' willingness to supply a good or service. *When a nonprice determinant of supply changes, the entire supply curve will shift*. Such shifts reflect a change in the quantity of goods supplied at *every* price.

The nonprice determinants of supply can be divided into five major categories:

- Prices of related goods.
- Technology.
- Prices of inputs.
- Expectations.
- The number of sellers.

LO 3.4 Draw a supply curve and describe the external factors that determine supply.

supply schedule a table that shows the quantities of a particular good or service that producers will supply at various prices

supply curve a graph that shows the quantities of a particular good or service that producers will supply at various prices

FIGURE 3-3
Supply schedule and the supply curve

(A) Supply schedule

Cell phones (millions)	Price ($)
270	180
240	160
210	140
180	120
150	100
120	80
90	60
60	40
30	20

This supply schedule shows the quantity of cell phones supplied each year at various prices. As prices decrease, suppliers want to produce fewer cell phones.

(B) Supply curve

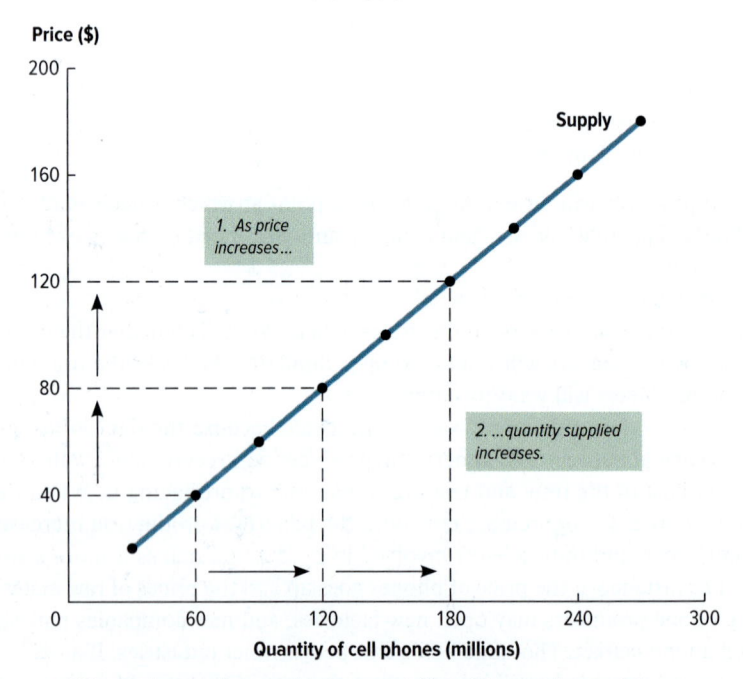

1. As price increases...
2. ...quantity supplied increases.

This supply curve is a graphic representation of the supply schedule for cell phones in the United States. It shows the quantity of cell phones that suppliers will produce at various prices.

TABLE 3-3
Determinants of supply

Determinant	Examples of an increase in supply	Examples of a decrease in supply
Price of related goods	The price of gas rises, so an automaker increases its production of smaller, more fuel-efficient cars.	The price of clean energy production falls, so the power company reduces the amount of power it supplies using coal power plants.
Technology	The installation of robots increases productivity and lowers costs; the supply of goods increases.	New technology allows corn to be made into ethanol, so farmers plant more corn and fewer soybeans; the supply of soybeans decreases.
Prices of inputs	A drop in the price of tomatoes decreases the production cost of salsa; the supply of salsa increases.	An increase in the minimum wage increases labor costs at food factories; the supply of processed food decreases.
Expectations	New research points to the health benefits of eating papayas, leading to expectations that the demand for papayas will rise. More farmers plant papayas, increasing the supply.	Housing prices are expected to rise, so builders hold back on new construction projects today (in order to build later when housing prices are higher), decreasing the supply of homes in the near future.
Number of sellers	Subsidies make the production of corn more profitable, so more farmers plant corn; the supply of corn increases.	New licensing fees make operating a restaurant more expensive; some small restaurants close, decreasing the supply of restaurants.

Each of these factors determines the opportunity cost of production relative to a given benefit (i.e., the price) and therefore the trade-off that producers face. Table 3-3 shows how the supply of various products responds to changes in each determinant.

Prices of related goods
Return to your factory, where you can produce either cell phones or laptops. Just as you chose to produce more laptops and fewer cell phones when the price of cell phones dropped, you would do the same if the price of laptops increased while the price of cell phones stayed constant.

The price of related goods determines supply because it affects the opportunity cost of production. When you choose to produce cell phones, you forgo the profits you would have earned from producing something else. If the price of that something else increases, the amount you forgo in profits also increases. For instance, imagine you can grow wheat or corn (or other crops, for that matter) on your land. If the price of corn increases, the quantity of wheat (the substitute crop) you are willing to grow falls. Why? Because each acre you devote to wheat is one fewer acre you can use to grow corn.

Technology
Improved technology enables firms to produce more efficiently, using fewer resources to make a given product. Doing so lowers production costs, increasing the quantity producers are willing to supply at each price.

Improved technology has played a huge role in the changing popularity of cell phones. As technological innovation in the construction of screens, batteries, and mobile networks and in the processing of electronic data has leapt forward, the cost of producing a useful, consumer-friendly cell phone has plummeted. As a result, producers are now willing to supply more cell phones at lower prices.

In 1980, this cutting-edge technology cost $4,000.
©Rubberball/Duston Todd/Getty Images

Prices of inputs The prices of the inputs used to produce a good are an important part of its cost. When the prices of inputs increase, production costs rise, and the quantity of the product that producers are willing to supply at any given price decreases.

Small amounts of silver and gold are used inside cell phones, for example. When the prices of these precious metals rise, the cost of manufacturing each cell phone increases, and the total number of units that producers collectively are willing to make at any given price goes down. Conversely, when input prices fall, supply increases.

Expectations Suppliers' expectations about prices in the future also affect quantity supplied. For example, when the price of real estate is expected to rise in the future, more real estate developers will wait to embark on construction projects, decreasing the supply of houses in the near future. When expectations change and real estate prices are projected to fall in the future, many of those projects will be rushed to completion, causing the supply of houses to rise.

Number of sellers The market supply curve represents the quantities of a product that a particular number of producers will supply at various prices in a given market. This means that the number of sellers in the market is considered to be one of the fixed parts of the supply curve. We've already seen that the sellers in the market will decide to supply more if the price of a good is higher. This does not mean that the number of sellers will change based on price in the short run.

There are, however, nonprice factors that cause the number of sellers to change in a market and move the supply curve. For example, suppose cell phone producers must meet strict licensing requirements. If those licensing requirements are dropped, more companies may enter the market, willing to supply a certain number of cell phones at each price. These additional phones must be added to the number of cell phones existing producers are already willing to supply at each price point.

Shifts in the supply curve

LO 3.5 Distinguish between a shift in and a movement along the supply curve.

Just as with demand, changes in price cause suppliers to move to a different point on the same supply curve, while changes in the nonprice determinants of supply shift the supply curve itself. A change in a nonprice determinant increases or decreases *supply*. A change in price increases or decreases the *quantity supplied*.

A change in one of the nonprice determinants increases or decreases the supply at any given price. These shifts are shown in panel A of Figure 3-4. An increase in supply shifts the curve to the right. A decrease in supply shifts the curve to the left. For instance, an improvement in battery technology that decreases the cost of producing cell phones will shift the entire supply curve to the right, from S_A to S_B; the quantity of phones supplied at every price is higher than before. Conversely, an increase in the price of the gold needed for cell phones raises production costs, shifting the supply curve to the left, from S_A to S_C.

As with demand, we differentiate these shifts in the supply curve from a movement along the supply curve, which is shown in panel B of Figure 3-4. If the price of cell phones changes, but the nonprice determinants of supply stay the same, we find the new quantity supplied by moving along the supply curve to the new price point.

Also, as with demand, economists use very specific terminology to distinguish between a shift in the supply curve and movement along the supply curve:

- We say that a change in one of the nonprice determinants of supply causes an "increase in supply" or "decrease in supply"—that is, a *shift* of the entire supply curve.
- To distinguish this from *movement along* the supply curve, we say that a change in price causes an "increase in the quantity supplied" or "decrease in the quantity supplied."

FIGURE 3-4
Shifts in the supply curve versus movement along the supply curve

(A) Shifts in the supply curve

When supply decreases, the supply curve shifts to the left.
When supply increases, the supply curve shifts to the right.

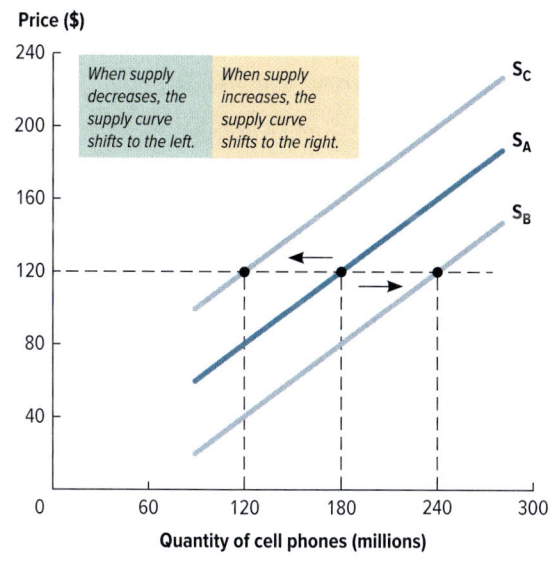

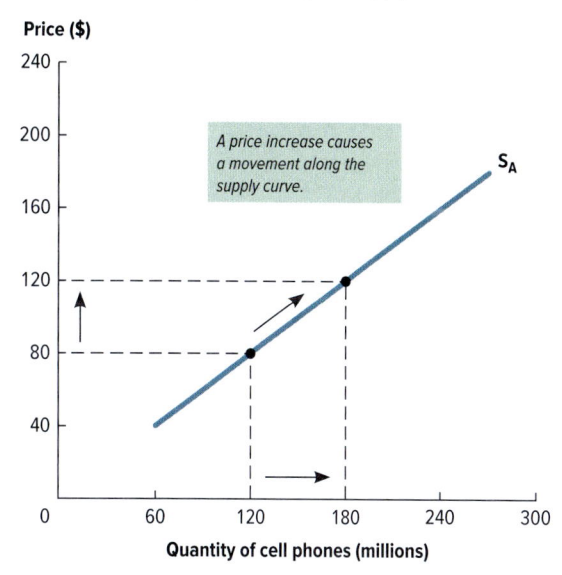

Changes in external factors cause the entire supply curve to shift. The shift from S_A to S_B represents an increase in supply, meaning that producers are willing to supply more cell phones at each price. The shift from S_A to S_C represents a decrease in supply, meaning that producers are willing to supply fewer cell phones at each price.

(B) Movement along the supply curve

A price increase causes a movement along the supply curve.

A price change causes a movement along the supply curve, but the curve itself remains constant.

✓ TEST YOURSELF

- ☐ What does the law of supply say about the relationship between price and quantity supplied? **[LO 3.4]**
- ☐ In which direction does the supply curve shift when the price of inputs increases? **[LO 3.5]**

Market Equilibrium

We've discussed the factors that influence the quantities supplied and demanded by producers and consumers. To find out what actually happens in the market, however, we need to combine these concepts. The prices and quantities of the goods that are exchanged in the real world depend on the *interaction* of supply with demand.

Graphically, this convergence of supply with demand happens at the point where the demand curve intersects the supply curve, a point called the market **equilibrium**. The price at this point is called the **equilibrium price** and the quantity at this point is called the **equilibrium quantity**.

Bear with us for a moment as we point out the obvious: There is no sale without a purchase. You can't sell something unless someone buys it. Although this point may be obvious, the implication for markets is profound. When markets work well, the quantity supplied exactly equals the quantity demanded.

We can think of this intersection, where quantity supplied equals quantity demanded, as the point at which buyers and sellers "agree" on the quantity of a good they are willing to exchange at a given price. At higher prices, sellers want to sell more than buyers want to buy. At lower prices,

equilibrium
the situation in a market when the quantity supplied equals the quantity demanded; graphically, this convergence happens where the demand curve intersects the supply curve

equilibrium price
the price at which the quantity supplied equals the quantity demanded

equilibrium quantity
the quantity that is supplied and demanded at the equilibrium price

FIGURE 3-5

Market equilibrium in the U.S. market for cell phones

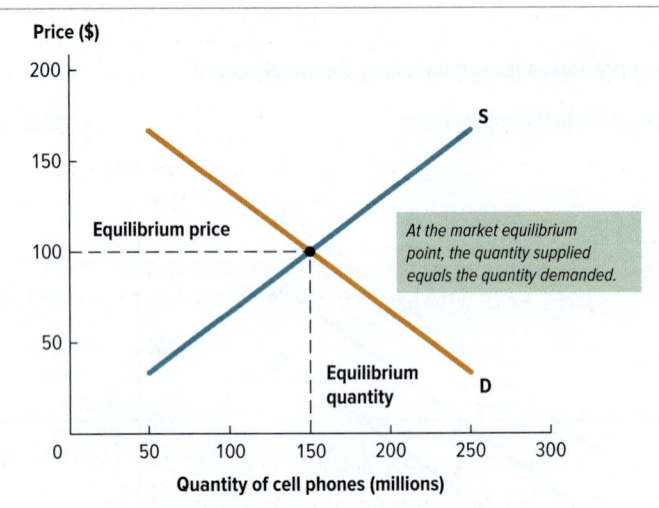

At the market equilibrium point, the quantity supplied equals the quantity demanded.

The point where the supply curve intersects the demand curve is called the equilibrium point. In this example, the equilibrium price is $100, and the equilibrium quantity is 150 million cell phones. At this point, consumers are willing to buy exactly as many cell phones as producers are willing to sell.

buyers want to buy more than sellers are willing to sell. Because every seller finds a buyer at the equilibrium price and quantity, and no one is left standing around with extra goods or an empty shopping cart, the equilibrium price is sometimes called the *market-clearing price*.

In reality, things don't always work so smoothly: Short-run "friction" sometimes slows the process of reaching equilibrium, even in well-functioning markets. As a result, smart businesspeople may hold some inventory for future sale, and consumers may need to shop around for specific items. On the whole, though, the concept of equilibrium is incredibly accurate (and important) in describing how markets function.

Figure 3-5 shows the market equilibrium for cell phones in the United States. It was constructed by combining the market supply and demand curves shown in Figures 3-1 and 3-3. In this market, the equilibrium price is $100, and the equilibrium quantity supplied and demanded is 150 million phones.

Reaching equilibrium

LO 3.6 Explain how supply and demand interact to drive markets to equilibrium.

How does a market reach equilibrium? Do sellers know intuitively what price to charge? No. Instead, they tend to set prices by trial and error, by past experience with customers, or by thinking through their costs and adding in a bit of profit. Irrespective of the firm's pricing process, typically the incentives buyers and sellers face naturally drive the market toward an equilibrium price and quantity.

Figure 3-6 shows two graphs, one in which the starting price is above the equilibrium price and the other in which it is below the equilibrium price. In panel A, we imagine that cell phone suppliers think they'll be able to charge $160 for a cell phone, so they produce 240 million phones. They find, though, that consumers will buy only 60 million. (We can read those quantities demanded and supplied at a price of $160 from the demand and supply curves.) When the quantity supplied is higher than the quantity demanded, we say that there is a **surplus** of phones, or an **excess supply**. Manufacturers are stuck holding extra phones in their warehouses; they want to sell that stock and must reduce the price to attract more customers. They have an incentive to keep lowering the price until quantity demanded increases to reach quantity supplied.

surplus (excess supply) a situation in which the quantity of a good that is supplied is higher than the quantity demanded

FIGURE 3-6
Reaching equilibrium in the market for cell phones

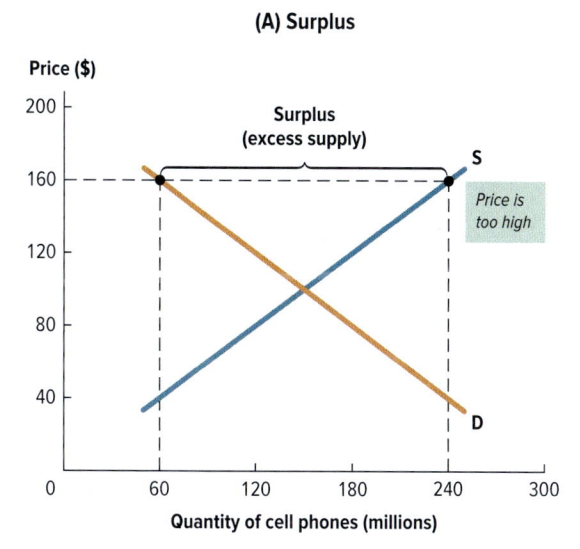

(A) Surplus

When the initial price for cell phones is above the equilibrium point, producers want to supply more cell phones than consumers want to buy. The gap between the quantity supplied and the quantity demanded is called a surplus, or excess supply.

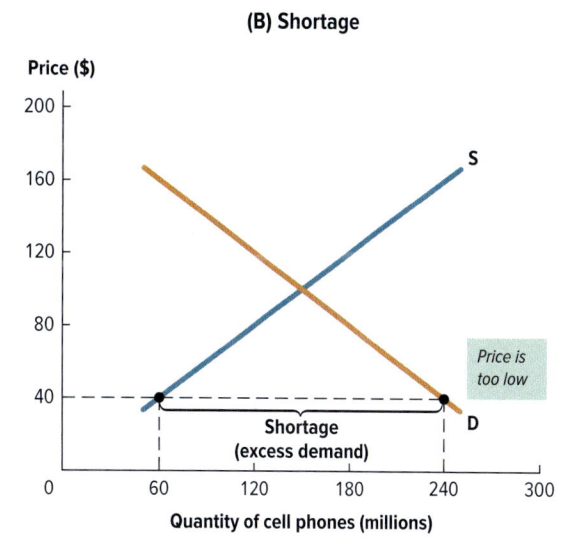

(B) Shortage

When the initial price for cell phones is below the equilibrium point, consumers want to buy more cell phones than sellers want to produce. The distance between the quantity demanded and the quantity supplied is called a shortage, or excess demand.

In panel B of Figure 3-6, we imagine that cell phone producers make the opposite mistake—they think they'll be able to charge only $40 per phone. They make only 60 million cell phones, but consumers actually are willing to buy 240 million cell phones at that price. When the quantity demanded is higher than the quantity supplied, we say there is a **shortage**, or **excess demand**. Producers will see long lines of people waiting to buy the few available cell phones; they will quickly realize that they could make more money by charging a higher price. They have an incentive to increase the price until quantity demanded decreases to equal quantity supplied, and no one is left standing in line.

Thus, at any price above or below the equilibrium price, sellers face an incentive to raise or lower prices. No one needs to engineer the market equilibrium or share secret information about what price to charge. Instead, money-making incentives drive the market toward the equilibrium price, at which there is neither a surplus nor a shortage. The Economics in Action box "The great Elmo shortage" describes a case in which a producer started out charging the wrong price, but the market solved the problem.

shortage (excess demand) a situation in which the quantity of a good that is demanded is higher than the quantity supplied

Changes in equilibrium

We've seen what happens to the supply and demand curves when a nonprice factor changes. Because the equilibrium price and quantity are determined by the interaction of supply and demand, a shift in either curve will also change the market equilibrium. Some changes will cause only the demand curve to shift; some, only the supply curve. Some changes will affect both the supply and demand curves.

LO 3.7 Evaluate the effect of changes in supply and demand on the equilibrium price and quantity.

The great Elmo shortage
Economics in Action

In 1996, American toymaker Tyco introduced "Tickle Me Elmo" in time for the winter holiday season. As the name suggests, the toy was a plush version of the famous furry red character from Sesame Street, which erupted in wild laughter when "tickled." Tyco expected only moderate sales, largely due to the expensive $30 price tag.

In October, though, actor Rosie O'Donnell plugged the new toy on her TV show, and sales of Tickle Me Elmo took off. By Thanksgiving, the toy was so popular that many stores ran out of stock. Tyco did its best to meet the surge in demand, even flying inventory from China in private jets. That wasn't enough. Faced with a shortage of Elmos, shoppers started taking drastic (and sometimes violent) measures. In Canada, a store employee was severely injured when a group of 300 shoppers noticed he was holding a Tickle Me Elmo and stampeded to get it. The *New York Times* even reported a story involving a Toys-"R"-Us store in Queens, NY, a case of Elmos, and a suspicious late-night shopping spree by members of a famous crime family. An Elmo even went missing from a New York City Police Station.

People offered to sell Elmos for hundreds or even thousands more than the $30 retail price. (That is exactly the economic result we'd expect when there is a shortage of a good.) Enterprising organizations and charities started raffling off Elmos; a radio station in Wichita, Kansas, solicited donations by threatening to destroy an Elmo along with a condemned building.

While it may seem a bit excessive, these types of "crazes" are often part of toy sales at the holidays. Unfortunately for producers and consumers, predicting the hot toy of the season is nearly impossible. If, like Tyco, they guess wrong, factories often can't catch up to surging demand, resulting in long lines, inflated prices, frustrated parents, and disappointed kids. However, the story of Tickle Me Elmo also shows that the "perfect" holiday gift will always be available to those who are willing and able to pay the price.

The shortage of Tickle Me Elmo dolls one holiday season demonstrated what happens to price in the case of excess demand.
©Meeyoung Son/Alamy

Sources: Dan Berry, "A Christmas Tale of the Gottis and Tickle Me Elmo," *The New York Times,* December 18, 1996, www.nytimes.com/1996/12/18/nyregion/a-christmas-tale-of-the-gottis-and-tickle-me-elmo.html; E.S. Huffman, "How 'Tickle Me Elmo' Caused Holiday Hysteria in 1996," *Uproxx,* December 16, 2015, https://uproxx.com/life/tickle-me-elmo-craze-history/; Jake Rossen, "Oral History: Tickle Me Elmo Turns 21," *Mental Floss,* November 16, 2017, http://mentalfloss.com/article/83563/oral-history-tickle-me-elmo-turns-20.

To determine the effect on market equilibrium of a change in a nonprice factor, ask yourself a few questions:

1. Does the change affect demand? If so, does demand increase or decrease?
2. Does the change affect supply? If so, does supply increase or decrease?
3. How does the combination of changes in supply and demand affect the equilibrium price and quantity?

Shifts in demand We suggested earlier that landline service is a *substitute* for cell phones and that if the price of landline service suddenly skyrockets, then demand for cell phones increases.

In other words, the demand curve shifts to the right. The price of landline service probably doesn't affect the supply of cell phones because it doesn't change the costs or expectations that cell phone manufacturers face. So the supply curve stays put.

Figure 3-7 shows the effect of the increase in landline price on the market equilibrium for cell phones. Because the new demand curve intersects the supply curve at a different point, the equilibrium price and quantity change. The new equilibrium price is $120, and the new equilibrium quantity is 180 million.

We can summarize this effect in terms of the three questions to ask following a change in a nonprice factor:

1. *Does demand increase or decrease?* Yes, the change in the price of landline phone service increases demand for cell phones at every price.
2. *Does supply increase or decrease?* No, the change in the price of landline phone service does not affect any of the nonprice determinants of supply. The supply curve stays where it is.
3. *How does the combination of changes in supply and demand affect equilibrium price and quantity?* The increase in demand shifts the demand curve to the right, pushing the equilibrium to a higher point on the stationary supply curve. The new point at which supply and demand "agree" represents a price of $120 and a quantity of 180 million phones.

TAKE NOTE...

Remember, when we say that supply or demand increases or decreases, we're referring to a *shift in the entire curve*. A change in quantity demanded or supplied would be a *movement* along the curve.

Shifts in supply What would happen if a breakthrough in battery technology enabled cell phone manufacturers to construct phones with the same battery life for less money? Once again, asking *How will others respond?* helps us predict the market response. We can see that the new

FIGURE 3-7
Shift in the demand for cell phones

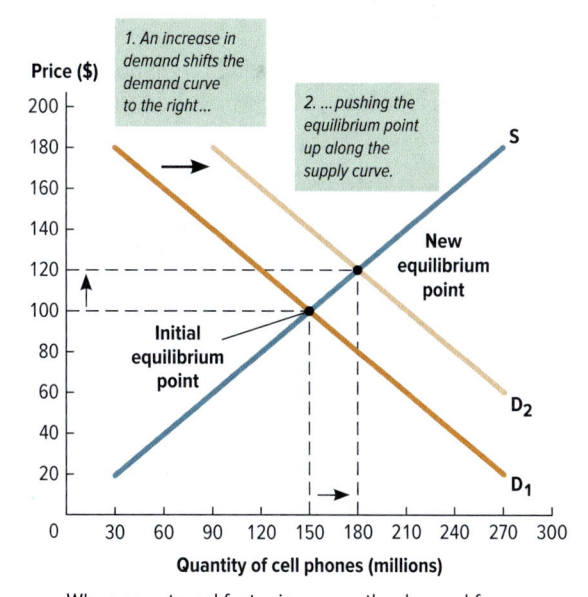

When an external factor increases the demand for cell phones at all prices, the demand curve shifts to the right. This increase in demand results in a new equilibrium point. Consumers purchase more cell phones at a higher price.

FIGURE 3-8
Shift in the supply of cell phones

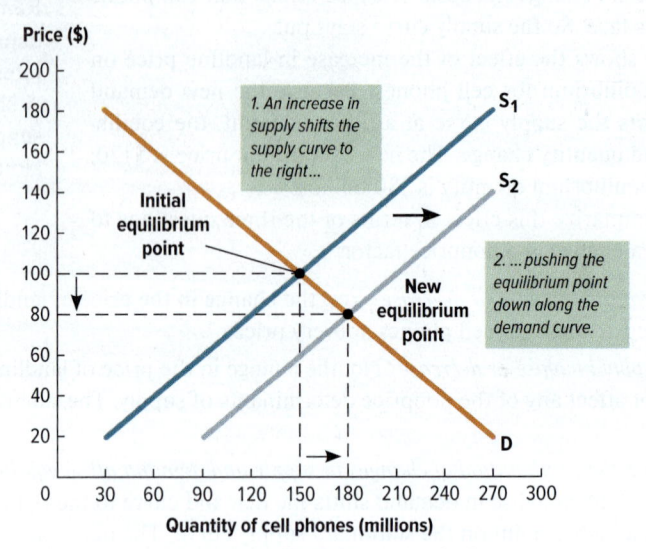

Price ($) vs *Quantity of cell phones (millions)*

1. An increase in supply shifts the supply curve to the right...
2. ...pushing the equilibrium point down along the demand curve.

Initial equilibrium point: $100, 150 million. New equilibrium point: $80, 180 million. Curves: S_1, S_2, D.

When an external factor affects the supply of cell phones at all prices, the supply curve shifts. In this example, supply increases and the market reaches a new equilibrium point. Consumers purchase more phones at a lower price.

---

technology does not have much impact on demand: Customers probably have no idea how much the batteries in their phones cost to make, nor will they care as long as battery life stays the same. However, cheaper batteries definitely decrease production costs, increasing the number of phones manufacturers are willing to supply at any given price. So the demand curve stays where it is, and the supply curve shifts to the right.

Figure 3-8 shows the shift in supply and the new equilibrium point. The new supply curve intersects the demand curve at a new equilibrium point, representing a price of $80 and a quantity of 180 million phones.

Once again, we can analyze the effect of the change in battery technology on the market for cell phones in three steps:

1. *Does demand increase or decrease?* No, the nonprice determinants of demand are not affected by battery technology.
2. *Does supply increase or decrease?* Yes, supply increases because the new battery technology lowers production costs.
3. *How does the combination of changes in supply and demand affect equilibrium price and quantity?* The increase in supply shifts the supply curve to the right, pushing the equilibrium to a lower point on the stationary demand curve. The new equilibrium price and quantity are $80 and 180 million phones.

Table 3-4 summarizes the effect of some other changes in demand or supply on the equilibrium price and quantity.

Shifts in both demand and supply In our discussion so far, we've covered examples in which only demand or supply shifted. However, it's possible that factors that shift demand and supply in the market for cell phones could coincidentally happen at the same time. For example, an increase in landline cost (a demand factor) could occur simultaneously with an improvement

TABLE 3-4

Effect of changes in demand or supply on the equilibrium price and quantity

Example of change in demand or supply	Effect on equilibrium price and quantity	Shift in curve
A successful "Buy American" advertising campaign increases the demand for Fords.	The demand curve shifts to the right. The equilibrium price and quantity increase.	
An outbreak of *E. coli* reduces the demand for spinach.	The demand curve shifts to the left. The equilibrium price and quantity decrease.	
The use of robots decreases production costs.	The supply curve shifts to the right. The equilibrium price decreases and the equilibrium quantity increases.	
An increase in the minimum wage increases labor costs.	The supply curve shifts to the left. The equilibrium price increases and the equilibrium quantity decreases.	

in battery technology (a supply factor). It's also possible that a single change could affect both supply and demand.

For instance, suppose that in addition to reducing the cost of production, the new battery technology makes cell phone batteries last longer. We already know that cheaper batteries will increase supply. As we saw before with increases in supply, price decreases while the quantity increases. Asking *how consumers will respond* allows us to see that the improvement in battery life will also increase demand: Longer-lasting batteries will make a cell phone more valuable to consumers at any given price. As a result, both the demand curve and the supply curve shift to the right. Panels A and B of Figure 3-9 both show that the effect of a double change is a new equilibrium point at a higher price and a higher quantity.

Even without looking at a graph, we could have predicted that in this case the equilibrium *quantity* would rise. Increases in demand and increases in supply both independently lead to a higher equilibrium quantity—and the combination will certainly do so as well.

Without more information, however, we cannot predict the change in equilibrium *price*. Holding all else equal, an increase in demand leads to an increase in price, but an increase in supply leads to a decrease in price. To find the net effect on equilibrium price, we would have to know whether the shift in demand outweighs the shift in supply shown in panel A of Figure 3-9, or vice versa, which is shown in panel B.

FIGURE 3-9
Shifts in both demand and supply

An increase in supply and demand shifts both curves to the right, resulting in a higher quantity traded. However, the direction of the price shift depends on whether supply or demand increases more.

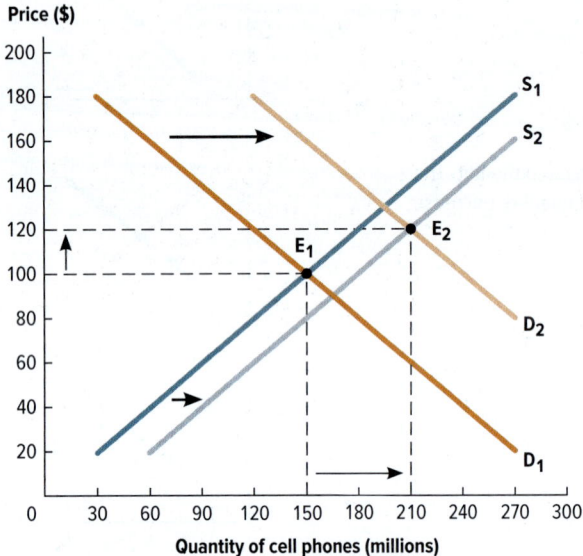

(A) Demand increases more

Sometimes, supply and demand shift together. In this example, both curves shift to the right, but demand increases more. At the new equilibrium point, E₂, consumers purchase more cell phones at a higher price.

(B) Supply increases more

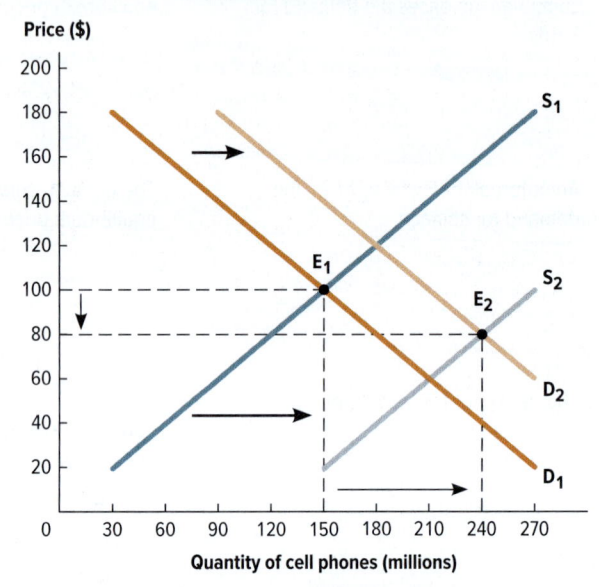

Sometimes, supply and demand shift together. In this example, both curves shift to the right, but supply increases more. At the new equilibrium point, E₂, consumers purchase more cell phones at a lower price.

We can state this idea more generally: When supply and demand shift together, it is possible to predict *either* the direction of the change in quantity *or* the direction of the change in price without knowing how much the curves shift. Table 3-5 shows some rules you can use to predict the outcome of these shifts in supply and demand. These rules are:

- When supply and demand shift in the *same* direction, we can predict the direction of the change in quantity but not the direction of the change in price.
- When supply and demand shift in *opposite* directions, the change in price is predictable, but not the change in quantity.

Thinking about the intuition behind these rules may help you to remember them. Any time you are considering a situation in which supply and demand shift at the same time, ask yourself,

TABLE 3-5
Predicting changes in price and quantity when supply and demand change simultaneously

Supply change	Demand change	Price change	Quantity change
Decrease	Decrease	?	↓
Decrease	Increase	↑	?
Increase	Increase	?	↑
Increase	Decrease	↓	?

"What do buyers and sellers agree on?" For instance, when both supply and demand increase, buyers and sellers "agree" that at any given price, the quantity they are willing to exchange is higher. The reverse is true when both supply and demand decrease: Buyers and sellers agree that at a given price, the quantity they are willing to exchange is lower.

Applying this reasoning to opposite shifts in supply and demand—when one increases but the other decreases—is trickier. To find out what buyers and sellers "agree" on, try rephrasing what it means for demand to increase. One way to say it is that consumers are willing to buy a *higher* quantity at the *same* price. Another way to say it is that consumers are willing to pay a *higher* price to buy the *same* quantity. So, when demand increases and supply decreases, buyers are willing to pay more for the same quantity; also, sellers are willing to supply the same quantity only if they receive a higher price. In other words, they can "agree" on a higher price at any given quantity. We can therefore predict that the equilibrium price will increase.

The opposite is true when demand decreases and supply increases. Buyers are willing to buy the same quantity as before only if the price is lower, and sellers are willing to supply the same quantity at a lower price. Because the two groups can "agree" on a lower price at any given quantity, we can predict that the price will decrease.

Of course, you can always work out the effect of simultaneous shifts in demand and supply by working through the three questions described in the previous section. Draw the shifts in each curve on a graph, as is done in two cases in panels A and B of Figure 3-9, and find the new equilibrium.

Before you finish this chapter, read the Economics in Action box "Give a man a fish" for some information about how cell phones affected supply and demand in one developing country.

Give a man a fish
Economics in Action

Cell phones can do many things: They can help you find the perfect restaurant, get directions, make new friends, or even manage your money. What if they could also help markets operate more efficiently?

That's what economist Robert Jensen found when he studied the market for fish in Kerala, a state on India's southern coast. Kerala is famous for its palm-lined beaches, and, not surprisingly, fishing is an important economic activity.

Initially, Jensen noticed that prices varied widely across different markets along the coast. Like most goods, these prices were governed by the laws of supply and demand. For example, if the fishing boats from one town had a great day and brought in huge hauls of fish, fish prices would plummet in that town. On the other hand, a special holiday in one town could inspire people to buy more fish, jacking up the price.

This variance in price created quite a problem for fishermen. Without information about the prices in other markets along the coast, fishermen had no way of knowing if it would be worth the time and extra fuel to check on prices somewhere else. The result was that fishermen usually sold at the going rate (if they could find buyers) in their home port, regardless of the price. On days of really bad luck, they would have to throw away fish because they were not be able to find a buyer at any price.

Jensen found that the fishermen solved this problem once cell phone service was introduced. While out on the ocean fishing, they could communicate with one another, and with people on land, and were able to find out where their catches would be most profitable that day. They used that information to travel to the right town to sell their fish. Supply began to better match the demand in each town, and prices became more uniform across towns.

(continued)

> Access to the right information allowed the market for fish to reach an efficient equilibrium. Sellers earned an average of 8 percent more in profits (due to fewer fish being thrown away), and buyers paid an average of 4 percent less for their fish. Fishermen increased their incomes, and consumers stretched their incomes further.
>
> As the saying goes, "Give a man a fish and he will eat for a day. Teach a man to fish and he will eat for a lifetime." To this wisdom, we might add, "Give people cell phones, and they might earn an 8 percent increase in profits."
>
> Source: R. Jensen, "Give a Man a Fish, " *The Quarterly Journal of Economics* 122, no. 3 (2007).

✓ TEST YOURSELF

- ☐ What is the market equilibrium? **[LO 3.6]**
- ☐ What happens to the equilibrium price and quantity if the supply curve shifts right but the demand curve stays put? **[LO 3.7]**

Conclusion

By the time you reach the end of this course, you'll be quite familiar with the words *supply* and *demand*. We take our time on this subject for good reason: An understanding of supply and demand is the foundation of economic problem solving. You'll be hard-pressed to make wise economic choices without it.

Although markets are not always perfectly competitive, you may be surprised at how accurately many real-world phenomena can be described using the simple rules of supply and demand. In the next chapters we'll use these rules to explain how consumers and producers respond to price changes and government policies.

Key Terms

market economy, p. 50
market, p. 50
competitive market, p. 50
price taker, p. 51
standardized good, p. 51
transaction costs, p. 51
quantity demanded, p. 52
law of demand, p. 52

demand schedule, p. 53
demand curve, p. 53
substitutes, p. 55
complements, p. 55
normal goods, p. 56
inferior goods, p. 56
quantity supplied, p. 59
law of supply, p. 59

supply schedule, p. 60
supply curve, p. 60
equilibrium, p. 63
equilibrium price, p. 63
equilibrium quantity, p. 63
surplus (excess supply), p. 64
shortage (excess demand), p. 65

Summary

LO 3.1 Identify the defining characteristics of a competitive market.

A market is the group of buyers and sellers who trade a particular good or service. In competitive markets, a large number of buyers and sellers trade standardized goods and services. They have full information about the goods, and there is no cost to participate in exchanges in the market. Participants in competitive markets are called price takers because they can't affect the prevailing price for a good.

LO 3.2 Draw a demand curve, and describe the external factors that determine demand.

A demand curve is a graph that shows the quantities of a particular good or service that consumers will demand at various prices. It also shows consumers' highest willingness to pay for a given quantity. The law of demand states that for almost all goods, the quantity demanded increases as the price decreases. This relationship results in a downward-sloping demand curve.

Several nonprice factors contribute to consumers' demand for a good at a given price: Consumer preferences, the prices of related goods, incomes, and expectations about the future all affect demand. On a marketwide level, the number of buyers also can increase or decrease total demand. When one of these underlying factors changes, the demand curve will shift to the left or the right.

LO 3.3 Distinguish between a shift in and a movement along the demand curve.

When one of the nonprice factors that drives demand changes, the entire curve *shifts* to the left or the right. With this shift, the quantity demanded at any given price changes. When demand increases, the curve shifts to the right; when demand decreases, it shifts to the left.

When the nonprice determinants of demand stay the same, a change in the price of a good leads to a *movement along* the curve, rather than a shift in the curve.

LO 3.4 Draw a supply curve and describe the external factors that determine supply.

A supply curve is a graph that shows the quantities of a particular good or service that producers will supply at various prices. It shows the minimum price producers must receive to supply any given quantity. The law of supply states that the quantity supplied increases as the price increases, resulting in an upward-sloping supply curve.

Several nonprice factors determine the supply of a good at any given price: They include the prices of related goods, technology, prices of inputs, expectations about the future, and the number of sellers in the market. If one of these underlying factors changes, the supply curve will shift to the left or the right.

LO 3.5 Distinguish between a shift in and a movement along the supply curve.

Just as with demand, a change in the nonprice determinants of supply will cause the entire supply curve to shift to the left or the right. As a result, the quantity supplied is higher or lower at any given price than it was before. When supply increases, the curve shifts to the right; when supply decreases, it shifts to the left.

A shift in the supply curve differs from movement along the supply curve. A movement along the curve happens when the price of a good increases but the nonprice determinants of supply stay the same.

LO 3.6 Explain how supply and demand interact to drive markets to equilibrium.

When a market is in equilibrium, the quantity supplied equals the quantity demanded. The incentives that individual buyers and sellers face drive a competitive market toward equilibrium. If the prevailing price is too high, a surplus will result, and sellers will lower their prices to get rid of the excess supply. If the prevailing price is too low, a shortage will result, and buyers will bid up the price until the excess demand disappears.

LO 3.7 Evaluate the effect of changes in supply and demand on the equilibrium price and quantity.

When one or more of the underlying factors that determine supply or demand change, one or both curves will shift, leading to a new market equilibrium price and quantity.

To calculate the change in the equilibrium price and quantity, you must first determine whether a change affects demand, and, if so, in which direction the curve will shift. Then you must determine whether the change also affects supply, and, if so, in which direction that curve will shift. Finally, you must determine the new equilibrium point where the two curves intersect.

Review Questions

1. Think about a competitive market in which you participate regularly. For each of the characteristics of a competitive market, explain how your market meets these requirements. **[LO 3.1]**
2. Think about a noncompetitive market in which you participate regularly. Explain which characteristic(s) of competitive markets your market does not meet. **[LO 3.1]**
3. Explain why a demand curve slopes downward. **[LO 3.2]**
4. In each of the following examples, name the factor that affects demand and describe its impact on your demand for a new cell phone. **[LO 3.2]**
    a. You hear a rumor that a new and improved model of the phone you want is coming out next year.
    b. Your grandparents give you $500.
    c. A cellular network announces a holiday sale on a data package that includes the purchase of a new smartphone.
    d. A friend tells you how great his new phone is and suggests that you get one, too.
5. Consider the following events:
    a. The price of cell phones goes down by 25 percent during a sale.
    b. You get a 25 percent raise at your job.

Which event represents a shift in the demand curve? Which represents a movement along the curve? What is the difference? **[LO 3.3]**

6. What is the difference between a change in demand and a change in quantity demanded? **[LO 3.3]**

7. Explain why a supply curve slopes upward. **[LO 3.4]**

8. In each of the following examples, name the factor that affects supply and describe its impact on the supply of cell phones. **[LO 3.4]**
   a. Economic forecasts suggest that the demand for cell phones will increase in the future.
   b. The price of plastic goes up.
   c. A new screen technology reduces the cost of making cell phones.

9. Consider the following events:
   a. A fruitworm infestation ruins a large number of apple orchards in Washington state.
   b. Demand for apples goes down, causing the price to fall.

   Which event represents a shift in the supply curve? Which represents a movement along the curve? What is the difference? **[LO 3.5]**

10. What is the difference between a change in supply and a change in quantity supplied? **[LO 3.5]**

11. What is the relationship between supply and demand when a market is in equilibrium? Explain how the incentives facing cell phone companies and consumers cause the market for cell phones to reach equilibrium. **[LO 3.6]**

12. Explain why the equilibrium price is often called the market-clearing price. **[LO 3.6]**

13. Suppose an economic boom causes incomes to increase. Explain what will happen to the demand and supply of phones, and predict the direction of the change in the equilibrium price and quantity. **[LO 3.7]**

14. Suppose an economic boom drives up wages for the sales representatives who work for cell phone companies. Explain what will happen to the demand and supply of phones, and predict the direction of the change in the equilibrium price and quantity. **[LO 3.7]**

15. Suppose an economic boom causes incomes to increase and at the same time drives up wages for the sales representatives who work for cell phone companies. Explain what will happen to the demand for and supply of phones and predict the direction of the change in the equilibrium price and quantity. **[LO 3.7]**

Problems and Applications

1. Consider shopping for cucumbers in a farmers' market. For each statement below, note which characteristic of competitive markets the statement describes. *Choose from:* standardized good, full information, no transaction costs, and participants are price takers. **[LO 3.1]**
   a. All of the farmers have their prices posted prominently in front of their stalls.
   b. Cucumbers are the same price at each stall.
   c. There is no difficulty moving around between stalls as you shop and choosing between farmers.
   d. You and the other customers all seem indifferent about which cucumbers to buy.

2. Suppose two artists are selling paintings for the same price in adjacent booths at an art fair. By the end of the day, one artist has nearly sold out of her paintings while the other artist has sold nothing. Which characteristic of competitive markets has not been met and best explains this outcome? **[LO 3.1]**
   a. Standardized good.
   b. Full information.
   c. No transaction costs.
   d. Participants are price takers.

3. Using the demand schedule in Table 3P-1, draw the daily demand curve for slices of pizza in a college town. **[LO 3.2]**

TABLE 3P-1

Price ($)	Quantity demanded (slices)
0.00	350
0.50	300
1.00	250
1.50	200
2.00	150
2.50	100
3.00	50
3.50	0

4. Consider the market for cars. Which determinant of demand is affected by each of the following events? *Choose from:* consumer preferences, prices of related goods, incomes, expectations, and the number of buyers. **[LO 3.2]**
   a. Environmentalists launch a successful One Family, One Car campaign.
   b. A baby boom occurred 16 years ago.
   c. Layoffs increase as the economy sheds millions of jobs.

d. An oil shortage causes the price of gasoline to soar.

e. The government offers tax rebates in return for the purchase of commuter rail tickets.

f. The government announces a massive plan to bail out the auto industry and subsidize production costs.

5. If a decrease in the price of laptops causes the demand for tablets to increase, are laptops and tablets substitutes or complements? **[LO 3.2]**

6. If rising incomes cause the demand for beer to decrease, is beer a normal or inferior good? **[LO 3.2]**

7. Consider the market for corn. Say whether each of the following events will cause a shift in the demand curve or a movement along the curve. If it will cause a shift, specify the direction. **[LO 3.3]**

   a. A drought hits corn-growing regions, cutting the supply of corn.

   b. The government announces a new subsidy for biofuels made from corn.

   c. A global recession reduces the incomes of consumers in poor countries, who rely on corn as a staple food.

   d. A new hybrid variety of corn seed causes a 15 percent increase in the yield of corn per acre.

   e. An advertising campaign by the beef producers' association highlights the health benefits of corn-fed beef.

8. The demand curve in Figure 3P-1 shows the monthly market for sweaters at a local clothing store. For each of the following events, draw the new outcome. **[LO 3.3]**

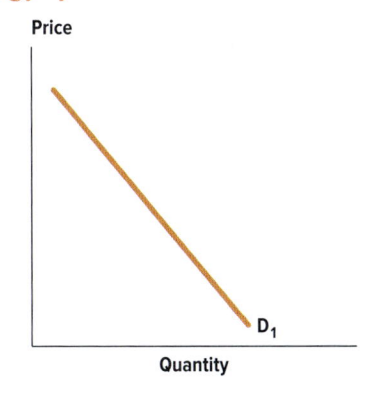

FIGURE 3P-1

Price / Quantity (curve labeled D_1)

   a. Sweaters fall out of fashion.
   b. There is a shortage of wool.
   c. The winter is particularly long and cold this year.
   d. Sweater vendors offer a sale.

9. Using the supply schedule found in Table 3P-2, draw the daily supply curve for slices of pizza in a college town. **[LO 3.4]**

TABLE 3P-2

Price ($)	Quantity supplied (slices)
0.00	0
0.50	50
1.00	100
1.50	150
2.00	200
2.50	250
3.00	300
3.50	350

10. Consider the market for cars. Which determinant of supply is affected by each of the following events? *Choose from:* prices of related goods, technology, prices of inputs, expectations, and the number of sellers in the market. **[LO 3.4]**

    a. A steel tariff increases the price of steel.
    b. Improvements in robotics increase efficiency and reduce costs.
    c. Factories close because of an economic downturn.
    d. The government announces a plan to offer tax rebates for the purchase of commuter rail tickets.
    e. The price of trucks falls, so factories produce more cars.
    f. The government announces that it will dramatically rewrite efficiency standards, making it much harder for automakers to produce their cars.

11. Consider the market for corn. Say whether each of the following events will cause a shift in the supply curve or a movement along the curve. If it will cause a shift, specify the direction. **[LO 3.5]**

    a. A drought hits corn-growing regions.
    b. The government announces a new subsidy for biofuels made from corn.
    c. A global recession reduces the incomes of consumers in poor countries, who rely on corn as a staple food.
    d. A new hybrid variety of corn seed causes a 15 percent increase in the yield of corn per acre.
    e. An advertising campaign by the beef producers' association highlights the health benefits of corn-fed beef.

12. The supply curve in Figure 3P-2 shows the monthly market for sweaters at a local craft market. For each of the following events, draw the new outcome. [LO 3.5]

FIGURE 3P-2

a. The price of wool increases.
b. Demand for sweaters decreases.
c. A particularly cold winter is expected to begin next month.
d. Demand for sweaters increases.

13. Refer to the demand and supply schedule shown in Table 3P-3. [LO 3.6]

TABLE 3P-3

Price ($)	Quantity demanded (slices)	Quantity supplied (slices)
0.00	350	0
0.50	300	50
1.00	250	100
1.50	200	150
2.00	150	200
2.50	100	250
3.00	50	300
3.50	0	350

a. If pizza parlors charge $3.50 per slice, will there be excess supply or excess demand? What is the amount of excess supply or excess demand at that price?

b. If pizza parlors charge $1.00 per slice, will there be excess supply or excess demand? What is the amount of excess supply or excess demand at that price?

c. What are the equilibrium price and quantity in this market?

The graph in Figure 3P-3 shows the weekly market for pizzas in a small town. Use this graph to answer Problems 14–16.

FIGURE 3P-3

14. Which of the following events will occur at a price of $20? [LO 3.6]
    a. Equilibrium.
    b. Excess demand.
    c. Excess supply.
    d. No pizzas supplied.
    e. No pizzas demanded.

15. Which of the following events will occur at a price of $10? [LO 3.6]
    a. Equilibrium.
    b. Excess demand.
    c. Excess supply.
    d. No pizzas supplied.
    e. No pizzas demanded.

16. What are the equilibrium price and quantity of pizzas? [LO 3.6]

17. The graph in Figure 3P-4 shows supply and demand in the market for automobiles. For each of the following events, draw the new market outcome and say whether the equilibrium price and quantity will increase or decrease. **[LO 3.7]**

FIGURE 3P-4

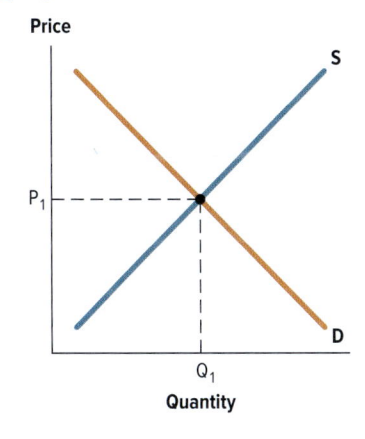

Price vs. Quantity graph showing supply curve S and demand curve D intersecting at point (Q_1, P_1).

a. Environmentalists launch a successful One Family, One Car campaign.
b. A steel tariff increases the price of steel.
c. A baby boom occurred 16 years ago.
d. An oil shortage causes the price of gasoline to soar.
e. Improvements in robotics increase efficiency and reduce costs.
f. The government offers a tax rebate for the purchase of commuter rail tickets.

18. Say whether each of the following changes will increase or decrease the equilibrium price and quantity, or whether the effect cannot be predicted. **[LO 3.7]**
    a. Demand increases; supply remains constant.
    b. Supply increases; demand remains constant.
    c. Demand decreases; supply remains constant.
    d. Supply decreases; demand remains constant.
    e. Demand increases; supply increases.
    f. Demand decreases; supply decreases.
    g. Demand increases; supply decreases.
    h. Demand decreases; supply increases.

Endnotes

1. http://www.gsmamobileeconomy.com/GSMA_Global_Mobile_Economy_Report_2015.pdf
2. http://www.ngrguardiannews.com/2015/06/africas-mobile-phone-penetration-now-67/

Appendix B

Math Essentials: Working with Linear Equations

Relationships between variables can be represented with algebraic equations, as well as graphs and tables. You should be comfortable moving among all three representations. We addressed graphs in Appendix A, "Math Essentials: Understanding Graphs and Slope"; if you didn't read it then, you might want to do so now.

Interpreting the Equation of a Line

If the relationship between two variables is linear, it can be represented by the equation for a line, which is commonly written as:

EQUATION B-1
$$y = mx + b$$

In this form, called the *slope intercept form*, m is the slope of the line and b is the y-intercept.

All linear equations provide information about the slope and y-intercept of the line. From our discussion in Appendix A, "Math Essentials: Understanding Graphs and Slope," we already know that slope is the ratio of vertical distance (change in y) to horizontal distance (change in x). So what does the y-intercept tell us? It is the point at which the line crosses the y-axis. Put another way, it is the value of y when x is 0. Knowing these values is useful in turning an equation into a graph. Also, as we'll see, they can allow us to get information about the real economic relationship being represented without even having to graph it.

Although you might see the equation for a line rearranged in several different forms, just remember that if y is on the left-hand side of the equation, whatever number is multiplying x (known as the *coefficient of* x) is your slope. If you don't see a number in front of x, the slope is 1. The number being added to or subtracted from a multiple of x is a constant that represents the y-intercept. If you don't see this number, you know that the y-intercept is zero. Take a look at a few examples in Table B-1.

LEARNING OBJECTIVES

LO B.1 Use linear equations to interpret the equation of a line.

LO B.2 Use linear equations to explain shifts and pivots.

LO B.3 Use linear equations to solve for equilibrium.

LO B.1 Use linear equations to interpret the equation of a line.

TABLE B-1

Examples of linear equations

The steepness and position of a line in the Cartesian coordinate system is determined by two things: its slope and its intercept. Slope refers to steepness; the intercept determines where the line is positioned.

Equation	Slope	y-intercept
$y = 6x + 4$	6	4
$y = -x - 2$	-1	-2
$y = 10 - 2x$	-2	10
$y = -4x$	-4	0

Turning a graph into an equation

To see how to translate a graph into an algebraic equation, look at Figure B-1. What is the equation that represents this relationship? To derive this equation, we need to find the values of the slope and the y-intercept. We can calculate the slope at any point along the line:

$$\text{Slope} = \frac{\Delta y}{\Delta x} = \frac{(y_2 - y_1)}{(x_2 - x_1)}$$

$$= \frac{(6 - 5)}{(4 - 2)} = \frac{1}{2} = 0.5$$

By looking at the graph to see where the line intersects the y-axis, we can tell that the y-intercept is 4. Therefore, if we write the equation in the form $y = mx + b$, we get $y = 0.5x + 4$. Our table, graph, and equation all give us the same information about the relationship between x and y.

Turning an equation into a graph

Let's work in the opposite direction now, starting with an equation and seeing what information it gives us. The following equation takes the form $y = mx + b$, with P and Q substituted for y and x, respectively.

$$P = -5Q + 25$$

We know from looking at this equation that it represents a line with a slope of -5 and a y-intercept of 25. Suppose that we know this equation represents supply or demand, but we're not sure which. How can we tell whether this is a demand equation or a supply equation? Easy. The slope is negative. We don't need a graph to tell us that the relationship between P and Q is negative and the line will be downward-sloping. Therefore, the equation must represent demand rather than supply.

Because the y-intercept in our equation is 25, we know that the demand curve will cross the y-axis at 25. This tells us that when price is 25, quantity demanded is 0. In order for consumers to demand a positive quantity, price must be lower than 25.

If we need to know more about the relationship represented by the equation, we can graph the demand curve. Since we know that 25 is the y-intercept, we can use the point (0,25) to begin plotting our graph as shown in Figure B-2.

It takes only two points to define a line, and we already have one from the y-intercept. To find a second point, we can plug in any value of Q and solve for the corresponding P (or vice versa). For example, if we let $Q = 2$ and solve for P, we get:

$$P = -5(2) + 25$$
$$P = -10 + 25$$
$$P = 15$$

We can now plot the point (2,15) and connect it to the y-intercept at (0,25).

Math Essentials: Working with Linear Equations ■ Appendix B   78C

FIGURE B-1

Translating a graph into an algebraic equation

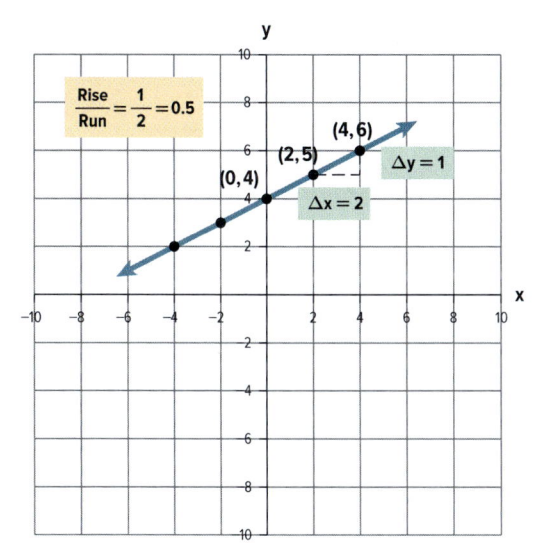

By using information provided on a graph, you can easily construct an equation of the line in the form $y = mx + b$. The slope, m, is calculated by taking the rise of a line over its run. The value of the y-intercept provides the b part of the equation.

FIGURE B-2

Translating an algebraic equation into a graph

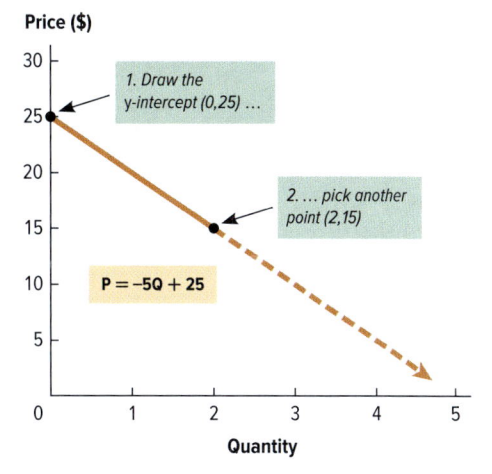

The first step in graphing the equation of a line in the form $y = mx + b$ is to plot the y intercept, given by b. Then pick another point by choosing any value of x or y, and solving the equation for the other variable to get an ordered pair that represents another point on the line. Connecting these two points gives the line.

Rather than plugging in random points, though, it is often useful to know the x-intercept as well as the y-intercept. On a demand curve, this will tell us what quantity is demanded when price is 0. To find this intercept, we can let $P = 0$ and solve for Q:

$$0 = -5Q + 25$$
$$-25 = -5Q$$
$$5 = Q$$

We can now plot the point (5,0) and connect it to (0,25) to graph the demand curve.

Finding intercepts is useful for interpreting other types of graphs as well. In a production possibilities frontier, the intercepts tell you how much of one good will be produced if all resources are used to produce that good and none are used to produce the other good. In the production possibilities frontier shown in Figure B-3, for example, we can find the y-intercept to see that by devoting all workers to making shirts and none to producing wheat, 2 million T-shirts can be produced. Alternatively, we can find the x-intercept to see that if all workers grow wheat and none make shirts, 4 million bushels of wheat can be produced.

We saw in Chapter 2, "Specialization and Exchange," that the slope of the frontier represents the trade-off between producing two goods. We can use our intercepts as the two points we need to calculate the slope.

$$\text{Slope} = \frac{\Delta y}{\Delta x} = \frac{(4 \text{ million} - 0)}{(0 - 2 \text{ million})} = \frac{4}{-2} = -2$$

You know that the slope of the frontier will be negative because it represents a trade-off: You can't make more wheat without giving up some shirts. Because an increase in wheat means a decrease in shirts, the two variables move in opposite directions and have a negative

FIGURE B-3
Using intercepts to interpret a production possibilities frontier

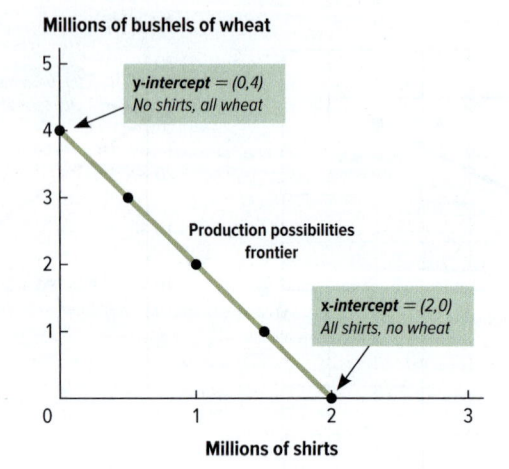

Millions of bushels of wheat (y-axis, 0 to 5)
Millions of shirts (x-axis, 0 to 3)

y-intercept = (0,4) — No shirts, all wheat
x-intercept = (2,0) — All shirts, no wheat
Production possibilities frontier

The intercepts of a production possibilities frontier give the maximum amount of a good a country can produce by dedicating all resources in the economy to the production of that good. In this case, with all workers dedicated to the production of one good or the other, the economy can make either 4 million bushels of wheat or 2 million shirts.

relationship. This frontier has a constant slope, which means that the trade-off between the two goods—which we can also think of as the opportunity cost of producing shirts in terms of wheat—is also constant.

Equations with *x* and *y* reversed

Thus far, we have represented demand and supply equations with P (or y) isolated on the left side of the equation. For example, our demand equation was given as $P = -5Q + 25$. You may find, however, that in some places, demand and supply equations are given with Q (or x) isolated on the left side of the equation instead.

When you see this, you cannot read the equation as giving you the slope and the y-intercept. Instead, when an equation is in this form, you have the inverse of slope and the x-intercept.

Look at our demand equation again. If we rearrange the equation to solve for Q, we have an equation of the form $x = ny + a$:

$$P = -5Q + 25$$
$$P - 25 = -5Q$$
$$-\frac{1}{5}P + 5 = Q \quad \text{or} \quad Q = -\frac{1}{5}P + 5$$

We know that the starting equation represents the same underlying relationship as the final equation. For instance, we know that our slope is -5, but in the rearranged form where we have solved for Q, the coefficient multiplying P is the inverse of slope, or $-\frac{1}{5}$. We can generalize this observation to say that when we have an equation of the form $x = ny + a$, $n = \frac{1}{m}$, where m is the slope of the line from the same equation expressed in the form $y = mx + b$. We also know that 25 is the

FIGURE B-4
Same line, different equation forms

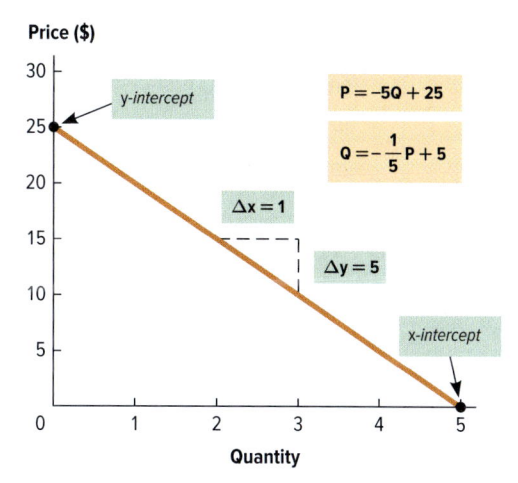

$$P = -5Q + 25$$
$$Q = -\frac{1}{5}P + 5$$

Regardless of whether you solve an equation for P or Q, the resulting line is the same.

y-intercept. But in our rearranged form, *a* represents the *x*-intercept, which is 5. The graph in Figure B-4 shows that these two equations represent different aspects of the same line.

Keep in mind that $P = -5Q + 25$ is the same equation as $Q = -\frac{1}{5}P + 5$; we have simply rearranged it to solve for Q instead of P.

Shifts and Pivots

Imagine that your campus cafeteria has a deli with a salad bar and that the price of a salad depends on the number of ingredients you add to it. This relationship is represented by the following equation:

$$y = 0.5x + 4$$

where

y = total price of the salad

x = number of added ingredients

Because our variables are the price of a salad and the number of ingredients, negative quantities do not make sense: You can't have negative carrots in your salad, and we doubt that the cafeteria is paying you to buy salads. Therefore, we can isolate the graph of this equation to the first quadrant, as shown in panel A of Figure B-5.

Our *y*-intercept of 4 represents the price of a salad if you add zero ingredients. In other words, a plain bowl of lettuce costs $4. The slope of 0.5 represents the cost of adding ingredients to the salad. Each additional ingredient costs 50 cents. The fact that (2,5) is a point along the line shows that the price of a salad with two added ingredients is $5.

How much is a salad with six added ingredients?

$$y = 0.5(6) + 4$$
$$y = 3 + 4$$
$$y = 7$$

A salad with six added ingredients is $7, and (6,7) is another point on the graph.

LO B.2 Use linear equations to explain shifts and pivots.

FIGURE B-5
Shifting a line to change the intercept

(A) Restrict the graph to Quadrant I

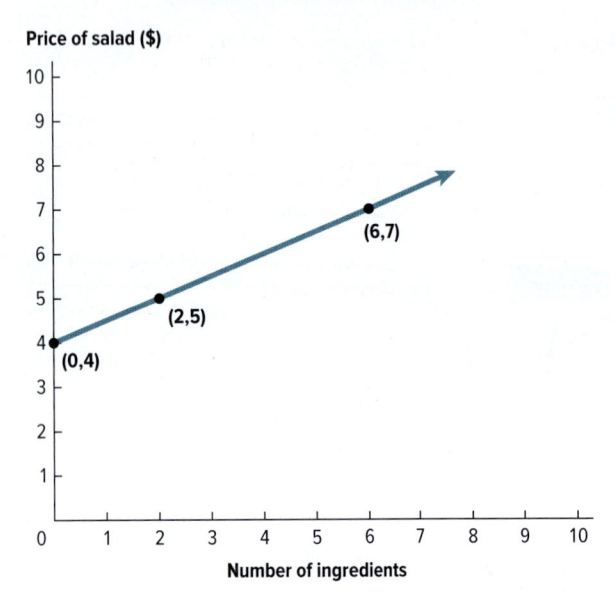

In order to easily change the intercept, first restrict the line to values in the first quadrant. This will clearly show the y-intercept of the line.

(B) Shift the line upward by moving the intercept

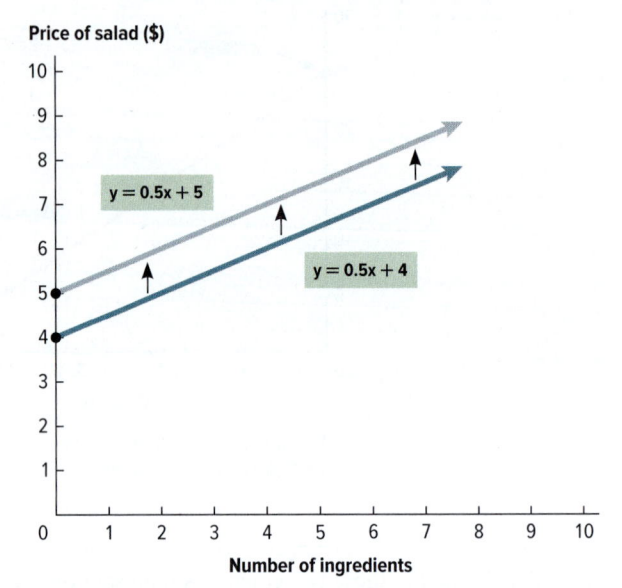

Once the y-intercept is clear, you can shift the line to the new intercept indicated by the equation of the line.

Now, let's see what happens to our graph when the baseline price of a bowl of lettuce without additional ingredients increases to $5. This baseline price is represented by the y-intercept, which changes from 4 to 5. The slope of the graph does not change because each additional ingredient still costs 50 cents.

Thus, our equation changes to $y = 0.5x + 5$. Rather than regraphing this new question from scratch, we can simply *shift* the original line to account for the change in the y-intercept, as shown in panel B of Figure B-5.

Suppose, instead, that the price of lettuce remains at $4, but the price of additional ingredients increases to $1 each. How will this change the graph and equation?

If the price of lettuce with zero additional ingredients remains at $4, the y-intercept will also stay the same. However, the slope will change, increasing from 50 cents to $1. Figure B-6 shows that this change of slope will *pivot* the line in our graph.

Our equation changes as well. This time, we substitute 1 in place of 0.5 for the slope. Thus, $y = x + 4$. (Remember that no coefficient on x indicates that the slope is 1.)

What happens if the baseline price of lettuce goes up to $5 *and* the price of toppings goes up to $1? We have to both *shift and pivot* the line to represent the change in the intercept and the slope. (Sounds like a fitness routine, doesn't it?) Figure B-7 shows both changes.

You will need to shift and pivot lines in many places throughout this book to represent changes in the relationship between two variables. For instance, we saw in Chapter 3, "Markets," that when a nonprice determinant of demand changes, you need to *shift* the demand curve to show that people demand a higher or lower quantity of a good at any given price. When consumers

Math Essentials: Working with Linear Equations ■ Appendix B 78G

FIGURE B-6
Pivoting a line to change the slope

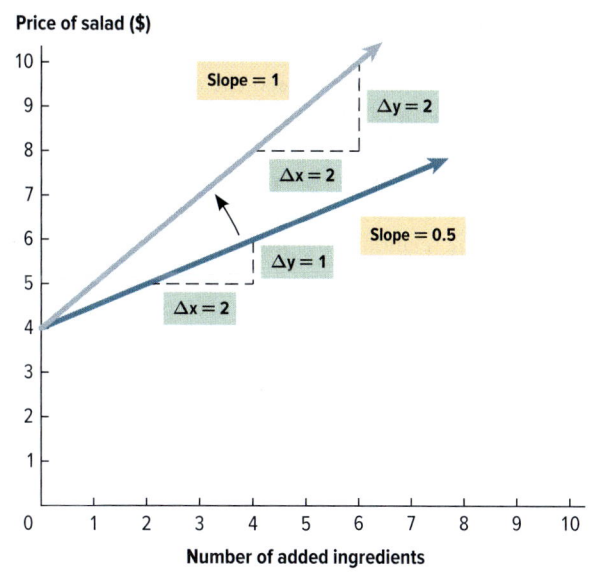

Changes in slope will pivot the equation of a line. Increases in slope will rotate the line upward; decreases in slope will rotate the line downward.

FIGURE B-7
Shift and pivot

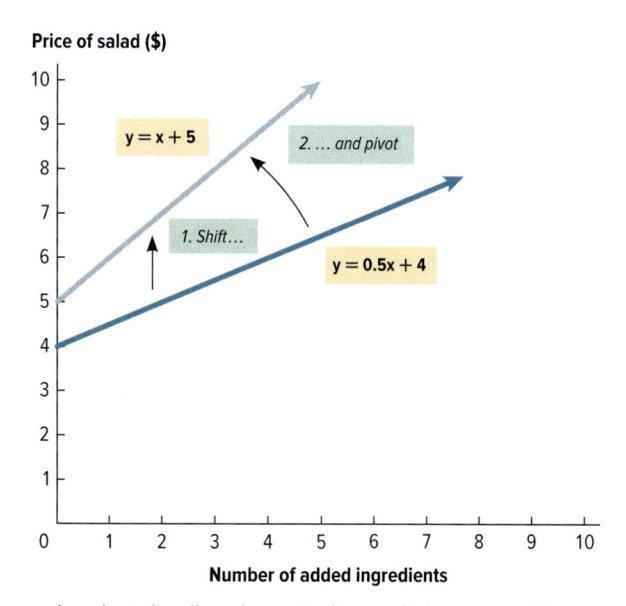

In order to handle a change in slope and intercept, you first shift the line to the new intercept and then pivot the line to reflect the new slope.

become more or less sensitive to changes in price, you need to *pivot* the demand curve to represent a change in slope.

Solving for Equilibrium

LO B.3 Use linear equations to solve for equilibrium.

One graph can show multiple relationships between the same two variables. The most frequent case we encounter in this book is graphs showing both the demand relationship and the supply relationship between price and quantity.

Panel A of Figure B-8 shows data from supply and demand schedules. Remember from Chapter 3, "Markets," that as P increases, the quantity *demanded* decreases. Since P and Q are moving in opposite directions, the relationship is negative. When these values are plotted in panel B, we have a downward-sloping line for the demand curve. Conversely, as P increases, the quantity *supplied* increases. Plotting these points yields an upward-sloping supply curve.

When we use one graph to show multiple equations of the same variables, we do so in order to show something meaningful about the relationship between them. For instance, when we show supply and demand on the same graph, we usually want to find the equilibrium point—the point at which the quantity supplied and the quantity demanded are equal to one another at the same price.

We can find the equilibrium point in several ways. If we have schedules showing both demand and supply data, the easiest way to find equilibrium is to locate the price that corresponds to *equal supply and demand quantities*. What is that price in panel A of Figure B-8? At a price of 80, Q is 60 in the demand schedule as well as in the supply schedule.

We can also find the equilibrium point easily by looking at a graph showing both supply and demand. The one-and-only point where the two lines intersect is the equilibrium.

FIGURE B-8

Graphing the supply and demand schedules

(A) Supply and demand schedules

Price ($)	Q_{demand}	Q_{supply}
20	180	0
30	160	10
40	140	20
50	120	30
80	60	60
90	40	70
100	20	80
110	0	90

The supply and demand schedules show the quantities demanded and supplied for a given price.

(B) Graphing the schedules

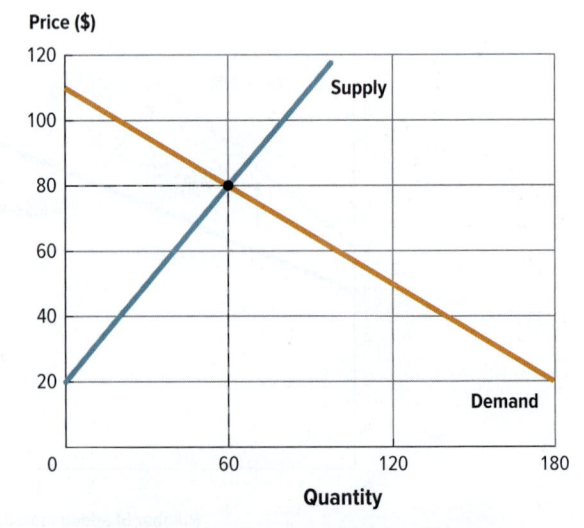

Graphing the values from the schedules gives a downward-sloping demand curve and an upward-sloping supply curve.

Sometimes, however, it is useful to find equilibrium from equations alone, without having to graph them or to calculate a whole schedule of points by plugging in different prices. Usually you'll want to use this method when you are given equations but no graph or schedule. However, just for practice, let's first derive the supply and demand equations from Figure B-8 and then figure out the equilibrium point.

We want to start by representing supply and demand as equations of the form $y = mx + b$. Let y = price and x = quantity. We need to determine the slope (m) and the y-intercept (b) for each equation.

First, the demand equation: What is the y-intercept? It is the value of y when x is 0. Looking at panel A in Figure B-8, we can see that when Q is zero, P is 110. The y-intercept of the demand equation is 110. Now we need the slope. Because this is a linear relationship and the slope is constant, we can determine the slope using any two points. Let's use the points (180,20) and (160,30).

$$\frac{\Delta y}{\Delta x} = \frac{(P_2 - P_1)}{(Q_2 - Q_1)} = \frac{(20 - 30)}{(180 - 160)} = \frac{-10}{20} = -0.5$$

Thus, our demand equation is: $P = -0.5Q + 110$.

We'll use the same procedure to derive the supply equation. Looking at the supply schedule, we can see that when Q is zero, P is 20. The y-intercept is 20. To determine slope, let's use the points (0,20) and (10,30).

$$\frac{\Delta y}{\Delta x} = \frac{(P_2 - P_1)}{(Q_2 - Q_1)} = \frac{(20 - 30)}{(0 - 10)} = \frac{-10}{-10} = 1$$

Thus, our supply equation is: $P = Q + 20$.

Now that we have our equations, we can use them to solve for equilibrium. Equilibrium represents a point that is on both the demand and supply curves; graphically, it is where the two curves intersect. This means that P on the demand curve must equal P on the supply curve, and the same for Q. Therefore, it makes sense that we find this point by setting the two equations equal to each other.

$$P_D = -0.5Q + 110$$
$$P_S = Q + 20$$
$$P_D = P_S$$

therefore,

$$-0.5Q + 110 = Q + 20$$

This allows us to solve for a numeric value for Q.

$$1.5Q + 20 = 110$$
$$1.5Q = 90$$
$$Q = 60$$

Now that we have a value for Q, we can plug it in either the supply or demand equation to get the value for P. Let's use our supply equation.

$$P = 20 + Q$$
$$P = 20 + 60$$
$$P = 80$$

Solving for equilibrium using the equations gives us the same point we found using the demand and supply schedules: $Q = 60$ and $P = 80$ (60,80).

Problems and Applications

1. Use the demand curve in Figure BP-1 to derive a demand equation. [LO B.1]

FIGURE BP-1

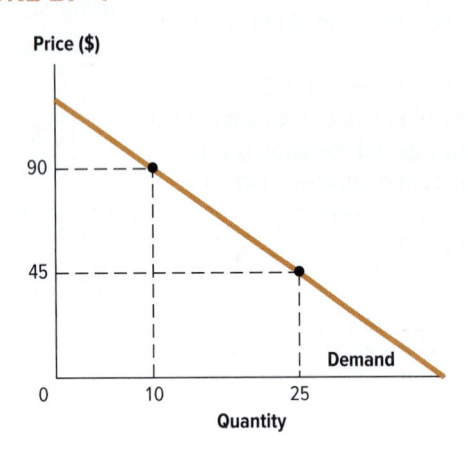

Price ($) axis with points at 90 and 45; Quantity axis with points at 10 and 25. Demand curve passes through (10, 90) and (25, 45).

2. Use the demand schedule in Table BP-1 to derive a demand equation. [LO B.1]

TABLE BP-1

Price ($)	Quantity
0	320
10	280
20	240
30	200
40	160
50	120
60	80
70	40
80	0

3. Use the supply curve in Figure BP-2 to derive a supply equation. [LO B.1]

FIGURE BP-2

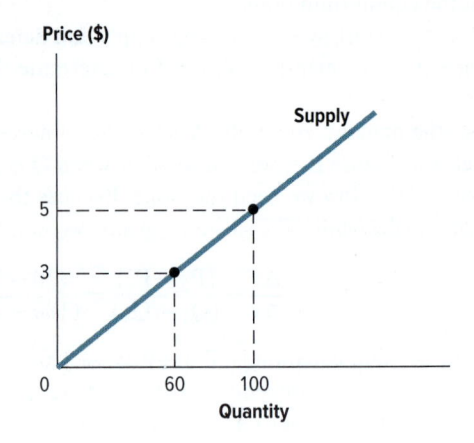

Price ($) axis with points at 5 and 3; Quantity axis with points at 60 and 100. Supply curve passes through (60, 3) and (100, 5).

4. Use the supply schedule in Table BP-2 to derive a supply equation. [LO B.1]

TABLE BP-2

Price ($)	Quantity
100	0
200	25
300	50
400	75
500	100
600	125

5. Graph the equation $P = 2Q + 3$. Is this a supply curve or a demand curve? [LO B.1]

6. Graph the equation $P = -8Q + 10$. Is this a supply curve or a demand curve? [LO B.1]

7. Rearrange the equation Q = 5 − 0.25P and sketch the graph. Is this a supply curve or a demand curve? [LO B.1]

8. Rearrange the equation Q = 0.2P and sketch the graph. Is this a supply curve or a demand curve? [LO B.1]

9. The entrance fee at your local amusement park is $20 for the day. The entrance fee includes all rides except roller coasters. Roller coasters cost an extra $2 per ride. [LO B.2]

   a. Write an equation that represents how much money you will spend on rides as a function of the number of rides you go on: S = total spending on rides; Q = the quantity of roller coaster rides.
   b. What is your total spending on rides if you ride 4 roller coasters?
   c. Draw a graph of the relationship between total spending on rides and the number of roller coaster rides.
   d. Redraw the graph from part (c) to show what changes if the entrance fee increases to $25.
   e. Rewrite the equation from part (a) to incorporate the increased entrance fee of $25.
   f. After the entrance fee increases to $25, what is your total spending on rides if you ride 4 roller coasters?

10. Use the following two equations: [LO B.3]

    (1) P = 12 − 2Q
    (2) P = 3 + Q

    a. Find the equilibrium price and quantity.
    b. Graph the demand and supply equations. Illustrate the equilibrium point.

11. With reference to Table BP-3: [LO B.3]

TABLE BP-3

Price ($)	Quantity demanded	Quantity supplied
0	12	0
20	10	4
40	8	8
60	6	12
80	4	16
100	2	20
120	0	24

a. Use the information from the table to create the demand and supply equations.
b. Use your demand and supply equations to solve for equilibrium.
c. Graph supply and demand curves. Illustrate the equilibrium point.

Chapter 4

Elasticity

Coffee Becomes Chic

In the 1990s, a coffeehouse craze rippled through middle-class communities in the United States, as a strong economy bolstered sales of high-priced espresso drinks. Soon, Americans were making daily pilgrimages to a place called Starbucks, where a cup of coffee had been transformed into the "Starbucks' experience," complete with soundtrack, mints, and charity-themed water bottles. For 15 years the Starbucks' business model was highly successful. From 1992 through 2007, the company expanded by over 15,000 stores.

When the U.S. economy stumbled in 2008, however, Starbucks's growth rate dropped to an all-time low. Competitors and customers began to ask, "How much is too much for a cup of coffee?" Presumably, Starbucks' executives had asked themselves that very question over the course of more than a decade. Given the company's phenomenal rate of expansion, they must have had the right answer—at least until the economy started having problems.

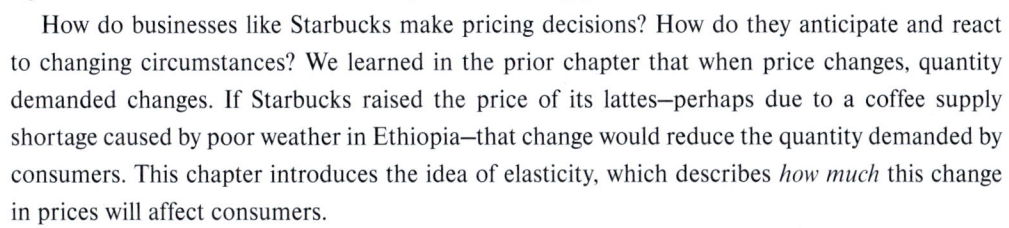

©amenic181/123RF

How do businesses like Starbucks make pricing decisions? How do they anticipate and react to changing circumstances? We learned in the prior chapter that when price changes, quantity demanded changes. If Starbucks raised the price of its lattes—perhaps due to a coffee supply shortage caused by poor weather in Ethiopia—that change would reduce the quantity demanded by consumers. This chapter introduces the idea of elasticity, which describes *how much* this change in prices will affect consumers.

Like the market for cell phones, the market for gourmet coffee is not perfectly competitive. Managers of a big company like Starbucks have some ability to set prices, and they try to choose prices that will earn the largest profits. They also try to respond to changing market conditions: How much will sales fall if the price of coffee beans drives up the cost of a latte? How much will people decrease their coffee consumption during a recession? How many customers will be lost if competitors like Dunkin' Donuts and McDonald's offer less-expensive coffee? Even in perfectly competitive markets, producers want to predict how their profits will change in response to economic conditions and changes in the market price.

Nonprofit service providers also often need to think about price elasticity. For instance, a nonprofit hospital wants to set the price of care so as to cover costs without driving away too many patients. Similarly, colleges and universities want to cover costs and keep education affordable for students.

The ability to address issues like these is critical for any public or private organization. Understanding how to price a Starbucks' latte requires the same kind of thinking as figuring out whether to raise entrance fees to national parks to cover the costs of maintaining the wilderness. Solving these challenges relies on a tool called *elasticity*, a measure of how much supply and demand will respond to changes in price and income.

LEARNING OBJECTIVES

LO 4.1 Calculate price elasticity of demand using the mid-point method.

LO 4.2 Explain how the determinants of price elasticity of demand affect the degree of elasticity.

LO 4.3 Calculate price elasticity of supply using the mid-point method.

LO 4.4 Explain how the determinants of price elasticity of supply affect the degree of elasticity.

LO 4.5 Calculate cross-price elasticity of demand, and interpret the sign of the elasticity.

LO 4.6 Calculate income elasticity of demand, and interpret the sign of the elasticity.

In this chapter, you will learn how to calculate the effect of a price change on the quantity supplied or demanded. You will become familiar with some rules that businesses and policy-makers follow when they cannot measure elasticity exactly. Using what you know about supply and demand, you will be able to categorize different types of goods by noting whether their elasticities are positive or negative. You will also learn how to use a rough approximation of price elasticity to tell whether raising prices will raise or lower an organization's total revenue.

What Is Elasticity?

If Starbucks raises the price of a latte, we can expect the quantity of lattes demanded to fall. But by how much? Although we saw in Chapter 3, "Markets," that price increases cause the quantity demanded to fall in a competitive market, we have not yet been able to say *how big* that movement will be. That question is the subject of this chapter.

Elasticity is a measure of how much consumers and producers will respond to a change in market conditions. The concept can be applied to supply or demand. Also, it can be used to measure responses to a change in the price of a good, a change in the price of a related good, or a change in income.

The concept of elasticity allows economic decision makers to anticipate *how others will respond* to changes in market conditions. Whether you are a business owner trying to sell cars or a public official trying to set sales taxes, you need to know how much a change in prices will affect consumers' willingness to buy.

There are several measures of elasticity:

- The most commonly used measures of elasticity are *price elasticity of demand* and *price elasticity of supply*. These two concepts describe how much the quantity demanded and the quantity supplied change when the price of a good changes.

elasticity
a measure of how much consumers and producers will respond to a change in market conditions

- The *cross-price elasticity of demand* describes how much the demand curve shifts when the price of another good changes. It tells us how much the quantity of coffee demanded changes, for example, when the price of tea increases.
- Another helpful measure, *income elasticity of demand*, measures how much the demand curve shifts when consumers' incomes change.

We'll examine these four elasticity concepts in this chapter. Let's begin with price elasticity of demand.

Price Elasticity of Demand

Price elasticity of demand describes the size of the change in the quantity demanded of a good or service when its price changes. We showed in Chapter 3, "Markets" that quantity demanded generally decreases when the price increases, but so far we have not been able to say *how much* it decreases. Price elasticity of demand fills this gap in our understanding of supply and demand.

Another way to think about price elasticity of demand is as a measure of consumers' sensitivity to price changes. Sensitivity to price changes is measured as more or less elastic:

- When consumers' buying decisions are highly influenced by price, we say that their demand is *more elastic*. By that, we mean that a small change in price causes a large change in the quantity demanded.
- When consumers are not very sensitive to price changes—that is, when they will buy approximately the same quantity, regardless of the price—we say that their demand is *more inelastic*.

price elasticity of demand
the size of the change in the quantity demanded of a good or service when its price changes

Calculating price elasticity of demand

Consider the challenge Starbucks faced in shoring up falling sales during the recession. In this situation, a business might lower its prices by offering a sale. But would a sale work? How much could Starbucks's managers expect purchases to increase as a result of the sale? In other words, *How will customers respond* to a sale? The ability to answer this question is a critical tool for businesses. To do so, we need to know the price elasticity of demand for Starbucks coffee.

Let's say that Starbucks usually charges $2 for a cup of coffee. What might happen if it offers a special sale price of $1.50? Suppose that before the sale, Starbucks sold 10 million cups of coffee each day. Now, say that consumers react to the sale by increasing the quantity demanded to 15 million cups per day. Figure 4-1 shows the quantity demanded before and after the sale as two points on the demand curve for coffee. Based on the results of this sale, what can we say about consumers' sensitivity to the price of coffee at Starbucks?

Mathematically, price elasticity is the percentage change in the quantity of a good that is demanded in response to a given percentage change in price. The basic formula looks like Equation 4-1.

LO 4.1 Calculate price elasticity of demand using the mid-point method.

EQUATION 4-1
$$\text{Price elasticity of demand} = \frac{\% \text{ change in Q demanded}}{\% \text{ change in P}}$$

To calculate percentage change, we will be using the **mid-point method**. The mid-point method measures the percentage change relative to a point *midway between the two points*. The mid-point method can be used to calculate the percentage change in quantity demanded, for example (the numerator in Equation 4-1). We do that by dividing the change in quantity demanded by the midpoint (average) quantity, as shown in Equation 4-2.

mid-point method
method that measures percentage change in quantity demanded (or quantity supplied) relative to a point midway between two points on a curve; used to estimate elasticity

EQUATION 4-2
$$\% \text{ change in Q demanded} = \frac{Q_2 - Q_1}{\text{Average of Q}} = \frac{Q_2 - Q_1}{\left(\frac{Q_2 + Q_1}{2}\right)}$$

FIGURE 4-1
Elasticity of the demand for coffee

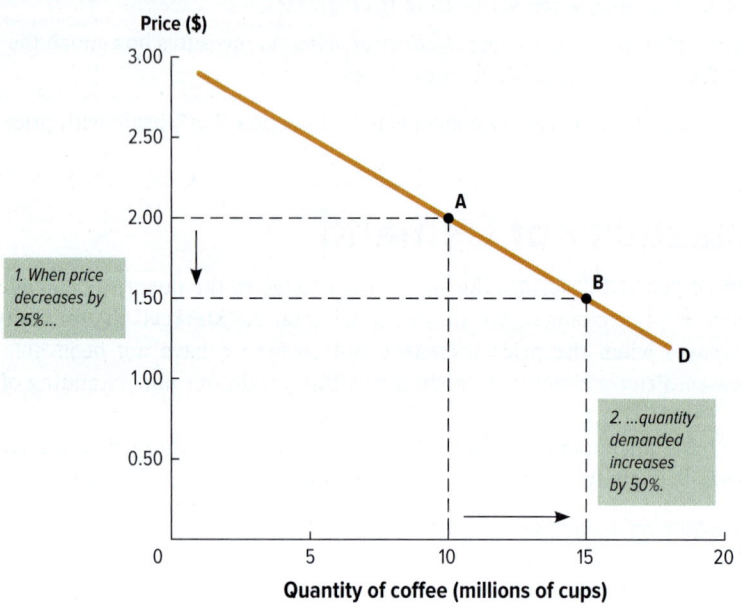

1. When price decreases by 25%...

2. ...quantity demanded increases by 50%.

When the price of coffee is $2 a cup, consumers demand 10 million cups. If the price falls to $1.50 per cup, the quantity demanded increases to 15 million cups.

In the denominator of this expression, the mid-point (average) quantity is equal to the sum of the two quantities divided by 2.

We can find the percentage change in price (the denominator of Equation 4-1) in the same way, as shown in Equation 4-3.

EQUATION 4-3
$$\% \text{ change in P} = \frac{P_2 - P_1}{\text{Average of P}} = \frac{P_2 - P_1}{\left(\frac{P_2 + P_1}{2}\right)}$$

Putting Equation 4-2 and Equation 4-3 together, we get Equation 4-4, which is the mid-point method for calculating the price elasticity of demand. This is a fully fleshed-out version of Equation 4-1.

EQUATION 4-4
$$\text{Price elasticity of demand} = \frac{(Q_2 - Q_1)/[(Q_2 + Q_1)/2]}{(P_2 - P_1)/[(P_2 + P_1)/2]}$$

Looking at our example, we find that the demand for coffee went from 10 million cups at $2 to 15 million cups at $1.50. So the average (mid-point) quantity demanded was 12.5 million cups. The average (mid-point) price was $1.75. If we plug the original and sale quantities and prices into Equation 4-4, what do we find? The price was cut by 29 percent and the quantity demanded rose by 40 percent. That tells us that the price elasticity of demand is −1.38.

$$\text{Price elasticity of demand} = \frac{\left(\frac{15 \text{ million} - 10 \text{ million}}{12.5 \text{ million}}\right)}{\left(\frac{1.50 - 2.00}{1.75}\right)} = \frac{0.40}{-0.29} = -1.38$$

⚠️ CAUTION: COMMON MISTAKE

Another way of calculating *percentage change* is to divide the difference between the starting and ending levels by the starting level. Using this method, the percentage change in quantity demanded would be expressed as:

$$\% \text{ change in quantity demanded} = \left[\frac{(Q_2 - Q_1)}{Q_1}\right]$$

Notice that the denominator of this expression is simply the starting value of quantity demanded. While you may have used this method before, this method causes a measurement problem when we use it to calculate elasticity: The elasticity changes depending on which direction we move along the demand curve. To avoid this problem, we will be using the mid-point method for calculating percentage change in this chapter.

What does it mean for the price elasticity of demand to be −1.38? Remember that the elasticity describes the size of the change in the quantity demanded of a good when its price changes. A measure of −1.38 price elasticity of demand for cups of coffee means that a 1 percent decrease in the price of coffee will lead to a 1.38 percent increase in the quantity of coffee cups demanded. (Alternatively, we could also say that a 1 percent *increase* in the price of coffee will lead to a 1.38 percent *decrease* in the quantity of coffee cups demanded.)

The *price elasticity of demand will always be a negative number*. Why? Because price and quantity demanded *move in opposite directions*:

- A positive change in price will cause a negative change in the quantity demanded.
- A negative change in price will cause a positive change in the quantity demanded.

In our example, the price of coffee decreased and the quantity demanded increased.

However, be aware that economists often drop the negative sign and express the price elasticity of demand as a positive number, just for the sake of convenience. Don't be fooled! Under normal circumstances, price elasticity of demand is always negative, whether or not the negative sign is printed.

⚠️ CAUTION: COMMON MISTAKE

Some texts include the negative sign, and others drop the negative sign. Another way to think of an elasticity measure is as an absolute value. The *absolute value* of a number is its distance from zero, or its numerical value without regard to its sign. For example, the absolute values of 4 and −4 are both 4. The absolute value of elasticity measures the "size" of the response, while the sign measures its direction. Sometimes only the absolute value will be printed, when it is assumed that you know the direction of the change.

You might be wondering why we work with percentages in calculating elasticity. Why not just compare the change in the quantity demanded to the change in price? The answer is that percentages allow us to avoid some practical problems. Think about what would happen if one person measured coffee in 12-ounce cups, while another measured it by the pot or the gallon. Without percentages, we would have several different measures of price elasticity, depending on which unit of measurement we used. To avoid this problem, economists use the *percentage change* in quantity rather than the *absolute change* in quantity. That way, the elasticity of demand for coffee is the same whether we measure the quantity in cups, pots, or gallons.

Determinants of price elasticity of demand

LO 4.2 Explain how the determinants of price elasticity of demand affect the degree of elasticity.

How would the quantity demanded of lattes (or your drink of choice) change if the price fell from $3 to $1.50? Now, how much would the quantity demanded of cotton socks change if the price fell from $10 per pack to $5? Although both represent a 50 percent price reduction, we suspect that the former might change your buying habits more than the latter. Socks are socks, and $5 savings probably won't make you rush out and buy twice as many. To state this more formally, we would say that the demand for lattes is more elastic than the demand for socks.

The underlying idea here is that consumers are more sensitive to price changes for some goods and services than for others. As said earlier, we can classify the degree of sensitivity to price changes by labeling the demand for a particular good as elastic or inelastic. More rigorous definitions of these terms will be given later, but for now remember this: When consumers are very responsive to price changes for a particular good, we say that the demand for that good is *more elastic*. When consumers are not very responsive to price changes for a particular good, we say the demand for that good is *more inelastic*.

Why isn't price elasticity of demand the same for all goods and services? Many factors determine consumers' responsiveness to price changes. The availability of substitutes, relative need and relative cost, and the time needed to adjust to price changes all affect price elasticity of demand.

Availability of substitutes   Recall from Chapter 3, "Markets," that substitutes are goods that are distinguishable from one another but have similar uses. When the price of a good with a close substitute increases, consumers will buy the substitute instead. If close substitutes are available for a particular good, then the demand for that good will be *more elastic* than if only distant substitutes are available. For example, the price elasticity of demand for cranberry juice is likely to be relatively elastic; if the price gets too high, many consumers may switch to grape juice.

Degree of necessity   When a good is a basic necessity, people will buy it even if its price rises. The demand for socks probably is not very elastic, nor is the demand for home heating during the winter. Although people may not like it when the prices of these goods rise, they will buy them to maintain a basic level of comfort. And when prices fall, they probably won't buy vastly more socks or make their homes a lot hotter.

In comparison, the demand for luxuries like vacations, expensive cars, and jewelry is likely to be much more elastic. Most people can easily do without these goods when their prices rise. Note, however, that the definition of a necessity depends on your standards and circumstances. In Florida, air conditioning may be a necessity and heating a luxury; the opposite is likely to be true in Alaska.

Cost relative to income   All else held equal, if consumers spend a very small share of their incomes on a good, their demand for the good will be less elastic than otherwise. For instance, most people can get a year's supply of ballpoint pens for just a few dollars. Even if the price doubled, a year's supply would still cost less than $10, so consumers probably would not bother to adjust their consumption of ballpoint pens.

The opposite is also true: If a good costs a very large proportion of a person's income, like going on a luxury three-week vacation to the beach, the demand for the good will be more elastic. If the price of rooms at high-end beachfront hotels doubles, then a lot of people will decide to do something else with their vacations.

Adjustment time   Goods often have much more elastic demand over the long run than over the short run. Often, adjusting to price changes takes some time. Consider how you might react to an increase in the price of gasoline. In the short run, you might cancel a weekend road trip, but you would still have to do the same amount of driving as usual to school, work, or the grocery store. Over a year, however, you could consider other choices that would further reduce your consumption of gas, such as buying a bus pass or a bicycle, getting a more fuel-efficient car, or moving closer to work or school.

Scope of the market A major caveat to the determinants just described is that each depends on how you define the market for a good or service. The price elasticity of demand for bananas might be high, but the price elasticity of demand for *fruit* could still be low because there are more substitutes for bananas than for the broader category of fruit. Similarly, although water might have a very low price elasticity of demand as a basic necessity, the demand for *bottled* water could be extremely elastic.

Using price elasticity of demand

When we make decisions in the real world, we often don't know the exact price elasticity of demand. But we don't always need to estimate elasticity precisely to know that consumers will react differently to price changes for lattes than for socks. Instead, businesses and other decision makers often know something general about the shape of the demand curve they are facing. Being able to place goods into several broad categories of elasticity can facilitate real pricing decisions in situations without full information.

At the extremes, demand can be perfectly elastic or perfectly inelastic. When demand is **perfectly elastic**, the quantity demanded drops to zero when the price increases even a minuscule amount. Thus, a perfectly elastic demand curve is horizontal, as shown in panel A of Figure 4-2. This graph indicates that consumers are very sensitive to price. When demand is **perfectly inelastic**, the quantity demanded is the same no matter what the price. Thus, the demand curve is vertical, as shown in panel B of Figure 4-2. These two extremes rarely occur in real life.

perfectly elastic demand
demand for which any increase in price will cause quantity demanded to drop to zero; represented by a perfectly horizontal line

perfectly inelastic demand
demand for which quantity demanded remains the same regardless of price; represented by a perfectly vertical line

FIGURE 4-2

Perfectly elastic and perfectly inelastic demand

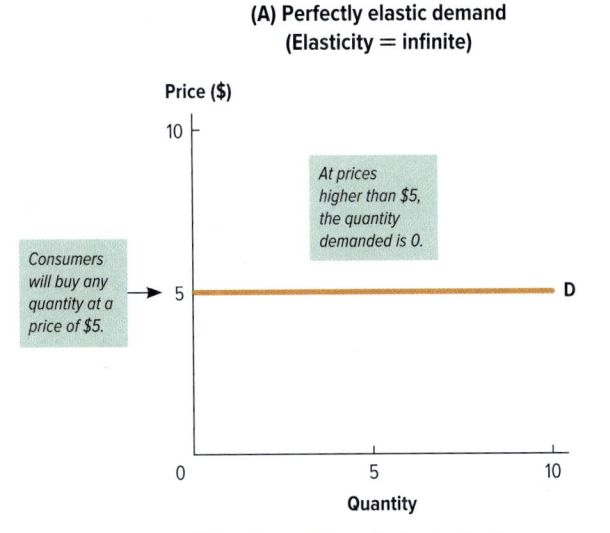

(A) Perfectly elastic demand (Elasticity = infinite)

Consumers will buy any quantity at a price of $5.

At prices higher than $5, the quantity demanded is 0.

When demand is perfectly elastic, the demand curve is horizontal. At prices above $5, consumers will not buy any quantity of the good.

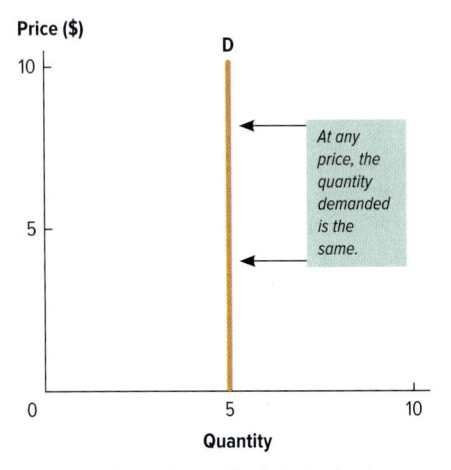

(B) Perfectly inelastic demand (Elasticity = 0)

At any price, the quantity demanded is the same.

When demand is perfectly inelastic, the demand curve is vertical. Consumers will always demand the same quantity of a good, regardless of the price.

elastic
demand that has an absolute value of elasticity greater than 1

inelastic
demand that has an absolute value of elasticity less than 1

unit-elastic
demand that has an absolute value of elasticity exactly equal to 1

Between these two extremes, elasticity is commonly divided into three quantifiable categories: elastic, inelastic, and unit-elastic. When the absolute value of the price elasticity of demand is greater than 1, we call the associated quantity demanded *elastic*. With elastic demand, a given percentage change in the price of a good will cause an even larger percentage change in the quantity demanded. For example, panel A of Figure 4-3 shows that for elastic demand, an 80 percent change in price could lead to a 150 percent change in the quantity demanded. Remember, we are using the mid-point method to calculate the percentage change here.

When the absolute value of the price elasticity of demand is less than 1, we say that demand is *inelastic*. With inelastic demand, a given percentage change in price will cause a smaller percentage change in the quantity demanded. Panel B of Figure 4-3 illustrates that for inelastic demand, an 80 percent change in price might lead to a 50 percent change in the quantity demanded.

If the absolute value of elasticity is exactly 1—that is, if a percentage change in price causes the same percentage change in the quantity demanded—then we say that demand is *unit-elastic*. Panel C of Figure 4-3 illustrates that for unit-elastic demand, an 80 percent change in price leads to an 80 percent change in the quantity demanded.

The concept of elasticity is not merely a theoretical tool. Businesses and policy decisions often depend on the value of particular elasticities. Table 4-1 displays actual estimates of price elasticities for a selection of goods. You can ask yourself why some price elasticities are larger than others. Why is the quantity demanded of air travel more elastic for leisure travel than business travel? Why is the quantity demanded of gasoline more elastic in the long run than the short run?

As we'll see later in this chapter, the terms *elastic*, *inelastic*, and *unit-elastic* can be used to describe any sort of elasticity, not just the price elasticity of demand. Although these categories may sound academic, they can have serious implications for real-world business and policy decisions. The Economics in Action box "Does charging for bednets decrease malaria?" describes a case in which knowing whether the price elasticity of demand is elastic or inelastic is a matter of life and death.

FIGURE 4-3

Elastic, inelastic, and unit-elastic demand

1. After price decreases by 80% under...

(A) Elastic demand — 2. ...quantity demanded increases by 150%.

(B) Inelastic demand — 2. ...quantity demanded increases by 50%.

(C) Unit-elastic demand — 2. ...quantity demanded increases by 80%.

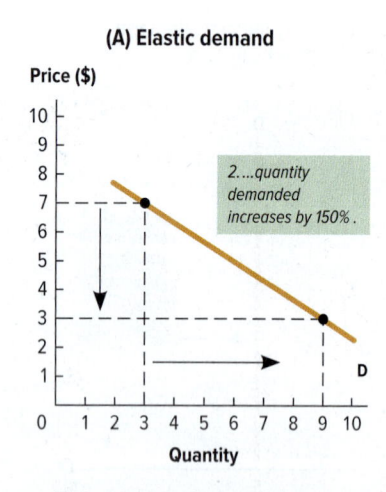

With an elastic demand curve, a small change in price leads to a big change in the quantity demanded. As a result, the price elasticity of demand is greater than 1.

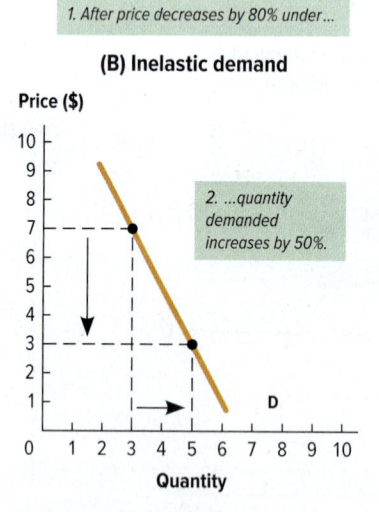

With an inelastic demand curve, even a large price change has a small effect on the quantity demanded. As a result, the price elasticity of demand is less than 1.

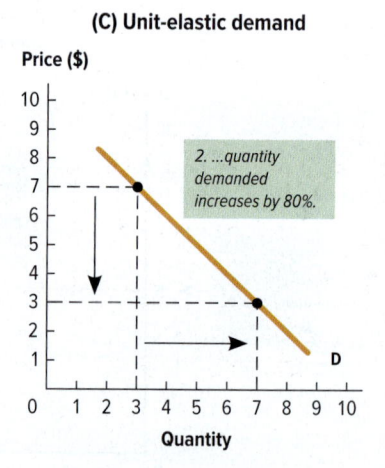

When demand is unit-elastic, the percentage change in price equals the percentage change in quantity, so that the price elasticity of demand is exactly 1.

TABLE 4-1
Estimated price elasticities of demand

Good	Estimated elasticities
Oil in the short run	−0.02
Eggs	−0.27
Gasoline in the short run	−0.05 to −0.6
Water (residential)	−0.41
Alcoholic drinks	−0.44
Gasoline in the long run	−0.25 to −0.7
Electricity	−0.38 to −0.61
Soft drinks	−0.7 to −0.8
Heroin	−0.8
Business air travel	−0.8
Leisure air travel	−1.6
NFL ticket resales	−2.94

Sources: T. Andreyeva, M. W. Long, and K. D. Brownell, "The impact of food prices on consumption: A systematic review of research on the price elasticity of demand for food," *American Journal of Public Health* 100, no. 2 (2010), p. 216; T. Helbling et al., "Oil scarcity, growth, and global imbalances," in International Monetary Fund, *World Economic Outlook*, April 2011, ch. 3, www.imf.org/external/pubs/ft/weo/2011/01/pdf/c3.pdf; S. M. Olmstead and R. N. Stavins, "Comparing price and nonprice approaches to urban water conservation," *Water Resources Research* 45, no. 4 (2009); T. A. Olmstead, S. M. Alessi, B. Kline, R. L. Pacula, and N. M. Petry, "The price elasticity of demand for heroin: Matched longitudinal and experimental evidence," *Journal of Health Economics* 41 (2015), pp. 59–71; P. Belobaba, A. Odoni, and C. Barnhart, eds., *The Global Airline Industry* (New York: Wiley & Sons, 2015), p. 61; M. A. Diehl, J. G. Maxcy, and J. Drayer, "Price elasticity of demand in the secondary market: Evidence from the National Football League," *Journal of Sports Economics* 16, no. 6 (August 2015), pp. 557–75; A. J. Ros, "An econometric assessment of electricity demand in the United States using panel data and the impact of retail competition on prices," *Insight in Economics*, June 9, 2015, www.nera.com/content/dam/nera/publications/2015/PUB_Econometric_Assessment_Elec_Demand_US_0615.pdf; P. Krugman, "Prices and gasoline demand," *The New York Times*, May 9, 2008, http://krugman.blogs.nytimes.com/2008/05/09/prices-and-gasoline-demand/?_r=0; L. Levin, M. S. Lewis, and F. A. Wolak, "High frequency evidence on the demand for gasoline," April 12, 2013, http://web.stanford.edu/group/fwolak/cgi-bin/sites/default/files/files/Levin_Lewis_Wolak_demand.pdf.

Does charging for bednets decrease malaria?
Economics in Action

It's hard to sleep when mosquitoes are buzzing. Most of the time, though, the worst outcome is waking up tired, dotted with a few itchy bites. But in some parts of the world, mosquitoes spread diseases like malaria that kill millions of young people every year.

Jessica Cohen and Pascaline Dupas, economics researchers working on a project in Kenya, saw some good news: The most dangerous mosquitoes come out only at night, and risks are cut sharply by sleeping under a bednet. The bad news is that many people, especially the poorest, don't have bednets.

Cohen and Dupas wanted to promote use of bednets, so they set up an organization to turn ideas into action (www.tamtamafrica.org). They faced a big, practical question: Should bednets be handed out for free? Or should providers sell them, perhaps at a discounted price?

(continued)

> One argument for selling bednets is that customers who buy them will probably value them more (and thus use them more) compared to people who get nets for free. If organizations sell bednets, they may also be able to distribute more of them.
>
> On the other hand, the law of demand states that the quantity demanded falls at higher prices. Charging for nets might dissuade some people—particularly, the very poorest families—from getting nets.
>
> As economists, Cohen and Dupas realized their practical question was: What's the price elasticity of the demand for bednets? To measure the elasticity, the two professors set up an experiment in western Kenya. Some people were offered bednets for free; others were offered bednets at a range of different prices. Cohen and Dupas found that charging a fee sharply reduced the quantity of the nets demanded. When the price increased from zero to just $0.75, the number of people wanting bednets dropped by 75 percent! Furthermore, the people who bought bednets did not use them more effectively than those who received them for free.
>
> If profit were the goal in this campaign, a few bednets sold at $0.75 would generate more revenue than a lot of bednets given away for free. But the goal was to help save lives, not to make a profit. Based on the high price elasticity, Cohen and Dupas concluded that for organizations with a social mission, free distribution of bednets beat charging a fee.
>
> Sources: J. Cohen and P. Dupas, "Free distribution or cost sharing? Evidence from a randomized malaria prevention experiment," *Quarterly Journal of Economics* 125, no. 1 (February 2010), pp. 1–45; T. Ogden, *Experimental Conversations: Perspectives on Randomized Trials in Development Economics* (Cambridge, MA: MIT Press, 2017).

Knowing whether the demand for a good is elastic or inelastic is extremely useful in business. That information allows a manager to determine whether a price increase will cause total revenue to rise or fall. **Total revenue** is the amount that a firm receives from the sale of goods and services, calculated as the quantity sold multiplied by the price paid for each unit. This number is important for an obvious reason: It tells us how much money sellers receive when they sell something.

An increase in price affects total revenue in two ways:

- It causes a *quantity effect*, or a decrease in total revenue that results from selling fewer units of the good.
- It causes a *price effect*, or an increase in total revenue that results from receiving a higher price for each unit sold.

total revenue the amount that a firm receives from the sale of goods and services; calculated as the quantity sold multiplied by the price paid for each unit

Figure 4-4 shows both the quantity effect and the price effect. When the quantity effect outweighs the price effect, a price increase will cause a drop in total revenue, as it does in Figure 4-4. When the price effect outweighs the quantity effect, a price increase will raise total revenue.

When demand is elastic, a price increase causes total revenue to fall. We already know that when demand is elastic, a change in price will cause a larger percentage change in quantity demanded. Another way of saying this is that the quantity effect outweighs the price effect. So when demand is elastic, a price increase causes a proportionally larger decrease in the quantity demanded, and total revenue falls.

Conversely, when demand is inelastic, the percentage change in price is larger than the percentage change in quantity demanded. The price effect outweighs the quantity effect, and total revenue increases. With inelastic demand, then, consumers will purchase less of a good when its price rises, but the change in the quantity demanded will be proportionally less than the change in price.

Figure 4-5 shows this trade-off between the price and quantity effects. As you can see, panel A shows an elastic demand in which a $1 change in price causes the quantity demanded to increase by 4,000. With the inelastic demand curve in panel B, a $2 decrease in price increases quantity demanded by only 1,000.

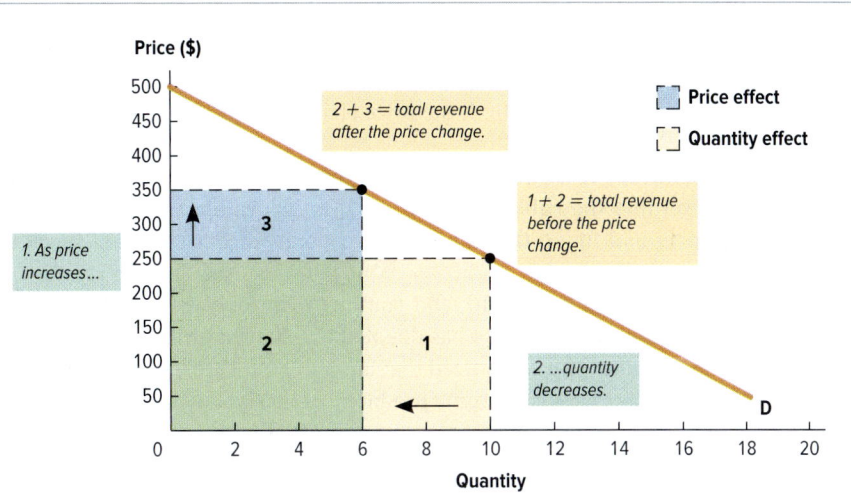

Elasticity ■ Chapter 4   89

FIGURE 4-4
Effect of a price increase on total revenue

The colored rectangles represent total revenue at two different prices. As the price increases from $250 to $350, total revenue is affected in two ways. The blue rectangle represents the increase in revenue received for each unit sold (the price effect). The yellow rectangle represents the decrease in total revenue as the number of units sold drops (the quantity effect). The elasticity of demand determines which effect is larger. In this case, the yellow area is larger than the blue area, meaning that the quantity effect outweighs the price effect, and total revenue decreases.

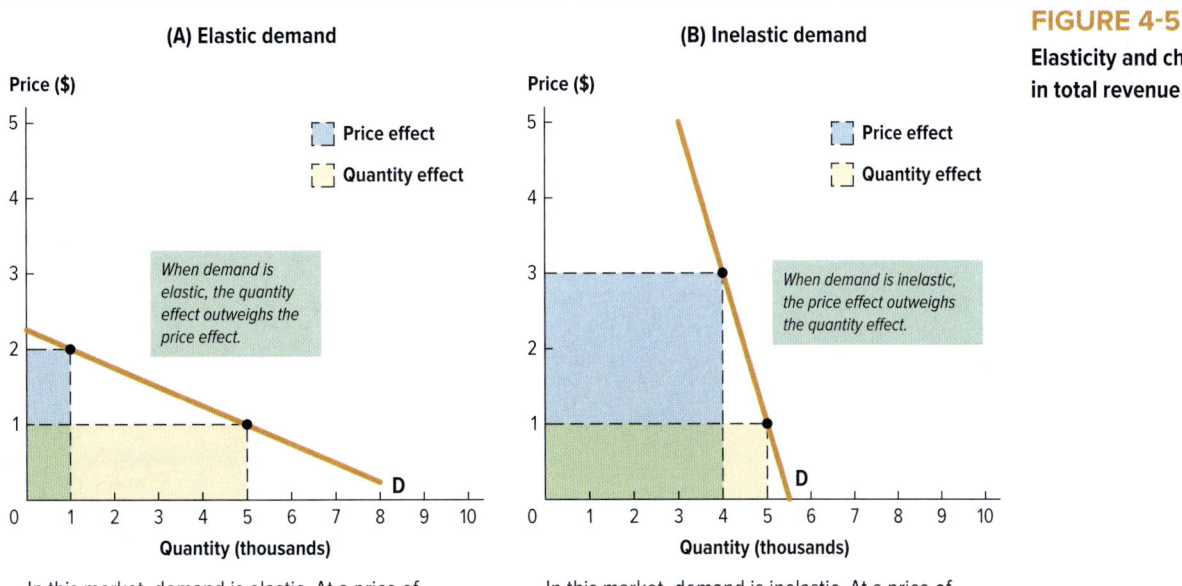

FIGURE 4-5
Elasticity and changes in total revenue

(A) Elastic demand

In this market, demand is elastic. At a price of $1, 5,000 units are sold for a total revenue of $5,000. If the price increases to $2, only 1,000 units are sold for a total revenue of only $2,000. The quantity effect outweighs the price effect.

(B) Inelastic demand

In this market, demand is inelastic. At a price of $1, 5,000 units are sold for a total revenue of $5,000. If the price increases to $3, the number of units sold drops by only 1,000, to 4,000 units. Because the price effect outweighs the quantity effect, total revenue climbs to $12,000, an increase of $7,000.

There is one final point to make. So far, everything we've said has described elasticity *at a particular spot on the demand curve*. For most goods, however, elasticity varies along the curve. So when we said that the price elasticity of demand for coffee was −1.38, we meant that it was −1.38 for a price change from $1.50 to $2 a cup. If the price changes from $2 to $2.50, the elasticity will be different.

The reasoning behind this fact is common sense. Imagine that the price of lattes plummets to 10 cents, and you get into the habit of buying one every morning. What would you do if you showed up one morning and found that the price had doubled overnight, to 20 cents? We bet you'd shrug and buy one anyway.

Now, imagine the price of lattes is $10, and you buy them only as occasional treats. If you arrive at the coffee shop and find the price has doubled to $20, what will you do? You'd probably consider very carefully whether you really need that latte. In both cases, you would be responding to a 100 percent increase in price for the same product, but you would react very differently. This makes perfect sense: In one case, the latte costs you only 10 more cents, but in the other, it costs an additional $10.

Your reactions to the latte illustrate a general rule: *Demand tends to be more elastic when price is high and more inelastic when price is low*. This brings us to an important caveat about the three graphs shown in Figure 4-3. Although the example of an elastic demand curve in panel A has a steeper *slope* than the inelastic demand curve in panel B, we now know that slope is not the same as elasticity.

In fact, the elasticity of demand is different at different points along a linear demand curve. The reasoning is nonintuitive, but straightforward when you think about it graphically. Look at Figure 4-6. The line in panel B has a constant slope, but the percentage changes in price and

FIGURE 4-6

Changes in elasticity along the demand curve

(A) Demand and revenue schedule

Price ($)	Quantity	Total revenue ($)
50	0	0
45	1	45
40	2	80
35	3	105
30	4	120
25	5	125
20	6	120
15	7	105
10	8	80
5	9	45
0	10	0

This table lists the data shown in the graphs in panels A and B. Quantity demanded always increases as price falls. Total revenue rises until the price falls to $25, then falls at lower prices.

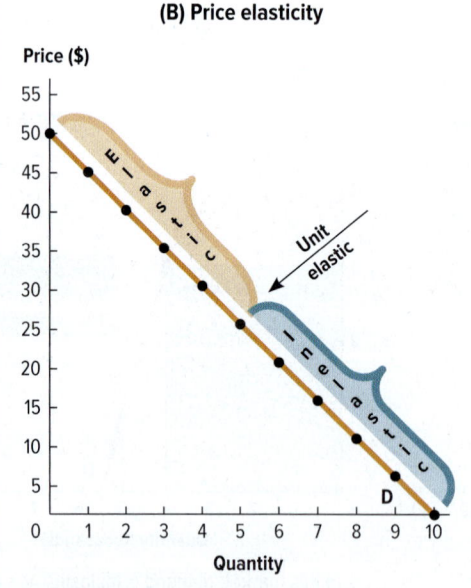

Price elasticity of demand varies along the demand curve. Above a certain price, demand is elastic; below it, demand is inelastic.

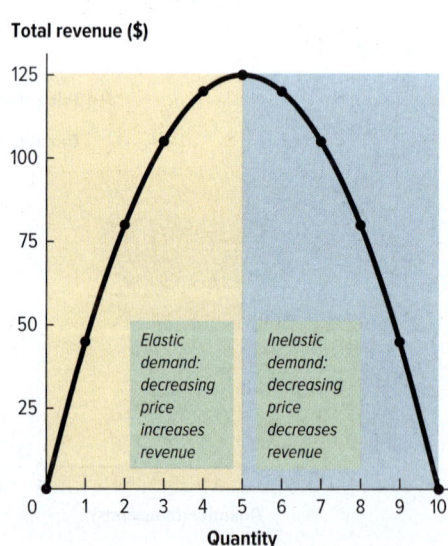

This graph shows total revenue along the demand curve shown above. Total revenue first rises, but then begins to fall as demand moves from elastic to inelastic.

quantity are very different at either end of the curve. For instance, going from $45 to $40 is a much smaller difference (in percentage terms) than from $10 to $5, but the slope of the curve is the same between both sets of points.

The result is that as we move along a linear demand curve starting from a price equal to zero, revenue first increases as the price increases, and then decreases with higher prices. (You can see this result in the "Total revenue" column in panel A.) The maximum revenue occurs where demand is unit-elastic.

Panel C of Figure 4-6 graphs out the total revenue curve associated with the demand curve in panel B, using calculations from the schedule in Panel A. Note that when the price is high, lowering the price will increase revenue. For example, when the price decreases from $45 to $40 (see the schedule), total revenue almost doubles, from $45 to $80. When the price is low, however, lowering it further decreases total revenue. Moving from $10 to $5, for example, decreases total revenue from $80 to $45.

Price elasticity of demand has all sorts of real-world applications. See, for example, the issue discussed in the What Do You Think? box "Should entrance fees at national parks be raised?"

For a refresher on slope versus elasticity, see Appendix C, "Math Essentials: Calculating Percentage Change, Slope, and Elasticity," which follows this chapter.

❓ Should entrance fees at national parks be raised?
What Do You Think?

America boasts 58 national parks spread across 84 million acres of the country's most famous natural spaces, including Yellowstone, the Grand Canyon, and the Florida Everglades. In 2017, 84 million people visited the parks—the most on record. These parks are feeling the strain; roads, trails, docks, and concessions at parks across the country need serious repairs. The U.S. Department of the Interior estimates that fully funding these fixes would cost $12 billion.

In October 2017, Interior Secretary Ryan Zinke proposed fee increases at 17 of the most popular national parks, including Zion, Joshua Tree, and Grand Canyon. During peak season, entrance fees for these parks would double to $70 per car, $50 per motorcycle, $30 per person. (For comparison, a ticket at Magic Kingdom in Orlando costs $129 on a "peak" day.) The Department of the Interior estimates that these increases could raise revenue at those parks by $70 million, a 34 percent increase.

During a 30-day public comment period, supporters and opponents of the plan weighed in on the issue. Many of these comments went straight to the bottom line: "This price hike is just too much. Having to pay $70 just to get in would definitely make me consider other options for our family vacation." Others noted that the price increases might make the parks unaffordable for families and individuals with low incomes.

The potential for a sharp decrease in overall visitors is especially concerning for business owners in areas around these parks. In 2015, visitors to national parks spent nearly $17 billion at businesses within 60 miles of park borders, supporting 295,000 jobs.

On the flip side, some commenters noted that facilities and ecosystems would get a much needed breather if fewer people visited. For example, Zion National Park, which received 4.3 million visitors in 2016, is often packed with tour buses in the summer, and rangers have found trails cut through sensitive environments. The problem has reached the point where the park has considered making a reservation system to allocate park visits.

After reviewing the comments, the U.S. Department of the Interior scrapped its original plan and is instead considering smaller rate increases and fees targeted at foreign visitors. Because parks need more revenue, the question isn't *if* rates will go up. Instead, the Department of the Interior is trying to balance the need for more revenue against the desire to keep wild areas accessible and local economies healthy.

(continued)

> **WHAT DO YOU THINK?**
>
> 1. Does the National Park Service (part of the U.S. Department of the Interior) have a responsibility to keep national parks accessible to families who cannot afford to pay higher fees?
> 2. Should the Park Service be concerned about the economic impact on surrounding communities of a reduced demand for visits?
> 3. How do your responses depend on assumptions about the price elasticity of demand for national park visits (i.e., whether higher fees will have a big or small effect on park use)? Think about the factors that affect price elasticity, such as the availability and price of substitutes.
>
> Sources: Darryl Fears, "Americans tell Interior to take a hike over proposed rate increases," *The Washington Post*, April 2, 2018, www.washingtonpost.com/news/energy-environment/wp/2018/04/02/americans-tell-interior-to-take-a-hike-over-proposed-national-park-fee-increase/?noredirect=on&utm_term=.76167aadfc6b.; Julie Turkewitz, "National Parks struggle with a mounting crisis: too many visitors," *New York Times*, September 27, 2017, www.nytimes.com/2017/09/27/us/national-parks-overcrowding.html.

✓ TEST YOURSELF

☐ What is the formula for calculating the price elasticity of demand? [LO 4.1]
☐ Why should you use the mid-point method to calculate the price elasticity of demand? [LO 4.1]
☐ If demand is inelastic, will an increase in price lead to more, less, or the same amount of revenue [LO 4.2]
☐ If demand is elastic, will an increase in price lead to more, less, or the same amount of revenue? [LO 4.2]
☐ If demand is unit-elastic, will an increase in price lead to more, less, or the same amount of revenue? [LO 4.2]

Price Elasticity of Supply

What happens when an increase in coffee consumption drives up the price of coffee beans? *How will the coffee market respond* to the price change? We can predict, based on the law of supply, that coffee growers will respond to an increase in price by increasing their production. But by how much will they increase production? The concept of price elasticity of supply can help us answer that question.

Price elasticity of supply is the size of the change in the quantity supplied of a good or service when its price changes. Price elasticity of supply measures producers' responsiveness to a change in price, just as price elasticity of demand measures consumers' responsiveness to a change in price.

Chapter 3, "Markets," showed that when prices rise, producers supply larger quantities of a good; when prices fall, they supply smaller quantities. Just as the price elasticity of demand for a good tells us how much the quantity demanded changes as we move along the demand curve, the price elasticity of supply tells us how much the quantity supplied changes as we move along the supply curve.

price elasticity of supply
the size of the change in the quantity supplied of a good or service when its price changes

Calculating price elasticity of supply

LO 4.3 Calculate price elasticity of supply using the mid-point method.

Price elasticity of supply, shown in Equation 4-5, is measured in the same way as price elasticity of demand: as the percentage change in quantity divided by the percentage change in price.

EQUATION 4-5
$$\text{Price elasticity of supply} = \frac{\%\text{ change in quantity supplied}}{\%\text{ change in price}}$$

To ensure that elasticity will be the same whether you move up or down the supply curve, you should use the mid-point method, as in Equation 4-6.

EQUATION 4-6
$$\text{Price elasticity of supply} = \frac{(Q_2 - Q_1)/[(Q_1 + Q_2)/2]}{(P_2 - P_1)/[(P_1 + P_2)/2]}$$

Suppose that when the price of coffee beans goes from $1 to $1.20 per pound, production increases from 90 million pounds of coffee beans per year to 100 million pounds. Using the mid-point method, the percentage change in quantity supplied would be:

$$\% \text{ change in quantity supplied} = \frac{(100 \text{ million} - 90 \text{ million})}{95 \text{ million}} = 11\%$$

The percentage change in price would be:

$$\% \text{ change in price} = \frac{1.2 - 1}{1.1} = 18\%$$

So the price elasticity of supply at this point on the supply curve is:

$$\text{Price elasticity of supply} = \frac{11\%}{18\%} = 0.6$$

As with the price elasticity of demand, we can describe the price elasticity of supply using three categories:

- *Elastic*, if it has an absolute value greater than 1.
- *Inelastic*, if it has an absolute value less than 1.
- *Unit-elastic*, if it has an absolute value of exactly 1.

We can also describe the extreme cases: Supply is *perfectly elastic* if the quantity supplied could be anything at a given price, and is zero at any other price. At the other extreme, supply is *perfectly inelastic* if the quantity supplied is the same, regardless of the price.

Going back to our example, an elasticity of 0.6 tells us that the supply of coffee beans is relatively inelastic, at least in the short run. Does this result make sense? As it turns out, coffee takes a long time to grow. Coffee plants don't produce a full yield for four to six years after they are planted. Because coffee growers can't increase production quickly, it makes sense that the supply of coffee would be inelastic. (What if prices had fallen from $1.20 to $1, instead of rising from $1 to $1.20? Using the mid-point method, the elasticity would be the same.)

There is one important difference between the elasticities of supply and demand: The price elasticity of demand is always negative and the price elasticity of supply is always positive. The reason is simple: The quantity demanded always moves in the *opposite direction* from the price, but the quantity supplied moves in the *same direction* as the price.

TAKE NOTE...

- Remember that the elasticity of *demand* is calculated by dividing a positive number by a negative number, or by dividing a negative number by a positive number, so the answer is always negative.
- The elasticity of *supply*, on the other hand, is calculated by dividing either a positive number by another positive number or a negative number by another negative number. In either case, the answer is always positive.

Remembering this rule can help you to check your arithmetic.

Determinants of price elasticity of supply

Whether supply is elastic or inelastic depends on the supplier's ability to change the quantity produced in response to price changes. Three factors affect a supplier's ability to expand production: the availability of inputs, the flexibility of the production process, and the time needed to adjust to changes in price. Recall that this last factor—time—is also a determinant of the elasticity of demand. Just as consumers take time to change their habits, suppliers need time to ramp up production.

LO 4.4 Explain how the determinants of price elasticity of supply affect the degree of elasticity.

Availability of inputs   The production of some goods can be expanded easily, just by adding extra inputs. For example, a bakery can easily buy extra flour and yeast to produce more bread, probably at the same cost per loaf. Increasing the supply of other goods is more difficult, however, and sometimes is impossible. If the price of Frida Khalo paintings goes up, there isn't much anyone can do to produce more of them.

In other words, the elasticity of supply depends on the elasticity of the supply of inputs. If producing more of a good will cost a lot more than the initial quantity did because the extra inputs will be harder to find or more costly, then the producer will be reluctant to increase the quantity supplied. Higher and higher prices will be needed to convince the producer to go to the extra expense.

Flexibility of the production process   The easiest way for producers to adjust the quantity supplied of a particular good is to draw production capacity away from other goods when its price rises, or to reassign capacity to other goods when its price falls. Farmers may find this sort of substitution relatively simple: When corn prices are high, they will plant more acres with corn; when corn prices are low, they will reassign acres to more profitable crops. Other producers have much less flexibility. If you own a company that manufactures specialized parts for Toyota, you might need to buy new machinery to begin making parts for Ford, let alone switch to another type of product entirely.

Adjustment time   As with demand, supply is more elastic over long periods than over short periods. That is, producers can make more adjustments in the long run than in the short run. In the short run, the number of hotel rooms at Disneyland is fixed; in the medium and long run, old rooms can be renovated and new hotels can be built. Production capacity can also increase or decrease over time as new firms start up or old ones shut down.

✓ TEST YOURSELF

☐ How would you calculate the price elasticity of supply? **[LO 4.3]**
☐ What are the three determinants of the price elasticity of supply? **[LO 4.4]**

Other Elasticities

The demand for a good is sensitive to more than just the price of the good. Because people are clever, flexible, and always on the lookout for ways to make the most of opportunities, demand also responds to changing circumstances, such as the prices of other goods and the incomes consumers earn. Let's consider two other demand elasticities, the *cross-price elasticity of demand* and the *income elasticity of demand*.

Cross-price elasticity of demand

LO 4.5 Calculate cross-price elasticity of demand, and interpret the sign of the elasticity.

Earlier we noted that price elasticities are affected by the availability of alternative options. For example, we might expect a Starbucks latte to have relatively price-elastic demand because some people will shift to buying coffee from Dunkin' Donuts when the price of a Starbucks latte rises. Once again, recalling the four economists' questions we presented in Chapter 1, "Economics and Life," asking *How will others respond?* is the key to understanding the situation.

What happens if the price of Dunkin' Donuts regular coffee falls but the price of a Starbucks latte stays the same? **Cross-price elasticity of demand** describes how much demand changes when the price of a *different* good changes. For example, because lattes and regular coffee are substitutes, we expect the demand for lattes to decrease when the price of regular coffee falls (as some people switch from lattes to coffee). The reverse also holds: If the price of a cup of

Dunkin' Donuts coffee rises, while the price of a Starbucks latte remains the same, we expect the demand for lattes to increase (as some people switch from coffee to the relatively cheaper latte). Equation 4-7 gives the formula for the cross-price elasticity of demand.

cross-price elasticity of demand
a measure of how the demand for one good changes when the price of a different good changes

EQUATION 4-7
$$\text{Cross-price elasticity of demand between A and B} = \frac{\%\text{ change in quantity of A demanded}}{\%\text{ change in price of B}}$$

Remember that nonprice determinants (like income or tastes) will shift a demand curve. In the case of cross-price elasticity, the price of a substitute or a complement is a nonprice determinant. Thus, the entire demand curve shifts. However, we still measure this change in demand by observing the change in the quantity demanded. But in this case, the initial quantity demanded is on one demand curve and the final quantity demanded is on another demand curve.

When two goods are substitutes, we expect their cross-price elasticity of demand to be positive. That is, an increase in the price of one will cause an increase in the quantity demanded of the other. On the other hand, a decrease in the price of one good will cause a decrease in the quantity demanded of the other. Just how elastic the demand is depends on how close the two substitutes are: If they are very close substitutes, a change in the price of one will cause a large change in the quantity demanded of the other, so that cross-price elasticity will be high. If they are not close substitutes, cross-price elasticity will be low.

Cross-price elasticity can also be negative. We saw that the price elasticity of demand is always negative and can be expressed as an absolute value. In contrast, cross-price elasticity can be positive or negative. Its sign tells us about the relationship between two goods:

- When two goods are substitutes, their cross-price elasticity will be positive.
- When two goods are complements (that is, when they are consumed together), cross-price elasticity will be negative.

For example, when people drink more coffee, they want more cream to go with it. Coffee and cream are complements, not substitutes. So when the demand for coffee increases, the demand for cream will increase, all else held equal. When two goods are linked in this way, their cross-price elasticity will be negative: an increase in the price of one good will decrease the quantity demanded of both goods. Again, the relative size of the elasticity tells us how strongly the two goods are linked. If the two goods are strong complements, their cross-price elasticity will be a large negative number. If the two goods are loosely linked, their cross-price elasticity will be negative but not far below zero.

Income elasticity of demand

People buy some goods in roughly the same amounts, no matter how wealthy they are. Salt, toothpaste, and toilet paper are three examples. These are not the sort of products people rush out to buy when they get a raise at work. Other goods, though, are very sensitive to changes in income. If you got a raise, you might splurge on new clothes or a meal at a fancy restaurant.

LO 4.6 Calculate income elasticity of demand, and interpret the sign of the elasticity.

The **income elasticity of demand** for a good describes how much demand changes in response to a change in consumers' incomes. Similar to cross-price elasticity, a change in income causes the demand curve to shift. We measure this change in demand by observing the change in the quantity demanded. As Equation 4-8 shows, the income elasticity of demand is expressed as the ratio of the percentage change in the quantity demanded to the percentage change in income:

income elasticity of demand
a measure of how much the demand for a good changes in response to a change in consumers' incomes

EQUATION 4-8
$$\text{Income elasticity of demand} = \frac{\%\text{ change in quantity demanded}}{\%\text{ change in income}}$$

Recall from Chapter 3, "Markets," that increases in income raise the demand for normal goods and lower the demand for inferior goods. Income elasticity tells us how much the demand for these goods changes.

For example, a Starbucks Frappuccino® is a normal good that might be fairly responsive to changes in income. When people become wealthier, they will buy more of a small luxury item like this. Therefore, we would guess that the income elasticity of demand for fancy iced coffee drinks is positive (because the drink is a normal good) and relatively large (because the drink is a non-necessity that has many cheaper substitutes).

Regular coffee is also generally a normal good, so its income elasticity should be positive. However, we might guess that it will be less elastic than a Frappuccino's. Many people consider their standard cup of coffee every day before work to be more of a necessity than a luxury and will buy it regardless of their incomes. Another way to put it is that the demand for Frappuccinos is income-elastic, while the demand for plain coffee is relatively income-inelastic.

For normal goods like these, income elasticity is positive because as incomes rise, demand increases. This then leads to an increase in quantity demanded. Both necessities and luxuries are normal goods, and although their income elasticities are positive, their sizes vary:

- If the good is a necessity, income elasticity of demand will be positive and less than 1.
- If the good is a luxury, income elasticity will be positive and greater than 1.

As with the cross-price elasticity of demand, the income elasticity of demand can be negative as well as positive. The income elasticity of demand is negative for inferior goods because quantity demanded decreases as incomes increase.

In 2009 Starbucks introduced a new retail product, VIA® Ready instant coffee. Although some coffee enthusiasts sneered, others thought it was a shrewd move at a time of economic hardship. Instant coffee mix may be an inferior good in some places: As incomes increase, people will drink more expensive beverages and *decrease* their consumption of instant coffee. During a recession, however, budgets tighten and people may increase their consumption of instant coffee as they cut back on more expensive drinks. At least, that is what Starbucks was hoping. In this scenario, the income elasticity of instant coffee would be small and negative. A less-appealing inferior good that people quickly abandon as they grow richer would have a large, negative income elasticity.

Once again, the sign and size of a good's elasticity tell us a lot about the good. Table 4-2 summarizes what we have learned about the four types of elasticity.

TABLE 4-2
Four measures of elasticity

Measure	Equation	Negative	Positive	More elastic	Less elastic
Price elasticity of demand	$\dfrac{\% \text{ change in quantity demanded}}{\% \text{ change in price}}$	Always	Never	Over time, for substitutable goods and luxury items	In the short run, for unique and necessary items
Price elasticity of supply	$\dfrac{\% \text{ change in quantity supplied}}{\% \text{ change in price}}$	Never	Always	Over time, with flexible production	In the short run, with production constraints
Cross-price elasticity	$\dfrac{\% \text{ change in quantity demanded of A}}{\% \text{ change in price of B}}$	For complements	For substitutes	For near-perfect substitutes and strong complements	For loosely related goods
Income elasticity	$\dfrac{\% \text{ change in quantity demanded}}{\% \text{ change in income}}$	For inferior goods	For normal goods	For luxury items with close substitutes	For unique and necessary items

If you find this discussion of price elasticity particularly interesting, you might want to consider work as a pricing analyst. In the near term, though, you can apply your knowledge about price elasticity when you buy airline tickets. You can read more about this in the Econ and YOU box "Finding a travel bargain."

Finding a travel bargain
Econ and YOU

Econ and YOU boxes show tips, strategies, and other ways that economics can inform choices—big and small—in your own life.

Are you fantasizing about traveling someplace warm for spring break? Taking a trip to see family or friends? If you've looked at airline prices, you'll know that some tickets can be really expensive and some much cheaper—even on the same routes. Why?

Airline prices are, of course, partly determined by the cost of getting you from point A to point B. If you fly from, say, Atlanta to Los Angeles, you'll pay more than when flying from Atlanta to Miami—simply because the cost of jet fuel and the time spent by pilots and flight attendants increase with distance. But even on the Atlanta to LA flight, you will pay different ticket prices depending on where you sit on the plane. When we checked the website of a major airline, for example, sitting in business class cost twice as much as sitting in economy because it costs the airline more to give you extra room and extra service.

But cost is not the whole story. Airlines know that different customers have different price elasticities. People traveling for business, for example, tend to have low price elasticities: they are less sensitive to cost than other fliers, especially when they need to get to important meetings and events. Airlines take advantage of that knowledge by raising prices for business travelers. (Similar principles apply to train travel and car rentals.)

In contrast, travelers who are flexible and on tight budgets, including many college students, tend to be sensitive to price. Their price elasticities for airline tickets are high, and they will make alternative plans if prices rise too much.

Airlines make the most profits when they can sort out which customers have high price elasticities, which have low elasticities, and which are in between. They do this by devising restrictions (no flexibility in seat choice for basic economy, for example) and amenities (more legroom in business class) that appeal to customers with different price elasticities. Cut-price airlines like Frontier, Spirit, Southwest, and JetBlue built their entire business models around serving customers with high price elasticities. On these airlines even the most basic amenities (carry-on bags, seat selection, and snacks and drinks) often cost extra. (The airlines also likely make money on people's being overly optimistic, when they make their reservations, that they will not spend money on the extra amenities, but then, as the day of the flight approaches, they do.)

On airlines with a wider variety of ticket options, finding a cheaper ticket may require signaling that you have a high price elasticity. That means making choices that are *not* typical for low-elasticity customers like business travelers. Staying over on Saturday night often signals low elasticity (since business travelers tend to head home for the weekend). Or buying tickets early (some say seven weeks is the sweet spot). Or accepting the restrictions, such as limited overhead bin access and restrictions on changing your ticket, that come with "basic economy" tickets. You might find that these trade-offs are worth it, but sometimes they can turn a great deal into a headache, with lots of extra fees for flight changes and baggage fees.

©kasto/123RF

✓ TEST YOURSELF

- ☐ Why is the cross-price elasticity of demand positive for substitutes? [LO 4.5]
- ☐ Why does the income-elasticity of demand depend on whether a good is normal or inferior? [LO 4.6]

Conclusion

Supply and *demand* may be the most common words in economics, but applying these concepts to the real world requires a bit of elaboration. Elasticity is the first of several concepts we will study that will help you to apply the concepts of supply and demand to business and policy questions. In this chapter we saw how elasticity can be used to predict how price changes will influence revenue. In the coming chapters we will use elasticity to predict the effects of government intervention in the market, and we will dig deeper into the consumer and producer choices that drive elasticity.

Key Terms

elasticity, p. 80
price elasticity of demand, p. 81
mid-point method, p. 81
perfectly elastic demand, p. 85

perfectly inelastic demand, p. 85
elastic, p. 86
inelastic, p. 86
unit-elastic, p. 86

total revenue, p. 88
price elasticity of supply, p. 92
cross-price elasticity of demand, p. 94
income elasticity of demand, p. 95

Summary

LO 4.1 Calculate price elasticity of demand using the mid-point method.

Elasticity is a measure of consumers' and producers' responsiveness to a change in market conditions. Understanding the elasticity for a good or service allows economic decision makers to anticipate the outcome of changes in market conditions and to calibrate prices so as to maximize revenues.

Price elasticity of demand is the size of the change in the quantity demanded of a good or service when its price changes. Elasticity should be calculated as a percentage using the mid-point method to avoid problems with conflicting units of measurement and with the direction of a change.

Price elasticity of demand is almost always negative because the quantity demanded falls as the price rises. It is usually represented as an absolute value, without the negative sign.

LO 4.2 Explain how the determinants of price elasticity of demand affect the degree of elasticity.

In general, demand is inelastic for goods that have no close substitutes, are basic necessities, or cost a relatively small proportion of consumers' income. Demand is also inelastic over short periods and for broadly defined markets.

When demand is elastic, a percentage change in the price of a good will cause a larger percentage change in the quantity demanded; the absolute value of the elasticity will be greater than 1. When demand is inelastic, a percentage change in price will cause a smaller percentage change in the quantity demanded; the absolute value of the elasticity will be less than 1. When demand is unit-elastic, the percentage changes in price and quantity will be equal, and the elasticity will be exactly 1.

LO 4.3 Calculate price elasticity of supply using the mid-point method.

Price elasticity of supply is the size of the change in the quantity supplied of a good or service when its price changes. Price elasticity of supply is almost always positive because the quantity supplied increases as the price increases.

LO 4.4 Explain how the determinants of price elasticity of supply affect the degree of elasticity.

Supply is generally inelastic when additional inputs to the production process are difficult to get and the production process is inflexible. Supply is also inelastic over short periods.

Supply is considered elastic when the absolute value of its price elasticity is greater than 1, inelastic when the absolute value is less than 1, and unit-elastic when it is exactly 1.

> **LO 4.5** Calculate cross-price elasticity of demand, and interpret the sign of the elasticity.

Cross-price elasticity of demand is the percentage change in the quantity demanded in response to a given percentage change in the price of a *different* good. The cross-price elasticity of demand between two goods will be positive if they are substitutes and negative if they are complements.

> **LO 4.6** Calculate income elasticity of demand, and interpret the sign of the elasticity.

Income elasticity of demand is the percentage change in the quantity of a good demanded in response to a given percentage change in income. Income elasticity of demand will be positive for normal goods and negative for inferior goods.

Review Questions

1. You are advising a coffee shop manager who wants to estimate how much sales will change if the price of a latte rises. You tell her that she should measure the change in sales using the percentage change in quantity of coffee sold rather than the number of cups of coffee or the total ounces of coffee sold. Similarly, you tell her that she should measure the price increase in percentage terms rather than in terms of absolute dollars. Explain why she should measure elasticity in percentage terms rather than in terms of dollars and cups. **[LO 4.1]**

2. Explain why the coffee shop manager should calculate elasticity using the mid-point method. **[LO 4.1]**

3. You are working as a private math tutor to raise money for a trip during spring break. First explain why the price elasticity of demand for math tutoring might be elastic. Then explain why the price elasticity of demand for math tutoring might be inelastic. **[LO 4.2]**

4. You are working as a private math tutor to raise money for a trip during spring break. You want to earn as much money as possible, and you think the demand for math tutors is currently inelastic. Should you increase or decrease the price you charge? Explain. **[LO 4.2]**

5. You have been hired by the government of Kenya, which produces a lot of coffee, to examine the supply of gourmet coffee beans. Suppose you discover that the price elasticity of supply is 0.85. Explain this number to the Kenyan government. **[LO 4.3]**

6. You have noticed that the price of tickets to your university's basketball games keeps increasing, but the supply of tickets remains the same. Why might supply be unresponsive to changes in price? **[LO 4.3]**

7. Which will have a more price-elastic supply over six months: real estate in downtown Manhattan or real estate in rural Oklahoma? Explain your reasoning. **[LO 4.4]**

8. Certain skilled labor, such as hair cutting, requires licensing or certification, which is costly and takes a long time to acquire. Explain what would happen to the price elasticity of supply for haircuts if this licensing requirement were removed. **[LO 4.4]**

9. Although we could describe both the cross-price elasticity of demand between paper coffee cups and plastic coffee lids and the cross-price elasticity of demand between sugar and artificial sweeteners as highly elastic, the first cross-price elasticity is negative and the second is positive. What is the reason for this? **[LO 4.5]**

10. Name two related goods you consume that would have a positive cross-price elasticity. What happens to your consumption of the second good if the price of the first good increases? **[LO 4.5]**

11. Name two related goods you consume that would have a negative cross-price elasticity. What happens to your consumption of the second good if the price of the first good increases? **[LO 4.5]**

12. In France, where cheese is an important and traditional part of people's meals, people eat about six times as much cheese per person as in the United States. In which country do you think the demand for cheese will be more income-elastic? Why? **[LO 4.6]**

13. Name a good you consume for which your income elasticity of demand is positive. What happens when your income increases? **[LO 4.6]**

14. Name a good you consume for which your income elasticity of demand is negative. What happens when your income increases? **[LO 4.6]**

Problems and Applications

1. When the price of a bar of chocolate is $1, the quantity demanded is 100,000 bars. When the price rises to $1.50, the quantity demanded falls to 60,000 bars. Calculate the price elasticity of demand using the mid-point method. **[LO 4.1]**

    a. Suppose the price increases from $1 to $1.50. Calculate the price elasticity of demand.

    b. Suppose the price decreases from $1.50 to $1. Calculate the price elasticity of demand.

2. If the price elasticity of demand for used cars priced between $4,000 and $6,000 is −1.2 (using the mid-point method), what will be the percent change in quantity demanded when the price of a used car falls from $6,000 to $4,000? **[LO 4.1]**

3. Three points are identified on the graph in Figure 4P-1. **[LO 4.2]**

FIGURE 4P-1

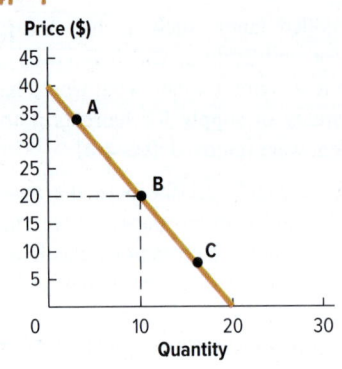

a. At point A, is demand inelastic, elastic, or unit-elastic?
b. At point B, is demand inelastic, elastic, or unit-elastic?
c. At point C, is demand inelastic, elastic, or unit-elastic?

4. Which of the following has a more elastic demand in the short run? **[LO 4.2]**
   a. Pomegranate juice or drinking water?
   b. Cereal or Rice Krispies®?
   c. Speedboats or gourmet chocolate?

5. In each of the following instances, determine whether demand is elastic, inelastic, or unit-elastic. **[LO 4.2]**
   a. If price increases by 10 percent and quantity demanded decreases by 15 percent, demand is _____.
   b. If price decreases by 10 percent and quantity demanded increases by 5 percent, demand is _____.

6. In each of the following instances, determine whether quantity demanded will increase or decrease, and by how much. **[LO 4.2]**
   a. If price elasticity of demand is −1.3 and price increases by 2 percent, quantity demanded will _____ by _____ percent.
   b. If price elasticity of demand is −0.3 percent and price decreases by 2 percent, quantity demanded will _____ by _____ percent.

Problems 7 and 8 refer to the demand schedule shown in Table 4P-1. For each price change, say whether demand is elastic, unit-elastic, *or* inelastic, *and say whether total revenue* increases, decreases, *or* stays the same.

TABLE 4P-1

Price ($)	Quantity demanded
80	0
70	50
60	100
50	150
40	200
30	250
20	300
10	350
0	400

7. Consider each of the following price increase scenarios. **[LO 4.2]**
   a. Price increases from $10 to $20. Demand is _____ and total revenue _____.
   b. Price increases from $30 to $40. Demand is _____ and total revenue _____.
   c. Price increases from $50 to $60. Demand is _____ and total revenue _____.

8. Price decreases from $60 to $50. Demand is _____ and total revenue _____. **[LO 4.2]**

Problems 9–12 refer to Figure 4P-2.

FIGURE 4P-2

9. Draw the price effect and the quantity effect for a price change from $60 to $50. Which effect is larger? Does total revenue increase or decrease? No calculation is necessary. [LO 4.2]

10. Draw the price effect and the quantity effect for a price change from $30 to $20. Which effect is larger? Does total revenue increase or decrease? No calculation is necessary. [LO 4.2]

11. Draw the price effect and the quantity effect for a price change from $60 to $70. Which effect is larger? Does total revenue increase or decrease? No calculation is necessary. [LO 4.2]

12. Draw the price effect and the quantity effect for a price change from $10 to $20. Which effect is larger? Does total revenue increase or decrease? No calculation is necessary. [LO 4.2]

13. Use the graph in Figure 4P-3 to calculate the price elasticity of supply between points A and B using the midpoint method. [LO 4.3]

FIGURE 4P-3

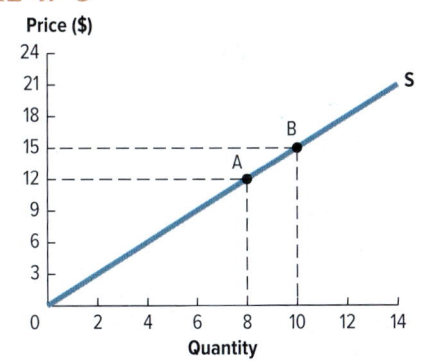

14. If the price of a haircut is $15, the number of haircuts provided is 125. If the price rises to $30 per haircut, barbers will work much longer hours, and the supply of haircuts will increase to 200. What is the price elasticity of supply for haircuts between $15 and $30? [LO 4.3]

15. Which of the following has a more elastic supply in the short run? [LO 4.4]
    a. Hospitals or mobile clinics?
    b. Purebred dogs or mixed-breed dogs?
    c. On-campus courses or online courses?

16. In each of the following instances, determine whether supply is elastic, inelastic, or unit-elastic. [LO 4.4]
    a. If price increases by 10 percent and quantity supplied increases by 15 percent, supply is _____.
    b. If price decreases by 10 percent and quantity supplied decreases by 5 percent, supply is _____.

17. In each of the following instances, determine whether quantity supplied will increase or decrease, and by how much. [LO 4.4]
    a. If price elasticity of supply is 1.3 and price increases by 2 percent, quantity supplied will _____ by _____ percent.
    b. If price elasticity of supply is 0.3 and price decreases by 2 percent, quantity supplied will _____ by _____ percent.

18. Suppose that the price of peanut butter rises from $2 to $3 per jar. [LO 4.5]
    a. The quantity of jelly purchased falls from 20 million jars to 15 million jars. What is the cross-price elasticity of demand between peanut butter and jelly? Are they complements or substitutes?
    b. The quantity of jelly purchased increases from 15 million jars to 20 million jars. What is the cross-price elasticity of demand between peanut butter and jelly? Are they complements or substitutes?

19. For each of the following pairs, predict whether the cross-price elasticity of demand will be positive or negative: [LO 4.5]
    a. Soap and hand sanitizer.
    b. CDs and MP3s.
    c. Sheets and pillowcases.

20. Suppose that when the average family income rises from $30,000 per year to $40,000 per year, the average family's purchases of toilet paper rise from 100 rolls to 105 rolls per year. [LO 4.6]
    a. Calculate the income-elasticity of demand for toilet paper.
    b. Is toilet paper a normal or an inferior good?
    c. Is the demand for toilet paper income-elastic or income-inelastic?

21. In each of the following instances, determine whether the good is normal or inferior, and whether it is income-elastic or income-inelastic. [LO 4.6]
    a. If income increases by 10 percent and the quantity demanded of a good then increases by 5 percent, the good is _____ and _____.
    b. If income increases by 10 percent and the quantity demanded of a good decreases by 20 percent, the good is _____ and _____.

Math Essentials: Calculating Percentage Change, Slope, and Elasticity

Appendix C

The math associated with the concept of elasticity covers a wide variety of topics. In order to be able to calculate elasticity, you need to be able to calculate percentage changes. In order to talk about shape of a line, and its elasticity, you need to be able to understand slope and the relationship between variables, particularly price and quantity.

LEARNING OBJECTIVES

LO C.1 Understand how to calculate percentage changes.

LO C.2 Use slope to calculate elasticity.

Percentage Change

In Chapter 4, "Elasticity," we calculated elasticity in all its forms. If you're not entirely comfortable calculating percentage change, though, elasticity can be a daunting idea. Percentage changes represent the relative change in a variable from an old value to a new one. In the chapter, and in this appendix, we use the mid-point method to calculate percentage change. The mid-point method measures the percentage change relative to a point *midway between the two points*.

Equation C-1 shows how to calculate percentage change using the mid-point method. There, X_1 represents the original value of any variable X, and X_2 is the new value of this variable.

LO C.1 Understand how to calculate percentage changes.

EQUATION C-1 $$\text{Percentage change} = \left[\frac{(X_2 - X_1)}{\left(\frac{X_2 + X_1}{2}\right)} \right] \times 100$$

Notice that the denominator is the *mid-point* between X_1 and X_2. In other words, it is the average of X_1 and X_2. Overall, you can use this method to calculate the percentage change in variables of various kinds. A percentage change in quantity, for example, would be expressed as:

EQUATION C-1A   Percentage change in quantity $= \left[\dfrac{(Q_2 - Q_1)}{\left(\dfrac{Q_2 + Q_1}{2}\right)} \right] \times 100$

where Q_2 represents the new value of quantity demanded and Q_1 the original quantity demanded.

Similarly, a percentage change in price would be expressed as:

EQUATION C-1B   Percentage change in price $= \left[\dfrac{(P_2 - P_1)}{\left(\dfrac{P_2 + P_1}{2}\right)} \right] \times 100$

Let's try an example for practice: For weeks, you have been watching the price of a new pair of shoes. They normally cost $90, but you see that the store has a sale and now offers them for $70. You find the percentage change in the price of the shoes by first subtracting the old price ($90) from the new one ($70) to find the change in price, which is −$20. To find how much of a change this is, you take this −$20 price change and divide it by the price midway between $70 and $90 ($80).

$$\dfrac{\$70 - \$90}{\left(\dfrac{\$70 + \$90}{2}\right)} = \dfrac{-\$20}{\$80} = -0.25$$

You then multiply by 100 to get the percentage change: −0.25 × 100 = −25%. In this case, the $20 price reduction was a 25 percent decrease in price. Not a bad sale!

Notice that in this case, the percentage change is negative, which indicates that the new value is less than the original. If the prices of shoes had increased instead, the associated percentage change would be a positive value.

The best way to do get comfortable with calculating percentage changes is through lots of practice. You can find a few extra problems to try on your own at the end of this appendix, and you also could challenge yourself to calculate price changes you see in your everyday life.

Slope and Elasticity

LO C.2 Use slope to calculate elasticity.

In Appendix A, "Math Essentials: Understanding Graphs and Slope," we showed that the direction of a slope tells us something meaningful about the relationship between the two variables we are representing:

- When *x* and *y* move in the *same direction*, they are said to have a *positive* relationship. Not surprisingly, this means that the slope of the line is a positive number. When the slope of a line is positive, we know that *y* increases as *x* increases, and *y* decreases as *x* decreases.
- Similarly, when *x* and *y* move in *opposite directions*, they are said to have a *negative* relationship. The slope of the line is a negative number. When the slope of a line is negative, we know that *y* decreases as *x* increases, and *y* increases as *x* decreases.

In Chapter 3, "Markets," we saw a positive relationship between price and quantity in the supply curve. We saw a negative relationship between price and quantity in the demand curve. Two variables (such as price and quantity) may have more than one relationship to each other, depending on whose choices they represent and under what circumstances.

The steepness of a slope is also important. Numerically, the closer the number representing the slope is to zero, the flatter the curve will be. Remember that both positive and negative numbers can be close to zero. So, a slope of −1 is equally steep as a slope of 1, although one slopes downward and the other upward. Correspondingly, a line with a slope of −5 is steeper than a line with a slope of −1 or one with a slope of 1.

You can tell just from looking at an equation how steep the line will be. If this idea is still a little hazy, you might want to page back to Appendix A, in the "Steepness of a slope" section, to refresh your memory. The steepness of slope is important to understanding the concept of elasticity.

Although the ideas of slope and elasticity are related, there are two basic mathematical distinctions between them:

1. Slope describes the change in y per the change in x, whereas elasticity measures are based on the change in x per the change in y.
2. We usually measure elasticity in terms of *percentage changes,* rather than absolute (unit-based) changes.

Why would we be interested in how much x changes in response to a one-unit change in y? To get at this difference, let's look at Figure C-1. It is similar to Figure A-10 (in Appendix A) but replaces the variables x and y with the quantity of a good (Q) and its price (P).

In Chapter 4, "Elasticity," you learned that *price elasticity* is a measure of the responsiveness of supply (or demand) to changes in price. In other words, it is a measure of how quantity (on the x-axis) responds to a change in price (on the y-axis). So this time, let's make the change in price (vertical distance) the same and look at how much quantity changes (horizontal distance).

Looking at Figure C-1, we can see that when price moves from P_1 to P_2, quantity supplied changes by less in panel A than it does in panel B. When price increases from P_1 to P_2 in panel A, quantity increases by 1 unit, from Q_1 to Q_2. In contrast, panel B shows an increase of 2 units from Q_1 to Q_2 for the same change in P. This means supply is less responsive to a price change in panel A compared to panel B.

FIGURE C-1

Measuring a change in Q in response to a change in P

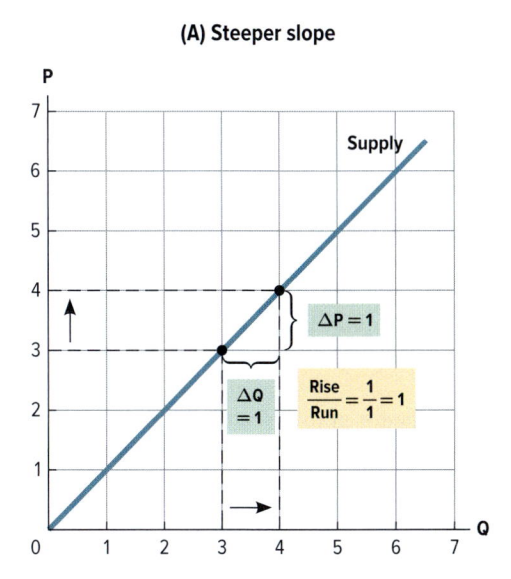

(A) Steeper slope

(B) Flatter slope

The steeper slope in panel A indicates that price changes less in panel A than in panel B in response to a change in quantity demanded.

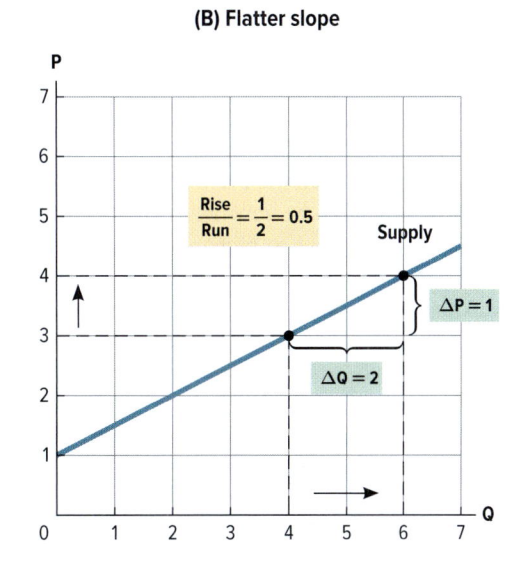

The flatter slope in panel B indicates that price changes more in panel B than in panel A in response to a change in quantity demanded.

FIGURE C-2
Slope versus elasticity of horizontal and vertical lines

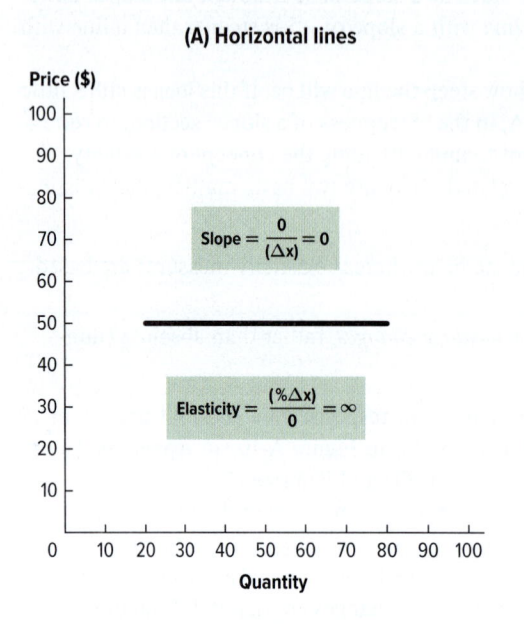

(A) Horizontal lines

Slope = $\dfrac{0}{(\Delta x)} = 0$

Elasticity = $\dfrac{(\%\Delta x)}{0} = \infty$

(B) Vertical lines

Slope = $\dfrac{(\Delta y)}{0} = \infty$

Elasticity = $\dfrac{0}{(\%\Delta y)} = 0$

When a line is horizontal, the slope is zero and the associated elasticity is infinite. In other words, demand or supply occurs only at a single price.

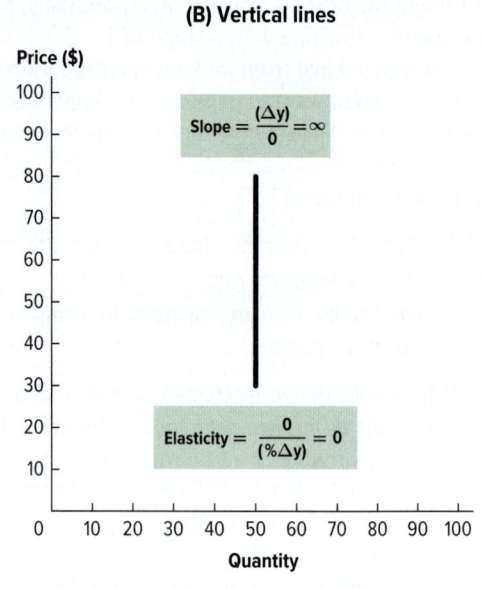

When a line is vertical, the slope is infinite and the elasticity is zero. Regardless of the price, quantity supplied or demanded is going to be the same.

X over Y, or Y over X?

We have noted that slope is indicated by $\frac{\Delta y}{\Delta x}$. In contrast, elasticity is commonly indicated by $\frac{\%\Delta Q}{\%\Delta P}$, which corresponds to $\frac{\Delta x}{\Delta y}$. In some sense, then, *elasticity is computed as the mirror image of slope*. The easiest way to picture this is to see the difference between slope and elasticity for vertical and horizontal lines.

In Figure C-2, the horizontal line pictured in panel A has a slope of zero. This is because a one-unit change in x results in zero change in y. Therefore, slope is calculated as $\frac{0}{\Delta x}$. Zero divided by any number is zero. If we think of the horizontal line as a demand curve mapping price to quantity demanded, however, the price elasticity is infinity.

How can slope be zero and elasticity infinity? Remember that slope measures how much y changes in response to a change in x. Elasticity, however, measures the sensitivity of P (on the y-axis) to a change in Q (on the x-axis). Whereas x is in the denominator when calculating slope, it is in the numerator when calculating elasticity. For a horizontal line, then, elasticity will be $\%\Delta Q/0$ since there is no change in P. Division by 0 is mathematically undefined, or known as infinity.

The reverse is true when we look at a vertical line. When a graph is vertical, there is zero change in x for any change in y. Therefore, slope is calculated as $\frac{\Delta y}{0}$. In this case, slope is undefined (infinity). But elasticity will be $0/\%\Delta P$. Again, zero divided by any number is zero.

Elasticity changes along lines with constant slope

The second important mathematical difference between slope and elasticity is that we usually measure slope in terms of absolute changes, but we measure elasticity in terms of percentage changes. This means that at different points along a straight line, slope is constant, but elasticity varies.

TABLE C-1
Demand schedule

Price ($)	Quantity
80	0
70	10
60	20
50	30
40	40
30	50
20	60
10	70
0	80

As an example, take a look at the demand schedule in Table C-1. First, let's calculate the slope between two different sets of points. Using the first two prices and quantities at the top of the demand schedule, we see that the slope between these points is −1.

$$\text{Slope \#1} = \frac{\Delta P_1}{\Delta Q_1} = \frac{(0 - 10)}{(80 - 70)} = \frac{-10}{10} = -1$$

Then, pick another two points. Using the quantities 30 and 20 and their respective prices, we can calculate that the slope is still −1.

$$\text{Slope \#2} = \frac{\Delta P_2}{\Delta Q_2} = \frac{(30 - 20)}{(50 - 60)} = \frac{10}{-10} = -1$$

No matter what two points along the demand curve we choose, the slope is the same. *Slope is constant because the demand curve is linear.*

Now let's calculate elasticity between these same two sets of points. We will use the mid-point method described in Chapter 4, "Elasticity," to calculate elasticity:

$$\text{Elasticity} = \frac{\%\Delta Q}{\%\Delta P} = \frac{\Delta Q/Q_{midpoint}}{\Delta P/P_{midpoint}}$$

Let's start with the top of the demand curve and calculate the price elasticity of demand for a price change from 80 to 70. Using the mid-point method, we have:

$$\frac{\Delta Q/Q_{midpoint}}{\Delta P/P_{midpoint}} = \frac{(0 - 10)/5}{(80 - 70)/60} = \frac{-10/5}{10/60} = \frac{-2}{0.17} = -11.8$$

Now let's calculate the price elasticity of demand at the bottom of the demand curve for a price change of 30 to 20.

$$\frac{\Delta Q/Q_{midpoint}}{\Delta P/P_{midpoint}} = \frac{(50 - 60)/55}{(30 - 20)/25} = \frac{-10/55}{10/25} = \frac{-0.18}{0.4} = -0.45$$

Even though both of these calculations represented a 10-unit change in quantity in response to a $10 change in price, along a linear demand curve, elasticity changes. Moving down along the demand curve means less elasticity. This is because the same change in Q or P is a different *percentage* of the midpoint at different points on the line.

Appendix C ▪ Math Essentials: Calculating Percentage Change, Slope, and Elasticity

Problems and Applications

1. Calculate the percentage change in each of the following examples using the mid-point method. **[LO C.1]**
   a. 8 to 12.
   b. 18 to 14.
   c. 130 to 120.
   d. 95 to 105.

2. Find the percentage change in price in each of the following examples using the mid-point method. **[LO C.1]**
   a. The price of a $4.50 sandwich increases to $5.50.
   b. A sale discounts the price of a sofa from $750 to $500.

3. Use the demand curve in Figure CP-1 to answer the following questions. Use the mid-point method in your calculations. **[LO C.2]**

FIGURE CP-1

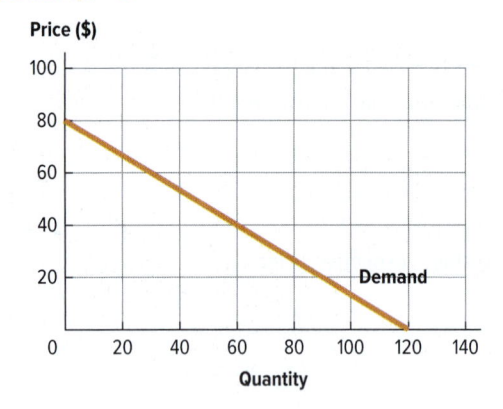

[Demand curve graph: Price ($) on vertical axis from 0 to 100, Quantity on horizontal axis from 0 to 140. Downward-sloping demand line from (0, 80) to (120, 0).]

   a. What is the price elasticity of demand for a price change from $0 to $20?
   b. What is the price elasticity of demand for a price change from $20 to $40?
   c. What is the price elasticity of demand for a price change from $40 to $60?

4. Use the demand schedule in Table CP-1 to answer the following questions. Use the mid-point method in your calculations. **[LO C.2]**
   a. What is the price elasticity of demand for a price change from $4 to $8?
   b. What is the price elasticity of demand for a price change from $8 to $16?
   c. What is the price elasticity of demand for a price change from $20 to $24?

TABLE CP-1

Price ($)	Quantity
0	60
4	50
8	40
12	30
16	20
20	10
24	0

5. Use the demand schedule in Table CP-2 to answer the following questions. Use the mid-point method when calculating elasticity. **[LO C.2]**

TABLE CP-2

Price ($)	Quantity
0	56
1	48
2	42
3	35
4	28
5	21
6	14
7	7
8	0

   a. What is the price elasticity of demand for a price change from $2 to $3? What is the slope of the demand curve for a price change from $2 to $3?
   b. What is the price elasticity of demand for a price change from $3 to $5? What is the slope of the demand curve for a price change from $3 to $5?
   c. What is the price elasticity of demand for a price change from $6 to $7? What is the slope of the demand curve for a price change from $6 to $7?

Chapter 5

Efficiency

A Broken Laser Pointer Starts an Internet Revolution

In 1995, a young software developer named Pierre Omidyar spent his Labor Day weekend building a website he called AuctionWeb. His idea was to create a site where people could post their old stuff for sale online and auction it off to the highest bidder. Soon after, he sold the first item on AuctionWeb for $14.83. It was a broken laser pointer, which he had posted on the site as a test, never expecting anyone to bid on it. When Pierre pointed out that the pointer was broken, the bidder explained that he was "a collector of broken laser pointers."

As you might have guessed, AuctionWeb became the wildly successful company we now know as eBay. In 2017, over 20 years after the site was first conceived, the total value of items sold on eBay was $88.4 billion, and 170 million people around the world were active buyers.[1]

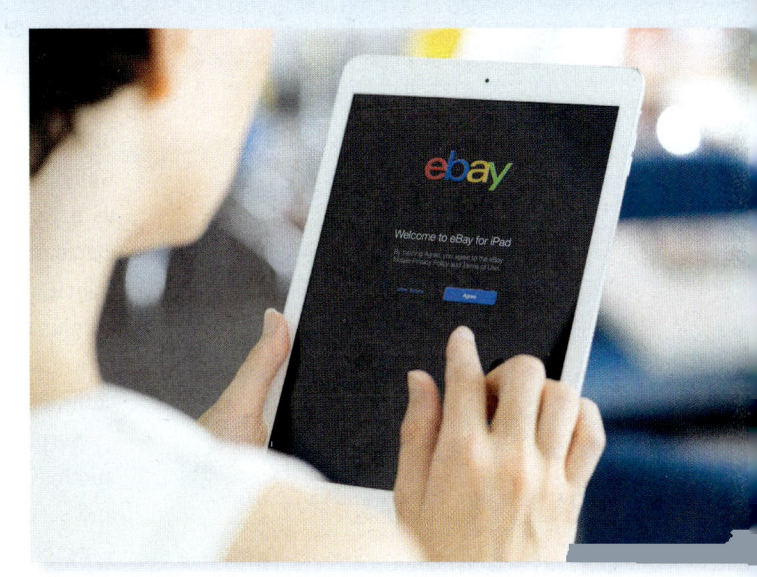

©bloomua/123RF

Like many creation stories, the tale of eBay's first sale gives us insight into what makes it tick. People are interested in some pretty odd things (like broken laser pointers), but given a big enough crowd, matches usually can be made between buyers and sellers. When buyers and sellers are matched up and they trade, each is made better off. The buyer gets an item he wants, and the seller gets money. Because both parties are willing participants, they benefit from engaging in such transactions. In fact, they even are willing to pay eBay to provide the marketplace where they can find one another. How else is someone with a broken laser pointer going to find an eager buyer?

eBay's success is based on one of the most fundamental ideas in economics: *Voluntary exchanges create value and can make everyone involved better off*. The importance of that idea stretches far beyond eBay. This principle drives a range of businesses—from grocery stores, to investment banks, to online retailers—that do not manufacture or grow anything themselves. Instead, they facilitate transactions between producers and consumers.

But this principle raises a question: How do we know that people are better off when they buy and sell things? Can we say anything about *how much* better off they are?

LEARNING OBJECTIVES

LO 5.1 Use willingness to pay and willingness to sell to determine supply and demand at a given price.

LO 5.2 Calculate consumer surplus based on a graph or table.

LO 5.3 Calculate producer surplus based on a graph or table.

LO 5.4 Calculate total surplus based on a graph or table.

LO 5.5 Define efficiency in terms of surplus, and identify efficient and inefficient situations.

LO 5.6 Describe the distribution of surplus, or benefits to society, that results from a policy decision.

LO 5.7 Calculate deadweight loss.

LO 5.8 Explain why correcting a missing market can make everyone better off.

To answer these questions, we need a tool to describe the *size of the benefits* that result from transactions and who receives said benefits. In this chapter we will introduce the concept of *surplus*. It can measure the benefit that people receive when they buy something for less than they would have been willing to pay. It also can measure the benefit that people receive when they sell something for more than they would have been willing to accept. *Surplus* is the best way to look at the benefits people receive from successful transactions.

Surplus also shows us why the equilibrium price and quantity in a competitive market are so special: They maximize the total well-being of those involved. Even when we care about outcomes other than total well-being (like inequality in the distribution of benefits), surplus gives us a yardstick for comparing different ideas and policies. For instance, calculations of surplus can clearly show who benefits and who loses from policies such as taxes and minimum wages. As we'll see, maximizing total surplus—an idea called *efficiency*—is one of the most powerful features of a market system. Even more remarkable is that it is achieved without centralized coordination.

Surplus also shows us how simply enabling people to trade with one another can make them better off. Often, creating a new market for goods and services (as the Grameen Bank did in Bangladesh, in the example in Chapter 1, "Economics and Life") or improving an existing market (as eBay did on the internet) can be a good way to help people. Knowing how and when to harness the power of economic exchanges to improve well-being is an important tool for businesspeople and public-minded problem solvers alike.

Willingness to Pay and Sell

LO 5.1 Use willingness to pay and willingness to sell to determine supply and demand at a given price.

eBay is an online auction platform that allows people to post items for sale that anyone else online can buy. People who want to buy the item make bids offering to pay a particular price. This decentralized marketplace supports all sorts of transactions: from real estate, to used cars, to rare books, to (in one extraordinary case) a half-eaten cheese sandwich said to look like the Virgin Mary (which sold for $28,000).[2]

Who uses eBay? What do they want? At the most basic level, they are people who want to buy or sell a particular good. We're not sure how many people want broken laser pointers or decade-old cheese sandwiches, so let's stick with something a little more typical. How about digital cameras? Just as we did in Chapter 3, "Markets," we'll make the simplifying assumption that there is just one kind of digital camera rather than thousands of slightly different models.

Imagine you see a digital camera posted for sale on eBay. Who might bid on it? What are their *wants and constraints?* Most obviously, people who bid will be those who *want* a camera. But they will also care about the price they pay: Why spend $200 for a camera if you can get it for $100 and spend the other $100 on something else? Potential buyers *want* to pay as little as possible, but on top of this general preference, each buyer has a maximum price she is willing to pay.

Economists call this maximum price the buyer's **willingness to pay** or the *reservation price*. Economists use these two terms interchangeably; in this text, we'll stick with "willingness to pay." This price is the point above which the buyer throws up her hands and says, "Never mind. I'd rather spend my money on something else." Each potential buyer wants to purchase a camera for a price that is as low as possible and no higher than her maximum *willingness to pay*.

On eBay, we can see willingness to pay in action. When the price of a product remains below a bidder's willingness to pay, he'll continue to bid on it. When the going price passes his willingness to pay, he'll drop out.

Of course, buyers are only half the story. Who posted the camera for sale on eBay in the first place? To create a functioning market for digital cameras, someone has to want to sell. Whereas buyers want to buy a camera for as low a price as possible, sellers want to sell for as high a price as possible. Why take less money if you could get more? Just as each potential buyer has a willingness to pay, each potential seller has a *willingness to sell*. **Willingness to sell** is the minimum price that a seller is willing to accept in exchange for a good or service. A seller always wants to sell for a price that is as high as possible, but never lower than his minimum.

We can see willingness to sell in action on eBay through the "reserve price" that sellers can set when they post an item. This reserve price sets a bar below which the seller will not accept any bids. If she doesn't get any higher bids, she simply keeps the item.

So far, so good: Buyers want to buy low; sellers want to sell high. What does this have to do with markets? We're about to see that willingness to pay and willingness to sell are actually the forces that drive the shape of demand and supply curves.

willingness to pay (reservation price) the maximum price that a buyer would be willing to pay for a good or service

willingness to sell the minimum price that a seller is willing to accept in exchange for a good or service

Willingness to pay and the demand curve

Let's return to potential camera buyers and take a closer look at how they choose to bid on the camera posted on eBay. To keep things simple, let's imagine that there are five potential buyers who are considering bidding on this particular camera.

- Bidder #1 is a bird watcher who cares passionately about having a good camera to document the rare birds she finds. She is willing to pay up to $500 for the camera.
- Bidder #2 is an amateur photographer. He has an outdated camera and is willing to pay $250 for this newer model.
- Bidder #3 is a real estate agent who will be willing to pay $200 or less to be able to take better pictures of her properties.
- Bidder #4 is a journalist. She wouldn't mind having a newer camera than the one her newspaper provided but would pay no more than $150 for it.
- Bidder #5 is a teacher who will spend no more than $100—the amount of the eBay gift certificate given to him by appreciative parents for his birthday.

We can plot on a graph each potential buyer's willingness to pay. In panel A of Figure 5-1, we've graphed possible prices for the camera against the number of buyers who would be willing to bid that price for it. Remember that each person's willingness to pay is a *maximum*—he or she would also be willing to buy the camera at any lower price. Therefore, at a price of $100, all five buyers are willing to bid; at $350, only one will bid.

If you look carefully, you might notice that the graph in panel A looks a lot like a demand curve: Price is on the *y*-axis, quantity is on the *x*-axis, and there's a line showing that quantity demanded increases as price decreases. In fact this *is* a demand curve, although it represents

FIGURE 5-1
Willingness to pay and the demand curve

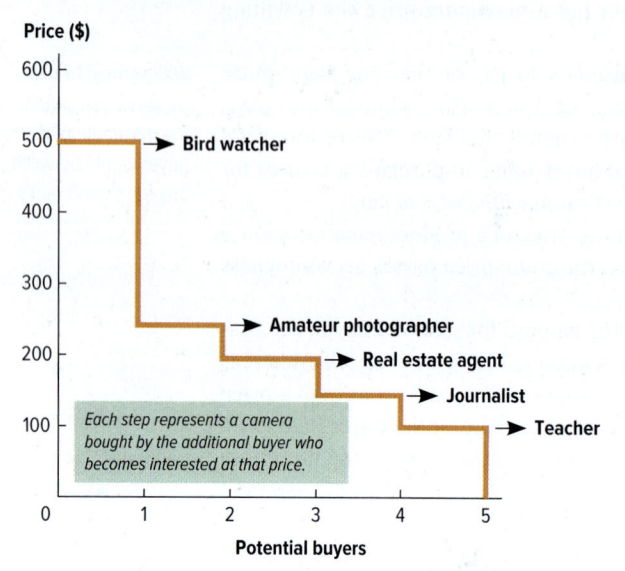

(A) Willingness to pay with few buyers

Each step represents a camera bought by the additional buyer who becomes interested at that price.

Labels on steps: Bird watcher ($500), Amateur photographer ($250), Real estate agent ($200), Journalist ($150), Teacher ($100).

At any given price, buyers with a higher willingness to pay will buy and those with a lower willingness to pay will not. If the price were $350, only one buyer would buy. If it were $50, all five people would buy. This demand curve has a step-like shape rather than a smooth line because there are a limited number of buyers whose prices are expressed in round dollar amounts.

(B) Willingness to pay with many buyers

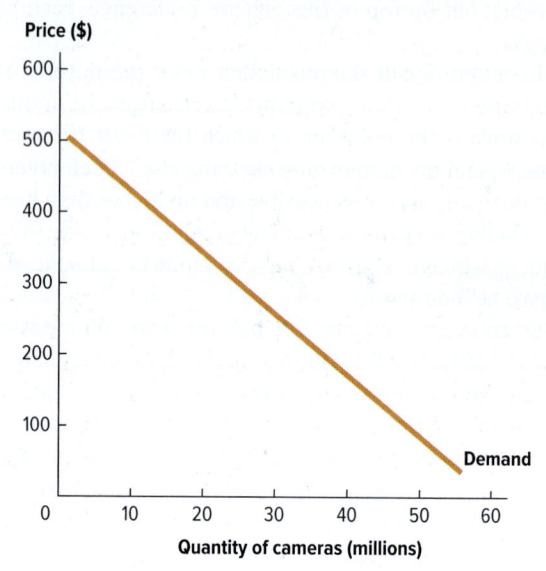

In the real market for a particular model of a digital camera, there are millions of cameras demanded at a particular price. The steps that we see in panel A get smaller and smaller until they disappear into a smooth curve.

---

only five potential buyers. We could conduct the same exercise in a bigger market and plot out the willingness to pay of millions of people rather than just five. In that case, we'd get a smooth demand curve, as shown in panel B of Figure 5-1. The individual steps that we see in panel A get smaller and smaller over the millions of cameras demanded, resulting in the smoothed-out curve.

Notice that although each buyer's willingness to pay is driven by different factors, we can explain the motivations behind all of their decisions by asking, *What are the trade-offs?* Money that is spent to buy a camera on eBay cannot be spent on other things. Willingness to pay is the point at which the benefit that a person will get from the camera is equal to the benefit of spending the money on another alternative—in other words, the opportunity cost. For instance, $250 is the point at which the enjoyment that the amateur photographer gets from a camera is the same as the enjoyment he would get from, say, spending $250 to upgrade his bicycle.

Since everyone has things they want other than cameras, the same opportunity cost logic applies to each of the potential buyers represented in the demand curve. At prices above the maximum willingness to pay, the opportunity cost is greater than the benefits. At lower prices, the benefits outweigh the opportunity cost.

To figure out which of our five individual buyers will actually purchase a camera, we have to know the market price. To find the market price, we have to know something about the supply of digital cameras. Therefore, we turn next to investigating the supply curve.

Willingness to sell and the supply curve

As you may have guessed, just as the shape of the demand curve was driven by potential buyers' willingness to pay, the shape of the supply curve for digital cameras is driven by potential sellers' *willingness to sell*. To simplify things, let's imagine five prospective sellers who have posted their cameras for sale on eBay.

- Seller #1 is a college student who was given a camera as a birthday present. All he really cares about is having money to see his favorite band, so he's willing to part with his camera for as little as $50.
- Seller #2 is a sales representative for a big company that makes digital cameras. She's authorized to sell a camera for $100 or higher.
- Seller #3 is a professional nature photographer who owns several cameras but won't sell for anything less than $200. At a lower price he'd rather give the camera as a gift to his nephew.
- Seller #4 is a sales representative for a small company that is just starting up in the camera industry and has much higher costs of production than the larger company; it can make money only by selling its cameras for $300 or more.
- Seller #5 is an art teacher who is sentimentally attached to her camera, given to her by a friend. She won't give it up unless she can get at least $400.

We can represent these five individuals by plotting on a graph their willingness to sell. Panel A of Figure 5-2 shows a graph of potential prices and the number of cameras that will be up for

FIGURE 5-2

Willingness to sell and the supply curve

(A) Willingness to sell with few sellers

Each step represents the additional camera sold by a seller who becomes interested as the price increases.

- Art teacher
- Sales rep (small company)
- Nature photographer
- Sales rep (big company)
- College student

(B) Willingness to sell with many sellers

At any given price, sellers with a lower willingness to sell will sell, while those with a higher willingness to sell will not. At a price of $400, all five people will sell their cameras, while at a price of $200, only three sell. This rough supply curve would look smooth if there were many sellers, each with a different willingness to sell.

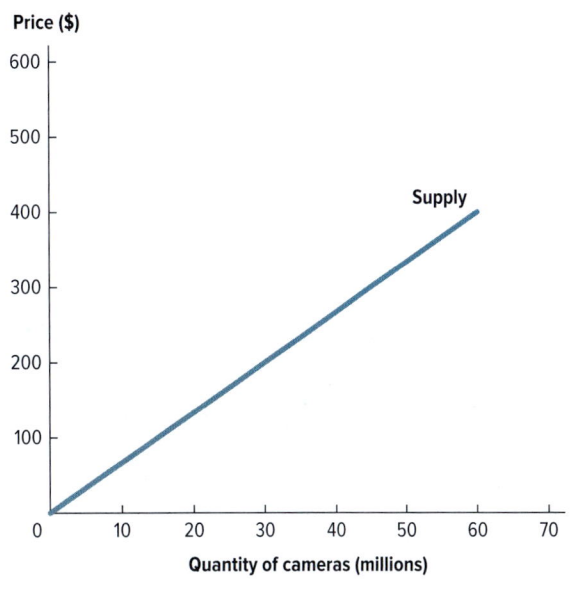

In the real market for a particular model of a digital camera, there are millions of cameras supplied at a particular price. The steps that we see in panel A get smaller and smaller until they disappear into a smooth curve.

bid at each price. This graph is a supply curve representing only five potential sellers. As with the demand curve, if we added all of the millions of digital cameras that are actually for sale in the real world, we see the smooth supply curve we're accustomed to, as in panel B.

Sellers' willingness to sell is determined by the *trade-offs* they face, and, in particular, the opportunity cost of the sale. The opportunity cost of selling a camera for sellers #1, #3, and #5 is the use or enjoyment that the seller could get from keeping the camera. In the case of the two camera manufacturers, sellers #2 and #4, the opportunity cost is whatever else the firm would do with the money that would be required to manufacture the camera—say, marketing the camera or researching new technology. The opportunity cost of each of the five sellers will be determined by different factors—not all of them strictly monetary, as in the case of the teacher, who is sentimentally attached to her camera.

For an item that a seller just wants to get rid of (like the broken laser pointer mentioned at the start of the chapter), the starting price might be one cent. If opportunity cost is zero, anything is better than nothing!

On the other hand, in a market where manufacturers are producing and selling new products, the minimum price will have to be high enough to make it worth their while to continue making new products. This would be the case for the two camera manufacturers. If the selling price didn't cover the costs of production, the manufacturers would simply stop making the item—otherwise, they would actually lose money every time they made a sale. (Occasionally, we do see manufacturers selling below the cost of production, but only when they've made a mistake and have to get rid of already-produced goods.)

Having met five potential buyers and five potential sellers, we're now in a position to understand what happens when the two groups come together in the market to make trades.

In the real world, transactions don't always sort so neatly. Sellers may post prices well above their true willingness to sell. Buyers, on the other hand, are always looking to get a better deal. In these cases, buyers and sellers may choose to negotiate on price. Take a look at the Econ and YOU box "It pays to negotiate" to consider a common version of such trading—salary negotiations.

It pays to negotiate
Econ and YOU

No matter which way you look at the data, women earn less than men. Overall, women working full-time earn just 77 percent of what male workers earn. Controlling for the fact that women and men often work in different kinds of jobs, there still is a 4-7 percent gap in pay.

There are many explanations for this gap, and the nature of wage negotiations tells part of the story. In some jobs, you're offered a wage and you take it or leave it. But often wages are decided by negotiation: Workers argue for the wage they want, and employers respond. The trouble is that it can be hard to know exactly how much a job should pay, and different people (with different talents, bargaining skills, and backgrounds) can end up with very different pay.

Economist Marianne Bertrand points to studies that find women are far less likely to negotiate their salary. Instead, they are more likely to accept the first wage offer presented by their employer. One survey of 200 workers found that men negotiated two to four times more often than women. The problem is that simply accepting the first offer puts women at a salary disadvantage.

Why were women in the survey more likely to take the first offer? One explanation is that women fear repercussions or worry about seeming greedy. Researchers Hannah Riley Bowles, Linda Babcock, and Lei Lai showed that women who tried to negotiate were more likely to be rated negatively by male evaluators and that male evaluators were more willing to work with women who accepted the first offer. However, when the evaluator was female, women did not get "punished" for asking.

Can employees help improve outcomes? One potential solution is to invite women to negotiate. Research by economists Andres Leibbrandt and John List randomly varied whether job searchers received ambiguous salary information or were told that the salary for a position was "negotiable." While men were three times more likely to try negotiating salary with ambiguous information, women and men were equally likely to try for more money when it was explicitly stated that the salary was "negotiable."

Alternatively, some firms have gone further and ended the practice of negotiations altogether. In 2015, Ellen Pao, the CEO of Reddit, a large internet community, cited the fact that men negotiate more often than women as a major part of her decision to end salary negotiations at the company. Whether changes like these will narrow the gender pay gap remains to be seen.

What should you do? The big lesson is: It pays to negotiate.

Sources: Marianne Bertrand, "Perspectives on gender," *Handbook of Labor Economics* (2011), Vol. 4, part B, pp. 1556–1562, edited by David Card and Orley Ashenfelter, www.fiwi.uni-jena.de/wfwmedia/Lehre/GenderEconomics/Bertrand+2011+New+Perspectives+on+Gender+In+Handbook+of+Labor+Economics+4+B-p-454.pdf; Hannah Riley Bowles, Linda Babcock, and Lei Lai, "Social incentives for gender differences in the propensity to initiate negotiations: Sometimes it does hurt to ask," *Organizational Behavior and Human Decision Processes* 103 (2007), pp.84–103, www.cfa.harvard.edu/cfawis/bowles.pdf; Andreas Liebbrandt and John A. List, "Do women avoid salary negotiations? Evidence from a large-scale natural field experiment," *Management Science* (2014), http://gap.hks.harvard.edu/do-women-avoid-salary-negotiations-evidence-large-scale-natural-field-experiment#method.

✓ TEST YOURSELF

- ☐ How is willingness to pay determined by opportunity cost? **[LO 5.1]**
- ☐ What is the relationship between willingness to pay and the demand curve? **[LO 5.1]**

Measuring Surplus

Surplus is a way of measuring who benefits from transactions and by how much. Economists use this word to describe a fairly simple concept: If you get something for less than you would have been willing to pay, or sell it for more than the minimum you would have accepted, that's a good thing. Think about how nice it feels to buy something on sale that you would have been willing to pay full price for. That "bonus" value that you would have paid if necessary, but didn't have to, is *surplus*. We can talk about surplus for both buyers and sellers, individually and collectively.

Surplus is the difference between the price at which a buyer or seller would be *willing* to trade and the actual price. Think about willingness to pay as the price at which someone is completely indifferent between buying an item and keeping his money. At a higher price, he would prefer to keep the money; at a lower price, he would prefer to buy. By looking at the distance between this "indifference point" and the actual price, we can describe the extra value the buyer (or the seller) gets from the transaction.

Surplus is a simple idea, but a surprisingly powerful one. It turns out that surplus is a better measure of the value that buyers and sellers get from participating in a market than price itself. To see why this is true, read the From Another Angle box "How much would you pay to keep the internet from disappearing?"

surplus
a way of measuring who benefits from transactions and by how much

How much would you pay to keep the internet from disappearing?

From Another Angle

Why is surplus a better measure of value than how much we pay for something? Consider the difference between what we pay for the internet versus a particular model of computer.

Most people can access the internet for very little, or even for free. You might pay a monthly fee for high-speed access at home, but almost anyone can use the internet for free at schools, libraries, or coffee shops. Once you're online there are millions of websites that will provide information, entertainment, and services at no charge.

Computer owners, on the other hand, pay a lot for particular types of computers. For instance, consumers might pay $999 for a MacBook laptop. Does this mean that we value access to the internet less than a MacBook? Probably not.

Simply measuring price falls short of capturing true value. To see why, think about how much you would pay to prevent the particular type of computer you own from disappearing from the market. You might pay something: After all, there's a reason you chose it in the first place, and you might be willing to cough up a bit extra to get your preferred combination of technical specifications, appearance, and so on. But if the price got very steep, you'd probably rather switch to another, similar type of computer instead of paying more money. That difference—the maximum extra amount you would pay over the current price to maintain the ability to buy something—is your *consumer surplus*. It is the difference between your willingness to pay and the actual price.

Now consider the same question for the internet. Imagine that the internet is going to disappear tomorrow, or, at least, that you will be unable to access it in any way. How much would you pay to keep that from happening? Remember, that means no e-mail, no Google search or maps, no Facebook, no Twitter, no YouTube, no video streaming, and no online shopping. We suspect that you might be willing to pay a lot. The amount that you're willing to pay represents the true value that you place on the internet, even though the amount that you currently spend on it might be very little. That's the magic of surplus.

Consumer surplus

LO 5.2 Calculate consumer surplus based on a graph or table.

consumer surplus the net benefit that a consumer receives from purchasing a good or service, measured by the difference between willingness to pay and the actual price

Let's go back to our five eBay buyers and calculate the surplus they would receive from buying a camera at a given price. This part of the transaction illustrates **consumer surplus**—the net benefit that a consumer receives from purchasing a good or service, measured by the difference between willingness to pay and the actual price.

Suppose it turns out that the going rate for cameras on eBay is $160. Using that amount, we can calculate the buyers' consumer surplus:

- The bird watcher was willing to bid up to $500. Therefore, her consumer surplus from buying the camera is $340—the difference between her willingness to pay and the $160 she actually pays.

Two other potential buyers will also buy a camera if the price is $160, and two will drop out:

- The amateur photographer is willing to pay $250, and the consumer surplus he receives is $90.
- The real estate agent is willing to pay up to $200, and the consumer surplus she receives is $40.
- The other two potential buyers will have dropped out of bidding when the price rose above $100 and then above $150, so they buy nothing and pay nothing. Their consumer surplus is zero.

We can add up each individual's consumer surplus to describe the overall benefits that buyers received in a market. (Somewhat confusingly, economists use the same term for individual and collective surplus, but you should be able to tell from the context whether we mean one person's consumer surplus or total consumer surplus for all buyers in the market.) If the market for digital cameras consisted only of our five individuals, then the total consumer surplus would be:

$$\$340 + \$90 + \$40 + \$0 + \$0 = \$470$$

On a graph, we represent consumer surplus as the area underneath the demand curve and above the horizontal line of the equilibrium price. Panel A of Figure 5-3 shows consumer surplus for these five individuals when the price is $160. (Because there are only five buyers in this market, the demand curve in panel A has the step-like shape we saw earlier.)

How does a change in the market price affect buyers? Since buyers would always prefer prices to be lower:

- a decrease in price makes them better off, and
- an increase in price makes them worse off.

Some people will choose not to buy at all when prices rise—which means that their surplus becomes zero. Those who do buy will have a smaller individual surplus than they had at the lower price. The opposite is true when prices fall. Measuring consumer surplus tells us *how much* better or worse off buyers are when the price changes.

For a refresher on the area under a linear curve, see Appendix D, "Math Essentials: The Area under a Linear Curve," which follows this chapter.

FIGURE 5-3
Consumer surplus

(A) Consumer surplus at $160

This graph shows consumer surplus in the camera market when price is $160. The shaded area is the difference between willingness to pay and the market price for each buyer. The more that a buyer would have been willing to pay, the greater the surplus at a lower price. At this price, total consumer surplus is $470, the sum of the individual surpluses shown.

(B) Consumer surplus at $100

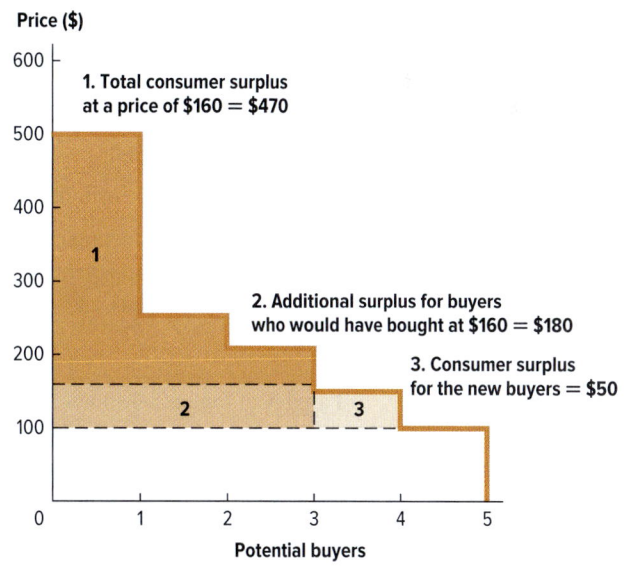

When the price of cameras falls to $100, consumer surplus increases. Area 1 is consumer surplus under the old price. Area 2 is the additional surplus received by people who were willing to buy at either price. Area 3 is the surplus received by the two new buyers who enter the market when price falls. The combination of the three areas is total consumer surplus when price is $100. When the price falls, total consumer surplus increases from $470 to $700.

Panel B of Figure 5-3 shows what happens to total consumer surplus if the going price of cameras on eBay falls to $100. You can see by comparing panel A with panel B that when the price level falls, the area representing consumer surplus gets bigger. When the price falls:

- The consumer surplus of each of the three buyers who were already willing to buy increases by $60 each.

Also, two more buyers join the market:

- The journalist's willingness to pay is $150, so she gains consumer surplus of $50.
- The teacher's willingness to pay is $100; he buys a camera but gains no consumer surplus because the price is exactly equal to his willingness to pay.

When the camera's price drops to $100, total consumer surplus among our five individuals totals $700 (an increase of $230):

$$\$470 + \$60 + \$60 + \$60 + \$50 + \$0 = \$700$$

Producer surplus

LO 5.3 Calculate producer surplus based on a graph or table.

producer surplus
the net benefit that a producer receives from the sale of a good or service, measured by the difference between the producer's willingness to sell and the actual price

Like buyers, sellers want to increase the distance between the price at which they are willing to trade and the actual price. Sellers are better off when the market price is higher than their minimum willingness to sell. **Producer surplus** is the net benefit that a producer receives from the sale of a good or service, measured by the difference between willingness to sell and the actual price. It's called *producer* surplus regardless of whether the sellers actually produced the good themselves or—as often happens on eBay—are selling it secondhand.

If our five potential sellers find that the going price of cameras on eBay is $160, two of them will sell because they will get more for their cameras than the minimum they were willing to accept, and three won't trade at that price:

- Seller #1 (the college student), whose willingness to sell is $50, has a producer surplus of $110.
- Seller #2 (the sales rep for the bigger camera company), whose willingness to sell is $100, has a surplus of $60.
- Potential sellers #3, #4, and #5 won't trade at a price of $160, so each has a surplus of zero.

Just as we did for consumer surplus, we can add up each seller's producer surplus to describe the overall benefits that sellers received in a market. If our five sellers are the only ones in the market, then total producer surplus at a price of $160 is:

$$\$110 + \$60 + \$0 + \$0 + \$0 = \$170$$

Panel A of Figure 5-4 shows producer surplus for the five sellers when the price is $160. (Again, because of the small size of this market, the supply curve in panel A has a step-like shape.)

A change in the market price affects sellers in the opposite way it affects buyers. Sellers would always prefer prices to be higher, so:

- a decrease in price makes them worse off, and
- an increase in price makes them better off.

Some sellers will choose not to sell at all when prices fall; their surplus becomes zero. Those who do sell will have a smaller individual surplus than at the higher price. The opposite is true when the market price rises, which makes sellers better off. Measuring producer surplus tells us *how much* better or worse off sellers are when the price changes.

On a graph, we represent producer surplus as the area below the horizontal line of equilibrium price and above the supply curve. Panel B of Figure 5-4 shows what happens to producer surplus if the price drops from $160 to $100. Sellers #1 and #2 still sell, but their surplus is reduced. Total producer surplus falls to $50.

FIGURE 5-4
Producer surplus

(A) Producer surplus at $160

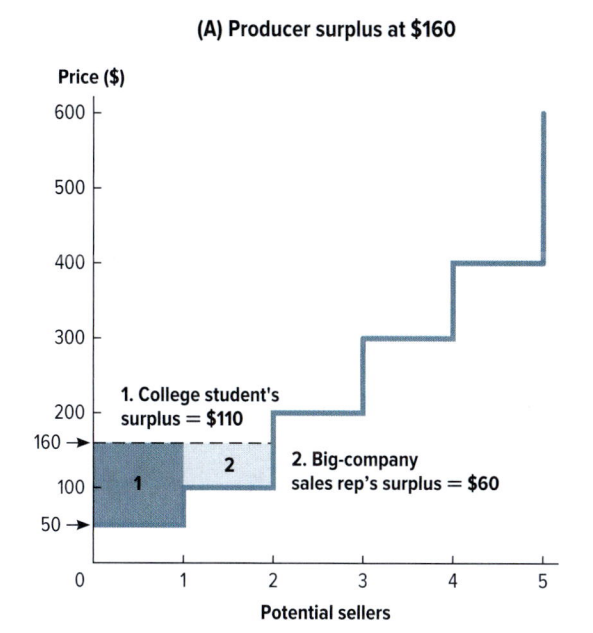

1. College student's surplus = $110
2. Big-company sales rep's surplus = $60

This shows the willingness to sell of all the potential sellers in our market. The shaded area (1 + 2) between the supply curve and the market prices shows total producer surplus of $170, the sum of the individual surpluses shown.

(B) Producer surplus at $100

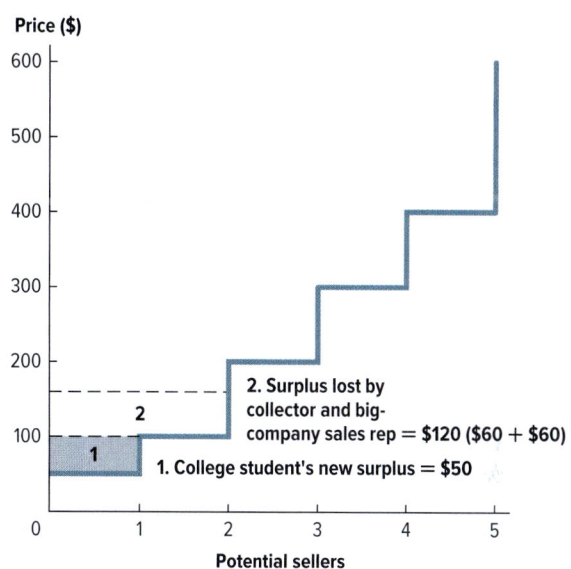

2. Surplus lost by collector and big-company sales rep = $120 ($60 + $60)
1. College student's new surplus = $50

Because sellers always prefer a higher price, producer surplus goes down when the price falls to $100. At $100, two sellers are still willing to sell, but are worse off because they receive less money for their cameras. Area 1 shows the new producer surplus: $50. Area 2 shows the reduction in surplus for the two sellers.

You can see by comparing panel A with panel B that when the price level falls, the area representing producer surplus gets smaller. On the other hand, the higher the price, the bigger the area, and the greater the producer surplus.

Total surplus

We now understand how to calculate consumer surplus and producer surplus at any given price. But what will the actual market price be? To find out, we have to put the demand and supply curves together and locate the point where they intersect.

Panel A of Figure 5-5 shows the demand curve for our five buyers and the supply curve for our five sellers. The two curves intersect at a price of $200. At this price, three buyers are willing to buy a camera and three sellers are willing to sell a camera. The consumer surplus of each buyer is shown as the area underneath the demand curve and above the horizontal line of the equilibrium price. Consumer surplus is:

$$\$300 + \$50 + \$0 + \$0 + \$0 = \$350$$

(Buyer #3 buys at her willingness to pay price, so she has no consumer surplus.) The producer surplus is shown as the area above the supply curve and beneath the equilibrium price.

Producer surplus is:

$$\$150 + \$100 + \$0 + \$0 + \$0 = \$250$$

(Seller #3 sells at his willingness to sell price, so he has no producer surplus.)

LO 5.4 Calculate total surplus based on a graph or table.

FIGURE 5-5

Surplus at market equilibrium

(A) Surplus at market equilibrium for the five-buyer and five-seller camera market

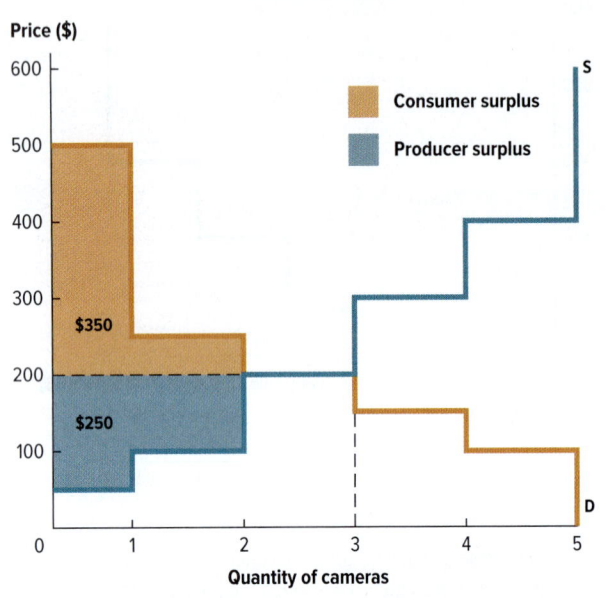

(B) Surplus at market equilibrium for the entire camera market

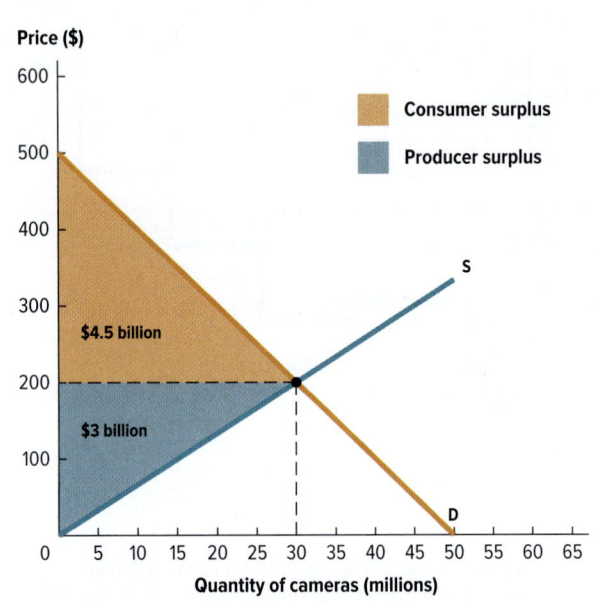

At the market equilibrium in our smaller market, the price of a camera is $200, and three are bought and sold. Consumer surplus is represented by the area between the demand curve and the market price, and is equal to $350. Producer surplus is represented by the area between the supply curve and the market price, and is equal to $250. Total surplus adds up to $600.

At the market equilibrium in our large market, the price of cameras is $200, and 30 million are bought and sold. Consumer surplus is represented by the area between the demand curve and the market price, and is equal to $4.5 billion. Producer surplus is represented by the area between the supply curve and the market price, and is equal to $3 billion. Total surplus adds up to $7.5 billion.

total surplus a measure of the combined benefits that everyone receives from participating in an exchange of goods or services

Just as we've found total consumer surplus and total producer surplus, we can find total surplus for an entire market. **Total surplus** is a measure of the combined benefits that everyone receives from participating in an exchange of goods or services. The total surplus is the benefit received by all market participants, the sum of both consumer and producer surplus. For our camera market of five buyers and five sellers, total surplus is:

$$\$350 + \$250 = \$600$$

To better understand total surplus, let's broaden our focus beyond just five buyers and five sellers to the entire market for digital cameras on eBay. To represent this big market, we can bring back the smooth demand and supply curves from Figures 5-1 and 5-2. When we put the two together in panel B of Figure 5-5, we find that the equilibrium price is $200, and the equilibrium quantity of cameras traded is 30 million. (We're assuming a standardized model of digital camera and all the other features of a competitive market outlined in Chapter 3, "Markets.")

Total consumer surplus is represented graphically by the area underneath the demand curve and above the equilibrium price. That's the area shaded gold in panel B of Figure 5-5. Total producer surplus is represented by the area of the graph above the supply curve and below the equilibrium price—the area shaded blue.

Added together, those two areas—consumer surplus and producer surplus—make up the total surplus created by those 30 million sales of digital cameras on eBay. Graphically, total surplus is equal to the total area between the supply and demand curves, to the left of the equilibrium quantity.

We can also think of total surplus as value created by the existence of the market. Total surplus is calculated by adding up the benefits that every individual participant receives ($300 consumer surplus for the bird watcher, plus $150 producer surplus for the college student, and so on, for every one of those 30 million sales). But these benefits exist only as a result of participation in exchanges in the market.

This is an important point because sometimes people mistakenly think of the economy as a fixed quantity of money, goods, and well-being, in which the only question is how to divide it up among people. That idea is referred to as a **zero-sum game**. A zero-sum game is a situation in which whenever one person gains, another loses an equal amount, such that the net value of a transaction is zero. Playing poker is an example of a zero-sum game: Whatever one player wins, another player, logically, has to lose.

The concept of surplus shows us that the economy generally does not work like a poker game. Voluntary transactions for buyers and sellers, like buying or selling cameras on eBay, do not have a winner or loser. Rather, *both the buyer and seller are winners* since each gains surplus. Everyone ends up better off than he or she was before. Total surplus cannot be *less* than zero—if it were, people would simply stop buying and selling.

As a rule, markets generate value, but the distribution of that value is a more complicated issue. In the following sections, we will look at what surplus can tell us about the well-being generated by market transactions and by deviations from the market equilibrium. Then, in the next chapter, we'll use these tools to evaluate the effects of some common government policies when they are implemented in a competitive market. Later in the text, we will revisit some of the assumptions about how competitive markets operate, and we will discuss what happens to surplus when those assumptions don't hold true in the real world.

> **zero-sum game**
> a situation in which whenever one person gains, another loses an equal amount, such that the net value of any transaction is zero

✓ TEST YOURSELF

- ☐ What consumer surplus is received by someone whose willingness to pay is $20 below the market price of a good? **[LO 5.2]**
- ☐ What is the producer surplus earned by a seller whose willingness to sell is $40 below the market price of a good? **[LO 5.3]**
- ☐ Why can total surplus never fall below zero in a market for goods and services? **[LO 5.4]**

Using Surplus to Compare Alternatives

In a competitive market, buyers and sellers will naturally find their way to the equilibrium price. In our eBay example, we expect that buyers and sellers of digital cameras will bargain freely, offering different prices until the number of people who want to buy is matched with the number of people who want to sell. This is the invisible hand of market forces at work. It doesn't require any eBay manager to coordinate or set prices. But as we're about to see, the magic of the invisible hand doesn't stop there.

Market equilibrium and efficiency

The concept of surplus lets us appreciate something very important about market equilibrium. It is the point at which transactions occur between the buyers willing to pay the most and sellers able to produce at the lowest cost. It is the point at which transactions maximize total surplus.

To see why this is so, let's look at what would happen to surplus if, for some reason, the market moved away from equilibrium. Suppose an eBay manager decides to set the price of cameras so that people don't have to go to the trouble of bidding. He decides that $300 seems like a reasonable price. How will potential buyers and sellers *respond* to this situation? Figure 5-6 shows us:

> **LO 5.5** Define efficiency in terms of surplus, and identify efficient and inefficient situations.

- There are now 10 million fewer cameras sold (the quantity sold falls from 30 million to 20 million). Buyers who wanted 10 million cameras at the equilibrium price of $200 are no longer willing to buy at $300, reducing their consumer surplus to zero.

FIGURE 5-6

Changing the distribution of surplus

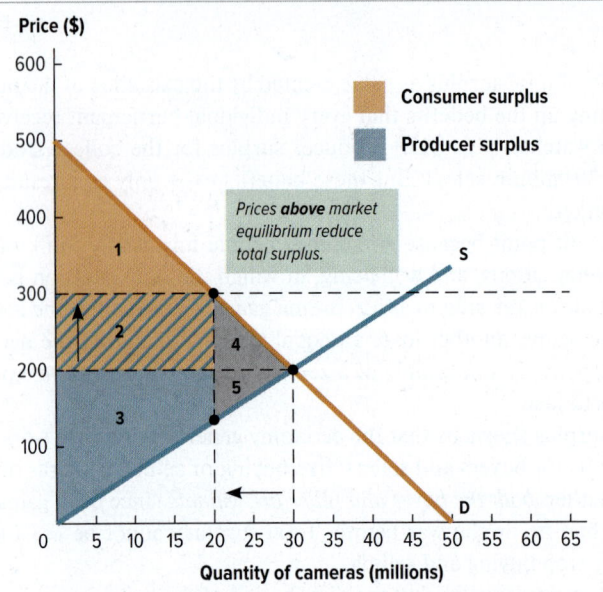

When the price rises above the market equilibrium, fewer transactions take place. The surplus shown in area 2 is transferred from consumers to producers as a result of the higher price paid for transactions that do still take place. The surplus in areas 4 and 5 is lost to both consumers and producers as a result of the reduced number of transactions.

*Prices **above** market equilibrium reduce total surplus.*

FIGURE 5-7

Surplus when price is below equilibrium

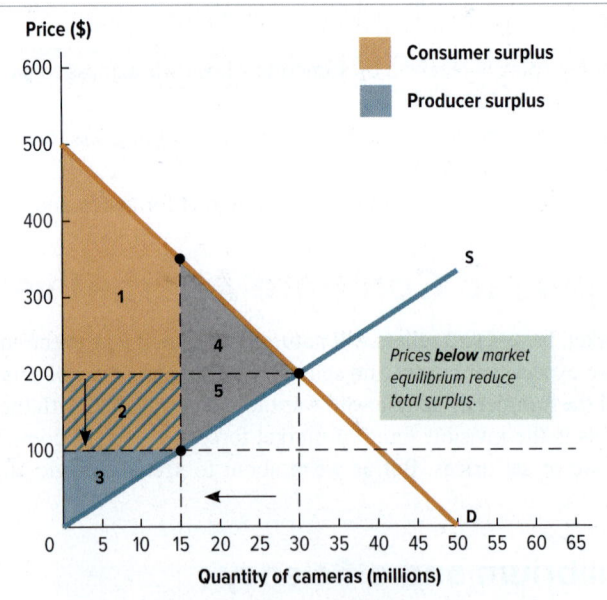

When the price of cameras drops to $100, buyers are willing to purchase 40 million, but sellers want to sell only 15 million. For those who do trade, successful buyers gain surplus of $1.5 billion (area 2) from buying at the lower price, while the sellers lose surplus of that same amount. The buyers and sellers who would have traded at equilibrium but no longer do so lose $1.875 billion of combined surplus. The surplus in areas 4 and 5 is lost to both consumers and producers as a result of the reduced number of transactions. Total surplus falls from $7.5 billion to $5.625 billion.

*Prices **below** market equilibrium reduce total surplus.*

- That means that sellers who would have sold those 10 million cameras to buyers also miss out and get producer surplus of zero.
- For the 20 million cameras that still are sold, buyers pay a higher price and lose surplus.
- The sellers of those 20 million cameras benefit from the higher price and gain the surplus lost by consumers.

Overall, total surplus in the market is lower than it was at the equilibrium price because 10 million fewer cameras are sold.

What happens if the interfering eBay manager instead decides to sell digital cameras for $100? As Figure 5-7 shows:

- Buyers are willing to purchase 40 million cameras at a price of $100. Sellers are willing to sell only 15 million at $100.
- Since 15 million fewer cameras sell (that is, 15 million instead of 30 million at equilibrium), buyers and sellers lose the surplus that would have been gained through their sale.
- For the 15 million transactions that still take place, consumers gain surplus of $1.5 billion ($100 × 15 million) from buying at a lower price (area 2). That consumer surplus is exactly equal to the surplus the remaining sellers lose from selling at a lower price.
- The buyers and sellers who would have traded at equilibrium but no longer do so lose $1.875 billion of combined surplus. Breaking this down, we find that the 15 million buyers no longer in the market lose $1.125 billion (area 4), and sellers lose $0.75 billion (area 5) in surplus.
- This $1.875 billion total (areas 4 + 5) in lost surplus is subtracted from the amount of total surplus before the price ceiling. Overall, total surplus falls from $7.5 billion to $5.625 billion.

In both cases—when the price is $300 (above the equilibrium price) or when it is $100 (below the equilibrium price)—total surplus decreases relative to the market equilibrium. In fact, we find this same result at *any price* other than the equilibrium price. The key is that a higher or lower price causes fewer trades to take place because some people are no longer willing to buy or sell. The value that would have been gained from these voluntary trades no longer exists. As a result, *the equilibrium in a perfectly competitive, well-functioning market maximizes total surplus.*

Another way to say this is that the market is **efficient** when it is at equilibrium: There is no exchange that can make anyone better off without someone becoming worse off. Efficiency is one of the most powerful features of a market system. Even more remarkable is that it is achieved without centralized coordination.

efficient market an arrangement such that no exchange can make anyone better off without someone becoming worse off

LO 5.6 Describe the distribution of surplus, or benefits to society, that results from a policy decision.

Changing the distribution of total surplus

A reduction in total surplus was not the only interesting thing that happened when the meddling eBay manager moved the price of digital cameras away from equilibrium. Another outcome was *reassignment of surplus* from customers to producers, or vice versa, for the transactions that did take place:

- When the price was raised, sellers gained some well-being at the expense of buyers.
- When the price was lowered, buyers gained some well-being at the expense of sellers.

In both cases, achieving this transfer of well-being from one group to the other came at the expense of *reduced total surplus*.

When an artificially high price is imposed on a market, it's bad news for consumer surplus. Consumers lose surplus due to the reduced number of transactions and the higher price buyers have to pay on the remaining transactions.

The situation for producers, though, is more complex. At the artificially high price, producers lose some surplus from the transactions that would have taken place under equilibrium and no longer do. On the other hand, they gain more surplus from the higher price on the transactions that do still take place. These two effects will compete with one another. Whichever effect "wins" will determine whether the producer surplus increases or decreases overall.

To see why, let's go back to Figure 5-6. Area 2 is surplus that is transferred from consumers to producers. Areas 4 and 5 represent surplus lost to consumers and producers, respectively, from transactions that no longer take place. Whether area 2 is bigger or smaller than area 5 will indicate whether producer surplus increases or decreases. That result depends on the shape of the demand curve and the supply curve. In this case, we can see that area 2 is bigger than area 5. The effect of the artificially high price was to make sellers better off (at the expense of making buyers even more worse off).

The opposite situation occurs when prices are lower than the market equilibrium, which you can see by looking again at Figure 5-7. Fewer transactions take place (because fewer producers are willing to sell), and so both producers and consumers lose some surplus from missed transactions. For the transactions that do still take place, consumers pay less and gain surplus at the expense of producers. Producers get paid less and lose surplus.

Thus, a price below the market equilibrium will always reduce producer surplus. That price might increase or decrease consumer surplus: The outcome depends on how much surplus is gained by those who buy at a lower price compared to what is lost to those who can no longer buy at all.

We don't expect eBay managers to start imposing their own prices any time soon—that would be contrary to the whole idea of eBay as a decentralized virtual marketplace. But there are times when governments or other organizations do decide to impose minimum or maximum prices on markets. That happens because efficiency is not the only thing we care about. Many fundamental public policy questions revolve around possible trade-offs between economic efficiency and other concerns such as fairness and equity. We'll look in much more detail at this idea in the next chapter.

Deadweight loss

LO 5.7 Calculate deadweight loss.

deadweight loss
a loss of total surplus that occurs because the quantity of a good that is bought and sold is below the market equilibrium quantity

An intervention that moves a market away from equilibrium might benefit either producers or consumers, but it always comes with a decrease in total surplus. Where does that surplus go? It disappears and becomes what is known as a **deadweight loss**. Deadweight loss is the loss of total surplus that occurs when the quantity of a good that is bought and sold is below the market equilibrium quantity. Any intervention that moves a market away from the equilibrium price and quantity creates deadweight loss. Fewer exchanges take place, so there are fewer opportunities for the generation of surplus.

We can calculate deadweight loss in two ways: One way is to subtract total surplus *after* a market intervention from total surplus at the market equilibrium *before* the intervention. Or we can calculate deadweight loss directly by determining the area of the triangle on a graph. This second method is usually the easiest.

Figure 5-8 shows what happens in the eBay camera market when the price is too low at $100. Only 15 million cameras are exchanged at this price, but the efficient quantity is 30 million. For the units between 15 million and 30 million, consumers have a willingness to pay that is higher than producers' costs. Thus, exchanging the units would create surplus, but because the units are not exchanged, this potential surplus is lost.

To calculate the exact size of this deadweight loss, we calculate the area between supply and demand for those units that aren't exchanged. The "base" of this triangle is measured along the y-axis from $100 to $350. The "height" is measured along the x-axis from 15 million to 30 million. Then, using the formula for the area of a triangle, the deadweight loss is:

$$\frac{b \times h}{2} = \frac{250 \times 15 \text{ million}}{2} = 1.875 \text{ billion}$$

We'll see in the next chapter that deadweight loss is an incredibly important concept for understanding the costs of government intervention in markets, through mechanisms such as taxes and controls on the prices of goods.

FIGURE 5-8
Deadweight loss

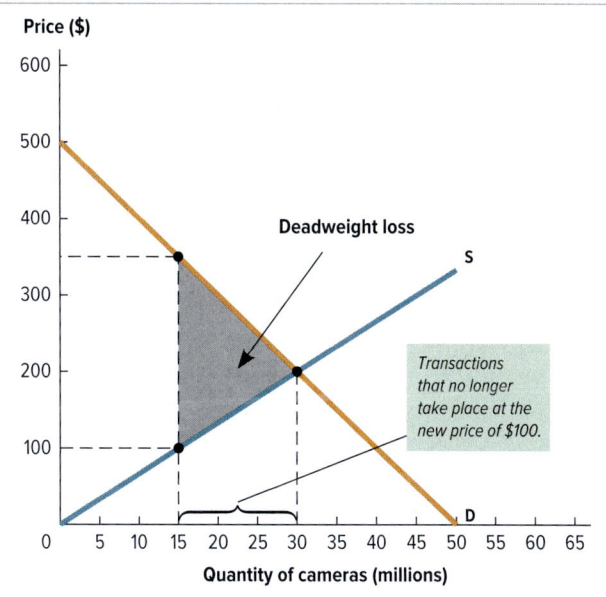

Deadweight loss represents the surplus that is lost to both producers and consumers as a result of fewer transactions taking place when the price moves away from equilibrium. Here, deadweight loss is equal to the gray shaded area.

Missing markets

When there are people who would like to make exchanges but cannot, for one reason or another, we miss opportunities for mutual benefit. In this situation, we say that a market is "missing." The term "missing" can be misleading. Sometimes a market exists, so it is not literally missing. But for some reason, some of the trades that potential buyers and sellers would *like* to make are not happening. Asking why a market is missing is important; the answer can provide guidance to policies and businesses that can allow more people to engage in trade for mutual benefit.

Markets can be missing for a variety of reasons:

- Sometimes public policy prevents the market from existing—for instance, when the production or sale of a particular good or service is banned.
- Or sometimes a particular good or service is taxed; the tax doesn't eliminate the market but does add a cost, which leads to fewer transactions.
- Markets can also be missing or shrunk due to other types of holdups: a lack of accurate information or communication between potential buyers and sellers, or a lack of technology that would make the exchanges possible.

LO 5.8 Explain why correcting a missing market can make everyone better off.

eBay and newer companies such as Airbnb, Uber, and Lyft are examples of how technology can generate new value by creating or expanding a market. Prior to the existence of such companies, people who wanted to offer a service or product, and people who wanted to buy it, often never found each other. For example, before eBay you could hold a garage sale to get rid of your extra stuff; you could go to your local stores or post an ad in a newspaper if you were looking to buy an unusual item. But it was quite difficult to find out if someone on the other side of the country was offering a rare product or a better price. eBay allows more buyers to find sellers and vice versa, encouraging more mutually beneficial trades.

The idea that we can increase total surplus by creating new markets and improving existing ones has important implications for public policy. Policies and technologies that help people share information and do business more effectively can increase well-being. For instance, ideas like creating a market for small loans by the Grameen Bank (see Chapter 1, "Economics and Life") or expanding access to cell phones in Indian fishing villages (see Chapter 3, "Markets") don't just redistribute pieces of the pie to help the poor. Instead, they make the whole pie bigger.

Think about the many situations in the world in which new technology, new strategies, and outreach to new clients have created a market that brings value to people. Also think about some controversial situations in which markets don't exist but could be created, as described in the What Do You Think? box "Kidneys for sale."

Kidneys for sale
What Do You Think?

When buyers and sellers come together to participate in voluntary transactions, the resulting markets create value that would not otherwise exist. The idea that well-functioning markets maximize surplus is an important descriptive fact.

But people may have moral and political priorities that go beyond maximizing surplus. In fact, many important public policy questions revolve around trade-offs between economic efficiency and other goals.

For instance, the law in the United States (and many other countries) prohibits certain types of market transactions. Consider the following cases:

- It's illegal to buy or sell organs for medical transplants.
- It's illegal to buy or sell certain drugs, such as cocaine and heroin.
- It's illegal to buy or sell children for adoption.
- It's illegal to buy or sell certain types of weapons, such as nuclear devices.

Looking at it from one angle, these are all examples of missing markets. You now know that when markets are missing, we miss opportunities to create surplus by enabling voluntary transactions to take place. For instance, a market for organs could make a lot of people better off. Some healthy people would gain surplus by selling their kidneys: They would rather have money and one remaining kidney than two kidneys and no money. Meanwhile, some people with kidney disease would happily pay for the donation of a healthy kidney. Because the law prevents this transaction from happening, both miss out on surplus.

If maximizing surplus is our highest goal, it's plausible that we should allow organs and other such goods to be traded on the market. But allowing markets for organs goes against many people's moral instincts—perhaps because they hold other goals higher than maximizing surplus.

WHAT DO YOU THINK?

1. Do you agree that the law should prevent trade in organs?
2. How about drugs, children, and nuclear weapons?
3. Are there any reasons that markets for these goods might not end up maximizing surplus?
4. What values and assumptions are driving your answers?

✓ TEST YOURSELF

- ☐ What can we say about the size and distribution of total surplus in an efficient market? **[LO 5.5]**
- ☐ How do price changes affect the distribution of surplus between consumers and producers? **[LO 5.6]**
- ☐ Why does an intervention that moves a market away from the equilibrium price and quantity create a deadweight loss? **[LO 5.7]**
- ☐ What does it mean to say that a market is "missing"? **[LO 5.8]**

Conclusion

In this chapter we've introduced the concepts of willingness to pay and willingness to sell, which help explain when individual buyers and sellers will choose to make a trade. We've also discussed what it means to measure consumer and producer surplus and shown that the market equilibrium is efficient because it maximizes total surplus.

As we'll see in the next chapter, surplus and deadweight loss are powerful tools for understanding the implications of business ideas and public policies. Who will benefit from the policy? Who will be harmed by it? What effect will it have on the economy overall? The language of surplus, efficiency, and distribution of benefits is particularly helpful for getting to the bottom of controversial decisions.

Later in the text, we will describe important cases in which the efficiency rule about market equilibrium does not always hold true, and we'll see how surplus can also help us understand these cases.

Key Terms

willingness to pay (reservation price), p. 105
willingness to sell, p. 105
surplus, p. 109
consumer surplus, p. 110
producer surplus, p. 112
total surplus, p. 114
zero-sum game, p. 115
efficient market, p. 117
deadweight loss, p. 118

Summary

LO 5.1 Use willingness to pay and willingness to sell to determine supply and demand at a given price.

Willingness to pay and willingness to sell describe the value that an individual places on a particular good or service. Willingness to pay (also sometimes known as the reservation price) is the maximum price that a buyer would be willing to pay for a particular good or service. Willingness to sell is the lowest price a seller is willing to accept in exchange for a particular good or service.

Consumers will buy only if the price is lower than their willingness to pay. Producers will sell only if the price is higher than their willingness to sell.

LO 5.2 Calculate consumer surplus based on a graph or table.

Surplus is a way of measuring who benefits from transactions and how much. Consumer surplus is the net benefit that consumers receive from purchasing a good or service, measured by the difference between each consumer's willingness to pay and the actual price. Graphically, it is equal to the area below the demand curve and above the market price.

LO 5.3 Calculate producer surplus based on a graph or table.

Producer surplus is a measure of the net benefits that a producer receives from the sale of a good or service, measured by the difference between the producer's willingness to sell and the actual price. Graphically, it is equal to the area above the supply curve and below the market price.

LO 5.4 Calculate total surplus based on a graph or table.

Total surplus is a measure of the combined benefits that everyone receives from participating in an exchange of goods or services. It is calculated by adding consumer surplus and producer surplus. Graphically, it is equal to the total area between the supply and demand curves, to the left of the equilibrium quantity.

LO 5.5 Define efficiency in terms of surplus, and identify efficient and inefficient situations.

A market is *efficient* if there is no exchange that can make anyone better off without someone becoming worse off. An efficient market maximizes total surplus but doesn't tell us how the surplus is distributed between consumers and producers. In a competitive market, efficiency is achieved only at the market equilibrium price and quantity; higher prices and lower prices will both decrease the quantity bought and sold and reduce total surplus.

LO 5.6 Describe the distribution of surplus, or benefits to society, that results from a policy decision.

Prices above or below the market equilibrium reduce total surplus but also redistribute surplus between producers and consumers differently. A price above the equilibrium always decreases consumer surplus. Also, at a price above equilibrium, some producers win and others lose; the overall effect on producer surplus depends on the shape of the supply and demand curves. A price below the equilibrium always decreases producer surplus; some consumers win and others lose.

LO 5.7 Calculate deadweight loss.

Deadweight loss is the loss of total surplus that occurs when the quantity of a good that is bought and sold is below the market equilibrium quantity. Any intervention that moves a market away from the equilibrium price and quantity causes deadweight loss. Fewer exchanges take place, so there are fewer opportunities for the generation of surplus.

LO 5.8 Explain why correcting a missing market can make everyone better off.

A market is "missing" when there is a situation in which people would like to engage in mutually beneficial trades of goods and services but can't because no market for them exists. A missing market is a special case of a market in which quantity is held below the equilibrium—in this case, at or close to zero. Missing markets can occur for many reasons, including government intervention or a lack of information or technology. When missing markets are filled, people are able to trade, which generates surplus.

Review Questions

1. Sangjay is a professional photographer. His camera is broken and he needs a new one within the next hour, or he will miss an important deadline. Keiko is a high-school student who doesn't have a camera but wants to get one to take pictures at her prom next month. Who do you think would have a higher willingness to pay for a particular camera today? Why? **[LO 5.1]**

2. You are in the market for a new couch and have found two advertisements for the kind of couch you want to buy. One seller notes in her ad that she is selling because she is moving to a smaller apartment, and the couch won't fit in the new space. The other seller says he is selling because the couch doesn't match his other furniture. Which seller do you expect to buy from? Why? (*Hint:* Think who would be the more motivated seller.) **[LO 5.1]**

3. Suppose you are at a flea market and are considering buying a box of vintage records. You are trying to bargain down the price, but the seller overhears you telling a friend that you are willing to pay up to $50. Why is your consumer surplus now likely to be lower than it would have been if the seller hadn't overheard you? **[LO 5.2]**

4. Consider a market in equilibrium. Suppose supply in this market increases. How will this affect consumer surplus? Explain. **[LO 5.2]**

5. You currently have a television that you want to sell. You can either pick a price and try to sell it at a yard sale or auction it off on eBay. Which method do you think will yield a higher producer surplus? Why? **[LO 5.3]**

6. Consider a market in equilibrium. Suppose demand in this market decreases. How will this affect producer surplus? Explain. **[LO 5.3]**

7. Consider the market for plane tickets to Hawaii. A bad winter in the mainland United States increases demand for tropical vacations, shifting the demand curve to the right. The supply curve stays constant. Does total surplus increase or decrease? (*Hint:* Sketch out a generic supply and demand curve and look at what happens to the size of the triangle that represents total surplus when the demand curve shifts right.) **[LO 5.4]**

8. You need to paint your fence, but you really hate this task. You decide to hire the kid next door to do it for you. You would be willing to pay him up to $100, but you start by offering $50, expecting to negotiate. To your great surprise, he accepts your $50 offer. When you tell your friend about the great deal you got, she is shocked that you would take advantage of someone. What can you tell your friend to assure her that you did not cheat the kid next door? **[LO 5.4]**

9. New York City has a long-standing policy of controlling rents in certain parts of the city—in essence, a price ceiling on rent. Is the market for apartments likely to be efficient or inefficient? What does this imply for the size of total surplus? **[LO 5.5]**

10. Total surplus is maximized at the equilibrium price and quantity. When demand increases, price increases. Explain how total surplus is still maximized if price increases due to an increase in demand. **[LO 5.5]**

11. When the price of gasoline was very high in the summer of 2008, several U.S. presidential candidates proposed implementing a national price ceiling to keep fuel affordable. How would this policy have affected producer and consumer surplus? How would it have affected total surplus? **[LO 5.6]**

12. Consider a policy to help struggling farmers by setting a minimum trade price for wheat. Will this be an effective way to increase their surplus? Explain. **[LO 5.6]**

13. If rent control creates deadweight loss for both consumers and suppliers of housing, why are consumers often in favor of this policy? **[LO 5.7]**

14. Suppose price is 5 percent above equilibrium in two markets: a market for a necessity and a market for a luxury good. All else equal (including supply conditions), in which market do you expect deadweight loss to be greater? Explain. **[LO 5.7]**

15. Your grandmother likes old-fashioned yard sales and doesn't understand why everyone is so excited about eBay. Explain to her why the creation of a market that enables people who don't live in the same town to buy and sell used goods increases total surplus over the yard-sale market. [LO 5.8]

16. At Zooey's elementary school, children are not allowed to trade lunches or components of their lunches with other students. Lunchroom monitors watch closely and strictly enforce this policy. Help Zooey make an argument about the inefficiency of this policy to her principal. [LO 5.8]

Problems and Applications

1. Use the information in Table 5P-1 to construct a step graph of the six consumers' willingness to pay. [LO 5.1]

TABLE 5P-1

Buyer	Willingness to pay for one unit ($)
Fadel	8
Ann	2
Morgan	16
Andre	12
Carla	2
Hanson	4

2. Use the information in Table 5P-2 to construct a step graph of the six sellers' willingness to sell. [LO 5.1]

TABLE 5P-2

Seller	Willingness to sell one unit ($)
Joseph	25
Juan	20
Kristin	60
Peter	10
Candice	25
Solomon	50

3. Answer the following questions based on Tables 5P-3 and 5P-4. [LO 5.1]
    a. What is the quantity demanded at $10? What is the quantity supplied at $10?
    b. What is the quantity demanded at $25? What is the quantity supplied at $25?

4. Based on Table 5P-5, calculate consumer surplus for each consumer when the price is $17. What is the total consumer surplus at this price? [LO 5.2]

TABLE 5P-3

Buyer	A	B	C	D	E	F	G	H	I
Willingness to pay for one unit	$35	$33	$27	$22	$21	$13	$13	$12	$6

TABLE 5P-4

Seller	A	B	C	D	E	F	G	H	I
Willingness to sell for one unit	$4	$9	$12	$14	$15	$21	$23	$30	$51

TABLE 5P-5

Buyer	A	B	C	D	E	F	G	H	I
Willingness to pay for one unit	$6	$27	$13	$21	$33	$35	$12	$13	$22

5. Use the demand curve represented in Figure 5P-1 to draw the consumer surplus when the market price is $8. What is the value of consumer surplus at this price? **[LO 5.2]**

FIGURE 5P-1

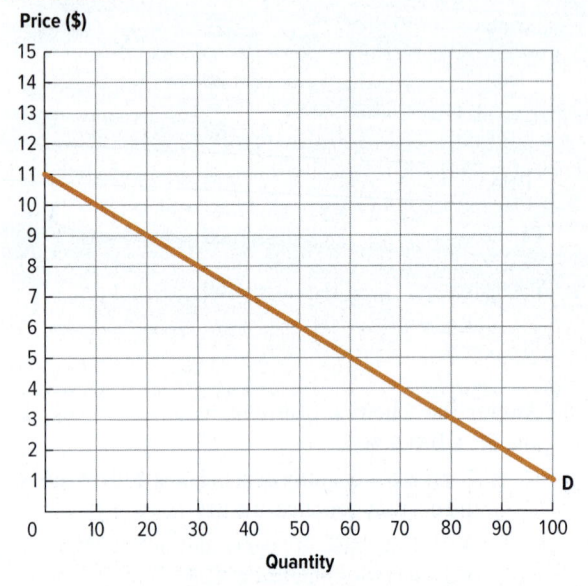

6. Based on Figure 5P-2, consumer surplus is $0 when price is greater than or equal to what price? **[LO 5.2]**

FIGURE 5P-2

7. Use the market represented in Figure 5P-2 to plot the equilibrium price and quantity and to draw the consumer surplus when the market is in equilibrium. What is the value of consumer surplus at the equilibrium price? **[LO 5.2]**

8. Use the market represented in Figure 5P-2 to draw the consumer surplus when the price is $5. What is the value of consumer surplus at this price? **[LO 5.2]**

9. Based on Figure 5P-2, producer surplus is $0 when price is less than or equal to what price? **[LO 5.3]**

10. Use the market represented in Figure 5P-2 to plot the equilibrium price and quantity and to draw the producer surplus when the market is in equilibrium. What is the value of producer surplus at the equilibrium price? **[LO 5.3]**

11. Use the market represented in Figure 5P-2 to draw the producer surplus if the price is $9. What is the value of producer surplus at this price? **[LO 5.3]**

12. Based on Table 5P-6, calculate producer surplus for each producer when the price is $20. What is total producer surplus at this price? **[LO 5.3]**

13. Use the supply curve represented in Figure 5P-3 to draw the producer surplus when the market price is $5. What is the value of producer surplus at this price? **[LO 5.3]**

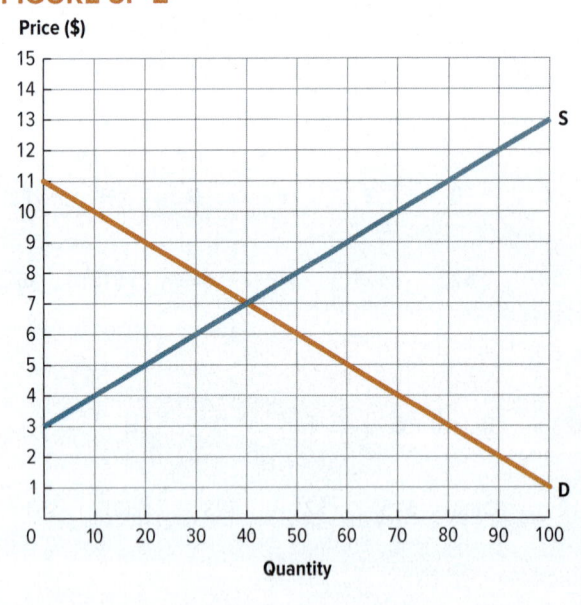

FIGURE 5P-3

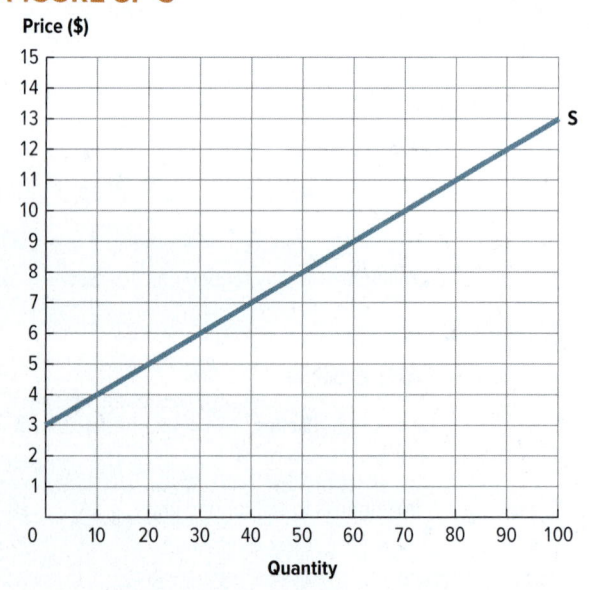

TABLE 5P-6

Buyer	A	B	C	D	E	F	G	H	I
Willingness to pay for one unit	$21	$4	$30	$14	$12	$15	$51	$9	$23

14. Use the market represented in Figure 5P-4 to draw the consumer and producer surplus when the market is in equilibrium. What is the value of total surplus at equilibrium? **[LO 5.4]**

FIGURE 5P-4

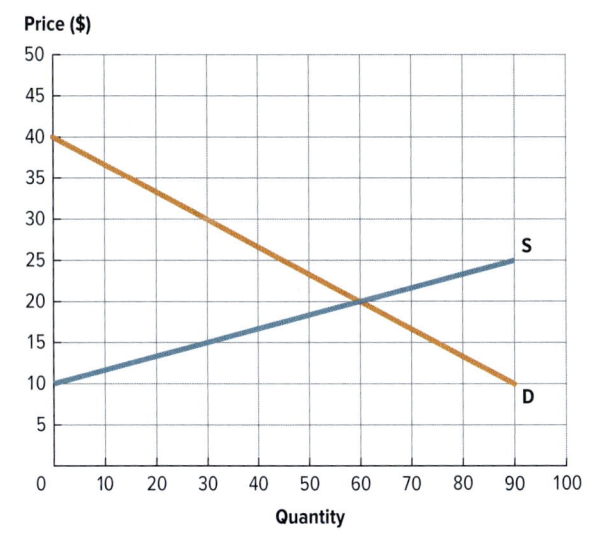

Price ($)

15. Consider the market represented in Figure 5P-5. **[LO 5.4]**

FIGURE 5P-5

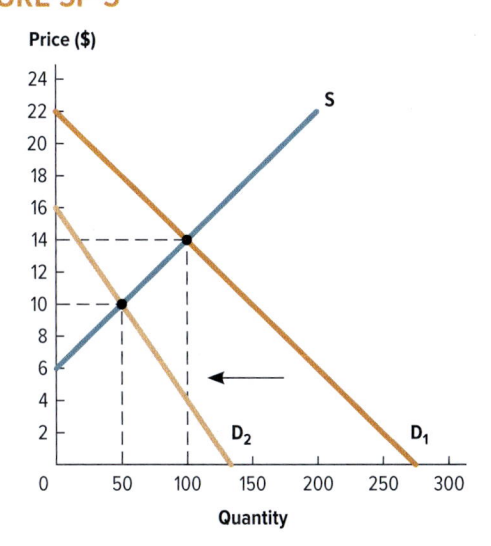

Price ($)

a. Calculate total surplus when demand is D_1.
b. Calculate total surplus when demand decreases to D_2.

16. Consider the market represented in Figure 5P-6. **[LO 5.4]**

FIGURE 5P-6

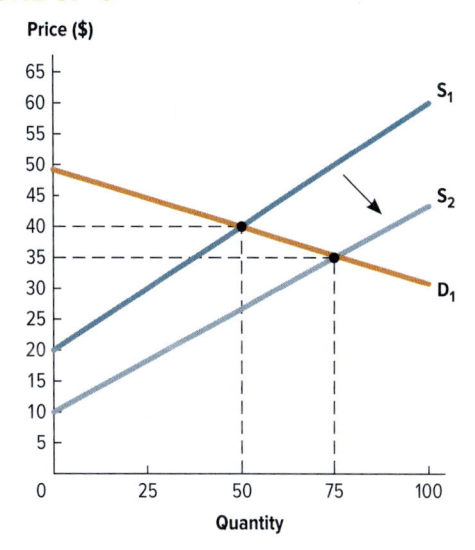

Price ($)

a. Calculate total surplus when supply is S_1.
b. Calculate total surplus when supply increases to S_2.

17. Consider the market represented in Figure 5P-7. **[LO 5.5]**

FIGURE 5P-7

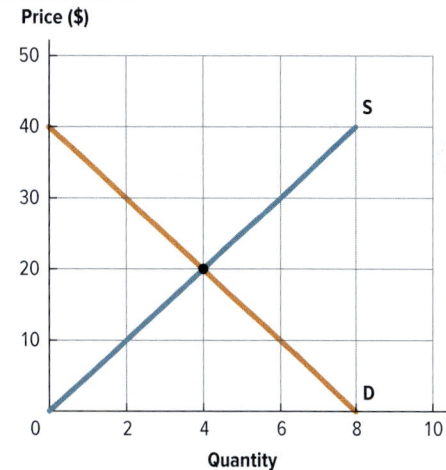

Price ($)

a. Draw the consumer surplus and the producer surplus at the equilibrium price and quantity. What is the value of total surplus at equilibrium?
b. Draw the consumer surplus and the producer surplus if the price is $30. What are the values of consumer surplus, producer surplus, and total surplus at this price?
c. Draw the consumer surplus and the producer surplus if the price is $10. What are the values of consumer surplus, producer surplus, and total surplus at this price?

18. Assume the market for wine is functioning at its equilibrium. For each of the following situations, say whether the new market outcome will be *efficient* or *inefficient*. **[LO 5.5]**

    a. A new report shows that wine is good for heart health.
    b. The government sets a minimum price for wine, which increases the current price.
    c. An unexpected late frost ruins large crops of grapes.
    d. Grape pickers demand higher wages, increasing the price of wine.

19. Based on Figure 5P-8, choose all of the following options that are true. **[LO 5.5, 5.6]**

FIGURE 5P-8

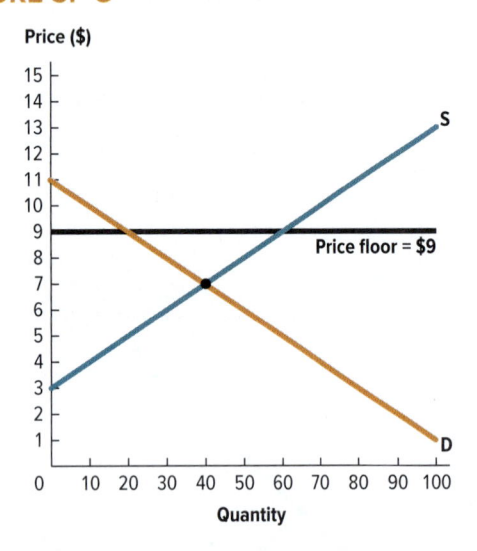

a. The market is efficient.
b. Total surplus is higher than it would be at market equilibrium.
c. Total surplus is lower than it would be at market equilibrium.
d. Producer surplus is lower than it would be at market equilibrium.
e. Consumer surplus is lower than it would be at market equilibrium.

20. In which of the following situations can you say, without further information, that consumer surplus decreases relative to the market equilibrium level? **[LO 5.6]**

    a. Your state passes a law that pushes the interest rate (i.e., the price) for payday loans below the equilibrium rate.
    b. The federal government enforces a law that raises the price of dairy goods above the equilibrium.
    c. Your city passes a local property tax, under which buyers of new houses have to pay an additional 5 percent on top of the purchase price.
    d. The government lowers the effective price of food purchases through a food-stamp program.

21. Use the areas labeled in the market represented in Figure 5P-9 to answer the following questions. **[LO 5.6]**

FIGURE 5P-9

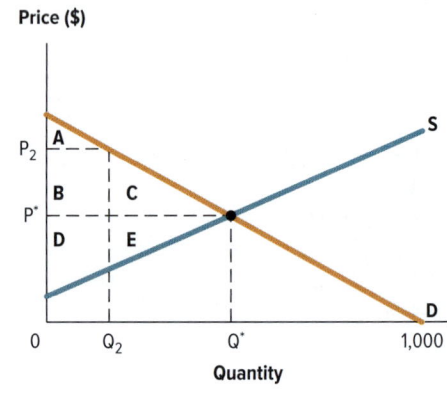

a. What area(s) are consumer surplus at the market equilibrium price?
b. What area(s) are producer surplus at the market equilibrium price?
c. Compared to the equilibrium, what area(s) do consumers lose if price is P_2?
d. Compared to the equilibrium, what area(s) do producers lose if the price is P_2?
e. Compared to the equilibrium, what area(s) do producers gain if the price is P_2?
f. Compared to the equilibrium, total surplus decreases by what area(s) if the price is P_2?

22. Figure 5P-10 shows a market for cotton, with the price held at $0.80 per pound. Draw and calculate the deadweight loss caused by this policy. **[LO 5.7]**

FIGURE 5P-10

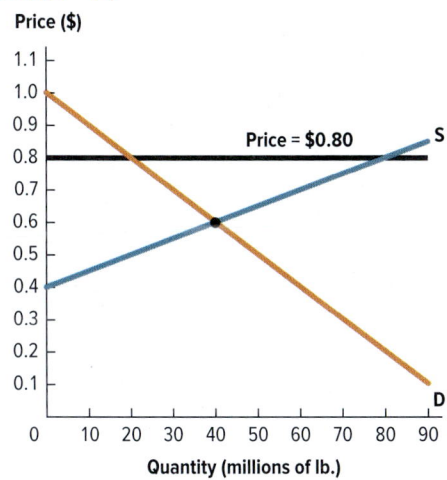

Price ($) vs Quantity (millions of lb.) graph showing supply and demand curves with equilibrium at approximately (40, $0.60) and a horizontal line at Price = $0.80.

23. Consider the market represented in Figure 5P-11. **[LO 5.7]**

FIGURE 5P-11

Price ($) vs Quantity graph showing supply and demand curves with equilibrium at (24, $20).

a. Suppose the government sets a minimum price of $25 in the market. Calculate the deadweight loss.
b. Suppose the government sets a maximum price of $25 in the market. Calculate the deadweight loss.

24. What is the value of the existence of the market represented in Figure 5P-12? **[LO 5.8]**

FIGURE 5P-12

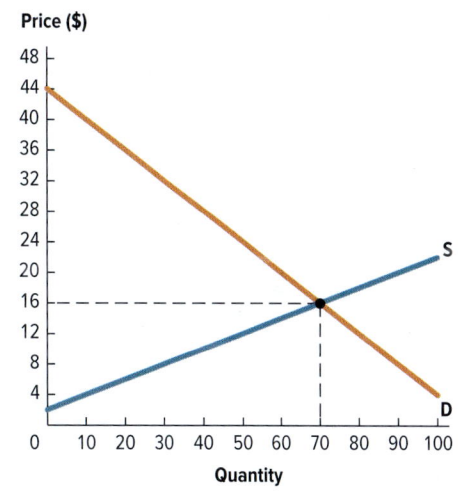

Price ($) vs Quantity graph showing supply and demand curves with equilibrium at (70, $16).

25. We can consider the market for traveling to Mars to be missing because no technology exists that allows this service to be bought and sold. Suppose that someone has invented space-travel technology that will enable this service to be provided. Figure 5P-13 shows the estimated market for trips to Mars. Calculate the surplus that could be generated by filling in this missing market. **[LO 5.8]**

FIGURE 5P-13

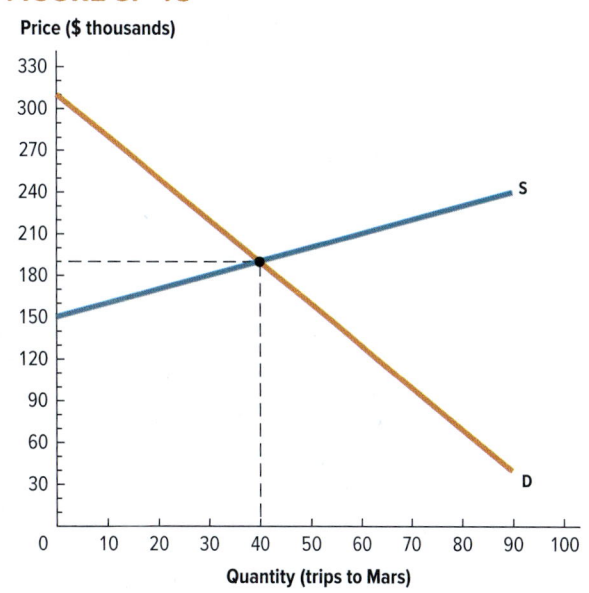

Price ($ thousands) vs Quantity (trips to Mars) graph showing supply and demand curves with equilibrium at (40, $190).

Endnotes

1. https://www.ebayinc.com/stories/news/ebay-inc-reports-fourth-quarter-and-full-year-2017-results/
2. http://news.bbc.co.uk/2/hi/4034787.stm

Math Essentials: The Area under a Linear Curve

Appendix D

Chapter 5 introduced you to the concept of surplus. Surplus measures the gains or losses in well-being resulting from transactions in a market. You will often need to calculate a numerical value for surplus. To do that, you need to know how to find the area under a linear curve, and, therefore, we will review a little geometry.

LEARNING OBJECTIVES

LO D.1 Calculate surplus by finding the area under a linear curve.

The Area under a Linear Curve

Graphically, surplus is represented as the area between a supply or demand curve and the market price. The area between these curves and the market price will take the form of a triangle. In order to find surplus, you are going to need to be able to calculate the area of a triangle:

LO D.1 Calculate surplus by finding the area under a linear curve.

EQUATION D-1

$$\text{Area of triangle} = \frac{1}{2} \times \text{Base of triangle} \times \text{Height of triangle} = \frac{1}{2}bh$$

The key, then, is to figure which length to use as the base and which as the height.

In panel A of Figure D-1, consumer surplus is the shaded triangle below the demand curve and above the market price. The base of this triangle is the *horizontal distance* from the equilibrium point to the y-axis, $(12 - 0) = 12$. The height is the *vertical distance* from the equilibrium price to the y-intercept of the demand curve, $(50 - 20) = 30$. Therefore, the area of the triangle—and the consumer surplus—is:

$$\frac{1}{2} \times (12 \times 30) = \$180$$

Producer surplus is the shaded area below the market price and above the supply curve in panel B of Figure D-1. The base of the triangle is again the *horizontal distance* from the equilibrium point to the y-axis, $(12 - 0) = 12$. The height is the vertical distance from the equilibrium price to the

128A

FIGURE D-1
Measuring the area under a curve

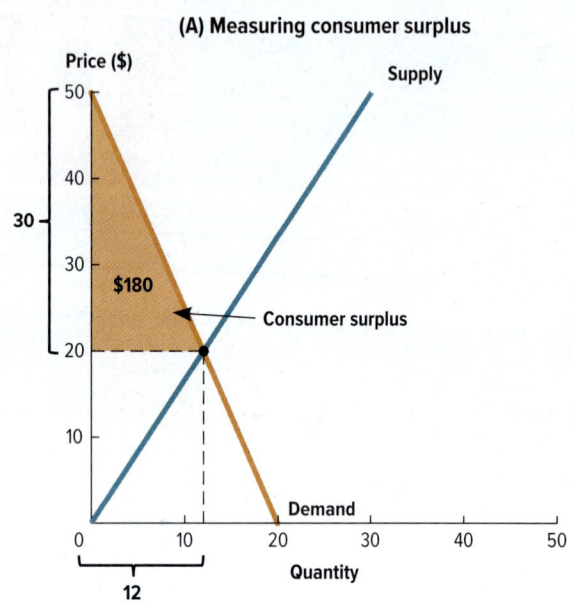

(A) Measuring consumer surplus

(B) Measuring producer surplus

Consumer surplus is found by taking the area of the triangle above the market price and below the demand curve.

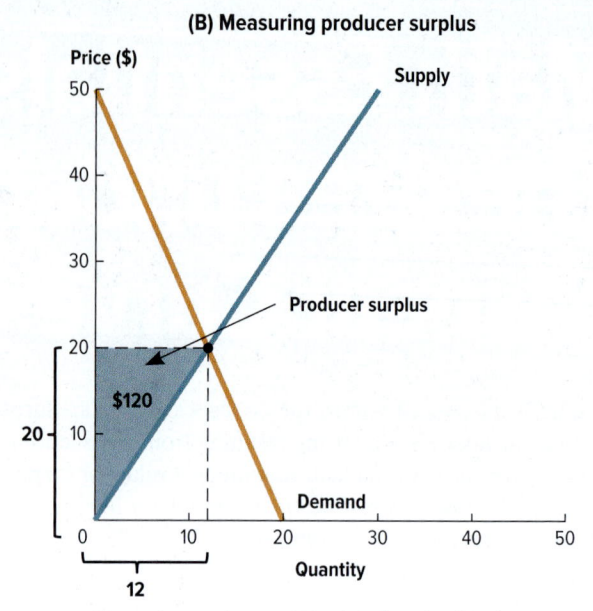

Measuring producer surplus, on the other hand, is found by taking the area of the triangle below the market price and above the supply curve.

y-intercept of the supply curve, $(20 - 0) = 20$. Therefore the area of the triangle—and the producer surplus—is:

$$\frac{1}{2} \times (12 \times 20) = \$120$$

You learned in Chapter 5 that total surplus is consumer surplus plus producer surplus:

$$\text{Total surplus} = \$180 + \$120 = \$300$$

We can also calculate total surplus directly by calculating the area of the larger triangle that encompasses both. This time, the calculation of this triangle is slightly different. The base is the amount of space in between the *y*-intercept of the supply and demand curves. This gives a base of 50. The height of the triangle, on the other hand, is the distance from the *y*-axis to the equilibrium point. The area is thus $\frac{1}{2} \times 50 \times 12 = \$300$, the same result as before.

Occasionally, you will see oddly shaped surplus areas. You can always calculate these by breaking them down into familiar rectangles and triangles. Then calculate the area of each using length times width (for a rectangle) and $\frac{1}{2}bh$ (for a triangle), and add the results to find the total area.

Problems and Applications

1. Use the graph in Figure DP-1 to answer the following questions. [LO D.1]
   a. What is the amount of consumer surplus?
   b. What is the amount of producer surplus?
   c. What is the amount of total surplus?

FIGURE DP-1

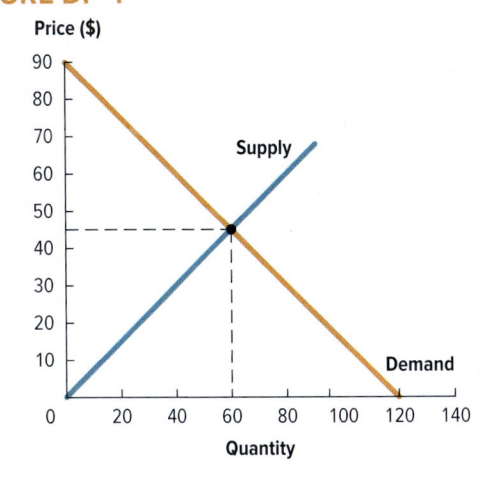

2. Use these two supply and demand equations to answer the following questions. [LO D.1]

$$P = 50 - 4Q$$
$$P = 2 + 2Q$$

   a. What is the equilibrium price? What is the equilibrium quantity?
   b. Draw a graph of supply and demand and illustrate the equilibrium.
   c. What is the amount of consumer surplus?
   d. What is the amount of producer surplus?
   e. What is the amount of total surplus?

Chapter 6

Government Intervention

Feeding the World, One Price Control at a Time

In the spring of 2008, a worldwide food shortage caused food prices to skyrocket. In just a few months, the prices of wheat, rice, and corn shot up as much as 140 percent. In the United States, the number of people living on food stamps rose to the highest level since the 1960s. By June, low-income Americans were facing tough choices, as the prices of basics like eggs and dairy products rose. Some reported giving up meat and fresh fruit; others said they began to buy cheap food past the expiration date.[1]

Rising food prices caused trouble all over the world. The *Economist* magazine reported on the political fallout:

©Abdurashid Abdulleaf/AFP/Getty Images

> [In Côte d'Ivoire,] two days of violence persuaded the government to postpone planned elections.... In Haiti, protesters chanting "We're hungry" forced the prime minister to resign; 24 people were killed in riots in Cameroon; Egypt's president ordered the army to start baking bread; [and] the Philippines made hoarding rice punishable by life imprisonment.[2]

Faced with hunger, hardship, and angry outbursts, many governments felt obliged to respond to the crisis. But what to do? Responses varied widely. Many countries made it illegal to charge

129

high prices for food. Other countries subsidized the price of basic necessities. In the United States, Congress passed a farm bill that increased the amount of money low-income families received to buy food. Were these responses appropriate? What, if anything, *should* governments do in such a situation?

Food is a tricky issue for policy-makers because it's a basic necessity. If prices rise too high, people go hungry. If prices fall too low, farmers go out of business, which raises the risk of food shortages in the future. So, while policy-makers aren't too concerned if the prices of many goods—like digital cameras or lattes—jump up and down, they often do care about food prices. But attempts to lower, raise, or simply stabilize prices can backfire or create unintended side effects. Sometimes the cure ends up being worse than the problem itself.

LEARNING OBJECTIVES

LO 6.1 Calculate the effect of a price ceiling on the equilibrium price and quantity.

LO 6.2 Calculate the effect of a price floor on the equilibrium price and quantity.

LO 6.3 Calculate the effect of a tax on the equilibrium price and quantity.

LO 6.4 Calculate the effect of a subsidy on the equilibrium price and quantity.

LO 6.5 Explain how elasticity and time period influence the impact of a market intervention.

In this chapter, we'll look at the logic behind policies that governments commonly use to intervene in markets. There are often both intended and unintended consequences—and economic models and data can help think through both. We will start with *price controls*, which make it illegal to sell a good for more or less than a certain price. Then we will look at *taxes* and *subsidies*, which discourage or encourage the production of particular goods. These tools are regularly applied to a broad range of issues, from unemployment to home ownership, air pollution to education. For better or worse, they have a huge effect on our lives as workers, consumers, businesspeople, and voters.

Why Intervene?

In Chapter 3, "Markets," we saw that markets gravitate toward equilibrium. When markets work well, prices adjust until the quantity of a good that consumers demand equals the quantity that suppliers want to produce. At equilibrium, everyone gets what he or she is willing to pay for. In Chapter 5, "Efficiency," we saw that equilibrium price and quantity also maximize total surplus. At equilibrium, there is no way to make some people better off without harming others.

So, why intervene? Why not let the invisible hand of the market determine prices and allocate resources? Some would argue that's exactly what should be done. Others believe the government has to intervene sometimes—and the fact is that every single government in the world intervenes in markets in some fashion.

Three reasons to intervene

The arguments for intervention fall into three categories: changing the distribution of surplus, encouraging or discouraging consumption of certain goods, and correcting market failures. As we discuss different policy tools throughout the chapter, ask yourself which of these motivations is driving the intervention.

Changing the distribution of surplus Efficient markets maximize total surplus, but an efficient outcome may still be seen as unfair. For example, even if the job market is efficient, wages can still drop so low that some workers fall below the poverty line while their employers make healthy profits. In such cases, some may argue for intervention in markets in order to change the distribution of surplus. The government might respond by intervening in the labor market to impose a minimum wage. This policy will change the distribution of surplus, reducing employers' profits (which may lead to higher prices) and lifting workers' incomes.

Of course, the definition of fairness is up for debate. Reasonable people can—and often do—argue about whether a policy that benefits a certain group (such as minimum-wage workers) is justified or not. Our focus will be on accurately describing the benefits and costs of such policies. Economics can help us predict whose well-being will increase, whose well-being will decrease, and who may be affected in unpredictable ways.

Encouraging or discouraging consumption
Around the world, many people judge certain products to be "good" or "bad" based on culture, health, religion, or other values. At the extreme, certain "bad" products are banned, such as many addictive drugs.

More often, governments use taxes to discourage people from consuming "bad" products, rather than simply banning them. Common examples are cigarettes and alcohol. Furthermore, in some cases consumption of a good imposes costs on others, such as second-hand smoke from cigarettes. In such cases the government may add a tax so that consumers or producers of the good have to pay more of the cost to society of consuming or producing that good. (Figuring out exactly what that cost is can be quite difficult, by the way.)

On the other hand, governments use *subsidies* to encourage people to consume "good" products or services. For instance, many governments provide public funding for schools to encourage education and for vaccinations to encourage parents to protect their children against disease.

Correcting market failures
Our model of demand and supply has so far assumed that markets work efficiently. In the real world, though, that's not always true. For example, sometimes there is only one producer of a good, who faces no competition and can charge an inefficiently high price. In other cases, one person's use of a product or service imposes costs on other people that are not captured in prices paid by the first person; an example is the pollution that others experience when smoke is ejected by your car (that is, the price you pay for the gas that is burned in your car imposes a cost on others when they must experience the pollution).

Situations in which the assumption of efficient, competitive markets fails to hold are called **market failures**. When there is a market failure, intervention can actually increase total surplus. We'll have much more to say about market failures in future chapters. In this chapter, we will stick to analyzing the effect of government interventions in efficient, competitive markets.

market failures situations in which the assumption of efficient, competitive markets fails to hold

Four real-world interventions

In this chapter we'll look at four real-world examples of how governments have intervened or could intervene in the market for food. For each, we'll consider the motives for the intervention and what its direct and indirect consequences were or could be. These four interventions are:

1. For many Mexican families, tortillas are an important food. What happened when the Mexican government set a *maximum price* for tortillas, in an effort to keep them affordable?
2. To ensure supplies of fresh milk, the U.S. government wanted to protect dairy farmers. What happened when the government set a *minimum price* for milk?
3. Many Americans struggle with health problems caused by overeating and poor nutrition. Several states have responded by banning the use of certain fats in food products; others require that restaurants post nutritional information about the foods they serve. What would happen if governments *taxed* high-fat or high-calorie foods?
4. What would happen if, instead of setting a maximum price for tortillas, the Mexican government *subsidized* tortillas?

As we walk through these examples of real policies, we want you to apply both positive and normative analysis. Remember the difference:

- *Positive analysis* is about facts: Does the policy actually accomplish the original goal?
- *Normative analysis* is a matter of values and opinions: Do you think the policy is a good idea?

Few policies are all good or all bad. The key question is, *What are the trade-offs* involved in the intervention? Do the benefits outweigh the costs?

✓ TEST YOURSELF

☐ What are three reasons that a government might want to intervene in markets?

Price Controls

Suppose you are an economic policy advisor, and food prices are rising. What should you do? If you live in a region with many low-income consumers, you might want to take action to ensure that everyone gets enough to eat. One policy tool you might consider using is a **price control**—a regulation that sets a maximum or minimum legal price for a particular good. The direct effect of a price control is to hold the price of a good up or down when the market shifts, thus preventing the market from reaching a new equilibrium.

Price controls can be divided into two opposing categories: *price ceilings* and *price floors*. We met this idea already in Chapter 5, "Efficiency," when we imagined an interfering eBay manager setting prices for digital cameras. In reality, eBay would never do such a thing, but governments often do, particularly when it comes to markets for food items. What are the effects of using price controls to intervene in a well-functioning, competitive market?

price control a regulation that sets a maximum or minimum legal price for a particular good

Price ceilings

A **price ceiling** is a maximum legal price at which a good can be sold. Many countries have price ceilings on staple foods, gasoline, and electricity because policy-makers try to ensure everyone can afford the basic necessities.

Here, we come to the first of the real-world interventions in the chapter: Historically, the government of Mexico has set a price ceiling for tortillas. The intent is to guarantee that this staple food will remain affordable. Panel A of Figure 6-1 illustrates a hypothetical market for tortillas without a price ceiling. The equilibrium price is $0.50 per pound and the equilibrium quantity is 50 million pounds.

Let's say that the government of Mexico responded to rising tortilla prices by setting a price ceiling of approximately $0.25 per pound, as shown in panel B of Figure 6-1. How would we expect consumers and producers to respond to this intervention?

LO 6.1 Calculate the effect of a price ceiling on the equilibrium price and quantity.

price ceiling a maximum legal price at which a good can be sold

- When the price falls, consumers will want to buy more tortillas. In this example, the price fell from $0.50 to $0.25, and as a result, quantity demanded increased from 50 million to 75 million pounds.
- Predictably, a lower price means fewer producers will be willing to supply tortillas. In this example, when the price fell to $0.25, the quantity supplied dropped from 50 million to 25 million pounds.

The lower price imposed by the price ceiling means higher quantity demanded but lower quantity supplied. Supply and demand were no longer in equilibrium. The price ceiling created a *shortage* of tortillas, equal to the 50-million-pound difference between the quantity demanded (75 million) and the quantity supplied (25 million).

FIGURE 6-1

A market with and without a price ceiling

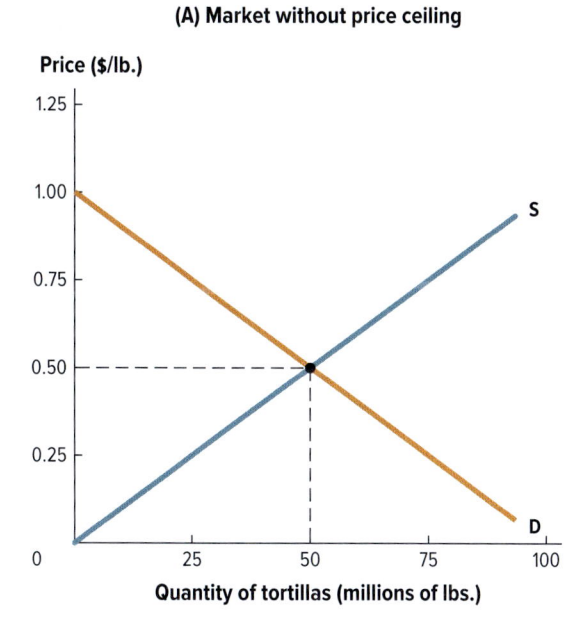

(A) Market without price ceiling

Without government intervention, the market for tortillas in Mexico would reach equilibrium at a price of $0.50 per pound and a quantity of 50 million pounds.

(B) Market with price ceiling

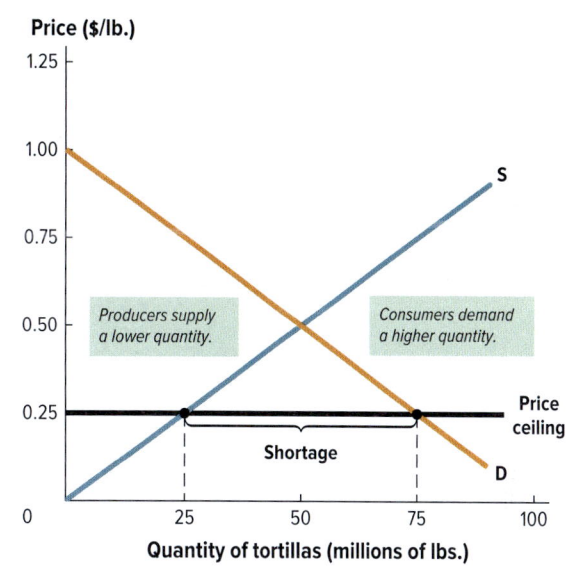

Producers supply a lower quantity.

Consumers demand a higher quantity.

After government intervention, a price ceiling of $0.25 keeps the price of tortillas below the equilibrium point. At this new price, consumers want to buy more tortillas (75 million pounds) than producers want to supply (25 million pounds), resulting in a shortage of tortillas.

Did the price ceiling meet the goal of providing low-priced tortillas to consumers? Yes and no. Consumers were able to buy *some* tortillas at the low price of $0.25 a pound—but they *wanted* to buy three times as many tortillas as producers were willing to supply.

We can assess the full effect of the price ceiling by looking at what happened to consumer and producer surplus. Even without looking at the graph, we already know that a price ceiling will cause producer surplus to fall: Sellers are selling fewer tortillas at a lower price.

We also know that total surplus—that is, producer and consumer surplus combined—will fall because the market has moved away from equilibrium. Some trades that would have happened at the equilibrium price do not happen. Also, the surplus that would have been generated by those mutually beneficial trades is lost entirely. This area is known as *deadweight loss* and is represented by area 1 in Figure 6-2.

As discussed in Chapter 5, "Efficiency," **deadweight loss** represents the loss of total surplus that occurs because the quantity of a good that is bought and sold is below the market equilibrium quantity. Economists refer to changes in the economic well-being of market participants, as measured by changes in consumer surplus or producer surplus like deadweight loss, as *welfare effects*.

What we can't tell without looking at the graph is whether consumer surplus will increase or decrease; that response depends on the shape of the supply and demand curves. In this instance, consumers lose surplus from trades that no longer take place (from the 25 million pounds of tortillas no longer supplied). But for the trades that still do take place, consumers gain surplus from paying $0.25 instead of $0.50. In those trades, producers lose the same amount of surplus from receiving the lower price. This direct transfer of surplus from producers to consumers is represented by area 2 (the cross-hatched area) in Figure 6-2.

deadweight loss
a loss of total surplus that occurs because the quantity of a good that is bought and sold is below the market equilibrium quantity

FIGURE 6-2
Welfare effects of a price ceiling

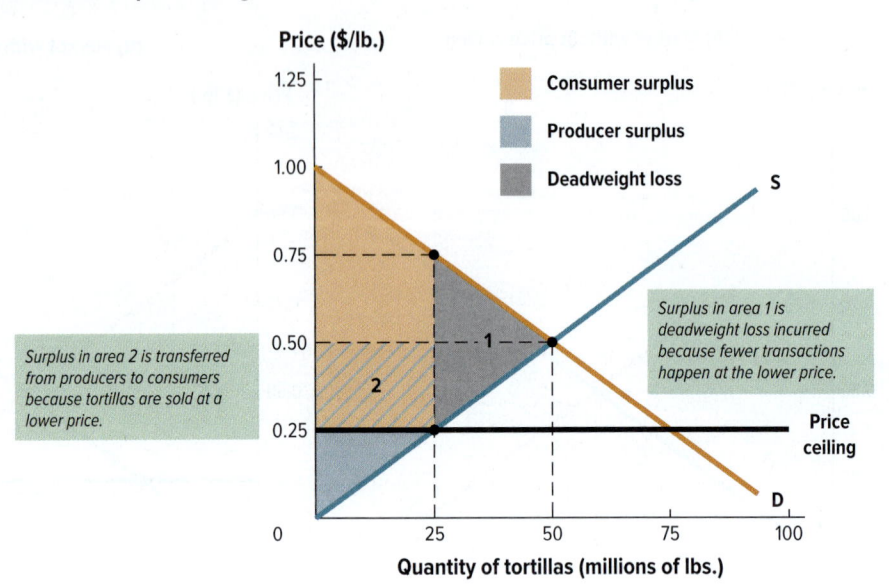

Surplus in area 2 is transferred from producers to consumers because tortillas are sold at a lower price.

Surplus in area 1 is deadweight loss incurred because fewer transactions happen at the lower price.

The price ceiling causes the total quantity of tortillas traded to fall by 25 million (from equilibrium at 50 million to 25 million). This results in deadweight loss. The price ceiling also causes surplus to be transferred from producers to consumers: Consumers win because they pay a lower price, and producers lose because they sell at a lower price ($0.25 instead of $0.50).

Did consumer surplus increase or decrease? Because area 2 in Figure 6-2 is larger than half of area 1 (the portion of deadweight loss that would have gone to consumers at equilibrium), we know that the intended goal of the price ceiling was achieved: a net increase in the well-being of consumers.

Was the policy worthwhile? On the one hand, consumers gained surplus. On the other hand, the surplus lost by producers was greater than that gained by consumers, meaning that total surplus decreased. Is it a price worth paying? That is a normative question about which reasonable people can disagree.

Another factor we may want to consider in our overall analysis of the price ceiling is how the scarce tortillas are allocated. Because a price ceiling causes a shortage, goods must be rationed. Rationing could be done in a number of ways:

- One possibility is for goods to be rationed equally, with each family entitled to buy the same amount of tortillas per week. This is what happened when food was rationed in the United States during World War II.
- Another possibility is to allocate goods on a first-come, first-served basis. This mode of rationing forces people to waste time standing in lines.
- In still other cases, rationed goods might go to those who are given preference by the government, or to the friends and family of sellers.
- Finally, shortages open the door for people to bribe whoever is in charge of allocating scarce supplies. Rationing via bribery results in even more deadweight loss than in the example shown in Figure 6-2. Economists call this *rent-seeking behavior*, and it is often cited as an argument against imposing price ceilings.

The What Do You Think? box "Put a cap on payday lending?" asks you to weigh the costs and benefits of a controversial price ceiling on the interest rates of payday loans.

Put a cap on payday lending?
What Do You Think?

Imagine the following scenario: You are on the way to work and your car breaks down, leaving you stranded on the side of the road. Soon, you are looking at a $300 bill for the tow truck and a new alternator. Coming up with $300 will be tough, and to make things worse, it's Monday and payday is a week away.

When faced with this type of emergency, some turn to a *payday loan,* a short-term cash loan of less than $1,000 that is intended to be repaid with the borrower's next paycheck. Many borrowers like these loans because they are quick (most centers will give you cash in 30 minutes or less) and convenient (in the United States, payday loan centers outnumber McDonald's).

Rather than charging interest rates, payday loan centers usually charge borrowers a "fee" in exchange for cash. For example, a 14-day loan of $300 might cost $35 in fees. That may not sound like a lot, but when calculated as an annual interest rate, it works out to over 300 percent. (For comparison, credit cards charge interest rates of about 20 percent.) Not only that, the loan comes due at the borrower's next paycheck, which may also be needed for food, gas, or rent. Failing to repay the $300 loan would require taking out a new loan of $335 and paying more fees. Many have a hard time finding enough money to break the cycle.

Citing these dangers, 14 states and the District of Columbia have banned payday loans altogether. Many more states have set caps on fees or the interest rate that lenders can charge. In economic terms, these caps constitute a price ceiling on payday loans. As with other price ceilings, decisions to cap interest rates and fees are controversial.

Supporters of greater regulation argue that limiting fees protects vulnerable consumers from "predatory" lenders who offer loans people can't afford. Payday lenders argue that their loans serve a real need.

Let's go back to the opening example of a broken-down car. If the car was the only way to get to work, failing to come up with $300 would mean losing your job. In that case, you might be happy to pay $35 in fees. Instead of protecting consumers, putting low caps on fees could drive some payday lenders out of business, hurting consumers who make informed decisions.

WHAT DO YOU THINK?

1. Considering that there are other ways to get money quickly, including credit cards, banks, or friends, can you think of a situation that would require visiting a payday loan center? Why might you not want to take advantage of the other ways? Can you think of "hidden" costs?
2. Price ceilings hold down interest rates and transfer surplus to consumers, but they also reduce the number of transactions that occur in a market. How would you determine whether price ceilings on payday loans are worth the cost?
3. Instead of implementing price caps, some states restrict the number of loans a borrower can take at a time or require that borrowers wait 24 hours (called a "cool-down" period) before taking out a new loan. Researchers Marianne Bertrand and Adair Morse found that providing customers with more information about the cost of loans decreased the amount and frequency of borrowing. How do you feel about these policies relative to a price ceiling?

Sources: Marianne Bertrand and Adair Morse, "Information disclosure, cognitive biases, and payday lending," *Journal of American Finance* 66, no. 6 (December 2011), pp. 1865–1863; "Payday lending state statutes," *National Conference of State Legislatures,* January 28, 2018, www.ncsl.org/research/financial-services-and-commerce/payday-lending-state-statutes.aspx

FIGURE 6-3
Nonbinding price ceiling

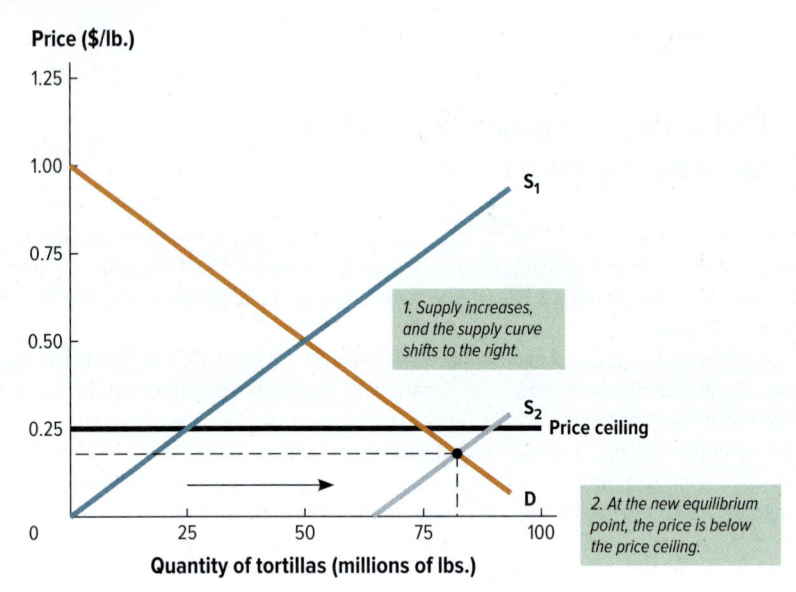

1. Supply increases, and the supply curve shifts to the right.

2. At the new equilibrium point, the price is below the price ceiling.

A price ceiling is intended to keep prices below the equilibrium level. However, changes in the market can reduce the equilibrium price to a level below the price ceiling. When that happens, the price ceiling no longer creates a shortage because the quantity supplied equals the quantity demanded.

Nonbinding price ceilings A price ceiling does not always affect the market outcome. If the ceiling is set above the equilibrium price in a market, it is said to be *nonbinding*. That is, the ceiling doesn't "bind" or restrict buyers' and sellers' behavior because the current equilibrium is within the range allowed by the ceiling. In such cases, the equilibrium price and quantity will prevail.

Price ceilings are usually binding when they are first implemented. (Otherwise, why bother to create one?) Over time, though, shifts in the market can render the ceilings nonbinding. Suppose the price of corn decreases, reducing the cost of making tortillas. Figure 6-3 shows how the supply curve for tortillas would shift to the right (from S_1 to S_2) in response to this change in the market (a change in the price of inputs). This shift causes the equilibrium price to fall below the price ceiling. The new equilibrium is 80 million pounds of tortillas at $0.20 a pound, and the price ceiling becomes nonbinding.

Price floors

LO 6.2 Calculate the effect of a price floor on the equilibrium price and quantity.

price floor a minimum legal price at which a good can be sold

A **price floor** is a minimum legal price at which a good can be sold. The United States has a long history of establishing price floors for certain agricultural goods. The rationale is that farming is a risky business—subject to bad weather, crop failure, and unreliable prices—but also an essential one, if people are to have enough to eat. A price floor is seen as a way to guarantee farmers a minimum income in the face of these difficulties, keeping them in business and ensuring a reliable supply of food.

We now come to the second of our four real-world interventions: The United States has maintained price floors for dairy products for over 65 years; the Milk Price Support Program began with the Agricultural Act of 1949. What effect has this program had on the market for milk?

FIGURE 6-4

A market with and without a price floor

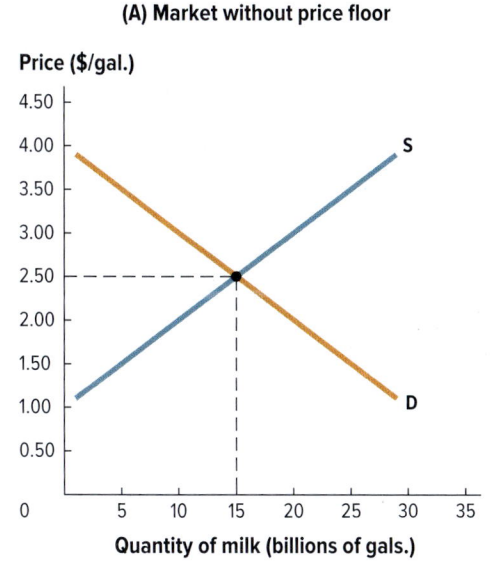

(A) Market without price floor

Without government intervention, the equilibrium point in the market for milk would be 15 billion gallons at a price of $2.50 per gallon.

(B) Market with price floor

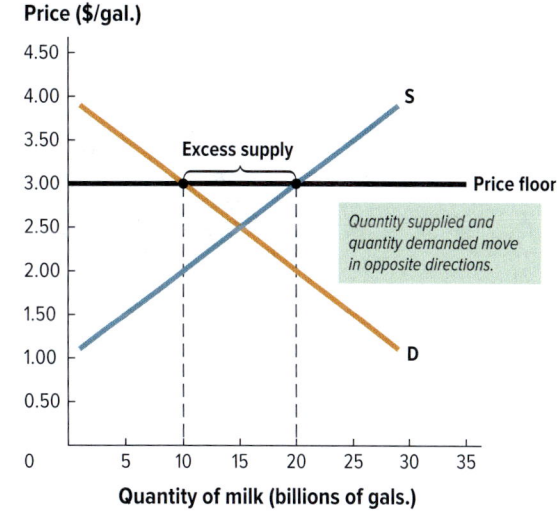

Quantity supplied and quantity demanded move in opposite directions.

A price floor raises the price of milk above the equilibrium point. At the new price of $3 per gallon, consumers want to buy less than suppliers want to produce, resulting in a 10-billion-gallon surplus.

In panel A of Figure 6-4, we show a hypothetical unregulated market for milk in the United States, with an annual equilibrium quantity of 15 billion gallons and an equilibrium price of $2.50 per gallon.

Now suppose the U.S. government implements a price floor, so that the price of milk cannot fall below $3 per gallon, as shown in panel B of Figure 6-4. How will producers and consumers respond?

- At $3 per gallon, dairy farmers will want to increase milk production from 15 to 20 billion gallons, moving up along the supply curve.
- At that price, however, consumers will want to decrease their milk consumption from 15 to 10 billion gallons, moving up along the demand curve.

As a result, the price floor creates an excess supply of milk that is equal to the difference between the quantity supplied and the quantity demanded—in this case, 10 billion gallons.

Has the government accomplished its aim of supporting dairy farmers and providing them with a reliable income? As with price ceilings, the answer is yes and no. Producers who can sell all their milk will be happy: They are selling more milk at a higher price. However, producers who cannot sell all their milk, because demand no longer meets supply, will be unhappy. Consumers will be unhappy because they are getting less milk at a higher price.

Again, we can apply the concept of surplus to formally analyze how this change in total surplus is distributed between consumers and producers. Before the price floor, 15 billion gallons of milk were supplied and bought; after the price floor, this number is only 10 billion. Five billion gallons of milk that could have been traded were not, reducing total surplus. This deadweight loss is represented by area 1 in Figure 6-5.

Like price ceilings, price floors change the distribution of surplus; in this case, producers win at the expense of consumers. When the price floor is in effect, the only consumers who buy are those whose willingness to pay is above $3. Their consumer surplus falls because they are buying

FIGURE 6-5
Welfare effects of a price floor

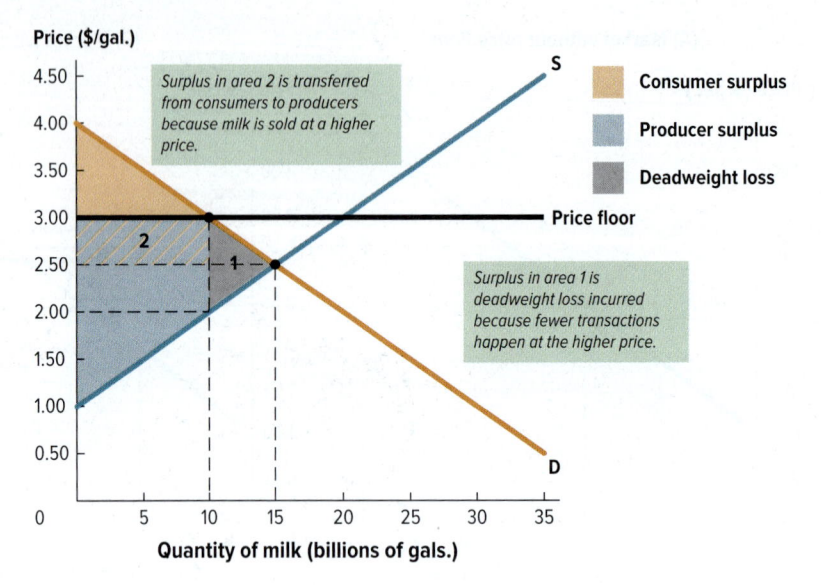

Surplus in area 2 is transferred from consumers to producers because milk is sold at a higher price.

Surplus in area 1 is deadweight loss incurred because fewer transactions happen at the higher price.

Legend: Consumer surplus, Producer surplus, Deadweight loss

The price floor causes the total quantity of milk traded to fall by 5 billion gallons relative to equilibrium. This results in deadweight loss. The price floor also causes surplus to be transferred from consumers to producers: In this example, producers win because they sell at a higher price, and consumers lose because they pay a higher price.

---

the same milk at a higher price. Consumers' lost surplus is transferred directly to the producers who sell milk to them. This transfer of consumer surplus is represented by area 2 (the cross-hatched area) in Figure 6-5.

Did producers gain or lose overall? The answer depends on whether the area of transferred consumer surplus is bigger or smaller than the producers' share of the deadweight loss. Area 2 (the transfer of consumer surplus) is larger than the section of area 1 lost to producers; in this case, the price floor policy increased well-being for producers.

Is the price of reduced total and consumer surplus worth paying to achieve increased producer surplus? One factor to consider is how the extra surplus is distributed among producers. Producers who are able to sell all their milk at the higher price will be happy. But producers who do not manage to sell all of their goods will be left holding an excess supply. They may be worse off than before the imposition of the price floor. With excess supply, customers may choose to buy from firms they like based on familiarity, political preference, or any other decision-making process they choose.

To prevent some producers from being left with excess supply, the government may decide to buy up all the excess supply of milk, ensuring that *all* producers benefit. In fact, that is how the milk price support program works in the United States. The Department of Agriculture guarantees producers that it will buy milk at a certain price, regardless of the market price. Of course, paying for the milk imposes a cost on taxpayers and is often cited as an argument against price floors. How much milk will the government have to buy? The answer is the entire amount of the excess supply created by the price floor. In the case of the hypothetical milk price floor, the government will have to buy 10 billion gallons at a price of $3. The cost to taxpayers of maintaining the price floor in this example would be $30 billion each year.

FIGURE 6-6
Nonbinding price floor

Price ($/gal.) vs Quantity of milk (billions of gals.)

2. At the new equilibrium point, the price is above the price ceiling.

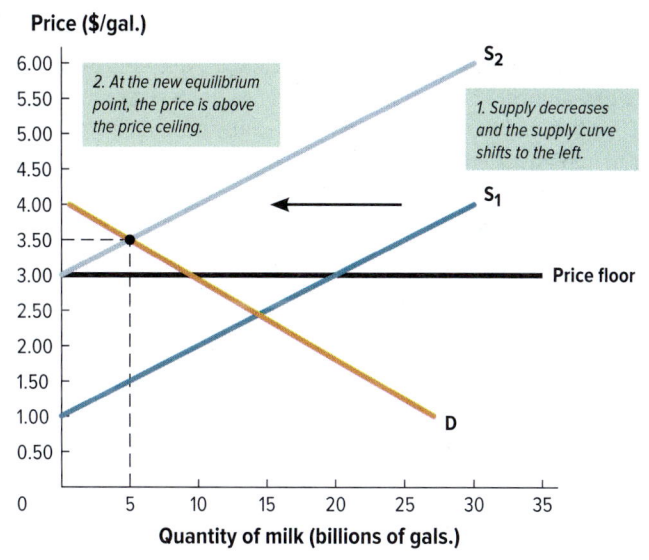

1. Supply decreases and the supply curve shifts to the left.

Curves: S_1, S_2, D, Price floor at $3.00, new equilibrium at $3.50 and 5 billion gals.

Although a price floor is usually set so as to raise prices above the equilibrium level, changes in the supply can raise the equilibrium price above the price floor. When that happens, the surplus that was created by the price floor disappears and the quantity supplied equals the quantity demanded.

Nonbinding price floors Price floors are not always binding. In fact, in recent years, the market prices for dairy products in the United States have usually been above the price floor. The price floor may become binding, however, in response to changes in the market. Figure 6-6 shows how such a decrease in supply could render a price floor nonbinding. Consider the effect of the increased demand for ethanol in 2007 on the market for milk. Ethanol is a fuel additive made from corn. The sudden rise in demand for ethanol pushed up the price of corn, which in turn pushed up the cost of livestock feed for dairy farmers. As a result of this change in the price of inputs, the supply curve for milk shifted to the left (from S_1 to S_2 in Figure 6-6). This shift pushed the equilibrium price for milk above the $3 price floor to $3.50.

✓ TEST YOURSELF

- ☐ Why does a price ceiling cause a shortage? **[LO 6.1]**
- ☐ What can cause a price ceiling to become nonbinding? **[LO 6.1]**
- ☐ Explain how a government can support a price floor through purchases. **[LO 6.2]**
- ☐ What can cause a price floor to become nonbinding? **[LO 6.2]**

Taxes and Subsidies

Taxes are the main way that governments raise revenue to pay for public programs. Taxes and subsidies can also be used to correct market failures and encourage or discourage production and consumption of particular goods. However, like price floors and price ceilings, they can have unintended consequences.

Taxes

LO 6.3 Calculate the effect of a tax on the equilibrium price and quantity.

We began this chapter by discussing hunger, which is usually a minor problem in wealthy countries. Indeed, the United States has the opposite problem: diseases associated with overeating and poor nutrition, such as obesity, heart disease, and diabetes. How can policy-makers respond to this new type of food crisis? This issue is the third of the real-world interventions in this chapter.

In 2008, the state of California banned the use of trans fats in restaurants in an effort to reduce heart disease and related problems. Trans fats are artificially produced ("partially hydrogenated") unsaturated fats. Used in many fried and packaged foods because they extend products' shelf lives, they are believed to be unhealthy if consumed in excess. For decades, trans fats have been the key to making commercially produced french fries crispy and pastries flaky.

Rather than banning trans fats, what would happen if California taxed them? When a good is taxed, either the buyer or seller must pay some extra amount to the government on top of the sale price. How should we expect people to *respond* to a tax on trans fats? Taxes have two primary effects:

- First, they discourage production and consumption of the good that is taxed.
- Second, they raise government revenue through the fees paid by those who continue buying and selling the good.

Therefore, we would expect a tax both to reduce consumption of trans fats and to provide a new source of public revenue.

Figure 6-7 illustrates this scenario by showing the impact of a trans-fat tax on the market for Chocolate Whizbangs. A delicious imaginary candy, Chocolate Whizbangs are unfortunately rather high in trans fats. Suppose that, currently, 30 million Whizbangs are sold every year, at

FIGURE 6-7
Effect of a tax paid by the seller

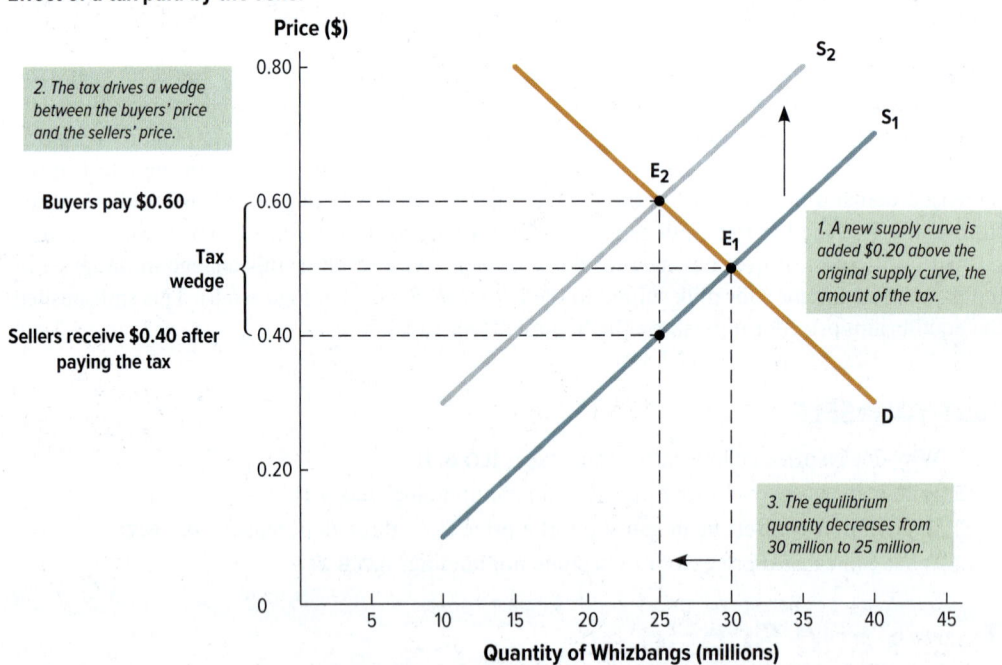

2. The tax drives a wedge between the buyers' price and the sellers' price.

Buyers pay $0.60

Tax wedge

Sellers receive $0.40 after paying the tax

1. A new supply curve is added $0.20 above the original supply curve, the amount of the tax.

3. The equilibrium quantity decreases from 30 million to 25 million.

A tax levied on the seller adds a new supply curve that is $0.20 higher than the original, which is the amount of the tax. As a result, the equilibrium quantity decreases and the equilibrium price increases. At the equilibrium quantity, the price paid by buyers is now different from the amount received by sellers after the tax is paid. This "tax wedge" is equal to the amount of the tax, or $0.20.

$0.50 each. To discourage consumption, a tax on Whizbangs has been proposed; the new tax could be imposed either on sellers or on buyers. Let's look at both options.

A tax on sellers Let's say that the government of California enacts a trans-fat tax of $0.20, which the seller must pay for every Whizbang sold. *How will buyers and sellers respond?* The impact of a tax is more complicated than the impact of a price control, so let's take it one step at a time.

1. **Does a tax on sellers affect supply?** *Yes, supply decreases.*

   When a tax is imposed on sellers (producers), they must pay the government $0.20 for each Whizbang sold. At any market price, sellers will behave as if the price they are receiving is actually $0.20 lower. Put another way, for sellers to be willing to supply any given quantity, the market price must be $0.20 higher than it was before the tax.

   Figure 6-7 shows this change in supply graphically, by adding a new supply curve (S_2). (Technically, this "shift" isn't really a shift of the curve but a way of showing the new equilibrium price; see the nearby Caution: Common Mistake box.) The new supply curve is $0.20 higher, the exact amount of the tax. At any given market price, sellers will now produce the same quantity as they would have at a price $0.20 lower before the tax: At $0.60 on curve S_2, the quantity supplied will be the same as at a price of $0.40 on curve S_1. At a price of $0.50 on curve S_2, the quantity supplied will be the same as at a price of $0.30 on curve S_1, and so on.

2. **Does a tax on sellers affect demand?** *No, demand stays the same.*

   Demand remains the same because the tax does not change any of the nonprice determinants of demand. At any given price, buyers' desire to purchase Whizbangs is unchanged. Remember, however, that the *quantity demanded* does change, although the curve itself doesn't change.

3. **How does a tax on sellers affect the market equilibrium?** *The equilibrium price rises and quantity demanded falls.*

   The new supply curve causes the equilibrium point to move up along the demand curve. At the new equilibrium point, the price paid by the buyer is $0.60. Because buyers now face a higher price, they demand fewer Whizbangs, so the quantity demanded falls from 30 million to 25 million. Notice that at the new equilibrium point, the quantity demanded is lower and the price is higher. Taxes usually reduce the quantity of a good or service that is sold, shrinking the market.

⚠ CAUTION: COMMON MISTAKE

In Chapter 3, "Markets," we distinguished between a curve *shifting* to the left or right and *movement along* the same curve. A shift represents a fundamental change in the quantity demanded or supplied at any given price; a movement along the same curve simply shows a switch to a different quantity and price point. The question here is, does a tax cause a *shift* of the demand or supply curve or a *movement along* the curve?

The answer is neither, really. Here's why: When we add a tax, we're not really shifting the curve; rather, we are adding a second curve. We still need the original curve to understand what is happening. This is because the price that sellers receive is actually $0.20 lower than the price at which they sell Whizbangs, due to the tax. So we need one curve to represent what sellers receive and another curve to represent what buyers pay.

Notice in Figure 6-7 that the price suppliers receive is on the original supply curve, S_1, but the price buyers pay is on the new supply curve, S_2. The original curve *does not actually move,* but we add the second curve to indicate that because of the tax, buyers face a different price than what the sellers will get. In order for the market to be in equilibrium, the quantity that buyers demand at $0.60 must now equal the quantity that sellers supply at $0.40.

Now let's look at the new equilibrium price in Figure 6-7. The price paid by buyers to sellers is the new market price, $0.60. However, sellers do not get to keep all the money they receive. Instead, they must pay the tax to the government. Since the tax is $0.20, the price that sellers receive once they have paid the tax is only $0.40. Ultimately, sellers do not receive the full price that consumers pay; the tax creates what is known as a *tax wedge* between buyers and sellers. A **tax wedge** is the difference between the price paid by buyers and the price received by sellers, which equals the amount of the tax. In Figure 6-7, the tax wedge is calculated as shown in Equation 6-1.

tax wedge
the difference between the price paid by buyers and the price received by sellers in the presence of a tax

EQUATION 6-1 $$\text{Tax wedge} = P_{\text{buyers}} - P_{\text{sellers}} = \text{Tax}$$

For each Whizbang sold at the new equilibrium point, the government collects tax revenue, as calculated in Equation 6-2.

EQUATION 6-2 $$\text{Government tax revenue} = \text{Tax} \times Q_{\text{post-tax}}$$

Specifically, the government receives $0.20 for each of the 25 million Whizbangs sold, or $5 million total. Graphically, the government revenue equals the green-shaded area in Figure 6-8.

Just like a price control, a tax causes deadweight loss and redistributes surplus. We can see the deadweight loss caused by the reduced number of trades in Figure 6-8. It is surplus lost to buyers and sellers who would have been willing to make trades at the pre-tax equilibrium price.

The redistribution of surplus, however, is a little trickier to follow. Under a tax, *both* producers and consumers lose surplus. Consumers who still buy pay more for the same candy than they

---

FIGURE 6-8

Government revenue and deadweight loss from a tax

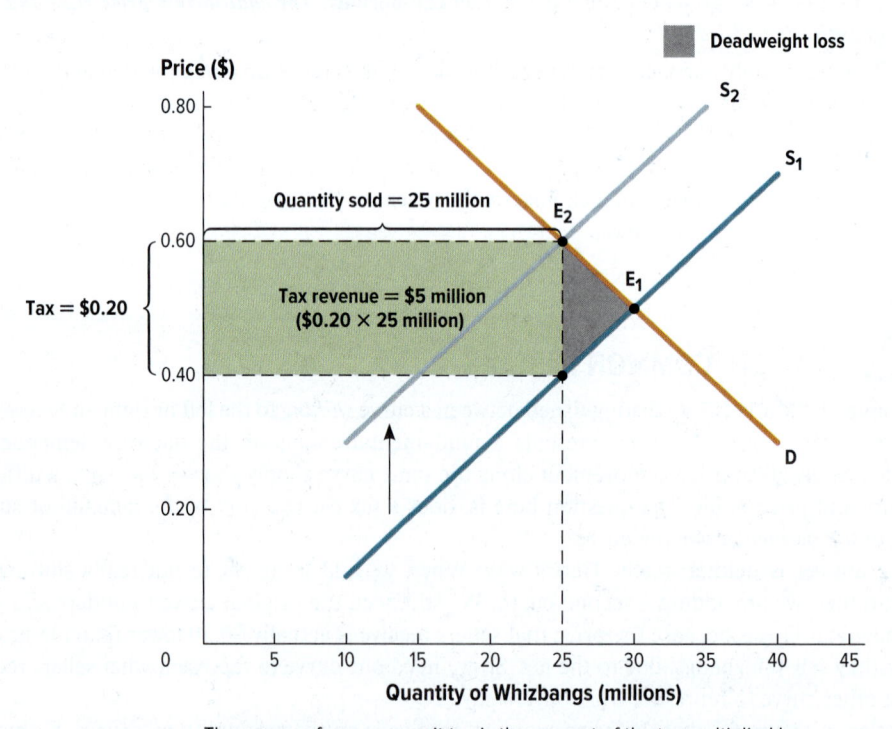

The revenue from a per-unit tax is the amount of the tax multiplied by the number of units sold at the post-tax equilibrium point. The amount of tax revenue directly corresponds to the surplus lost to consumers and producers. The trades that no longer happen under the tax represent deadweight loss.

would have under equilibrium, and producers who still sell receive less for the same candy. The difference between this lost surplus and deadweight loss, however, is that it doesn't "disappear." Instead, it becomes government revenue. In fact, the area representing government revenue in Figure 6-8 is exactly the same as the surplus lost to buyers and sellers still trading in the market after the tax has been imposed. This revenue can pay for services that might transfer surplus back to producers or consumers, or both, or to people outside of the market.

A tax on buyers What happens if the tax is imposed on buyers instead of sellers? Surprisingly, the outcome is exactly the same. Suppose California enacts a sales tax of $0.20, which the buyer must pay for every Whizbang bought. In this case, as Figure 6-9 shows, the demand curve (rather than the supply curve) moves by the amount of the tax, but the resulting equilibrium price and quantity are the same.

To double-check this result, let's walk step by step through the effect of a tax levied on buyers.

1. **Does a tax on buyers affect the supply curve?** *No, supply stays the same.*

   The supply curve stays the same because the tax does not change the incentives producers face. None of the nonprice determinants of supply are affected.

2. **Does a tax on buyers affect the demand curve?** *Yes, demand decreases.*

   Demand decreases because the price buyers must pay per unit, including the tax, is now $0.20 higher than the original price. As Figure 6-9 shows, we take the original demand curve D_1 and factor in the amount of the tax; the result is a second demand curve D_2, which represents the price buyers pay under the tax. At any given price, buyers will now behave as if the price were actually $0.20 higher. For example, at $0.40 on curve D_2,

---

FIGURE 6-9
Effect of a tax paid by the buyer

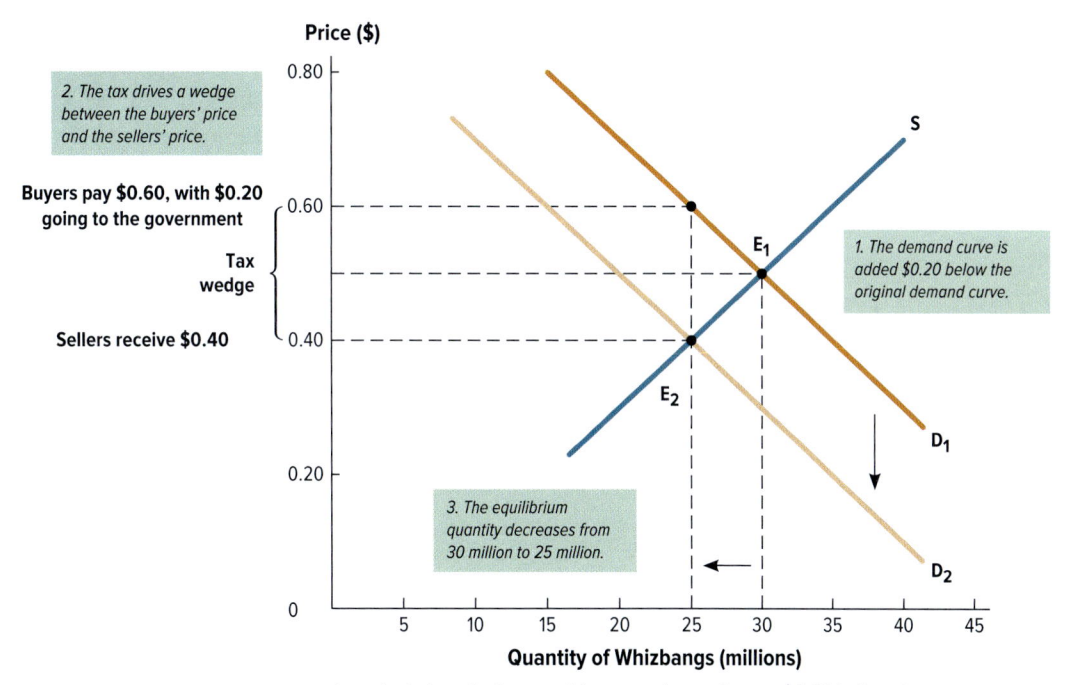

2. The tax drives a wedge between the buyers' price and the sellers' price.

Buyers pay $0.60, with $0.20 going to the government

Tax wedge

Sellers receive $0.40

1. The demand curve is added $0.20 below the original demand curve.

3. The equilibrium quantity decreases from 30 million to 25 million.

A tax levied on the buyer adds a new demand curve $0.20 below the original curve. As a result, the equilibrium quantity decreases and the equilibrium price paid by the buyer increases. These results are the same as those of a tax levied on the seller.

the quantity demanded is as if the price were $0.60 on curve D_1. At $0.30 on curve D_2, the quantity demanded is as if the price were $0.50.

3. **How does a tax on buyers affect the market equilibrium?** *The equilibrium price and quantity both fall.*

As a result, the equilibrium point with the new demand curve is further down the supply curve. The equilibrium price falls from $0.50 to $0.40 and the quantity demanded and supplied falls from 30 million to 25 million. Although the market equilibrium price goes down instead of up, as it does with a tax on sellers, the actual amount that buyers and sellers pay is the same no matter who pays the tax. When buyers pay the tax, they pay $0.40 to the seller and $0.20 to the government, or a total of $0.60. When sellers pay the tax, buyers pay $0.60 to the seller, who then pays $0.20 to the government. Either way, buyers pay $0.60 and sellers receive $0.40.

As Figure 6-9 shows, a tax on buyers creates a tax wedge just as a tax on sellers does. At the new equilibrium point, the price sellers receive is $0.40. The buyer pays $0.40 to the seller and then the $0.20 tax to the government, so that the total effective price is $0.60. Using Equation 6-1, once again the tax wedge is $0.20, exactly equal to the amount of the tax.

$$\text{Tax wedge} = \$0.60 - \$0.40 = \$0.20$$

Furthermore, the government still collects $0.20 for every Whizbang sold, just as under a tax on sellers. Again, using Equation 6-2, the post-tax equilibrium quantity is 25 million, and the government collects $5 million in tax revenue.

$$\text{Government tax revenue} = \$0.20 \times 25 \text{ million} = \$5 \text{ million}$$

What is the overall impact of the tax on Whizbangs? Regardless of whether a tax is imposed on buyers or sellers, there are four effects that result from all taxes:

1. *Equilibrium quantity falls.* The goal of the tax has thus been achieved—consumption of Whizbangs has been discouraged.
2. *Buyers pay more for each Whizbang and sellers receive less.* This creates a tax wedge, equal to the difference between the price paid by buyers and the price received by sellers.
3. *The government receives revenue equal to the amount of the tax multiplied by the new equilibrium quantity.* In this case, the California state government receives an additional $5 million in revenue from the tax on Whizbangs—which could be used to offset the public health expenses caused by obesity-related diseases.
4. *The tax causes deadweight loss.* The value of the revenue the government collects is always less than the reduction in total surplus caused by the tax.

In evaluating a tax, then, we must weigh its goal—in this case, reducing the consumption of trans fats—against the loss of surplus in the market.

Who bears the burden of a tax?

We've seen that the outcome of a tax does not depend on who pays it. Whether a tax is levied on buyers or on sellers, the cost is shared. But which group bears more of the burden?

In our example, the burden was shared equally:

- Buyers paid $0.50 for a Whizbang before the tax; after the tax, they pay $0.60. Therefore, buyers bear $0.10 of the $0.20 tax burden.
- Sellers received $0.50 for each Whizbang before the tax; after the tax, they receive $0.40. Therefore, sellers also bear $0.10 of the $0.20 tax burden.

tax incidence
the relative tax burden borne by buyers and sellers

The shaded rectangles in panel A of Figure 6-10 represent graphically this 50-50 split. The relative tax burden borne by buyers and sellers is called the **tax incidence**.

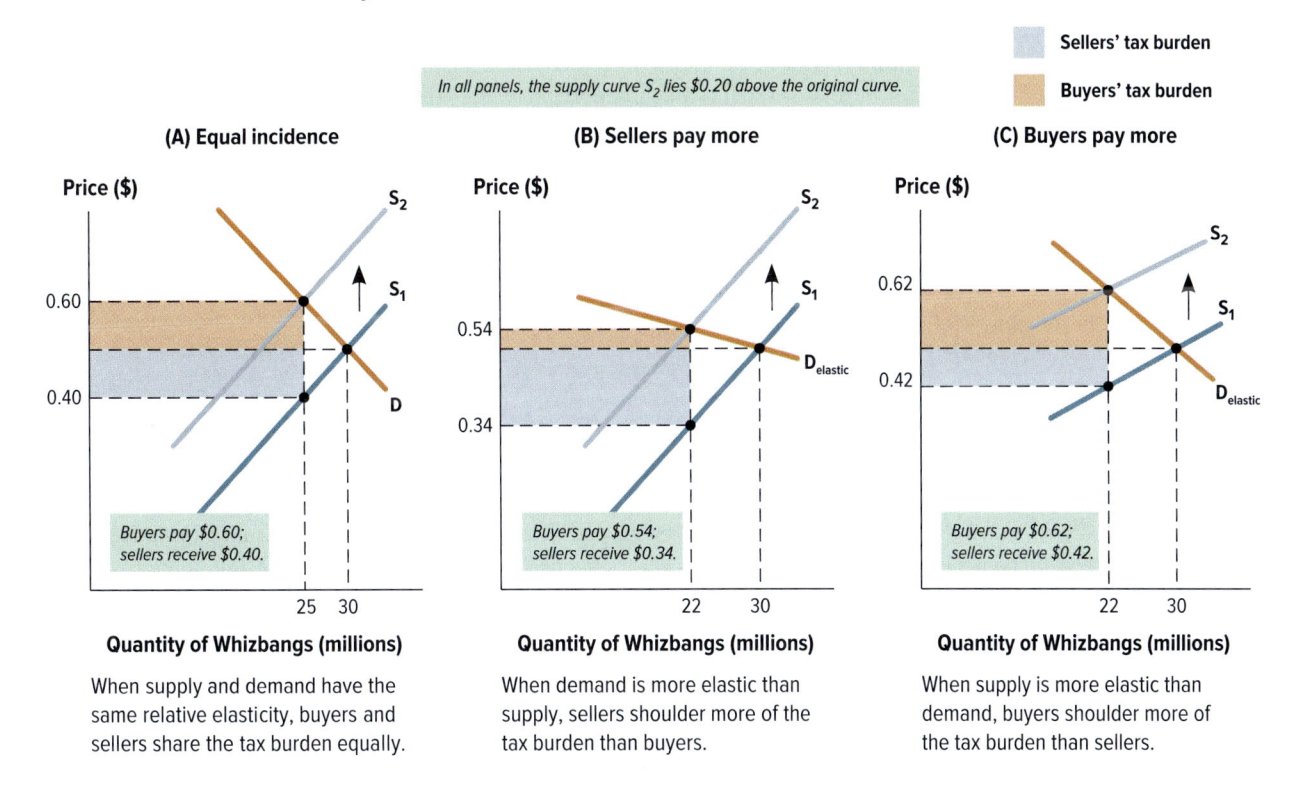

FIGURE 6-10
Tax incidence and relative elasticity

In all panels, the supply curve S_2 lies $0.20 above the original curve.

Legend: Sellers' tax burden | Buyers' tax burden

(A) Equal incidence

Price ($): 0.60, 0.40; Quantity 25, 30
Buyers pay $0.60; sellers receive $0.40.

When supply and demand have the same relative elasticity, buyers and sellers share the tax burden equally.

(B) Sellers pay more

Price ($): 0.54, 0.34; Quantity 22, 30
Buyers pay $0.54; sellers receive $0.34.

When demand is more elastic than supply, sellers shoulder more of the tax burden than buyers.

(C) Buyers pay more

Price ($): 0.62, 0.42; Quantity 22, 30
Buyers pay $0.62; sellers receive $0.42.

When supply is more elastic than demand, buyers shoulder more of the tax burden than sellers.

Often, however, the tax incidence is not split equally. Sometimes one group carries much more of it than the other. Compare the example just given to another possible market for Whizbangs, represented in panel B of Figure 6-10. In this case:

- Buyers paid $0.50 before the tax. After the tax, they pay $0.54, so their tax burden is $0.04 per Whizbang.
- Sellers, on the other hand, receive only $0.34 after the tax, so their tax burden, at $0.16 per Whizbang, is four times as large as that of buyers.

Panel C of Figure 6-10 shows the opposite case, in which buyers bear more of the burden than sellers. Thus, buyers pay $0.62 and sellers receive $0.42.

What determines the incidence of a tax? The answer has to do with the relative elasticity of the supply and demand curves. Recall from Chapter 4, "Elasticity," that price elasticity describes how much the quantity supplied or demanded changes in response to a change in price. Since a tax effectively changes the price of a good to both buyers and sellers, the relative responsiveness of supply and demand will determine the tax burden. Essentially, *the side of the market that is more price elastic will be more able to adjust to price changes and will shoulder less of the tax burden.* For example:

- Panel B of Figure 6-10 imagines a market in which demand is more elastic: Many consumers easily give up their Whizbang habit and buy healthier snacks instead. In that case, Whizbang producers pay a higher share of the tax.
- Panel C of Figure 6-10 imagines a market in which demand is less elastic: Consumers are so obsessed with Whizbangs that they will buy even at the higher price. In that case, Whizbang buyers pay a higher share of the tax.

Recall that the market outcome of a tax—the new equilibrium quantity and price—is the same regardless of whether a tax is imposed on buyers or on sellers. Thus, the tax burden will be the same no matter which side of the market is taxed. Note in panel C of Figure 6-10 that buyers bear the greater part of that burden, even though the tax is imposed on sellers. The situation in panels B and C shows there can be a difference between *economic incidence* (the economic effect of a tax on either buyers or sellers) and *statutory incidence* (the person who is legally responsible for paying the tax). The actual economic incidence of a tax is unrelated to the statutory incidence.

This is an important point to remember during public debates about taxes. A politician may say that companies that pollute should be held accountable for the environmental damage they cause, through a tax on pollution. Regardless of how you may feel about the idea of taxing pollution, remember that levying the tax on companies that pollute does not mean that they will end up bearing the whole tax burden. Consumers who buy from those producers will also bear part of the burden of the tax, through higher prices. Policy-makers have little control over how the tax burden is shared between buyers and sellers.

Subsidies

LO 6.4 Calculate the effect of a subsidy on the equilibrium price and quantity.

subsidy
a requirement that the government pay an extra amount to producers or consumers of a good

A **subsidy** is the reverse of a tax: It is a requirement that the government pay an extra amount to producers or consumers of a good. Governments use subsidies to encourage the production and consumption of a particular good or service. They can also use subsidies as an alternative to price controls to benefit certain groups without generating a shortage or an excess supply.

Let's return to the Mexican dilemma—what to do when hungry people cannot afford to buy enough tortillas. This is the last of the four real-world interventions in the chapter, and here we ask a different question: What would happen if the government *subsidized* tortillas rather than imposed a price ceiling on them?

Figure 6-11 shows the tortilla market we discussed earlier in the chapter. The figure shows that before the subsidy, the market is in equilibrium at a price of $0.70 per pound and a quantity of 50 million pounds. Now suppose the government offers tortilla makers a subsidy of $0.35 per pound. *How will buyers and sellers respond to the subsidy?* They will respond in the opposite way that they respond to a tax:

- With a tax, the quantity supplied and demanded decrease, and the government collects revenue.
- With a subsidy, the quantity supplied and demanded increase, and the government spends money.

We can calculate the effect of a $0.35 tortilla subsidy by walking through the same three steps we used to examine the effect of a tax.

1. **Does a subsidy to sellers affect the supply curve?** *Yes, supply increases.*

   When producers receive a subsidy, the real price they receive for each unit sold is higher than the market price. At any market price, therefore, they will behave as if the price were $0.35 higher. Put another way, for sellers to supply a given quantity, the market price can be $0.35 lower than it would have to be without the subsidy. As a result, the new supply curve is drawn $0.35 below the original. In Figure 6-11, S_2 shows the new supply curve that is the result of the subsidy.

2. **Does a subsidy to sellers affect the demand curve?** *No, demand stays the same.*

   The demand curve stays where it is because consumers are not directly affected by the subsidy.

3. **How does a subsidy to sellers affect the market equilibrium?** *The equilibrium price decreases and the equilibrium quantity increases.*

   The equilibrium quantity with the new supply curve increases as consumers move down along the demand curve to the new equilibrium point. At the new, post-subsidy

FIGURE 6-11
Effect of a subsidy to the seller

Price ($/lb.)

- 3. Sellers receive the equilibrium price plus the subsidy, $0.88.
- 0.88
- 1. A new supply curve is added $0.35 below the original, the amount of the subsidy.
- 0.70 — E₁
- 2. Buyers pay the equilibrium price, $0.53.
- 0.53 — E₂
- 4. The equilibrium quantity increases from 50 million lbs. to 62 million lbs.
- 50   62
- **Quantity of tortillas (millions of lbs.)**

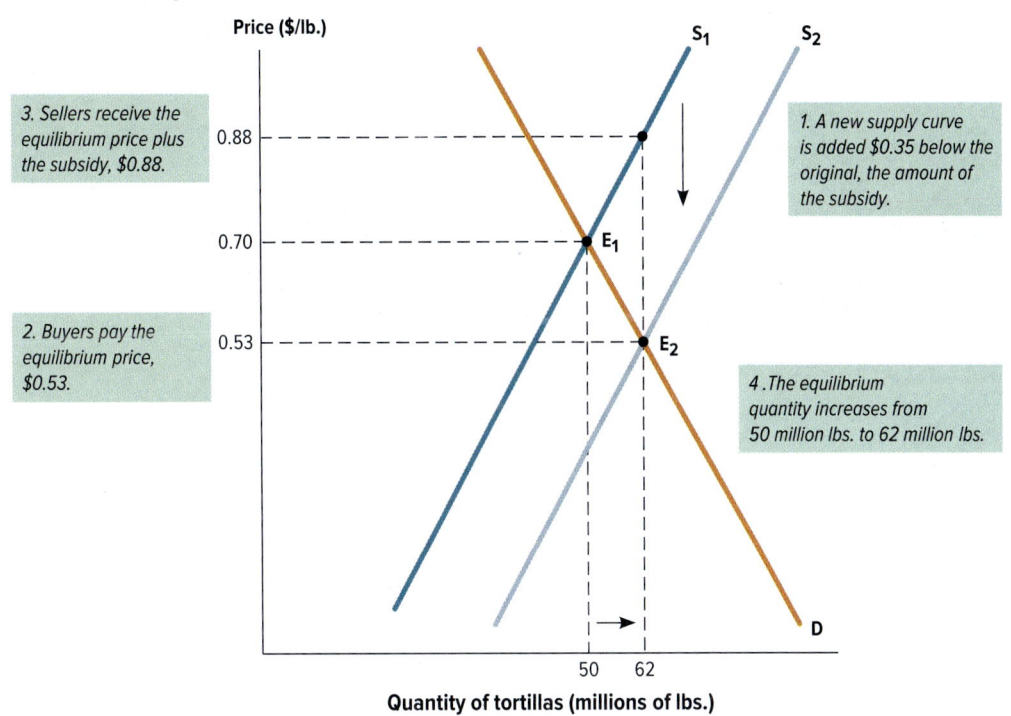

A subsidy has the opposite effect of a tax. A new supply curve is added $0.35 below the original supply curve. This decreases the equilibrium price and increases the equilibrium quantity supplied and demanded.

equilibrium, the quantity supplied increases from 50 million pounds of tortillas to 62 million pounds. As with a tax, the price buyers pay for tortillas differs from the price sellers receive after the subsidy because the subsidy creates a wedge between the two prices. This time, however, sellers receive a *higher* price than the pre-subsidy equilibrium of $0.70, and buyers pay a *lower* one. Buyers pay $0.53 per pound and sellers receive $0.88 per pound. The government pays the $0.35 difference.

The government subsidizes each pound of tortillas sold at the new equilibrium point. To calculate the total amount of government expenditure on a subsidy, we can use Equation 6-3. The government spends $0.35 for each of the 62 million pounds of tortillas sold, or $21.7 million total.

EQUATION 6-3   Government subsidy expenditure = Subsidy × $Q_{\text{post-subsidy}}$

Like taxes, subsidies also cause deadweight loss and redistribute surplus. Panel A of Figure 6-12 shows the deadweight loss caused by the overproduction and overconsumption of tortillas. If there is no subsidy, 50 million pounds is the equilibrium quantity. Any more, and the cost to produce them would be higher than the benefit to consumers. Thus, it would be inefficient to exchange more than 50 million pounds of tortillas. The subsidy lowers the cost to the producer, thus causing producers and consumers to exchange 12 million more pounds of tortillas than is efficient. This leads to a deadweight loss.

Panel B of Figure 6-12 shows the total government expenditure on the subsidy. You may wonder why only part of the government expenditure is counted as deadweight loss. If the government is funding 12 million more pounds of tortillas than is efficient, shouldn't the entire expenditure

FIGURE 6-12
Deadweight loss from a subsidy

(A) Deadweight loss from tortilla subsidy

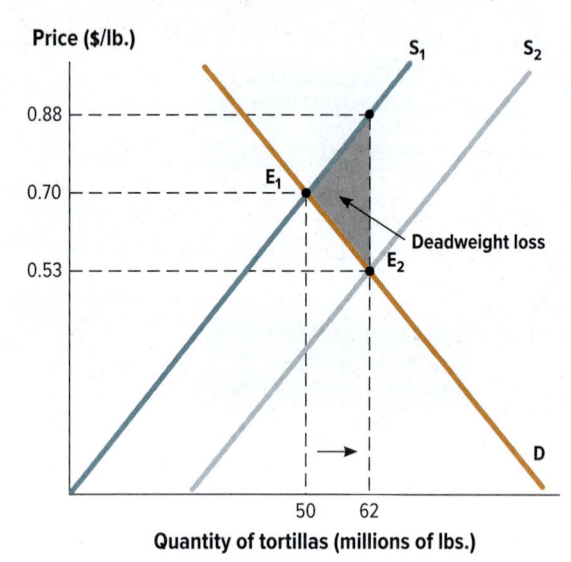

Price ($/lb.) vs. Quantity of tortillas (millions of lbs.)
- Prices marked: 0.88, 0.70, 0.53
- Quantities marked: 50, 62
- Curves: S_1, S_2, D
- Points: E_1, E_2
- Deadweight loss shaded region

For the 12 million pounds of tortillas produced due to the subsidy, supply exceeds demand. Thus, the exchange of these tortillas causes deadweight loss.

(B) Government spending on tortilla subsidy

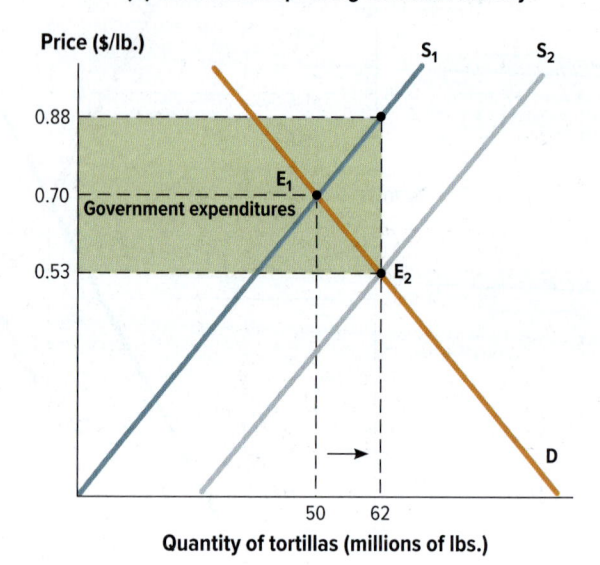

Price ($/lb.) vs. Quantity of tortillas (millions of lbs.)
- Prices marked: 0.88, 0.70, 0.53
- Quantities marked: 50, 62
- Curves: S_1, S_2, D
- Points: E_1, E_2
- Government expenditures shaded region

The government subsidy expenditure is the amount of the subsidy multiplied by the post-subsidy equilibrium quantity. The subsidy increases both consumer surplus and producer surplus but imposes a cost on the government, which ultimately is paid for by taxes on consumers and producers.

---

be deadweight loss? The answer is no, because the government is increasing both consumer and producer surplus with its expenditures. However, the deadweight loss arises because not all of the expenditure becomes surplus.

Figure 6-13 shows the consumer surplus and producer surplus from a subsidy. Notice that both consumer surplus and producer surplus increase with a subsidy. However, recall that the increase in surplus is funded by the government, as shown in panel B of Figure 6-12. Notice that the amount of government expenditure is less than the total increase in producer and consumer surplus. Ultimately, that expenditure is passed on to taxpayers (both producers and individuals) in the form of more taxes.

Are the benefits to consumers and producers worth the cost? That depends on how much we value the increased production of tortillas and their reduced cost to consumers versus the opportunity cost of the subsidy—that is, whatever other use the government or taxpayers might have made of that $21.7 million.

In addition, as the Economics in Action box "The unintended consequences of biofuel subsidies" shows, the obvious benefits of a subsidy can sometimes be swamped by unexpected costs.

As with a tax, the effect of a subsidy is the same regardless of whether it is paid to producers or consumers. If consumers received a $0.35 subsidy for every pound of tortillas they bought, their demand curve would be $0.35 above the original, and the supply curve would remain unchanged. In that case, the equilibrium outcome would be the same as if producers received the subsidy: Quantity increases from 50 million pounds to 62 million pounds, buyers pay $0.53 per pound, and sellers receive $0.88 per pound.

Also as with a tax, the way in which the benefits of a subsidy are split between buyers and sellers depends on the relative elasticity of the demand and supply curves. *The side of the market*

FIGURE 6-13
A subsidy's effect on surplus

(A) Consumer surplus from tortilla subsidy

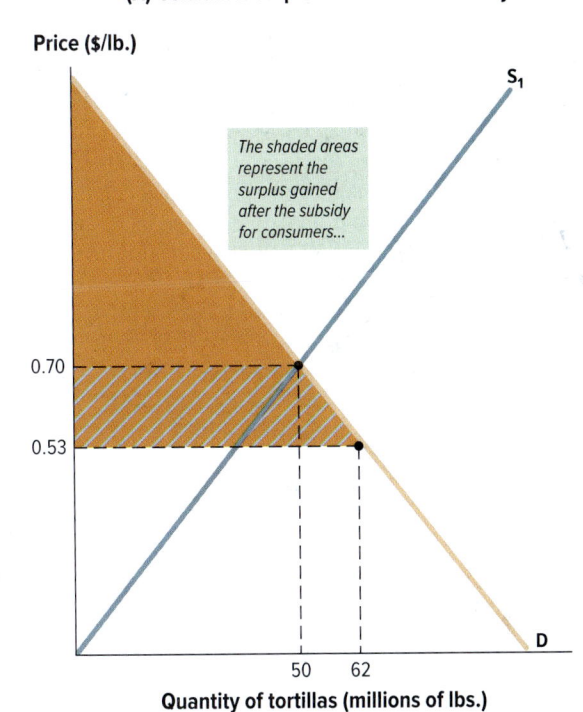

The shaded areas represent the surplus gained after the subsidy for consumers...

Price ($/lb.): 0.70, 0.53
Quantity of tortillas (millions of lbs.): 50, 62

(B) Producer surplus from tortilla subsidy

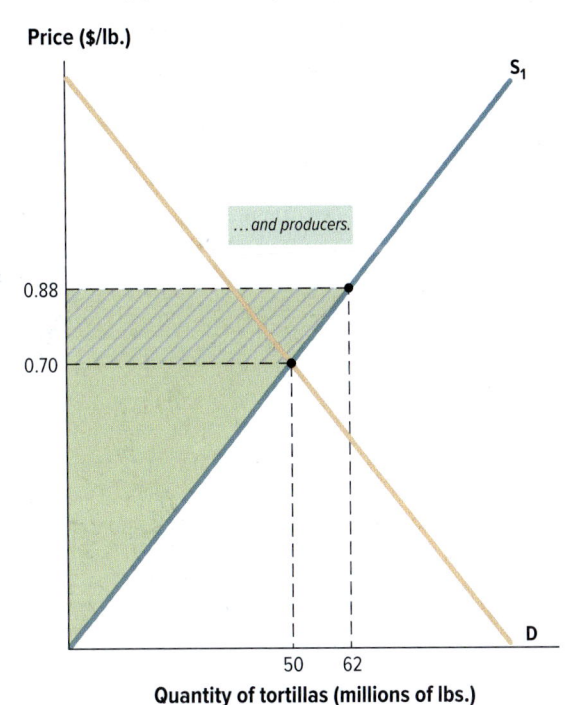

...and producers.

Price ($/lb.): 0.88, 0.70
Quantity of tortillas (millions of lbs.): 50, 62

The post-subsidy price paid by consumers ($0.53) is lower than the initial equilibrium price ($0.70), and the post-subsidy quantity (62 million pounds) is higher than the initial equilibrium quantity (50 million pounds). This results in an increase in consumer surplus.

The post-subsidy price received by sellers ($0.88) is higher than the initial equilibrium price ($0.70), and the post-subsidy quantity (62 million pounds) is higher than the initial equilibrium quantity (50 million pounds). This results in an increase in producer surplus.

that is more price inelastic receives more of the benefit. In our example, both have almost the same benefit: Buyers are better off by $0.17 per pound of tortillas, and producers by $0.18.

As with taxes, it is important to note that who gets what share of benefit from the subsidy does not depend on who receives the subsidy. Sometimes in debates about subsidies you will hear someone argue that a subsidy should be given either to buyers or sellers because they "deserve it more." This argument doesn't make much sense in a competitive market (although it might in a noncompetitive market).

In sum, a subsidy has the following effects, regardless of whether it is paid to buyers or sellers:

1. Equilibrium quantity increases, accomplishing the goal of encouraging production and consumption of the subsidized good.
2. Buyers pay less and sellers receive more for each unit sold. The amount of the subsidy forms a wedge between buyers' and sellers' prices.
3. The government has to pay for the subsidy, the cost of which equals the amount of the subsidy multiplied by the new equilibrium quantity.

✓ TEST YOURSELF

☐ What is a tax wedge? **[LO 6.3]**
☐ What determines the incidence of a tax? **[LO 6.3]**

> ### The unintended consequences of biofuel subsidies
> **Economics in Action**
>
> In the United States, cars partly run on corn. "Gasoline" often contains ethanol, a "biofuel" that is a cleaner fuel than gasoline. Ethanol is fermented from starch, most often from corn in the United States.
>
> The U.S. government subsidizes ethanol production in part to reduce pollution; as hoped, the subsidy has caused a huge increase in the production of ethanol. Unfortunately, it has also had some unintended effects. Scientists find that, indirectly, biofuels can actually increase pollution.
>
> Researchers find that the problem is simple, and yet something policy-makers didn't anticipate. In order to grow the products that ethanol is created from, farmers need land—a need that can lead to the destruction of forests, wetlands, and grasslands. Pollution can also be created in the process of growing and fermenting corn and when distilling the ethanol. These activities can lead to the opposite effect of the hoped-for reduction in air pollution.
>
> In addition, some organizations (including United Nations agencies, the International Monetary Fund, and the World Bank) have warned that biofuels could push food prices higher in the future (although it is not yet clear how much and when).
>
> Unfortunately, unintended consequences aren't always just a postscript to market interventions. Sometimes, they can change the story.
>
> Sources: Christopher W. Tessuma, Jason D. Hill, and Julian D. Marshall, "Life cycle air quality impacts of conventional and alternative light-duty transportation in the United States," *Proceedings of the National Academy of Sciences* 111, no.52 (December 30, 2014). *The New York Times* had a discussion in its environmental blog: http://green.blogs.nytimes.com/2008/11/03/the-biofuel-debate-good-bad-or-too-soon-to-tell/. Also, www.theguardian.com/global-development/poverty-matters/2011/jun/01/biofuels-driving-food-prices-higher. The US Energy Information Administration provides a perspective on ways to limit side-effects: www.eia.gov/energyexplained/index.php?page=biofuel_ethanol_environment.

- ☐ How does a subsidy affect the equilibrium quantity? How does it affect the price that sellers receive and the price that buyers pay? **[LO 6.4]**
- ☐ Does it matter whether a subsidy is paid to buyers or sellers? Why or why not? **[LO 6.4]**

Evaluating Government Interventions

LO 6.5 Explain how elasticity and time period influence the impact of a market intervention.

We began this chapter with a discussion of three reasons why policy-makers might decide to intervene in a market: to change the distribution of surplus, to encourage or discourage consumption, and to correct market failures. To decide whether policy-makers have achieved their goals by implementing a price control, tax, or subsidy, we need to assess the effects of each intervention, including its unintended consequences.

We've established a few rules about the expected outcomes of market interventions. Table 6-1 summarizes the key effects of price controls, taxes, and subsidies. In general, we can say the following:

- Price controls have opposing impacts on the quantities supplied and demanded, causing a shortage or excess supply. In contrast, taxes and subsidies move the quantities supplied and demanded in the same direction, allowing the market to reach equilibrium at the point where the quantity supplied equals the quantity demanded.
- Taxes discourage people from buying and selling a particular good, raise government revenue, and impose a cost on both buyers and sellers.
- Subsidies encourage people to buy and sell a particular good, cost the government money, and provide a benefit to both buyers and sellers.

In the following sections we will consider some of the more complicated details of market interventions. These details matter. Often the details of an intervention make the difference between a successful policy and a failed one.

TABLE 6-1

Government interventions: A summary

Intervention	Reason for using	Effect on price	Effect on quantity	Who gains and who loses?
Price floor	To protect producers' income	Price cannot go below the set minimum.	Quantity demanded decreases and quantity supplied increases, creating excess supply.	Producers who can sell all their goods earn more revenue per item; other producers are stuck with an unwanted excess supply.
Price ceiling	To keep consumer costs low	Price cannot go above the set maximum.	Quantity demanded increases and quantity supplied decreases, creating a shortage.	Consumers who can buy all the goods they want benefit; other consumers suffer from shortages.
Tax	To discourage an activity or collect money to pay for its consequences; to increase government revenue	Price increases.	Equilibrium quantity decreases.	Government receives increased revenue; society may gain if the tax decreases socially harmful behavior. Buyers and sellers of the good that is taxed share the cost. Which group bears more of the burden depends on the price elasticity of supply and demand.
Subsidy	To encourage an activity; to provide benefits to a certain group	Price decreases.	Equilibrium quantity increases.	Buyers purchase more goods at a lower price. Society may benefit if the subsidy encourages socially beneficial behavior. The government and ultimately the taxpayers bear the cost.

How big is the effect of a tax or subsidy?

Regardless of the reason for a market intervention, it's important to know exactly *how much* it will change the equilibrium quantity and price. Can the effect of a tax or subsidy on the equilibrium quantity be predicted ahead of time? The answer is yes, *if* we know the price elasticity of supply and demand.

A general rule applies: *The more elastic supply or demand is, the greater the change in quantity.* This rule follows directly from the definition of price elasticity, which measures buyers' and sellers' responsiveness to a change in price—and a tax or subsidy is effectively a change in price.

Figure 6-14 shows the effect of a $0.20 tax on the quantity demanded under four different combinations of price elasticity of supply and demand—again, for Whizbangs. It's worthwhile to walk through each combination, one by one:

- In panel A, both supply and demand are *relatively inelastic:* In this case the tax causes the equilibrium quantity to decrease, but not by much. Both buyers and sellers are willing to continue trading, even though they now must pay the tax.
- In panel B, *demand is more elastic than supply:* When the supply curve is $0.20 higher, the change in quantity is much larger than in panel A.
- In panel C, *supply is elastic but demand is relatively inelastic:* Again, because suppliers are highly responsive to the cost of the tax, the quantity changes more than in panel A.
- In panel D, *supply and demand are both elastic:* In this case, the quantity goes down even more than in the second and third examples.

To predict the size of the effect of a tax or subsidy, then, policy-makers need to know the price elasticity of both supply and demand. As we have seen, they can also use that information to determine who will bear more of the burden or receive more of the benefit.

FIGURE 6-14
Price elasticity and the effect of a $0.20 tax

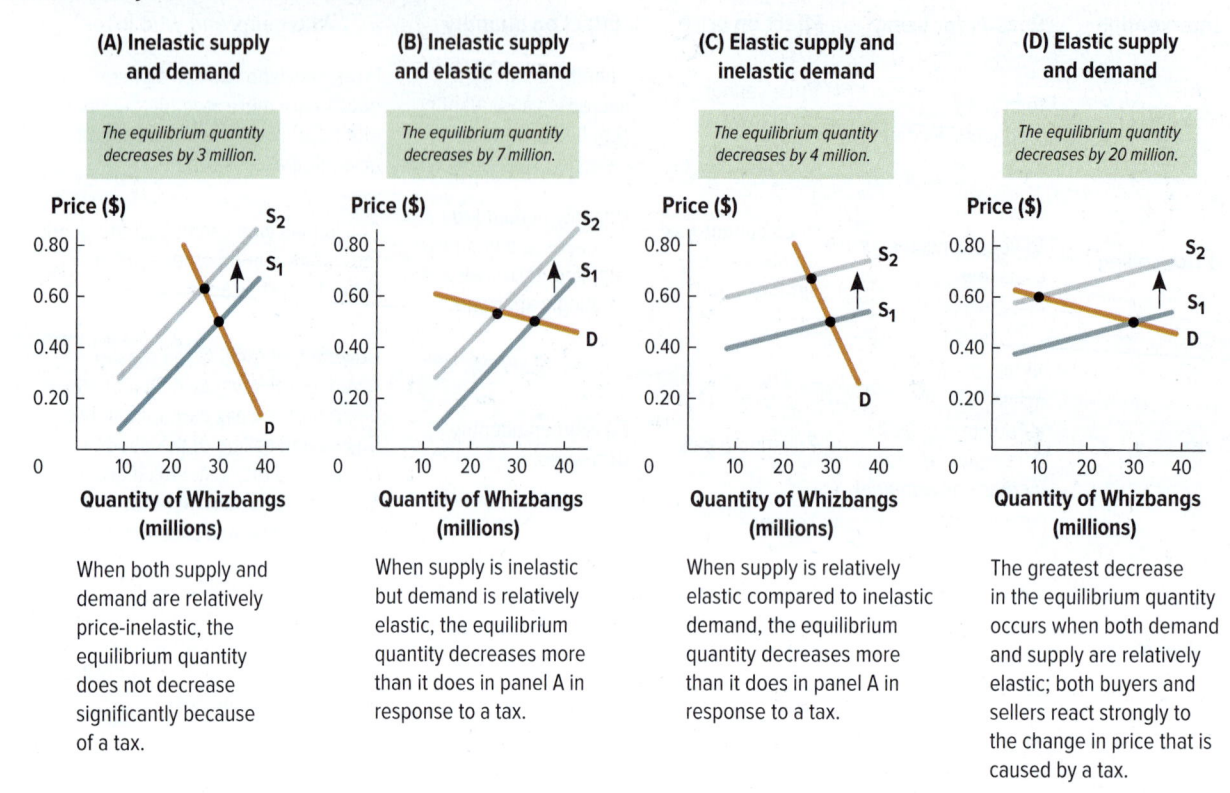

(A) Inelastic supply and demand
The equilibrium quantity decreases by 3 million.

When both supply and demand are relatively price-inelastic, the equilibrium quantity does not decrease significantly because of a tax.

(B) Inelastic supply and elastic demand
The equilibrium quantity decreases by 7 million.

When supply is inelastic but demand is relatively elastic, the equilibrium quantity decreases more than it does in panel A in response to a tax.

(C) Elastic supply and inelastic demand
The equilibrium quantity decreases by 4 million.

When supply is relatively elastic compared to inelastic demand, the equilibrium quantity decreases more than it does in panel A in response to a tax.

(D) Elastic supply and demand
The equilibrium quantity decreases by 20 million.

The greatest decrease in the equilibrium quantity occurs when both demand and supply are relatively elastic; both buyers and sellers react strongly to the change in price that is caused by a tax.

Sometimes, who pays the tax can depend on who is paying attention to true cost. The Econ and YOU box "Out of sight, out of mind" discusses research that looked into what happened when stores posted tax-inclusive prices of certain goods.

Out of sight, out of mind
Econ and YOU

Forty-five of the 50 states charge a sales tax on consumer goods. In most places, the sales tax is added on at the cash register. If the tax is 5 percent, for example, you'll be charged $21 for a book that has a $20 price tag. If you live in a place where advertised prices don't include taxes—and especially if you shop in a hurry—you might find that it's easy to focus on the number on the price tag and forget that you will end up paying more for that good.

If this happens to you, you're not alone. Economists Raj Chetty, Adam Looney, and Kory Kroft ran an experiment in a grocery store to test whether shoppers "forget" about sales tax when they look at the number on the price tag. In this experiment, price tags in some aisles listed both pre- and post-tax prices on goods. By showing both amounts, researchers would be able to compare sales of the same items at other stores that did not use the unique tags. Standard theory maintains that the different tagging shouldn't make a difference; when taxes are not posted, perfectly rational consumers should do the math on each item and make buying decisions based on the full, tax-inclusive prices.

However, the researchers found that customers weren't doing the math. So, when tax was included in the posted price of items, rather than added at the register, quantity demanded decreased by 8 percent. Clearly, something wasn't adding up.

It wasn't that people didn't know about the sales tax when it wasn't included in the posted price. When asked, most shoppers were able to correctly identify how much tax they would owe on what sort of goods. Rather, the tax simply wasn't at the top of their minds while they shopped; instead, they defaulted to thinking that the listed price was the true cost.

One result is that buying decisions were sensitive to changes in the prices on the price tags, but their decisions were not very sensitive to changes in tax rates. In terms of elasticities, demand was inelastic with respect to changes in taxes.

In this case, the quirks of human behavior—in this case, "out of sight, out of mind"—undermine our assumptions about rational, informed response to incentives. We don't expect you to start bringing a calculator to the grocery store. But stopping to spend a little more time thinking about taxes (especially on big-ticket items) can help make you make more rational decisions about what to buy.

Source: Raj Chetty, Adam Looney, and Kory Kroft, "Salience and Taxation: Theory and Evidence," *American Economic Review* 99, no. 4 (2009), p. 1145–1177.

Short-run versus long-run impact

We have seen that in addition to changing the price of a good or service, price controls cause shortages or excess supply. Because buyers and sellers take time to respond to a change in price, sometimes the full effect of price controls becomes clear only in the long run.

Suppose the U.S. government imposes a price floor on gasoline in an attempt to reduce air pollution by discouraging people from driving. Panel A of Figure 6-15 shows the short-run impact of a price floor in the market for gasoline. In the short run, the quantity of gas demanded might not change very much. Although people would cut down on unnecessary driving, the greater part of demand would still be based on driving habits that are difficult to change, such as commuting to school or work or going to the grocery store. And unless gasoline producers have a lot of unused oil wells sitting around, sellers might have trouble ramping up production quickly. In the short run, demand and supply are not very elastic, so the price floor results in only a small excess supply.

Recall that for both supply and demand, one of the determinants of price elasticity is the period over which it is measured. On both sides of the market, elasticity is often greater over a long period than over a short one:

- On the demand side, consumers might make small lifestyle changes over the medium term, such as buying a bus pass or shopping closer to home. Over the long run, they might make even bigger changes. When they need to buy a new car, for example, they will be inclined to buy a model that offers high gas mileage. If they move to a new job or home, they may place more weight than in the past on commuting distance.

- Supply will also be more elastic over the long run. Because a higher price gives suppliers an incentive to produce more, they may invest in oil exploration, dig new wells, or take steps to increase the pumping capacity of existing wells. Panel B of Figure 6-15 shows the long-run impact of a price floor in the market for gasoline. Because both supply and demand are more elastic in the long run than in the short run, the excess supply of gasoline is much larger in the long run than in the short run.

If the goal of the price floor was to reduce air pollution by giving consumers an incentive to cut down on driving, the impact might look disappointing in the short run: The quantity of gas burned

FIGURE 6-15
Government intervention in the short and long run

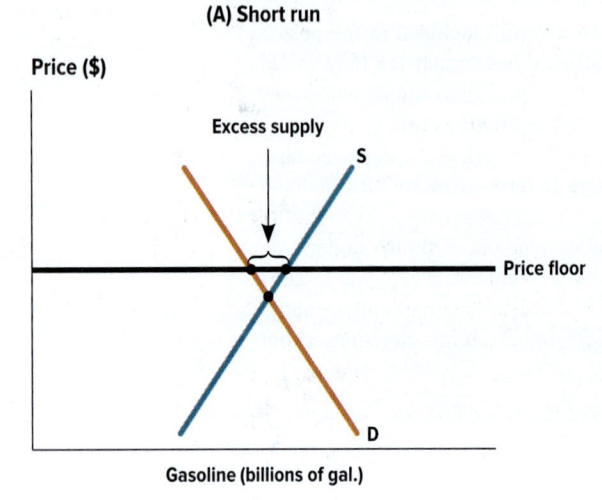

(A) Short run

In the short run, neither the supply nor the demand for gasoline is very elastic, so the effect of a price floor on the quantity supplied is relatively small.

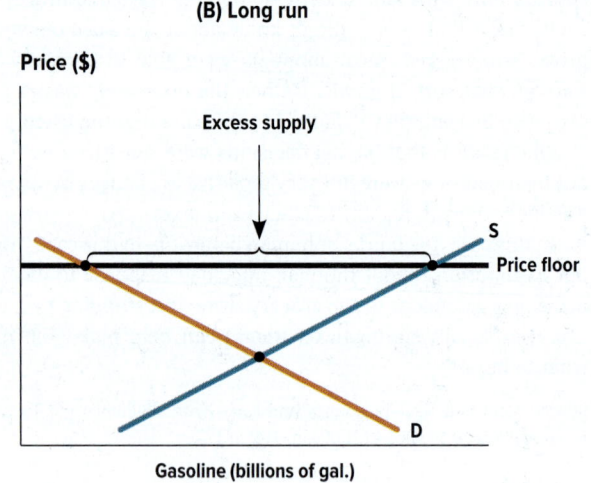

(B) Long run

In the long run, both the supply and the demand for gasoline will change in response to price controls. As a result, the long-run effect on the quantity supplied is much greater than the short-run effect.

will decrease very little. Over the long run, however, the quantity of gas burned will decrease further, and the policy will look more successful.

If, on the other hand, the reason for the price floor was to support gasoline suppliers, the short-run response would look deceptively rosy because suppliers will sell almost the same quantity of gas at a higher price. As the quantity falls over the long run, however, more producers will be stuck with an excess supply and the policy will start to look less successful.

The federal minimum wage is an example of a controversial price floor. Some advocate raising it all the way to $15 per hour. Read the full debate in the What Do You Think? box "Fight for $15."

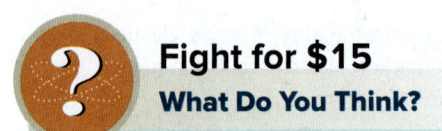

Fight for $15
What Do You Think?

In 2013, 200 fast-food workers in New York City walked off the job, protesting low wages and poor working conditions. This walkout was the first major action of The Fight for $15 Movement, a nationwide campaign advocating for higher wages. The movement quickly gained momentum. A year later, the mayor of Seattle signed a bill to gradually increase Seattle's minimum wage to $15 per hour by 2021. Pittsburgh, Los Angeles, San Francisco, and other cities followed with similar policies. In October 2018 Amazon raised its minimum wage to $15 for all U.S. employees and challenged other companies to follow suit. Some have (such as Disney, Charter Communications), and others (such as Target) have committed to do so within a short time frame.

The biggest "Fight for $15" centers on the federal minimum wage. Raising the federal minimum wage would affect 2.6 million workers, or roughly 2 percent of the U.S. workforce who earn the minimum wage or below. Just under half are 25 or younger, and two-thirds are employed in service industries.

Advocates of the Fight for $15 argue that the current federal minimum wage of $7.25 is far too low. Working at the minimum wage 40 hours a week, 52 weeks a year, yields a yearly income of $15,080. That's above the poverty line for single people but below the $18,769 mark set for an adult supporting two children. In 2015, the National Employment Law Project reported that 42 percent of the U.S. workforce earned less than $15 per hour, a group disproportionately made up of women and workers of color. Supporters note also that in most states a worker would need to earn at least $15 an hour to afford a two-bedroom apartment. Raising the minimum wage could pull many workers and families out of poverty, allowing them to live healthier and less stressful lives.

Critics say that raising the minimum wage to $15 is a blunt tool that could actually hurt low-income workers. They cite the textbook model of supply and demand, which shows that a price floor would reduce the quantity of labor demanded by firms. A higher minimum wage would then give employers incentives to cut jobs, give workers fewer hours, and automate more operations. Critics of the $15 wage also note that living costs are not the same around the country. Money goes much further in Iowa City, Iowa, than in Seattle, for example: $15 in Iowa City is equivalent to $26 in Seattle. A minimum wage of $15 that might seem reasonable in Seattle looks unreasonably high in Iowa City.

What do the data say? Overall, most research into minimum-wage increases finds that workers benefit and the quantity of labor demanded tends to fall some, but not a lot (at least in the short run). In particular:

- A group of economists at the University of Washington found that increasing the minimum wage from $10.50 to $13 per hour in Seattle caused businesses to reduce employee hours by 9 percent, while incomes increased by 3 percent.
- Economists at the University of California, however, found no reduction in employment when focusing just on Seattle's food-service sector (a big employer of minimum-wage workers).

The answer to whether raising the minimum wage is a good policy clearly depends on who, where, and when.

WHAT DO YOU THINK?

1. Advocates argue that minimum-wage laws help give workers a fairer deal in the face of declining unions and the decreasing bargaining power of workers relative to employers. Can you think of other policies (other than raising the minimum wage by law) which could ensure that workers get a fair deal?
2. In an interview with the *Washington Post,* economist Josh Vigdor describes how he would think about the issue: "If I'm a voter, I want to ask three questions about a proposed minimum-wage increase: How far [how high a wage?], how fast [would the increase be implemented in steps?], and in what kind of economy?" How would you answer these questions in your region? How do different answers to these questions change your thoughts about the Fight for $15?
3. How might the impact of $15 initiatives affect different jobs and sectors? For example, would the owner of a farm respond the same way that a restaurant owner would? What might a manufacturing firm do in response to higher labor costs?
4. Critics argue that a higher minimum wage would surely raise the price of goods and services. Is this cost to consumers worth the benefit of higher wages to workers?

Sources: "About us," Fight for $15, https://fightfor15.org/about-us/; Christopher Ingraham, "The effects of 137 minimum wage hikes, in one chart," *The Washington Post Wonkblog,* February 5, 2018, www.washingtonpost.com/news/wonk/wp/2018/02/05/raising-the-minimum-wage-doesnt-cost-jobs-multiple-studies-suggest/?noredirect=on&utm_term=.95529f5e8896; Irene Tung, Paul K Sonn, and Yannet Lanthrop, "The growing movement for $15," *National Employment Law Project Report,* November 4, 2015, www.nelp.org/publication/growing-movement-15/.

✓ TEST YOURSELF

- ☐ If the demand for a good is inelastic, will a tax have a large or small effect on the quantity sold? Will buyers or sellers bear more of the burden of the tax? [LO 6.5]
- ☐ Would you expect a tax on cigarettes to be more effective over the long run or the short run? Explain your reasoning. [LO 6.5]

Conclusion

If you listen to the news, it might seem as if economics is all about business and the stock market. Business matters, but many of the most important, challenging, and useful applications of economic principles involve public policy.

This chapter gives you the basic tools you need to understand government interventions and some of the ways they can affect your everyday life. Of course, the real world is complicated, so this isn't our last word on the topic. Later, we discuss how to evaluate the benefits of both markets and government policies. We'll also discuss market failures and whether and when governments can fix them.

Key Terms

market failures, p. 131

price control, p. 132

price ceiling, p. 132

deadweight loss, p. 133

price floor, p. 136

tax wedge, p. 142

tax incidence, p. 144

subsidy, p. 146

Summary

LO 6.1 Calculate the effect of a price ceiling on the equilibrium price and quantity.

The government usually intervenes in a market for one or more of the following reasons: to change the distribution of a market's benefits, to encourage or discourage the consumption of particular goods and services, or to correct a market failure. Governments may also tax goods and services in order to raise public revenues.

A price ceiling is a maximum legal price at which a good can be sold. A binding price ceiling causes a shortage because at the legally mandated price, consumers will demand more than producers supply. This policy benefits some consumers because they are able to buy what they want at a lower price, but other consumers are unable to find the goods they want. Producers lose out because they sell less at a lower price than they would without the price ceiling.

LO 6.2 Calculate the effect of a price floor on the equilibrium price and quantity.

A price floor is a minimum legal price at which a good can be sold. A price floor causes an excess supply because at the minimum price, sellers will supply more than consumers demand. This policy benefits some producers, who are able to sell their goods at a higher price, but leaves other producers with goods they can't sell. Consumers lose because they buy less at a higher price. Maintaining a price floor often requires the government to buy up the excess supply, costing taxpayers money.

LO 6.3 Calculate the effect of a tax on the equilibrium price and quantity.

A tax requires either buyers or sellers to pay some extra price to the government when a good is bought and sold. A tax shrinks the size of a market, discouraging the consumption and production of the good being taxed. The effect is the same regardless of whether the tax is levied on buyers or sellers. The tax burden is split between consumers and producers, and the government collects revenues equal to the amount of the tax times the quantity sold.

LO 6.4 Calculate the effect of a subsidy on the equilibrium price and quantity.

A subsidy is a payment that the government makes to buyers or sellers of a good for each unit that is sold. Subsidies increase the size of a market, encouraging the consumption and production of the good being subsidized. The effect is the same regardless of whether the subsidy is paid to buyers or sellers. Both consumers and producers benefit from a subsidy, but taxpayers must cover the cost.

LO 6.5 Explain how elasticity and time period influence the impact of a market intervention.

In evaluating the effects of a government intervention in the market, it is important to consider both the intended and unintended consequences of the policy. The size of the impact of a tax or subsidy and the distribution of the burden or benefit will depend on the price elasticities of supply and demand. Furthermore, the impact of a government intervention is likely to change over time, as consumers and producers adjust their behavior in response to the new incentives.

Review Questions

1. You are an advisor to the Egyptian government, which has placed a price ceiling on bread. Unfortunately, many families still cannot buy the bread they need. Explain to government officials why the price ceiling has not increased consumption of bread. **[LO 6.1]**

2. Suppose there has been a long-standing price ceiling on housing in your city. Recently, population has declined and demand for housing has decreased. What will the decrease in demand do to the efficiency of the price ceiling? **[LO 6.1]**

3. Suppose the United States maintains a price floor for spinach. Why might this policy decrease revenues for spinach farmers? **[LO 6.2]**

4. Suppose Colombia maintains a price floor for coffee beans. What will happen to the size of the deadweight loss if the price floor encourages new growers to enter the market and produce coffee? **[LO 6.2]**

5. Many states tax cigarette purchases. Suppose that smokers are unhappy about paying the extra charge for their cigarettes. Will it help smokers if the state imposes the tax on the stores that sell the cigarettes rather than on smokers? Why or why not? **[LO 6.3]**

6. Consider a tax on cigarettes. Do you expect the tax incidence to fall more heavily on buyers or sellers of cigarettes? Why? **[LO 6.3]**

7. In the United States, many agricultural products (such as corn, wheat, and rice) are subsidized. What are the potential benefits of subsidizing these products? What are the costs? **[LO 6.4]**

8. A subsidy will increase consumer and producer surplus in a market and will increase the quantity of trades. Why, then, might a subsidy (such as a subsidy for producing corn in the United States) be considered inefficient? **[LO 6.4]**

9. Suppose the government imposes a price ceiling on gasoline. One month after the price ceiling, there is a shortage of gasoline, but it is much smaller than critics of the policy had warned. Explain why the critics' estimates might still be correct. **[LO 6.5]**

10. A state facing a budget shortfall decides to tax soft drinks. You are a budget analyst for the state. Do you expect to collect more revenue in the first year of the tax or in the second year? Why? **[LO 6.5]**

Problems and Applications

1. Many people are concerned about the rising price of gasoline. Suppose that government officials are thinking of capping the price of gasoline below its current price. Which of the following outcomes do you predict will result from this policy? Check all that apply. **[LO 6.1]**
    a. Drivers will purchase more gasoline.
    b. Quantity demanded for gasoline will increase.
    c. Long lines will develop at gas stations.
    d. Oil companies will work to increase their pumping capacity.

2. Consider the market shown in Figure 6P-1. The government has imposed a price ceiling at $18. **[LO 6.1]**

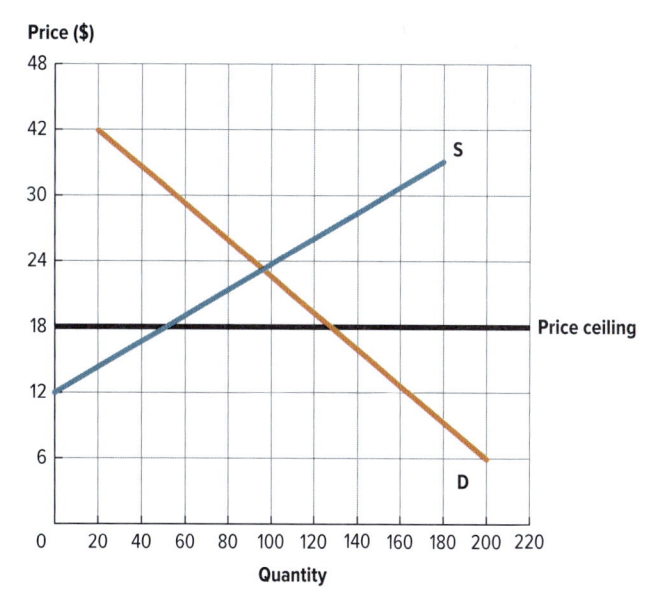

FIGURE 6P-1

    a. At a price ceiling of $18, what is quantity demanded? Quantity supplied?
    b. At this price ceiling, is there a shortage or a surplus? By how many units?

3. Figure 6P-2 shows a market in equilibrium. **[LO 6.1]**

FIGURE 6P-2

a. Draw a price ceiling at $12. What is the amount of shortage at this price? Draw and calculate the deadweight loss.
b. Draw a price ceiling at $4. What is the amount of shortage at this price? Draw and calculate the deadweight loss.

4. Decades of overfishing have dramatically reduced the world supply of cod (a type of whitefish). Farm-raised halibut is considered a close substitute for ocean-fished cod. Figure 6P-3 shows the market for farm-raised halibut. **[LO 6.1]**

FIGURE 6P-3

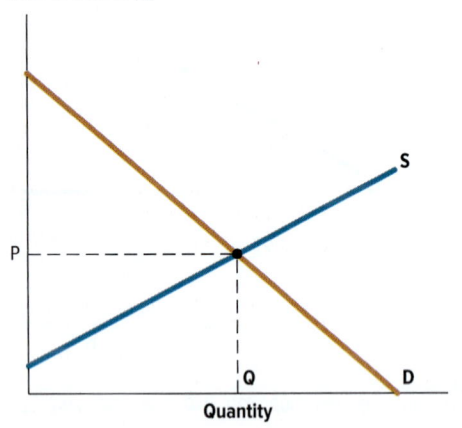

a. What effect will overfishing cod have on the price of cod? On the graph, show the effect of overfishing cod on the market for farmed halibut.
b. A fast-food chain purchases both cod and halibut for use in its Fish 'n' Chips meals. Already hurt by the reduced supply of cod, the fast-food chain has lobbied aggressively for price controls on farmed halibut. As a result, Congress has considered imposing a price ceiling on halibut at the former equilibrium price—the price that prevailed before overfishing reduced the supply of cod. What will happen in the market for farmed halibut if Congress adopts the price control policy? Draw and label the price ceiling, quantity demanded, quantity supplied, and deadweight loss.

5. Consider the market shown in Figure 6P-4. The government has imposed a price floor at $36. **[LO 6.2]**

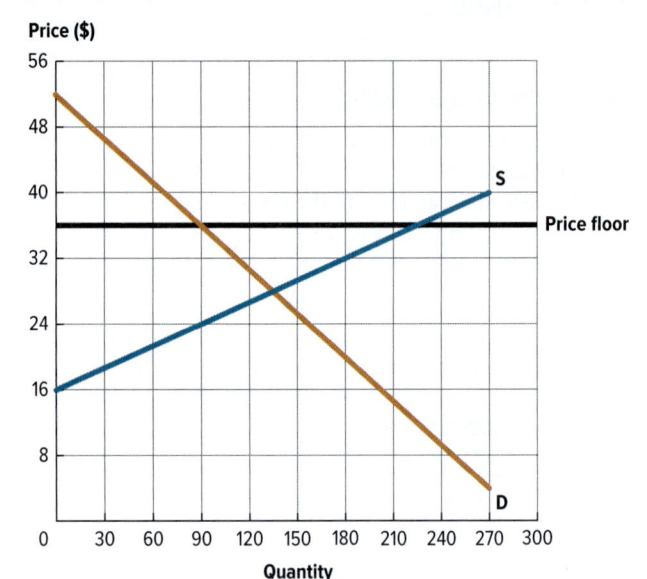

FIGURE 6P-4

a. At a price floor of $36, what is quantity demanded? Quantity supplied?
b. At this price floor, is there a shortage or a surplus? By how many units?

6. The Organization for the Promotion of Brussels Sprouts has convinced the government of Ironia to institute a price floor on the sale of brussels sprouts, at $8 per bushel. Demand is given by $P = 9 - Q$ and supply by $P = 2Q$, where Q is measured in thousands of bushels. **[LO 6.2]**
    a. What will be the price and quantity of brussels sprouts sold at market equilibrium?
    b. What will be the price and quantity sold with the price floor?
    c. How big will be the excess supply of brussels sprouts produced with the price floor?

7. The traditional diet of the citizens of the nation of Ironia includes a lot of red meat, and ranchers make up a vital part of Ironia's economy. The government of Ironia decides to support its ranchers through a price floor,

which it will maintain by buying up excess meat supplies. Table 6P-1 shows the supply and demand schedule for red meat; quantities are given in thousands of pounds. **[LO 6.2]**

TABLE 6P-1

Price ($)	Quantity demanded (thousands of lbs.)	Quantity supplied (thousands of lbs.)
6	5	80
5	20	70
4	35	60
3	50	50
2	65	40
1	80	30

a. How many thousands of pounds of meat would you recommend that the government purchase to keep the price at $4/pound?

b. How much money should the government budget for this program?

8. The market shown in Figure 6P-5 is in equilibrium. Suppose there is a $15 per unit tax levied on sellers.

FIGURE 6P-5

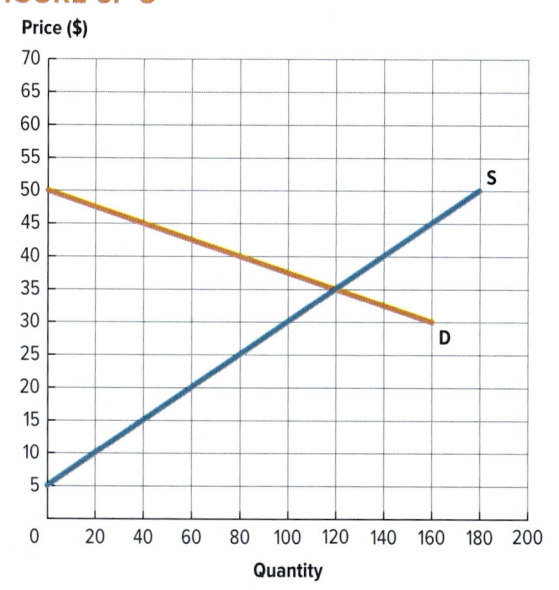

a. Draw the after-tax supply curve.
b. Plot the after-tax price paid by consumers and the after-tax price paid by sellers.

9. The market shown in Figure 6P-6 is in equilibrium. Suppose there is a $1.50 per unit tax levied on sellers. **[LO 6.3]**

FIGURE 6P-6

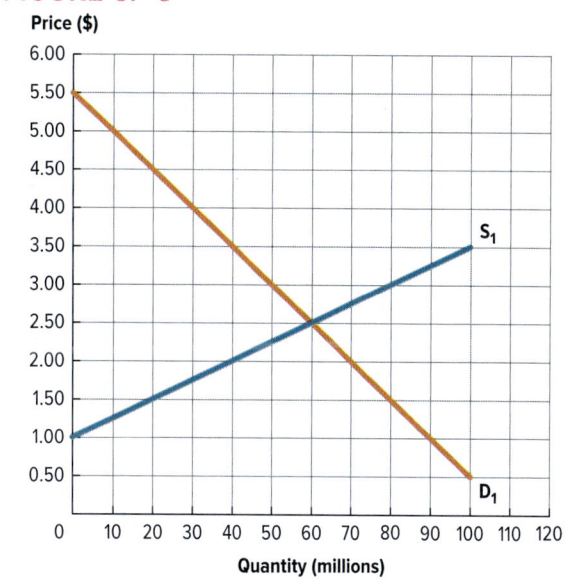

a. Draw the after-tax supply curve.
b. Plot the after-tax price paid by consumers and the after-tax price paid by sellers.
c. Draw consumer surplus, producer surplus, tax revenue, and deadweight loss after the tax.
d. Calculate deadweight loss.
e. Calculate total surplus.

10. Suppose the government is considering taxing cigarettes. Because it is often politically more popular to tax the producers of cigarettes than the consumers of cigarettes, the government first considers the impact on the market as a result of taxing the producers of cigarettes. Figure 6P-7 shows the market in equilibrium. **[LO 6.3]**

FIGURE 6P-7

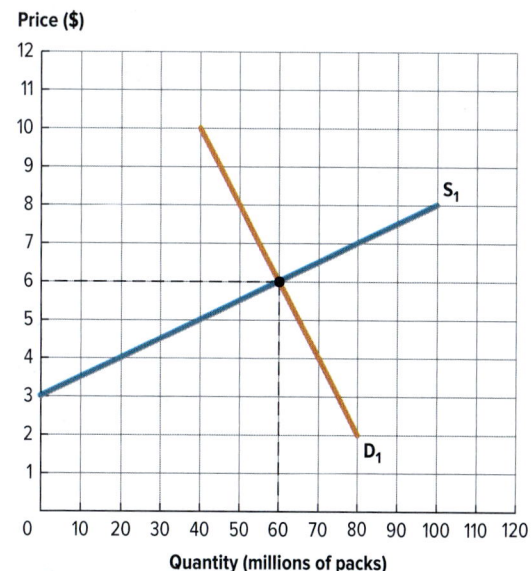

a. Draw the after-tax supply curve if the government chooses to tax cigarette producers $2.50 per pack of cigarettes.
b. Plot the after-tax price paid by consumers and the after-tax price received by sellers.
c. Do consumers or producers bear the greater burden of this tax?
d. Now suppose the government considers taxing the consumers of cigarettes instead of the producers of cigarettes. Draw the after-tax supply curve if the government chooses to tax cigarette consumers $2.50 per pack of cigarettes.
e. Plot the after-tax price paid by consumers and the after-tax price received by sellers.
f. Do consumers or producers bear the greater burden of this tax?
g. Is the price sellers receive when the government taxes consumers of cigarettes more than, less than, or the same as the price sellers receive when the government taxes producers of cigarettes?
h. Is the price buyers pay when the government taxes consumers of cigarettes more than, less than, or the same as the price buyers pay when the government taxes producers of cigarettes?

11. Suppose you have the information shown in Table 6P-2 about the quantity of a good that is supplied and demanded at various prices. **[LO 6.3]**

TABLE 6P-2

Price ($)	Quantity demanded	Quantity supplied
45	10	160
40	20	140
35	30	120
30	40	100
25	50	80
20	60	60
15	70	40
10	80	20
5	90	0

a. Plot the demand and supply curves on a graph, with price on the y-axis and quantity on the x-axis.
b. What are the equilibrium price and quantity?

c. Suppose the government imposes a $15 per unit tax on sellers of this good. Draw the new supply curve on your graph.
d. What is the new equilibrium quantity? How much will consumers pay? How much will sellers receive after the tax?
e. Calculate the price elasticity of demand over this price change.
f. If demand were less elastic (holding supply constant), would the deadweight loss be smaller or larger? **[LO 6.5]**

12. The weekly supply and demand for fast-food cheeseburgers in your city is shown in Figure 6P-8. In an effort to curb a looming budget deficit, the mayor recently proposed a tax that would be levied on sales at fast-food restaurants. **[LO 6.3]**

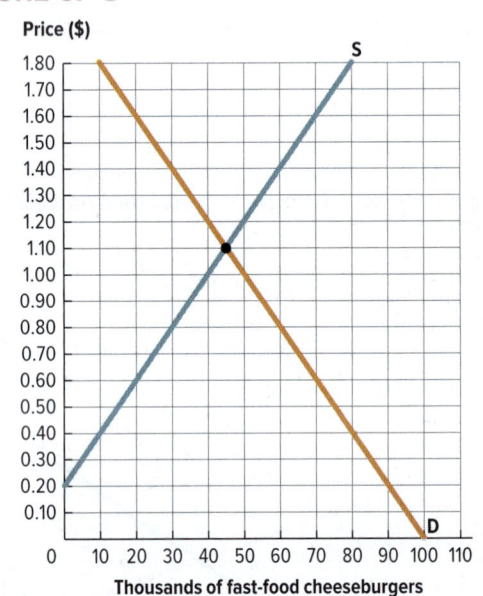

FIGURE 6P-8

a. The mayor's proposal includes a sales tax of 60 cents on cheeseburgers, to be paid by consumers. What is the new outcome in this market (how many cheeseburgers are sold and at what price)? Illustrate this outcome on your graph.
b. How much of the tax burden is borne by consumers? How much by suppliers?
c. What is the deadweight loss associated with the proposed tax?
d. How much revenue will the government collect?
e. What is the loss of consumer surplus from this tax?

13. The market shown in Figure 6P-9 is in equilibrium. Suppose there is a $15 per unit subsidy given to buyers. **[LO 6.4]**

FIGURE 6P-9

a. Draw the after-subsidy demand curve.
b. Plot the after-subsidy price paid by consumers and the after-subsidy price paid by sellers.

14. The market shown in Figure 6P-10 is in equilibrium. Suppose there is a $15 per unit subsidy given to sellers. **[LO 6.4]**

FIGURE 6P-10

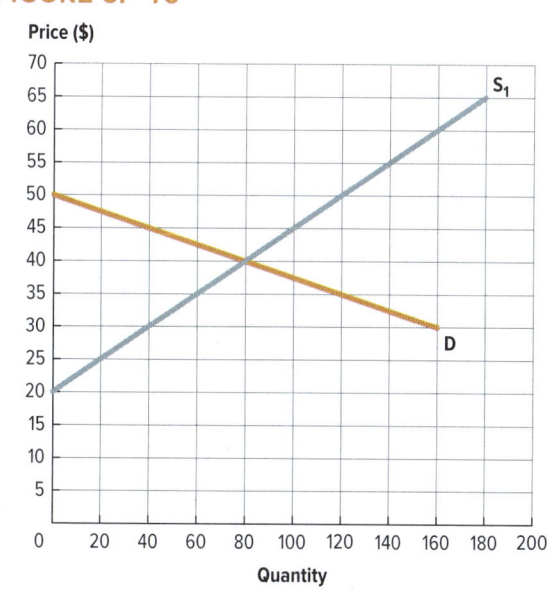

a. Draw the after-subsidy supply curve.
b. Plot the after-subsidy price paid by consumers and the after-subsidy price paid by sellers.

15. Demand and supply of laptop computers are given in Figure 6P-11. The quantity of laptops is given in thousands. Suppose the government provides a $300 subsidy for every laptop computer that consumers purchase. **[LO 6.4]**

FIGURE 6P-11

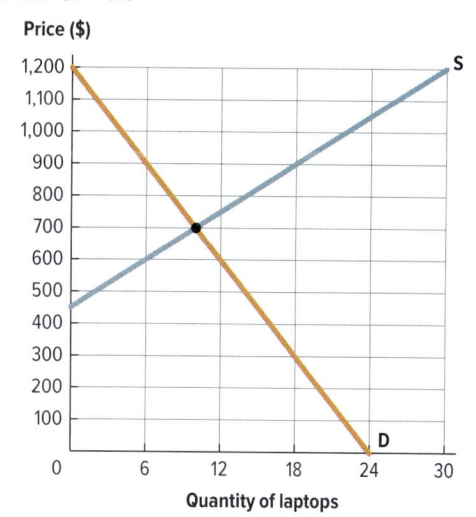

a. What will be the quantity of laptops bought and sold at the new equilibrium?
b. What will be the price consumers pay for laptops under the subsidy?
c. What will be the price that sellers receive for laptops under the subsidy?
d. How much money should the government budget for the subsidy?

16. The market shown in Figure 6P-12 is in equilibrium. Suppose there is a $1.50 per unit subsidy given to buyers. **[LO 6.4]**

FIGURE 6P-12

a. Draw the after-subsidy demand curve.
b. Plot the after-subsidy price paid by consumers and the after-subsidy price paid by sellers.
c. Draw government expenditures for the subsidy.
d. Calculate government expenditures.

17. The market shown in Figure 6P-13 is in equilibrium. Suppose there is a $3 per unit subsidy given to buyers. **[LO 6.4]**

FIGURE 6P-13

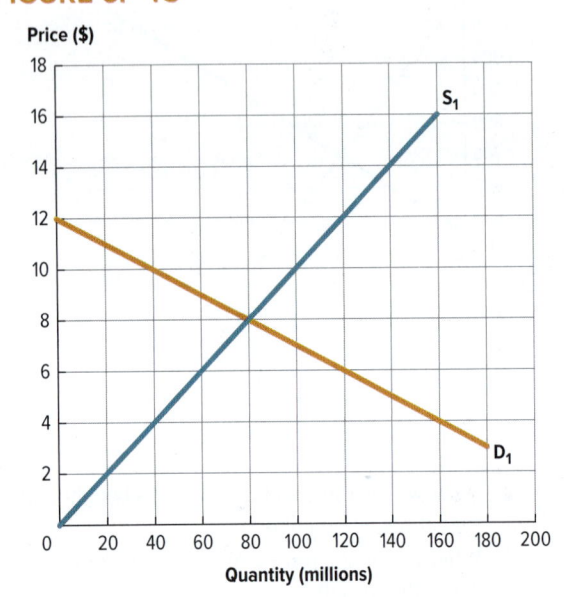

Price ($) vs Quantity (millions); supply curve S_1 and demand curve D_1 intersect at (80, 8).

a. Draw the after-subsidy demand curve.
b. Plot the after-subsidy price paid by consumers and the after-subsidy price paid by sellers.
c. Draw the deadweight loss after the subsidy.
d. Calculate deadweight loss.

18. Suppose government offers a subsidy to laptop sellers. Say whether each group of people gains or loses from this policy. **[LO 6.4]**
    a. Laptop buyers.
    b. Laptop sellers.
    c. Desktop computer sellers (assuming that they are different from laptop manufacturers).
    d. Desktop computer buyers.

19. Suppose that for health reasons, the government of the nation of Ironia wants to increase the amount of broccoli citizens consume. Which of the following policies could be used to achieve the goal? **[LO 6.1, 6.4]**
    a. A price floor to support broccoli growers.
    b. A price ceiling to ensure that broccoli remains affordable to consumers.
    c. A subsidy paid to shoppers who buy broccoli.
    d. A subsidy paid to farmers who grow broccoli.

20. The following scenarios describe the price elasticity of supply and demand for a particular good. In which scenario will a subsidy increase consumption the most? Choose only one. **[LO 6.5]**
    a. Elastic demand, inelastic supply.
    b. Inelastic demand, inelastic supply.
    c. Elastic demand, elastic supply.
    d. Inelastic demand, elastic supply.

21. The market shown in Figure 6P-14 is in equilibrium. **[LO 6.5]**

FIGURE 6P-14

Price ($) vs Quantity; supply curve S and demand curve D intersect at approximately (4.5, 5).

a. If a tax was imposed on this market, would buyers or sellers bear more of the burden of the tax? Why?

22. The following scenarios describe the price elasticity of supply and demand for a particular good. All else equal (equilibrium price, equilibrium quantity, and size of the tax), in which scenario will government revenues be the highest? Choose only one. **[LO 6.5]**
    a. Elastic demand, inelastic supply.
    b. Inelastic demand, inelastic supply.
    c. Elastic demand, elastic supply.
    d. Inelastic demand, elastic supply.

Endnotes

1. http://www.time.com/time/magazine/article/0,9171,1727720,00.html and http://www.nytimes.com/2008/06/22/nyregion/22food.html.
2. "The new face of hunger," *The Economist*, April 17, 2008.

The Data of Macroeconomics

PART THREE

The two chapters in Part 3 will introduce you to . . .

the topic of macroeconomics and two important macroeconomic concepts: gross domestic product and consumer prices.

How well off do you think you will be in 10 years? In 20 years? Your answers probably depend on choices that you may already be considering—especially choices about where to live, family plans, and your career.

Of course, your future financial position will also depend on forces outside of your control. Some of those forces will be economic, like how many jobs are available, how housing prices change, and how fast prices rise over time. These forces are the focus of macroeconomics, the study of how billions of daily decisions made by individuals add up to shape the overall economy. It's the study of economic growth, inflation, booms and busts, and unemployment.

Chapter 7, "Measuring GDP," covers the calculation of gross domestic product (GDP), the most useful metric of macroeconomics, which sums up the amount of economic activity in a country. It's the first number economists look at when tracking overall economic growth and the ups and downs of the economy.

Chapter 8, "The Cost of Living," covers another important part of macroeconomic record-keeping: consumer prices. A century ago, a bottle of Coke cost a nickel and and a brand-new car could be purchased for hundreds of dollars. Both items cost a lot more today, but that doesn't mean that we're worse off—our incomes have risen along with prices. As you'll see, accounting for consumer prices gives an important part of the macro picture.

As we progress through the study of macroeconomics, the concepts of GDP and changing price levels will come up over and over again; they are useful tools for answering questions about the health and direction of the economy. These two chapters offer insight into forces that will affect your job and income, as well as the wealth and well-being of the whole country.

Measuring GDP

Chapter 7

It's More than Counting Peanuts

If we made a list of the economic changes that are most dramatically reshaping the world, the rapid growth of China's economy would likely top it. In 1978, when China's leaders moved to open up its economic system, it was the world's 15th-largest economy. The size of China's economy doubled. Then it doubled, and doubled, and doubled again. By 2011, China's economy checked in at about $6 trillion, passing Japan's to become the second-largest economy in the world. This progress is about more than numbers. Rapid economic growth can create jobs, reduce poverty, and improve standards of living. In China, the fraction of the population living below the international poverty line ($1.90 per person per day) fell from 88 percent in 1981 to 6.5 percent in 2012, and to just 0.7 percent in 2015.[1]

Economic growth has increased living standards all over the world in recent decades, although typically in less dramatic fashion than in China. Over the same time of China's explosive growth, the proportion of people worldwide living on less than $1.90 fell from 42 percent to 10 percent in 2015.

The health of the national economy has a powerful effect on everyday life in any country. When the economy is doing well, jobs are plentiful and most people can live well and securely. When the economy does poorly, jobs are scarce, businesses close down, and people struggle. It's no wonder that politicians spend a lot of energy debating the best plan to expand the economy. Over the next few chapters, we'll discuss many of the ideas and terms used in those debates.

But, first, we need to answer a basic question: How do we measure the "size" of an economy? If we can answer that, we can compare China's economy to economies of other nations. We also can determine whether an economy is growing or not over time. What does it really *mean* to say that China has a $12 trillion economy?

The answers to these questions require some careful accounting. As a start, think about just one of the many transactions that take place in the U.S. economy. Say you bought a jar of peanut butter when you went to the grocery store. Although small, your purchase contributed to the size of the economy.

©McGraw-Hill Education/Elite Images

Consider some of the things that happened before that jar of peanut butter made it into your shopping cart: A farmer grew the peanuts, perhaps on a small farm in Georgia. The farmer sold his peanuts to a wholesaler in Atlanta. The wholesaler then sold the peanuts to a peanut butter factory in Ohio, which combined the peanuts with other ingredients to produce a jar of peanut butter. The factory then sold that jar to a grocery store chain, which delivered it to your neighborhood store.

Many people were employed to produce that peanut butter: farmers, accountants, truck drivers, custodians, and grocery-store cashiers. Many firms earned profits from the jar of peanut butter, too: the peanut farm, the wholesaler, the factory, the shipping company, and your local store. Clearly, the activities that went into making and buying the jar of peanut butter added value to the economy. Can we measure how much?

The peanuts passed through many stages: from seed, to harvested nut, to peanut butter, to a jar on the grocery store shelf. At each stage, the peanuts were sold as an *output* of one firm and purchased as an *input* by another firm. Should we add up all of these sales individually to calculate the value the jar of peanut butter added to the economy? No—if we did that, we'd be overcounting the value of your purchase. All of the sales were just steps toward one end product: your peanut butter. How then *do* we calculate the total value of your jar of peanut butter to the economy?

LEARNING OBJECTIVES

LO 7.1 Understand the importance of using the market value of final goods and services to calculate GDP, and explain why each component of GDP is important.

LO 7.2 Explain the equivalence of the expenditure and income approaches to valuing an economy.

LO 7.3 Explain the three approaches that are used to calculate GDP, and summarize the categories of spending that are included in the expenditure approach.

LO 7.4 Explain the difference between real and nominal GDP.

LO 7.5 Calculate the GDP deflator.

LO 7.6 Use GDP per capita to compare economies and calculate the real GDP annual growth rate.

LO 7.7 Discuss some limitations to GDP, including its measurement of well-being, home production, the underground economy, and environmental degradation.

This is the problem that economists faced in the 1920s and 1930s when they first attempted to calculate the value of the U.S. economy. How can you add up all economic activity to arrive at an overall value for the economy, *without double-counting* items that are resold more than once before they reach the consumer?

The solution is a system called *national income accounting*, created by Nobel Prize winners Simon Kuznets and Richard Stone. In this chapter, we'll see how to use this system to calculate the value of a national economy. We'll see why it's so useful to measure a country's total output and also why gross domestic product (GDP), the most commonly used measure, has some limitations. In later chapters, we'll put these ideas to work to explain economic growth, unemployment, and economic booms and slowdowns.

Valuing an Economy

Economics has traditionally been divided into two broad fields, microeconomics and macroeconomics. *Microeconomics* is the study of how individuals and firms manage resources. In microeconomics, we zero in on a single person's budget, or one firm's cost of production, or the price of a particular good.

Macroeconomics, on the other hand, is the study of the economy on a broad scale, focusing on issues such as economic growth, unemployment, and inflation. In macroeconomics, we talk about consumption, production, and prices in the *aggregate*, on a national level, and we look at the effects of those aggregate forces on the whole economy.

Compared to microeconomics, the concepts of macroeconomics may seem distant from decisions we make and challenges we face. But macroeconomic issues can have profound impacts on our daily lives. Periods with steady economic growth, stable prices, and low unemployment create solid platforms for progress. On the flip side, long periods of stagnation, inflation, and high unemployment can do great damage to family finances and communities.

At the start of the chapter, we introduced one of the most important macroeconomic phenomena of our time: the incredible growth of the Chinese economy. Thinking about the Chinese economy raises some questions:

- How do we know how big the Chinese economy is?
- How do we know that it is larger than Japan's but smaller than the United States's?
- What does it mean to say that the size of China's economy doubled?

To talk about these critical issues, we need a tool for measuring the "size" or "value" of a national economy.

The most commonly used metric for measuring the value of a national economy is **gross domestic product**, or **GDP**. Gross domestic product is the sum of the market values of all final goods and services produced within a country in a given period of time. Economists divide these goods and services into different categories, called *consumption, investments, government purchases,* and *net exports,* to make it clear what is being produced in the economy. We'll cover these categories in more detail later. For now, we'll unpack the definition of GDP using examples of consumption.

GDP is one of the most important and commonly used data points in macroeconomics. It gives us a sense of the well-being of the average person in a country. It also allows us to gauge the direction an economy is headed, by looking at changes over time. Before we look at how economists calculate GDP, though, let's unpack the component parts of the definition.

Unpacking the definition of GDP

The definition of GDP has four important pieces:

- the *market value*
- of *final goods and services*
- produced *within a country*
- in a *given period of time*.

Let's take each piece one at a time and explain its importance.

Market values If we measured the output of economies by simply listing every single good and service, we wouldn't learn much—680 million jars of peanut butter, 103 million copies of Microsoft Word, 421 million haircuts, and so on. The list would go on for thousands of pages. It wouldn't be very interesting. Nor would it be useful for comparing the overall size of different national economies, which tend to make different things. For example, how would we compare the size of the U.S. economy with the Mexican economy—which produces its own set of petrochemicals, cars, crops, and other goods and services?

Clearly, we need to translate the production of peanut butter, software, haircuts, and all the other goods and services into a common unit so we can add them up. That common unit is their *market value*—which in the United States is measured in dollars (and pesos in Mexico). So we know from this part of the definition that GDP is going to be a *number measured in the local currency.* (Though for comparison across countries, these local currency calculations are then later translated to a value in a common currency.)

Final goods and services Consider the 800 or so peanuts that end up in your jar of peanut butter. Suppose our Georgia peanut farmer sells them to the Atlanta wholesaler for 12 cents. The wholesaler sells them to the Ohio peanut butter factory for 25 cents. The peanut butter factory

---

macroeconomics
the study of the economy as a whole, and how policy-makers manage the growth and behavior of the overall economy

gross domestic product (GDP)
the sum of the market values of all final goods and services produced within a country in a given period of time

LO 7.1 Understand the importance of using the market value of final goods and services to calculate GDP, and explain why each component of GDP is important.

sells the 18-ounce jar of peanut butter to the grocery store for $1.85. Finally, the grocery store sells it to you for $3.40. How much does this process contribute to GDP?

If we simply add up all the transactions, we might think that the jar of peanut butter contributed $5.61 to GDP ($0.12 + $0.25 + $1.85 + $3.40). But, if that were true, producing the jar of peanut butter would contribute more to GDP than its final selling price. That can't be right. If it were, we could grow the economy just by trading the same jar of peanut butter for the same dollar, over and over again, and adding up each "transaction."

The problem here is that by adding each of the transactions, we are double-counting, giving us too big a total. To avoid double-counting, we should *ignore the price of intermediate* goods and services—that is, goods and services used only to produce something else, like the raw peanuts that were sold to the peanut butter factory.

©Inge van Mill/Hollandse Hoogte/Redux

Instead, we want to count only expenditures on *final goods and services*—those that get sold to the consumer. In this case, the only final good was the jar of peanut butter you bought at the store. Its price was $3.40—so that is how much your purchase contributed to GDP.

Produced within a country The goods and services that count toward GDP are defined in terms of the *location of production*, not the citizenship of the producer. So:

- If a U.S. company owns a factory in Mexico, the value of the goods produced in that factory will count toward Mexican GDP, not U.S. GDP.
- A U.S. citizen working in France will contribute to French GDP.
- Likewise, a French or Mexican citizen working in the United States will contribute to U.S. GDP.

What if we want to measure the value of what is produced by all U.S. companies regardless of their location? In this case, we use a different metric, called **gross national product (GNP)**. GNP is the sum of the market values of all final goods and services produced by a country's businesses within a given period of time. It is similar to GDP except that it

1. includes the *worldwide* value of all final goods and services produced by a country's businesses and
2. excludes production by foreign businesses within the country.

gross national product (GNP)
the sum of the market values of all final goods and services produced by citizens of a country within a given period of time

Given period of time As a measure of income, GDP tracks production over the course of a year. Measuring production within a certain space of time allows for clear calculation.

In theory, we could calculate the output of the economy over any time period—a day, a month, a year. When you hear people talking about GDP, they're often referring to an annual figure. However, a year is a long time to wait for an update on how the economy is doing, so GDP is usually calculated on a *quarterly* basis—that is, four times a year.

Typically, what we really want to know is an estimate of annual GDP, using the most recent quarterly information. We can't just multiply this quarter's GDP by four, however, because the economy seldom rolls along at the same pace all year. For instance, December usually has more economic activity than other months due to people buying presents and traveling.

Therefore, we need to adjust quarterly GDP estimates to account for these seasonal patterns. That's why quarterly GDP is typically shown as a *seasonally adjusted estimate at an annual rate*. By taking account of predictable seasonal patterns, we can have a good guess at what annual GDP will be if the economy continues at its current pace.

Production equals expenditure equals income

Now that we have defined the term *gross domestic product*, how do we go about measuring it? The example of peanut butter was just a start – the economy is dynamic, producing a whole range of "stuff."

Economists use two terms interchangeably—*output* or *production*—to refer to this "stuff," which includes both goods and services. Indeed, about three-quarters of U.S. output is services, not goods. In the previous section, we saw that the final value of goods or services sold makes up GDP. However, there are three ways to calculate that final value. We'll look at the first two ways briefly here (and then look at all three in more detail in the next section).

First, the *expenditure approach:* The market value of a good or service is the price at which it is bought and sold. If we add up all the money people spend buying final goods and services—being careful to omit spending on intermediate goods so as not to double-count—the sum will be the market value of all output sold in the economy. In other words, we can use the expenditure approach to measure total output by *measuring total expenditure*.

Second, the income approach: Every transaction, of course, has not only a buyer who spends on a good or service but also a seller who earns income from the sale. Thus, expenditures by one person translate directly into *income* for someone else. So, we can also measure production using the income approach by *adding up everyone's income*.

This approach may sound familiar if you remember the *circular flow model* of the economy that was presented in Chapter 1, "Economics and Life," and is repeated here in Figure 7-1.

Households buy things from firms in the market for goods and services. Firms then use some of the money they earn in revenue to pay wages to workers and rent to landowners in the market for the factors of production. In each of these transactions, expenditures by one party are income for another.

The circular flow model is a major simplification of the economy. (We're ignoring, for now, the money paid in taxes or the money that is saved instead of spent, for example.) Yet it shows that we should get to the same figure for GDP regardless of whether we measure expenditure or income in an economy:

National production = National expenditure = National income

This equality is a crucial idea in the study of macroeconomics.

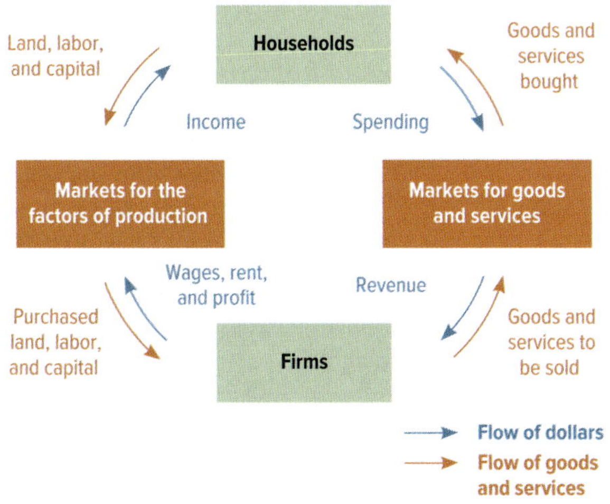

LO 7.2 Explain the equivalence of the expenditure and income approaches to valuing an economy.

FIGURE 7-1

Circular flow diagram

✓ TEST YOURSELF

☐ Why are only final goods and services counted under GDP? Why are sales of used goods not counted? [**LO 7.1**]

☐ Why is total income in a country equal to total expenditures on goods produced in that country? [**LO 7.2**]

Approaches to Measuring GDP

LO 7.3 Explain the three approaches that are used to calculate GDP, and summarize the categories of spending that are included in the expenditure approach.

We just saw that national production equals national expenditure equals national income. The equality of production, expenditure, and income would hold true in a literal, straightforward way if we lived in a *closed economy*—an economy in which all goods were produced and sold domestically and everything was consumed as soon as it was made. The actual economy is more complicated, but the basic equality still holds—as long as we're a little more careful about how we define each part.

We'll need to consider two complications in particular:

- One complication is international trade. Once we start to consider imports and exports, we see that expenditure in one country can translate into income in *another* country.
- The second complication is unsold inventories. What happens when goods are produced but not sold?

In this section, we will consider three approaches to measuring GDP—the expenditure approach, the income approach, and the value-added approach. Looking at the different approaches, we will see how economists deal with the complications of international trade and unsold inventories.

Why are there three approaches? Each focuses on a different piece of GDP and so provides a slightly different look at how those different pieces make up the big picture. It turns out, though, that all three approaches end up with roughly the same GDP number.

After reading the next three sections, you'll understand the details of how they differ. For now, it's enough to give this broad overview of the differences:

- The *expenditure approach* highlights the importance of consumer spending versus government purchases.
- The *income approach* emphasizes information about the relative importance of different factors of production.
- The *value-added approach* is especially useful for tracking how goods are sold and resold.

Some countries use all three approaches to calculate GDP so that policy-makers and researchers can get a full picture of economic activity.

The expenditure approach

To measure output using the *expenditure method*, we start by breaking down expenditure into categories. Remember that we don't want to double-count, so we *don't* include intermediate products, like raw peanuts and the labor of peanut factory workers, which firms buy only to transform into final goods and services. It turns out that all expenditures can be classified in one of of four categories: final goods and services, goods bought as investment, government purchases, and net exports. To find total expenditure, we add together those four categories:

$$\text{Consumption (C)} + \text{Investment (I)} + \text{Government purchases (G)} + \text{Net exports (NX)} = \text{Total expenditure}$$

Let's look at each in more detail.

consumption (C) spending on goods and services by private individuals and households

Consumption (C) The first category, **consumption (C)**, measures spending on goods and services by private individuals and households. It includes almost anything you'd buy for yourself, from basic, nondurable goods (like food and clothing), to durable goods (like computers and cars), to services (like haircuts, tutoring, and plumbing). If you pay rent or college tuition, those expenses are also included in consumption.

Note that what is consumed has to be *new*. This requirement avoids the illogical conclusion that we could grow the economy simply by reselling the same jar of peanut butter over and over again. If you buy a *used* camera on eBay, for example, the camera itself is not counted toward the size of the economy; the original purchase of the camera was already recorded in GDP when it was sold new. However, the fee the seller pays to eBay *is* counted as consumption and so is the price the seller pays FedEx to deliver the camera to you.

Investment (I) The second category, **investment (I)**, includes spending on productive inputs, such as factories, machinery, and inventories. That means goods bought by people or firms who plan to use those purchases to produce other goods and services in the future, rather than consuming them. It includes *capital goods*, which are items like machines or tools that will be used for production of other goods or services. It also includes buildings and structures, like warehouses, that will be involved in providing goods and services.

investment (I)
spending on productive inputs, such as factories, machinery, and inventories

It's worth noting that newly built houses are also counted as investment. In contrast, if you rent a house, that expenditure falls under consumption. Why the difference? A newly built house will provide a place to live (or to rent out) now and for years to come, just as a newly built factory will generate output now and in future years. But when you *rent* a house, you are paying its owner for the service of letting you live there. You are consuming "place-to-live" services, but you're not making an investment because the house belongs to someone else and won't generate future revenues for you.

Again, note that investment goods are counted only if they are *new*. We don't count buying an existing factory or secondhand tools as investment. Nor do we count an individual's purchase of an existing house. The services of the real estate agent selling you the house, though, would be counted toward consumption.

⚠ CAUTION: COMMON MISTAKE

You may have heard people talk about their "investments"—stocks, bonds, mutual funds, and other products bought and sold in the financial markets. While it may seem as if these financial products should be counted under the "I" (investment) term in GDP, *they do not get counted as a part of GDP*. There are two reasons for that:

- First, if you buy a share of General Motors stock through the New York Stock Exchange, your money does not go to General Motors. Instead, you are buying stock from some other investor who has decided to sell her stock in General Motors. (We'll cover how economists think about buying stocks and making other financial "investments" in Chapter 14, "The Basics of Finance.")
- Second, including stock purchases in GDP calculations would be another type of double-counting. If we added to GDP every time someone bought shares, we could make the economy seem to be growing simply by having people resell the same shares over and over again—just like selling the same jar of peanut butter multiple times.

Although sales of stocks do not count in GDP, the money raised in initial public offerings (IPOs) of stocks may still be counted in other ways. Since the money raised by stock offerings goes to the company that sells stock, they may make investments or purchases with the money, increasing GDP.

inventory
the stock of goods that a company produces now but does not sell immediately

Finally, our definition of investment also includes a less-obvious type of "purchase": spending on inventories. Earlier in the chapter, when we equated production, income, and expenditure, we raised the question of how to deal with goods that are produced but not sold. Inventory is the answer: It's the stock of goods that a company produces now but keeps to sell at a future time. If Ford manufactures a car this year, but the car sits on the lot until next year, the car becomes part of Ford's inventory. If Apple makes a batch of iPhones but keeps them in a warehouse until it's time to release the new model for public sale, they become part of Apple's inventory.

When a good is added to a company's inventory, we treat it as if the *producing company* has "bought" that item to keep in stock for the future. The value of the company's purchase is included in our calculation of investment for the year. What happens next year when a consumer buys the new-model iPhone? We don't want to count the same iPhone toward GDP in two different years. So, its value will be subtracted from Apple's inventory at the same time as it is counted as consumption. These two transactions cancel out, meaning the consumer's purchase of the phone results in no net increase in GDP.

government purchases (G)
spending on goods and services by all levels of government

Government purchases (G) The next category of spending, **government purchases (G)**, represents goods and services bought by all levels of government. This includes both:

- "Consumption"-type purchases of goods (for instance, buying new bulbs to go in streetlights) and services (buying the labor of government workers who repair streetlights).
- "Investment"-type purchases (for instance, buying a truck that government workers will use to repair streetlights in the future).

In fact, the technical name for this category of spending is "government consumption expenditures and gross investment." We'll stick with the term *government purchases* because it's less of a mouthful. In the United States, government purchases were $4.4 trillion in 2018, or 21 percent of GDP.

However, one important category of government spending does *not* count as a government purchase: spending that simply *transfers resources* to individuals, through Social Security or similar programs. For example, the Social Security payment from the government to a retired person does not count toward government purchases. When that person spends money from his or her Social Security payment to buy groceries, the spending will then be counted as private consumption.

net exports (NX)
exports minus imports; the value of goods and services produced domestically and consumed abroad minus the value of goods and services produced abroad and consumed domestically

Net exports (NX) The three categories of spending we've considered—consumption, investment, and government purchases—include spending on goods and services produced abroad as well as those produced domestically. Let's think about the GDP of the United States. Our calculation of consumption will include instances when people in the United States buy goods made abroad—say, a sweater imported from Scotland. If we're trying to measure the value of the goods produced *within the United States*, we don't want to count this spending. On the flip side, we don't want to miss spending by people in other countries on goods or services made in the United States and exported for sale abroad—say, a Harley-Davidson motorcycle.

These two forces work in opposite directions: Domestic spending on imports should get subtracted from our GDP calculations, while international spending on exports should get added. We can simplify these international transactions by combining exports and imports into one term, called **net exports (NX)**. Net exports represent the value of goods and services produced domestically and consumed abroad minus the value of goods and services produced abroad and consumed domestically. If exports are higher than imports, NX will be positive. If imports are higher than exports, NX will be negative. Figure 7-2 shows how we can think about the role of net exports using a visual tool.

Summing spending categories When we add together spending in all four categories—consumption, investment, government purchases, and net exports—the total will be equal to

FIGURE 7-2

Adding up expenditures when there are imports and exports Everything that is produced domestically is added to GDP, whether it is purchased for consumption, for investment, by the government, or by people abroad (exports). Goods that are produced internationally but bought domestically, otherwise known as imports, are subtracted from GDP because they represent expenditures leaving the country. Transactions between foreign producers and foreign buyers do not involve domestic production or expenditure and therefore do not figure into GDP calculations.

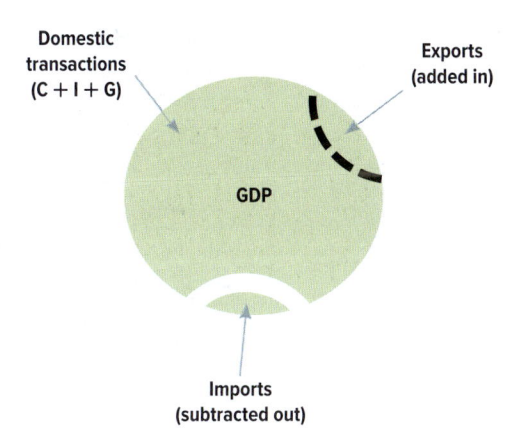

expenditure on all goods and services produced in a country. As we learned in the previous section, the total of those national expenditures is equal to the value of national production. This equation is represented as follows.

EQUATION 7-1 $$\text{Expenditure} = C + I + G + NX = \text{Production}$$

As you can see in Figure 7-3, consumption is by far the largest single category of expenditure in the United States, but investment and government purchases are also significant.

We can also see in Figure 7-3 that U.S. residents *buy* more goods from abroad than they *sell* to people abroad. That's why the value for net exports is a negative number, -3.2 percent of total 2018 GDP. In other words, in 2018 U.S. consumers spent more abroad than U.S. producers earned from foreigners buying U.S.-made goods, and the size of that difference was equal to 3.2 percent of GDP. If exports had been higher than imports, this number would have been positive.

Figuring out what goes into GDP and what isn't counted in the expenditure method takes a little practice. To help you keep track, Table 7-1 summarizes some of the examples presented in this chapter.

The income approach

A different way to think about the value of a national economy is to add up the *income earned by everyone in the country*. The income approach thus brings together information on the different factors of production.

To value an economy using the income approach, we add up all the types of income earned by people in a country:

- wages earned by workers,
- interest earned on capital investments,
- rents earned on land and property, and
- profits earned by firms (plus a couple of additional technical adjustments).

FIGURE 7-3

U.S. GDP breakdown
This figure shows the *expenditure method* of calculating GDP, which adds together consumption, investment, government purchases, and net exports (exports minus imports). In the United States, imports are currently higher than exports, so the value of net exports is negative and is subtracted from the total.

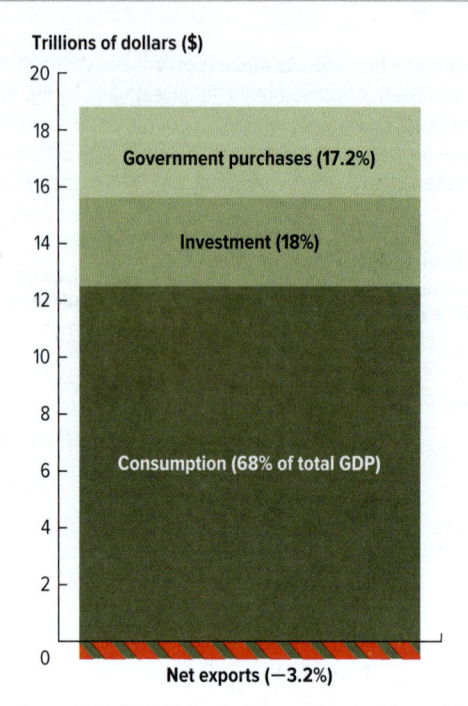

Trillions of dollars ($)

- Government purchases (17.2%)
- Investment (18%)
- Consumption (68% of total GDP)
- Net exports (−3.2%)

Source: Bureau of Economic Analysis, Domestic Product and Income, https://apps.bea.gov/iTable/iTable.cfm?reqid=19&step=2#reqid=19&step=2&isuri=1&1921=survey

TABLE 7-1
Is it GDP?

Situation	GDP Category	Why?
Buying a new digital camera	Consumption	Purchasing a *new* good or service always counts toward GDP.
Buying a used camera on eBay	Not counted	As a used good, the camera does not count toward GDP as it was already counted when new. The fees paid to eBay for selling the camera count as consumption, though.
Buying a new house	Investment	Since buying a house will provide a place to live for years into the future, it makes sense to think of it as an investment.
Renting an apartment	Consumption	You are paying the owner of the house for a service, so it is counted as consumption.
Apple makes a new batch of iPhones but doesn't sell them until next year	Investment	Counted as a part of investment as Apple is holding these phones as a part of its inventory.
Buying shares of General Motors stock	Not counted	Shares of stock are a transfer of money from one owner of the stock to another. Including stocks would cause a double-counting problem.
TSA buys plastic bins for airport security	Government spending	Any consumption or investment purchases made by the government are counted in GDP as government spending.
Babysitting for your neighbor	Not counted	In principle, it should be included in GDP, but such income is often not reported to the IRS, and thus it can't be included in official statistics.

Under this approach, national income can be shown in an equation as:

EQUATION 7-2   National income = Wages + Interest + Rental income + Profits

In an economy without any imports and exports, this income approach will give us the same result as the expenditure approach. Why? Because in every transaction, there is not only a buyer who spends but also a seller who earns the same amount in income. If you spend $20 on gasoline, that same $20 is both expenditure to you and income to the owner of the gas station. The expenditure approach added up everything on one side of this transaction. The income approach adds up everything on the *other side* of the transaction, which comes out to the same amount.

But what happens when there is foreign trade? When goods produced in the United States are exported, the transaction is expenditure by other countries and income for the United States. When people in the United States spend money on goods made in another country, the transaction is expenditure in the United States and income for the other country.

The "value-added" approach

Finally, we come to the third approach that economists sometimes use to measure economic output: the *value-added approach*. We have seen that the expenditure approach solves the double-counting problem by considering only transactions that represent final, and not intermediate, goods and services. For example, we count a consumer's purchase of a jar of peanut butter from a store but not a peanut butter factory's purchase of peanuts from a peanut wholesaler. What if, instead, we were to look at *all* transactions, but count only the *value they add* to the economy?

To see the reasoning behind this approach, let's stick with peanut butter. At each stage of the peanut butter production process, let's look at the difference between the sale value of the product and the value of the inputs that went into it. This difference represents the "value added" at that stage of production. For instance:

- The farmer *adds value* to the economy by taking seeds, land, and water and growing peanuts. Just for simplicity, imagine the farmer didn't pay anything for his inputs. The value added to the economy is the $0.12 the farmer gets from selling his 800 or so peanuts to the wholesaler, minus the value of the inputs, which we are imagining to be zero.
- If the wholesaler buys those $0.12 in peanuts and sells them to a peanut butter factory for $0.25, then the wholesaler has added $0.13 ($0.25 − $0.12) in value to the economy by helping to link up farmers and factories.
- The peanut butter factory adds value by pressing the peanuts into butter and pouring it into jars. If the factory is able to get $1.85 per jar, it has added $1.60 ($1.85 − $0.25) in value to the economy.
- The grocery store adds value by transporting jars to a convenient location in your neighborhood, where clerks are on hand to allow you to purchase it for the final price of $3.40 per jar, a value added of $1.55 ($3.40 − $1.85).

To see the final value added, simply sum up the value added at each stage of the process:

$$\$0.12 + \$0.13 + \$1.60 + \$1.55 = \$3.40$$

You'll notice that this is the same as the final price of the peanut butter in the store—which is the amount that is counted in the expenditure method. The value-added approach is an alternative, and equally valid, way of avoiding the problem of double-counting the peanuts. It lets us break down the total value paid and see how much value was created at each step of the production process.

The value-added approach is especially useful when thinking about services involved in the resale of existing goods. We've already seen, for example, that resale of used cameras, existing houses, and shares of company stock do not count toward GDP—but the related services provided by eBay, real estate agents, and stockbrokers do. The concept of added value helps us to think about why this is so. A stockbroker adds value by handling the paperwork associated with purchasing shares of stock. A real estate agent adds value by publicizing the fact that a house is for sale, showing potential purchasers around, and helping negotiate a sale. eBay adds value by connecting buyers with sellers.

In general, any intermediary involved in the sale of used goods adds value by sourcing those goods and making them available for sale in a convenient way.

✓ TEST YOURSELF

- ☐ What is the difference between consumption spending and investment spending? [**LO 7.3**]
- ☐ Under which category of expenditure do inventories fall? [**LO 7.3**]
- ☐ Does the sale of intermediate goods count toward GDP in the expenditure approach? [**LO 7.3**]
- ☐ How do the expenditure approach and income approach capture two sides of the same transactions? [**LO 7.3**]
- ☐ How do GDP calculations account for the value added in the sale of an existing house by a realtor? [**LO 7.3**]

Using GDP to Compare Economies

U.S. GDP increased from $12.5 trillion in 2005 to nearly $21 trillion in 2018. Does this mean that people in the United States produced more goods and services in 2018 than in 2005? Or does it mean that we just paid more for the same things because prices were higher? The calculation of real and nominal GDP allows us to get to the heart of the question.

Real versus nominal GDP

LO 7.4 Explain the difference between real and nominal GDP.

GDP is a function of *both* the quantity of goods and services produced (output) and their market value (prices). For this reason, economists look at two different calculations of production: real GDP and nominal GDP.

Both numbers are important, but economists are generally more interested in *real GDP* because it gives a sense of how the size of the economy moves over time. Tracking *real GDP* gives a clearer view of changes in the amount of "stuff" (goods and services) that the economy produces.

real GDP
GDP calculation in which goods and services are valued at constant prices

The term *real GDP* refers to GDP measurement that focuses *solely on output*, controlling for price changes. Formally, **real GDP** is calculated based on goods and services valued at *constant prices*. Those constant prices are given for a specific year. We might, for example, measure real GDP by valuing output in 2018 at the prices that prevailed in 2010.

nominal GDP
GDP calculation in which goods and services are valued at current prices

If we report GDP *without controlling for price changes*, we are talking about *nominal GDP*. **Nominal GDP** is calculated based on goods and services valued at *current prices* (current at the time they are produced). Thus, in nominal GDP measurement, output for 2018 would be valued in 2018 prices.

Calculating nominal and real GDP To see the difference between real and nominal GDP measures in practice, let's imagine an economy with only two goods: pizza and spaghetti. For ease of discussion, let's call this fictional economy "Pizzetta."

Suppose that in 2015, Pizzetta produced 5 million pizzas at a price of $10 each and 20 million plates of spaghetti at a price of $8. Table 7-2 shows this output. In 2016, the number of pizzas and plates of spaghetti increased to 6 million and 22 million, respectively; prices stayed the same. In 2017, Pizzetta produced the same number of pizzas and plates of spaghetti, but prices increased. In 2018, both quantity and prices increased.

In order to calculate nominal GDP, we simply multiply the quantity of each good produced in a given year by its price in that year, as shown in column 6 of Table 7-2. We can see that Pizzetta's nominal GDP increased between 2015 and 2016 and again in 2017 and 2018.

What doesn't nominal GDP tell us? If we looked just at nominal GDP, we couldn't tell the cause of the increase. We wouldn't see that in 2016 the increase was due to larger output, or that in 2017 the increase was due only to an increase in prices with no increase in output. Instead, looking at real GDP helps us see the different causes of the changes in GDP in the two years.

To calculate real GDP (GDP valued at constant prices), we have to choose a *base year*. In the base year, nominal GDP and real GDP are equal. In every other year, we multiply the quantity of a good produced in that year by its price in the base year. In essence, we are holding prices constant while allowing quantities to rise and fall. This method isolates increases in output from increases in prices.

Looking at the Pizzetta example, suppose we pick 2015 as our base year. We can see in Table 7-2 that in 2016, the increase in real GDP is actually the same as the increase in nominal

TABLE 7-2
Calculating real versus nominal GDP growth

Nominal GDP is the sum of the market values of all final goods and services, which we calculate by multiplying the quantity of each output by its market price in the current year. To calculate *real GDP*, we want to value those goods and services at their prices in the base year. When prices stay the same, nominal GDP and real GDP increase at the same rate. If prices rise, nominal GDP will be higher than real GDP.

(1) Year	(2) Pizzas (millions)	(3) Price of pizza ($)	(4) Spaghetti (millions)	(5) Price of spaghetti ($)	(6) Nominal GDP (millions of $)	(7) Real GDP in 2015 prices (millions of $)	(8) What's happening
2015 (base year)	5	10	20	8	(5 × $10) + (20 × $8) = $210	(5 × $10) + (20 × $8) = $210	In the base year, nominal GDP and real GDP are equal by definition.
2016	6	10	22	8	(6 × $10) + (22 × $8) = $236	(6 × $10) + (22 × $8) = $236	When output rises and prices stay constant, nominal and real GDP rise at the same rate.
2017	6	12	22	10	(6 × $12) + (22 × $10) = $292	(6 × $10) + (22 × $8) = $236	When prices rise and output stays constant, nominal GDP rises, but real GDP does not.
2018	7	13	25	11	(7 × $13) + (25 × $11) = $366	(7 × $10) + (25 × $8) = $270	When both output and prices rise, nominal and real GDP rise at different rates.

GDP ($236 million). That makes sense: Prices didn't change between the two years, so base-year prices are the same as current-year prices.

Between 2016 and 2017, however, the difference between nominal and real GDP shows up. Nominal GDP increases because prices increased. (Prices of pizza and spaghetti increased by $2 each.) But real GDP stays constant because output stayed constant.

Between 2017 and 2018, *both* nominal *and* real GDP increase because both prices *and* output increased. However, the increase in real GDP ($34 million) is smaller than the increase in nominal GDP ($74 million). What does that tell us? It indicates that only $34 million of the $74 million growth in nominal GDP is due to rising output; the rest is due to rising prices.

In summary:

- Real GDP isolates changes in an economy's output.
- Nominal GDP encompasses changes in both output and prices.

As a result, because economists and policy-makers are often most interested in changes in output, they typically use *real GDP numbers* as a reference point.

When economists and policy-makers do want to focus on changes in prices, they turn to another measure—the GDP deflator.

The GDP deflator

LO 7.5 Calculate the GDP deflator.

We just saw that the difference between nominal and real GDP is the difference between current prices and base-year prices. If we want to know about how prices have changed, we *could* directly compare the price of each good in the current and base years. But that would be much like listing every good and service instead of reporting total GDP: It's not incorrect, but it's long and boring and doesn't do much to summarize what's going on in the economy as a whole. The GDP deflator is one way of summarizing how prices have changed across the entire economy.

GDP deflator
a measure of the overall change in prices in an economy, using the ratio between real and nominal GDP

The **GDP deflator** is a measure of the overall change in prices in an economy, using the ratio between real and nominal GDP. To compute the index, we first need to have measures of nominal GDP and real GDP from the current year. Then, we calculate the GDP deflator as follows:

EQUATION 7-3
$$\text{GDP deflator} = \frac{\text{Nominal GDP}}{\text{Real GDP}} \times 100$$

The GDP deflator equation gives us the ratio between the base-year value of current output (the real GDP number) and the current-year value of current output (the nominal GDP number). The equation has three direct implications:

- In the base year, the GDP deflator is always equal to 100 because current prices *are* base-year prices. Thus, in the base year, nominal GDP equals real GDP.
- If prices have risen such that nominal GDP is now higher than real GDP, the deflator will be greater than 100. So, for example, if the GDP deflator is 115 in a given year, we infer that the overall price level is 15 percent higher than it was in the base year.
- If prices have fallen such that nominal GDP is now lower than real GDP, the deflator will be less than 100. Similarly, if we are looking at a year before the base year, when prices were lower, the deflator will be less than 100.

Table 7-3 shows the GDP deflator for the imaginary country Pizzetta in 2015–2018.

The GDP deflator gets its name from its relationship to inflation. Inflation is an idea we'll discuss at length in future chapters; in fact, Chapter 16, "Inflation," is entirely devoted to the topic. For now, it's enough to note that *inflation* describes how fast the overall level of prices is changing. Inflation is defined in terms of a year-to-year increase in prices, rather than an increase over a base year.

TABLE 7-3

Calculating the GDP deflator and inflation rates

Using the values of nominal and real GDP, we can calculate the GDP deflator, a measure of price changes over time. It is set to 100 for a base year; as prices increase, the value of the deflator increases as well. With the GDP deflator we can calculate inflation, the percentage change of prices.

Year	Nominal GDP (millions of $)	Real GDP (millions of $)	Deflator	Inflation
2015	210	210	$\frac{\$210}{\$210} \times 100 = \mathbf{100}$	—
2016	236	236	$\frac{\$236}{\$236} \times 100 = \mathbf{100}$	$(100 - 100)/100 = 0\%$
2017	292	236	$\frac{\$292}{\$236} \times 100 = \mathbf{124}$	$(124 - 100)/100 = 24\%$
2018	366	270	$\frac{\$366}{\$270} \times 100 = \mathbf{136}$	$(136 - 124)/124 = 9.7\%$

We can calculate inflation by looking at the increase in the GDP deflator between any two years using the equation below:

EQUATION 7-4
$$\text{Inflation rate} = \left[\frac{\text{Deflator}_{\text{Year 2}} - \text{Deflator}_{\text{Year 1}}}{\text{Deflator}_{\text{Year 1}}}\right] \times 100$$

For instance, as shown in Table 7-3, the inflation rate in Pizzetta between 2017 and 2018 is:

$$\text{Inflation rate} = \left[\frac{\text{Deflator}_{2018} - \text{Deflator}_{2017}}{\text{Deflator}_{2017}}\right] \times 100$$
$$= \frac{136 - 124}{124} \times 100$$
$$= 9.7\%$$

The GDP deflator is one simple way of measuring changes in the price level. It allows us to "deflate" nominal GDP by controlling for price changes.

In official government statistics, the GDP deflator is actually calculated using a somewhat more elaborate method called a *chain-weighted index*. The basic intuition is the same as the simpler approach we've described here.[2] We'll return to the idea of changes in the overall price level in Chapter 8, "The Cost of Living."

Using GDP to assess economic health

How do we use GDP to compare economies? We could, of course, simply look at the GDPs of two countries side by side to see their relative sizes. High GDP means a big economy. Figure 7-4 shows the GDPs of a number of countries around the world. As you can see, the United States has the largest economy by far, followed by China.

LO 7.6 Use GDP per capita to compare economies and calculate the real GDP annual growth rate.

However, if what we really want to know is the income of an *average individual* in these countries, GDP will paint a misleading picture. The reason is that the populations of the countries are quite different sizes. For example:

- China's GDP is just over one-half as high as that of the United States, but its population is more than four times as large. India has just under four times as many people as the United States but only about one-tenth the GDP. The total income earned in China and India is spread across far more people, so the average person has a lower income.
- Meanwhile, Norway has a much smaller economy than the United States, but because its population is also much smaller, the average Norwegian is actually richer than the average American.

To compare average income across countries, we need to know GDP per capita.

FIGURE 7-4

GDP around the world (in 2018 dollars) The top 10 countries in terms of GDP in current dollars include rich countries—with both large populations (the United States) and small (the United Kingdom)—as well as some poorer countries with large populations (China and India).

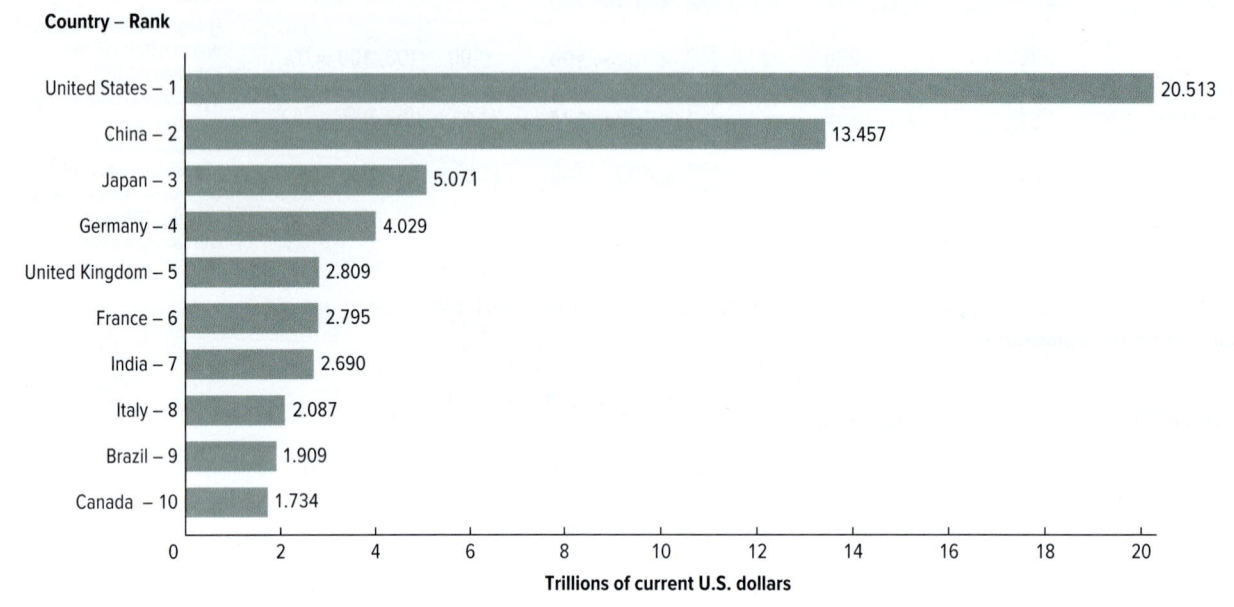

Country – Rank

Country – Rank	Trillions of current U.S. dollars
United States – 1	20.513
China – 2	13.457
Japan – 3	5.071
Germany – 4	4.029
United Kingdom – 5	2.809
France – 6	2.795
India – 7	2.690
Italy – 8	2.087
Brazil – 9	1.909
Canada – 10	1.734

Source: http://statisticstimes.com/economy/countries-by-projected-gdp.php.

GDP per capita
a country's GDP divided by its population

GDP per capita If we want get an idea of how much is produced *per person* in a country, we need to divide GDP by population size. This measure is called **GDP per capita**. ("Per capita" simply means for each person.) Figure 7-5 shows GDP per capita in each country in the world. When we compare this map to Figure 7-4, the most noticeable pattern is that the wealthy but small countries of Europe and the Middle East rise to the top, while populous countries like China, Brazil, and India move down.

GDP per capita is a useful measure. Knowing, for example, that GDP per capita in Switzerland is $58,087 while in Haiti it is only $1,750 suggests a lot about differences in life in these two countries.

However, GDP per capita doesn't tell us everything. First, it is a measure of *average* income; it doesn't tell us anything about how that income is distributed. A country with deep poverty and a rich elite could have higher GDP per capita than a country where everyone has a moderate standard of living.

Second, it doesn't tell us what you can buy with a given amount of money in that country. The same goods might be more expensive in some countries than in others. For instance, GDP per capita in the United States in 2017 was about $59,500 and Hong Kong's GDP per capita was about $46,200, but many goods and services are less expensive in Hong Kong than in the United States. A dollar in Hong Kong will buy you more, on average, than it would in the United States. When we account for this difference in the cost of living, the real value of GDP per capita in Hong Kong rises to about $61,500, which is *higher* than in the United States.[3]

Many poor countries are cheaper to live in than rich ones. This doesn't mean that every single thing costs less but that, overall, the cost of living is lower. Looking at GDP per capita without accounting for differences in the cost of living makes poor countries look even poorer than they really are. In the United States, for example, it would be almost impossible to survive on an income of $3,000 per year. In parts of Tanzania or Bangladesh, on the other hand, that income would buy you a decent basic lifestyle.

We will return to the subject of how to account for these differences in price levels in the next chapter. For now, just remember that GDP per capita is only a start in understanding people's real ability to consume goods and services.

FIGURE 7-5
Global GDP per capita (in 2017 U.S. dollars)

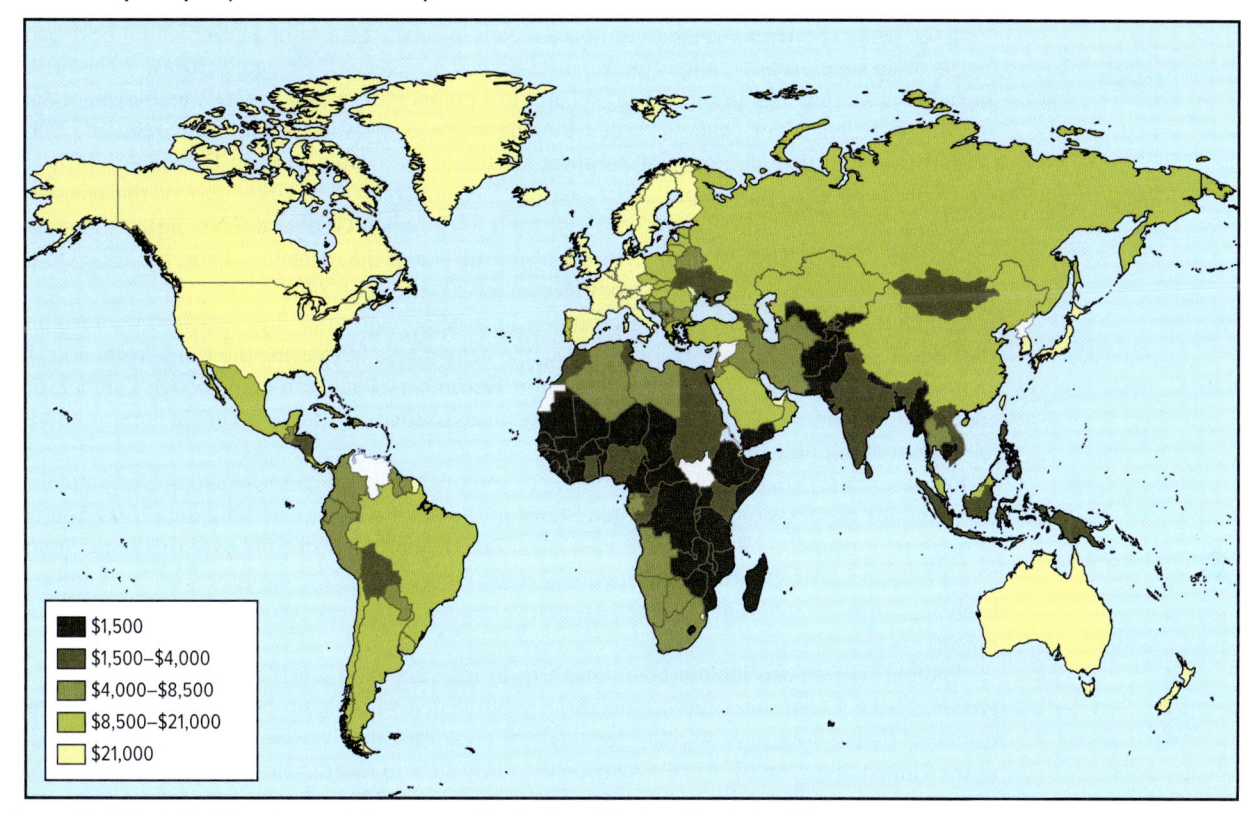

Legend:
- $1,500
- $1,500–$4,000
- $4,000–$8,500
- $8,500–$21,000
- $21,000

Source: World Bank, *World Development Indicators*, http://databank.worldbank.org/data/embed/GDP-per-capita-(2017)-fig-24-5/id/18f24527.

GDP growth rates One of the most common uses of GDP is to track changes in an economy over time. We usually talk about changes in GDP in terms of the *growth rate*. This is often measured as the percent change in real GDP from one time period to the next, typically annually or quarterly at an annual rate, calculated as:

EQUATION 7-5

$$\text{GDP growth rate} = \left[\frac{\text{GDP in Year 2} - \text{GDP in Year 1}}{\text{GDP in Year 1}}\right] \times 100$$

For instance, if U.S. real GDP grew from $14 trillion in one year to $14.5 trillion (in constant dollars) the next, the annual growth rate would be:

$$\text{GDP growth rate} = \left[\frac{\$14.5 \text{ trillion} - \$14 \text{ trillion}}{\$14 \text{ trillion}}\right] \times 100 = 3.6\%$$

If the economy shrinks, the growth rate will be negative. For instance, the U.S. economy shrunk between 2008 and 2009, with a negative annual real GDP growth rate of −2.4 percent.

We can think about GDP growth rates in several ways. Let's think first about how economic growth changes year to year for the same country. A shrinking economy is a big deal. It means that people are actually producing less than they did the year before.

We have special terms for a period in which the economy contracts:

- A **recession** is a period of significant decline in economic activity. A recession is usually marked by falling GDP, rising unemployment, and an increased number of bankruptcies.
- A **depression** is a severe or extended recession.

recession
a period of significant economic decline

depression
a particularly severe or extended recession

Although there is no hard-and-fast rule rule about when a recession becomes a depression, an old joke, heard from both Harry Truman and Ronald Reagan, says that a recession is when your neighbor loses his job; a depression is when you lose yours.

In the United States, a recession or depression is officially determined by a committee of economists at an organization called the *National Bureau of Economic Research (NBER)*. The NBER looks for economic high points ("peaks") and low points ("troughs") in GDP, employment data, and other statistics. For example, when looking at these statistics during the Great Recession, the NBER found that employment numbers started to fall from a peak in December 2007, and GDP followed shortly afterward. That peak in December 2007 was the start of the recession. The overall economy didn't bottom out until June 2009, when GDP and GNI started to increase again. The NBER declared this as the trough and the end of the recession. Thus, according to the NBER, the Great Recession lasted from December 2007 to June 2009.

People often feel the effects of a recession long before and after they register in government statistics. In the 2008 recession, for instance, the news media were using the word "recession" for almost a year before the NBER confirmed it in December 2008. And even though the recession ended in the middle of 2009, the economy continued to shed jobs for another six months and the job market didn't fully recover for 5 years.

Recessions are actually not as uncommon as you might think. Figure 7-6 shows that there were eight periods of recession in the United States in the 56 years between 1960 and 2016. You can also see that, overall, U.S. real GDP grew significantly and quite steadily over this same period. The 1990s and early 2000s were particularly recession-free decades, with only two brief and relatively mild dips in GDP. The 2008 recession involved a much deeper dip in GDP and lasted much longer.

Another way we can look at economic growth is to compare how fast different countries are growing. High growth rates are not necessarily associated with high total GDP or high GDP per capita, as Figure 7-7 shows. We can see that real GDP growth in the world's rich countries, such as the United States and Europe, has been relatively slow in recent years (although from a much higher starting level). Much more rapid growth has occurred in middle-income and poorer countries, led by China and followed by South Asia and East Africa.

FIGURE 7-6

U.S. real GDP over time   Real GDP has been steadily rising since 1960, and has more than quadrupled in value over the past 56 years. The gray bars show recessions, when economic activity slows.

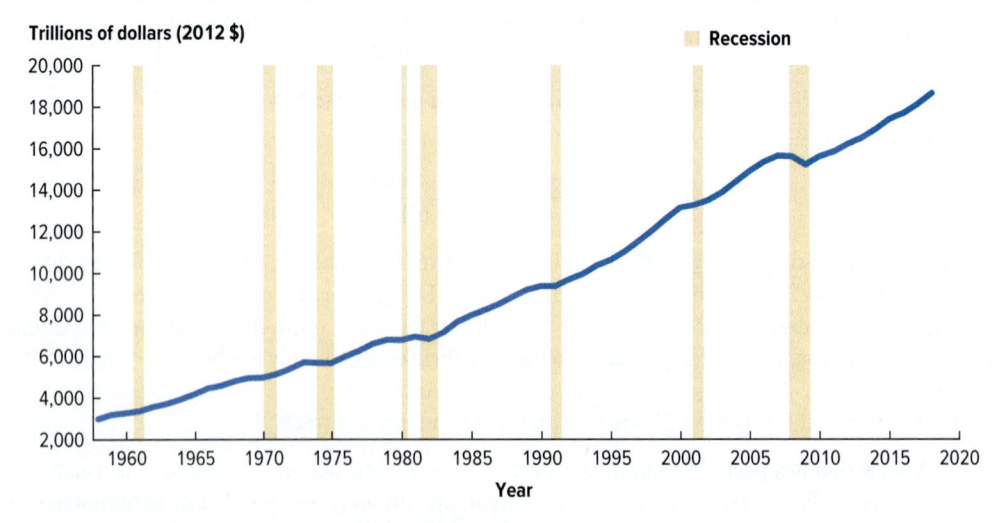

Sources: Federal Reserve Bank of St. Louis, https://research.stlouisfed.org/fred2/series/GDPC1#.

FIGURE 7-7

Global real GDP growth rates (2017) In contrast with the map of overall income, poorer countries grew faster than more developed countries, on average.

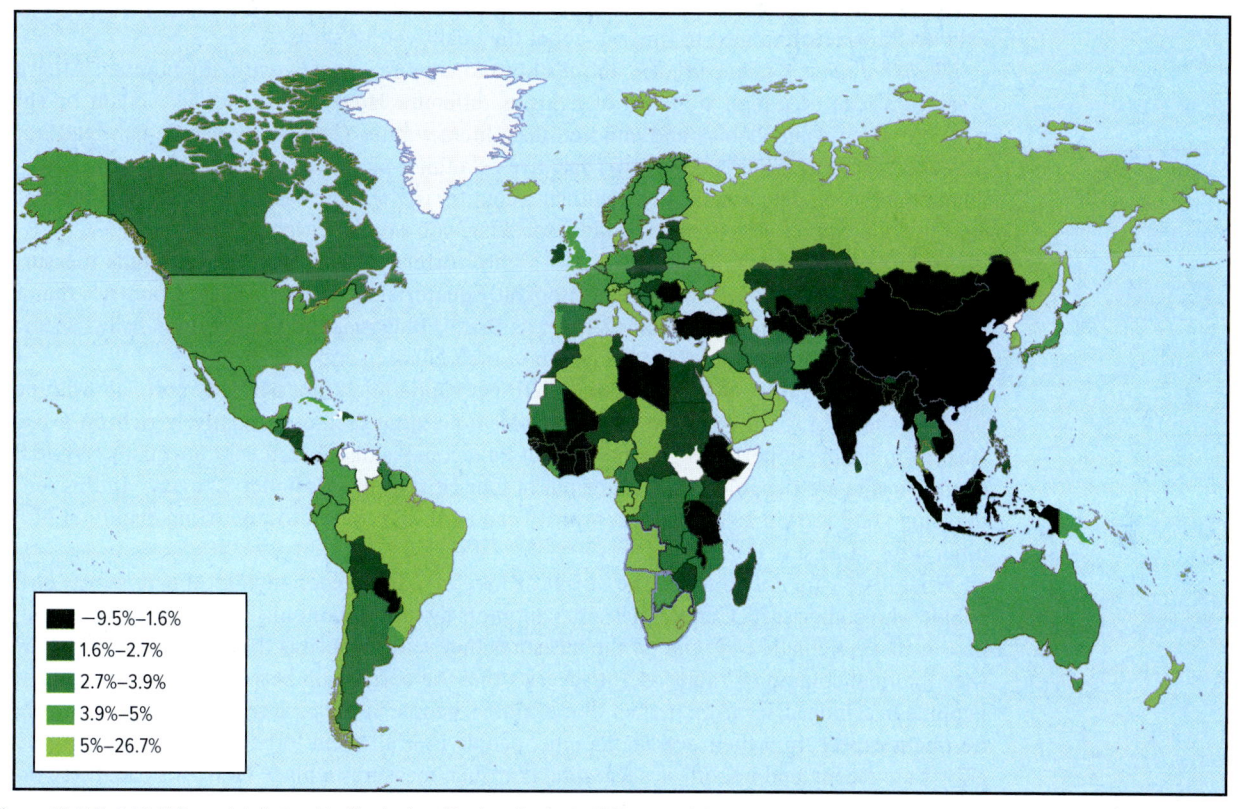

Legend:
- −9.5%–1.6%
- 1.6%–2.7%
- 2.7%–3.9%
- 3.9%–5%
- 5%–26.7%

Source: World Bank, World Economic Indicators, http://databank.worldbank.org/data/embed/GDP-growth--(2017)-Fig-24-7/id/4f7e0778.

✓ TEST YOURSELF

- ☐ What is the difference between real and nominal GDP? **[LO 7.4]**
- ☐ To calculate the GDP deflator, why do we divide nominal GDP by real GDP from the *same* year? **[LO 7.5]**
- ☐ What does it mean if country A has higher GDP than country B, but country B has higher GDP per capita? **[LO 7.6]**

Limitations of GDP Measures

GDP is a powerful and versatile way of measuring the size of an economy. It helps answers such questions as: How much do people produce in different countries? What is the average income per person? Is the economy growing? How quickly? The uses of GDP in answering these questions make it one of the most important measures in a macroeconomist's toolbox.

Although GDP is a powerful metric, it does not measure some important parts of overall well-being. In this section, we'll look at which aspects of economic and societal well-being are and are not captured by GDP. We'll also talk about some types of economic activity that are, by design, excluded from GDP.

GDP provides a powerful start on describing the health and direction of an economy, but we can get an even richer picture by supplementing it with other metrics.

LO 7.7 Discuss some limitations to GDP, including its measurement of well-being, home production, the underground economy, and environmental degradation.

GDP vs. well-being

GDP tells us a lot about the living standards in a country, but it can't tell us everything. Suppose you are offered the chance to live in a country that you know nothing about. You could quickly learn more by finding out the country's average income as measured by its GDP per capita. Which data would you turn to next to find out about the quality of life there?

Quality of life is a nuanced idea, and it's hard to capture perfectly with any number. After all, everyone's idea of a high standard of living is different. However, metrics like infant or child mortality (how many babies and children die), literacy rates (how many people can read), and life expectancy (how long people live) can give us a fuller picture of the well-being of a country's inhabitants. You might assume the wealthier a country is, the more easily it can afford good health care and education for its people. Broadly speaking, you would be right.

As Table 7-4 shows, GDP per capita *is* highly correlated with these quality-of-life measures. However, the correlation is not perfect: Look at Equatorial Guinea in Africa. Countries that are much poorer than Equatorial Guinea—such as Brazil, Bulgaria, and China—nonetheless seem to do a much better job of caring for the health of their children and elderly.

There are good reasons to expect that GDP per capita might not perfectly correlate with people's well-being. Let's take an obvious example: Equatorial Guinea is relatively rich on average (thanks to having important oil reserves), but its income is distributed very unequally. While the country's elite are rich, more than three out of four citizens live on under $2 a day.[4] In this sense, pursuing GDP growth as the highest priority can be in opposition to improving quality of life in other ways, at least in the short term.

What if we care not so much the *output* or *well-being* of an economy but the *happiness* of the people who comprise it? Can we measure happiness directly? Economists and others are trying to do this in a systematic way. One of the measures they've developed is the Life Satisfaction Index. (See the final column in Table 7-4.) It suggests that the correlation between GDP per capita and happiness is, indeed, far from perfect. For example, people in Bulgaria seem to be less happy than we might expect from their average income; people in Mali seem to be happier. However, these efforts are recent, and nobody is suggesting that such measures replace GDP. Instead, these measures are designed to paint a more complete picture of well-being in different countries.

TABLE 7-4
GDP compared with other measures of well-being

While GDP is commonly used to measure average income in a country, it can't capture all aspects of quality of life. Overall, metrics of well-being and quality of life like infant mortality, literacy, and life expectancy are correlated with GDP per capita, but in extreme cases, like that of Equatorial Guinea, they can diverge dramatically.

Country	GDP per capita (current U.S. $)	Literacy rate (% of population over 15)	Life expectancy at birth (years)	Child mortality (deaths per 1,000 under age 5)	Life Satisfaction Index (0 to 10)
Norway	75,504.6	[No data]	82	3	7.5
United States	59,531.7	[No data]	79	7	6.9
Equatorial Guinea	9,850.0	95.3	58	92	3.6
Brazil	9,821.4	92.6	74	16	6.6
Bulgaria	8,031.5	98.4	75	8	4.8
China	8,827.0	96.4	76	10	5.3
Mali	824.5	38.7	58	110	4.0

Sources: https://ourworldindata.org/happiness-and-life-satisfaction; http://databank.worldbank.org/data/source/world-development-indicators#.

For a deeper look at how these metrics might translate to individual happiness, read the Economics in Action box "Can money buy you happiness?"

Can money buy you happiness?
Economics in Action

Everyone has heard the saying, "Money can't buy you happiness." But is that actually true? The answer depends on two things: how much money, and how you define happiness.

Generally speaking, research shows that income is correlated with greater happiness. Countries with higher GDP are generally happier than those with lower income. However, countries do not necessarily get happier as they get richer. Researchers have found that Americans are not noticeably happier than they were 50 years ago, even though per capita GDP is much higher today than it was in 1970. One possible explanation for this puzzle is that people naturally tend to compare their lifestyles and material wealth to those of their peers, rather than to their parents or grandparents.

Research in the United States has also found that there is a positive correlation between individual happiness and money—up to an income level of about $75,000 per year. For people earning less than $75,000, more money is related to higher levels of happiness on average. Above that income level, it's much less clear.

Turns out an extra wrinkle is added to the picture when researchers change how they measure happiness. Typically, researchers use two distinct methods. One is to ask something like, "How satisfied are you with your life as a whole these days?" This measure, usually called *life satisfaction*, continues to rise with income. In other words, someone earning $750,000 is likely to tell a researcher that she is more satisfied than someone earning $75,000.

The other method is to ask people about the emotions they felt *on the previous day*. For example, did you feel happiness yesterday? Enjoyment? Anger? Stress? Worry? Here, we find that overall someone earning $75,000 is more likely to have experienced positive emotions than someone earning $25,000. But despite what you would think, someone earning $750,000 did not report more positive emotions, and less negativity, than someone earning $75,000. Although money doesn't always buy happiness, it seems to help up to a certain point.

Sources: Angus Deaton, "Income, Health, and Well-Being around the World: Evidence from the Gallup World Poll," *Journal of Economic Perspectives* 22, no. 2 (2008), pp. 53–72; http://economix.blogs.nytimes.com/2009/03/10/the-happiest-states-of-america/; www.princeton.edu/~deaton/downloads/deaton_kahneman_high_income_improves_evaluation_August2010.pdf.

Data challenges

When critics argue that we should look beyond GDP, they point out that GDP calculations leave out some important types of economic activity. GDP measures the market value of final goods and services, but it does not include anything that is not traded in a market or that isn't reported to the government.

As a result, three major categories of economic activity are not counted as part of GDP: home production, the underground economy, and nonmarket externalities such as environmental degradation.

Home production Goods and services that are both produced and consumed within one household are called *home production*. In general, home-production goods and services are not included in GDP:

- If you eat out, your meal is part of GDP. If you eat at home, it's not.
- If you hire a cleaning service to clean your home, that's part of GDP. If you clean your own home, it's not.

Similarly, the same goods might or might not be part of GDP, depending on whether you sell them or consume them yourself:

- If you grow vegetables in your garden and sell them at a farmers' market, that's part of GDP. If you eat them yourself, it's not.
- If your grandmother knits a sweater and gives it to you for your birthday, that's not part of GDP. If your grandmother sells her knitting on eBay or Etsy, it is.

Home production is a major component of economic activity in most places. In relatively poor countries, many people grow their own food on small farms and may make their own tools and clothes. In these instances, the official GDP measure may be missing a significant percentage of real production. Even in wealthy countries, much of the value of caretaking work—raising children or caring for elderly parents—is uncounted. Because home production varies from place to place, it can change how one country compares to another.

Some economists have made efforts to quantify the value of this work. For more detail, read the From Another Angle box "Not everything that counts can be counted."

Not everything that counts can be counted
From Another Angle

GDP doesn't count everything in the economy. Consider this example close to home: A mother or father who stays home to look after children and cooks dinner contributes nothing to GDP. But when she or he goes out to work for pay, hires someone to look after the children, and takes the family to eat out, those activities add to GDP.

The distinction matters when we ask: Does faster GDP growth mean that life is getting better? Not necessarily. Between the 1970s and the 1990s, for example, the U.S. economy as measured by GDP grew faster than Germany's. But digging deeper shows that life did not get proportionately better in the United States during that period relative to life in Germany.

In the 1970s, about the same proportion of Germans and Americans were in paid employment. But then American women started entering the labor force in increasing numbers. As a result, a much higher proportion of Americans had jobs by the 1990s, a difference largely explained by the rising rate of female participation in the U.S. labor force. A larger workforce makes for a larger GDP.

But the larger GDP did not necessarily mean that the United States was better off. The women who stayed at home in the 1970s weren't sitting around doing nothing. They were running households and raising families, growing and making goods for home consumption, doing volunteer work in their communities, and so on. Although these are valuable activities, they are not counted in GDP.

So we can't automatically conclude from the rise in U.S. GDP relative to Germany's that more goods and services were being produced in the United States in the 1990s. Some goods and services simply moved from the uncounted area of home production to the documented area of GDP. When you add up paid work, home production, and volunteer work, Americans and Germans put in about the same number of hours per week, but workers in Germany spent 5.3 hours less on paid work and 6 hours more on household production than did Americans. Estimating home production suggests that a lower German employment rate did not necessarily imply lower overall production or a lower standard of living.

Taking account of home production can also change the way we view recessions. U.S. GDP dropped during the 2008 recession, but home production went up. Feeling a financial squeeze, people substituted home-cooked meals for restaurant meals, planted vegetable gardens, and did their own repairs rather than hire someone. When the economy was doing well, people's choices suggested that they preferred to hire others to do these tasks. So the 2008 recession clearly reduced people's well-being. But economist Nancy Folbre, who has led efforts to quantify the value of home production, argues that it might not have reduced well-being by nearly as much as official GDP statistics suggest.

Sources: http://economix.blogs.nytimes.com/2009/05/04/including-home-production-gdp-might-not-look-so-bad; http://www.nber.org/papers/w8797.pdf; http://scholar.harvard.edu/files/alesina/files/work_and_leisure_in_the_u.s._and_europe.pdf.

The underground economy Many goods and services are sold below the radar, outside of official records. These transactions make up the *underground economy*.

On the extreme end, there is trade in goods and services that are themselves illegal—banned drugs, restricted weapons, endangered animals and plants, and so on. Sales of illegal goods and services are part of what is called the *black market*.

In principle, black-market activities belong in the GDP calculation. Remember GDP is the market value of *all* final goods and services produced within a country in a given period of time. While illegal trade isn't desirable, selling a restricted plant or animal, for example, fits that definition. However, because black-market transactions are illegal, they are, of course, not reported to the government or tax authorities. As a result, they don't show up in government statistics, and they don't get counted as part of the official GDP.

Even though black-market transactions are not counted, they may influence GDP in other ways. For example, if a city noticed an uptick in illegal trade, it might decide to hire more police officers to combat crime. This decision would add to the government spending component of GDP. In this case, GDP has increased, even though the city is worse off because of the crime.

At the less-extreme end are economic transactions that are otherwise legal but are sometimes not reported to the government. Failure to report can be either accidental or deliberate (to avoid paying taxes). For instance, were you ever hired to mow a neighbor's lawn, or babysit, or run errands for a few bucks when you were in high school? If you didn't report those amounts to the IRS,[5] you were participating in what's known as the *gray market*—so called because it sits somewhere between the black market and the documented economy.

Gray-market transactions aren't counted in GDP for the same reason that black-market transactions aren't counted: If it's not reported, it doesn't show up in government statistics. And, if it doesn't show up in government statistics, it can't be counted in GDP.

Even though black- and gray-market transactions don't get reported, researchers try to quantify them to get a sense of what's missing in our GDP calculations. After all, production of goods and services is production, regardless of whether it is counted.

It turns out that the underground economy accounts for a significant portion of the total economy in many countries. On average across the world, the underground economy is worth about one-third of GDP. This average hides wide variations, though:

- In the United States, for example, the underground economy has been valued at only around 7 or 8 percent of GDP. (Still, 8 percent of current U.S. GDP is more than $1.5 trillion dollars.)
- It is estimated at more than half of GDP in Nigeria and more than two-thirds in some Latin American countries.[6]

The typical explanation for this pattern reflects the cost of doing business legally. In some countries you have to pay extremely high taxes or pay bribes to officials to cut through bureaucratic red tape. When the cost of doing business legally is high, people are much more likely to conduct their business through other channels. In such countries, GDP may significantly underestimate the true size of the economy. In the case of Nigeria, it would mean increasing the official GDP figure by 50 percent.[7]

Environmental externalities   Suppose an electricity company causes air pollution by burning coal. The electricity generated ends up being counted in GDP. It may appear in the price paid by households for their electricity. Or it may be wrapped up in the price of goods and services that other firms make using the electricity as an input.

Some economists feel that GDP, as a metric, is missing the costs associated with pollution. They argue that we need to account for the *negative externalities* of economic activities. In a sense, we can think of the value of negative externalities as *negative output*. They are final "goods" that do harm to people, and therefore have negative value, but don't otherwise get counted in production or expenditure measures.

Increasingly, those who deal with economic statistics are trying to incorporate the value of negative externalities into GDP. Some countries have tried to calculate **Green GDP**. This alternative measure of GDP subtracts the environmental costs of production from the positive outputs normally counted in GDP.

In some countries that are growing rapidly, such as China and India, there are few regulations to guard against environmental degradation. When the Chinese government attempted to calculate Green GDP in 2007, it came up with some shocking results. Once adjusted for pollution, the soaring GDP growth rates in many provinces in China dropped to almost zero. This was such an inconvenient finding that the government abandoned the Green-GDP project.[8]

The Chinese government is not alone in its concerns about the political implications of GDP measures. For more about the intersection of politics and national accounting, read the From Another Angle box "Green GDP."

Green GDP
an alternative measure of GDP that subtracts the environmental costs of production from the positive outputs normally counted in GDP

Green GDP
From Another Angle

GDP is widely viewed as the measure of the overall health of the economy. It's meant to capture the total production of goods and services. But what if the economy produces "bads" along with all the goods? Specifically, how can GDP be adjusted to account for pollution and the depletion of resources? That's the aim of efforts to calculate "Green GDP."

Recognizing that GDP may not capture the negative externalities of environmental production, in 1993 officials in the U.S. Bureau of Economic Analysis (BEA) started to work on how to calculate a more "complete" measure of economic activity. This idea started off with the typical GDP equation:

$$C + I + G + NX$$

What made the new GDP calculation "green" was that it would weigh the value of this production against its overall environmental costs. Included in those costs would be the consumption of nonrenewable resources—such as pumping oil and mining coal—and some of the costs from pollution.

You may have noticed that we don't see this figure reported in the news. Why not? The BEA needed funding to continue the project, which needed the approval of Congress. The National Academy of Science supported the proposal, but a member of Congress from West Virginia nixed it in 1995, worried that the numbers would hurt the coal industry.

Efforts to calculate Green GDP in China started in 2004, but they too lost favor. The project ended in 2009, in part because it proved difficult to reliably estimate the costs of pollution.

Part of the difficulty is that goods like cars and ships are fundamentally different from "bads" like pollution and environmental degradation. When goods are sold on the market, we can see their prices; those prices can then be used to put a value on the goods' production. But "bads" like pollution are not bought and sold, so there is nothing like a price for them. Putting a (negative) value on "bads" remains technically challenging—and, for now, controversial.

Sources: Jon Gertner, "The Rise and Fall of the GDP," *New York Times Magazine*, May 13, 2010, http://www.nytimes.com/2010/05/16/magazine/16GDP-t.html?pagewanted=all; Justin Fox, "The Economics of Well-Being," *Harvard Business Review*, January-February 2012, https://hbr.org/2012/01/the-economics-of-well-being; Shi Jiang-tao, "Green GDP Drive Grinds to a Halt," *South China Morning Post*, March 12 2009, https://www.scmp.com/article/672949/green-gdp-drive-grinds-halt.

✓ TEST YOURSELF

- ☐ What is home production? **[LO 7.7]**
- ☐ Why might GDP fall if environmental damages caused by production were taken into account? **[LO 7.7]**
- ☐ What supplemental metrics are commonly used to measure quality of life alongside GDP per capita? **[LO 7.7]**

Conclusion

GDP is a powerful and versatile metric. There are good reasons that it is one of the most commonly used tools in macroeconomics. It gives a simple measure of the size of an economy and the average income of its participants. It also allows us to make comparisons over time or across countries. The system of national income accounts gives us a picture of how output, expenditure, and income are linked, and a framework for adding up the billions of daily transactions that occur in an economy.

Comparing nominal and real GDP allows us to disentangle the role of increasing prices versus increasing output in a growing economy. The GDP deflator and the inflation rate track changes in overall price levels over time—which, as we'll see in the next chapter, is a major task in macroeconomics.

GDP per capita gives us a sense of the average income within a country, although it doesn't tell us about the distribution of income or quality of life. Finally, calculating real GDP growth rates shows us in which direction the economy is moving, and is an important indicator of recession or depression.

In the next chapter, we'll dig deeper into the tools that economists use to measure price changes and the cost of living. When we combine these tools with GDP, we have a menu of macroeconomic metrics that will allow us to describe and analyze national and international economies.

Key Terms

macroeconomics, p. 166	inventory, p. 172	GDP deflator, p. 178
gross domestic product (GDP), p. 167	government purchases (G), p. 172	GDP per capita, p. 180
gross national product (GNP), p. 168	net exports (NX), p. 172	recession, p. 181
consumption (C), p. 170	real GDP, p. 176	depression, p. 181
investment (I), p. 171	nominal GDP, p. 176	Green GDP, p. 188

Summary

LO 7.1 Understand the importance of using the market value of final goods and services to calculate GDP, and explain why each component of GDP is important.

Most goods and services go through several production steps and may pass through multiple firms before ending up in the hands of the consumer. However, when calculating GDP, we should consider only the value of the final good or service, in order to avoid double-counting. The value added by each step of the production process will be included in the price of the final product.

The most commonly used variable for measuring the value of a national economy is gross domestic product, or GDP. GDP is the sum of the market values of all final goods and services produced within a country in a given period of time. The goods and services that count toward GDP are defined in terms of the location of production, not the citizenship of the producer.

GDP is usually calculated on both annual and quarterly (three-month) bases; only new goods and services being produced within that time period are counted. Quarterly GDP estimates are typically given as a seasonally adjusted annual rate, which projects what annual GDP will be based on the current quarter's output if the economy continues to follow expected seasonal patterns.

LO 7.2 Explain the equivalence of the expenditure and income approaches to valuing an economy.

Economists can think about the size of a national economy in three different ways: how much is produced (output), how much is spent (expenditure), and how much income is earned (income). All three of these methods add up to the same thing. Total output is the *value* of the things produced in an economy in dollar terms, which is the same as the price for which those outputs sell, which is the same as what people spent to buy those outputs. Therefore, the value of output is equal to expenditures. Every transaction has both a buyer and a seller, so expenditures by one person translate directly into income for someone else; therefore, income equals expenditure.

LO 7.3 Explain the three approaches that are used to calculate GDP, and summarize the categories of spending that are included in the expenditure approach.

The *expenditure* approach of calculating the size of an economy involves adding up all spending on goods and services produced in an economy and subtracting spending on imports.

We can break expenditures into four categories: *Consumption (C)* measures spending on goods and services to be consumed by private individuals and families. *Investment (I)* includes any goods that are bought in order to produce other goods and services in the future. *Government purchases (G)* are goods and services bought by all levels of government, for either consumption or investment. Finally, *net exports (NX)* are foreign spending on domestically produced goods and services minus domestic spending on foreign-produced goods and services. The sum of these categories and the equivalence of income (Y) and expenditure gives us the equation $Y = C + I + G + NX$.

The *income* approach adds up the income earned by everyone in a country—including wages (earned by workers), interest (earned on capital investments), rental income (earned on land and property), and profits (earned by firms).

The *value-added* approach accounts for the value that is added at each stage of production in the economy. This approach allows economists to investigate the contribution of each transaction in the economy to overall GDP. It also solves the double-counting problem; only part of the value of each transaction is registered, and it does not register the total price of intermediate goods and services.

Many countries use all three approaches to calculate GDP so that policy-makers and researchers can get a full picture of economic activity.

LO 7.4 Explain the difference between real and nominal GDP.

GDP is a function of both the quantity of goods and services produced (output) and their market value (prices); an increase in GDP can result from growth in either or both components. To isolate the role of growing output, we can control for price changes. *Real GDP* is calculated based on goods and services valued at constant prices. *Nominal GDP* is calculated based on goods and services valued at current prices.

LO 7.5 Calculate the GDP deflator.

One way to measure price changes is by calculating the GDP deflator. The *GDP deflator* summarizes the overall increase in prices in an economy using the ratio between real and nominal GDP in a given year. If prices have risen such that nominal GDP is now higher than real GDP, the deflator will be greater than 100. If prices have fallen such that nominal GDP is now lower than real GDP, the deflator will be less than 100. The GDP deflator allows us to "deflate" nominal GDP by controlling for price changes.

LO 7.6 Use GDP per capita to compare economies and calculate the real GDP annual growth rate.

GDP per capita is total GDP divided by the population of a country. It tells us the average income or productivity per person in the economy. To track changes in an economy over time, we can calculate the *real GDP growth* rate, measured as the percent change in real GDP from one time period to the next, typically annually or quarterly at an annual rate. When the economy shrinks, the growth rate is negative and is one of the major indicators used to determine whether the economy is in a recession or depression.

LO 7.7 Discuss some limitations to GDP, including its measurement of well-being, home production, the underground economy, and environmental degradation.

GDP is a rough measure of the average standard of living in a country, but it does not tell us about the distribution of wealth. Higher GDP is often associated with other indicators of higher well-being, such as health, education, and life satisfaction, but does not guarantee those things.

Three other important measures of the economy are not included in GDP by design: home production (goods and services that are produced and consumed within a household), the underground economy (illegal transactions, or legal transactions that simply aren't reported to the government), and externalities (such as pollution) that are not fully accounted for in regular production or consumption measures.

Review Questions

1. U.S. car dealers sell both used cars and new cars each year. However, only the sales of the new cars count toward GDP. Why does the sale of used cars not count? **[LO 7.1]**

2. There is an old saying, "You can't compare apples and oranges." When economists calculate GDP, are they able to compare apples and oranges? Explain. **[LO 7.1]**

3. When Americans buy goods produced in Canada, Canadians earn income from American expenditures. Does the value of this Canadian output and American expenditure get counted under the GDP of Canada or the United States? Why? **[LO 7.2]**

4. Economists sometimes describe the economy as having a "circular flow." In the most basic form of the circular flow model, companies hire workers and pay them wages. Workers then use these wages to buy goods and services from companies. How does the circular flow model explain the equivalence of the expenditure and income methods of valuing an economy? **[LO 7.2]**

5. In 2017, the average baseball player earned $4 million per year. Suppose that these baseball players spend all of their income on goods and services each year, and they save nothing. Argue why the sum of the incomes of all baseball players must equal the sum of expenditures made by the baseball players. **[LO 7.2]**

6. Determine whether each of the following counts as consumption, investment, government purchases, net exports, or none of these, under the expenditure approach to calculating GDP. Explain your answer. **[LO 7.3]**
    a. The construction of a courthouse.
    b. A taxicab ride.
    c. The purchase of a taxicab by a taxicab company.
    d. A student buying a textbook.
    e. The trading of municipal bonds (a type of financial investment offered by city or state governments).
    f. A company's purchase of foreign minerals.

7. If car companies produce a lot of cars this year but hold the new models back in warehouses until they release them in the new-model year, will this year's GDP be higher, lower, or the same as it would have been if the cars had been sold right away? Why? Does the choice to reserve the cars for a year change which category of expenditures they fall under? **[LO 7.3]**

8. The value-added method involves taking the cost of intermediate outputs (i.e., outputs that will in turn be used in the production of another good) and subtracting that cost from the value of the good being produced. In this way, only the value that is added at each step (the sale value minus the cost of the goods that went into producing it) is summed up. Explain why this method gives us the same result as the standard method of counting only the value of final goods and services. **[LO 7.3]**

9. Imagine a painter is trying to determine the value she adds when she paints a picture. Assume that after spending $200 on materials, she sells one copy of her painting for $500. She then spends $50 to make 10 copies of her painting, each of which sells for $100. What is the value added of her painting? What if a company then spends $10 per copy to sell 100 more copies, each for $50? What is the value the painter adds then? If it's unknown how many copies the painting will sell in the future, can we today determine the value added? Why or why not? **[LO 7.3]**

10. In a press conference, the president of a small country displays a chart showing that GDP has risen by 10 percent every year for five years. He argues that this

growth shows the brilliance of his economic policy. However, his chart uses nominal GDP numbers. What might be wrong with this chart? If you were a reporter at the press conference, what questions could you ask to get a more accurate picture of the country's economic growth? **[LO 7.4]**

11. Suppose that the GDP deflator grew by 10 percent from last year to this year. That is, the inflation rate this year was 10 percent. In words, what does this mean happened in the economy? What does this inflation rate imply about the growth rate in real GDP? **[LO 7.5]**

12. An inexperienced researcher wants to examine the average standard of living in two countries. In order to do so, he compares the GDPs in those two countries. What are two reasons why this comparison does not lead to an accurate measure of the countries' average standards of living? **[LO 7.4, LO 7.6]**

13. In 2018, according to the International Monetary Fund, India had the world's 7th-highest nominal GDP, the 142th-highest nominal GDP per capita, and the 7th-highest real GDP growth rate. What does each of these indicators tell us about the Indian economy and how life in India compares to life in other countries? **[LO 7.6]**

14. China is a rapidly growing country. It has high levels of bureaucracy and business regulation, low levels of environmental regulation, and a strong tradition of entrepreneurship. Discuss several reasons why official GDP estimates in China might miss significant portions of the country's economic activity. **[LO 7.7]**

15. Suppose a college student is texting while driving and gets into a car accident causing $2,000 worth of damage to her car. Assuming the student repairs her car, does GDP rise, fall, or stay constant with this accident? What does your answer suggest about using GDP as a measure of well-being? **[LO 7.7]**

Problems and Applications

1. Suppose a gold miner finds a gold nugget and sells the nugget to a mining company for $500. The mining company melts down the gold, purifies it, and sells it to a jewelry maker for $1,000. The jewelry maker fashions the gold into a necklace that it sells to a department store for $1,500. Finally, the department store sells the necklace to a customer for $2,000. How much has GDP increased as a result of these transactions? **[LO 7.1, LO 7.3]**

2. Table 7P-1 shows the price of inputs and the price of outputs at each step in the production process of making a shirt. Assume that each of these steps takes place within the country. **[LO 7.1, LO 7.3]**

TABLE 7P-1

	Cotton farmer ($)	Fabric maker ($)	Sewing and printing ($)
Inputs	0	1.10	3.50
Value of output	1.10	3.50	18.00

a. What is the total contribution of this shirt to GDP, using the standard expenditure method?

b. If we use a value-added method (i.e., summing the value added by producers at each step of the production process, equal to the value of output minus the price of inputs), what is the contribution of this shirt to GDP?

c. If we mistakenly added the price of both intermediate and final outputs without adjusting for value added, what would we find that this shirt contributes to GDP? By how much does this overestimate the true contribution?

3. The U.S. government gives income support to many families living in poverty. How does each of the following aspects of this policy contribute to GDP? **[LO 7.2]**

a. Does this government's expenditure on income support count as part of GDP? If so, in which category of expenditure does it fall?

b. When the families buy groceries with the money they've received, does this expenditure count as part of GDP? If so, in which category does it fall?

c. If the families buy new houses with the money they've received, does this count as part of GDP? If so, in which category does it fall?

4. Given the following information about each economy, either calculate the missing variable or determine that it cannot be calculated. **[LO 7.2, LO 7.3]**

a. If C = $20.1 billion, I = $3.5 billion, G = $5.2 billion, and NX = −$1 billion, what is total income?

b. If total income is $1 trillion, G = $0.3 trillion, and C = $0.5 trillion, what is I?

c. If total expenditure is $675 billion, C = $433 billion, I = $105 billion, and G = $75 billion, what is NX? How much are exports? How much are imports?

5. Using Table 7P-2, calculate the following. **[LO 7.2, LO 7.3]**

TABLE 7P-2

Sector	Value (millions)
Consumption	$770,000
Investment	$165,000
Government spending	$220,000
Net exports	− $ 55,000
Population	50

    a. Total gross domestic product and GDP per person.
    b. Consumption, investment, government purchases, and net exports, each as a percentage of total GDP.
    c. Consumption, investment, government purchases, and net exports per person.

6. Determine which category each of the following economic activities falls under: consumption (C), investment (I), government purchases (G), net exports (NX), or not included in GDP. [LO 7.3]
    a. The mayor of Chicago authorizes the construction of a new stadium using public funds.
    b. A student pays rent on her apartment.
    c. Parents pay college tuition for their son.
    d. Someone buys a new Hyundai car produced in South Korea.
    e. Someone buys a used Hyundai car.
    f. Someone buys a new General Motors car produced in the United States.
    g. A family buys a house in a newly-constructed housing development.
    h. The U.S. Army pays its soldiers.
    i. A Brazilian driver buys a Ford car produced in the United States.
    j. The Department of Motor Vehicles buys a new machine for printing drivers' licenses.
    k. An apple picked in Washington in October is bought at a grocery store in Mississippi in December.
    l. Hewlett-Packard produces a computer and sends it to a warehouse in another state for sale next year.

7. Table 7P-3 shows economic activity for a very tiny country. Using the expenditure approach, determine the following. [LO 7.3]

TABLE 7P-3

Activity	Total value (thousands of $)
Families buy groceries	600
Electronics company sells HD projectors to households	100
Personal trainer gives Zumba class	5
Custard stand sells pistachio ice cream	2
Police department buys new cars	500
Mayor leads creation of new education budget	300
Elevator construction company builds new factory	600
Local businessperson purchases corn from Mexico	400
Sports-gear company sells hockey gloves to Canadian team	200
Bike store sells used carbon-fiber bikes	200
Local stockbroker executes trades for clients	2,000

    a. Consumption.
    b. Investment.
    c. Government purchases.
    d. Net exports.
    e. GDP.

8. During the 2008 recession sparked by financial crisis, the U.S. economy suffered tremendously. Suppose that, due to the recession, the U.S. GDP dropped from $14 trillion to $12.5 trillion. This decline in GDP was due to a drop in consumption of $1 trillion and a drop in investment of $500 billion. The U.S. government, under the current president, responded to this recession by increasing government purchases. [LO 7.3]
    a. Suppose that government spending had no impact on consumption, investment, or net exports. If the current presidential administration wanted to bring GDP back up to $14 trillion, how much would government spending have to rise?
    b. Many economists believe that an increase in government spending doesn't just directly increase GDP, but that it also leads to an increase in consumption. If government spending rises by $1 trillion, how much would consumption have to rise in order to bring GDP back to $14 trillion?

9. Assume Table 7P-4 summarizes the income of Paraguay. **[LO 7.3]**

TABLE 7P-4

Category	Value (billions of $)
Wages	8.3
Interest	0.7
Total business expenditures	21.0
Total business revenues	30.0

a. Calculate profits.
b. Calculate the GDP of Paraguay using the income approach.
c. What would GDP be if you were to use the value-added approach?
d. What would GDP be if you were to use the expenditure approach?

10. Table 7P-5 provides information about the cost of inputs and the value of output for the production of a road bike. Note there are four different stages of production. **[LO 7.3]**

    a. What value is added by the supplier of the raw materials?
    b. What value is added by the tire maker?
    c. What value is added by the maker of the frame and components?
    d. What value is added by the bike mechanic?
    e. What value is added by the bike store?
    f. What is the total contribution of the bike to GDP?

11. Imagine that the United States produces only three goods: apples, bananas, and carrots. The quantities produced and the prices of the three goods are listed in Table 7P-6. **[LO 7.4]**

TABLE 7P-6

Goods	Quantities produced	Prices ($)
Apples	5	2.00
Bananas	10	1.00
Carrots	20	1.50

a. Calculate the GDP of the United States in this three-goods version of its economy.
b. Suppose that a drought hits the state of Washington. This drought causes the quantity of apples produced to fall to 2. Assuming that all prices remain constant, calculate the new U.S. GDP.
c. Assume, once again, that the quantities produced and the prices of the three goods are as listed in Table 7P-6. Now, given this situation, carrot sellers decide that the price of carrots is too low, so they agree to raise the price. What must be the new price of carrots if the U.S. GDP is $60?

12. Suppose that the British economy produces two goods: laptops and books. The quantity produced and the prices of these items for 2017 and 2018 are shown in Table 7P-7. **[LO 7.4, LO 7.5]**

TABLE 7P-7

Year	Quantities produced	Price($)
2017	Laptops = 50 Books = 1,000	Laptops = 200 Books = ?
2018	Laptops = 100 Books = ?	Laptops = $150 Books = 10

TABLE 7P-5

Raw materials	Manufacturing	Construction	Sale by the retailer
• Rubber for one tire ($20) • Aluminum for the frame ($80) • Other component materials ($70)	• Tire maker sells tires for $30 each • Frame maker sells bike frame and components for a total of $250	• Bike mechanic puts everything together and sells the bike for $350	• Retailer sells the bike for $500

TABLE 7P-8

Year	Quantity of oranges	Price of orange ($)	Quantity of beach balls	Price of beach ball ($)	Nominal GDP ($)	Real GDP ($)	GDP deflator	Inflation rate (%)
2016	500	1.00	850	5.00				
2017	600	1.50	900	7.50				
2018	750	1.65	1,000	8.25				

TABLE 7P-9

	2017			2018		
Country	Nominal GDP (billions of $)	Real GDP (billions of $)	Population	Nominal GDP (billions of $)	Real GDP (billions of $)	Population
Argentina	554.10	458.25	44,044,811	625.92	446.731	44,494,502
Egypt	332.48	271.710	96,442,593	253.25	286.149	98,423,595
Germany	3,479.23	3,883.870	82,657,002	4,211.64	3,939.23	82,927,922
Ghana	42.78	50.620	29,121,471		53.79	29,767,108
United States	18,624.95	17,348.63	325,147,121	20,412.87	17,844.28	327,167,434

a. Let's assume that the base year was 2017, so that real GDP in 2017 equals nominal GDP in 2017. If the real GDP in Britain was $15,000 in 2017, what was the price of books?

b. Using your answer from part *a*, if the growth rate in nominal GDP was 10 percent, how many books must have been produced in 2018?

c. Using your answers from parts *a* and *b*, what is the real GDP in 2018? What was the growth rate in real GDP between 2017 and 2018?

13. Based on Table 7P-8, calculate nominal GDP, real GDP, the GDP deflator, and the inflation rate in each year, and fill in the missing parts of the table. Use 2016 as the base year. **[LO 7.4, LO 7.5]**

14. Based on Table 7P-9, calculate nominal GDP per capita in 2017 and 2018, and the real GDP growth rate between the two years. Which countries look like they experienced recession in 2017–2018? **[LO 7.6]**

15. Table 7P-10 describes the real GDP and population of a fictional country in 2017 and 2018. **[LO 7.6]**

TABLE 7P-10

Year	Real GDP (billions of $)	Population (millions)
2017	10	1.0
2018	12	1.1

a. What is the real GDP per capita in 2017 and 2018?

b. What is the growth rate in real GDP?

c. What is the growth rate in population?

d. What is the growth rate in real GDP per capita?

TABLE 7P-11

Country	C ($)	I ($)	G ($)	Net exports ($)
Bohemia	9,800,000,000	230,000,000	950,000,000	−120,000,000
Silesia	450,000,000	78,000,000	100,000,000	13,000,000
Bavaria	2,125,000,000	319,000,000	597,000,000	134,000,000
Saxony	2,750,000,000	75,000,000	1,320,000,000	−45,000,000
Ottoman Empire	6,225,000,000	567,000,000	1,435,000,000	1,000,000

Country	Population	Home production ($)	Underground economy ($)	Environmental externalities ($)
Bohemia	1,200,000	1,250,000,000	5,770,000,000	−1,560,000,000
Silesia	160,000	75,000,000	128,000,000	−45,000,000
Bavaria	425,000	386,000,000	1,450,000,000	−523,000,000
Saxony	760,000	146,000,000	250,000,000	−820,000,000
Ottoman Empire	800,000	432,000,000	654,000,000	−396,300,000

16. Table 7P-11 shows fictional data on population and expenditures in five countries, as well as the value of home production, the underground economy, and environmental externalities in each. [LO 7.6, LO 7.7]
    a. Calculate GDP and GDP per capita in each country.
    b. Calculate the size of home production, the underground economy, and environmental externalities in each country as a percentage of GDP.
    c. Calculate total and per capita "GDP-plus" in each country by including the value of home production, the underground economy, and environmental externalities.
    d. Rank countries by total and per capita GDP, and again by total and per capita "GDP-plus." Compare the two lists. Are the biggest and the smallest economies the same or different?

17. Suppose a parent was earning $20,000 per year working at a local firm. The parent then decides to quit his job in order to care for his child, who was being watched by a babysitter for $10,000 per year. Does GDP rise, fall, or stay constant with this action, and how much does GDP change (if at all)? [LO 7.7]

Endnotes

1. http://databank.worldbank.org/data/reports.aspx?source=2&country=CHN&series=&period= http://www.nytimes.com/2010/08/16/business/global/16yuan.html?_r=0.
2. To find out more about the chain-weighted index, see this explanation from the Federal Reserve: http://www.frbsf.org/publications/economics/letter/2002/el2002-22.pdf.
3. World Bank World Development Indicators. http://databank.worldbank.org/data/reports.aspx?source=2&series=NY.GDP.PCAP.CD#advanced DownloadOptions.
4. http://data.worldbank.org/country/equatorial-guinea.
5. Below certain thresholds, some earnings from self-employment don't need to be reported, so failure to report isn't necessarily against the tax laws. In any case, if they're not reported, those activities are not captured in GDP calculations.
6. https://openknowledge.worldbank.org/bitstream/handle/10986/3928/WPS5356.pdf?sequence=1.
7. Ibid.
8. http://www.nytimes.com/2007/08/26/world/asia/26china.html?pagewanted=2.

The Cost of Living

Chapter 8

Thank You for Not Smoking

Tucked in among the signs and ads on commuter trains in Massachusetts is a small notice that says, "No smoking—General Laws Chapter 272, Sec 43A—Punishable by imprisonment for no more than 10 days or a fine of no more than one hundred dollars, or both such fine and imprisonment." It's the kind of sign that you'd glance at and quickly forget. But when you think about the crime and the two possible punishments (10 days in jail or paying $100 cash), it's a pretty imbalanced trade-off. Although the judge ultimately gets to determine the consequences, most people would choose to pay $10 a day to avoid jail if they could. What is the point of giving both options when one is clearly worse than the other?

To understand the reasoning behind the two punishments, it helps to know one fact: The no-smoking law was written in 1968. Back then, a Hershey Bar cost 5 cents and a box of cornflakes cost 29 cents. Today a box of cornflakes costs about $2.99. Back then, it would take nearly eight days working at McDonald's to earn $100. Today it would take about two days at the current federal minimum wage of $7.25 per hour.

Clearly, prices and wages are much higher today than they were in 1968. When the fine was originally set, $100 went a long way. It also took a long time to earn. As prices increased over time, $100 bought less and less, and the opportunity cost of paying the $100 fine fell. In contrast, 10 days is still 10 days. As a result, what might have been a tough choice when the law was written—the fine or the jail time—now seems an easy trade-off.

©Hershey Community Archives, Hershey, PA

The smoking fine draws our attention to an important idea: A dollar now is very different from a dollar in the past. More generally, it reminds us that a "dollar" is just a word or a piece of paper. What really matters is what we can buy with the dollar—and what we can buy with a dollar changes over time.

When we talk about what a dollar actually buys, we are talking about the *cost of living*. When we say the cost of living has gone up, we mean that, looking broadly over a range of goods and services, a dollar buys less today than it used to buy.

LEARNING OBJECTIVES

LO 8.1 Understand the importance of a market basket in tracking price changes.

LO 8.2 Calculate and use a price index to measure changes in the cost of living over time.

LO 8.3 Name the two main challenges the BLS faces when measuring price changes, and outline how it responds to these challenges.

LO 8.4 Calculate the inflation rate and recognize alternative measures.

LO 8.5 Use a price index to adjust nominal variables into real variables.

LO 8.6 Understand how indexing keeps the real value of a payment constant over time.

LO 8.7 Explain what purchasing power parity is.

LO 8.8 Use a price index to calculate PPP-adjusted variables, and compare the cost of living across different places.

In this chapter we'll describe the most important measures of changing prices. In the first part of the chapter, you'll see how to measure changes of prices over time. In the second part, you will see why prices differ among countries and how to measure these differences. Along the way, you'll get a sense of how the cost of living factors into everything from how far your paycheck will stretch, to debates over the size of Social Security, to how many poor people live on the planet.

The Cost of Living

In Chapter 7, "Measuring GDP," we discussed how to measure output on a national level. Now we turn our attention to the second pillar of macroeconomic data: prices. Before, we calculated real GDP to see how output increases over time, independent of price changes. We also looked at nominal GDP to see how changes in the price level influenced the overall valuation of the economy. Now, we want to focus on both real and nominal price changes and how that effects the cost of everyday goods and services.

Real values of goods and services are determined by the economy. Throughout previous chapters, we have seen how various factors of supply and demand influence the eventual price of a good. A shortage of labor, for example, may make it more expensive to produce a good, raising its price. Or demand may fall, causing its price to fall.

Nominal price changes, on the other hand, occur when the value of money changes. These price changes tend to be widespread, and they change how we count the value of "stuff" in general. The important thing to remember is that this type of price change does not change the *real value* of what is bought and sold.

Measuring prices in a national economy helps us answer the question, "What's a dollar (or euro or yen or peso) worth?" This question is trickier than it sounds. What a dollar will buy changes from year to year as the prices of goods rise or fall (but usually rise) over time. Most people earn more money now than people earned in the 20th century, but they also tend to face higher prices today.

It also matters where you live. People tend to earn more in New York City than they do in Iowa City. But prices are also higher in New York. As we describe in the box below, sometimes you can buy more with a lower income if you live in a cheaper place. The key to understanding the cost of living is to look at the full picture.

If all prices and incomes rose at the same rate everywhere in the world, tracking the cost of living would be a simple accounting question. What makes it an interesting and important macroeconomic topic is the fact that, in the real world, prices change at different speeds across time and place. Those differing speeds have effects on people's economic behavior. For example:

- At any given time, wages might be rising more slowly than the price of consumer goods. That difference effectively shrinks your ability to buy things.
- Or if you have $5,000 in student debt, rising price levels mean that the real value of that debt (in terms of the quantity of goods and services you have to give up in order to pay back the loan) is getting smaller over time.
- Or suppose you have competing job offers in New York City and Iowa City, Iowa. You will want to consider not only the salaries offered but also the costs of living in both places.

The cost of living can differ greatly, even for two cities in the same country, as shown in the Economics in Action box "The costs of living in New York City vs. Iowa City."

> ### The costs of living in New York City vs. Iowa City
> **Economics in Action**
>
> "I want to wake up in that city that doesn't sleep," sang Frank Sinatra. "I want to be a part of it, New York, New York."
>
> Waking up in the city that doesn't sleep isn't cheap, though. Today, New York City is the most expensive city in America. A simple one-bedroom apartment can cost thousands of dollars a month in rent. In fact, the median price of homes in Manhattan is almost $1.2 million; the U.S. median is about $276,000. Other things are quite expensive as well. According to online price-tracker Numbeo, "cheap" eats in New York City will cost you about $20. A swankier three-course dinner is going to cost at least $80 per person.
>
> Using the same price-tracker, we can compare the relative expense of living in different U.S. cities. It turns out that groceries in Manhattan cost around 75 percent more on average than in Iowa City, and rent costs about 233 percent more. You can rent a one-bedroom apartment in Iowa City for about $840, less than you would pay for a walk-in-closet-sized apartment in Manhattan.
>
> As you would expect, though, people also get paid more in New York City. The latest data from the U.S. Census show the median NYC household income is $60,879. Iowa City has a median income of $50,320. That's a difference in incomes of about 20 percent.
>
> The income difference is pretty substantial, but it's less than half of the difference in prices. In other words, the median household in Iowa City is substantially better off than the median household in New York City, at least in terms of the quantity of goods and services they can afford to buy.
>
> Why, then, do people choose to live in New York City? Why doesn't everyone prefer to move to places like Iowa City? We can deduce that people who choose to live in Manhattan get some kind of additional utility from their choice, worth many thousands of dollars a year to them. But if living in a "city that doesn't sleep" isn't your thing, you're likely to find greater happiness—and cheaper meals—in another part of the country.
>
> Sources: www.numbeo.com; www.bestplaces.net/col; www.zillow.com/home-values/; www.dailymail.co.uk/news/article-2971028/Life-90-square-foot-box-Woman-s-apartment-takes-cramped-New-York-living-extreme-does-pay-750-West-Village.html; http://factfinder.census.gov/faces/nav/jsf/pages/index.xhtml.

As these examples show, changing price levels can have real effects on people's incentives and choices. They determine the relative value of your salary, of saving or borrowing, of living in one city or another, and a multitude of other decisions. When you add up all of these microeconomic choices, you can get big macroeconomic effects.

Measuring Price Changes over Time

What does it mean to track how "prices" change? After all, people buy many different goods and services, and each has its own price. For the things you routinely buy, some prices go up and some go down. Some prices move a lot, while some don't budge. For example:

- Perhaps your rent went up over the past year, but the price of gasoline held steady.
- Maybe it became cheaper to buy an older iPhone once the new iPhone came out.
- Maybe the price of clothing rose only slightly since last year, but cable bills went through the roof.

In addition, the scope of the price change matters. A price change in some goods and services will matter more to a given consumer than other price changes. For example, a 10 percent increase in rent (often a big budget item) hurts much more than a 10 percent jump in the price of your favorite shampoo. The most important factors are how much the price changed (and in what direction) and whether the item is a big part of one's total budget.

Consumers can get a rough sense of how changes in prices affect them overall by:

- First considering how much of their spending goes to which items.
- Then using that knowledge to weigh the importance of individual price changes.

The same idea translates to thinking about changes in prices in the overall economy: The idea is to track how individual prices move over time, giving the most weight to the items that account for the biggest shares of a typical consumer's budget. That process can give a measure of how the *overall* cost of living has changed. The aim is a single number that summarizes changes in the prices of many goods, not just one at a time.

But how do we know which goods and services to look at in the first place? How do we weigh the importance of rent versus shampoo for the whole economy? The idea of a "market basket" gives us a method for comparing prices over time and locations.

The market basket

LO 8.1 Understand the importance of a market basket in tracking price changes.

market basket
a list of specific goods and services in fixed quantities

When comparing the cost of living across time and place, we have to consider the prices of many different goods and services—housing, food, clothing, transportation, entertainment, and so on. To accomplish this, we construct something that looks like a really long shopping list, called a **market basket**. The list includes specific goods and services that roughly correspond to a typical consumer's spending. (Who's a "typical" consumer? Good question. We'll come back to that later.)

The goal of creating the market basket is to see how the cost of buying the goods and services on the list changes over time. To do so, economists keep the goods and quantities included in the market basket relatively constant. This strategy ensures that any change in the total cost of the basket is caused by a change in prices, rather than the type or amount of things being consumed.

To see how this method works, imagine that you noticed changes from last year to this year in the prices of four items you typically buy at the grocery store:

	Price last year ($)	Price this year ($)
Bread (per loaf)	2.60	2.73
Milk (per gallon)	3.00	3.06
Beef (per pound)	4.00	4.16
Carrots (per pound)	1.00	1.25

TAKE NOTE...

Remember the formula for calculating a percentage change is $\left[\frac{(X_2 - X_1)}{X_1}\right] \times 100.$)

How much did the price of groceries increase since last year? It depends on which type of food you look at. The price of bread rose by 5 percent, milk by 2 percent, beef by 4 percent, and carrots by a whopping 25 percent.

Suppose we want to know how much the *overall cost of your groceries* rose—a very reasonable and practical question. To answer it, we have to know how much of each food you typically buy. For instance, if you typically buy a loaf of bread, a gallon of milk, three pounds of beef, and a pound of carrots, then:

$$\text{Cost last year} = (\$2.60 \times 1) + (\$3.00 \times 1) + (\$4.00 \times 3) + (\$1.00 \times 1) = \$18.60$$
$$\text{Cost this year} = (\$2.73 \times 1) + (\$3.06 \times 1) + (\$4.16 \times 3) + (\$1.25 \times 1) = \$19.52$$
$$\text{Price increase from last year to this year} = \left[\frac{(\$19.52 - \$18.60)}{\$18.60}\right] \times 100 = 4.95\%$$

This is the *basket approach*. It measures changes in the cost of your shopping basket, assuming that you buy the same items in the same quantities. This approach gives us a *single number* to measure how much your total costs rise over time.

Someone might ask, "Why not just average the increase in the price of each grocery item (bread, 5%; milk, 2%; beef, 4%; carrots, 25%)?" If we did that, we would get a completely different—and wrong!—answer:

$$= \frac{(5\% + 2\% + 4\% + 25\%)}{4}$$
$$= 9\% \text{ (Remember, this answer is wrong!)}$$

Why would this calculation be wrong? Most people don't spend nearly as much on carrots as they do on beef or milk or bread. Therefore, the relatively big increase in the price of carrots doesn't affect consumers as much as the average of the percentage increases would suggest. After all, we want a meaningful answer to the original question, "How much did the price of groceries increase since last year?" To get that answer, what we really want to know is how much more it will cost when you take your usual basket of groceries to the store checkout.

Of course, most people don't buy exactly the same thing all the time, especially when they see that prices are changing. In fact, we know that when prices rise, quantity demanded usually falls. In reality, you might decide to buy less beef and switch from carrots to potatoes. However, these short-term fluctuations don't change the market basket, unless there's a permanent reason for consumers to buy more potatoes.

Later in the chapter we'll come back to ways of dealing with this challenge. For now, the basket approach gives us a way to capture lots of different price changes in a single number that (approximately) represents the purchases of a typical consumer.

Consumer Price Index (CPI)

The basket approach allows us to track changes in the cost of living. To summarize these changes, we construct a **price index**. It measures how much the cost of a market basket has risen or fallen relative to the cost in a base time period or location.

The most commonly used index tool for tracking changes in the cost of living in the United States is the **Consumer Price Index**, or **CPI**. The CPI tracks changes in the cost of a basket of goods and services purchased by a typical U.S. household. It is calculated by the Bureau of Labor Statistics (BLS), a statistical agency in the U.S. federal government.

The method for calculating the CPI is relatively simple. First, the BLS comes up with a basket of goods and services purchased by a typical household. Then, every month it collects data on the prices of those goods and services in a variety of places around the country. Using these data, the BLS calculates the cost of buying that market basket.

The CPI measures the increase in the cost of the market basket relative to the cost in a given base year. For instance, suppose that the cost of the market basket was $40,000 in 2017

price index
a measure showing how much the cost of a market basket has risen or fallen relative to the cost in a base time period or location

Consumer Price Index (CPI)
a measure that tracks changes in the cost of a basket of goods and services purchased by a typical U.S. household

LO 8.2 Calculate and use a price index to measure changes in the cost of living over time.

(the base year) and $40,400 in 2018. To find the index for 2018 relative to 2017, we use the following formula:

EQUATION 8-1

$$\text{CPI} = \frac{\text{Cost of desired-year basket in base-year prices}}{\text{Cost of base-year basket in base-year prices}} \times 100$$

$$= \left(\frac{\text{Basket}_{\text{desired-year}}}{\text{Basket}_{\text{base-year}}}\right) \times 100$$

$$= \left(\frac{\text{Basket}_{2018}}{\text{Basket}_{2017}}\right) \times 100$$

$$= \left(\frac{\$40,400}{\$40,000}\right) \times 100 = 101$$

In the base year, by definition, the index will always be 100. In future years:

- If the cost of the basket rises higher than the base-year cost, the index will be more than 100.
- If the cost of the basket falls below the base-year cost, the index will be less than 100.

In our example, with 2017 as the base year, the CPI increases from 100 to 101. This change implies a 1 percent increase in the basket of consumer goods. That 1 percent increase also means a 1 percent increase in the cost of living for a typical household.

The BLS's stated goal for the CPI is to answer the question, "What is the cost, at this month's market prices, of achieving the standard of living attained in the base period?" In other words, the CPI helps us understand how the cost of living today compares with the cost of living at some time in the past. In the (hypothetical) example above, the CPI tells us that the cost of living in 2018 was 1 percent higher than it was in 2017. However, in reality, as Figure 8-1 shows, the CPI has risen consistently over the last hundred years.

TAKE NOTE

Figure 8-1 happens to use 1984 as the base year. In other words, the index for 1984 was 100, and the indexes for other years are numbers relative to 1984. An index of 105, for example, means prices were 5 percent higher than in 1984.

What would happen to the graph if a different base year had been chosen? The shape of the graph would be exactly the same, though the index numbers would be scaled to a different base year.

The challenges in measuring price changes

LO 8.3 Name the two main challenges the BLS faces when measuring price changes, and outline how it responds to these challenges.

The idea behind the CPI is straightforward, but turning that idea into reality requires addressing two big challenges:

- The first is to figure out which goods should go into the market basket so that the CPI reflects the average purchases of the widest group of people.
- The second is how to measure changes over time. Take this simple question as an example: Is it a price increase if a computer costs 10 percent more but is also 10 percent faster?

In this section, we'll address both of these challenges in turn.

Which goods? The first question is, *which goods* should go into the market basket to measure price changes? Your next-door neighbor may love carrots, and you may love beef. As a result,

FIGURE 8-1

CPI from 1913 to 2018 Prices are much higher now than in the early part of the 20th century. Over time, the slope of the line shows the rate of price increases. For example, the particularly steep portion of the line between 1973 and 1980 reflects high inflation during that time.

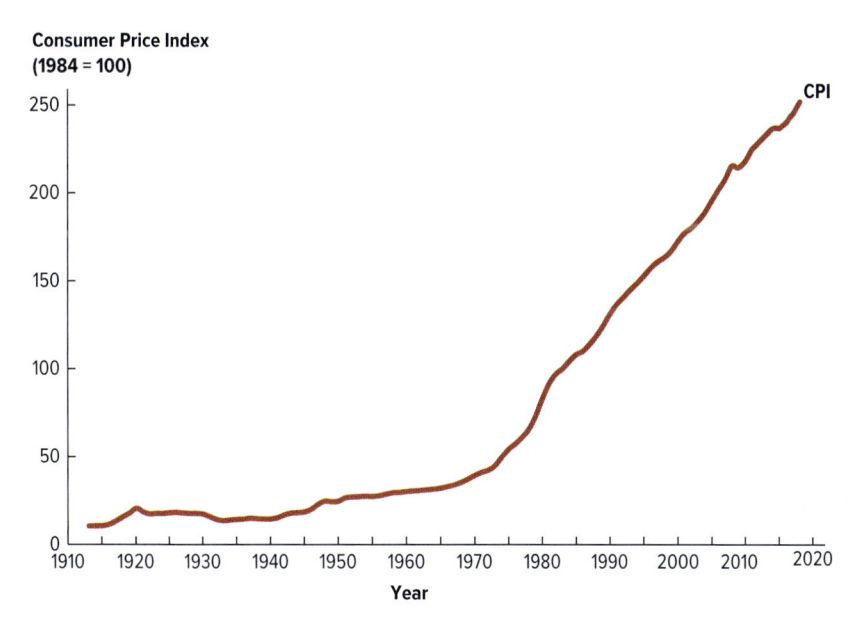

Source: http://inflationdata.com/Inflation/Consumer_Price_Index/HistoricalCPI.aspx?reloaded=true.

your grocery bills will probably look very different, and they will increase at different rates as the prices of carrots and beef change. There is no way to have a single number that perfectly describes changes in the cost of living for everyone because people buy different things. The best we can do is to come up with a basket that tries to represent a "typical" household.

Who is typical? The CPI is based on an average of the goods and services purchased by "urban consumers"—anyone living in a city of 2,500 or more. (This measure is technically called the CPI-U, for "urban.") The CPI accounts for 93 percent of the U.S. population; it includes people in all sorts of jobs as well as unemployed and retired people. It doesn't, however, include people living in rural areas, members of the military, or the "institutionalized" population (mostly people living in prisons or mental hospitals).

The CPI tries to balance out the consumption of different types of people in different life stages and situations. Rather than representing the exact consumption of any particular household, it is an average across a very large group of U.S. consumers. A particular family's cost of living might increase more or less than the CPI, depending on exactly how much of which things the family buys. Figure 8-2 shows the breakdown of spending in 2017 in the average urban-consumer household across eight major categories.

Changes over time: Substitution and innovation Earlier, we noted that a price index like the CPI measures pure price changes only if the types and quantities of goods in the market basket remain relatively constant. However, there is an accuracy trade-off involved: Keeping the basket fixed accurately isolates price changes from behavior changes. However, when real people's behavior has changed enough, keeping the basket fixed also means that it will no longer accurately represent the consumption of a typical household.

FIGURE 8-2

Spending by urban consumers represented in the CPI This bar chart shows how much prices in certain sectors are weighted in the calculation of the Consumer Price Index. By far, the largest component of the Consumer Price Index is housing costs, at over 41 percent. The next two largest components are transportation, followed by food and beverage, which together make up about a third of the CPI. The rest of the categories together comprise the final quarter.

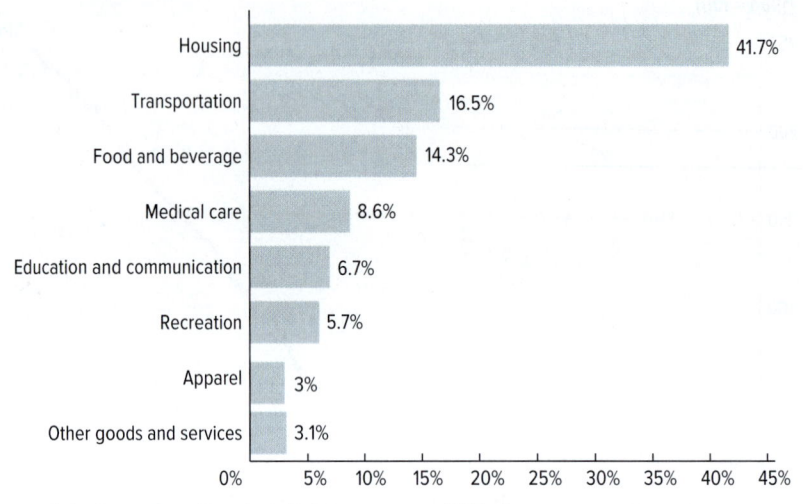

Category	Percent
Housing	41.7%
Transportation	16.5%
Food and beverage	14.3%
Medical care	8.6%
Education and communication	6.7%
Recreation	5.7%
Apparel	3%
Other goods and services	3.1%

Source: U.S. Bureau of Labor Statistics, www.bls.gov/cpi/tables/relative-importance/2017.pdf.

Price indexes have to deal with the fact that as tastes and prices change, households tend to buy different goods and services. There are two main reasons for changes in consumption patterns over time—substitution and innovation.

Substitution is the idea that people switch between similar goods and services when relative prices shift. For example:

- If the price of carrots goes up by 25 percent while the prices of other vegetables increase by a smaller amount, people will tend to buy fewer carrots and more other vegetables.
- If the price of going out to the movies goes up and the price of streaming video goes down, people will tend to watch more videos at home and fewer at the movie theater.

If the market basket doesn't reflect the fact that people buy less of particular goods as they get more expensive, it will overstate actual changes in the cost of living.

The second reason why the market basket has to change over time is *innovation:* As new goods and services become available, people change what they consume. When the CPI was first calculated during World War I, for example, it did not include refrigerators, washing machines, telephones, computers, and many other goods that almost all households today purchase at one time or another. Some of these things couldn't be bought at any price because they hadn't been invented. Others existed but hadn't made it into the general consumer market yet.

The BLS does occasionally update the basket used to calculate the CPI, to account for both substitution and new products. These updates undermine the idea of comparing a *constant* basket of goods and services. But the underlying aim is to capture the cost of achieving a certain *standard of living*. Creating a basket that balances these competing goals requires some tricky judgment calls.

Similar judgment calls are required when products get better. For example, cars today are far safer, are more reliable, and offer more features than did those in the 1950s. So if cars are more expensive now than they were in the 1950s, how do we tease apart the fact that the price of the basic product has increased from the fact that car quality is now higher? If a higher price represents higher quality, the true cost of living may not actually have increased.

In trying to make these judgment calls, the BLS has to attempt something called *hedonic quality adjustment*. While the math gets tricky, the general idea is to break a product into a list of features, and then determine how much utility consumers get from each feature to determine how these features influence well-being.

Computer technology provides a great example of how this works in practice. Although an iMac computer from 1998 cost about the same as an iMac today (about $1,800), it was far more limited both in screen resolution and computing power. Without hedonic price adjustment, it would appear that people buying computers are about as well off as two decades ago; in reality, though, the Retina 5K display and terabyte of hard-drive storage give consumers of new iMacs a lot more for their money.

TEST YOURSELF

- What is the purpose of a market basket? **[LO 8.1]**
- What is a price index? **[LO 8.2]**
- Does the CPI show price changes for people living in rural areas? **[LO 8.3]**
- Name the two challenges that complicate the calculation of inflation. **[LO 8.3]**

Using Price Indexes

Now that we know how to measure price changes over time, what do we *do* with that knowledge? As we saw with GDP in Chapter 7, "Measuring GDP," many economic variables give an incomplete picture when expressed in nominal terms—that is, without accounting for price differences. To solve this problem, we can use price indexes to turn nominal variables into real ones.

Using price indexes, we can isolate changes in prices from changes in fundamentals like income and output and can express those changes in constant dollars relative to a base year. Those changes are captured in the **inflation rate**, which represents the size of the change in the overall price level. The inflation rate is one of the central concepts in macroeconomics. In this section we'll discuss how to calculate the inflation rate and how to use it.

inflation rate the size of the change in the overall price level; the percent change in a price index such as the CPI from year to year

LO 8.4 Calculate the inflation rate and recognize alternative measures.

The inflation rate

The inflation rate is the percent change in the CPI from year to year, calculated as follows:

EQUATION 8-2
$$\text{Inflation rate} = \left[\frac{(CPI_{year2} - CPI_{year1})}{CPI_{year1}}\right] \times 100$$

Table 8-1 shows increases in the CPI from 2008 to 2018, using an average of prices in 1982–84 as the base period (when the CPI = 100). If we want to know how much prices have increased since the base period, the change in the CPI provides a direct answer. For instance, the 2008 CPI of 215.3 means that price levels in 2008 were 115.3 percent higher than they were in the base period, 1982–84.

When you read about inflation in the news, it is typically expressed as an increase over the *previous year*. For example, what if we want to compare 2018 to 2017, rather than to 1982–84? We can calculate the percent increase in prices from year to year as follows:

$$\text{Inflation rate}_{2018} = \left(\frac{CPI_{2018} - CPI_{2017}}{CPI_{2017}}\right) \times 100$$
$$= \left(\frac{251.1 - 245.1}{245.1}\right) \times 100 = 2.4\%$$

TABLE 8-1

Calculating the inflation rate

To calculate the inflation rate, subtract the CPI of the previous year from the current year and then divide by the CPI of the previous year. In most years, prices have increased, but in 2009, there was negative inflation, or deflation.

Year	CPI	Calculation	Inflation rate (%)
2008	215.3	—	3.9
2009	214.5	$\frac{214.5 - 215.3}{215.3} \times 100$	−0.4
2010	218.1	$\frac{218.1 - 214.5}{214.5} \times 100$	1.7
2011	224.9	$\frac{224.9 - 218.1}{218.1} \times 100$	3.1
2012	229.6	$\frac{229.6 - 224.9}{224.9} \times 100$	2.1
2013	233.0	$\frac{233.0 - 229.6}{229.6} \times 100$	1.5
2014	236.7	$\frac{236.7 - 233.0}{233.0} \times 100$	1.6
2015	237.0	$\frac{237.0 - 236.7}{236.7} \times 100$	0.1
2016	240.0	$\frac{240.0 - 237.0}{237.0} \times 100$	1.2
2017	245.1	$\frac{245.1 - 240.0}{240.0} \times 100$	2.1
2018	251.1	$\frac{251.1 - 245.1}{245.1} \times 100$	2.4

Source: The base period (when the CPI = 100) is 1982–1984. U.S. Bureau of Labor Statistics and https://inflationdata.com/Inflation/Consumer_Price_Index/HistoricalCPI.aspx?reloaded=true.

An inflation rate of 2.4 percent means that the overall price level increased at that rate between 2017 and 2018.

If you follow news reports on the economy, you may hear discussion of two different inflation measures:

- **Headline inflation** measures price changes for the entire market basket of the average urban consumer. It's simply another term for inflation measured using the CPI.
- **Core inflation** measures price changes minus food and energy costs, which are traditionally volatile.[1]

headline inflation
measure of inflation that measures price changes for all of the goods in the market basket of the average urban consumer

core inflation
measure of inflation that measures price changes minus food and energy costs, which are traditionally volatile

Why have two different measures? Compared to many goods, energy and food prices go up and down a lot. Because they might be very high or very low at the time the CPI is calculated, including them might over- or understate the real change in overall prices. On the other hand, most Americans spend a large part of their income on food and gas. Any basket that does not include these goods is missing a large part of the cost-of-living picture. Looking at both headline and core inflation can give us a more accurate sense of what's really happening in the economy.

Alternative inflation measures The difference between headline and core inflation suggests a more general idea: We can measure inflation using *any* basket of goods or price index we want. The resulting measures of inflation will reflect changes in the prices of different sets of goods. The CPI focuses on prices *paid by consumers*.

What if we are more interested in the costs that businesses, rather than consumers, are facing? An alternative price index, the *Producer Price Index (PPI)*, measures the prices of goods and services purchased *by firms*. The PPI includes things that are not part of the typical person's consumption basket, such as industrial machinery. Because increases in input prices eventually make it to consumers when they buy the final product, the PPI is considered a good predictor of *future* consumer prices. Regardless of whether we use the CPI or the PPI, inflation is measured as a *percent increase in the index from one year to the next*.

Another alternative is to calculate the inflation rate using the *GDP deflator*, as we did in Chapter 7, "Measuring GDP." The GDP deflator measures price changes for *everything produced*

FIGURE 8-3

U.S. inflation rates, as measured by the CPI, PPI, and GDP deflator, 1960–2018 This graph shows the three main measures of inflation over the past 58 years. All three show similar trends in the rise and fall of prices. The Producer Price Index shows the most dramatic ups and downs, while the GDP deflator shows more restrained changes.

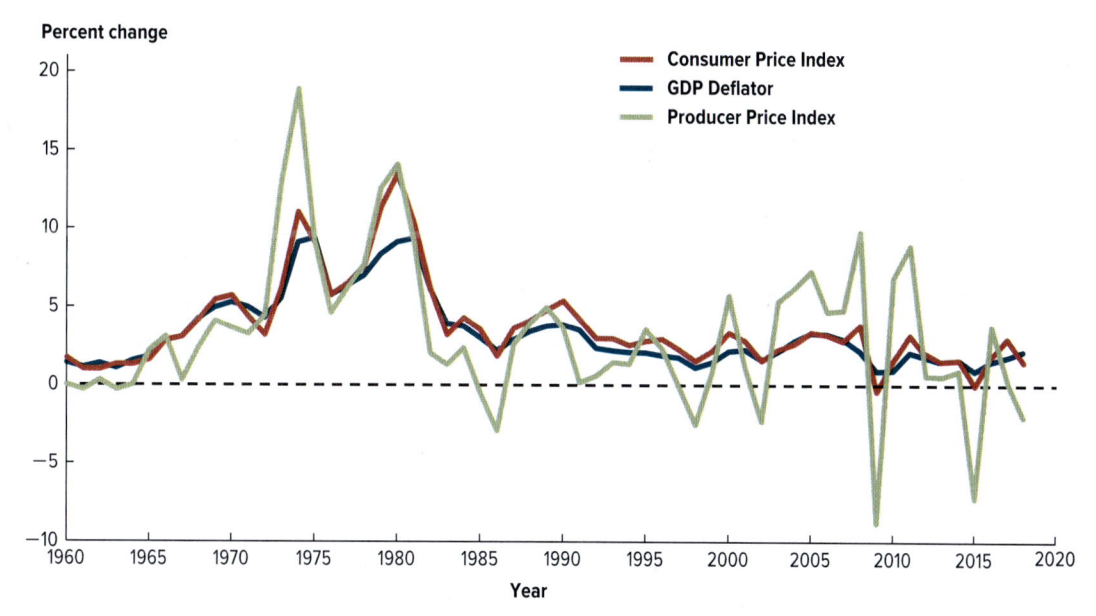

Source: U.S. Federal Reserve Bank of St. Louis—FRED, http://fred.stlouisfed.org; Bureau of Labor Statistics, https://data.bls.gov/timeseries/WPSFD4?output_view=pct_1mth.

in the country. It doesn't, though, include goods produced abroad that might have a real effect on the typical household's cost of living, such as oil. Another key difference is that the GDP deflator is computed using the actual quantities that are produced in the economy each year, rather than using a "fixed" basket of goods.

All three measures of inflation—CPI, PPI, and GDP deflator—are useful; they simply measure different things. In practice, inflation rates calculated using the three methods track each other quite closely. Figure 8-3 shows inflation rates in the United States using each measure over the last 55 years.

Deflating nominal variables

Often, we want to study how the real value of a variable, such as income, has changed over time. To do this, we can use the CPI (or another price index) to "deflate" the nominal variable and state it in constant, real terms.

You might be surprised, or even shocked, if your grandparents told you how much money they made in their younger days. For instance, in 1969, a salary of $20,520 would have allowed your grandparents to live a comfortable life, send their kids to college, and put away a little for retirement. When your grandparents retired 45 years later, in 2014, that income would have been below the federal poverty line for a family of four.

Suppose we want to know how much money your grandparents would have to earn now to have purchasing power equivalent to their income in 1969. To compare changes in purchasing power over time, we can translate nominal income in any past year into constant, real dollars. Equation 8-3 shows how any dollar amount from the past can be translated into its current value.

LO 8.5 Use a price index to adjust nominal variables into real variables.

EQUATION 8-3 Value of year-X income in year-Y dollars

$$\text{Real value}_{\text{yearY}} = \text{Nominal value}_{\text{yearX}} \times \left(\frac{\text{CPI}_{\text{yearY}}}{\text{CPI}_{\text{yearX}}}\right)$$

Let's apply this equation to find the purchasing power of $20,520 in 2014 dollars. We multiply $20,520 by the ratio of the CPI in 2014 and 1969:

$$\text{Real value}_{2014} = \text{Nominal value}_{1969} \times \left(\frac{\text{CPI}_{2014}}{\text{CPI}_{1969}}\right)$$

$$= \$20{,}520 \times \left(\frac{236.7}{36.7}\right)$$

$$= \$132{,}346$$

What does this result mean? It means that in 2014 you would have needed $132,346 to buy the amount of goods and services your grandparents would have been able to buy with $20,520 in 1969. It turns out that they were doing pretty well, after all.

We can make this same calculation with any base year and any nominal variable. For instance, suppose we want to know how much of the increases in the incomes of the wealthy are attributable to inflation and how much they represent an increase in real wealth. Take a look at Table 8-2:

- The first two columns show average income for the top 20 percent of the population in nominal terms.
- The third column shows the CPI for each decade.
- The fourth column uses the CPI to translate income into a direct comparison of purchasing power in 2014 dollars.

These data show that although the cost of living has increased, the income of the wealthiest 20 percent of Americans has increased faster. How do we know that? We can see that real—inflation-adjusted—income of the group has grown steadily, except in 2009. So, income must have grown faster than prices. If they had grown at exactly the same rate, real income in 1969 would equal real income in 2014. In other words, increased nominal incomes are partly due to inflation but also partly due to a real increase in purchasing power.

TABLE 8-2
Calculating the deflation of nominal variables

At first glance, the average income of those living in 1969 looks much lower than in 2014. When 1969 incomes are inflated so that the value of these dollars is the same between the two decades, the gap decreases.

Year	Average income of top 20 percent ($)	CPI (1982–84 = 100)	Value in 2014 dollars
1969	20,520	36.7	$\$20{,}520 \times \left(\frac{236.7}{36.7}\right) = $ **$132,346**
1979	43,265	72.6	$\$43{,}265 \times \left(\frac{236.7}{72.6}\right) = $ **$141,058**
1989	85,529	124.0	$\$85{,}529 \times \left(\frac{236.7}{124.0}\right) = $ **$163,263**
1999	135,250	166.6	$\$135{,}250 \times \left(\frac{236.7}{166.6}\right) = $ **$192,158**
2009	170,844	214.5	$\$170{,}844 \times \left(\frac{236.7}{214.5}\right) = $ **$188,526**
2014	217,021	236.7	217,021

Sources: Income data from the U.S. Census, www.census.gov/hhes/www/income/data/historical/families; CPI data from http://inflationdata.com/Inflation/Consumer_Price_Index/HistoricalCPI.aspx?reloaded=true.

Inflation adjustment can make a huge difference in how we perceive things that happen *now* relative to things that happened *in the past*, as discussed in the From Another Angle box "The wealthiest American?"

The wealthiest American?
From Another Angle

Who would you say is the richest American in history? Bill Gates, maybe? Gates created software giant Microsoft and was worth over $101 billion at his wealthiest. In 2017, however, Jeff Bezos, founder of Amazon.com, moved ahead, with a net worth of $112 billion. Whether that makes Bezos the richest American ever, though, all depends on how you look at it.

Going backward through history, we find that the nominal wealth of the richest people in a generation keeps shrinking:

- At his death in 1937, John D. Rockefeller's wealth was a puny-sounding $1.4 billion.
- Cornelius Vanderbilt, famous for wealth gained through railroads and shipping, finished with a fortune of $100 million in 1877.
- John Jacob Astor, who had a virtual monopoly on the fur trade, had a final wealth of $20 million in 1848.

If all we did was consider *nominal* dollar amounts, Jeff Bezos looks vastly wealthier than all of them.

If we adjust those fortunes for inflation, we get a different picture. It's not exactly easy to compare the cost of living of today's multibillionaires with those of yesteryear. Technically, we'd need a constant basket of the kind of goods a typical multibillionaire might purchase. But we can't ask how much it might have cost Astor to buy a Bugatti sports car in 1848 or what Vanderbilt might have paid for a private jet in 1877. Those things didn't exist.

Still, some economists took a stab at translating the fortunes of history into constant 2006 dollars. The result?

- Rockefeller tops the inflation-adjusted list, by a lot. He would have been able to buy $305 billion worth of Cristal champagne and private Caribbean islands had he been alive in 2006.
- Not far behind, at $281 billion, is steel magnate Andrew Carnegie.
- Vanderbilt comes in third at $168 billion.
- Astor's $20 million in 1848 money would buy him $110 billion worth of luxury if he could have spent it in 2006.

As it turns out, Bill Gates and Jeff Bezos don't tower over the super-rich from previous eras after all.

Sources: www.forbes.com/2007/09/14/richest-americans-alltime-biz_cx_pw_as_0914ialltime_slide_2.html; http://archive.fortune.com/magazines/fortune/fortune_archive/2007/03/05/8401299/index.htm; http://time.com/money/4746795/richest-people-in-the-world/.

Adjusting for inflation: Indexing

How can we be sure that wages will keep up with inflation? One fundamental theory in macroeconomics says that, with enough time, wages should naturally rise to offset the effects of inflation, so in the end inflation should not matter to people's well-being and their choices. However, most economists agree that there are times when some prices are changing so fast that the rest of the economy struggles to keep up.

If prices increase faster than wages, for instance, people will experience a drop in their standard of living. Everyone will face a very strong incentive to buy things *now* if they are afraid prices will be higher next week or next month. In that economic environment, inflation can distort economic choices. We'll talk a lot more about problems like these in later chapters, particularly in Chapter 16, "Inflation." For now, let's look at how *measuring* inflation can be an important step toward solving problems that inflation causes.

LO 8.6 Understand how indexing keeps the real value of a payment constant over time.

One very practical application of the CPI is to index payments to inflation. Ida May Fuller was the first-ever recipient of monthly Social Security benefits. When she retired in 1940, she received a check for $22.54. For the next decade, her benefits stayed constant, at $22.54 every month. By 1950, the real value of her Social Security check had fallen by almost half, due to inflation. In 1950, her $22.54 check could buy only $13.37 worth of goods and services, when translated into the purchasing power of 1940.

In the early years of Social Security, no accommodation was made for inflation. Retirees expected to receive the same nominal dollar amount monthly for the rest of their lives. In 1950, Congress looked at the problem faced by elderly people like Ms. Fuller. In signing the Social Security Act in 1935, President Franklin D. Roosevelt had expressed his intent that the law would "give some measure of protection to the average citizen . . . against poverty-ridden old age." With the real value of benefits dwindling every year as the cost of living rose, Social Security's success in protecting the elderly against poverty and hardship was limited. In response, Congress revised the law, to nearly double the value of monthly benefits.[2]

From 1950 to 1974, Congress amended the Social Security Act every few years. Each time, it increased the level of benefits in accord with the cost of living. However, these increases were sporadic and required a concerted effort on the part of lawmakers.

Starting in 1975, Congress implemented a different solution: indexing. **Indexing** automatically increases payments in proportion to the cost of living. Such payments are said to be *indexed to inflation*. Congress indexed Social Security benefits directly to the CPI: If the CPI increases 5 percent, so does the nominal value of monthly benefits. As a result, the dollar amount of benefits has increased most years since 1975, keeping pace with changes in the cost of living.

Indexed payments are usually referred to as *cost-of-living adjustments*, or *COLAs*. In the United States, few salaries or income payments are indexed to inflation (except for those with union contracts, where they are more common). Social Security does have a COLA and affects millions of retirees. Indexing is much more common in other countries. In much of Europe, government employees' salaries receive automatic COLAs, as do retirees' pensions.

The reasoning behind indexing is straightforward: If you want the real value of a payment to stay constant over time, make the adjustment for inflation automatic. The alternative is to rewrite a law or a contract every year—a process that involves more work and less certainty.

However, indexing is not without controversy. In particular, some have argued that the the minimum wage should be indexed to inflation to ensure that it pays an equal real amount over time. For more, read the Economics in Action box "Poverty and the minimum wage."

indexing
the practice of automatically increasing payments in proportion to the cost of living

Poverty and the minimum wage
Economics in Action

Elizabeth Warren was 12 in 1961 when her father had a heart attack and had to take a pay cut. Warren's mother took a job answering phones at Sears to help support the family and pay for mounting medical bills. At one point, their car was repossessed, yet the family was still able to scrape by. Warren claims, however, that this would not be possible today.

Back in 1961, it took $2,383 for a family of three (two parents and a child) to cross the poverty line.* A lot has changed since the early 1960s, but the real value of the federal poverty line in the United States has kept up with inflation. Every year, the line is updated using the Consumer Price Index. As a result, in 2019, a family with two parents and a child would need to earn at least $21,330 to stay above the federal poverty line.

Although the federal poverty line increases each year, the federal minimum wage is not changed unless Congress decides to do so—which happens rarely. As you can see in Figure 8-4, increases in the minimum wage have not kept up with prices.

The result is that the real value of the minimum wage has declined by $3 since the 1960s. A worker earning the minimum wage of $1.15 an hour in 1961 would have earned $2,392 a year,

FIGURE 8-4

The real value of the minimum wage Since the 1940s, the real value of the minimum wage has fluctuated as Congress has adjusted its nominal value to try to keep pace with inflation. Overall, the real value of the minimum wage climbed steadily between 1938 and the 1960s but has generally fallen since that time.

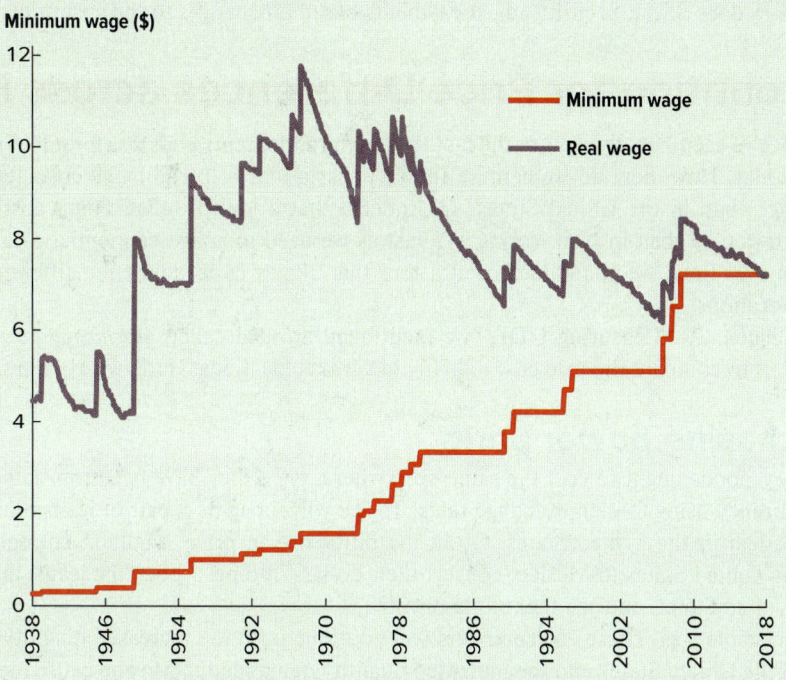

Source: Federal Reserve Bank of St. Louis, FRED—https://fred.stlouisfed.org/series/FEDMINNFRWG;

just enough to stay out of poverty. By 2018, the federal minimum wage was $7.25 an hour, and a full-time worker earned $15,080 in a year. That's no longer enough to stay out of poverty if supporting a family of three.

Nearly 60 years later, Elizabeth Warren is a U.S. Senator from Massachusetts with presidential aspirations, and she's telling her story as part of an argument to increase the minimum wage. But not everyone thinks she's telling the full story about changes in earnings and poverty over the past decades.

The first issue is that the Consumer Price Index captures price changes, but it's less good at reflecting changes in the quality of what we buy. Harvard economist Jeffrey Miron writes: "Consider that people in poverty now often have indoor plumbing, modern medical care, cell phones, access to the internet, and so on. Being at the poverty level is much less bad than during Warren's childhood." Miron also points out that "households at or below the poverty level are now eligible for two significant government transfers that did not exist in Warren's early childhood." These are the Earned Income Tax Credit (which provides a big transfer to low-income workers in the form of a tax refund) and Medicaid (which provides subsidized healthcare).

Warren is right that the federal minimum wage has lagged behind inflation. And Miron is right that simple historical comparisons give a limited view on the conditions of poverty. Economists will continue to debate the appropriate level for the minimum wage—and how to measure poverty in a changing economy.

*For the sake of argument, Warren uses the example of a family of three, even though she was the fourth child in her family.

Sources: Glenn Kessler, "Fact Checker: Elizabeth Warren's Claim that Minimum Wage Supported Her Family in the 1960s," *Washington Post*, January 11, 2019; Jeffrey Miron, "Elizabeth Warren's Claim about Minimum Wage," Cato At Liberty Blog, www.Cato.org, January 14, 2019; Elizabeth Warren, *A Fighting Chance* (New York: Metropolitan Books, 2014).

TEST YOURSELF

- [ ] What is the role of the base period when measuring inflation? **[LO 8.4]**
- [ ] When is PPI, rather than CPI, the appropriate measure of inflation? **[LO 8.4]**
- [ ] How do differences between real and nominal variables reveal changes in prices over time? **[LO 8.5]**
- [ ] How does Social Security adjust payments based on changes to the cost of living? **[LO 8.6]**

Accounting for Price Differences across Places

So far, we've seen how to capture the fact that our grandparents paid less for a loaf of bread than we do today. Now, how do we capture the fact that a loaf of bread *today* costs less on average in Mexico than in the United States? Or, indeed, that a loaf of bread might cost less on average in Iowa City than in New York City? Just as we need to adjust economic variables for price changes over time, we sometimes need a tool that allows us to adjust for differences in prices across locations.

In Chapter 7, "Measuring GDP," we mentioned an idea called *purchasing power parity* that enables us to compare the true cost of living in various locations. Here, we explain how it works.

Purchasing power parity

LO 8.7 Explain what purchasing power parity is.

In theory, goods ought to cost the same everywhere, once they have been translated into a common currency using foreign exchange rates. To see why, imagine a pair of jeans that costs less in Mexico than in the United States. Given the difference in price, wouldn't entrepreneurs travel from the United States to Mexico, convert their dollars into pesos, buy the jeans, take them back to the United States, and sell them for a profit?

In principle, yes. These entrepreneurs will continue until the increased quantity of jeans supplied in the United States and the increased quantity demanded in Mexico cause the prices in the two countries to equalize. At that point, no one has an incentive to buy jeans abroad. The result is that purchasing power should theoretically be the same everywhere, when stated in a common currency. This idea is called **purchasing power parity (PPP)**.

purchasing power parity (PPP) the theory that purchasing power in different countries should be the same when stated in a common currency

In reality, PPP almost never holds exactly. Overall price levels are lower in Mexico. For most goods, $100 exchanged into pesos buys you more in Mexico than $100 would buy you in the United States. Why? There are three main factors: transaction costs, non-tradable goods and services, and trade restrictions. Let's briefly consider them.

- **Transaction costs:** One reason that PPP doesn't hold is transportation costs: It costs money to move goods from place to place. However, the difference in PPP is usually larger than what would be explained by transport costs alone; there are other transaction costs also. For example, it costs time and money to find sellers in another country. If the price difference is small and the costs of making transactions in another country are high, the *trade-off* involved may not be worth it. As a result, the entrepreneurs will decide not to bring in less-expensive jeans from Mexico.

- **Non-tradables:** Some goods and services just can't be taken from place to place very easily, or at all. For instance, you can't buy an apartment in Iowa City and transport it to Manhattan. You can't buy a pizza in Italy and transport it to North Dakota. (Well, you could, but it wouldn't be worth eating when you got it there.) You can't buy a haircut in India if you live in New Orleans. (Of course, you could fly to India to get your hair cut, but the transaction costs would be extremely high relative to the few dollars you'd save.) These types of goods and services are called *non-tradables*.

- **Trade restrictions:** Finally, international trade isn't free. There are often tariffs and trade restrictions that increase the cost or difficulty of making exchanges across national borders. Such restrictions discourage people from fully taking advantage of lower prices in other countries.

For these three reasons, we frequently see substantially different prices for individual goods and services, as well as different overall price levels, across countries or locations within a country. For example, the purchasing power of a dollar is higher in Mexico than in the United States and lower in Switzerland.

If we want to compare incomes or costs across different countries, we're going to need to adjust nominal prices in different places. This is similar to what we do when comparing standards of living in different time periods. To compare prices in different places, economists have developed the idea of *purchasing power indexes*.

Purchasing power indexes

Just as we can use a price index to account for changes in prices over time, we can also construct a price index that describes differences in prices across locations. The methodology is quite similar:

- First, we need to find a market basket of goods and services that we can compare across countries.
- Next, we measure the price of the goods in the basket in each country and calculate the overall cost of purchasing it in each country.
- Then, we build an index showing how much the basket costs in each country relative to some base.

LO 8.8 Use a price index to calculate PPP-adjusted variables, and compare the cost of living across different places.

For a simple example, let's think about the price of Big Macs around the world. *The Economist* magazine measures these prices in 120 countries in what it calls the Big Mac Index. The Big Mac isn't a basket that represents the full cost of living, of course. But it has the advantage of being similar in each country, due to McDonald's international production and sourcing policies. It also requires a variety of inputs, such as beef, bread, lettuce, labor, advertising, and real estate.

The Big Mac Index uses the United States as the base country and compares the cost of a Big Mac there to the cost in another country. In the United States, the price of a Big Mac in 2018 was $5.51; in Mexico it was 50 pesos. Remember the theory of purchasing power parity—that purchasing power in different countries should be the same when stated in a common currency. If that theory holds true, Big Macs would have the same real price in the United States and Mexico. In that case, the exchange rate between dollars and pesos should be 9.07 pesos per dollar (50 pesos ÷ $5.51).

In reality, the official exchange rate between pesos and dollars in November 2018 was 20.1 pesos per dollar. We can calculate the Big Mac Index by comparing the official exchange rate (20.1) to the exchange rate predicted by PPP (9.07):

$$\text{Big Mac Index for Mexico} = \frac{(9.07 - 20.1) \times 100}{20.1}$$
$$= \frac{11.03 - \times 100}{20.1} = -54\%$$

What does a negative Big Mac Index for Mexico tell us? It means that price levels in Mexico are lower than we'd expect if PPP held true. As a result, real purchasing power is higher in Mexico than it is in the United States. That is, if you exchange your dollars for pesos, they'll go further at a McDonald's in Mexico than one in the United States.

A positive Big Mac Index (as in expensive countries like Sweden and Switzerland) would imply that price levels are higher than predicted by PPP. Therefore, real purchasing power is lower in such places than in the United States.

Figure 8-5 shows how price levels differ across a number of countries, using the Big Mac Index and with the United States as the base level.

The Big Mac Index is a simple, and fun, way of looking at price differences. The main measure that economists actually use for international price comparisons is the World Bank's *International Comparison Program (ICP) index*. It uses a broad market basket that tries to represent the full cost of living across countries.

FIGURE 8-5

The Big Mac Index (in U.S. dollars) The Big Mac Index is one way to measure differences in purchasing power across countries. According to the index, Egypt and Malaysia have a low cost of living. Rich countries generally have costs of living that are similar to that in the United States or even higher.

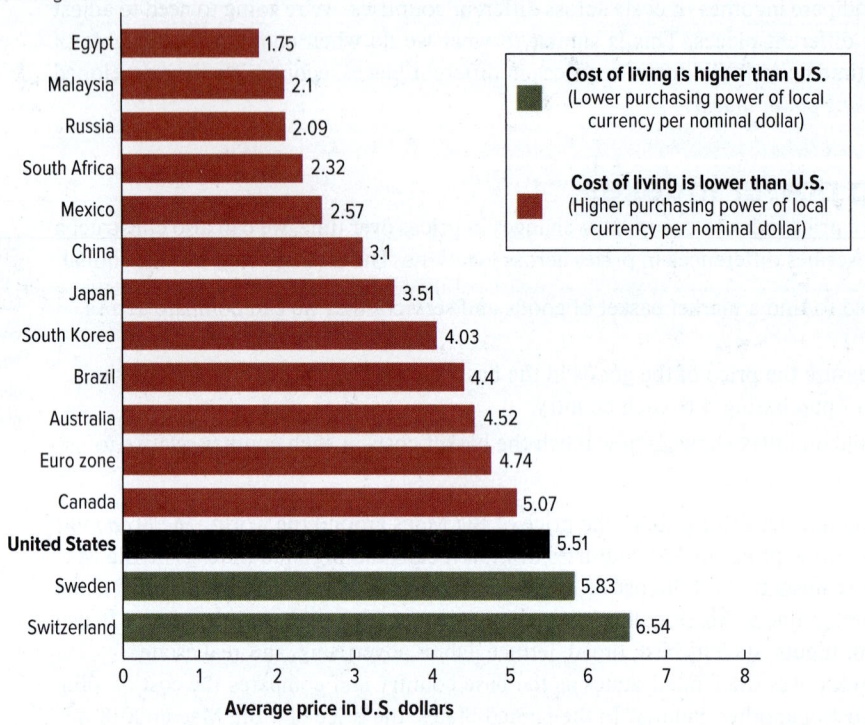

Country	Average price in U.S. dollars
Egypt	1.75
Malaysia	2.1
Russia	2.09
South Africa	2.32
Mexico	2.57
China	3.1
Japan	3.51
South Korea	4.03
Brazil	4.4
Australia	4.52
Euro zone	4.74
Canada	5.07
United States	5.51
Sweden	5.83
Switzerland	6.54

Cost of living is higher than U.S. (Lower purchasing power of local currency per nominal dollar)

Cost of living is lower than U.S. (Higher purchasing power of local currency per nominal dollar)

Source: www.statista.com/statistics/274326/big-mac-index-global-prices-for-a-big-mac.

The question is how to construct that market basket. People in different places consume different things depending on their culture, climate, religion, and so on. As a result, it's impossible to create a market basket that is "typical" everywhere. The methods behind the idea of purchasing power parity are still being improved, but for now, even imperfect PPP data are better than no data at all.

PPP-adjustment

Suppose that we are comparing GDP per capita around the world. What we want from this statistic is some sense of the differences in the average standard of living across countries. If the cost of living varies, the nominal level of GDP per capita will actually mean very different things in different countries.

PPP-adjustment involves recalculating economic statistics to account for differences in price levels across countries. When we do this, we say that we are calculating *PPP-adjusted* variables. PPP-adjustment using a price index is quite similar to adjusting for cost of living increases using a price index like the CPI.

For example, let's calculate PPP-adjusted GDP per capita in the United States and Mexico. In 2017, nominal GDP per capita in the United States was $59,532; in Mexico it was $8,903.[3] The U.S. figure is about 6.6 times larger than that for Mexico. But because prices are generally lower in Mexico, we turn to data from the World Bank's International Comparison Program (ICP) index to account for differences in how much one's income can purchase in the two economies.

PPP-adjustment recalculating economic statistics to account for differences in price levels across countries

To find PPP-adjusted GDP per capita of any country relative to the United States, we can use Equation 8-4.

EQUATION 8-4 *PPP-adjustment*

$$\text{PPP-adjusted GDP} = \text{Nominal dollars}_{\text{country A}} \times \left(\frac{1}{1 - \text{Price-level adjustment}_{\text{country A}}} \right)$$

We can plug the numbers for Mexico into this equation. The price level adjustment comes from comparing data from the World Bank International Comparison Project (ICP) to market exchange rates. In this case, the peso can buy about 50 percent more in Mexico than it could in the United States:

$$\text{PPP-adjusted GDP} = \$8{,}903 \times \left(\frac{1}{1 - 0.514} \right)$$

$$= \$8{,}903 \times 2.0576 = \$18{,}318.93$$

If we look only at the nominal figure ($8,903), we might think that the average person in Mexico has a standard of living comparable to someone earning that amount in the United States. In reality, as the PPP-adjusted figure shows us, the average Mexican lives about as well as someone who earns $18,318.93 in the United States.

PPP-adjustment gives us a more realistic sense of differences in living standards around the world. In general, price levels are lower in poorer countries, so PPP-adjustment lets us see that poorer countries are not quite so poor as suggested by their nominal GDP per capita.

Making international comparisons of purchasing power is not straightforward. This is especially true when trying to get a realistic sense of how the living standards of the world's poorest citizens translate into dollar terms. The much-quoted "dollar-a-day" figure for international poverty comes from the World Bank's attempts to figure out the true purchasing power of the poor. For insight into some of the challenges with this measure, and how economists are tackling those challenges, read the Economics in Action box "What can you buy for $1.90?"

What can you buy for $1.90?
Economics in Action

What can you buy for $1.90 in your town? Maybe some gum, or a chocolate bar, or a few vegetables at the grocery store. Could you live on $1.90 a day? It's probably pretty difficult to imagine. Yet close to 900 million people around the world do live on $1.90 per day, or less. It is the current level of the World Bank's absolute poverty measure, the most common measure of international poverty.

If you've traveled to low-income countries, you'll know that prices are very different than in the United States. Perhaps you might think that $1.90 is not too bad, after all. Sometimes, $1.90 (converted into local currency) can buy you lunch in a nice café or even some clothes. But that $1.90 poverty measure is a *PPP-adjusted* number. In other words, it measures the equivalent of what $1.90 would buy in the United States—which might be a chocolate bar or a few vegetables.

It's hard to believe that almost a billion people in the world are trying to survive on the equivalent of what $1.90 would buy in the United States. Could it be that the impossibility of living on $1.90 in the United States suggests that there may be something wrong with how we adjust the incomes of the poor in local currencies to get to that figure in U.S. dollars?

(continued)

Economists Angus Deaton of Princeton University and Olivier Dupriez, senior economist-statistician at the World Bank, think so. They argue that precisely because no one in the United States is living in the same degree of absolute poverty as the poorest households in India or Ethiopia, we need to be particularly careful how we compare the cost of living for poor households in poor countries to "typical" households in the United States. Rather than calculating the cost of living for typical households in a country, we need to determine what the typical *poor* household buys. We then would use this basket of goods to get a more meaningful estimate of the cost of living for the poor. Deaton and Dupriez call this the "poverty-weighted purchasing power parity indexes"—known as *PPPP*, or simply *P4*.

Using P4 addresses two problems of using standard PPP to calculate the cost of living of the poor. The first is one we're familiar with: The official price indexes in poor countries are based on consumption baskets of typical urban families, not the poorest.

A second problem is that even when the indexes focus on goods typically bought by the poor, the poor may not pay as much as the index suggests. For example, the same foods can cost a lot more at stores in the capital city (where customers tend to be richer) than they do at markets in the suburbs or the provinces. That cost difference helps income go much further in rural areas. Alternatively, poor households may pay more for many items, because local stores don't face much competition and keep prices high.

Yet, despite the difference in methods, the numbers for the overall amount of poverty turn out to be similar when using either the original PPP or the newer P4 measures.

There is more research to do to understand patterns of prices and their role, but the broad message is clear: When figuring out the extent of global poverty, it turns out that the cost of living is an important part of the calculation.

Source: www.princeton.edu/~deaton/downloads/Global_Poverty_and_Global_Price_Indexes.pdf.

✓ TEST YOURSELF

- ☐ How can transaction costs partially explain differences in purchasing power parity? **[LO 8.7]**
- ☐ What does the Big Mac Index show? **[LO 8.7]**
- ☐ Why do economists adjust international statistics based on purchasing power? **[LO 8.8]**

Conclusion

What can a dollar buy? The answer today is not the same as it will be next year, and it's not the same in New York City as it is in Iowa City. The result is that a nominal dollar amount in a particular time or place is just part of the answer. What we really care about is the *purchasing power*, or real value, of that dollar amount. That's what determines how much you can buy at the store.

In this chapter, we've developed tools that allow us to track changes in the overall price level. These tools help us understand how the purchasing power of a dollar changes over time and across locations. Using the cost of a constant market basket allows us to construct a price index that shows relative price levels over time, such as the CPI. It also allows us to construct price indexes that show relative purchasing power in different places, such as the World Bank's International Comparison Program (ICP) index.

Using price indexes, we can adjust economic variables such as wages, income, GDP, and interest rates to see the difference between their nominal and real values. Remember, real values are determined by market forces, while nominal changes influence how we count things. Adjusting for real values lets us answer questions like "What would today's salaries have bought in our grandparents' time?" or "How rich are people in other countries relative to the United States?" It can also help us make better choices when deciding how to invest money, write contracts, or set up policies that account for the effects of inflation.

This chapter and the previous one have introduced the basic language and metrics of macroeconomics. We've discussed output and prices, and how to measure both the size of an economy and the cost of living there. In the next chapter, we'll move to another fundamental economic concern: how to maintain steady employment levels and avoid periods of high unemployment.

Key Terms

market basket, p. 200

price index, p. 201

Consumer Price Index (CPI), p. 201

inflation rate, p. 205

headline inflation, p. 206

core inflation, p. 206

indexing, p. 210

purchasing power parity (PPP), p. 212

PPP-adjustment, p. 214

Summary

LO 8.1 Understand the importance of a market basket in tracking price changes.

To understand how the overall cost of living has increased, we need a way to measure the combined change in the prices of multiple goods, whose individual prices may be changing at different rates. To accomplish this, we can construct a market basket that includes specific goods and services in fixed quantities. By keeping goods and quantities constant, we can be sure that any change in the total cost of the basket is caused by a change in prices, rather than the type or amount of things being consumed.

LO 8.2 Calculate and use a price index to measure changes in the cost of living over time.

To summarize changes in price levels, we can construct a price index, which measures how much the cost of a market basket has risen or fallen relative to the cost in the base year or location. The most commonly used tool for measuring the cost of living in the United States is the Consumer Price Index, or CPI. It tracks the cost of a basket of goods and services that is representative of the purchases of U.S. households.

The price index in a given year is equal to the ratio of the cost of the market basket in that year to the cost in the base year, multiplied by 100. In the base year, the index will always be 100. In future years, if the price of the basket rises, the index will be more than 100. If the price of the basket falls below that in the base year, the index will be less than 100. An index of 120 implies a 20 percent increase in price levels over the base year.

LO 8.3 Name the two main challenges the BLS faces when measuring price changes, and outline how it responds to these challenges.

The BLS faces two major challenges in constructing a basket: how to decide which consumption should be measured and how to account for changes in consumption over time.

To deal with the first challenge, the CPI is based on an average of the goods and services purchased by "urban consumers," which ends up representing 81 percent of the U.S. population. It also presents two broad measures of this basket, headline inflation (another term for the CPI) and core inflation. Core inflation measures price changes for the CPI market basket, but with food and energy costs taken out. Removing those costs may miss a large part of the inflation picture.

The second challenge comes from changes to consumption and products over time. If the market basket doesn't change to reflect the substitutions consumers make as prices change, it will overstate the effect due to the rising prices. Finally, in trying to measure changes in the standard of living, economists need to tease out differences between mere changes in prices of products versus changes in quality as a result of innovation and technological advances.

LO 8.4 Calculate the inflation rate and recognize alternative measures.

The inflation rate describes the size of changes in the overall price level year to year. It is calculated by measuring the percent change in a price index from one year to the next. *Headline inflation* measures the changes in prices for the entire market basket of urban consumers. *Core inflation* measures price changes with food and energy taken out.

Inflation estimates based on the CPI measure price changes paid by consumers. Estimates based on the Producer Price Index (PPI) measure the prices of goods and services purchased by firms. Estimates based on the GDP deflator measure price changes for everything produced within a country (and thus exclude imports). Unlike the CPI and PPI, estimates based on the GDP deflator do not use a "fixed" basket of goods. In practice, inflation rates based on the CPI, PPI, and GDP deflator track each other quite closely.

LO 8.5 Use a price index to adjust nominal variables into real variables.

One of the most important applications of price indexes is the ability to be able to determine the purchasing power of money from a different time period. This gives the power to see the value of what a certain amount of dollars from the past could buy today, or how much a certain amount of dollars today would be worth in the past.

To translate a nominal amount from year X into a constant, real amount in year Y, multiply the nominal value for year X times the ratio of the CPI of year Y divided by the CPI of year X.

LO 8.6 Understand how indexing keeps the real value of a payment constant over time.

Indexing is an important application of the need to adjust nominal values into their real purchasing power. Recognizing that the purchasing power of money changes over time, payments and paychecks can be automatically indexed to inflation, so that their purchasing power stays equal even as prices change. Indexed payments are often referred to as cost-of-living adjustments (COLAs).

LO 8.7 Explain what purchasing power parity is.

Purchasing power parity (PPP) is the idea that price levels in different countries should be the same, once they have been stated in a common currency. For a number of reasons—including transaction costs, non-tradable goods and services, and trade restrictions—PPP doesn't typically hold true; the real purchasing power of a dollar differs from place to place.

LO 8.8 Use a price index to calculate PPP-adjusted variables, and compare the cost of living across different places.

When we recalculate economic variables to account for differences in purchasing power across countries, we say that we are calculating *PPP-adjusted variables*. To measure this difference in purchasing power, we can calculate a price index by comparing the cost of purchasing a market basket in each country. If the cost of living is lower than the base country, then PPP-adjusted GDP will be higher than nominal GDP. If the cost of living is higher than the base country, then PPP-adjusted GDP will be lower than nominal GDP.

Review Questions

1. If we want to measure changes in the cost of living, why don't we track differences in each household's *actual* expenditures from one year to the next, rather than the difference in the cost of a market basket? Offer several reasons why this method would fail to capture changes in the overall price level accurately. **[LO 8.1]**

2. There are many different types of market baskets that economists measure. For example, the market basket for consumers—called the Consumer Price Index—tracks the prices associated with the typical consumer's purchases of goods and services. The Producer Price Index tracks the prices of the goods and services purchased by firms. A third type of market basket is the Home Price Index, which tracks the value of residential housing. In what scenarios would each of these market baskets be useful? **[LO 8.1]**

3. Why is the list of the highest-grossing films of all time dominated by movies made within the last 10 years? (*Hint:* Did *Black Panther*, released in 2018, really sell considerably more movie tickets than the classic *Gone with the Wind*, or is something else going on?) **[LO 8.2]**

4. How would you use the concept of the Consumer Price Index to compare prices across different locations? **[LO 8.2]**

5. What types of goods and services would a basket measuring the inflation rate for farmers include? Why doesn't the BLS calculate the price levels for a market basket approximating the purchases of farmers? **[LO 8.3]**

6. Does the CPI represent the actual change in the cost of living for any given household? Explain why or why not. **[LO 8.3]**

7. Suppose wages rise in China, leading to an increase in the price of toys imported from China. How would this change affect the CPI, PPI, and the GDP deflator in the United States? **[LO 8.4]**

8. If the growth rate in nominal income is larger than the inflation rate (as measured by the change in the CPI or the GDP deflator), has the real value of income grown? **[LO 8.4]**

9. What is the better measure of inflation to determine how much should be paid to employees for cost-of-living adjustments: the Producer Price Index (PPI) or the CPI? Why? **[LO 8.5]**

10. Why are people unlikely to buy Big Macs in the places where they are relatively cheap according to purchasing power parity and sell them where they are relatively more expensive, in order to make a profit? **[LO 8.4, LO 8.6]**

11. In many poor countries, even middle-class families may have full-time servants, a luxury reserved for only the very wealthiest households in rich countries like the United States. How does the existence of low-cost domestic help affect PPP-adjusted GDP statistics in poor countries? **[LO 8.7, LO 8.8]**

12. Would Kentucky, a state with a very low cost of living, have a PPP-adjusted GDP higher or lower than its GDP calculated without PPP-adjustment? Why? **[LO 8.8]**

Problems and Applications

1. Subscribing to the theory that life is indeed a beach, the residents of La Playa spend all of their money on three things: Every year, they collectively buy 250 bathing suits, 600 tubes of sunscreen, and 400 beach towels. Using the data in Table 8P-1, calculate the following. **[LO 8.1]**

TABLE 8P-1

Item (amount purchased)	Price 2015 ($)	Price 2016 ($)	Price 2017 ($)	Price 2018 ($)
Bathing suits (250)	10.00	12.00	15.00	18.00
Sunscreen (600)	4.00	5.00	5.00	6.00
Beach towels (400)	5.00	5.50	7.00	9.00

   a. The total cost of this basket each year from 2015 through 2018.

   b. How much the price of this basket has changed from year to year in percentage terms.

2. Suppose a typical American consumer purchases three goods, creatively named good A, good B, and good C. The prices of these goods are listed in Table 8P-2. **[LO 8.1]**

TABLE 8P-2

Good	Price in 2017 ($)	Price in 2018 ($)
A	10	15
B	6	5
C	2	3

   a. If the typical consumer purchases two units of each good, what was the percentage increase in the price paid by the consumer for this basket between 2017 and 2018?

   b. If the typical consumer purchases 10 units of good B and 2 units of both good A and good C, what was the percentage increase in the price paid by the consumer for this basket?

   c. Given your answers to parts a and b, what is the relationship between the market basket and the percentage price change?

3. Using the data in Table 8P-3, calculate the CPI and the inflation rate in each year, using 2013 as a base year. **[LO 8.2]**

TABLE 8P-3

Year	Price of basket ($)	CPI	Inflation rate
2013	20,000	100	—
2014	21,400		
2015	22,800		
2016	26,150		
2017	28,840		
2018	32,600		

4. Table 8P-4 lists the prices and quantities consumed of three different goods from 2016–2018. **[LO 8.2]**

TABLE 8P-4

	2016		2017		2018	
Good	Price ($)	Quantity	Price ($)	Quantity	Price ($)	Quantity
A	10	10	16	8	18	5
B	5	18	3	30	4	25
C	1	10	2	5	5	10

   a. For 2016, 2017, and 2018, determine the amount that a typical consumer pays each year to purchase the quantities listed in the table.

   b. Using the amounts you found in part a, calculate the percentage change in the amount the consumer paid from 2016 to 2017, and from 2017 to 2018.

   c. Why is it problematic to use your answers to part b as a measure of inflation?

   d. Suppose we take 2016 as the base year, which implies that the market basket is fixed at the 2016 consumption levels. Using 2016 consumption levels, now find the rate of inflation from 2016 to 2017 and from 2017 to 2018. (*Hint:* First calculate the cost of the 2016 market basket using each year's prices and then find the percentage change in the cost of the basket.)

   e. Repeat the exercise from part d, now assuming that the base year is 2017.

   f. Why were your answers from parts d and e different?

5. Which of the following goods have likely required hedonic quality adjustment over time if they were included in the Consumer Price Index (CPI)? **[LO 8.3]**

   a. Laptop computers.
   b. Cellphones.
   c. Salt.
   d. Televisions.
   e. Housing.
   f. Tennis rackets.

6. Use Table 8P-5 to calculate core and headline inflation in each time frame relative to the base year, assuming that each category is weighted equally in the calculation of headline inflation. **[LO 8.2, LO 8.4]**

TABLE 8P-5

	Food and energy	Other goods and services
2014	116	102
2018	105	107

   a. 2014 to a base year.
   b. 2018 to a base year.
   c. 2014 to 2018.

7. Table 8P-6 shows the GDP deflator and the CPI over five recent years for Vortexia. By what percent did prices change between years for each measure? Calculate the annual inflation rate and then the inflation rate across the entire time period. **[LO 8.4]**

TABLE 8P-6

Year	GDP deflator	Change in GDP deflator	CPI	Change in CPI
2014	100		100	
2015	105		104	
2016	112		110	
2017	123		113	
2018	127		120	
2014–2018	–			

8. The median American household earned $9,387 in 1973 and $60,336 in 2017. During that time, though, the CPI rose from 44.4 to 245.1. **[LO 8.5]**
   a. Calculate the total growth rate in nominal median household income from 1973 to 2017.
   b. Calculate the total growth rate in real median household income from 1973 to 2017.

9. Using Table 8P-7, find the real value of a $1,200 payment to be received each year given the following CPI values. Next, find the amount that this $1,200 should be adjusted to, in order to keep its real value at $1,200. **[LO 8.5, LO 8.6]**

TABLE 8P-7

Year	CPI	Real value of $1,000	Cost-of-living adjusted payment
2015	100	1,000	0
2016	103		
2017	105		
2018	110		

10. Suppose General Electric paid its line workers $10 per hour in 2017 when the Consumer Price Index was 100. Suppose that deflation occurred and the aggregate price level fell to 80 in 2018. **[LO 8.5, LO 8.6]**
    a. What did GE need to pay its workers in 2018 in order to keep the real wage fixed?
    b. What did GE need to pay its workers in 2018 if it wanted to increase the real wage by 10 percent?
    c. If GE kept the wage fixed at $10 per hour in 2018, in real terms, what percentage increase in real wages did its workers get?

11. Suppose Table 8P-8 shows the prices of a tall Starbucks latte in countries around the world. Using the data, and the fact that a latte costs $3 in the United States, calculate how much a country's currency is under- or overvalued according to purchasing power. First, calculate the implied exchange rate for each country. Next, calculate the "latte index" for each country using the Big Mac index formula from the chapter. **[LO 8.7]**

TABLE 8P-8

Country	Price	Official exchange rate
Thailand	60 baht	30 baht/dollar
Argentina	15 pesos	6 pesos/dollar
United Kingdom	2 pounds	0.5 pound/dollar
Japan	450 yen	80 yen/dollar

12. An employee asks her boss whether she can transfer offices so that she can work in a different part of the country. The boss responds positively and says that the employee can choose to work in Cleveland, Miami, or New York City. The boss then hands the employee a list, as shown in Table 8P-9, of the salaries that she would earn in the different cities and the average price levels in those same cities. [LO 8.7, LO 8.8]

TABLE 8P-9

Office location	Salary ($)	CPI
Cleveland	85,000	100
Miami	125,000	160
New York City	165,000	205

a. From a standpoint of maximizing the employee's consumption possibilities, which office should she choose?
b. What would be the minimum salary in New York City the boss could offer the employee to make the employee indifferent between moving to Cleveland and to New York City?

13. Calculate the PPP-adjusted GDP for each of four countries, using the information found in Table 8P-10. [LO 8.8]

TABLE 8P-10

Country	GDP ($)	Price level (%)
Ona	10,000	6
Rye	12,700	−27
Zolfo	14,100	−10
Avon	23,400	20

Endnotes

1. The Federal Reserve's preferred measure of inflation is a related measure that uses the core Personal Consumption Expenditure (PCE) Index. The core PCE Index is like the core CPI but includes data from businesses, and it encompasses a wider range of household purchases.
2. www.ssa.gov/history/briefhistory3.html.
3. http://data.worldbank.org/indicator/NY.GDP.PCAP.CD?order=wbapi_data_value_2014+wbapi_data_value+wbapi_data_value-last&sort=desc.

Labor Markets and Economic Growth

PART FOUR

The two chapters in Part 4 will introduce you to . . .

labor markets and economic growth. As we explore labor markets, we turn to the forces that shape employment patterns in both the long run and the short run. Moving on to economic growth, we turn to the forces that determine why some countries are richer and others are poorer.

Chapter 9, "Unemployment and the Labor Market," discusses how the unemployment rate reflects the struggles of individuals looking for work and why it is considered to be an important barometer of the overall health of the economy. A strong economy has many benefits: Factories and business create new jobs, people find it relatively easier to get work, and unemployment is usually low. But when the economy falters, firms lay off workers to cut production and unemployment is high. Because it acts as a signal of the state of the economy, the unemployment rate is tracked closely from month to month and is influential in government policy and political debates.

Chapter 10, "Economic Growth," focuses on one of the great challenges in economics: How can policy and resources be combined to create healthy economic growth? Growth increases economic opportunities, creates a dynamic business environment, and generates new wealth that allows people to lead more comfortable, secure lives. In recent years, economic growth has lifted hundreds of millions of people around the world out of poverty. In the search for the combination of policies that will lead to economic growth, we look to success stories like the astounding advances in China in the last few decades, and we take cautionary lessons from countries that still search for ways to lift living standards.

Chapter 9

Unemployment and the Labor Market

What Does It Mean to Be Unemployed?

Rick Alexander is a master builder who spent three decades running a successful home-restoration business in Connecticut. When his elderly parents fell ill in 2008, he gave up his business and moved to Florida to help them. He thought it would be easy to find work—after all, he had a certified trade and many years of experience. He looked first for a job as a supervisor at construction sites but didn't find anything. Lowering his sights, he next looked for work at wholesalers and lumberyards, and then he applied for any job at hardware stores. Still, he experienced a constant stream of rejections. He tried to start his own business, but in the struggling housing market in Florida, he couldn't generate enough sales to make it profitable. Tired of the search, Rick Alexander gave up looking for work.[1]

Alexander's story is frustratingly common, especially during a recession. In tough times, jobs are hard to find. In October 2009, four months after the official end of the "Great Recession," the unemployment rate in the United States rose to close to 10 percent. Unemployment was even higher for certain groups of the population. For young men without a high-school degree, the unemployment rate was close to 30 percent.[2] Even many college graduates struggled to find work and ended up living back at home with their parents.

©Sean De Burca/Getty Images

Of course, unemployment exists even when the economy is not in a recession. After the "Great Recession," the job market boomed, adding 194,000 jobs per month from March 2010 to December 2018. Even so, the natural churning of the labor market caused people to be unemployed for short periods as they moved between jobs. That churn is a normal part of economic life. So is the type of regional unemployment that occurs as factories close and when the needs of local employers shift. Such unemployment is made worse when laid-off workers find that their skills no longer match the jobs that are available. Ironically, policies designed to protect workers—like minimum wage laws and unionization—also can lead to unemployment. Although they help existing workers, they often make it harder for those out of work to find jobs.

Some unemployment may be unavoidable, but too much of it can have serious consequences, both for the economy as a whole and on a personal level. One consequence of unemployment is that some of the productive potential of the economy—the time and skills of the unemployed—is not being put to use.

Another consequence is much more personal. Prolonged unemployment, like what happened to Rick Alexander, can be one of the most difficult experiences that a person suffers. It creates uncertainty about the future and can bring on feelings of hopelessness, especially when trying to support oneself and one's family. Studies show that being unemployed is correlated with higher rates of depression and lower assessments of self-worth. Unemployment is an economic problem with potentially serious social and psychological consequences.

LEARNING OBJECTIVES

LO 9.1 Explain how economists measure employment and unemployment.

LO 9.2 Explain how wage rates above equilibrium cause unemployment.

LO 9.3 Explain why there is a natural rate of unemployment in an economy.

LO 9.4 Explain why there is a cyclical component of unemployment.

LO 9.5 Identify factors that may stop wages from falling to the equilibrium level.

LO 9.6 Recognize how unemployment insurance and related policies can affect rates of unemployment.

Being unemployed can take a mental toll, but the reality is that the difficulties of finding a job are in large part shaped by macroeconomic forces outside of an individual's control. What are these forces? Why does unemployment exist in the first place? These questions pose a puzzle for economists.

We start by assuming that a market reaches an equilibrium where quantity demanded is equal to quantity supplied at the prevailing price. Applying that idea to labor demand and labor supply, the fact that unemployment exists suggests that people want to supply more labor at the prevailing wage than firms are demanding. Why don't wages drop until unemployment is eliminated? In this chapter, we'll investigate the reasons why wages might not drop to an equilibrium level. We'll also see why some unemployment will exist even when the labor market is in equilibrium. As we distinguish between different sources of unemployment, we'll see the logic of different strategies to address the underlying problems.

Defining and Measuring Unemployment

LO 9.1 Explain how economists measure employment and unemployment.

Measuring unemployment turns out to be more complicated than simply counting those who aren't working. The chapter-opening story illustrates some of the complexity: On the one hand, we want to count Rick Alexander as unemployed when he's actively searching for a job. On the other hand, Alexander's retired parents don't have jobs, but they're not interested in getting them. How do we differentiate those two forms of being unemployed? And how do we represent the situation when someone like Alexander gets so discouraged that he stops looking for work? Defining unemployment in a clear and consistent way is an important step toward getting a handle on the underlying issues. In general, **unemployment** occurs when someone wants to work but cannot find a job.

People are unemployed for many reasons:

- Job seekers may be holding out for high salaries.
- Job seekers may lack relevant skills.
- Sometimes job seekers have the right skills and appropriate ambitions but still can't land a job in the current market.

unemployment situation in which someone wants to work but cannot find a job in the current market

The government's definition of unemployment attempts to capture all of these situations. The Bureau of Labor Statistics, the government agency in charge of collecting employment statistics, defines unemployment in this way:

> Persons aged 16 years and older who had no employment during the reference week, were available for work, except for temporary illness, and had made specific efforts to find employment sometime during the 4-week period ending with the reference week.[3]

This definition means that the United States counts people as being unemployed *only if they meet three criteria*:

1. They didn't work at all in the prior week.
2. They were available to work if they had been offered a job.
3. They were making efforts to look for a job.

Measuring unemployment

In this section, we will put together all the pieces you need to understand the sort of unemployment figures you might see or hear in a news report or a Bureau of Labor Statistics (BLS) official report. These reports are extremely influential in the worlds of business and politics. Everyone wants to know what the latest information about unemployment says about the health of the economy.

First, we need to define some key groups of people. The *working-age population* is the civilian, noninstitutional population aged 16 and over. This category means all adults except those who are in the armed forces (such as soldiers) or who are inmates in an institution (such as prisons or mental facilities).

However, not everyone who is over 16 *wants to work*. In the official definition of unemployment, we want to count only those people who are "available for work" and "making specific efforts to find employment." That means we don't count as unemployed the following categories of people:

- Full-time students.
- Parents who are staying home to look after their children.
- People who cannot work because of a disability.
- People who have inherited wealth and choose to live off that wealth rather than work.
- Retirees. (Some countries define the "working-age population" as 16 to 64, but the BLS does not impose an upper age limit.)

When we want to refer to people of working age excluding those in the categories listed above (full-time students, stay-at-home parents, retirees, and so on), we instead talk about the *labor force*.

The **labor force** consists of people in the working-age population who are either currently working ("employed") or who would like to work and are actively trying to find a job ("unemployed"). That is,

EQUATION 9-1
$$\text{Labor force} = \text{Employed} + \text{Unemployed}$$

(The labor force does not include those people in the categories listed above who are in the working-age population but not wanting to work.)

The unemployment rate We now have the numbers we need to define the **unemployment rate**, which is the number of unemployed people divided by the labor force:

EQUATION 9-2
$$\text{Unemployment rate} = \frac{\text{Number of unemployed}}{\text{Labor force}} \times 100$$
$$= \frac{\text{Unemployed}}{\text{Employed} + \text{Unemployed}} \times 100$$

labor force
people who are in the working-age population and are either employed or unemployed; people who are currently working or who are actively trying to find a job

unemployment rate
the number of unemployed people divided by the number of people in the labor force

TABLE 9-1
U.S. employment statistics

Between 2006 and 2018, the working-age population and the number of people in the labor force increased. The number of people employed also rose, while the number of unemployed fell.

Month	Working-age population (non-institutionalized)	Labor force	Employed	Unemployed
December 2006	230,108,000	152,732,000	145,970,000	6,762,000
December 2018	258,888,000	163,240,000	156,945,000	6,294,000

Source: https://www.bls.gov/news.release/empsit.t01.htm

Table 9-1 shows the official unemployment and employment numbers for the U.S. economy for December 2006 and December 2018. The first date, December 2006, is near the end of an economic expansion. The figures for December 2018 followed 10 years of job creation. In total, December 2018 had about 468,000 fewer people unemployed, in a larger labor force.

Table 9-1 also shows the number of people in the labor force. Dividing the number of unemployed by the size of the labor force gives us the unemployment rate at both dates:
Unemployment rate, December 2006:

$$\frac{6{,}762{,}000}{152{,}732{,}000} \times 100 = 4.4 \text{ percent}$$

Unemployment rate, December 2018:

$$\frac{6{,}294{,}000}{163{,}240{,}000} \times 100 = 3.9 \text{ percent}$$

The December 2018 unemployment rate tells us that at the end of 2018, approximately 3.9 percent of Americans who wanted to work couldn't find work.

The unemployment rate describes what is going on in the national economy as a whole but doesn't tell us much about *who* is affected. In general, the unemployment rate varies greatly by educational status, gender, age, and race. On average, younger people have higher unemployment rates than older people, and people with less education are more likely to be unemployed than people with more education. Figure 9-1 shows some comparisons of unemployment among different types of people in the years 2006–2018.

The labor-force participation rate We can also learn something interesting about the state of the economy by looking at the **labor-force participation rate**, which is the number of people in the labor force divided by the working-age population:

labor-force participation rate
the number of people in the labor force divided by the working-age population

EQUATION 9-3 $$\text{Labor-force participation rate} = \frac{\text{Labor force}}{\text{Working-age population}} \times 100$$

This figure tells us what fraction of the population *wants* to be working, whether or not they actually have a job.

During recessions we usually see the labor-force participation rate fall. Some people who are unemployed eventually give up looking for work, like Rick Alexander in our chapter-opening example. Once these people stop actively looking for work, they are no longer considered part of the labor force. Other people may drop out of the labor force in a recession because they choose to go back to school, or take early retirement, or become homemakers instead of looking for work.

FIGURE 9-1
Unemployment rates by demographic group

(A) Unemployment rate by sex

Until the start of the great recession, unemployment rates were the same for men and women. Afterwards, men were far more likely to be unemployed, although this has stabilized in recent years.

(B) Unemployment rate by age

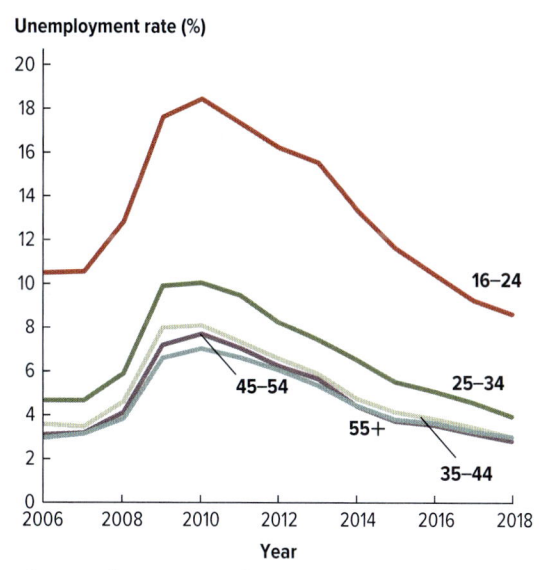

In general, younger people are more likely to be unemployed.

(C) Unemployment rate by race/ethnicity

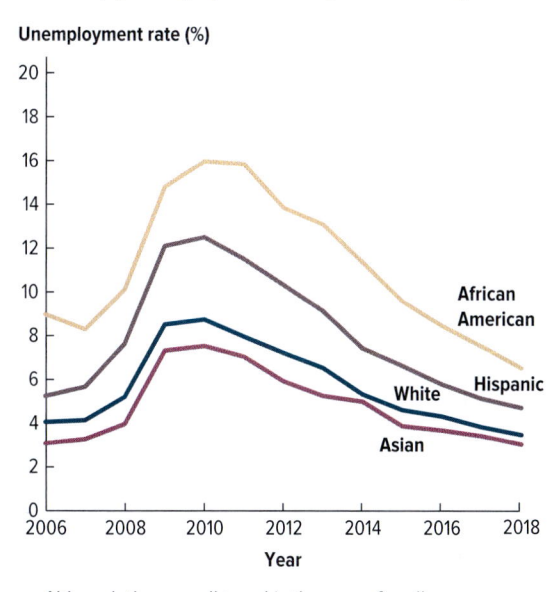

Although the overall trend is the same for all races, African Americans have a much higher rate of unemployment.

(D) Unemployment rate by education level

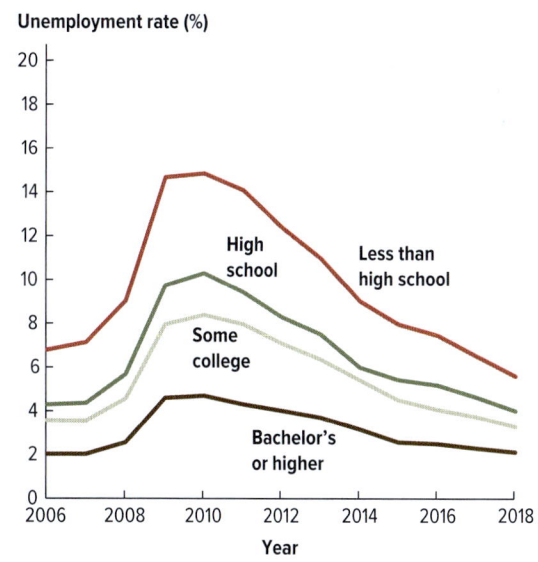

The more education a person has, the more likely he or she is to have a job.

Source: Federal Reserve Bank of St. Louis, FRED—https://fred.stlouisfed.org/categories/32447?t=education&rt=education&ob=pv&od=desc.

TABLE 9-2

Employment in the United States, 2006 and 2018

The unemployment rate in 2018 was lower than in 2006. At the same time, however, the percentage of the population participating in the labor force fell between 2006 and 2018.

	Unemployment rate (%)	Labor-force participation rate (%)
December 2006	4.4	66.4
December 2018	3.9	63.1
Change	−0.5	−3.3

Source: Bureau of Labor Statistics (accessed June 22, 2016), http://www.bls.gov/cps/tables.htm.

However, the impact of the Great Recession on the labor force participation rate has persisted well beyond the duration of the downturn. Let's take a look at the data from Table 9-1, to compare the labor-force participation rate in December 2006 against the rate in 2018:

$$\frac{152{,}732{,}000}{230{,}108{,}000} \times 100 = 66.4 \text{ percent}$$

This means that 66.4 percent of the total working-age population was in the labor force in December 2006.

In December 2018 the labor-force participation rate was:

$$\frac{163{,}240{,}000}{258{,}888{,}000} \times 100 = 63.1 \text{ percent}$$

Over the twelve-year period, 3.3 percent of the working-age population stopped participating in the labor force. It is likely that at least some of these people would have been unemployed if they had stayed in the labor force. So the unemployment rate of 3.9 percent in December 2018 may understate the effect of the recession on employment.

Table 9-2 summarizes the two different measures of the U.S. labor market in 2006 and 2018.

⚠ CAUTION: COMMON MISTAKE

When discussing unemployment, people often talk about *percentage point* changes—such as the unemployment rate decreasing by 0.5 percentage *points*, from 4.4 percent to 3.9 percent. Sometimes people talk loosely about unemployment, referring to such a change as unemployment going down by "0.5 percent" rather than by "0.5 percentage point." There is a big difference, although people may guess what is meant by the loose talk.

If we want to, we could, of course, talk about changes in unemployment in terms of percent, rather than percentage points. For example, from 4.4 to 3.9 is a decrease of about 11 percent. That would be technically accurate, but you rarely hear economists talk this way.

Talking in percentage *points* makes a change easier to conceptualize: If you hear that the unemployment rate decreased by "0.5 percentage point," for example, it means that 5 people out of every 1,000 in the labor force have found a job.

On the other hand, if you hear that an economy's unemployment rate decreased by "11 percent," you have no way of knowing how bad the change really is. Maybe the decrease was from 1 percent unemployment to 0.89 percent, which would be considered a small change. Or maybe unemployment went from 10 percent to 8.9 percent, which would be considered a more substantial change.

This is why statisticians and economists report changes in percentage points, not percentages, when discussing unemployment.

Beyond the unemployment rate

People often use the unemployment rate to summarize the state of the labor market, but it has significant limitations. Most obviously, it doesn't include people like Rick Alexander, introduced at the start of the chapter. While Alexander was actively looking for work, he was counted as unemployed. Once he gave up hope of finding a job, he was deemed to have dropped out of the labor force and was no longer counted as unemployed.

There are six different measures of unemployment. Do you know what they are?
©DNY59/Getty Images

This seems like a semantic trick. Why should we count Alexander as unemployed when he's feeling optimistic and spends his days sending out résumés, but not when he turns pessimistic and gives up the search? In fact, the Bureau of Labor Statistics (BLS) has a term for people like Alexander: **discouraged workers**. Discouraged workers are people who have looked for work in the past year but have given up looking because of the condition of the labor market. Thinking about discouraged workers gives a broader view of who is affected by a recession.

What about people who have part-time jobs but would like to work full time? Such people are defined as being **underemployed**. So are workers who are in jobs that are not matched to their skill level—for example, a law-school grad who can't get a job in law and takes work as a barista at Starbucks. The BLS collects data on the first kind of underemployment (working fewer hours than you would like), but unfortunately not on the second kind (working in a job for which you are overqualified).

In fact, the BLS collects *six* different measures of unemployment, as shown in Table 9-3:

- The first two are "narrow" unemployment rates, counting only people who have been unemployed for a long time (U1) and those who have recently lost their jobs or done temporary work (U2).
- The "official" unemployment rate is the one shown in the table as U3.
- The fourth measure (U4) combines unemployed plus discouraged workers.
- The fifth measure (U5) adds "marginally attached" workers. These people are like discouraged workers in some respects—they would *like* to work, and they have looked for work

discouraged workers people who have looked for work in the past year but have given up looking because of the condition of the labor market

underemployed workers who are either working less than they would like to or are working in jobs below their skill level

TABLE 9-3

Six measures of unemployment

Total unemployment in an economy can be measured using narrower or broader definitions. The BLS reports six main measures, ranging from the narrowest (U1), which includes only those who are chronically unemployed, to the broadest (U6), which includes everyone from the chronically unemployed to those who are already working part time but want to be working full time. The "official" unemployment rate typically cited in the news media is U3.

Category of unemployment	Rate in December 2006 (%)	Rate in December 2018 (%)
U1: Long-time unemployed (more than 15 weeks)	1.4	1.3
U2: Job losers + those who completed temporary work	2.1	1.7
U3: Unemployed	4.4	3.7
U4: Unemployed + discouraged workers	4.6	3.9
U5: Unemployed, discouraged workers + marginally attached workers	5.2	4.7
U6: Unemployed, discouraged workers, marginally attached workers + underemployed	7.9	7.6

Source: https://www.bls.gov/news.release/empsit.t15.htm

at some point in the last year. But they don't meet the strict definition of unemployed because, for whatever reason, they haven't looked for a job in the last four weeks.
- The final definition, U6, includes underemployed people with part-time work who seek full-time jobs.

Adding extra dimensions to unemployment measures helps to paint a more complete picture of the labor market. On the whole, unemployment (U3) decreased from 2006 to 2018, dropping from 4.4 percent to 3.7 percent, and the share of the labor force in many other categories fell as well.

However, both long-term unemployment (U1) and the broadest measure of unemployment (U6) in 2018 stayed close to 2006 levels. The Great Recession in 2009 could be part of the explanation. In 2009, headline unemployment reached 10 percent, and U6 was over 17 percent. Although the job market added nearly 200,000 positions per month from March 2010 to December 2018, some workers were still left out.

Where do the data come from?

The main source of information on unemployment in the United States is a household survey that asks people if they are working and how much they are earning. This survey, performed by the Bureau of Labor Statistics, is called the Current Population Survey. Every month, employees of the BLS survey about 60,000 households. It's not exact—it would be prohibitively expensive to survey every single U.S. household every month—but the sample size is big enough to give a reliable estimate for the economy as a whole.

The survey is collected year-round, allowing the BLS to analyze and adjust for changes in unemployment that are due to the season. If you're a trained ski instructor, for example, you'll more easily find work in February than in August. Farm workers and construction workers are also affected by seasonal changes. The BLS publishes statistics that are *seasonally adjusted* in order to help distinguish these expected seasonal patterns from deeper shifts in economic conditions. The data we show in the tables here are all seasonally adjusted.

✓ TEST YOURSELF

☐ How is the labor-force participation rate calculated? **[LO 9.1]**
☐ Are discouraged workers counted as being unemployed? **[LO 9.1]**
☐ How is underemployment different from unemployment? **[LO 9.1]**

Equilibrium in the Labor Market

LO 9.2 Explain how wage rates above equilibrium cause unemployment.

The existence of *any* amount of unemployment is a bit of a puzzle. Labor is bought and sold in a market, just like other goods and services. There is demand for labor (from firms wanting to hire workers), a supply of labor (from individuals looking for jobs), and a price (called the wage). In most markets, we expect the price to adjust until the market reaches equilibrium, a point at which the quantity supplied equals the quantity demanded.

The existence of unemployment suggests that this simplest of models can't fully explain what goes on in the labor market. In this section, we explore the predictions of the simple model. In the next section, we'll add nuance to show that unemployment can arise when the wage is held above the equilibrium level or when real-world frictions prevent labor supply or labor demand from adjusting perfectly to changes in the economy.

As in any other market, the labor market features a demand curve and a supply curve. The demand for labor comes from firms, who need labor to produce output. The **labor demand curve**, depicted in panel A of Figure 9-2, shows the relationship between the total quantity of labor demanded by all the firms in the economy and the wage rate. All things being equal, firms will want to hire more labor when wages are lower and less labor when wages are higher.

labor demand curve a graph showing the relationship between the total quantity of labor demanded by all the firms in the economy and the wage rate

FIGURE 9-2
Labor demand and labor supply

(A) Firms and the labor market

Labor demand curve (downward sloping), Wage vs. Units of labor

As the price of labor, or the wage, decreases, the amount of labor demanded by firms increases. This relationship is shown by the curve above.

(B) Workers and the labor market

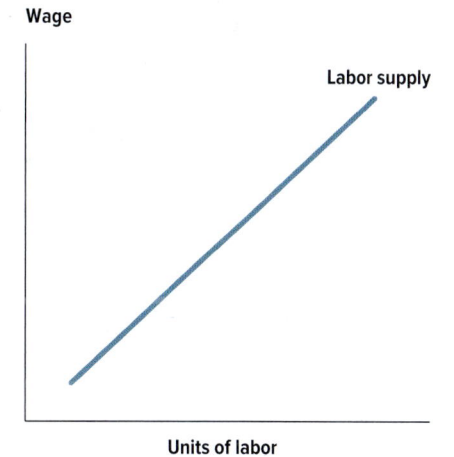

Labor supply curve (upward sloping), Wage vs. Units of labor

Conversely, as the wage rate increases, workers are increasingly willing to supply labor. This relationship is shown by the curve above.

The supply of labor comes from people who are able to work and who choose to participate in the labor market. As we have seen, not everyone who could potentially work wants to work. Other things being equal, we expect that across the economy as a whole, people will be willing to supply more labor at higher wage rates and less labor at lower wage rates. The **labor supply curve**, pictured in panel B of Figure 9-2, shows the relationship between the total quantity of labor supplied in the economy and the wage rate.

Together, the labor demand and labor supply curves describe the national labor market, as shown in Figure 9-3. As in any other market, equilibrium occurs at the intersection of the supply and demand curves. At the equilibrium wage, quantity demanded equals quantity supplied: Everyone who wants to work at prevailing wages and has the required skills is able to find a job.

Our definition of unemployment—people wanting to work but being unable to find a job at the prevailing wage—is easy to rephrase in the language of supply and demand: The quantity of labor supplied at the prevailing wage (people wanting to work at that wage) is greater than the quantity of labor demanded (jobs offered by firms wanting to hire at that wage). In other words, there is a *surplus* of labor.

Surplus arises in a market when the prevailing price is higher than the equilibrium price. (Look back to Chapter 6, "Government Intervention," if you need to confirm this statement.) Figure 9-4 shows how unemployment occurs when the wage rate is W_1—that is, higher than the equilibrium level of W^*. In this very simple model, unemployment is the gap between the number of people who want to work and the number of jobs offered at the prevailing wage. (However, we'll see in a minute that when a little nuance is added to the model, we can get unemployment even when the wage is not above the equilibrium level.)

Here's the puzzle: Why would wages remain above the equilibrium level? We know what *should* happen in a market when the price is too high: The price should fall until the market reaches equilibrium. Why don't firms offer lower wages, or unemployed people offer to work for lower wages, until the equilibrium wage is reached? In the next section we'll look at several reasons why this might not happen, as well as reasons unemployment occurs even at the equilibrium wage.

labor supply curve a graph showing the relationship between the total labor supplied in the economy and the wage rate

FIGURE 9-3
The labor market in equilibrium

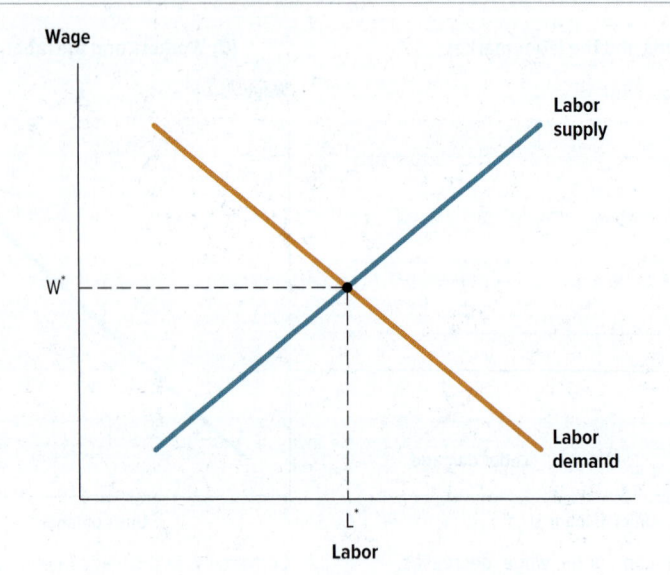

When the labor demand and labor supply curves are put together, this forms a labor market of people willing to buy and sell labor. Like any other market, where the two curves intersect, the market is at an equilibrium, with a stable wage (price) and amount of labor bought and sold.

FIGURE 9-4
The labor market with unemployment

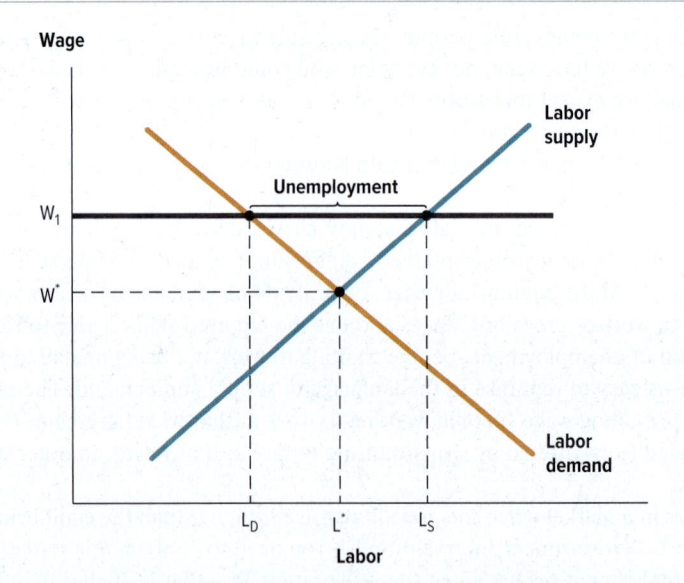

When people are willing to supply more labor than firms are willing to hire, the labor market has a surplus of workers, which is also known as unemployment.

✓ TEST YOURSELF

- ☐ What is the equilibrium price of labor also called? **[LO 9.2]**
- ☐ What two curves intersect at the labor market equilibrium? **[LO 9.2]**

Categories of Unemployment

To start understanding the causes of unemployment, it's helpful to separate out two categories of unemployment:

- First is unemployment explained by the *natural* rate of unemployment. This is the normal level of unemployment that persists in an economy in the long run.
- Second is *cyclical* unemployment, which describes short-term fluctuations around this long-run norm.

We'll see that some unemployment is an unavoidable part of a dynamic economy, but also that the amount of unemployment is affected by public policy.

Natural rate of unemployment

The simplified model of the labor market described in Figure 9-3 suggests that we might reasonably expect to see *zero* unemployment when the market is in long-run equilibrium. The data in the first half of the chapter, however, showed that this is never the case (even when the economy is doing well, as it was around 2005).

Instead, all economies experience some level of unemployment, regardless of how well or badly the economy is doing in the short term. We refer to this normal level of unemployment that persists in an economy in the long run as the **natural rate of unemployment**. The natural rate of unemployment is also sometimes called the *equilibrium rate of unemployment*.

Three contributors lead to the natural rate of unemployment: frictional, structural, and real-wage (classical) unemployment.

LO 9.3 Explain why there is a natural rate of unemployment in an economy.

natural rate of unemployment the normal level of unemployment that persists in an economy in the long run

Frictional unemployment
The first contributor to the natural rate of unemployment is **frictional unemployment**. It is unemployment caused by workers who are changing their location, job, or career. When people search for new jobs, it takes time to search for openings, submit applications, interview, move to a new city, and so on.

How long it takes to make a job transition can depend on a lot of factors. These include things like:

- how well-informed workers are about job openings,
- how picky workers are about waiting to find the job that is the best possible match, and
- what resources workers can draw on to support them while they search.

Some amount of frictional unemployment is unavoidable—it's a natural and healthy part of life in a dynamic economy. Jobs in one company open up while others close, and ambitious workers leave their jobs to seek out better positions.

frictional unemployment unemployment caused by workers who are changing location, job, or career

Structural unemployment
The second contributor to the natural rate of unemployment is **structural unemployment**. It is unemployment that results from a mismatch between the skills workers can offer and the skills that are in demand. Consumer preferences are constantly shifting, and new technologies are being invented all the time. As a result, skills that are in demand today may not be in demand next year.

If people could switch effortlessly from a job in a shrinking industry (like auto manufacturing) to one in a booming industry (like online services), then structural unemployment wouldn't exist. However, the reality is that people have educational qualifications, job experiences, and family and community ties that are hard to change in the short run. These qualifications and ties make them better suited for jobs in some sectors and locations than others. A changing economy can lead to a mismatch between the types of jobs that firms are offering and the types of jobs for which people are qualified.

structural unemployment unemployment that results from a mismatch between the skills workers can offer and the skills in demand

For example, consider the job of travel agent. If you want to book a flight, you probably just go online, right? A couple of decades ago, you would have gone to a travel agent, who would have used a special database of routes and prices to propose an itinerary. The advent of websites such as Travelocity, Kayak, Priceline, and Expedia allows customers to do the travel agent's job for themselves easily and quickly. As a result, demand for the services of travel agents has plummeted; people who trained as travel agents lost their jobs and couldn't find new ones using the same knowledge and skills.

Some degree of structural unemployment is inevitable in an ever-changing economy, but governments can take steps to minimize it. One way is to provide information to unemployed people about which professions are experiencing rising demand for labor. Another way is to subsidize retraining programs for unemployed workers to learn new skills, improving their chances of finding work.

These programs can help, but the changes can take years. If you were a middle-aged, unemployed auto worker, could you imagine moving to a different part of the country to start a new career from scratch?

Real-wage (classical) unemployment The third contributor to the natural rate of unemployment is **real-wage** or **classical unemployment**. This idea captures the effect of wages remaining persistently above the market-clearing level. It's what we saw in Figure 9-4: Anything that acts like a price floor in the labor market will create surplus labor, which we call unemployment. Explanations include minimum wage laws, bargaining by unions, and strategic choices by employers to pay wages above the equilibrium rate. We'll explore each of these possible explanations later in the chapter.

> **real-wage or classical unemployment** unemployment that results from wages being higher than the market-clearing level

The common thread in these three different contributors to the natural rate of unemployment—frictional unemployment, structural unemployment, and real-wage unemployment—is that they reflect underlying features of the economy. As you'd guess, the features can change over time, which can raise or lower the natural rate. For instance:

- A new policy dramatically raising the minimum wage by $10 an hour would surely raise the natural rate of unemployment.
- An educational system that retrains laid-off workers could lower the natural rate.

The natural rate of unemployment, however, doesn't go up and down with every boom and bust in the economy. Those short-term fluctuations in unemployment need a different explanation, which we turn to next.

Cyclical unemployment

> **LO 9.4** Explain why there is a cyclical component of unemployment.

The economy goes through ups and downs over time, which are reflected by changes in GDP growth. Economists call this pattern of ups and downs the *business cycle*, a topic we'll discuss further in Chapter 12, "Aggregate Demand and Aggregate Supply." The business cycle matters for unemployment because it affects the demand for labor:

- When the economy is going strong, demand for workers increases as firms expand their operations.
- When the economy slows down, demand for workers decreases as firms downsize.

Cyclical unemployment is unemployment caused by these short-term economic fluctuations. Because GDP growth tends to go in *cycles*, speeding up and slowing down in a regular pattern, we call the related unemployment *cyclical*, too.

> **cyclical unemployment** unemployment caused by short-term economic fluctuations

Imagine the effect of an economic slowdown as a reduction in the total demand for labor at any wage. In other words, the labor demand curve shifts to the left. In the simple labor-market

FIGURE 9-5

Cyclical unemployment in the United States In general, unemployment tends to be higher when GDP growth is low, although this is not always true. Unemployment tends to lag behind overall GDP growth, meaning it will change soon after, but not at the same time as, GDP growth changes.

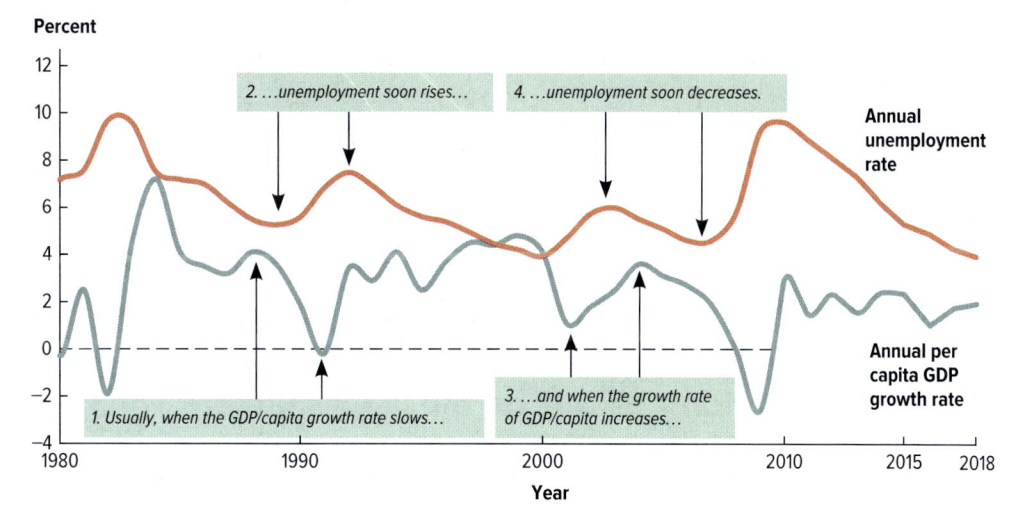

[Graph showing Annual unemployment rate and Annual per capita GDP growth rate from 1980 to 2018, with annotations:
1. Usually, when the GDP/capita growth rate slows...
2. ...unemployment soon rises...
3. ...and when the growth rate of GDP/capita increases...
4. ...unemployment soon decreases.]

Source: https://data.bls.gov/timeseries/LNU04000000?periods=Annual+Data&periods_option=specific_periods&years_option=all_years (unemployment rates); https://fred.stlouisfed.org/series/A939RX0Q048SBEA (GDP per capita growth rates).

model, this change would cause the equilibrium to move down along the supply curve, reaching a new equilibrium at a lower quantity of labor and lower wage. Why don't wages simply fall during a cyclical slowdown, so that the market still clears and cyclical unemployment is zero? The typical explanation is that wages are "sticky" in the real world, meaning that they are slow to respond to shifts in the economy.

There are many possible reasons for wage stickiness: Some workers may be on contracts that are difficult to change, or employers may choose not to raise and lower wages all the time because it will upset workers and cause them to not work as hard. The degree of wage stickiness in the real world is a controversial topic, even among economists.

The result of wage stickiness is that actual wages are temporarily above the market-clearing level, which causes cyclical unemployment. When the economy swings back toward the boom part of the business cycle, labor demand will recover and cyclical unemployment will decrease.

Figure 9-5 shows the relationship between GDP and unemployment in the U.S. economy over the last 35 years. When growth goes down, unemployment tends to go up shortly after, and vice versa.

The slight delay, or time lag, makes unemployment what we call a *lagging* or *trailing* indicator. It takes time for changes in the economy to translate into changes in employment. Employers wait to see how bad a recession looks before making the difficult decision to lay off workers. They also wait to see how solid a recovery looks before committing to take on new employees. While playing wait-and-see, firms may first try to decrease or increase the hours of existing employees.

✓ TEST YOURSELF

- ☐ What is the natural rate of unemployment? **[LO 9.3]**
- ☐ Contrast frictional and structural unemployment. **[LO 9.3]**
- ☐ With what measure does cyclical unemployment tend to move? **[LO 9.4]**

Public Policies and Other Influences on Unemployment

Addressing issues relating to unemployment can be tough. Unemployment is an important indicator of the overall health of the economy. It is also a very personal issue for those who experience it. As a result, discussions about the causes of unemployment—particularly those that have implications for public policy—can get heated.

In this section, we'll break down some of the policies and other factors in the economy that can influence the level of unemployment. Before we get into the details, consider one example of a controversial unemployment-related debate: Do immigrants cause unemployment by taking jobs? See the From Another Angle box "Immigration's effects on the labor market" to see why economists generally disagree that this is the case.

Immigration's effects on the labor market
From Another Angle

Imagine an American worker—we'll call him John. John lives in Charlotte, North Carolina. He's 35 years old and works as a construction worker. Now, imagine a would-be immigrant—we'll call him José. José is a 35-year-old worker who lives in Lima, Peru; he makes about a quarter of what John earns.

José moves to Charlotte and finds a job working on a roofing crew for minimum wage. It's a great deal for the company, which will save money on wages. It's a great deal for José, who more than doubles his salary. Unfortunately, it's lousy for John, who loses his job unless he wants to take a pay cut. (We assume that John's company is fairly cutthroat in its business practices, and can hire and fire at will).

This is the kind of plausible scenario that lies behind the rhetoric you often hear about immigrants taking U.S. jobs. It looks like a straightforward case, right? Well, no. Applying some economic logic, we can add important details to the story.

First of all, economists debate whether immigrants directly compete with native workers for work—in other words, how often immigrants like José take jobs from workers like John. Some research suggests that immigrants tend to find employment in industries that native workers don't want to do, such as agriculture, or that don't pay a high enough wage for local workers. Others suggest immigrants do compete with native workers in fields such as food preparation, hospitality, or construction.

The answer to that debate ultimately makes a big difference when looking at the impact of immigrants on the labor market and overall economy. To start, let's look at it from Jose's perspective. Now that José is living in Charlotte, he is also spending money in Charlotte. Also, some of the money the roofing company saves on wages will likely end up reflected in lower costs, saving customers money. Some of the money customers save will get spent elsewhere, in other businesses.

However, these benefits are offset by John's losses. If he is unable to find another job, the costs will be quite high, both because he's not spending as much and because of lost skills. Furthermore, if immigration is high enough and more workers like José move to Charlotte, the change could drive down wages in the construction field, affecting the welfare of thousands of workers.

Of course, this simplified example hides a good deal of complexity in the real-world effects of immigration on labor markets. Transition is painful, and it may not be easy for John to find a new job. Nor is it easy for local economies to adapt if many workers are displaced.

The point is that immigration can cause disruptions. But over time immigration also can expand the economy, rather than just steal jobs from current workers. Thus, economists generally reject the simple assertion that immigration necessarily causes unemployment. Instead, there are winners and losers, depending on the industry, as immigrants tend to compete for some kinds of jobs more than others.

Rhetoric and emotion can get in the way of seeing the full picture. The political debate tends to focus on immediate job losses, like the one suffered by John. And it's often hard to put numbers on society's longer-term gains, which tend to be diffuse. Economists see their role as trying to assess all of these trade-offs with as much balance as possible.

Source: Michael Clemens et al., "The Place Premium: Wage Differences for Identical Workers across the U.S. Border" (Center for Global Development Working Paper, 2008).

Factors that may stop wage rates from falling

In the previous section, we noted that unemployment can be influenced by forces that prevent wages from falling to the market-clearing level, either in the long run (through the natural rate of unemployment) or in response to short-term economic fluctuations (though cyclical unemployment). Why don't wages fall so that everyone with the skills and desire gets a job? In this section we will look at three possible explanations:

LO 9.5 Identify factors that may stop wages from falling to the equilibrium level.

- The government might prevent it, through minimum-wage legislation.
- Labor unions might prevent it, through bargaining backed by the threat to strike.
- Firms themselves might prevent it, by voluntarily choosing to pay higher wages than necessary.

Let's consider these three explanations in turn.

Minimum wage   A *minimum wage* is the lowest wage that a firm is legally allowed to pay its workers. In the United States, the federal minimum wage in 2018 was $7.25 per hour. Some states mandate a higher minimum wage. New York, California, Massachusetts, Washington D.C., and others, have passed laws to raise the minimum wage to $15 by 2023.[4]

The $7.25 per hour wage is approximately the wage that entry-level workers at a fast-food restaurant earn.[5] A worker who earns $7.25 an hour and works 40 hours a week earns just over $15,000 a year, before taxes. In 2016, that annual wage was not enough to keep a two-person household above the poverty line.

Supporters of minimum-wage legislation argue that workers deserve a basic standard of living. They say it is not fair to allow firms to pay workers a wage that would leave them struggling to escape poverty. But even those who support the idea of a higher minimum wage do not agree on the optimal level: $12 per hour? $15 per hour? Lower? Higher?

Opponents of minimum wage legislation point to graphs like the one we showed in Figure 9-4, which suggests that if the minimum wage is higher than the equilibrium wage, then we would expect unemployment to result. Of course, if the minimum wage is set at a level *below* the equilibrium wage, it will have no effect; this is called a *nonbinding* minimum wage.

Does a minimum wage cause unemployment? The question can't be resolved by a theoretical analysis alone. We need to look at data. Economists have found evidence both for and against the idea that a minimum wage causes unemployment:

- Evidence from fast-food restaurants in different U.S. states indicates that raising the state minimum wage did not cause fast-food chains to lay off employees. This implies that the real-world labor market does not work exactly like the model shown in Figure 9-4.

- In other cases, economists have found that minimum wages do appear to cause a small amount of unemployment or a change in *who* is employed, as firms substitute more skilled, older workers for unskilled, younger workers.

Another possibility some economists raise, given that the minimum wage applies only to people hired legally, is that it could drive jobs "under the table." That is, firms might respond to minimum-wage legislation by employing undocumented migrants at below-minimum wages or paying workers cash without telling the government.

Views on minimum wages vary greatly. If the minimum wage does indeed cause unemployment, people who can't find jobs will lose out, while people lucky enough to be in jobs will benefit. If it *doesn't* cause unemployment, then all workers will benefit, while firms lose out by making lower profits. The debate rages on.

What if the federal government stepped in to guarantee workers a job that paid $15 per hour? See the Economics in Action box "Employment guaranteed" for the economic arguments for and against a very controversial policy.

Employment guaranteed
Economics in Action

Politicians spend a lot of time talking about how to create jobs and get Americans "back to work." Policies include subsidies and tax breaks to employers and job-training programs for workers. Economists, including Stephanie Kelton, Darrick Hamilton, and William Darity, want to take a simpler (and more radical) approach. They say: Simply guarantee work to any American who needs it. It's a new version of an idea that Martin Luther King Jr. and Franklin Delano Roosevelt promoted decades ago.

"It's pretty simple at its core level," Kelton says. The idea is that having a decent job should be a fundamental right. "You don't have to prove anything, you don't have to meet certain requirements," Kelton explains. "It's just an open-ended offer of employment for anyone seeking work, and that's the end of it."

While a job guarantee has many possible versions, the core idea is the same: Offer all workers a job at a set wage, usually $15 per hour, to work in the public sector (building roads, installing solar panels, etc.). Proponents believe that the policy would provide a solid fallback option for workers, strengthen workers' bargaining power, and help ensure that all workers' are paid their fair share.

The idea is a long way from reality. Policy-makers still fiercely debate proposals to increase the minimum wage. A federal job guarantee would go further; not only would it effectively raise the minimum wage, it would offer an actual job at that wage. Progressive Democrats, including Senators Bernie Sanders (VT), Kristen Gillibrand (NY), Cory Booker (NJ), Kamala Harris (CA), and Elizabeth Warren (MA), have jumped on board. Rep. Alexandria Ocasio-Cortez called for a Green New Deal, which would offer displaced factory workers and others the ability to help build renewable energy infrastructure. New Jersey's Cory Booker proposed legislation that would offer $15 per hour jobs in 15 trial districts around the country.

Although it faces big political hurdles, a jobs guarantee has some clear economic pros and cons. First, the costs: Like many government proposals, a job guarantee costs money. One proposal, crafted by researchers Mark Paul, William Darity, and Darrick Hamilton, would cost $543 billion *per year*. Proponents say that it would be funded with money that previously went to support government "welfare" programs and tax credits, such as TANF, SNAP, or the EITC. The idea is that offering employment at a "living" wage would decrease the number of people using these services, decreasing their cost. However, the savings still would not cover a robust jobs program; some proposals, such as the one from Rep. Ocasio-Cortez, suggest that it could be paid for by raising taxes on the wealthiest Americans.

> Second, a jobs guarantee would undoubtedly cause disruption in the labor market, for better and worse. Offering federal jobs at $15 per hour would put pressure on private employers to match that rate, affecting 44 million workers, or about 30 percent of the American workforce. The impact would be like an increase in the minimum wage. To cover the increased wage, businesses would have to increase costs, or get by with fewer workers or hours worked. These increased costs might even force some businesses to shut down.
>
> Third, it's not clear that the government could efficiently create the jobs at the heart of the proposal. Nor is it clear that there would be support for the government to step in to compete with the private sector. Most economists believe that the government should promote free enterprise, not create alternatives to it.
>
> There could be strong benefits, however. Advocates hope that the government investments would jump-start or revitalize parts of the economy, such as infrastructure or renewable energy, that would not get the same kind of attention from the private sector. Not only that, steady employment at $15 per hour would move millions of Americans out of poverty, which would provide long-term benefits to workers and their families.
>
> What does the evidence say? Although there are few modern analogues, a decade-old program in India offers some evidence about the potential of a jobs guarantee. The Mahatma Ghandi National Rural Employment Guarantee Act offered 100 days of employment at a basic daily rate (roughly about $3 per day in state of West Bengal). An evaluation of the program found that despite some concerns of corruption and uneven implementation, the program increased rural wages, reduced the gender wage gap, and reduced migration to urban areas to find work.
>
> Whether a policy in America would offer the same benefits is far from guaranteed, however.
>
> Sources: Jayati Ghosh, "India's Rural Employment Programme Is Dying a Death of Funding Cuts," *The Guardian*, February 5, 2015, www.theguardian.com/global-development/2015/feb/05/india-rural-employment-funding-cuts-mgnrega; Gregory Krieg, "Why a 'Federal Jobs Guarantee' Is Gaining Steam with Democrats," *CNN*, April 26, 2018, www.cnn.com/2018/04/26/politics/federal-jobs-guarantee-gaining-steam-democrats/index.html; Laura Paddison, "What Is a Federal Jobs Guarantee?" *HuffPost*, July 6, 2018, www.huffingtonpost.com/entry/federal-job-guarantee-explained_us_5b363f4ae4b007aa2f7f59fc; David Weigel and Jeff Stein, "Democrats, Emboldened by GOP Cuts and Policies, Back Bigger Government," *The Washington Post*, May 27, 2018, www.washingtonpost.com/powerpost/democrats-emboldened-by-gop-cuts-and-policies-back-bigger-government/2018/05/27/9a6a4928-4a2d-11e8-9072-f6d4bc32f223_story.html?utm_term=.0b54871f6a5c.

Unions and bargaining

In 2007, television and screenplay writers went on strike. They picketed outside the major Hollywood studios and Broadway theaters, refusing to work until they were offered a bigger share of the profits from the shows they worked on. The writers' strike meant that production had to shut down for many TV shows; the writers gave up $285 million in lost wages. The strike was resolved after 100 days, with the writers gaining a pay increase and a bigger share of profits, especially from TV shows streamed over the internet and mobile devices.

Strikes like this are made possible by the existence of labor unions. In this case the writers were part of a union called the Writers' Guild. **Labor unions** are groups of employees who join together to bargain with their employer(s) over salaries and working conditions.

Unions benefit their members by being able to bargain as a group. If just a few disgruntled writers had gone on strike, then other writers could easily have been brought in to cover for them. But if workers strike together, they can bring an industry to a halt. This threat enables workers to drive a harder bargain with employers on wages and working conditions, such as benefits like health insurance, pension plans, and vacation time.

In the United States, the power of unions is falling. In the 1950s, about one-third of U.S. workers were in unions. The proportion is far lower today: As of 2017, about 10.7 percent of all wage and salary workers, or just under 15 million Americans, are in unions. About 35 percent of these union members work for government entities.[6] In some countries independent unions are restricted or banned altogether.

labor unions
groups of employees who join together to bargain with their employer(s) over salaries and work conditions

What does the existence of labor unions mean for the labor market and for unemployment? If labor unions drive a hard enough bargain, wage rates can rise above the equilibrium level. Then, the effect of labor unions is the same as with the minimum wage. To the extent that the labor market behaves like any other market, when unions manage to negotiate higher wages for their members, employers will in theory respond by employing fewer people. That means that being in a union is good for its own members but can be harmful for the unemployed looking for work.

There's some evidence, though, that the presence of unions pushes wages upward even for workers who are not in a union (if they work in a sector with a strong union presence). One reason is that employers with nonunion workers want to keep their employees happy enough that they do not feel the need to form a union.

Opinions about the role of unions on wages depend on whether you think that labor markets do a good job of determining fair wages, and how much weight you put on the well-being of unemployed people versus people with jobs.

Efficiency wages Another reason why wages might be above the market-clearing level is that some firms may *want* to pay their workers more than the going wage. Why would they do this? There are two related reasons:

- First, paying a higher wage will make workers less likely to quit, saving the expense of advertising for, interviewing, and training new people.
- Second, workers are more likely to fear losing their jobs and might work harder to keep the jobs they have.

Thus, it could be efficient for a firm to pay workers more than the going wage rate, especially in sectors where skills are scarce and worker motivation really matters. The idea is to give positive incentives to maximize productivity: Job transitions, from one worker to another, harm productivity. Also, workers exerting more effort to keep their jobs obviously also improves productivity. Paying wages above market-clearing levels may simply be a smart decision by firms.

The idea of deliberately setting wages above the market rate in order to increase productivity is captured by the term **efficiency wages**. Henry Ford is famous for instituting an efficiency wage at the Ford car factories in Detroit. He doubled his workers' wages in 1914 in order to reduce costly turnover and absenteeism, a move that turned out to be quite profitable.

How might efficiency wages prevent wages from falling in a recession? Imagine that you are running a firm with 10 employees, and a recession causes the wage rate for labor to drop by 10 percent. Which would you rather do: force all your employees to take a 10 percent pay cut or fire one employee?

You might calculate that the latter option is better. Sure, it would leave you with one fewer employee, but all nine remaining employees would be highly motivated to work hard and keep their jobs, knowing they are earning above the going rate. Among them, the nine employees may even end up producing more for the firm than 10 employees, disgruntled because of a pay cut, would have produced.

In addition, the fact that efficiency wages can create unemployment can strengthen their impact. When employers fire workers (rather than cut pay), the rising level of unemployment worsens the consequence of losing a job. When workers fear an extended period of unemployment (rather than just having to work at a lower wage), they are likely to push themselves that much harder.

There is little clear evidence so far about how much of unemployment can be explained by efficiency wages. Some economists think that it's a key feature of labor markets; others argue that simply raising wages is unlikely to increase productivity.

Recently economists have built on the efficiency-wage idea that workers' effort is also determined by whether wages are seen as being "fair." Needing to maintain "fair" wages might also limit employers' flexibility in cutting wages. The idea has support from laboratory-style economic experiments that explore made-up situations, and the idea awaits rigorous study in the real labor market.

---

efficiency wages wages that are deliberately set above the market rate to increase productivity

Unemployment insurance

Unemployment insurance is money that is paid by the government to people who are unemployed. The main goal of unemployment insurance is to provide insurance against a major loss of income. Such a loss can be tough to sustain without help. There are usually certain conditions that determine eligibility for unemployment insurance—such as actively looking for work and reporting work-related activities.

But does unemployment insurance influence the overall level of unemployment? Some economists and policy-makers believe that unemployment insurance increases unemployment because it removes the incentive to really look for work (beyond the requirement at least). Other economists believe that unemployment insurance does not change the amount of time it takes someone to find a job—the benefits of finding stable employment outweigh the benefits from a few weeks of insurance.

The amount and duration of unemployment insurance varies widely across countries. In the United States, unemployment insurance is based on how much an individual earned over the previous year, up to a maximum level. The standard duration of unemployment benefits is 26 weeks. However, this time period can be extended in times of unusually high unemployment. For example, during the recession of 2008–2009, the maximum limit was extended to 99 weeks for most states.

What happens if you don't have a job when your unemployment insurance runs out? In the United States, people can move onto other government welfare programs such as food and housing assistance. In European countries, unemployment benefits typically last longer and replace a greater percentage of average work income.

LO 9.6 Recognize how unemployment insurance and related policies can affect rates of unemployment.

unemployment insurance money paid by the government to people who are unemployed

Other factors

Unemployment insurance is just one policy we can expect to affect rates of unemployment. What are some others?

Taxes on wage income are important as well. We would expect, all else equal, that lower taxes would reduce unemployment. Why? The reasoning is that lower taxes give people more incentive to find a job, knowing they will keep more of the income they earn from the job. The magnitude of the impact taxes have on job-search effort, however, is inconclusive.

Another factor is the use of internships, which have exploded in the past few decades. However, internships do not always offer the same protections offered to full employees. For a a deeper look into the ethics and economics of internships, read the Econ and YOU box "Are internships experience or exploitation?"

Are internships experience or exploitation?
Econ and YOU

David Hyde, a 22-year-old from New Zealand, was elated to start an unpaid internship at the United Nations offices in Geneva, Switzerland. The catch? After failing to find affordable housing, he was forced to spend his nights in a tent set up along the banks of the river. "I guess my budget was not realistic in the end," he says. "It was way more expensive than I imagined. I thought I could find a really budget way to live, but to be honest, I've ended up living in a tent."

David's story is part of a larger debate about unpaid internships. In 2011, Eric Glatt and Alex Footman, two interns who worked on the set of the movie *Black Swan*, sued Fox Searchlight Pictures, alleging that their work was really a form of employment and should have been

(continued)

compensated. Similar lawsuits hit publishers Hearst and Condé Nast, as well as NBCUniversal and Warner Music. Yet in 2017 the U.S. Department of Labor loosened the guidelines for acceptable internships.

Despite their challenges, internships are an economic reality for many students. Almost 60 percent of college students in the class of 2017 held an internship, and approximately 40 percent of those internships were unpaid. Does that give an unfair advantage to students who can afford to work at a job that doesn't pay? In some cities, like Los Angeles, New York, and Washington, D.C., unpaid internships are common, but living costs are high. That can make it hard for students from less-advantaged backgrounds to gain experience and connections in their chosen fields.

There are other problems as well. Since unpaid interns do not receive wages, they are not protected by federal laws enforced by the U.S. Equal Employment Opportunity Commission (EEOC). These laws include protections against workplace discrimination and sexual harassment. Without employment status, interns have little recourse if they have an issue on the job.

However, there is high demand for internships of all types. Interns note that they develop real skills in a real professional environment. The data on job-market outcomes suggest that employers recognize these benefits. According to the NACE Class of 2017 Student Survey, students with a paid internship on their resume were far more likely than others to receive a job offer, and they were offered a higher salary on average. (The difference persisted across all sectors represented in the survey, and can't be explained by the fact that paid internships are more likely to be found in higher-paying industries.)

What about the impacts on the labor market? Anywhere from 500,000 to 1 million people work for free as interns every year. The increasing number of people willing to work without pay puts downward pressure on wages and makes it harder for workers without a college degree to find work, since many internships replace entry-level jobs.

Sources: www.naceweb.org/about-us/press/2018/type-of-internship-experience-affects-job-offer-rates-salary/; Imogene Foulkes, "How a UN Intern Was Forced to Live in a Tent in Geneva," *BBC News, Geneva*, August 12, 2015, www.bbc.com/news/world-europe-33893384; Rebecca Greenfield, "Unpaid Internships Are Back, with the Labor Department's Blessing," *Los Angeles Times*, January 13, 2018, www.latimes.com/business/la-fi-unpaid-internships-20180112-story.html; Derek Thomas, "The Murky Ethics (and Crystal-Clear Economics) of the Unpaid Internship," *The Atlantic*, May 19, 2012, www.theatlantic.com/business/archive/2012/05/the-murky-ethics-and-crystal-clear-economics-of-the-unpaid-internship/256940.

✓ TEST YOURSELF

- ☐ Why do some governments set a minimum wage? **[LO 9.5]**
- ☐ Why would an employer pay an efficiency wage? **[LO 9.5]**
- ☐ What are the trade-offs in the effect of unemployment insurance? **[LO 9.6]**

Conclusion

Most of our adult lives are spent working, and finding a great job can be a key to happiness. At the same time, not being able to find the right job—or not being able to find any job at all—can be one of the toughest life experiences.

The labor market is in many ways like any other market. It's driven by the forces of supply and demand, and we can describe an equilibrium wage rate at which the quantity of labor supplied equals the quantity of labor demanded. But there are differences too: Minimum wages, bargaining by labor unions, and efficiency wages can all cause the wage rate to be above the market-clearing level for extended periods, which leads to unemployment.

We've discussed how the official unemployment rate is measured. Since the unemployment rate doesn't always give a full picture of labor-market conditions, economists and policy-makers often pore over other measures, such as the labor-force participation rate.

We've described the main reasons for unemployment. Frictional and structural unemployment occur naturally; they will exist in any labor market regardless of policy. They are caused by people switching between jobs or shifting from one sector to another.

Another type of unemployment, cyclical unemployment, mirrors the overall health of the economy and the business cycle. In boom times, jobs get created and cyclical unemployment is small. But jobs are lost when the economy weakens, and cyclical unemployment rises.

Economists debate how much the rules of the labor market affect the overall rate of unemployment. We've seen that labor-market policies often come with important trade-offs:

- Policy-makers have to decide how generous to make unemployment benefits. Providing more support for the unemployed may be desirable from a social perspective, but when benefits are *too* generous, incentives to actively search for a job are diminished.
- Similarly, raising minimum wages helps workers on the bottom rungs of the labor market, but raising minimum wages can also make it harder for unemployed workers to find jobs.

Unemployment is not something that occurs in isolation from the rest of the economy. In fact, one of the most powerful ways to reduce unemployment is to generate sustained economic growth in the overall economy. In the next chapter, we focus on this important economic challenge: How can policy and resources be combined to create healthy economic growth?

Key Terms

unemployment, p. 226
labor force, p. 227
unemployment rate, p. 227
labor-force participation rate, p. 228
discouraged workers, p. 231
underemployed, p. 231
labor demand curve, p. 232
labor supply curve, p. 233
natural rate of unemployment, p. 235
frictional unemployment, p. 235
structural unemployment, p. 235
real-wage or classical unemployment, p. 236
cyclical unemployment, p. 236
labor unions, p. 241
efficiency wages, p. 242
unemployment insurance, p. 243

Summary

LO 9.1 Explain how economists measure employment and unemployment.

To be considered unemployed, a person needs to meet three conditions: (1) be part of the working-age, civilian population; (2) not have worked in the previous week; and (3) be actively looking for work. Economists measure unemployment with the *unemployment rate*. This is the number of people who are unemployed, divided by the labor force.

The *labor force participation rate* is the fraction of the working age population that is working or looking for work. People who are not working but who are not actively looking for work—for example, students, homemakers, or *discouraged workers*—are not considered part of the labor force. Those, on the other hand, who are working jobs that don't utilize their skills or knowledge are considered to be *underemployed*.

LO 9.2 Explain how wage rates above equilibrium cause unemployment.

Like other markets, the labor market features a demand curve and a supply curve. The *total* demand for labor from all the firms in the economy is represented by the *labor demand curve*. On the whole, firms will want to hire more labor when wages are cheaper and less labor when wages are expensive, which means the labor demand curve slopes downward.

The total labor supply is represented by the *labor supply curve*. We would expect that people will be willing to supply more labor at higher wage rates and less labor at lower wage rates. This relationship gives the labor supply curve a positive slope.

Equilibrium in the market for labor is reached at the wage (price of labor) where the labor demand and labor supply curves meet. Unemployment results when the market wage rate remains above the market equilibrium; it is effectively a surplus of labor at the inflated wage rate.

LO 9.3 Explain why there is a natural rate of unemployment in an economy.

We think of the economy having a long-run natural level of unemployment. This *natural rate of unemployment* is the amount of unemployment that is unavoidable in a dynamic economy.

There are two reasons why we expect the economy to have some unemployment when everything else is normal: Some unemployment comes from *frictional* reasons, such as people changing jobs or locations. Some unemployment comes from *structural* reasons, such as government policies that affect how easily the wage rate can adjust. Structural unemployment also includes people who are unemployed because of technological development in the economy that results in a mismatch between the skills demanded by firms and the skills the labor force has.

LO 9.4 Explain why there is a cyclical component of unemployment.

There is also unemployment that is related to changes in GDP in the economy. When GDP is higher than normal, unemployment is lower than the equilibrium rate. When GDP is lower than normal, unemployment is above the equilibrium rate. This type of unemployment is called *cyclical unemployment*.

LO 9.5 Identify factors that may stop wages from falling to the equilibrium level.

Many factors affect the level of unemployment rate. Three reasons why the wage rate may not fully adjust to the equilibrium wage rate in the labor market are a minimum wage that is above the equilibrium wage rate, labor unions that negotiate a wage rate above the equilibrium wage rate, and *efficiency wages* (wages paid by firms, above the equilibrium wage rate).

LO 9.6 Recognize how unemployment insurance and related policies can affect rates of unemployment.

The design of the unemployment insurance programs is ultimately a balance of trade-offs. When benefits are not generous, losing a job can become a devastating financial hardship. When benefits are *too* generous, incentives to actively search for a job are diminished. In the United States, unemployment benefits last only a short time and pay only a fraction of people's average working wages, so as to minimize the incentive to shirk the job search.

Review Questions

1. During the 1960s societal norms regarding working women were changing, and many women who had been housewives began working outside the home. How would you expect this new norm to change the labor-force participation rate? What about the unemployment rate? **[LO 9.1]**

2. List at least five types of people who do not have paid jobs but would nevertheless *not* be considered unemployed. **[LO 9.1]**

3. Compare two countries, one that has unlimited unemployment insurance and one in which workers are eligible for 26 weeks of unemployment insurance. Explain one reason why the country with more unemployment insurance may have a higher equilibrium unemployment rate. **[LO 9.2]**

4. Suppose the president of a country comes to you to ask your advice. The country is currently at 8 percent unemployment, and the president wishes to reduce unemployment in the country to 3 percent. As an economist, you determine that the country's natural rate of unemployment is 5 percent. What advice would you give the president? **[LO 9.3]**

5. Innovation often requires "creative destruction," in which the new product or technology makes previous products or technologies obsolete. For example, when the personal computer was invented, typewriters became useless; hence, the personal computer "destroyed" the typewriter. This process of creative destruction often results in structural unemployment because workers who knew how to build and maintain the old products have skills that are no longer in demand. Do you think the government has a role in either limiting how often new products are created or in helping those workers who are displaced because of the new product? **[LO 9.3]**

6. Suppose the National Bureau of Economic Research (NBER) just came out with a report suggesting that the economy will soon dip into recession. How do you think the levels of frictional, structural, and cyclical unemployment will change as the recession begins? What will happen to the labor-force participation rate? **[LO 9.4]**

7. What happens to a country's levels of frictional, structural, and cyclical unemployment, as well as its

labor-force participation rate, as a recession drags on for an extended period of time? [LO 9.4]

8. What happens to a country's levels of frictional, structural, and cyclical unemployment, as well as its labor-force participation rate, as a country begins to recover from a deep recession? [LO 9.4]

9. Give two reasons why it may be rational for a firm to offer wages above the minimum wage. [LO 9.5]

10. In France, labor laws typically made it very difficult or even illegal for firms to fire workers during economic downturns. How would these laws affect cyclical unemployment as well as frictional and structural unemployment? (*Hint*: Think about how these laws affect firms' decisions to hire workers in the first place.) [LO 9.4, LO 9.5]

11. Unemployment is often called a lagging or trailing indicator because unemployment tends to rise some time after the economy begins to slow down, and unemployment begins to fall again after the economy begins to rebound. In other words, unemployment trails GDP. Why do you think this might be the case? [LO 9.5]

12. The traditional goal of a government is to maximize its citizens' welfare. Given this goal, would you suggest getting rid of unemployment insurance? How would your answer change if the goal of the government is to maximize employment? [LO 9.6]

13. In the United States during regular economic times, the maximum length of time a worker can collect unemployment insurance is 26 weeks. During recessions, however, Congress often increases the length of time in which workers can collect benefits. During the recent financial crisis, workers could collect benefits for up to 99 weeks in some states. Comment on the advantages and disadvantages of this system. [LO 9.6]

Problems and Applications

1. For each of the following situations, would the Bureau of Labor Statistics count Rick Alexander (from the chapter-opening story) as employed, unemployed, or not in the labor force? [LO 9.1]

   a. Alexander is self-employed in his old job as a carpenter.
   b. Alexander moves to Florida and begins looking for work.
   c. Alexander feels discouraged looking for work and stops applying for jobs.
   d. Alexander starts looking for work again.
   e. Alexander starts work at a new job.

2. Consider the economy whose data appear in Table 9P-1. [LO 9.1]

TABLE 9P-1

Group of people	Number of people in group
Working-age population	130,000
Labor force	65,000
Unemployed	12,000

   a. What is the unemployment rate?
   b. What is the labor-force participation rate?

3. Table 9P-2 uses data for the year 2018, adjusted to be comparable to each other. All population values are in thousands.

   a. Fill in the blanks in the table. [LO 9.1]
   b. In part *a*, you should have found that the unemployment rates of the three countries differ significantly from one another. Suggest three possible reasons to explain why the countries might have different unemployment rates. [LO 9.3, LO 9.4]

4. Assume the equilibrium wage rate is $6. Draw a graph of the labor market to answer the following questions. [LO 9.2]

   a. When the government introduces a minimum wage of $5.50, does unemployment increase, decrease, or stay the same compared to unemployment at the equilibrium wage?
   b. When the government introduces a minimum wage of $6.50, does unemployment increase, decrease, or stay the same compared to unemployment at the equilibrium wage?

TABLE 9P-2

Country	Working-age population	Labor force	Employed	Unemployed	Unemployment rate (%)	Labor-force participation rate (%)
Japan	75,469		67,130	1,730		
France		30,399		2,874		72.2
Germany	53,484	43,401			5.1	

5. Assume that the labor demand equation for a fictional country is $L_d = 60 - 2w$, where w is the wage per hour worked and L_d is the number of workers demanded by firms. Assume also that the labor supply equation for that country is $L_s = 0.4(w)$, where L_s is the number of people willing to work. **[LO 9.2, LO 9.5]**
   a. Find the equilibrium wage and quantity of labor employed.
   b. At the equilibrium wage, how many people are unemployed?
   c. How would the number of unemployed change if the supply of workers increased?

6. Suppose a firm's labor demand equation is $L_d = 60 - 2(w)$ and the labor supply equation that it faces is $L_s = -20 + 3(w)$, where w is the wage per hour worked, L_d is the number of workers demanded by firms, and L_s is the number of people willing to work. **[LO 9.2, LO 9.5]**
   a. Find the equilibrium wage and quantity of labor employed.
   b. The workers, thinking that their wages are too low, decide to strike. After tense negotiations, the firm decides to raise the wage by 50 percent. After the wage increase, how many people are unemployed?

7. Classify each of the following situations as either frictional, structural, or cyclical unemployment. **[LO 9.3, LO 9.4]**
   a. Maria has started looking for work after taking time off to have a baby.
   b. Juan left high school without graduating and can't find any jobs he is qualified for.
   c. Rohit had a job working on Wall Street but lost his job during the financial crisis.
   d. Adam has just arrived in a new city and is looking for work.
   e. Max wants to work as an air steward, but because the airline industry is heavily unionized there are very few jobs available.
   f. Jada has just lost her job in a web start-up that was affected by a downturn in the economy.

8. For each of the following situations, would the unemployment rate increase, decrease, or stay the same? **[LO 9.5]**
   a. A company begins paying efficiency wages above the equilibrium wage rate.
   b. The number of workers covered by union contracts falls.
   c. The government extends the duration of unemployment insurance.

9. Suppose a country has a 26-week limit on the duration that an unemployed person receives unemployment benefits. You collect some data and notice that workers in their 26th week of unemployment benefits somehow manage to find jobs at a much higher rate than other unemployed workers. What would this statistic tell you about the incentives involved with unemployment insurance? **[LO 9.6]**

10. Understanding that unemployment benefits give workers the incentive to not look for work until their benefits run out, suppose an economist suggested that instead of giving workers up to 26 weeks of unemployment benefits that end once the person finds work, a person who loses his or her job would just get a single big check for 26 weeks of benefits, regardless of how long the worker is unemployed. What are the advantages and disadvantages of this idea? **[LO 9.6]**

Endnotes

1. Rick Alexander's story is from Michael Luo, "Out of Work, and Too Down to Search On," *The New York Times*, September 7, 2009, p. A1, New York edition.
2. http://www.nytimes.com/2009/09/07/us/07worker.html?pagewanted=2.
3. Bureau of Labor Statistics: http://www.bls.gov/bls/glossary.htm#U.
4. www.usatoday.com/story/money/2018/12/27/minimum-wage-2019-which-states-increasing-next-year/2377035002/.
5. http://www.payscale.com/research/us/employer=mcdonald%27s_Corporation/Hourly_rate.
6. www.bls.gov/news.release/union2.nr0.htm.

Economic Growth

Chapter 10

Why Economic Growth Matters

Between 2005 and 2015, a miracle occurred: Over 650 million people around the world rose out of poverty, cutting the number of the global poor by nearly half. These people moved from worrying about where their next meal was coming from to being able to worry instead about finding a better place to live or a more satisfying job.

What triggered this miracle? It wasn't a humanitarian intervention or massive government program. It was two numbers: an annual (compounded) growth rate of average GDP per person of 8 percent for China and 5 percent for India.[1]

If you had traveled through those countries in recent years, you'd have found them buzzing with entrepreneurial spirit. Buildings and infrastructure sprouted like mushrooms in many parts of both countries. Highways carried people and goods between enormous cities. The bridge of new wealth connected millions of people to the internet and a global consumer culture.

High rates of economic growth have produced more than just tall buildings and smoother roads. The newly minted middle classes in China and India have cash to spend, buying the latest cell phones and flooding the roads with new cars. The middle class in China alone is bigger than the entire population of the United States. The bright lights of Shanghai and Mumbai also offer promise to millions of people who have migrated from poorer rural areas hoping to land jobs in factories or hotels, trading rural lifestyles for urban ones. Wages are rising, and poverty rates are falling.

It is easy to get excited by these transformations and to proclaim that we're ending global poverty. But saying that economic growth is the solution to poverty is a bit like saying that brilliant medical research cures diseases or that scoring lots of touchdowns wins football games. Of course, it's important, but how do you make it happen? That's the hard part.

LEARNING OBJECTIVES

LO 10.1 Calculate the growth rate of real GDP per capita, accounting for changes in price levels and population.

LO 10.2 Describe the relationship between productivity and growth, and discuss the factors that determine productivity.

LO 10.3 Explain the difference between a country's level of income and its rate of growth.

LO 10.4 Use the growth accounting framework to describe how technology, labor, and capital contribute to economic growth.

LO 10.5 Assess the empirical evidence for and against convergence theory.

LO 10.6 Discuss policies that could promote growth, and relate them to productivity.

LO 10.7 Explain how government policy and economic openness lay the foundation for growth.

Leaders all over the world seek economic growth. It translates to wealthier, healthier, and better-educated citizens enjoying more comfortable lives. It also results in higher tax revenues for governments and enticing opportunities for investors. Sadly, we have no magic formula for economic growth. Decades of research have helped us see why some countries are rich and others poor. But history has also shown that it's not easy for policy-makers to translate this understanding into action.

The search for a recipe for economic growth captivates economists. It is simultaneously one of the most important and fascinating questions in economics, and one about which we're still learning. In this chapter, we will describe three aspects of the study of growth. First, we'll discuss how growth is measured and show the patterns that have emerged around the world in the last century. Second, we'll create a basic framework for understanding why growth happens, and how savings, capital, labor, and technology contribute to it. Finally, we'll dig into details on how public policy choices can affect growth.

Economic Growth through the Ages

Over the past 70 years, real GDP per capita in the United States has grown at an average rate just under 2 percent per year. That might not sound so impressive compared to the 8 percent and 5 percent growth experienced, respectively, by China and India recently. In the context of history, however, it's revolutionary. In this section, we'll explore two reasons why this is so.

History of world growth

LO 10.1 Calculate the growth rate of real GDP per capita, accounting for changes in price levels and population.

Imagine you were living in 1800. Almost anywhere in the world at that time, income per person was not much different from what it had been a millennium earlier. The possibility of growth has always been around, of course, but very little of it actually happened until a century or two ago. Rapid economic growth is a modern phenomenon.

Look at Figure 10-1, which shows world population and income per person over the last 3,000 years. Historical records and archaeological evidence allow us to get a general sense of prices and standards of living in ancient days. Notice that for the first 2,800 of the last 3,000 years, *very little was happening*. The population was growing slowly, and the economy was growing just fast enough to keep up with the snail's pace of the population. The result was that real income per person barely changed at all.

FIGURE 10-1

History of world economic growth: Real GDP per capita, 1000 BC to AD 2000   For the first 2,800 years of this graph, real global GDP per capita was essentially constant. Then, in 1800, with the Industrial Revolution, incomes in Europe began to increase rapidly. In the last 50 years, real global GDP per capita quadrupled. Note that the numbers on the vertical axis refer to both real GDP per capita (calculated as if the entire world was one economy and deflated using PPP exchange rates) and to the number of people on earth—which rose to over 6 billion people (6,000 × 1 million) by 2000.

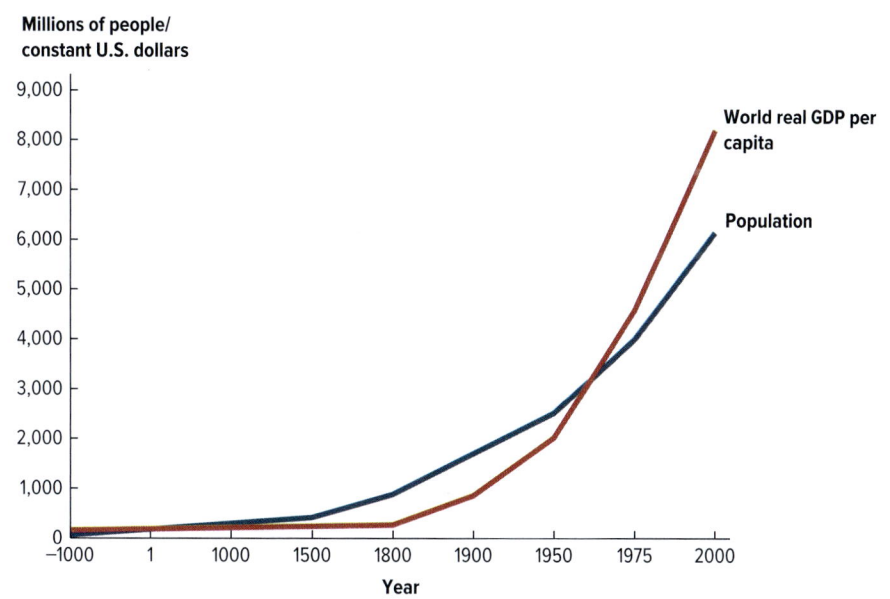

Source: www.j-bradford-delong.net/macro_online/ms/ch5/chapter_5.pdf.

Suddenly, in the 1800s, the nature of the global economy underwent a radical transformation. After staying about the same size for thousands of years, it started to grow. This growth was even more striking given that the world's population exploded at roughly the same time. The red line in Figure 10-1 shows real GDP per capita, calculated as if the entire world was one economy. The blue line shows world population growth. The figure shows that even though population grew at a historically fast pace in the twentieth century, real GDP per capita grew even faster.

The growth rate of real GDP per capita is typically the number we care about. It describes the change in actual purchasing power for each person. In order to get an accurate picture of the real GDP per capita growth rate, we need to subtract changes in both prices and population from the nominal GDP growth rate, as follows:

EQUATION 10-1

$$\text{Real GDP per capita growth rate} = \text{Nominal GDP growth rate} - \text{Inflation rate} - \text{Population growth rate}$$

Just from glancing at Figure 10-1, you can see that the fast rise of GDP growth in the last few centuries means that nominal GDP must have grown much faster than inflation and population combined. As a result, the purchasing power of the average person in the world today is more than 30 times as high as it was 200 years ago. This represents a transformative change in the way people live. A growth rate like 2 percent may not sound revolutionary, but it is a big jump from what had been essentially zero growth for centuries before.

> **TAKE NOTE**
>
> Growth rates usually compare the level of a variable in one year to its level the previous year (though growth rates can be calculated for other time frames too). To get a concrete sense of an annual growth rate, here's how to calculate the United States' real GDP per capita growth rate at the start of 2018: First, find the level of U.S. real GDP per capita in 2018 ($55,964 in early 2018) and the level in 2017 ($54,945 in early 2017).[2] Then subtract to find the absolute change, an increase of $1,019. The growth rate is then calculated as the absolute change between 2017 and 2018 expressed as a percentage of the level in 2017:
>
> $$\left(\frac{\$1,019}{\$54,945}\right) \times 100 = 1.85 \text{ percent}$$

Compounding and the rule of 70

The second reason that the historical U.S. growth rate of 2 percent per year is more impressive than it sounds is that economic growth builds on itself over time. This process is the same as the *compounding of interest* in a savings account—earlier interest payments get added to the account and earn interest in turn.

Similarly, a relatively modest annual growth rate can add up to a large change in the economy over time. In fact, real per capita GDP in the United States is roughly *four times* what it was seventy years ago. Figure 10-2 shows this growth in real purchasing power.

Compounding results in total changes in GDP over time that are bigger than the annual growth rate would at first suggest. The key insight is that the base from which growth is measured gets bigger every year. To see how this works, let's call U.S. GDP in 2000 "Y." If the economy is growing at 2 percent per year, then in 2001, GDP will be:

$$GDP_{2001} = Y + (0.02 \times Y) = 1.02Y$$

To simplify the math, notice that a 2 percent growth rate means that every year GDP is 1.02 times GDP in the previous year. In 2002, the base is now larger, 1.02Y rather than just Y:

$$GDP_{2002} = 1.02 \times GDP_{2001} = 1.02 \times 1.02Y = (1.02)^2 Y$$

And, in 2003:

$$GDP_{2003} = 1.02 \times GDP_{2002} = 1.02 \times (1.02)^2 Y = (1.02)^3 Y$$

Are you seeing the pattern? Because 2003 is three years after 2000, we find GDP in 2003 by multiplying the base 2000 GDP by one plus the growth rate three times—that is, by 1.02 to the power of three.

FIGURE 10-2

U.S. real GDP per capita, 1947–2018 (valued in 2012 dollars)   Since 1947, the trend of GDP has been overwhelmingly positive, with some exceptions. The most recent was the Great Recession (late 2007 to mid-2009).

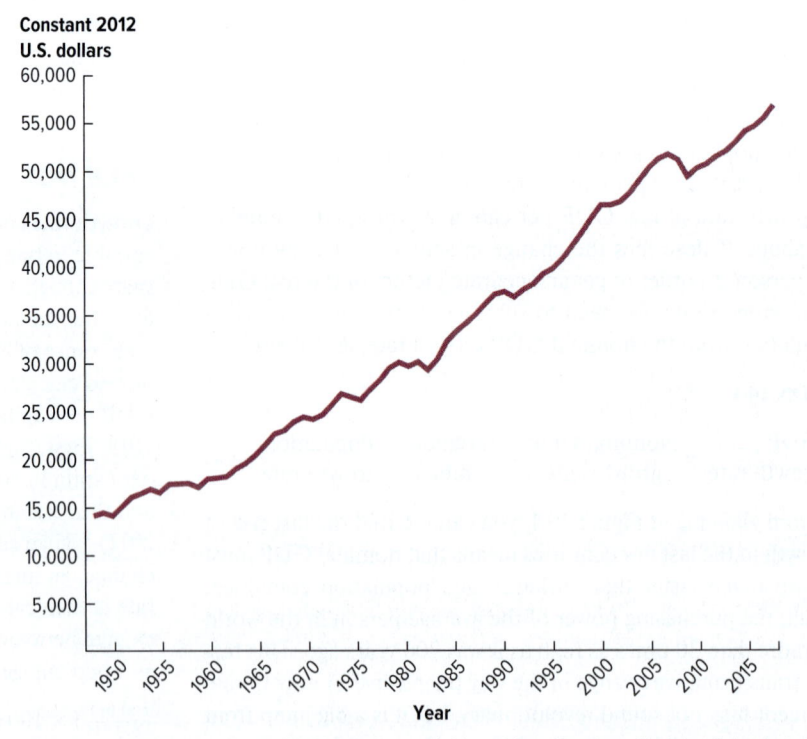

Source: FRED, Federal Reserve Bank of St. Louis, Chained 2012 Dollars, Seasonally Adjusted Annual Rate, https://fred.stlouisfed.org/series/A939RX0Q048SBEA#0.

If we generalize this formula, we can predict GDP per capita in any year, A. We start from year B and multiply by 1 plus the growth rate, as many times as there are years between B and A:

EQUATION 10-2
$$\text{GDP}_{\text{yearA}} = \text{GDP}_{\text{yearB}} \times (1 + \text{Growth rate})^{(\text{yearA}-\text{yearB})}$$

Let's apply this equation to the 70 years between 1948 and 2018. In 1948, real per capita GDP in the United States was roughly $14,316.[3] Plugging that amount for $\text{GDP}_{\text{yearB}}$ into Equation 10-2, we calculate that real GDP per capita in 2018 would have been roughly $57,258 if the growth rate during that whole period had been a steady 2 percent per year:

$$\text{GDP}_{2018} \approx \$14,316 \times (1 + 0.02)^{70} = \$57,258$$

It turns out that the actual real per capita GDP was $55,964 at the start of 2018, so the approximation of steady 2 percent growth was high, but not far off.

A different way to calculate the implications of steady growth is to use the *rule of 70*. It states that the number of years it will take for income to double at a given annual growth rate is approximately equal to 70 divided by the annual growth rate:

EQUATION 10-3
$$\text{Years until income doubles} = \frac{70}{\text{Annual growth rate}}$$

Thinking of growth in terms of "years to doubling" makes it easier to appreciate how small differences in growth rates can add up to huge differences in income over time. For example, what if the growth rate in the United States increased from around 2 percent to about 3.5 percent? That might not sound like a big difference, but consider:

- At a growth rate of 2 percent, income doubles every 35 years. So over 70 years, income doubles and then doubles again.
- At a growth rate of 3.5 percent, income doubles every 20 years instead of every 35. So over 70 years, income doubles, doubles again, doubles yet again, and keeps growing toward another doubling. So, starting with $14,316 in 1948, instead of earning an average $57,258 by 2018 (at 2 percent growth per year), Americans would be earning an average of about $159,091—about $145,000 a year more thanks to the 3.5 percent growth rate. That's more than 11 times the average income in 1948.

To see the effect that differences in growth rates can make, consider the incredible economic story of East Asia. Starting in 1960, Hong Kong, Singapore, Taiwan, and South Korea managed growth rates of over 8 percent per year. That implies that real incomes doubled more than once every 10 years! In just 50 years, this impressive economic growth managed to vault many people out of poverty. For insight into the debate about why this "Asian miracle" hasn't happened elsewhere, see the Economics in Action box "What a difference 50 years makes."

What a difference 50 years makes: The story of Korea and Ghana

Economics in Action

Samsung, LG, Hyundai, and Kia—you probably recognize these global brands, all based in South Korea, one of the world's major manufacturing forces. South Korea makes sophisticated, high-end electronics and cars, and today it is a relatively wealthy country, with a GDP per capita over $28,000.

Fifty years ago, few would have predicted that outcome. An early World Bank report on the country called South Korea's growth plan "ridiculously optimistic" and predicted sluggish growth. Its citizens were quite poor, with most of the population eking out livings on small farms.

(continued)

Ghana, on the other hand, was seen as a promising economy. Fifty years ago, most economists thought it was poised to grow by at least 7 percent per year. Ghana's economy did grow in the subsequent decades, though much more slowly than Korea's. And, since Ghana's population grew even more quickly than its economy, the average income per capita in Ghana was actually *higher* in 1960 than in 2000.

Today, Ghana is one of the richer countries in Africa, but it is much less well-off than South Korea. Ghana's GDP per capita in 2014 was a little over $1,400 per person. Over half of its workforce is still employed in the agricultural sector, either growing export crops such as cocoa or subsistence crops such as cassava and maize.

Why did Korea take off while Ghana failed to meet its early promise? The story is complicated, but an important part of it is that Ghana suffered years of political instability after 1960. Government intervention in the economy was heavy-handed and discouraged foreign trade.

South Korea, on the other hand, focused relentlessly on educating its citizens and encouraging people to save. The government gave firms generous incentives to export, including tax benefits and low-interest loans. South Korea's expanding manufacturing sector led it to an average growth rate of real GDP per capita of 5.4 percent in the half-century between 1961 and 2011.

The rule of 70 estimates that Korea doubled in size about every 13 years. Put another way, in the 50 years between 1961 and 2011, Korea doubled its income nearly four times. The result: The current generation of young adults in Korea have incomes that are about 13 times that of their grandparents, after adjusting for inflation.

Economists don't have a foolproof formula for creating growth miracles. But by studying how Korea grew and why Ghana didn't, we can get closer to a real understanding of economic growth.

Sources: http://siteresources.worldbank.org/DEC/Resources/84797-1275071905763/Lessons_from_Korea_Lim.pdf; http://countrystudies.us/south-korea; www.nber.org/chapters/c8548.pdf; www.cimmyt.org/; http://economistsview.typepad.com/economistsview/2006/03/amartya_sen_dem.html; http://data.worldbank.org/indicator/NY.GDP.PCAP.CD.

✓ TEST YOURSELF

☐ What was the overall trend of economic growth in the world before 1800? **[LO 10.1]**
☐ What is the rule of 70? **[LO 10.1]**

Determinants of Productivity

Growth may seem like an abstract concept, but it has a big impact on people's standard of living. If you happen to have been born in the United States or South Korea, for instance, you likely enjoy a standard of living much higher than that of your grandparents and great-grandparents. You are probably taller, healthier, better-educated, and more widely traveled and have more luxury and comfort in your life. Other regions of the world have grown much more slowly or not at all. As a result, in those regions people live in ways relatively similar to earlier generations.

What determines the dramatic differences between countries and their growth paths over time? In this section, we will build a framework to understand factors that determine the level of income in a country and the rate at which it grows over time. With this framework, we will have a basis for discussing the historical circumstances and policy choices that cause some economies to grow and others to stagnate.

Productivity drives growth

Imagine a single household—say, a family that lives away from others, on a farm in a remote place. The only goods available to this family are things its members can produce. If the family wants food or clothes or toys or a house, it will have to grow or make them. Suppose some family members learn to sew more quickly; they will make clothes more quickly and have more time left over to make toys for their children. Or suppose they build a plow that allows them to plant vegetables more easily, freeing up time and energy to build an extra room in their house. The total amount of goods they produce will increase, and so will their standard of living.

In fact, the *only* way that the family can consume more and enjoy a higher standard of living is to increase the amount each person produces. We call that output **productivity**. Productivity can be measured in various ways, but it's typically measured as output per worker.

From Chapter 7, "Measuring GDP," we know that *output per person on a country level* is the same thing as *GDP per capita*. Just like the farm family, we can think of a country as a self-contained economic unit: It can earn and consume only as much as it produces. Thus, a country's income—like that of the farm family—depends on how productive its workers are.

Of course, hardly any family or country today consumes exactly what it produces itself. Typically, both sell some of the goods and services they produce. They then use the money they earn to buy goods and services that others produce. Still, the underlying relationship holds: The more a country produces, the more it can consume. In the short term, it can temporarily push consumption higher than production by borrowing money. But in the long run, debts have to be paid, and the only way to get to consume more is by producing more.

As a result, the standard of living in a country is driven by the average productivity of its people. *Increases in productivity per person* lead to *increases in per capita income*, which we call *economic growth*. So now the question is: What makes a country's people more productive?

productivity
output produced per worker

Components of productivity

To answer the question of what makes people more productive, we'll go back to the enterprising farm family. What determines how many vegetables they can grow in a year? The answer depends on several other questions: How skilled and experienced are they at farming? How fertile is their land, and what is the climate like? Do they have plows and fertilizer? Do they have state-of-the-art computerized irrigation systems, or do they depend on rainfall? Do they use the latest high-yield seed varieties?

Most of us are not farmers. But the factors that determine our productivity as workers fall into the same categories: *physical capital* (like plows and tractors), *human capital* (farming experience), *natural resources* (land quality and rainfall), and *technology* (high-tech tools and crop varieties). Let's walk through each determinant to see how it affects productivity.

LO 10.2 Describe the relationship between productivity and growth, and discuss the factors that determine productivity.

Physical capital
Most types of production require tools, and better tools allow workers to be more productive. A farmer with a sturdy horse-drawn plow will outperform a farmer with a shovel but won't do as well as his neighbor with a tractor. These are examples of **physical capital**, the stock of equipment and structures that allow for the production of goods and services. Elsewhere in the economy, examples of physical capital include a manufacturer's factory and machines, a cellular network's towers and cables, and so on.

We calculate the amount of physical capital in an economy by adding up the value of all tools, equipment, and structures. Every year, some new physical capital is added through investment (farmers buy new tractors). Likewise, some old physical capital wears out or becomes obsolete (old tractors stop working). Taking into account both new investment and the retirement of older capital, we can tell how much physical capital has been added to the economy on net.

Where does the money for investment in physical capital come from? It largely comes from the savings of ordinary households. You put away money in the bank, and the bank then loans funds to farmers and factories and cellular networks so that they can purchase new equipment. Thus, the *level of savings* in an economy can be an important determinant of investment in capital, and through that mechanism, a determinant of future productivity. In countries with low levels of savings, firms have trouble finding the money they need to invest in their factories and businesses. We will look in more detail at the relationship between savings and investment in later chapters.

physical capital
the stock of equipment and structures that allow for production of goods and services

human capital
the set of skills, knowledge, experience, and talent that determine the productivity of workers

Schools around the world aim to build human capital. Here, a school in Kenya shows attentive students in a jam-packed classroom.
©Feije Riemersma/123RF

Human capital Having new machines is usually a plus for productivity, but only if workers know how to use them. **Human capital** refers to the set of skills, knowledge, experience, and talent that determine the productivity of workers.

Education is one of the main ways that we think about people building human capital. By taking an economics course, you are learning things that will make you more productive in the workplace. Human capital can also be acquired through training or job experience.

Human capital contributes to growth because it helps workers in the economy produce more with the same amount of physical capital. In other words, people can work smarter.

A large increase in human capital is one explanation for the growth in the U.S. economy over the last 100 years. A century ago, the average person in America completed only around 8 years of school; today, the average is more than 12 years of school. The average worker today knows more than the average worker at the start of the century and so will be more productive.

Countries with low levels of GDP per capita usually also have low levels of schooling. For example, the average person in Malawi or India has approximately five years of schooling. Helping people to invest in their human capital through better access to schools and job training is a priority for many developing countries.

Note that an individual's, or a nation's, human capital is not always improving—it can also become outdated or deteriorate. People who are unemployed for long periods of time can forget some of the skills that were valuable in the workplace, for instance.

Natural resources *Natural resources* are production inputs that come from the earth—lakes, mineral deposits, forests, and so on. Natural resources can be split into two categories: renewable or nonrenewable.

- *Renewable resources* can be replenished naturally over time. For instance, after cutting down a tree for lumber, you can plant another one to grow in its place. Likewise, when a hydroelectric plant harnesses the power of a river to generate electricity, it doesn't "use up" the river, which continues to flow. Of course, some things take longer to renew than others. The river renews immediately, but the trees take many years to replenish.
- Mineral deposits such as coal, oil, and gold, on the other hand, are *nonrenewable*. When you take them out of the ground and use them, they do not get replenished.

The availability of natural resources can account for some of the differences in economic development around the world. The United States has been blessed with a lot of fertile land, for example. Britain got a big boost from having easily accessible coal to power its manufacturing.

But natural resources aren't everything. Japan and Switzerland are wealthy countries without an abundance of natural resources; Guinea and Kazakhstan are poor countries despite having many natural resources.

Technology The word *technology* may conjure up the image of a sleek new consumer gadget. When we think of how technology contributes to productivity, though, we need to understand the term more broadly. Technology comes in all forms and sizes. It can be big developments such as the invention of the internet or cell phones. It can also be seemingly small advances like a more efficient water pump for irrigating crops or an engine design that allows cars to travel further on the same amount of fuel.

Big or small, technology means that the same inputs will produce more outputs. In other words, countries with better technology will be able to produce more with the same amount of physical and human capital.

It is hard to overstate the importance of technology for understanding economic growth. Technology is fundamentally different from other factors of production, such as land, resources, capital, and labor. Whereas these other factors are in scarce supply and run into diminishing returns, technology can be shared relatively easily, with good ideas leading to even better ideas. Growth economist and Nobel laureate Paul Romer of New York University emphasized that ideas are like recipes: While the ingredients may be scarce, the instructions for combining the ingredients can be shared at low cost. Thus, if one country develops a better way to combine existing resources, that same idea can spread quickly to other countries and lead to faster economic growth worldwide.

One of the most striking examples of the power of technology is the transformation of agriculture in Asia starting in the 1960s. Scientists developed new varieties of seeds for crops like rice and wheat, which produced much higher yields than traditional seeds. These high-yielding seed varieties doubled the amount of food that could be produced on a plot of land. This "Green Revolution" not only erased the prospect of famine but also set the stage for the incredible overall growth that has occurred in Asia over the past five decades. We'll come back to this story later in the chapter.

Rates versus levels

Imagine that you're driving a car and merging onto the highway, pressing the accelerator pedal to the floor. Your speedometer says you are doing 15 mph, then a second later 20 mph, then a second later 25 mph. Your *level* of speed is fairly low, but your *rate of change* is high. Now imagine you are on the highway and cruising at 55 mph. You are at a high *level* of speed, but the speed is constant—your *rate of change* is zero.

LO 10.3 Explain the difference between a country's level of income and its rate of growth.

This analogy is useful for thinking about the differences between wealthy countries and fast-growing countries:

- Switzerland, for example, has high levels of physical and human capital and access to sophisticated technology. Consequently, it has high productivity and standards of living. Its current *rate* of growth is low, but it's starting from a high *level*. It's like the driver cruising along on the highway.
- By contrast, China has lower *levels* of physical and human capital and less widespread access to the latest technologies. As a result, Chinese workers have lower productivity than Swiss workers, and GDP per capita in China is lower than in Switzerland. However, incomes are increasing very rapidly in China. They have not yet achieved the same level as Switzerland, but they are moving quickly in that direction. China is like the car merging onto the highway, not yet going as fast as the cars already on the highway, but with a high *rate of change*. Its level of speed is increasing all the time.

As we discuss policies that can influence future growth, the distinction between the *level of income* and the *rate of increase in income* is crucial. The factors that took a country to its current economic level may or may not be related to those that can lead to future growth. For instance, Kuwait has grown rapidly in the last few decades and enjoys high productivity and incomes. This growth was almost entirely due to its incredible natural endowment of oil. But Kuwait would be foolish to base its future economic growth strategy only on exploiting its oil reserves. The people of Kuwait might hope that there are untapped oil reservoirs hiding somewhere in the desert, but there's nothing they can do to make more oil than already exists.

Similarly, we saw in Chapter 7, "Measuring GDP," that increasing participation of women in the labor market partially explained U.S. growth rates from the 1970s to the 1990s. But clearly, as with Kuwait's oil, it would not be sensible to think you can grow an economy forever by encouraging more and more stay-at-home parents to get jobs or current workers to work longer hours.

The spread of technology is a key driver of economic growth and can speed up rates of convergence. This Bedouin youth talks on a mobile phone as he leads a camel in southern Iraq.
©*Essam Al-Sudani/AFP/ Getty Images*

Sooner or later there will be no stay-at-home parents left, and no more hours in the day for people to work overtime. Such one-time changes in the economy can cause growth spurts that lead to higher income *levels*, but they cannot sustain a higher *rate of change* over time.

In contrast, improvements in technology *can* sustain high rates of change. Sure, when an inventor creates a new gizmo, that invention is a one-time change. If technology stops improving, the economy won't continue to grow. But often, improvements in technology lead to *more* improvements in technology. For example, computing capacity has approximately doubled every two years since the invention of computers, a phenomenon called *Moore's law*. People are constantly finding better and more effective ways to do things, and as a result, their productivity is continuously increasing.

Accounting for growth

Now that we've seen the main ingredients of growth, it's natural to ask which ones are the most important. It turns out that we can separate the growth rate of output per person into the contributions of capital, labor, and technology. When we describe the determinants of output, we often use a *production function*, an equation that captures the relationship between the quantity of inputs and the resulting quantity of outputs.

Here, instead, we want to capture the relationship between the *growth rate* of inputs and the resulting *growth rate* of outputs. Economists call this *growth accounting*. In particular, economists use an equation like this:

LO 10.4 Use the growth accounting framework to describe how technology, labor, and capital contribute to economic growth.

EQUATION 10-4 Growth accounting equation

$$g_Y = g_A + \alpha g_K + (1 - \alpha) g_L$$

where the g's with subscripts denote the percentage change in the variable indicated by the subscript:

$g_Y =$ the growth rate of output

$g_A =$ the growth rate of technology

$g_K =$ the growth rate of capital

$g_L =$ the growth rate of labor

$\alpha =$ the share of GDP that is distributed to the owners of capital

$1 - \alpha =$ the share of output that is distributed to labor

The growth accounting equation tells us that the growth rate of GDP is equal to the growth rate of technology plus the growth rates of capital and labor, weighted by their shares of output. Sometimes, the growth accounting equation will break capital down into separate variables for both human and physical capital.

Growth accounting also offers a way to estimate the role of technology in economic growth. Output, labor, and capital are relatively straightforward to define and measure. In contrast, technology is hard to measure. It can take the form of new innovations in information technology, better management practices, or simply reduced government distortions. Measuring technology directly would therefore be close to impossible.

Growth accounting, however, provides an *indirect* route to measuring technology. Since we can directly measure the growth of output, labor, and capital, and we also have a rough idea how large the capital and labor shares are, we can simply compute the growth of technology as a *residual* in the equation above. Indeed, this residual is exactly what macroeconomists have in mind when they talk about technology—it's the unexplained part of economic growth!

As an example of how growth accounting works in practice, let's consider China's growth experience from 1978 to 2004, an era that generated the highest sustained period of growth on record. China's GDP grew at an average annual rate of 9.3 percent; employment grew at around 2 percent; capital grew at about 10 percent.[4] The capital share of output in China was about 40 percent during this period, while the labor share was around 60 percent. Substituting these values into our growth accounting equation (Equation 10-4), we can solve for the implied growth rate of technology:

$$0.093 = g_A + (0.4 \times 0.10) + (0.6 \times 0.02)$$
$$g_A = 0.093 - (0.4 \times 0.10) - (0.6 \times 0.02) = 0.041$$

Thus, even though China experienced a rapid increase in its physical capital stock over the 30 years since the beginning of the reform era, 44 percent of the total growth in GDP came from "technology" (since 0.041/0.093 = 0.44). The quotes around "technology" are there to remind you that technology includes all changes that lead the economy to use inputs more efficiently; this includes the effects of reduced government distortions, for example, as well as new management practices and modernized factories.

Advancements in technology can be fantastic, but they can also be fickle. The "Green Revolution," which introduced new agricultural technologies, was a rousing success in Asia but has been more complicated in Africa. The Economics in Action box "Feeding the world" provides details of this story.

Feeding the world
Economics in Action

In 1961, India was at risk of famine. The population was booming, and no more farmland was available. How would everyone be fed? Incredibly, by 1985 the specter of famine had all but disappeared, not only in India but across Asia. In just 25 years, crop yields had doubled, easily outpacing the growth of the population.

This transformation in agriculture, called the *Green Revolution*, was the result of research and development funded by private charities such as the Rockefeller Foundation. It resulted in new crop varieties, such as so-called "miracle rice," developed in 1968 by the International Rice Research Institute in the Philippines. "Miracle rice" required more

New crop varieties, such as "miracle rice" developed in 1968, resulted from research and development funded by private charities.
©Dick Swanson/The LIFE Images Collection/Getty Images

(continued)

intensive fertilizer and irrigation treatments than traditional varieties but produced about double the amount of rice per plant.

Many economists believe that the Green Revolution partly explains why Asia's economies have grown quickly in the last half century: When you don't need as many workers to grow food, they can do something else instead, such as work in factories in the city.

Today, economists and agricultural experts are working to create a green revolution in Africa. It has proved to be a daunting challenge. Unlike Asia, many places in Africa do not have strong government institutions to support agriculture. Nor do they have distribution networks for getting seeds and other inputs to farmers or transportation systems to move food to markets. The result? Many African farmers today still farm as their grandparents did, and as farmers in Asia did 50 years ago, with little fertilizer and limited tools.

There are some positive notes. Economists Esther Duflo and Micheal Kramer have found that offering farmers fertilizer at harvest time increases the amount they are able to purchase and use during the next growing season, increasing yields. The Drought Tolerance Maize for Africa project, which ended in 2015, helped 5.4 million households earn 20–30 percent higher yields when rains failed.

This new work may not be as immediate or dramatic as the Asian Green Revolution, but it may lead to innovations that put ample food in every bowl—and help Africa along the path to greater prosperity.

Convergence

LO 10.5 Assess the empirical evidence for and against convergence theory.

Are poor countries doomed to stay poor, like cars poking along forever at 10 or 20 mph? Or does the fact that a country now is poor just mean that we are seeing it early in the development process, like a car moving slowly but accelerating toward highway speed? Will China and other low-income but fast-growing countries eventually reach a similar level of wealth to the United States and Switzerland? If they do, will they keep accelerating forever, or will they eventually see their rates of growth slow and settle in on the highway alongside the world's rich countries?

One classic model of economic growth suggests the "settling in" story is the correct one. This model relates to the idea of *decreasing marginal returns* to factors of production: Countries that start with very little physical capital will get a higher return from adding a unit of capital than will a country that starts at a higher initial level. This leads to the general hypothesis that countries starting at low levels of income (which correspond to low levels of capital) will tend to grow at much faster rates than those starting with high levels of income. Each additional unit of capital provides larger gains when you're coming from behind.

This idea is called **convergence theory** (or the *catch-up effect*). It says that poor countries will grow faster than rich ones, until they catch up and all countries "converge" to the same growth rate. The theory predicts that even if countries differ in their rates of savings, population growth, and other features, they will still converge to the same *growth rate*, although not the same *level of income*. In other words, countries that start out poor should initially grow faster than ones that start out rich but will eventually slow to the same growth rate.

convergence theory the theory that countries that start out poor will initially grow faster than rich ones but will eventually converge to the same growth rate

In some ways, convergence theory fits the evidence from the real world. Figure 10-3 shows the differences between growth rates in different regions of the world from 1980 to 2018. Looking at the map, you'll see that:

- Richer countries have mostly been growing slowly.
- Though uneven, countries in developing regions of Asia and after 2000, countries in sub-Saharan Africa have grown quickly.

Many economists think convergence theory explains the incredible growth of the East Asian countries. Those countries experienced very high marginal returns as they began to accumulate

FIGURE 10-3

Regional growth rates, 1980–2018 The graph shows that while developed countries averaged growth rates of about 2 percent, developing countries in Asia grew much faster. Starting in about 2000, countries in sub-Saharan Africa also grew at a high rate.

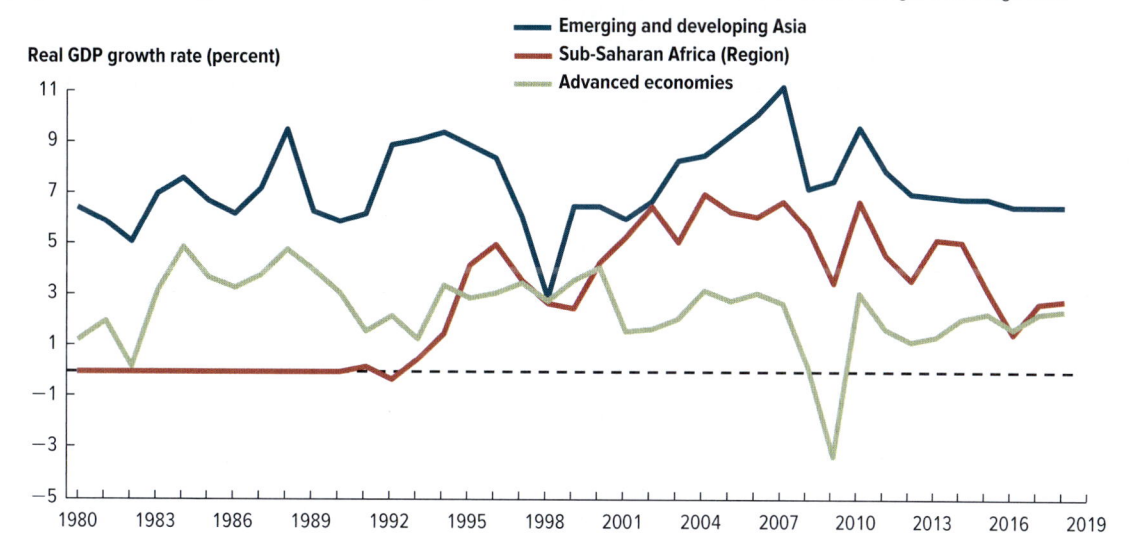

Source: IMF *World Economic Outook*, October 2018, www.imf.org/external/datamapper/NGDP_RPCH@WEO/OEMDC/ADVEC/WEOWORLD.

physical and human capital. They also were well positioned to take advantage of technologies and capital flows from wealthier countries.

In other places, however, convergence is uneven. Most African countries started at levels of physical and human capital as low as East Asia's half a century ago, but they did not experience the same sustained growth spurt. In fact, some actually became poorer during the 1980s and early 1990s. Since then, however, convergence is looking better. Between 2000 and 2018, countries in sub-Saharan Africa averaged a real GDP growth rate of nearly 5 percent and per income doubled.

While convergence has lifted millions out of poverty, the gains have occurred unevenly. In 1980, the richest 1 percent held 16 percent of the world's income. By 2016, that figure had increased to about 20 percent. Over the same time, the poorest 50 percent held about 9 percent of the world's income. This shift in the income distribution shows a slight increase in global inequality.

Even though per capita incomes around the world have increased, some countries are converging faster than others, while some countries stagnate. To understand why, we need to consider how public policy affects economic growth.

✓ TEST YOURSELF

- ☐ What are the main determinants of productivity? **[LO 10.2]**
- ☐ How are rates different from levels when talking about economic growth? **[LO 10.3]**
- ☐ How do economists measure the impact of technology on economic growth? **[LO 10.4]**
- ☐ What does convergence theory predict about growth rates? About income levels? **[LO 10.5]**

Growth and Public Policy

Billions of people around the world still live in conditions that are unimaginable to those living in wealthy countries. Recent history has shown that a few decades of strong economic growth like that experienced by South Korea could transform their lives. What can be done to spark and sustain that growth? Unfortunately, no one has a simple answer to this question.

Investment and savings

LO 10.6 Discuss policies that could promote growth, and relate them to productivity.

If physical capital increases productivity, why don't countries simply put as much money as possible into infrastructure, machinery, and other capital investments? In some cases, this is precisely what they do. However, there is an opportunity cost involved. For a country to acquire more physical capital, someone has to pay for it, which means that there is less money to spend on consumption. This problem is called the **investment trade-off**—a reduction in current consumption to pay for the investment in capital intended to increase future production (and, ultimately, future consumption). Savings that pay for capital investment can come either from within a country or from outside it.

investment trade-off a reduction in current consumption to pay for investment in capital intended to increase future production

domestic savings savings for capital investment that come from within a country; equal to domestic income minus consumption spending

Investment funds from within a country   Savings that come from within a country are called **domestic savings** and are equal to domestic income minus consumption spending. They can come from three sources:

- private households earning more than they spend,
- corporations earning profit beyond what they give to shareholders as dividends, and
- governments generating surpluses (that is, government revenues exceed government spending).

Savings rates vary enormously across countries, as Figure 10-4 shows. On one end of the spectrum, we have China, where the economy typically puts away a whopping 47.3 percent of GDP. In contrast, the United States saves just 16.8 percent, and households contribute a small share of that saving. In 2017, the U.S. household savings rate was just above 6 percent.[5]

FIGURE 10-4

Gross savings rates among countries in 2017   Savings rates vary a lot around the world. For example, China saves a whopping 47 percent of GDP, India saves almost 31 percent, and the United States saves nearly 17 percent. Gross savings are calculated as national income less total consumption plus net transfers.

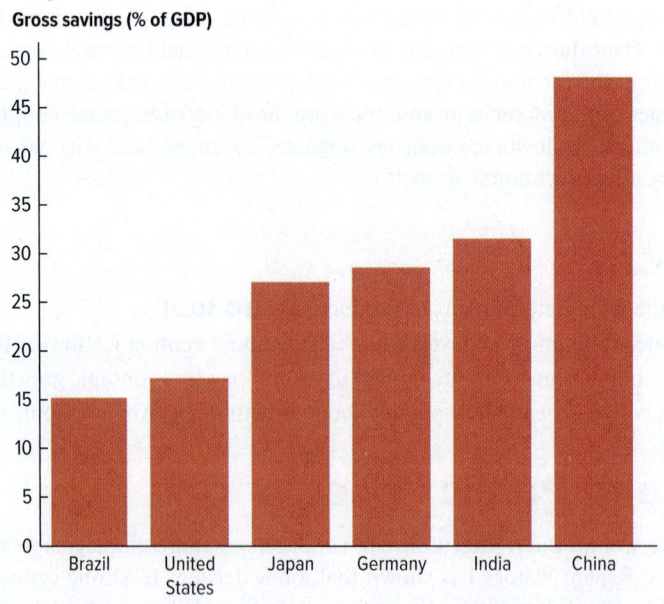

Gross savings (% of GDP)

Country	Gross savings (% of GDP)
Brazil	15
United States	17
Japan	27
Germany	28.5
India	31.5
China	48

Source: www.ceicdata.com/en/indicator/united-states/gross-savings-rate; www.ceicdata.com/en/indicator/japan/gross-savings-rate; and https://data.worldbank.org/indicator/ny.gns.ictr.zs.

Investment funds from outside a country Funds for capital investment can also come from outside a country. **Foreign direct investment (FDI)** is investment that occurs when a firm runs part of its operation abroad or invests in another company abroad. For example, when Toyota operates a plant in the U.S. state of Georgia, the Japanese firm owns the machinery and buildings, even though the production takes place in the United States. Similarly, factories owned by U.S. firms on the Mexican side of the United States–Mexico border are an important source of FDI in Mexico.

Many governments actively work to attract FDI, hoping it will build up their capital stock when domestic savings aren't sufficient. Another benefit of FDI is that when foreign companies invest in local firms, they can transfer human capital to local managers and workers. Perhaps managers from the foreign country travel to oversee the investment. In doing so, they can train local staff or set up more efficient procedures. In fact, the Chinese government will require foreign firms to transfer technology to local partners as part of the price of doing business in the country.

However, FDI has its critics. Foreign firms with money to invest often have numerous governments competing to attract the investment. The firm can drive a hard bargain, demanding special tax breaks or legal exemptions that governments cannot easily afford. If foreign managers oversee operations without training up local talent, the transfer of knowledge or technology may not happen to the extent some in the local country would wish. As a result, some argue that a policy of attracting FDI might not ultimately be as beneficial as it first appears.

foreign direct investment (FDI) investment that occurs when a firm runs part of its operation abroad or owns all or part of another company abroad

Public policy

Government policy can shape economic growth in many ways. As we've discussed, one way is to promote saving and investment by households and businesses. Likewise, government spending can directly contribute to current public consumption, transfer payments, and investments in infrastructure.

Governments also fund education and health, invest in infrastructure and industrial policy, and encourage development of technology. And they play an essential role by making and enforcing laws, maintaining property rights, and fostering economic openness.

LO 10.7 Explain how government policy and economic openness lay the foundation for growth.

Education and health In rich countries, we take free basic education for granted. In many countries, however, schools may be few and far between, charge unaffordable fees to students, or simply provide very low-quality education. One of the major efforts of the Sustainable Development Goals—a collection of targets set by the United Nations to tackle aspects of poverty in low-income countries by 2030—has been to push countries to provide free elementary school education.

Free availability of high-quality public education for all children is one of the most important ways a country can increase its stock of human capital. Education teaches skills such as literacy, basic math, and communication—all essential to perform more than the most elementary jobs. High-quality education also builds the pool of scientists, thinkers, and entrepreneurs who develop new technologies and business models.

Using public policy to promote health can also contribute to growth. Workers who are in good health will be more productive and less likely to miss work days. Some economic benefits of improved health are less visible, especially in low-income countries. For instance, health economists have found that reducing vitamin and mineral deficiencies such as anemia (the result of a diet with not enough iron in it) and parasites such as worms can improve people's mental and physical energy. Treatment for such health problems increases the ability to focus, making it easier for children to learn in school and for adults to do their best at work.

It's hard to accumulate greater levels of human capital when health problems and lack of educational opportunities combine. Most of us would agree that we are more productive when we're working with other highly educated workers. In some places, like California's Silicon Valley, this creates a positive feedback loop in productivity: Talented computer programmers and business managers can multiply their productivity by working with other talented programmers and managers.

In low-income countries, however, this cycle can work in the opposite direction: The productivity of skilled workers can diminish due to the lower average levels of skill of their co-workers. Public policy can help to push a country out of this negative cycle by improving public health services and the quality of education.

Infrastructure and industrial policy Infrastructure is a critical component of the growth equation. Governments often fund the underlying infrastructure that private companies rely on for their operations, such as roads, bridges, ports, and sewer systems. This infrastructure can have a major effect on growth. In many low-income countries, for example, even if farmers could grow more, poor roads make it hard to get their goods to market. Also, many governments are currently investing heavily in communications infrastructure such as high-speed internet, in the expectation that it will improve private companies' productivity.

Governments can also focus resources on industries they believe can contribute the most to national growth. Some people attribute the rapid growth of the East Asian economies in the 1980s and 1990s to the success of their "industrial policies." Through these policies, governments picked industries to support with investments and favorable tax and trade policies. The idea that governments can effectively plan growth by "picking winners" is controversial, though. Consider the arguments on either side in the Economics in Action box "Planning for growth."

Planning for growth
Economics in Action

"We are fifty or a hundred years behind the advanced countries. We must make good this distance in ten years. Either we do it, or they will crush us." These words were delivered by Joseph Stalin, leader of the Soviet Union, in 1931.

Russia's new Communist leaders had inherited a country whose economy was far behind its neighbors to the west. They wanted economic growth in a hurry. Rather than relying on the invisible hand of the market to guide the economy, Russia created a five-year plan that called for the government to directly determine inputs and outputs in state-run factories and farms.

The plan was ambitious, centering on the goal of an increase in overall industrial production of 250 percent. Unsurprisingly, the goals were not met. Still, the early results were impressive: production of many industrial goods doubled, and electrical production nearly tripled. These successes inspired similar economic planning around the world. Communist countries from Cuba to Hungary developed their own five-year plans.

Some market-oriented economies also created plans. They turned to industrial policy, investing public funds in industries the government considered strategically important. But most planning did not go well. One reason is that politicians worried about getting re-elected, so they ended up focusing on short-term gain rather than long-term strategy. As a result, they propped up old industries to save existing jobs rather than helping young industries create new jobs. Another problem was that it was simply hard to predict which industries had the capacity to grow.

By the 1980s, industrial policy had fallen out of fashion in most Western economies. Planning in the Soviet Union was judged an economic failure too. When the Soviet Union collapsed in 1989, Russia's per capita income was just $9,200, compared with $21,000 in the United States.

In East Asia, however, industrial policy was more successful. The so-called "Asian Tigers" relied heavily on the market but also promoted some sectors directly with subsidies and planning. China's rapid economic growth was credited to a mix of markets and planning. After decades of recommending against industrial policy, the World Bank took a fresh look at industrial policy and argued that—in the right contexts and with the right incentives—it could be worth considering.

Sources: www.umsl.edu/services/govdocs/wofact90/world12.txt; http://planningcommissionarchive.nic.in; www.economist.com/node/16741043; J. Stalin, "The Tasks of Economic Executives," speech delivered at the First All-Union Conference of Leading Personnel of Socialist Industry, February 4, 1931, from J. V. Stalin, *Problems of Leninism* (Peking: Foreign Languages Press, 1976), pp. 519-31; Joseph E. Stiglitz, Justin Yifu, and Celestin Monga, 2013, *The Rejuvenation of Industrial Policy* (English), Policy Research working paper, no. WPS 6628, Washington, DC: World Bank, http://documents.worldbank.org/curated/en/350481468331907193/The-rejuvenation-of-industrial-policy.

Technological development A lot of research and development takes place at private institutions—in firms, private laboratories, and so on. However, public policy can also encourage technological development—through the educational system, funding for research and study, and tax structures that encourage firms to develop and adopt new technologies. In the United States, under 3 percent of GDP is spent on research and development. Less than a third of that amount is spent by the federal government to support universities and research institutes. Most research and development spending is done by business.[6]

You might be wondering why the government should be involved in research and development in areas other than military spending and public works. Recall that technology is fundamentally about ideas, which once created can be adopted at low cost by others. This means that there is a *positive externality* associated with innovation: Part of the benefit associated with a firm's investment in new ideas goes to competing firms. As a result, there is a "free-rider" problem associated with innovation.

The economy as a whole would be better off with more innovation. But firms underproduce innovation because they care only about the direct benefits of innovation for their own bottom line. They do not care about the indirect benefits to other firms in the economy. The tendency to underproduce innovation creates a reason for the government to keep supporting research and development.

Laying the groundwork: Good government, property rights, and economic openness Imagine that you live in a country where, if someone steals your truck, there is nothing you can do about it. The police won't help you, unless you bribe them. Even if you could get police help, it might take five years and a lot of money to prosecute someone in court. Would you still buy a truck? You might, if you thought that the potential benefits were high enough to outweigh the risk of losing your investment. But you'd certainly be less inclined to invest in trucks and other expensive capital goods than you would if you thought that your property would be protected.

This is just one example of the ways in which enforceable laws and effective, trustworthy government services are critical to a well-functioning economy. Most countries have mechanisms to punish those who violate the property rights of others and to enforce contracts between buyers and sellers. Institutions like police forces, courts of law, and government bureaucracies are meant to protect property, settle disputes, and provide a predictable legal framework in which people can make plans and agreements. However, these institutions are more effective and reliable in some countries than in others.

Stability in leadership and institutions is important, as is effectiveness. Would you want to build an expensive new factory if you thought there was a good chance of new leaders coming to power who might seize it? Would you risk investing in a business if the tax policies or laws that determine its profitability change from month to month?

Many economists believe that good government has a major impact on economic growth. The degree of government effectiveness can help us understand why some economies have grown rapidly and others have stagnated. How to improve government is a tricky question, though. It is challenging to design effective policies to tackle corruption, make courts more efficient, limit the powers of politicians, and so on.

Government policy also determines how open a country will be to trade. Firms often argue that governments need to protect them from competition by placing tariffs on foreign goods. However, the "Asian miracle" countries succeeded by combining industrial policy with "outward-oriented" policies to gear their economies toward exporting goods. Later in the text, we'll discuss free trade and why most economists believe that there are important gains to keeping economies open.

The juggling act

As with many things in life, there are *trade-offs* between different ways of promoting growth through public policy. Most governments—especially those in poor countries—can't pay for education *and* health *and* highways *and* better police all at the same time. Unfortunately, this is a vicious cycle: The richer you are, the better able you are to pay for things that will help you be even richer in the future. The poorer you are, the less able you are to pay for the things that can make you richer.

Earlier in the chapter, we noted the trade-off between current consumption and investment in physical capital, human capital, and research that will contribute to growth and to higher future income. The poorer the country, the tougher this trade-off becomes. It's harder for people who live close to the edge on a dollar or two a day to save a given amount of money or pay more taxes than it would be for wealthier people. This logic leads to the vicious cycle described above. If you can't afford to pay for a good court system or to invest in a tractor or a computer, you will find it harder to climb out of poverty. This "poverty trap" is one of the main justifications for foreign aid that provides loans or funding for infrastructure and human capital development.

Why don't countries take one element at a time—for example, focusing limited resources first on infrastructure, and then on education or health, and so on? Unfortunately, it's not usually that simple. Growth often requires concurrent improvements in many aspects of the economy. For instance, translating new technology into growth often requires a population with sufficient human capital to take advantage of it, and sometimes specific infrastructure.

Imagine a country trying to build an internet-based economy. This would be difficult, if not impossible, if much of the population can't read, or if the electrical grid experiences regular blackouts due to insufficient power generation. Harnessing the power of the internet to promote commerce, and thus growth, would require simultaneous improvements in literacy, computer skills, the power grid, a trustworthy postal service, and payment mechanisms.

Another trade-off that governments face is how much to sacrifice their natural environment in pursuit of economic growth. The What Do You Think? box "Is it okay to pollute one's way to progress?" explores this particular trade-off.

Is it okay to pollute one's way to progress?
What Do You Think?

During the European Industrial Revolution, factories spewed pollution into the atmosphere as they rolled out a steady stream of textiles, steel, and other goods. Power plants fueled by dirty coal dotted cities throughout Western Europe and eventually the United States. Miners and factory workers alike often died of lung diseases and other health problems associated with dirty air and unsafe working conditions. After many years of unchecked pollution, conditions got so bad that London suffered from chronic smog that would settle over the city for days, blotting out the sun. In 1952, one particularly severe smog episode killed over 4,000 people. In retrospect, the environmental and health consequences of Europe's industrialization seem awful. At the time, though, they were simply part and parcel of a massive increase in wealth and economic power.

In the past 50 years, technologies have been developed that allow firms to produce goods and energy with far less pollution. Low-income countries today don't necessarily have to go through the same painful arc that marked earlier industrial transformations. Despite this, China's economic explosion has been accompanied by smog and the release of toxic chemicals into rivers. Occasionally, actual explosions at factories have killed thousands of people and filled the atmosphere with pollutants. Why haven't firms in China chosen to use the new, cleaner technology now available?

There are two reasons:

- Acquiring clean technologies is not always straightforward, due to stringent trade policies or intellectual property laws.
- Even when these technologies are accessible, they may be very expensive.

The reason factories and power plants in Europe and the United States are now relatively clean is not because the new technologies are always cheaper than the older, dirtier methods. Rather, it's often because governments in those countries have introduced strict regulations requiring firms to mitigate their environmental impact and protect the health and safety of their workers and neighbors.

The questions for China and other low-income countries are:

- Is it better to introduce strict environmental laws, forcing companies to use expensive clean technology?
- Or is it better to grow our economy as quickly as possible by using cheaper ways of doing things, even if they are environmentally damaging?

Production in low-income countries is releasing vast amounts of greenhouse gases, which affect other countries, too. For example, even though China's economy is barely a third the size of the U.S. economy, China emits more carbon than the U.S. and European Union *combined*. The negative effects, through climate change, are felt across the whole world. Many people feel that fast-growing countries such as India and China should have to protect the environment by using the cleaner technologies now available.

Low-income countries, on the other hand, counter that being forced to use the cleaner technologies would make their goods more expensive and less competitive in the world market. They argue that developed countries created the problem of climate change by releasing greenhouse gases during their own industrial revolutions. It's not fair, they say, to expect poorer countries to pay the penance. It's also not clear what the more "humane" policy is: We've seen that economic growth can decrease poverty and alleviate suffering, and stricter regulations likely mean slower growth and slower poverty reduction.

To help solve this impasse, the United Nations launched a "Green Climate Fund" to distribute money to low-income countries, partly to help them acquire and pay for cleaner technologies. The fund may help countries avoid some of the pollution associated with economic growth, but probably won't solve the whole problem.

WHAT DO YOU THINK?

1. Should all countries be held to the same environmental standards?
2. Do rich countries have a responsibility to help poorer countries acquire cleaner technologies?
3. Is it worth implementing cleaner technologies if it means slower economic growth?

Sources: www.reuters.com/article/2011/04/15/us-climate-fund-idUSTRE73E3WG20110415; www.cnbc.com/id/43139649; http://news.bbc.co.uk/2/hi/uk_news/england/2545759.stm; www.nytimes.com/2010/07/29/world/asia/29china.html; http://www.law.duke.edu/journals/dltr/articles/2009dltr001.html.

✓ TEST YOURSELF

- ☐ What determinant of economic growth is influenced by domestic saving? [**LO 10.6**]
- ☐ Why do police protection and efficient courts matter for economic growth? [**LO 10.7**]

Conclusion

Economic growth can make the rich richer. It also is a powerful way to make the poor richer too. In this chapter, we looked at how we define and measure economic growth and why growth is so important. Because of compounding, even a small increase in the growth rate will have a large impact on the level of income in the long run. A country that is growing at 3.5 percent, instead of 2 percent, will end up approximately four times richer after 100 years.

In order to grow, a country needs to be able to put together the ingredients:

- savings that can be invested into physical capital,
- healthy and skilled workers,
- appropriate technology, and
- supportive public policies and institutions.

All governments face tough trade-offs: How much should the country invest in health, education, and infrastructure? How can the government create a secure legal environment for people to invest? The goal is a positive cycle in which people gain human capital, invent better technology, become more productive at their jobs, get richer and be able to afford more physical capital, and so on.

This process is not easy, but it is important. If policy-makers, businesses, and workers come together effectively to build the right environment for investment, their contributions can deliver a foundation for the prosperity of future generations.

Key Terms

productivity, p. 255
physical capital, p. 255
human capital, p. 256
convergence theory, p. 260
investment trade-off, p. 262
domestic savings, p. 262
foreign direct investment (FDI), p. 263

Summary

LO 10.1 Calculate the growth rate of real GDP per capita, accounting for changes in price levels and population.

The fact that growth compounds over time makes it hard to tell just from looking at the annual growth rate what the total effect on incomes will be. GDP growth rates are often stated without taking population growth into account and sometimes without taking inflation into account. To find the rate of real GDP growth, take the nominal growth rate and subtract both population growth and inflation growth rates.

National economic growth builds on itself over time. The result is that a relatively modest annual growth rate, like 2 percent, actually adds up to quite a large total growth rate over time. The rate at which GDP increases incomes can be found through the *rule of 70:* To find how long it takes incomes to double within a country, divide 70 by the rate of real GDP growth.

LO 10.2 Describe the relationship between productivity and growth, and discuss the factors that determine productivity.

The only way that a country can consume more and enjoy a higher standard of living is to increase its *productivity*—the amount it produces per worker. Productivity can be measured for any unit of labor, whether that unit is an hour of time worked or how much one worker produces; it is typically measured as output per person. The factors that influence labor productivity are physical capital, human capital, technology, and natural resources.

LO 10.3 Explain the difference between a country's level of income and its rate of growth.

There are two important distinctions to make in terms of economic development. One is about the *level* of well-being. Countries like the United States or Switzerland that have very high amounts of physical and human capital are said to be at a high level of development. The other distinction is about the *rate* of economic growth. While the United States may have a high level of development, the rate of growth in U.S. GDP is not nearly as fast as China's. Level matters because it tells how wealthy a country currently is. Rates matter because they tell how quickly a country is increasing its wealth.

LO 10.4 Use the growth accounting framework to describe how technology, labor, and capital contribute to economic growth.

The growth accounting framework is a way to explain the growth rate of GDP as the sum of the growth rate of technology plus the growth rates of capital and labor, weighted by their shares of output. The framework helps us see how much of growth is due to using more inputs (capital and labor) versus using existing inputs more efficiently (via technology).

While labor and capital are relatively straightforward to measure, it's much harder to measure technology. Fortunately, the framework gives a way to estimate the importance of technology in economic growth by calculating it indirectly as a residual. The evidence shows that technology (defined broadly) is often extremely important in explaining growth.

LO 10.5 Assess the empirical evidence for and against convergence theory.

Convergence theory predicts that countries that are starting at lower levels of income will grow at a faster rate than those starting at higher levels, until they catch up and converge to the same growth rate.

In some ways, convergence theory fits evidence from the real world. The four East Asian countries that experienced incredible growth since the 1960s started from low levels of physical and human capital but were well positioned to take advantage of technologies and capital flows from wealthier countries. However, most African countries had similar or even lower levels of physical and human capital than did East Asia half a century ago but have not experienced high growth rates.

LO 10.6 Discuss policies that could promote growth, and relate them to productivity.

Countries face an investment trade-off, in which they must reduce current consumption to pay for the capital investment needed to increase future production. Funds to pay for capital investment can come either from domestic savings or from foreign direct investment (FDI) from outside the country.

LO 10.7 Explain how government policy and economic openness lay the foundation for growth.

A variety of policies can promote economic growth. Education teaches skills such as literacy, basic math, and communication, which are essential to perform more than the most elementary jobs. Public health systems can also contribute to growth by increasing the portion of the population that is fit, healthy, and able to work.

Public policy can also encourage technological development through the education system, funding for research and study, and tax structures that encourage firms to develop and adopt new technologies. Education is also a way to develop the training and skills that countries need to be able to undertake technological research and development.

Governments also often invest in underlying infrastructure, such as transportation systems and high-speed internet. This infrastructure can have a major effect on growth. Governments can also focus resources on industries they believe can contribute the most to national growth.

Finally, enforceable laws and effective, trustworthy government services are critical to a well-functioning economy. The most important is the provision of property rights, giving people the ability to have control over the resources they own. Most countries have institutions and infrastructure designed to protect property rights. Courts enforce the contracts between buyers and sellers. They also are responsible, through the criminal justice system, for punishing people who are accused of violating the property rights of others.

Review Questions

1. Explain why inflation reduces the real value of nominal GDP per capita. **[LO 10.1]**

2. When policy-makers discuss policies that encourage long-run growth in per capita real GDP, they often mention policies aimed at reducing the growth rate in the population. If effective, why might these policies improve long-run growth? Also, what are the potential costs associated with these policies? **[LO 10.1]**

3. Does the rule of 70 predict greater increases in the amount of income for richer or poorer countries when both have the same growth rate? Why? **[LO 10.1, LO 10.3]**

4. Explain why many rich countries are able to continuously grow, even though they already have very high levels of physical and human capital. [LO 10.2]

5. At a young age, would you rather have a large level of savings or a pool of savings that was increasing at a faster rate? [LO 10.3]

6. If a country's labor and capital grow at the same rate, is this likely to have the same impact on the growth rate of output? Why or why not? [LO 10.4]

7. Measuring the growth in technology directly is almost impossible. How does the growth accounting equation allow economists to calculate an implied growth rate for technology? [LO 10.4]

8. Using the growth rates for countries found in Figure 10-3, is there evidence that poorer countries in Africa and Asia are converging to the level of income found in Western Europe? Why or why not? [LO 10.5]

9. Southern states in the United States are, on average, poorer than northern states. Southern states also have higher growth rates in real GDP per capita, on average, than northern states. Use these facts to draw a conclusion about whether the theory of convergence is correct. What other factors should be considered? [LO 10.5]

10. Many believe that technology is very costly to create but cheap to transfer. For example, think of the personal computer: The technology underpinning the personal computer took a generation of time and a ton of money to create. However, now that the personal computer has been created, it is easy for others to purchase and reap the benefits. Given this insight, what do you believe will be the growth implications for the United States (traditionally more apt to create new technology) and China (traditionally more apt to adopt technologies created elsewhere)? [LO 10.5, LO 10.7]

11. How might low rates of saving in the United States limit the accumulation of physical capital? [LO 10.6]

12. Realizing that poor countries must solve many problems at once has shifted donors away from the idea of giving multiple small payments to the idea of a "Big Push." This Big Push entails giving a very large sum of money that could be used to fix multiple problems at once. In fact, the amount of money required might be so large that other countries might be the only ones who could afford the donation. What are the trade-offs associated with this idea? [LO 10.6]

13. How is it possible that Switzerland, a landlocked country with almost no natural resources, is one of the richest countries in the world while the Democratic Republic of the Congo, a huge country with vast deposits of many strategically important minerals, is one of the poorest? [LO 10.2, LO 10.6, LO 10.7]

14. Why could a free press be important for economic growth? (Think about the connection between the press and government.) [LO 10.7]

Problems and Applications

1. Fill in the blanks in Table 10P-1. [LO 10.1]

2. Equation 10-1 states that Real GDP per capita growth rate = Nominal GDP per capita growth rate − Inflation rate − Population growth rate.

    This equation is an approximation of the exact rate of growth of GDP per capita, and so it results in some errors when calculating this rate. However, the simplified equation both is easy to use and results in small error terms when inflation, nominal GDP growth, and population growth are low, and so it is a useful approximation. Table 10P-2 lists a fictional country's nominal GDP, real GDP, GDP deflator, and population over two years. [LO 10.1]

    a. Use your knowledge from Chapter 8, "The Cost of Living," to verify that the real GDP figures in Table 10P-2 are accurate.

TABLE 10P-1

Country	Nominal GDP growth (%)	Population growth (%)	Inflation (%)	Real GDP growth per capita (%)
Svea	4	3		−1
Bonifay	3	1	0	
Chaires		2	6	4
Drifton	5	1	−2	
Estiffanulga	7		2	4

TABLE 10P-2

Year	Nominal GDP ($)	GDP deflator	Real GDP ($)	Population
2017	1,000,000	1.00	1,000,000	1,000
2018	1,050,000	1.03	1,019,417	1,005

    b. Calculate this country's real GDP per capita for both 2017 and 2018.

    c. Calculate the growth rate in this country's real GDP per capita between 2017 and 2018.

    d. Calculate the growth rates in the nominal GDP, GDP deflator, and the population.

3. For each growth rate below, use the rule of 70 to calculate how long it will take incomes to double. **[LO 10.2]**

    a. 4 percent.

    b. 7 percent.

    c. 2.5 percent.

    d. 10 percent.

    e. 3 percent.

4. For each part below, determine whether the following actions will increase or decrease productivity, and name the component of productivity that each affects. **[LO 10.2]**

    a. The local government builds a new school.

    b. Teachers in the new school hold classes for young students.

    c. A manufacturer installs robots on its assembly line.

    d. A research team designs a more efficient system of irrigation.

    e. A soda company discovers a new source of underground water that can be used to make its products.

    f. A professor writes a new and improved economics text.

    g. A large number of people have less access to health care.

    h. A worker receives on-the-job training to be a mechanic.

5. Which of the countries shown in Table 10P-3 had the highest level of per capita income in 2018? Which had the highest rate of income growth from 2013 to 2018? Do incomes in these countries appear to be converging? **[LO 10.3, LO 10.5]**

TABLE 10P-3

Country	GDP per capita 2013 ($)	GDP per capita 2018 ($)
Boliv	3,664	4,592
Chi	4,102	7,519
Ghala	2,007	2,615
Artinia	10,860	15,854
Plazi	8,603	11,239

6. In 2017 the median household income in Louisiana was approximately $43,903 per year, while the income per household in Massachusetts was about $74,167. However, suppose the growth rate of per capita real GDP in Louisiana is higher than in Massachusetts (3 percent versus 2 percent). **[LO 10.3, LO 10.5]**

    a. From the perspective of trying to maximize your income per capita, which state will have higher increases in income over the next few years?

    b. From the perspective of trying to maximize your income per capita, which state will have higher increases in income in the long run?

7. Will the three countries in Table 10P-4 converge to the same level of economic development given enough time? **[LO 10.3, LO 10.5]**

TABLE 10P-4

Country	Income per capita ($)	Real per capita GDP growth rate (%)
Ansonia	5,000	7.0
Trumbull	7,500	4.5
Shelton	10,000	2.0

8. Indicate whether each of the following statements is true or false and explain your answer. **[LO 10.4]**

    a. Country A's labor share is 60 percent, Country B's labor share is 70 percent, and labor is growing at a rate of 3 percent in both countries. All else the same, Country B has a higher growth rate of output.

    b. Country A's labor share is 40 percent, Country B's labor share is 70 percent, and labor is

TABLE 10P-5

Scenario	Growth rate of output (%)	Growth rate of labor (%)	Growth rate of capital (%)	Implied growth rate of technology (%)
A	3.0	2	2	
B	4.2	3	3	
C	3.0	1	5	
D	4.2	1	4	

growing at a rate of 10 percent in country A and 6 percent in country B. All else is the same, Country A has a higher growth rate of output.

c. Labor is growing at a negative rate in country A and a positive rate in country B, so country B must have a higher growth rate of output.

d. Labor and capital are both growing more quickly in Country A than in Country B, so Country A must have a higher growth rate of output.

9. Calculate the implied growth rate of technology in each scenario in Table 10P-5. Assume labor's share of output is 60 percent and capital's share of output is 40 percent. **[LO 10.4]**

10. For each of the following examples, state whether this activity would likely hinder or promote economic growth, and name a component of productivity each produces or reduces. **[LO 10.2, LO 10.7]**

    a. Not requiring students to attend school.
    b. Granting patents on new inventions.
    c. Building a solid infrastructure system.
    d. Allowing local rivers and streams to become polluted.

11. Policy-makers in the U.S. government have long tried to write laws that encourage growth in per capita real GDP. These laws typically do one of three things, as listed below. For each of the three points, name a law or government program with that intention. **[LO 10.7]**

    a. They encourage firms to invest more in research and development in order to boost technology.
    b. They encourage individuals to save more in order to boost the physical capital stock.
    c. They encourage individuals to invest more in education in order to boost the stock of human capital.

12. Name the type of institution that is responsible for promoting a stable environment for the economy regarding each of the following situations. **[LO 10.7]**

    a. Someone steals your car, but is caught.
    b. You claim that your employer violated the terms of your employment contract.

Endnotes

1. Calculated using the series at http://data.worldbank.org/indicator/NY.GDP.PCAP.CD.
2. https://fred.stlouisfed.org/series/A939RX0Q048SBEA. The income data in the example are in constant 2012 dollars to adjust for inflation, seasonally adjusted.
3. https://fred.stlouisfed.org/series/A939RX0Q048SBEA. The income data in the example are in constant 2012 dollars to adjust for inflation, seasonally adjusted.
4. Barry Bosworth and Susan M. Collins, "Accounting for Growth: Comparing China and India," *Journal of Economic Perspectives* 22, no. 1 (Winter 2008), pp. 45–66, www.aeaweb.org/articles?id=10.1257/jep.22.1.45.
5. https://fred.stlouisfed.org/series/PSAVERT; and www.ceicdata.com/en/indicator/united-states/gross-savings-rate.
6. https://data.worldbank.org/indicator/gb.xpd.rsdv.gd.zs https://nces.ed.gov/fastfacts/display.asp?id=75.

The Economy in the Short and Long Run

PART FIVE

The three chapters in Part 5 will introduce you to . . .

a basic model of the entire economy. The preceding four chapters introduced the key economic concepts used to measure the health of the economy and how the economy changes over time. Now, we'll put the pieces together.

Chapter 11, "Aggregate Expenditure," focuses on the forces responsible for recessions and booms. The chapter develops a model of *aggregate expenditure*, which shows how an economy can get "stuck" producing below potential output. We build intuition without describing a complete model of the economy. To keep things simple, the chapter investigates what happens when the price level doesn't change in the short run.

Chapter 12, "Aggregate Demand and Aggregate Supply," introduces a more complete framework that describes the state of the national economy as a whole. All of the transactions in the economy—from the snack you bought on the way to class to the purchase of new computer servers by Amazon—can be represented by a single demand curve, called *aggregate demand*. On the other side, everything that firms produce is represented by a single supply curve, called *aggregate supply*. We can use these two curves, together, to investigate changes in the entire economy, through booms and busts. Aggregate demand and aggregate supply are the main concepts used in macroeconomics to provide fundamental insights into changes in the broader economy.

Using the aggregate demand/aggregate supply model, we can start to analyze how policy choices affect the national economy. Government decisions about taxes and spending make up *fiscal policy*, which is the focus of Chapter 13, "Fiscal Policy." The chapter compares the effects of taxes and government spending on the economy. It turns out that one dollar of government spending doesn't add just one dollar to overall GDP. Thanks to the effect of a *multiplier*, when the government spends money or changes taxes, the effect of the dollar gets magnified throughout the economy. If you understand the role of the multiplier, you're a long way toward understanding what policy can and can't do.

Aggregate Expenditure

Chapter 11

The Big Crash

During most of 1929, stock prices had been rising steadily. Investors were feeling rich. That fall, a famous economist, Irving Fisher, remarked, "Stock prices have reached what looks like a permanently high plateau." Unfortunately, Fisher could not have been more wrong.

Shortly after Fisher's optimistic prediction, stock prices in the United States started falling fast, bottoming out in July 1932 at a level 90 percent below the high of September 1929. Millions of Americans lost their investments. Worse yet, the stock market crash was followed by a devastating drop in output, employment, and prices in the United States and around the world, known as the Great Depression.

People alive during the Great Depression of the 1930s shared stories of bread lines and having to make do with very little. The novelist John Steinbeck wrote of people with "muscles aching to work, minds aching to create," but jobs were hard to find. The Great Depression started in 1929 and the worst part lasted through 1933, but it took over a decade for the economy to recover.

In contrast, the Great Recession of 2007–2009 was another sharp, global economic downturn, but it was shorter and less severe than what happened in the 1930s. Although millions lost their jobs and unemployment reached 10 percent, by 2014 many indicators had returned to pre-recession levels.

Depressions and recessions are puzzling. People are *willing* to work at the prevailing wage, but they can't find a job. Firms *can* supply more output, but there simply isn't enough demand. Workers lose their jobs, machines run idle, inventories accumulate, and output falls sharply. A lot of people suffer.

©General Photographic Agency/Stringer/Getty Images

It's no surprise that economists want to know why things go so wrong. More importantly, they want to know what policy-makers can do to get an economy back on track. In most economic models, prices rise or fall to keep markets in equilibrium. When prices adjust like that, there should be no food shortages, no unemployment, and nothing resembling the Great Depression. The standard models were useful for understanding standard cases, but they couldn't explain something as extraordinary as the Great Depression.

In the 1930s, however, the British economist John Maynard Keynes (pronounced "canes") introduced *price frictions* into a model of the economy. Keynes's model showed that rather than freely adjusting, prices were actually "sticky" and rarely decreased enough during recessions to restore demand. That revolutionary idea placed the focus on aggregate demand. Macroeconomists have now extended many of Keynes's original insights, and his basic ideas continue to help explain economic booms and busts in the United States and abroad.

LEARNING OBJECTIVES

LO 11.1 Identify the factors that affect the consumption component of aggregate expenditure.

LO 11.2 Identify the factors that affect the investment component of aggregate expenditure.

LO 11.3 Identify the factors that affect the government spending component of aggregate expenditure.

LO 11.4 Identify the factors that affect the net exports component of aggregate expenditure.

LO 11.5 Describe the difference between planned aggregate expenditure and GDP, and show their relationship graphically.

LO 11.6 Describe autonomous expenditure and how it differs from the rest of planned aggregate expenditure.

LO 11.7 Show how to find equilibrium aggregate expenditure when given the relationship between planned aggregate expenditure and actual aggregate expenditure.

LO 11.8 Explain the importance of the aggregate expenditure equilibrium model to understanding the behavior of the economy.

LO 11.9 Illustrate how any initial change in aggregate expenditure can have a multiplier effect on the overall level of aggregate expenditure.

In this chapter we'll use a simple model to explore Keynes's explanation for economic downturns. The model shows how it's possible for an economy to get stuck at a short-run level of output that lies below potential. In human terms, the model explains how widespread unemployment can persist, even when people are willing and able to work. The model also points to practical solutions to help economies escape a recessionary rut.

The Components of Aggregate Expenditure

When economies face downturns, both spending and production fall. To understand that drop in spending (and to understand how policy should respond), we need to start with the components of aggregate expenditure. Chapter 7, "Measuring GDP," showed that all activity in the economy can be summarized by gross domestic product (GDP), and one way of calculating GDP is by aggregating all expenditure in the economy. **Aggregate expenditure (Y)** can be divided into four primary components of spending: consumption (C), investment (I), government spending (G), and net exports (NX).

If we use Y to denote aggregate expenditure, we can write the relationship simply as:

EQUATION 11-1 $$Y = C + I + G + NX$$

This tells us that everything that was produced must have been purchased by a combination of households (C), firms (I), the government (G), and foreigners (NX). The equation is just an accounting identity. It doesn't depend on assumptions about the behavior of decision makers, and it can't tell us much about how the economy actually works.

To get further, we need to understand how the key players in the economy—especially households and firms—make decisions. With that knowledge, we can start to build a simple model of the economy. The model starts with a set of statements that we know to be true (like $Y = C + I + G + NX$). Then we'll use our understanding of economic relationships to make things more realistic. As Albert Einstein reportedly said, we're going to build a model that tries to "make things as simple as possible, but no simpler." At the end of the chapter, the model will help us see how policy can address downturns, get people back to work, and help businesses.

Consumption (C)

The starting point is *consumption*. Consumption makes up two-thirds to three-quarters of GDP in most countries. Because it accounts for such a large share, consumption accounts for much of the variation in aggregate economic activity.

Since you make consumption choices every day, you probably already understand the basics of consumption. You decide how much to spend on food, travel, entertainment, transportation, and housing. You also decide how much to save for later (that is, you choose how much *not* to consume now). Like most people making these choices, you likely consider four factors:

- current income
- wealth
- expected future income
- the interest rate on saving and borrowing

These basic factors are the building blocks of our model of consumption expenditures.

Current income People who earn more tend to consume more. For example, most investment bankers live in nicer houses and drive fancier cars than teachers do. Of course, the exact relationship between earnings and consumption depends on the details: It matters whether your income will *always* be high or if it's likely to fall in the future. If you win the lottery this year, for example, you might save a big chunk of the winnings to spend later when your income goes back to normal. Alternatively, a young family may want to borrow to buy a house or car early on, especially if they expect that their future income will grow over time.

These details matter a lot when considering particular households. They matter much less when thinking about the *basic patterns* that hold across all households. When we think about households in general, we can streamline things by assuming that households simply consume a constant fraction of disposable income (income after taxes and transfers). This fraction is called the **marginal propensity to consume**, abbreviated as **MPC**.

If a household receives an extra $10,000 in disposable income, for example, and its marginal propensity to consume is 60 percent (MPC = 0.6), then the household will consume $6,000 (= 0.60 × $10,000) of the extra disposable income. The marginal propensity to consume plays a central role in the model of aggregate expenditure that we're developing.

Wealth Wealth takes many forms. Examples of wealth include money held in savings and checking accounts; holdings of stocks, bonds, and mutual funds; and the value of houses. From those assets are subtracted the amount of any debt, such as credit card debt, mortgages (home loans), and student loans.

Wealthier households tend to spend more, so we assume that increased wealth leads to increased consumption (and decreased wealth leads to lower consumption). That should make sense. After all, higher-wealth households can afford to consume more for any given level of income. This is confirmed by the evidence: When the level of savings rises in an economy, aggregate consumption tends to rise as well. This occurs because households can dip into savings to fund consumption rather than being limited by their income. Indeed, changes in stock-market and housing wealth have driven some of the most dramatic movements in consumption in the past 20 years.

Often, policy-makers also want to know which households are likely to have a larger marginal propensity to consume. As we've noted, income and wealth matter. It is commonly assumed,

---

aggregate expenditure (Y) the level of aggregate expenditure that consists of consumption, government spending, net exports, and actual investment by firms

LO 11.1 Identify the factors that affect the consumption component of aggregate expenditure.

marginal propensity to consume (MPC) the amount that consumption increases when after-tax income increases by $1

for example, that poor households have a relatively high marginal propensity to consume out of income. Why? Because, by definition, poor households often do not have enough income. As a result, they are likely to spend a relatively big share of any income they receive. Recent research finds a surprising pattern: Some wealthy households also act like they're poor. To see why, read the Economics in Action box "The wealthy hand-to-mouth."

The wealthy hand-to-mouth
Economics in Action

The expression "living hand-to-mouth" means that you're spending all of your paycheck, with nothing left over to save. Not surprisingly, many poor families live hand-to-mouth. One implication is that, as a group, poor families have a high marginal propensity to consume out of disposable income.

But you don't have to *be* poor to *feel* poor. In a 2014 study, economists from Princeton University and New York University found that some relatively wealthy people live hand-to-mouth too. About a third of U.S. households were estimated to live hand-to-mouth, but only one-third of those were actually poor. The other two-thirds were relatively wealthy but still had to watch their budgets carefully.

These wealthy hand-to-mouth households were often young; many have assets that are tied up in forms that are hard to draw upon, such as a house or a retirement account, for example. As a result, they felt financially squeezed. They too have a high marginal propensity to consume out of disposable income. This means that wealth alone is not a good predictor of the marginal propensity to consume—nor of how wealthy families feel.

Figure 11-1 shows that the same pattern was even more pronounced in other countries. The research found that in each country, most people "living hand-to-mouth" were actually relatively wealthy.

FIGURE 11-1

Percentage of people living hand-to-mouth in various countries

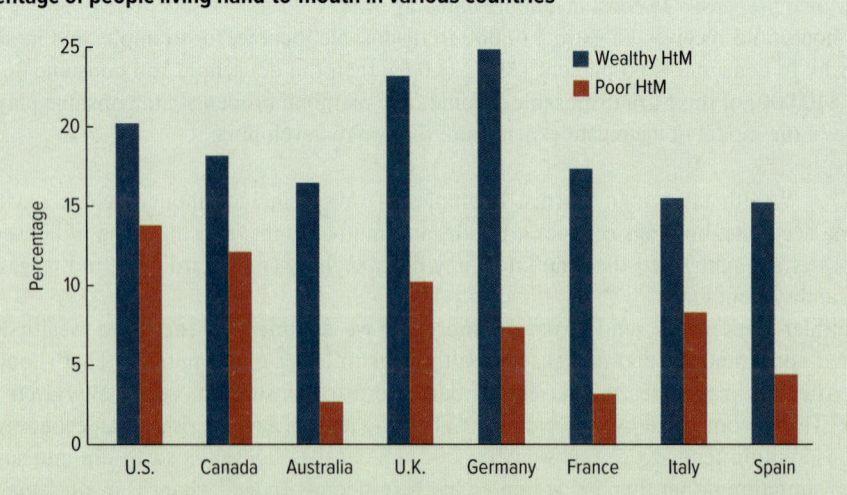

Source: Greg Kaplan, Giovanni L. Violante, and Justin Weidner, "The Wealthy Hand-to-Mouth," *Brookings Papers on Economic Activity*, Spring 2014, http://www.brookings.edu/~/media/projects/bpea/spring-2014/2014a_kaplan.pdf.

Expected future income Most people try to keep their spending fairly steady even when their income rises and falls. (This is referred to as the desire to "smooth consumption" over time.) As a result, expected future income influences current consumption in much the same way that current income does:

- If you expect your income (specifically, expected future disposable income) to rise in the future, you tend to be more willing to borrow or to dip into savings in order to fund a higher level of consumption today.
- Similarly, if you expect your income to be lower in the future, you tend to consume less now in order to save more for later.

As a result, there is a positive relationship between expected future income in an economy and current aggregate consumption.

The interest rate The interest rate is also known as the "price of money." For savers, it is the price received for letting a bank use money for a specified period of time. For borrowers, it is the price of using money for a specified period of time. Thus, the interest rate determines the financial return on saving and the cost of borrowing.

The interest rate (specifically, the "real" interest rate, which is the interest rate adjusted for inflation) influences consumption:

- A higher interest rate generally encourages saving, which in turn decreases consumption.
- In the same way, a high interest rate discourages people from borrowing on credit cards and taking other loans to pay for purchases; this decreases consumption too.

Therefore, there is a *negative relationship* between the interest rate and consumption on an aggregate level.

Table 11-1 shows how increases in these four determinants of aggregate consumption directly affect consumption. We can usually predict whether an increase in a determinant will increase or decrease consumption.

interest rate the "price of money," typically expressed as a percentage per dollar per unit of time; for savers, it is the price received for letting a bank use money for a specified period of time; for borrowers, it is the price of using money for a specified period of time

Investment (I)

When you hear people talking about investing, they are often talking about buying and selling shares in the stock market. But when economists talk about investing, they often use the word "investment" in a more specific way. Economists use "investment" to refer to *changes in capital*—including changes in machines, structures, software, and even residential housing. The determinants of investment are thus the factors that change the benefits and costs of adding physical capital—specifically:

- expected profitability
- the interest rate
- business taxes

These are the building blocks of our model of investment expenditure.

LO 11.2 Identify the factors that affect the investment component of aggregate expenditure.

Increase in determinant	Effect on consumption (C)
Current income	Increase
Wealth	Increase
Expected future income	Increase
Interest rate	Decrease

TABLE 11-1

Increases in determinants of aggregate consumption

LO 11.3 Identify the factors that affect the government spending component of aggregate expenditure.

Expected profitability   Profit-maximizing firms, not surprisingly, make capital investments they think will increase profits. (Likewise, they avoid capital investments that they think will lose money.) When firms expect their projects will be profitable, they will invest more to grow their businesses. Therefore, there is a *positive relationship* between expected profitability and the current level of aggregate investment.

Not surprisingly, innovations that open up new spheres for profit usually spur high rates of investment in physical capital. For example, the development of 5G cellular technology (available starting in 2020) has pushed carriers to start making investments in new technology. Since 5G signals cannot travel as far as previous standards, the new technology will require more towers to provide the same coverage.

The interest rate   One big way that businesses invest is by borrowing financial capital. The interest rate (again, the "real" interest rate, adjusted for inflation) can be thought of as the cost of borrowing. When the cost of borrowing decreases, the amount of borrowing increases. Therefore, there is a *negative relationship* between the interest rate and the amount of aggregate investment in an economy.

In fact, this relationship exists even if firms finance their investment by retaining earnings from their profits (rather than distributing them to shareholders). A lower interest rate reduces the returns that investors expect, which encourages firms to keep more funds for investment rather than distribute them.

In the same way, investment in housing is stimulated by a lower interest rate: When the interest rate is lower, it's less expensive for households to take out mortgages to fund home purchases. (Remember: this applies only to new-home purchases; sales of previous construction are not counted in GDP.) A lower interest rate generally results in an increase in mortgage borrowing.

(In practice, lenders may charge somewhat different interest rates, depending on the specific context. It's usually okay, though, to simplify by talking about "the interest rate," as a way to capture the role of interest rates in general.)

Business taxes   Business taxes reduce profits. Thus, when business taxes rise, firms have less incentive to invest. Conversely, when business taxes fall (as happened in 2017), firms generally feel encouraged to invest. This dynamic creates a *negative relationship* between business taxes and aggregate investment in an economy.

Table 11-2 shows how increases in these determinants of aggregate investment directly affect investment. We can usually predict whether an increase in a determinant will increase or decrease investment.

Government spending (G)

Government spending is not like the other components of aggregate expenditure. It is different because the government chooses how much to spend based on beliefs about what citizens need (roads, schools, and the like). The government may also choose spending levels as a way to stimulate or restrain the economy. (That is, government spending is a tool of fiscal policy.) Therefore, in the short run, government spending is not directly affected by standard macroeconomic factors

TABLE 11-2
Increases in determinants of aggregate investment

Increase in determinant	Effect on investment (I)
Interest rate	Decrease
Expected profitability	Increase
Business taxes	Decrease

such as aggregate income, wealth, and the interest rate, so we take government spending as given in our model of aggregate expenditure.

Note that we're focused here on spending by the federal government (not on spending by state or city governments). Note also that transfer payments to individuals are not included in government spending. *Transfer payments* include spending on unemployment insurance and Social Security benefits—payments the federal government makes to households without receiving any goods or services in return. Those transfer payments are often negatively correlated with aggregate income. For instance, more people tend to qualify for unemployment benefits during recessions (a time when aggregate income is relatively low and unemployment rises).

Net exports (NX)

The *net exports* component of aggregate expenditure is exports (the value of goods and services sold to foreign consumers) minus imports (the value of goods and services purchased domestically from foreign producers). The factors that increase net exports, therefore, are forces that increase exports and decrease imports. These forces are:

- domestic income
- foreign income
- exchange rates
- tastes for foreign goods
- trade policies

LO 11.4 Identify the factors that affect the net exports component of aggregate expenditure.

These are the building blocks of our model of net-exports expenditure.

Domestic income   *Domestic income* is the income earned by those living within a country. As domestic income rises, so does consumption.

- An increase in consumption generally leads to an increase in purchases of imports (along with increased purchases of goods and services produced domestically).
- When imports increase, net exports decrease (because imports are subtracted out in the calculation of net exports).

Thus, domestic income and net exports are usually *negatively related*.

Foreign income   *Foreign income* is income earned by those living outside a country. We just saw that increases in domestic income tend to increase the consumption of imports. Similarly, increases in foreign income tend to increase exports: As income increases in a foreign economy, citizens there increase consumption of goods from outside. The result is increasing exports to the foreign economy.

Therefore, foreign income and net exports are usually *positively related*.

Exchange rates   Exchange rates—specifically, the **real exchange rate**—are discussed in detail in Chapter 18, "Open-Market Macroeconomics." For now, it is sufficient to keep in mind that the *real exchange rate* is the value of goods in one country expressed in terms of the same goods in another country. Real exchange rates represent conversions between the cost of foreign and domestic goods that incorporates both currency exchange rates (that is, nominal exchange rates) and differences in foreign versus domestic price levels.

real exchange rate the value of goods in one country expressed in terms of the same goods in another country

When real exchange rates increase, domestic goods get more expensive relative to foreign goods. That usually leads to an increase in imports and a decrease in exports. Since imports are subtracted out when calculating net exports, real exchange rates are *negatively associated* with net exports.

Of course, an economy has many real exchange rates, one for each country it does business with. Therefore, it is helpful to think of a change in real exchange rates as the direction that the overall set of exchange rates moves on average.

TABLE 11-3
Increases in determinants of net exports

Increase in determinant	Effect on net exports (NX)
Domestic income	Decrease
Foreign income	Increase
Exchange rates	Decrease
Tastes for foreign goods	Decrease
Trade policies	Depends

Tastes for foreign goods When tastes for foreign goods increase (when people find foreign goods more attractive than they did previously), domestic consumption expenditure shifts toward consumption of imports. This shift increases imports and, as a result, decreases net exports.

Therefore, tastes for foreign goods are *negatively associated* with the level of net exports.

Trade policies In part, the effects of trade policies are reflected in exchange rates and other macroeconomic variables rather than influencing the level of net exports directly. That said, trade policies can be analyzed on a case-by-case basis to determine whether they have a direct effect on net exports as well. For example, a new free trade agreement may increase or decrease net exports depending on factor distribution and current exchange rates of counties involved in the deal.

Table 11-3 shows how increases in different factors directly affect net exports. We can usually predict whether an increase in a determinant will increase or decrease net exports.

TABLE 11-4
Summarizing all determinants of aggregate expenditure

This chart summarizes Tables 11-1 through 11-3. It shows at a glance how increases in the determinants of aggregate expenditure directly affect all components of aggregate expenditure. We can usually predict an increase or decrease.

Increase in determinant	Effect on C	Effect on I	Effect on G	Effect on NX	Effect on aggregate expenditure (Y)
Domestic income	Increase	—	—	Decrease	Generally increase
Wealth	Increase	—	—	—	Increase
Expected future income	Increase	—	—	—	Increase
Interest rate	Decrease	Decrease	—	—	Decrease
Expected profitability	—	Increase	—	—	Increase
Business taxes	—	Decrease	—	—	Decrease
Foreign income	—	—	—	Increase	Increase
Exchange rates	—	—	—	Decrease	Decrease
Tastes for foreign goods	—	—	—	Decrease	Decrease
Trade policies	—	—	—	Depends	Depends

A summary of the determinants of aggregate expenditure

Table 11-4 summarizes the determinants of all the components of aggregate expenditure. They'll be essential when we use the model for policy analysis. It's important to keep in mind that these relationships hold "all else being equal." Also, you should recognize that changes in macroeconomic factors can have both direct and indirect effects. For example, an increase in interest rates affects consumption and investment directly and also affects consumption indirectly because higher interest rates affect levels of wealth and expected future income.

✓ TEST YOURSELF

- ☐ What happens to the level of consumption in an economy when interest rates decrease? **[LO 11.1]**
- ☐ What happens to the level of (planned) investment in an economy when businesses become more cautious regarding future profitability? **[LO 11.2]**
- ☐ Suppose that business taxes decrease in an economy. Which components of aggregate expenditure are directly affected? **[LO 11.2]**
- ☐ What happens to the level of government spending in an economy when the level of wealth in an economy increases? **[LO 11.3]**
- ☐ What happens to the level of net exports in an economy when other countries experience rapid economic growth? **[LO 11.4]**

Aggregate Expenditure Equilibrium and the Keynesian Equilibrium

The Great Depression of the 1930s was the longest-lasting economic crisis in U.S. history, so it's not surprising that economists have spent a lot of time trying to understand it. Millions of families lost their wealth; almost half of U.S. banks failed. At the worst point, one in four workers was unemployed. As the U.S. economy reeled, other parts of the world suffered too. International trade fell by a third. Economists couldn't figure out how to help get people back to work, and the United States remained in a downturn through the 1930s.

In Britain, the economist John Maynard Keynes made the case that insufficient spending was the main culprit. He argued that low spending could explain how economies got stuck in a pattern of output and income below their long-run productive capacity—that is, below potential GDP. Attention then turned to the components of aggregate expenditure described in the previous section—consumption, investment, government spending, and net exports. The questions were: How can aggregate expenditure be increased? And what would be the effect on the economy and unemployment?

LO 11.5 Describe the difference between planned aggregate expenditure and GDP, and show their relationship graphically.

Keynes's insight has had a lasting influence on policy-makers and economists. Governments around the world have used Keynesian solutions to stimulate economies that had fallen into deep recessions. "Keynesian" ideas were widely discussed (and often debated) during the 2007–2009 economic crisis, for example. In this section, we show the core of Keynes's insight.

LO 11.6 Describe autonomous expenditure and how it differs from the rest of planned aggregate expenditure.

Actual versus planned aggregate expenditure

In the previous section, we described the elements of GDP and ways that different events in the economy can change the values of these components. In this section, we'll compare these components to *planned* aggregate expenditure. Doing so will allow us to see how the economy gets stuck.

FIGURE 11-2

The investment schedule Investment spending is the same for each level of GDP.

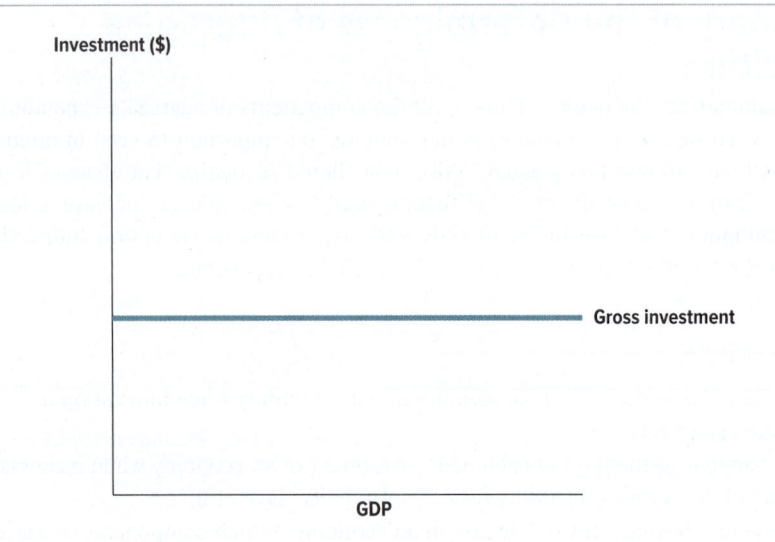

[Graph showing a horizontal line labeled "Gross investment" with "Investment ($)" on the y-axis and "GDP" on the x-axis]

Planned aggregate expenditure is like GDP in many ways, but with one major difference: While GDP is spending and production that has already occurred, **planned aggregate expenditure (PAE)** looks at the amount of spending and production that businesses, households, and others are planning to make. It consists of planned consumption, investment, government spending, and net exports.

To get a feel for planned aggregate expenditure, let's first look at planned expenditure in a closed, private economy. This economy has only two elements—consumption and investment. As in the previous section, firms in this closed, private economy make decisions about how much to invest based on the interest rate, expectations about the economy, and business taxes. For example, higher interest rates will discourage investment; lower interest rates will promote investment. Once firms know the interest rate and tax rate, and have expectations for the strength of the economy, they decide how much to invest. This investment choice will be the same for all levels of GDP, as shown in Figure 11-2. In the figure, the *x*-axis is GDP, also referred to as Y (see the CAUTION: Common Mistake box).

Consumption on the other hand, has two different parts: a certain amount of spending that happens "automatically" and an amount of spending that depends on income. Think of your personal budget. Each month, a certain amount of spending, such as rent or a car payment, happens automatically. These expenses are baked into your budget. Other spending, such as going out to eat at a restaurant or updating your wardrobe, will depend in part on your income—the more income you have, the more you can spend on these items.

When considering the entire economy, aggregated consumption decisions have the same form as your personal budget. The consumption schedule intercepts the *y*-axis (the amount of spending) at the amount of automatic spending. It then slopes upward, reflecting the portion of spending that increases with income. This consumption schedule can be found in Figure 11-3.

Now let's move beyond a private, closed economy and add net exports to the model:

- Exports add production—and consequently income and employment—to an economy, so they need to be added to planned aggregate expenditure.
- Imports, on the other hand, increase the production elsewhere so they need to be subtracted.

This math gives us net exports.

Net exports add to planned aggregate expenditure for each level of GDP. For the sake of simplicity, we are assuming that net exports are constant for each level of income in this model.

---

planned aggregate expenditure (PAE) the amount of spending and production that businesses, households, and others are planning to make, consisting of planned consumption, investment, government spending, and net exports

> ### ⚠ CAUTION: COMMON MISTAKE
>
> *Aggregate expenditure. National income. National production. Total output. GDP. Y.* What's the difference among these terms? None. For our purposes in this chapter, they are all the same.
>
> In the "Production equals expenditure equals income" section of Chapter 7, "Measuring GDP," we showed that these concepts are equivalent. We get the same number for gross domestic product (GDP) whether we measure all the expenditure or the income in an economy. We showed then that
>
> National production = National expenditure = National income
>
> This is an important simplification, but it is also potentially confusing because there are many interchangeable terms. We have noted that *national production* and *total output* refer to the same thing. Further, GDP = Y, and Y also refers to *national income*—which is also *aggregate expenditure*, which is also *national expenditure!*
>
> One important difference would arise if we consider international investment. Then, the national income of the United States includes the income of U.S. companies earned abroad (but it excludes earnings by foreign companies from sales in the United States). We discuss the implications of this consideration in Chapter 18, "Open-Market Macroeconomics."
>
> In this chapter, however, we've simplified by assuming that:
>
> GDP = Y = National production = Total output = National expenditure
> = Aggregate expenditure = National income
>
> To reduce confusion, we aim here to use "planned aggregate expenditure" for *planned production and spending decisions* and "GDP" or "Y" to refer to the *actual goods and services produced.*

(In reality, spending on imports often increases as GDP increases.) The relationship of net exports to planned aggregate expenditure looks like the flat investment schedule shown in Figure 11-2.

Government spending is the final thing we'll add to the model. In the model, government spending does not depend on the amount of GDP in the economy. Higher levels of government spending will push PAE higher for each level of GDP; lower levels of government spending will decrease PAE.

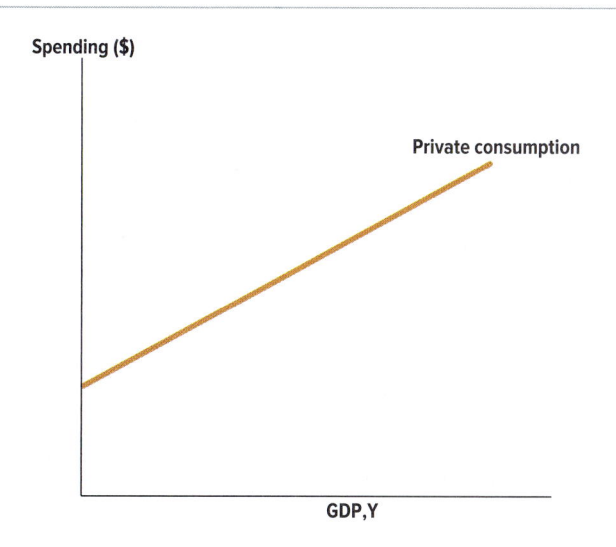

FIGURE 11-3

Consumption and GDP Consumption spending is made up of two parts: autonomous spending, which occurs independent of GDP, and spending that increases as GDP increases.

FIGURE 11-4

Planned aggregate expenditure This figure shows planned aggregate expenditure as a function of income.

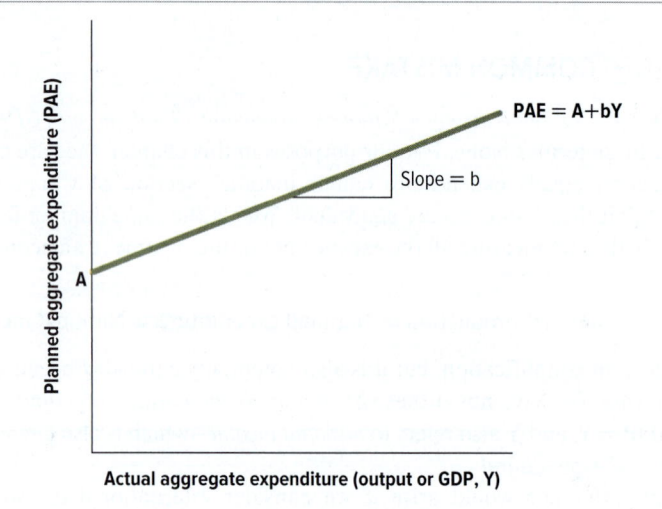

With each of these features, we can then build a model of the entire economy:

EQUATION 11-2 $$PAE = (a + bY) + I + G + NX$$

In this equation, a equals the amount of "automatic" spending that occurs only within consumption spending, and b is consumption spending that depends on GDP.

As explained above, investment (I), government spending (G), and net exports (NX) do not change with GDP. As a result, the constant values of I, G, and NX can be added to the constant amount of consumption spending to form a simplified equation:

autonomous expenditure spending that is not directly influenced by income; it is instead independent of the current level of aggregate income in the economy

EQUATION 11-3 $$PAE = A + bY$$

where

A = a constant that represents **autonomous expenditure**—spending that is not directly influenced by income. Think of this spending as including basics (basic food and housing, for example) and other expenditure categories (investment, government spending, and net exports) whose levels don't change with income. In this equation, A is influenced by a diverse set of factors explained in the previous section, including real interest rates, financial and housing wealth, government spending, export demand, and taxes.

b = a positive coefficient that relates spending to national income. In this model, b will simply be equal to the marginal propensity to consume (MPC).

Y = national income.

planned aggregate expenditure curve planned aggregate expenditure as a function of actual aggregate expenditure, holding all other factors constant

Figure 11-4 is a graphic representation of the planned aggregate expenditure equation. The sloped line is the **planned aggregate expenditure curve**. Remember, autonomous expenditure happens independent of GDP, and it is represented as the point where the PAE curve hits the y-axis. The slope, b, shows how quickly planned expenditures increase as GDP increases.

LO 11.7 Show how to find equilibrium aggregate expenditure when given the relationship between planned aggregate expenditure and actual aggregate expenditure.

Keynesian equilibrium

Keynes's big insight was that firms don't always produce the most they *can* at a given price. Instead, they produce what they can *sell* at a given price. So when demand is weak and prices don't fall, firms end up producing only what gets sold. The problem is that the economy could be producing more if prices adjusted. Because prices fail to adjust, the economy can get stuck below potential output. We'll develop this idea more fully later in the chapter, but for now, we need to build out the rest of Keynes's model.

FIGURE 11-5
The Keynesian cross

The model that Keynes used to show his insight about stuck economies includes two pieces. One is the idea of planned aggregate expenditure (PAE). To that curve, Keynes added another line representing all the points where PAE matches GDP, which we will call PAE = Y. Because the model has *planned* aggregate expenditure on the *y*-axis and GDP (or equivalently, *actual* aggregate expenditure) on the *x*-axis, this line rises at a 45-degree angle from the origin of the graph. This 45-degree line represents an aggregate supply curve, along which anything demanded in the economy will be supplied.

The two lines in Keynes's model together are often called the *Keynesian cross* for the way they intersect, as shown in Figure 11-5. The point of intersection yields the unique equilibrium where planned aggregate expenditure is just equal to actual aggregate expenditure. We call this point **equilibrium aggregate expenditure**.

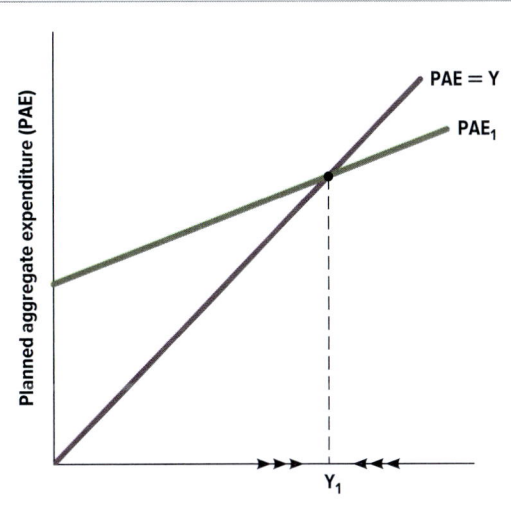

However, there are cases when planned expenditure and what is actually produced (i.e., GDP) do not line up. To bridge the gap, firms dip into inventories and then adjust production to match. Let's look at some fictional values of an economy to see how the economy finds equilibrium in those cases. Table 11-5 shows values of GDP and its components against aggregate expenditure in a hypothetical country.

Let's look at some data in Table 11-5:

- At the top of the table, planned aggregate expenditure ($19 trillion) is higher than GDP ($17 trillion). When this occurs, goods will fly off shelves, and firms will have $2 trillion in an unplanned change to inventories. Seeing that inventories are getting low, firms will be likely to increase production, expanding hiring and increasing income, until GDP matches levels of planned aggregate expenditure.
- At $21 trillion in the table, you can see that firms have no incentive to change production.
- When planned aggregate expenditure is lower than GDP, as shown at the bottom of the table ($22.5 trillion PAE versus $24 trillion GDP), extra goods produced will sit unsold in warehouses, and firms will cut production to match. Consequently, income and employment will fall.

Figure 11-6 captures the results of the table graphically:

- When planned aggregate expenditure (PAE) is higher than GDP (given by the PAE = Y line), firms are surprised by the lower-than-expected inventories, and they respond by increasing production over time. The increase in production in response to lower-than-expected inventory investment is indicated by the arrowheads to the left of Y_1 on the *x*-axis.

equilibrium aggregate expenditure
the level of aggregate expenditure where unplanned investment is equal to zero, or, equivalently, where planned aggregate expenditure is equal to actual aggregate expenditure

TABLE 11-5
Finding equilibrium aggregate expenditure (in trillions of dollars)

Real GDP	Consumption	Investment	Government spending	Net exports	Aggregate expenditure	Unplanned change in inventories	Production decision
17	12.5	4	3	−0.5	19	−2	Increase
18	13	4	3	−0.5	19.5	−1.5	Increase
19	13.5	4	3	−0.5	20	−1	Increase
20	14	4	3	−0.5	20.5	−0.5	Increase
21	14.5	4	3	−0.5	21		
22	15	4	3	−0.5	21.5	0.5	Decrease
23	15.5	4	3	−0.5	22	1	Decrease
24	16	4	3	−0.5	22.5	1.5	Decrease

- When planned aggregate expenditure (PAE) is lower than GDP, firms are accumulating more inventory than planned, and they will decrease production in response. This is indicated by the arrowheads to the right of Y_1 on the *x*-axis.

Equilibrium in this model is not set in stone. It naturally depends on the levels of the nonincome determinants of the components of aggregate expenditure:

- Economic environments that correspond to higher levels of planned aggregate expenditure (for a given level of Y) have PAE curves that are higher on the expenditure diagram. Examples include times with lower interest rates, favorable expectations about the economy, and increased government spending.

FIGURE 11-6
Disequilibrium in the Keynesian cross

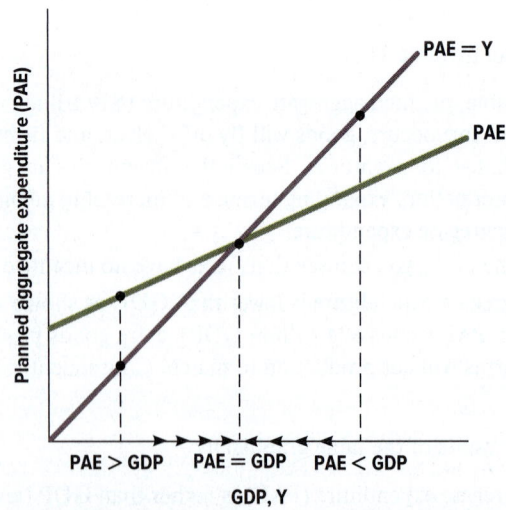

The left side of the graph shows planned aggregate expenditure higher than GDP, At this point, firms lose inventory and increase production. On the right side of the graph, GDP is above planned aggregate expenditure, leading firms to cut production.

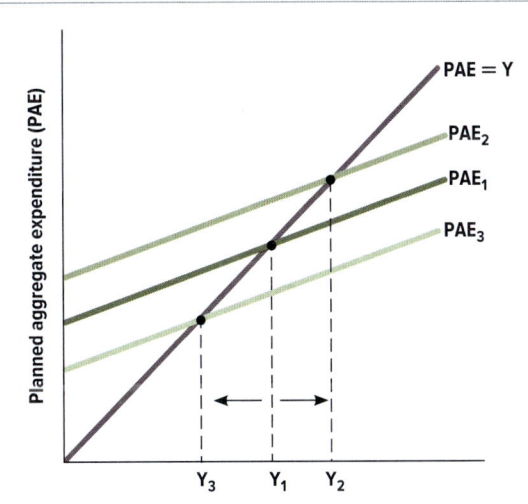

FIGURE 11-7

Nonincome determinants and changes in aggregate expenditure equilibrium

- Economic environments that correspond to lower levels of planned aggregate expenditure (for a given level of Y) have PAE curves that are lower on the expenditure diagram. Examples of factors that would prompt lower levels of spending include an increased demand for imports or higher interest rates.

For example, in Figure 11-7, planned aggregate expenditure curve PAE_2 corresponds to an environment with lower interest rates, more business optimism, or other features that increase PAE relative to curve PAE_1. In the same way, the planned aggregate expenditure curve PAE_3 corresponds to an environment with less government spending, higher exchange rates, or other features that decrease PAE relative to curve PAE_1. Not surprisingly, higher PAE curves result in higher levels of equilibrium aggregate expenditure, and lower PAE curves result in lower levels of equilibrium aggregate expenditure.

Output gaps

Crucially, the model provides an explanation for how an economy can get stuck at a level of equilibrium aggregate expenditure that is either below or above the full-employment level of output. This requires adding in one final element of the model—the level of GDP representing full employment in the economy. *Full employment* occurs when there is no cyclical unemployment in the economy; there is still frictional unemployment, which in recent history creates unemployment rates of about 4 percent.

A **recessionary output gap** occurs when equilibrium aggregate expenditure is below the level needed for full employment. Graphically, the amount of the recessionary output gap is shown by the distance between Y_1 and Y_{FE} in Figure 11-8. (Full employment output is given by Y_{FE}.) Showing that there are instances when an economy is at equilibrium but below full employment is one of the most valuable insights of Keynes's model. Unless some other variable, such as a change in expectations about the economy or a decrease in interest rates, is able to increase planned aggregate expenditure, the economy will be stuck in a recession.

Equilibrium aggregate expenditure can also be above the level needed for full employment. In that case, an **inflationary output gap** occurs when the current level of output is above the level corresponding to full employment.[1] Graphically, an inflationary output gap is shown by the distance between Y_1 and Y_{FE} in Figure 11-9. (Full employment output is given by Y_{FE}.) Inflation occurs in the economy because firms have to increase wages to attract workers, and this increase in wages trickles through the economy as higher prices.

LO 11.8 Explain the importance of the aggregate expenditure equilibrium model to understanding the behavior of the economy.

recessionary output gap
an output gap that occurs when equilibrium aggregate expenditure is below the level needed for full employment

inflationary output gap
an output gap that occurs when equilibrium aggregate expenditure is above the level needed for full employment

FIGURE 11-8
A recessionary output gap

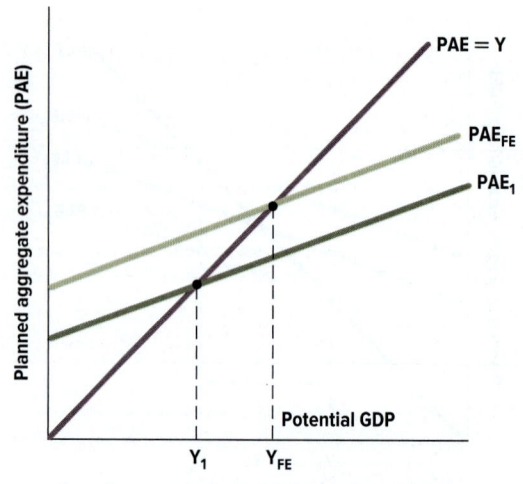

FIGURE 11-9
An inflationary output gap

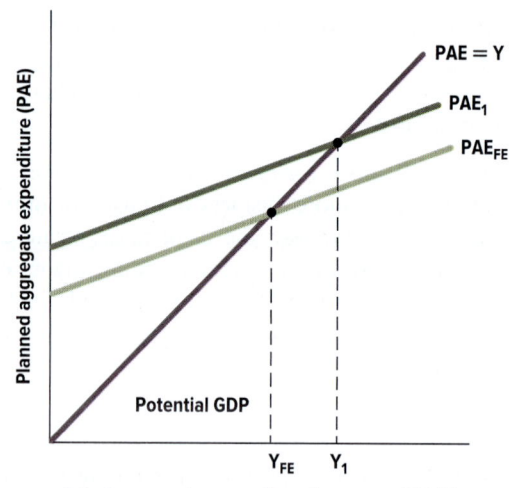

The multiplier effect

LO 11.9 Illustrate how any initial change in aggregate expenditure can have a multiplier effect on the overall level of aggregate expenditure.

Another important insight that comes from the Keynesian model is that a change in autonomous expenditure (e.g., government spending) can have a *multiplier effect*. What does that mean?

A **multiplier effect** is an increase in consumer spending that occurs when spending by one person causes others to spend more too, increasing the impact on the economy of the initial spending. The initial consumer spending ripples through the economy such that the overall change in output is larger than the initial change in expenditure.

To see the intuition behind the multiplier effect, consider what happens when you make a purchase: Let's say you hire a builder to construct a new deck for your backyard. The total bill is $5,000. This decision adds $5,000 to GDP, right? Yes, but that's not the end of the story.

Let's say the builder decides to take her family on a two-week beach vacation, which she couldn't have afforded before you employed her to build your deck. The money she spends on her vacation, including $3,000 on her family's hotel stay, also counts toward GDP. So, your decision to build a deck has added $8,000 to GDP, not $5,000. But that's still not the end of the story.

Thanks to the builder's stay at the hotel, the hotel owner feels able to buy a painting for the hotel lobby for $1,500. And so on. Your decision has sent ripples through the economy, increasing

multiplier effect the increase in consumer spending that occurs when spending by one person causes others to spend more too, increasing the impact on the economy of the initial spending

GDP by considerably more than the $5,000 you paid your builder. If you hadn't built the deck, none of this would have happened.

This extra spending occurs because there is a positive marginal propensity to consume (MPC). A positive MPC means that an initial change in government spending or consumption due to a change in taxes will have two effects: It will affect aggregate expenditure directly, *and* it will start a cycle in which changes in expenditure cause changes in consumption. Those changes in consumption will in turn cause changes in expenditure, and so on.

Mathematically, with the help of a simple numerical example we can see how the multiplier effect works in our model. In particular, suppose that initially Y = PAE and then an increase in government expenditure causes PAE to increase above Y by $100. But the process doesn't stop there. Why? Because the increased output increases incomes by $100, and we know that b fraction of the increased incomes get spent, so that PAE is now $100 + (b \times \$100)$ more than Y. (This is the same b that's in Equation 11-2.)

Firms again respond—this time by increasing output by $b \times \$100$. That increase then generates $b \times b \times \$100$ of additional consumption spending, so that firms once again find themselves increasing output, this time by $b \times b \times \$100$. This process continues, and eventually the gap between planned and actual aggregate expenditure shrinks to almost nothing.

The surprising result of the example above is that the final change in output will be larger than one-for-one. In the example, output changed according to:

$$\Delta Y = \$100 + b \times \$100 + b^2 \times \$100 + b^3 \times \$100 + \ldots = \$100 \times \left(1 + b + b^2 + b^3 + \ldots\right)$$

The sum in the parentheses is the sum of an infinite geometric series, which for $b < 1$ is simply equal to $1/(1-b)$. Thus, the final change in output above is equal to

EQUATION 11-4
$$\Delta Y = \$100 \times \frac{1}{1-b}$$

If, for example, $b = 0.8$, then $1 \div (1-b) = 5$. So, the final change in output would be *five times* as large as the initial change in aggregate expenditure. The factor by which output increases in response to an initial change in aggregate expenditure is known as the **expenditure multiplier**.

The expenditure multiplier can also be seen graphically. The multiplier effect is illustrated by the fact that the distance between old and new equilibrium values of GDP is greater than the distance between the corresponding old and new PAE curves. In Figure 11-10, the overall change in equilibrium aggregate expenditure is given by the length of the horizontal arrow. Likewise, the initial change in planned aggregate expenditure is given by the length of the vertical arrow. The strength of the multiplier effect depends on the relative sizes of the two arrows.

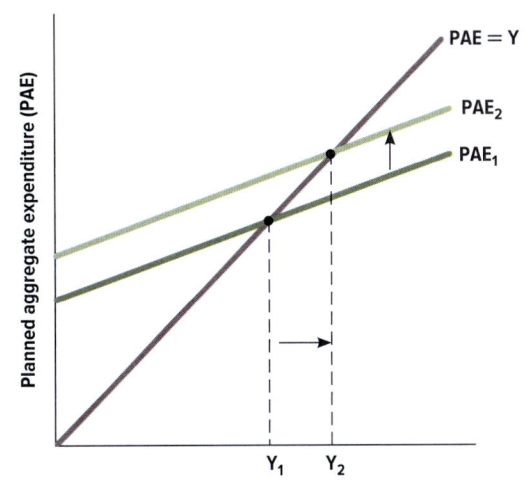

expenditure multiplier the factor by which output increases in response to an initial change in aggregate expenditure

FIGURE 11-10

Overall change in equilibrium aggregate expenditure
The multiplier can be approximated by comparing the length of the horizontal arrow to the length of the vertical arrow. In the case drawn here, the multiplier is greater than 1, because the horizontal arrow is longer.

The expenditure multiplier turns out simply to equal the length of the horizontal arrow divided by the length of the vertical arrow. In the example given in the figure, the horizontal arrow is longer than the vertical arrow, implying an expenditure multiplier greater than 1.

The expenditure multiplier is a powerful idea in macroeconomics. As shown in the example above, the expenditure multiplier is critical in determining the impact of government spending on the economy. Knowing the size of the multiplier is important for economic policy. The multiplier's size is an empirical matter, and it is a major subject of study. If the multiplier is large, even limited policy interventions can have big impacts.

The 2008 recession gives one example of how complex it can be to figure out how the multiplier effect works in the real world. Christina Romer of the University of California, who at the time was an economic advisor to President Obama, suggested a huge increase in government spending; other economists argued for tax cuts, partly because they didn't trust the government to spend effectively. One focus of the debate was on the size of the multiplier for government spending. To see how this debate played out, read the Economics in Action box "The great multiplier debate."

The great multiplier debate
Economics in Action

At the end of 2008, the economy was in crisis, and economists debated how to bring it out of recession. The debate got heated. Much of the disagreement turned out to be about numbers: What's the best assumption about the size of the multipliers for government spending and tax cuts?

- On the optimistic end, the Congressional Budget Office predicted that the government-spending multiplier on "shovel-ready" projects, like building roads or schools, would be 1.5.
- More pessimistically, Robert Barro, an economist at Harvard University, argued that the government-spending multiplier was below 1. He thought that each dollar of government spending would add no more than 80 cents to GDP.

A multiplier of 1.5 may not sound that different from a multiplier of 0.8, but the choice makes a huge difference to the economic impact you would expect from a policy to combat the recession. The difference in the expected impact of the stimulus under a multiplier of 1.5 versus 0.8 is about $440 billion more in GDP increases and 4 million more jobs created.

Why is there such a large difference between different estimates of the multiplier? There are three big reasons:

First, the multiplier is determined by overall economic conditions. Suppose the government employs 100 workers to build a bridge at a time when the economy is doing pretty well and most of those 100 workers would have had little trouble finding other employment. In the worst case, the workers might actually get pulled into bridge-building from another, potentially higher-priority job. In that case, the impact of government spending on GDP would be small. If instead those 100 workers had been sitting at home hoping for a job, the impact could be big.

Second, different *kinds* of government spending and tax cuts will each have different multipliers. Should the government invest in "shovel-ready" public works? Or should the money instead go to help low-income families buy food? Would it be better to cut taxes on workers or taxes on companies? The overall multiplier for government spending depends on which *specific* programs are under consideration.

Third, economists hotly debate whether government spending has a positive or negative impact on private-sector investment. Some argue that stimulus spending will inspire confidence in the economy and encourage firms to invest more, which would increase GDP. Others counter that government borrowing may drive up interest rates. As the government increases its demand for money in order to finance its spending, all else equal, the cost of borrowing—that is, the interest rate—will increase too. When faced with higher interest rates, firms may choose to invest less, decreasing GDP. This phenomenon is known as *crowding out*. This is one reason that some economists argue that the multiplier may be less than 1.

While it may seem like just another number, different views about multiplier effects reflect how different economists see the economy as a whole. So, one thing you can always count on: Expect debate.

Sources: www.cbo.gov/blog; http://online.wsj.com/article/SB123258618204604599.html.

With the idea of output gaps and the multiplier, we can put the Keynesian model to powerful use. What happens if the economy enters a period in which demand is low and prices refuse to fall? As in Figure 11-8, this equilibrium would set up a recession, with output stuck at a level below full employment. In traditional models, the economy would be stuck until prices fell and demand was restored. But in the Keynesian model, the economy is not stuck—the government could play a unique role in helping the economy regain full employment without waiting for prices to have an effect. To see how, let's start the economy in a period of reduced demand (or recession), about $300 billion below full employment.

If the government decides to get involved, it would want to provide $300 billion in additional expenditure. Of course, it isn't so simple as just adding $300 billion of extra spending or tax cuts. For one thing, the depth of a recession can't be measured in such precise amounts, making it hard to know exactly how much spending will restore full employment. Second, $300 billion in government spending doesn't always translate into $300 billion in aggregate expenditure. The government spending may end up crowding out private investment, reducing other parts of aggregate expenditure. At the same time, as we saw above, the multiplier effect makes it hard to pin down how much demand $300 billion in spending will actually create. Because of the multiplier effect, restoring demand probably requires less than $300 billion in government spending.

There are many other hurdles, such as the time it takes to put together a stimulus plan, and there are questions about how to pay for the extra government spending. We'll cover those issues in later chapters. For now, the central idea to remember is that the Keynesian model offers a revolutionary way of looking at the overall economy, and it gives practical insights about how to restore demand during a recession.

✓ TEST YOURSELF

- ☐ If planned and actual aggregate expenditure are always equal, what is the slope of the planned aggregate expenditure curve? **[LO 11.5]**
- ☐ In reality, do net exports count as autonomous expenditure? What about in our aggregate expenditure model? **[LO 11.6]**
- ☐ What is the value of unplanned investment expenditure in an aggregate expenditure equilibrium? **[LO 11.7]**
- ☐ What important feature of the economy does the aggregate expenditure equilibrium analysis help to explain? **[LO 11.8]**
- ☐ Why can an increase in spending lead to a change in aggregate expenditure that is larger than the initial increase? **[LO 11.9]**

Conclusion

Keeping the economy running at capacity is one of the most important concerns of economics. A well-running economy doesn't just mean more production—it also generates income and jobs. But sometimes the economy fails to operate as well as it could. Our focus here has been on problems connected to aggregate demand.

In order to understand why aggregate demand and fiscal policy behave the way that they do, we developed a model of aggregate expenditure in the economy. We first outlined the drivers of aggregate expenditure and then used a simplified model to show how the drivers work. That helped show why even an economy with plentiful productive resources can still get stalled and not operate at its full potential.

The aggregate expenditure equilibrium model is the main building block for understanding the demand side of the macro economy. In the next chapter, we connect aggregate demand to aggregate supply to see a broader range of options available to policy-makers.

Key Terms

aggregate expenditure (Y), p. 276
marginal propensity to consume (MPC), p. 277
interest rate, p. 279
real exchange rate, p. 281
planned aggregate expenditure (PAE), p. 284
autonomous expenditure, p. 286
planned aggregate expenditure curve, p. 286
equilibrium aggregate expenditure, p. 287
recessionary output gap, p. 289
inflationary output gap, p. 289
multiplier effect, p. 290
expenditure multiplier, p. 291

Summary

LO 11.1 Identify the factors that affect the consumption component of aggregate expenditure.

Other than the price level, there are a number of factors that affect the current level of aggregate consumption (C) in an economy. Current income and consumption are positively related through the marginal propensity to consume. The levels of wealth and consumption are positively related. Expected future income and consumption are positively related. Interest rates and consumption are negatively related.

LO 11.2 Identify the factors that affect the investment component of aggregate expenditure.

Other than the price level, there are a number of factors that affect the current level of planned investment (I) in the economy. Expected future profitability and investment are positively related. Interest rates and investment are negatively related. The level of business taxes and investment are negatively related. There is a relationship between the levels of saving and investment in an economy, but there doesn't have to be perfect parity between the two when government budgets aren't balanced and international trade is present.

LO 11.3 Identify the factors that affect the government spending component of aggregate expenditure.

The level of government spending on goods and services in an economy (G) is an explicit policy choice and therefore is not directly determined by macroeconomic factors. That said, macroeconomic factors may enter into the policy discussion in an indirect fashion.

LO 11.4 Identify the factors that affect the net exports component of aggregate expenditure.

Other than the price level, there are a number of factors that affect the current level of net exports (NX) in an economy. Domestic income and net exports are negatively related. Foreign income and net exports are positively related. Exchange rates and net exports are negatively related. Tastes for foreign goods and net exports are negatively related. Trade policies can have an effect on net exports, but the analysis of the relationship must be done on a case-by-case basis since increases and decreases are not always well defined.

LO 11.5 Describe the difference between planned aggregate expenditure, and GDP and show their relationship graphically.

Planned aggregate expenditure (PAE) is the sum of consumption, planned investment, government spending, and net exports, where planned investment is the level of investment in productive capital and strategic inventory accumulation that firms choose before aggregate expenditure is realized. *Actual aggregate expenditure*, by definition, is equal to aggregate output and income, and it is the sum of consumption, actual investment, government spending, and net exports. Actual investment includes not only planned investment but also unexpected investment in the form of accumulation of unsold inventory or divestiture of existing inventory.

Graphically, the relationship between actual and planned aggregate expenditure results in an upward-sloping curve with a slope equal to the marginal propensity to consume.

LO 11.6 Describe autonomous expenditure and how it differs from the rest of planned aggregate expenditure.

Autonomous expenditure is spending that is not directly influenced by income. It includes spending on basics, such as food and housing, that are needed even when income is zero. It also includes other categories (investment, government spending, and net exports) whose levels don't change with income. In the planned aggregate expenditure analysis, all expenditure categories other than consumption are considered autonomous.

LO 11.7 Show how to find equilibrium aggregate expenditure when given the relationship between planned aggregate expenditure and actual aggregate expenditure.

The *equilibrium aggregate expenditure* can be found by calculating the level of unplanned investment for various levels of output and finding the level of output where unplanned investment is equal to zero.

Graphically, the level of output where planned and actual aggregate expenditure are equal can be found by drawing a 45-degree line on the planned aggregate expenditure diagram and finding the point where this 45-degree line intersects the planned aggregate expenditure curve.

LO 11.8 Explain the importance of the aggregate expenditure equilibrium model to understanding the behavior of the economy.

The aggregate expenditure equilibrium model is important because it shows how an economy can persist at a level of output that deviates from full-employment potential GDP. Specifically, the model explains how *recessionary expenditure gaps* can occur where equilibrium aggregate expenditure is below what is needed to sustain potential GDP. In addition, the model explains how *inflationary expenditure gaps* can occur where equilibrium aggregate expenditure is larger than what is needed to sustain potential GDP. Lastly, the model explicitly shows how the different parts of the model come together to create the *multiplier effect* of initial changes in aggregate expenditure.

LO 11.9 Illustrate how any initial change in aggregate expenditure can have a multiplier effect on the overall level of aggregate expenditure.

The determinants of the components of aggregate expenditure show that there is a circular relationship between current income and current consumption: Current income is a determinant of current consumption, but current consumption is also a determinant of current income. Therefore, any initial change to a determinant of aggregate expenditure is going to flow through to this consumption/income cycle. The result is an overall impact that is larger than the initial change. This overall impact can't be infinitely large, however, since the effect of the initial change on aggregate expenditure gets smaller with each iteration of the cycle.

Review Questions

1. What effect does an increase in current income have on current consumption? What effect does an increase in expected future income have on current consumption? **[LO 11.1]**

2. What effect does an increase in the interest rate have on current consumption? What effect does an increase in wealth have on current consumption? **[LO 11.1]**

3. How does a change in expected profitability affect aggregate investment? How does a change in business taxes affect aggregate investment? **[LO 11.2]**

4. How does a change in the interest rate affect aggregate investment? What if firms prefer to pay for investment spending out of retained earnings? Does a change in the interest rate still affect aggregate investment? **[LO 11.2]**

5. Does the amount of government spending in an economy respond directly to changes in aggregate income, wealth, or interest rates? Does it respond indirectly to changes in these variables? **[LO 11.3]**

6. What are government transfer payments? Are they included as part of the government spending component of GDP? **[LO 11.3]**

7. What happens to the level of net exports in an economy when income in that economy increases? What happens to the level of net exports in an economy when income in other economies increases? **[LO 11.4]**

8. You read in the paper that the dollar has strengthened in value relative to the euro. How is this change in the exchange rate value of the dollar likely to affect exports to Europe and imports from Europe? **[LO 11.4]**

9. The investment category of GDP measures three different types of expenditures. What are they? Why is planned investment sometimes different from actual investment? **[LO 11.5]**

10. What causes a movement along the planned aggregate expenditure curve? What causes the planned aggregate expenditure curve to shift? **[LO 11.5]**

11. Which components of aggregate expenditure do not directly depend on current income? **[LO 11.6]**

12. In a Keynesian equilibrium will the economy always be producing at its level of potential output? Why or why not? **[LO 11.7]**

13. Suppose planned aggregate expenditure is greater than actual aggregate expenditure. In this case, what do you think will happen to output over time? **[LO 11.7]**

14. Suppose the economy is experiencing a recessionary output gap. What has happened to planned aggregate expenditure? What might have caused this change? **[LO 11.8]**

15. Suppose that an increase in business confidence increases investment expenditure by one million dollars. How do you expect this increase in investment expenditure to affect equilibrium output? Will equilibrium output increase by exactly one million, more than one million, or less than one million? **[LO 11.9]**

16. Define the relationship between the expenditure multiplier and the marginal propensity to consume. If the marginal propensity to consume increases, what happens to the expenditure multiplier? **[LO 11.9]**

Problems and Applications

1. "People who earn more income tend to have higher levels of consumption spending, so the value of their marginal propensity to consume must be greater than that of lower income people." Do you think this is a true statement? Why or why not? **[LO 11.1]**

2. Do you think there is a predictable relationship between the business cycle and aggregate investment spending? Why or why not? **[LO 11.2]**

3. "During a recession more people qualify for unemployment insurance. This will increase the government spending category of GDP and help reduce the severity of the recession." Do you agree with this statement? Why or why not? **[LO 11.3]**

4. "When one country in the world falls into a recession, this tends to cause other countries to also fall into a recession." Do you agree with this statement? Why or why not? **[LO 11.4]**

5. For each of the following shocks, identify what component(s) of planned aggregate expenditure is/are directly affected and in which direction. **[LO 11.1, LO 11.2, LO 11.3, LO 11.4]**
    a. Tax rates increase.
    b. China experiences an economic boom.
    c. People become more optimistic regarding their future prospects.
    d. Congress decides to increase funding for education.
    e. German fashion designs become popular among celebrities.

6. Draw a planned aggregate expenditure curve as described in the chapter. Then show what happens to the planned aggregate expenditure curve in each of the following scenarios. **[LO 11.5]**
    a. Government spending increases.
    b. Business taxes increase.
    c. Aggregate income decreases.

7. Draw a planned aggregate expenditure curve for an economy where autonomous expenditure is $500 billion and the marginal propensity to consume is equal to 0.75. **[LO 11.5, LO 11.6]**

8. Which of the following would be classified as an autonomous change to planned aggregate expenditure? **[LO 11.6]**
    a. Interest rates in an economy decrease.
    b. Current income in an economy increases.
    c. Domestic goods become more expensive relative to foreign goods.
    d. Congress decides to undertake an infrastructure repair project.

9. Consider the planned expenditure curve in Figure 11P-1. What is the level of autonomous expenditure in this economy? **[LO 11.5, LO 11.6]**

FIGURE 11P-1

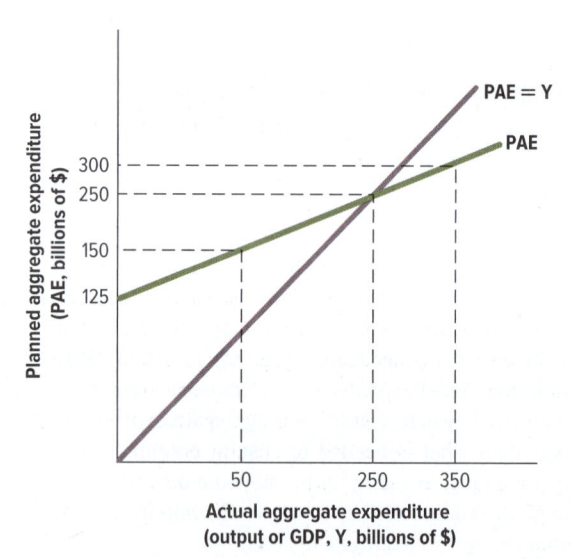

10. Consider the data presented in Table 11P-1. **[LO 11.7]**
    a. What is the marginal propensity to consume for households in this economy?
    b. Based on the assumptions of our aggregate expenditure model, fill in the columns for planned investment, government spending, and net exports. What is this type of expenditure called?
    c. For each level of actual aggregate expenditure, calculate unplanned inventory investment.

TABLE 11P-1

Actual aggregate expenditure or output (Y) (billions of $)	Consumption (C) (billions of $)	Planned investment (billions of $)	Government spending (G) (billions of $)	Net exports (NX) (billions of $)	Unplanned investment (inventory change) (billions of $)	Future output tendency
350	200	60	90	60		
400	220					
450	240					
500	260					
550	280					

d. What is the equilibrium level of aggregate expenditure in this economy? How do you know?

e. For each level of actual aggregate expenditure, label the future output tendency as "increase," "decrease," or "same" based on what you expect to happen to future output. What relationship does this categorization have to your answer in part *d*?

11. Suppose that an economy is at an aggregate expenditure equilibrium at an output level of $300 billion. **[LO 11.7]**

    a. Show this point on a planned versus actual aggregate expenditure graph.

    b. Label a point on the planned aggregate expenditure curve where the economy will decrease its output next year. (To do this, pick a specific level of output that makes sense.)

    c. Label a point on the planned aggregate expenditure curve where the economy will increase its output next year. (To do this, pick a specific level of output that makes sense.)

12. Consider the data presented in Table 11P-2. **[LO 11.7, LO 11.8]**

    a. For each level of actual aggregate expenditure, calculate unplanned inventory investment.

    b. What is the equilibrium level of aggregate expenditure in this economy? How do you know?

    c. Suppose that planned investment increases by $50 billion. What is the new equilibrium level of aggregate expenditure in this economy?

    d. What is the marginal propensity to consume in this economy?

    e. What is the expenditure multiplier in this economy?

TABLE 11P-2

Actual aggregate expenditure or output (Y) (billions of $)	Consumption (C) (billions of $)	Planned investment (billions of $)	Government spending (G) (billions of $)	Net exports (NX) (billions of $)	Unplanned investment (inventory change) (billions of $)
500	300	150	100	50	
600	350				
700	400				
800	450				
900	500				

13. Consider the graph in Figure 11P-2, where the full-employment level of output is given by Y_{FE} and is the equilibrium level of aggregate expenditure for curve PAE_1. [**LO 11.8**]

FIGURE 11P-2

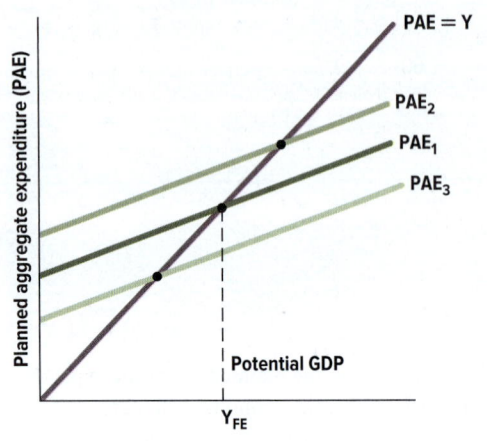

a. Which planned aggregate expenditure curve will result in a recessionary output gap? Label the size of the recessionary output gap on the graph.
b. Which planned aggregate expenditure curve will result in an inflationary output gap? Label the size of the inflationary output gap on the graph.

14. Consider the graph in Figure 11P-3. [**LO 11.9**]

FIGURE 11P-3

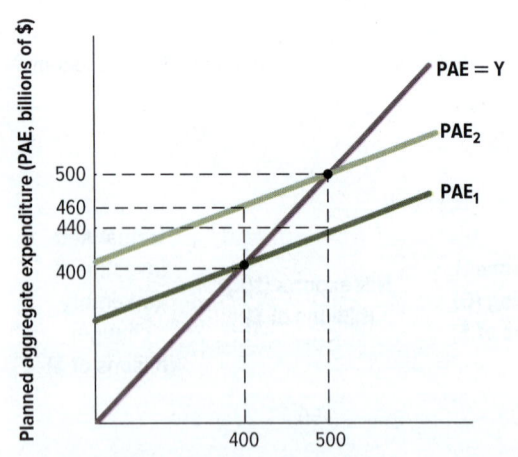

a. What is the expenditure multiplier in this economy?
b. What is the marginal propensity to consume in this economy?

15. In each of the following scenarios, describe and calculate the overall effect on aggregate expenditure. [**LO 11.9**]

   a. A recent stock market boom has increased household wealth by $20 billion, which increases consumption by $10 billion, and the marginal propensity to consume in the economy is equal to 0.5.
   b. Rising interest rates reduce domestic consumption by $3 billion and reduce investment by $4 billion, and the marginal propensity to consume in the economy is equal to 0.5.

Endnotes

1. The inflationary output gap is sometimes called an *expansionary gap*.

Appendix E

Math Essentials: Algebra and Aggregate Expenditure

In Chapter 11, "Aggregate Expenditure," we showed how to find the equilibrium level of aggregate expenditure by using graphs to analyze planned versus actual aggregate expenditure. We can also solve for equilibrium aggregate expenditure using algebra, if we make some assumptions about what functional form the components of aggregate expenditure take. This appendix takes that approach.

Using Algebra to Find Equilibrium Aggregate Expenditure

The aggregate expenditure model that we developed in Chapter 11, "Aggregate Expenditure," implies that the functions for consumption, planned investment, government spending, and net exports depend on factors such as income, interest rates, and wealth. It is possible to include all of these factors in a model of the economy, but it helps to start by simplifying. We'll begin with a simplified model of the economy in which consumption depends only on disposable income plus a constant—the constant captures the roles of all other components of aggregate expenditure.

Consider a model economy, for example, represented by the following values for planned consumption, investment, government spending, net exports, and taxes net of transfers:

$$C = 0.75(Y - T) + 30$$
$$I_{planned} = 50$$
$$G = 100$$
$$NX = 30$$
$$T = 100$$

LEARNING OBJECTIVES

LO E.1 Represent the components of planned aggregate expenditure algebraically, and use these expressions to find equilibrium aggregate expenditure.

LO E.2 Illustrate the multiplier effect of aggregate expenditure using the algebraic form of the aggregate expenditure equilibrium.

LO E.1 Represent the components of planned aggregate expenditure algebraically, and use these expressions to find equilibrium aggregate expenditure.

298A

(To be closer to reality, think of these numbers as representing billions of dollars.) Note that the expressions for planned investment, government spending, and net exports are constant values. The expression for consumption, on the other hand, has not only a constant component but also a component that depends on the level of current income in the economy.

We can combine the expressions to find planned aggregate expenditure:

$$PAE = Y_{planned} = C + I_{planned} + G + NX = 0.75(Y - 100) + 30 + 50 + 100 + 30$$
$$PAE = 0.75Y + 135$$

As stated earlier, the equilibrium level of aggregate expenditure is the level where planned and actual aggregate expenditure are equal. In algebraic terms, the equilibrium condition translates to the following:

EQUATION E-1
$$PAE = Y$$

We can solve this equation for Y by plugging in the expression we found for planned aggregate expenditure:

$$0.75Y + 135 = Y$$
$$0.25Y = 135$$
$$Y = 540$$

Solving the equation tells us that the equilibrium level of aggregate expenditure in this economy is $540 billion.

We can generalize this analysis by separating the components of planned expenditure into those that depend on output, Y, and those that do not. Let A denote all of the components of planned expenditure that do not depend on output, and let b denote the slope of the planned expenditure function against output. (In the previous example, $A = 135$, and $b = 0.75$.) The Keynesian equilibrium requires that planned aggregate expenditure equals output, or:

EQUATION E-2
$$Y = PAE = A + bY$$

We can now find the equilibrium level of aggregate expenditure by performing the same steps as before:

$$Y = PAE = A + bY$$
$$Y - bY = A$$
$$Y(1 - b) = A$$
$$Y = \frac{A}{1 - b}$$

Using this expression, we can find the equilibrium level of aggregate expenditure by simply plugging in the relevant values for the constant components of aggregate expenditure and the slope coefficient on income in an economy.

Using algebra to derive the expenditure multiplier

LO E.2 Illustrate the multiplier effect of aggregate expenditure using the algebraic form of the aggregate expenditure equilibrium.

One of the main purposes of the equilibrium aggregate expenditure model is to determine the overall impact of an initial change in a component of aggregate expenditure. Therefore, it makes sense to extend our algebra to analyze this impact as well.

Writing our equilibrium aggregate expenditure expression in changes rather than levels form gives the following:

EQUATION E-3
$$\Delta Y = \frac{1}{1 - b} \Delta A$$

As before, a $1 change in autonomous expenditure results in a $1/(1 - b)$ change in equilibrium aggregate expenditure.

Continuing the model economy used above, we can analyze the impact of a $10 billion increase in government spending by plugging the relevant values into Equation E-3:

$$\Delta Y = \frac{1}{1 - 0.75} \times 10 = \frac{1}{0.25} \times 10 = 4 \times 10 = 40$$

Note that many of the terms in Equation E-3 drop out because all changes other than the change in G are equal to zero. In this case, equilibrium aggregate expenditure increases by $40 billion, from $540 billion to $580 billion.

What if we instead considered a $10 billion decrease in taxes? Will this increase output by the same amount as the $10 billion increase in government spending described above? The answer is no. Each $1 reduction of taxes increases disposable income by $1, but only 0.75 times (which is the marginal propensity to consume) that increase in disposable income gets spent. Thus, the change in A is not $10 billion, but $10 billion times 0.75, or $7.5 billion. The change in output is:

$$\Delta Y = \frac{0.75}{1 - 0.75} \times 10 = \frac{1}{0.25} \times 7.5 = 30$$

But notice that as long as you correctly compute the change in autonomous expenditure A, you will always be able to find the change in output as the change in A times the multiplier. This means that there is a reliable way to solve for *both* the equilibrium value of output and the change in output due to a change in one of the expenditure components in just two steps:

1. Figure out the slope coefficient on income, b. In simple versions of the model, it will just be the marginal propensity to consume (MPC). But in other versions, it might reflect the MPC as well as factors like the tendency to consume more imports when income rises.

2. Sum up all the other components of aggregate expenditure that do not depend on income, which yields A. The multiplier will always equal $1/(1 - b)$. The equilibrium level of output will always equal A times the multiplier. And the change in output due to a change in one of the components of expenditure will always equal the change in the component times the multiplier.

✓ TEST YOURSELF

- ☐ Based on the model assumptions, which components of aggregate expenditure are represented by constants? **[LO E.1]**

- ☐ Algebraically, what is the equilibrium condition for aggregate expenditure? When the economy has reached this equilibrium, is it necessarily the case that output has reached potential? Explain. **[LO E.1]**

- ☐ Why does a $1 decrease in taxes have a smaller expansionary impact on the economy than a $1 increase in government spending? **[LO E.2]**

- ☐ The model economy in this section assumed that taxes net of transfers were a lump sum, with $T = 100$. Suppose instead that taxes net of transfers depended on income, so that $T = 100 + 0.1Y$. Solve for the expenditure multiplier in this case and say whether it is larger, smaller, or the same as the original multiplier. Provide a brief intuition for your answer. **[LO E.2]**

Problems and Applications

1. Consider the following components of the aggregate expenditure equilibrium model:

$$C = 0.6(Y - 200) + 150$$
$$I_{planned} = 175$$
$$G = 200$$
$$NX = 50$$

Assume all model parameters are in billions of dollars. [LO E.1, LO E.2]

a. What is the marginal propensity to consume in this economy?

b. What is the level of taxes in this economy? (You can assume that the functional forms above are consistent with those described earlier.)

c. What is the equilibrium level of aggregate expenditure in this economy?

Now suppose that planned investment decreases by $25 billion.

d. Find the overall change in equilibrium aggregate expenditure that results from this initial change by finding the new level of equilibrium aggregate expenditure and comparing this new level to the initial level.

e. Again, find the overall change in equilibrium aggregate expenditure that results from the initial change, but this time use the changes formulation of the equilibrium aggregate expenditure expression directly.

Chapter 12

Aggregate Demand and Aggregate Supply

"Pop!" Goes the Bubble

Home prices in the United States increased by over 80 percent between 2000 and 2007. Seeing that house prices were increasing, banks started making more mortgage loans, even to people who didn't earn enough to easily make their scheduled payments. The banks calculated that if these "subprime" customers got into trouble, the homes could be sold and the loans could be repaid from the profit.

Homeowners started feeling flush as they saw the value of their homes increase. With that feeling of wealth, they started to spend on other things—a new car, a new kitchen, a holiday shopping splurge. In short order, the economy was heating up.

Unfortunately, the housing boom turned out to be an example of what is called an *asset-price bubble*. Bubbles happen when people buy assets for no reason other than that they think the price will go up. There are, of course, good reasons why you might pay a lot for a house—say, if you're willing to pay to get a house you like in the location you want. But during the housing boom, many people were willing to pay hefty prices simply because they believed prices would keep going up and they'd be able to sell for a profit.

©feverpitched/123RF

But—inevitably—housing prices stopped rising. Between the end of 2007 and the middle of 2009, house prices fell by 25 percent. Banks found that many customers couldn't afford to repay the money they'd borrowed to buy their houses. Suddenly, the "subprime" mortgages that banks had been so eager to approve became a massive burden. Worse still, in many cases the houses were now worth less than the amount the bank had loaned; even foreclosing and taking possession of the house wouldn't fill the gap.

Facing huge losses, banks tightened down on credit of all sorts. As a result, homebuyers weren't the only ones finding that loans were scarcer and more expensive than before—businesses also began to find borrowing more difficult. Homeowners who had been happily spending on other things, confident that they could afford it because their houses were growing in value, suddenly got cold feet and stopped buying. This double whammy—the loss of cheap lending *and* a sharp decrease in consumer spending—hit businesses hard. The result was that GDP fell, unemployment rose, and the economy entered the period that some call the Great Recession.

LEARNING OBJECTIVES

LO 12.1 Show how the aggregate expenditure equilibrium model can be used to trace out the aggregate demand curve, and understand why the aggregate demand curve slopes downward.

LO 12.2 List factors that could cause the aggregate demand curve to shift.

LO 12.3 Explain how changes in government spending and taxes can have a multiplier effect on aggregate demand.

LO 12.4 Explain the difference between the short run and long run in the economy.

LO 12.5 Demonstrate a shift in the short-run aggregate supply curve, and list factors that cause it to shift.

LO 12.6 Demonstrate a shift in the long-run aggregate supply curve, and list factors that cause it to shift.

LO 12.7 Explain the short-run and long-run effects of a shift in aggregate demand.

LO 12.8 Explain the short-run and long-run effects of a shift in aggregate supply.

LO 12.9 Use the AD/AS framework to determine whether an observed change in output and prices was due to a demand shock or a supply shock.

LO 12.10 Describe the policy options the government can use to counteract supply and demand shocks.

How can we explain what happened to the national economy during this turbulent period? What is the connection between home prices, consumer spending, business investment, and the overall health of the economy? In Chapter 11, "Aggregate Expenditure," we focused on issues specific to aggregate expenditure. In this chapter, we add more pieces. We will create a framework, called the *aggregate demand and aggregate supply (AD/AS) model*, for understanding how the economy operates as a whole.

So far in this text we've looked at supply and demand in an individual market, for a particular good or service. As macroeconomists, however, we need to think about *all* the goods and services in the economy. The aggregate demand and aggregate supply model is a way of adding up everything, leading to an "equilibrium" that describes the state of the national economy. We will use this model to understand how three important macroeconomic variables—output, prices, and employment—are determined and how they affect each other.

This bird's-eye view lets us see the economy from the perspective of policy-makers and businesspeople, who need to consider macroeconomic shifts and frame strategies to respond to them. When President Barack Obama began the first term of his presidency in 2009, the economy was already in deep trouble. One of the first challenges he faced was figuring out how the government should respond. In this chapter and the next, we'll see which policies are available to a president and how they can affect the national economy.

Building a Model of the Economy

In recent chapters, we've developed tools for measuring the major features of the macroeconomy: output (GDP), prices, and unemployment. We also investigated aggregate expenditure. But these aspects of the economy don't exist in isolation. Instead, they are different faces of one big, complex system. You probably have some intuitive sense of how they are tied together in determining the health of the economy. For instance, when we say the economy is "doing badly," most of us have a mental picture of both falling production *and* high unemployment. Similarly, you might associate crashing or skyrocketing prices of important goods, such as houses or gasoline, with economic troubles.

In this chapter, we're going to build an economic model using that intuition. The model shows how the condition of the economy—described in terms of GDP and overall price levels—can be seen as an equilibrium outcome. In that equilibrium, the total demand for all goods and services equals the total supply. In some superficial ways, this will look like a microeconomic model of demand and supply. As in the microeconomic model, the *macroeconomic* model works with both price and quantity:

- *Price* is the overall price level, calculated as a weighted average of the prices of all goods and services.
- *Quantity* is represented by GDP, the measure of the value of all goods and services produced by the economy. It is the economy's total output.

However, new forces come into play when we start to *aggregate* (add up) demand and supply across many different goods and services. Employment, for one, is tightly linked with output. As output falls, firms close factories and lay off workers—unemployment rises. As output increases, firms will expand their workforces.

By putting together all of these elements, the model provides a prediction of what happens when the economy is hit by an event like the popping of the housing bubble or a natural disaster. The model allows us to see the likely consequences for the price level, output, and employment.

Aggregate Demand

This section will develop a picture of the demand side of the macroeconomy. The term *aggregate demand* describes the total demand for all goods and services in the economy. That means adding up demand across all of the individual markets for goods and services.

Fortunately, we've already developed a tool for dealing with this problem. In Chapter 7, "Measuring GDP," we introduced the concept of GDP, which adds up all the goods and services in the economy by translating them into a common unit: market value. Thus, *aggregate demand* measures the total quantity of goods and services demanded in the economy, *in terms of their market value*.

LO 12.1 Show how the aggregate expenditure equilibrium model can be used to trace out the aggregate demand curve, and understand why the aggregate demand curve slopes downward.

aggregate demand curve a curve that shows the relationship between the overall price level in the economy and total demand

The aggregate demand curve

The **aggregate demand curve** shows the relationship between the overall price level and the level of total demand in the economy. When we graph aggregate demand, the price level is shown on the vertical axis, and output (or, equivalently, aggregate expenditure, Y, or GDP) is on the horizontal axis.

The aggregate demand curve slopes downward, just like the demand curves for televisions, haircuts, and any other individual good or service. But the reason for the similarity is not as obvious as it might seem. Here's the difference:

- When we draw the downward-sloping demand curve for televisions, for example, we assume that the price of all other goods is held constant. Thus, the demand curve shows the change in the quantity of TVs that are demanded when *only* TV prices drop.
- With *aggregate* demand, though, we can't change the price of one good and hold the prices of all the other goods constant. By definition, aggregate demand represents *all* goods, so we're interested in what happens when the prices of *all* goods go up or down—as measured by the price index, or inflation level.

TAKE NOTE

Remember from Chapter 7, "Measuring GDP," that aggregate expenditure is equal to output, and that Y and GDP reflect the same quantity. In Chapter 11, "Aggregate Expenditure," we put aggregate expenditure on the horizontal (x) axis. Since in this chapter we will bring together aggregate demand and aggregate supply, we will most often label the horizontal axis as "output"—which is equivalent to aggregate expenditure.

Why does the aggregate demand curve slope downward? So why *does* the aggregate demand curve slope downward? In Chapter 11, "Aggregate Expenditure," we learned how each of the main components of output—consumption, investment, government spending, and net exports—are affected by important economic variables. To understand why the aggregate demand curve slopes downward, we need to examine how each component reacts to changes in the *overall price level* of the economy. Keep in mind that we are interested in how the *real* values of these variables change in response to the price level. (We do not have to worry about a mechanical relationship between the price level and the nominal values of the expenditure components.)

Since we're interested in real values, first note that if firms raise wages whenever prices increase (to perfectly offset inflation), the purchasing power of those wages will stay the same. Real wages will be constant. When that happens, changes in the price level can't affect aggregate demand through real wages.

But changes in the price level *do* influence the aggregate demand curve in three other ways: through the wealth or *real-balances effect*, the *interest-rate effect*, and the *exchange-rate effect*.

Let's start with the *real-balances effect*. In general, changes in the price level will change the real value of people's money balances. Those money balances include, for example, the money they hold in checking or savings accounts, cash in wallets, and other dollar-denominated assets whose value does not necessarily increase along with inflation. A rise in the overall price level means that a given number of those dollars won't buy as much in terms of real goods and services. If prices were to double, for example, the $1,000 in your checking account could buy only half of what it previously could. When people are less wealthy, they reduce their consumption, creating a negative relationship between the overall price level and spending. This relationship, called the *wealth* or *real-balances effect*, gives us one way to explain the downward-sloping aggregate demand curve.

Second is the *interest-rate effect*. When prices rise, the interest rate—roughly speaking, the price of borrowing—also tends to rise. Why do interest rates rise? We'll cover this in more detail in later chapters, but can answer the question in a simple way here: In the short-run, the amount of money available in the economy is fixed. When prices are higher, it takes more money to buy the same amount of stuff, and with more money needed, the price of money—the interest rate—will be higher. Higher interest rates make it more expensive for consumers and firms to borrow. This change in the price of borrowing means that fewer households will decide to purchase goods that require financing, such as houses or cars, and firms will invest less in factories or working capital. (We'll come back to this idea in Chapter 14, "The Basics of Finance.") The increased borrowing costs create an indirect negative relationship between the price level and investment spending.

Third is the *exchange-rate effect*. This effect refers to the changes in international trade that occur as a result of the price level. When prices in the United States increase, U.S. goods become relatively more expensive than goods from other countries, assuming that price levels stay the same in the other countries. (We assume, in other words, that exchange rates do not adjust to the new price levels.) As a result of the increase in prices of U.S. goods, we would expect exports to decrease and imports into the United States to increase. This means that when the price level increases, net exports (exports minus imports) should decrease. Thus, there is a negative relationship between the price level and net exports, augmenting the downward slope of the aggregate demand curve.

In short, changes in the price level affects the GDP equation as follows:

- There is a negative relationship between price level and national expenditure for three of the four expenditure components—C, I, and NX.
- There is no relationship between the price level and the fourth expenditure component—G.

Economists debate about how strong the three negative relationships are. Some economists don't believe that the effects are very strong; as a result, they conclude that the quantity of aggregate demand is not likely to change very much when the price level changes. Others explain the downward-sloping aggregate demand curve by pointing to explanations having to do with the money supply (which we will get to in future chapters). But all agree there is a negative overall

FIGURE 12-1
The aggregate demand curve

Price level

1. A decrease in the price level...

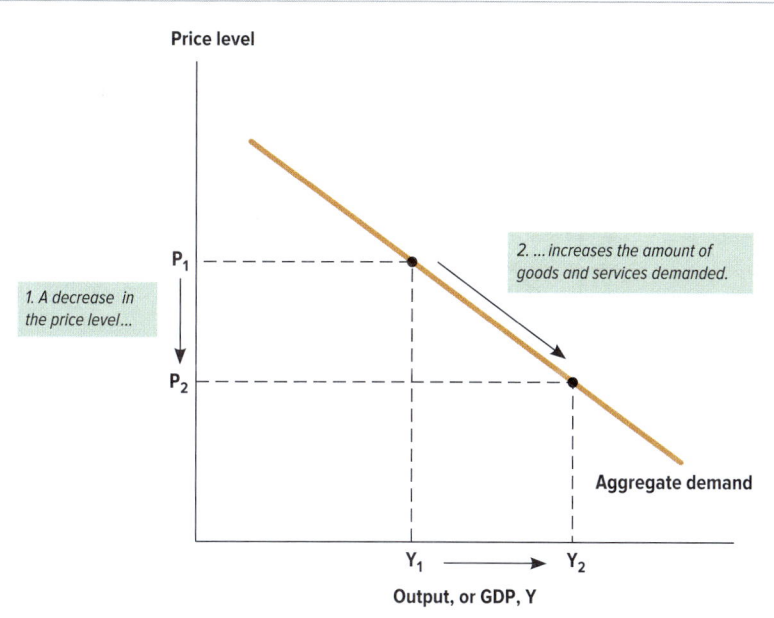

2. ...increases the amount of goods and services demanded.

Aggregate demand

Output, or GDP, Y

The aggregate demand curve shows the relationship between the price level and the quantity of output demanded by households, firms, the government, and the rest of the world. This relationship shows that as prices decrease, the quantity of aggregate output demanded increases.

relationship between the price level and aggregate expenditure or GDP. In other words, we end up with a downward-sloping aggregate demand curve, as shown in Figure 12-1.

Let's connect this model to the planned aggregate expenditure curve introduced in the previous chapter. In the model, planned expenditure is broken down into two components: The first is *autonomous spending*, which happens automatically, independent of income. The second is spending that depends on the income level.

Figure 12-2 shows that increases in the price level decrease the amount of planned expenditure for each level of income. In the top portion of the figure, PAE_1 is the lowest price, PAE_2 represents a price increase from PAE_1, and PAE_3 represents a price increase from PAE_2. We can then use the equilibrium aggregate expenditure points to trace out the aggregate demand curve, as shown in the bottom portion of Figure 12-2.

In the next section, we show how the aggregate demand curve shifts.

Shifting the aggregate demand curve

Price changes generate movements *along* the aggregate demand curve. We saw that when the price level increases, for example, the wealth effect drives people to spend less, and overall output falls.

However, the entire aggregate demand curve can also *shift* in response to *nonprice changes* in any of the four components of aggregate demand—consumption, investment, government spending, and net exports. Such nonprice changes move the entire curve to the left or right, making aggregate demand lower or higher at any given price level.

Big changes to the national economy can sometimes be described as shifts in the aggregate demand curve. Consider, for instance, the story of the housing bubble. People felt confident when housing prices were rising steadily until late 2007. Homeowners could see the value of their

LO 12.2 List factors that could cause the aggregate demand curve to shift.

FIGURE 12-2

How price-driven shifts in planned aggregate expenditure trace out the aggregate demand curve

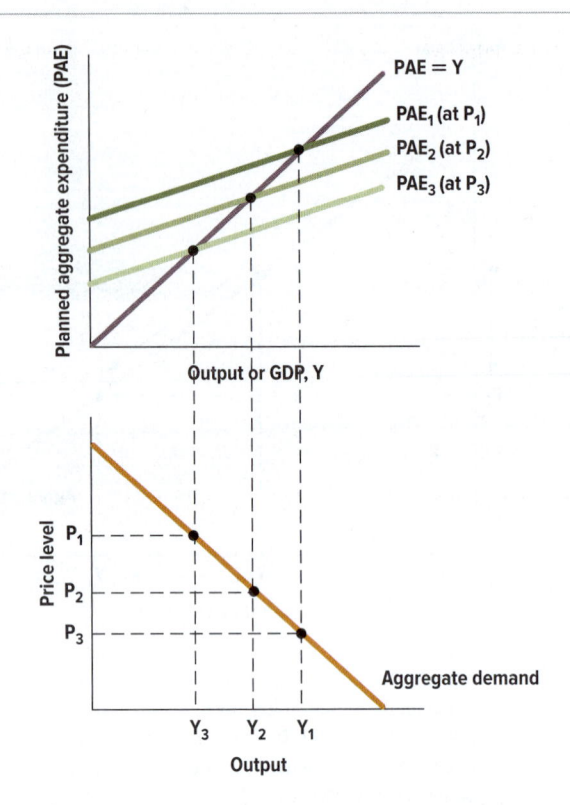

houses increasing, which made them feel better off and more optimistic, so they consumed more. That additional spending made all kinds of firms throughout the economy also feel good about their future prospects, so they invested more.

The total effect of this boost in consumer and company confidence was to shift the aggregate demand curve to the right, increasing aggregate demand at any price level, as shown in panel A of Figure 12-3.

Unfortunately, the housing prices bubble popped in late 2007. House prices started to fall, and people worried that they were not as wealthy as they thought they were. This concern reduced consumer confidence, and people bought less. In turn, managers of companies worried that they would not sell as many goods and services in the future, so they became less willing to invest. Together, this drop in confidence throughout the economy shifted aggregate demand to the left, as shown in panel B of Figure 12-3.

Confidence is a fuzzy concept, but as the example of the housing bubble shows, it can be critical to both consumption and investment:

- If people feel positive about their prospects for future income, they will be more likely to consume more.
- Similarly, if businesses are optimistic about the direction of the economy, they will want to invest more in new factories, warehouses, and machinery.

Increasing consumer and business confidence will therefore shift the aggregate demand curve to the right.

Much the same reasoning applies to the loss of confidence in the economy:

- If people feel worried about losing their jobs, they will probably start consuming less and saving more for a rainy day.

FIGURE 12-3
Shifts in the aggregate demand curve

(A) A rightward shift of aggregate demand

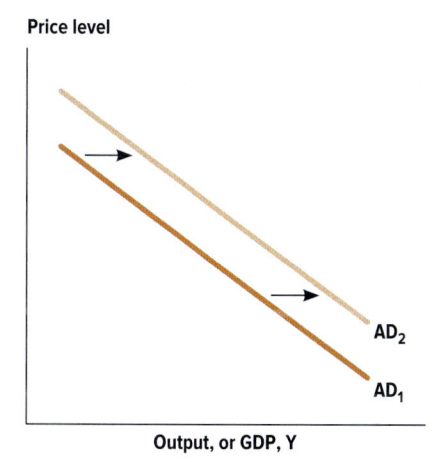

Price level

AD_2
AD_1

Output, or GDP, Y

When the aggregate demand curve shifts out (to the right) due to an overall increase in consumption, GDP is higher at every price level.

(B) A leftward shift of aggregate demand

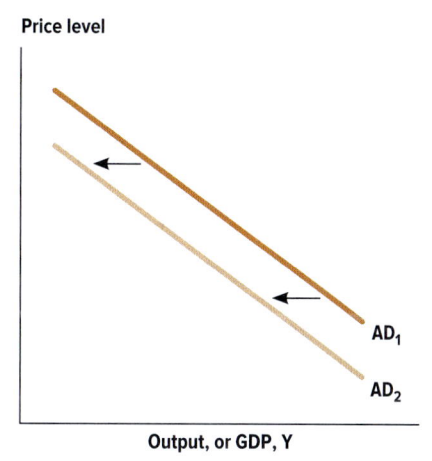

Price level

AD_1
AD_2

Output, or GDP, Y

When the aggregate demand curve shifts in (to the left), the opposite is true. At each price level, GDP is lower.

- If prospects for the economy start to look bleak, business managers will be less interested in expanding and increasing capacity, and will invest less.

Decreasing confidence shifts the aggregate demand curve to the left.

Some government policies, such as taxes and government spending, can also shift the aggregate demand curve:

- Cutting taxes on consumers is likely to increase consumption because people keep more of the money they earn and so are in effect wealthier. Increased consumption spending shifts the aggregate demand curve to the right.
- By the same logic, raising taxes can dampen the desire to spend by leaving consumers with less money. Higher taxes shift the aggregate demand curve to the left.

The government can also affect aggregate demand through its own spending:

- Government spending increases aggregate demand directly, through the "G" in the demand equation. (But as we'll see in detail in the next chapter, government spending can also have indirect effects on demand by encouraging more consumer spending.) In the face of a recession, government can increase spending in order to shift the aggregate demand to the right. For example, this strategy could mean the construction of federal highways and other infrastructure, more spending for the military, or added spending for schools.
- If, instead, the government sharply cut its spending during a recession, it risks a decline in aggregate demand. In that case, the aggregate demand curve would shift to the left.

Table 12-1 shows examples of changes that can cause shifts in the aggregate demand curve. The middle column lists several factors that would increase aggregate demand, shifting the aggregate demand curve to the right. The right-hand column lists factors that would decrease aggregate demand, shifting the aggregate demand curve to the left.

TABLE 12-1
What causes the aggregate demand curve to shift?

Category	Increase (shift right)	Decrease (shift left)
Consumption	• High expectations about future income increase consumer spending. • Tax cuts increase consumer spending.	• Low expectations about future income lead to greater saving and less spending. • Higher interest rates discourage borrowing.
Investment	• Confidence in the future of the economy leads firms to expand their businesses. • A tax credit for small businesses inspires firms to buy new equipment.	• Firms cut back on spending in order to weather a recession. • Taxes on capital increase, leaving less money for investment.
Government spending	• Increase in government spending spurs spending after a recession.	• Decrease in government spending in response to concerns about increasing debt leads to less spending.
Net exports	• The WTO ends European Union tariffs and trade regulations on some U.S. goods. • Economic growth abroad in China increases demand for U.S. goods and services.	• Other countries increase their tariffs on U.S. goods, making the goods more expensive. • The dollar strengthens, making U.S. goods and services more expensive for international consumers, decreasing demand.

Stimulus spending or tax cut?

LO 12.3 Explain how changes in government spending and taxes can have a multiplier effect on aggregate demand.

In Chapter 11, "Aggregate Expenditure," we introduced the *multiplier effect*. It means that each additional dollar of expenditure in the economy leads to more than one dollar of output. This principle has important consequences for economic policy.

Imagine that you're the U.S. president, and you've just entered office. The economy is in a recession, and you are considering how to use economic policy to stimulate the economy and create jobs. Your economic advisors are divided over the best route to take:

- Some advise you to cut taxes. They reason that employees will take home more money, and some of it will be spent, which will boost demand.
- Others advise you to increase government spending. Since millions are out of work, these advisors argue, the government should create jobs by spending on infrastructure projects. The money paid to government agencies or companies that do the work and the income paid to the workers they hire will flow into the economy. The workers in turn spend their new income on food, clothes, housing, energy, and other things. The spending on the infrastructure projects will provide an immediate boost to GDP.

Both plans will stimulate the economy, but you want to ensure that you use government resources as efficiently as possible. Which policy gives you the "bigger bang" for the government's buck?

First, let's consider the case of *stimulus spending*, as proposed by your second set of advisors. Suppose that government agencies buy new computers. Here's what happens:

- The government pays $500 million to the computer manufacturer. Immediately, this expenditure increases GDP by $500 million since government spending is one of the contributors to overall GDP.
- The computer manufacturer in turn uses the money to pay workers and make new capital investments, such as building a factory.
- The people employed to build the factory, in turn, spend money on goods and services elsewhere in the economy, and so on.

In the end, the $500 million injection of spending will increase GDP by $500 times the multiplier.

In Chapter 11, "Aggregate Expenditure," we defined the expenditure multiplier as $1/(1-b)$. If the marginal propensity to consume out of disposable income is 0.6, then $b = 0.6$ and the multiplier is $1/(1-b) = 2.5$. Given a multiplier of 2.5, the stimulus spending on the new computers would result in $500 million × 2.5 = $1,250 million in additional GDP.

Now imagine that, instead of spending that $500 million on new computers, the government decides to cut taxes by $500 million. The tax cut puts money in people's pockets, which they can use for consumption. The multiplier effect comes into play under this policy, too. This policy *seems* like it should have exactly the same impact as the direct increase in government spending, but that is not actually the case.

Again, the impact can be found by multiplying the initial spending increase by the expenditure multiplier. But note that in the case of the tax cut, the initial spending increase is not the full $500 million. Some people will decide to save, rather than spend, some of the money they receive as a tax cut. As a result, because the marginal propensity to consume is less than 1, only a fraction, b, of the $500 million tax cut results in a first round of new consumption spending. Continuing to assume that $b = 0.6$, then the *initial* increase in aggregate expenditure with the tax cut is only $500 million × 0.6 = $300 million. This is less than the case of direct government spending, for which the entire $500 million was spent.

The tax cut still creates a multiplier effect, though. Because the expenditure multiplier is still 2.5, the total increase in output in the case of the tax cut would be $300 million × 2.5 = $750 million. More generally, each dollar *reduction* in lump-sum taxes will result in $b × 1/(1-b)$ additional dollars of GDP.

Note that you do not need to memorize two different formulas for understanding the impact of government spending versus tax cuts. As long as you correctly compute the initial change in aggregate expenditure due to the policy, you still multiply that change by the same expenditure multiplier. The only difference with tax cuts is that the initial change in expenditures is smaller (in absolute value) than the full change in taxes.[1]

When the economy is slumping because consumer confidence is down, politicians often try to get things moving again by asking people to spend more. When times are good, though, they give very different advice, as seen in the From Another Angle box "Save . . . no, spend!"

Save . . . no, spend!
From Another Angle

When Barack Obama started his first term as president in January 2009, U.S. households were feeling the pinch. Worried about the future, they had cut back on their spending and started to save more. On an individual level, it's a good idea to save in times of economic trouble. Unfortunately, though, the overall health of the economy is tightly linked with how much people spend. In fact, over 70 percent of total GDP in the United States comes from consumption spending. That's why, in a speech to Congress in 2009, in the middle of the Great Recession, Obama noted that the best path to recovery was for everyone to spend a little more:

> That's what [the stimulus] is about. It's not about helping banks—it's about helping people. Because when credit is available again, that young family can finally buy a new home. And then some company will hire workers to build it. And then those workers will have money to spend, and if they can get a loan too, maybe they'll finally buy that car, or open their own business. Investors will return to the market, and American families will see their retirement secured once more. Slowly, but surely, confidence will return, and our economy will recover.*

Just five years previously, U.S. consumers had heard a very different message. In a 2004 speech, Federal Reserve Board Vice Chairman Roger Ferguson called on households to stop

(continued)

spending so much and start saving more. He explained that this saving would mean banks had more funds to lend to U.S. companies:

> Probably nothing is more critical to the long-run well-being of the U.S. economy than ensuring high rates of productivity growth. Productivity growth requires adequate levels of investment. While foreign saving is currently a feasible source of investable resources, it would be more economically advantageous in the longer run if we could raise the amount of household and government savings and close the gap between domestic investment and national savings.*

©Freeograph/Shutterstock

Why would policymakers give totally different advice, just five years apart? The U.S. economy had changed sharply in the time between the two speeches. In 2004, the economy was doing well. U.S. firms were eager to invest, which meant borrowing money, but because U.S. households were saving so little, investment funds from domestic sources were scarce. The logic was that if households would save more, banks would have more money to loan out, and firms would be able to make more investments to improve their businesses. Ferguson had his eye on increasing long-run aggregate supply.

By 2009, though, the economy was in a rough spot. Consumers weren't spending very much. This lack of spending meant that firms were no longer as interested in borrowing to invest. Now the focus had to be on aggregate demand. If households could be persuaded to *spend* more instead of saving, the AD curve would shift to the right. In 2009 the logic was that when firms saw that demand was increasing, they would want to employ more people and invest again. Consumer spending would kick-start economic recovery.

In both cases, the aim of the advice was to improve the health of the economy. When times are good, saving makes sense as a way to help firms make needed investments to secure the future. When times are bad, extra spending can help move the economy out of a rut and toward recovery.

*Sources: http://www.federalreserve.gov/boarddocs/speeches/2004/20041006/default.htm; http://www.whitehouse.gov/the_press_office/Remarks-of-President-Barack-Obama-Address-to-Joint-Session-of-Congress/.

✓ TEST YOURSELF

- ☐ What four components of spending make up aggregate demand? **[LO 12.1]**
- ☐ Is the relationship between price level and aggregate demand generally positive or negative? **[LO 12.1]**
- ☐ Would the construction of a new interstate highway by the U.S. Department of Transportation shift aggregate demand to the left or right? **[LO 12.2]**

- ☐ Does a decrease in consumer spending after a tax increase shift aggregate demand to the left or right? **[LO 12.2]**
- ☐ Why does a tax cut have a different multiplier effect than an equally costly increase in public spending? **[LO 12.3]**

Aggregate Supply

Now that we've described the demand side of the economy, we'll turn to the other side. *Aggregate supply* is the sum total of the production of all the firms in the economy. Production occurs when factor inputs—technology, capital, and labor—are combined to produce output.

The **aggregate supply curve** shows the relationship between the overall price level in the economy and total production by firms (output). The aggregate supply curve is similar to a market supply curve, with two key differences:

1. The aggregate supply curve represents production in the economy *as a whole* rather than just one good or service.
2. At the macroeconomic level, there is a difference between how the economy operates in the short run and how the economy operates in the long run.

Because of the difference between the short run and the long run, there are actually *two* different aggregate supply curves:

- One describes aggregate supply in the long run; it is called the **long-run aggregate supply (LRAS) curve**.
- The second describes how firms decide how much to produce in the short run; it is called the **short-run aggregate supply (SRAS) curve**.

We'll look at both in this section.

The difference between short-run and long-run aggregate supply

In order to understand the two aggregate supply curves, we need to explore the difference between the short run and the long run in the economy.

Short-run aggregate supply
The *short run* refers to the hourly, daily, or weekly decisions that firms have to make. If you're running a fast-food burger joint, short-run decisions include choices about how much beef and lettuce you want to order for the week or how many hours you want each employee to work. In choosing these inputs, you are essentially deciding how much food you want to produce.

In the short run, the aggregate supply curve slopes upward, as Figure 12-4 shows. This means that as overall price levels increase, firms are willing to produce more. Why is this so? Because the prices of final goods and services—like burgers—tend to increase more quickly than the prices of inputs. (Below, we explain why.) So, the burger joint is able to increase revenues faster than the increases in its costs. As a result, it is willing to produce more.

Why do prices of final goods and services increase more quickly than inputs? The key idea is that when the price level increases, input prices don't all increase immediately. Instead, some prices are *"sticky,"* meaning that they adjust slowly in response to changes in the economy.

Wages are a prime example of sticky input prices. To understand why sticky wages cause the short-run aggregate supply curve to slope upward, think about a sudden increase in the price of a burger. The burger joint is going to earn more revenue because the prices of its products are higher. However, wages don't adjust right away. In the short run, the burger stand can make higher profits because its revenues have increased but labor costs haven't. Because of the sticky wages,

aggregate supply curve a curve that shows the relationship between the overall price level in the economy and total production by firms

long-run aggregate supply (LRAS) curve a curve that shows the relationship between the overall price level in the economy and total production by firms in the long run

short-run aggregate supply (SRAS) curve a curve that shows the relationship between the overall price level in the economy and total production by firms in the short run

LO 12.4 Explain the difference between the short run and long run in the economy.

FIGURE 12-4

The short-run aggregate supply curve

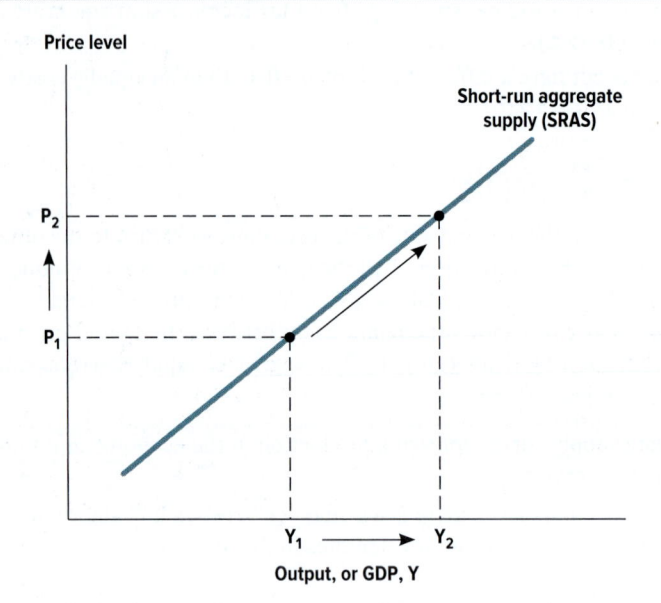

In the short run, the aggregate supply curve reacts to price changes. This means that firms are willing to change how much they supply based on price.

firms will be prepared to hire new workers and produce more output, earning higher revenues in the short run.

But why are input prices sticky, yet the prices of final goods and services can change quickly? Contracts or informal practices make wages and the prices of other inputs sticky. For instance:

- Many firms reevaluate wages only once a year. Unionized firms typically have formal labor contracts that often determine wage levels for several years at a time. If an employee wants higher wages or an employer wants to implement a pay cut, they will have to wait until the next period in which wages are adjusted or when the present contract expires.
- Also, raw materials often are supplied on the same basis. For example, a fast-food chain might have a contract with a beef supplier setting out how much it will pay for beef over the coming year.

Although contracts are common for input prices, the prices of final goods are rarely dictated by contract. It's not likely, for example, that a fast-food stand would ever get its customers to agree to a long-term contract that specifies how many burgers and fries they'll buy over a year. Instead, customers grab a burger whenever they're hungry, paying the price on the current menu. To change the price, the fast-food stand simply changes its menu.

Although changing final prices isn't always easy, in general, we assume that final prices can change far more easily than input prices.

Long-run aggregate supply Now let's look at the long run. The first thing to know is that *the long run is not a set amount* of time, like one year, two years, or 10 years. Instead, it is however long it takes for prices of inputs—such as wages, rent, and raw materials—to *fully adjust to changes in economic conditions*. In the long run, a burger stand can renegotiate the rent on its building, hire new employees, and negotiate new wages.

The adjustment process between the short and long run in macroeconomics differs from the adjustment process studied in microeconomics. In microeconomics, we focus on individual markets, and *the key adjustment problem is one of quantities*. Some costs are "fixed" because the quantity of an input cannot be adjusted in the short run; others are "variable" costs because the quantity used can easily be adjusted in the short run.

For example, back to the burger stand, basic equipment like deep fryers and heat lamps are fixed costs in the short run. In the long run, new equipment can be purchased and installed. In contrast, the amount of beef used is more likely to be a variable cost, which can be increased or decreased as weekly burger sales dictate.

In macroeconomics, the focus is on how long it takes for *prices to adjust through the whole economy*, rather than the flexibility of quantities within an individual firm.

To see what happens to the shape of the supply curve in the long run, let's return to our example of the fast-food stand. In the short run, the burger stand's owners are making extra profits because revenues have risen but costs have not. That situation can't go on forever. Since goods are now more expensive, fry cooks and cashiers are going to ask for higher wages. Input prices, which have been under contract, will increase when the contracts are renegotiated.

Once these input prices adjust, the burger stand no longer makes higher profits. Its revenues may be higher, but its costs also are higher. As a result, profits go back to where they were before the price increase. *This same process happens throughout the economy.* Once wages and input costs adjust to the new price level, the economy will go back to where it started.

In the long run, when input prices can adjust, our model says that changes in the prices of goods and services paid by consumers have no effect on aggregate supply. The long-run aggregate supply curve is a vertical line, showing that the same amount of output is supplied at *any* price level. Figure 12-5 shows an example of a long-run aggregate supply curve.

If it's not prices, what does determine the quantity of output supplied in the long run? The long-run aggregate supply curve represents *potential output* in the economy—the level of *output possible if the economy is operating at full capacity*. It may help to think of the long-run aggregate supply curve as a production function. The production function shows how society's natural resources, labor, and capital can be combined to produce the greatest output.

Changes in the long-run aggregate supply curve happen because something changes in the way that society's resources create output. Maybe there has been a new technological invention or the discovery of new resources, like a new oil reserve. The process of steadily pushing the long-run

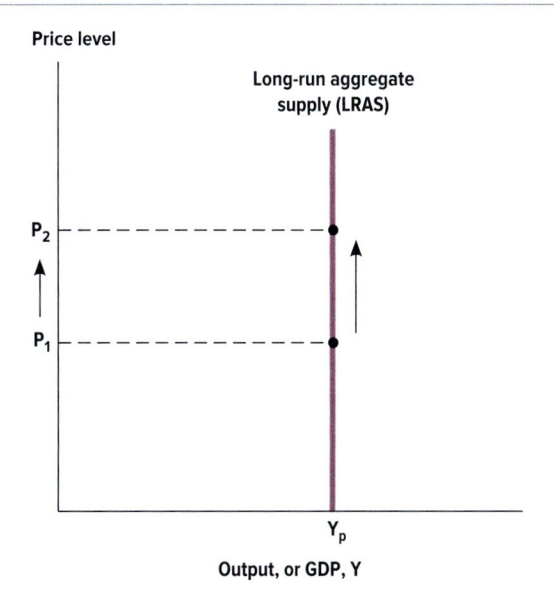

FIGURE 12-5

The long-run aggregate supply curve

In the long run, the aggregate supply curve is fixed. Changes in the overall level of prices do not influence the level of output in the economy.

aggregate supply curve to the right—that is, *increasing potential output*—is the *main driver of economic growth*.

The business cycle The economy does not always produce its potential output. Sometimes less output is produced, and sometimes more:

- When output is higher than potential output, the economy is in a boom.
- When output is below potential, the economy is in a recession.[2]

business cycle
Fluctuations of output around the level of potential output in the economy

We call these fluctuations around the level of potential output the **business cycle**. Figure 12-6 shows the business cycle for the United States over the past 58 years.

You might be wondering: How can there ever be a boom? Using the model of aggregate demand and aggregate supply, how can short-run supply ever exceed the economy's level of potential output? It turns out that in the short run, production can be expanded beyond long-run potential by pressing all of the factors of production beyond their normal capacity. For instance, if firms ask workers to take on extra hours or run their factories around the clock, output can be temporarily pushed beyond the level of potential output.

To understand how this works, think about what happens at school during exam time. You may put in lots of extra hours to cram for a test. In doing so, you are operating beyond your long-run capacity for schoolwork. You may be able to study 18 hours a day for a few weeks before midterms, but that schedule is probably not sustainable over an entire semester. Cramming for exams racks up costs that wouldn't occur with a normal schedule. These include the stress that comes from worrying about final grades or the health costs of eating too much junk food, not getting enough exercise or sleep, and not having enough leisure time. Once exams are over, these costs will push you to return to a normal workload in the beginning of the next semester. In other words, you will go back to your potential output.

In the same way that you incur costs by operating above capacity during exam time, firms incur costs by operating beyond potential output in the aggregate supply and aggregate demand model. When the economy is below capacity, ramping up production is easy. Firms can hire workers who were unemployed and rent warehouses that were sitting empty. This isn't the case when the economy is operating at full capacity. Since wages and input prices are fixed in the short run, firms often have to pay current employees overtime to work longer hours, or hire workers who may not be fully qualified for the job.

FIGURE 12-6
The business cycle

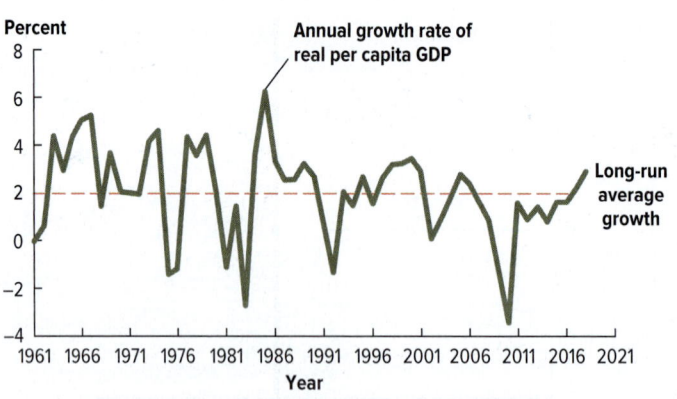

This graph shows the U.S. business cycle since 1961. Although the average real GDP per capita growth rate over this time is about 2 percent, the yearly average fluctuates quite a bit, with periods of expansion and recession.

Sources: The World Bank Data, GDP per capita growth (annual %), http://data.worldbank.org/indicator/NY.GDP.PCAP.KD.ZG/countries; and (for 2017 and 2018) www.imf.org/external/datamapper/NGDP_RPCH@WEO/USA.

Eventually, the intense demand for labor and capital when an economy is operating above capacity will drive prices upward. Hard-pressed workers will demand raises or leave to work for firms that are willing to pay them more money. As a result:

- input prices will increase,
- profits will shrink back to the original level, and
- supply will fall back to the long-run level.

The end result of this short-term boost in output is higher prices in the long run.

Shifts in the short-run aggregate supply curve

The short-run aggregate supply curve can shift—for example, if the costs of production change. Imagine that oil prices rise all of a sudden. Firms will feel the pinch. When oil prices rise, many firms will find that producing output is much more expensive. It's more costly for farmers to harvest and transport their crops, and transportation costs will make it more expensive to purchase the inputs that are needed for production. Such changes shift the short-run aggregate supply (SRAS) curve to the left, as firms choose to supply fewer goods at any given price level. Figure 12-7 shows this shift.

The short-run aggregate supply (SRAS) curve will also shift with other significant events that directly affect production—often called **supply shocks**. An example would be a major flood that disrupts the power grid and ruins crops.

LO 12.5 Demonstrate a shift in the short-run aggregate supply curve, and list factors that cause it to shift.

supply shocks significant events that directly affect production and the aggregate supply curve in the short run

Shifts in the long-run aggregate supply curve

In the long run, firms produce an amount dictated by available inputs, regardless of the overall price level. But that doesn't mean that the long-run aggregate supply curve never moves.

Remember that the long-run aggregate supply (LRAS) curve is like a production function: A combination of land, technology, capital, and labor will produce a certain amount of output. Anything that affects the output possible using these factors will shift the LRAS curve, as follows:

- The LRAS curve will shift to the right if the potential output of the economy expands.
- The LRAS curve will shift to the left if the economy loses productive capacity.

LO 12.6 Demonstrate a shift in the long-run aggregate supply curve, and list factors that cause it to shift.

FIGURE 12-7
Shifts in the short-run aggregate supply curve

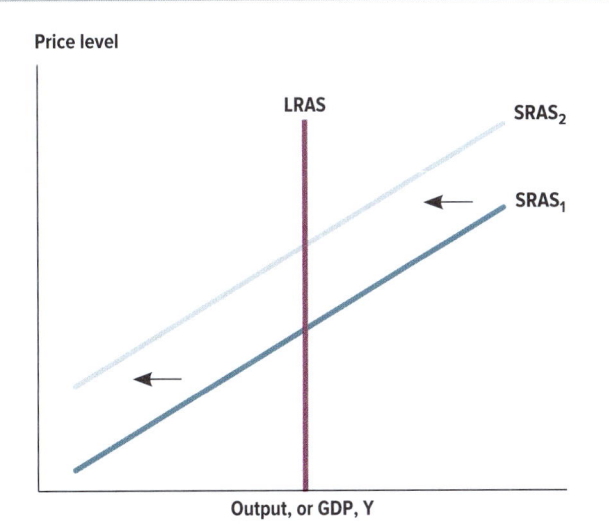

With an increase in the price of oil, prices increase for the same amount of production, so the aggregate supply curve shifts in (to the left).

> ⚠️ **CAUTION: COMMON MISTAKE**
>
> You may wonder at this point why a change in the world price of oil causes a shift of the SRAS instead of a movement along the curve. The reason has to do with the distinction between prices and costs. An increase in the *cost of production* is different from an increase in the *price level*:
>
> - An increase in the *cost of production* shifts the SRAS curve leftward, reducing the quantity of output produced at a given price level.
> - In contrast, an increase in the *price level itself*—the weighted average of the prices of all goods and services we produce—would cause us to move from one point on the SRAS curve to another point on the same (unmoving) curve.
>
> As oil prices rise, as we said, it's the increase in the *cost of inputs*, and therefore more costly production, that cause the SRAS to shift.

Factors that will shift the LRAS curve include new technologies, improved transportation systems, management innovations, and so on. Consider the case of a new technology. When firms throughout the economy adopt a new technology, they can use the same amount of resources to produce more output than before. Historical examples include the power loom during the nineteenth-century Industrial Revolution and the internet in the past 30 years. These innovations shift the LRAS curve out to the right, as illustrated in Figure 12-8.

The long-run aggregate supply curve also shifts with changes in the factors of production in the economy. For example:

- An increase in foreign investment will increase the capital stock of an economy. That will allow production to increase and will shift the long-run aggregate supply curve to the right.
- In contrast, if levels of investment are low and existing capital is not replaced as it wears out, we would see the opposite effect: Potential output decreases, and the long-run aggregate supply curve shifts to the left.

Table 12-2 gives some examples of changes that will shift the long-run aggregate supply curve.

FIGURE 12-8

Shifts in the long-run aggregate supply curve

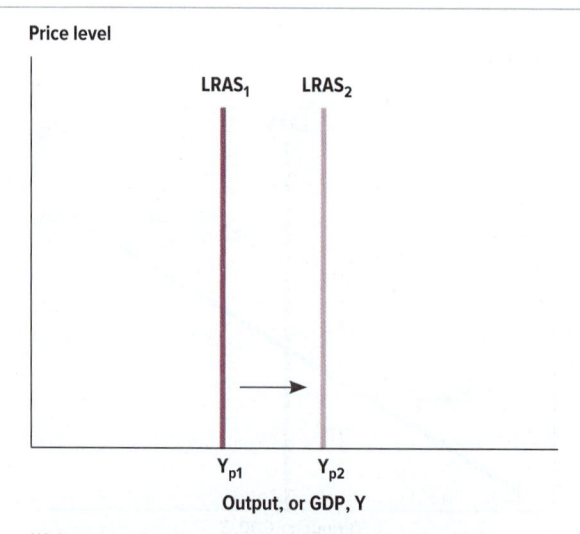

With an increase in technology, firms can produce more goods with the same amount of inputs. This shifts the long-run aggregate supply curve, the potential output of an economy, outward (to the right).

TABLE 12-2
What causes the LRAS curve to shift?

A variety of factors can shift the long-run aggregate supply curve by changing the potential output in an economy.

Factor	Increases LRAS	Decreases LRAS
Technology	Technological innovation allows for greater production using the same amount of inputs.	A new law stripping away intellectual property rights reduces the incentive to innovate.
Capital	Foreign investment in factories and machines increases available capital.	Depreciation and wear break down capital.
Labor	Immigration increases the available supply of labor.	Aging population takes workers out of the labor force.
Education	Universal primary education gives everyone a chance to go to school.	Reduction of federal college grants makes it more difficult for some to go to college.
Natural resources	New energy sources allow factories to produce more with the same inputs.	Climate change permanently reduces the amount of land that can be farmed.

Do the LRAS and SRAS always shift together? Do the long-run and short-run aggregate supply curves always shift together? No. On one hand, *everything that shifts the LRAS curve will also shift the SRAS curve*. The reason is that the available factors of production and technology that determine the position of the LRAS will also drive short-run supply. For instance, the spread of the internet in the past 30 years shifted both the LRAS and the SRAS.

However, the opposite is not true. Not everything that shifts the SRAS curve will also shift the LRAS curve. Specifically, *changes in expectations about future price levels affect* only *the SRAS curve*.

Before we discuss why this is so, it's a good idea to remind ourselves that although this situation involves the price level, it shifts the aggregate supply curve (a change in aggregate supply) rather than causing a movement along the curve (a change in aggregate quantity supplied). Why? Because we are focusing on *expected* changes in prices, not *actual* changes in prices. The principle is this: *There must be an actual change in those prices to cause a movement along a curve, whether in the short run or long run*.

Expectations about prices, on the other hand, are just guesses about the future. These expectations affect firms' production plans. Firms don't want to be caught unaware by changes in prices. When they expect the prices of what they sell to rise at some future point, for example, they may reduce the quantity supplied in order to sell more later when prices have risen. As a result, in the short-run firms reduce production in the short-run at any given current price level, shifting the SRAS curve to the left.

Why don't changes in expected prices shift the LRAS curve? We can look at this in two ways. The first comes from our definition of the LRAS—as a representation of the production function, located at the economy's potential output. The only things that can shift the LRAS are those factors that affect how we produce—such as the amount of labor, capital, natural resources such as land, and technology. Expected prices aren't included in the production function, so they cannot cause the LRAS to shift.

The second way to think about this is to consider our definition of the long run versus the short run. In the long run, expectations are fully incorporated into economic variables such as the price level. Since our expectations are fully accounted for, no shift occurs.

No matter how we look at it, while all other factors we mentioned shift the SRAS and LRAS curves in the same manner, *changes in expected prices shift* only *the SRAS curve:*

- In only the short run, an expected increase in prices shifts the SRAS curve leftward.
- In the long run, these expectations are incorporated into the LRAS curve, and so we see no change at all.

Changes in expected prices will not affect the LRAS curve if they do not affect the number of workers, the amount of capital, or the amount of land and technology in the economy. In the long run, prices will fully adjust to take into account any changes in policies or expectations.

✓ TEST YOURSELF

- ☐ Why is the long-run aggregate supply curve vertical? **[LO 12.4]**
- ☐ What is the business cycle? **[LO 12.4]**
- ☐ Which way does the short-run aggregate supply curve shift when the cost of inputs decreases? **[LO 12.5]**
- ☐ Does the SRAS curve shift when the availability of land, labor, or capital decreases? If yes, in which direction does it shift? **[LO 12.5]**
- ☐ Does the LRAS curve shift when the availability of land, labor, or capital decreases? If yes, in which direction does it shift? **[LO 12.6]**
- ☐ How do changes in expected prices shift the SRAS? Why isn't the LRAS curve affected? **[LO 12.6]**

Economic Fluctuations

Now we have all the ingredients for a full model of the national economy: aggregate demand, short-run aggregate supply, and long-run aggregate supply. It's time to put them together.

Equilibrium in the national economy is the point at which aggregate demand equals aggregate supply. Short-run equilibrium is given by the intersection of the aggregate demand and short-run aggregate supply curves. In long-run equilibrium, the aggregate demand curve crosses the long-run aggregate supply and short-run aggregate supply curves *at the same point*. This means that prices are at expected levels and the short-run level of output is the same as long-run potential output. Figure 12-9 shows the macroeconomy in equilibrium: The intersection of the AD, LRAS, and SRAS curves gives the equilibrium price level and output.

A variety of shocks can push the economy out of long-run equilibrium. These shocks can shift either the aggregate demand curve or the short-run aggregate supply curve, causing the economy to shift away from potential output in the short run. In the long run, prices will adjust and the economy will return to its long-run equilibrium.

In reality, it's not always immediately clear whether a particular shock is shifting the aggregate demand curve or the aggregate supply curve. In this section, we will show that supply-side shocks and demand-side shocks produce different implications for output and prices, which can help us to distinguish them.

Effects of a shift in aggregate demand

LO 12.7 Explain the short-run and long-run effects of a shift in aggregate demand.

Aggregate demand can either increase or decrease. Let's look, first, at what happens when AD increases.

Increases in aggregate demand Let's return to the example of the housing bubble. From 2000 to 2007, house prices were increasing, and people who owned homes felt that their wealth was increasing as well. Consumer confidence increased throughout the economy, and consumption rose.

FIGURE 12-9

A model of the macroeconomy

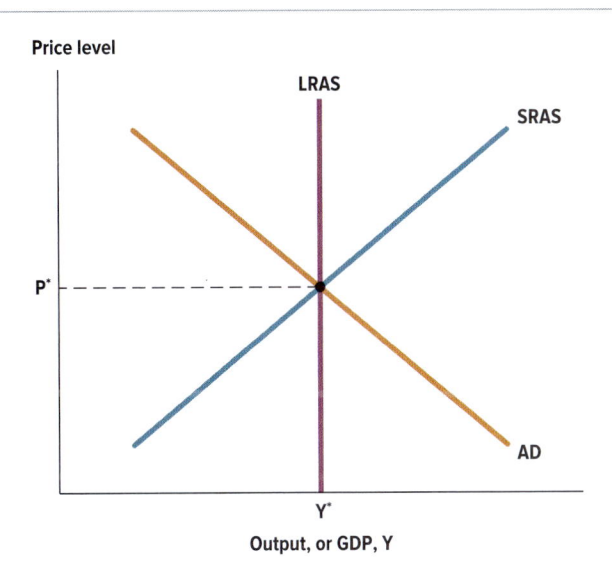

When the aggregate demand and supply curves are put together, we get a model of the entire economy. The intersection of these curves is the equilibrium, which represents a stable level of prices and output.

We saw earlier in the chapter that increased consumption shifts the aggregate demand curve to the right. How will an increase in consumption affect the economy in the short run and the long run?

Panel A of Figure 12-10 shows how the increase in consumption during a housing bubble affects the economy in the short run. When the AD curve shifts to the right, the short-run equilibrium moves from point E_1 (the intersection of the AD, LRAS, and SRAS curves) to point E_2 (the intersection of the new AD curve and the AS curve). Point E_2 shows the effect of the housing boom: Output was above the long-run potential level, and prices increased.

Point E_2 is an equilibrium point, but it is only a short-run equilibrium. How do we know this? *The long-run equilibrium is determined by the productive factors* in the economy, and this increase in consumption didn't change any of the land, labor, or capital that was available for production. Therefore, we know that the LRAS curve hasn't moved.

How does the economy return to the long-run equilibrium? The SRAS curve has to shift again to restore the long-run equilibrium. As we'll see, this is where our model diverges from what actually happened during the housing boom. If the economy had come down naturally, wages and other resource prices would have started to increase gradually because of inflation, causing an increase in input costs for firms and therefore shifting aggregate supply. As contracts were negotiated and wages increased, the SRAS curve would have gradually shifted to the left until equilibrium was restored, as shown in panel B of Figure 12-10.

If you compare point E_1 to point E_3 in panel B of Figure 12-10—the movement from the initial long-run equilibrium to the new long-run equilibrium—you'll see that output didn't change, but the price level increased. So, the effects of an increase in consumption differ in the short and long runs:

- In the short run, absent any other changes, the effect of a shift in the AD curve due to an increase in consumer confidence will be to increase both prices and output.
- In the long run, the gains to output retreat, output returns to its former level, and the only change that is left is higher prices.

FIGURE 12-10
The effect of an increase in aggregate demand

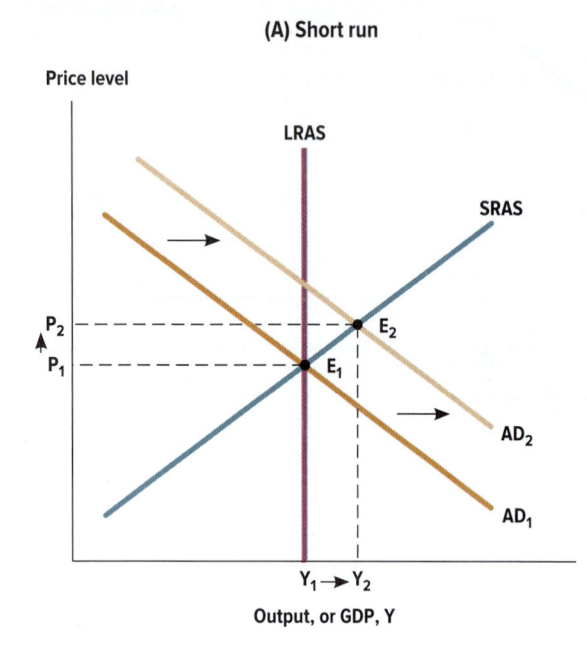

(A) Short run

When people buy more as a result of increased consumer confidence, the aggregate demand curve shifts out. This results in a new short-run equilibrium at point E₂. At this new equilibrium, output and prices are higher.

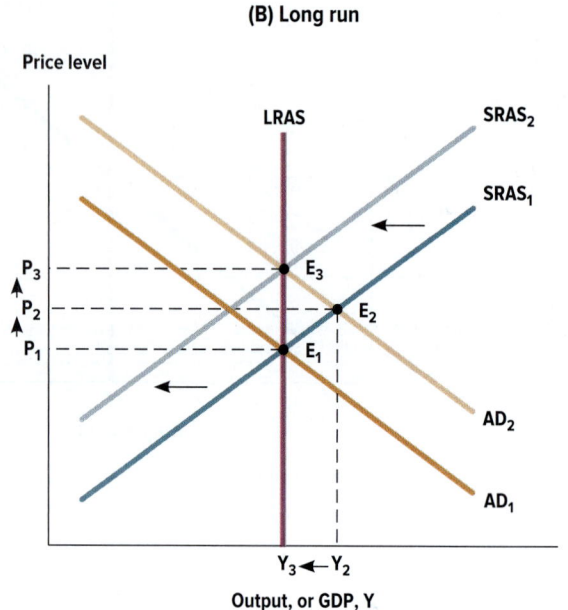

(B) Long run

As wages and prices increase due to the shift in aggregate demand, it becomes more costly to produce goods, so the short-run aggregate supply curve shifts to the left. This brings production back to its original level, but prices increase again.

Decreases in aggregate demand The economy is in an opposite situation when a negative shock shifts aggregate demand to the left, as shown in Figure 12-11. For example, suppose the economy is humming along at equilibrium. Then, all of a sudden, housing prices collapse. Consumer confidence falls, and consumption decreases, shifting the AD curve to the left.

In the short run, shown in panel A of Figure 12-11, output will be below the potential level of output. However, this change exerts downward pressure on prices. As prices adjust and inputs get cheaper, firms will increase their output—shifting the SRAS curve to the right, as shown in panel B. The new long-run equilibrium will be at the original level of output, but with a lower price level (point E₃).

If you compare point E₁ to point E₃ in panel B of Figure 12-11—the movement from the initial long-run equilibrium to the new long-run equilibrium—you'll see that output didn't change, but the price level decreased. So, the effects of a decrease in consumption differ in the short and long runs:

- In the short run, absent any other changes, the effect of a shift in the AD curve due to a decrease in consumer confidence will be to decrease both prices and output.
- In the long run, as prices adjust and inputs get cheaper, output increases to its former level, and the only change that is left is lower prices.

Table 12-3 summarizes the effects of a change in aggregate demand in the short run and long run. The key is this: Demand-side shifts change only the price level in the long run, while output eventually returns to its long-run potential level.

FIGURE 12-11
The effect of a decrease in aggregate demand

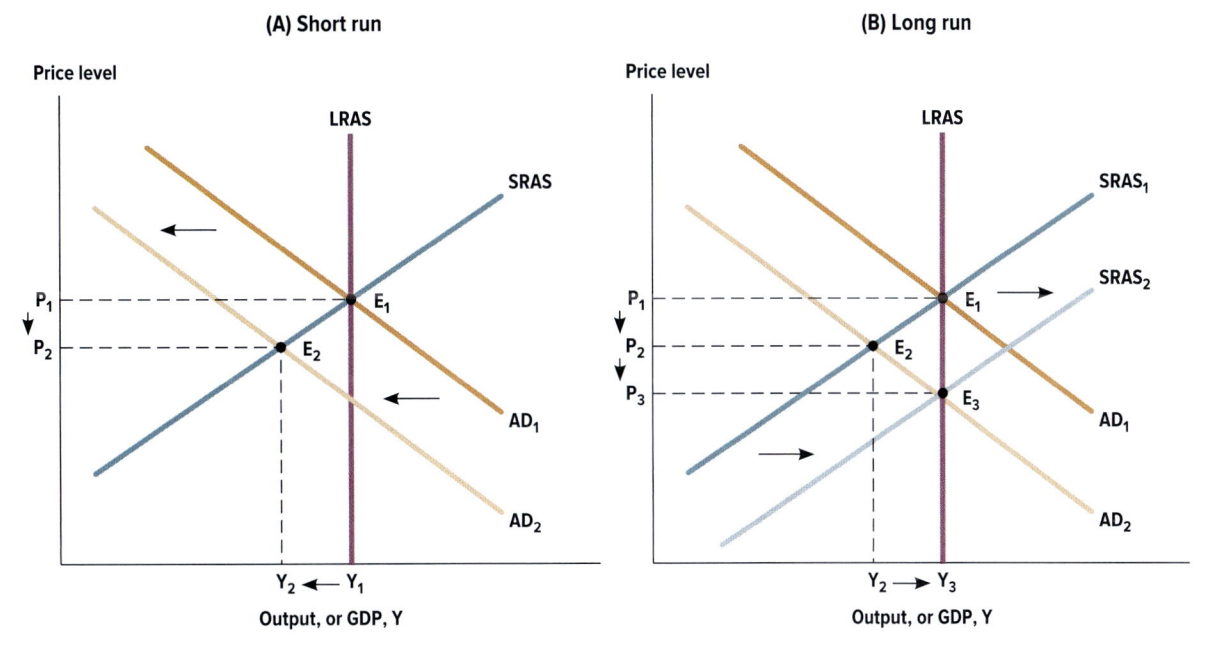

(A) Short run

When aggregate demand shifts in due to a decrease in aggregate demand, the new short-run equilibrium moves to point E_2. At point E_2 both prices and output are lower.

(B) Long run

Lower prices of inputs make it cheaper for firms to produce goods so the aggregate supply curve shifts out. This shift restores the economy to a long-run equilibrium with the same original level of output, but with lower prices.

Effects of a shift in aggregate supply

The other type of shocks the economy can face is shocks to the supply side. Supply-side shocks may be either temporary or permanent:

- When such changes are temporary, *only the SRAS curve* will shift.
- When the changes are permanent, *both the LRAS curve and the SRAS curve* will shift.

LO 12.8 Explain the short-run and long-run effects of a shift in aggregate supply.

Temporary supply shocks   Let's first consider a temporary shock. Suppose there is a year-long drought in the Midwest and a lot of corn is damaged. This shock will shift the SRAS curve to the left, as shown in panel A of Figure 12-12. The economy will move from its long-run equilibrium at point E_1 to the new short-run equilibrium at point E_2. Prices will be higher and output will be lower. How does the economy adjust?

TABLE 12-3
Changes in aggregate demand in the short run and the long run

The impacts of a shift in demand can be separated into two main paths. An increase in AD will increase both prices and output in the short run. In the long run, only prices will be higher as output slides back to the original equilibrium level. The opposite is true for a decrease in aggregate demand.

Shift	Example	Short run	Long run
Increase in AD	Increase in government spending: increases G	Output increases Price increases	Output unchanged Price increases
Decrease in AD	Reduction in consumer confidence: reduces C	Output decreases Price decreases	Output unchanged Price decreases

FIGURE 12-12

The effect of a decrease in short-run supply: A drought in the Midwest

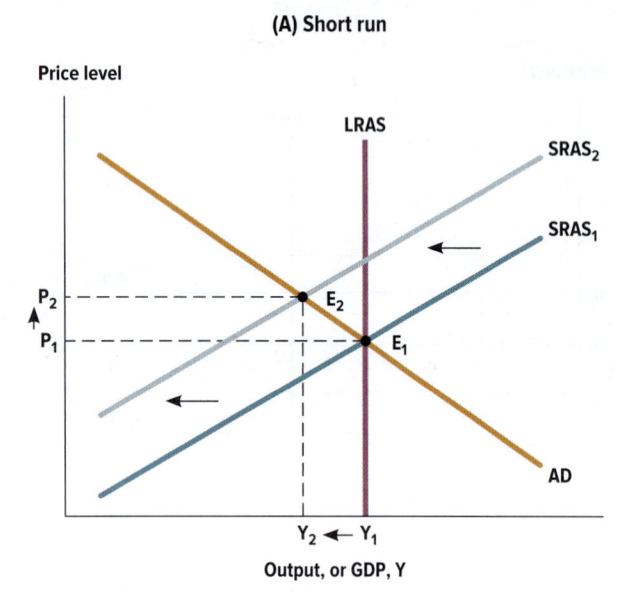

(A) Short run

A drought that destroys much of the corn crop will shift the short-run aggregate supply curve in. In the short run, prices will be higher, and output falls.

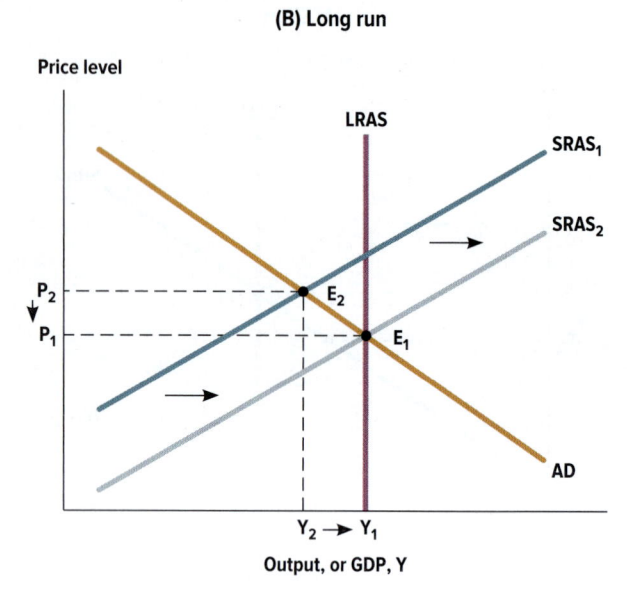

(B) Long run

As the rainfall returns and wages fall due to increased unemployment, the short-run aggregate supply curve will slide out. This means that prices and output return to their original levels.

A situation in which output decreases while prices increase is often referred to as *stagflation*—economic stagnation coupled with high inflation. Adjustment from this short-run equilibrium is not easy. A drop in wages would help, but employees are usually reluctant to accept lower wages. We say that wages are generally "sticky downward," meaning that it takes a long time for them to fall. Sticky input prices contribute to keeping the economy in this undesirable equilibrium.

When the economy is producing at a level less than the potential output and wages are slow to fall, firms will lay off workers; unemployment will be higher than its natural rate. If the unemployment rate remains high, wages will eventually begin to fall (as workers decide it's better to accept a lower-paying job than none at all). As labor becomes cheaper, the costs of production for firms will decrease. The short-run aggregate supply curve shifts back to the right, as shown in panel B. Eventually, costs will decrease to the point where the SRAS is back to its original level, and the economy will be back at its old long-run equilibrium (point E_1). In the long run, both prices and output return to their initial level.

Permanent supply shocks Now let's think about a permanent supply shock. Instead of just a short-term drought, imagine that cataclysmic climate change makes it impossible to grow corn or anything else with yields similar to what farmers now get in the Midwest. Since the Midwest is integral to U.S. food production, there simply isn't enough other land to make up the difference. With a loss of one of the factors of production (in this case, land), the LRAS curve will shift to the left, as in panel A of Figure 12-13.

This change has effects in the short run as well. Corn grown in the Midwest is important in the production of goods throughout the economy. Everything from the cereal you eat for breakfast to the gas you put in your car likely contains some corn or product derived from corn. The increase in food and other prices means that the costs of production will also rise, shifting the SRAS to the left. The SRAS curve may not shift immediately to the new long-run equilibrium point. In the short run, the equilibrium may move only to point E_2 in panel A of Figure 12-13.

FIGURE 12-13

The effect of a decrease in long-run supply: Climate change

(A) Short run

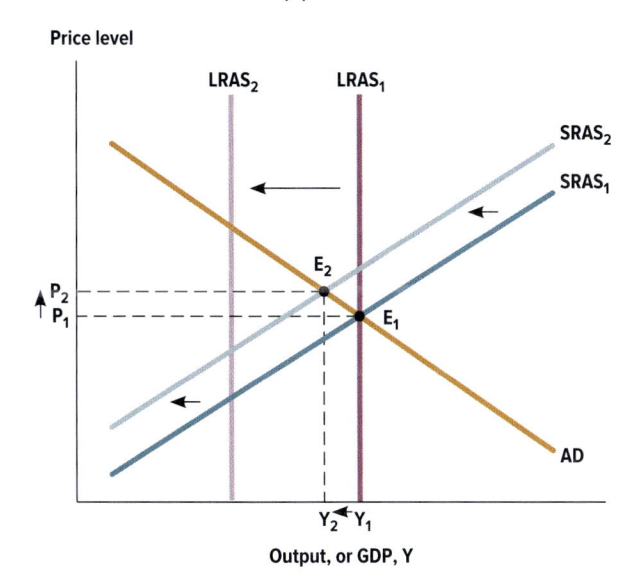

With climate change, the impact to the economy is initially similar to what occurs with a shock like a drought. The aggregate supply curve shifts in. At the new short-run equilibrium, point E_2, prices are higher and output falls.

(B) Long run

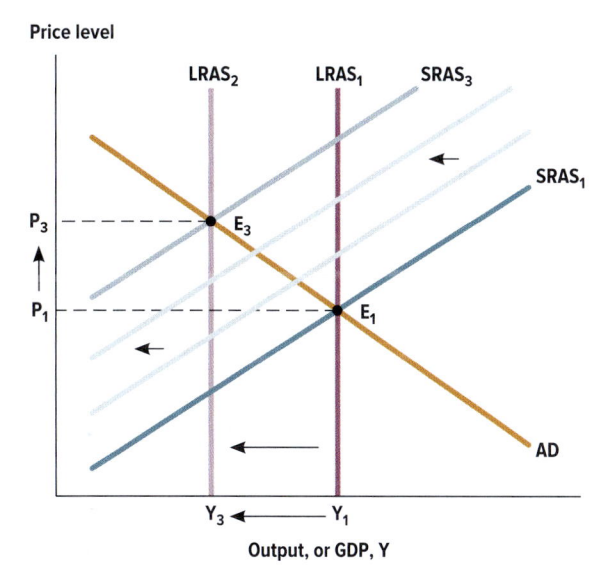

Since the effects of climate change are permanent, the long-run supply curve shifts to the left. With continually increasing prices, the short-run aggregate supply curve will shift to the left until it reaches the new long-run equilibrium at point E_3. At this point, prices are much higher and output lower than the original equilibrium.

As long as prices are above the long-run equilibrium level, the SRAS will continue to shift to the left, as shown in panel B. This process continues until the economy reaches a new long-run equilibrium (at point E_3), with higher prices and a lower level of potential output.

Comparing demand and supply shocks

The AD/AS model is a powerful tool for understanding overall economic conditions and figuring out how to formulate policy response to shocks. Successful economic policy hinges on being able to tell the difference between a demand and a supply shock. If you apply a policy designed to fight the effects of one kind of shock and it turns out to be the other, you could potentially make things even worse.

This section describes the two main challenges that arise when using the AD/AS model to analyze events in the economy:

- If you see a specific shock, can you tell which side of the economy it is going to affect?
- If you see a change in the economy, can you work backward to figure out what type of shock might have caused it?

LO 12.9 Use the AD/AS framework to determine whether an observed change in output and prices was due to a demand shock or a supply shock.

First, think through whom a shock will affect and what role they play in the economy. For example:

- Higher oil prices are going to affect businesses that use oil to produce goods. This means that an oil-price change will be a shock to the *supply side* of the economy. Because the shock has to do with prices rather than real factors of production, it will affect only the *short-run aggregate supply curve*, and not the long-run curve.

TABLE 12-4

Comparing demand and supply shocks

The first task to determine how an event will affect the overall economy is to decide whether it is a demand or a supply shock. This means figuring out whom the shock most affects and what their role is in the economy.

Event	What kind of shock?
Temporary increase in the price of oil	Short-run supply shock
Technological innovation	Long-run supply shock
Drop in consumer confidence	Demand shock
Sudden increase in immigration	Long-run supply shock

- In contrast, if you see a shock that affects consumers or government spending, it is likely to affect consumption. It therefore will act on the *demand side* of the economy.

Table 12-4 shows some examples of demand and supply shocks. For each shock, think about (1) which group of people the shock will affect, (2) whether it is a demand-side or a supply-side shock, and (3) whether it is a long-run or a short-run shock.

When thinking in the other direction—when working backward from effect on the economy to figuring out the cause—there are clear predictions about how different types of shocks will affect prices and output; these give clues about what the main shock must have been. For example, when output falls in the short run, the cause could be either a reduction in aggregate demand or a reduction in short-run aggregate supply.

The two cases are shown in Figure 12-14 (which actually recalls panels from Figure 12-11 and Figure 12-12). By comparing the two panels of Figure 12-14, we can see very different effects on prices:

- The demand-side shock will reduce prices (panel A).
- The supply-side shock will increase the price level (panel B).

So, an economy in which output has decreased and prices have decreased would suggest a decrease in demand. On the other hand, an economy in which output has decreased and prices have increased would suggest that there has been a supply-side shock.

Sometimes, however, there can be a complex combination of overlapping shocks to untangle. For example, when the U.S. housing bubble popped in 2007, banks and other financial institutions faced large losses from the bad loans they had made. Their need to cover those losses and their growing pessimism about the economy made them less willing to lend to businesses. For firms, borrowing became harder and more expensive. The effect was shocks to both aggregate supply and aggregate demand in the short run:

- The increase in the cost of doing business was a short-run supply-side shock; it shifted the short-run aggregate supply curve to the left.
- That was on top of the demand shock that happened when consumers reduced their spending after the housing bubble popped. The demand shock led to a further decrease in the level of output in the economy.

Demand-side and supply-side shocks can also differ in the long run:

- Demand-side shocks will cause a change to the price level in the long run since the short-run supply curve will shift in to restore the long-run equilibrium output.
- For a supply-side shock, there are no long-run changes to the price level. If the short-run supply curve initially shifts to the left, for example, prices will adjust to restore the long-run equilibrium.

We summarize the difference between supply-side and demand-side shocks in Table 12-5.

Aggregate Demand and Aggregate Supply ■ Chapter 12   323

FIGURE 12-14

Different short-run impacts of decreases in aggregate demand versus aggregate supply   When the economy experiences a decrease in aggregate demand, both prices and output decrease in the short run. But when the economy experiences a decrease in aggregate supply, prices rise and output falls in the short run.

(A) Decrease in aggregate demand

(B) Decrease in aggregate supply

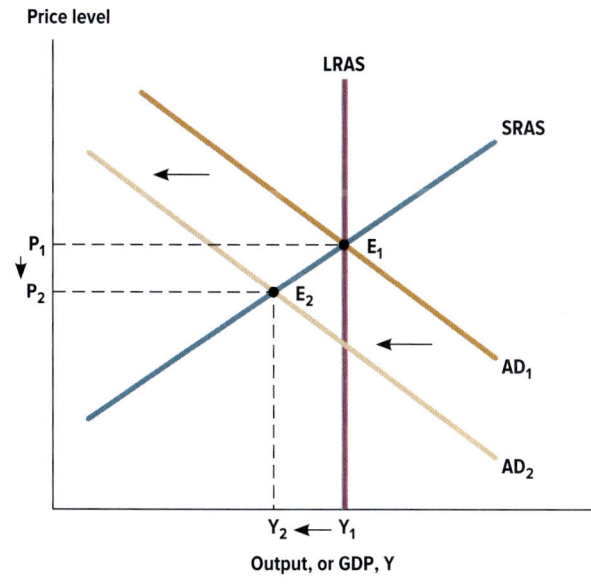

When aggregate demand shifts in due to a decrease in aggregate demand, the new short-term equilibrium moves to point E_2. At point E_2 both prices and output are lower.

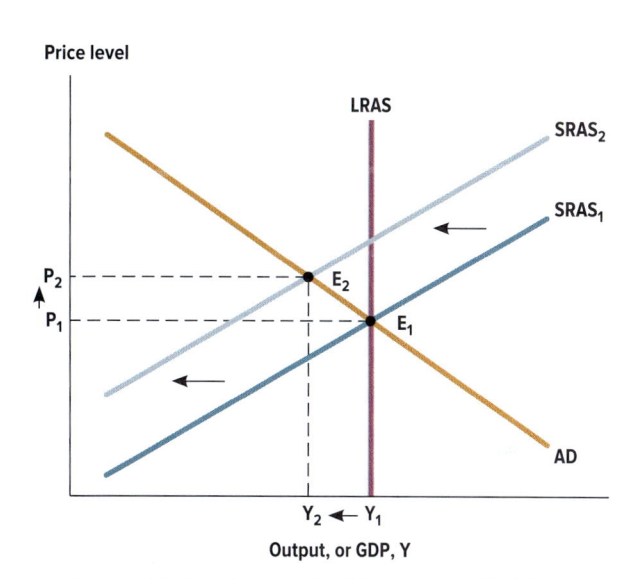

A drought that destroys much of the corn crop will shift the short-run aggregate supply curve in. In the short run, prices will be higher, and output falls.

TABLE 12-5

Demand-side versus supply-side shocks

This table summarizes the impacts of a shock on the demand and supply sides of an economy. Each shock has a different effect on the economy in the long and short run.

Supply or demand?	Positive shock	Negative shock
Demand side	**Short run:** Output increases Price increases	**Short run:** Output decreases Price decreases
Demand side	**Long run:** No change in output Price increases	**Long run:** No change in output Price decreases
Temporary shock: Supply side	**Short run:** Output increases Price decreases	**Short run:** Output decreases Price increases
Temporary shock: Supply side	**Long run:** No change in output No change in price	**Long run:** No change in output No change in price
Permanent shock: Supply side	**Long run:** Output increases Price decreases	**Long run:** Output decreases Price increases

For an example of economic detective work to tease out whether shifts in supply or demand were responsible for observed effects in an economy, see the Economics in Action box "The Kobe earthquake and aggregate supply."

The Kobe earthquake and aggregate supply
Economics in Action

In January 1995, a large earthquake rocked the port city of Kobe, Japan. Many people lost their lives. Buildings and infrastructure were destroyed. The value of Japan's stock market dropped substantially. It was one of the most expensive natural disasters the world had ever seen, with a final damage bill equal to about 2.5 percent of Japan's GDP.

However, amazingly, only 15 months after the disaster, Japanese manufacturing was back to 96 percent of the pre-earthquake trend. How well can the aggregate supply and aggregate demand model explain the recovery of the Japanese economy?

George Horwich, an economist at Purdue, studied this question. The earthquake destroyed a large amount of capital, and so we would expect the short-run aggregate supply curve to shift to the left. This shift would push the price level higher and would reduce output, increasing unemployment. However, when Horwich looked at the data, he saw a different picture. Surprisingly, the price level was relatively stable, and employment was constant.

How can we match up those data with the predictions of the AD/AS model? There are two possibilities in Kobe: Either the aggregate supply curve shifted quickly back out again in the months after the earthquake or the aggregate demand curve shifted out.

We have a way to figure out what actually happened. If an increase in aggregate demand occurred, the price level would increase. But the data showed that the price level stayed constant, or even decreased. This suggests that there wasn't an aggregate demand response. Instead, Horwich argues, the aggregate supply curve shifted back out.

Although the damage in Kobe was significant, it seems that the Japanese economy was able to adjust to this very large shock in one part of the economy by rearranging how resources were used. In this process of adjustment, the aggregate supply curve shifted back out, returning the economy to its original position. The response to the Kobe earthquake tells us that the macroeconomy can sometimes adjust surprisingly quickly, even after large supply-side shocks.

Source: George Horwich, "Economic Lessons of the Kobe Earthquake," *Economic Development and Cultural Change* 48, no. 3 (April 2000), pp. 521–542.

✓ TEST YOURSELF

☐ Will a positive demand shock lead to increased or decreased output in short-run equilibrium? What about in long-run equilibrium? **[LO 12.7]**

☐ How do prices and output change with a leftward shift in aggregate supply? **[LO 12.8]**

☐ How do changes in the price level help distinguish between a demand-side shock to the economy and a supply-side shock? **[LO 12.9]**

The Role of Public Policy

LO 12.10 Describe the policy options the government can use to counteract supply and demand shocks.

It can take a long time for the economy to fully adjust to demand and supply shocks, and waiting for adjustments often isn't comfortable for people who experience changing prices and unemployment. When the economy hits a recession, voters often call upon politicians to "do something."

We will examine the role of government in the economy in more detail when we look at fiscal policy and monetary policy in later chapters. For now, we will consider just one channel through which the government can try to boost the economy out of a recession: government spending.

Government spending to counter negative demand shocks

Imagine that things are going badly in the economy: Newspapers are full of stories about falling home prices, mass layoffs, and factory closings. With the steady beat of bad news, consumer confidence decreases and consumption falls. As we've seen in this chapter, such changes cause the aggregate demand curve to shift to the left, shown in panel A of Figure 12-15. Output and the price level decrease.

As discussed in the earlier example of stimulus spending, the government can try to counter this negative demand shock by increasing government spending. As we have seen, the effect of an increase in government spending is to shift the aggregate demand curve to the right. For policy-makers, the goal is to counteract the negative shock to aggregate demand with a positive one, and restore the curve to its original position.

This is not so easy to do. In practice, it can be hard to gauge the overall effect of government spending on aggregate demand. Even worse, it's rare to perfectly design government policy so that spending occurs at just the right amount to restore aggregate demand to its original level. Panel B of Figure 12-15 shows a case in which the policy is partly, but not entirely, successful: The increase in government spending shifts the AD curve only part of the way back to its previous position.

What about the long run? We know that for any demand-side shock, there can't be an effect on long-run output. According to our AD/AS model, if the government did nothing, then eventually prices would adjust downward until output rose to its previous level. This occurs through changes on the supply side, as cheaper prices reduce the costs of production, shifting the aggregate supply curve to the right.

FIGURE 12-15

Government response to a negative demand shock: The housing crash

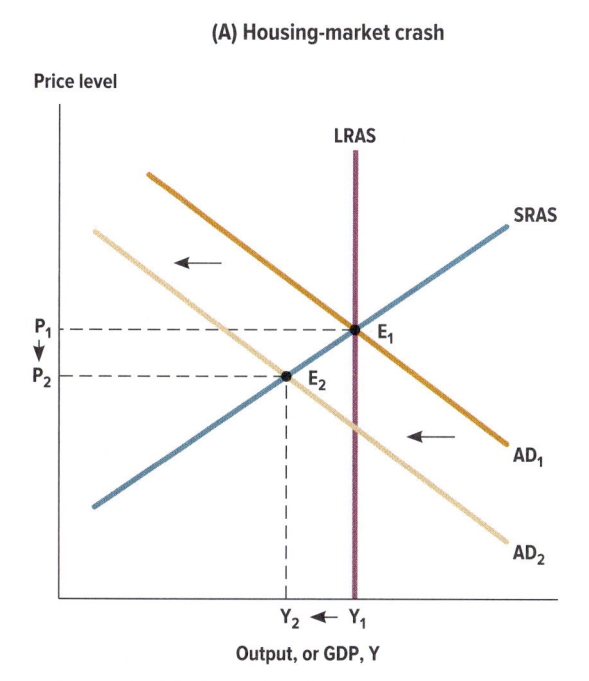

(A) Housing-market crash

In a crash of the housing market, aggregate demand drops sharply, shifting the curve in. The new short-term equilibrium has lower prices and output.

(B) Government stimulus

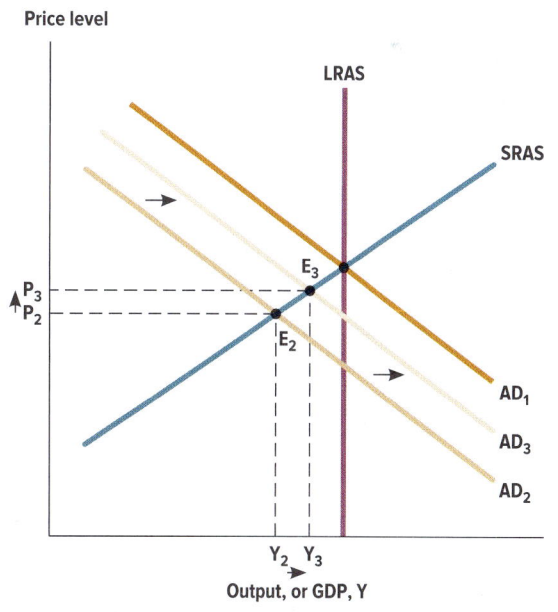

If the government increases spending in response to the housing crash, aggregate demand will shift back out. The new equilibrium is at a higher level of prices and output, but still below the levels under the long-run equilibrium.

If, instead of doing nothing, the government increases spending to stimulate the economy, the end result will be slightly different. In this example, government policy was only partly successful, so the economy still has to adjust before reaching long-run equilibrium. The process of adjustment is still the same as before, except that, now, SRAS doesn't have as far to go as it did when the government hadn't acted. In the end, the long-run effect of the government's increase in spending is that the previous level of output will be restored, but at a slightly higher price level than if the government hadn't acted, holding all else constant. The result is that with a given income or wealth, people can buy less.

This trade-off between increasing the speed of adjustment and allowing higher prices is a genuine challenge the government faces in setting policies to fight downturns in the economy.

Government spending to counter negative supply shocks

Now imagine a short-run supply-side shock: A terrible drought has reduced the corn harvest by 80 percent. The short-run aggregate supply curve has shifted to the left, as in panel A of Figure 12-16. The economy is now at point E_2: The level of output has fallen, and prices have risen.

In this case, policy-makers are in a bind. If they choose to do nothing, the economy will be stuck in a period of higher prices and lower output (stagflation). (We'll talk more about the challenges of stagflation in Chapter 16, "Inflation.") For now, imagine a period in which prices increase but with large amounts of unemployment and low output. It's a very hard situation to get out of. Remember that prices can be very sticky, especially when they have to adjust downward.

Instead of waiting for the aggregate supply curve to shift back out to the right, the government could choose to increase government spending in order to shift the aggregate demand curve. This action and effect are shown in panel B of Figure 12-16. With the shift in aggregate demand, the

FIGURE 12-16

Government response to a negative supply shock: Extreme drought in the Midwest

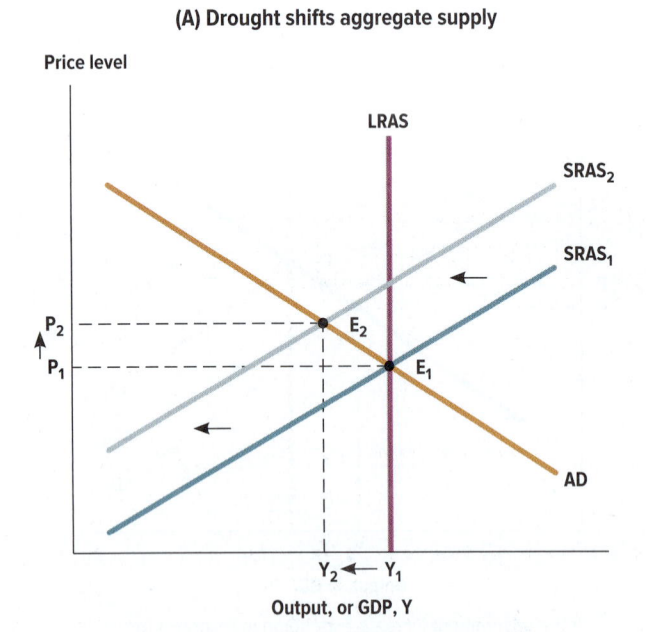

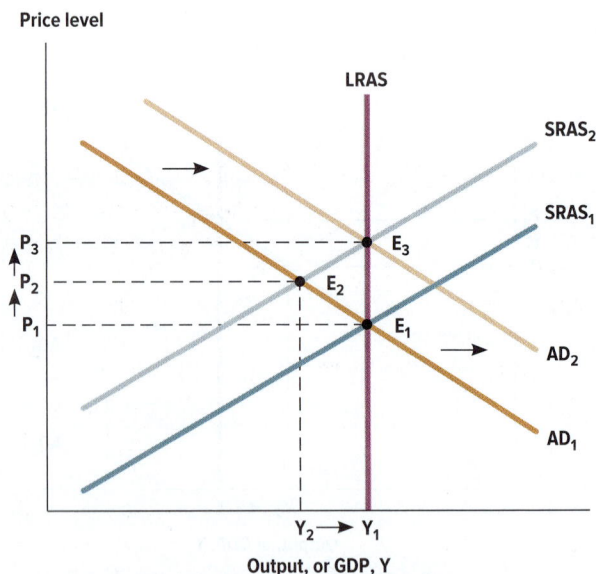

Like before, a drought shifts the short-run aggregate supply curve in, which pushes the economy toward a new short-run equilibrium with higher prices and lower output.

In response to the drought, the government increases spending, which shifts the aggregate demand curve out. Instead of falling back to the original equilibrium, the new long-run equilibrium is at a higher prices level.

economy moves to a new short-run equilibrium at point E_3. While this shift solves the problem of low output and unemployment, it actually drives prices even higher.

In both examples, the long-run result of government intervention is higher prices at the same level of output. So, why would the government ever choose to intervene? One reason concerns the speed of the recovery. Without the increase in government spending, adjustment might have been a long and painful process. In addition, lower prices are not always a good thing. As we will see in Chapter 16, "Inflation," falling prices, called *deflation*, carry another set of challenges for the economy.

The bottom line is that government spending is a *short-term* policy action that is often applied to address short-term demand shocks. Government spending is less effective in countering negative supply shocks, but political pressures can sometimes drive government action even when it's not a great solution.

✓ TEST YOURSELF

☐ What is the long-term effect on prices and output when the government counters a negative demand shock with an increase in spending? **[LO 12.10]**

Conclusion

In this chapter, we created a model of the whole economy. This model is relatively simple, yet ambitious. It helps us to understand what drives key macroeconomics outcomes such as prices, unemployment, and GDP.

The AD/AS model breaks the economy down into two sides. The *demand side* is composed of all the components of expenditure in the economy: consumption, investment, government spending, and net exports. The aggregate demand curve identifies the relationship between overall price levels and aggregate demand in the economy. On the *supply side* of the economy, the aggregate supply curve identifies the relationship between overall price levels and total production in the economy.

In the short run the economy responds to changes in the price level by increasing or decreasing output, so the short-run aggregate supply curve is upward-sloping.

In the long run, production is determined by the availability of inputs for production and the technology to convert inputs to outputs. In the long run, there is no relationship between the price level and output. The long-run equilibrium occurs at the intersection of the aggregate demand and long-run aggregate supply curves.

We used the model of aggregate demand and aggregate supply to understand the recession that engulfed the United States after the housing bubble popped in 2007, shifting the aggregate demand curve to the left. We also used it to understand the government's response, a stimulus package whose aim was to shift the aggregate demand curve back out and stimulate output and employment.

In the next chapter, we'll talk about policy responses to economic shocks in more depth and explore the different effects of spending versus taxes.

Key Terms

aggregate demand curve, p. 301
aggregate supply curve, p. 309
long-run aggregate supply (LRAS) curve, p. 309

short-run aggregate supply (SRAS) curve, p. 309
business cycle, p. 312

supply shocks, p. 313

Summary

LO 12.1 Show how the aggregate expenditure equilibrium model can be used to trace out the aggregate demand curve, and understand why the aggregate demand curve slopes downward.

The aggregate demand and supply model captures the relationship between prices and output in the economy. It comprises two parts: the *aggregate demand* curve, which shows the relationship between the price level and total demand in the economy, and the *aggregate supply* curve, which shows the relationship between the price level and the total supply in the economy. The aggregate demand curve can be traced out by graphing how equilibrium planned aggregate expenditure changes as the price level changes. The aggregate demand curve is downward-sloping because consumption, investment, and net exports all decline when the price level rises.

LO 12.2 List factors that could cause the aggregate demand curve to shift.

Since the aggregate demand curve is derived from the definition of GDP—$Y = C + I + G + NX$—anything that affects any of the components of GDP will shift the aggregate demand curve. For example, if government spending increases, the aggregate demand curve will shift out; if net exports decrease, the aggregate demand curve will shift in. When the aggregate demand curve shifts, there will be a short-run change in output, but no long-run shift in output. The price level will change in both the short run and the long run.

LO 12.3 Explain how changes in government spending and taxes can have a multiplier effect on aggregate demand.

When the government increases spending, it sets into motion a series of additional rounds of expenditure in the economy. Each time aggregate expenditure increases, disposable incomes go up and households respond by spending more. The increased spending causes another round of increased aggregate expenditure, and the process continues. With taxes, the story is similar. A reduction in taxes increases disposable income, triggering a chain of higher spending, increased incomes, and further spending.

There is, however, an important difference between the impact of taxes and government spending. Whereas government spending increases aggregate expenditure dollar-for-dollar in the first round of the multiplier process, a portion of the tax cut gets saved. Thus, the multiplier associated with a given dollar value of tax cuts will tend to be smaller than the multiplier associated with the same dollar increase in spending.

LO 12.4 Explain the difference between the short run and long run in the economy.

The aggregate supply curve is actually two different curves: a *long-run aggregate supply* (LRAS) curve and a *short-run aggregate supply* (SRAS) curve. The long-run aggregate supply curve shows what the economy can produce if all the factors of production are being utilized. This doesn't depend on prices, so the LRAS is vertical. The SRAS is an upward-sloping curve between prices and output. There are factors that affect only the cost of production and do not change the amount of factors available for production. These changes will shift only the SRAS curve.

LO 12.5 Demonstrate a shift in the short-run aggregate supply curve, and list factors that cause it to shift.

If the prices of *inputs* change, the entire aggregate supply curve will shift. Any change that makes production more expensive for firms will shift the supply curve in (to the left). Any change that makes production cheaper for producers will shift the aggregate supply curve out (to the right).

LO 12.6 Demonstrate a shift in the long-run aggregate supply curve, and list factors that cause it to shift.

Anything that affects the output possible using these factors will shift the long-run aggregate supply curve. If the potential output of the economy expands, the long-run aggregate supply curve will shift out. If the production possibility frontier for the economy contracts, the long-run aggregate supply curve will shift in.

LO 12.7 Explain the short-run and long-run effects of a shift in aggregate demand.

When there is a positive shock in aggregate demand, prices and output increase in the short run. Eventually, input prices and wages catch up to the increase in the price level. The SRAS curve slowly adjusts to the right; in the end, this adjustment further increases prices while decreasing output. The final result is that output falls back to its original level, and prices are higher than they were originally.

For a negative shock, the aggregate demand shifts to the left. Prices and output fall. The adjustment of the SRAS curve to the right brings output back to its original level, but prices fall even further.

LO 12.8 Explain the short-run and long-run effects of a shift in aggregate supply.

The aggregate supply curve is a relationship between total supply in the economy and price level. Anything that affects the factors of production or the level of technology will affect both the long-run aggregate supply curve and the short-run aggregate supply curve; this shift is a permanent supply shock. Anything that affects the prices of inputs or the costs of doing business will affect the short-run aggregate supply curve, but not the long-run aggregate supply curve; this shift is a temporary supply shock.

When there is a temporary supply shock, the price level and output change in the short run but not in the long run. For a permanent supply shock, both the price level and output change in the long run.

LO 12.9 Use the AD/AS framework to determine whether an observed change in output and prices was due to a demand shock or a supply shock.

In reality, we do not observe aggregate supply and demand curves shifting. Instead, what we see are changes in output and the price level. With the help of the AD/AS model, we can infer whether the changes in the economy were more likely to be caused by a shift in supply or demand and whether the shock was temporary or permanent.

A situation where output falls and prices rise is likely due to a backward shift of the aggregate demand curve. If, however, output falls and prices rise, it's likely that the culprit is an upward shift in aggregate supply. Temporary shifts in demand and supply do not cause permanent changes in output and prices. Permanent shifts leave output unchanged, but they can lead to permanent changes in the price level. If, for instance, there is a permanent upward shift in the supply curve, long-run output will eventually return to potential, but prices will be permanently higher.

LO 12.10 Describe the policy options the government can use to counteract supply and demand shocks.

Depending on the type of shock, the government can choose to increase or reduce government spending in response. The government often chooses to act because action is preferable to waiting for the economy to adjust after a shock. Shortfalls in aggregate demand can be corrected by increasing spending. The same is true of aggregate demand, although the government might want to be careful in this situation. Regardless of the shock, increases in government spending will produce higher prices in the long run.

Review Questions

1. Identify the four components of aggregate demand. Explain the relationship between aggregate demand and the price level. **[LO 12.1]**

2. The demand curves for individual goods are typically downward-sloping, due both to the substitution effect as well as to the income effect. Why does the substitution effect not affect the aggregate demand curve? **[LO 12.1]**

3. What is the relationship between the equilibrium level of aggregate expenditure in an economy and the aggregate demand curve? According to the aggregate expenditure equilibrium model, why does the aggregate demand curve slope downward? **[LO 12.1]**

4. What effect does rising business optimism and confidence have on the aggregate demand curve? What effect does falling optimism and confidence in business prospects have on the aggregate demand curve? **[LO 12.2]**

5. List several events that could cause a "demand-side" recession (i.e., a recession caused by a fall in aggregate demand). **[LO 12.2]**

6. Everything else equal, which will have a larger effect on aggregate demand and GDP: a $100 million reduction in taxes or a $100 million increase in government spending? Is everything else equal in practice? Why or why not? **[LO 12.3]**

7. Suppose the economy is in a recession and the president wants to stimulate production and create jobs. To do this, he has decided to increase government spending. Some of his economic advisors are suggesting the marginal propensity to consume (MPC) has a value of 0.9 and others are suggesting the value is 0.8. How will this difference in the value of the MPC affect the president's decision regarding the dollar amount of the increase in government spending? **[LO 12.3]**

8. Which typically can change faster: the components of aggregate demand or the components of aggregate supply? Explain. **[LO 12.4]**

9. Explain the difference between sticky wages and sticky prices. How do these two ideas explain the upward slope of the short-run aggregate supply curve? Why don't sticky wages or sticky prices affect the long-run aggregate supply curve? **[LO 12.4]**

10. List several events that could cause a "supply-side" recession (i.e., a recession caused by a fall in aggregate supply). **[LO 12.5]**

11. In the late 1990s, the United States experienced very high GDP growth, record low unemployment rates, and virtually nonexistent inflation. Based on the conclusions of the AD/AS model, what could explain this combination of good economic results? **[LO 12.5, LO 12.6]**

12. Why is long-run economic growth generally positive rather than negative? **[LO 12.6]**

13. Explain the mechanism through which the economy adjusts in the short run and the long run when consumer confidence falls. **[LO 12.7]**

14. Suppose a country is in the midst of an economic boom and is running large budget surpluses. The president suggests that due to the good economic conditions, the time is ripe for a large tax cut. What are the arguments for and against this position? **[LO 12.7, LO 12.10]**

15. Suppose a country is in the midst of a serious recession, with high unemployment and large government deficits. The president suggests that in times like this the government has the obligation to "tighten its belt" and cut spending since so many families around the country have to do the same thing. Do you agree with the president? Why or why not? **[LO 12.7, LO 12.10]**

16. Using the aggregate demand and aggregate supply model, explain the difference between a one-year drought and permanent climate change. What happens to the price level and output in the short run and in the long run for each type of shock? **[LO 12.5, LO 12.6, LO 12.8]**

17. A government official observes that there has been a short-run increase in the price level. Is it possible for her to determine whether this was caused by a demand shock or a supply shock? Why or why not? **[LO 12.9]**

18. A government official observes that there has been a long-run increase in the price level but no change in the level of potential output. Is it possible for her to determine whether this was caused by a demand shock or a supply shock? Why or why not? **[LO 12.9]**

19. Why does the government have a harder time counteracting shifts in AS than in AD? **[LO 12.8, LO 12.10]**

20. Whenever AD or AS shifts, putting the economy out of long-run equilibrium, AS has a natural tendency to shift in such a way as to bring the economy back into long-run equilibrium. If the economy always eventually comes back to long-run equilibrium, why would the government ever try to implement policies to bring the economy into equilibrium through government means? **[LO 12.10]**

Problems and Applications

1. Is there a negative, positive, or no relationship between the price level and the following components of aggregate demand? **[LO 12.1]**
   a. Consumption.
   b. Investment.
   c. Government spending.
   d. Net exports.

2. If the government cuts taxes, what components of aggregate demand are affected? **[LO 12.1]**

3. Consider the planned aggregate expenditure lines in Figure 12P-1. **[LO 12.1]**

FIGURE 12P-1

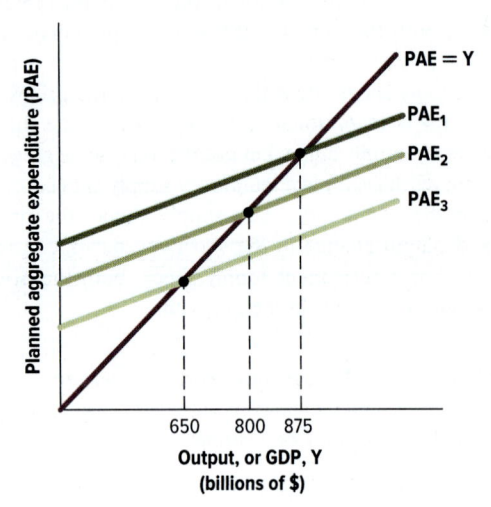

a. Suppose that the planned aggregate expenditure lines correspond to price levels of 100, 110, and 120. Which line corresponds to which price level?

b. Use the information in the expenditure diagram to trace out the aggregate demand curve for this economy.

4. For each of the following shocks, say whether it is a demand-side shock or a supply-side shock. **[LO 12.2, LO 12.5]**
   a. Consumer confidence falls.
   b. Government spending increases.
   c. The price of foreign goods increases.
   d. The price of oil increases.
   e. A cyclone destroys manufacturing plants.

5. In the late 1990s, the U.S. experienced a technology boom. In part the boom was due to a revolution in communication technology that resulted in a massive expansion of the internet; in part the boom was due to households and firms purchasing new computer equipment in anticipation of Y2K. What two curves of the model would be affected by these events? **[LO 12.2, LO 12.5]**

6. Suppose the marginal propensity to consume (MPC) is either 0.55, 0.95, or 0.75. **[LO 12.3]**
   a. For each value of the MPC, calculate the expenditure multiplier, or the impact of a one-dollar increase in government spending on GDP.

b. For each value of the MPC, calculate the impact on GDP of a $250 million increase in government spending.

c. Explain the relationship between the MPC and the impact of a change in government spending on GDP.

7. Suppose the marginal propensity to consume (MPC) is either 0.75, 0.80, or 0.90. **[LO 12.3]**

   a. For each value of the MPC, calculate the impact of a one-dollar decrease in taxes on GDP.

   b. For each value of the MPC, calculate the impact on GDP of a $250 million decrease in taxes.

   c. Explain the relationship between the MPC and the impact of a change in taxes on GDP.

8. Say whether the following statements are true or false. **[LO 12.4]**

   a. In the long run, prices don't affect output.

   b. In the short run, prices may affect output.

9. Say whether the following statements are true or false. **[LO 12.4]**

   a. If the prices of all final goods and services are sticky, then the short-run aggregate supply (SRAS) curve is horizontal at the given price level.

   b. If the prices of inputs and wages are not fixed by contracts, and instead adjust more quickly to demand and supply shocks, then the SRAS curve is more vertical.

10. "Fracking" is a relatively new technology that allows drillers to extract significantly larger quantities of natural gas from existing deposits than was previously possible. How is this discovery likely to affect the economy? (*Hint:* Think about whether this will have a short-run or long-run effect.) **[LO 12.5, LO 12.6]**

11. Throughout the nineteenth and twentieth centuries, the U.S. economy experienced frequent ups and downs, but over the past 200 years, the real GDP in the United States rose from roughly $8.2 billion to over $16.1 *trillion*, an increase by a factor of nearly 2,000 times. This growth represents a change in which curve? **[LO 12.6]**

12. Suppose that a statement by the chair of the Federal Reserve Board about the state of the economy causes a loss of consumer confidence. What will be the long-run impact on the economy if the government allows the economy to adjust without a policy response? **[LO 12.7]**

    a. Output will fall below its initial level in the long run and the price level will decline.

    b. Output will return to its initial level in the long run, but the price level will be lower.

    c. Output will return to its initial level in the long run, but the price level will be higher.

    d. Output will rise above its initial level in the long run and the price level will rise.

13. For each of the following situations, use an AD/AS model to describe what happens to price levels and output in the United States in the short run. In each case, assume the economy starts in long- and short-run equilibrium, and describe the appropriate shifts in the AS or AD curves. **[LO 12.7, LO 12.8]**

    a. A stock market crash reduces people's wealth.

    b. The spread of democracy around the world increases consumer confidence in the United States.

    c. The European economy crashes.

    d. The United States enters into an arms race with China, resulting in a significant increase in military spending.

    e. A revolution in Iran results in a significant reduction in the world's supply of oil.

    f. Terrorist activities temporarily halt the ability of Americans to engage in certain productive activities such as transportation and finance.

    g. Intel develops a new computer chip that is faster and cheaper than previous chips.

    h. A summer of perfect weather in the Midwest leads to record harvests of corn, wheat, and soybeans.

14. For each of the following scenarios, say whether the shock was a demand-side shock, a supply-side shock, or a combination of both shocks. **[LO 12.9]**

    a. The price level and GDP both fell. GDP then increased, but the price level fell even further.

    b. In the long run, the economy had the same level of output but a higher price level.

    c. In the short run, the price level increased, but GDP fell.

    d. In the long run, GDP increased, and the price level fell.

    e. In the long run, GDP increased, and the price level was constant.

15. In 2009, during the height of the U.S. financial crisis, real GDP fell 3.5 percent, and the Consumer Price Index fell from 215.3 to 214.9. Was this recession likely caused by a shift in aggregate demand or aggregate supply? **[LO 12.9]**

16. In 1974, GDP fell by 0.6 percent, and inflation increased from 6.2 percent to 11.0 percent. Was this recession likely caused by a shift in aggregate demand or aggregate supply? **[LO 12.9]**

For questions 17–20, use an AD/AS model to answer the following questions. In each case assume the economy starts in long- and short-run equilibrium, and show the appropriate shifts in the AS or AD curves.

17. Suppose a stock market crash reduces people's wealth. **[LO 12.7, LO 12.8, LO 12.10]**
    a. Show what happens to price levels and output in the United States in the short run.
    b. Suppose the government takes no action to help the economy. What happens to price levels and output in the long run?
    c. Suppose, instead, the government decides to take action to help the economy. What action(s) would you recommend? Why?
    d. If the U.S. government makes the appropriate policy response, what happens to price levels and output in the long run?

18. Suppose the spread of democracy around the world increases consumer confidence in the United States. **[LO 12.7, LO 12.8, LO 12.10]**
    a. Show what happens to price levels and output in the United States in the short run.
    b. Suppose the government takes no action to help the economy. What happens to price levels and output in the long run?
    c. Suppose, instead, the government decides to take action to help the economy. What action(s) would you recommend? Why?
    d. If the U.S. government makes the appropriate policy response, what happens to price levels and output in the long run?

19. Suppose a revolution in Iran results in a significant reduction in the world's supply of oil. **[LO 12.7, LO 12.8, LO 12.10]**
    a. Show what happens to price levels and output in the United States in the short run.
    b. Suppose the government takes no action to help the economy. What happens to price levels and output in the long run?
    c. Suppose, instead, the government decides to take action to help the economy. What action(s) would you recommend? Why?
    d. If the U.S. government makes the appropriate policy response, what happens to price levels and output in the long run?

20. Suppose a summer of perfect weather in the Midwest leads to record harvests of corn, wheat, and soybeans. **[LO 12.7, LO 12.8, LO 12.10]**
    a. What happens to price levels and output in the United States in the short run?
    b. Suppose the government takes no action to help the economy. Show what happens to price levels and output in the long run.
    c. If the U.S. government reacts to the record harvests by increasing taxes or decreasing spending, what happens to price levels and output in the long run?
    d. What is the problem associated with the government reacting to the record harvests by increasing taxes or decreasing spending?

Endnotes

1. The impact of increasing government transfers to households can be analyzed similarly to the impact of a tax cut.
2. Although potential output is often used to track economic booms and recessions, the National Bureau of Economic Research (NBER), a group of economists tasked with tracking the business cycle, marks a recession as the time between a peak and trough in major economic indicators.

Chapter 13

Fiscal Policy

From Housing Bubble to Great Recession

By 2008, the warning signs were everywhere: Unemployment was increasing. Business confidence was down. The economy was at the start of a recession. What, if anything, could the U.S. government do to give the economy a boost?

The two political parties had different answers: Democrats argued that increasing government spending would kick-start the economy. To that end, they advocated for construction projects and other public investments, with the intention of creating badly needed jobs. Republicans argued that since times were tough, the government should tighten its belt, as individuals do when they face money problems. Their favored solution was to lower taxes, allowing people to keep a larger share of their income, to encourage people to spend more, boosting demand.

©karen roach/Shutterstock

In the end, both sides got a little of what they wanted. One of the first acts of newly elected President Barack Obama was to sign the American Recovery and Reinvestment Act of 2009, more commonly known as the "stimulus plan." That plan included both tax cuts and a sizable increase in government spending. Its total cost was nearly $800 billion—slightly more than 5 percent of U.S. GDP.

Despite the big sum spent, the recovery was slow. When economists looked back four years later (at the end of 2012), the economy had still not fully recovered. In the meantime, millions of people had lost their jobs and homes, and many businesses had closed. Things looked better after another four years (at the end of 2016). While the unemployment rate had hit 10 percent at its peak in 2009, by 2016 the unemployment rate had fallen to about where it was before the recession, under 5 percent. The increased spending and decreased tax revenues, though, had put the U.S. government further into debt. By 2012, the dollar value of the debt had climbed past 100 percent of GDP. In 2016 the debt was 104 percent of GDP.[1]

So, was the stimulus plan a success? We can't judge this simply by looking at what happened before and after it was signed into law. Instead, we need to ask: What *would have* happened if the stimulus plan had *not* been enacted? Or what would have happened if the government had chosen an alternative balance of tax cuts and government spending? Would the level of unemployment and the health of the economy have been better, worse, or just the same?

LEARNING OBJECTIVES

LO 13.1 Explain the difference between contractionary fiscal policy and expansionary fiscal policy.

LO 13.2 Explain how fiscal policy can counteract short-run economic fluctuations.

LO 13.3 Identify the time lags that complicate the formulation of fiscal policy.

LO 13.4 Discuss how stabilizers can automatically adjust fiscal policy as the economy changes.

LO 13.5 Describe the theory and evidence about Ricardian equivalence and what it implies for the effectiveness of fiscal policy.

LO 13.6 Describe how revenue and spending determine a government budget and how the U.S. budget deficit occurs.

LO 13.7 Explain the difference between the government deficit and debt.

LO 13.8 Understand how Treasury securities work and why people value them.

LO 13.9 Identify the benefits and costs of government debt.

fiscal policy government decisions about the level of taxation and public spending

To answer some of these questions, we'll create a framework for thinking about how taxation and government spending affect the national economy, based on the aggregate demand and aggregate supply (AD/AS) model you saw in Chapter 12, "Aggregate Demand and Aggregate Supply." By the end of this chapter you should be able to discuss the pros and cons of different policies in terms of their effect on both short-run economic fluctuations and longer-run issues such as the national debt. These questions have been hotly debated since 2007, as policy-makers tried to steer the economy out of the Great Recession, and they continue to have critical implications for the national economy today.

Fiscal Policy

Each February, the U.S. president and Congress begin the process of deciding how much to spend on the varied functions of the federal government: how much to spend on building bridges, supporting the military, investing in medical research, and so on. Occasionally, Congress changes tax policy (as it did in the 2017 Tax Cuts and Jobs Act), which determines how much revenue the government collects. Government decisions about the level of taxation and public spending are called **fiscal policy**. Fiscal policy also includes the effects of programs that grow and shrink automatically as the economy changes. An example is unemployment insurance, which expands during economic downturns as people lose their jobs and shrinks as people find work during an economic recovery. Policies that grow or shrink along with the economy are called *automatic stabilizers*. We'll discuss automatic stabilizers in more detail later in the chapter.

Fiscal policy and aggregate demand

Fiscal policy is more than just simple budgeting. Choices about how much to spend, how to spend it, and how to raise the necessary funds can have dramatic impacts on the economy.

Recall from Chapter 7, "Measuring GDP," that government spending is one of the components of GDP. It is also part of the way we calculate the demand side of the economy in the aggregate demand and aggregate supply (AD/AS) model:

$$\text{Aggregate demand} = C + I + G + NX$$

Fiscal policy affects the economy by increasing or decreasing aggregate demand. As we saw in the previous chapter, shifts in the aggregate demand curve translate into higher or lower output and price levels throughout the economy. Fiscal policy affects aggregate demand through two channels: government spending and tax policy.

LO 13.1 Explain the difference between contractionary fiscal policy and expansionary fiscal policy.

Effects on aggregate demand Government spending *directly* affects the "G" in the aggregate demand equation (above):

- An increase in government spending will generally shift the aggregate demand curve out (to the right).
- A decrease in government spending will shift the aggregate demand curve in (to the left).

Government spending can also have *indirect* effects on the "C" (consumption) and "I" (investment) components of aggregate demand. These effects come through mechanisms called the *multiplier effect* and *crowding out*, which we discuss in detail in later chapters.

The second channel through which fiscal policy drives aggregate demand is tax policy. Before anyone gets a paycheck, the government takes some money in taxes. Consumption therefore depends not on total income but, rather, on *disposable income*—what's left after taxes:

- If the tax rate increases, workers will take home less disposable income, and we can expect them to reduce their consumption. As a result, the aggregate demand curve will shift in (to the left).
- If, on the other hand, the tax rate decreases, workers take home more money and will consume more. The decrease in the tax rate will shift the aggregate demand curve out (to the right).

This effect acts on aggregate demand directly through consumption, or the "C" part of the aggregate demand equation. It can also indirectly affect the other components, such as investment.

Expansionary or contractionary policy We differentiate two types of fiscal policy—*expansionary* or *contractionary*. The first aims to increase aggregate demand, and the second is used to decrease aggregate demand.

The term **expansionary fiscal policy** describes the overall effect of decisions about government spending and taxation intended to increase aggregate demand. Increased government spending and lower taxes both have expansionary effects: They shift the aggregate demand curve to the right, as shown in panel A of Figure 13-1.

In contrast, the term **contractionary fiscal policy** describes the overall effect of decisions about government spending and taxation intended to decrease aggregate demand. Decreased government spending and higher taxes both have contractionary effects, shifting the aggregate demand curve in to the left, as shown in panel B of Figure 13-1.

expansionary fiscal policy
decisions about government spending and taxation intended to increase aggregate demand

contractionary fiscal policy
decisions about government spending and taxation intended to decrease aggregate demand

Policy response to short-run economic fluctuations

One of the most important ways that policy-makers use fiscal policy is to try to smooth out fluctuations in the economy that might hurt consumers and businesses. In this section, we'll show how policy-makers use fiscal policy to counteract the effects of economic shocks through the aggregate supply and aggregate demand model.

In Chapter 12, "Aggregate Demand and Aggregate Supply," we saw how a shock like the collapse of the U.S. housing market in late 2007 can affect the national economy. The most immediate consequence of the steep drop in housing prices was that homeowners felt poorer. This response shifted the aggregate demand curve to the left. Panel A of Figure 13-2 shows the leftward shift of the aggregate demand curve, from AD_1 to AD_2. (If this figure looks familiar, it's because you saw a version of it before—as Figure 12-15, in a discussion of government response to a negative demand shock.) The decrease in aggregate demand caused the economy to produce below its level of potential output. The result was lower GDP (output) and higher unemployment, seen in panel A as a reduction in output from Y_1 to Y_2.

LO 13.2 Explain how fiscal policy can counteract short-run economic fluctuations.

FIGURE 13-1

Expansionary or contractionary fiscal policy

(A) Expansionary fiscal policy shifts the AD curve to the right

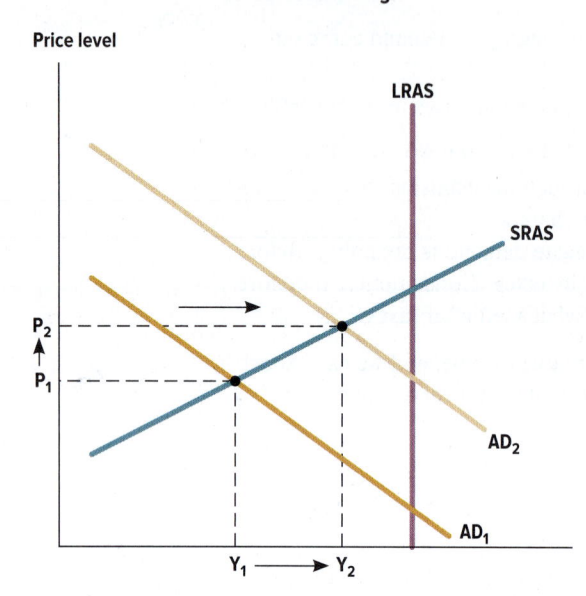

Increasing government spending and lowering taxes are fiscal policies with expansionary effects, shifting the aggregate demand curve out to the right from AD_1 to AD_2. This has the effect of increasing output and price levels.

(B) Contractionary fiscal policy shifts the AD curve to the left

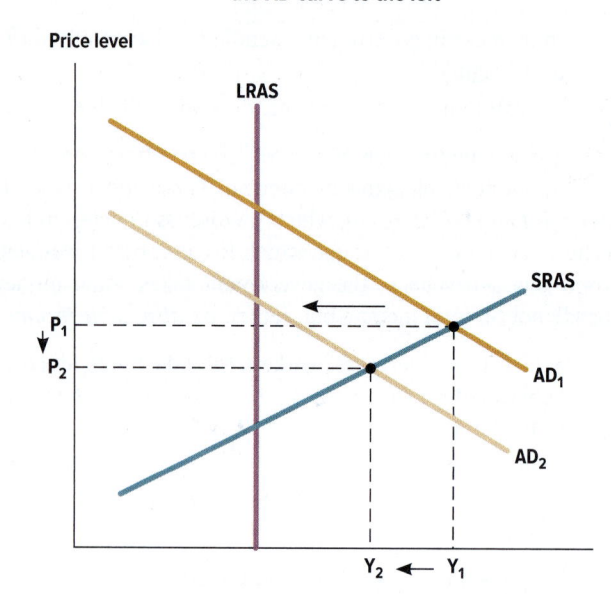

Decreasing government spending and raising taxes are fiscal policies with contractionary effects, shifting the aggregate demand curve in to the left from AD_1 to AD_2. This has the effect of decreasing output and price levels.

According to the AD/AS model, if nothing else happened, the economy would have automatically corrected itself—eventually. Wages would have fallen in response to unemployment, and lower production costs would bring other prices down. This response would cause the short-run aggregate supply curve to shift to the right until the economy returned to its original level of potential output level at Y_1. In the long run, output would have recovered to its previous level, with lower overall prices in the economy.

Why didn't lawmakers simply wait for this to happen? Because it could have been a very slow and painful process. The wage rate would have had to fall along with other prices; we saw in Chapter 9, "Unemployment and the Labor Market," some reasons why that might not happen quickly or easily.[2] When businesses fail and people lose their jobs, they want their government to do something about it. They don't want just to hear that the economy will work the problems out if they wait long enough. As economist John Maynard Keynes (pronounced "canes") once said, "In the long run, we are all dead."

We'll show in this chapter that fiscal policy can have real effects on the economy even in the short run. Ideally, the government can counterbalance shocks like the collapse of the housing market, minimizing the damages to consumers and businesses without having to wait for the economy to correct itself in the long run. However, we'll also see that the government may not always be able to improve matters—it might even make things worse, for reasons we describe in the next section.

But if the government *is* going to act, for better or for worse, what should it do? Let's look at examples of both expansionary and contractionary policy responses.

FIGURE 13-2
Effect of expansionary fiscal policy

(A) Initial market response to fall in AD

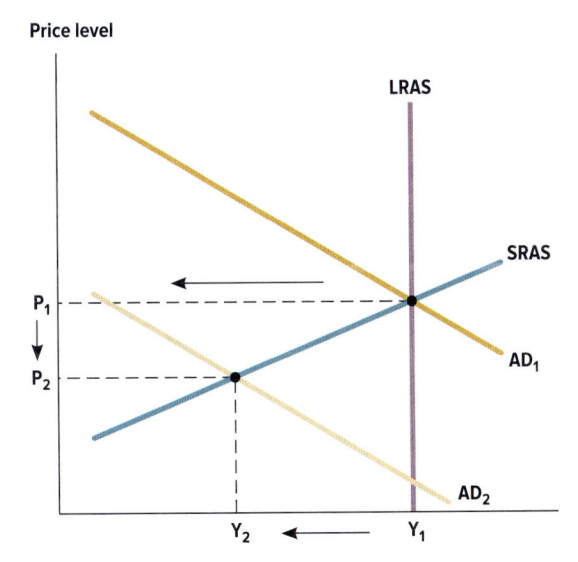

Initially, with a decrease in aggregate demand the AD curve shifts to the left. At the new equilibrium, prices and output are lower than before.

(B) Expansionary fiscal policy restores some AD

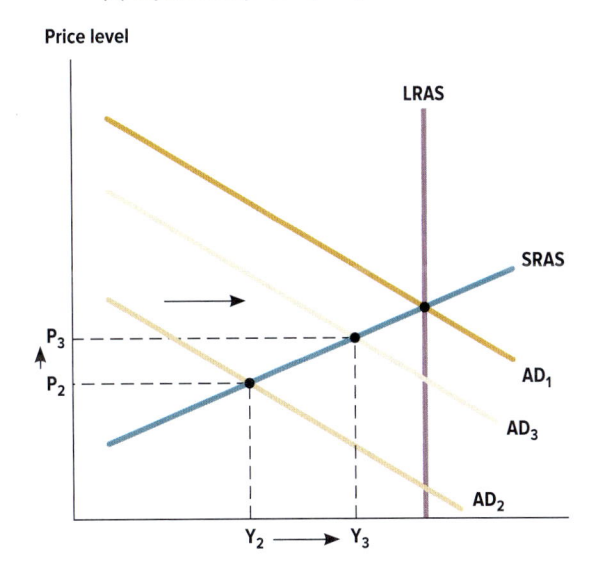

If the government decides to pursue expansionary fiscal policy, it will increase spending, which shifts the AD curve rightward (here, AD_2 to AD_3). The amount of the shift depends on the amount of spending. Here, the government's spending increases output and the price level, but not to their levels before the original fall in AD.

Expansionary policy response To counteract a decrease in aggregate demand like that caused by the 2007 housing-market collapse, the government can try to boost demand, either by spending more or taxing less. This kind of expansionary policy is often called "Keynesian" (pronounced "canes-e-an") in recognition of John Maynard Keynes, who championed the strategy after the Great Depression of the 1930s.

The challenge is finding the dosage of fiscal policy that restores aggregate demand to its prerecession level. As shown in panel B of Figure 13-2:

- A completely successful stimulus plan would shift the AD curve all the way back from AD_2 to its original position, AD_1.
- If the stimulus is only partly successful, then it would move the curve only part of the way back, from AD_2 to AD_3.

However, even a partially successful stimulus may be better than nothing since it pushes the economy toward a better outcome (and the economy can continue adjusting toward the long-run equilibrium over time).

Contractionary policy response What should the government do when the economy is suffering from the opposite problem—that is, when the economy is growing too quickly? People are often happy when the economy is booming, but government policy-makers worry that big booms can get out of hand and the economy can suffer high inflation or asset-price bubbles before a large crash. Implementing contractionary fiscal policy to slow down the economy is a lot like turning down the music at a raging party because you are worried that the neighbors might start to complain. It can be the smart thing to do, even though there will be plenty of grumbling.

FIGURE 13-3
Effect of contractionary fiscal policy

(A) Economy overheats from too much AD

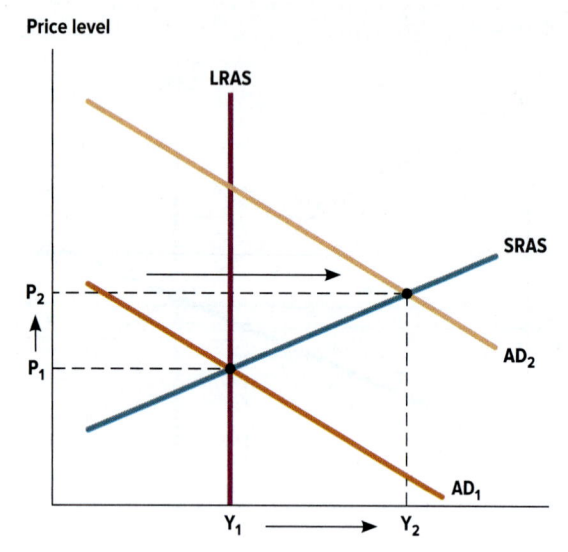

In an overheating economy, prices and output are above the long-run equilibrium in the economy.

(B) Contractionary fiscal policy lowers prices and output

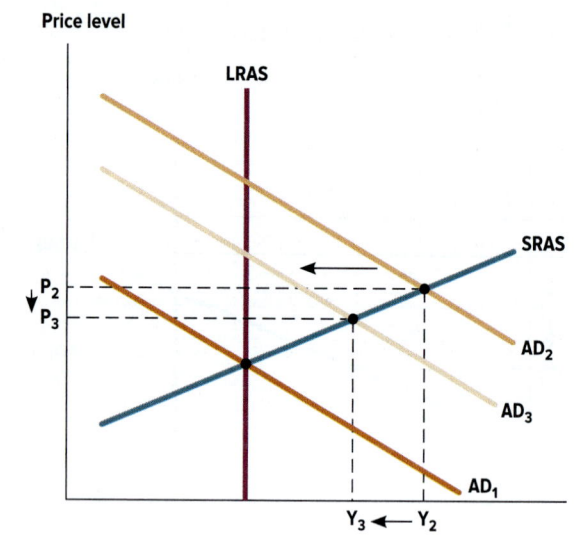

In order to slow down the economy, the government can cut spending or raise taxes, shifting the AD curve leftward. When this happens, prices and output fall, although the economy is still above long-run equilibrium.

A surge in aggregate demand—like that caused by the housing market boom of the early and mid-2000s—increases output and the price level, as shown in panel A of Figure 13-3. Contractionary fiscal policy slows down the economy by cutting government spending or increasing taxes, shifting the aggregate demand curve back in to the left, as shown in panel B of Figure 13-3.

Real-world challenges

LO 13.3 Identify the time lags that complicate the formulation of fiscal policy.

Fiscal policy might sound like a golden solution: Why should any government wait for the economy to correct itself in a slow and painful way when it can do the work much more quickly?

The analysis so far suggests that fiscal policy is a potent tool. After all, we saw in Chapter 12, "Aggregate Demand and Aggregate Supply," that increasing direct government spending has a larger multiplier effect on output than a similarly costly reduction in taxes net of transfers. Looking at the math alone, it seems that there's a strong case for tackling a recession through government spending instead of tax cuts.

Unfortunately, it's not so simple. The analysis rests on some big simplifying assumptions that do not always hold. In the real world, things are more complicated. For instance, we've assumed that government spending doesn't *crowd out* (i.e., reduce) private-sector spending. **Crowding out** is the reduction in private borrowing that is caused by an increase in government borrowing. As we show in greater detail in Chapter 14, "The Basics of Finance," one common form of crowding out happens when the government borrows in order to finance extra spending. The government's borrowing tends to push interest rates upward, which then can decrease investment by the private sector. The decrease in private investment undermines the positive impact of government spending.

Even without this kind of crowding out, fiscal policy can be hard to get right. Fiscal policy choices often amount to no more than educated guesses, made without the benefit of all the

crowding out
the reduction in private borrowing caused by an increase in government borrowing

relevant information. Furthermore, time lags between when policies are chosen and when they are implemented mean that sometimes it is too late to do any good.

To see some of the difficulties of implementing fiscal policy, imagine that the economy is a bus. You're the driver and it's your job to prevent the bus from stalling if it comes to an uphill section of road or from running out of control if it comes to a downhill section. You can step on the gas (in terms of the economy, use expansionary fiscal policy). Or you can step on the brakes (use contractionary fiscal policy). Sounds easy enough, right? But here's what you face as you attempt to drive the bus:

- Imagine that the windshield is blacked out so you can't see the road ahead. In addition, the speedometer indicates how fast you were going three blocks ago rather than how fast you're going now.
- Even worse, imagine that the bus is run as a democracy, so you also have to get the agreement of a majority of the passengers before you can hit the brakes or the gas, and they typically argue the matter for at least four blocks.
- Finally, once you actually hit the brakes or gas, it takes six to 12 blocks for that action to take effect.

This is how policy-makers can feel when deciding about fiscal policy. Lags in the policy-making process come from three main sources:

1. *Information lag:* Understanding what the current economic situation is. (You can't see out of the front of the bus, and the speedometer is three blocks delayed.)
2. *Formulation lag:* The process of deciding on and passing legislation. (If the president is the bus driver, lawmakers in Congress are the arguing passengers.)
3. *Implementation lag:* The time it takes for the policy to affect the economy. (Once you push the gas or the brakes, it takes several blocks until the acceleration or braking engages.)

Information lag   The first issue involves an *information lag*. It might seem pretty clear that the economy is in a recession or boom, just as it might seem pretty clear from looking out of the back window of a bus that you've started to go up or down a hill. But it can take a long time to collect data that tell policy-makers about GDP, unemployment, and inflation. GDP figures, for example, are released every three months, and they report on economic activity that was happening three or four weeks before. These early numbers aren't always accurate, so it may be six months or more before the true figures are known.

Three to six months is a short time to register a trend in the overall economy. You certainly don't want to be the one who raises the alarm about a huge mountain up ahead of the bus, only to find that it was actually a tiny hill. It took an entire year's worth of data to trigger the announcement by the National Bureau of Economic Research that the U.S. economy was in a recession in 2008. By then, the economy had lost over 1 million jobs.

Just as it takes time to find out how bad things are, it also takes time to find out if the economy has reached the end of a recession. There will be news reports of companies hiring more workers, but it can take months to discover if this has translated into real gains for the economy. In both cases, policy-makers have to make important decisions for the future, but they only know where the economy was a few months ago.

Formulation lag   The second issue is *formulation lag*—the time it takes to decide on and pass legislation. First, a policy needs to be drafted and proposed in Congress, where it becomes a bill. The bill is first debated in the House of Representatives. If at least half of the representatives approve it, it then moves to the Senate. If a majority (or 60 if the other party decides to filibuster the legislation) of the 100 senators approve, the president can sign the bill into law, or veto it, in which case the whole process has to start again. The 535 members of Congress can take a while to make up their minds: It was clear in September 2008, with the collapse of the investment bank Lehman Brothers, that the economy was in real trouble. But the stimulus act wasn't passed until after President Obama and a new Congress had been inaugurated in January 2009.

Implementation lag   The last hurdle for fiscal policy is *implementation lag*. Even after a policy has been proposed and passed, it may take time for it to take effect. It takes time for funds to be disbursed, employees hired, and materials purchased. Even tax cuts can take some time to kick in. In 2008, the government sent U.S. taxpayers a tax rebate as part of a first response to the recession, but it took three months to print and mail the 130 million checks. Even after receiving the checks, it took time for people to spend the money.

These three lags in the policy process—information lag, formulation lag, and implementation lag—make conducting good fiscal policy a tough endeavor. In fact, the lags may be so large that by the time the policy takes effect, the economy might have corrected itself, making the policy unnecessary.[3] In the worst case, the economy might even have started to face the opposite problem, making the policy actively harmful—like slamming on the brake when it turns out the bus is just starting to go uphill, or stepping on the gas when it's now going downhill.

In addition to challenges in formulation and implementation, it also turns out that the effectiveness of a stimulus depends on how people receive their money. The Economics in Action box "A check in the mail, or more in your paycheck?" investigates the implementation differences between stimulus packages in 2008 and 2009.

A check in the mail, or more in your paycheck?
Economics in Action

When the economy is doing badly, governments often try to stimulate demand by giving citizens money to spend. So, in 2008 and 2009 the U.S. government disbursed "stimulus payments" and encouraged Americans to spend the money.

It might seem that money is money, and people will spend extra money no matter how they receive it. But the government disbursed the stimulus payments in two very different ways:

- One way to deliver the stimulus money was through a simple, one-time check or a one-time transfer of electronic funds directly into people's bank accounts. Recipients got a big chunk of money all at once.
- The second way to deliver the stimulus money involved splitting the payment into small installments that were received each payday. (In practice, this second way involved reducing the amount of taxes withheld from people's paychecks.)

How people received the stimulus money partly determined their spending choices.

Some experts predicted that the people who received the big, one-time chunk would save more of it (that is, they would spend less of it), compared with people who received the money as regular, small installments. The reasoning was that the small installments would hardly be noticed by most people, and they would just spend the extra money without thinking much about it. Those people who got a big, one-time chunk would surely pay attention, and they would be more likely to pause, plan, and deliberately save some of it for important uses in the future. The reasoning was based on psychological theories about how we pay attention.

It turns out that the exact opposite happened. Economists Claudia Sahm, Matthew Shapiro, and Joel Slemrod surveyed people who received the stimulus payments. Their survey revealed that twice as many of the people getting the big chunks (25 percent) said they would spend most of the money, compared with the people who got the money in small installments (13 percent of whom said they would spend most of it).

Why? One possibility is that people were generally reluctant to spend during the hard economic times. Thus, those people who got a bit of extra money in each paycheck were reluctant to spend that too. But people who got the big, one-time chunk of money were more likely to view it as a special opportunity—so they grabbed the chance to buy something meaningful.

Sahm and her colleagues show that when it comes to debates about stimulus payments, the policy question is not just, "How much to give?" but also, "How?"

Source: Claudia R. Sahm, Matthew D. Shapiro, and Joel Slemrod, "Check in the Mail or More in the Paycheck: Does the Effectiveness of Fiscal Stimulus Depend on How It Is Delivered?" *American Economic Journal: Economic Policy* 4, no. 3 (2012), pp. 216–250, http://dx.doi.org/10.1257/pol.4.3.216.

Policy tools—discretionary and automatic

The 2009 stimulus bill is an example of targeted, or *discretionary*, fiscal policy. This is policy that the government actively *chooses* to adopt. Even if there had been no stimulus act at all, though, fiscal policy would still have had some effect on the economy due to already-existing taxes and spending policies. These taxes and government spending that affect fiscal policy without specific action from policy-makers are called **automatic stabilizers**. Let's look at how both taxes and government spending act as automatic stabilizers.

LO 13.4 Discuss how stabilizers can automatically adjust fiscal policy as the economy changes.

automatic stabilizers taxes and government spending that affect fiscal policy without specific action from policy-makers

Taxes as automatic stabilizers
Any income tax system that has people pay higher tax rates as their earnings rise creates automatic stabilizers. Although this section focuses on individual rates, corporate taxes also create automatic stabilizers.

In the U.S., income tax laws require you to pay a given percentage on each portion of your income that falls between certain ranges (often called "tax brackets"). For example, in 2018 single Americans paid the following rates:

- 10 percent in taxes on the portion of their income from $0 to $9,525
- 12 percent from $9,526 to $38,700
- 22 percent from $38,701 to $82,500, and so forth.[4]

People can end up paying a different proportion of their income as taxes, simply because as their income changes, they face different tax obligations. For instance, if you earned $38,000 in 2018, the highest tax rate you faced was 12 percent. But if instead you changed jobs (or got an amazing raise) that bumped your income to $44,000 in 2018, you would have had to pay a greater proportion of your income as taxes in 2018 because part of your income would now automatically be charged at 22 percent.

Unlike discretionary fiscal policy, automatic stabilizers are not affected by information, formulation, or implementation lags. In addition, automatic stabilizers work to push the economy in the same direction that correctly timed and correctly formulated discretionary policy would. For example:

- When the economy is booming, people earn more and move into higher income ranges, so they pay taxes at higher tax rates automatically—without any new intervention from policy-makers. When that happens, the increased taxes that people must pay put a slight check on overall spending. This slight check cools down aggregate demand by taking away dollars that might have otherwise been spent—just as would happen if policy-makers had intentionally increased taxes as a contractionary fiscal policy.
- When the economy is in a recession, people earn less on average, and so they automatically end up paying lower tax rates as they move to lower income ranges. The reduced taxes at lower tax brackets put some extra money in people's pockets (compared with what

they would have had to pay if tax rates hadn't changed), encouraging a little extra spending. This stabilization spurs aggregate demand slightly, just as would happen if the government had intentionally decreased taxes to implement an expansionary fiscal policy.

Government spending as an automatic stabilizer Some aspects of government spending also work as automatic stabilizers. Unemployment insurance benefits and welfare programs such as food assistance and Medicaid have set eligibility criteria based on low income or unemployment status. Their effects reflect the health of the economy:

- When the economy is booming, fewer people are eligible for these programs, so government spending on them decreases. With reduced government spending, the aggregate demand curve shifts to the left. This has a contractionary effect similar to discretionary policy that lowers government spending, reducing aggregate demand.
- In a recession, more people qualify for unemployment insurance and food assistance, so spending on those programs automatically rises. With higher government spending, the aggregate demand curve shifts to the right. This has an expansionary effect similar to discretionary policy that raises government spending, increasing aggregate demand.

In sum, when the U.S. economy hits a recession, fiscal policy *automatically* becomes expansionary: Average tax rates go down and spending on welfare programs goes up. In a booming economy, fiscal policy *automatically* becomes contractionary: Tax rates rise and welfare payments fall. The kind of *discretionary* stimulus bill approved in 2009 comes on top of these automatic effects.

Limits of fiscal policy: The money must come from somewhere

LO 13.5 Describe the theory and evidence about Ricardian equivalence and what it implies for the effectiveness of fiscal policy

Politicians often cut taxes in response to recessions. The idea is that people will spend more money when they have more cash in their hands, increasing aggregate demand. That spending, in turn, will raise business profits, create jobs, and help the economy recover.

But it's not always so simple. Those tax cuts don't come for free. Economic theory suggests that the government will eventually have to find a way to make up for the lost tax revenue, especially if the economy is sluggish and cannot expand revenue to cover the gap. That means either cutting an equivalent amount of government spending or, more frequently, raising taxes in the future to pay for debt incurred today.

What happens if people see that today's tax cuts just mean higher taxes tomorrow? In that case, people won't want to spend as much from their tax cuts, and the stimulus strategy will be less effective. This idea is known as *Ricardian equivalence*. This theory predicts that if governments cut taxes but not spending, people will *not* change their behavior. Why not? Because people realize that the government will have to borrow money to cover the financial shortfall created by cutting taxes. They realize that at some point in the future, they—or their children or grandchildren—will eventually have to repay the extra government debt through future tax increases. In other words, taxpayers understand that the money to maintain government spending must come from somewhere.

Because taxpayers realize that the debt will eventually have to be repaid through future taxes, today's tax cut will feel more like a loan than a real windfall. According to the Ricardian equivalence theory, rational people should save what they receive rather than spend it today, in order to meet the financial obligation of future taxes. But if people save rather than spend, consumption does not increase, and the tax cut will be unsuccessful in increasing aggregate demand.

Of course, in reality, people may not be so rational and forward-looking. When they get a tax cut, they may go ahead and spend it (or part of it). If they do, Ricardian equivalence will fail to hold, and the fiscal policy *will* have the intended expansionary effect.

Nonetheless, the theory of Ricardian equivalence is a good reminder that people often respond to changes in government policy by adapting their behavior. Good policy has to take those responses and the unintended consequences that stem from them into account. In some cases, rational responses by individuals may be strong enough to make a well-intentioned policy fail. In practice, however, most people seem not to think about future tax increases when they open that envelope containing a tax rebate, as described in the Economics in Action box "Spending your stimulus check."

Spending your stimulus check
Economics in Action

In early 2008 it had become clear that the economy was ailing. President George W. Bush's administration took steps to address the problem with the Economic Stimulus Act, which sent taxpayers a "stimulus check"—a check that came in the mail, no strings attached, for the household to spend as it pleased. About 130 million households got checks, for a total of $100 billion across the nation. Individuals received between $300 and $600, and couples received twice that, plus $300 per child.

The government hoped that families would spend the checks, increasing consumption and shifting the aggregate demand curve to the right. But there was no requirement that people spend the money rather than just save it. In fact, the theory of Ricardian equivalence predicts that a rational family would save the money. This was the chance that the government took when sending out the stimulus checks.

What happened in practice? It turned out that families spent most of their windfall. They purchased cars and trucks and went back to the shopping mall. The average spending response amounted to between 50 and 90 percent of the value of the checks. The increase in overall household spending did shift the aggregate demand curve to the right and helped stimulate the economy back toward its previous higher level of output.

In short, people did not respond in the way predicted by Ricardian equivalence theory—they spent a good chunk of the money, although not all of it. The economy wasn't out of the woods yet, but the stimulus checks served their intended purpose as an early counterstrike against the contractionary effects of the recession.

Source: Jonathan Parker, Nicholas Souleles, David Johnson, and Robert McClelland, "Consumer Spending and the Economic Stimulus Payments of 2008," *American Economic Review* 103, no. 6 (2013), pp. 2530-2553.

Fiscal policy can be a powerful tool, enabling the government to counteract short-run fluctuations in the economy by increasing spending or cutting taxes. However, there is a catch: The government has to pay for all the roads and bridges and tax rebates somehow.

Where does the money come from? It comes from taxpayers. If spending increases without a comparable increase in taxes, or if taxes are cut without a comparable decrease in spending, the government often goes into debt. The following section discusses how fiscal policy interacts with the government budget.

✓ TEST YOURSELF

- ☐ What are decisions about the level of government spending and taxation called? **[LO 13.1]**
- ☐ What type of fiscal policy increases aggregate demand? **[LO 13.2]**
- ☐ What are the three types of time lags involved in implementing fiscal policy? **[LO 13.3]**
- ☐ Are income taxes an example of discretionary or automatic fiscal policy? **[LO 13.4]**

- ☐ Why might citizens experience a tax cut more like a loan than a real windfall? And how would that affect fiscal policy? [LO 13.5]
- ☐ What does the evidence say about Ricardian equivalence? [LO 13.5]

The Government Budget

We've seen why the government may want to influence the economy by changing the amount it spends or taxes. If spending is higher than revenue, which is the current situation in the United States and in most other countries, the government will have a **budget deficit**—an amount of money a government spends beyond the revenue it brings in. And although it happens more rarely at the federal level, it is also possible for the government to have a **budget surplus**—an amount of revenue a government brings in beyond what it spends.

In practice, budget deficits can require borrowing money. When governments persist in running budget deficits year after year, the amounts borrowed to cover the deficits can pile up over time. These accumulations are the *public debt*. In the remainder of this chapter, we'll discuss the government budget and the effect that public debt can have on the economy.

budget deficit an amount of money a government spends beyond the revenue it brings in

budget surplus an amount of revenue a government brings in beyond what it spends

LO 13.6 Describe how revenue and spending determine a government budget and how the U.S. budget deficit occurs.

Revenue and spending

At a glance, how a government budget works is pretty simple: Money comes in as tax revenues and goes out through government purchases and transfer payments. (*Transfer payments* refer to payments from government accounts to individuals for programs, like Social Security, that do not involve a purchase of goods or services. As such, these payments are not reflected in GDP.)

What's *not* simple about a government budget is the enormous amount of money involved. Total U.S. government expenditure in 2018 was around $4.11 trillion. The government took in, through tax revenue, approximately $3.33 trillion. The gap between revenue and spending—the budget deficit—was an incredible $779 billion.[5]

The size of the 2018 deficit actually represents an improvement: In 2011, the U.S. government deficit was as high as $1.3 trillion. The last time the deficit had been that large as a percentage of GDP was during the run-up of spending on tanks and airplanes necessary to fight World War II.

It's important to keep in mind that government decisions about spending, income, and borrowing differ fundamentally from households' decisions when it comes to recessions:

- When households face tough times, they usually think about belt-tightening and building up resources for a rainy day.
- When the government faces a downturn, it sometimes makes sense to *increase* spending and reduce taxes in order to stimulate aggregate demand.

Indeed, the government has a role in undoing the negative demand externality that occurs when households all "do the right things" for themselves (cut consumption), but which ends up reducing overall demand in the economy at a time when *greater* demand is in fact needed to help improve the economy.

The U.S. budget deficit

Figure 13-4 shows the U.S. budget deficit for the last 78 years. In almost every year since 1940 there has been a budget deficit. Deficits have been especially large in times of war, as government spending on the military increases. The amount of the budget deficit for 2018 was approximately $779 billion.

Economists usually express the deficit as a *percentage of GDP* to emphasize the relationship between the deficit and the size of the economy. As Figure 13-4 also shows, during World War II, the deficit reached 30 percent of GDP. Much smaller spikes in spending corresponded with the 1990–1991 Gulf War and the period after September 11, 2001, when the wars in Iraq and Afghanistan were launched.

FIGURE 13-4

U.S. budget deficit since 1940 With the exception of World War II (the big upward spike in the 1940s comes from military spending), the U.S. budget was relatively balanced until about 1970. For a few decades afterward, there was a modest budget deficit. After a short period of surplus, the government again started running deficits due to tax cuts and efforts to spend the economy out of the Great Recession.

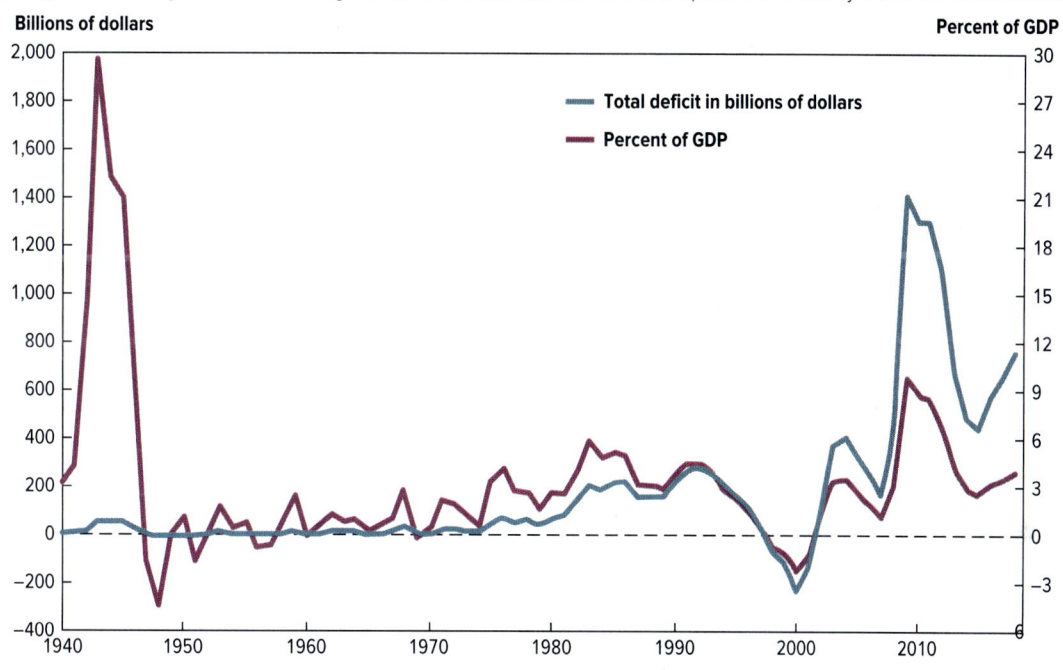

Source: https://fred.stlouisfed.org/series/FYFSD, and https://fred.stlouisfed.org/series/FYFSGDA188S.

Spending increases can lead to larger deficits, but so can decreases in tax revenues. You may notice that the deficit was pretty high—on average 4 percent of GDP—during the 1980s, a time of economic growth and peace. This was due to changes on the revenue side of the government budget, as tax rates were lowered by President Ronald Reagan and the government took in less money. A similar thing happened after the 2017 tax cut. Although it is tough to pinpoint the exact impact of a specific policy, the CBO projected that the legislation would add $1.854 trillion to the deficit over 10 years, after factoring in the boost lower taxes would add to the economy.

Recessions also tend to increase deficits, as can be seen in the sharp spike from 2007 onward. During a recession, government spending often increases as part of an expansionary fiscal policy, while revenues tend to decrease because people are earning and spending less.

For an account of how increases in government spending and reductions in revenue contributed to a gaping budget deficit, see the Economics in Action box "From surplus to deficit."

From surplus to deficit
Economics in Action

By the end of the 2018 fiscal year, the U.S. government deficit was $779 billion. The government spent much more than it took in through taxes and other revenue. It hasn't always been like that. When President Bill Clinton left office in 2001, the government was running a surplus. Every year since 1997, the federal government had been taking in more in revenue than it spent, and

(continued)

it was steadily reducing the public debt. Looking at these surpluses, the Congressional Budget Office (CBO) predicted that the government would be able to repay all of its debt by 2006.

That prediction turned out to be far from reality. Starting in 2002, the government began running deficits, and those deficits led to increases in the public debt. Rather than falling to zero by 2006, government debt had increased from $5.4 trillion to $8 trillion. By 2019, the government debt was over $16 trillion. What happened to cause the government to run deficits after 2001, when it had been running surpluses beforehand?

In short: wars, tax cuts, and a recession. The terrorist attacks of September 11, 2001, led President George W. Bush to announce a "War on Terror" and embark on a protracted conflict in Afghanistan and then in Iraq. As of 2010, the war in Iraq had cost $704 billion; between them, Iraq and Afghanistan account for 10 percent of the error in the CBO's 2001 debt projection.

What else did the CBO not see coming? President Bush passed two deep tax cuts, in 2001 and 2003, and President Barack Obama passed one in 2010. Proponents of the tax cuts argued that they would actually increase overall tax revenue, as they would spur faster economic growth. Increases in revenues due to economic growth, they argued, would be enough to cover the decrease in revenue due to lower rates. This did not happen—instead, the amount of tax revenue collected by the government fell. It fell by so much, in fact, that the level of revenue collected in 2000 was not reached again until 2006. The two Bush tax cuts, along with the further tax-relief package passed by President Obama in 2010, account for another 30 percent of the 2001 prediction error. At the end of 2017, President Trump signed another large tax cut.

Also, there was recession: first, a short recession in 2001 and then the Great Recession of 2007–2009. The Great Recession had three important impacts on government finances:

- First, the government did not collect nearly as much revenue as the CBO had projected.
- Second, spending on government programs such as unemployment benefits and food stamps increased.
- Third, the government bailed out the banks and automakers while simultaneously stimulating the economy with government spending.

This spending came on top of other increases, including a historic expansion of the federal Medicare program under the Bush administration.

If predictions can be so far off the mark, why does the CBO bother making them? Decision makers need a general idea of how policies such as tax cuts and economic-stimulus packages might affect the economy. When these unexpected events happen, the CBO updates its initial predictions—something it has had to do more than 30 times since 2001.

Source: www.pewtrusts.org/~/media/legacy/uploadedfiles/wwwpewtrustsorg/fact_sheets/economic_policy/driversfederaldebtsince2001pdf.pdf.

✓ TEST YOURSELF

- ☐ What is the term for when the government collects more revenue than it spends? **[LO 13.6]**
- ☐ Name three reasons why the budget deficit might increase during a recession. **[LO 13.6]**

The Public Debt

Just a few blocks from the flashy billboards and dazzling displays of Times Square in New York City is a far more humble digital counter that keeps tabs on the debt incurred by the U.S. federal government. Every time the government runs a deficit, the **public debt**—the total amount of money that a government owes at a point in time—increases.

In the rare years when the government runs a surplus, the debt decreases. When the public debt decreased at the end of the 1990s, the clock's owner had to shut down the clock temporarily because he hadn't programmed it to be able to count backwards.

public debt
the total amount of money that a government owes at a point in time; the cumulative sum of all deficits and surpluses

The upward trend soon resumed. The next time the debt clock had to be shut down, the reason was to add another digit as the debt passed $9,999,999,999,999. By 2019, the clock had rolled past the $22 trillion mark and shows little sign of slowing. This $22 trillion is the equivalent of almost $67,492 of debt per citizen.[6]

Seymour Durst, who put up the NYC debt clock, said, "It'll be up as long as the debt or [New York City] lasts," adding, "If it bothers people, then it's working."[7] How bothered *should* we be about the size of the public debt? Throughout the rest of the chapter, we'll present statistics and both sides of the story to help you decide for yourself.

Since this photo was taken at the Republican National Convention in June 2018, the U.S. national debt has crossed the $22 trillion threshold, with little sign of slowing.
©Michael Brochstein/SOPA Images/LightRocket/Getty Images

Size of the debt

In 1792, Alexander Hamilton convinced the only two banks in the country to lend the newly formed United States of America $19,608.61. This is the first known entry on the ledger of the country's public debt.

Although people sometimes confuse the terms *debt* and *deficit*, they are different, and the distinction between them is an important one:

- The *deficit* tells us how much the government revenues fall short of spending *each year*.
- The *debt* is the *total* amount that the government owes those from whom it has borrowed money.

In other words, the debt is the cumulative sum of all deficits and surpluses.

Figure 13-5 demonstrates the *cumulative effect* of the annual deficits depicted in Figure 13-4. This figure shows the public debt since 1940, in real-dollar terms (blue line) and as a share of GDP (red line).

LO 13.7 Explain the difference between the government deficit and debt.

FIGURE 13-5

U.S. government debt since 1940   The total amount of U.S. government debt was held below $1 trillion through 1980 due to low yearly deficits. Afterward, the debt began to increase dramatically. As a share of GDP, the total debt decreased after 1948. Then government debt started to increase as a share of GDP, especially in 2008 due to large deficits.

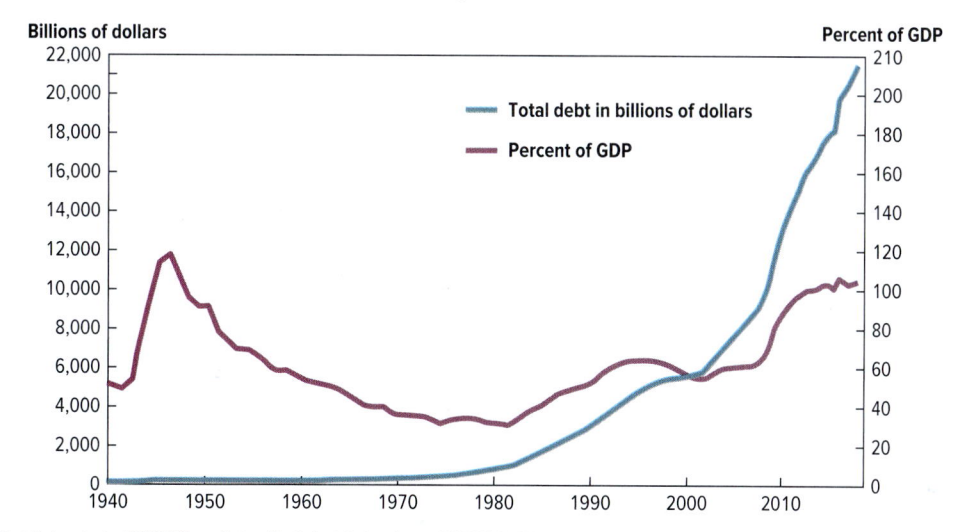

Source: https://fred.stlouisfed.org/series/GFDEBTN, and https://fred.stlouisfed.org/series/GFDEGDQ188S.

FIGURE 13-6

Debt in various countries, 2018 There is a wide discrepancy in the amount of debt owed among countries. In 2018, Japan's debt was the highest in relation to GDP, at 236.6 percent of its GDP. Most countries have a level of debt that ranges between 20 and 80 percent of their GDP.

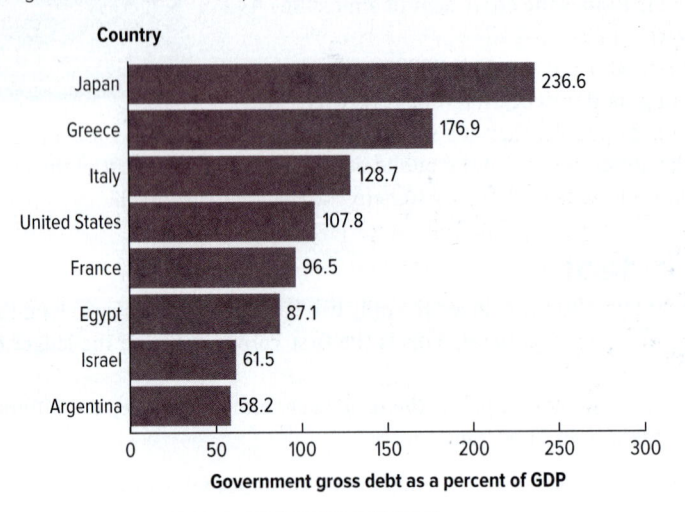

Country	Government gross debt as a percent of GDP
Japan	236.6
Greece	176.9
Italy	128.7
United States	107.8
France	96.5
Egypt	87.1
Israel	61.5
Argentina	58.2

Source: www.imf.org/external/datamapper/GGXWDG_NGDP@WEO/EURO/EU/USA/JPN/CHN.

To see why it's useful to think of the public debt as a share of GDP, consider it in terms of personal finances. Which would you prefer:

- To be making $20,000 a year and owe $10,000 in debt?
- To be making $100,000 a year and owe $30,000 in debt?

In the first case, your debt is smaller but amounts to 50 percent of your annual income. In the second case, your debt is three times as large, but only 30 percent of your annual income. Even though you owe more in the second case, you'd be less worried about your ability to repay it.

Similar logic explains why debt as a share of GDP actually shrank between 1950 and 1980, even though in dollar terms the debt was going up: The economy grew quickly during these years, much faster than the growth in the debt. After 2009, in contrast, debt as a share of GDP increased quickly as the government spent money while the economy remained sluggish after the Great Recession.

Almost every country in the world has debt, some much more than the United States as a percentage of GDP. Figure 13-6 shows the amount of debt owed by various countries. Four of them—Japan, Greece, Italy, and the United States—owe more than 100 percent of GDP.

How does the government go into debt?

LO 13.8 Understand how Treasury securities work and why people value them.

Treasury securities debt-financing arrangements made by the U.S. government

How exactly does government spending lead to debt? The process is more complicated than simply putting purchases on a charge card or getting a loan at a local bank. The government borrows money from people by selling **Treasury securities** (simply called "Treasuries" for short). The details of Treasuries can be complex, but the basic idea is that the U.S. government accepts money from people with an obligation to pay them back by a certain date.

Some Treasuries are short-term promises (the government will pay back the money after one month or one year); others operate on much longer time frames and don't get repaid for 30 years:

- The shortest-term Treasury securities are *Treasury bills*, also known as *T-bills*. These are loans to the government that mature in less than a year. When you buy a T-bill, you're buying a promise that the government will pay you a set amount of money on a fixed date—for example, $1,000, three months from today. People bid for T-bills when they are issued, so depending on the state of the market for T-bills, you might pay, say, only $997 for this particular promise. The $3 difference is the equivalent of interest earned on a savings account. The return on these loans is usually quite low, but they are liquid (your money is tied up in the bond for less than a year). Most important, investors consider them to be very safe, and they thus appeal as a place to securely park money.

- For longer-term investments, the government issues *Treasury notes* in 2-, 3-, 5-, 7-, and 10-year increments. When you purchase a Treasury note, every six months you receive an interest payment at a set rate. The return on 10-year Treasury notes is often cited as an indicator of the country's overall macroeconomic health. It is the most liquid and most widely traded bond in the world. These notes pay more in interest than do T-bills, since liquidity and interest paid are inversely related. (Chapter 14, "The Basics of Finance," addresses this relationship in more detail.)

- For those who are even more patient, the government offers its longest-term option: *Treasury bonds* mature in 30 years and pay a specified amount of interest every 6 months.

Who buys Treasury securities? They are purchased as financial investments by individuals and by other governments and banks, both in the United States and abroad. The Federal Reserve also holds about $2.2 trillion of U.S. Treasury securities. Almost half of the privately held government debt is held by people who live outside the United States. At the end of 2018, the top eight foreign holders of U.S. debt, from largest to smallest, were China, Japan, Brazil, Ireland, the United Kingdom, Switzerland, Luxembourg, and the Cayman Islands.[8] Due to the large export imbalance China and Japan have with the United States, together they hold just under a quarter of U.S. debt.

Why would people, banks, and governments want to hold U.S. government debt? The main reason lies in the relative safety of the investment, especially when compared with other investments. When you invest in real estate, the housing market can crash. When you invest in a company's stock, the company can lose market value or go bankrupt. Governments can declare themselves bankrupt, too, and refuse to pay back money that people have loaned them. But investors generally believe that the odds of the U.S. government doing this are quite low, essentially zero.

In the shakiest part of the Great Recession, investors flocked to short-term U.S. Treasuries to escape risks in the stock market and real estate market. Demand was so strong that for a while interest rates were negative, meaning that investors were willing to lose money in return for the safety of buying the debt of the United States.

Is government debt good or bad?

In the summer of 2011, more than 100,000 people marched in the streets of Athens. They were protesting "austerity" measures that would cut government spending in the hope of taming Greece's astronomical debt burden. At 1.5 times the size of GDP, debt had become a serious worry to its creditors and the European Union, who were behind the drive to cut spending. (By 2015, Greece's debt had risen above 175 percent.)[9] However, most economists believe that debt is necessary to the smooth functioning of government. What are the benefits and costs of government debt?

LO 13.9 Identify the benefits and costs of government debt.

Benefits of government debt
There are two main benefits of government debt: flexibility and investment for growth.

The first benefit of debt is that it allows the government to be flexible when something unexpected happens. Hurricane Katrina, which devastated the Gulf Coast in 2005, cost the U.S. government $105 billion, or almost 4 percent of government spending that year. If the choice is between borrowing to cover the costs of responding to an emergency or not responding at all, many people would say it's better to borrow.

The second benefit of debt is that it can pay for investments that will lead to economic growth and prosperity (and, presumably, higher tax revenues) in the long run. Just as you might decide to borrow to fund your college education because you expect it to lead to a better job and higher salary down the road, it can make sense for governments to borrow to invest in the education system or to construct roads and other infrastructure that will help the economy to grow more quickly.

Costs of government debt On the other hand, there are both *direct* and *indirect* costs of government debt. The *direct cost* is the interest the government has to pay to the people it has borrowed from.

Interest payments on the debt are substantial. In the past, interest payments on the U.S. debt have amounted to the fourth-largest budget expense, just behind spending on transfer payments (consisting of Social Security and means-tested transfer payments such as Medicare, the first- and third-largest budget categories, respectively) and defense (the second-largest budget category).

The direct cost of debt depends on the interest rate. If the interest rate increases, the government debt becomes more expensive to pay. The interest rate, in turn, depends on investors' confidence in the government's ability to pay back the debt. This can become a vicious cycle: If investors doubt that a government will be able to repay its debt, they will demand a higher interest rate before they are willing to lend to that government. That higher interest rate increases the burden of debt, making it even more doubtful whether the government can pay it back.

This self-reinforcing spiral of investor doubt and a higher interest rate has, in the past, forced defaults by some governments when they could no longer afford the direct costs. Although few people think there is a serious risk of this happening to the U.S. government, in 2011 the major rating agency Standard & Poor's downgraded its rating of U.S. debt from AAA to AA+. This downgrade implied some degree of doubt about whether U.S. politicians would be able to meaningfully tackle the tough choices required to shrink the government debt.

There are also *indirect costs* of government debt. In some circumstances, government debt can distort the credit market and slow economic growth. We have already noted the possibility that government borrowing can *crowd out* private borrowing: When the government borrows money, it increases the demand for credit, and so increases the price of credit—the interest rate—in the wider economy. A higher interest rate increases the cost of borrowing for businesses that want to invest and for consumers who want to buy new homes or cars, slowing aggregate demand. (We describe this mechanism more extensively in Chapter 14, "The Basics of Finance.")

Finally, there is the question of who bears the burden of government debt. People today benefit when the government borrows to spend more on services or cut taxes, but people tomorrow will have to repay the loans. The costs of services are being kicked down the road to the country's children and grandchildren.

✓ TEST YOURSELF

- ☐ What is the difference between government debt and deficit? **[LO 13.7]**
- ☐ How do Treasury securities provide financing for the U.S. government's debt? **[LO 13.8]**
- ☐ What is one possible effect of government debt on the amount of private investment? **[LO 13.9]**

Conclusion

We started this chapter by looking at why the government might want to change fiscal policy to counteract economic fluctuations. When the economy is in a recession, expansionary fiscal policy—cutting taxes, increasing spending, or both, as with the 2009 stimulus plan—can increase aggregate demand and speed up recovery. Unemployment remained high even in the first years after the stimulus, but ultimately there is no way of knowing for certain whether it would have been even higher without it.

We also looked at how the government can borrow and how deficits lead to public debt. Debt adds to government flexibility, but it can be costly and slow down economic growth. It also raises questions about the fairness of expecting future generations to bear the burden of paying off the debt.

Governments have an alternative to fiscal policy when they want to influence the economy: *monetary policy*. Monetary policy works through the financial system, so before we get into monetary policy, we will cover the basics of finance in the next chapter.

Key Terms

fiscal policy, p. 334
expansionary fiscal policy, p. 335
contractionary fiscal policy, p. 335
crowding out, p. 338
automatic stabilizers, p. 341
budget deficit, p. 344
budget surplus, p. 344
public debt, p. 346
Treasury securities, p. 348

Summary

LO 13.1 Explain the difference between contractionary fiscal policy and expansionary fiscal policy.

Together, the level of taxation and government spending is called *fiscal policy*. We say that fiscal policy is either expansionary or contractionary.

Expansionary fiscal policy involves changes to fiscal policy that cause the aggregate demand curve to increase (shift out to the right). It is expansionary because it expands demand. Expansionary fiscal policy occurs because either government spending increases or the level of taxation decreases and is a response to recessionary conditions.

On the other hand, *contractionary fiscal policy* involves changes to fiscal policy that contract aggregate demand, causing the aggregate demand curve to decrease (shift in to the left). Contractionary fiscal policy occurs when government spending decreases or when taxation increases, and is a response to an overheating economy with the accompanying threat of excessive inflation.

LO 13.2 Explain how fiscal policy can counteract short-run economic fluctuations.

The government can use fiscal policy to counteract business-cycle fluctuations. When the economy is sluggish, the government can conduct expansionary fiscal policy to stimulate demand. This will lead to a faster recovery than without the fiscal policy. On the other hand, if the economy is overheating, the government can undertake contractionary fiscal policy to reduce aggregate demand. This action also returns the economy closer to the long-run equilibrium level.

LO 13.3 Identify the time lags that complicate the formulation of fiscal policy.

Time lags can mean that sometimes a fiscal policy choice is too late to do any good. Time lags come in many forms. There are *information* lags (how long it takes to get the right information about the overall health of the economy), *formulation* lags (getting everyone to agree on the right policy), and *implementation* lags (how long it takes fiscal policy to have an effect on the economy).

LO 13.4 Discuss how stabilizers can automatically adjust fiscal policy as the economy changes.

To get around time lags, *automatic stabilizers* can affect fiscal policy without specific action from policy-makers. These features of government policy can automatically stimulate or slow the economy.

The tax system is designed so that people who earn more income should pay higher average tax rates. One consequence is that when the economy is booming, people move into higher income ranges, which means they automatically face higher tax rates. The automatically increased taxes have a contractionary effect by slightly checking overall spending and aggregate demand. When the economy is in a recession, people move to lower income ranges, which have lower tax rates. The automatically reduced taxes have an expansionary effect, encouraging spending and spurring aggregate demand.

Government spending can also work as an automatic stabilizer. When the economy is booming, fewer people are eligible for unemployment insurance benefits and welfare programs; government spending on those programs falls, reducing aggregate demand and having a contractionary effect. In a recession, more people are eligible for these programs and spending on them automatically rises, increasing aggregate demand and having an expansionary effect.

> **LO 13.5** Describe the theory and evidence about Ricardian equivalence and what it implies for the effectiveness of fiscal policy.

Ricardian equivalence predicts that if governments cut taxes but not public spending, people will recognize that the government will have to borrow money to cover the financial shortfall that's been created. People will then figure that, at some point in the future, taxes will have to go back up to repay the extra government debt incurred through tax cuts. Since people see that a tax cut today will just mean higher taxes in a few years (or maybe decades), they are reluctant to spend so freely after the tax cut. The theory says that, as a result, tax cuts will have no impact on spending: People will continue to save rather than spend, consumption will not increase, and the tax cut will be unsuccessful in changing aggregate demand.

Recent empirical evidence, however, shows that people do spend extra when taxes are cut, increasing aggregate demand. Ricardian equivalence is an important theoretical idea, but the data show it is not a good guide to predicting the actual effect of tax cuts.

> **LO 13.6** Describe how revenue and spending determine a government budget and how the U.S. budget deficit occurs.

The government budget includes all of the revenue it collects in taxes and all of the money it spends on government programs. When the government spends more than it collects in revenue, it runs a *deficit*. When it collects more revenue than it spends, it has a *surplus*.

In most years, the government spends more than it collects in revenue. Deficits tend to increase during recessions and, more generally, when spending rises and tax revenues fall.

> **LO 13.7** Explain the difference between the government deficit and debt.

Deficits occur when annual spending is more than annual revenue. A *surplus* occurs when annual spending is less than annual revenue. The *public debt* is the total amount of money that the government has borrowed (but not yet repaid) over time.

The debt and the deficit are closely related: The budget deficit tells us how much the government borrows each year, and the debt tells us the total that the government has borrowed and not paid back over time. In other words, the debt is the cumulative sum of all deficits and surpluses.

> **LO 13.8** Understand how Treasury securities work and why people value them.

The government borrows money from others by selling *Treasury securities*. They are debt-financing arrangements made by the United States with obligations to pay back the money over varying lengths of time (often for a year or less, but sometimes for as long as 30 years).

Individuals, other governments, and banks, both abroad and in the United States, purchase Treasuries as financial investments. They are typically seen as relatively safe investments, and investors around the world flocked to these during the Great Recession and its aftermath.

> **LO 13.9** Identify the benefits and costs of government debt.

A deficit allows the government to spend more than its revenue. Allowing the government to run a deficit permits the government to respond to unexpected events and to undertake expansionary fiscal policy.

However, there are also costs of running deficits. Interest needs to be paid on the debt, the government may not spend the money efficiently, and high government deficits may increase interest rates and thus reduce investment in the economy.

Review Questions

1. What is the best fiscal policy for a country suffering from high inflation? **[LO 13.1]**

2. If the government wants to reduce GDP by $500 million, should it increase or decrease its spending? Must it increase or decrease spending by exactly $500 million, some amount more than $500 million, or some amount less than $500 million? Would this be expansionary or contractionary fiscal policy? **[LO 13.1]**

3. President Obama said the following in November 2010 when announcing a two-year pay freeze for civilian federal employees: "After all, small businesses and families are tightening their belts. Their government should too." What do you think the intended effect of this policy would be, assuming the economy was in a recession at the time? Do you think it was the appropriate response? Why or why not? **[LO 13.2]**

4. If unemployment is high and spending is sluggish, what type of fiscal policy should be enacted? How would this be enacted via taxes? Via government spending?

What is the intended effect of this policy on aggregate demand? **[LO 13.2]**

5. "The problem with democracy," your friend tells you as you debate politics, "is the time it takes to get approval for every action the government takes. If the president didn't have to spend so much time arguing back and forth with Congress, policy wouldn't take so long to affect the economy." Is your friend right or wrong? What would your response be? **[LO 13.3]**

6. Explain the difference between tax rates and tax revenues, and how each is related to recession and policy enacted to counteract it. Do you expect to see tax rates rise or fall during recession? What about tax revenues? Explain your answer. **[LO 13.4]**

7. The government decides to reduce income taxes due to a recession in the economy over the past nine months. Will the reduction in income taxes boost spending in the economy? Why or why not? **[LO 13.5]**

8. Use the theory of Ricardian equivalence to explain why cutting taxes during a recession may not always be an effective expansionary fiscal policy. **[LO 13.5]**

9. Why have budget deficits been so high in the United States since 2007? **[LO 13.6]**

10. You hear on the nightly news that the president has vowed to decrease the nation's debt. "We'll have to buckle down and learn to do without, both the government and private citizens," he says. How can a nation lower its debt? How will the government and private citizens be affected? **[LO 13.6]**

11. A friend of yours looks at the state of the U.S. debt in 2018 and tells you, "Since the debt is so high, we must be running an incredibly large deficit every year." Is your friend's analysis valid? Why or why not? **[LO 13.7]**

12. Is it possible for a nation's government to run a budget deficit in some years but not have national debt? Explain your answer. **[LO 13.7]**

13. Explain the differences and similarities among Treasury bills, Treasury notes, and Treasury bonds. **[LO 13.8]**

14. Your friend thinks buying Treasury bills is riskier than leaving money in a savings account. You disagree. Who is right? **[LO 13.8]**

15. Taxpayers are clamoring for their government to be more responsible, and many strongly support a balanced-budget amendment. This would mean the country could no longer spend more than it takes in each year. Discuss the primary advantages and disadvantages of such a law. **[LO 13.9]**

16. Is government debt good or bad for the economy and the nation as a whole? Give one argument for each side of the debate. **[LO 13.9]**

Problems and Applications

1. Is each of the following policies an example of expansionary or contractionary fiscal policy? Explain your answers in terms of the effect on aggregate demand. **[LO 13.1]**
    a. The government slashes funding for the Environmental Protection Agency, without changing any other spending.
    b. The government raises taxes on households making more than $250,000.
    c. The government decides to fill gaps in Medicare by making it available to more people.

2. The economy is growing far too quickly, as high aggregate demand is causing inflation. What fiscal policy should be pursued in this instance—expansionary or contractionary? What will be the effect of the appropriate policy on aggregate demand? **[LO 13.1]**

3. Assuming that unemployment is high and spending is low, answer the following questions. **[LO 13.2]**
    a. Should the government pursue expansionary or contractionary fiscal policy?
    b. What will the appropriate policy do to the aggregate demand curve? Will the curve shift to the right or to the left?
    c. Through which component(s) of aggregate demand (C, I, G, or NX, or some combination of the preceding) will the change occur?

4. The diagram in Figure 13P-1 shows aggregate demand for New Caprica last year (AD_1) and this year (AD_2). If you were to advise the president of New Caprica on economic policy, how would you answer the following? **[LO 13.2]**

FIGURE 13P-1

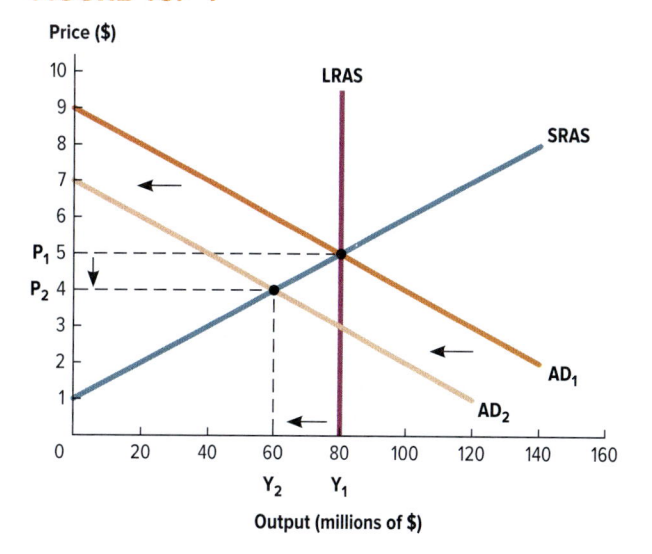

a. How large is current output? How large is potential output? What is the difference, if any, between the two?

b. Is New Caprica in a recession or a boom?

c. Given your findings, should the president enact expansionary or contractionary fiscal policy, or no policy at all?

d. In which direction would the aggregate demand curve shift if the president used contractionary fiscal policy?

5. "Our fiscal policy was unsuccessful," an economic analyst says, "due to partisan bickering in Congress that delayed the passing of the appropriate measures and our failure to realize we were headed into recession until it was too late." What type of lags is the analyst describing? **[LO 13.3]**

6. Assume that the government in some nation intended to respond to low employment via fiscal policy. What type of policy would this require? Assume that this policy ended up having an undesirable outcome. How could this happen in terms of formulation and implementation lags? **[LO 13.3]**

7. Saabira earns $68,000 a year and pays an average tax rate of 15 percent. **[LO 13.4]**

a. Calculate Saabira's disposable income and the amount of tax she pays to the government.

b. Suppose a recession hits the economy and Saabira's income falls to $60,000 per year due to the fact that she is earning a smaller annual bonus. If she now pays an average tax rate of 12 percent, what is her disposable income and the amount of tax she pays to the government?

c. Calculate how much Saabira's annual salary and disposable income fell by due to the recession.

d. Explain how income taxes are an automatic stabilizer in this example.

8. True or false? If the amount of time a person is eligible for unemployment compensation is reduced from 26 weeks to 4 weeks, people will have an incentive to quickly find a new job. This occurs because unemployment compensation is an important automatic stabilizer for the economy. **[LO 13.4]**

9. Consider three countries. The first country runs small budget surpluses each year. The other two countries run large budget deficits each year. In one of the deficit countries the national debt-to-GDP ratio has been steady, whereas in the other deficit country the national debt-to-GDP ratio has been rising. Suppose each of these countries decides to reduce income taxes. Is Ricardian equivalence likely to hold in all of these countries? Why or why not? **[LO 13.5]**

10. A country is in the midst of a recession with real GDP estimated to be $2.7 billion below potential GDP. The government's policy analysts believe the current value of the marginal propensity to consume (MPC) is 0.90. **[LO 13.5]**

a. If the government wants real GDP to equal potential GDP, by how much should it increase government spending? Alternatively, by how much should it reduce taxes?

b. Suppose that during the recession people have become less confident and decide they will spend only 50 percent of any additional income. In this case, if the government increases spending by the amount calculated in part a, will real GDP end up less than, greater than, or equal to potential GDP? By how much?

c. With the same decrease in consumer spending described in part b, if the government decreases taxes by the amount calculated in part a, will real GDP end up less than, greater than, or equal to potential GDP? By how much?

d. Why is it difficult for the government to predict exactly how a change in spending or taxes will affect GDP?

11. If in some year a nation's budget deficit is $9.49 trillion and government spending is $12.26 trillion, how much must it have earned in tax revenue this year? **[LO 13.6]**

12. "The government shouldn't borrow so much," your uncle claims. "Look at that national debt! It's no different from someone borrowing on credit cards they can't pay." **[LO 13.6]**

a. Is your uncle right?

b. How is government debt spending like someone borrowing on a credit card?

c. How is government debt spending different from someone borrowing on a credit card?

13. Econo Nation started 2015 with no national budget debt or surplus. By the end of 2015, it had a budget surplus of $304 million; in 2016, it had a budget deficit of $452 million; in 2017 it had a budget surplus of $109 million. The amount of its budget deficit or surplus in 2018 is unknown. If at the end of 2018 Econo Nation's national debt totaled $50 million, did it run a deficit or surplus in 2018? How much? **[LO 13.7]**

14. "Though the national debt has increased, don't worry," the president says in a televised speech. "We will not have to pay these funds back to bond buyers." How is this possible? How must the government have financed its debt in this case? **[LO 13.7]**

15. You buy a Treasury note for $950. Every 6 months you receive a payment of $40. **[LO 13.8]**
    a. What is the annual rate of return?
    b. What would be the annual rate of return if the payment was instead $30?
    c. What would be the annual rate of return if the payment was instead $45?

16. Your friend believes buying Treasury bills or Treasury notes will offer protection against rising inflation in comparison to buying stocks or mutual funds, because the rate of return on the Treasury bills and notes is known at the time of purchase. Do you agree? Why or why not? **[LO 13.8]**

17. Which of the following are examples of the negative effects associated with government debt? **[LO 13.9]**
    a. Increased interest rates.
    b. Increased taxes or lower spending in the future.
    c. Increased investment in the economy.

18. If the government could borrow as much as it liked with a 0 percent interest rate, would the government debt be cost-free? Explain your answer. **[LO 13.9]**

Endnotes

1. http://data.bls.gov/timeseries/LNS14000000 and www.tradingeconomics.com/united-states/government-debt-to-gdp.
2. In Chapter 16, "Inflation," we will also see that there are other reasons to be concerned about *deflation*, or falling prices in an economy.
3. It turns out that many recessions last less than a year. The official length of the 2007–2009 recession was 14 months. Of course, it's impossible to know how long the recession would have lasted without the government's expansionary policy.
4. www.irs.gov.
5. www.usgovernmentspending.com/federal_deficit.
6. www.usgovernmentdebt.us.
7. http://content.time.com/time/business/article/0,8599,1850269,00.html#ixzz1OtKQCoQM.
8. U.S. Treasury, http://ticdata.treasury.gov/Publish/mfh.txt.
9. http://blogs.wsj.com/briefly/2015/07/03/greeces-debt-the-numbers.

The Financial System and Institutions

PART SIX

The four chapters in Part 6 will introduce you to . . .

the financial and monetary systems and the institutions that make them work. In Part 6, we'll discuss everything from the traders on Wall Street to the humble dollar bill in your wallet.

Chapter 14, "The Basics of Finance," runs through the basics of financial markets and describes the roles that individuals and institutions play in them—including everyone from a family buying a first house to the traders making million-dollar bets on Wall Street. Financial markets connect savers and borrowers, helping money flow to the parts of the economy where it is the most valuable at any given time and allowing people to manage their money over time and minimize the risks they face.

Chapter 15, "Money and the Monetary System," is all about money. Money helps the economy operate smoothly. As a *medium of exchange*, it enables you to buy a pack of gum, a car, or an entire tropical island. It is more than just bills and coins, though. In the United States, the Federal Reserve is the main institution responsible for creating and managing the overall money supply. This power gives it a unique ability to steer the economy through good times and bad.

Chapter 16, "Inflation," covers the delicate relationship between inflation and unemployment. Policy-makers at central banks, like the U.S. Federal Reserve, have the task of controlling fluctuations in the value of money. They can also use the tools of monetary policy to influence the overall level of unemployment. With this power comes great responsibility: Recent history is filled with examples of how countries have suffered from inflation and unemployment caused by poor monetary policy.

Although financial markets usually run smoothly, there are times when the system fails to efficiently manage risk and fund new ventures. Investigating how financial systems break down provides unique insights into how they actually work. In Chapter 17, "Financial Crisis," we'll pick through the details of the worst financial crisis for generations: the problems that followed the 2007 crash in the U.S. housing market, which plunged the U.S. economy and others around the world into deep recession.

Chapter 14

The Basics of Finance

Henry Lehman and His Brothers

In 1844, Henry Lehman opened a dry-goods store in Montgomery, Alabama. At first, he sold groceries and basic supplies to local farmers. Soon, his brothers joined the firm, and the business began to expand. The Lehman brothers started acting as go-betweens for local planters, buying their cotton and then selling it in more distant markets. Business boomed, and they opened an office in New York City, adding coffee and other commodities to their cotton brokerage.

With its southern roots, the company was hard hit by the U.S. Civil War. At the end of the war, it regrouped and soon had a contract with the state of Alabama to help manage its finances and debt payments. By the end of the nineteenth century, the Lehman Brothers brokerage house had become one of the largest and most powerful institutions on Wall Street.

©Kiyoshi Ota/Getty Images

Lehman Brothers survived the Civil War, the Great Depression, World War II, an ill-fated merger with a rival, and the September 11, 2001, destruction of its headquarters, located just across the street from the World Trade Center towers. Despite all of that, on September 15, 2008, Lehman Brothers declared bankruptcy. The failure of such a large, long-standing, reputable firm was almost unimaginable. Global markets panicked. How could such a seemingly sturdy organization, which less than a year earlier had earned record profits, suddenly go broke?

The story of Lehman's collapse, the housing market crash that led to it, and the financial-system implosion and Great Recession that followed is one of the most fascinating economic tales of our time. To understand these events, we have to begin with an understanding of the financial system itself.

LEARNING OBJECTIVES

LO 14.1 Define a financial market, and describe the information asymmetry problems that can occur in them.

LO 14.2 Discuss the three main functions of financial markets.

LO 14.3 Describe the market for loanable funds, including the price of loanable funds, and differentiate between savings and investment.

LO 14.4 List the factors that affect the supply and demand of loanable funds.

LO 14.5 Understand how interest rates on loans vary with the length of the loan and the riskiness of the transaction.

LO 14.6 Describe why it is important for the financial system to intermediate between buyers and sellers, provide liquidity, and diversify risk.

LO 14.7 Differentiate between debt and equity, and define the major types of assets in each category.

LO 14.8 Name the main institutions in financial markets, and describe the role that each plays.

LO 14.9 Explain the trade-off between risk and return in financial assets, and describe how risk can be measured.

LO 14.10 Give arguments for and against the assumption that markets are efficient.

LO 14.11 Describe why savings equals investment in a closed economy and how government spending and foreign capital flows affect the saving-investment relationship.

Traditional markets in goods and services are relatively straightforward—they help to match prospective buyers with those willing to sell. In comparison, *financial markets* can seem abstract and remote. What do they do? What exactly are Wall Street firms selling and on whose behalf are they selling it? How did old-fashioned cotton brokers like the Lehman brothers end up on Wall Street? Why do we have a financial system?

In fact, the basic purpose of financial markets is similar to any other market—they match people who want money to spend now (buyers) with people who want to save their money for later (sellers). In doing so, they also help people manage their money over time and protect themselves against risk. The *financial system* brings together savers and borrowers in a set of interconnected markets in which people trade a variety of financial products.

The basic premise of a financial market is simple, but actual transactions can be quite complex. Financial markets offer a wide variety of financial products, targeted to people with different investment or saving needs. Just as wholesalers and grocery stores mediate between farmers and hungry consumers, there are many different firms and institutions that mediate between savers and borrowers in financial markets.

Businesses, governments, nongovernmental organizations, and individuals depend on the financial system to achieve their goals. The system helps people get the money they need, in the right amount, at the right time, with as little uncertainty as possible. If you have a savings account, checking account, credit card, student loan, home mortgage, or car loan, then you benefit from access to financial markets. People tend to take these services for granted. But the global disruptions surrounding the Lehman bankruptcy showed just how valuable a well-functioning financial system is, and how much it matters.

In this chapter, we'll start by looking at the role of *financial markets* and the value they provide to savers and borrowers. We build a simple model of the market in which savers and borrowers participate. Then we look at the *financial system* from three angles: the functions it serves, the players involved in it, and the assets they trade. Finally, we'll look at some general features of financial products, like risk and return.

The Role of Financial Markets

The high-tech, elaborate dealings we associate with Wall Street are a relatively recent phenomenon, but basic financial markets existed at least as far back as ancient Greece. Money-lenders, based in temples, accepted deposits, changed money for travelers, and (as their name implies) made loans. A person's show of wealth went from precious metals, which were weighed, to coins stamped by the nation-state, which were counted. Stock markets we would recognize today first appeared in the seventeenth century. Why have financial markets been such a natural and useful institution in different societies throughout history? What do they do?

What is a financial market?

In a **financial market**, people trade future claims on funds or goods. These "claims" can take many different forms:

- If you take out a loan, a bank gives you money now, in return for an agreement that you will repay the bank, with interest, in the future.
- If you buy stock in a company, you have a right to a share of any profits earned in the future.
- If you buy an insurance policy, you make regular premium payments, and the insurance company agrees to pay out, if and when something bad happens to you in the future.

We'll talk about the details of these and other types of financial assets later in the chapter. The important thing to notice, for now, is that they are all agreements that allow people to move funds around, *from one time, place, or situation to another*.

The key idea behind financial markets is that, at any given time, the people who have spare funds are not necessarily the same people who have the most valuable ways to spend those funds. Financial markets allow funding to flow to the places where it is most highly valued at the moment. A well-functioning market makes everyone better off, by matching buyers and sellers who both have something to gain from a trade.

In financial markets:

- Buyers are people who want to spend money on something of value right now but don't have cash on hand. Among the buyers in financial markets are students paying for college, families buying new houses, corporations building new factories, entrepreneurs starting new ventures, and (often) the government when it needs to finance public spending.
- Sellers are people who have cash on hand and are willing to let others use it, for a price. Sellers in financial markets are individuals, corporations, and government entities willing to forgo some spending right now in return for repayment down the road.

Information asymmetries and financial markets

An **information asymmetry** arises when one participant in a transaction knows more than another participant. You may have already encountered examples of information asymmetries in microeconomics. For example, the people selling used cars often know more about the quality of the cars than the people buying them. People buying health insurance, on the other hand, usually know more about their own health issues than the companies selling insurance. And so on.

But perhaps nowhere are information asymmetries more prevalent than in financial markets: The people seeking loans tend to know more about the potential uses (and misuses!) of the funds than the lenders. Information asymmetries are so fundamental to financial markets that they have essentially determined the structure of modern financial systems. As protection against information asymmetries, banks, stock markets, bond markets, and regulatory agencies restrict the activities of both borrowers and lenders.

To get a sense of why information asymmetries are so important in financial markets, let's consider the two classic problems that arise when parties have access to different amounts of information: adverse selection and moral hazard.

Adverse selection Adverse selection refers to a state that occurs when buyers and sellers have different information about the quality of a good or the riskiness of a situation, and this asymmetric information results in failure to complete transactions that would have been possible if both sides had the same information. For example:

- Mortgage borrowers might know that the actual market value of their house is much lower than the public assessment.

LO 14.1 Define a financial market, and describe the information asymmetry problems that can occur in them.

financial market
a market in which people trade future claims on funds or goods

information asymmetry
a condition in which one participant in a transaction knows more than another participant

adverse selection
a state that occurs when buyers and sellers have different information about the quality of a good or the riskiness of a situation, and this asymmetric information results in failure to complete transactions that would have been possible if both sides had the same information

- Executives of a company issuing *stock* (an asset that represents partial ownership in the company) might know that the company is much closer to bankruptcy (in which case the stockholders would receive nothing) than could be judged based on public information.

In either case, the problem that arises is that market participants cannot "separate the wheat from the chaff"—that is, they cannot separate the reliable borrowers from the reckless or the genuinely promising company from the frauds. Without tight regulation on the provision of public information, adverse selection would lead to sharp decreases in the market prices of company stock (since investors would worry about drawing a bad apple) and higher interest rates on bank loans.

Moral hazard Moral hazard refers to the tendency for people to behave in a riskier way or to renege on contracts when they do not face the full consequences of their actions. It's an asymmetric information problem that arises once a transaction takes place. Once drivers have purchased car insurance, for example, they face smaller (financial) consequences of getting in an accident. As a result, they might be more likely to speed or try to pass other cars in risky situations.

In the financial context, moral hazard arises in almost all transactions. For example:

- When a borrower has secured a loan, he might be tempted to make riskier investments than promised in the loan agreement. The upside of the investment belongs to the borrower, encouraging the greater risk, while the downside is borne by the lender.
- A company might believe that the government is likely to provide support in the event of a financial crisis. In this case, taxpayers are providing the company with implicit insurance against catastrophic risk. The company (which might be a bank or financial firm) might then take advantage of this "insurance" by engaging in riskier practices.

Sometimes the consequences of these information asymmetries are so severe that financial transactions are impossible. But more often, the participants find ways to limit the problems. Financial innovators (like Muhammad Yunus, the microfinance pioneer from Bangladesh described in Chapter 1, "Economics and Life") have been creative in developing new ways of banking that help financial markets overcome moral hazard and adverse selection (and, in the process, have helped millions of people get better access to banks).

Functions of banks and financial markets

These days, financial markets are extremely complicated—so complicated that when Lehman Brothers fell apart in 2008, very few people really had the full picture of what was going on. But the origins of financial markets are not so complicated. A financial market starts with a bank, savers, and borrowers.

Imagine a world without banks. People face a problem: The times when you need to spend money almost never match up perfectly with the times when you earn money. This problem crops up in a lot of different ways. Some mistiming is long term, reflecting the cycle of your whole life:

- You might want to pay for a college degree or a house or a car early in life, before you've had a chance to do much earning.
- You might want to earn more than you spend during your working years and then live on the savings during retirement.

Other types of mistiming are shorter term:

- You might earn a paycheck once a month, but you want to buy things in various places and times throughout the month.
- If you run a business (such as a farm), your revenues might come in during one season (harvest) but most of your expenses come in another (planting).

moral hazard
the tendency for people to behave in a riskier way or to renege on contracts when they do not face the full consequences of their actions

LO 14.2 Discuss the three main functions of financial markets.

A bank helps to solve these problems: It takes in savings from people who are earning more than they're spending at the moment. It gives out loans to people who currently want to spend more than they earn.

Why do we need banks for that? Why not just stuff cash under your pillow as you earn it and lend to or borrow from family and neighbors as needed? In fact, that *is* the old-fashioned way of managing money. Even today, billions of people around the world don't have good access to modern banks, and they still rely on those simple methods. But for those who have access to them, banks—and, more broadly, financial markets, of which banks are one example—serve three main functions: They intermediate between savers and borrowers, provide liquidity, and diversify risk.

Intermediating between savers and borrowers   The first function of a bank is that it acts as an *intermediary* between savers and borrowers. Without a bank, you'd have to make the rounds every time you need a loan, trying to cobble together bits and pieces of savings from the people you know. If they don't happen to have savings at the moment, you might just be out of luck. That sort of bad luck isn't unlikely if the people you know are similar to you in some way. If they are about your age or work in similar jobs or farm the same crops, then they're likely to be short on cash at the same times that you are.

A bank connects you to a much wider range of people who might have savings when you need to borrow. It also saves you (and them) the time and effort of managing dozens of small, person-to-person transactions. A bank is an easy, one-stop clearinghouse for everyone, whenever they need to save or to borrow.

Providing liquidity   Second, a bank makes it easier to have access to cash when and where you want it. In the old days, people had to have cash on hand to be able to buy something. They had to carry heavy gold or silver coins around, and worry about having them lost or stolen. What's more, it was risky to let others borrow or invest your coins (even beyond the risk of not being repaid) because the coins wouldn't be available if you needed them back in a hurry. For instance, if you made a loan to your neighbor and then your child got sick, you might have trouble getting your coins back right away to pay the doctor. It was safer to keep some coins around, doing nothing, just in case they were needed. A bank lets people enjoy the benefits of *liquidity*—having cash easily available when you want it—without the downsides of holding cash.

Some of the liquidity benefits are logistical. With banks and the tools they provide, like ATMs, checkbooks, debit accounts, and credit cards, it's simple and inexpensive to have access to cash when you want it. And you don't have to worry about protecting your cash when you don't need it. The real value is that you can deposit your savings at the bank and feel reasonably sure that you will be able to withdraw them if a need comes up.

This works because there are many depositors at the bank, and it's very, very unlikely that all of them will need to withdraw their savings at once. So, the bank can keep just a small amount of cash on hand and can loan out most of the deposits, to be put to use in productive investments. The borrowers pay the bank interest on the loans and the bank can pay savers interest on their deposits—all without losing the benefits of liquidity for individual savers.

Diversifying risk   Finally, banks help savers and borrowers to *diversify risk*. Suppose that in the pre-bank system you made a big loan to your cousin who wanted to open a store. If the store did well, you'd get paid back and everything would be fine. But if the store went bankrupt—as small businesses often do—you might be financially ruined. When you borrow and save on a person-to-person level, there's no getting around the risk involved in having a lot of your eggs in one basket, even if everyone is well-intentioned and trustworthy.

In contrast, a bank spreads your eggs around to many different baskets. Because the bank has a big pool of borrowers, the risk of everyone failing to pay back their loans at once is very small. A few borrowers will default on their loans, but most will repay, and no individual saver will have to bear the full burden of a failed investment.

In fact, it's not only banks that provide these benefits. The whole financial system—made up of many institutions, including banks, insurance companies, investors, stock exchanges, and government agencies—is designed to *intermediate* between savers and borrowers, *provide liquidity*, and *diversify risk*. We'll come back to these ideas over and over again throughout the chapter.

In the next section, we look at how these buyers and sellers come together in a simplified type of financial market we call the "market for loanable funds."

✓ TEST YOURSELF

- ☐ What is traded in a financial market? **[LO 14.1]**
- ☐ What are adverse selection and moral hazard, and how do they create problems in financial markets? **[LO 14.1]**
- ☐ What are the three main functions that banks, and the financial system in general, provide for savers and borrowers? **[LO 14.2]**

The Market for Loanable Funds: A Simplified Financial Market

LO 14.3 Describe the market for loanable funds, including the price of loanable funds, and differentiate between savings and investment.

Consider a whole country of people earning and spending. At any given time, some of them want to borrow and others want to save. How much do they want to borrow, and how much are they willing to save? If the amount people want to borrow is higher than the amount saved, what determines which loans get approved? Financial markets mediate the forces of supply and demand *by determining the price* at which the quantity of funds saved will be equal to the quantity invested.

Real-world financial markets involve many products, with different prices, targeted at different types of buyers and sellers. You can get the flavor of this variety just by browsing the business section of a newspaper or looking at the types of accounts and loans offered by any bank. We'll dig into some of this nuance later in the chapter. For now, let's simplify all saving and borrowing into one market, which we'll call the *market for loanable funds*.

market for loanable funds
a market in which savers supply funds to those who want to borrow

savings
the portion of income that is not immediately spent on consumption of goods and services

investment
spending on productive inputs, such as factories, machinery, and inventories

Savings, investment, and the price of loanable funds

The **market for loanable funds** is a market in which savers, who have money to lend, supply funds to those who want to borrow for their investment spending needs. "Loanable funds" are the dollars that are on the table between them to be lent out and borrowed.

When talking about savings and investment, we have to be careful with terminology. Economists differentiate between savings and investment:

- **Savings** is the portion of income that is not immediately spent on consumption of goods and services.
- **Investment**, or, more properly, *investment spending*, refers to spending on productive inputs, such as factories, machinery, and inventories.

TAKE NOTE ✏️

When people put money into a 401(k) account for retirement or purchase stocks, they often say they are "investing" the money. But to an economist, these are examples of *savings*, not investment.

Using the economists' definitions of savings and investment, we can build a simple model of the market for loanable funds. Remember:

- The supply of loanable funds comes from savings.
- The demand for loanable funds comes from investment.

Just as in any market, savings (supply) and investment (demand) are brought into equilibrium at the price at which the quantity supplied and the quantity demanded are equal. For sellers and buyers in the market for loanable funds:

- Saving is like *selling the right to use your money* for a time. The quantity of savings that people are willing to supply will depend on the price they receive.
- Borrowing is like *buying the right to use someone else's money*. The quantity of investment funding that people demand also will depend on the price they receive.

For both savers and borrowers, the "price of money" is usually called the **interest rate**. It is typically expressed as a percentage per dollar per unit of time. Specifically:

- For savers, the interest rate is the price received for letting a bank use their money for a specified period of time.
- For borrowers, the interest rate is the price of borrowing money for a specified period of time. It is the price a lender charges a borrower for the use of funds until the loan is repaid.

The interest rate determines the total amount that a borrower must pay back on a loan in addition to paying back the original amount borrowed (called the *principal*). For instance, if you take out a one-year loan of $1,000 with a 10 percent annual interest rate, you'll have to repay the $1,000 principal plus $100 ($1,000 × 0.10) in interest.[1]

Just as in any market, the intersection of the downward-sloping demand curve and the upward-sloping supply curve determines the equilibrium interest rate and quantity of loanable funds. The market for loanable funds is shown in Figure 14-1.

Why is the supply (savings) curve upward-sloping? This shape implies that the amount the population is willing to save increases as the interest rate increases. In markets for *goods and services*, the higher the price, the more people will find it profitable to supply the good. The relationship between price and quantity supplied in the market for *loanable funds* is essentially the same. The key is to realize that there is an opportunity cost of saving: Saving money means that you can't consume as much right now. People rationally calculate those trade-offs.

interest rate
the "price of money," typically expressed as a percentage per dollar per unit of time; for savers, it is the price received for letting a bank use money for a specified period of time; for borrowers, it is the price of using money for a specified period of time

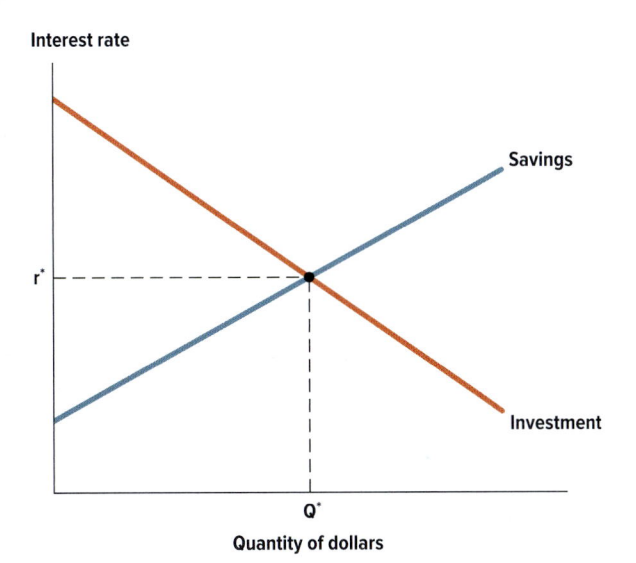

FIGURE 14-1

The market for loanable funds

The typical market for loanable funds is at equilibrium at the point where the savings curve intersects the investment curve. From this point, one can determine the equilibrium interest rate (r*) and the amount of money traded in the market (Q*).

For example, if you save $100, you are trading off $100 worth of consumption now for the promise of getting some amount of money in the future. If the interest rate is zero, you will get just your $100 back. Some people will be willing to save even with zero interest—maybe they know they would rather consume $100 when they are retired than another $100 now.

The higher the interest rate, the more people will find it worthwhile to delay their consumption in order to increase their future earnings. So, if you wouldn't save $100 in exchange for $101 a year from now, you might be willing to do it for $110. Even more people would save $100 if they were guaranteed to get $200 back in a year, and so on as the interest rate goes up.

On the other side of the market for loanable funds, the demand (investment) curve is downward-sloping. This is because the cost of borrowing decreases as the interest rate decreases, making more and more investment opportunities worth the cost.

When deciding whether to borrow, firms or households that are contemplating an investment—say, building a factory or buying a new home—must first try to estimate the rate of return on that investment.[2] The *rate of return* describes the expected profit that the project will generate per dollar invested. The investment decision then becomes a matter of comparing benefits and costs:

- If the rate of return (the benefit of borrowing) is lower than the cost of borrowing, then the investor will lose money on net after paying back the loan. In that case, the investment probably isn't worth making.
- If the rate of return is above the interest rate, the investment will yield a profit, and it makes sense to borrow the money.

In the real world, there are a range of investment opportunities that offer different rates of return. At higher interest rates, fewer and fewer of these opportunities will have a rate of return higher than the costs involved in borrowing, and so the quantity of loanable funds demanded will decrease. The result is the familiar downward-sloping demand curve.

Changes in the supply and demand for loanable funds

LO 14.4 List the factors that affect the supply and demand of loanable funds.

The underlying factors that determine how much people want to save and invest can change over time or differ from country to country. These determinants shift the supply and demand curves in the market for loanable funds, changing the quantity of funds supplied or demanded at any given interest rate. As a result, the equilibrium interest rate and quantity will change. In this section, we'll discuss some of the important underlying determinants of savings and investment.

Determinants of savings Savings decisions reflect the *trade-off* people face between spending their income on consumption now and saving that money for later. The upward-sloping supply curve reflects the fact that as the interest rate increases, the value of saving relative to consuming increases. As the interest rate increases, people supply more savings.

However, factors other than the interest rate can also affect this choice. What are the underlying factors that determine how much people want to save at a given interest rate? Of course, many factors help determine individuals' choices about savings. In this chapter, however, we are concerned with factors that affect the economy on a macro level—issues that will cause the population of the country *as a whole* to want to save more or less. These factors can change over time within a country, but they can also help to explain differences across countries.

The following are important factors that drive the supply of savings:

- **Wealth.** Studies show that richer households tend to save more of their income than others.
- **Current economic conditions.** When we think about how people's savings decisions respond to economic conditions, it's important to distinguish between *current* economic conditions and how current conditions might change expectations about the *future*. If expectations about the future don't change at all, then an economic downturn will generally decrease savings at a given interest rate. (That is, it will shift the supply curve for loanable funds to

the left.) When times are bad and people lose jobs or have lower incomes, they will be less inclined to save and may even spend down past savings to pay for current expenses. In the 2007-2009 recession, however, the savings rate actually went up. To explain this puzzle, we have to turn to . . .

- **Expectations about future economic conditions.** People often view a recession as a bad sign about how the economy will be doing in the future, as well as how it is doing at the moment. This expectation about the future can affect the savings rate: When people expect their income to be lower in the future, they will be more inclined to save, all else equal, to make sure that they have enough down the road.
- **Uncertainty.** When savers are uncertain about what the future holds, they are more likely to save extra as a precaution, just in case things turn out badly.
- **Borrowing constraints.** At any given interest rate, there will always be households and firms that would like to borrow at that interest rate but cannot. Banks and other lenders are typically willing to lend only to potential borrowers who have sufficient collateral (an asset that can be seized if the borrower is unable to pay) or sufficiently high expected incomes. When borrowing is difficult, households and firms are more likely to save to finance large purchases and investments. Borrowing constraints can change with loosening or tightening of regulations, changes in expectations about the future direction of incomes, and collateral values.
- **Social welfare policies.** Incentives to save at any given interest rate can be affected by public policies that determine the benefits people will receive if they lose their jobs, become sick or disabled, fall into poverty, or simply grow old. For instance, individuals in China may save more because they expect to bear more of the burden for their own health care and retirement costs in the future. In contrast, U.S. citizens expect to receive retirement benefits through Social Security and Medicare, reducing the need for some households to save. (Of course, tax contributions to Social Security could be thought of as forced saving for retirement—but that type of "saving" isn't counted in the savings rate.)
- **Culture.** Different cultures and traditions place varying weights on being frugal, showing your wealth through material goods, leaving an inheritance for future generations, and so on. These cultural expectations are difficult to quantify but at times help explain differing savings rates across countries.

A change in these underlying determinants of savings will shift the supply curve in the market for loanable funds.

Imagine a change that makes people want to save less at any given interest rate. For instance, suppose people become more optimistic that the economy will be doing well over the next decade. Because they feel more confident that they will have jobs and earn plenty of money in the future, they become less concerned about saving now. This change in expectations will shift the supply curve to the left, as shown in panel A of Figure 14-2. The equilibrium in the market for loanable funds moves up along the demand curve, to a new point with a higher interest rate and a lower quantity of funds saved and invested.

In contrast, a change that increased the quantity people want to save at any given interest rate would shift the supply curve to the right, as shown in panel B of Figure 14-2. The new equilibrium would have a lower interest rate and a higher equilibrium quantity of funds saved and invested.

Diving further into the relationship between current economic conditions and expectations about future economic conditions, we can understand why average U.S. household savings rates *fell* dramatically when the economy was doing well through most of the 1980s, 1990s, and early 2000s, as shown in Figure 14-3. By 2005, households on average were hardly saving at all—the average savings rate was less than 2 percent.[3] Although we might think that good current conditions would make people willing to save more, it also made them optimistic about the future, which made them *less* inclined to save and more inclined to borrow. In addition, the strong economic times and housing boom meant that households saw an increase in their net worth, which

FIGURE 14-2

A change in the underlying determinants of saving shifts the supply curve for loanable funds

(A) Decrease in quantity of savings

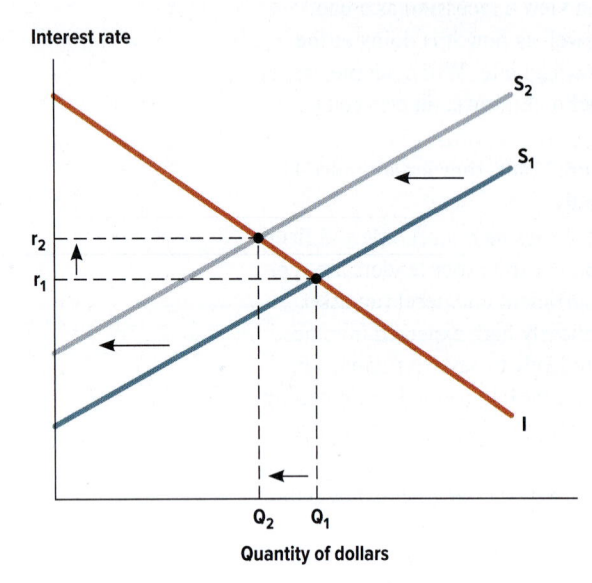

When the level of savings shifts dramatically to the left due to a change in one of the determinants of savings, the equilibrium interest rate is higher and the quantity of loanable funds in the market is lower.

(B) Increase in quantity of savings

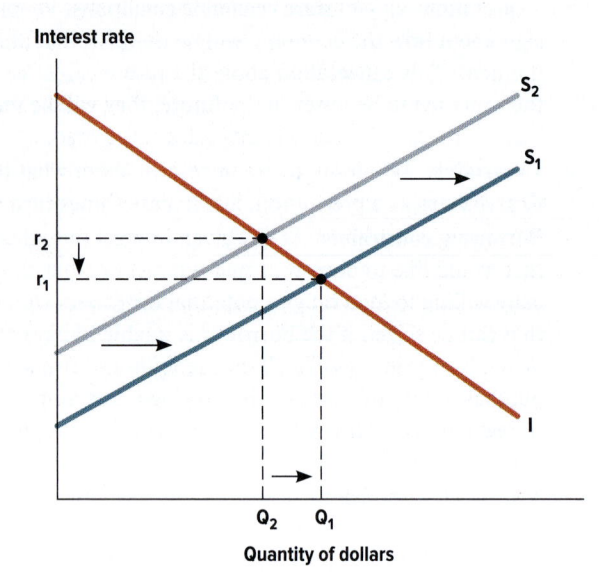

When the level of savings shifts dramatically to the right due to a change in one of the determinants of savings, the equilibrium interest rate is lower and the quantity of loanable in the market is higher.

FIGURE 14-3

Savings rate in the United States since 1980 In the early 1980s, the savings rate in the United States was rather high, ranging from 8 to 10 percent. After this, the savings rate decreased steadily until it was about 2 percent in the mid-2000s. After the crash of the housing market in 2007, the savings rate jumped by about 5 percent.

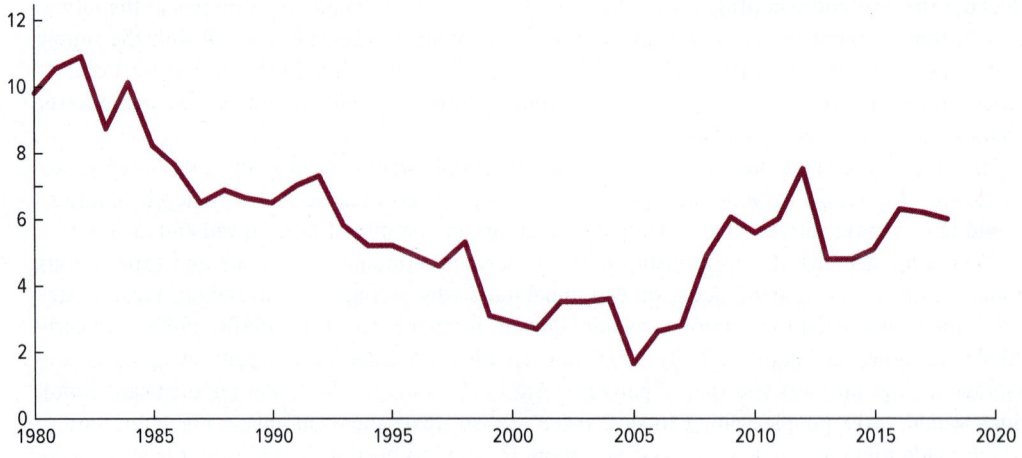

Source: Federal Reserve Bank of St. Louis, FRED, https://fred.stlouisfed.org/series/PSAVERT.

further reduced saving. When the economy hit a big bump, the savings rate moved back up, starting around 2008, in the depths of the financial crisis. This suggests that people took the recession as a negative sign about the future, and in response they saved more and borrowed less.

Determinants of investment   Investment decisions are based on the *trade-off* between the potential profits that could be generated by an investment and the cost of borrowing money to finance that investment. The downward-sloping demand curve in the market for loanable funds reflects the fact that as the interest rate increases, fewer and fewer potential investments will generate returns high enough to make the cost of paying back a loan worthwhile.

Just as on the supply side of the market for loanable funds, there are other factors that affect the demand for loanable funds. What underlying factors determine how much people want to invest at a given interest rate? They include:

- **Expectations about future profitability and future economic conditions.** Apart from the interest rate, the primary factor affecting the demand for loanable funds is expectations about the future profitability of investments made today. This view about future profitability usually goes hand in hand with overall expectations about future economic conditions.

For example, in 2018 the economy was strong and consumer demand was high. A strong economy can make investors eager to borrow money because they expect ventures like new companies, products, shops, and real estate developments to earn large profits. This expectation shifts the demand curve to the right, as firms want to borrow more at any given interest rate. The opposite was true when the housing market soured in late 2007. Since consumer demand was weak throughout the economy, there was little incentive to take out a loan to expand production or start a new business.

- **Uncertainty.** When investors are uncertain about the likely path of the economy, the demand for loanable funds will fall. Uncertainty especially reduces demand when it's costly to change investment strategies once fresh information arrives.
- **Changes in the government's budget deficit.** When the government borrows more, it increases the demand for loanable funds. This is simply because the total demand for loanable funds consists of both public and private demand.

These factors change the set of investment opportunities in the economy, increasing or decreasing the number of investments that are worth making at any given interest rate.

For example, a change that increases the value of potential investments throughout the economy will increase the quantity of loanable funds demanded at every interest rate, shifting the whole demand curve to the right, as shown in panel A of Figure 14-4. As a result, the equilibrium will move up along the supply curve to a new point with a higher interest rate and higher equilibrium quantity of funds saved and invested.

On the other hand, if investors are uncertain about the path of the economy, their desire to borrow will decrease, and this will shift the demand curve for loanable funds to the left, as shown in panel B of Figure 14-4.

Investment decisions are also affected by external forces that determine the *supply* of loanable funds and the level of the interest rate. At any given interest rate, there will be households and firms that would like to borrow at that interest rate but cannot. Banks and other lenders are typically willing to lend only to potential borrowers who have sufficient collateral or sufficiently high expected incomes. We noted above that borrowing constraints can affect saving decisions; much more directly, borrowing constraints reduce the supply of loanable funds. Borrowing constraints can change with loosening or tightening of regulations, changes in expectations about the future direction of incomes, and collateral values.

Earlier we discussed government borrowing, and how changes in the government's budget deficit can affect the demand for loanable funds. Some have suggested that when the government borrows more, it can *crowd out* private investment. **Crowding out** is the reduction in private borrowing

crowding out
the reduction in private borrowing caused by an increase in government borrowing

FIGURE 14-4
A change in the underlying determinants of investment opportunities shifts the demand curve for loanable funds

(A) Increase in quantity of investment

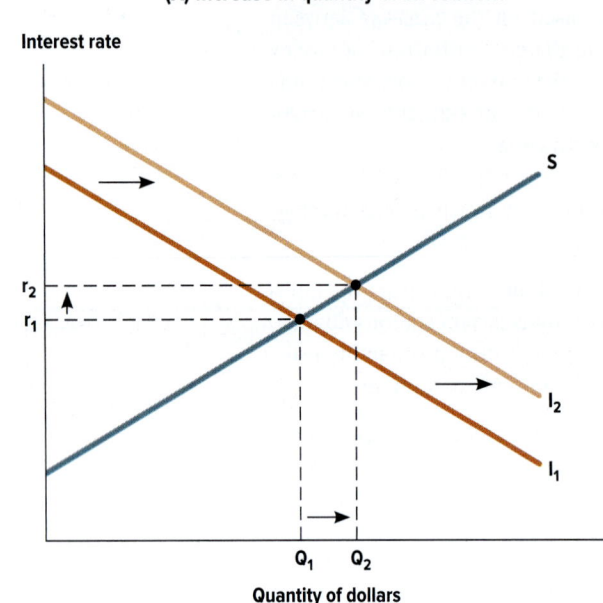

When the demand for investment increases, people are willing to invest more money at every interest rate. This takes the market for loanable funds to a new equilibrium, with higher rates and a greater quantity of loanable funds traded.

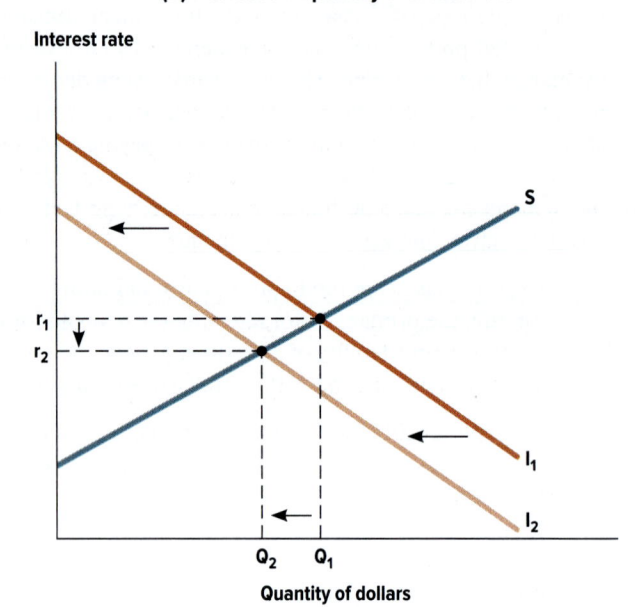

(B) Decrease in quantity of investment

A weak economy decreases the demand for loanable funds. At every interest rate, people are less interested in making investments, fearing such investments will not work out. At this new equilibrium, the interest rate is lower, and the quantity of loanable funds traded is lower.

that is caused by an increase in government borrowing. The government's increased demand for borrowing can shift the demand curve to the right, forcing up interest rates, as shown in panel A of Figure 14-4. This shift in the demand curve, in turn, increases the cost of borrowing and so reduces private investment.

Such crowding out of private investment is always a fear when the government intervenes in the market. Evidence from the Great Recession suggests that crowding out was minimal then, but it is always a possibility that policy-makers need to take seriously.

A price for every borrower: A more realistic look at interest rates

LO 14.5 Understand how interest rates on loans vary with the length of the loan and the riskiness of the transaction.

The simple model of the market for loanable funds illustrates the basic relationships between supply and demand in financial markets. In reality, however, *there is no such thing as a single interest rate* that is paid by all prospective borrowers. Different borrowers pay different interest rates:

- An individual may have to pay a higher interest rate to borrow money than an established company would. Almost everyone has to pay a higher rate than the U.S. government.
- Also, the same borrower may also pay different rates on different kinds of transactions. For example, the interest rate will be less on a mortgage than on a credit card for a given individual.

How is the interest rate for a particular loan determined? Two basic factors drive differences in interest rates: length of time and degree of risk.

The first factor is the *length of time* the borrower has to repay the loan. The reason for this is not immediately obvious. Isn't a lender already being compensated for lending over a longer period by earning interest over that longer period? Only partially. Think of it this way: Lenders want to be compensated for the *opportunity cost* of being unable to get their money back quickly. When they lend money for 20 years at a fixed interest rate, they've tied up their money for that length of time; they must pass up any better investment opportunities and interest rates that could emerge in those 20 years. Since there's more uncertainty about potential future investment opportunities over a longer period of time, lenders generally want a higher interest rate to compensate them for the added opportunity cost when loans stretch over a longer period.

The second factor that drives differences in interest rates is the *riskiness* of the transaction. To understand why, ask yourself a simple question: To whom would you rather loan money—a stranger on the street or the local bank? Regardless of your answer, you probably had a simple criterion for deciding: Who was more likely to pay you back?

Lenders in the financial markets make this same calculation when they consider the likelihood that a borrower may default on a loan. A **default** happens when a borrower fails to pay back a loan according to the agreed-upon terms. If lenders think that a particular borrower might default, they will demand a higher interest rate to make it worth taking that risk.

default the failure of a borrower to pay back a loan according to the agreed-upon terms

Sometimes, loans are secured against an asset (called *collateral*), such as a house. If a borrower defaults on a mortgage loan, the lender takes ownership of the house as compensation for the loss. This explains why mortgages generally are made at a lower interest rate than credit card loans: If a mortgage borrower defaults, the lender can sell the house to get some money back (although usually not the full value of the loan). In contrast, credit cards aren't backed with valuable assets, so the lender's losses are higher if someone defaults.

The risk of a borrower defaulting on a loan is known as *credit risk*. It is measured against the **risk-free rate**—the interest rate at which one would lend if there were no risk of default. The risk-free rate is usually approximated by interest rates on U.S. government debt because the U.S. government is considered extremely unlikely to default. All other borrowers must pay higher rates to compensate lenders for the higher possibility that they will default.

risk-free rate the interest rate at which one would lend if there were no risk of default; usually approximated by interest rates on U.S. government debt

The difference between the risk-free rate and the interest rate a particular investor has to pay is called the *credit spread* or *risk premium*. The difference can be quite large, both among investors and over time. The recession and financial crisis of 2007–2009, for example, caused credit spreads to rise dramatically, as borrowers of all kinds suddenly became more likely to default.

Armed with data about the length of time of a loan and roughly how likely it is for the borrower to default, we can get an idea what price a particular borrower might face for a particular transaction in the market for loanable funds. In general, the longer the term of a loan and the more likely the risk of default, the higher above the risk-free rate will be the interest rate of that loan.

✓ TEST YOURSELF

- ☐ What is another name for the price of money in the market for loanable funds? **[LO 14.3]**
- ☐ What are factors that can cause the supply curve to shift right in the market for loanable funds? **[LO 14.4]**
- ☐ In the market for loanable funds, which factors can cause the demand curve to shift right? **[LO 14.4]**
- ☐ Describe the factors that explain why interest rates on loans to households and firms are not all the same. **[LO 14.5]**

The Modern Financial System

Now that we've covered the basic *theory* of financial markets, we'll turn our attention to some key *realities* of the modern financial system. We've already noted that the idea of a single market for loanable funds is an oversimplification. In reality, people and firms face different interest rates based on the length and riskiness of their loans.

financial system
the group of institutions that bring together savers, borrowers, investors, and insurers in a set of interconnected markets where people trade financial products

LO 14.6 Describe why it is important for the financial system to intermediate between buyers and sellers, provide liquidity, and diversify risk.

The **financial system** consists of institutions that bring together savers, borrowers, investors, and insurers in a set of interconnected markets where people trade financial products. This section looks at the role the financial system plays in helping people manage their money and risk. It also defines some of the most important types of products that are traded in the financial system and identifies the people and institutions that trade them.

Functions of the financial system

At the beginning of the chapter, we saw how financial markets—banks, in particular—can help to fill three basic roles in the economy: *intermediating* between savers and borrowers, providing *liquidity*, and *diversifying risk*. In this section, we expand on these ideas and show how the *financial system as a whole* contributes to achieving them.

Matching up buyers and sellers: Intermediation
Imagine you want to borrow to start a small business. How are you going to get together enough money? You could go to everyone you know and ask them to lend you whatever amount they can afford. This approach won't necessarily fund your business, unless you happen to know a lot of people with spare cash sitting around. But even if you managed to pull it off, the process of arranging and keeping track of all of those loans would be incredibly time-consuming and complicated.

The existence of banks lowers the *transaction costs* of the borrowing process. When banks exist, there is only one person you need to persuade to lend you the entire sum of money—the bank loan officer. This saves you—and the friends and family you'd otherwise be pestering for loans—time and money by replacing a lot of small, informal transactions with one big, professionalized one.

Various institutions act as **financial intermediaries**—they channel funds from people who have them to people who want them. A bank is one kind of intermediary. A different kind of intermediary is a stock exchange, which matches people wanting to buy ownership shares of companies with people wanting to sell those shares. This intermediation reduces transaction costs, by centralizing information about share prices and providing a broad and dynamic marketplace for transactions. The financial system offers savers and borrowers a wide set of interconnected markets in which to find financial intermediaries.

Financial intermediaries, such as the Chicago Board of Trade shown here, centralize information about prices and provide a marketplace for transactions.
©Felix Lipov/123RF

financial intermediaries
institutions that channel funds from people who have them to people who want them

liquidity
a measure of how easily a particular asset can be converted quickly to cash without much loss of value

Providing liquidity
A second critical function of the financial system is to provide liquidity. Earlier in the chapter, we talked informally about why people value liquidity. Formally, **liquidity** is a measure of how easily a particular asset can be converted quickly to cash without much loss of value. We say that an asset is *liquid* if it can be sold for cash quickly without much loss of value and is *illiquid* if it can't.

Consider two types of assets that many people own: cars and houses. If you needed cash quickly, which would you sell? A car is relatively easy to sell quickly. You can simply drive into a car dealership and ask the dealer to make you a cash offer. You won't get the best possible price, of course—but you'll get much of what the car is worth, in cash, right away. The house, on the other hand, is much harder to sell. You can't walk into most real estate agencies and expect a cash offer on the spot. The real estate agent will instead help you find a buyer, which can take time, and even then there are still mountains of paperwork and things that could go wrong.

In other words, the car is a more liquid asset than the house. Why is there such a difference in liquidity? Houses are more difficult to value and are legally complex to purchase. Before you decide how much to pay for a house, you should do a thorough check of every part of it—make sure it doesn't have a leaky roof and that there aren't plans to build a waste-processing facility nearby. Cars are much easier to value. An experienced dealer can accurately size up a car from a peek under the hood. That's why there are car dealers fulfilling the role of liquidity providers but few equivalents in the real estate market. A *liquidity provider* is someone who helps make a market more liquid by being always ready to buy or sell an asset.

Various players in the financial system are liquidity providers, helping ensure that markets are liquid. The very structure of financial assets such as stocks and bonds (as we'll define and discuss below) also serves to increase liquidity. If you want to sell a share of company stock or a government bond, there is almost always someone in the financial system willing to buy it from you. Often that someone is your bank or your broker; it may also be a mutual fund or simply a large financial investor. We sometimes call these people *market makers*—they, in effect, "make a market" by being always ready to buy or sell, just like the car dealer.

Liquidity is important because it affects people's willingness to save. Savers generally want to know that their money will be there for them when they need it. If markets were not liquid, you couldn't count on being able to sell your assets quickly in order to get your money back.

As a result, you'd probably be extremely cautious about lending out money for investment in the first place. That reluctance would reduce the supply of loanable funds, which would drive up interest rates, reduce the amount of investment, and lead to slower growth in the economy.

Diversifying risk   The third major role played by the financial system is that it spreads risk. Imagine that, as a saver, you could lend your money directly only to other individuals or companies. If the borrower defaulted, you would lose everything.

If you lend your money to a bank, however, you know that the bank will pool your money with that of other savers and make thousands of loans to different borrowers. Some of those borrowers will default, but the bank won't lose everything at once, and neither will its savers. The bank has *diversified* the risk. **Diversification** is the process by which risks are shared among many different assets or people, reducing the impact of a particular risk on any one individual. The financial system helps share risk even more broadly than an individual bank.

Diversification is critical for the functioning of the economy. People are more willing to save money, and entrepreneurs are more willing to start new ventures, if they don't have to worry too much about the risk of losing everything.

diversification
the process by which risks are shared across many different assets or people, reducing the impact of any particular risk on any one individual

Major financial assets

How does the financial system fulfill its roles of intermediation, providing liquidity, and diversifying risk? It does so by creating financial assets that can be bought and sold within the financial markets. There are far more varieties of financial assets than we could possibly cover in this text; we'll focus on just the major ones: equity, debt, and derivatives.

LO 14.7 Differentiate between debt and equity, and define the major types of assets in each category.

Equity   When you own part of a company and share in its profits, we say that you *have equity* in that company. Financial assets that represent this partial ownership are called *equities*. A "stock"—the financial asset you probably hear the most about—is the common name for an equity asset.

What exactly are stocks? A **stock** is a financial asset that represents partial ownership of a company. If a company has issued 100,000 shares of stock, then the owner of each share (called a *shareholder* or *stockholder*) owns 1/100,000 of the company.

stock
a financial asset that represents partial ownership of a company

Why do companies issue stock? For one thing, issuing stock allows a company to raise capital without borrowing. Imagine you are a store owner who wants to expand your business by opening a new store but you need money to do so. You have two choices:

- You could borrow money from the bank, but you'd have to pay interest and pay back the loan even if the new store fails.

- Alternatively, you might choose to sell some equity in your company. People who buy the shares of stock will become part owners of the company. As part owners, they take on the risk of losing money if the new store fails, and they expect a percentage of the profits if it succeeds.

Stock is also a mechanism for turning an illiquid asset (ownership of a private company) into a liquid one (a share that can be sold on the stock market). Ownership of an entire business is not easy to sell. Just like buying a house, there are many complicated things that a potential buyer will want to understand beforehand.

On the other hand, stock in *public companies*—so called because anyone can buy a share—is a liquid asset.[4] Stock can be easily bought and sold in small, standardized increments on the stock market. The news media report figures from the stock market every day, such as the Dow Jones Industrial Average, the Standard & Poor's (S&P) 500, and the Nasdaq. There even are television networks dedicated to following every move of these stock market indexes.

Stockholders, as partial owners, are usually entitled to vote on certain aspects of how the company is run. They elect the board of directors, for example. Stockholders also are entitled to receive a portion of the company's profits, proportional to the size of their ownership stake, in the form of dividends. A **dividend** is a payment made periodically, typically annually or quarterly, to all shareholders of a company.

dividend
a payment made periodically, typically annually or quarterly, to all shareholders of a company

loan
an agreement in which a lender gives money to a borrower in exchange for a promise to repay the amount loaned plus an agreed-upon amount of interest

Debt The main alternative to equity is *debt*. The most basic and familiar type of debt is a loan. A **loan** is an agreement in which a lender gives money to a borrower in exchange for a promise to repay the amount loaned plus an agreed-upon amount of interest. Banks make loans to individuals to make purchases like houses and cars, and they lend to businesses that want to make investments.

Making a loan is generally both less risky and less potentially rewarding than buying stock:

- A borrower might default on a loan. People who have loaned money to a company that goes bankrupt do have some protection: They have the first legal claim on that company's assets and will be paid as much as possible before stockholders earn anything.
- Buying stock in a company comes with a higher risk of losing everything if the company fails. But if the company does very well and earns huge profits, stockholders are usually entitled to a share of those profits, in the form of dividends and an increase in the price of the stock. With a loan, no matter how successful the company gets, the lender will never receive more than the amount specified in the original loan agreements.

Like any other financial asset, loans can be bought and sold. Imagine that a bank lends you money to buy a house. You sign a contract, and you have a legal obligation to pay the loan back at a specified interest rate by a specified date. The bank could then sell that obligation to somebody else. The buyer of the loan would pay the bank for the right to collect the money from you, according to the terms of the loan deal.

To make loans even more liquid, they can be standardized into a more easily tradable asset, called a *bond*. A **bond** represents a promise by the bond issuer to repay the loan, at a specified maturity date, and to pay periodic interest at a specific percentage rate. (Because of the set interest rate, bonds are often referred to as *fixed-income securities*.) In general, bonds work like this:

bond
a form of debt that represents a promise by the bond issuer to repay the face value of the loan, at a specified maturity date, and to pay periodic interest at a specific percentage rate

- The owner of the bond (*bondholder*) is legally entitled to receive scheduled interest payments (called *coupon* payments). These coupon payment are generally paid every three or six months.[5]
- The bondholder also receives a final payment of the original loan amount for the bond (the *principal*, also sometimes called the *face value*, of the bond) at the maturity date.
- Bonds are issued in varying maturities. *Corporate bonds* typically have maturities of 10 to 30 years. *Government bonds* (issued by the U.S. Treasury, government agencies, and states and municipalities) generally range from one to 10 years.

Governments and big companies often sell bonds as a way to borrow large sums of money, typically from a large number of lenders. Because bonds are standardized, it is easy for bondholders to sell them, making them a more liquid asset than regular loans.

Since a bond is essentially a loan, the basic risk-reward trade-off that applied to loans also applies to bonds: They are generally safer than stocks but also less rewarding. While returns can vary (and historical returns do not necessarily predict future returns), government bonds have historically averaged a real (inflation-adjusted) return of about 2 percent per year, while a broad index of stocks indicates a real return of nearly 7 percent per year over the same period.[6]

Why might savers be interested in buying government bonds, with so much lower returns, instead of stocks? Because stocks are more risky. They can easily go down in value, whereas the government is very unlikely to default on a bond.

Wouldn't it be useful if there were a way to take nonstandard loans—say, loans to people to buy homes—and turn them into standardized, bond-like instruments that can be easily traded? It turns out there *is* such a process, called *securitization*. Securitization turns a group of many loans into a single larger asset, thus reducing the risk to the lender of any individual borrower defaulting on the loan.

Securitization became popular in the early 2000s. Financial assets of all types, from student loans to mortgage loans, were securitized to create liquid assets that would be appealing to a wide array of lenders. In Chapter 17, "Financial Crisis," we'll show how securitization played a starring role in the financial crisis that sparked the Great Recession and the fall of Lehman Brothers.

Despite its involvement in the financial crisis, debt is not bad when done right. As we've mentioned, debt is behind many of the transactions we take for granted. When you're able to drive off the lot with a new car, or a firm is able to build a new factory, it's likely that debt helped make those investments possible.

Derivatives Stocks, loans, and bonds are examples of financial contracts in which one person or firm agrees to pay another a certain amount, under certain circumstances. If you get creative, you can come up with much more complex arrangements, based on the same fundamental idea. For instance, you can create a contract based on the future value of particular assets or goods, like mortgages, stocks, or the price of oil.

Financial contracts based on the value of some other asset represent a special category of financial assets, called **derivatives**. A derivative is an asset whose value is based on (or "derived from"–hence the term *derivative*) the value of another asset, such as a home loan, stock, bond, or barrel of oil.

derivative
an asset whose value is based on the value of another asset

The best example of this type of arrangement is a *futures contract*. The buyer of a futures contract agrees to pay the seller a set amount today based on the *expected future price* of some asset. For example, through a futures contract you could sell all or part of your farm crop in advance at a set price. Here's what could happen with the futures contract:

- At harvest, if the price of the crop ends up being worth more than the contract price, the person to whom you sold the futures will be able to sell the crop for a profit.
- If crop prices fall, the buyer of your crop will lose out, but you will still get the contract price.

In effect, you have managed your risk by transferring both good and bad risks about the future price of the crop to your contract partner. In general, derivatives are meant to transfer risk to people who are more willing to bear it.

Major players in the financial system

So far, we've seen the functions of the financial system and the major assets that get traded. We'll now look at four key players without whom there couldn't be a well-functioning financial system: banks and other intermediaries, savers and their proxies, entrepreneurs and businesses, and speculators.

LO 14.8 Name the main institutions in financial markets, and describe the role that each plays.

Banks and other financial intermediaries
We've already mentioned that banks play a crucial intermediary role. Digging deeper, we can divide banks into two categories: *commercial banks* and *investment banks*.

Commercial banks Commercial banks are probably what you think of when someone says "bank." When you make a deposit at a bank or get a mortgage or student loan from a bank, you are interacting with a commercial bank. As well as being an intermediary between savers and borrowers, commercial banks help to create liquidity. The loans they make are relatively illiquid assets, typically taking years to be repaid.

Most savers, however, don't want their money to be tied up for years. How can banks "lend long" (make loans of long duration) while also "borrowing short" (using the money gained from deposits to make loans that allow them to be ready to give depositors their money back at short notice)? Crucially, banks assume that not all depositors will try to get their money back at once, so they keep on hand only a fraction of all deposits. If too many depositors want their cash back at once, the bank would run out of funds—a potentially disastrous situation known as a bank run. (We'll further explore the topic of fractional lending in Chapter 15, "Money and the Monetary System.")

Investment banks Investment banks are part of what is commonly referred to as "Wall Street"—banks like Goldman Sachs and the now-bankrupt Lehman Brothers. These banks don't take deposits and they don't make loans in the traditional sense. Instead, they provide liquidity to financial markets by acting as market makers. They help companies issue stocks and bonds by guaranteeing to buy any that remain unsold (a process known as *underwriting*).

Most banks are either a commercial bank or an investment bank, but not both at once. This fact is due to a law passed in the 1930s, the Glass-Steagall Act, which banned banks from taking on both roles. However, Congress repealed this law in 1999, and a few of the largest banks—such as JP Morgan Chase and Bank of America—have taken on both roles simultaneously.

Savers and their proxies
Most savers don't approach financial markets directly. Instead, they operate through a *proxy*—that is, they give their money to someone else to decide whom to lend it to. These proxies include banks, mutual funds, pension funds, and life insurance companies.

According to the Federal Reserve, by 2017 U.S. mutual fund companies held $18.75 trillion in assets; life insurance and private pension companies held $15 trillion in assets.[7] (Remember that in economic terminology, buying assets like stocks and bonds is a form of savings, not "investing.")

mutual fund
a portfolio of stocks, bonds, and other assets managed by a professional who makes decisions on behalf of clients

Mutual funds A mutual fund is a portfolio of stocks, bonds, and other assets managed by a professional who makes decisions on behalf of clients. Savers entrust their money to mutual funds to save themselves the hassle of researching the thousands of stocks and bonds they could buy; instead, they let a professional make the decisions.

There are many different types of mutual funds. Two popular types are specialized funds and index funds:

- Managers of *specialized funds* try to beat the performance of the market by researching specific companies and picking stocks they believe will earn higher returns than the market average.
- *Index funds* buy all the stocks represented in a broad market like the Standard & Poor's (S&P) 500, with the goal of mirroring the same average return as the market.

Mutual funds charge a fee for their services that can be as little as a tenth of a percent of assets (such as with a simple index fund) or as much as 3 or 4 percent (in the case of a fund that spends a lot on stock research).

Surprisingly enough, the simplest approach to mutual funds may be the best, as outlined in the Econ and YOU box "The incredible index fund."

The incredible index fund
Econ and YOU

Entire TV networks dedicate their efforts to reporting the rise and fall of asset prices, from stocks to the price of gold. Books are filled with advice on playing the stock market. If you're lucky enough to have money to put in the stock market, how can you make sense of this noisy information? Can you find a way to outperform the market?

Maybe you shouldn't even try. Many savers have embraced *index funds*, such as the pioneering Vanguard Index Fund. Index funds, now offered by a wide range of financial companies, attempt to replicate the exact movements of a given stock market index. One such index is the S&P 500, which is comprised of stocks in 500 leading U.S. companies.

Index funds have a big advantage over traditional, actively managed mutual funds: They cost much less to maintain. One reason for their lower costs is that index funds don't need to employ highly paid asset managers to research which stocks have the highest probability of "beating the market." Instead, the goal is to simply mimic the market average.

A second benefit of index funds is that they minimize the capital gains taxes that are owed when stocks are bought or sold. This occurs because the stocks that comprise an index like the S&P 500 don't change much, so there is much less buying and selling of stocks.

Perhaps you've spotted the most common objection to index funds: Professional fund managers point out that since index funds attempt to duplicate the exact movements of what is essentially the *average* performance of the market, they can miss out on large returns earned by specific subsets of the market. In the dot-com boom during the late 1990s, for example, the returns for some mutual funds that specialized in up-and-coming technological firms far outstripped the returns for index funds.

Who's right? Consider all the mutual funds (portfolios of stocks) actively managed by professional analysts and that invest in a broad range of stocks. Since 2002, only 5 percent of those funds have beat the returns of the overall market—the returns reflected by proxy index funds.

Sources: Richard A. Ferri, *All about Index Funds: The Easy Way to Get Started*, 2nd ed. (New York: McGraw-Hill Education, 2007); http://www.fool.com/mutualfunds/indexfunds/indexfunds01.htm; Edwart Wyatt, "John C. Bogle, Founder of Financial Giant Vanguard, Is Dead at 89," *New York Times*, January 17, 2019, p. A23.

Pension funds Pension funds are also a major outlet for individual savings. Usually linked to one's employer, a **pension fund** is a professionally managed portfolio of assets intended to provide income to retirees. Two main categories of pension funds exist:

- *Defined-benefit* plans guarantee a fixed payout to employees who have met certain entry requirements, such as working a certain number of years with the company.
- *Defined-contribution* plans do not guarantee retirees a defined level of pension. Employees pay in a certain (defined) amount each year and their employers may match some portion of that contribution; the fund provides payouts that depend on how the stock market performs. The most common defined-contribution plan is the *401(k) plan*, in which contributions grow tax-deferred until they are withdrawn.

In the past, defined-benefit plans were the norm. Today, defined-contribution plans such as 401(k)s are much more common.

Life insurance policies Life insurance policies are also a significant form of savings. The savings people put into these policies are called *premiums*, and as with mutual funds and pension funds, a professional decides how to use them in financial markets. Unlike mutual funds (from which you can take money out at any time) and pension funds (which you can access when you retire), life insurance policies pay out to your dependents only when you die.

pension fund
a professionally managed portfolio of assets intended to provide income to retirees

These three proxies—mutual funds, pension funds, and life insurance policies—are by no means the only ways in which individuals can entrust their savings to a third-party manager. Other options include hedge funds, private-equity firms, and venture-capital funds.

Entrepreneurs and businesses   Entrepreneurs and businesses also are major players in financial markets because they are often looking to borrow money to finance their latest ventures. Strictly speaking, these are the people who engage in economic investment, often with the advice of specialized investment banks that channel savers' money to them. Without these borrowers, much of the financial system would simply cease to exist.

Speculators   The last group of major players in the financial system is speculators, who play a unique and controversial role in the financial system. A *speculator* is anyone who buys and sells financial assets purely for financial gain.

You may ask what's controversial about that—aren't the other three key players we've considered (intermediaries, savers, and entrepreneurs) also out for financial gain? Yes, but what sets speculators apart is that they are neither a "natural" buyer nor a seller but are willing to play either role in an effort to make a profit.

There is fierce debate over whether speculators are good for the health of the financial markets, as summarized in the From Another Angle box "Are speculators a good influence on markets?"

Are speculators a good influence on markets?
From Another Angle

From 2006 to 2008, prices of many staple commodities, such as wheat and corn, practically doubled. The sharp increase in food prices came after poor harvests, combined with increases in demand for food by consumers.

Opinion is divided about whether speculation on corn and wheat enables markets to find the "correct" price for these key food commodities.
©smereka/Shutterstock

However, speculators may also have played a role. Some say that speculators predicted rising prices and grabbed the opportunity to profit by buying food and then selling it again at a higher price. Pope Benedict XVI, former leader of the Catholic Church, gave voice to a number of critics when he asked, "How can we be silent before the fact that food has become an object of speculation, or tied to happenings in a financial market that, lacking any certain rules and devoid of moral principles, appears to be still rooted to the sole object of profit?"

Speculators defend themselves by pointing to their important role in price discovery—that is, they help markets to find the "correct" price for an asset, reflecting all available information. What might the price of wheat be six months from now? Because speculators are trying to earn a profit, they will spend huge amounts of research energy on understanding every nuance of this kind of question. Their goal is to figure out if they should be buying or selling wheat futures at the current price. Many believe that this is a valuable service, saving wheat farmers, bakeries, and grocery stores from needing to do this research themselves. Instead, they can be confident that the market price already reflects the best information available.

Others believe, however, that speculation can have the opposite effect. They say that speculation can cause prices to swing wildly away from the "correct" levels. Such swings magnify small fluctuations in the market and create potentially destabilizing bubbles and busts. Consider the housing boom of 2000–2007, which was driven in part by speculators buying houses in expectation that the price of real estate would continue going up. Critics argue that something similar happened with the prices of corn and wheat: Speculators bid up the prices because they expected the price to continue to go up, creating a self-fulfilling prophecy.

This sounds like a puzzle. If speculators research the market thoroughly, wouldn't they realize that wheat was overpriced and want to sell, thereby returning wheat to its correct price? Some say that's what happens. Others believe that speculators might still want to buy overpriced wheat today under certain conditions: For example, they may feel confident that the wheat will be even *more* overpriced tomorrow, and they'll be able to sell again for a profit before the inevitable crash comes. The "correct" price will be found in the end, but perhaps only after a period of hysteria and at the risk of damage to consumers and savers.

Sources: www.nytimes.com/2008/04/10/opinion/10thu1.html; https://fee.org/articles/the-benefits-of-speculation/; Getaw Tadesse, Bernardina Algieri, Matthias Kalkuhl, and Joachim von Braun, "Drivers and Triggers of International Food Price Spikes and Volatility," *Food Policy* 47 (2014), pp. 117–128.

✓ TEST YOURSELF

☐ Why is it important that the financial system provides liquidity? **[LO 14.6]**
☐ Which type of financial asset is included in the Dow Jones Industrial Average? **[LO 14.7]**
☐ Why would an investor wish to diversify his or her financial investments? **[LO 14.7]**
☐ What are the two different types of banks? **[LO 14.8]**
☐ What is a pension fund? **[LO 14.8]**

Valuing Assets

We've touched on one particular question a few times so far: *How do buyers and sellers in the market for financial assets reach agreement on the correct price?* We've already looked at how businesses balance the expected rate of return on an investment with the cost of borrowing. How do the *suppliers* of funds—that is, savers—decide whether to deposit money in a bank or to purchase stocks or bonds? And if they choose to purchase stocks or bonds, how do they decide what to buy? In this section, we'll explore some of the basic principles of *asset valuation*, which help savers make these decisions.

LO 14.9 Explain the trade-off between risk and return in financial assets, and describe how risk can be measured.

The trade-off between risk and return

The basic trade-off in valuing any asset is between risk and return: If you face a high risk of losing your money, you're going to want the chance of a high return to make it worth taking that risk.

Figure 14-5 shows the historical risk and return profile for various major financial assets. As you can see:

- Cash and bond investments (both fixed-income and inflation-adjusted) are on the low-risk, low-return end of the spectrum.
- Stocks (equities of various types) are on the high end of the spectrum, both carrying a hefty amount of risk but generally also providing larger returns.

FIGURE 14-5

Risk and reward of various financial assets There is clearly a strong correlation between the expected risk and expected return in financial assets. Assets such as cash and fixed-income bonds carry very low risk and reward. At the upper end of the scale, financial assets in developing countries carry a return that is high, but they also are quite risky.

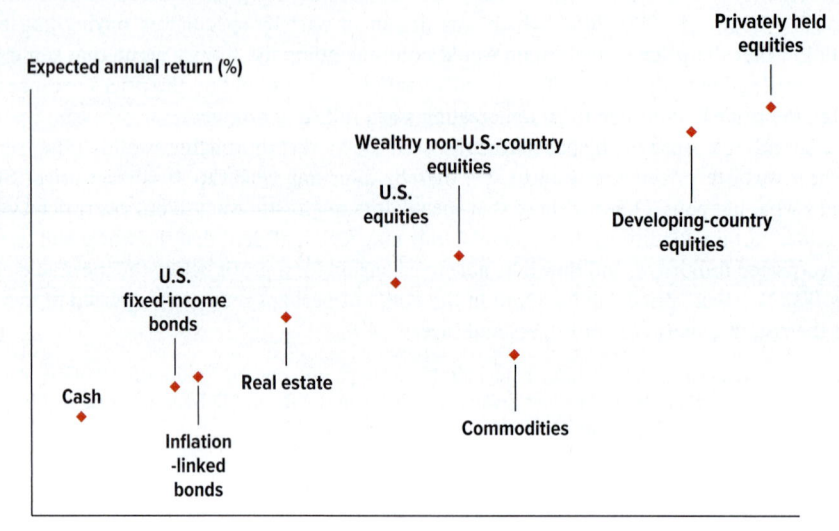

[Scatter plot with Expected risk on x-axis and Expected annual return (%) on y-axis, showing the following assets ordered roughly from low to high risk and return: Cash, U.S. fixed-income bonds, Inflation-linked bonds, Real estate, U.S. equities, Wealthy non-U.S.-country equities, Commodities, Developing-country equities, Privately held equities.]

Source: http://www.nepc.com/writable/research_articles/file/2010_03_risk_parity.pdf/.

Different individuals have different appetites for risk: Some savers may prefer to keep their money in low-risk bonds. Speculators enjoy chasing high rewards at the risk of losing everything.

Diversification, market risk, and idiosyncratic risk

One way to manage risk is to hold assets like cash and fixed-income bonds that have low risk but low return. Another way to manage risk but improve return is through diversification:

- If you put all your money in one company's stock and that company goes bankrupt, you've lost everything.
- If you buy stock in many companies, especially those in different industries, they're unlikely all to go bankrupt at the same time.

A *portfolio*—a collection or group of many different assets—will often have a higher return for a given level of risk than any individual asset could offer. To better understand how diversification works, let's look at two different types of risk that exist with financial assets.

First, **market risk**, also called *systemic risk*, refers to any risk that is broadly shared by the entire market or economy. An example would be the risk of unexpected inflation. Of course, some businesses will be more affected than others by unexpected inflation, but all businesses will face the consequences of the rising prices. For this reason, market risk is harder to eliminate via diversification.

In contrast, **idiosyncratic risk** is unique to a particular company or asset. For example, the risk that a particular company will make a bad business decision, causing the value of its stock to fall, is idiosyncratic to that company. Idiosyncratic risks are the easiest to lower or even eliminate via diversification. If you buy stock in many different companies, it's unlikely that they're all going to fail at the same time.

A portfolio composed of many stocks succeeds in diversifying away idiosyncratic risks. As more stocks are added to the portfolio, idiosyncratic risk goes down without reducing the expected performance of the portfolio.

---

market (systemic) risk any risk that is broadly shared by the entire market or economy; also called *systemic risk*

idiosyncratic risk any risk that is unique to a particular company or asset

Index funds are the natural extreme of diversifying to eliminate idiosyncratic risk: By investing in essentially all the stocks in the market, index funds achieve a very high level of diversification and face little to no idiosyncratic risk. A certain amount of market risk, just from having money in the financial market, remains in all portfolios and cannot be diversified away.

Measuring risk   How is risk measured? The most commonly used measure of risk in financial markets is a simple tool borrowed from statistics: the standard deviation. The **standard deviation** is a measurement of the amount of variation in a set of numbers.

In financial markets, the simplest way to measure risk is to look at the standard deviation of an asset's return over time. That means that we keep track of how much money it makes each day or month or year, and then measure how widely these numbers differ from period to period. For example:

- The stock market has historically returned about 7 percent per year after inflation *on average*, but the actual returns in a *particular* year have ranged anywhere from −80 percent to +120 percent. A 20-30 percent increase or decrease in any given year would not be particularly surprising. For example, in 2008 the stock market lost 37 percent of its value but then rebounded in 2009 to gain 26.5 percent.[8]
- Government bonds, on the other hand, have historically gained about 2-3 percent per year after inflation on average. Rarely have they experienced more than a 10 percent gain or loss.

In other words, government bonds have a much smaller standard deviation—meaning they have much less risk than the stock market. Those historical figures don't necessarily give a good prediction of average levels of future stock prices, but they do show the bigger point: Higher average returns usually come with substantially higher risk.

> **standard deviation**
> a measurement of the amount of variation in a set of numbers

Predicting returns: The efficient-market hypothesis

Imagine you were asked to pick the stock most likely to go up in value over the next year. How would you do it? There are three basic approaches you could take: fundamental analysis, technical analysis, and the idea of market efficiency.

> **LO 14.10** Give arguments for and against the assumption that markets are efficient.

Fundamental analysis   The first approach is through *fundamental analysis*. This approach involves trying to predict how much profit a company will make in the future and using that as a basis for calculating how much the company is worth now. Fundamental analysis is a fancy way of describing extensive research on an individual company: poring over financial statements, studying how the company is run, understanding the industry the company is in and who its competitors are, and so on. Specialized investment funds often employ hundreds of analysts to do such research.

Once we have a prediction of future profits, we can use interest rates to translate between the *present value* and *future value* of money. If you estimate the future value of the profits the company will make, you can translate it into the company's **net present value** (often abbreviated as NPV). Net present value is a measure of the current value of a stream of cash flows expected in the future. This tells you the "correct" price of shares in the company.

> **net present value (NPV)**
> a measure of the current value of a stream of cash flows expected in the future

Technical analysis   The second approach is called *technical analysis*. It ignores any attempt to predict future profits or calculate NPV, or indeed to learn anything whatsoever about the stock in question. Instead you analyze the *past* movements of a stock's price to try to predict future movements; you look for patterns in the data that could point to what's going to happen next. This method is usually done with the help of highly sophisticated computer software.

Efficient-market hypothesis

This is all pretty hard work. Is there an easier way? Well, yes. Here's the third approach: Make a list of all the stocks, pin it to a wall, and throw a dart at it. Wherever it lands, that's your choice. This doesn't sound like a great plan, does it? But if many academic researchers in the finance world are right, this approach is often just as good over time as either of the first two approaches, as well as being a whole lot cheaper, quicker, and simpler.

The idea underlying this third approach is called the **efficient-market hypothesis (EMH)**. It states that market prices always incorporate *all available information* and therefore represent true value as correctly as is possible. Notice the difference between fundamental and technical analysis and the EMH:

- Both fundamental and technical analysis are ways of trying to outsmart the market; they work only if you find a stock whose current price is either higher or lower than the "correct" price.
- The EMH implies that finding incorrectly priced stocks is impossible. If prices already represent the best-possible information about the true value of a stock, then all stocks are already correctly priced, and so there is no additional information you can use to predict which stocks will gain value.

The intuition behind this idea is pretty straightforward. Imagine that careful observers of the stock market have information that a particular company will announce high profits tomorrow. Such an announcement generally causes a stock's price to rise, so it makes sense to buy the stock today in the hope of selling at a profit tomorrow. The effect is to drive up the price of the stock today, until it reaches the price expected for tomorrow. The expectation of tomorrow's announcement is now *priced in*.

So what will happen to the stock's price tomorrow? According to the efficient-market hypothesis, the stock's expected movements might go in any direction—described as a *random walk*. This idea brings us back to our dart-throwing plan: If you can't possibly predict stock returns, you might as well just pin a list of stocks on the wall and throw darts at them.

Not surprisingly, the efficient-market hypothesis isn't popular with the Wall Street brokers and analysts who are paid handsomely for their attempts to pick winning stocks. They argue that some analysts simply have better information than others or at least a better ability to put together all the complex pieces.

However, the number of people who have consistently outsmarted the markets over a long period is vanishingly small. Over the course of one year, only about 50 percent of managed funds beat the market. After 15 years, however, only *5 percent* of managed funds had a higher rate of return.[9] The efficient-market hypothesis is exactly the reason why we should not be surprised that index funds consistently outperform actively managed funds. Since index funds earn the same return as the overall market, they generally beat actively managed funds in the long run. In addition, actively managed funds charge higher fees that erode their net rates of return.

One argument against the efficient-market hypothesis is that occasionally the same financial asset can be traded at different prices in different markets. That's evidence that the market isn't efficiently using all its information. If you can manage to simultaneously sell that asset in one place while buying it in another, you can make a risk-free profit.

The process of taking advantage of market inefficiencies to earn profits is called **arbitrage**. Some fund managers specialize in scouring different markets in search of arbitrage opportunities. However, it takes a huge amount of effort to spot these opportunities, and if you get the timing even slightly wrong, you can end up losing a lot of money.

Over the past couple of decades, some academic economists in a field called behavioral finance have also started questioning the validity of the efficient-market hypothesis because they believe it might be possible to exploit the mistakes of Wall Street analysts. See the Economics in Action box "Behavioral finance" for more.

---

efficient-market hypothesis (EMH) the idea that market prices always incorporate all available information and therefore represent true value as correctly as is possible

arbitrage the process of taking advantage of market inefficiencies to earn profits

Behavioral finance
Economics in Action

The efficient-market hypothesis says that people have good information and make smart choices when buying and selling shares on the stock market. If that happens, it's difficult to systematically make money in the stock market. Other investors will have already snapped up bargains, and there will be no undiscovered gems overlooked by others.

But what if people don't use their information well and don't make good choices? Then, it could be possible to make money systematically by taking into account how they actually make choices—and then creating strategies that exploit their mistakes.

This is the thinking behind *behavioral finance*, a branch of behavioral economics. Behavioral economists study the ways in which people fall short of fully rational behavior. What sorts of irrational behavior might play a role when people are playing the stock market? One possibility is that people pay too much attention to recent events. For instance, if a stock has recently been going up, they might be too quick to conclude that it will continue to go up. This tendency is called *herding*. People naturally like to feel that they're part of the crowd; they feel more confident in their decisions if they see that other people around them agree.

Other investors feel that it might be a winning strategy to study what the herding consensus seems to be and go against it: If stock market analysts are optimistic about a company's prospects and it's getting great coverage in the financial media, perhaps that is leading people to overbuy it. If so, you should sell the company's stock, not buy it. This strategy is known as *contrarian investing*.

In the 1990s, some investment banks launched mutual funds based on the insights of behavioral economics. The investment bank JP Morgan and leading behavioral economist Richard Thaler (the 2017 Economics Nobel Memorial Prize winner) started the JP Morgan Undiscovered Managers Behavioral Value Fund. The fund uses a variety of behavioral tactics to find "undervalued" stocks.

How did such funds perform? Although the Undiscovered Managers Behavioral Value Fund has outperformed its benchmark index between 2008-2018, the overall set of funds that employ behavioral finance have not done quite so well. In a 2013 study, researchers looked at mutual funds that used principles of behavioral economics and found that the funds "neither outperform nor underperform the market."

Of course, just because a fund says it is employing behavioral finance approaches does not mean it is doing it well. The debate on whether anyone can consistently beat the market remains open. We can say, however, that as long as fortunes can be made outsmarting other investors, people will try to find systems and patterns that aim to beat the market.

Sources: www.iijournals.com/doi/abs/10.3905/jii.2010.1.2.056; https://am.jpmorgan.com/us/en/asset-management/gim/adv/products/d/undiscovered-managers-behavioral-value-fund-l-904504842.

Bubbles

According to the efficient-market view, markets are rational, in the sense that asset prices incorporate all relevant information at any given point in time. There are times, however, when asset prices rise far above historically justified levels and then subsequently collapse, a phenomenon known as a *bubble*.

One of the earliest examples of a bubble was the Dutch Tulip Mania of 1634-1637. At the top of that market, a single tulip sold for as much as a house. More recent examples include the stock-market boom in the 1920s, the internet bubble in the late 1990s, and the housing bubble that ended with the onset of the global financial crisis of 2009. (See Chapter 17, "Financial Crisis," for further discussion of some famous bubbles.)

What exactly is a bubble? Robert Shiller, one of the leading scholars in behavioral finance and a Nobel laureate, described a bubble as:

> [a] situation in which news of price increases spurs investor enthusiasm, which spreads by psychological contagion from person to person, in the process amplifying stories that might justify the price increase. This attracts a larger and larger class of investors, who, despite doubts about the real value of the investment, are drawn to it partly through envy of others' successes and partly through a gambler's excitement.[10]

Thus, bubbles in asset prices can be seen as social epidemics, in which the excitement surrounding rapidly growing asset prices infects people with a "bug" to buy in the hope of selling at ever higher prices. Since this process can't continue indefinitely, bubbles will eventually pop and prices will plummet, often causing severe economic damage in the process.

✓ TEST YOURSELF

- ☐ What is the general relationship between risk and return in financial markets? **[LO 14.9]**
- ☐ How does idiosyncratic risk differ from market risk? **[LO 14.9]**
- ☐ Is a stock that has a net present value lower than the current market price a good buy? **[LO 14.9]**
- ☐ What is the prediction of the efficient-market hypothesis? **[LO 14.10]**
- ☐ Does the possibility for arbitrage suggest that a market is efficient? **[LO 14.10]**

A National Accounts Approach to Finance

LO 14.11 Describe why savings equals investment in a closed economy and how government spending and foreign capital flows affect the saving-investment relationship.

Earlier in the chapter, we showed that when the market for loanable funds is in equilibrium, savings (supply) must equal investment (demand). This applies the microeconomic logic of market equilibrium to the financial system.

We also can approach the analysis from a purely macroeconomic angle. By looking at savings and investment through the lens of the national income accounting method introduced in Chapter 7, "Measuring GDP," we can track the quantity of funds on a national level and separate out different sources of savings.

The savings-investment identity

Start by imagining a simplified economy with no government and no international trade. All transactions happen within the borders of the country, among its residents. How could the residents of our simple economy use the money they earn? They have only two possible uses for their income: They can *consume it* (spend it now) or they can *save it* (keep it for later). In other words, income is equal to the sum of consumption and savings:

EQUATION 14-1   Income = Consumption + Savings

private savings the savings of individuals or corporations within a country

In this simple economy, with no government or international trade, all savings are **private savings**—the savings of individuals or corporations within a country.

Now, let's think about how people in this simple economy earn their income. Since there are no governments or foreign countries to interact with, they earn income only when other people in the country purchase goods or services from them. We can categorize all of these purchases as spending on *consumption* (things like meals, clothes, and cars) or as spending on *investment goods* (productive inputs like factories and machines). Income in the closed economy is equal to total spending, which is equal to consumption plus investment:

EQUATION 14-2   Income = Consumption + Investment

This result is related to the national accounts framework we developed in Chapter 7, "Measuring GDP."

Next, to relate savings to investment, we can put together Equations 14-1 and 14-2. Equation 14-1 says that consumption plus savings equals income. Equation 14-2 says that income also equals consumption plus investment. Putting the two together, we see that

$$\text{Consumption} + \text{Savings} = \text{Income} = \text{Consumption} + \text{Investment}$$

Since consumption appears on both sides of this equation, we can cancel it out and immediately see the *savings-investment identity:*

EQUATION 14-3 $$\text{Savings} = \text{Investment}$$

which is commonly written:

$$S = I$$

The savings-investment identity tells us that savings always equals investment in an economy with no government and no trade.

Private savings, public savings, and capital flows

Our simple economy is of course missing a large reality: government. When we add government to the picture, we also add taxes:

- If government takes in more through taxes than it spends, it can run *budget surpluses*. These government surpluses are another form of saving: The government receives income in the form of taxes and saves it by not spending it right away.
- On the other hand, if government spends more than it takes in taxes, it runs a *budget deficit*. That deficit is a form not of saving but of *dissaving*. In that case, the government must borrow money from the rest of the economy in order to spend more than it collects in taxes.

If we look at how much the government takes in through tax revenue and subtract what it spends, that difference is **public savings**. Mathematically, that's

EQUATION 14-4 $$\text{Public savings} = \text{Taxes} - \text{Government spending}$$

Adding public savings to private savings, we get **national savings**, which is the sum of the private savings of individuals and corporations plus the public savings of the government:

EQUATION 14-5 $$\text{National savings} = \text{Private savings (of individuals)} \\ + \text{Public savings (of government)}$$

When the government runs a deficit, national savings will be lower than private savings; the opposite is true when the government runs a surplus.

Now, there are *three* things that citizens of our simple economy could do with the income they earn: They can consume, save privately, or pay taxes to the government. We can show this by adding taxes to Equation 14-1:

EQUATION 14-6 $$\text{Income} = \text{Consumption} + \text{Private savings} + \text{Taxes}$$

There is also an additional way for citizens to earn income: They can sell goods and services to or receive benefits from the government. We can show this new income source as a variation on Equation 14-2:

EQUATION 14-7 $$\text{Income} = \text{Consumption} + \text{Investment} + \text{Government spending}$$

public savings
the difference between government tax revenue and government spending

national savings
the sum of the private savings of individuals and corporations plus the public savings of the government

Just as we did before, we can put together these two ways of arriving at "income" (from Equations 14-6 and Equation 14-7):

$$\text{Income} = \text{Consumption} + \text{Private savings} + \text{Taxes}$$
$$= \text{Consumption} + \text{Investment} + \text{Government spending}$$

Canceling consumption from both sides, this reduces to:

$$\text{Private savings} + \text{Taxes} = \text{Investment} + \text{Government spending}$$

Now, let's rearrange that equation to isolate investment:

EQUATION 14-8 $\quad\quad\quad \text{Investment} = \text{Private savings} + \text{Taxes} - \text{Government spending}$

But we know (from Equation 14-4) that taxes minus government spending equals public savings. So, we can simplify further:

EQUATION 14-9 $\quad\quad\quad\quad\quad\quad \text{Investment} = \text{Private savings} + \text{Public savings}$

And we know that national savings equals private savings plus public savings. Therefore,

$$\text{Investment} = \text{National savings}$$

In other words, *national savings are equal to the total investment in the economy*.

Note that we are still assuming no international trade. The identity between national savings and investment holds only in a **closed economy**—an economy that does not interact with other countries' economies.

The final piece of real-world complexity we need to add to our model is opening it up to international interactions. This is called an **open economy**. When money is allowed to move freely across borders, two different types of international financial transactions can happen:

- A *capital outflow* occurs when the money saved *domestically* (within the home country) is invested in another country.
- Conversely, a *capital inflow* occurs when savings from another country finance domestic investment.

The difference between capital inflows and capital outflows is **net capital flow**. A net capital inflow occurs in countries where investment is higher than national savings. In the opposite case, when national savings are higher than domestic investment, there is a net capital outflow.

For an *open* economy, national savings can be more or less than investment. But for the *global economy as a whole*, savings must be equal to investment. This means that any excess savings in one country have to be soaked up as investment elsewhere.

In the From Another Angle box "Savings glut?" we evaluate this possibility in practice.

closed economy
an economy that does not interact with other countries' economies

open economy
an economy that interacts with other countries' economies

net capital flow
the net flow of funds invested outside of a country; specifically, the difference between capital inflows (investment financed by savings from another country) and capital outflows (domestic savings invested abroad)

Savings glut?
From Another Angle

As children, we were often reminded of the virtue of saving. Many of us dutifully put our allowances in piggy banks, looking forward to blowing it all on a bigger and better toy or treat down the road.

For the past decade, though, people in the United States haven't been saving much. The government has, for the most part, run large deficits. Households save only a small percentage of their income on average. Many actually spend more than they earn, financing the difference by credit cards and loans. In addition, the country has long been running a sizable *current-account deficit*, meaning that it imports far more than it exports. All of these patterns suggest that people in the United States are spending way too much.

But could the problem be that other countries are *saving* way too much? This hypothesis, called the *global savings glut*, ties recent U.S. economic ills to high savings rates in Asia and Latin America.

When economies are open to cross-border capital flows, savings no longer have to equal investment within a given country. It's possible for a nation to save more than its firms and individuals want to invest. When that happens, these excess funds end up searching for the best returns in other investments around the world. Most of these funds end up in the United States, largely because it is seen as a safe place to invest. In fact, economist Kenneth Rogoff estimated that in 2007, a full two-thirds of excess savings in the world ended up invested in the United States.

This represents a huge sum of money. In the years before the 2007 financial crisis, net capital inflows—the amount of money coming in minus the amount the United States invested around the world—were around 6 percent of U.S. GDP. Ben Bernanke, the Federal Reserve chair at the time, argued that this large inflow of money kept interest rates low, which translated to cheap borrowing for Americans. Cheap borrowing enabled the housing boom during the mid-2000s, when people borrowed heavily to buy houses they wouldn't have been able to afford at higher interest rates.

Could the U.S. housing bubble really have been caused in part by industrious savers in Asia and Latin America? It seems hard to believe, but it's possible that this played a role.

Sources: www.federalreserve.gov/newsevents/speech/bernanke20110218a.htm; Kenneth Rogoff, "Betting with the House's Money," *The Guardian*, February 7, 2007, www.guardian.co.uk/commentisfree/2007/feb/07/bettingwiththehousesmoney.

✓ TEST YOURSELF

- ☐ What are the components of national savings? **[LO 14.11]**
- ☐ What is it called when the amount of capital leaving a country is greater than the amount going in? **[LO 14.11]**

Conclusion

In this chapter we've explored the basic framework of financial markets and the financial system: how buyers find sellers, how interest rates set the price of borrowing and the return on lending, and how the various players interact. We've also learned about a few of the major financial-asset classes and explored some of the ways that investors attempt to evaluate the risk and return potential of their investments.

You've seen that financial markets mostly operate like other markets. However, financial markets can sometimes behave in mysterious and opaque ways. We'll see more examples in Chapter 17, "Financial Crisis."

Now that we've covered the basics of how financial markets and the financial system work, it's time to look at the bigger picture: how the financial system fits into the overall economy. In the next chapter, we'll look at the origins of money and how the modern financial system is responsible for both creating and destroying money. We'll also learn about the people who oversee much of the financial system, including influencing the money supply, and how their actions affect economic growth in ways both enormous and subtle.

Key Terms

financial market, p. 361
information assymetry, p. 361
adverse selection, p. 361
moral hazard, p. 362
market for loanable funds, p. 364
savings, p. 364
investment, p. 364
interest rate, p. 365
crowding out, p. 369
default, p. 371
risk-free rate, p. 371
financial system, p. 372

financial intermediaries, p. 372
liquidity, p. 372
diversification, p. 373
stock, p. 373
dividend, p. 374
loan, p. 374
bond, p. 374
derivative, p. 375
mutual fund, p. 376
pension fund, p. 377
market (systemic) risk, p. 380
idiosyncratic risk, p. 380

standard deviation, p. 381
net present value (NPV), p. 381
efficient-market hypothesis (EMH), p. 382
arbitrage, p. 382
private savings, p. 384
public savings, p. 385
national savings, p. 385
closed economy, p. 386
open economy, p. 386
net capital flow, p. 386

Summary

LO 14.1 Define a financial market, and describe the information asymmetry problems that can occur in them.

A *financial market* is one in which people trade future claims on funds or goods. Financial markets help ensure that the world's wealth is channeled to the individuals and organizations that can most effectively take advantage of it. A well-functioning financial market matches buyers and sellers as efficiently and effectively as possible. In financial markets, buyers are people who want to spend money on something of value right now but don't have cash on hand. Sellers are people who have cash on hand and are willing to let others use it, for a price.

An *information asymmetry* arises when one participant in a transaction knows more than another participant. Adverse selection and moral hazard are two types of information asymmetry problems of financial markets. *Adverse selection* refers to a state that occurs when buyers and sellers have different information about the quality of a good or the riskiness of a situation, and this asymmetric information results in failure to complete transactions that would have been possible if both sides had the same information. *Moral hazard* refers to people's tendency, after a transaction takes place, to behave in a riskier way or to renege on contracts when they do not face the full consequences of their actions.

LO 14.2 Discuss the three main functions of financial markets.

Financial markets—including banks, which are one example—serve three main functions. First, they act as *intermediaries*, bringing together savers and borrowers in an easy, one-stop clearinghouse. Second, they provide the benefits of *liquidity*—having cash easily available when you want it—without the downsides of holding cash. Third, they help savers to *diversify risk* by providing funds to a big pool of borrowers. No individual saver will bear the full burden of a failed loan or investment.

LO 14.3 Describe the market for loanable funds, including the price of loanable funds, and differentiate between savings and investment.

The market for loanable funds is a hypothetical marketplace that brings together everyone looking to lend money (savers) and everyone looking to borrow money (anyone with investment-spending needs). The market for loanable funds clears at a price where supply and demand meet. This price is known as the *interest rate*. A key determinant of the supply curve for loanable funds is how much people decide to save.

Economists differentiate between savings and investment: *Savings* is the portion of income that is not immediately spent on consumption, whereas *investment* is spending on productive inputs.

LO 14.4 List the factors that affect the supply and demand of loanable funds.

Many factors influence the supply and demand curves for loanable funds. Factors that determine how much people save include wealth, current economic conditions, expectations about future economic conditions, borrowing constraints, social welfare policies, and culture. Factors that determine investment decisions include expectations about future profitability and future economic conditions, borrowing constraints, and crowding out (reduction in private borrowing that is caused by an increase in government borrowing).

LO 14.5 Understand how interest rates on loans vary with the length of the loan and the riskiness of the transaction.

Two basic factors drive differences in interest rates: length of time and degree of risk. Lenders generally want a higher interest rate to compensate for the added opportunity cost when loans stretch over a long period and for taking on additional risk. The interest rate at which one would lend if there were no risk of default is the *risk-free rate* (generally approximated by interest rates on U.S. government debt). In the market for loanable funds, loans with longer terms and higher risks of default will have interest rates further above the risk-free rate.

LO 14.6 Describe why it is important for the financial system to intermediate between buyers and sellers, provide liquidity, and diversify risk.

Financial systems provide features similar to financial markets: intermediating between savers and borrowers, providing liquidity, and diversifying risk. In financial systems, various institutions act as *financial intermediaries*, channeling funds from people who have them to people who want them. Intermediation in financial systems reduces transaction costs by centralizing information about prices and providing a broad and dynamic marketplace for transactions.

Various players in the financial system are liquidity providers, helping ensure that markets are liquid. Some of these we even call *market makers* because they are always ready to buy or sell assets. The very structure of financial assets such as stocks and bonds also serves to increase liquidity. Liquidity is important because it affects people's willingness to save.

Finally, the financial system spreads risk even more broadly than a financial market does: Savers can diversify into different savings products and across geographic areas; borrowers have access to loans from the funds provided by many more savers.

LO 14.7 Differentiate between debt and equity, and define the major types of assets in each category.

The major types of financial assets are debt and equity. *Equity* is ownership in a company, and the most common form of such ownership is *stock*. As partial owners, stockholders are entitled to receive a portion of a company's profits, in the form of dividends, in proportion to the size of their ownership.

The most basic type of debt is a *loan*. *Loans* are an agreement between a lender and a borrower in which the lender lends money to the borrower in exchange for a promise to repay the amount loaned (the *principal* of the loan) plus an agreed-upon amount of interest. A *bond* is a loan that has been standardized into a more easily tradable and liquid asset. Bonds are a type of debt issued by corporations or governments as a way to borrow large sums of money. Stocks and bonds are liquid assets that are easily bought and sold in financial markets.

Financial contracts based on the value of some other asset represent a special category of financial assets, called *derivatives*. The best example of a derivative is a futures contract.

LO 14.8 Name the main institutions in financial markets, and describe the role that each plays.

There are many different players in the financial market. There are banks, which can be divided into two categories: *commercial banks* and *investment banks*. When you make a deposit at a bank, or get a mortgage or student loan from a bank, you are interacting with a commercial bank. *Investment banks* focus on providing liquidity to the financial markets themselves, by acting as market makers, helping companies to issue stocks and bonds (a process known as *underwriting*).

Individual actors in the financial market have to operate through a *proxy*—they give their money to someone else to invest for them. These proxies include *mutual funds* (professionally managed portfolios of stocks and other assets), *pension funds* (professionally administered portfolios of assets intended to provide income to retirees), and life insurance policies (in which people pay *premiums* that pay out to dependents upon the death of the insured).

Entrepreneurs and businesses are also major players in financial markets, as are speculators.

LO 14.9 Explain the trade-off between risk and return in financial assets, and describe how risk can be measured.

In general, there is a direct relationship between risk and reward in the financial market. The riskier the investment, the higher its potential return. Typically, the investments with the lowest risk—and lowest return—are government bonds. Stocks are a considerably more risky investment, but also offer the possibility of higher returns.

Two different types of risk exist for financial assets—*market risk* (risk that is broadly shared by the entire market) and *idiosyncratic risk* (risk unique to a particular asset or company). A *portfolio* of assets can help diversify away idiosyncratic risk; a certain amount of market risk remains in all portfolios.

In financial markets, the most commonly used method of measuring this risk is a simple tool borrowed from statistics: the standard deviation. The *standard deviation* is a measurement of the amount of variation in a set of numbers.

> **LO 14.10** Give arguments for and against the assumption that markets are efficient.

The efficient-market hypothesis holds that markets are *efficient*—that market prices incorporate all available information and, as a result, accurately predicting stock returns is impossible.

Supporters of the efficient-market hypothesis describe the expected movements of a stock as a *random walk*, a term from statistics that describes any variable (like the price of a stock) that moves in a completely unpredictable (random) way from one moment to the next.

Those who argue against market efficiency suggest that some people simply have better information than others or a better ability to put all the complex pieces together to predict stock price. Occasionally markets have certain information inefficiencies that savvy investors, through *arbitrage*, can exploit to profit from the differences between prices in different markets.

> **LO 14.11** Describe why savings equals investment in a closed economy and how government spending and foreign capital flows affect the saving-investment relationship.

In a *closed economy*, one with no international trade, citizens can consume or save. The amount of savings within an economy is necessarily the amount of investment that can occur. Thus, savings and investment spending (the supply and demand of the financial markets) are always equal, a relationship called the *savings-investment identity*.

Review Questions

1. In financial markets, who are the sellers? Who are the buyers? **[LO 14.1]**
2. Identify the two types of information asymmetry defined in the chapter. What is the difference between them? **[LO 14.1]**
3. Explain why a country with poorly developed financial markets might have a hard time sustaining economic growth. **[LO 14.2]**
4. Is it savings or investment when Collins Inc. uses the proceeds from issuing bonds to purchase equipment needed to start a new product line? If Daisy buys some of the Collins Inc. bonds, is her purchase savings or investment? **[LO 14.3]**
5. When the real interest rate increases, what happens to the quantity of loanable funds supplied? What happens to the quantity of loanable funds demanded? **[LO 14.3]**
6. Why might a government want to encourage saving among its citizens? If the government enacts a successful policy aimed at encouraging saving, what would be the likely effect on the interest rate and the quantity of investment? **[LO 14.4]**
7. The government of a small country has enacted new regulations that make it more difficult to obtain a loan from a bank. How does this affect savings, investment, and the interest rate in the country? **[LO 14.4]**
8. Using the concept of default, explain why the interest rate on credit card debt is higher than the interest rate on a mortgage. **[LO 14.5]**
9. Your friend claims that there is no such thing as a risk-free interest rate because all loans are risky. Do you agree? Why or why not? **[LO 14.5]**
10. Is the stock exchange an example of a financial intermediary? Why or why not? **[LO 14.6]**
11. In a famous bet known as the Simon-Ehrlich wager, Paul Ehrlich bet that over the course of 10 years, the prices of five commodities would be higher than they were at the start of the decade; Julian Simon believed the price of these goods would be lower. The loser had to pay the difference of the price from the starting point. What type of financial asset does this wager resemble? Why? **[LO 14.7]**
12. What is securitization? How did it contribute to the recent housing-market crisis? **[LO 14.7]**
13. How do economists generally define a bank? What kind of bank exemplifies this definition? Does an investment bank meet this definition? **[LO 14.8]**
14. What is an index fund, and why would a financial investor consider buying one? **[LO 14.8]**
15. Which is likely to have more risk, a government bond from a developing country or one from France? Which should have a higher return? **[LO 14.9]**
16. Define diversification and comment on how successful it is at managing market risk and idiosyncratic risk. **[LO 14.9]**
17. During the 1990s, securities related to technology and other dot-com firms experienced skyrocketing market prices, but around 2000 the market crashed. Was

that crash an example that supports or offers evidence against the efficient-market hypothesis? **[LO 14.10]**

18. Describe the difference between fundamental analysis and technical analysis. Which, if any, does the efficient-market hypothesis suggest financial investors engage in? **[LO 14.10]**

19. Does the level of taxation in a closed economy have an impact on national savings? Explain. **[LO 14.11]**

20. Explain how a persistent government budget deficit can hurt a closed economy's ability to engage in economic investment. **[LO 14.11]**

Problems and Applications

1. For each scenario, indicate whether it is an example of moral hazard or adverse selection. **[LO 14.1]**
   a. You decide to buy a new car instead of a used car because you are worried about the quality of the used car.
   b. You sell your condominium because you fear there will be a large special assessment next year. There has been no official notice of an upcoming assessment.
   c. The owner of a company has just secured a new line of credit from the bank. He decides to change his business plan and open a second office in a foreign country.
   d. A firm that has purchased a large insurance policy becomes careless about setting the security alarm.
   e. A number of households find themselves owing more on their mortgages than their houses are currently worth. Some of them decide to abandon the house and walk away.
   f. The owners of a company suspect there will be more competition from foreign producers in upcoming years. They have just issued new shares of stock in their company.

2. The chapter discusses three main functions of a banking system. Classify each of the following by the function it best represents. **[LO 14.2]**
   a. Wyatt can get cash out of the ATM at any time of day or night.
   b. Instead of lending all her savings out to one borrower, Xander's bank makes the money in his savings account available to a variety of firms, with different characteristics and risk profiles, wishing to invest.
   c. When Yao's car suddenly breaks down, she can quickly withdraw funds from her savings account to pay the mechanic and rent a car.
   d. Zirwat can get start-up funds for her new hair salon from a bank, instead of having to find people in her neighborhood willing to lend their extra money.

3. After graduating, you take an unusual job: consulting with the queen of a small, newly populated island in the middle of the sea. You've provided advice to her on matters related to government and the economy, and while she has taken your advice most of the time, she has so far turned down your suggestion to have a banking system. She claims that banks will make the economy more complicated and do little to make the lives of her subjects easier.

    Over the past several months, though, the queen has discussed with you several issues that have arisen in the newly formed economy. For each of the three quotes from the queen below, refer to one of the three functions of banks discussed in this chapter to explain how a banking system could help with the issue described. **[LO 14.2]**
   a. "When my subjects have money left over after spending, they want to keep it somewhere safe and earn some interest on it. But that's hard for most of them because they have no way of finding out who wants to borrow and whether it would be a good idea to lend to them."
   b. "My subjects are lucky that we have very little crime, so they can safely keep their extra money inside their houses and take only what cash they need for a day's spending. However, many of them have complained that if an emergency occurs when they're all the way on the other side of the island, they can't access their funds."
   c. "Some of my subjects who are in the know about good borrowers have been making loans and earning interest. But lately there have been a couple of borrowers who defaulted on loans, and when they did, the lenders were totally out of luck. All that money just disappeared! And those bad experiences have made other potential lenders afraid, so that now borrowing and lending have dried up almost completely. If only there were some easy way for them to divide their savings among several different borrowers, they might feel safe enough to start lending again!"

4. Categorize each of the following as a type of savings or investment in the economic sense. **[LO 14.3]**
   a. You buy 100 shares of Apple Computer stock.
   b. You place part of your income in a mutual fund.
   c. A delivery service buys 1,000 new trucks.
   d. You put $1,000 in a certificate of deposit by giving money to the bank in exchange for a set amount of return.

5. Use the following words to fill in the blanks in the statements below about the market for loanable funds. *Choose from:* demanded, supplied; left, right; higher, lower. **[LO 14.4]**
   a. A change that makes people want to save less will shift the quantity of loanable funds _____ to the _____. The resulting new equilibrium in the market for loanable funds would be a _____ interest rate and a _____ quantity of funds saved and invested.
   b. A change that makes people want to save more will shift the quantity of loanable funds _____ to the _____. The resulting new equilibrium in the market for loanable funds would be a _____ interest rate and a _____ quantity of funds saved and invested.
   c. A change that makes people want to invest more will shift the quantity of loanable funds _____ to the _____. The resulting new equilibrium in the market for loanable funds would be a _____ interest rate and a _____ quantity of funds saved and invested.
   d. A change that makes people want to invest less will shift the quantity of loanable funds _____ to the _____. The resulting new equilibrium in the market for loanable funds would be a _____ interest rate and a _____ quantity of funds saved and invested.

6. Consider the market for loanable funds. Graphically illustrate the impact on the equilibrium interest rate and the equilibrium quantity of funds saved and invested in each of the following scenarios. **[LO 14.3, LO 14.4]**
   a. Due to slow growth in the economy, fewer workers are receiving pay increases and more workers are losing their jobs.
   b. The government decides to reduce the number of weeks a person is eligible for unemployment compensation.
   c. Numerous firms remain concerned about growth prospects in the economy.
   d. The government decides to reduce income tax rates, and this reduction leads to an increase in the size of the budget deficit.

7. You go to the bank and purchase a $1,000 certificate of deposit (CD). **[LO 14.5]**
   a. Who is doing the borrowing? Who is doing the lending?
   b. Which is higher, the interest rate paid on the 6-month CD or the 2-year CD? Why?

8. What does the risk premium measure? During a recession, what is likely to happen to the risk premium? **[LO 14.5]**

9. You have a sum of funds sitting in a savings account earning a modest interest rate of 3 percent. A good friend wants to borrow half of this sum, and he has agreed to pay you an interest rate of 5 percent. Should you lend your friend the money? Why or why not? **[LO 14.6]**

10. In your spare time, you help out with a magazine for high schoolers that focuses on current events related to economics and politics. While the magazine aims to be readable and entertaining, it also wants to use terminology correctly. Knowing that you've taken an economics class, the editor turns to you to look over a paragraph in a story focusing on the roles of saving and investment after the recent crisis in the housing market. Go through the following quotation and correct any errors in economic vocabulary, including an explanation for the editor about why the original was incorrect. **[LO 14.3, LO 14.6]**

    When Americans invest by buying securities such as stocks and bonds or putting money in a bank, they provide funds for firms wishing to engage in diversification by buying assets used to produce goods and services. Households with extra money left over after buying things they want or need consume by purchasing securities or putting their funds in savings accounts, and banks help transfer those funds to firms. By matching and working with these borrowers and lenders, banks act as a source of liquidity.

11. In each of following examples, name the financial product being described. **[LO 14.7]**
    a. A family borrows money to pay for a house.
    b. A new tech start-up offers investors the ability to purchase a small part of the company to raise needed capital.
    c. The U.S. government offers to pay investors a 3 percent return rate next year if they finance its debt today.

12. Evaluate each of the following statements and say whether it describes a loan, a bond, and/or a stock. **[LO 14.7]**
    a. It implies ownership in the issuing firm.
    b. Small businesses use these to raise funds for investment.
    c. This is also known as equity financing.
    d. We can think of this as a more liquid version of a loan.
    e. It pays some form of interest, and principal is paid at maturity.

13. Match each of the following players in the financial system with the financial product(s) they are most associated with. **[LO 14.8]**

a. Commercial banks.   i. Stocks.
b. Savers.   ii. Bonds.
c. Investment banks.   iii. Loans.

14. Rank the following actors in financial markets by the level of liquidity they are providing. [LO 14.8]
    a. Entrepreneurs offering equity in their businesses.
    b. The Federal Reserve offering banks the chance to borrow short-term money through the discount window.
    c. Investment banks offering shares in mutual funds, which penalize you if you withdraw your money within 30 days.
    d. A bank offering you a no-minimum reserve requirement checking account.

15. Rank the following assets based on their expected return. Then repeat the exercise, this time ranking the assets based on their expected risk. [LO 14.9]
    a. Real estate.
    b. Commodities.
    c. U.S. equities (stocks).
    d. Cash.
    e. U.S. fixed-income bonds.

16. Evaluate whether the following statements are true or false. [LO 14.9]
    a. Risk is measured by looking at the expected value (average) of an asset's returns over time.
    b. Market risk can be minimized with a well-diversified portfolio.
    c. Idiosyncratic risk is unique to a particular asset, rather than to the market as a whole.
    d. A portfolio of well-diversified assets will often be less risky for the same level of return when compared to an individual asset.

17. "Listen," your buddy says. "Have you ever noticed that you can get the same type and size of tire for $30 cheaper in the next county over? I've got a way to make profits for years—we'll buy the tires where they're cheaper and bring them back here to sell." What is the term for the transaction your friend wants to make? Would the efficient-market hypothesis predict it will be as profitable as he says? Explain. [LO 14.10]

18. In each of the following examples say whether the market is behaving within the principles of the efficient-market hypothesis. [LO 14.10]
    a. The day after unrest in the Middle East, the source of supply for much of the world's oil, the price of oil falls.
    b. Investors find very few opportunities for arbitrage in the foreign exchange market.
    c. The Dow Jones Industrial Average, a major stock market index, changes in value by 5 percent for an entire week, even though very little economic news is released.

19. In 2018, U.S. government spending was $3.90 trillion, tax revenue was $4.50 trillion, GDP was $14.02 trillion, and total consumer spending was $10.75 trillion. If the economy has no exports or imports, what was the national savings in 2018? How much was public savings? How much was private savings? [LO 14.11]

20. A country's government has been running a deficit for the past few years. Suppose this country decides to increase its government spending. [LO 14.4, LO 14.11]
    a. Compare the impact of the increase in government spending in a closed economy and an open economy.
    b. Are you more likely to observe crowding out in a closed economy or an open economy? Explain.

21. Consider the U.S. market for loanable funds in a closed-economy model. Answer the following questions about each scenario. [LO 14.4, LO 14.11]
    a. The government starts offering a national savings bond to increase private savings, which pays a higher return than many other options available on the market. Which way will the supply of loanable funds curve shift? Will the interest rate increase or decrease? Will there be more or less borrowing?
    b. Suppose the economy is now open. Due to rapid economic expansion in China, the Chinese government decides to invest in U.S. Treasury notes with some of its surplus. Which way will the supply curve shift?
    c. A new computer software program is introduced into the market that offers businesses that purchase it promising returns on their investment. Which curve will shift? Which way will it shift?
    d. The government reduces the capital gains tax, which taxes earnings on assets in the stock market. Which curve will shift? Which way will it shift?

Endnotes

1. For the moment, we are talking about the real interest rate. In Chapter 16, "Inflation," we'll talk about how the nominal interest rate can differ from the real interest rate when there is inflation; don't worry about that for now.

2. In Chapter 16, "Inflation," we will also see that there are other reasons to be concerned about *deflation*, or falling prices in an economy.

3. The savings rate is measured as the difference between disposable income and spending. The measure thus reflects how much money people put in the bank minus how much they borrow. Economists estimate that changes in how much people borrow explains much of the recent variation in the measured savings rate shown in Figure 14-3. See http://www.frbsf.org/economic-research/files/el2011-01.pdf.

4. Note that the word *public* in *public companies* indicates that ownership is open to the general public; it does not imply anything about government, as in the term *public*–government–*spending*.

5. In the past, bonds had actual coupons that bondholders would clip and return to the bond issuer in exchange for interest payments. Those coupons were quite different in purpose from the ones that people use to get price reductions on goods and services.

6. The average inflation-adjusted stock return in the 50 years between 1965 and 2015 was about 7 percent. A better measure of returns is the compound annual growth rate, which shows a gain of about 5.5 percent in the same period. If you're interested in looking further into data trends, you can try the stock market return calculator at http://www.moneychimp.com/features/market_cagr.htm.

7. www.statista.com/statistics/255518/mutual-fund-assets-held-by-investment-companies-in-the-united-states/.

8. www.thebalance.com/stock-market-returns-by-year-2388543.

9. http://www.aei.org/publication/more-evidence-that-its-very-hard-to-beat-the-market-over-time-95-of-financial-professionals-cant-do-it/.

10. Robert Shiller, *Irrational Exuberance*, 2nd ed. (Princeton University Press, 2005).

Chapter 15

Money and the Monetary System

Cigarette Money

During World War II, millions of soldiers were captured and sent to prisoner-of-war (POW) camps. With no formal currency and little connection with the outside economy, the camps initially functioned with little more than an internal trading system: If a soldier had an extra bar of soap and really wanted a can of tuna, he would have to find someone who had a spare can of tuna and really wanted a bar of soap. Finding these kinds of trading possibilities sometimes worked, but it was time-consuming and inefficient.

Over time, a solution evolved: Prisoners began to use cigarettes as a common currency. A simple system of exchange with standardized prices developed: Cans of food could be bought for a set quantity of cigarettes, soap for another quantity.

Why did the prisoners start using cigarettes as money? To start with, they were a lot easier to carry around than bars of soap or cans of salmon. Unlike food, cigarettes didn't spoil. And there was a fairly stable supply. Cigarettes came into the camps in shipments of food and other supplies from the Red Cross humanitarian agency and were distributed among the prisoners.

©Hulton Archive/Getty Images

Sometimes, though, there would be a sudden influx of cigarettes—say, if the Red Cross managed to send an extra shipment one week. Soldiers, having an abundance of cigarettes, would go on spending sprees. They would outbid each other to get the things they wanted. As you might predict, that bidding would send prices skyrocketing. Soldiers would then need a lot more cigarettes to buy a bar of soap.

But what would happen if war troubles caused the Red Cross to miss a few shipments? There would be a steady decrease in the number of cigarettes in circulation, as prisoners smoked them. Prices would plummet, and overall economic activity would fall, as trading slowed to a halt. Why would this happen? The reason is obvious if you think about it: With fewer and fewer cigarettes in circulation, and uncertainty about when the next shipment might arrive, cigarettes would become increasingly rare and valuable. This would give prisoners greater incentive to hoard rather than spend their cigarettes.

This unique system of money and trade was described by a British officer named R. A. Radford, who was captured by the Nazis and sent to a series of prisoner-of-war camps, where he remained until his rescue by Allied forces. After his return to Great Britain in 1945, Radford wrote a now-classic paper, "The Economic Organisation of a P.O.W. Camp." His paper showed that money—in whatever form it might take, even cigarettes—is an intrinsic part of any economic system.

LEARNING OBJECTIVES

LO 15.1 Describe the three main functions of money.

LO 15.2 Describe the characteristics that make something a good choice as money, and distinguish between commodity-backed and fiat money.

LO 15.3 Explain the concept of fractional-reserve banking and the money multiplier.

LO 15.4 Describe M1 and M2.

LO 15.5 Understand the role of a central bank, and discuss the idea of the Federal Reserve's dual mandate.

LO 15.6 Explain the tools the Federal Reserve uses to conduct monetary policy.

LO 15.7 Understand how monetary policy affects the prevailing interest rate and supply of money.

LO 15.8 Explain how expansionary or contractionary monetary policy influences the broader economy.

The challenges that made World War II prisoners adopt cigarettes as their currency are the same as those faced in any economy. What is money? What functions does it serve and what problems does it solve? What makes a particular item (such as cigarettes) a good or bad choice for use as money? How does the supply of money influence the broader economy, and who controls the supply?

In this chapter, we'll see how and why money works in the economy. And we'll show how the tools of economics are being used to make sure the dollar in your pocket keeps its value.

What Is Money?

We all have an intuitive grasp of what money is—we use it every day. But what is it that separates the cash we hold in our hands from any of the other items we own that have value? Economies used to work on a system in which one person could trade a few eggs from her chicken for some milk from a neighbor's cow. Why did civilization long ago abandon that system for one based on the exchange of small pieces of precious metal? And how did sheets of printed paper come to substitute for that shiny metal and then give way to records kept in a bank's computer?

To answer these questions, we'll need a more formal understanding of the functions money plays in society and what makes something good as money.

Functions of money

LO 15.1 Describe the three main functions of money.

money the set of all assets that are regularly used to directly purchase goods and services

How much money do you have? When asked that question, you might answer by counting just the cash in your wallet and maybe the amount in your bank account. You also might count the total value of your car (if you own one) or any stocks, bonds, real estate, or any other assets you may be fortunate enough to own. By most definitions, money consists only of what you typically use to buy something—which includes the cash in your wallet and the balance in your bank account, but not the stocks, bonds, real estate, car, or any other asset. More precisely, **money** is the set of all assets that are regularly used to directly purchase goods and services.

Money typically serves three major functions: it is a *store of value*, a *medium of exchange*, and a *unit of account*.

A store of value   We say that money is a **store of value** because it represents a certain amount of purchasing power that money retains over time. To have $100 or $1,000 or $1 million is to have the ability to acquire a certain quantity of goods. Money stores value in the sense that if you put a $100 bill in a safe, you can expect to be able to purchase roughly $100 worth of goods when you take the bill out, whenever that is. The value won't be absolutely the same, of course—we'll learn more shortly about how changes in prices create changes in the value of money—but holding money is nearly always the most convenient way to hold onto wealth over time. If, by contrast, you stored all your wealth in bananas, you would lose most of that wealth quickly, as the fruit spoiled.

store of value
a certain amount of purchasing power that money retains over time

A medium of exchange   Of course, items other than money also generally store value pretty well, such as stocks and land. So we need to add to our list of money's functions its role as a **medium of exchange**—that is to say, the fact that you can use it to purchase goods and services. That is, you can make a transaction by exchanging your money for the goods or services you want to buy.

medium of exchange
the ability to use money to purchase goods and services

First, imagine a world without money, where the only way to acquire something you wanted would be to engage in **barter**—to directly offer a good or service (maybe your jacket or bike, or maybe the value of your labor) in exchange for some good or service you want. The reason barter is extremely inefficient is that you have to find someone who both has what you want and wants what you have.

barter
directly offering a good or service in exchange for some good or service you want

Now add money to the world. Money makes life much easier because you need only find someone who wants what you have (say, your labor). You accept money in exchange for the labor because you are confident that, once you have money, the person who has what you want (say, groceries) will also, in turn, accept that money in exchange. There's no longer any need to find one person who fits both requirements.

Not surprisingly, an economy that uses money is dramatically more efficient than a society based on directly trading one good for another. Without money people and firms would have to search constantly for mutually agreeable trades. Using money reduces transaction costs immeasurably.

Some businesses are getting rid of physical money altogether, refusing to accept cash. Although going cashless can make business sense, this system leaves out those who do not have access to alternative methods of payment. The What Do You Think? box "No card, no service?" addresses the arguments for and against a cashless—though not moneyless—economy.

A unit of account   The final role of money is also important, though it is easily overlooked: Money provides a common **unit of account**—a standard unit of comparison. Imagine that you live in an economy without money and have to choose between two competing job offers:

unit of account
a standard unit of comparison

- A farmer offers to pay you 12 big crates of eggs a week.
- A shoemaker offers weekly wages of a pair of fine leather shoes.

Which is the better option? It's hard to tell. But if one offered you $300 a week and the other offered you $400 for the same amount of work, you could easily compare the offers. By giving us a standard unit of comparison, money allows us to make more informed decisions.

LO 15.2 Describe the characteristics that make something a good choice as money, and distinguish between commodity-backed and fiat money.

What makes for good money?
Now that we understand the functions played by money, we can ask a related question: What makes for good money? Economists differ on the exact answer, but two basic considerations offer a good starting point. Something makes for good money if it has *stability of value* and *convenience*.

No card, no service?
What Do You Think?

You probably pay for things in many ways apart from cash. Increasingly, purchases are shifting online, where cash isn't an option, and more consumers at brick-and-mortar stores are paying with cards or apps.

Some businesses now simply want to get rid of cash—and are refusing to accept coins and paper money. For businesses, there's less risk of crime when they're not handling cash. And some evidence shows that we spend more when using cards rather than paper bills: spending can feel easier—for better and worse—when you're not literally handing over the contents of your wallet.

Still, cash is an important part of the economy. In 2017, the Federal Reserve found that U.S. adults used debit cards for 32 percent of transactions, cash accounted for 27 percent, and credit cards for 23 percent.

Cash is used especially heavily by people who are "underbanked"—those without great access to financial services, roughly 7.5 percent of the U.S. population. The underbanked are more likely to be poorer and people of color. Cash is also useful for people who are trying to stick to budgets or whose credit cards have hit their maximums.

As a result, some politicians are trying to prevent businesses from banning cash. Ritchie Torres, a city councilman from the Bronx, New York, introduced a bill to ensure that cash always remains an option in New York City businesses. A similar bill failed in Chicago; another has been introduced in New Jersey.

Are we on our way to a cashless society, and if so, is that a good thing?
©Marcus Clackson/Getty Images

Torres grew up poor in public housing, and he worries that banning cash will effectively ban certain customers. Torres remarked, "It is bad enough that the poor are already so stigmatized, and now we are stigmatizing them even further for the way they consume goods and services." For Torres, "this amounts to intentional discrimination, because these businesses that don't accept cash know exactly who they are keeping out."

Businesses, however, say that getting rid of cash is a simple business decision: it is more efficient and will help raise profits.

WHAT DO YOU THINK?
1. Should businesses be allowed to ban the use of cash by customers?
2. Does banning cash seem discriminatory?
3. Is it okay for the government to pass laws that overrule business decisions like this?

Sources: www.nytimes.com/2018/12/06/nyregion/how-the-cashless-economy-shuts-out-the-poor.html; www.frbatlanta.org/banking-and-payments/consumer-payments/research-data-reports/2018/the-2016-and-2017-surveys-of-consumer-payment-choice-summary-results.aspx?panel=4.

Stability of value We saw the importance of stability in our chapter-opening example, in which prisoners used cigarettes as a form of money. As long as shipments arrived predictably from the Red Cross, the value of a cigarette remained fairly stable. If there was either a sudden influx or a prolonged shortage of cigarettes, the functioning of the camp economy was disrupted.

Like cigarettes in the POW camp, the earliest forms of money were chosen primarily because they offered stability of value. These early versions of money generally took the form of a physical material that is durable and has *intrinsic value*, or value unrelated to its use as money. Goods that have intrinsic value will keep a more steady value; even if their value as money falls, the good is still useful to people for other reasons.

Gold is the traditional example of intrinsic value: In early societies, gold had intrinsic value because it was durable and people liked wearing it as shiny jewelry. That's still true today. The cigarettes in the chapter opener also had intrinsic value. After all, the reason the cigarettes were being shipped to the POW camp in the first place was that many soldiers smoked.

There is no reason, though, why money needs to have intrinsic value. A dollar bill has practically no intrinsic value: People don't typically eat it, smoke it, or wear it as a necklace. We accept dollar bills because we know that everyone else values them too. Wide acceptance comes largely from the fact that dollars have stable value.[1]

Gold is the traditional example of intrinsic value: it is durable and people like wearing it as jewelry.
©Comstock Images

Convenience How and why did we go from gold coins to dollar bills? Paper money is more *convenient*. Compared to paper money, gold coins are heavy and hard to use for small purchases. A solid gold coin weighing just one ounce would be worth about $1,325 at the time of this writing, making it hard to use to pay for a package of gum or a soda.[2]

Ultimately, as time goes on, technology allows for the development of more convenient forms of money. For an ingenious example of making money even more convenient in the developing world, read the Economics in Action box "Banking with a cell phone."

Banking with a cell phone
Economics in Action

You probably didn't grow up in a village in rural Kenya. But imagine that you did and that you then moved to the capital city to find work. You want to send money back to your village to support your family, but how do you do it? Your village does not have a bank branch—the nearest is hours away. You could take a wad of banknotes back to the village yourself, but that would involve a long day's travel in a crowded bus. Or you could entrust the money to someone else who is traveling back to your village, but what if no one's going soon? Besides, both options carry the very real risk your money will get lost or stolen along the way.

A Kenyan mobile phone company called Safaricom came up with a solution to this problem. It's called M-Pesa—the M stands for mobile, while *Pesa* is the local word for money. The system allows people to transfer money simply by sending a text message. The process works on even the simplest mobile flip phone; it doesn't have to be an iPhone or Android. It requires only the ability to send a text message.

(continued)

The M-Pesa system expands the banking area to rural Kenyans, enabling safe transfers of money via text messages.
©Tony Karumba/AFP/Getty Images

The process is amazingly simple: You go to an M-Pesa outlet (a small store usually located in the village marketplace) and deposit money into an account. This becomes your *e-float*, essentially an electronic representation of money. In this way, it's not all that different from a deposit at a traditional bank. You can then use a text message to transfer, say, $15 worth of e-float to the account of another M-Pesa user. (The transfer costs a small fee, but that's a much smaller transaction cost than the time and money of traveling back to the village.) The recipient then goes to the local M-Pesa outlet and withdraws the e-float as cash, paying another small fee.

With this ease of use, and the fact that M-Pesa outlets outnumber bank branches five to one, M-Pesa quickly became wildly popular. In 2018, M-Pesa had over 23 million active users—more than three-quarters of Kenya's adult population. Annual transfers were equal to over half of Kenyan GDP, or $43 billion. Using an e-float account is safer than carrying cash and much more accessible than a traditional bank account. Most M-Pesa members say they use their e-float accounts not just to transfer money but also to save money. Safaricom has now added a product called M-Schwari that includes interest-paying savings accounts and greatly expands access to banking services in rural areas.

M-Pesa is used for many purposes. Economists William Jack and Tavneet Suri show that households that use M-Pesa are better able to cope during emergencies and other bad shocks. When they got into trouble, M-Pesa users were more likely to receive financial help from others and could tap a wider network of sources. As a result, the households with M-Pesa maintained consumption levels despite the shocks, while nonusers experienced consumption dips averaging 7 percent.

M-Pesa shows how new technologies can connect underserved areas and change the concept of money. Inspired by the success in Kenya, more and more banking around the world is going mobile.

Sources: William Jack and Tavneet Suri, "Risk Sharing and Transactions Costs: Evidence from Kenya's Mobile Money Revolution," *American Economic Review* 104, no. 1 (2014), pp. 183–223; www.forbes.com/sites/tobyshapshak/2018/11/27/how-mobile-money-continues-to-boom-in-africa/#5808dcda205; http://siteresources.worldbank.org/AFRICAEXT/Resources/258643-1271798012256/M-PESA_Kenya.pdf; www.bbc.co.uk/news/business-11793290; www.safaricom.co.ke/personal/m-pesa/do-more-with-m-pesa/m-shwari.

Commodity-backed money versus fiat money

The earliest forms of paper money could be converted at a bank into a specified amount of a named commodity. **Commodity-backed money** is any form of money—usually paper money—that can be legally exchanged into a fixed amount of an underlying commodity, generally gold.

In the United States, the dollar was fully commodity-backed for half a century, from shortly after the Civil War until 1933. During that time, anyone could go to a designated "reserve bank" and exchange those dollar bills for a fixed amount of gold, whenever they wanted to. By law, the bank was required to make that exchange.[3]

commodity-backed money
any form of money that can be legally exchanged into a fixed amount of an underlying commodity

While the ability to exchange dollars for gold reassured people of the stability of the currency, commodity-backed money has a *resource cost*. To start, it costs money to dig gold out of the ground and prepare it for use as money. Not only that, commodities used as money have other uses. For example, gold is often used in medicine and dentistry, and in electronics. When used for money, the commodities become more expensive for those uses.

What of the post-1971 world? If our money is no longer backed by the value of a commodity like gold, where does its value come from? What is it backed by? Well, it's backed by nothing—nothing tangible, at least. Instead, the U.S. dollar today is backed by "the full faith and credit of the United States government." In other words, the U.S. dollar has value only to the extent that people trust the U.S. government to keep using dollars and to keep their value roughly constant. The formal term for this type of money is **fiat money**. Fiat money is money created by rule, without any commodity to back it. (*Fiat* is a Latin term that roughly translates to "it shall be.")

When we say "to the extent that people trust the U.S. government," what exactly are we trusting it to do or not do? Essentially, we're trusting the government to maintain a reliable system of money—in short, to not create lots of new money. Creating lots of new money would reduce the value of existing money—just as, in our chapter-opening example, an unexpectedly large shipment of cigarettes into the POW camp reduced the value of existing cigarettes.

fiat money
money created by rule, without any commodity to back it

✓ TEST YOURSELF

- ☐ What kind of exchange happens when people trade goods without using money? **[LO 15.1]**
- ☐ How are cigarettes a good example of commodity-backed money? **[LO 15.2]**
- ☐ What kind of money is the U.S. dollar? What kind was it 60 years ago? **[LO 15.2]**

Banks and the Money-Creation Process

We discussed how using actual gold coins in payment was eventually replaced by paper money that was backed by gold. We considered one obvious advantage of this: It's easier to carry around a piece of paper saying "10 gold coins" than it is to carry around 10 gold coins.

Here's another, less obvious, implication: Paper money made it possible for banks to *create money*, through a process called *fractional-reserve banking*. This is one of the most important, yet intuitively challenging, facts about our modern financial system. It's worth taking some time to make sure you understand it.

"Creating" money

The easiest way to understand how banks create money is to picture an economy making the transition from gold coins to paper money. To start with, imagine that you live in ancient times and all transactions are carried out using actual gold coins. How much money exists in the economy? That's an easy question to answer: It's simply the amount of gold.

Next, imagine that banking is invented, and now you're offered the chance to store your gold coins so you don't have to carry them around. When you deposit a gold coin in the bank, the bank gives you a piece of paper (a banknote) saying "one gold coin." At any time, you could go to the bank, give the bank back this piece of paper, and get a gold coin.

But you don't need to do this because merchants are happy to accept the banknote instead of the gold coin. They know that the note is as good as the coin itself. At any point *they* could take the note to the bank to get a coin. And people find it so much more convenient to use notes than lug around heavy gold coins.

Now put yourself in the bank's shoes (sandals): As a banker, you observe that on any given day, out of the 1,000 coins that are in your bank vault, people come in and ask for only 100 of them. The other 900 are just sitting there. Why not lend them out, charge an interest rate to the borrowers on these loans, and make a profit?

LO 15.3 Explain the concept of fractional-reserve banking and the money multiplier.

TABLE 15-1
Simple money-creation process

Gold coins in bank	Money (banknotes) in the economy
1,000 coins deposited in bank	1,000 banknotes issued in exchange for initial deposit
−900 coins loaned out (with 100 held in reserve)	
+900 coins that were loaned out and then deposited by workers	+900 banknotes issued in exchange for workers' deposits
1,000 coins in bank	**1,900 banknotes**

So, you decide to lend out the other 900 coins to people who want to use them to buy things—say, to pay workers to build a house. When the workers receive their coins as wages, the workers all decide to deposit them in the bank for safe keeping. For every coin they deposit, the bank gives them a piece of paper saying "one gold coin."

How much money is in the economy now? To answer that question, let's consider both the gold coins in the bank and the banknotes now available in the economy. As Table 15-1 shows, the bank again has 1,000 gold coins. But it has now issued 1,900 banknotes saying "one gold coin." Because people are just as happy to trade banknotes as actual gold coins—and, thus, we can meaningfully consider the banknotes to be *money*—we can say that by making loans, the bank has *created money*. It has created 900 gold coins worth of money, to be exact. It did so simply by lending a portion of the money it had on deposit.

Money creation in today's economy How does the money-creation process work in today's economy? Let's work through another simple example with the aid of some basic accounting tools.

Let's say that you walk into a bank with $1,000 in cash and you make a deposit. The bank takes your cash, puts it in a vault, and records $1,000 as your account balance. You can get your $1,000 back any time you ask the bank for it. Because of that fact, such deposits are called **demand deposits**—funds held in bank accounts that can be withdrawn ("demanded") by depositors at any time without advance notice.

From an accounting point of view, the $1,000 cash deposit represents two things for the bank:

- Cash is an *asset*—a resource the bank possesses.
- It also is a *liability*—an amount the bank owes. The bank owes you that amount and has promised that you can get your cash back at any time.

The primary way that banks earn money is by lending funds and collecting interest on those loans. So the bank wants to lend out as much of your $1,000 deposit as it (safely) can. As we saw in the example of the gold-coin bank, it's not necessary to keep on hand the total amount of the demand deposits. Instead, the bank decides to keep a certain amount on hand and to lend the rest.

We call the cash that a bank keeps in its vault its **reserves**. In practice, modern banks keep reserves either as cash or as deposits at the Federal Reserve ("the Fed"), the U.S. government's central bank. As before, lending funds enables banks to "create" money.

The Federal Reserve requires banks to keep a certain proportion of their deposits as reserves. When expressed as an amount, it is called the **required reserves**. Of course, a bank can choose to hold more in reserves than the required minimum. Any additional amount, beyond the required reserves, that the bank chooses to keep in reserve is called **excess reserves**. As with the earlier gold-coin example, banks "create" money by lending funds not kept as reserves.

---

demand deposits
funds held in bank accounts that can be withdrawn ("demanded") by depositors at any time without advance notice

reserves
the money that a bank keeps on hand, either in cash or in deposits at the Federal Reserve

required reserves
the minimum fraction of deposits that banks are legally required (by the Federal Reserve) to keep on hand

excess reserves
any additional amount, beyond the required reserves, that a bank chooses to keep in reserve

When the reserve requirement is expressed as a fraction, it is called the **reserve ratio**. The reserve ratio is calculated as the amount of cash kept as reserves divided by the total amount of demand deposits. We'll assume throughout our discussion that the bank keeps a reserve ratio of 10 percent.

In the example above, we saw that the $1,000 cash deposit created both an asset and a liability for the bank. Financial accounting is based on the *basic accounting equation*, which says that assets must equal the total of liabilities plus owners' equity (the claim the owners of a firm have on assets):

$$\text{Assets} = \text{Liabilities} + \text{Owners' equity}$$

Companies periodically report the balances of their assets, liabilities, and owners' equity in a financial statement called a *balance sheet*. One common form of a balance sheet is called the *account form* of the balance sheet; it mimics the accounting equation by showing assets on the left and liabilities and owners' equity on the right. We'll use that form to visualize the bank's transactions. In the example we work through here, we will assume owners' equity of zero. Thus, we will assume that for the bank, assets must equal liabilities.

Panel A of Figure 15-1 shows, in a simple account-form balance sheet format, what happens to the bank's assets and liabilities when you make a $1,000 deposit. The left-hand side shows the bank's assets—in this case, the $1,000 cash deposit. The right-hand side shows the bank's liabilities (the amount owed to you, the depositor)—in this case, the demand deposits of $1,000.

Now, let's see what happens when a new customer comes into the bank wanting to *borrow* $900—say, to purchase a new refrigerator. After completing the loan-approval process, the banker takes $900 in cash out of the vault and hands over the money to the customer as a $900 loan. Panel B of Figure 15-1 shows the bank's new situation: Because the loan is an asset for the bank (an amount it will collect from the borrower at some time in the future), the bank still has $1,000 in assets: $100 in required cash reserves plus the loan of $900. The assets and liabilities both still total $1,000, though the composition of the assets has changed.

> **reserve ratio**
> the fraction of deposits a bank must hold as reserves; calculated as the amount of cash kept as reserves divided by the total amount of demand deposits

FIGURE 15-1

How banks create money As the money comes in to the bank and then is lent out again, new money is created. In this example, by the time the money is lent out twice, the bank has created $1,900 from $1,000.

(A) Modern Bank

Assets		Liabilities	
Cash	$1,000	Demand deposits	$1,000
Total	$1,000	Total	$1,000

(B) Modern Bank

Assets		Liabilities	
Required reserves	$100	Demand deposits	$1,000
Loan	900		
Total	$1,000	Total	$1,000

(C) Modern Bank

Assets		Liabilities	
Required reserves	$100	Demand deposits	$1,900
Loan	900		
New cash deposit	900		
Total	$1,900	Total	$1,900

(D) Modern Bank

Assets		Liabilities	
Required reserves*	$190	Demand deposits	$1,900
Loans**	1,710		
Total	$1,900	Total	$1,900

*10% × $1,900
**90% × $1,900

The bank has less actual cash on hand ($100 required reserves) than the total of its deposits ($1,000). Is this reckless on the bank's part? It's not, if you remember the thinking of our ancient bank that stored gold coins: Observing that only a small number of customers wanted to convert banknotes into coins on any given day, it was happy to keep only 10 percent of its coins in its vault and lend out the rest. In the same way, modern banks count on the fact that not all of their customers will try to withdraw cash at the same time.

Here's where things get even more interesting: The appliance store sells the refrigerator and gets paid $900 in cash. The store owner goes to the bank and deposits that amount in the store's bank account. Panel C of Figure 15-1 shows the bank's position now. It now has the following assets: the $100 required cash reserves, a loan of $900, and the new cash deposit of $900, for a total of $1,900. Demand deposits total the same amount, $1,900. (The bank's assets equal its liabilities.)

After the new cash deposit, what happens to the required reserves? Let's say our modern bank keeps in its vault as required cash reserves 10 percent of what its customers have deposited. Experience indicates that that amount will be enough to cover day-to-day requests from its depositors for cash withdrawals.[4] With $1,900 in liabilities ($1,000 in the original deposit and the store owner's deposit of $900), the bank will now want to keep 10 percent of $1,900, or $190, required cash reserves in the vault. That means it will be happy to lend money up to the amount of $1,710 (90 percent of $1,900). The bank has already made loans of $900 and now lends another $810 to another customer in order to have lent a total of $1,710. This new situation is shown in panel D of Figure 15-1.

How far can this process continue? The bank will continue lending and taking deposits. Over time, the bank can end up creating as much as $9,000 in new loans. Why $9,000? Because you originally deposited $1,000, and the bank has to hold 10 percent of that (= $100) as required cash reserves. It then lends the rest, and eventually gets the loans back as deposits (assuming Modern Bank is the only bank in the economy).

Those deposits, in turn, create reserve requirements. By the time the bank has lent a total of $9,000, it can expect $9,000 in deposits—which creates a need for 10 percent of those deposits to be held as cash reserves too (= $900). The total sum of required cash reserves is thus $100 + $900. Thanks to your original $1,000 cash deposit, the bank has enough cash to cover that. But that's all the bank has in cash, so it can't lend more.

With $9,000 in loans and $1,000 in reserves, there is no money left for new loans. Still, your original $1,000 has had quite a run: The bank has used it to create $9,000 in new money, effectively turning $1,000 into $10,000.

From one bank to an entire economy
So far, we have assumed that there's only one bank in the economy—everyone has to use that bank to borrow and save. In practice, of course, modern economies have many banks. The logic of the example still holds, though, if we think of the bank in our example as representing the *entire banking system:* The first deposit might be made into Bank of America, for example, and the next into Chase. The next might go to Citi. The key is that all money loaned out eventually gets put back into some bank within the banking system.

Let's round off our discussion with some formal terminology. In our example, the bank kept 10 percent of its deposits as reserves. If the reserve ratio were 100 percent (a situation known as *full-reserve banking*), no lending would have happened in the example. Your entire original $1,000 deposit would just sit in the bank's vault. If banks aren't lending, it would be very hard to get the money needed to buy a house or car. The entire financial system would grind to a halt.

Rarely if ever do we observe full-reserve banking. Instead, we have **fractional-reserve banking**, a banking system in which banks keep on reserve less than 100 percent of their deposits. (That is, the reserve ratio is less than 100 percent.) Fractional-reserve banking allows the bank to lend out a portion of the money deposited in the bank.

We call the ratio of money created by the lending activities of the banking system to the money created by the government's central bank the **money multiplier**. The size of the reserve determines

fractional-reserve banking
a banking system in which banks keep on reserve less than 100 percent of their deposits

money multiplier
the ratio of money created by the lending activities of the banking system to the money created by the government's central bank

the size of the money multiplier: As a simple approximation, we can calculate the money multiplier as $\frac{1}{R}$, where R is the reserve ratio. In practical terms, the money multiplier will also depend on cash in the hands of the public. Any cash that people hold onto will not enter the banking system, reducing the size of the money multiplier.

EQUATION 15-1
$$\text{Money multiplier} = \frac{1}{\text{Reserve ratio}}$$
$$= \frac{1}{R}$$

Thus, a reserve ratio of 10 percent (or, equivalently, 0.10) means the money multiplier is 10:

$$\text{Money multiplier} = \frac{1}{0.10}$$
$$= 10$$

With $1,900 in liabilities ($1,000 in the original deposit and the store owner's deposit of $900), the bank will want to keep $190 required cash reserves in the vault (10 percent of $1,900). That means it will be happy to lend money up to the amount of $1,710 (90 percent of $1,900)—the situation shown in panel D of Figure 15-1.

The bank has already made loans of $900 and now lends another $810 to another customer in order to have lent a total of $1,710. The approximation in Equation 15-1 works exactly, as long as two things occur:

- People don't hold any money as cash outside the bank and
- Banks lend out as much as they can beyond what's legally required for them to hold as reserves.[5]

Of course, in reality people hold some money outside of banks (in wallets, under mattresses, etc.), and banks sometimes hold onto more reserves than they legally must. As a result, the actual multiplier is somewhat smaller than the approximation.

Ultimately, the system of fractional reserve banking is what makes possible the existence of banks as we know them. However, you may be wondering if there are big risks involved.

What if too many customers turn up at the bank asking for their dollar bills at the same time? When that happens, a *bank run* occurs—the situation that arises from fear that the bank is in danger of running out of money. Read the Economics in Action box "Bank runs and the banking holiday" for some real-life examples.

Bank runs and the banking holiday
Economics in Action

In 2007, hundreds of panicked customers lined up outside branches of the British bank Northern Rock in a desperate attempt to get money out of their accounts. The media had just reported that Northern Rock had made big investments in financial products created during the U.S. housing bubble. Those investments were now nearly worthless, and the losses pushed the bank toward bankruptcy. Not surprisingly, customers suddenly wanted their money out of the bank.

British banking regulations at the time offered some protection to savers: The government pledged that customers wouldn't lose the value of their savings at Northern Rock, with a guarantee up to a limit of £35,000 (about $55,000). But many customers decided they'd prefer to withdraw their money immediately rather than risk it. About £2 billion of cash was withdrawn in just two days.

(continued)

Bank runs are a problem because under a fractional-reserve system, banks don't hold enough cash to pay out more than a fraction of their depositors' money. Ironically, a bank run can *create* the very thing customers are afraid of—the bank going bust—even if their fears are unfounded. If enough customers demand their deposits back all at once, a bank will inevitably go bankrupt, no matter its initial condition.

The most important response to a bank run, therefore, is to try to reassure savers and create time for their panic to subside. During the Great Depression, in March 1933, the governor of Michigan feared that one of the largest banks in the state, the Guardian Trust Company of Detroit, was on the edge of shutting down for good. In order to keep the bank from failing, the governor took the drastic measure of stopping transactions at all of the 800 banks in the state, leaving people to get by on only the cash they had in their pockets. The move backfired. Far from quelling the panic, it only sparked greater concern. Many reasoned that if the banks could be saved only by preventing all transactions, the entire system must be in danger of collapse.

Word of bank trouble spread throughout the country, and bank runs threatened to spiral out of control, destroying people's savings and crippling the economy. In response, Congress quickly passed what became known as the "Bank Holiday," closing all banks in the country for four days (later stretched out to a week). Right before the banks were due to reopen, President Roosevelt talked to Americans through radio broadcasts known as "fireside chats" to explain what was going on. Furthermore, the Federal Reserve pledged to supply unlimited currency to banks that reopened, and so depositors essentially had 100 percent insurance on their deposits.

Amazingly, it worked. When the banks reopened, the panic had abated, and Americans replaced two-thirds of the money they had drawn out in the bank runs. The outgrowth of this holiday was the creation of the Federal Deposit Insurance Commission (FDIC) through the Glass-Steagall Act. It reassured savers that if their bank fails, the government will protect any deposit less than $100,000 (later increased to $250,000).

What happened to Northern Rock? After a second day of lines outside the bank's branches, the British government stepped in and announced that it would refund the entire value of customers' savings accounts if the bank went bust. The panic abated, and Northern Rock lived to see another day. (However, it lost so much money in the U.S. housing crash that the British government eventually had to take it over to keep it going.)

These experiences remind us that bank runs—widely thought to have been consigned to the history books—can still happen in today's economy.

Sources: www.nber.org/papers/w12717; www.bostonfed.org/-/media/Documents/education/pubs/closed.pdf.

Measuring money

LO 15.4 Describe M1 and M2.

Now that we know how money is created by the banking system, let's revisit our earlier question: How much money *is* there?

If you are thinking to yourself, "That depends on what type of money you are asking about," you are exactly right. It is the job of the Federal Reserve to manage the **money supply**—the amount of money available in the economy—and the Fed provides the most common definitions of the money supply.

The Fed classifies different types of money by their *liquidity*—that is, by how easy an asset is to convert immediately to cash without losing value. The most common classifications of money are the monetary base, M1, and M2:

- The **monetary base** is the sum of currency in circulation and reserves held by banks at the Federal Reserve.
- **M1** includes currency held by the public ("cash") plus checking account balances (demand deposits, which are not exactly cash but are readily accessible for most people).

money supply
the amount of money available in the economy

monetary base
the sum of currency in circulation and reserves held by banks at the Federal Reserve

M1
definition of money that includes cash plus checking account balances

- **M2** is broader still. M2 includes everything in M1 plus savings accounts and other financial instruments where money is locked away for a specified period of time. Since these forms of savings can't be accessed quickly without penalty fees, they are slightly less liquid than other forms of money. (Certificates of deposit are an example of a less-liquid form of money.)

All three are legitimate measures of the money supply. Which one we use depends on our goals:

- If we want to look at spending (liquidity), we use M1.
- If we want to look at the money multiplier, we would use M2. Comparing M2 to the monetary base (the sum of currency and reserves) can give you some sense of what the money multiplier actually is at a given point in time.

Figure 15-2 shows that the money multiplier was relatively stable over time, until the huge change sparked by the 2008 financial crisis. At that point, the monetary base rose dramatically due to actions by the Federal Reserve to combat the financial crisis by adding to banks' reserves. But banks were nervous in the face of the crisis and reluctant to lend to others. As a result, there were relatively small increases in M1 and M2, despite the big expansion in reserves.

At this point, you might wonder who decides how much money is going to exist. Obviously, based on our earlier discussion of money creation, the banks play a large role in M1 and M2. But who decides how much hard money there is to multiply in the first place? And who sets the required reserves ratio? We address these questions in the next section.

M2
definition of money that includes everything in M1 plus savings accounts and other financial instruments where money is locked away for a specified amount of time; less liquid than M1

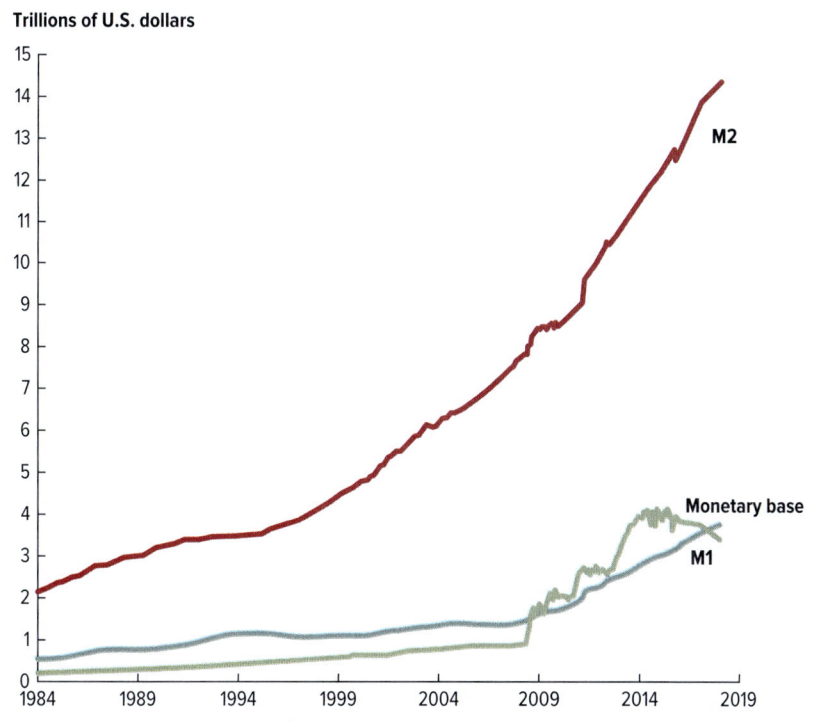

FIGURE 15-2

Monetary base, M1, and M2 over time In nominal terms, all three measures of money steadily increased over this period of time, although the rate of increase of M2 sped up dramatically starting around 1995. The monetary base ("hard money") increased dramatically in 2008 as part of the effort to combat the financial crisis.

Source: Federal Reserve Economic Data, FRED:

Monetary base: https://fred.stlouisfed.org/series/BOGMBASE?utm_source=series_page&utm_medium=related_content&utm_term=related_resources&utm_campaign=categories.

M1: https://fred.stlouisfed.org/series/MANMM101USA189S.

M2: https://fred.stlouisfed.org/series/M2SL?utm_source=series_page&utm_medium=related_content&utm_term=related_resources&utm_campaign=categories.

TEST YOURSELF

- [ ] What is a reserve requirement of 100 percent called? **[LO 15.3]**
- [ ] How does the money multiplier create money in the economy? **[LO 15.3]**
- [ ] What type(s) of money includes demand deposits (amounts in checking accounts)? **[LO 15.4]**

Managing the Money Supply: The Federal Reserve

On October 24, 1907, the United States was in the middle of one of the most severe financial crises in its history. Tens of thousands of depositors were descending upon banks across the country, creating a bank run of such proportions that no one was safe. Even some of the largest banks were in jeopardy and struggling to survive day to day.

In this flurry of activity, a single man took responsibility for the survival of the U.S. financial system: John Pierpont Morgan, president of J.P. Morgan & Co. and the most powerful banker of the time. With many banks already near collapse, at 1:30 p.m. on October 24th, news reached Morgan that the New York Stock Exchange was simply out of money. Even someone willing to pay 100 percent interest for a loan couldn't find a lender. Stock prices were plummeting. Absent any action, all stock on the exchange would become worthless.

With only a few hours to act, Morgan convened nearly every major figure in the U.S. financial world of the time—all of the leading bankers and industrial capitalists. Even the Secretary of the Treasury, George Cortelyou, came running to see if the most powerful banker in the country could save the U.S. economy from collapse. The system needed cash—lots of it. In the face of catastrophe, the U.S. government pitched in $25 million. John D. Rockefeller offered $10 million immediately and up to $40 million if extra funds were needed. By 2:30 p.m., Morgan had collected enough money to save the system.

The reliance on a single titan of industry to save the nation from collapse was a stark reminder that the nation was ill-prepared for crisis. Six years later, in 1913, President Woodrow Wilson signed the Federal Reserve Act into law, creating the Federal Reserve. Since then, the Fed has been the centralized institution responsible for coordinating the operations of the U.S. financial system.[6]

The role of the central bank

LO 15.5 Understand the role of a central bank, and discuss the idea of the Federal Reserve's dual mandate.

central bank the institution ultimately responsible for managing the nation's money supply and coordinating the banking system to ensure a sound economy

monetary policy actions by the central bank to manage the money supply, in pursuit of certain macroeconomic goals

Almost every major nation has a central bank. A **central bank** is the institution ultimately responsible for managing the nation's money supply and coordinating the banking system to ensure a sound economy. In the United States, the central bank is the Federal Reserve. Like any central bank, the Federal Reserve has two essential functions:

- managing the money supply and
- acting as a lender of last resort.

Before we explain the two functions of a central bank, it may help to explain what a central bank *is not*. It is not the government's finance arm. In the United States, the financial operations of the government—collecting taxes, paying bills, issuing debt, and generally managing the nation's finances—are conducted by the Treasury Department. The Fed is responsible for deciding how much physical currency should be printed, but the printing itself is done by the Treasury Department's Bureau of Engraving and Printing.

In short, the Treasury Department executes *fiscal policy*, while the Federal Reserve conducts *monetary policy*. Formally, **monetary policy** consists of actions by the central bank to manage the money supply, in pursuit of certain macroeconomic goals.

So, a central bank's most important function is to manage the money supply. A bit later, we'll learn more about the ways that the Fed does that. First, though, it's worth asking whether we in fact *need* a central bank to manage the money supply. Why not leave it to the private market to issue currency and control it? In principle at least, there is no reason why a privately issued currency should not gain wide acceptance. For more about one attempt to create a new currency, see the From Another Angle box "Is bitcoin the currency of the future?"

Is bitcoin the currency of the future?
From Another Angle

Will cryptocurrencies, like bitcoin, eventually replace our traditional currency?
©REDPIXEL.PL/Shutterstock

In 2009, a mysterious programmer using the fake name Satoshi Nakamoto created a new virtual currency—bitcoin—that proposed a solution to the problem of currency inflation. Instead of the central government printing money, the supply of bitcoins increases at a rate predetermined by mathematical algorithm. Because trades rely on cryptography to (ideally) prevent counterfeiting and fraudulent transactions, currencies such as bitcoin are called *cryptocurrencies*.

In its early days, people were skeptical, and the value of a bitcoin was a tiny fraction of a cent. The first real-world purchase was made, for fun, by a Florida programmer named Laszlo Hanyecz, who paid 10,000 bitcoins to get two Papa John's pizzas delivered. (He transferred the bitcoins to another enthusiast, who paid in dollars.) Soon, however, bitcoins attracted the attention of the media, and their value took off.

By the end of 2017, bitcoins were selling for nearly $20,000 each. Cryptocurrency seemed to be the wave of the future. But various sites that manage bitcoins reported hacks and other security issues. The value of bitcoins started to plummet, falling to $3,000 by February 2019. That's a net loss of 85 percent, a major blow for a currency that prides itself on stability.

Will bitcoin be able to overcome security and viability concerns and start to challenge traditional money? (And in June 2019, Facebook announced its intent to create a cryptocurrency of its own, called Libra, to be launched in 2020.) The bitcoin saga shows that even in the digital age, we still need to take seriously the very old problem of how to maintain stable, trustworthy currencies.

Sources: www.wired.com/magazine/2011/11/mf_bitcoin/all/1; www.dailytech.com/Digital+Black+Friday+First+Bitcoin+Depression+Hits/article21877.htm; www.economist.com/blogs/babbage/2011/06/virtual-currency.

Another role played by a central bank is the *lender of last resort*. What does this mean? Think back to the story of J.P. Morgan, who almost single-handedly saved the banking system in 1907. When nobody else was willing to lend to banks facing a bank run, J.P. Morgan, along with others he rallied to the table, stepped in as lenders of last resort. They became the last line of defense before an imminent financial collapse. These days, that's the Fed's job. As we'll see in Chapter 17, "Financial Crisis," the Fed played exactly this role during the U.S. financial crisis in 2008.

How does the Federal Reserve work?

Now that you know what the role of a central bank is, let's look more closely at how the Federal Reserve—the United States's central bank—actually works. We will focus on two topics: the organizational structure of the Federal Reserve and the key principles that guide the Fed in its policy-making.

Federal Reserve ("the Fed")
the system consisting of a seven-member Board of Governors and 12 regional banks that act as the central bank of the United States

How the Fed is organized The entity we popularly call the **Federal Reserve**, or **Fed** for short, is actually not one organization but an entire system. The Federal Reserve System consists of 12 regional banks and a seven-member Board of Governors that act as the central bank in the United States. The seven-member Board of Governors and its staff, based in Washington, DC, are responsible for the overall governance of the system.

Supporting the efforts of the Board of Governors are 12 regional Federal Reserve banks scattered in major cities across the country, as shown in Figure 15-3. These 12 banks conduct the day-to-day affairs of the central bank. Under them are the so-called *member banks*, which include most of the banks in the United States. These banks are considered to be members of the Federal Reserve System and are subject to its regulations.

The Board of Governors is made up of experts in finance, banking, and monetary policy who are appointed by the U.S. president and confirmed by the Senate for 14-year terms. In addition, the president appoints one member of the Board of Governors to be chair for a four-year term. The chair of the Federal Reserve is one of the most important economic positions in the United States, if not the world. The chair has significant direct control over the conduct of monetary policy by the central bank.

Each of the regional Federal Reserve banks, for their part, is led by a president. The regional presidents are generally selected from the banking and business community in the region. They are responsible for overseeing the day-to-day actions of the regional banks, including regulatory oversight and implementation of monetary policy.

FIGURE 15-3

The Federal Reserve System The Federal Reserve System is made up of 12 regional banks spread across the country, headed by the Board of Governors in Washington, DC.

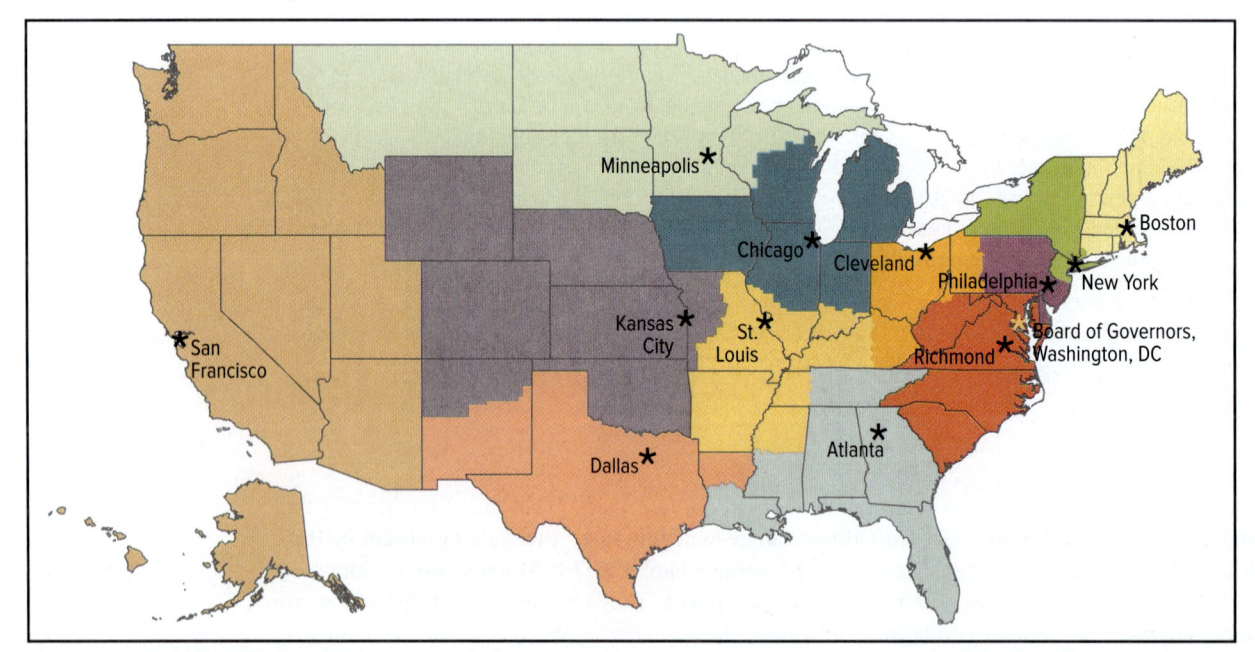

Source: http://www.federalreserve.gov/otherfrb.htm.

In addition, five of the 12 regional bank presidents serve on the *Federal Open Market Committee*, or FOMC. Four of these regional presidents serve on a rotating basis; the president of the New York regional bank is always a member, emphasizing how important the financial industry in the New York metropolitan area is to the nation's monetary and financial policy. The five regional bank presidents are joined on the FOMC by the seven-member Board of Governors (for a total of 12 members). The FOMC is the most important policy-making body of the Federal Reserve System. It carries full responsibility for setting the overall direction of monetary policy and guiding the money supply.

You may notice that for a governmental agency, the Federal Reserve has little connection with the rest of government. Though appointed by the government, the members of the Board of Governors enjoy the security of serving long terms, which helps them to be independent of politics. This is no accident. Politicians of all parties know the power of monetary policy. Giving the Fed a high degree of independence means that the Fed governors will not be as tempted by political pressure as someone with less independence. The Fed's independence, for example, makes it less likely to expand the money supply simply to make it cheaper for the government to repay its debt. In addition, knowing that technocrats rather than politicians are in charge tends to increase people's trust in the stability of the dollar.

The three most recent chairs of the Federal Reserve: Jerome Powell (2018–present), Janet Yellen (2014–2018), and Ben Bernanke (2006–2014).
©Jessica McGowan/Getty Images

How the Fed makes policy But what exactly does it mean to manage monetary policy for the benefit of the country? The Federal Reserve has twin responsibilities—what is commonly known as a **dual mandate**: The first part of this mandate is to *ensure price stability* and the second is to *maintain full employment*.

The first responsibility is what many think of when talking about monetary policy. It involves maintaining a stable money supply that meets the needs of the economy, while keeping prices relatively constant over time. For many central banks, this is as far as the mandate goes. (Maintaining price stability is, for instance, the only mandate of the European Central Bank, which manages monetary policy for much of Europe.)

In the United States, however, the Federal Reserve also has been given the second part of the mandate—to use monetary policy to maintain full employment. Monetary policy can have powerful effects on the economy. This second responsibility means using that power to keep the economy strong and stable. In the next few sections, we'll show how the Fed works to fulfill this second part of its mandate. In Chapter 16, "Inflation," we'll see how the two parts of the dual mandate can be fundamentally in conflict and how the Fed manages the tension between them.

dual mandate
the twin responsibilities of the Federal Reserve, to use monetary policy to ensure price stability and to maintain full employment

Tools of monetary policy

To fulfill its dual mandate, the Fed manages the supply of money. In order to change the money supply, the Fed has a number of different options at its disposal. In this section, we'll walk through the three traditional ones to show how the Federal Reserve generally conducts business. These tools, from least commonly used to most, are

- Reserve requirements.
- The discount window.
- Open-market operations.

Open-market operations are the most frequently used tool of monetary policy; the others are backup tools, rarely used.

LO 15.6 Explain the tools the Federal Reserve uses to conduct monetary policy.

Reserve requirements Although it is seldom used, the most powerful tool available to the Federal Reserve is its ability to adjust the **reserve requirement**—the regulation that sets the minimum fraction of deposits banks must hold in reserve.

reserve requirement
the regulation that sets the minimum fraction of deposits banks must hold in reserve

You'll recall that the reserve ratio a bank maintains is one of several determinants of how much money is available in the economy, and by extension how much lending occurs. If it wanted to, the Fed could even eliminate fractional-reserve banking altogether by mandating that banks hold 100 percent of their deposits in reserve, though that wouldn't be a very good idea.

Although changing the reserve requirement is a powerful tool, it is *too* powerful in most situations. Meaningfully controlling the money supply through reserve requirements would mean dramatically changing the amount of money banks are required to hold, an action almost certain to have significant and unpredictable consequences. Bank managers make their plans depending in part on a certain reserve requirement. Rapid change in the requirement would make it harder for them to manage their money. Rapid change also would have ripple effects throughout the entire economy, affecting the availability of credit and confidence in the banking system.

Despite the dangers of changing reserve requirements, some countries, most notably China, have used adjustments to the required reserve ratio as a primary tool of monetary policy (and have had mixed success). In the United States, changes to the reserve requirements are rarely used for policy unless there's a crisis. Think of changing the reserve requirement as a big shove; most of the time, monetary policy changes aim for more of a gentle push.

The discount window

The second tool used by the Fed is the discount window. The **discount window** is a lending facility that allows any bank to borrow reserves from the Fed. The discount window is one of the Fed's primary tools for providing liquidity to the markets and acting as a lender of last resort. When a bank is in trouble (because of a bank run, perhaps), the discount window can be a guaranteed source of emergency funds. The interest rate charged for these loans is called the **discount rate**.

Historically, although the discount window is key to the Fed's responsibility as lender of last resort, loans from the discount window are rarely used for monetary policy. The reason is that the discount rate has generally been somewhat higher than interest rates available in the market. As a result, banks tend to look elsewhere for loans. Because of that, any bank that makes use of the window opens itself up to significant speculation about its financial health. If the bank needs to borrow on unfavorable terms to stay alive, the thinking goes, it's likely that the bank is in trouble. Such stigma makes banks reluctant to use the discount window.

Sometimes, though, banks lack better options. The stigma of discount-window loans fell away during the 2008 financial crisis: Banks in desperate need of cash were forced to put aside their reputational concerns and turn to the only place willing to lend to them. In just one week in October 2008, banks borrowed $117 billion in emergency funds from the discount window.[7]

Open-market operations

The final, most used, and most important tool in the Fed's traditional toolbox is open-market operations. **Open-market operations** are sales or purchases of government securities, by the Fed to or from banks on the open (public) market. The actual process is a bit more indirect than we'll present it here, but the ultimate end is the same: The Fed sells bonds to a bank or buys bonds from it.

Open-market operations directly result in an increase or decrease in the money supply:

- *Increasing the money supply:* When the Fed wants to increase the money supply, it can purchase a bond from one of the large banks it trades with. This purchase translates into larger deposits and reserves in the commercial bank.
- *Decreasing the money supply:* On the other hand, if the Fed wants to decrease the money supply, it sells bonds, accepting as payment reserves from the buying bank. The Fed then effectively destroys the money it receives, which decreases the amount of the monetary base in existence.

How exactly do open-market operations affect the larger economy? This tool works two ways. The Fed can *buy* government bonds to pursue **expansionary monetary policy**—actions that increase

---

discount window
the lending facility run by the Fed that allows any bank to borrow reserves

discount rate
the interest rate charged by the Fed for loans of reserves through the discount window

open-market operations
sales or purchases of government bonds by the Fed, to or from banks, on the open market

expansionary monetary policy
actions that increase the money supply in order to increase aggregate demand

the money supply in order to increase aggregate demand. When the Fed buys bonds from a bank, it pays for those bonds by increasing the bank's deposit in the Fed, which increases the bank's reserves. The bank can then lend more and set off a ripple effect that increases other banks' lending. This maneuver enables the Fed to increase the growth rate of the money supply and pursue expansionary monetary policy.[8]

When the Fed *sells* bonds to a bank, the bank pays for the transaction with money that it keeps on deposit at the Fed. The sale thus reduces the bank's reserves. This in turn reduces the bank's ability to lend. Through the multiplier effect, the reduction in lending sets off a ripple effect with other banks' lending and slows down the growth rate of the money supply. This is an important way to conduct **contractionary monetary policy**—actions that reduce the money supply in order to decrease aggregate demand.

Open-market operations have a couple of advantages over other tools of monetary policy. First, the transactions—the buying and selling of bonds—take place on a *daily* basis. Since the Fed commonly wants to make small adjustments rather than sweeping changes in the economy, the frequency of these transactions adds to this tool's flexibility. The ability to act on a day-to-day basis helps maintain the Fed's reputation for steady, credible policy.

The second advantage of open-market operations is that they affect the *federal funds rate*, the interest rate that banks charge when one bank makes a very-short-term (usually overnight) loan of reserves to another bank. The Fed uses this rate as a target in open-market operations, pushing it upward by selling bonds and pushing it downward by buying bonds.

The federal funds rate and money supply

The Federal Reserve rarely describes its policies in terms of changes in the money supply. Instead, it focuses on interest rates. Technically, the Fed announces a "target" for the **federal funds rate**—the interest rate at which banks choose to lend reserves held at the Fed to one another, usually just overnight.

Banks are required to maintain a certain level of reserves. Thus, when a bank finds itself short at the end of the day, it may choose to make up the shortfall by borrowing from another bank that has excess reserves. Since both banks have an account with the Federal Reserve, it is easy and safe to borrow money this way.

How does the Fed affect the federal funds rate? In contractionary policy, as we saw, the Fed sells bonds, taking reserves from banks as payment. This decrease in the supply of reserves pushes the federal funds rate upward. Why? By reducing the supply of reserves, the price of borrowing reserves rises, just as in the standard analysis of supply and demand in a market for goods. Other interest rates move in the same direction as the federal funds rate, so interest rates rise in general, discouraging spending on houses, cars, new machinery, and other things. Raising the federal funds rate thus helps meet the goal of contractionary policy—which is to slow the economy down.

A similar chain of logic applies to expansionary policy, in which the goal is to reduce interest rates to stimulate the economy. In expansionary policy, the logic works in the opposite direction: The Fed buys bonds, injecting reserves into the banking system, and lowers the federal funds rate.

The one caveat with expansionary monetary policy is that there is a natural limit to how low the federal funds rate (or any other nominal interest rate) can go. Since anyone in the economy can always hold cold, hard cash, which offers a zero-percent interest rate, it is nearly impossible to push nominal interest rates on any other asset below zero. The natural lower limit on interest rates is known as the **zero lower bound**, and it has played a central role in the recent economic crises in the United States, Japan, and Europe.

These three tools—reserve requirements, the discount window, and open-market operations—comprise the traditional strategies of the Federal Reserve.

We'll discuss examples of more unorthodox techniques in Chapter 17, "Financial Crisis." These innovations were used in the recent financial crisis to help shore up the entire financial system. Through use of such new policies, the Federal Reserve has rapidly adapted its toolkit to meet the changing demands of the global economy.

---

contractionary monetary policy actions that reduce the money supply in order to decrease aggregate demand

federal funds rate the interest rate at which banks choose to lend reserves held at the Fed to one another

zero lower bound the natural lower limit on interest rates

✓ TEST YOURSELF

- ☐ What is the name of the part of the Federal Reserve in Washington, DC, that oversees the Fed's operations? **[LO 15.5]**
- ☐ What is the dual mandate of the Federal Reserve? **[LO 15.5]**
- ☐ What is the most common tool that the Federal Reserve uses to conduct monetary policy? What makes this tool more appealing than the other two? **[LO 15.6]**

The Economic Effects of Monetary Policy

To understand why the Federal Reserve's control over the money supply is so powerful, we need a better understanding of the mechanism by which monetary policy affects the economy. Some economists, known as *monetarists*, argue that over the *long run*, monetary policy is irrelevant because prices will adjust to a high or low supply of money, without any change in overall economic output. (Consequently, monetarists say that "money is neutral.") However, most economists agree that in the *short run*, at least, the Federal Reserve's control over monetary policy allows it to combat recessions and cool an overheating economy. But how does this mechanism work?

Monetary policy primarily influences the economy through changes in the interest rate. Changes in the interest rate, in turn, affect the desire to borrow and lend, which can have significant impacts on the economy. In this section, we'll walk through the connections in this process as well as some of the challenges of implementing monetary policy.

Interest rates and monetary policy: The liquidity-preference model

LO 15.7 Understand how monetary policy affects the prevailing interest rate and supply of money

When the central bank increases or decreases the money supply, it changes the balance of money supplied versus money demanded. If the words "supply" and "demand" make you think about the supply-demand graphs we've used so far, you're on the right track.

To understand how the relationships work, we first describe the nature of the supply and demand of money using an idea, first proposed by economist John Maynard Keynes in 1936, called the *liquidity-preference model*.

The demand for money   As you know, economists use the term "liquid" to describe the ease of turning assets into cash. Cash is highly liquid by definition, and checking accounts (demand-deposit accounts) are nearly as liquid as cash. We need cash and easy-to-access bank accounts to be able to meet our daily spending needs. In other words, we have a preference for liquidity. This preference for liquidity forms the most basic determinant of money demand. Money demand is dictated by the amount of stuff people want to buy.

The other determinant of money demand is interest rates. To see why, let's compare cash and certificate of deposit (CD) accounts. In contrast to cash, CD accounts are not very liquid. The accounts have a fixed "maturity" date, which could be six months away, for example; some are as long as 10 years. The longer the date until maturity, the higher the interest rate, in general. In order to take money out of a CD before the maturity date, the holder has to officially request the funds and pay penalties for the privilege. Of course, these savings accounts have an important advantage over cash: they earn interest. The advantage of earning interest is weighed against the disadvantage of not being very liquid:

- When the interest rates earned on CDs are high, most people will try to save more in CDs and hold less cash.
- When the interest rates on CD accounts are low, their advantage is reduced, making cash relatively more attractive. When you don't earn much interest on CDs, you may as well hold your money in cash and other liquid forms.

This relationship is the central idea of the **liquidity-preference model**, which explains that the quantity of money people want to hold is a function of the interest rate. In this model, the money-demand curve slopes downward, showing a negative relationship between the interest rate and how much money is demanded. Why? Think of "money" here as cash—specifically, cash as opposed to other assets such as bonds that pay interest. (No matter how high interest rates are, though, you'll still have to hold onto some money to complete day-to-day transactions.)

On the whole, the liquidity-preference model means that people aren't going to demand much money when interest rates are high; they will demand more and more money as interest rates decrease.

A change in the quantity of money demanded in response to a change in the interest rate is represented by movement along the money demand curve:

- When the interest rate rises, we demand a lower quantity of money, moving leftward along the curve.
- When the interest rate falls, we demand a higher quantity of money, moving rightward along the curve.

Not all changes in the quantity of money demanded result from movement along the demand curve. Some factors instead cause the demand curve itself to shift.

One such factor is the price level in the economy. The demand for money in the United States is much higher today than it was 50 years ago, for the simple reason that almost everything is far more expensive today than it was then. Higher prices mean a greater need for money to meet the everyday needs of life, and that means more money demanded at every level of the interest rate. This increase in demand is represented by shifting the money demand curve to the right.

Increases or decreases in real GDP have a similar effect on money demand:

- Increases in real GDP—more production and income—mean more money is needed to purchase goods and services.
- Decreases in real GDP would have the opposite effect: With less activity in the economy, less money will be needed to purchase goods and services.

In addition to these economic factors, technological advancements can also play a role. Easier use of credit cards and greater availability of ATMs, for instance, reduce the demand for money. With these tools, people need to carry around far less cash in their wallets at any given time in order to make day-to-day purchases.

liquidity-preference model
idea that the quantity of money people want to hold is a function of the interest rate

Money supply In the simple version of the liquidity-preference model, the supply of money is considered to be set only by the Federal Reserve. Regardless of the interest rate, the Fed will ensure that there is a constant quantity of money supplied in the economy. As Figure 15-4 shows, this means that the money supply curve can be represented as a vertical line in the liquidity-preference model. It also means that the only way the supply of money can change is when the Fed does so for policy reasons.

Figure 15-4 shows the basic relationship between money supply and money demand in the liquidity-preference model. The point where the supply of money meets the demand for money (r*) will determine the *nominal interest rate*, or stated price of money in the economy.

This simple model assumes that the Fed has complete control over the supply curve, but in reality an economy's money supply comes from a variety of sources. As the model currently stands, the Fed dictates the supply of the monetary base. Banks decide how much money is eventually created from the base money through the impact their lending decisions have on the money multiplier. As we'll see later, the Fed's ability to target the money supply and interest rates is not nearly as precise as this model suggests. Still, the assumption of a fixed money supply controlled by the Fed is useful for introducing the model.

FIGURE 15-4
The liquidity-preference model

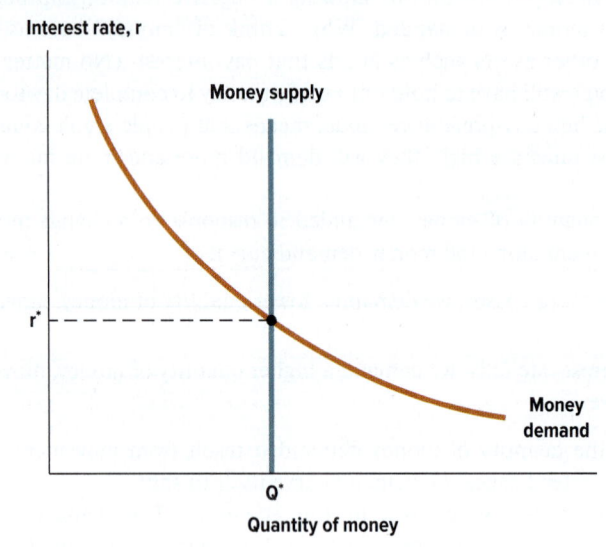

The liquidity-preference model shows the basic relationship between money supply and money demand. In this model we assume that the money supply is completely fixed by the Fed. The money demand curve slopes downward as a function of the interest rate. With high interest rates, people demand a small quantity of money, but as interest rates decrease, people demand more.

Earlier, we discussed the tools the Fed has to adjust the money supply. These adjustments can be represented by shifts in the money supply curve, depending on whether the Fed wants to increase or decrease the money supply. In short:

- Any actions that increase the money supply will shift the money supply curve to the right. These actions include decreasing the reserve requirement, decreasing the discount rate, or buying government bonds on the open market.
- In contrast, any actions that decrease the money supply will shift the money supply curve left. These actions include increasing the reserve requirement, increasing the discount rate, or selling government bonds on the open market.

As you can see in Figure 15-5, changes in the money supply increase or decrease interest rates.

Knowing the slope of the money demand curve is important: The slope of the money demand curve determines how a change in the money supply will change the interest rate. If the quantity of money demanded is really responsive to changes to the interest rate (a flat, elastic demand curve), changes to the money supply will have a smaller effect on interest rates than if demand is less responsive (steeper, more inelastic). You can see this visually in Figure 15-6.

LO 15.8 Explain how expansionary or contractionary monetary policy influences the broader economy.

Interest rates and the economy

The liquidity-preference model explains how the Federal Reserve's actions can change interest rates. The Fed can cause interest rates to fall by increasing the money supply, or it can cause interest rates to rise by decreasing the money supply. But why does the Fed care about the interest rate? The answer is that the interest rate has important effects in the economy. Many of the large purchases we make—buying a house, a car, or an expensive appliance—are made using money

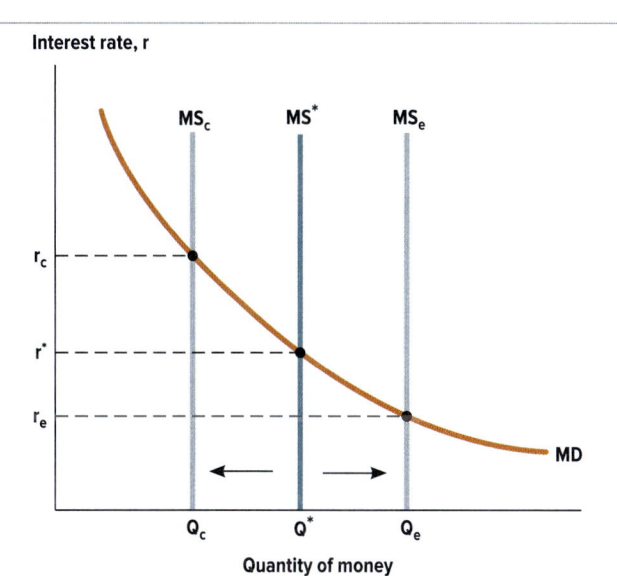

FIGURE 15-5

Shifts in the money supply curve and their effects on the interest rate

Shifting the money supply curve to the right (expanding the money supply) is called expansionary monetary policy (denoted with an e). The result is a greater amount of money in the economy, at lower interest rates. Shifting the curve to the left represents a decrease in the money supply. The result is less money in the economy, at higher interest rates.

FIGURE 15-6

The slope of the money supply curve affects the amount of change in the interest rate

(A) Elastic money demand curve

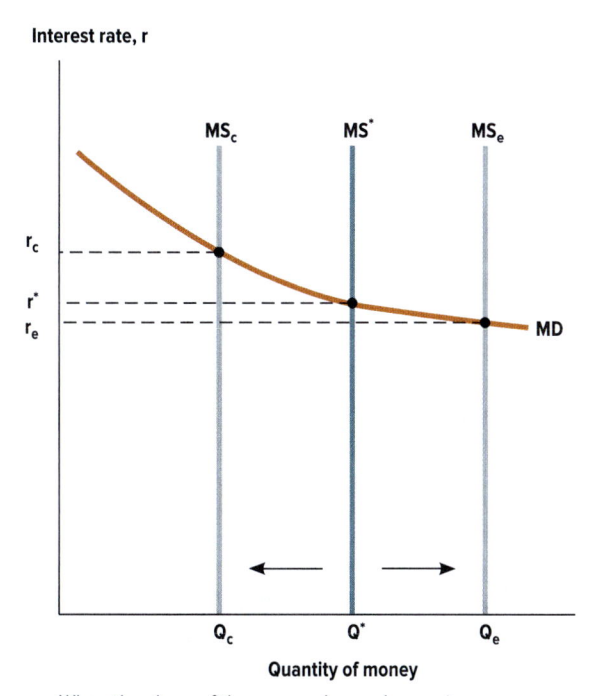

When the slope of the money demand curve is more elastic, changes in the money supply will have a smaller effect on interest rates.

(B) Inelastic money demand curve

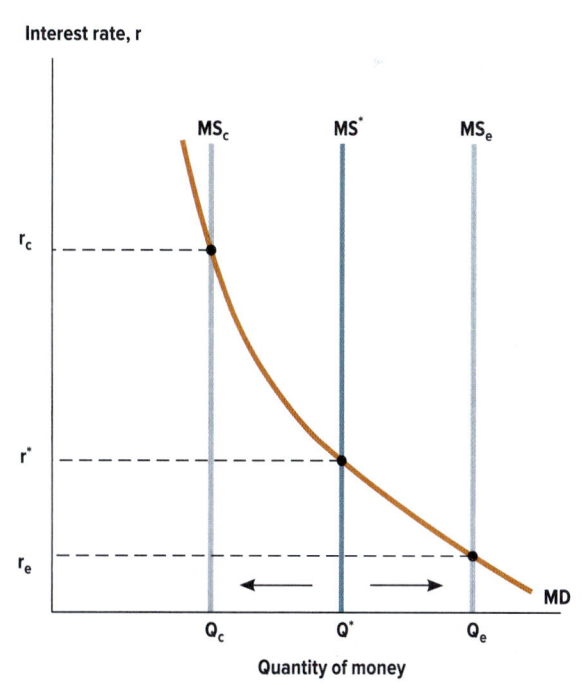

When the slope of the money demand curve is more inelastic, changes in the money supply will have a greater effect on interest rates.

we've borrowed. Likewise, corporations borrowing to make investments must also pay the price dictated by the interest rate.

Expansionary monetary policy Changes in interest rates affect aggregate demand and supply in an economy: Lower interest rates make it cheaper to borrow money, and less rewarding to save money. At lower interest rates, people will spend on big-ticket items instead of save, further increasing the consumption part of aggregate demand. Monetary policy is thus an important way for policy-makers to respond to changes in the health of the economy.

For an example, let's say that the economy is in a recession. Aggregate demand is low. The economy is in a short-run equilibrium marked by sluggish output and lower prices. The Fed knows that lower interest rates would spur increased borrowing and spending—shifting the aggregate demand curve to the right. The Federal Reserve chairman announces that the Fed will lower the federal funds rate. So the Fed conducts open-market operations to increase the supply of money in the economy. This action is called *expansionary monetary policy*. As you can see in panel A of Figure 15-7, lower interest rates are the result of this action. It is important to keep in mind that the lower interest rates affect the rates of return on assets throughout the economy:

- When the Fed purchases bonds on the open market, it increases the demand for those bonds, drives up their prices, and therefore lowers their expected rates of return (since investors now have to pay more for the same stream of payments).
- Since investors no longer find Treasuries as attractive as before, they shift their portfolios toward other assets, like private stocks and bonds and real estate.
- This portfolio shift then increases the prices of the other assets in the economy and reduces *their* rates of return.

FIGURE 15-7
Expansionary monetary policy

(A) Expansionary monetary policy

(B) Expansionary monetary policy and the AD/AS model

Expansionary money supply pushes interest rates lower and puts more money into the economy.

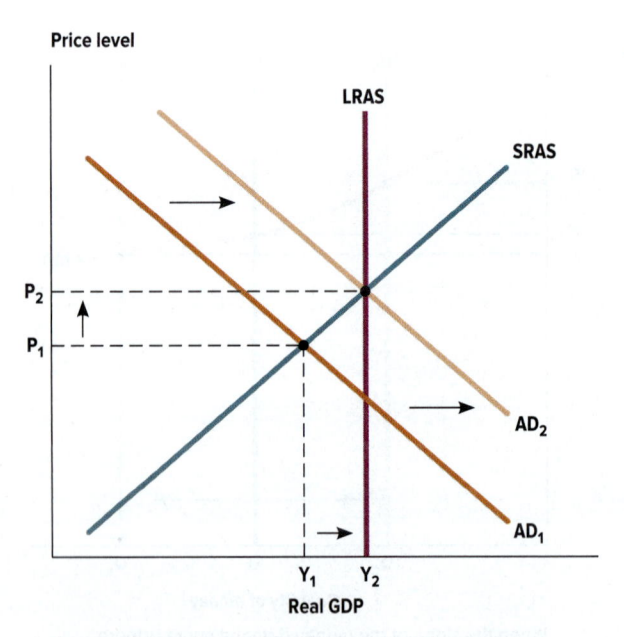

As a result people spend and borrow more, increasing aggregate demand. In this case, monetary policy was able to pull the economy out of recession.

Thus, the Fed's decision to lower *an* interest rate—the federal funds rate—results in an economy-wide increase in asset prices and rates of return.

This increase in asset prices leads to what is known as the *balance sheet channel* of monetary policy. The idea is that a rise in asset prices causes firms and households to perceive an increase in their net worth. Then, when they feel an increase in net worth, they tend to increase spending. The causes of the additional spending differ for households and firms:

- In the case of households, the most important asset tends to be the house itself. For them, the balance sheet channel refers to spending out of an increase in housing wealth.
- In the case of firms, corporations tend to hold much of their business savings in the form of financial assets. When firms see an increase in their net worth due to increased asset prices, they are usually more willing to spend on new projects. They can use those larger internal savings to self-finance their investments. (Also, of course, the opportunity cost of using those funds is lower because the interest rate is lower.)

So, lower interest rates spur borrowing and spending. They also discourage saving. With increases in consumption spending and investment, aggregate demand increases. The aggregate demand curve shifts to the right as shown in panel B of Figure 15-7. Ultimately the effect is the same as that of the expansionary *fiscal* policy we discussed in Chapter 14, "The Basics of Finance." Both prices and output increase, taking the bite out of the recession.

Contractionary monetary policy Conversely, what should the Fed do when the economy is booming, as it was in the housing bubble of 2006? Since the system was flush with cash, the aggregate demand curve was way to the right, and price levels were high. Output was also high, which made the decision of what needed to be done in this situation slightly tougher.

On the one hand, strong economic activity is obviously a good thing. On the other hand, it is possible for the economy to be operating beyond its means. When short-run output moves above long-run equilibrium, the price level will inevitably increase. Such increases in the price level are contrary to the central bank's mandate to maintain stable price levels. We'll go into this responsibility in more depth in Chapter 16, "Inflation," but for now, let's say that the Fed would be worried that these rising price levels would begin to adversely affect the economy.

When the Fed decides that the economy is a little too active—economists often call this "overheating"—it often moves to increase interest rates, as it did throughout the housing bubble. This increase in interest rates shifts the aggregate demand curve leftward, leading to lower prices and equilibrium output in the short run. That result, shown in panel B of Figure 15-8, is the effect of a contractionary monetary policy, shown in panel A of the same figure.

You'll note that we left both of these examples in the short run. In the long run, the economy will adjust to changes in the money supply, leaving only changes in the overall price level. This fact leads to one of the challenges facing the Federal Reserve: how to maintain stable price levels while also ensuring full employment. As you'll see in Chapter 16, "Inflation," these two goals are often in fundamental conflict.

Challenges and advantages of monetary policy The examples of the use of monetary policy, above, show how policy can work in ideal cases. It is rare for the world to work so cleanly. When we discussed fiscal policy, we noted that policy-makers face practical challenges, such as time lags and imperfect information, when they try to make policy. The Fed faces the same problems as it seeks to steer the economy using monetary policy.

Although monetary policy usually does not take as long to implement as fiscal policy, a few months can pass before the Fed's actions start to have their desired impact. By that time, the state of the economy might have changed. A boost in the money supply could push the economy past the level of long-run equilibrium output, for example, and cause the economy to overheat. Even worse, the Fed could inadvertently contract the money supply just as the economy starts sliding into a recession. This mistiming of policy would make the ensuing recession even worse.

FIGURE 15-8

Contractionary monetary policy

(A) Contractionary monetary policy

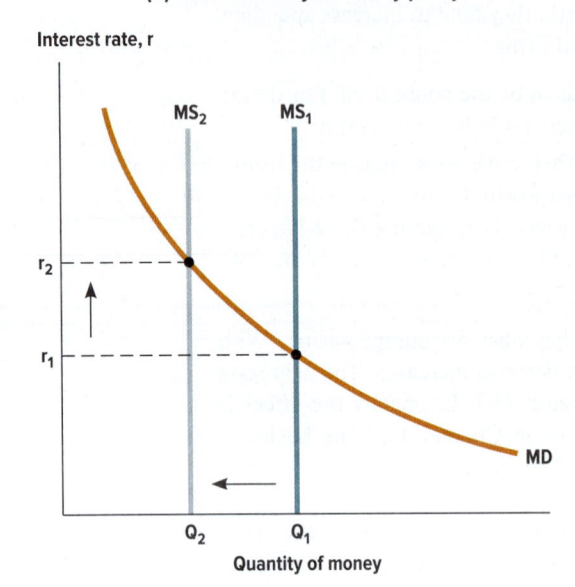

Contractionary monetary policy decreases the money supply, increasing interest rates.

(B) Contractionary monetary policy and the AD/AS model

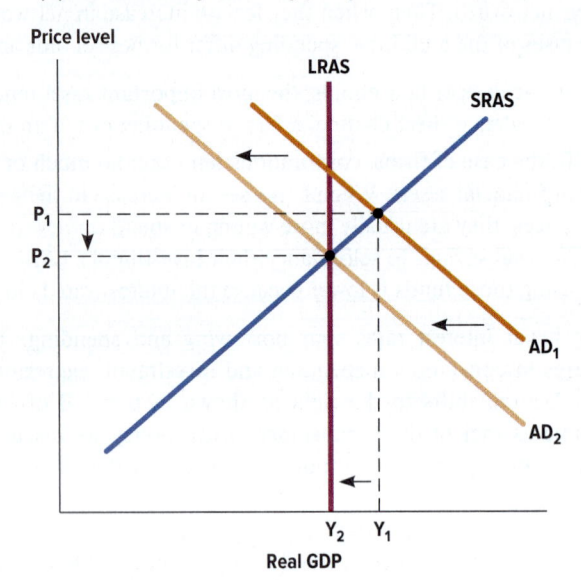

Decreasing the money supply can cool down the economy when it overheats.

Even so, monetary policy does have advantages compared to traditional fiscal policy. The Fed does not have to wait for politicians to come to a consensus about the best policy to help the economy. Instead, the Fed Board of Governors and Open Market Committee typically meet every six weeks or so. They can, if necessary, change monetary policy then and there.

Also, the Fed is made up of prominent economic policy-makers whose job is to make sure they fully understand the nuances of the overall economy in order to apply the right policy at the right time. It does not need to make specific decisions about spending and tax policy; it merely lowers or raises interest rates and lets the market determine spending decisions.

Benefits like these make monetary policy a vitally important weapon against low employment and excessive inflation.

✓ TEST YOURSELF

- ☐ What is the federal funds rate? **[LO 15.7]**
- ☐ What should the central bank do to fight low aggregate demand during a recession? **[LO 15.8]**

Conclusion

In this chapter, we've explored one of the most fundamental concepts in modern economics: money. We've looked at the roles money plays in the economy. We've also looked at how central banks and the private banking system interact to determine the size of the money supply. Finally, we've seen some of the tools the central bank has to manage the money supply and how those tools allow it to exert considerable influence over the broader economy.

This unique power gives the Fed (and central banks in other countries) incredible responsibility for the economy. As you'll see in the next few chapters, this responsibility usually comes down to two main tasks: keeping price levels stable and acting as a lender of last resort. The Fed is the last line of defense when a financial crisis threatens an economy.

Key Terms

money, p. 396
store of value, p. 397
medium of exchange, p. 397
barter, p. 397
unit of account, p. 397
commodity-backed money, p. 400
fiat money, p. 401
demand deposits, p. 402
reserves, p. 402
required reserves, p. 402
excess reserves, p. 402

reserve ratio, p. 403
fractional-reserve banking, p. 404
money multiplier, p. 404
money supply, p. 406
monetary base, p. 406
M1, p. 406
M2, p. 407
central bank, p. 408
monetary policy, p. 408
Federal Reserve ("the Fed"), p. 410
dual mandate, p. 411

reserve requirement, p. 411
discount window, p. 412
discount rate, p. 412
open-market operations, p. 412
expansionary monetary policy, p. 412
contractionary monetary policy, p. 413
federal funds rate, p. 413
zero lower bound, p. 413
liquidity-preference model, p. 415

Summary

LO 15.1 Describe the three main functions of money.

The three main functions of money are as a store of value, a medium of exchange, and a unit of account. Money derives much of its true importance from its role as a medium of exchange—from the fact that you can use it to purchase the goods and services you desire. Money is also important as a way to register the value of transactions.

LO 15.2 Describe the characteristics that make something a good choice as money, and distinguish between commodity-backed and fiat money.

Money needs to have *stability of value* and *be convenient*. Items whose value varies from one day to the next will not be a good store of value, and so are not suitable as money. Money also needs to be widely accepted in order to fulfill its function as a medium of exchange. The earliest forms of paper money could be legally exchanged into a specific amount of a named commodity (generally gold), making it *commodity-backed money*. Since 1971, U.S. money has been *fiat money*, which is money created by rule rather than backed by a commodity.

LO 15.3 Explain the concept of fractional-reserve banking and the money multiplier.

Banks keep on hand a portion of the money deposited, in case depositors want to withdraw money. This money is known as the bank's *reserves*, and the ratio of the original deposit to the amount kept as reserves is the *reserve ratio*. If the reserve ratio were 100 percent (a situation known as *full-reserve banking*), no lending would take place; all deposits would sit in the banks' vaults, and the financial system would grind to a halt. *Fractional-reserve banking* allows a reserve ratio of less than 100 percent, enabling banks to lend a portion of the money that has been deposited. By means of that lending, banks "create" money. The ratio of money created by the lending activities of the banking system to the money created by the government's central bank is the *money multiplier*.

LO 15.4 Describe M1 and M2.

The Fed classifies different types of money by their *liquidity*—by how easy an asset is to convert immediately to cash without losing value. Cash and reserves physically held at the Fed are *hard money*, which can be used in transactions without delay. *M1* includes hard money plus checkable deposits (which are not exactly cash but are fairly readily accessible for most people). *M2* includes everything in M1 as well as things like savings accounts and CDs (certificates of deposit) that are generally harder to access immediately and so slightly less liquid than other forms of money.

LO 15.5 Understand the role of a central bank, and discuss the idea of the Federal Reserve's dual mandate.

In any nation, the central bank's duties generally include maintaining the money supply and coordinating the banking system. In the United States, the central bank is known as the Federal Reserve—a system consisting of a Board of Governors and 12 regional banks. It has a dual mandate: to use monetary policy to ensure price stability and maintain full employment. *Price stability* means maintaining a stable money supply that meets the needs of the economy, while keeping the purchasing power of a dollar relatively constant over time by preventing destabilizing levels of price changes. Full employment can be affected through monetary policy to stimulate or cool aggregate demand.

LO 15.6 Explain the tools the Federal Reserve uses to conduct monetary policy.

The Federal Reserve has three tools to conduct monetary policy. The first is changing the *reserve requirement*, or the regulation that sets the minimum fraction of deposits that banks must hold. It is usually seen as a rather blunt tool—powerful but inappropriate for most day-to-day economic maintenance.

The second is the *discount window*, a lending facility run by the Fed that allows any bank to receive cash in exchange for certain noncash assets like government bonds; the interest rate charged for these loans is the *discount rate*. The discount window is one of the Fed's primary tools for providing liquidity to the markets and acting as a lender of last resort.

The final and most-used tool is *open-market operations*, in which the Federal Reserve sells or buys government bonds in the open market. Use of this tool alters bank reserves and influences overall interest rates.

LO 15.7 Understand how monetary policy affects the prevailing interest rate and supply of money.

The *liquidity-preference model* explains that the quantity of money people want to hold (the demand for money) is a function of the interest rate, which the Federal Reserve controls. As the quantity of money supplied changes, the price of that money, reflected in interest rates, will change as well. Increasing the money supply (such as by buying government bonds on the open market) decreases interest rates. Decreasing the money supply (such as by selling government bonds) will increase interest rates.

LO 15.8 Explain how expansionary or contractionary monetary policy influences the broader economy.

Depending on the circumstances, the Fed may want to engage in either expansionary or contractionary monetary policy. *Expansionary monetary policy* involves lowering interest rates; the lower rates increase aggregate demand, helping to expand the economy. This action is generally taken in response to recessionary forces. *Contractionary monetary policy* involves raising interest rates, which shrinks aggregate demand and slows the economy; it generally is taken in response to inflationary forces.

Review Questions

1. Describe how money contributes to economic activity and allows for a more complex society than barter does. **[LO 15.1]**
2. Explain how cigarettes fulfilled the three functions of money in the POW camps during World War II. **[LO 15.1]**
3. Throughout time, metals such as gold have been popular choices for money across various societies. Explain why this might be, using our criteria for what makes good money. **[LO 15.2]**
4. On the Yap Islands in the middle of the Pacific Ocean, giant stone wheels, weighing as much as a small car, were used as currency. What were some of the likely problems with this currency? **[LO 15.2]**
5. Explain why keeping a reserve ratio of zero could be a very bad idea. **[LO 15.3]**
6. If banks keep 100 percent of deposits on hand as reserves, what would this imply about the reserve requirement and the multiplier? What would it imply about banks' ability to create new money? **[LO 15.3]**
7. Explain the role of base money and the money multiplier in the Federal Reserve System's enactment of monetary policy. **[LO 15.4]**
8. Give an example where depositors changing the way they hold assets could increase the M1 measure of the money supply while leaving M2 unchanged. **[LO 15.4]**
9. What is one key way in which the mission of the Federal Reserve differs from the mission of the European Central Bank? **[LO 15.5]**
10. What do we mean when we say that the Federal Reserve System is politically independent, and how might this independence be a good thing for the U.S. economy? **[LO 15.5]**
11. Explain why using changes in reserve requirements to conduct monetary policy is generally not a good idea for the United States. **[LO 15.6]**
12. Which tool of monetary policy is used most frequently by the Federal Reserve System? What makes this tool the best choice in most circumstances? **[LO 15.6]**
13. Are there any differences in the effects of fiscal policy versus monetary policy on aggregate demand in the short-run aggregate demand and supply model? **[LO 15.7]**
14. Describe the slope of the money supply curve in the liquidity-preference model. Are the assumptions behind the supply curve realistic? **[LO 15.7]**
15. Under the liquidity-preference model, how would the slope of the money demand curve affect the power of a central bank to conduct monetary policy? **[LO 15.8]**

16. Use the liquidity-preference model to explain how the Federal Reserve can react to the threat of exceedingly high inflation via monetary policy. Be sure to include the intended effect on the interest rate and quantity of money. **[LO 15.8]**

Problems and Applications

1. Determine whether each of the following would fulfill the three functions of money. If the item does not fulfill all three, name at least one function of money that it violates. **[LO 15.1]**
    a. Salt.
    b. The barter system.
    c. Baseball cards.

2. Imagine you own a lawn-mowing business. Identify the main function of money exhibited in each situation below. **[LO 15.1]**
    a. You swipe your debit card to purchase gasoline for your lawn mower.
    b. You stuff your earnings from mowing lawns into a piggy bank.
    c. You pay your friend Cornelius $5 to help you mow lawns.
    d. You calculate your net earnings for the year on your tax return.
    e. You determine how much value your new lawn mower has added to your business.

3. From 2004 to 2009 the country of Zimbabwe underwent hyperinflation, in which prices rise rapidly. The government began printing bills as large as 100 billion Zimbabwe dollars. Explain how this situation would have affected the characteristics of good money discussed in this chapter. **[LO 15.2]**

4. Suppose you live in a country perfect for growing tulips and governed by King Balthazar, who proposes that you use the tulips for your currency. After all, says Balthazar, they are widely accepted in the community, they've been valuable for years, and they are highly portable. If you were Balthazar's economic advisor, would you recommend using the tulips? If yes, list the traits of good money they satisfy. If no, list the trait(s) of good money they do not satisfy. **[LO 15.2]**

5. You decide to take $500 out of your piggy bank at home and place it in the bank. If the reserve requirement is 5 percent, how much can your $500 increase the amount of money in the economy? **[LO 15.3]**

6. Assume that $1 million is deposited in a bank with a reserve requirement of 15 percent. What is the money supply as a result? What would change if the government decides to raise the reserve requirement to 30 percent? **[LO 15.3]**

7. Say whether each of the following are types of M1 or M2, or both. **[LO 15.4]**
    a. Checkable deposits.
    b. Dollar bills.
    c. Money in your checking account.
    d. Money in your savings account.
    e. Certificates of deposit under $100,000.
    f. Traveler's checks.

8. Which of the following statements are true regarding the differences between M1 and M2? Check all that apply. **[LO 15.4]**
    a. M1 includes cash and reserves, whereas M2 does not.
    b. M2 represents a broader measure of the money supply compared to M1.
    c. Numerically, M1 is larger than M2.
    d. All items in M1 are more liquid than all items in M2.
    e. M2 includes savings deposits, whereas M1 does not.
    f. Checking account balances are part of M2 but not M1.

9. The following quotation comes from remarks given by Ben Bernanke, former chairman of the Federal Reserve. The Federal Reserve has a dual mandate. Which mandate does the quote below refer to? **[LO 15.5]**

    > The substantial ongoing slack in the labor market and the relatively slow pace of improvement remain important reasons that the Committee continues to maintain a highly accommodative monetary policy.[9]

10. Look back to the POW camps described at the beginning of this chapter. Who played the role of the central bank? **[LO 15.5]**

11. Which tool of monetary policy is most likely being described by each of the following statements? **[LO 15.6]**
    a. It's the major way the Federal Reserve System enacts monetary policy.
    b. This tool is good for emergency situations that require major, large-scale action.
    c. This tool goes through the Federal Reserve's role as lender of last resort.
    d. This tool is best for everyday monetary policy.

e. A major disadvantage of this tool is that it requires that banks want to borrow from the Fed.

f. Even if they aren't interested in buying, selling, or borrowing from the Fed, changes in this tool may inconvenience bank managers.

12. Name the monetary policy tool being used in each of the following examples. **[LO 15.6]**

    a. The central bank buys government securities from banks.

    b. The central bank raises the cost of borrowing money.

    c. The central bank changes the amount of money banks must hold from their depositors.

13. The economy is in recession and the Federal Reserve wants to increase the money supply. Should it increase or decrease the following? **[LO 15.6]**

    a. Reserve requirements.

    b. The discount rate.

    c. Purchases of bonds in the open market.

14. Using Figure 15P-1, answer the following questions. **[LO 15.7]**

FIGURE 15P-1

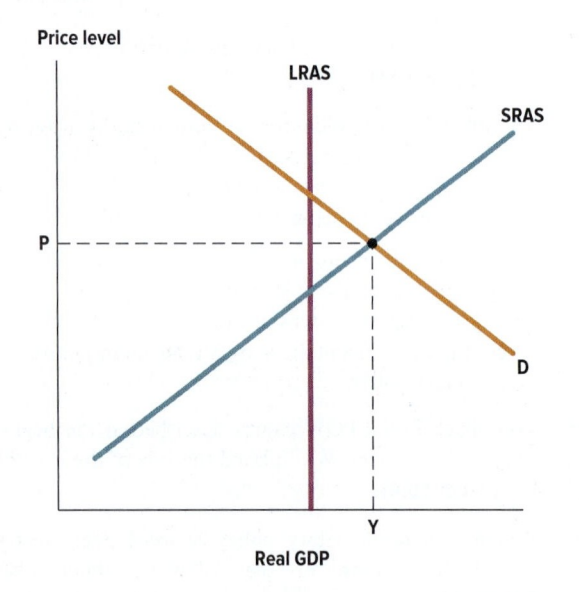

Price level

LRAS

SRAS

P

D

Y

Real GDP

a. Is this economy in recession, just right, or overheating?

b. What is the correct monetary policy in this situation—expansionary or contractionary?

c. What is the effect on prices of that policy—will they increase or decrease?

15. What would happen to each of these components of the liquidity-preference model if the Federal Reserve decides to raise the reserve requirement? **[LO 15.8]**

    a. Money supply.

    b. Interest rates.

    c. Quantity of money in the economy.

    d. Money demand curve.

16. For each of the following situations, identify whether the Federal Reserve is likely to pursue an expansionary or a contractionary monetary policy. **[LO 15.8]**

    a. The unemployment rate is at 0.5 percent.

    b. The economy is experiencing record growth in GDP.

    c. The unemployment rate is at 15 percent.

    d. Inflation has reached 10 percent, a recent high.

    e. A hurricane recently demolished a major city, causing a major recession.

Endnotes

1. This wasn't always the case: In the early days of the United States, there was no universal U.S. dollar; banks in each state produced their own currencies. In 1792 the United States started slowly phasing out the competing state currencies in favor of a standard form of money for the entire country. This was a critical decision in U.S. economic history.

2. www.jmbullion.com/charts/gold-price.

3. The change in 1933 applied only to domestic transfers. From 1933 to 1971, foreign holders of currency could still exchange dollars for gold.

4. The bank has two reasons to hold reserves. First, the Federal Reserve *requires* the bank to hold a certain percentage of deposits as reserves. It's simply the law. In the example, the Fed's reserve requirement is 10 percent. The second reason is that banks have to meet customers' needs for *liquidity*, independent of the banks' legal requirements to hold reserves. Sometimes banks find it strategic to hold extra reserves over and above the legal requirement. In the example here, the bank's legal requirement and its own judgment of customers' needs happen to coincide. So, for both reasons, the bank chooses to hold 10 percent of deposits as reserves.

5. In reality, some dollars might get held as cash rather than being deposited, but usually we're safe to ignore those very small amounts relative to the total, especially in the United States and other economies with well-developed banking systems. In some parts of the world today, however, much more money is held outside of banks and that fact would need to be taken into account.

6. Robert F. Bruner and Sean D. Carr, *The Panic of 1907: Lessons Learned from the Market's Perfect Storm* (Hoboken, NJ: John Wiley & Sons, 2007).

7. Binyamin Appelbaum and Jo Craven McGinty, "The Fed's Crisis Lending: A Billion Here, a Thousand There," *The New York Times*, April 1, 2011, p. B1, www.nytimes.com/2011/04/01/business/economy/01fed.html.

8. The Fed also buys bonds directly from the public—not just banks. Some of the money from the sales of those bonds gets put into banks as deposits. Those deposits increase the banks' reserves, and we see the same result as we do when the Fed buys the bonds directly from banks.

9. Source: Speech by Chairman Ben S. Bernanke of the Federal Reserve at the New York Economic Club, New York, New York, November 20, 2012 ("The Economic Recovery and Economic Policy"), http://www.federalreserve.gov/newsevents/speech/bernanke20121120a.htm.

Chapter 16

Inflation

A Land of Opportunity... and Inflation

The story is a familiar one: In the closing years of the 1800s, millions of immigrants sought out the promised land—a country rich in natural resources and with the highest standards of living in the world. These immigrants sought a new life in one of the world's great cities—a modern, cosmopolitan city where the blending of cultures led to vibrancy nearly unrivaled in the world. At its peak, nearly 50 percent of the city's residents were immigrants.

These immigrants were not greeted by the Statue of Liberty. They did not pass through New York's Ellis Island. They didn't set foot in Manhattan or anywhere else in the United States. Instead, they went to Buenos Aires—their promised land was Argentina. From the late 1800s to the early 1900s, more than 5 million immigrants from across Europe arrived in Argentina, a country with seemingly limitless opportunity. In 1910, Argentina's per capita GDP was relatively high, four-fifths that of the United States.

©Photodisc/Getty Images

In the century that followed, though, Argentina lagged behind economically. Its per capita GDP is now less than a third of that in the United States. What caused this divergence in fortunes? You could point to the political instability that led to a series of military coups and populist dictatorships. But dig a little deeper and you will find a common thread that came to define daily life in Argentina: steadily rising prices throughout the economy—in other words, out-of-control *inflation*.

More than almost any other country in the world, Argentina has struggled with rising prices. Over the past 75 years, Argentina experienced three separate *hyperinflations* (extremely long and painful inflationary periods). The worst of these, in the late 1980s and early 1990s, saw inflation peak at over 20,000 percent per year. (In other words, prices were doubling every month or two.)

427

If this were to happen in the United States today, an iPod costing $100 at Christmas would cost $200 in February, $400 in March, and more than $20,000 by the following Christmas.

In between the periods of hyperinflation, Argentina has seen sustained high inflation unlike almost any other country in the world. In fact, the average annual inflation rate over the last 75 years is over 200 percent—a tripling of prices every year! Argentina brought inflation down to about 25 percent per year recently—which seems modest compared to historical levels, despite being one of the highest inflation rates in the world.[1]

A century ago, Argentina seemed on the cusp of challenging the United States for supremacy in the Americas. Of course, the difference in inflation rates was not the only policy or geographic difference between the United States and Argentina. But it does help explain why that dream is gone. What is so damaging about inflation for a nation's economy? And why do most economists believe that its opposite—deflation—is even worse?

LEARNING OBJECTIVES

LO 16.1 Define inflation, deflation, headline inflation, and core inflation.

LO 16.2 Explain the neutrality of money.

LO 16.3 Describe and illustrate the classical theory of inflation.

LO 16.4 Explain the quantity theory of money, and relate it to inflation and deflation.

LO 16.5 Analyze the economic consequences of inflation.

LO 16.6 Analyze the economic consequences of deflation.

LO 16.7 Describe disinflation and hyperinflation, and explain the role of monetary policy in creating both situations.

LO 16.8 Understand why policy-makers favor a small amount of inflation over zero inflation.

LO 16.9 Explain the relationship between inflation, the output gap, and monetary policy.

LO 16.10 Explain how the relationship between inflation and unemployment is modeled by the Phillips curve and integrated into the non-accelerating inflation rate of unemployment.

In the chapter on money and the monetary system, we saw how money creation and the supply of money can have an enormous impact on the overall economy, and in particular on interest rates. In this chapter, we will look at the topic of inflation from various angles—theories about changing price levels, inflation in its various forms, and the effects of inflation on monetary policy.

Changing Price Levels

The price level, and especially changes in it, is one of the most important concepts in macroeconomics. The economy is driven by billions of frequently changing prices. Some of these price changes matter for the economy more than others.

There are a few key questions economists address: How should we summarize the most important price changes? What causes the price level to change? And how do changes in the price level affect the economy?

Measuring inflation

Price levels go up and down:

- An overall rise in prices in the economy is called **inflation**.
- An overall fall in prices in the economy is called **deflation**.

As we saw in Chapter 8, "The Cost of Living," the U.S. government's Bureau of Labor Statistics (BLS) measures overall prices in the economy by creating a consumption basket designed to resemble the purchases of the average urban consumer. This measure of overall prices is called the *Consumer Price Index (CPI)*. Measuring inflation or deflation is done by calculating the percentage change in the CPI ratio of the cost of the market basket to the cost of that basket in a base year (as we saw in Equation 8-2 in Chapter 8):

LO 16.1 Define inflation, deflation, headline inflation, and core inflation.

$$\text{Inflation rate} = \left[\frac{(CPI_{year2} - CPI_{year1})}{CPI_{year1}}\right] \times 100$$

The BLS measures two inflation numbers:

- The measure of inflation that includes *all* of the goods that the average consumer buys is called **headline inflation**. It measures the changes in prices for *all of the goods* in the market basket of the average urban consumer.
- **Core inflation** is a measure of inflation that measures price change minus food and energy costs, which are traditionally volatile. It is the BLS's official measure of changes in prices through the CPI.

The reason to calculate core inflation is that changes in price levels due to goods with volatile prices might simply reflect shocks to individual product markets rather than any sort of economy wide inflation. In 2018, for example, the price of gasoline dropped by 10 percent, while core inflation was positive 2.4 percent.[2]

When economists are interested in the underlying rate of inflation in the economy, they often differentiate between headline inflation and core inflation. Although headline inflation gives a more complete picture of how changing prices are affecting the average consumer, it's useful to subtract out food and gasoline if we want to get a better feel for underlying economic trends. Figure 16-1 clearly shows how much more stable core inflation (as represented by the core CPI) is than overall or headline inflation (as represented by the CPI).

inflation
an overall rise in prices in the economy

deflation
an overall fall in prices in the economy

headline inflation
measure of inflation that measures price changes for all of the goods in the market basket of the average urban consumer

core inflation
measure of inflation that measures price changes minus food and energy costs, which are traditionally volatile

FIGURE 16-1

Running annual change in CPI and core CPI, January 2001–January 2019 The figure shows actual annual inflation rates, as represented by CPI (representing headline or overall inflation) and core CPI (representing core inflation). Core inflation is much more stable than headline inflation.

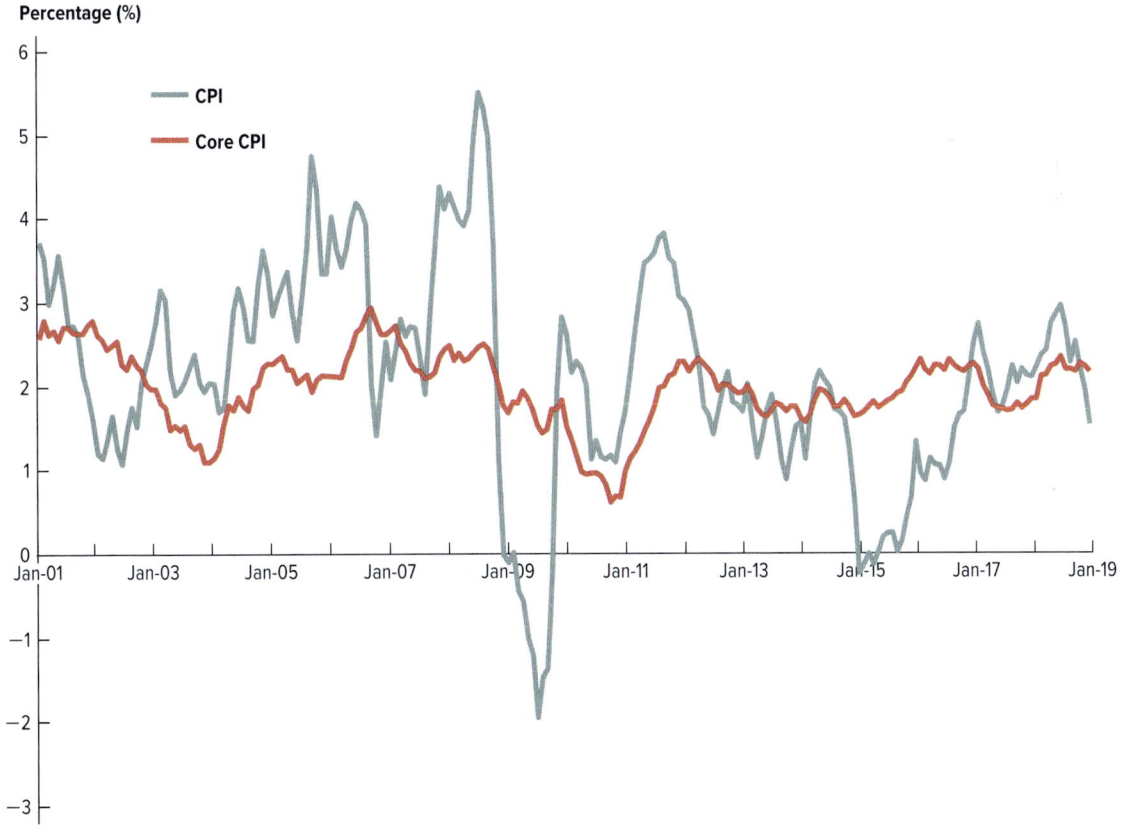

Sources: Federal Reserve Bank of St. Louis, FRED Economic Data, https://fred.stlouisfed.org/series/CPIAUCSL (CPI data); and https://fred.stlouisfed.org/series/CPILFESL (core CPI data).

LO 16.2 Explain the neutrality of money.

The neutrality of money

When we say that the price level changes, what do we mean? To answer the question, it helps to think about what "output" really is. A country's GDP is simply an accounting of all of the purchases and sales that take place over a given period. In each transaction, somebody gives money to somebody else. All output, then, can be tied to the movement of money. But how do we measure that output?

It seems intuitive to measure output in terms of money, but this can become problematic. Imagine that the government were to simply add two zeros to every piece of money—automatically turning $1 into $100 and $100 into $10,000. Prices would jump, and the measured "value of output" in the economy would increase tremendously. But we would know that the real output, the goods and services traded, didn't actually change—only the numbers did. What we want to measure is the output in terms of *real, tangible* goods and services: How many cans of soda or tons of steel did the country create?

As you may recall from earlier chapters, we use the terms *real* and *nominal* to differentiate the quantity of tangible goods and services from the numbers associated with them:

- We call quantities measured in terms of real, tangible goods and service *real values*. They represent an accounting for the actual amount of something that is produced. That accounting is independent of how many pieces of paper with a certain number of zeros on it you would need to purchase that output.

- In contrast, values measured in terms of how much money it would take to purchase something are called *nominal values*.

We use changes in the *price level* to get from one measure to the other.

In Chapter 8, "The Cost of Living," we described the concept of a *deflator*—the idea of using a price index like the CPI or the GDP deflator to adjust between nominal and real prices. These indexes allow us to convert nominal measures of output into real measures of output. In other words, they let us measure how much real stuff we get for our money. The **aggregate price level** is a measure of the average price level for GDP. In practice, it is measured by either the CPI or the GDP price deflator.

aggregate price level a measure of the average price level for GDP; in practice, the CPI or GDP price deflator

Now, back to the hypothetical: What if the government one day decided to add two zeros to the figure on every new and existing dollar bill (and added two zeroes to every financial account)? Doing this would essentially increase the money supply by 100 times. After a period of spending-spree chaos, if nothing else changed in the economy, you can predict that a store-owner who previously sold a bottle of water for $1 would raise the price to $100. Your $20 haircut would soon cost $2,000. And you would push for a raise from $10 an hour to $1,000 an hour in your job at the library. With that new wage, the change in the price of goods and services really wouldn't make much of a difference. You could still buy the same things you bought before, even though their prices now have the additional two zeroes.

neutrality of money the idea that, in the long run, changes in the money supply affect nominal variables, such as prices and wages, but do not affect real outcomes in the economy

In this example, the change in the price level (prices and wages being 100 times higher than before) didn't dent your purchasing power because the *real value* of your money hasn't changed. When all prices (including wages) increase proportionately, what you could buy when you made $10 an hour is the same as what you can buy when you make $1,000 an hour. The change in the price level—that is, the change in the unit of measurement used to account for something—changed only *nominal values*.

This is the basic intuition behind what is called the **neutrality of money**—the idea that, in the long run, changes in the money supply affect nominal variables, such as prices and wages, but do not affect real outcomes in the economy. The underlying mechanism is described in the next section.

LO 16.3 Describe and illustrate the classical theory of inflation.

The classical theory of inflation

In Chapter 15, "Money and the Monetary System," we touched on the idea that the level of prices in an economy is affected by the quantity of money in an economy. It's time to explain formally how this process happens, using the *classical theory of inflation*. The classical theory of inflation illustrates the relationship between money supply, output (or GDP), and the overall level of prices. It also shows the neutrality of money in the long run.

Figure 16-2 illustrates the basic framework of the classical theory using the now-familiar aggregate demand and aggregate supply (AD/AS) perspective. Suppose the economy is in long-run equilibrium at point E_1 in the figure. Short-run aggregate demand matches short-run aggregate supply, which matches the long-run potential aggregate supply of the economy.

What happens if the Federal Reserve increases the money supply, as in expansionary monetary policy? The increased money supply will result in lower interest rates and higher levels of borrowing; in turn, aggregate demand will increase. In that case, as Figure 16-2 shows, aggregate demand shifts right, creating a new temporary equilibrium where the new short-run aggregate demand curve intersects the short-run aggregate supply curve and increasing output (real GDP). The economy is at point E_2.

We know from the idea of the neutrality of money, however, that this situation can't survive for long. Eventually, prices will rise in proportion with the increase in the money supply. In practice, this can take a little bit of time, since prices are relatively *sticky* (slow-moving). (Remember, for example, you don't get to renegotiate your wages immediately when prices go up; you have to wait until your contract is up for renewal or the time is right to renegotiate your wage.)

While it might take time for prices to rise, as long as money is neutral we know they will eventually tick upwards. The increase in prices, especially in nominal wages, in turn leads to a leftward shift in the short-run aggregate supply curve. Why? Because the higher input prices of labor and other goods used in production make it more expensive to produce a given level of output.

The economy eventually reaches a new equilibrium, indicated by point E_3 on the figure: Aggregate supply and short-run aggregate demand once again meet at exactly the level of the long-run aggregate supply curve, and real GDP has fallen back to exactly the point at which it started.

FIGURE 16-2

Increase in the money supply under the classical theory of inflation

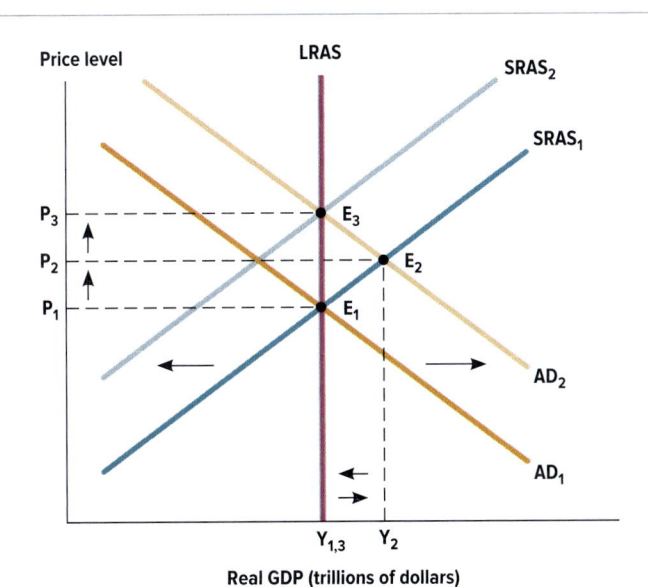

According to the classical theory of inflation, in the long run, increases in the money supply will lead to an increase in prices only; output will stay the same. In the short run, output and prices increase as aggregate demand shifts to the right. However, workers then begin to negotiate for a higher wage, which shifts the aggregate supply curve to the left. Output returns to the original level, while prices increase even more.

(This point is often called *potential output*, a concept we'll explore later in the chapter.) In fact, the only difference is that now *the price level is higher*—reflecting the lower value of money due to the increased money supply. In other words, it will now take a higher number of dollars to buy a given good or service. (Again, think back to the effect of more cigarettes in the POW camp in Chapter 15, "Money and the Monetary System.")

The neutrality of money holds in many cases. But in extreme situations, such as the story of Argentina that we discussed in the chapter opener, the neutrality of money does break down. Extreme and sustained inflation can wreak havoc in the economy, leading to slower growth. At a minimum, stores would need to constantly reprice items. When prices change more rapidly, consumers and firms face uncertainty, and the cost of discovering (and updating) information about new prices rises.

It's important to emphasize that the classical theory of inflation describes a long-run equilibrium. Some economists have used the eventual neutrality of money to argue that the Federal Reserve can't meaningfully guide the economy through monetary policy. Others cite empirical evidence that suggests that there is considerable scope for the Federal Reserve to affect the economy in the short run through expansionary or contractionary policy. This is one reason our analysis may yield different answers in the short run versus the long run.

The quantity theory of money

LO 16.4 Explain the quantity theory of money, and relate it to inflation and deflation.

The classical theory of inflation is strongly connected to a related theory: the **quantity theory of money**.

The framework begins with the **quantity equation** which says that the money supply (M) multiplied by the velocity of money (V) equals the price level (P) multiplied by the quantity of goods and services in the economy (Y):

EQUATION 16-1
$$M \times V = P \times Y$$

The left side of the equation captures the money in the economy used to pay for stuff. The right side of the equation is the value of all the goods and services that are purchased. The equation says that there has to be enough money (the left-hand side of the equation) to pay for all the stuff purchased in the economy (shown on the right-hand side). This relationship holds by definition.

quantity theory of money
theory that the value of money (and thus the aggregate price level) is determined by the overall quantity of money in existence (the money supply); it states that changes in the price level (inflation or deflation) are primarily the result of changes in the quantity of money

Note that the money available to pay for stuff is not simply the money supply (that is, the total amount of money in circulation on average during the period). After all, a given dollar can be used more than once. The money supply is thus multiplied by the **velocity of money**. The velocity of money reflects the number of times the entire money supply turns over in a given period. It approximates the number of transactions in which a typical dollar is used during the given period.

For example, if you and friends go out for tacos, some of the dollars you spent to purchase your meal goes to the waitress, another part goes to the cook, and yet other parts go to the farmers who raised the fillings in the tacos. Some of the dollars also go to the dozens of other suppliers who provided everything from the taco shells to the booth you are sitting in. In other words, your consumption spending is someone else's income, and that person can (and usually does) go on to spend at least part of that income on something else. Intuitively, the velocity of money is a simple concept. If the average dollar is spent five times a year, then the velocity of money for that year would be five.

quantity equation
the equation $M \times V = P \times Y$, which relates the money supply and velocity of money to the price value of real output

Rearranging Equation 16-1 allows us to show important facts about different variables of the equation. To start, we can mathematically calculate the velocity of money (V) as equal to the price level (P) multiplied by real output (Y), divided by the money supply (M):

velocity of money
the number of times the entire money supply turns over in a given period

EQUATION 16-2
$$V = \frac{P \times Y}{M}$$

For example, if an economy produces 1,000 units of output (so that Y = 1,000) with a price level of $1 (P = $1) and the money supply (M) is $500, velocity is

$$\frac{\$1 \times 1{,}000}{\$500} = 2$$

That means that over the course of the year, each dollar in the money supply was spent twice on average in order to generate $1,000 worth of output.

What does the quantity theory of money mean for inflation? To find out, we need to rearrange Equation 16-1 to isolate price levels on one side of the equation. It turns out that the price level (P) in an economy is the money supply (M) multiplied by velocity (V) divided by the real value of output (Y):

EQUATION 16-3
$$P = \frac{M \times V}{Y}$$

In order to understand what causes changes in prices, let's look at the variables on the right-hand side of the equation. To start, economists assume that the velocity of money tends to be fairly stable over time. But is that true in practice? Figure 16-3 shows information on the velocity of money in the United States through history. As you can see, velocity has been relatively stable historically, though the recent financial crisis temporarily caused some significant changes.

When production is at its long-run equilibrium level, real output (Y) is relatively stable as well. If Y and V are stable in Equation 16-3, the only pieces that can move are M and P. That means that when the money supply (M) increases, the price level (P) must rise too. In equilibrium, then, changes in the price level (inflation or deflation) are primarily the result of changes in the quantity of money:

- An increase in M (the money supply) has to eventually lead directly to an increase in P (the aggregate price level). In other words, *an increase in the money supply leads to an increase in prices (inflation)*, as there are more dollar bills spent on the same number of goods and services.

- Likewise, a decrease in M would result in a decrease in P. In other words, *a decrease in the money supply leads to a decrease in prices (deflation)*, as there are just as many goods and services but fewer dollars with which to purchase them.

FIGURE 16-3

Velocity of M1 in the United States For much of the early part of this graph, the velocity of money, reflected by the amount of money spent compared to nominal GDP, slowly heats up. After oscillating between six and eight times GDP in the '80s and early '90s, money velocity increases to over 10 times GDP at the height of the housing boom. The speed of money through the economy then slowed in the recession.

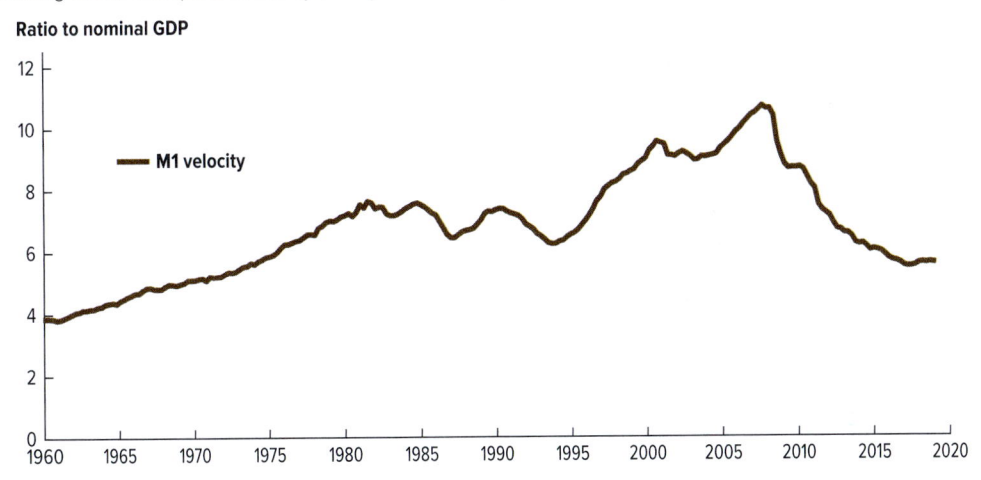

Source: Federal Reserve Bank of St. Louis, FRED economic data, https://fred.stlouisfed.org/series/M1V.

In short: Increasing the money supply leads to inflation, and decreasing the money supply leads to deflation.

Of course, velocity and output do often change. What happens to the quantity theory of money then? When either of these variables changes, the close relationship between prices and the money supply no longer holds. With rapid increases or decreases in the amount of money changing hands in the economy, it would be possible for the money supply to double while people spend their money half as fast. Rather than increasing prices, as we would otherwise expect when the money supply doubles, the amount of money moving around in the economy would stay the same, and prices would stay roughly the same as well. If the velocity of money had not declined during this period (as shown in Figure 16-3), the result would have been far more inflation than was actually observed.

As an example of this situation, the Fed increased the size of the monetary base quite substantially in an attempt to stimulate the economy following the 2007–2009 recession. If the velocity of money had not declined during this period (as shown in Figure 16-3), the result would have been far more inflation than was actually observed.

An implication of the quantity theory of money is that deflation occurs if the money supply remains constant but real output increases. Logically, the effect is the same as if real output stayed constant and the money supply declined. As we saw in Chapter 15, "Money and the Monetary System," this relationship between output and the money supply is one of the main arguments against the gold standard. Barring a sudden discovery of gold, the supply of gold-backed money is relatively fixed. If M is constant, when the economy expands (that is, when Y increases), then either the velocity of money must go up or the price level must go down (or a combination of these two events will occur). And if velocity is relatively constant, then there is only one option: The price level must fall, a situation known as *deflation*. We will see in more detail later in this chapter why deflation can be extremely damaging to an economy.

The Where's George? website brings to life the idea of velocity. The site allows users to enter the serial number of a dollar bill and see where it has been (assuming other holders of that dollar have entered the bill). See the Economics in Action box "Where's George?" for more.

Other causes of changing price levels

We've looked at how the quantity theory of money explains changes in price levels: In the long term, an increase in the money supply will result in an increase in the price level. Similarly, in the long term, a decrease in the money supply will decrease the price level. In addition, the price level can change temporarily by (1) the actions of the business cycle or (2) sudden supply shocks to a key resource in production.

We've actually discussed the changes in the price level resulting from the action of the business cycle many times before, in other chapters. Recall what happens in the aggregate demand and aggregate supply (AD/AS) framework:

- When an economy goes through a boom, companies look to expand rapidly to meet rising demand and competition for scarce resources heats up. It becomes harder to find workers, leading employers to bid against each other for the best talent, increasing wages. This demand pulls prices higher, as too much money is spent chasing too few goods. This is *demand-pull inflation*.
- Of course, the opposite is also true. When economic activity is slow, fewer dollars are spent on the same amount of goods, pushing prices downward. This kind of demand-related deflation is relatively rare.

These two effects combine to create a rise in price levels during the boom periods and, potentially, a fall in price levels during busts. We'll explore the relationship between inflation and the business cycle, and in particular unemployment, in more detail a bit later.

The other type of change in price levels occurs when the price of any key input increases suddenly. Known as *cost-push inflation*, the rising cost causes firms to increase prices in order to

Where's George?
Economics in Action

Have you ever looked at a crumpled dollar bill and wondered where that piece of paper had been before it got to you? You might even have noticed a stamp on a dollar bill leading you to the Where's George? website (www.wheresgeorge.com). Now that you know more about how money works, you might find it interesting to see what happens there: Users track the adventures of millions of bills as they travel through the economy. Tracking those travels captures what economists mean when they talk about velocity.

The website works like this: Users input the serial number found at the corner of any U.S. bill. If the bill has already been entered on the site, you can see where the bill has been and how long it took for it to get around. If you are the first person to enter the serial number, the bill becomes part of the database that will record the story of that bill.

How far could a dollar bill travel in a year?
©David A. Tietz/Editorial Image, LLC

Statistics from the site can give a pretty interesting picture of who holds money in the United States. Overall, more than 263 million unique Georges have been added. The most bills are entered in California, New York, and Florida. This is not too surprising as these states are within the top five in total population.

The individual stories can also tell a lot about how money moves through the economy. The site records such statistics as the distance the bills traveled between being recorded in the site, which is also converted into a miles per day figure. Most bills travel about five miles per day on average.

One of the more intrepid Georges visited 14 cities in a 7,686-mile, four-year jaunt around the country that took it from the fast-food chain Whataburger in Tallahassee, Florida, to Aiken, South Carolina, via flashy Times Square and the hip streets of Portland, Oregon.

Most trips are far more mundane: 57 percent of the bills on the site travel only between 30 and 500 miles in the course of nine months. The website depends on users to add bills, and it has captured only a sliver of the 11.4 billion dollar bills in circulation. Still, the site reminds us that those crumpled dollars in your pocket might have already had some interesting adventures.

Sources: www.wheresgeorge.com; www.federalreserve.gov/paymentsystems/coin_currcircvolume.htm.

---

maintain profits. A serious bout of cost-push inflation occurred in the mid-1970s in the United States when OPEC, the organization that controls most of the world's supply of oil, decided to cut the amount of oil they produced. Oil in its many forms is absolutely essential not only to the production of gasoline but also to many other goods, from corn to plastics. The shortage caused an increase in the price of oil, and the increase in the price of oil increased the prices of goods throughout the economy.

✓ TEST YOURSELF

- ☐ What is included in headline inflation that is left out of core inflation? **[LO 16.1]**
- ☐ Do changes in the aggregate price level change overall real output? **[LO 16.2]**
- ☐ According to the classical theory of inflation, will inflation increase or decrease if the Federal Reserve pursues expansionary monetary policy? **[LO 16.3]**
- ☐ What is the velocity of money? **[LO 16.4]**

Why Do We Care about Changing Price Levels?

At this point you may find yourself wondering why changes in the price level matter. After all, we've seen from the theory of money neutrality that the economy should adjust itself to different levels of nominal prices, leaving no change in overall output. So why be concerned about price levels?

As we'll see in this section, while the price level itself is immaterial, *changes* in the price level can have a big effect on economic behavior. We'll also see why many economists believe a modest and predictable level of inflation is a good thing, but high or unpredictable levels of inflation—and any level of deflation—are economically damaging.

Inflation

LO 16.5 Analyze the economic consequences of inflation.

We've defined inflation as an overall rise in prices (an increase in the aggregate price level). If the average price level rises 10 percent every year (that is, the prices of all the things in the economy go up by an average of 10 percent), we say that the economy is experiencing an inflation rate of 10 percent per year.

Figure 16-4 shows inflation rates for regions around the world from 1980 to 2017. Note that over the last four decades, the inflation rate has generally decreased.

Despite the generally decreasing inflation rate in the past four decades, inflation is always a threat. That makes it important to understand the costs of predictable inflation and the problems of unpredictable inflation.

Costs of inflation If money is neutral in the long run, why is it bad if prices go up? Won't the rest of the economy adjust to any price change? As we'll see shortly, arguably the most damaging economic consequence of inflation is the *uncertainty* it can create. Such uncertainty is increased when the amount or timing of inflation is *unpredictable*.

But even if inflation is predictable—say, if you are sure that prices will go up by about 20 percent every year—it still imposes three types of costs on the economy: menu costs, shoe-leather costs, and tax distortions.

Menu costs refer to the costs of changing prices to keep pace with inflation. Such costs are measured in money, time, and opportunity. The term *menu costs* comes from the simple idea that

menu costs
the costs (measured in money, time, and opportunity) of changing prices to keep pace with inflation

---

FIGURE 16-4

Inflation around the world, 1980–2017

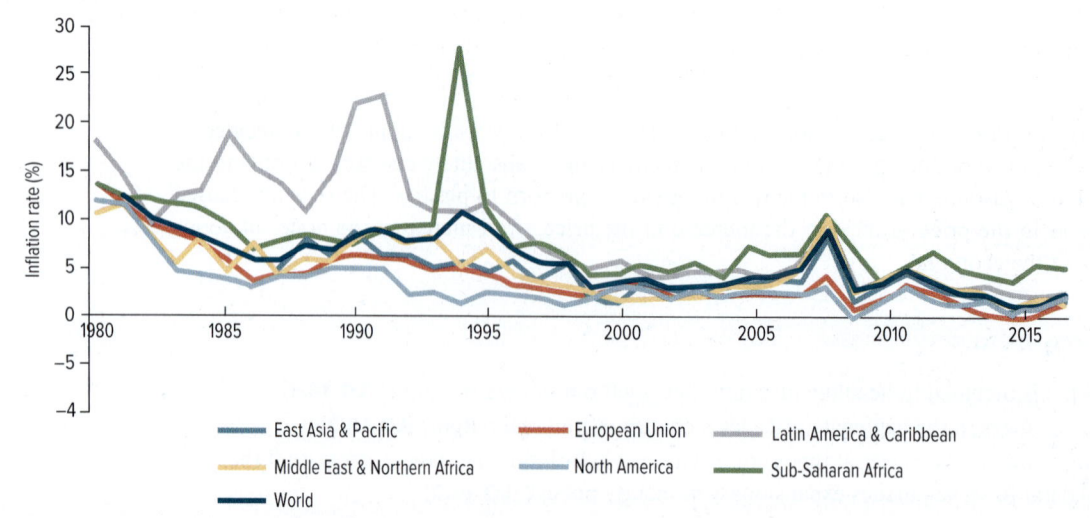

Source: World Bank World Development Indicators, 2019, http://data.worldbank.org/data-catalog/world-development-indicators.

for restaurants, changing prices likely means reprinting menus. Consider a company that runs vending machines and has to send someone out to reprogram every machine when it wants to raise the price of a can of soda. Even if a company has to update only a website, it takes some time and effort.

Inflation also imposes **shoe-leather costs** on the economy. That term refers to the time, money, and effort one has to spend *managing cash* in the face of inflation. Imagine you run a business that involves handling a lot of cash—a grocery store, say. You are likely to handle cash in different ways depending on how stable you think prices are:

- If you know prices are fairly stable, you will be relaxed about keeping cash on your premises if it's more convenient (and safe) to do so. If prices aren't going up much, you won't lose much buying power by holding the cash.
- But if you know prices are going up quickly, you will want to keep as much money as possible in an interest-bearing bank account. You'll earn at least a bit of interest to help offset the loss in buying power due to rising prices. In addition to other hassles, you'll likely waste a lot of time traveling back and forth to the bank to deposit and withdraw cash—wearing out your shoes, hence the name. (And even though with online banking your actual shoes may not wear so thin, the time you spend transferring assets from one form to another could be spent in more profitable ways.)

The third type of cost that inflation imposes on the economy is *tax distortion* (also sometimes called *bracket creep*). This one is a bit more subtle than menu costs and shoe-leather costs but can be costly all the same. Tax distortions happen because tax laws take into consideration only nominal income—not what you can buy with that income. It's easiest to show the consequences with an example. Let's assume that those who earn less than $60,000 a year pay a 10 percent tax on their entire income, and those who earn $60,000 or more pay a 15 percent tax on their entire income. If a family earns $50,000 a year, they pay $5,000 in tax to the government.

But imagine that inflation is 20 percent per year, and the family's income adjusts to exactly keep up with inflation. They now earn $60,000, but their purchasing power is unchanged. All the same, they now have to pay a 15 percent tax rate because they just entered the higher tax bracket. Their bill to the government has now increased to $9,000. The tax system is essentially penalizing the family for inflation.

In theory, the government can adjust tax brackets for inflation. In practice this doesn't always happen. In the United States, the *alternative minimum tax* (AMT) is an example of a tax that has been subject to bracket creep. The AMT was designed to impose taxes on only very wealthy individuals. But because the cutoffs were not adjusted for inflation, millions of Americans who were not super-rich were eventually hit by the tax. In 2013, Congress created new rules that automatically adjust the AMT cutoffs for inflation. The 2017 tax-cut law changed the AMT, substantially cutting the number of taxpayers expected to be hit with the alternative tax (and returning the AMT closer to its original purpose).

Problems of unpredictable inflation We've just considered three costs that occur even when inflation is stable and predictable. While these costs also apply when inflation is unpredictable, there are even worse problems to worry about when inflation is *not* predictable.

In many businesses, the profit margin (the difference between the cost of producing a product and the amount it can be sold for) is less than 10 percent. If the company can't be sure whether the prices of the inputs used to make its product will go up by 5 percent, 10 percent, or 20 percent over the next year, planning becomes tough. Businesses become hesitant to invest in new ideas and to hire workers.

Uncertainty also lies behind a more complex "cost" of inflation, which occurs because changing prices affect interest rates. In general, interest rates will be higher when inflation is higher. Yet this does not mean that savers earn more when inflation is high. To see why, it might help to consider the difference between *nominal* and *real* interest rates:

shoe-leather costs
the costs (measured in time, money, and effort) of managing cash in the face of inflation

nominal interest rate
the reported interest rate, not adjusted for the effects of inflation

- The **nominal interest rate** is the everyday notion of the interest rate. It is the reported interest rate, not adjusted for the effects of inflation. For example, the percentage that the bank pays you for saving (or, if you're borrowing, the percentage that you pay the lender) is the nominal interest rate. Examples of the nominal interest rate can be found in the financial pages of a newspaper such as *The Wall Street Journal* or *The New York Times* or in a loan contract.

real interest rate
the interest rate adjusted for the effects of inflation

- The **real interest rate** is the interest rate adjusted for the anticipated effects of inflation. As we know, inflation means that each dollar becomes less valuable over time.

Since investors do not know, however, the exact inflation rate that will prevail over the duration of the transaction, they need to adjust nominal interest rates for the *expected* rate of inflation. When you're deciding how much to save, you need to look at two things that work in opposite directions:

- How interest will add to the value of your savings.
- How inflation will erode the purchasing power of each dollar in your savings account.

To know which effect is dominant—that is, whether the real value of your money will increase or decrease over time—you can calculate the real interest rate by subtracting the expected inflation rate from the nominal interest rate. Since both rates are typically stated as an annual percentage of the base level, the formula for calculating the real interest rate is simple:

EQUATION 16-4   Real interest rate = Nominal interest rate − Expected inflation rate

To see how important the difference between the nominal and real interest rates can be, look at Table 16-1. It shows an example of the same savings account with two different inflation rates. Suppose that in 2013 you had deposited $1,000 into an account with a nominal annual interest rate of 4 percent, keeping it there for five years. Here's what would happen with varying rates of inflation:

- If there is no inflation, then your real return is equal to the nominal interest rate. In that case you would end up with $1,217 in both 2018 dollars and 2013 dollars.
- If inflation runs at 3 percent per year over the five years, your real interest rate is only 1 percent (4% nominal interest rate − 3% inflation rate). Then, in 2018, you will still have $1,217 in 2018 dollars, but they are worth only $1,051 in 2013 dollars.
- If inflation is 5 percent per year, then the *real* interest rate is negative: 4% nominal interest rate − 5% inflation rate = −1%. In this case, the money in your savings account actually loses value. You again end up with $1,217 at the end of the five-year period in 2018 dollars, but in this case it's worth only $951 in 2013 dollars.

Of course, the reverse situation applies to *borrowers*. Suppose you borrowed $1,000 in 2013 and agreed to pay it back at a rate of 4 percent interest. High inflation is now your friend: If inflation

TABLE 16-1

Real and nominal interest rates

Without inflation, the real and nominal interest rates are the same, so the interest rate you see is what you actually get. With inflation, the real interest you are earning is less than the nominal rate; if inflation is greater than the nominal interest rate, the investment actually becomes worth less in real value than the original investment.

Value in 2013 ($)	Nominal interest rate (%)	Inflation rate (%)	Real interest rate (%)	Nominal 2018 value ($)	Real value in 2018 in 2013 dollars
1,000	4	0	4	1,217	1,217
1,000	4	3	1	1,217	1,051
1,000	4	5	−1	1,217	951

turns out to be 5 percent, then the real value of what you end up paying back is less than the amount you borrowed. That is good news for you!

In other words, when the inflation rate is higher than nominal interest rates, the value of both savings and debts decreases:

- Savers become worse off, as the value of what they have put in the bank becomes less valuable over time.
- Borrowers gain from inflation since inflation reduces the value of dollars; a loan made today will have a smaller value in real terms later. This debt will be easier to repay as its real value decreases.

Effectively, we can say that *high inflation redistributes wealth from those who save to those who borrow*. (We should note, however, that borrowers may eventually suffer if savers/lenders stop making loans entirely because of these losses.)

If inflation is predictable, then this redistributive effect need not happen. Even if inflation is high—say, 20 percent—savers will not lose out as long as banks offer nominal interest rates above 20 percent. However, changes in the inflation rate often come as a surprise, and it can take time for nominal interest rates to adjust. (Storekeepers cannot immediately change all prices, nor can employers immediately change wages.). And as we discussed earlier, there are other costs of inflation that apply even when its timing and amount are predictable.

These same ideas about the economic consequences of inflation apply to governments that have taken on debt and need to repay it. The only difference is that a government can control inflation, at least to some degree, through monetary policy. A government may thus be tempted to slowly "inflate away" the amount of debt it owes. The pros and cons of such a strategy are discussed in the Economics in Action box "Just print money!"

Deflation

Inflation has a natural opposite: deflation. *Deflation* is an overall fall in prices (a decrease in the aggregate price level)—negative inflation, essentially.

LO 16.6 Analyze the economic consequences of deflation.

Periods of deflation occur far less often than inflation, and they generally occur in only the very worst economic circumstances. Deflation characterized the Great Depression of the 1930s, when aggregate prices in the United States fell by nearly half in a few years. More recently, Japan experienced a so-called lost decade of deflation in the 1990s, which continues to pose challenges for its economy.

Why is deflation such a problem? For one thing, it increases the burden of debt. As we saw in the discussion of the problems of unpredictable inflation, most loans are made in nominal terms: If you borrow $100 at an annual interest rate of 5 percent for one year, you will owe $105 at the end of the year. If the price level has gone down due to deflation, the *real* value of that $105 will be even higher. Since paying back loans eats up a greater part of what you can buy in real terms, consumption will decrease.

Of course, the flip-side is that if you are a saver in deflationary times, your savings will be worth more in real terms. In that case, won't savers spend more, given that deflation causes their savings to increase in value? Probably not. If people *expect* deflation, they will likely want to spend less. It's easy to see why: Suppose you expect prices to be 10 percent lower in a few months than they are now. Will you buy that new car now or wait a few months?

The expectation that prices will fall explains at least in part why deflation can cripple an economy. In addition, companies that expect deflation to continue will be less willing to borrow money to invest. They expect the money they borrow will be worth more in real terms when they have to pay it back.

With consumption and investment both down in response to deflation, the net result of expected deflation is to *reduce the level of aggregate demand* in the economy. This, in turn, reduces prices, causing deflation to continue. This self-reinforcing cycle is referred to as a *deflationary spiral*, or deflationary trap.

Just print money!
Economics in Action

Picture this: You're the president of a country in an economic bind. Tax revenues are down. The prospect of economic growth is bleak. You face a growing government debt.

What do you do? You could cut government spending or raise taxes, but both of these options are destined to make you unpopular. Fortunately, your chief economic advisor has an idea: "Just print money! That can solve your debt problems," he says. "With the money we print, we can pay the government's bills."

Zimbabwe, a country in southern Africa, used this scheme to increase military spending, despite a troubled economy. To get out of the bind, the regime headed by Robert Mugabe decided to print more Zimbabwean dollars. Lots more. In 2006, the government printed 21 trillion Zimbabwean dollars (roughly $210 million U.S.) to pay off loans, and another 60 trillion ($600 million U.S.) to pay civil servants and the military.

Did the strategy work? In a sense, yes. The government paid its bills. The problem was that it also unleashed one of the most dramatic episodes of hyperinflation (that is, really, really high rates of inflation) ever seen. Experts estimate that inflation in Zimbabwe reached an incredible *500 billion percent* in 2008! At the worst point, prices were doubling every day. The hyperinflation caused utter chaos that crippled the Zimbabwean economy, leading to an unemployment rate of more than 80 percent.

With inflation spiraling out of control, the government also sharply reduced the real value of the debt the country owed (at least the part of the debt denominated in Zimbabwean dollars). It had successfully inflated away that part of the debt, but the costs for Zimbabwe's population were enormous.

A 100-trillion Zimbabwean dollar note—not enough to buy a gallon of milk!
©Finnbarr Webster/Alamy Stock Photo

Inflating away the debt is not always such a recipe for disaster, though. On a more modest scale, this strategy can have some success. In the 1940s, for example, the United States emerged from World War II with a debt-to-GDP ratio of 108.6 percent. In other words, even if all of the country's income earned during a year was used to pay off the national debt, there still would have been some unpaid debt remaining. According to economists Joshua Aizenman and Nancy Marion, thanks to inflation—which reached 14.4 percent in 1947—that debt ratio was cut by more than a third within a decade. In the meantime, the economy, buoyed by postwar economic activity, posted strong gains.

Even when the economy stays strong, inflation is not an ideal way for a country to reduce debt (although an inflation rate of 14.4 percent is better than 500 billion percent). Debt represents a promise made to lenders, and they stand to lose money if the government decides to print its way out of debt. In the end, nobody is going to want to lend money to a government that has a track record of inflating away its debts.

Still, it's easy to see the attraction of the idea: If you could simply print money to reduce the real value of your personal debts, wouldn't you be just a little bit tempted?

Sources: www.forbes.com/sites/stevehanke/2017/10/28/zimbabwe-hyperinflates-again-entering-the-record-books-for-a-second-time-in-less-than-a-decade/#1c7f7dcb3eed; http://allafrica.com/stories/200602170023.html; http://economix.blogs.nytimes.com/2010/02/18/inflation-wont-solve-our-debt-problems; www.nber.org/papers/w15562.

As we saw in Chapter 15, "Money and the Monetary System," the risk of deflation is an argument against tying a currency to gold. Indeed, the pain caused by deflation was a major populist issue at end of the nineteenth century in America. Under the gold standard, prices were decreasing at the rate of 1 to 2 percent per year. This decrease consistently expanded the debts of borrowers, who were mostly poor farmers. At the 1896 Democratic Party convention, William Jennings Bryan railed against the power of the gold standard to the advantage of savers at the expense of borrowers, in what is now known as the "Cross of Gold" speech. He ended by saying, "You shall not press down upon the brow of labor this crown of thorns, you shall not crucify mankind upon a cross of gold."

Bryan instead advocated for returning to a bimetallic standard, in which silver and gold were both used as money. That change would have resulted in a substantial increase in the money supply and overall prices. This increase would have enabled farmers and workers to be able to pay off their debt more easily. In the end, Bryan's opponent, William McKinley, won the election and formally entrenched the gold standard as official policy of the United States in 1900.

Controlling inflation, or not: Disinflation and hyperinflation

Controlling inflation is a critical role of the Federal Reserve in managing the money supply, part of its dual mandate. When central banks succeed at controlling inflation, *disinflation* occurs. When central banks fail to control runaway inflation, *hyperinflation* occurs. Here, we look at both situations.

LO 16.7 Describe disinflation and hyperinflation, and explain the role of monetary policy in creating both situations.

Disinflation
Let's say the Federal Reserve wants to reduce inflation from 7 percent to 2 percent. If it succeeds, the result is **disinflation**, the term for a period during which overall inflation rates, while still positive, are falling. (Be sure not to get this concept confused with *deflation*, in which inflation rates are negative.)

In general, disinflation is usually discussed in the context of a central bank aggressively trying to contain inflation via contractionary monetary policy. In the United States, the Federal Reserve famously applied disinflationary tactics to slow the increase in prices experienced as a result of the OPEC oil embargo in the 1970s, when inflation hit about 10 percent per year. Efforts to reduce the ballooning inflation rate made little progress—until President Jimmy Carter appointed Paul Volcker as chairman of the Federal Reserve in 1979.

In a direct reversal of his predecessor's policies, Volcker advocated for "shock therapy" to gain control over the double-digit inflation. He bumped the official federal funds rate from 10 percent to 20 percent. Unsurprisingly, because the economywide rise in interest rates made it very expensive to borrow money, this increase in interest rates plunged the economy deep into recession. In protest, a group of farmers drove tractors onto C Street, in the heart of Washington, DC, and blockaded the main entrances of the Federal Reserve building. However, the shock therapy eventually worked. Inflation fell from 10.4 percent in 1981 to below 5 percent in 1983 and has stayed low ever since. Volcker's bold vision caused short-run pain, but it fixed the inflation problem in the long run.

Economists differ over how high inflation has to be before it becomes enough of a problem to merit such painful measures. Some countries have successfully coped with very high inflation (as much as 30 or 40 percent a year) for long periods of time without too much adverse effect on their economy. This is a high-risk situation, though: At such a high rate, inflation is extremely unstable, and it doesn't take much for an economy to slip further toward higher and higher inflation rates.

disinflation
a period in which inflation rates are falling, but still positive

Hyperinflation
When inflation begins to spiral out of control, we say that a country is experiencing **hyperinflation**—extremely long-lasting and painful increases in the price level. Such increases are usually enough to render the currency completely valueless or close to it.

hyperinflation
extremely long-lasting and painful increases in the price level

In one of his first major involvements in public policy, John Maynard Keynes attended the meetings at Versailles that formally ended World War I. During these negotiations, the Allied powers demanded extensive reparation payments from Germany, despite objections from Keynes. Keynes left the Versailles meetings and returned to England to write *The Economic Consequences of the Peace* (1919). This popular work argued that the Versailles treaty demanded more in reparation payments from Germany than the German economy was capable of producing. Keynes predicted that it could lead to political and economic instability and the possibility of hyperinflation in Germany.

Keynes's predictions materialized. While this was not the first or most severe hyperinflation experienced in Europe, it had far-reaching consequences: The resultant political and economic instability helped lead to the collapse of the Weimar Republic and the rise of Nazi Germany.

The worst hyperinflation ever recorded happened in Hungary in 1946. With the economy in ruins after World War II, and tax revenues covering only 15 percent of expenditures, the government began to print money to finance the gap. In January 1946, there were 16,500,000 *pengos* in circulation. By July 1946, there were 1,730,000,000,000,000,000. Prices were doubling approximately every 15 hours. Clearly, this situation was not sustainable. In August 1946 the government abandoned the *pengo* and introduced a new currency, the *forint*, which is still in circulation today. By backing the new currency with gold, the government instilled confidence that it would not print huge amounts of forints.

Expectations can also perpetuate hyperinflation. In Brazil during the 1990s, prices rose in part because everyone simply expected them to keep rising. The increase was slowed only by an unorthodox plan that included an entirely fake currency. The story can be found in the Economics in Action box "A *real* plan—with fake currency."

Imagine the complications of hyperinflation in daily life. This Zimbabwean man, at the height of the country's hyperinflation, is carrying enough money to buy some milk.
©Tsvangirayi Mukwazhi/AP Images

A *real* plan—with fake currency
Economics in Action

In 1993, President Itamar Franco of Brazil appointed Fernando Henrique Cardoso to be the country's fourth finance minister within seven months. As the rate of turnover suggests, it was not an enviable job. Price levels in Brazil had been steadily rising for seven years, and the inflation rate was approaching 2,000 percent per year. If he wanted to keep his job, Cardoso had to tackle the hyperinflation quickly. No one had high hopes for his success, though. Cardoso was a professor of sociology, with little training in economics. Furthermore, years of failed efforts had convinced Brazilians that the hyperinflation was invincible to government efforts.

Cardoso sought help from an academic economist named Edmar Bacha, who had been debating with colleagues about how to tame Brazil's stubbornly high inflation. Observing that the traditional tactics used to fight inflation—freezes on prices and wages—had been unsuccessful, they proposed an elegant, if slightly unorthodox solution: Brazil would create a system of fake money, called "units of real value," or URVs for short.

The plan, dubbed *Plano Real* in Portuguese or "Real Plan," worked as follows: Cardoso required everyone in the economy—grocery stores, the government, retail outlets, and all other businesses—to quote prices in both *cruzeiros* (the Brazilian currency at the time) and URVs. Even contracts with promises for future payment had to quote the payment in URVs as well as *cruzeiros*. People would pay in *cruzeiros* but would always see the price in URVs as well.

Changing conversion rates would ensure that the URV price remained stable: If prices doubled, the conversion rate between *cruzeiros* and URVs would halve, so that prices in URVs would remain the same. For example, the price shown on a pint of milk might increase from 1,000 *cruzeiros* to 2,000 *cruzeiros*, but the price in URVs shown alongside would remain the same.

How could this simple accounting trick possibly help to get inflation under control? The genius of the idea is that it tackled what economists call the *psychological inertia* of hyperinflation. As inflation rises and rises, and all government efforts visibly fail to reduce it, people simply get used to the idea that things can only get worse. Businesses raise prices merely because they expect that prices will keep rising. When enough businesses do this, it becomes a self-fulfilling prophecy. A vicious cycle ensues.

The *Plano Real* broke this cycle. Since prices in URVs were stable, people began to trust that they would *stay* stable. Once trust in the stability of URVs developed, the government simply traded out the untrustworthy *cruzeiros* for a new currency called the *real*, which is still in use today. The government explained that one *real* was worth one URV. Convinced through experience that URV prices were stable, people expected *real* prices to be stable as well. And because they *expected* prices to be stable, they were—relatively speaking, at least. In the first few years after the *real* was introduced, inflation fell to under 20 percent.

And what of Fernando Henrique Cardoso, whose job prospects as finance minister originally seemed so uncertain? A grateful nation promptly elected him president.

Sources: www.econ.puc-rio.br/gfranco/rptpd.pdf; http://uk.reuters.com/article/2011/07/02/uk-brazil-president-idUKTRE76119A20110702.

Why a little inflation is good

If deflation is bad and inflation is bad, then central banks must try to achieve perfect price stability with an inflation rate of zero, right? Wrong. In fact, for most central banks around the world, the preferred monetary policy is to promote modest positive inflation—something around 2 or 3 percent per year.

Why do most economists believe it's better to aim for modest inflation than completely stable prices? There are three main reasons.

The first reason to favor modest inflation over completely stable prices is that allowing for a little inflation reduces the risk of deflation. If the inflation rate tends to hover around zero percent, and the central bank miscalculates by making monetary policy too contractionary, the result would be deflation—which can have serious impacts on the economy. Keeping inflation at a modest positive level gives a central bank some leeway to make mistakes, without running the risk of tipping the country into a deflationary spiral.

Second, keeping inflation at a modest positive level leaves more room for the central bank to engage in expansionary monetary policy. To understand why, we can work through a simple example. Suppose that inflation is at a healthy 3 percent per year. Investors are going to want an interest rate that is at or above the inflation rate to ensure that the real rate of return they earn on their money is positive. For monetary policy, this means that the overall interest rate will likely end up somewhere at or above 3 percent. This gives the Federal Reserve some room to reduce interest rates before hitting the *zero lower bound* (the natural lower limit on the interest rate).

By contrast, if inflation was zero percent, nominal interest rates would be close to zero as well. In the case of a recession, a central bank would have very little leeway to further reduce interest

LO 16.8 Understand why policymakers favor a small amount of inflation over zero inflation.

rates in an effort to stimulate the economy. (This situation is sometimes referred to as a *liquidity trap*. It has been a major problem in Japan for more than a decade.)

In fact, during the latest financial crisis, Olivier Blanchard, the former chief economist of the International Monetary Fund (IMF), advised central banks to increase their inflation target from the traditional 2 percent to 4 percent. That extra room, he argued, could mean the difference between effectively fighting a deep recession and hitting the zero lower bound while the economy could still use some help from monetary policy.[3]

A third reason for having a positive inflation target is that the target makes it easier for firms to adjust real wages in the labor market in response to changing labor demand and supply conditions. Reductions in labor demand or labor supply result in reductions in the equilibrium real wage. If prices are stable, reducing the real wage requires employers to reduce the nominal wage; workers may respond to a 1 percent reduction in their nominal pay by reducing their work effort. But workers generally seem less bothered if they receive a 2 percent wage increase when there is 3 percent inflation. The effect is the same—a 1 percent reduction in income—but the cause of the reduced income seems different.

Furthermore, in cases in which there is a formal labor contract, nominal wages cannot be reduced during the life of the contract. With a low inflation rate, though, all that is required for firms to lower real wages is to increase nominal wages more slowly than the inflation rate. Thus, a low and stable inflation rate may help to "grease the wheels" of the labor market, allowing for more flexible real wages and more efficient labor markets.

✓ TEST YOURSELF

- ☐ Why would people at the highest income level not worry about bracket creep? **[LO 16.5]**
- ☐ Why do people spend less in the present when deflation is expected in the future? **[LO 16.6]**
- ☐ What is a reduction in the overall rate of inflation known as? **[LO 16.7]**
- ☐ Why would lenders favor unexpected deflation, while borrowers favor unexpected inflation? **[LO 16.7]**
- ☐ Why does the "zero lower bound" cause problems for macroeconomic policy? **[LO 16.8]**

Inflation and Monetary Policy

We've discussed the Federal Reserve's dual mandate in conducting monetary policy: maintaining price stability and ensuring full employment. Maintaining price stability is, of course, another way of saying that inflation rates should be consistently low. Ensuring full employment simply means that the economy experiences only frictional and structural unemployment and no cyclical unemployment. For a review of these terms, you can flip back to Chapter 9, "Unemployment and the Labor Market."

LO 16.9 Explain the relationship between inflation, the output gap, and monetary policy.

The competing goals of the dual mandate

In practice, the goals of the dual mandate are often incompatible. That's because prices and employment move in the same direction—prices generally will not increase while employment decreases, and vice versa. To understand why maintaining strong employment and low prices is difficult, it helps to think about how inflation rates change through a typical business cycle.

During a recession, inflation is typically very low. Why is that? During an economic downturn, the economy is operating well below its potential. Economists refer to an economy's **potential output** as the total amount of output the country could reasonably produce if all of its people and capital resources (i.e., machines and factories and the like) were fully engaged. In practice, this means that only frictional and structural unemployment—no cyclical unemployment—occur when the economy is achieving its potential output.

potential output the total amount of output a country could produce if all of its resources were fully engaged

The output gap and inflation However, an economy's actual output can differ from its potential output at some point in time. When that occurs, we say that the economy is experiencing an **output gap**. An output gap can be negative or positive:

- If output is below potential, then the output gap is *negative*. Resources—either factories or workers—are not being fully used. Workers are unemployed and factories are sitting idle, waiting for work.
- When an economy is working above capacity, we say that it has a *positive* output gap. Factories and workers are not only fully employed but also working overtime.

> **output gap**
> the difference between actual and potential output in an economy

Figure 16-5 shows the historical output gap for the United States. For the most part, actual output has been below potential output (a negative output gap).

What is going on when an economy has a negative output gap? As we've said, resources are not being fully used. Workers are unemployed and factories are sitting idle. In other words, the economy is experiencing recessionary conditions. During recessionary periods, there is typically little threat of a rise in inflation (unless the economy is hit by an oil crisis or similar external shock). Low rates of inflation occur in part because there is so little demand for money in an economy experiencing recession:

- Borrowers, for example, are less interested in taking out loans for big-ticket items during a recession since they are less confident in their ability to pay back the loans.
- Firms have little incentive to borrow in an effort to expand their businesses when overall demand for goods and services is low. Why produce if you don't assume there will be buyers for the output you make?

As long as the supply of money stays the same in a recession, decreased demand causes the overall price level to fall.

But what happens when the economy is experiencing a positive output gap? With nearly everyone employed (and working overtime):

- Hiring new workers can become very expensive. Employers have to compete for workers, who can eventually command higher salaries to switch jobs.

FIGURE 16-5

The output gap in the United States The output gap registers the difference between the actual GDP and the potential GDP at full employment. For the most part, actual output has stayed below potential output.

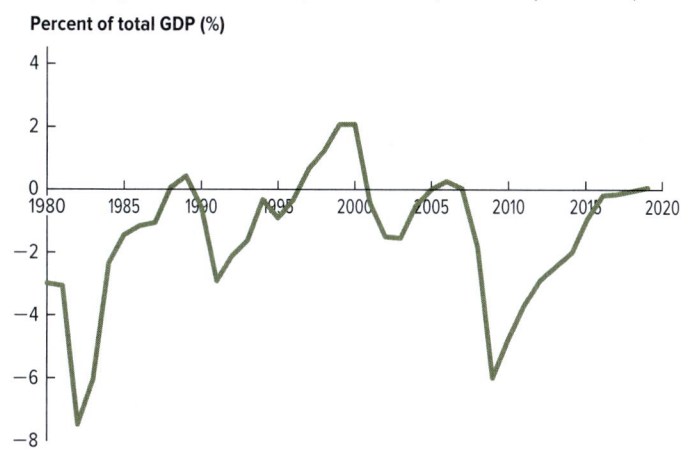

Sources: IMF World Economic Outlook database, http://data.okfn.org/data/core/imf-weo#data; www.quandl.com/data/ODA/USA_NGAP_NPGDP-United-States-Output-Gap-of-potential-GDP.

- Likewise, firms are competing to buy machines, factories, or other inputs to meet soaring demand for their products. That competition leads to a rise in the prices of those inputs as well.

Rising prices across the economy, of course, mean inflation.

The output gap and monetary policy   As you can see, there is typically a strong relationship between the output gap and inflation. What does this have to do with monetary policy? To answer that question, we'll have to go back to what happens when the Fed conducts monetary policy.

We'll start with *expansionary monetary policy*. In a recession, an output gap implies that employment is low. A central bank knows that it can fix this problem by engaging in expansionary monetary policy: It increases the money supply and lowers interest rates. As a result, borrowing may increase, which may then help the economy rebound. An increase in economic activity puts more people back to work, which fulfills the mandate: Prices have increased only a little bit, and employment is high.

But as you know, this is only a short-run equilibrium. The increased demand for goods and services will put upward pressure on prices. With an increase in the money supply, more money will be spent chasing the same amount of goods. The economy will eventually fall back to the long-run equilibrium. Employment will decrease, but prices will remain elevated. So what does a central bank do? It could continue to pump money into the economy in an effort to increase employment, but these gains will be short lived and inflation will worsen.

The opposite scenario occurs when inflation is above normal. When inflation is pulled high by demand, money in the economy is spent chasing a limited amount of goods. Firms want to buy machines and inputs in an effort to expand operations, while workers receive higher wages. In this case, employment is at full, or even beyond full, capacity. If a central bank decides that it needs to curb inflation, it will pursue *contractionary monetary policy:* It will reduce the growth rate of the money supply to work toward a higher interest rate. As we described earlier, this action slows the economy. The higher interest rate makes borrowing more expensive, and firms slow investment. Although inflation decreases, the slowing of the economy increases unemployment. Eventually, though, as the economy adjusts to lower prices and we move into the long run, employment will return to full-output levels, leaving just the decrease in overall prices.

So, you can see that central banks, no matter how they conduct monetary policy, inevitably *affect only price levels*, with no lasting impact on employment in the long run:

- Attempts to stimulate the economy through expansionary monetary policy will increase the inflation rate.
- Attempts to slow the economy through contractionary policy will lower the inflation rate, and risk causing deflation.

The Federal Reserve has to navigate this trade-off carefully.

Inflation and unemployment

LO 16.10 Explain how the relationship between inflation and unemployment is modeled by the Phillips curve and integrated into the non-accelerating inflation rate of unemployment.

We've seen that there is a trade-off between inflation and unemployment in the short run, which poses a challenge for the Federal Reserve's dual mandate. Ensuring full employment is really another way of saying "keeping actual output near potential output." Fulfilling this mandate through expansionary monetary policy, however, risks violating the Fed's other mandate, that of price stability. How can the Fed calculate the best way to make this trade-off?

The Phillips curve   In 1958, an economist named A. W. Phillips plotted the change in prices against unemployment over a 95-year period in Great Britain. A distinct pattern emerged:

- As inflation ran higher, unemployment was low.
- When inflation was low, unemployment was high.

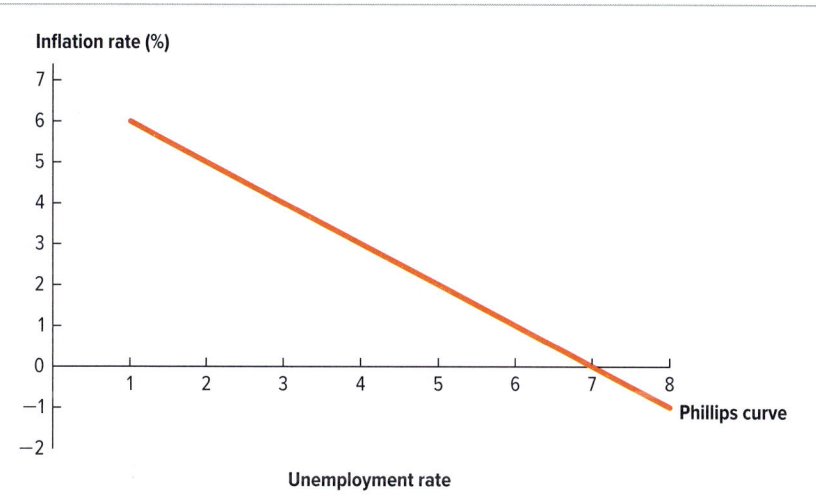

Inflation ■ Chapter 16   447

FIGURE 16-6
Hypothetical short-run Phillips curve for an economy

[Graph: Inflation rate (%) on y-axis ranging from -2 to 7; Unemployment rate on x-axis from 1 to 8. A downward-sloping orange line labeled "Phillips curve" runs from approximately (1, 6) to (8, -1).]

The short-run Phillips curve shows a direct relationship between the inflation rate and the unemployment rate. In an economy that is humming along, prices will increase at a faster rate, although unemployment will be low. As the unemployment rate increases, prices increase far more slowly.

The line showing that relationship is now called the **Phillips curve**, and it forms the basis of a model that shows the connection between inflation and unemployment in the short run.

Figure 16-6 shows the most basic form of the Phillips curve. The curve, based on hypothetical data, shows that if the central bank of this economy wants zero inflation, then it will have to accept 7 percent unemployment. If it wants to target a modest positive rate of inflation of, for example, 3 percent, then it will have to accept 4 percent unemployment. If it wants to get unemployment down as low as 1 percent, it will have to accept a rate of inflation of 6 percent. And so on.

We can now further investigate this relationship using the aggregate demand and aggregate supply (AD/AS) model in the short run, as shown in panels A and B of Figure 16-7. If the economy is at short-run equilibrium with 4 percent unemployment and 3 percent inflation, an increase in aggregate demand above expectations is going to cause the economy to be at a point higher and to the left on the Phillips curve.

However, this basic Phillips curve fails to consider an important factor: the role of *inflation expectations*. In any economy, people often come to expect whatever level of inflation has prevailed over the past few years. If inflation has been about 3 percent over the past few years, then the expectation of 3 percent inflation typically becomes "baked into" prices. If prices are rising by 3 percent per year, employees will expect raises of at least 3 percent as a matter of course, and 3 percent inflation becomes sort of a "default" for the economy.

Why does this matter? Let's assume that the economy represented in Figure 16-5 is humming along at a *long-run equilibrium* of 4 percent unemployment and 3 percent inflation. Now imagine that the central bank decides to try to reduce unemployment, accepting a slightly higher inflation rate as a result: By expanding the money supply, unemployment falls to 1 percent and inflation increases to 6 percent.

So far, the central bank has achieved the results it hoped for. However, we know that the economy was in long-run equilibrium at 4 percent unemployment. And we know from Figure 16-1, earlier in the chapter, what happens if a central bank pursues expansionary monetary policy when the economy is already at long-run equilibrium: It can increase output (and, hence, reduce unemployment), but *only in the short run*. In the long run, output returns to its earlier equilibrium, and so do levels of employment.

Phillips curve
a model that shows the connection between inflation and unemployment in the short run

FIGURE 16-7
Aggregate demand and the Phillips curve in the short run

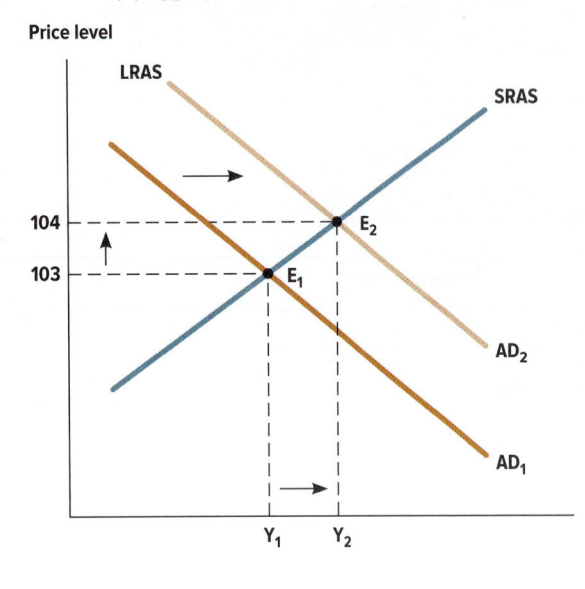

(A) Aggregate demand and aggregate supply

(Graph showing Price level vs. Real GDP (trillions of dollars). Curves: LRAS, SRAS, AD₁, AD₂. Equilibrium points E₁ at price 103, output Y₁, and E₂ at price 104, output Y₂.)

(B) Phillips curve

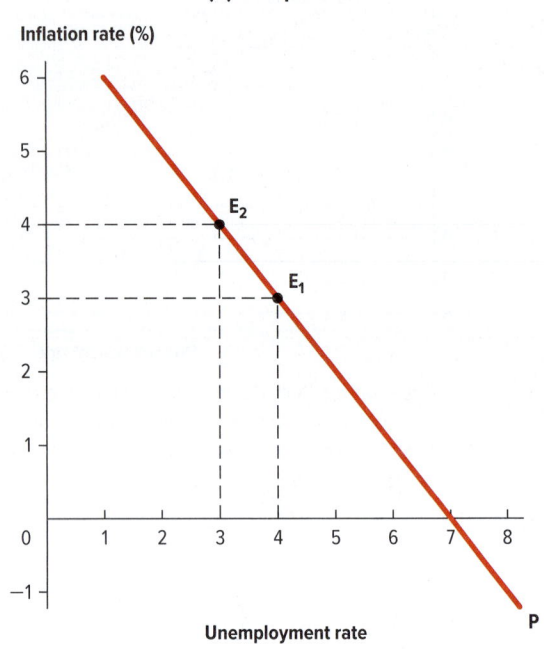

(Graph showing Inflation rate (%) vs. Unemployment rate. Downward-sloping red curve labeled P. Point E₂ at (3, 4) and point E₁ at (4, 3).)

Panel A shows the result of two different aggregate demand curves. E₁ shows a short-run equilibrium with lower prices and output than point E₂ on a higher aggregate demand curve.

With more economic activity, point E₂ on the Phillips curve shows higher inflation and lower unemployment than point E₁, which represents the short-run equilibrium with lower economic activity.

Our hypothetical central bank finds that unemployment is now back at 4 percent, but inflation is now running at 6 percent. Effectively, by pursuing expansionary monetary policy when the economy was already at long-run equilibrium, it has shifted the Phillips curve upward, as shown in Figure 16-8.

People in our hypothetical economy now *expect* inflation of 6 percent. What happens if the central bank, stubbornly, has another go at reducing unemployment to 1 percent? It will succeed in the short run, but as we can see from the new Phillips curve, inflation will go up to 9 percent (see point D). And in the long run, unemployment will rise again to 4 percent, but inflation will remain stubbornly at 9 percent because people will have adjusted their inflation expectations upward once again.

Eventually, the central bank's efforts would simply spiral out of control, leading to more and more inflation and the unemployment rate never staying at the bank's goal in the long run.

Realizing this effect, economists proposed an improved version of the Phillips curve—one that also shows the long-run effect of changing inflation expectations. We'll now call the traditional Phillips curve the *short-run* Phillips curve. The new, improved version we call the *long-run* Phillips curve.

Figure 16-9 shows two short-run Phillips curves (P₁ and P₂) and the long-run Phillips curve (the vertical line) for two different levels of inflation expectations. The vertical line in the figure is the long-run Phillips curve, which is at 4 percent. This line represents the idea that in the long run in our hypothetical economy, it is impossible to get the level of unemployment below 4 percent. Economists call this minimum level of unemployment the **non-accelerating inflation rate of unemployment (NAIRU)**. The NAIRU is sometimes also called the *natural rate of unemployment* or simply *full employment* (even though it's not technically 0 percent unemployment).

non-accelerating inflation rate of unemployment (NAIRU) the lowest possible unemployment rate that will not cause the inflation rate to increase

Inflation • Chapter 16 • 449

FIGURE 16-8
The Phillips curve responds to inflation expectations

1. When the central bank increases short-run aggregate demand, unemployment initially falls (A→B).

2. However, once the economy returns to the long-run equilibrium, unemployment returns to the same level while inflation stays the same (B→C).

3. If the central bank again tries to reduce unemployment, it will succeed in the short run, but inflation will go up (C→D). The economy would return to long-run equilibrium and the pattern would continue with every effort.

With preset expectations in the economy, the Phillips curve shifts upward by the amount of expected inflation. This means that the amount of inflation at any given amount of unemployment rises in the long run by the amount of expected inflation.

FIGURE 16-9
The long-run Phillips curve (NAIRU)

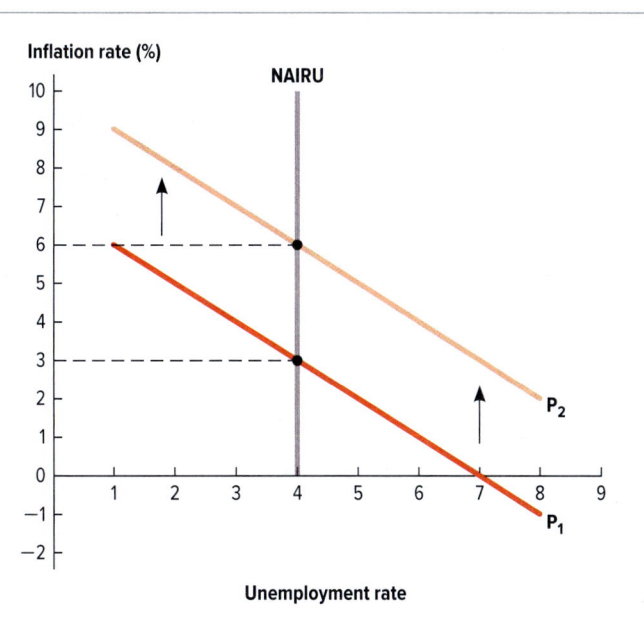

The long-run Phillips curve represents the fact that there is no trade-off between inflation and unemployment in the long run.

The NAIRU can change over time. Take, for example, the introduction of the internet to job searches. This innovation reduced structural unemployment (and the NAIRU) on two fronts:

- It increased opportunities available to searchers. Before the availability of sites like monster.com and indeed.com (which allow you to search millions of job listings), job hunters had to scour local classifieds and attend job fairs. They essentially confined their searches to opportunities within a very narrow geographical range. With the internet, that range has been greatly expanded.
- The internet has also been a boon to employers. Today, a job posting on the internet will be seen by more job seekers and bring forward a wider pool of high-quality applicants.

Both job seekers and employers have a wider range of opportunities, with an attendant reduction in the NAIRU.

In practice, calculating the exact NAIRU is difficult. It differs among economies and over time due to variations in the structural components of unemployment, the regulatory and competitive environment, and a multitude of other factors. As a result, it can be difficult to know whether an economy is truly at full employment at any given time—which is a challenge for Federal Reserve policy-makers looking to fulfill their dual mandate. Though we may not know the *exact* location of the NAIRU, we can fairly quickly determine if we are above or below it, though:

- If unemployment is below the NAIRU, inflation generally accelerates.
- If we observe involuntary unemployment rising, unemployment is above the NAIRU.

The Phillips curve and NAIRU in practice To understand how the NAIRU and Phillips curve work in practice, we'll return to the story from earlier in the chapter of monetary policy after the OPEC oil embargo. When the oil embargo hit, the aggregate supply curve shifted sharply to the left. At that short-run equilibrium, prices were higher and output lower. Obviously, this combination was not desirable for policy-makers; it meant either permitting high rates of inflation, in order to keep unemployment in check, or slowing the economy even further in order to rein in inflation.

During the 1970s, the Federal Reserve chose the first path. The Fed thought that unemployment was a greater danger to the economy than was inflation. The Fed even expanded the money supply to try to pick up the economy after the supply shock. As time wore on, inflation pushed higher and higher, but unemployment stayed relatively the same. You now know why: The economy had shifted to a higher Phillips curve. Since inflation was *expected* in the economy, further attempts to boost the economy simply pushed the trade-off between inflation and unemployment even higher.

By the end of the 1970s, inflation was running at double digits, with high unemployment. Figure 16-10 shows this adjustment upward toward higher Phillips curves, from an inflation rate of about 4 percent in the early 1970s to the double-digit rate by 1979. While inflation in this period was high, demand was sluggish and the U.S. economy experienced two periods of recession. Observers coined the term *stagflation* (a combination of the words "stagnant" and "inflation") to describe the phenomenon of high inflation despite low economic growth and high unemployment.

When Paul Volcker became Fed chairman in 1979, he realized that shock therapy was needed to wean the economy off the expectation that inflation would continue to increase at relatively high rates. He employed the traditional tool used to fight inflation: Volcker decreased the money supply through increases in interest rates.

This blunt policy worked. Since people knew that the Fed was going to take a tough stand on inflation, expectations for price increases in the future evaporated. In just five years, the overall economy was in a position with a far more favorable trade-off between inflation and unemployment. In Figure 16-11 you can see the change in Phillips curves over this time period, resulting from a decrease in the inflation rate of about 14 percent in 1980 to a much tamer rate of about 4 percent in 1985.

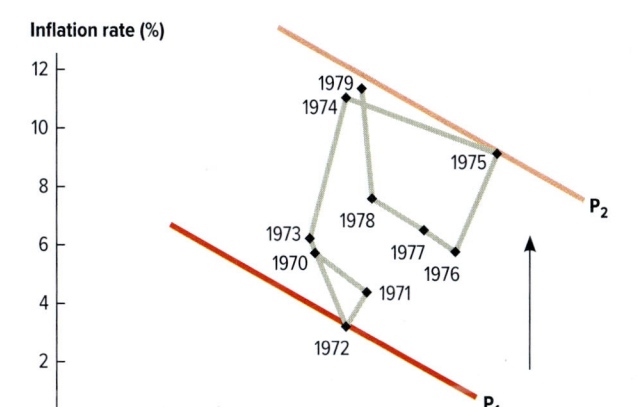

FIGURE 16-10
The Phillips curve winds upward

When the Fed tried to battle unemployment by allowing higher inflation, it eventually found that it had simply put the economy on a higher Phillips curve (P_2), as shown above.

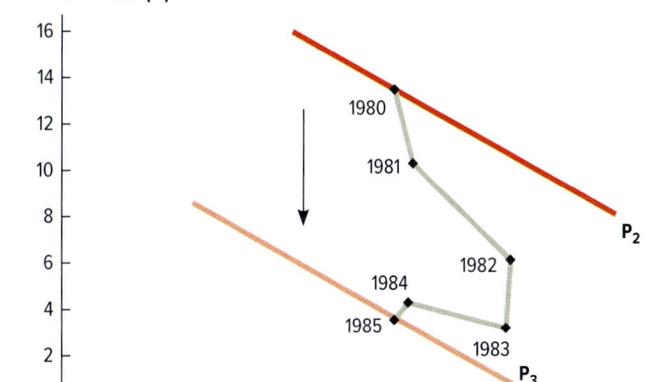

FIGURE 16-11
The Phillips curve adjusts downward

When Paul Volcker became Fed chairman, inflation was running above 12 percent. In the early 1980s, he led an effort to raise interest rates, thereby decreasing the money supply and bringing down inflation. By 1985, the economy was on a lower Phillips curve (P_3).

The Phillips curve remains an essential tool for understanding how the Fed's dual mandate works in practice. Effectively, fulfillment of the mandate for full employment means ensuring that employment remains as close to the NAIRU as possible at all times. Pushing unemployment below that level all but guarantees that inflation will get out of control, violating the dual mandate by failing to maintain price stability. On the other hand, allowing unemployment to remain at a higher level than NAIRU would mean failing to maintain full employment, also violating the dual mandate.

The Fed's aim, then, is to keep unemployment levels near the NAIRU and inflation reasonably under control. As the story of the oil embargo shows, managing this trade-off is no easy task.[4]

✓ TEST YOURSELF

☐ What does it mean for the output gap to be positive? What will eventually happen if that occurs? [**LO 16.9**]

☐ What happens if unemployment is lower than the NAIRU? [**LO 16.10**]

Conclusion

In this chapter we've explored one of the most complex issues in economics: inflation. We've seen how mismanagement of the money supply can lead to runaway inflation, how even relatively modest inflation can have far-reaching consequences for healthy economies, and why deflation is a problem. We've also seen that expectations of inflation help determine whether savings will hold their value and whether it's a good time to borrow.

We've seen too that when people expect inflation to continue, those beliefs can, in themselves, perpetuate inflation. Thus, inflation can be a self-fulfilling prophecy. Getting runaway inflation under control thus requires the right monetary policy plus convincing people that inflation will indeed fall.

Key Terms

inflation, p. 428
deflation, p. 428
headline inflation, p. 429
core inflation, p. 429
aggregate price level, p. 430
neutrality of money, p. 430
quantity theory of money, p. 432

quantity equation, p. 432
velocity of money, p. 432
menu costs, p. 436
shoe-leather costs, p. 437
nominal interest rate, p. 438
real interest rate, p. 438
disinflation, p. 441

hyperinflation, p. 441
potential output, p. 444
output gap, p. 445
Phillips curve, p. 447
non-accelerating inflation rate of unemployment (NAIRU), p. 448

Summary

LO 16.1 Define inflation, deflation, headline inflation, and core inflation.

Inflation is an overall rise in prices in the economy. *Deflation* is an overall fall in prices in the economy. Economists measure inflation or deflation by calculating the percentage change in the CPI. This is the ratio of the cost of the market basket in a given year to the cost of that same basket in a base year.

Two different measures of inflation are used: *Headline inflation* is the measure of inflation that includes all of the goods that the average consumer buys. *Core inflation* is the measure of inflation minus goods with historically volatile price changes (energy and food). The BLS's official measure uses core inflation because it is less likely to reflect shocks to individual product markets and more likely to show economywide inflation.

LO 16.2 Explain the neutrality of money.

Prices denote the nominal value of goods; the price level reflects prices when aggregated across the economy. The *neutrality of money* suggests that the money supply affects price levels throughout the economy, but in the long run has no effect on real variables in the economy, such as output. The neutrality of money implies that if the money supply suddenly doubled, nominal GDP would double as well, but real GDP would remain the same.

LO 16.3 Describe and illustrate the classical theory of inflation.

The *classical theory of inflation* describes the relationship between the money supply, output, and the price level. The theory argues that the money supply has no effect on output in the long run. However, it shows how adjusting the money supply can change output in the short run. If the Federal Reserve adopts expansionary policy, it could increase the money supply, shifting the aggregate demand curve to the right and causing output and prices to increase. The effect on the cost of production and anticipation that these high prices will continue causes the aggregate supply curve to shift leftward until it intersects the demand curve at the original level of output.

LO 16.4 Explain the quantity theory of money, and relate it to inflation and deflation.

The *quantity theory of money* shows the relationship between the value of money in terms of the output we can buy and the quantity of it. Mathematically, the quantity theory of money indicates that the product of the velocity of money and the money supply (total spending) is identical to the product of the price level and real output (nominal GDP).

Changes in the quantity of money affect the price level: An increase in the money supply leads to inflation; a decrease in the money supply leads to deflation.

LO 16.5 Analyze the economic consequences of inflation.

Inflation is an increase in the price level in an economy. Over the long run, inflation is often caused by increases in the money supply. In the short run, it is more often a result of the business cycle. If inflation rates are unstable, they introduce uncertainty into the market, often causing a decline in output. Even a stable rate of inflation can impose costs on the economy, including *menu costs, shoe-leather costs*, and *bracket creep*.

LO 16.6 Analyze the economic consequences of deflation.

In contrast to inflation, deflation is a fall in the price level of an economy. Deflation is considered more dangerous than inflation. When prices are falling, borrowers have a more difficult time paying back their debts; deflation makes the debt more expensive over time, often causing borrowers to default. High default rates, in turn, lower prices, causing further defaults. A deflationary spiral often ensues, halting the economy.

LO 16.7 Describe disinflation and hyperinflation, and explain the role of monetary policy in creating both situations.

When central banks succeed at controlling inflation, disinflation often occurs. *Disinflation* happens when inflation rates are positive but falling. A famous example of disinflation was Paul Volcker's efforts to stem inflation in the 1980s.

When central banks fail to control inflation, hyperinflation can occur. *Hyperinflation* is an extreme rise in price levels. It can cause economic crisis and drastically reduce the value of a country's currency.

LO 16.8 Understand why policy-makers favor a small amount of inflation over zero inflation.

Although you might think that central banks want to achieve perfect price stability with an inflation rate of zero, most central banks around the world actually prefer modest positive inflation of around 2 or 3 percent per year. There are a few reasons for this. For starters, a little inflation reduces the risk of deflation, giving the central bank some leeway in case their monetary policy is too contractionary. Second, keeping inflation at a modest positive level leaves more room for the central bank to engage in expansionary monetary policy. Finally, positive inflation makes it easier for firms to adjust real wages in response to changing labor demand and supply conditions.

LO 16.9 Explain the relationship between inflation, the output gap, and monetary policy.

The central bank uses monetary policy to control inflation. Central banks prefer to keep inflation low but positive. When full employment occurs, the economy is said to be producing at its *potential output*, the total amount of output a country can produce if its resources are used efficiently.

The *output gap* is the difference between potential and actual output. When the output gap is negative, inflation will decrease. Central banks will then pursue expansionary monetary policy by lowering interest rates, allowing inflation to rise and bringing back full employment. When the output gap is positive, inflation will increase.

LO 16.10 Explain how the relationship between inflation and unemployment is modeled by the Phillips curve and integrated into the non-accelerating inflation rate of unemployment.

This relationship between employment and inflation in the short run is modeled by the *Phillips curve*. The curve shows that a decrease in unemployment will be accompanied by an increase in inflation in the short run. The relationship does not hold over the long run, in part because of inflation expectations. If central banks pursue aggressive expansionary policy to reduce unemployment, inflation may spiral out of control.

The level of unemployment at which inflation will remain stable is called the *non-accelerating inflation rate of unemployment (NAIRU)*, or full employment.

Review Questions

1. What is the difference between the Consumer Price Index and the inflation rate? **[LO 16.1]**

2. What is the difference between core inflation and headline inflation? Why do economists calculate both types of inflation? **[LO 16.1]**

3. Your uncle comes to you with an investment idea. He tells you that the nominal GDP of Paradisia quadrupled over the past year and suggests that you invest there. Unemployment is at 20 percent, and inflation over the last year was 500 percent. Do you think it's a good idea to invest? Draw on the neutrality theory of money to explain why or why not. **[LO 16.2]**

4. Why might we want to measure GDP in dollar terms? In output terms? How does the neutrality of money relate to your answer? [LO 16.2]

5. Suppose a country's currency is a gold coin. One day, speculators find a large gold mine, which doubles the supply of gold coins in the economy. What will happen to output in the short run? What about price levels? What will happen to output in the long run? What about price levels? [LO 16.3]

6. Explain how some analysts might use the short-run and long-run effects on the aggregate demand–aggregate supply model to argue that monetary policy can't affect employment in the long run. [LO 16.3]

7. Why might the velocity of money increase around the holidays? If the Federal Reserve wants to avoid inflation in those times, what should it do? [LO 16.4]

8. Use the quantity theory of money to explain how expansionary monetary policy can be inflationary. [LO 16.4]

9. Imagine you own an ice cream store in New York City. Write a brief note to your senators explaining two ways in which unpredictable inflation hurts your business. [LO 16.5]

10. Is inflation harmful only when it's unexpected? If yes, why? If no, name two costs that occur with even predictable inflation. [LO 16.5]

11. Your senators now claim that lowering prices would be good for everyone—"Who doesn't like lower prices, after all?" They tell you they plan to lobby for deflation. Explain why falling prices could lead to a bad situation. [LO 16.6]

12. When does inflation become hyperinflation? What causes hyperinflation? [LO 16.6]

13. What could have happened to prices and inflation in the years during and after the 2007–2009 recession if the government and the Federal Reserve had not intervened in the economy? How would this have affected the economy? [LO 16.7]

14. Are deflation and disinflation the same thing? Why or why not? [LO 16.7]

15. Would you expect nominal interest rates to be higher in countries that have higher target inflation rates? Why or why not? [LO 16.8]

16. Your friend claims that a target inflation rate of zero is a good policy because this will keep prices stable. You claim a positive target inflation rate is preferred because the country will be able to better avoid a liquidity trap. Who is right? [LO 16.8]

17. In the 1960s, policy based on the simple short-run Phillips curve worked better than similar attempts in the 1970s. How might better information availability have contributed to this result? [LO 16.9]

18. When we have a negative output gap, what is the proper monetary policy response in the short run? What are its intended effects on interest rates and employment? [LO 16.9]

19. Explain the effect contractionary monetary policy will have on the output gap, inflation, and unemployment if unemployment is currently at the non-accelerating inflation rate of unemployment. [LO 16.10]

20. Compare and contrast the effect of increased unemployment on inflation in the short and long run. [LO 16.10]

Problems and Applications

1. Two series of hypothetical price index values used to calculate headline and core inflation for 2014 through 2018 are found in Table 16P-1. [LO 16.1]

TABLE 16P-1

Year	Series 1	Series 2
2014	134.00	125.00
2015	137.22	127.56
2016	141.26	129.68
2017	146.24	132.72
2018	148.81	135.72

a. Calculate the annual inflation rate for each series.

b. Which series represents core inflation and which represents headline inflation? How do you know?

c. Is there inflation or deflation in each year?

2. Determine whether each of the following events is likely to cause deflation, disinflation, no change in the price level, or inflation. [LO 16.1]

a. A bubble in the biomedical industry just burst.

b. A new technology is introduced into the economy, sparking an economic boom.

c. The Federal Reserve conducts contractionary monetary policy.

d. The Federal Reserve is successful at meeting its dual mandate of full employment and price stability.

3. Which of the following can be affected by the money supply in the long run? [LO 16.2]

a. Nominal GDP.
b. Real GDP.
c. Inflation.
d. Unemployment.

4. The average individual in a country earns an annual salary of $62,000, of which $24,800 is spent on housing, $11,160 on food, $11,160 on transportation, and $14,880 on other goods and services. Suppose the government in this country mandates that all salaries and the prices of all goods and services be reduced by 40 percent. **[LO 16.2]**

   a. How much does the average individual now earn?
   b. How much does the average individual now spend on housing, food, transportation, and other goods and services?
   c. What happened to the average individual's real salary?

5. To increase the self-esteem of dieters everywhere, powerful fashion designers lobby Congress to redefine "five pounds" as "one pound." Under this system, what would have previously been five pounds of bananas will now be one pound of bananas and a 500-pound gorilla would now weigh only 100 pounds. **[LO 16.3]**

   a. How much would someone who originally weighed 180 pounds now weigh as a result of this redefinition?
   b. Has there been a nominal change in the person's weight? A real change?
   c. How is this story similar to contractionary monetary policy via a decrease in the money supply in the long run? (*Hint:* Congress essentially shrunk the "pounds supply" by redefining the word.)

6. "Monetary policy is incredible," your friend says. "Just a little manipulation of the money supply and interest rates, and we end up at just the right price level and amount of output." Is your friend overstating the Fed's control over price levels and output? Why or why not? **[LO 16.3]**

7. Your dormitory Griffingate has appointed you central banker of its economy, which deals in the currency of wizcoins. Assume that the velocity of wizcoins in Griffingate is constant at 10,000 transactions per year. Right now, real GDP is 1,000 wizcoins and there are 2,000 wizcoins in existence. **[LO 16.4]**

   a. What will be the value of each of the variables that make up the quantity equation—M, V, and P?
   b. Now indicate how the other variables will respond to each of the following scenarios, taking each case separately and assuming that velocity remains constant.
      i. *Real GDP:* You increase the money supply to 4,000, and prices increase twofold.
      ii. *Price level:* Start with the initial values. Real GDP drops to 500 wizcoins, and the money supply remains constant.
      iii. *Real GDP:* Start with the initial values. Prices increase threefold because of a sudden scarcity of soda, and you decide to keep the supply of wizcoins constant.
      iv. *Real GDP:* Start with the initial values. You increase the money supply to 5,000 wizcoins, and prices rise by 350 percent.

8. Express the following relationships using the equation for the quantity theory of money. **[LO 16.4]**

   a. The money supply is given by nominal GDP divided by the velocity of money.
   b. The relationship of the money supply to the price level is the same as the relationship between real GDP and velocity. (*Hint:* Start by dividing the money supply by the price level.)
   c. Real GDP is given by the flow of money divided by the price level.
   d. The price level of an economy can be found by dividing the product of the money supply and its velocity by real GDP.

9. Identify whether the following individuals will be affected by bracket creep next year given the rates of taxation and levels of inflation found in Table 16P-2. **[LO 16.5]**

TABLE 16P-2

Marginal tax rate (%)	Income level ($)
10	0–10,000
15	10,001–30,000
18	30,001–50,000
20	50,001–100,000
23	100,001–150,000
25	150,001 and up

   a. Gabriela makes $9,500, and inflation is at 5 percent.
   b. Cooper makes $160,000, and inflation is at a record high of 20 percent.
   c. Shawna makes $140,000, and inflation is at 8 percent.
   d. Samuel makes $45,000, and inflation is at 6 percent.
   e. Marguerite makes $96,000, and inflation is at 6 percent.

10. Cookie Monster has decided to channel his love of cookies into a new business, "Me Want Cookies Inc.," a new partnership he has formed with Miss Piggy. They are considering different countries in which to start their venture and would like to rank the countries based on the inflationary environment. They decide to give a country 10 "menu-cost" points for each percent

TABLE 16P-3

Country	Projected inflation (%)	Actual inflation (%)	Uncertainty points	Menu-cost points	Total points	Rank
Kermikopia	2	4				
Gonzoland	4	5				
Elmostan	7	8				
Oscaria	10	13				
Bertico	14	14				

of actual inflation in the last year since inflation will cause their menu costs to increase. They also dislike unstable inflation, so they will give a country 20 "uncertainty" points for each percent difference in the actual inflation rate when compared to the projected inflation rate. Countries with the least total points will receive the highest rankings. Complete Table 16P-3 for Cookie Monster. **[LO 16.5]**

11. Jack recently took out a loan from Diane at an interest rate of 6 percent. Diane expected this year's inflation rate to be 3 percent and the real interest rate to be 3 percent. The loan is due at the end of this year. Complete Table 16P-4, showing the real interest rate for each possible inflation rate. For each situation, determine whether the unexpected inflation level benefits Jack or Diane. **[LO 16.5]**

TABLE 16P-4

This year's actual inflation rate (%)	Actual real interest rate (%)	Who benefits?
1		
2		
−1		
−3		

12. Assume the prices shown in Table 16P-5 are the prices of Big Macs in 2030, 2031, and 2032, and that changes in the price of Big Macs tend to closely keep up with inflation. For each of the four instances, determine the following. **[LO 16.6, LO 16.7]**

    a. The percentage changes in price levels between each consecutive year.
    b. Whether the economy was experiencing inflation, deflation, disinflation, or hyperinflation over each period. (Assume that inflation above 100 percent constitutes hyperinflation.)

TABLE 16P-5

	Price in 2030 ($)	Price in 2031 ($)	Price in 2032 ($)
a.	1.00	1.02	1.03
b.	1.00	0.99	0.97
c.	0.01	0.05	1.00
d.	1.00	1.10	1.15

13. Assuming that inflation above 100 percent is hyperinflation, categorize each of the inflation rates in Table 16P-6 as deflation, disinflation, inflation, or hyperinflation as we move from one year to the next. **[LO 16.6, LO 16.7]**

TABLE 16P-6

	Year	Inflation rate (%)	Description
a.	1900	90	
b.	1901	80	
c.	1902	120	
d.	1903	40	
e.	1904	−2	

14. Suppose you live in Frigidia, a country near the North Pole that is experiencing hyperinflation. You work for a U.S. company that pays you a monthly income of $100 U.S. Today, you can exchange those dollars for frigids, the currency of Frigidia, at a rate of 1,000 frigids/dollar. You pay a monthly heating bill that costs $10 U.S. Instead of paying the heating bill, you could simply burn Frigidia notes (which you can obtain in one-frigid

denominations) at a rate of 1 million per month to supply heating. What would the exchange rate between frigids and U.S. dollars have to be for you to decide to burn bills instead of paying for heating? What level of inflation does this represent, assuming the real exchange rate remains the same? **[LO 16.7]**

15. "The problem wasn't having the wrong idea about interest rates," a sheepish central bank official says at a conference, "but rather not having the right idea about inflation rates." What does the official mean? How does the inflation rate affect the central bank's interest rate target, and how can a wrong prediction about inflation make monetary policy go awry? **[LO 16.7]**

16. In which scenario is monetary policy likely to be more effective? Explain. **[LO 16.8]**

    Scenario A—The inflation rate in the country has hovered close to zero for the last three years.

    Scenario B—The inflation rate in the country has averaged 3 percent for the last three years.

17. Consider a country that has experienced a decline in labor demand that results in a 2 percent reduction in the equilibrium real wage. **[LO 16.8]**
    a. If the inflation rate in the country has been at zero percent, what has to happen to the nominal wage to restore labor market equilibrium?
    b. If the inflation rate in the country has been at 4 percent, what has to happen to the nominal wage to restore labor market equilibrium?
    c. Do you think workers and employers would prefer to have a zero percent inflation rate or a 4 percent inflation rate in this case? Explain.

18. Determine whether the Federal Reserve would pursue contractionary monetary policy, expansionary monetary policy, or no change in policy in each of the following situations. **[LO 16.9]**
    a. Inflation is 10 percent, above its average of 3 percent in the last several years.
    b. The output gap is positive.
    c. Unemployment is at a record high.
    d. The economy is experiencing full employment.
    e. The economy is on the brink of deflation.
    f. A new technology causes output to surge.

19. Answer each of the following questions assuming the economy is experiencing a positive output gap. **[LO 16.9]**
    a. Is inflation decreasing, increasing, or stable?
    b. Is actual output greater than or less than potential output?
    c. Is unemployment rising or falling?
    d. Is the Federal Reserve more likely to pursue expansionary or contractionary monetary policy?
    e. Is the economy likely experiencing an expansion or contraction?

20. Answer each of the following questions assuming the economy is experiencing a negative output gap. **[LO 16.9]**
    a. Is inflation decreasing, increasing, or stable?
    b. Is actual output greater than or less than potential output?
    c. Is unemployment rising or falling?
    d. Is the Federal Reserve more likely to pursue expansionary or contractionary monetary policy?
    e. Is the economy likely experiencing an expansion or contraction?

21. Assume the Phillips curve is given by the simple equation $U = -I + 15$. The non-accelerating inflation rate of unemployment is 8 percent. If inflation changes to 14 percent, what will be the unemployment rate in the short run? What will it be in the long run? **[LO 16.10]**

22. Using what you know about the Phillips curve, determine whether the following quantities will increase, decrease, or remain the same. **[LO 16.10]**
    a. Unemployment in the short run after an increase in inflation.
    b. Unemployment in the long run after an increase in inflation.
    c. Inflation in the short run after a decrease in unemployment.
    d. Inflation in the long run after a decrease in unemployment.

Endnotes

1. "Argentina's Inflation Problem: The Price of Cooking the Books," *The Economist*, February 25, 2012, http://www.economist.com/node/21548229.

2. https://tradingeconomics.com/united-states/gasoline-prices; www.in2013dollars.com/inflation-rate-in-2018

3. Bob Davis, "IMF Tells Bankers to Rethink Inflation," *The Wall Street Journal*, February 12, 2010, http://online.wsj.com/article/SB10001424052748704337004575059542325748142.html.

4. Marco A. Espinosa-Vega and Steven Russell, "History and Theory of the NAIRU: A Critical Review," *Economic Review* (Federal Reserve Bank of Atlanta), 1997, https://www.frbatlanta.org/-/media/Documents/research/publications/economic-review/1997/vol82no2_espinosa-russell.pdf.

Financial Crisis

Chapter 17

A Financial Storm

At 8:00 a.m. on a Friday in September 2008, Ben Bernanke, the chair of the Federal Reserve, joined Hank Paulson, the Secretary of the U.S. Treasury Department, for breakfast. They usually ate breakfast together once a week, but this morning was very different. A financial storm was brewing: Some of the country's biggest banks and financial companies were in desperate trouble. The firms had made risky bets about the future of the housing market, and now it was becoming clear how risky those bets were—and how badly they were turning out. What started as a simple breakfast turned out to be the beginning of a week of tense meetings about how to save the economy from disaster.

Two days earlier, the investment firm Lehman Brothers announced that it had lost a staggering $4 billion on its bets. All weekend, officials at the Treasury and Federal Reserve scrambled to find a way to rescue Lehman, but the pieces didn't come together. Three days later, Lehman declared bankruptcy.

©Mike Olbinski Photography/Getty Images

The storm soon intensified: It became clear that Merrill Lynch, a major Wall Street Bank, also needed rescuing. So too did AIG, the insurance giant, and Washington Mutual, America's largest savings-and-loan bank. One crisis was leading to another, and related problems were increasing in Europe. Within the month, the U.S. stock market was in free fall.

What started as a banking crisis was felt by people, rich and poor, across the country. Between 2007 and 2009, retirees saw the value of the stocks in their pensions collapse; investments built up over decades evaporated. Families lost their most valuable assets, their homes. All in all, household wealth was cut in half, and workers lost jobs, nearly 9 million in all.

Over the next ten years, the economy started coming back, the stock market began rising again, and companies created new jobs. But the effects of the 2007–2009 financial crisis are still being felt. This chapter tells the story of that financial storm—how the economy got into trouble and what economics teaches about tackling future crises.

LEARNING OBJECTIVES

LO 17.1 Describe the role of irrational expectations and leverage in the creation of financial crises.

LO 17.2 Discuss the causes of two famous historical financial crises.

LO 17.3 Trace the role of mortgage-backed securities and tranching in the rise of subprime lending.

LO 17.4 Analyze the factors that led to the housing bubble and rising levels of household debt.

LO 17.5 Explain how the collapse of the housing bubble created a credit crisis and subsequent contraction in output.

LO 17.6 Describe the monetary and fiscal policy responses to the financial crisis of 2008.

LO 17.7 Describe the different tools that can be used to stimulate the economy when interest rates are at the zero lower bound.

Markets are a powerful tool for the efficient allocation of scarce resources. Financial markets are in many ways the purest expression of the market mechanism. Relatively free from government intervention, financial markets are a global marketplace in which sophisticated investors make billion-dollar decisions nearly every second of the day.

So, how do financial markets go so very wrong as they did in the 2007–2009 crisis? And why do the failings of financial markets reverberate through the broader economy? Developing an understanding of the common causes of financial crises has become an urgently important task.

In this chapter, we'll introduce a few of the basic concepts of financial crises. We'll talk about why things sometimes go wrong in financial markets and how those problems might be corrected. In particular, we will take a close look at the crisis that began in December of 2007 after the collapse of the housing market.

The Origins of Financial Crises

Financial crises often occur as the result of a financial bubble. As discussed in Chapter 14, "The Basics of Finance," a **bubble** involves trade in an asset whose price has risen unsustainably far above historically justified levels.

bubble trade in an asset whose price has risen unsustainably far above historically justified levels

The first recorded example of a financial bubble is a "tulip mania" that afflicted investors in Holland in 1636–1637. At the time, a single tulip bulb was worth more than a handful of diamonds. Investors paid incredible sums for bulbs, hoping to profit by selling later at even higher prices. After a few years, however, the mania surrounding tulips died out, and prices plummeted. Those who had invested in tulips lost fortunes.

This pattern has since been repeated many times. Prices go up and up and up, way higher than seems to make any rational sense, and then suddenly crash. Why does this happen? Two interconnected concepts lie at the heart of many financial crises: irrational expectations and leverage.

Irrational expectations

LO 17.1 Describe the role of irrational expectations and leverage in the creation of financial crises.

In Chapter 14, "The Basics of Finance," we talked about how financial markets are supposed to allocate funds efficiently. Ideally, they allow money to flow to the places where it is most highly valued at any given time. What's more, the efficient-market hypothesis says that financial markets should incorporate all available information, and so prices should represent the true value of an asset as correctly as possible. Where, in all of that, is there room for bubbles and crashes?

In reality, markets sometimes appear to be very irrational. The price of an asset can become inflated beyond the point where anyone can explain precisely why it should be so valuable. How does that happen? One hypothesis is that investors sometimes follow a "herd instinct," investing in something simply because everyone else is doing it. Investors are just people—albeit often well-informed people with a financial interest in making good investments. They can get caught up in the moment and act emotionally, just like anyone else. A bubble starts to inflate when investors become irrationally optimistic that an asset's price will continue to rise.

Where do irrational expectations come from? One possible explanation is a well-established cognitive bias called the *recency effect*. There is a basic human tendency to overvalue recent experience when trying to predict the future. When investors and speculators do this, it can lead to enormous miscalculations.

For example, consider a company that has enjoyed some spectacular years of success: Apple Computer. In 2008, Apple's net income (income minus expenses, or total profit) was just over $6.1 billion. Then, it launched the MacBook, followed by the iPhone, and then the iPad. In 2018, Apple reported net income of almost $60 billion.

With Apple's products still flying off the shelves in 2019, would an investor be justified in believing that Apple might continue its incredible run for another five or 10 or 15 years? By 2028, after another 10 years of tenfold growth, Apple would be earning more than $600 billion a year. By 2038, Apple would be earning $6 trillion annually—more than the current GDP of Japan! When you look at it that way, it becomes clear that there will come a time for Apple when future growth simply can't resemble past growth.

Although it's unlikely that anyone would project something quite that extreme, trends do influence our thinking. For example, in the housing markets, decades of rising house prices persuaded many Americans that it was inconceivable that they could ever fall, but between 2007 and 2012, the Case-Shiller U.S. National Home Price Index fell by about 25 percent.[1]

However, not all investors in a bubble are necessarily caught up in irrational expectations. Some may be aware that assets are overpriced but gamble on riding the rise in prices as close to the top as possible in the hope of selling at maximum profit, just before the inevitable crash. This high-stakes game is described in the From Another Angle box "Timing is everything."

Timing is everything
From Another Angle

The thing about bubbles is that they usually pop. That's true of stock bubbles and housing bubbles too. When a financial bubble exists—when prices for stocks or real estate are unsustainably and irrationally high—it would seem that investors should stay away. After all, when the bubble pops, investors know that the value of their investments will collapse.

But that's not the full story. The other thing about bubbles is that no one knows *when* exactly they will pop. If your timing is right and you're lucky, you can make a lot of money investing during a bubble—as long as you sell early enough. The trouble is that timing is everything.

The housing price bubble that collapsed spectacularly in 2007 in the United States was not a complete surprise to many people. In fact, on June 16, 2005, *The Economist* magazine ran a story entitled "After the Fall." The magazine spelled out clearly why the fast-rising real estate prices around the world were a bubble that would burst, sooner or later:

> It is impossible to predict when [housing] prices will turn. Yet turn they will. Prices are already sliding in Australia and Britain. America's housing market may be a year or so behind.

Many investors in real estate *knew* that the market was a bubble and that prices were too high to make economic sense. But they invested anyway. Why? Because there were enough other people who were still in the game, willing to keep betting that housing prices would continue upward.

As it happened, housing prices in the United States stayed astronomically high for *another two years* after *The Economist*'s warning. Between 2005 and 2007, many investors were playing a high-stakes game. Selling too soon would mean missing out on ever higher prices.

(continued)

Investors who waited too long got badly burned; house prices fell sharply between 2007 and 2012. Bubbles pop when a critical mass of investors decides that, finally, the time is right to sell. This mass decision causes prices to dip. Everyone who had been sitting tight will rush to sell as well, turning the dip into a plummet. If you haven't managed to sell before this moment comes, you'll struggle to find anyone who wants to buy. What seemed like a good bet can, in just a few weeks, turn into a major loss.

The bursting of the housing bubble led to countless foreclosures.
©feverpitched/123RF

Sources: www.princeton.edu/~markus/research/papers/bubbles_crashes.pdf; "After the Fall: Soaring House Prices Have Given a Huge Boost to the World Economy. What Happens When They Drop?" © The Economist Newspaper Limited, London (June 16, 2005).

Leverage

Irrational expectations help explain how prices get so inflated during a bubble, but we have to go further to understand why the crash is so damaging after a bubble bursts. One culprit is the extensive use of leverage, which multiplies the effect of gains and losses in financial markets. In finance, **leverage** is the practice of using borrowed money to pay for investments.

The use of leverage means that a person or company can make an investment that is much larger in value than the amount they actually own:

- If the investment does well, you pay back the loan and get to keep the profits, which will be larger than what you would have earned if you could invest only the cash you had on hand.
- If the investment does badly, you still have to pay back the loan, and that can require digging deep into your own resources.

When financial markets are booming, leverage multiplies the gains; when they crash, leverage magnifies the losses.

On a personal level, people can leverage their funds through a "margin account." A margin account allows you to use your existing investments as collateral to either buy more financial assets or withdraw cash. For example, if you have $100 in an account that offers "2x" margin, you can effectively buy $200 worth of stocks even though you put in only $100. When stocks rise, you will earn twice as much profit, minus interest payments.

But what happens if the stock you bought goes down? Let's say it goes down 10 percent. If you did not buy on margin, your account value would go down to only $90. If you did buy on margin, however, you are going to lose $20, which would bring your account value down to $80. That doesn't sound so bad, but what if the stock goes down 50 percent? You would lose all your money since 50 percent of $200 is your entire original $100. If the stock goes down more than 50 percent, you could actually end up owing money to your broker! In both cases, your percentage win or loss doubles.

leverage
the practice of using borrowed money to pay for investments

In practice, brokers exercise a "margin call" to ensure that *they* don't lose money. If it looks like you are in danger of running through your money, the broker will force you to sell your stock and use the money to pay back the loan. Since this probably means selling at the worst possible time—just as the market is collapsing—this situation is both bad for you and potentially destabilizing for the market as a whole. A rapidly falling stock price can trigger a flood of margin calls, leading to massive sales of the stock, which pushes the price down even more.

Companies and banks can also leverage their funds. Such transactions can lead to losses on a much larger scale than personal margin accounts. For instance, an investment bank or hedge fund might use $5 million as collateral in order to buy a claim on $50 million worth of oil futures.[2] Gains or losses on that investment will be multiplied by the use of leverage in exactly the same way that they are on a personal level. If the value of the investment goes down by a lot, the company can end up owing more than it is able to pay. Just before it went bankrupt during the crash in 2008, Lehman Brothers investment bank was highly leveraged. Its total assets were valued at levels about 30 times the actual funds it owned, depending on exactly how one calculates it.

The amount of leverage a company takes on can be expressed in terms of the **leverage ratio**. That measure is the ratio of a company's assets to its equity, where equity is defined as the firm's assets minus its liabilities. In the case of Lehman Brothers, a leverage ratio of 30 implies that a 10 percent increase in the value of its assets would generate a 300 percent increase in the value of its equity.[3]

leverage ratio the ratio of a company's assets to its equity, where equity is defined as the firm's assets minus its liabilities

This magnification of returns may sound attractive when we're considering positive changes in asset prices, but the logic also works in reverse: Small decreases in asset values can lead to catastrophic losses for highly leveraged institutions.

Leverage alone is not necessarily a dangerous thing—so long as it is limited and investors understand the risks well. Unfortunately, leverage combined with irrational expectations about a market can be a brutal combination. Imagine you believed that Apple would keep growing at 60 percent a year for the next decade, and borrowed heavily to leverage your investment. When the price of Apple stock inevitably fell back to earth, you would take a huge loss.

The two-headed monster of leverage and irrational expectations is at the heart of most financial crises.

Two famous historical financial crises

Before we dive into a case study of the Great Recession, let's take a quick look back at how the twin dangers of irrational expectations and leverage have played out in two famous historical financial crises.

LO 17.2 Discuss the causes of two famous historical financial crises.

The South Seas Bubble In the late seventeenth century, stock markets in England were in their infancy. In 1688, the East India Company made one of the first issuances of stock: Investors would be given a cut of the profits on a forthcoming voyage to India. By 1695, 140 companies were offering similar arrangements in London's Exchange Alley.

The South Seas Company took form in this new environment. The company was granted a government monopoly on trade between England and South America. Interest in the company's stock was intense. In just a single day, the price of South Seas Company stock rose from £130 to over £300. The company issued more stock, and the price jumped from £300 to £325 as investors used their existing stock as collateral to buy more. By June 1720, the bubble was in full swing, with stock of the South Seas Company trading at a price over £1,000 a share.

It was never entirely clear how the South Seas Company was going to earn enough profit to justify this fantastic share price. After all, there wasn't much trade between England and South America, which at the time was made up of colonies that were mostly controlled by Spain. The company depended on an agreement with Spain to be able to run trading ships, and Spain allowed it to run only one ship a year. Still, wild rumors circulated of the fabulous profits that would one day flow from the South Seas. Investors were caught up in the frenzy.

Con artists saw the high prices that investors were willing to pay for shares in the South Seas Company and decided to cash in on the frenzy. They concocted their own companies, which promised investors riches through fanciful schemes. One company claimed to be building a wheel of perpetual motion. Another famously invited investors to buy stock in "a company for carrying out an undertaking of great advantage, but nobody to know what it is." Eventually, the English Parliament realized the dangers and moved to regulate companies that traded stock publicly, through a law known as the Bubble Act.

Inevitably, sanity returned, and the price of stock in the South Seas Company plunged back to earth. Many investors were ruined. Sir Isaac Newton, the great mathematician and one of the investors, lost £20,000—the equivalent of about $5 million today. Kicking himself, Newton grumbled that he could "calculate the motion of heavenly bodies, but not the madness of people."

The Great Crash of 1929

While the South Seas Bubble could be considered the first financial crisis of the modern stock market era, the worst was arguably the infamous stock market crash of October 1929. This event led to the Great Depression, which wreaked havoc throughout the 1930s. Production slowed and unemployment in the United States exceeded 25 percent.

The Great Crash and resulting Great Depression had their roots in another bubble, a period of flashy exuberance known as the "Roaring Twenties." From 1922 to 1929, the total value of the stock market more than tripled, averaging an annual growth rate of over 18 percent. There was some foundation for this increase in share prices: U.S. soldiers, home from World War I, had boosted production with additional manpower. New technologies such as movies, radio, and mass-produced automobiles were causing widespread excitement. Many people began buying stocks on the margin.

If stock prices continued to rise, as many figured they would, buying on the margin could increase profits substantially. For most of the 1920s, that seemed a pretty good bet. Economist Irving Fisher infamously assured everyone that the stock market had reached a "permanently high plateau." Secretary of the Treasury Andrew Mellon stated on October 14, 1929, that there was "no cause to worry. The high tide of prosperity will continue."

Ten days later, the stock market fell apart. On October 24, 1929—"Black Thursday"—the leading index of stock prices dropped by 9 percent. Bankers tried to shore up confidence by buying up the stocks of large companies. But this buying couldn't stem the avalanche of selling as investors unloaded shares in an unprecedented, panicked sell-off. Once prices started to drop, everyone wanted to sell before the price dropped further. Of course, this rush of sales *caused* the price to drop further, making the panic a self-perpetuating problem.

The Great Crash of 1929 wreaked havoc on Wall Street—a loss the U.S. economy took 25 years to recover from.
©MPI/Getty Images

On the following Monday, the stock market posted a loss of 13 percent. The next day, the market fell again by 12 percent. As more panic set in, the volume of shares traded reached a record-setting 16.4 million—more than four times the typical number.

By the time prices bottomed out in July 1932, 90 percent of the entire value of the stock market had been wiped away in just three years. It took until 1954—a full 25 years later—for the stock market to return to the peak reached in September 1929.

✓ TEST YOURSELF

- ☐ Why does leverage exacerbate the effect of a financial crash? **[LO 17.1]**
- ☐ What is the name of the period of sluggish economic activity that followed the Great Crash of 1929? **[LO 17.1]**
- ☐ Why did the initial stock sell-off create further panic during the Great Crash of 1929? **[LO 17.2]**

The Great Recession: A Financial-Crisis Case Study

In the 1930s, Congress passed several laws intended to prevent crises similar to the Great Crash and Great Depression:

- The Glass-Steagall Banking Act of 1933 required the separation of investment and commercial banks.[4]
- The Federal Deposit Insurance Corporation (FDIC) insured bank deposits against possible bank failures, among other things.
- The Securities and Exchange Act of 1932 formed the Securities and Exchange Commission (SEC), which regulates the securities industry today.

These reforms contributed to a long period of relative stability in financial markets. For decades, the U.S. economy chugged along without a major financial crisis or contraction in output. It seemed that the stock market crash of 1929 might go down in history as the beginning of a new and more predictable era. Perhaps the global economy had moved on from the days of bubbles and panics. By the mid-2000s, this idea, sometimes dubbed "the Great Moderation," had support in the academic and policy-making community.

However, by 2008 we were in the midst of the greatest global economic downturn since the Great Depression. Industrial and financial giants from General Motors to Merrill Lynch were under threat of collapse. Millions of people saw their life savings evaporate as housing prices collapsed and markets around the world plummeted.

In this section, we'll explore the origins of the financial crisis and the extraordinary monetary and fiscal response from the world's governments, using the macroeconomics concepts we've explored over the last few chapters. We will focus on the United States—in many ways the epicenter of the crisis—but the global crash was not just the result of problems in the United States spreading to the rest of the world. Countries from Spain to Ireland and the United Kingdom also faced enormous challenges of their own that helped feed the global crisis.

In order to really understand how the U.S. economy collapsed so suddenly, we'll start by looking at some interrelated components of the U.S. economy: subprime lending, the housing and mortgage market, and the broader world of consumer debt.

Subprime lending

To understand the financial crisis that rocked the country in 2008, we have to start with the housing market. From World War II to the onset of the financial crisis—a period of more than 60 years—housing prices had never fallen across the entire United States. Housing prices on the whole had stayed steady, even when the rest of the economy went into recession. Buying a house was considered the safest investment anyone could make—a path to stability, wealth, and the American Dream.

LO 17.3 Trace the role of mortgage-backed securities and tranching in the rise of subprime lending.

Even the federal government joined the bandwagon in promoting home ownership: It implemented policies ranging from tax deductions on home mortgage interest to government-created companies like Fannie Mae and Freddie Mac, which are intended to spread access to mortgage financing.

Yet some people still couldn't obtain a traditional mortgage loan—because of poor credit, low income, or lack of a job. Financial innovators opened a new path to home ownership through the growing availability of subprime mortgages. A *subprime mortgage* is a mortgage loan made to a borrower with a low credit score—that is, to someone who has a history of missing payments or otherwise struggling with debts. (The word *subprime* is in contrast to *prime* borrowers, who have better credit scores.) At first, subprime mortgages were seen as a triumph: They enabled even more Americans to pursue the dream of home ownership for the first time.

securitization
the practice of packaging individual debts into a single uniform asset

Why were lenders willing to lend to subprime borrowers? The loans, after all, are especially risky. Banks had long been wary of lending to subprime-rated borrowers. That all changed with the advent of securitization. **Securitization** is the practice of packaging individual debts, like mortgage loans or credit card debts, into a single uniform asset that can be easily bought and sold. In the late 1990s, investment banks began purchasing mortgages from the local banks that had created them. They, in turn, then securitized those loans: They packaged them as *mortgage-backed securities*, which were tradable assets made up of collections of individual mortgages, whose value was tied to the revenues of those mortgages.

Securitization of mortgages allowed *local banks* to reduce their exposure to risk by effectively selling their mortgage debt to investors. The investors got the revenues from mortgage payments, but if borrowers defaulted, the investors would experience a loss.

For investors, the mortgage-backed security seemed to promise diversification: By combining many mortgages into one security, the risks specific to individual mortgages (called *idiosyncratic risk*) would be diluted. As a result, the combination of mortgages would have lower total risk than any individual mortgage. The reasoning was similar to that of a bank or insurance company pooling risks, as discussed in Chapter 14, "The Basics of Finance":

- If you make a single loan and the borrower defaults, you lose everything at once.
- If, however, you make a thousand loans, it's very unlikely that everyone will default at once. A bank can take a thousand loans, estimate that *on average* 150 of them will default, and set prices so that it can still earn a profit on the total package.

An investor could go out and buy a thousand different individual mortgages to diversify risk. Doing that, though, takes time: It would involve scrutinizing each mortgage to guess how likely a particular homeowner is to default and ensuring that the thousand mortgages are not highly correlated. Instead, the mortgage-backed security was supposed to be a single, uniform asset that pooled risk while still being easy to buy and sell quickly. It allowed local banks to pass the risk involved in holding mortgage debts on to investors with higher risk tolerance.

Diversification is valuable, but the logic of pooling risks depends crucially on the degree to which the loans in the pool are correlated with one another. If for any reason the risks associated with a set of loans are highly correlated, then it is much harder to diversify away the default risk. (An example of high correlation of mortgage risk, for example, would be if many loans are issued to households who could make payments only if interest rates stayed low.) Worse yet, if investors are unaware that the underlying risks are in fact highly correlated, then they might unintentionally take on more risk than they want.

Some banks went one step further: They divided packages of debts into slices (called *tranches*), each with different risk and return characteristics. Packages of reliable, low-risk mortgages could be sold to more risk-averse investors; higher-risk subprime mortgages could be sold to risk-loving investors.

What was the point of this financial repackaging? It allowed local banks and mortgage companies to chase higher profits by making loans that they would have rejected as too risky in the past. Now they could sell those mortgages to investment banks, which in turn could chase profits by packaging them as mortgage-backed securities and selling them on.

Investors had such an appetite for mortgage-backed securities that local banks couldn't make loans fast enough. Real estate agents started pushing larger mortgages to customers, even to borrowers who wouldn't traditionally have been able to afford them. Some mortgage brokers cut corners in paperwork to be able to pump out more loans. By 2006, a full 20 percent of the mortgage market consisted of subprime loans, a category that barely even existed a decade before. The sudden explosion of subprime mortgages is shown in Figure 17-1.

LO 17.4 Analyze the factors that led to the housing bubble and rising levels of household debt.

The creation of the housing bubble

The sudden explosion of cheap and readily available mortgages encouraged people to buy bigger and better homes. A mortgage is a form of leverage—you make a down payment that is only a

FIGURE 17-1

Growth of the subprime loan market This figure shows subprime mortgages as a percentage of all new mortgages from 2001 through 2007. Traditionally, new subprime mortgages comprised less than 10 percent of the total new mortgages in any given year. This changed in 2004, when the number of new subprime mortgages more than doubled as a share of new mortgages. Then, in 2007, the housing market collapsed, and lenders reacted by sharply reducing subprime loans.

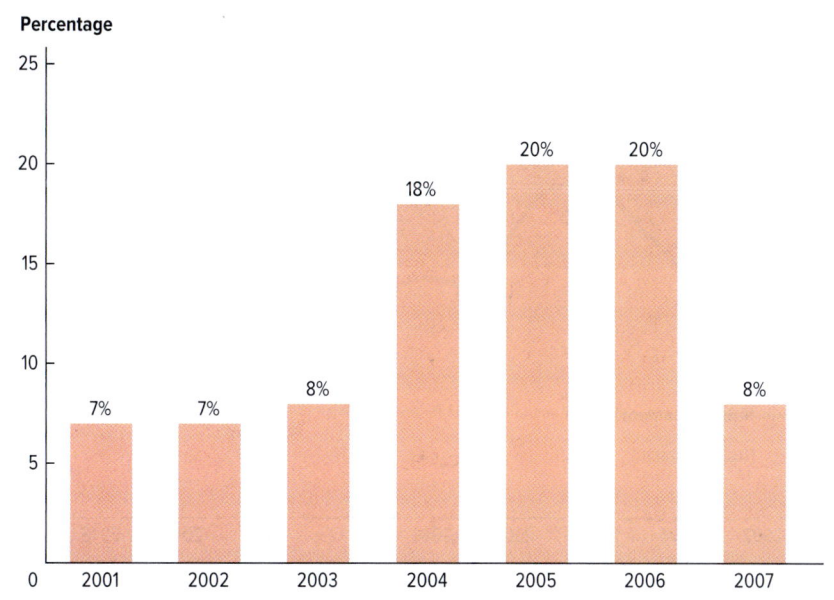

Year	Percentage
2001	7%
2002	7%
2003	8%
2004	18%
2005	20%
2006	20%
2007	8%

Source: *The State of the Nation's Housing,* Harvard University Joint Center for Housing Studies, 2008.

fraction of the value of the asset (i.e., the house) that you are buying, and you borrow the rest. As down-payment requirements got smaller and loans got cheaper, many homeowners became more and more leveraged.

The frenzy of highly leveraged demand for houses was accompanied by a sharp run-up in housing prices. Figure 17-2 shows the rapid rise in U.S. home prices during this period and the number of *housing starts* (a term that means new home construction—an indicator of increasing supply in the housing market) in the same period. At the height of the real estate bubble, American homeowners were much like Lehman Brothers, with a very high ratio of home "value" to money actually paid.

When housing prices stopped rising, however, millions of homeowners found themselves with payments to make on highly leveraged housing properties.

Why did these loans get made? Economists continue to debate this question, but in many ways, the enormous run-up in housing prices was a classic bubble. People bought houses with the expectation that they would continue to go up in value. Banks began to offer special types of mortgages that allowed borrowers to defer payments for the first few years of the loan. Or they offered "teaser" interest rates that would increase to much higher levels a few years down the road. As long as home prices kept going up, borrowers would simply "refinance" their homes when the bills came. That is, they would use the new, higher value of the home as collateral to take out a new mortgage with friendlier terms. Banks and borrowers both got caught up in the moment. Convinced that housing prices would never go down, both agreed to incredibly risky loans.

When housing values went down, however, high leverage became a real problem. Signers of risky loans couldn't refinance. At the same time, others found it hard to keep up with expensive mortgage payments when they lost their job. And some homeowners who found themselves "underwater" (having a loan worth more than their house) simply chose to default. The default rate rose well above what investment firms were able to handle.

FIGURE 17-2

The housing bubble pops The chart shows the rapid increase of housing prices from 2000 to 2006, and then the decline and recovery after the recession. As you can see, prices peaked in early 2007 and then quickly plummeted. The bubble was large nationally (as seen by the national composite index, represented by the blue line), as prices doubled on average in the span of seven years. The bursting of the bubble is shown by the sudden decrease in housing starts, followed by a sharp reduction in price of houses. By 2018, housing starts remained stable, but the housing price index had recovered to exceed its 2007 high.

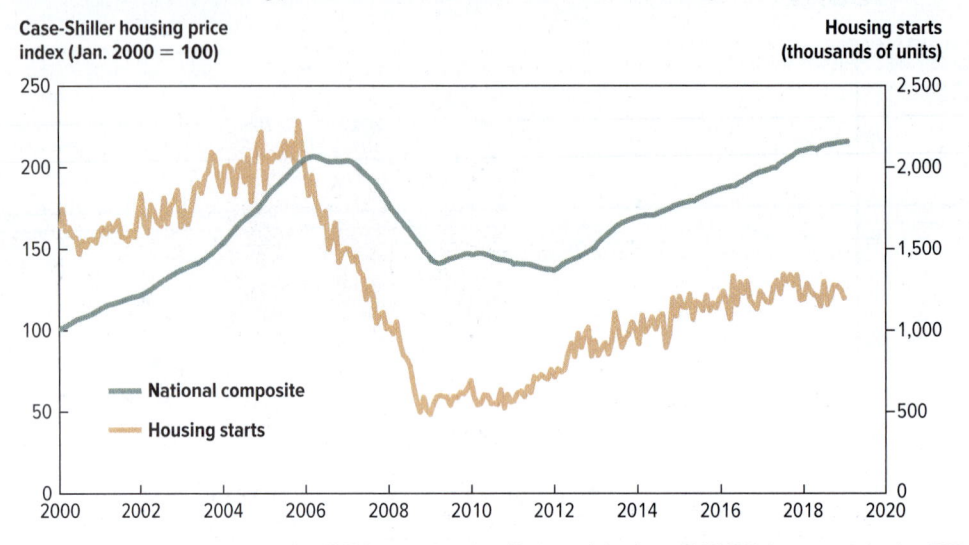

Sources: Case-Shiller housing price index data from FRED Economic Data, https://fred.stlouisfed.org/series/SPCS20RSA; housing starts data from FRED Economic Data, https://fred.stlouisfed.org/series/HOUST.

Securitization encouraged the process by removing most of the risk from the lenders who created the original mortgage. This removal of risk from the original lender also may have contributed to misaligned incentives to properly assess risk:

- Investment banks on Wall Street relied on the local banks to assess each individual borrower. But local banks had the incentive to make as many loans as possible since they earned fees for each loan.
- Wall Street bankers made money not by ensuring local banks were making good loans, but by buying as many loans as possible, packaging them into mortgage-backed securities, and selling them to investors.

At some point up the chain, the people creating and buying complicated assets that were several steps removed from the original mortgage may not have fully understood what they were paying for.

There was plenty of blame to go around:

- Investors relied on the reassuringly high AAA ratings given to many of these assets by credit-rating agencies.
- However, the ratings agencies attracted business in part by keeping Wall Street happy. The ratings turned out to be much too optimistic.
- Politicians were driven by a vision of broader home ownership but failed to pay enough attention to the economics.

The same tools that were intended to allocate funds and spread risk more efficiently made it difficult for everyone to stay fully informed; they diluted the incentive to do the research and to say no to bad risks.

Effects of the housing bubble collapse

As housing prices continued to rise, consumers were simultaneously saving less and borrowing (and spending) more. Flush with the feeling of wealth from their inflated home values, many consumers used the value of their homes to secure loans and higher limits on their credit cards, taking on more and more debt to support their spending habits.

In addition, consumers had become accustomed to *refinancing* their mortgages—paying off the existing mortgage and taking out a new mortgage based on the increased value of the home. Often the new mortgage was structured to result in lower payments (at least for a while), and often the appreciated value of the home enabled the homeowner to borrow some cash in the refinancing deal.

These consumer responses to the housing bubble ultimately led to a credit crisis and a new equilibrium in the economy in which both prices and output had fallen.

Buying on credit Personal debt levels in the United States had steadily been rising for decades, since the mid-1980s. As the housing market took off in the early 2000s and consumers began borrowing more, the growth in household debt accelerated rapidly, hitting a peak by the end of 2008. Figure 17-3 shows the historical trajectory of personal debt in the United States.

To understand consumer debt, economists look at a concept known as debt service. **Debt service** is the amount that consumers have to spend to pay their debts, often expressed as a percentage of disposable income. Figure 17-4 shows total debt service for consumers in the United States. Over the two decades leading up the 2008 crisis, falling interest rates made borrowing—and therefore going into debt—much cheaper. Consumers could take on more debt without significantly increasing the amount of debt service they had to pay.

Unfortunately, the high level of debt was sustainable only as long as interest rates remained low and home values remained high. Consumers would be facing serious trouble if anything unexpectedly went wrong—which is exactly what happened when the housing bubble popped.

LO 17.5 Explain how the collapse of the housing bubble created a credit crisis and subsequent contraction in output.

debt service the amount that consumers have to spend to pay their debts, often expressed as a percentage of disposable income

FIGURE 17-3

Historical personal debt trends in the United States Since the 1960s, personal debt in the United States has almost doubled its share of GDP, from around 45 percent to about 80 percent of GDP today. During the financial crisis, personal debt was almost 100 percent of GDP.

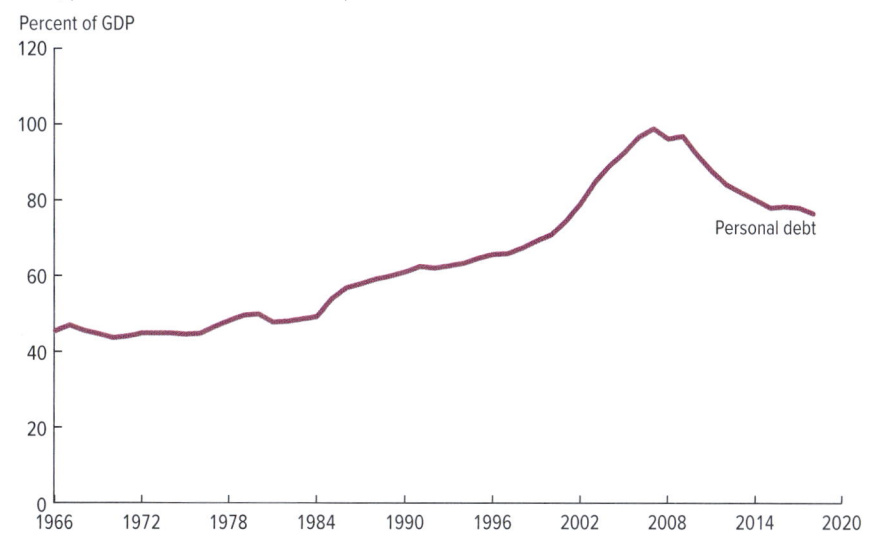

Source: http://stats.bis.org:8089/statx/srs/table/f3.1.

FIGURE 17-4

Household debt service as a percent of income This graph shows household financial obligations (which include payments during the year for mortgages, credit cards, property tax, and leases). Despite the fact that household debt has risen considerably (as shown in Figure 17-3), household payments on this debt have not increased very much, as low interest rates have kept the price of debt low.

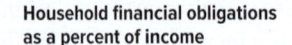

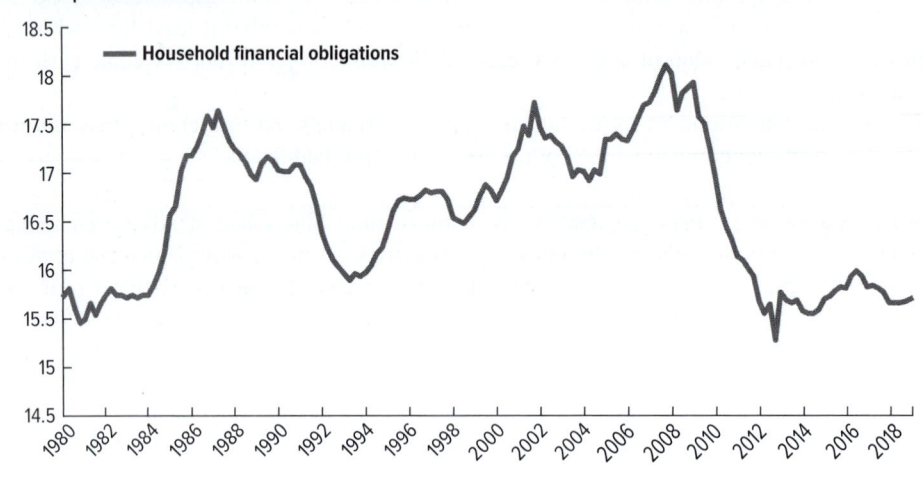

Source: FRED Economic Data: https://fred.stlouisfed.org/series/FODSP.

As home prices fell, consumers were unable to refinance mortgages, and a cycle of defaults and falling prices followed, eventually engulfing the entire economy.
©OJO Images/Getty Images

A domino effect toward reduced output

When housing prices stopped rising and began to fall in places like Nevada, Arizona, California, and Florida, consumers found themselves unable to refinance their loans. The housing collapse began in the subprime housing market. It was like a domino trail, in which the first domino that tips starts a cascading effect:

- Faced with impossibly high payments relative to their incomes, a massive wave of mortgage defaults occurred. Millions of people found themselves in *foreclosure:* Their homes became the property of the bank when they defaulted on a mortgage loan. Often, the bank would then evict the homeowner and try to sell the house.
- The wave of foreclosed properties hit the market, creating a big increase in the supply of housing. The increase in supply depressed housing prices even further, leading to another wave of defaults.
- Consumers who had used second and third mortgages or borrowed in other ways to extract wealth from their homes suddenly found themselves "underwater," owing more in mortgage debt than their houses were worth. A vicious cycle of defaults and falling prices began; it would ultimately cause home values to fall by more than 50 percent in the hardest-hit areas.
- Riskier real estate investments became worthless. Even the supposedly "safe," AAA-rated investments were badly affected. Banks lost trillions of dollars.
- Because of the opaque and complicated nature of mortgage-backed securities, it was difficult to tell which banks had been hit the hardest by the crash. As a result,

the *entire* borrowing and lending engine of the economy ground to a halt. Nobody wanted to lend to anybody, in case they turned out to be a bad risk.
- Even the most venerable banks teetered on the edge of collapse. Large institutions and companies that had deposited money with Wall Street's banks began withdrawing their funds, leading to a run on bank assets. Two of the largest and most respected banks—Bear Stearns and Lehman Brothers—collapsed, and the rest were perceived to be at risk as well. Figure 17-5 shows the dramatic collapse in stock prices of the largest banks.
- Because banks were unwilling to lend, many businesses were suddenly unable to get access to credit for their day-to-day needs. Even simple tasks like buying inventory or taking delivery of a container ship full of imported goods became nearly impossible for many companies. Effectively, the aggregate productive capacity of the entire world was reduced almost overnight.
- The combination of increasing interest rates and pessimism about future economic prospects decreased investment spending: Businesses could no longer obtain credit to invest, and most would not have wanted to invest as the economy weakened anyway.
- Households found themselves struggling to pay back debts, and some faced reduced income and poor job prospects. The fall in home prices meant they were no longer as wealthy as they thought they were, and people reduced their consumption accordingly.
- With demand flagging, businesses had to cut back further. Some employees were laid off, and others saw their wages or hours cut.
- Lower incomes led naturally to lower spending and still more layoffs.

Figure 17-6 shows the combined impact of these forces: As a result of the housing-market crash, both aggregate demand and aggregate supply shifted to the left. The combined shifts put the economy at a new equilibrium, with dramatically reduced output. Prices fell because the effect of the leftward shift in the aggregate demand curve was stronger than the effect of the leftward shift in aggregate supply. The combined effect left the economy reeling.

FIGURE 17-5

Stock prices of major banks As a result of the housing boom, the financial sector performed well in the years leading up to the crisis. This ended when many of the banks announced that they held large amounts of toxic assets. Beginning in February 2007, prices began to fall. Come September 2008, prices of stocks throughout the financial sectors plummeted as the crisis hit.

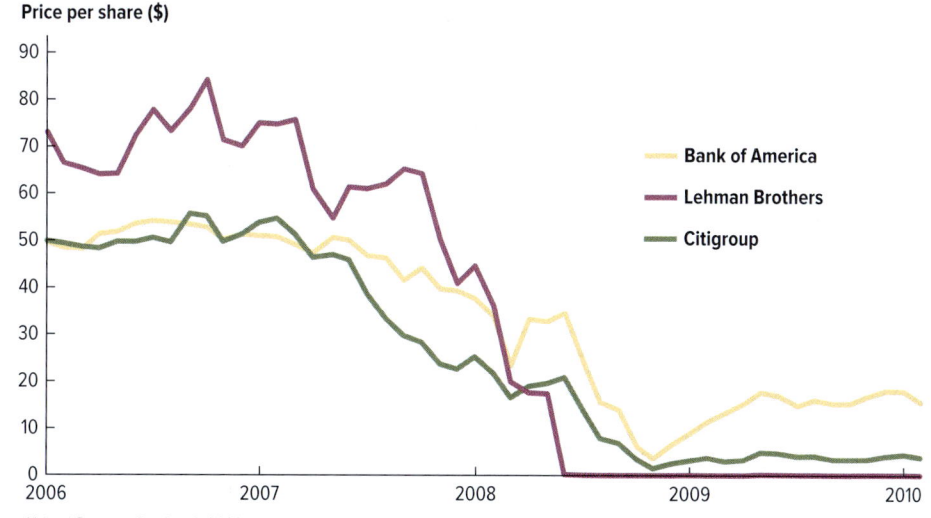

Source: Yahoo! Finance, October 4, 2011.

FIGURE 17-6
The financial crisis in AD/AS terms

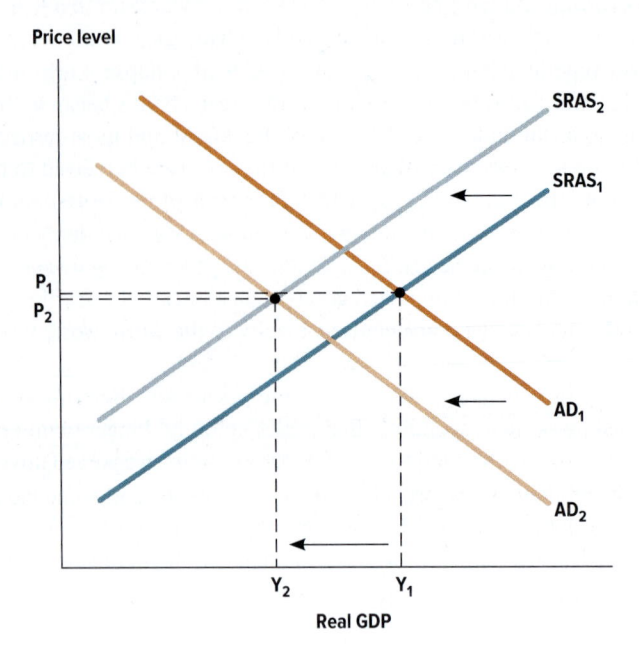

As a result of the housing-market crash, both aggregate demand and aggregate supply shifted to the left. This put the economy at a new equilibrium, with lower prices and dramatically reduced output.

It took barely two years for the bursting of a real estate bubble to tip the global economy into its worst downturn in over 75 years. Once housing prices collapsed and the bad loans in the financial system were revealed for what they were, it was only a matter of time before the convulsions on Wall Street led to job losses and economic pain on Main Street.

The immediate response to the crisis

LO 17.6 Describe the monetary and fiscal policy responses to the financial crisis of 2008.

With the private sector reeling from the impact of the shifts in both aggregate demand and aggregate supply, many looked to the government to provide stability and ensure that the situation did not become even worse. We've talked about how the government can use monetary and fiscal policy to impact the economy. During the financial crisis, policy-makers used these tools to try to avert a catastrophic economic collapse.

The challenges facing the financial system stemmed from the two fundamental issues of liquidity and solvency. The more pressing of the two was liquidity. There was great uncertainty about which banks were facing losses and which would most likely go bankrupt next. As a result, banks were not willing to lend to each other. The lack of liquidity meant that there wasn't enough money moving through the system to keep transactions going. Concerns about the amount of the liquidity in the market were reflected in interest rates: In the depths of the financial crisis, interest rates on even the most secure loans soared.

Addressing the liquidity problem fell to the world's central banks, and primarily to the U.S. Federal Reserve in its role as "lender of last resort." When a similar financial crisis shook the United States in the early 1900s, one man—J.P. Morgan—had stepped in to act as the lender of last resort, averting a national financial collapse. Six years after that event, the Federal Reserve was created.

In 2008, the existence of the Fed meant that the situation played out very differently. Shortly after Lehman Brothers' collapse, the Fed leapt into action: It offered nearly unlimited short-term financing to any bank that suddenly found itself short on cash. The European Central Bank and the Bank of England quickly followed suit, trying to help the financial system from seizing up completely.

Figure 17-7 shows the effect of this monetary policy response: a dramatic spike in the size of the Federal Reserve's balance sheet in September 2008. The Fed greatly expanded its holdings of financial products, doubling the assets over the span of a month. The intent of the policy was to compensate for the loss of capital in the financial markets. By buying various assets, the Fed added nearly $1.5 trillion in new money to the U.S. economy. Even though you may not recognize every asset on the Fed's balance sheet, notice the rise in mortgage-backed securities beginning in early 2009, which the Fed began purchasing as a way to support the housing market.

At the same time, the U.S. Treasury began the difficult task of dealing with banks that had a solvency problem. "Solvency problem" is a gentle way of referring to banks that had lost so much money that they would inevitably go bankrupt. Hundreds of banks were allowed to fail during this period. However, certain banks were deemed **"too big to fail"**—that is, so large in terms of assets or customers or so historically important that banking regulators allow the bank to keep operating despite insolvency. The failure of one of these big banks carried the risk of causing a domino effect in the highly integrated financial system, causing widespread loss and credit seize-up.

Banks considered "too big to fail" were eventually bailed out through fiscal policy—that is, through increased government spending. The bulk of this effort came through the *Troubled Asset Relief Program*, commonly known as *TARP*. This program represented the first wave of the federal government's fiscal policy response to the crisis. The first wave invested more than $700 billion in failing institutions. The recipients ranged from major banks like Citigroup to insurance companies like AIG. General Motors and Chrysler, two automakers that were floundering in the weak economy, also received bailouts from the Treasury.

This one-two punch of monetary and fiscal policy averted a systemic collapse and brought stability to the global financial system. By shoring up the capital of the most heavily damaged banks

"too big to fail" so large in terms of assets or customers or so historically important that banking regulators allow the bank to keep operating despite insolvency

---

FIGURE 17-7

The Federal Reserve's balance sheet Responding to the crisis, the Fed in fall 2008 doubled the assets on its balance sheet, over the span of just a month. Notice the rise in mortgage-backed securities beginning in early 2009, which the Fed began purchasing as a way to support the housing market.

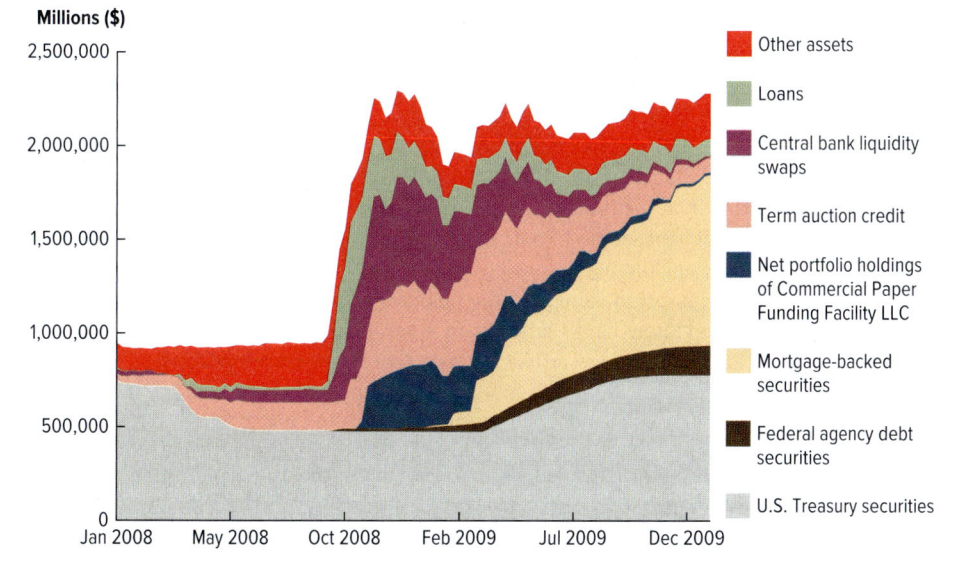

Source: Board of Governors of the Federal Reserve System, http://www.federalreserve.gov/releases/h41/current/, updated July 5, 2012.

and flooding the system with liquidity, the Treasury and the Federal Reserve worked together to restore the lines of credit within the economy.

Many officials argued that the bailouts were absolutely necessary to save the economy. Debate swirled around TARP as it made its way through government. Chief among the concerns was the fear that blanket bailouts would create a class of banks that *knew* they were considered to be "too big to fail" and so would continue to take unnecessary risks. This debate is covered in the Economics in Action box "Too big to fail?"

Too big to fail?
Economics in Action

Imagine going to a casino and knowing that if you lose everything, your parents will bail you out. Wouldn't you be more willing to gamble than if you had to bear all of the consequences yourself?

That's also a big worry for government regulators when banks get in trouble. Should the government bail out banks that took risks and lost their financial bets?

In 1984, the Continental Illinois Bank based in Chicago was headed for bankruptcy. The government and financial regulators had a choice: They could let the seventh-largest bank in the country fail and risk damaging the financial sector. Or they could bail out the bank by giving it the cash it needed to stay in business. In the end, the government stepped in to save Continental Illinois. The government feared the consequences of letting such a big bank fail.

That might have been the right choice in the moment, but the government worried that it had created a dangerous precedent. This "heads I win, tails you lose" problem creates a dilemma for government:

- On the one hand, the government doesn't want bank collapses to have negative effects on the economy.
- On the other hand, the government doesn't want to encourage risky behavior by bailing out banks whenever they get into trouble.

This dilemma came into sharp focus again when Lehman Brothers, the fourth-largest investment bank in the United States, faced bankruptcy in 2008. After many emergency meetings, the government ultimately decided *not* to bail out Lehman Brothers.

That decision sent shockwaves through the financial sector. Many analysts had assumed that Lehman would be deemed "too big to fail." If Lehman was allowed to fail, financiers wondered how many other banks would also fold. Though concerned about the consequences of a Lehman bankruptcy, the government decided it was more important to send a signal that it wasn't automatically going to help every bank that got itself into trouble.

The very next day, the insurance giant AIG was about to fail. This time, the government *did* step in to bail it out, to the tune of $85 billion. AIG was the country's largest insurer of commercial and industrial outfits. Policy-makers calculated that AIG could not go bust without inflicting extensive damage throughout the financial system.

Where does that leave banks today? Some have suggested that the solution to the "too big to fail" dilemma is to break up "too big" banks into smaller chunks. Those smaller banks could be allowed to fail without widespread damage to the financial system. So far, regulators have simply chosen to regulate more closely banks larger than a certain size (measured by their financial assets). Such regulation is intended to reflect the risks that taxpayers are bearing.

As things stands, the dilemma remains: Any bank that faces going bust will have to wait (nervously) to discover if the government considers it to be truly "too big to fail." Will that bank be considered more like a Lehman Brothers or an AIG?

Sources: www.nytimes.com/2008/10/02/business/02crisis.html; www.cnn.com/2018/10/31/business/federal-reserve-bank-loosen-rules/index.html.

Financial Crisis ■ Chapter 17   475

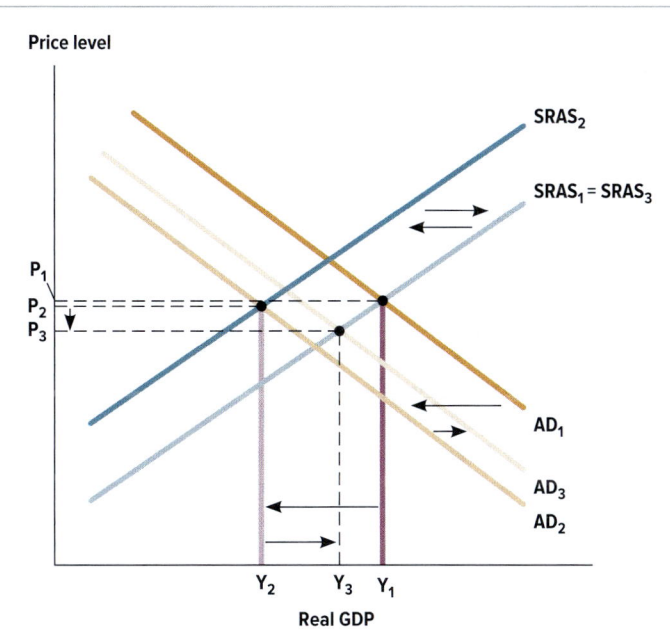

FIGURE 17-8

Fed and Treasury intervention restores aggregate supply

The Fed and the Treasury both responded to the sharp reduction of credit available in the market. Their responses provided enough money in the market to spur aggregate supply and demand, although due to sluggish aggregate demand, output was still well below pre-crash levels (Y_1).

The effect of the monetary and fiscal actions in the aggregate demand and aggregate supply model is shown in Figure 17-8, which builds from Figure 17-6:

- The Federal Reserve lowered interest rates to respond to the sharp reduction in the amount of credit available in the market:
- The Treasury through the TARP provided money in the market.

These two actions restored aggregate supply to its original level.

Once order was restored in the credit market, businesses were again able to finance their inventories and continue to grow their operations. This restoration pushed the SRAS curve back toward its original pre-crisis position.

These actions also supported aggregate demand. As credit markets began to function again, firms started making investments; some consumers who had been putting off purchases in a time of uncertainty opened their wallets. However, due to sluggish aggregate demand, output was still well below pre-crash levels (Y_1).

You might be wondering why all of that capital failed to have much effect on aggregate demand. The short answer is that these programs did not have the same goal as traditional monetary policy conducted through the federal funds rate. Most of the offerings, instead, were used only by banks that faced problems getting the capital they needed to function normally—emergency programs for an extraordinary situation. So even as the financial sector stabilized, the United States found itself with the classic problem of most economic downturns: depressed aggregate demand.

Stimulus at the zero lower bound

LO 17.7 Describe the different tools that can be used to stimulate the economy when interest rates are at the zero lower bound.

The policy prescriptions for fixing low aggregate demand are relatively straightforward:

- The Federal Reserve can pursue expansionary monetary policy, lowering interest rates to encourage borrowing and investment spending, which pushes the aggregate demand curve to the right.
- Alternatively, the government can engage in stimulus through fiscal policy, increasing aggregate demand through tax cuts or increases in government spending.

In fact, both routes were pursued in the 2007–2009 crisis. Congress and President Obama passed fiscal stimulus legislation intended to support demand. The Federal Reserve slashed the federal funds rate from a little more than 5 percent before the crisis to 2 percent. As demand stayed weak—even after stimulus spending—the Fed continued to cut the federal funds rate.

By 2009, the economy was in an unusual situation. Interest rates were near zero, and the economy had still not recovered. Households were trying to pay down their debts; there was little desire to borrow for consumption—even when borrowing was essentially free. With consumption weak, businesses were in no mood to invest in expanding their productive capacity. With interest rates already at zero, it seemed as though monetary policy was out of ammunition. After all, the Fed couldn't lower interest rates below zero (the *zero lower bound*). What *could* it do?

What came out of this impasse was a prescription for unorthodox monetary policy: quantitative easing. **Quantitative easing** involves policies that are designed to directly increase the money supply by a certain amount. As a policy, it contrasts with the more common practice of indirectly adjusting the money supply through interest rates. The Fed accomplished quantitative easing by purchasing long-term government bonds. The aim was to get more money into the economy. In all, the Fed purchased more than $1 trillion worth of long-term bonds with newly created money, thus adding $1 trillion to the money supply.

quantitative easing policies that are designed to directly increase the money supply by a certain amount

In choosing quantitative easing, the Fed wanted to avoid what happened in Japan after a housing bubble inflated in the 1980s and then popped. For years, the Japanese economy was weak, and deflation was a recurring problem. The Economics in Action box "The walking dead" tells the story.

The walking dead
Economics in Action

Zombies are never a good thing, as countless TV shows demonstrate. Imagine an economy where many financial institutions are essentially zombies—not dead, but also not really able to contribute to the economy in a meaningful way. That's exactly what happened in Japan during the 1990s.

During the 1980s, the Japanese economy was one of the strongest in the world. But by the end of the decade, the Bank of Japan decided the economy was moving too fast and raised interest rates to slow things down. Instead of slowing, however, the economy went into freefall. Housing prices fell 87 percent from their peak. This shock ravaged the Japanese stock market. Japan ended up losing the equivalent of three years of GDP, one of the largest peacetime losses of wealth in human history.

In response, the government embarked on an ambitious fiscal stimulus plan that mostly built bridges and roads in rural areas. The Japanese government also bailed out banks that were in danger of collapse. Banks got enough capital to keep them afloat, but the money wasn't enough for normal day-to-day lending. In an especially drastic measure, the central bank dropped interest rates from 8 percent all the way down to zero. When these measures didn't work, the central bank said there was little else it could do—it had reached the *zero lower bound* on interest rates and spent large sums of money propping up the economy.

Japan's economy stagnated. Homeowners who had borrowed to purchase their houses when prices were high cut back on their spending so they could pay back debt. As a result, the economy became so weak that prices started to fall. The resulting deflation further damaged the economy. Consumers held onto their money, knowing that they would be able to buy more in the future as prices dropped. That reluctance to spend drove prices even further downward.

However, one economist who closely studied Japan's experience suggested that much of this "walking-dead"–style stagnation was avoidable. The government could have let some of the zombie banks fail, continued stimulus spending, and tried alternative monetary policy measures, such as quantitative easing, to stimulate the economy.

Who was the economist who proposed these measures? It was Ben Bernanke, chairman of the Federal Reserve during the U.S. financial crisis.

Sources: www.nytimes.com/2010/05/21/opinion/21krugman.html; www.time.com/time/magazine/article/0,9171,1884815,00.html.

After the Fed's first round of quantitative easing, the overall money supply remained nearly unchanged. When the economy continued to stagnate, however, the Fed engaged in a second round of quantitative easing. The second round dramatically increased the overall level of the money supply. By mid-2011, the money supply stood at nearly $3 trillion, more than triple its level going into the crisis.

This enormous increase in the money supply was unprecedented. Critics feared that it would cause very high inflation. With the economy stagnating, however, the increase in the money supply led to only a slight increase in borrowing. Why did this happen? The money multiplier collapsed as banks were unwilling to lend and consumers and businesses were not very interested in, or capable of being approved for, borrowing.

There is still debate about whether quantitative easing was successful in boosting demand. It appears, though, that the Fed's efforts at least prevented an outright fall in borrowing and lending, which would have further damaged an already weak economy.

✓ TEST YOURSELF

- ☐ What is a subprime mortgage? **[LO 17.3]**
- ☐ Why did mortgage-backed securities lead to an increase in subprime lending? **[LO 17.4]**
- ☐ How did the 2007 financial crisis affect aggregate demand? **[LO 17.5]**
- ☐ What is the dilemma involved in deciding whether to bail out a bank that is considered "too big to fail"? **[LO 17.6]**
- ☐ Why would a central bank implement quantitative easing? **[LO 17.7]**

Conclusion

This chapter began with a simple question: Why do financial crises occur? Usually, financial crises arise from a combination of irrational expectations and leverage, which create bubbles that burst with dire consequences for the real economy. Crises have been around since the very first financial markets, as the example of the South Seas Company in the 1700s shows.

These forces surfaced once again when innovations in the subprime lending market led to a dramatic increase in home ownership and housing prices. When the real estate bubble burst in 2007, a financial crisis struck again, challenging economists' belief that economic crises had become a thing of the past.

Recent events show that we still have much to learn about the macroeconomy. Can we permanently moderate the business cycle? How will increasing global interdependency affect future crises? What can governments do to make financial markets work better? There are no quick and easy answers to these questions, but we are starting to better understand the complexity of the challenges. The unfortunate reality is that economies can collapse almost overnight, but they often take a lot longer to recover.

Key Terms

bubble, p. 460
leverage, p. 462
leverage ratio, p. 463
securitization, p. 466
debt service, p. 469
"too big to fail," p. 473
quantitative easing, p. 476

Summary

LO 17.1 Describe the role of irrational expectations and leverage in the creation of financial crises.

The existence of financial crises challenges the efficient-market hypothesis, showing that markets may not always accurately reflect all available information. Irrational expectations, often based on overly optimistic projections for the future, frequently lead to overvaluations of companies' stocks. Combined with leverage, irrational expectations can create or fuel financial crises.

LO 17.2 Discuss the causes of two famous historical financial crises.

The twin dangers of irrational expectations and leverage played out in two famous historical financial crises. The South Seas Bubble of the eighteenth century is one example: Unrealistic expectations about access to trade with South America led to dramatic overvaluation of companies and spawned fanciful investment schemes. Centuries later, the optimism and rush to invest in the stock market following the Roaring Twenties gave way to the Great Crash of 1929 and a decade of economic decline during the Great Depression.

LO 17.3 Trace the role of mortgage-backed securities and tranching in the rise of subprime lending.

Securitization in the market for mortgage loans created a wave of subprime lending. Investment banks packaged these loans into larger mortgage-backed securities, which pooled the risk of subprime loans and enabled more loans to be made. Eventually, banks began tranching these securities, dividing them into segments with different risk and return characteristics. This process allowed the banks to tailor mortgage-backed securities to their clients' investment needs. It also contributed to asymmetric information problems, which later contributed to the crisis.

LO 17.4 Analyze the factors that led to the housing bubble and rising levels of household debt.

Securitization of mortgage loans encouraged banks to offer more subprime mortgages, increasing demand for housing and pushing up prices. At the same time, homeowners found themselves with more wealth because the price of their homes had risen. Feeling wealthier, people increased their household debt, taking out more loans at attractive low interest rates, to pay for higher levels of consumption.

LO 17.5 Explain how the collapse of the housing bubble created a credit crisis and subsequent contraction in output.

Eventually, the housing bubble popped. Many subprime borrowers defaulted on their loans after teaser rates expired; home prices dropped, and banks found themselves with mortgage-backed securities worth a fraction of their original estimate. Many banks stopped lending and many failed; credit markets dried up. Businesses were no longer able to finance economic investments. Households, facing a negative shock to wealth due to depressed housing prices, began saving more and consuming less. Both aggregate demand and aggregate supply shifted to the left. At the new equilibrium, output was dramatically lower. Prices fell because the effect of the leftward shift in the aggregate demand curve was stronger than the effect of the leftward shift in aggregate supply. The economy entered a recession.

LO 17.6 Describe the monetary and fiscal policy responses to the financial crisis of 2008.

In response to the crisis, the federal government acted quickly to stabilize the financial system. The Federal Reserve, in its role as the lender of last resort, offered short-term financing to banks that couldn't access credit otherwise. This provided liquidity to the market, a crucial step in raising aggregate supply. The government also tackled solvency issues by bailing out several large banks through the Troubled Assets Relief Program (TARP). Once the crisis gave way to a contraction in output, the government used fiscal policy to increase aggregate demand by passing stimulus measures.

LO 17.7 Describe the different tools that can be used to stimulate the economy when interest rates are at the zero lower bound.

When the monetary policy hit the zero lower bound, the Fed undertook quantitative easing, designed to increase the money supply by a certain amount. In two rounds of quantitative easing, it directly purchased a total of $3 trillion in long-term government bonds, thus adding that amount to the money supply.

Review Questions

1. Your best friend comes to you for financial investment advice. She is wondering whether she should invest in (a) a sector of the economy that has been performing extremely well in the last five years relative to historical levels or (b) one that has been performing extremely poorly in the last five years relative to historical levels. What would you advise? How might irrational expectations affect your recommendations? **[LO 17.1]**
2. What is leverage, and how can it make an asset pricing bubble worse? **[LO 17.1]**
3. What causes a stock market bubble to form? **[LO 17.2]**
4. History suggests that all stock market bubbles will eventually pop and cause severe financial loss for many of those who purchased stock. Given this history, do you think that stock market bubbles will continue to occur? Why or why not? **[LO 17.2]**
5. Explain why it's possible for tranching to make investing in a mortgage-backed security more risky than investing in a single subprime loan. **[LO 17.3]**
6. Explain how a mortgage-backed security can increase loan availability to those with little credit or bad credit. **[LO 17.3]**
7. Explain the role that leverage played in the recent housing bubble. **[LO 17.4]**
8. How did government policies and asymmetric information problems make the recent housing bubble worse? **[LO 17.4]**
9. Many subprime borrowers entered into "adjustable-rate mortgages" with low teaser rates. These mortgages allowed borrowers to pay a low interest rate for the first two years on their mortgage, before the rate jumped to market levels. But the loan documents sometimes made it difficult for borrowers to understand that the rate would increase. Explain why this practice could lead to a bubble in housing prices. **[LO 17.5]**
10. How did the recent housing crisis affect the aggregate demand curve? **[LO 17.5]**
11. Imagine what would have happened if the Federal Reserve was not in place to act as a lender of last resort during the financial crisis. Absent government involvement, what would be the likely effect on aggregate supply? Why? What would be the likely effect on aggregate demand? Why? **[LO 17.6]**
12. As the Federal Reserve responded to the recent housing crisis, how did this affect its balance sheet? Can you think of what caused the balance sheet's size to change so much? **[LO 17.6]**
13. What is the "zero lower bound" that must be considered in monetary policy, and how can it cause problems in enacting such policy? **[LO 17.7]**
14. What is quantitative easing, and when might it be used? **[LO 17.7]**

Problems and Applications

1. Determine whether or not each of the following is an example of irrational expectations. **[LO 17.1]**
    a. The price of Amazon's stock rises after tech blogs reveal that the company plans to release a new tablet, rumored to be competitive with Apple's iPad.
    b. The CEO of a new start-up producing applications for tablets is quoted as proclaiming a new era of media, in which thirst for content will rise indefinitely as information becomes more and more convenient for people to digest. An economics blog continues the discussion a year later, discussing returns to investment that have never before been contemplated. Stock prices for media companies are consistently outperforming historical levels by 50 percent and seem to be on a permanent rise.

TABLE 17P-1

Margin account level	Account value in a stellar market	Account value in a fair market	Account value in a terrible market
No margin			
60%			
100%			
150%			
200%			

c. After an unusually cool summer, investors in Papa's Cool-Pops decide to sell, believing demand for frozen treats will never reach historic levels again because of the weather.

d. The Justice Department reveals allegations against the CEO of a food and beverage company, alleging misconduct within the company. A trial could cost the company millions of dollars. The stock price falls by 5 percent by the day's end.

2. Ike, an investor, is considering opening a margin account and investing $1,000 in Mike's mutual fund. The terms of the account require that he pay back the amount he borrowed on the margin by the end of the year with 10 percent interest. Ike is trying to decide what level of margin he wants. For example, if he chooses an account at the level of 50 percent, the bank will let him borrow and invest an additional $500, or 50 percent of his original $1,000. Complete Table 17P-1 by filling in Ike's account value at the end of the year, given varying levels of the margin account and mutual fund performance. Assume that Mike's mutual fund will return 40 percent per year in a stellar market and 5 percent per year in a fair market, and that in a terrible market, it will lose 30 percent. [LO 17.1]

3. Consider a stock whose value increases across an 8-year period as shown in Table 17P-2. [LO 17.2]

    a. Calculate the percentage change in the value of the stock from year to year.
    b. Calculate the percentage change in the value of the stock across the entire 8-year period.
    c. Do you think this qualifies as a bubble? Why or why not?

4. Assume that a subprime mortgage involves a loan of $1,000 and is to be paid back in full with 30 percent interest after one year. [LO 17.3]

    a. Sometimes borrowers will not be able to pay off the entire mortgage or may default entirely. Calculate the final amount of money an investor

TABLE 17P-2

Year	Stock value ($)	Percentage change
1	70.00	n/a
2	76.00	
3	82.00	
4	90.00	
5	100.00	
6	187.02	
7	330.00	
8	570.00	

earns under the payback rates shown in Table 17P-3. (Note that a rate of 130 percent means that the whole loan is paid off, plus the additional 30 percent of interest.)

b. Assume investors are unwilling to invest in these loans unless the expected rate of return is

TABLE 17P-3

Amount paid (%)	Final value	Probability
130		0.6
110		0.1
100		0.1
50		0.1
0		0.1

10 percent. Calculate the expected rate of return for this loan by adding up all of the products of the final value and the probability that that value will occur. Will investors want to invest in this loan?

5. A single bank is considering two options: First, it can make a $200,000 mortgage loan for a customer with a 10 percent probability of default or, second, it can buy a $200,000 security representing a bundle of 100 mortgage loans, which break down as shown in Table 17P-4. You can calculate the weighted risk for each firm category by multiplying the percentage of loans represented (for example, the first tier includes 40 loans, which is $\frac{40}{100}$ = 40% of the total) times the probability of default on loans of that category. Do so for each type of loan, then add together the weighted risks to come up with an overall expected default risk for this financial investment. If the bank is willing to take on only projects for which the default risk is 6 percent or less, which option(s) should it choose? [LO 17.3]

TABLE 17P-4

Number of loans	Probability of default (%)	Weighted risk
40	3.0	40% × 3% = 1.2%
25	11.0	
15	1.5	
20	5.0	

6. Table 17P-5 shows hypothetical levels of average household debt and debt service payments in two years, 2015 and 2018. At what annual interest rate would consumers have had to borrow for the debt-service payments in 2018 to equal the debt-service payments in 2015, despite the increase in household debt? Assume households are paying only interest on their debt and not part of the principal. [LO 17.4]

TABLE 17P-5

	2015	2018
Household debt	$40,000	$70,000
Annual debt-service payments	700	?

7. Imagine that your personal finances are summarized by the account balances shown in Table 17P-6. Assume also that your decision to save is a function of your income and net worth. More specifically, assume that your savings each year will be equal to: 0.2I − NW, where I is your income and NW is your net worth. [LO 17.4]

TABLE 17P-6

Assets		Liabilities	
Home	$100,000	Mortgage	$90,000
Checking account	15,000	Student loans	20,000
Car	10,000	Credit card	10,000
Total assets	$125,000	Total liabilities	$120,000

a. If your income is $60,000, how much will you save this year?
b. Assume the value of your house decreases by 20 percent. What is your net worth now? How much will you save?

8. Table 17P-7 gives information on income and debt for a small nation for the years 2015 through 2018. The nation had average household debt of $34,000 at the end of 2014. Use this information to fill in the blanks. [LO 17.4]

TABLE 17P-7

Year	Household income ($)	Financial obligations ($)	Financial obligations as % of income	Household debt ($)	Debt as % of income
2015	35,000	4,200			
2016	38,000	4,100			
2017	41,000	5,100			
2018	45,200	6,100			

9. If the rate currently payable on 10-year Treasury bonds is 4.8 percent and the risk spread is 3 percent, what is the average rate on other forms of commercial lending? **[LO 17.5]**

10. Which of the following policies were used in response to the latest financial crisis? Of those used, which are examples of monetary policy? Of fiscal policy? **[LO 17.6]**
    a. Aggressive controlling of inflation by raising interest rates.
    b. Providing short-term financing directly to small businesses to jump-start investment.
    c. Bailing out banks that have large amounts of risky mortgage-backed securities.
    d. Purchasing long-term bonds to increase the money supply.
    e. Raising the Social Security eligibility age by five years to encourage people to work.

11. Table 17P-8 shows the balance sheet of a bank in millions of dollars. **[LO 17.6]**

TABLE 17P-8

Assets (in millions)		Liabilities (in millions)	
Cash	$ 800	CDs	$2,000
Commercial loans	2,000	Savings accounts	1,500
Consumer loans	600	Long-term debt	1,000
Prime mortgages	800		
Subprime mortgages	500		
Total assets	$4,700	Total liabilities	$4,500

a. What is the bank's net worth?
b. Assume housing prices increase and defaults on subprime mortgages rise, causing the bank's assets in subprime mortgages to decrease from $500 million to $350 million. What are total assets now? What is the bank's new net worth?
c. How far would the value of subprime mortgages have to fall to cause the bank to be insolvent (that is, for liabilities to be greater than assets)?

12. Japan's economic situation throughout its Lost Decade and beyond can be explained in terms of problems with monetary policy via interest rates. Explain what happened. Identify what Japan's central bank should have done. **[LO 17.7]**

13. Consider an economy with $12 billion in base money and a multiplier of 3. The money supply is currently $12 billion × 3 = $36 billion. Now let's say that the amount of base money rises by 50 percent, to $18 billion. How must the multiplier change for the money supply to remain unaffected by this change in base money? **[LO 17.7]**

Endnotes

1. https://fred.stlouisfed.org/series/CSUSHPISA.
2. *Futures* are standardized financial contracts that obligate the buyer to either buy or sell a specified amount of some asset at a particular price at a specific future date. There are two main motivations for buying futures. One is "hedging": Companies and individuals use futures contracts to reduce uncertainty about prices in the future. The other is "speculating": Other investors use futures contracts as a way to make bets on the direction of price changes—and, they hope, to make profits by betting correctly.
3. Holding liabilities constant, equity increases by exactly as much as assets. Since assets are 30 times the size of equity, a 10 percent increase in assets amounts to a 300 percent increase in equity.
4. This provision was effectively reversed by the Gramm-Leach-Bliley Act in 1999.

International Policy Issues

PART SEVEN

The two chapters in Part 7 will introduce you to . . .

the international financial system and development policy.

Chapter 18, "Open-Market Macroeconomics," covers the *international financial system*. If you've ever traveled abroad and traded your dollars for another currency, you've participated in one part of the international financial system. Yet it goes much further than that. Anything that was originally produced internationally and imported into the United States was made possible by the international trade of money. In this chapter, we'll introduce the markets that make this trade possible. Like the domestic financial system, the international financial system is vitally important to the smooth operation of the U.S. economy. We'll describe how it works and where it can get into trouble.

Chapter 19, "Development Economics," turns to a large and pressing question: Why is the world filled with poverty amid so much wealth? This is one of the basic questions in *development economics*. We'll describe how understandings of economic development have changed over time. We'll review the current state of research and introduce promising new methods to rigorously evaluate policies and innovations that aim to reduce poverty. Finally, we'll give some examples of solutions that draw on ideas developed in this text—solutions that are making a practical difference in people's lives.

Throughout the text we've seen how economics sheds light on many questions, decisions, and policy issues. Some (such as tax policy) are more obviously about "economics" and some less so. We hope that in reading, you've learned how to apply the economic toolkit to help you solve everyday problems at home and investigate questions about the world around us.

Chapter 18

Open-Market Macroeconomics

From Factory to Figures

The Apple iPhone has been a runaway success. Since its release in June 2007 to November 2018, Apple has sold over 2.2 billion phones around the world.[1] You might think of the iPhone as an all-American success story, given that Apple is a U.S. company. Technically, though, the iPhone counts as an import. That's because, like so many consumer goods, the iPhone's component parts are put together in a factory in China before the finished product is shipped to the United States.

The fact that the iPhone is an import means that every iPhone bought in the United States contributes to the trade deficit the United States has with China. In 2018, American consumers bought $493 billion worth of goods and services from China, while American firms sold only $111 billion worth of goods and services to consumers in China.

The result is an astronomical $382 billion *trade gap* between what America is buying from China and what it is selling there.

To see what this trade gap really means, imagine for a moment that China bought exactly as much from the United States as it sold to the United States. What would happen? Americans would convert $493 billion U.S. into the Chinese currency, the yuan, and use it to buy Chinese goods. In turn, Chinese people would then buy $483 billion worth of American goods. Everything would balance out.

In reality, though, the Chinese spend only $111 billion to buy American goods. So there must be $382 billion still sloshing around the Chinese economy. Presumably the Chinese don't just keep this money under their mattresses. Where does it end up?

Some of this money is spent or invested at home (as yuan) or abroad, searching for the best return. A lot of them end up being invested in U.S. government debt, meaning the Chinese make *loans to* the U.S. government. Overall, as of December 2018, the U.S. government has borrowed $1.12 trillion directly from Chinese investors by selling U.S. Treasury securities.[2] The web of international financial connections is something to think about the next time you see an iPhone.

LEARNING OBJECTIVES

LO 18.1 Define the balance of trade, and describe the general trends of U.S. trade.

LO 18.2 Define portfolio investment and foreign direct investment.

LO 18.3 Explain the connection between the balance of trade and net capital outflow.

LO 18.4 Describe the determinants of international capital flows using the demand and supply for international loanable funds.

LO 18.5 Show how the international market for loanable funds can be used to explain events in the international financial system.

LO 18.6 Describe exchange rate appreciation and depreciation, and understand their effects on trade.

LO 18.7 Describe the determinants of demand and supply in the forex market.

LO 18.8 Explain fixed and floating exchange rates.

LO 18.9 Describe why monetary policy is ineffective when maintaining a fixed exchange rate.

LO 18.10 Describe the difference between the real and nominal exchange rates.

LO 18.11 Describe the role of the IMF and how financial crises are created by excessive debt and unsustainable exchange rates.

LO 18.1 Define the balance of trade, and describe the general trends of U.S. trade.

What explains trade flows? How and why does the United States accrue debt to China? Why would China lend to the United States? What determines the rate at which dollars can be converted into yuan? This chapter will answer those questions by exploring international economics. We examine the flow of goods and money around the world and then discuss related shifts in the value of a country's currency.

By showing how to understand the macroeconomy in an international context, this chapter sheds light on important policy debates about exchange rates, trade balances, and capital flows across countries.

International Flows of Goods and Capital

International trade is not a new thing. More than 3,000 years ago, China was exporting textiles along the famed Silk Road to the Mediterranean and Persian empires. Over 1,500 years ago, spices were traveling from India to the Roman Empire along the Spice Route. The voyage of Christopher Columbus was inspired by the desire to find a quicker route to the riches of India. Today, modern communications and ease of transportation have allowed international flows of goods and capital to reach unprecedented levels: Consumers in Europe buy freshly cut flowers from Kenya, Americans dine on shrimp from Thailand, and Chinese utility companies ship in coal from Colombia.

In this section, we look at the different ways in which goods and capital flow around the global economy today.

Imports and exports

First, let's look at some patterns of trade in the United States. Figure 18-1 shows trade flows over the last nearly 60 years. You can see that both exports and imports have increased dramatically over this period as the economy has grown. In 2018, exports of goods and services were $2.5 trillion, or approximately 12.4 percent of GDP. Imports the same year were $3.1 trillion, or approximately 12 percent of GDP.[3]

It is interesting to look at the flows in and out, but the number that economists care the most about is the net value of these flows. Called the **balance of trade**, it is the value of exports minus the value of imports.

The balance of trade can be either negative or positive:

- If a country imports more than it exports, the balance of trade is negative. Economists call this situation a **trade deficit**. For nearly every year since 1970, the United States has had a trade deficit. In 2018, the trade balance was −$621 billion, or about 2 percent of GDP.[4]

- If a country exports more than it imports, the balance of trade is positive. In that case, the country is said to have a **trade surplus**. Countries like Japan, China, and Germany run large trade surpluses. For example, the 2018 trade surplus in Germany was worth 8 percent of its GDP.[5]

FIGURE 18-1

Imports, exports, and the balance of U.S. trade since 1960 Until 1980, trade by the United States was relatively balanced; imports were roughly equal to exports. Shortly thereafter, the amount of imports grew faster than the amount of exports, which led to a negative trade balance. Now, the trade deficit stands at almost $956 billion.

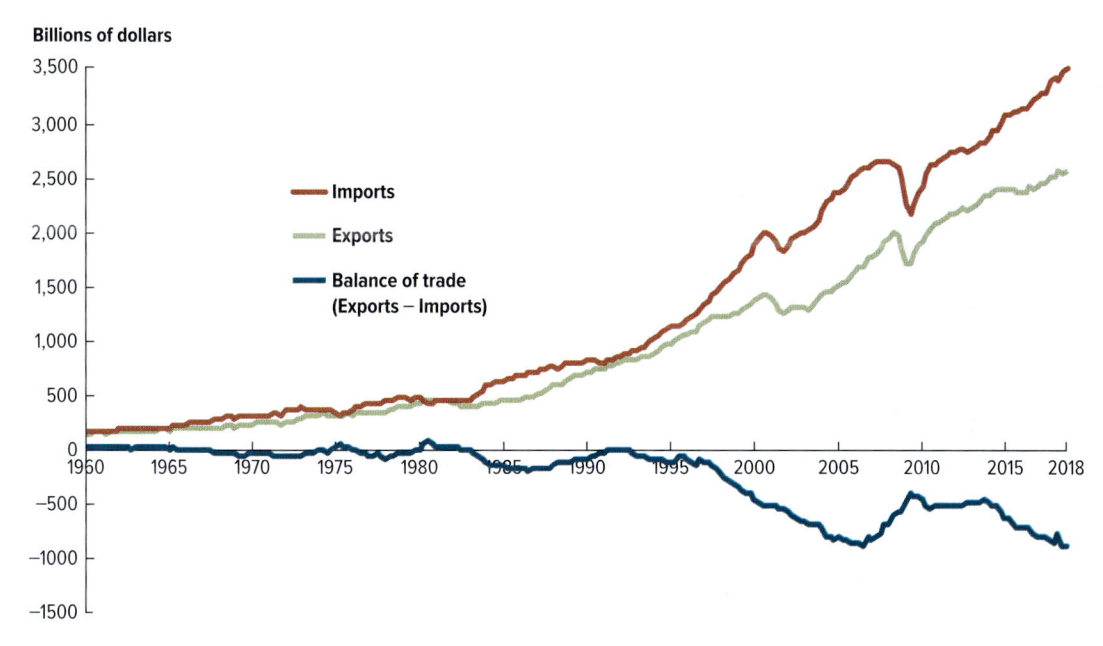

Source: https://fred.stlouisfed.org, exports (EXPGSC1) and imports (IMPGSC1).

Figure 18-1 shows the total trade balance of the United States with all the other countries in the world. If you had to guess, which countries would you expect to be the main trading partners of the United States? Because trade requires transporting goods, which costs money, countries tend to trade with their neighbors. This holds true for the United States. Two of its biggest trading partners are its neighbors: Canada to the north and Mexico to the south. In addition to being neighbors, trade has expanded because of the North American Free Trade Agreement (NAFTA), a pact that eliminates many barriers to trade and investment among these neighbors.

Of course, as Figure 18-2 shows, not all trade partners are neighbors. In fact, the United States imports more goods from China than from any other country, including its neighbors Mexico and Canada. Also, the United States imports much more from China than it exports to it. This difference generates a negative trade balance with China that makes up about 66 percent of the total U.S. trade deficit for goods. As we go through this chapter, we'll examine explanations for the trade deficit with China. One factor is that Chinese products tend to be low in price. We'll also look at less-obvious factors such as the amount of savings in China and its exchange-rate policies.

We've seen how much the United States is trading and with whom—but *what* is it trading? As we described in Chapter 2, "Specialization and Exchange," there are *gains from trade* when countries specialize in producing particular goods and then trade with others to meet their other needs. Looking at trade statistics shows exactly where the gains from trade in the United States come from. Figure 18-3 shows the main categories of goods that the United States exports and imports, and the contribution to the trade balance for each category.

The largest category of U.S. exports is capital goods—goods used to produce other goods, such as factory machines. The United States exported $562 billion in capital goods in 2018. At the same time, it imported $693 billion worth of capital goods, mostly computers and telecommunications equipment. The balance of trade in capital goods was about −$131 billion.

balance of trade
the value of exports minus the value of imports

trade deficit
a negative balance of trade; a greater amount of imports than exports

trade surplus
a positive balance of trade; a greater amount of exports than imports

FIGURE 18-2
Major U.S. trading partners

Much of U.S. trade occurs with its closest neighbors, Canada and Mexico. However, the United States's biggest trading partner is China, even though it is far away. Trade between the United States and China consists mostly of imports into the United States.

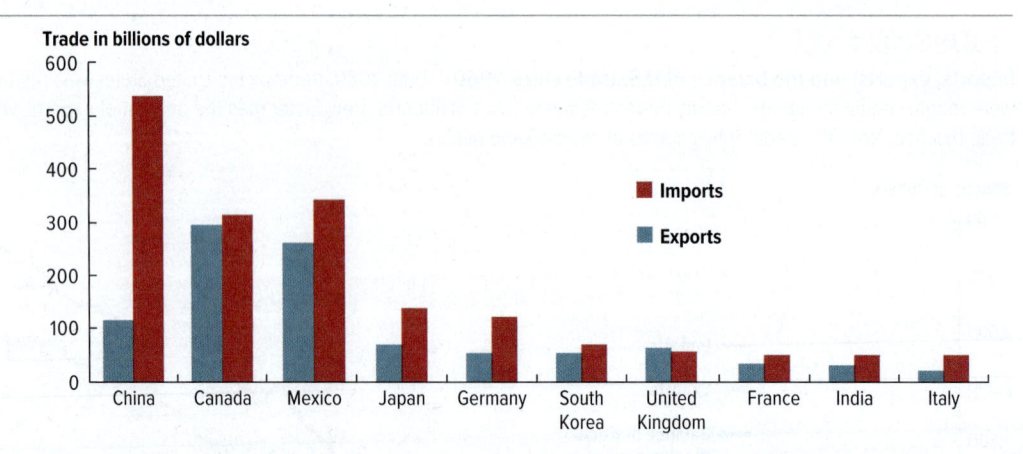

Source: U.S. Census Bureau, Top Trading Partners, December 2018, www.census.gov/foreign-trade/statistics/highlights/top/top1812yr.html.

FIGURE 18-3
What goods does the United States trade?

The United States imports a large amount of capital goods—things that are used to produce other goods—which also constitute the largest U.S. export. The largest difference between imports and exports in 2018 was in the category of consumer goods, as the United States imported far more consumer goods than it exported.

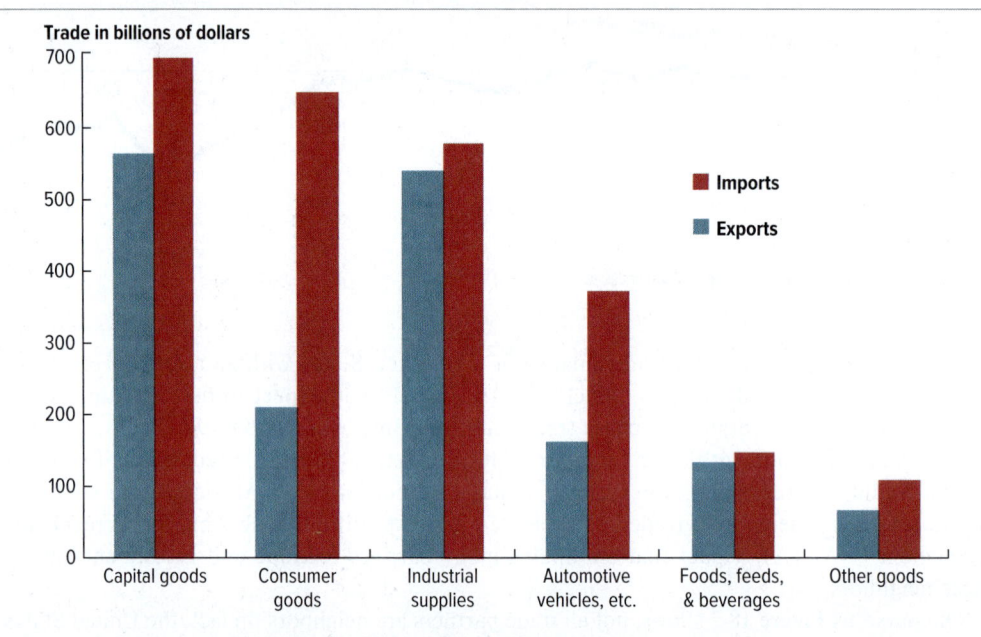

Source: U.S. Census Bureau, www.bea.gov/system/files/2019-03/trad0119.pdf, Table 6.

While the amount the United States imports and exports is pretty close for capital goods, consumer goods are dominated by imports—goods such as clothing, smartphones, pharmaceuticals, and toys. The balance of trade in consumer goods was −$442 billion, with imports of about $648 billion and exports of about $206 billion in 2018. In fact, as of December 2018, the United States was running a negative trade balance in all categories. The "Foods, feeds, and beverages" category had the smallest trade deficit; the high value of U.S. exports of soybeans and corn explained this.

The picture looks very different when we turn to trade in services. Unlike trade in goods, the United States generates surpluses in many categories of traded services. As Figure 18-4 shows, travel is the largest export. When foreign visitors come to the United States and spend on restaurants and hotels, they're adding to U.S. exports. In 2018, non-residents spent $214 billion on U.S.-related travel, which is about $70 billion more than U.S. residents spent on travel in other countries. The United States also ran large trade surpluses for financial services, the use of intellectual property (i.e., licenses for using patented inventions), and other business services.

FIGURE 18-4

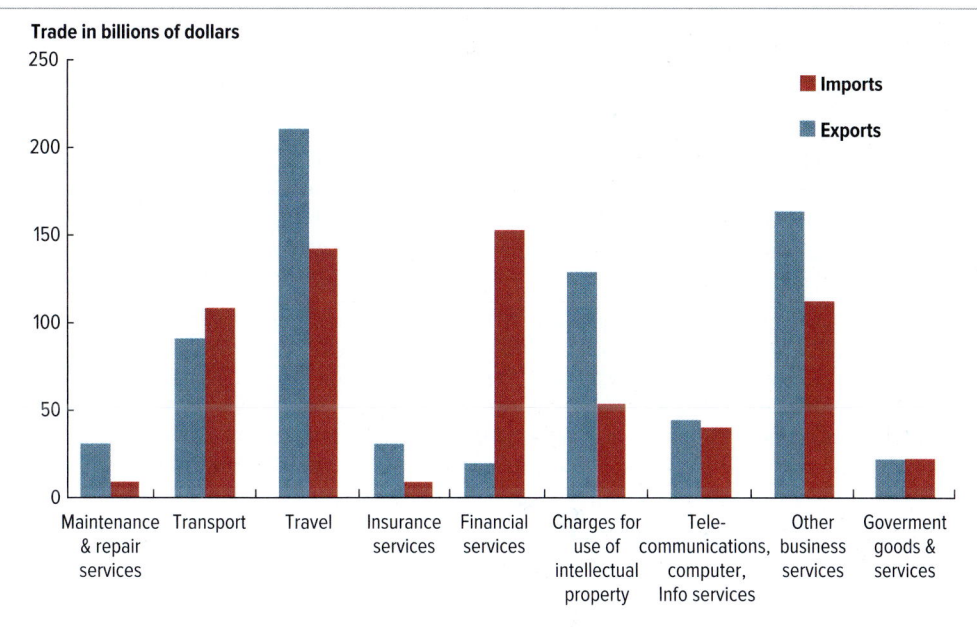

What services does the United States trade?

U.S. exports exceed imports in many categories of traded services. The two largest surpluses in services in 2018 were in the categories of travel and charges for the use of intellectual property.

Source: U.S. Census Bureau, www.bea.gov/system/files/2019-03/trad0119.pdf, Tables 3 and 4.

Foreign investment

Imports and exports are the most visible and straightforward aspects of international economics. Countries interact in other ways as well, including through investment. Here we look at two forms of foreign investment: *foreign direct investment* and *foreign portfolio investment*.

LO 18.2 Define portfolio investment and foreign direct investment.

Foreign direct investment (FDI)
The investment that occurs when a firm runs part of its operation abroad or owns all or part of another company abroad is called **foreign direct investment (FDI)**. Foreign direct investment often makes economic sense for businesses—it helps broaden markets and can cut wage costs, for example.

Some people object that foreign direct investment can encourage "sweatshops" abroad, where workers work for long hours under worse conditions than would be allowed in the United States. For a discussion of some of the issues surrounding foreign investment, see the What Do You Think? box "Are sweatshops good or bad?"

foreign direct investment (FDI) investment that occurs when a firm runs part of its operation abroad or owns all or part of another company abroad

Foreign portfolio investment
Of course, investment abroad doesn't have to be just in tangible assets such as factories. Often, investors also want to buy financial assets, such as stocks or government-issued securities, of other countries. We call this type of investment *foreign portfolio investment*. **Foreign portfolio investment** is investment in domestic financial assets, funded by foreign sources. Portfolio investment allows investors to hold financial assets that deliver greater profit and reduce overall risk relative to financial investments available at home.

Foreign portfolio investment can generally flow across borders quickly because it mainly involves transfers between bank accounts. When a country is small, the rapid movement of money across borders can easily overwhelm the country's financial markets. Foreign direct investment doesn't move as fast. You cannot just pick up a factory and move it across the border.

One of the largest foreign portfolio investments comes from Chinese purchases of U.S. government debt. Part of the reason for this investment is that Chinese investors have a large reserve of U.S. dollars, so they want to buy assets that are U.S. dollar-denominated. Why do they have a large reserve of U.S. dollars? Because, as noted earlier, every time we buy Chinese goods, someone had to sell dollars in exchange for *yuan* to pay for these products. One option for what to do with all these dollars is to use them to buy U.S. Treasury securities.

foreign portfolio investment investment in domestic financial assets, funded by foreign sources

Are sweatshops good or bad?
What Do You Think?

In 2001, an MIT graduate student named Jonah Peretti ordered a pair of sneakers from the NIKE iD service, which allows customers to personalize their shoes with a word of their choice. Peretti asked that his be emblazoned with the word "sweatshop." Nike refused, claiming that the word violated the NIKE iD terms and conditions because it was "inappropriate slang."

Peretti e-mailed back, with false innocence:

> After consulting Webster's Dictionary, I discovered that "sweatshop" is in fact part of standard English, and not slang. The word means: "a shop or factory in which workers are employed for long hours at low wages and under unhealthy conditions" and its origin dates from 1892. . . . Your web site advertises that the NIKE iD program is "about freedom to choose and freedom to express who you are." I share Nike's love of freedom and personal expression. . . . I hope that you will value my freedom of statement and reconsider your decision to reject my order.

Nike again refused, doubtless not wanting the bad publicity. But Nike got bad publicity anyway when the e-mail exchange with Peretti went viral, sparking media coverage around the globe. Peretti had a pointed goal—to shame Nike for the use of "sweatshop" labor to make its shoes. (Nike, for its part, has since taken steps to improve labor standards and monitor conditions.)

Yet here is the irony: Although they are bad for publicity, it's not entirely clear that sweatshops are always such a bad thing. Economists, including Jeffrey Sachs of Columbia University, argue that some kinds of sweatshops are good for an economy. After all, the fact that people choose to work in sweatshops indicates that these jobs are better for them than their other options. Outside of working in the factories, the only alternative may be backbreaking agricultural work that pays even less than the low wages offered by sweatshops. By bringing people out of agriculture, sweatshops provide a source of relative financial security and contribute toward the growth of the economy.

Those who forwarded Peretti's e-mail exchange with Nike presumably felt uneasy with Sachs's argument. Critics of sweatshops think it's wrong that workers can toil for as long as 80 hours per week for what most Americans would consider a tiny wage. Often, it is not just that wages are low by U.S. standards. In addition, workers may be unknowingly exposed to hazardous chemicals and dangerous machinery. Such a problem could be a market failure due to information asymmetry if employees are not fully aware of the risks they are taking. Even where safety regulations exist, workers may be unable to report violations to local authorities without fear of retribution.

WHAT DO YOU THINK?

1. Why do rich countries tend to have stricter labor standards than poor counties? How do you think these labor standards developed?
2. If consumers feel uneasy about buying goods made in overseas sweatshops, should they support efforts to enact minimum wage and worker safety legislation all over the world? Why or why not?

Source: "Making Nike Sweat," *Village Voice*, February 13, 2001.

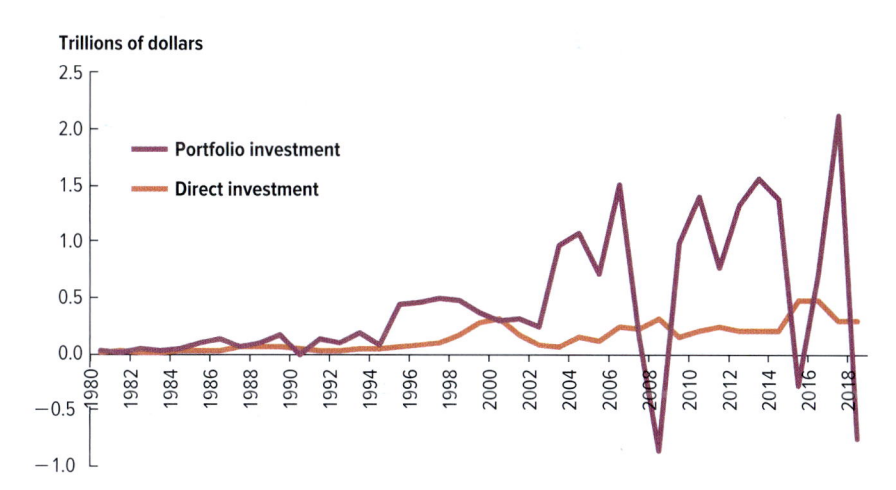

FIGURE 18-5

Net capital flows for the United States

For a long time, foreign portfolio and foreign direct investment flows in the United States were small. Then, starting with the tech bubble, portfolio investment began to ramp up, blipped downward before the bubble popped, and then completely exploded in the housing bubble. The falloff from this crash was severe: In the span of one year, portfolio investment fell from $1.4 trillion to an outflow of $200 billion. Variations since the housing bubble have sometimes been equally dramatic.

Source: FRED Economic Data, https://fred.stlouisfed.org.

Net capital flow When the total amount of foreign direct investment and foreign portfolio investment is tallied, we can find the net investment position of a country. The **net capital flow** is the net flow of funds invested outside of a country. Specifically, net capital flow is the difference between capital inflows and capital outflows:

- *Capital inflows* are investments financed by savings from another country. Countries that have a trade deficit have a *net capital inflow*.
- *Capital outflows* are domestic savings invested abroad. Countries that have a trade surplus have a positive *net capital outflow*.

Figure 18-5 shows net capital outflow for the United States over 30 years. You can see that the capital outflow is broken down into the two types of foreign investment: direct investment and portfolio investment.

The trade in goods, services, and capital comprises trillions of dollars around the world. Keeping track of the trade balance and net capital flows helps organize these transactions. In general, the accounting for trade in goods and capital is known as the *balance of payments*.

net capital flow
the net flow of funds invested outside of a country; specifically, the difference between capital inflows (investment financed by savings from another country) and capital outflows (domestic savings invested abroad)

Balance of payments

The United States imports much more than it exports. The result is a large trade deficit with the rest of the world (the gap was $891 billion in 2019). How can the United States sustain the deficit?

To answer that, we need to look at what's happening to the capital of trading partners like China. It turns out that trade in tangible goods and different types of capital must balance each other out, balancing trade deficits with capital surpluses. The short answer is that the United States can run a big trade deficit because it also runs a big capital surplus.

This is shown through the **balance-of-payments identity**, an equation that shows that the value of net exports equals the net capital outflow. To find the balance-of-payments identity we start with the definition of GDP from Chapter 7, "Measuring GDP." We defined total expenditure in an economy as the sum of four parts:

LO 18.3 Explain the connection between the balance of trade and net capital outflow.

balance-of-payments identity
an equation that shows that the value of net exports equals net capital outflow

$$\text{Consumption (C)} + \text{Investment (I)} + \text{Government purchases (G)} + \text{Net exports (NX)} = \text{Total expenditure}$$

If total expenditure in the economy is **Y,** we can write the relationship more simply as:

$$Y = C + I + G + NX$$

If we then rearrange this equation, we find that savings equals investment plus net exports. This finding relies on the fact that in an open economy, savings equals overall output minus consumption and government spending.

(1) $I + NX = Y - C - G$
(2) $S = S_{private} + S_{public} = Y - C - G$
(3) $S = I + NX$

Finally, assume that people can choose where they want to invest:

- They can invest in the home country; those investments we'll call I, as before.
- Or they can invest in the rest of the world; those investments we'll call NCO, which stands for "net capital outflow."

The total amount of money that a country has to invest, its savings (S), must add up to I + NCO. Using this equation and (3) above, we find that net capital outflows to all other countries equal net exports to all other countries:

(4) $S = I + NCO$
(5) $S = I + NX$
(6) $I + NCO = I + NX$
(7) $NCO = NX$

The result—that net capital outflows equal net exports (NCO = NX)—is the balance-of-payments identity. It answers the question posed in the beginning of this section: *How are countries able to sustain large deficits in trade?* A country that exports more goods than it imports, like China, will necessarily also send out more capital than it receives. That's because China's high net exports must be balanced by high net capital outflows. The capital outflows allow countries to sustain trade imbalances for long periods of time. This idea may seem tricky, so let's work through a simplified example.

Let's assume that China and the United States are both initially closed economies; their savings equal domestic investment. Then, one day, a firm in the United States decides to buy a specialized battery made in China. The Chinese firm sends the battery to the United States, and the U.S. firm gives the Chinese firm a $100 bill.

What will the Chinese firm do with the $100 bill? It can do two things:

- Option 1: It can keep the money in America (for instance, by depositing it in a bank account in the United States, or buying bonds or stocks or financial securities in the United States).
- Option 2: It can buy something in America—say, a collection of economics books—and ship them back to China.

If the Chinese firm decides that it wants to keep the $100 in America, then it has made an investment in the U.S. economy. In other words, the *net capital outflow* from China to the United States is $100. The value of exports—the battery—from China to the United States is $100. Net exports are equal to net capital outflow (NX = NCO).

What if, instead of investing the $100, the Chinese firm decides to use to it buy the books and import them back to China (option 2)?

- Net exports for China are zero: The Chinese firm exported a $100 battery and imported $100 worth of books.
- Net capital outflow for China is also zero because the money earned from the batteries was used to buy books, rather than being invested in the United States. Thus, none of its money remains in the United States.

FIGURE 18-6

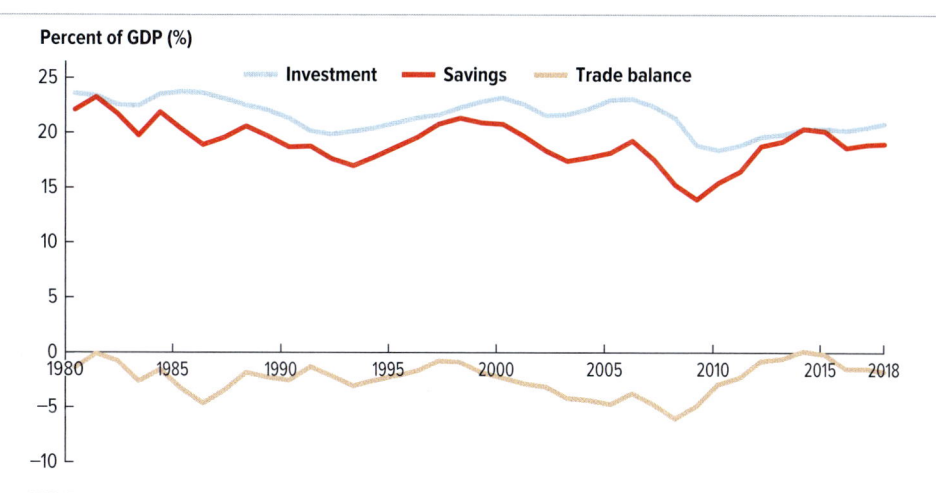

Investment, savings, and net exports in the United States

The gap between savings and investment in the overall economy is shown by the trade balance. When investment is larger than savings, as it is in the United States, an economy will have a negative trade balance.

Sources: FRED Economic Data, https://fred.stlouisfed.org.

So, for China in option 2, NX = NCO.

Now let's look at the same transaction from the U.S. perspective:

- Option 1: The United States has $100 of its currency owned by China; the U.S. net capital outflow is −$100. Because the U.S. firm bought the battery from China, the United States has net exports of −$100. Net capital outflow equals net exports for the United States as well.
- Option 2: When the United States initially imported the battery, it had NX of −$100. But then it exported $100 worth of books, so NX became zero. No capital has been invested in or from China, so NCO is zero. For the United States, too, NX = NCO.

Remember that the balance-of-payments identity tells us that the *net capital outflow of a country equals the value of its net exports*. Figure 18-6 shows savings, investment, and net exports in the United States in recent years. Notice that the gap between savings and investment is almost exactly the trade balance. (There may be small differences, which stem from the complexities of measurement.) In general, savings equals investment plus net exports, as we saw in the equations above.

✓ TEST YOURSELF

- ☐ Which country is the United States's largest trading partner? **[LO 18.1]**
- ☐ What is portfolio investment? **[LO 18.2]**
- ☐ What is the relationship between net capital outflow and net exports in the balance-of-payments identity? **[LO 18.3]**

International Capital Flows

For the last three decades, seas of money have surged into the U.S. economy from abroad, in search of profitable investment opportunities. Why does capital flow into some economies and out of others? In this section, we'll develop a model to explain international capital flows.

LO 18.4 Describe the determinants of international capital flows using the demand and supply for international loanable funds.

Determinants of international capital flows

In Chapter 14, "The Basics of Finance," we developed a model of the market for loanable funds in a closed economy. In that model, the equilibrium interest rate was determined by the intersection of the domestic investment curve and the domestic savings curve—the demand and supply of domestic loanable funds.

How does this model change in an open economy? The basic idea is the same: There still is a demand for and supply of loanable funds. Exactly as before, the *supply of loanable funds* is the sum of national savings. Savings has a positive relationship with the interest rate: As the interest rate increases, savers will supply a greater quantity of loanable funds to the market.

The *demand for loanable funds* (investment) comes from two sources:

- *Domestic investment* is the same as it was in the domestic market for loanable funds, when we considered the economy to be closed.
- *International investment* comes in two forms: capital inflow (when money from abroad is invested domestically) and capital outflow (when domestic money is invested internationally).

For the sake of this model, we will assume that all investment transactions occur through loanable funds. When we subtract capital inflows from capital outflows, we get *net capital outflows (NCO)*. This NCO plus domestic investment form the demand for loanable funds in the open economy. What does this demand curve look like?

We can start with the fact that domestic investment has a negative relationship with the interest rate. (That is, lower interest rates make it cheaper for firms to invest in equipment and factories.) Let's use that knowledge to think about the intuition behind how capital inflows and outflows will be affected by U.S. interest rates.

Suppose the domestic interest rate declines:

- People in the United States will start to look overseas for opportunities to earn more interest on their money. The result will be higher capital outflows.
- Meanwhile, people overseas will be less keen to invest in the United States because of the lower returns, so there will be lower capital inflows.

Higher outflows and lower inflows both push *net* outflows in the same direction: *higher*.

Now suppose the interest rate goes up. In that case, the opposite happens:

- People in the United States will be more willing to keep their savings in the country; outflows will go down.
- At the same time, people overseas will send their financial investments to the United States in pursuit of better returns; inflows will go up.

Lower outflows and higher inflows both push net outflows in the same direction: *lower*.

When we put this result together with domestic investment, as shown in Figure 18-7, we get the combined I + NCO curve—which is the *demand for loanable funds in the open economy*. In the open economy, the equilibrium interest rate is found at the intersection of national savings and the combined I + NCO curve.

Effects of foreign investment

LO 18.5 Show how the international market for loanable funds can be used to explain events in the international financial system.

Using our model of international capital flows, we can begin to examine the impact of foreign investment—and understand why it's often economically beneficial. In short, foreign investment can

- Increase the GDP of the host country by giving it access to additional resources.
- Increase the GDP of the investing country by providing it with ways to earn higher returns on its capital.
- Make the world a more efficient place by moving capital from places with low returns to places with high returns.

To see how this works, imagine that financial troubles abroad trigger a "flight to quality," where investors suddenly find lower-risk U.S. government bonds more attractive as a safe haven for savings. Figure 18-8 shows what happens in this case. The shift in preferences toward investing in the

FIGURE 18-7

Expanded market for loanable funds

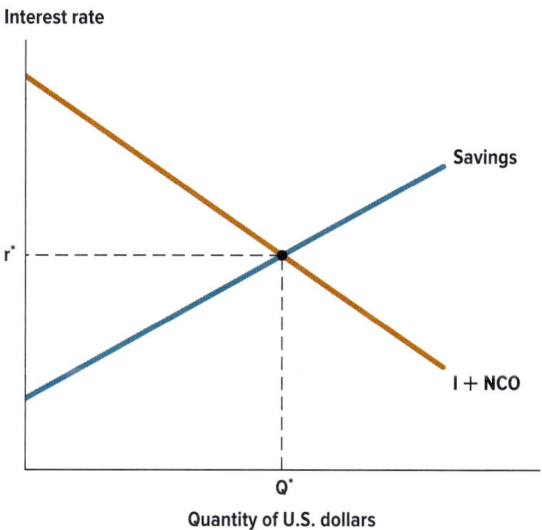

The market for loanable funds in the open economy is determined by both domestic and international investment as well as the amount of domestic savings. Domestic and international investment is reflected in the I + NCO curve. The interest rate is determined by the intersection of the savings curve and the combined investment + net capital outflow curve.

FIGURE 18-8

Effect of a "flight to quality" (purchase of government bonds) in the U.S. economy

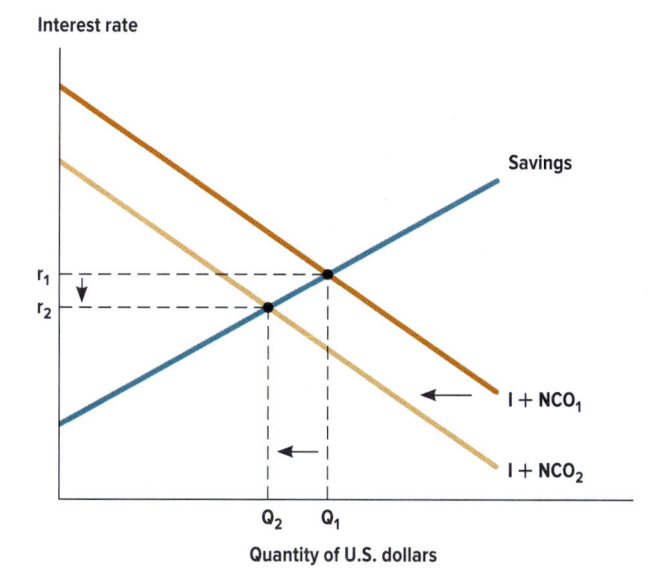

If investors at home and abroad suddenly find lower-risk U.S. government bonds more attractive, the combined investment plus net capital outflow (I + NCO) curve shifts to the left. The result is a lower interst rate, more dollers invested in physical capital, and lower national saving.

United States means that the demand curve for loanable funds in the open economy will shift to the left, for two reasons:

- First, foreign investors are now more eager to purchase U.S. assets than they were before, so net capital outflows contract ($NCO_1 > NCO_2$).
- In addition, the existence of better investment opportunities in the United States means that domestic investors are also going to keep more of their money at home, which again contributes to the leftward shift of the loanable funds curve.

How does this contraction in net capital outflows affect interest rates, saving, and investment in the United States?

- The increase in demand for U.S. assets means that people are now willing to pay *more* for the same stream of payments (and investors are now paying more for the same asset), so the rate of return on these assets (that is, the interest rate) falls.
- The lower rate of return on financial assets makes saving less attractive for people in the United States, which can be seen as the leftward movement along the blue savings curve in Figure 18-7.
- However, the lower interest rate also makes it cheaper for firms to finance capital projects; as a result, investment demand increases. The increase in investment due to the lower interest rates helps explain why the quantity of loanable funds demanded does not fall by the full leftward shift of the I + NCO curve.

Investment is a key component of GDP, so the U.S. economy benefits when foreign investment increases. Foreign investors also benefit from better investment opportunities in the United States, adding to the GDP of their countries.

We can also examine the relationship between foreign investment and public savings. Doing so will bring us closer to understanding the trade imbalance between the United States and China. Recall that the savings curve for the economy reflects the sum of private and public savings. In order to see the connection, let's look at the case of a government budget deficit, which causes a decrease in public savings:

- When the government runs a deficit, the savings curve shifts to the left, as in Figure 18-9. When this happens, the new equilibrium interest rate is higher than before.
- With a higher interest rate, there is more incentive to invest in the United States. Less capital flows out and more capital flows in. Net capital outflow decreases and the quantity of loanable funds saved and invested in equilibrium drops.
- Although net capital outflow is lower, the higher interest rate in the economy due to a decrease in savings instead means that there is a lower level of domestic investment. Foreign and domestic savings are used to finance the government budget, instead of being used to finance domestic investment.

We say that the government deficit "crowds out" domestic investment; the higher interest rate reduces firms' investment in the economy.

As mentioned before, China funds much of the U.S. government deficit by buying Treasury securities. But where does all of that money come from? Ben Bernanke, a Princeton economist and former chair of the Federal Reserve, argues that China is simply saving too much.

Can a country save too much?

Saying that it is possible to save too much is like claiming that it's possible to eat too much broccoli. It's true only at the most ridiculous extremes. But perhaps China's saving rate is at that extreme. After all, it currently saves nearly 50 percent of its GDP! In comparison, the United States saves only 18 percent of its total income.[6] High domestic savings can keep demand for local products low, as people consume less. There are empty malls and vacant housing projects in

FIGURE 18-9
Effect of an increase in the government deficit

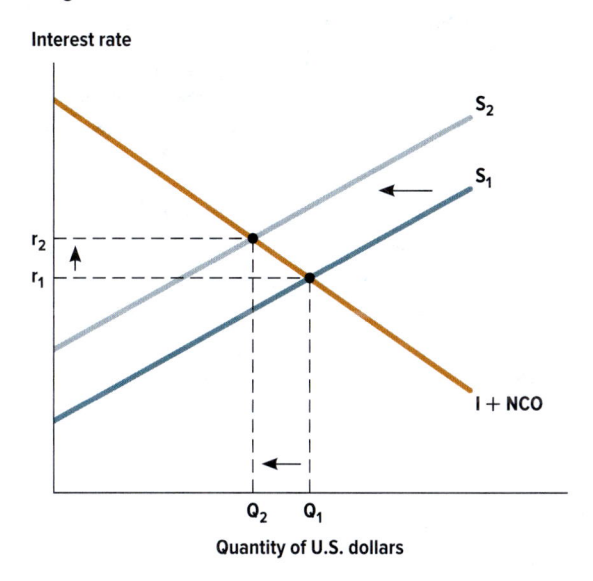

When the government spends more than it collects in revenue, it has to borrow money. This pushes the savings curve left, which results in an increase in the interest rate and lower quantity of investment.

China, simply waiting for customers to open their wallets. Saving too much can also lead to trade imbalances.

We mentioned this idea in Chapter 14, "The Basics of Finance," but now we have the tools to evaluate the effects of a "global savings glut." A growing propensity to save shifts out the savings curve, decreasing the equilibrium interest rate. Low interest rates in China relative to other markets encourage capital to flow abroad, raising net capital outflow—which explains why China has so much invested in the United States.

The massive net capital outflow from China requires that large quantities of Chinese currency are exchanged into U.S. currency. The flip-side is the massive trade imbalance between China and the United States, which requires that large quantities of U.S. currency are exchanged into Chinese currency in order to buy the goods.

If this explanation of the trade imbalance is right, how could it be corrected? Consider a couple of possible solutions:

- One solution could be for China to reduce its savings levels and increase consumption. So long as some of this spending purchases goods or services from the United States, Chinese imports will rise.

- Another solution could be for the United States to increase its own savings levels and spend a little less. The U.S. economy saves 18 percent overall, but the rate of household savings is low (usually less than 5 percent). The rate of government saving is actually negative (the government is running a budget deficit). If the United States were to increase its total savings, either because households or the government saves more, then capital outflow would increase from the United States, reducing the imbalance.

There's another story, however. Others, particularly politicians, suggest that the trade deficit between the United States and China stems from China's fixed exchange rate, an idea we explore next.

TEST YOURSELF

☐ Which two curves make up the international market for loanable funds? **[LO 18.4]**
☐ What is the difference between the closed- and open-economy versions of the market for loanable funds? **[LO 18.5]**
☐ Which way does the savings curve shift when the government reduces its deficit? **[LO 18.5]**

Exchange Rates

If you arrive in a foreign country with a pocketful of U.S. dollars, chances are you won't be able to use them locally. Most local shops and restaurants will require local currency, which you can get by exchanging your dollars at a bank or a specialized foreign currency dealer. The price at which the exchange happens is the *exchange rate*. Sometimes the exchange rate gives you lots of local currency for your dollars. Other times, the exchange rate requires you to give more of your dollars for the same amount of local currency. How does the market for currency work?

The foreign-exchange market

LO 18.6 Describe exchange rate appreciation and depreciation, and understand their effects on trade.

exchange rate
the value of one currency expressed in terms of another currency

The market for buying and selling foreign currencies is often referred to as the "forex" market, short for *foreign exchange*. Every weekday people engage in trillions of dollars of transactions around the clock. They trade dollars for euros or euros for Mexican pesos, for example.

In the forex market, like any other market, there are supply, demand, price, and quantity traded. We'll return to the other elements of the forex market, but for now, we'll talk about the price of different currencies, called the exchange rate. The **exchange rate** is the value of one currency expressed in terms of another currency. For example, in January 2019, one U.S. dollar—abbreviated USD—could be exchanged for 0.88 euro, 6.79 Chinese yuan, 1.33 Canadian dollars, or 19.17 Mexican pesos.

Exchange rates can be expressed in two ways: either in terms of the domestic currency or in terms of the foreign currency. When we examine the exchange rates between two nations' currencies, the exchange rates will be reciprocals of each other.

If 1 unit of domestic currency is worth 6 units of a foreign currency, then we can express this equivalently as the foreign currency being worth $\frac{1}{6}$ of a unit of the domestic currency.

In the real world, foreign exchange rates are often expressed in decimal form rather than fraction form, but the same idea applies:

- If $1 U.S. is worth 0.88 euro, then 1 euro is worth $1.136 U.S. ($1 ÷ 0.88).
- If $1 U.S. is worth $1.33 Canadian, then $1 Canadian is worth $0.75 U.S. ($1 U.S. ÷ $1.33).

TAKE NOTE

Recall that the *reciprocal* of a fraction or ratio is just that fraction or ratio "turned upside down" or "flipped over": The numerator (portion above the fraction line) becomes the denominator (portion below the fraction line), and the denominator becomes the numerator. The reciprocal of $\frac{3}{4}$ is $\frac{4}{3}$, and the reciprocal of 2 (equivalent to $\frac{2}{1}$) is therefore $\frac{1}{2}$.

From this point forward, we will express exchange rates *from the point of view of the United States, using the dollar as the domestic currency*. That means that exchange rates will be expressed in terms of *units of foreign currency required to "buy" one dollar*.

Of course, we could also look at things from the perspective of another nation—for example, from Japan's point of view. In that case, the yen would be considered the home currency, and exchange rates would be expressed in terms of the units of foreign currency—dollars, yuan, euro, and so forth—required to "buy" one yen. All concepts discussed in the chapter apply no matter which nation's point of view we assume.

You might wonder if discrepancies between the forex markets, located in so many places, might arise. Is it possible for a trader to make money by taking advantage of discrepancies in currency exchange rates? For example, could a trader convert dollars to pesos in a Mexican forex market, pesos to yuan in a Chinese forex market, yuan to euro in a European forex market, and euro back to dollars in an American forex market and end up with more dollars than she started with?

This possibility is known as *arbitrage*, gaining financially by taking advantage of discrepancies in currency exchange rates. Yes, it is possible that money *can* be made on such trades. Because of that possibility, forex traders have sophisticated software constantly scouring information from the world's different forex markets to see if any discrepancies exist. If they find them, they instantly trade the currencies until the discrepancy no longer exists. As a result, any opportunities for arbitrage are fleeting.

Although the forex market is made up of many different currencies, one currency, the U.S. dollar, plays an extremely large role in the everyday functioning of international trade and finance. The Economics in Action box "The almighty dollar" explores why the U.S. dollar holds such a lofty position and some possible alternatives.

U.S. dollars can be used all over the world but need to be changed into local currency by currency exchangers. Sometimes this means a bank, and sometimes it is just a small shop, like this one in Manila.
©*Joel Nito/AFP/Getty Images*

The almighty dollar
Economics in Action

If you live in the United States, you don't think twice about using dollars to buy things, to save, and to invest. Why would you use a currency other than the one from your country? It seems a silly question.

Yet around the world, many people do not always use their own currencies. In fact, around the world, the U.S. dollar is king: American tourists who don't want to exchange for local currency can often get by using U.S. dollars when abroad. Global investors looking for a stable place to stash money use dollars to buy Treasury securities issued by the U.S. government. Much of international trade is transacted in U.S. dollars, even when the trade is not occurring with the United States. In total, 62 percent of the money held by central banks around the world is in the form of U.S. dollars. This widespread use of the U.S. dollar enables the United States to borrow and trade more easily. It also enables other countries to transact in a relatively stable currency.

Gita Gopinath, the chief economist of the International Monetary Fund (and a Harvard economics professor), shows that the widespread use of the U.S. dollar in international trade has some downsides for other countries. She argues that since so much trade is transacted in dollars, when a country's currency weakens relative to the dollar, the impact on the country's level of inflation can be very big. This happens because it becomes more costly to buy things sold in dollars—and because so much of imports are valued in dollars.

Why is the dollar king? To start, Americans buy a lot of things abroad. In 2018 alone, $2.7 trillion were used to import goods and services. At the same time, Treasury securities offered by the U.S. government offer investors a reliable return and safe place to store money. However, ballooning U.S. debt ($22 trillion in 2019) and a weaker economy mean that the dollar is not invincible. But which other currency could take the dollar's place?

The euro is one possible replacement for the dollar on the world stage. Most countries in Europe now use the euro, including Germany, France, Italy, and Spain. The euro shares two key

(continued)

factors with the United States dollar. The economy of the European Union is huge, and the value of the euro has also been relatively stable over time.

The euro has its own problems, however. Most important, governments like Germany's simply do not borrow as much as the Unites States. That means that investors have far fewer options for buying government debt denominated in euros. And while the value of the euro has been relatively stable, the European Union has had its share of trouble. A debt crisis in Greece and a vote in the United Kingdom to leave the European Union (so-called "Brexit") have led to some worry about the overall stability of the currency.

China has also made major investments in increasing the influence of its currency, the *renminbi* (also called *yuan* and denoted RMB). China has launched a plan known as the "Belt and Road Initiative" that involves a pledge to spend over US$1 trillion funding infrastructure projects all over the world. China has also signed contracts with Canada, the UK, and others to trade in renminbi.

Even with this investment, however, the renminbi makes up only about 2 percent of the money held by central banks. That's because slowing economic growth in China and worries about the strong centralized authority of the Chinese government scare away potential interest in making renminbi the main currency for the world. "We're stuck with the dollar," concludes Mark Blyth, an economist at Brown University.

Catherine Schenk, an economic historian at Oxford University, comes to the same conclusion about the euro. Given the challenges faced by the European Union, she concludes that, for now, the euro "doesn't look like a very safe haven to go to from the U.S. dollar."

Until there are better alternatives, the dollar remains king.

Sources: Peter S. Goodman, "The Dollar Is Still King. How (in the World) Did That Happen?" *The New York Times*, February 22, 2019, www.nytimes.com/2019/02/22/business/dollar-currency-value.html; Douglas Clement, "Interview with Gita Gopinath," *The Region*, Federal Reserve Bank of Minneapolis, December 20, 2019, www.minneapolisfed.org/publications/the-region/interview-with-gita-gopinath.

Exchange rate appreciation and depreciation Another way in which speculators try to make money from forex is by betting on the direction that an exchange rate will move over time. The value of one currency relative to another can either increase (appreciate) or decrease (depreciate).

When the value of a currency *increases* relative to the value of another currency, we say that a currency experiences **exchange-rate appreciation**. When the currency appreciates, it can "buy" more of another currency. For example, if the U.S. dollar appreciates against the euro—say from 0.7 to 0.8 euro—the result is that one dollar can buy 0.1 more euro than before.

Who benefits when the dollar appreciates against the euro? The U.S. dollar can buy more goods that are denominated in euro, so people who have U.S. dollars and want to buy goods from Europe will benefit. For instance, American tourists in Paris will find that things are cheaper as the dollar appreciates against the euro:

- A French hotel room with a nightly rate of 70 euro would cost $100 at an exchange rate of 0.7 euro per dollar: $\left[70 \text{ euro} \times \left(\frac{\$1}{0.7 \text{ euro}} \right) = \$100 \right]$.

- After the dollar appreciates against the euro, and the new exchange rate is 0.8 euro per dollar, the hotel room would cost only $87.50: $\left[70 \text{ euro} \times \left(\frac{\$1}{0.8 \text{ euro}} \right) = \$87.50 \right]$.

On the other hand, a U.S. company that sells Alaskan salmon to chefs in France likely will find that it has fewer customers:

- A $25 pound of salmon would sell for 17.50 euro in Paris at an exchange rate of 0.7 euro per dollar: $\left[\$25 \times \left(\frac{0.7 \text{ euro}}{\$1} \right) = 17.50 \text{ euro} \right]$.

exchange-rate appreciation
an increase in the value of a currency relative to the value of another currency

- After the dollar appreciates against the euro, and the new exchange rate is 0.8 euro per dollar, the $25 pound of salmon would sell for 20 euro: $\left[\$25 \times \left(\frac{0.8 \text{ euro}}{\$1}\right) = 20 \text{ euro}\right]$.

In contrast, when the value of a currency *decreases* relative to other currencies, we say that a currency experiences **exchange-rate depreciation**. When the currency depreciates, it can "buy" less of another currency. In our example, when the dollar appreciates against the euro, logic tells us that the euro has *depreciated* against the dollar. Or imagine the U.S. dollar goes from being worth 6.5 yuan to 6 yuan. We say the U.S. dollar has depreciated—it now buys fewer yuan than it did before.

Who's going to be happy if the dollar depreciates against the yuan? U.S. consumers will have to pay more for Chinese goods, which they won't like. On the other hand, U.S. exporters will have an easier time selling to Chinese consumers.

exchange-rate depreciation
a decrease in the value of a currency relative to other currencies

The exchange rate and net exports
Exchange rates affect nearly every dimension of international economics. The flow of goods is one example:

- When the U.S. dollar appreciates against a foreign currency, U.S. goods become more expensive to people abroad, and foreign goods become cheaper for Americans. As a result, we would expect *net exports to decrease*.
- When the U.S. dollar depreciates against a foreign currency, foreign goods become more expensive for Americans, and American goods become cheaper for foreign consumers. We would expect *net exports to increase*.

Does this expectation hold empirically? Figure 18-10 shows U.S. net exports plotted against an exchange-rate index. That index represents the average value of the U.S. dollar against its main trading partners. Just as we would expect:

- When the U.S. dollar goes up in value against other currencies, net exports tend to go down soon afterward. When net exports fall, the trade deficit rises. That's why we see that when the exchange rate rises (as represented by the "Real effective exchange rate index" line in Figure 18-10), the trade deficit will usually rise too.
- Similarly, when the U.S. dollar drops in value, exports tend to go up, which reduces the trade deficit. When the exchange rate falls, so will the trade deficit.

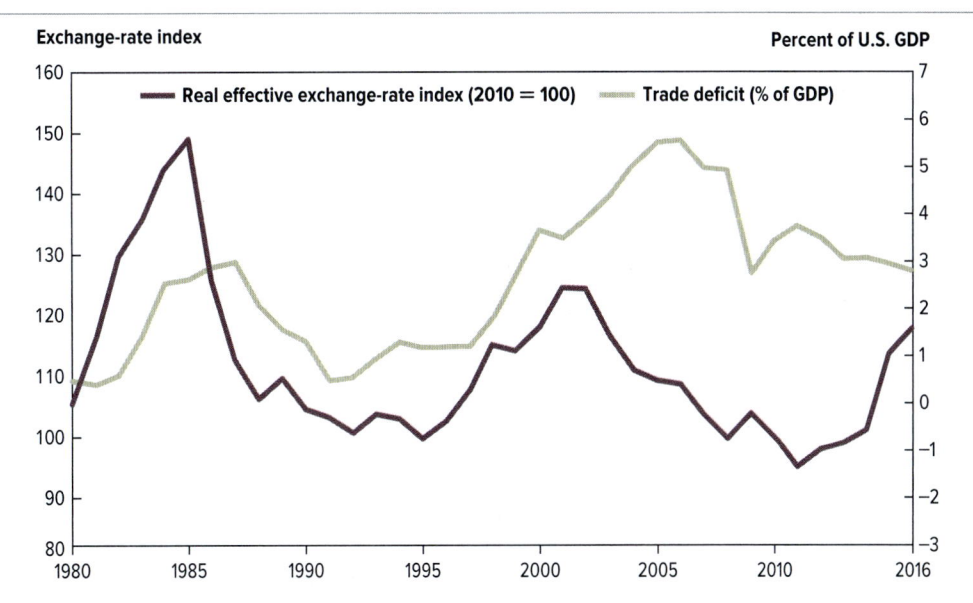

FIGURE 18-10
Trade deficit and the exchange rate in the United States

In the United States, there is a distinct relationship between the exchange rate (shown here relative to its 2010 level) and the trade deficit. When the exchange rate falls, the trade deficit decreases, although this effect operates on a lag, meaning that it takes time for trade to respond to changes in the exchange rate.

Sources: The World Bank, http://data.worldbank.org/indicator/NE.RSB.GNFS.ZS?end=2015&locations=US&start=1990 and http://data.worldbank.org/indicator/PX.REX.REER.

A model of the exchange-rate market

LO 18.7 Describe the determinants of demand and supply in the forex market.

As we mentioned, the foreign-exchange market is a market like any other: There is demand for a currency and a supply of that currency. An equilibrium price and quantity are determined by the intersection of supply and demand. What determines demand and supply in the forex market?

Demand for foreign currency Let's start with *demand*. Why would foreigners demand foreign currency? Three key factors affect such demand:

- Consumer preferences.
- Interest rates.
- Perceived risk.

The first determinant of demand for currency comes from *consumer preferences*—from foreign consumers, businesses, and governments that want to use the currency to buy goods or services in the domestic currency. For example, a British family might demand dollars to be able to vacation in Florida. A Japanese shop might demand dollars to import U.S.-made furniture for sale to Japanese consumers. The Chinese government might demand dollars to be able to purchase financial assets such as U.S. Treasury debt.

The demand for dollars also depends on *interest rates*, both in the United States and abroad:

- High interest rates in the United States *relative to overseas* will attract foreign capital. These assets need to be paid for in U.S. dollars, so demand for U.S. dollars will increase.
- On the other hand, if foreign interest rates are high *relative to those in the United States*, demand for dollars will decrease. Investors will sell their dollars to buy foreign currency for investment.

The last key variable in determining the demand for a country's currency is the *perceived risk* of investing in that country against the perceived risk of investing in other countries. Generally, the United States is seen as a safe place to invest. However, if investors feel confident about putting money into emerging economies such as Brazil, India, or Thailand, they will invest more there, all else equal. If investors decide it is risky to invest in such countries compared to the United States, then more people will want to invest more in the United States, increasing the demand for U.S. dollars.

To make an investment, one has to have the right currency. Anything that motivates investors to invest in a particular country will therefore increase demand for the currency of that country.

Supply of foreign currency What about factors affecting the *supply* of foreign exchange? The same three factors affect the supply:

- First, *consumer preferences* play a role. If U.S. consumers prefer foreign goods, they will sell their dollars to obtain foreign currency, increasing the supply of U.S. dollars in the forex market.
- If the U.S. *interest rate* is low relative to foreign interest rates, financial investors holding U.S. assets will want to sell them and purchase foreign assets.
- Finally, *perceived risk* plays a role: If investors' *confidence* in foreign economies increases, the supply of U.S. dollars will increase as investors sell off U.S. assets.

The equilibrium exchange rate Panel A of Figure 18-11 shows how the supply of and demand for dollars determines the equilibrium exchange rate against any other given currency. The "price" of the currency is the exchange rate. As the exchange rate increases, the quantity supplied of dollars increases and the quantity demanded of dollars decreases

Panel B of Figure 18-11 shows how the equilibrium exchange rate in turn determines the level of net exports:

- When the price of dollars is high, foreigners will buy fewer goods from the United States and Americans will buy more goods from overseas. As a result, net exports are low and may even be negative.

FIGURE 18-11
The foreign-exchange market in equilibrium

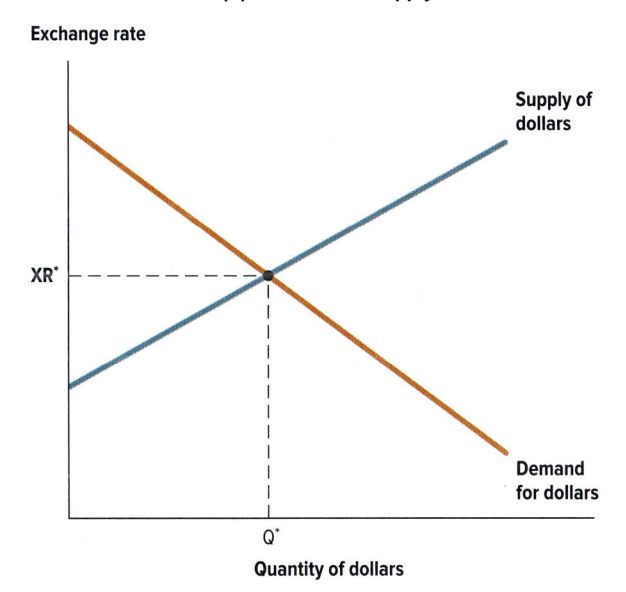

(A) Demand and supply

Like any other market, there is supply and demand for foreign currency. The quantity supplied of dollars increases as the exchange rate increases, and the quantity demanded decreases as the price of currency increases. The price of the currency is known as the exchange rate.

(B) Exchange rate and net exports

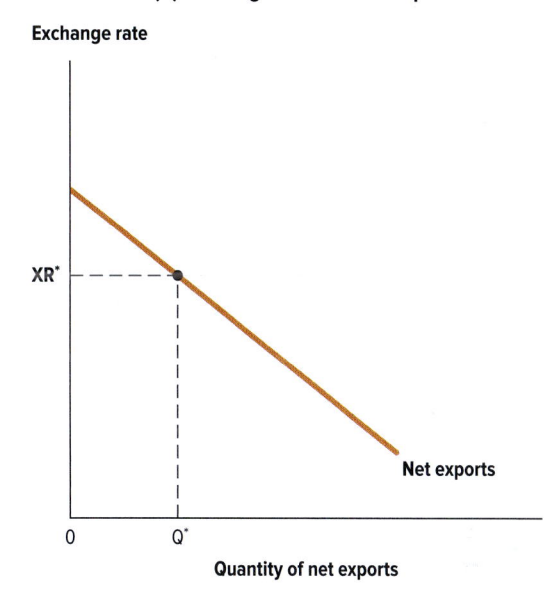

As the exchange rate from local to foreign currency decreases, the quantity of net exports decreases. With the lower price of goods, local goods will become attractive to foreigners, and foreign goods will be more expensive locally.

- When the price of dollars is low, the reverse happens: It's cheap for foreigners to buy U.S. goods and expensive for Americans to buy foreign goods, so net exports will be high.

An example: Prius imports Let's look at an example of how this model works in practice. When the Toyota Prius was released to the U.S. market in 2003, many people wanted to get their hands on the first mass-produced hybrid gas/electric vehicle. Because the Prius was manufactured by Toyota in Japan, U.S. dealers had to exchange dollars for Japanese yen to be able to buy and import Priuses. This led the supply curve of U.S. dollars to shift to the right. The exchange rate from the U.S. dollar to the Japanese yen fell as a result. The new equilibrium is shown in panel A of Figure 18-12.

What effect would the fall in the exchange rate have on net exports for the United States? As we have seen, the net export curve is a demand curve; it shows the demand for net exports at different prices (in this case, those prices are exchange rates). Just like a standard demand curve, shifts in preferences shift the net export curve. Actually, two shifts occur:

- When U.S. consumers decide they want to buy Priuses rather than cars made in America, this shift in preferences moves the net export curve to the left (because more imports mean fewer exports).
- However, something else is also going on at the same time: Because the value of U.S. dollars depreciated, U.S. exports would become cheaper, which would increase the quantity of net exports.

Panel B of Figure 18-12 shows the combined effects of these two shifts: The effects of a greater preference for Japanese cars are counterbalanced by the effects of the depreciation in the exchange

FIGURE 18-12
Increase in demand for Prius cars

(A) Foreign-exchange market

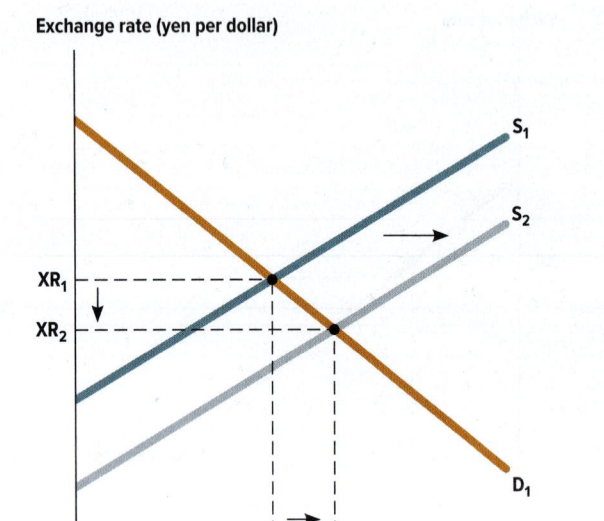

[Graph showing Exchange rate (yen per dollar) on y-axis and Quantity of dollars on x-axis. Supply curve shifts from S₁ to S₂ (rightward), with demand curve D₁. Equilibrium moves from (Q₁, XR₁) to (Q₂, XR₂).]

When the demand for Priuses shifts to the right, the supply of dollars at equilibrium increases as more people are trying to sell dollars in order to purchase yen. This shift increases the quantity of dollars traded, but lowers the exchange rate.

(B) Exchange rate and net exports

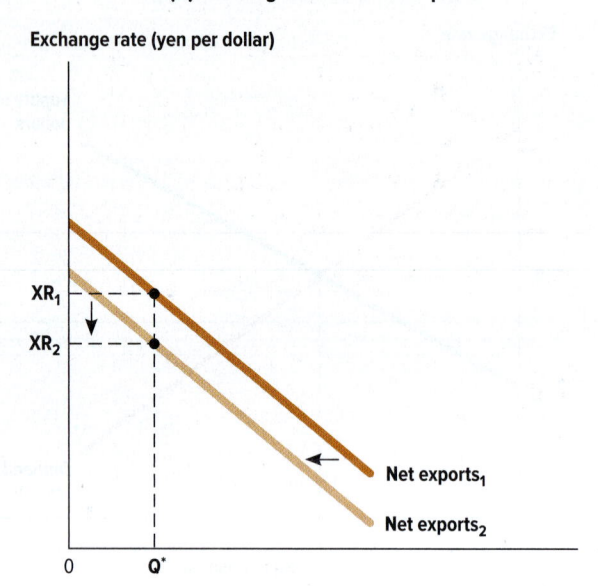

[Graph showing Exchange rate (yen per dollar) on y-axis and Quantity of net exports on x-axis. Net exports curve shifts leftward from Net exports₁ to Net exports₂. Exchange rate falls from XR₁ to XR₂ at the same quantity Q.]*

Since Americans are now importing far more cars, the net exports curve shifts to the left. At the same time the exchange rate falls. Depending on the size of these two changes, the quantity of net exports could be higher or lower than it was before; in this instance the two cancel each other out.

rate. Depending on *which effect is bigger*, the quantity of net exports could end up being higher *or* lower than before the Prius was introduced. In this case, the graph depicts the effects as canceling each other out exactly.

Another example: A rising interest rate
Now imagine another scenario: The Federal Reserve decides to tighten monetary policy by increasing the interest rate. This increase is going to affect both the demand for and the supply of U.S. dollars:

- Because the return to investment is higher in the United States as a result of the higher interest rate, foreign investors want to buy U.S. foreign assets; the demand for U.S. dollars increases.
- At the same time, U.S. investors would rather invest in their own economy instead of buying financial assets abroad, reducing the supply of U.S. dollars.

As shown in panel A of Figure 18-13, these shifts will cause the exchange rate to appreciate. Although the figure does not show a change in the quantity of U.S dollars traded, this result could change depending on whether the demand or supply response is stronger. For example, a smaller shift left in the supply curve would result in a larger quantity of dollars available for foreign markets. Nothing in this story will shift the net exports curve, however. Therefore, panel B shows that the higher exchange rate translates directly into a reduction in net exports.

We can also look at the change in monetary policy in another way. We know that net exports equal net capital outflows (NX = NCO), so the higher exchange rate has also caused a reduction

FIGURE 18-13
Effects of tighter monetary policy in the United States

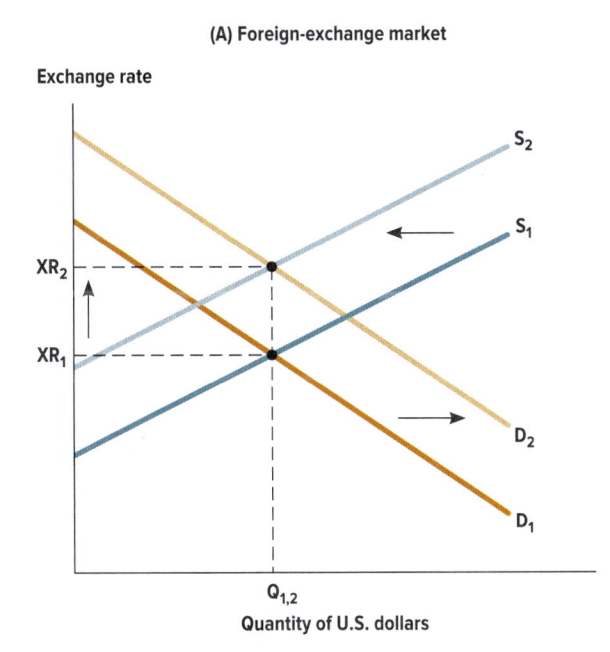

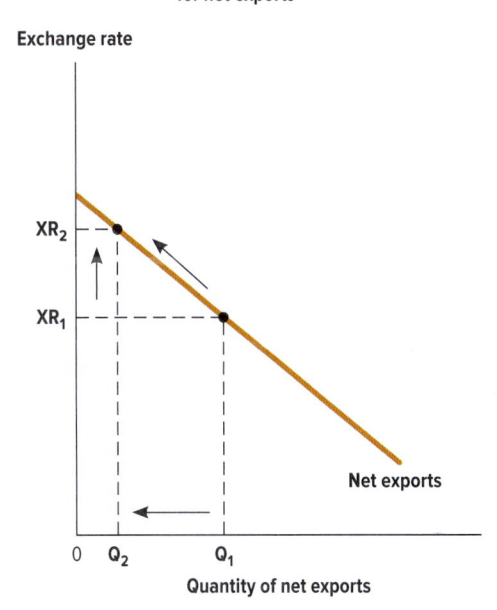

(A) Foreign-exchange market

(B) Decrease in quantity demanded for net exports

When the Federal Reserve tightens the money supply, the price of the dollar initially rises and supply decreases. Demand shifts out as well, and the price of the dollar rises and the quantity of dollars traded returns to the initial amount.

With an increase in the exchange rate of the dollar, the quantity of net exports falls, as U.S. goods are now more expensive for foreigners.

in NCO. In other words, it has caused more capital *inflows*. We know that there will be more capital flowing into the United States when interest rates go up, as foreign savers take advantage of the opportunity to get a better return.

Our model of the foreign-exchange market has shown us that monetary policy works on aggregate demand in two ways: reducing investment and reducing net exports. Remember, by raising the interest rate, the Fed is trying to cool off the economy. So:

- A higher interest rate makes borrowing more expensive, reducing investment.
- Increasing the interest rate also causes the exchange rate to appreciate, which reduces net exports.

Because net exports are also part of aggregate demand, reducing net exports further reduces aggregate demand.

However, this result holds only in an open economy where the exchange rate is determined by the market. As we shall now see, some governments do not allow the market to determine the exchange rate for their currency.

Exchange-rate regimes

The euro is used by 23 European countries, each of which previously had its own currency. Since many European countries are small, different currencies made life difficult. A 150-mile trip from Dusseldorf, Germany, to Brussels, Belgium, with a stop in Maastricht in The Netherlands, would require the use of three separate currencies—the German mark, Dutch guilder, and Belgian franc.

LO 18.8 Explain fixed and floating exchange rates.

Now, with the euro, tourists no longer have the hassle of exchanging money (and paying a commission to do so) every time they cross a border. Businesses that do a lot of trade with neighboring countries no longer have to worry about exchange-rate fluctuations changing the prices they have to pay for their inputs or will receive for their products.

There are also disadvantages, however. In being so tightly joined to other economies, the members of the euro zone give up some of their ability to conduct independent macroeconomic policy. For example, let's say that:

- Germany has low unemployment: Wages are rising, and so are concerns about inflation. We know that to tackle inflation, a central bank would usually tighten monetary policy—that is, increase interest rates.
- At the same time Italy is experiencing *high* unemployment. There, a central bank would usually loosen monetary policy—that is, lower interest rates.

When Germany used the mark and Italy used the lira, these differing monetary policies would cause their currencies' exchange rates to change. In our example, the lira would depreciate and the mark would appreciate. The result? Italian products would become cheaper for other countries to buy, helping to boost aggregate demand in Italy and tackle unemployment. Meanwhile, just as we saw in the U.S. example presented in Figure 18-13, the appreciating German mark would help to reduce net exports in Germany and also aggregate demand, easing the upward pressure on prices. When countries gave up their own currencies and joined the euro, however, they could no longer pursue their own monetary policies to tackle their specific macroeconomic situations.

Why this isn't a problem among U.S. states? What if Wisconsin is experiencing high demand for labor and rising prices and wages, whereas Nebraska is experiencing high unemployment? The problem solves itself without any need for separate currencies and exchange rate changes: We would expect unemployed Nebraskans to move to Wisconsin in search of higher wages, and Wisconsin-based businesses to relocate to Nebraska in search of cheaper labor.

The difference with the euro zone is that, unlike people in Nebraska and Wisconsin, Germans and Italians speak different languages and have distinct cultures. In theory, Italian laborers can seek work in Germany and German businesses can relocate to Italy. But in practice it's not so easy—certainly not as easy as moving from one state to another in the United States.

Not all countries that share a currency are neighbors. In fact, Ecuador, a small country in South America, now uses U.S. dollars exclusively. The barriers seem even greater than between Italy and Germany: Ecuador and the United States are much farther apart geographically, and unemployed Ecuadorans don't have the legal right to seek work in the United States, as Italians do in Germany. Still, that hasn't stopped Ecuador from adopting the U.S. dollar as its currency, as the Economics in Action box "Dollarization: When not in the U.S. . . ." discusses.

Dollarization: When not in the U.S. . . .
Economics in Action

In 1998 and 1999, Ecuador experienced a wrenching financial crisis that caused the value of the Ecuadoran currency, the sucre, to fall by 50 percent in just two months. Within two years, 70 percent of Ecuador's financial institutions went out of business, sending shockwaves throughout the rest of the economy. When the crisis was over, the country's GDP, at $10 billion, was half of what it had been two years earlier.

Rather than try to reboot the sucre, the government decided to "dollarize"—to replace all sucres with U.S. dollars. This move immediately stabilized the Ecuadoran economy. In just three years, the annual inflation rate in Ecuador dropped from 20 percent to 2.7 percent.

However, dollarization has a drawback: It tied Ecuador's economy to that of the United States, for better or worse. In exchange for a stable currency and lower inflation, the government had to give up control of monetary policy. Ecuador's government cannot print U.S. dollars if the country's economy is in recession. Nor can it reduce the amount of U.S. dollars in circulation if it wants to cool an overheating economy. Only the U.S. Federal Reserve can do those things, and the Fed is not likely to take much account of Ecuador's macroeconomic needs when making decisions. If the U.S. economy is doing well while Ecuador is struggling, a contraction in the money supply would further damage the Ecuadoran economy.

Ecuador is one of a few countries that have decided to dollarize. They have given up their own national currency and thrown in their lot with the United States in terms of monetary policy and exchange rates. Most of these countries are scattered throughout the Pacific (such as Palau and Micronesia) or Latin America (Panama and El Salvador, along with Ecuador). Zimbabwe, in southern Africa, also dollarized (although not so successfully).

It is a rather dramatic step, but for countries where inflation or financial instability is a persistent problem, the price of giving up control over monetary policy is one that may be well worth paying.

Source: www.imf.org/external/pubs/ft/issues/issues24.

Fixed and floating rates Exchange rates either can float in response to market conditions or can be fixed at a certain level.

The dollar, euro, Mexican peso, and Japanese yen are all examples of currencies with a **floating exchange rate**. Their value is determined by the market. The exchange rate of floating-rate currencies is set by the intersection of the supply and demand curves for foreign exchange, shown in panel A of Figure 18-14. Floating-rate currencies can be freely traded by market participants.

Some currencies, however, have a **fixed exchange rate**—one that is set by the government, usually with reference to the U.S. dollar or some composite index of major global currencies. A fixed exchange rate can be fixed at a price that is above the market equilibrium rate or below the market equilibrium rate, as shown in panel B of Figure 18-14.

Why might a government decide to fix its currency's exchange rate? The thinking is similar to Ecuador's decision to dollarize. The theory is that a fixed rate allows for more predictability and stability. More stability helps attract foreign investment and gives businesses that depend on overseas trade more confidence to invest.

How is a fixed exchange rate kept above or below market rates? To maintain a fixed exchange rate, the government needs to be prepared to intervene in the foreign-exchange market, either buying or selling foreign currency. For example, let's say that all of a sudden consumers develop a greater appetite for imported goods. What would happen under each type of exchange-rate regime?

- If the exchange rate were allowed to float, the increased supply of local currency would push the exchange rate downward.
- When the exchange rate is fixed, though, the exchange rate is not allowed to depreciate. The government then has to step into the foreign-exchange market and buy up local currency to

floating exchange rate
an exchange rate whose value is determined by the market

fixed exchange rate
an exchange rate that is set by the government, instead of determined by the market

FIGURE 18-14
Floating versus fixed exchange rates

(A) Floating exchange rate

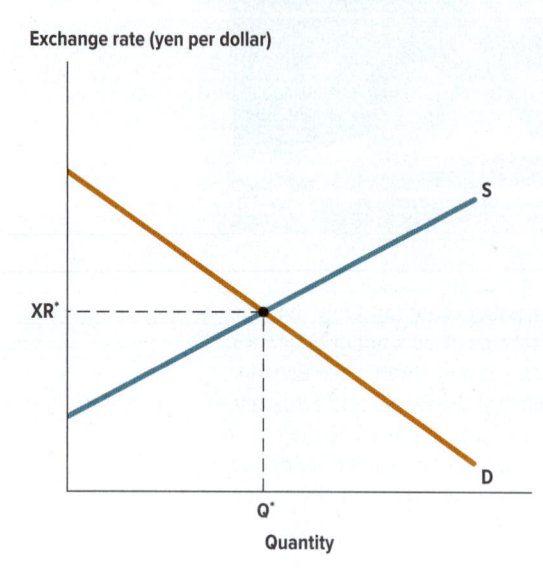

When the exchange rate is allowed to float, the market for foreign exchange will operate at the equilibrium price and quantity.

(B) Fixed exchange rate

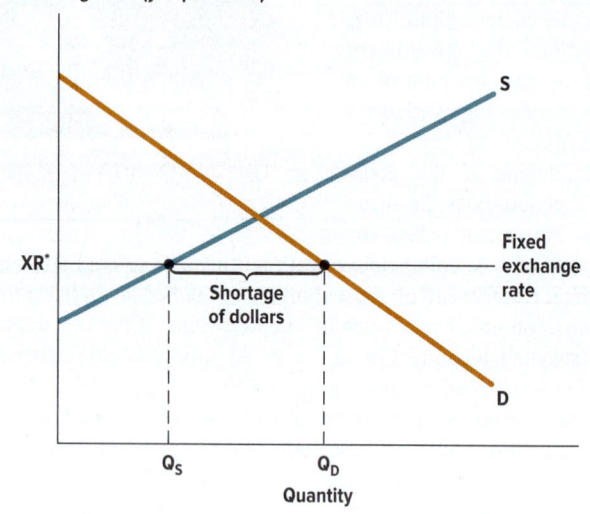

On the other hand, when there is a fixed exchange rate that is set too low, there is excess demand for the currency, which the government must cover by buying foreign currencies and selling the local currency.

> **TAKE NOTE**
>
> Economists use a slightly different vocabulary to describe changes in the exchange rate when the exchange rate is fixed. Instead of saying that a currency depreciates, we say that it is *devalued* if the government lowers the level at which the fixed exchange rate is set. Likewise, instead of saying that a currency appreciates, we say that the fixed exchange rate is *revalued* if the fixed exchange rate is set higher.

balance out the increased supply. Governments generally try to increase demand for their currency by using their own reserves of foreign currencies to buy the domestic currency.

Maintaining a fixed exchange rate can be tough, especially when investors begin to doubt the overall health of an economy. Then investors will start to sell their investments, increasing the supply of local currency. To counter that, the government will be forced to spend large amounts of foreign reserves to prop up demand for its currency.

Some investors, called *speculators*, look for these kinds of situations. The moment they begin to doubt the ability or the resolve of a country to maintain its fixed exchange rate, they will sell that currency, converting it into a different currency, like dollars. If they dump a lot of the currency quickly, they may cause the government to run out of its stock of dollars and other foreign reserves.

If that happens, the government has to give up its efforts to maintain the fixed exchange rate. The value of the currency usually drops fast. At that point, the speculators come back in and buy the cheapened currency. They pocket a profit from having sold the currency at a high price and then buying it back at a low price. When this activity is happening, we say that a currency is experiencing a *speculative attack*.

In 1997, for example, the Thai baht came under intense speculative attack from investors. The Thai government had a fixed-exchange-rate policy; when the attack began, it needed to use foreign reserves to buy baht. The government spent more than $33 billion (about 90 percent of the country's foreign reserves) trying to protect the currency. It also increased domestic interest rates to

FIGURE 18-15
Speculative attack on the Thai baht

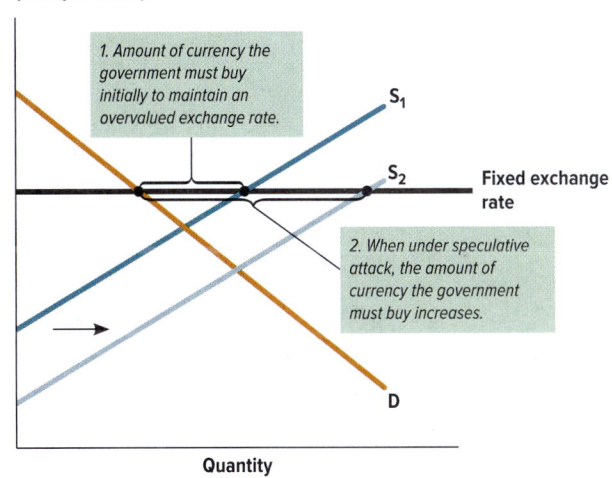

When a country suffers from a speculative attack, the supply of currency available shifts right. This lowers the equilibrium exchange rate even further, forcing the government to spend even more to defend the fixed exchange rate.

encourage investors to keep money in the country. However, the attack continued, and the government eventually could not continue to defend the baht. The only choice was to untether the currency from the fixed exchange-rate system and let the baht float. Or, rather, sink: When the rate was allowed to float, the baht lost half its value.[7]

We show in Figure 18-15 how a speculative attack on the currency puts pressure on the exchange rate.

Macroeconomic policy and exchange rates

Now that we have outlined the difference between floating and fixed exchange rates, we'll look at monetary policy under the two exchange-rate regimes. The key message: Monetary policy is effective *only* under a flexible (floating) exchange rate.

LO 18.9 Describe why monetary policy is ineffective when maintaining a fixed exchange rate.

To see why, imagine there's a recession and the Federal Reserve wants to increase the money supply to stimulate aggregate demand. Recall what is likely to happen under a floating-rate system:

- The lower interest rates that follow this action will make investing in the United States less attractive. Since the return on investment is lower, demand for U.S. dollars will fall.
- At the same time, the supply of U.S. dollars will increase as investors sell their U.S. financial assets and look to buy assets abroad instead.
- Under a floating exchange-rate system, the exchange rate depreciates and net exports increase.

Figure 18-16 depicts what would happen if the exchange rate were fixed:

- Increasing the money supply would naturally cause the value of the dollar to fall.
- Since the government must maintain the exchange rate, however, it must buy its own currency in the foreign-exchange market. This purchase of dollars must be exactly the same as the increase of the money supply in order to maintain a fixed exchange rate.
- The end result is no change in the overall money supply.

FIGURE 18-16
Loosening monetary policy with fixed exchange rates

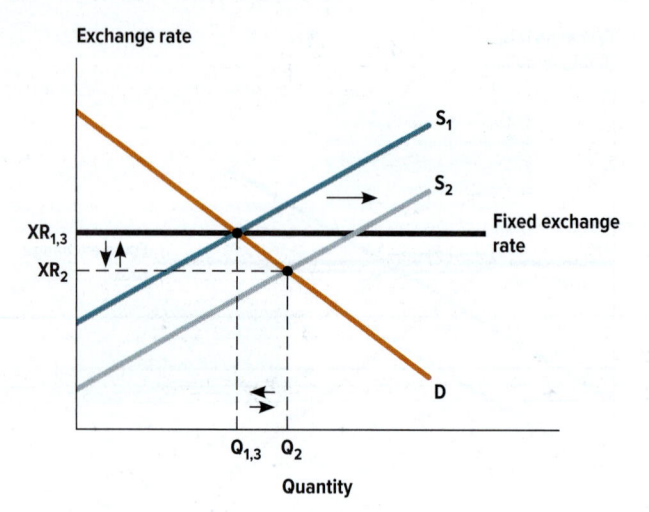

With a fixed exchange rate, monetary policy cannot be successful. When a country expands the money supply, the supply of currency increases and the exchange rate falls. Since this is unacceptable in a fixed exchange-rate regime, the government is forced to buy back the local currency on foreign markets, restoring the exchange rate.

This example leads to a key point about fixed exchange rates: It is impossible to conduct monetary policy *and* maintain a fixed exchange rate.

Is the Chinese currency undervalued? Our discussion of monetary policy and exchange rates leads us to the second explanation for the large trade deficit between China and the United States, which we mentioned at the beginning of this chapter. During China's great economic expansion, China maintained a fixed exchange rate, keeping its currency pegged at 6.5 yuan per dollar.[8] This rate was *below* what the market would likely set. Why did China want to do that? Its goods would be cheap when measured in other currencies, so there would be lots of demand for Chinese exports.

The Chinese government kept its currency's value low by selling piles of renminbi in the foreign-exchange market, and it uses a portion of those dollars to buy U.S. Treasury debt. The effect was to make China's exports more attractive to U.S. consumers and make it harder for U.S. companies to export to China.

Today, the Chinese government lets the renminbi float to some extent, and it currently trades a bit below the previous fixed rate of 6.5 yuan per dollar. However, some U.S. legislators, officials, and U.S. President Donald Trump argue that China's currency is still intentionally undervalued. As of 2018, China was one of six countries on a U.S. Treasury Department "monitoring list" that focused attention on their currency practices.

Our model of the currency markets suggests that when the Chinese renminbi appreciated, as it did between 2015 and 2019, Chinese exports became more expensive and imports became cheaper, which could help reduce the trade balance between the two countries.

The effect on the United States's overall trade balance is not so straightforward, however. The United States would likely import less from China, but it is possible that consumers in the United States would instead choose to import from other countries.

Suppose China is undervaluing its currency to promote its exports. If having a low exchange rate is good for exports, we should ask, *"Why isn't everyone already doing it?"* To start, it's expensive. In order to maintain a long-term devaluation, a country has to buy up huge amounts of foreign reserves, to put more local currency on the market. Second, currency devaluation means that savers tend to send their money to be invested overseas rather than domestically, just as much of China's savings end up in the United States. This loss of capital may not be the best way to develop the domestic economy.

Another cost is that an undervalued currency makes imported foreign goods more expensive. For example, an undervalued Chinese currency makes goods imported from the United States relatively more expensive for Chinese consumers.

Sometimes, though, countries determine the costs of an undervalued currency are worth it. When a group of countries are trying to boost their economies by lowering interest rates, the strategy is known as *competitive devaluation*, or a currency war. In 2009, the fact that many central banks were slashing interest rates in response to recession raised fears that countries worldwide would get caught in a competition to make their exports competitive on the world market.

The real exchange rate

As we saw in Chapter 8, "The Cost of Living," it's not only currency exchange rates that determine the relative price of goods in different countries. Even after converting exchange rates, the exact same Big Mac might be more expensive in Switzerland than in the United States, and more expensive in the United States than in China.

Up until now, we have been talking about the **nominal exchange rate**—the stated rate at which one country's currency can be traded for another country's currency. To really understand international trade, we also need to take into account the prices in two different countries by looking at the *real* exchange rate. The **real exchange rate** expresses the value of goods in one country in terms of the same goods in another country.

To take a simplified example, let's consider only one good—an apple. Say that you can buy an apple in the United States for $1, and in China an apple costs 3 yuan. If the nominal exchange rate is 6 yuan per dollar, then the *real* exchange rate is 2. We'll provide a standard formula for calculating the real exchange rate in a few paragraphs, but for now, let's concentrate on the intuition behind this answer. Since $1 can be exchanged for 6 yuan, and 6 yuan can buy two apples (6 yuan/3 yuan per apple = 2 apples), the dollar that can buy only one apple in the United States can buy two apples in China. Note that our dollar "goes further" (buys more) in real terms in China than in the United States—you can buy twice as many apples with that dollar in China than in the United States.

Of course, people want to buy and sell more than apples. To calculate the real exchange rate properly, we need to look at *all the prices* in the United States and compare this total to *all the prices* in China. To do so, we need to look at the *price index* in both countries—the index that measures a typical basket of goods bought by a household.

The real exchange rate uses the price level in each country to convert the exchange rate into a value that is in "real" terms. Similar to what we did with the apple example, to calculate the real exchange rate, we divide the price level at home by the price level in the foreign country, and then multiply by the nominal exchange rate. Mathematically:

EQUATION 18-1 $$\text{Real exchange rate} = \left(\frac{\text{Domestic price level}}{\text{Foreign price level}}\right) \times \text{Nominal exchange rate}$$

Note that the nominal exchange rate in this formula is expressed in terms of the foreign currency per dollar, as we've done throughout the chapter.

So, for example, let's say that the price of a typical basket of goods in the United States (the domestic price level) is $100; in China the price of a typical basket of goods (the foreign price level) is 300 yuan. Further, let's assume that the nominal exchange rate expressed in terms of yuan

---

LO 18.10 Describe the difference between the real and nominal exchange rates.

nominal exchange rate the stated rate at which one country's currency can be traded for another country's currency

real exchange rate the value of goods in one country expressed in terms of the same goods in another country

per dollar is 6; in other words, 1 dollar can be traded for 6 yuan. With this information, we can calculate the real exchange rate to be 2:

EQUATION 18-1A

$$\text{Real exchange rate} = \left(\frac{\text{Domestic price level}}{\text{Foreign price level}}\right) \times \text{Nominal exchange rate}$$

$$= \left(\frac{\$100}{300 \text{ yuan}}\right) \times 6 \text{ yuan}/1 \text{ dollar} = 2$$

The *real* exchange rate is another way of saying "the exchange rate adjusted for *purchasing power*," an idea we discussed in Chapter 8, "The Cost of Living." If there were parity in purchasing power—that is, if an apple cost the same in China as in the United States, after adjusting for nominal exchange rates—then the real exchange rate would be 1.

The same factors that complicate calculations of purchasing power parity also complicate calculations of the real exchange rate. Consumers in China purchase different kinds of goods than do U.S. consumers—more rice, for example, and fewer burgers—so it's not easy to compare price levels using typical baskets of goods. Still, the real exchange rate is a useful way of comparing how far your money will go in another country.

✓ TEST YOURSELF

- ☐ Does exchange-rate appreciation mean that the home currency gets stronger or weaker relative to other foreign currencies? **[LO 18.6]**
- ☐ When demand for a foreign good increases, what happens in the market for foreign exchange? **[LO 18.7]**
- ☐ How does the relative level of the U.S. interest rate affect the supply of foreign currency? **[LO 18.7]**
- ☐ What measurement gives the prices of the same goods in two different countries? **[LO 18.8]**
- ☐ Which variable can monetary policy affect under a flexible exchange rate that cannot be affected under a fixed exchange rate? **[LO 18.9]**
- ☐ What is another name for the real exchange rate? **[LO 18.10]**

Global Financial Crises

LO 18.11 Describe the role of the IMF and how financial crises are created by excessive debt and unsustainable exchange rates.

Although the international financial system works well most of the time, occasionally it falls out of order. In general, these crises can be labeled as one of two types: debt crises and exchange-rate crises. Throughout this section, you'll see how foreign direct investment and international flows can be fickle, which can destabilize economies when things go wrong.

The role of the IMF

Before working through some examples of disruptions in the financial system, we'll introduce the institution that is responsible for keeping the system together—the *IMF*, or *International Monetary Fund*. The IMF was created at the end of World War II. Although it's an international agency like the United Nations and World Bank, the IMF headquarters is in Washington, DC, a few blocks from the U.S. Federal Reserve headquarters and the U.S. Treasury Department.

Initially, when many countries had fixed exchange rates tied to gold, the IMF had the task of helping countries maintain their fixed rates. When countries ran into trouble maintaining their currencies, the IMF would step in and provide a loan to patch up a balance-of-payments deficit.

Now that most exchange rates are flexible (floating), the IMF's role has changed. Today, the IMF often steps in as a lender of last resort, making loans to countries when private investors flee. The loans can help to stabilize the economy and keep fears from building on themselves.

As recent financial crises in Greece, Russia, and Turkey show, international financial crises still occur, and the IMF is needed to help when things go wrong.

However, the IMF is not a magic solution for countries in need. Many IMF loans are made on the condition that the governments make certain policy changes. For example, a recipient country may be required to make efforts to reduce its budget deficit as a signal that it is committed to reform. In many cases, the IMF has been criticized for requiring economies to undertake contractionary fiscal policy and tighter monetary policy during the crisis itself. These policies usually depress the economy further and can exacerbate the crisis.

The role of the IMF and other global institutions is an area of ongoing debate. As globalization poses more risks of contagious collapse, how can the international system design institutions that will be able to prevent crises?

Debt crises

When countries need to finance their expenses, they often turn to international capital markets. The result is that a large share of government debt is often held by foreign investors. If those investors begin to worry whether the government will be able to repay the debt, the investors begin to move their money out of the country in a hurry. Why? If the government defaults, everyone who had invested in that debt stands to lose their money.

One such instance of investors losing confidence in the government's ability to repay debt occurred in Argentina in 2001. The setting for the debt crisis in Argentina started with heavy financing of a variety of industrial development projects during the 1960s and 1970s. The government then accumulated more debt in a war against the United Kingdom for control of the Falkland Islands.

As Argentina accumulated more debt, paying the interest on its debt formed a larger proportion of its budget. That wasn't the only problem, though. In an effort to curb inflation, Argentina had created a fixed exchange rate tied to the U.S. dollar, but the currency became overvalued. Domestic industry and large amounts of trade went to Argentina's neighbors, where products were cheaper. In addition, the financial crisis in Russia in 1998 made investors far more skeptical of investing money in "emerging markets" like Argentina. The combination of overvalued currency and loss in confidence raised interest rates, making it harder and more expensive to borrow more.

To try to stop the flight of capital, the Argentine government announced several attempts to reduce government spending. As you might have guessed, these promises were not kept. What followed was a painful economic spiral: Increased capital outflows from the country led to higher and higher interest rates. The increasing rates made debt payments more expensive, which created further government deficits. By 2001, the problem had spun into a full-on crisis, with bank runs and public protests. Unemployment came close to 20 percent. The government finally defaulted on its debt, unable to meet the increasingly high debt payments.[9]

We can analyze this scenario using the open-economy loanable-funds market set up earlier in the chapter. Figure 18-17 illustrates the stages of this debt crisis:

- When foreign investors started pulling their money out of the country, the net capital outflow curve shifted to the right.
- Interest rates then increased to r_2, which reduced investment. The higher interest rates also made the government's debt more expensive, and the government deficit increased.
- As the government deficit increased, this shifted the national savings curve to the left, increasing the interest rate again (to r_3) and reducing investment yet again.

Exchange-rate crises

Loss of confidence in a government's ability to defend an exchange rate can also spook investors. If a government devalues an exchange rate, it essentially represents a loss for those holding investments in the country.

FIGURE 18-17
The Argentine debt crisis

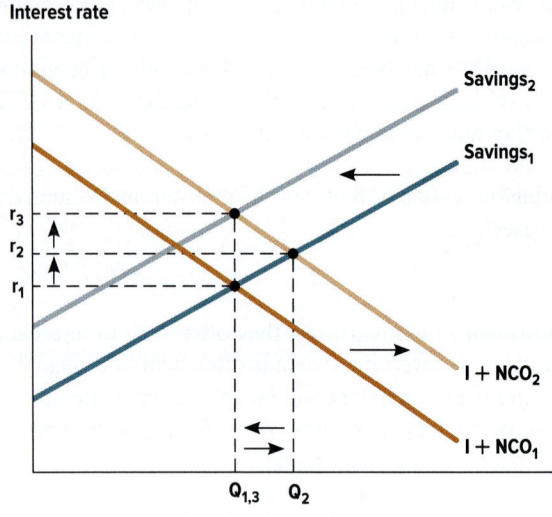

Once investors got word that the Argentine government was in danger, they pulled their investments out of the country, shifting the combined investments and net capital outflow curve to the right, increasing the interest rate. This higher interest rate made the government debt more expensive, which decreased savings. This led to a further increase in the interest rate, and a repetition of the cycle.

With this in mind, we turn to the story of the Asian financial crisis. In the early 1990s, emerging economies in Asia—Thailand, Indonesia, Malaysia, the Philippines—received a lot of capital from global investors. The influx of investment contributed to a remarkable spurt of growth. With all that fresh capital, banks wanted to put that money to productive use, and they started making loans to riskier entrepreneurs. Soon the signs of good fortune were fading. In Thailand, especially, most economic indicators started to create worries, and investors began pulling their money out of the country.

But the crisis didn't end there. Because the world is so interconnected, crises can easily spread in a chain reaction called a *contagion*. The virus imagery is fitting. When Thailand got into trouble, investors immediately became nervous about other countries in the area, regardless of their economic condition. Soon, fearful investors were pulling their money out of the surrounding countries as well, creating financial crises in those countries. In other words, the crisis was contagious.

After the financial fall of Thailand in 1997, speculative attacks spread to Indonesia, the Philippines, South Korea, and Malaysia. Like Thailand, each of these countries was unable to defend its fixed currency. Not surprisingly, their currencies rapidly depreciated once the fixed exchange-rate policies were abandoned and exchange rates were made flexible. GDP in these five countries fell about 10 percent between 1997 and 1998.

The crisis lasted for about a year, and millions of people suffered. The overriding lesson of the Asian financial crisis was that the combination of fast-moving capital and fixed exchange rates can lead to devastating speculative attacks with the power to shake to whole continents.[10]

Following crises like these, the question is how the destructive forces of contagion can be contained without losing the benefits of the free movement of capital. Among the many proposals to slow the flight of capital is the *Tobin tax*, which would apply a minuscule tax to all foreign-capital transactions, as described in the From Another Angle box "Cooling down hot money."

Cooling down hot money
From Another Angle

The largest financial market in the world is the market for foreign currency, with around $5.1 trillion exchanged daily. A large proportion of this trade is pure speculation, by traders making bets about the future price of currencies all over the world. As a result, trades in currency happen very quickly; short gaps in time can mean the difference between making money and losing it all.

These currency flows can be extremely destructive. Think about a country that experiences an event—financial or otherwise—that seriously undermines traders' faith in the value of a currency. Thanks to speculators making quick bets, the initial event can quickly blow up into a massive crisis.

A typical pattern starts with traders predicting that the value of a currency will fall. They then try to get rid of the sickly currency as fast as possible in order to cut losses. These first movers scare others into thinking the currency is not stable, so others start selling their assets denominated in the currency. In a short time, citizens and businesses who have capital inside the country rush to get rid of their assets too, moving their money into safer currencies.

This process often leaves a lot of wreckage. Countries that suffered through the capital flight in the Asian financial crisis saw GDP shrink by 10 percent in a year.

In response, two economists have proposed measures to slow down the lightning-fast transaction of foreign currencies.

One proposal is the *Tobin tax*, devised by the Nobel Prize–winning economist James Tobin. He proposed a small levy on the trading of currency, on the order of 0.5 percent of the overall volume of trade. This tax would slow some of the capital flight.

A problem, though, is that the tax would apply to *all* transactions of currency, whether made by speculators or investors. The challenge is that it's hard to slow down currency speculators (which is the real aim) without slowing down investors and traders too. A big retailer like Best Buy, for example, would get hit by the tax each time it purchases Sony televisions from Japan. By taxing all of these transactions identically and at all times, the Tobin tax could impede international trade and investment.

Rather than taxing all currency-market transactions all the time, Paul Bernd Spahn proposed an alternative: Any tax on international financial transactions would stay dormant until a country experienced a speculative currency attack like those experienced during the Asian financial crisis. When trouble occurs, transactions would incur a slightly higher tax. In theory, this higher tax rate would dissuade flighty investors from moving large sums of money on a whim.

Putting sand in the gears of currency trading with measures like those proposed by Tobin and Spahn introduces a trade-off. In exchange for slowing down currency trading, markets would gain some stability. To date, the price of slowing down the electronic herd, though, has been too costly. The Tobin tax has been around since 1976 and the Spahn tax since 1995, and some countries have cautiously adopted the ideas. But neither idea has attracted global interest—yet.

Sources: www.ft.com/intl/cms/s/0/6210e49c-9307-11de-b146-00144feabdc0.html; www.wiwi.uni-frankfurt.de/profs/spahn/pdf/publ/7-041.pdf.

✓ TEST YOURSELF

☐ What is a lender of last resort? **[LO 18.11]**
☐ Why are fixed exchange rates vulnerable to speculative attack? **[LO 18.11]**

Conclusion

In this chapter, we opened up the national economy to understand how countries trade and invest with each other. When we add net exports to our GDP equation, we get an interesting result: The difference between what a country buys and sells is also equal to the level of foreign investment. In effect, if a country is buying more than it is selling, it needs to borrow money from abroad to pay for its imports. This important equality is called the *balance-of-payments identity*. The tight link between the trade balance and capital flows is the key to understanding issues such as the U.S. trade deficit and the U.S. debt with China.

We looked at two explanations for the trade deficit with China, which turn out to be different sides of the same coin. The first explanation is that the United States is not saving nearly as much as China and is relying on investment from other countries. From the balance-of-payments identity, we know that if foreign investment is high, then there must also be a trade imbalance.

The second explanation is that exports from China are artificially cheap because the Chinese currency is set at a price below what it should be—that is, below its market price. Cheap Chinese exports mean that the balance of trade is negative, and the United States needs to borrow money to pay for its spending.

In extreme cases, we saw how international debt and fixed exchange rates can tip countries into economic crises. As the world continues to become more and more interlinked, economic policy in one part of the world will have global effects.

Macroeconomics may seem more abstract than microeconomics, with lots of moving parts. Yet trade policy, government fiscal policy, monetary policy, and the decision of how to set the exchange rate affect the daily lives of every citizen, usually in ways that are hard to see.

In the concluding chapter, we will apply the lessons you've learned throughout the text to one of the most stubborn problems in economics—international poverty.

Key Terms

balance of trade, p. 486
trade deficit, p. 486
trade surplus, p. 486
foreign direct investment (FDI), p. 489
foreign portfolio investment, p. 489

net capital flow, p. 491
balance-of-payments identity, p. 491
exchange rate, p. 498
exchange-rate appreciation, p. 500
exchange-rate depreciation, p. 501

floating exchange rate, p. 507
fixed exchange rate, p. 507
nominal exchange rate, p. 511
real exchange rate, p. 511

Summary

LO 18.1 Define the balance of trade, and describe the general trends of U.S. trade.

The *balance of trade* is the value of exports less the value of imports. It is also called *net exports*. Net exports respond to the value of the exchange rate: When the exchange rate is high, domestic goods are expensive and foreign goods are cheap, so net exports are low. When the exchange rate is low, net exports are high. The United States exports and imports both goods and services, though services are only a fraction of the amount of goods traded.

LO 18.2 Define portfolio investment and foreign direct investment.

There are two types of foreign investment. *Portfolio investment* is investment in financial securities, such as stocks or bonds, so that domestic residents still operate firms. *Foreign direct investment (FDI)* occurs when a firm invests abroad with an active interest—for example, by building a factory and managing the factory. Together, portfolio investment and foreign direct investment give the *net capital outflow* of the country, a measure of the money a country invests outside its border.

LO 18.3 Explain the connection between the balance of trade and net capital outflow.

The balance of trade and net capital outflow are related through the balance-of-payments identity, which states that NX = NCO. This identity is an accounting identity: If a country has an imbalance of trade (positive net exports), it means that it has lent money to the rest of the world (positive capital outflow) to pay for these goods.

LO 18.4 Describe the determinants of international capital flows using the demand and supply of international loanable funds.

Net capital outflows are determined by the demand and supply for net capital outflow. The supply of net capital outflows is national savings less domestic investment. The demand for net capital outflow is determined by the domestic interest rate and the foreign interest rate. When the domestic interest rate is high, net capital outflow is low because foreign money flows into the country. When the foreign interest rate is high, net capital outflow is high because money flows out of the country to take advantage of high returns.

LO 18.5 Show how the international market for loanable funds can be used to explain events in the international financial system.

Various events can influence the international supply and demand for loanable funds. An increase in confidence in an economy will cut net capital outflows and lower the interest rate. A decrease in savings from an increase in the government deficit will shift the supply curve for loanable funds to the left, increasing the interest rate and decreasing net capital outflows.

LO 18.6 Describe exchange rate appreciation and depreciation, and understand their effects on trade.

The *exchange rate* is the value of one currency expressed in terms of another currency. Exchange rates can be expressed in two ways: either in terms of the domestic (home) currency or in terms of the foreign currency. Exchange rates can appreciate or depreciate, as the currencies strengthen or weaken against each other.

LO 18.7 Describe the determinants of demand and supply in the forex market.

The exchange rate is determined by demand and supply for domestic currency. Demand and supply are influenced by preferences for domestic and foreign goods and services, the domestic interest rate, the foreign interest rate, and the perceived riskiness of domestic and foreign investment.

LO 18.8 Explain fixed and floating exchange rates.

A *fixed exchange rate* is an exchange rate that is set by the government, not the market. Usually fixed exchange rates are set to maintain a steady relationship with another stable currency. A government maintains a fixed exchange rate by intervening in the foreign-exchange market, by either buying or selling foreign currency.

A *floating exchange rate* is set by the market. Floating exchange rates are set by the intersection of supply and demand for foreign exchange.

LO 18.9 Describe why monetary policy is ineffective when maintaining a fixed exchange rate.

A fixed exchange rate necessarily means that monetary policy will not have an effect—any change to the money supply has to be counteracted by government actions on the foreign-exchange market to maintain the exchange rate. Monetary policy is more effective under a flexible exchange rate because the flexible rate can affect both investment and net exports.

LO 18.10 Describe the difference between the real and nominal exchange rates.

The *real exchange rate* is the nominal exchange rate corrected for the price levels in the domestic and foreign country. The real exchange rate is measured in terms of goods instead of currency. If the real exchange rate is 1, then a good can be exchanged in one country directly for a good in another country. If this is the case, we say there is purchasing power parity between the two countries.

LO 18.11 Describe the role of the IMF and how financial crises are created by excessive debt and unsustainable exchange rates.

Although the financial system works well most of the time, financial crises can occur. The International Monetary Fund (IMF) often steps in as a *lender of last resort* when this happens, making loans to countries when private lenders flee. However, this is not always an ideal solution. Crises exist because countries often turn to international capital markets to finance expenses, therefore meaning investors own the countries' debts. This can backfire if investors worry that the government won't be able to repay the debt or if they lose confidence in the government's ability to defend the exchange rate.

Review Questions

1. What happens to the U.S. balance of trade as oil prices rise? **[LO 18.1]**
2. Suppose a presidential candidate criticizes his opponent by saying his opponent's economic policies have made the dollar weaker and cost U.S. factory workers their jobs. What would be your response? **[LO 18.1]**
3. Why would a company want to make a direct investment in countries where the company's home currency has higher purchasing power? **[LO 18.2]**
4. Part of the North American Free Trade Agreement (NAFTA) opened the Mexican stock market to U.S. and Canadian investors for the first time. How would this affect direct and portfolio foreign investment in Mexico? **[LO 18.2]**
5. If many factories that once made goods in the United States move to Mexico, what must also happen in order to correct the balance of payments in the United States? **[LO 18.3]**
6. Critics of NAFTA argued that opening our borders to free trade with Mexico would result in U.S. firms moving all of their factories to Mexico and the United States running large trade deficits with Mexico. Comment on the concerns of these critics using your knowledge of international trade and net capital flows. **[LO 18.3]**
7. Rating agencies rate countries on the perceived riskiness of investing in their economies. Standard and Poor's, one of the main rating agencies, downgraded the credit rating for U.S. Treasury bonds in 2011. According to this chapter, what impact should the downgrading have had on net capital outflows and interest rates? Why? **[LO 18.4]**
8. The interest rate on 10-year U.S. Treasury bonds just before Standard and Poor's downgraded the U.S. credit rating was 2.47 percent. One year later, the interest rate on these bonds had fallen to 1.60 percent. How can one explain this result that seems to contradict the findings of this chapter? **[LO 18.4]**
9. List three policies that a government could engage in that would reduce interest rates. (*Hint:* Look back to Figures 18-6 through 18-8.) **[LO 18.5]**
10. A country doubles its rate of saving. How is this likely to affect the equilibrium interest rate and net capital outflow? What is the impact on the trade balance? **[LO 18.5]**
11. Suppose the exchange rate value of the dollar depreciates. Who wins and who loses? **[LO 18.6]**
12. Suppose the exchange rate was 104 yen per dollar in 2017 and 110 yen per dollar in 2018. Did the dollar appreciate or depreciate? What about the yen? **[LO 18.6]**
13. Identify the main reasons why people convert one currency into another currency. **[LO 18.7]**
14. During a recession the central bank lowers interest rates. How does this affect the exchange rate and net exports? **[LO 18.7]**
15. A country has a fixed exchange rate. If world interest rates rise, what will the country have to do to maintain its fixed exchange rate? Has the fixed exchange rate become relatively more undervalued or overvalued? **[LO 18.8]**
16. Suppose that in response to a severe recession, a country with an overvalued currency and a fixed exchange rate moves to a floating exchange-rate system. Who are the winners and losers in this move? **[LO 18.8]**
17. A country operates under a flexible exchange rate system. When the central bank lowers the interest rate during a recession, how does this affect investment and net exports, and ultimately aggregate demand? What if the exchange rate was fixed instead? **[LO 18.9]**
18. What are the advantages to fixing the exchange rate at an undervalued level? What are the disadvantages? **[LO 18.9]**
19. Discuss what would happen to the real exchange rate between the U.S. and Australia if oil prices fell, which dramatically reduced the cost of transporting goods. **[LO 18.10]**
20. Is it ever possible for a country's nominal exchange rate to be depreciating while its real exchange rate is appreciating? Explain. **[LO 18.10]**
21. Foreign investors in a country become worried about the stability of the government due to its rising debt level. What do you expect to happen to the interest rate and the exchange rate value of the country's currency, assuming the country has a floating exchange rate? **[LO 18.11]**
22. Foreign investors in a country become worried about the stability of the government due to its rising debt level. How might the IMF help avert a financial crisis in this country? **[LO 18.11]**

Problems and Applications

1. Suppose total U.S. exports in the month of June were $123.1 billion and total imports from foreign countries were $192.2 billion. What was the balance of trade? **[LO 18.1]**
2. Suppose a country has total GDP (Y) = $10 trillion, consumption = $8 trillion, government spending = $2 trillion, investment = $3 trillion, and taxes = $1.6 trillion. What is the level of net exports or balance of trade? What is the level of public savings? What is the level of private savings? What is the level of net capital outflow? **[LO 18.1, LO 18.3]**
3. Assume that U.S. investors purchased $50 billion in foreign assets, and foreigners purchased $100 billion in

U.S. assets such as stocks and Treasury bills. In addition, U.S. businesses invested $150 billion in foreign factories and operations, while foreign companies invested $100 billion in U.S. factories and operations. What was the net capital outflow for the United States? **[LO 18.2]**

4. Define each of the following as direct or portfolio foreign investment. **[LO 18.2]**
   a. Nike (a U.S. company) builds new factories in Cambodia.
   b. A U.S. hedge fund purchases 30 percent of the shares of a Brazilian paper manufacturer.
   c. Mercedes-Benz (a German company) builds a new manufacturing plant in Alabama.
   d. Intel (a U.S. company) sets up a new call center in India.
   e. A British chocolate maker buys a smaller U.S. rival.
   f. Hilton Hotels (a U.S. company) builds a new resort in Hawaii.

5. Tom is stuck with his friends on an island that uses coconuts for currency, but they recently discovered Wilson's Island nearby. Tom's Island agrees to make only one transaction with Wilson's Island: It sells a fishing boat to Wilson's for 15 coconuts. Answer the following questions, assuming that yearly consumption on Tom's Island equals 500 coconuts and domestic investments in huts and farm equipment equals 150 coconuts. **[LO 18.3]**
   a. What are net exports for Tom's Island?
   b. What is the total national savings for Tom's Island?
   c. Suppose Tom's Island imports a volleyball net from Wilson's Island for 5 coconuts. What is the total national savings now?
   d. Now Tom purchases 1 coconut tree on Wilson Island at a cost of 10 coconuts. What is the balance of payments? (*Hint:* A coconut tree produces coconuts like a factory produces goods.)

6. Over the last five years, Portlandia's average income has risen and caused the supply curve of loanable funds to increase and shift right. **[LO 18.4, LO 18.5]**
   a. Would the domestic interest rate have increased or decreased?
   b. Given the change in the interest rate, would General Motors (GM) be more or less likely to open a car manufacturing plant in the country?
   c. If Portlandia hits a recession and interest rates fall, which way must the demand curve for loanable funds have shifted?

7. Describe what happens to the supply and/or demand curves for U.S. dollars under the following scenarios. In each scenario, does the U.S. exchange rate appreciate or depreciate, and what happens to the U.S. balance of trade? **[LO 18.6, LO 18.7]**
   a. A drought in Russia destroys the wheat crop, resulting in increased purchases of wheat from the United States.
   b. Bollywood movies become extremely popular in the United States, increasing demand for foreign movies.
   c. The U.S. government forces all government offices to purchase American-made computer products, instead of importing them.

8. Suppose there is major unrest in the labor market in the United States, making European investors nervous about investing in the United States. **[LO 18.6, LO 18.7]**
   a. Draw the supply and demand curves for U.S. dollars, and show the appropriate shift(s) in supply and demand for U.S. dollars associated with the labor unrest.
   b. Did the value of the U.S. dollar depreciate or appreciate?

9. A government has been running budget deficits for many years and decides to balance its budget. Explain how each of the following are affected under a floating exchange-rate regime. **[LO 18.5, LO 18.6, LO 18.7]**
   a. The interest rate.
   b. The exchange rate.
   c. The trade balance.

10. Suppose the CEO for Apple Inc. decides to produce all the company's products in the United States instead of China. **[LO 18.7]**
    a. Which way will the supply for U.S. dollars shift?
    b. Which way will the demand for U.S. dollars shift?
    c. Does the value of the U.S. dollars depreciate or appreciate?

11. Suppose that in the United States last season's hot holiday gift was the iPad (which is made primarily in China), while this season's big gift is media content for the iPad (which is made in the United States). Determine whether there will be an increase, decrease, or no change for each of the following variables compared to last year. **[LO 18.6, LO 18.7]**
    a. Supply and demand for dollars.
    b. Exchange rate between the United States and China.
    c. Net exports for the United States.
    d. Net capital outflows for the United States.

12. In March 2009 the Canadian dollar was worth US$0.78. In April 2011 the Canadian dollar was worth US$1.06. What effect would this increase have on the

trade balance between the United States and Canada? Why? **[LO 18.6]**

13. Hiro has $10,000 to invest in the foreign-exchange market. He's interested in trading U.S. dollars (USD) for euro (EUR) and Japanese yen (JPY). Using Table 18P-1, determine the arbitrage profit/loss Hiro will make in each of the following scenarios. (*Note:* Any value less than $10 should be considered zero.) **[LO 18.6]**

TABLE 18P-1

Exchange rate	USD	EUR	JPY
USD	1.00000	0.78230	81.200
EUR	1.27830	1.00000	103.796
JPY	0.01232	0.00963	1.000

    a. USD → EUR → JPY → USD.
    b. USD → JPY → EUR → USD.
    c. Now look up the current exchange rates among any three currencies. Show that there are no arbitrage opportunities for the three currencies you chose.

14. Some politicians argue for imposing trade restrictions in the hope that doing so will reduce the trade deficit of the United States. Assuming the United States has a floating exchange rate, answer the following questions regarding the impact of the trade restrictions. **[LO 18.7]**
    a. What is the impact in the foreign exchange market for dollars?
    b. What is the impact in the market for foreign currency (euros, yen, etc.)?
    c. What happens to the exchange rate of the dollar?
    d. What happens to net exports?

15. Suppose the U.S. economy slips into a recession. In response, the Federal Reserve cuts the federal funds rate in order to avoid unemployment. Consider what happens to the following under a floating exchange-rate regime. **[LO 18.8]**
    a. Domestic investment.
    b. Capital inflow.
    c. Capital outflow.
    d. Exchange rate.
    e. Net exports.
    f. Aggregate demand.

16. Reevaluate the previous problem assuming the U.S. economy follows a fixed exchange-rate regime. **[LO 18.8, LO 18.9]**

17. A country that has been operating under a fixed exchange-rate regime falls into recession. All attempts at using fiscal policy to lift the economy out of recession have failed. **[LO 18.9]**
    a. Can monetary policy be effective in this case? Why or why not?
    b. Should the country allow the exchange rate to float? Why or why not?

18. In Windsor, Ontario, a Big Mac from McDonald's costs C$4.17 (Canadian dollars), and across the border in Detroit it costs $3.56 in U.S. dollars. **[LO 18.10]**
    a. Suppose the nominal U.S. exchange rate with Canada is US$0.70 per Canadian dollar. Does purchasing power parity hold between the two countries?
    b. What is the purchasing power parity exchange rate for the United States?

19. Suppose the current U.S.–UK exchange rate is 0.64 pound (the pound is the UK currency) per dollar, and the aggregate price level is 175 for the United States and 138 for the UK. What is the real exchange rate? What does this real exchange rate mean in terms of the relative purchasing power of the dollar and the pound? **[LO 18.10]**

20. Imagine there are only two trading nations in the world. For each of the following scenarios, determine whether goods in one country will become more attractive relative to goods in the other country given their inflation rates and a shift in the nominal exchange rates. **[LO 18.10]**
    a. Inflation is 8 percent in the UK and 4 percent in Germany, but the UK pound–euro exchange rate remains the same.
    b. Inflation is 3 percent in the United States and 7 percent in Japan, but the exchange rate for U.S. dollars to Japanese yen increases from 70 to 80 Japanese yen.
    c. Inflation is 10 percent in the United States and 6 percent in Mexico, and the price of the Mexican peso rises from US$0.08 to US$0.15.

21. Over several years, foreign investors poured billions of dollars into a country due to its favorable growth prospects. They have now become concerned about the return on their investments because growth in the country is stagnating. As a result they are pulling their money out. Will this country be better able to withstand the financial crisis if it has a fixed or a floating exchange rate? Explain. **[LO 18.11]**

Endnotes

1. In November 2018, Apple announced dit would stop reporting iPhone sales data. www.lifewire.com/how-many-iphones-have-been-sold-1999500.
2. www.thebalance.com/u-s-debt-to-china-how-much-does-it-own-3306355.
3. Exports of goods and services: https://fred.stlouisfed.org/series/EXPGSA; Imports of goods and services: https://fred.stlouisfed.org/series/IMPGSA .
4. www.bea.gov/news/blog/2018-09-19/us-current-account-deficit-decreases-second-quarter-2018.
5. https://tradingeconomics.com/germany/current-account-to-gdp.
6. http://data.worldbank.org/indicator/NY.GNS.ICTR.ZS.
7. http://fas.org/man/crs/crs-asia2.htm.
8. Note that the word "yuan" is like saying "dollar." It's a unit of money in China. The actual currency is officially called renminbi (RMB).
9. http://fpc.state.gov/documents/organization/8040.pdf.
10. http://fas.org/man/crs/crs-asia2.htm.

Chapter 19

Development Economics

Poverty amid Plenty

In the macroeconomics chapters, we've talked a lot about economic growth. But economic growth is not an end in itself. An economy can grow but still leave many people behind. Although the average level of real GDP per capita tripled in the second half of the twentieth century across the world as a whole, many people today still don't have enough resources for much of anything.

About 731 million of the 7.2 billion people on earth live on just $1.90 per day, the World Bank's measure of extreme poverty.[1] Billions more live on only slightly higher incomes. The depth and breadth of global poverty are not just a compelling humanitarian concern but also an economic puzzle: How can such poverty persist amid such plenty?

Some who have a more pessimistic outlook believe that poverty will always be a part of life. They point to a decades-long legacy of hopelessly failed bureaucracies and wasted foreign-aid budgets.

Others who are more optimistic point to evidence of progress: Thanks to sustained efforts by governments, nongovernmental organizations, and communities, many more children are attending school than even a decade or two ago. Infant mortality has dropped by half since 1960. Each year, about 9 million more kids live to celebrate their first birthday than would have if the mortality rate had stayed at the 1960 level.

©shibu bhattacharjee/Getty Images

Impressively, such improvements have occurred even in places where average incomes failed to grow. So although growth is good in general, the poorest can do better even if there is little growth. Nor does lots of growth necessarily mean higher incomes for the poorest. In more technical words, overall growth and income for the poorest are correlated, but not perfectly.

So what can help the poorest lead better lives? One important step is improving access to markets and institutions that can expand opportunities and give more choices. Think of how you rely on a basic bank account to pay bills and save money. About 30 percent of the adults in the world live their lives without access to a bank. By expanding access to banks, millions would be helped to save, invest, and provide for their families.

The same goes for access to improved markets for transportation, health care, education, and other basic services, backed by responsive legal and political institutions to maintain fair practices.

LEARNING OBJECTIVES

LO 19.1 Explain how the capabilities approach relates to economic development.

LO 19.2 Explain the relationship between economic growth and economic development.

LO 19.3 Describe how improvements to health and education can develop human capital.

LO 19.4 Explain the importance of institutions and good governance in development economics.

LO 19.5 Evaluate the role of industrial policy and clusters in development.

LO 19.6 Evaluate how migration and remittances promote development.

LO 19.7 Describe the aims of foreign aid, the role of poverty traps, the main institutions delivering aid, and criticisms of foreign aid.

LO 19.8 Understand how impact investing provides a new tool for creating social impact.

LO 19.9 Explain the need for impact evaluation, and analyze the role of randomized controlled trials in measuring impact.

These are the issues taken up in the field of *development economics*, the topic of this chapter. Development economists tackle a series of questions that span several core economic issues: What makes some people—and some countries—richer than others? What makes others poorer? How can markets be made more efficient and wide-reaching in low-income countries? How should donors and investors choose among good options, given that resources are scarce?

Speaking personally, these are some of the questions that drew both of the text's authors into economics. They're the kinds of questions that have been the focus of our research, whether studying saving behavior in Peru or political economy in China. We hope that this chapter shows how the economic tools introduced in this text can lead to better outcomes globally, in ways big and small.

In the first part of this chapter, we examine the relationship between economic growth and economic development. Then we look at the basics of economic development, taking a fresh perspective on some ideas we've encountered already in this book—human capital, good governance, investment, trade, and migration. In the final part of the chapter, we consider foreign aid—its history, the arguments for and against such aid, and how development economists are striving to understand what works.

Development and Capabilities

So far, we've talked a lot about economic *growth*. In this chapter, we talk about economic *development*. The concepts are intertwined, but distinct. Economic *growth* involves increases in GDP. However, GDP doesn't necessarily tell us much about what it's like to live in a country—its levels of inequality and poverty, what opportunities there are to better yourself if you're in the middle or at the bottom of the heap, how well basic institutions like courts and hospitals work, how many people can read and write, and so on. These are the kinds of things we're concerned about when we talk about economic *development*.

Development economics looks beyond GDP growth to ask about the *quality of life* for all sectors of society. A helpful way to think about what matters comes from an idea called the *capabilities approach*.

LO 19.1 Explain how the capabilities approach relates to economic development.

The capabilities approach

The capabilities approach was developed by Amartya Sen, a Harvard professor who won the 1998 Nobel Prize in Economics. His idea provides a framework for economists to think about poverty, inequality, and human development.

A **capability** is something a person is able to be or do. Examples of capabilities include being able to live a long and healthy life, have adequate food and shelter, get an education, speak one's mind, travel freely, live free of the fear of violence, be able to find secure and meaningful work, and be able to enjoy recreational and cultural activities. In all, capabilities represent a vast spectrum of life—from basic survival and good health to self-expression and engagement in culture.

Whereas economic growth focuses on expanding the economy, the capabilities approach to economic development instead looks to constantly improve what individuals can be and can do. Institutional and market failures restrict what people can do, and the restriction of capabilities often affects poorest citizens the most.

You might be wondering why we need a fancy new term like "capabilities" here. Aren't all of the things we've mentioned also simply things that increase utility? Why do we need to depart from the traditional economic framework of maximizing utility? Read the What Do You Think? box "Utility versus capabilities" for more on that question.

capability
something a person is able to be or do, such as to engage fully in life, including having economic and political freedoms

Utility versus capabilities
What Do You Think?

What does a good society look like? Many economists would say that it's a place that has maximized the total "utility" of all its citizens. Roughly, that means that the society has delivered the greatest satisfaction to the greatest number of people. By "satisfaction," economists mean that people get more of what they want. Who could disagree?

The economist and philosopher Amartya Sen disagrees, making the case in a series of books and essays. Sen argues that when we think about what makes a good society, we should worry less about "utility" and worry more about what he calls "capability." Capability captures the idea of being able to live life to its full potential—to be educated and healthy and to have the freedom to speak, write, meet with others, and pursue important goals. Unlike utility, it is not about how you *feel* or whether you're happy. Capability is, instead, about your freedom to live and function. Development economists often focus especially on Sen's idea of "basic capabilities" which are limited to the most fundamental capabilities like being literate, well-nourished, and having basic political freedoms. Sen captures these ideas in his book *Development as Freedom*.

One criticism of a simple utility-maximizing approach is that it does not have a natural way to address the idea of fundamental rights. For example, what if slave owners received more utility from slave ownership than the utility that slaves would get from being freed? Should society therefore allow slavery? Most people would say there are some rights, like not being enslaved, that are worth preserving even if it means accepting lower utility across society as a whole. As Amartya Sen says, "Happiness or desire fulfillment represents only one aspect of human existence. The capabilities approach attempts to fill the gap by looking at a much broader conception of life" (as quoted by Clark, 2011).

Second, simply trying to maximize utility ignores the *distribution* of that utility. Imagine that a business executive feels gnawing envy when she sees other CEOs flying around in private jets. It drives her insane with jealousy. Her utility from owning a private jet could be so great that it would outweigh the combined utility gained from spending the same money to build a new health clinic that serves a district of poorer citizens. Should we, then, buy the president a private jet instead of improving health care? After all, buying the jet would be the choice that maximized society's total utility for the given budget. There seems to be something wrong with accepting this conclusion at face value.

On the other hand, by moving too far away from the utility approach, do we risk paternalistically giving the poor what we think they *ought* to want instead of what they really *do* want? In their book *Poor Economics*, Abhijit Banerjee and Esther Duflo tell of a man in a remote, dusty

(continued)

village in Morocco who owned a television and a DVD player although his family didn't have enough to eat. "Oh," he told the researchers, "television is more important than food."

WHAT DO YOU THINK?
1. Should the World Bank and local governments be building bridges, schools, and clinics in low-income countries if citizens would rather have TVs?
2. Should development economists put more focus on capabilities or utility?

Sources: Abhijit Banerjee and Esther Duflo, *Poor Economics* (New York: Public Affairs, 2011); David A. Clark, "The Capability Approach: Its Development, Critiques and Recent Advances," www.gprg.org/pubs/workingpapers/pdfs/gprg-wps-032.pdf (accessed November 7, 2011).

Economic growth and economic development

LO 19.2 Explain the relationship between economic growth and economic development.

We saw in an earlier chapter that growth in countries such as China has slashed poverty rates. The average person in China now earns about $12,500 a year, compared with just $250 three decades ago.[2] Average levels of education and health have increased dramatically, too. That's not surprising. After all, when people have more money, you would expect them to spend more on improving their health and educating their children.

However, there is nothing inevitable about GDP growth improving health and education for everyone. For example, survey data show that in India, the rate of children suffering from malnutrition essentially didn't change over the span of two health surveys conducted in 1998 and 2005, even as GDP per capita growth averaged about 4.75 percent.[3] Clearly, it is possible for a country to experience strong economic *growth* without comparably strong economic *development*. There needs to be additional attention paid to policy mechanisms that can help to translate higher average incomes into improved capabilities for the poorest citizens.

What about the other direction of the relationship? Does economic *development* lead to economic *growth*? There are plenty of reasons to think it does. As we saw in Chapter 10, "Economic Growth," economists hotly debate the fundamentals of economic growth. There is general agreement, though, that those fundamentals include such things as property rights, the rule of law, and human capital. After all, an economy without healthy, educated workers is obviously going to have a hard time growing.

We will turn now to considering in more depth some of the basic aspects of economic development.

✓ TEST YOURSELF

☐ What are some examples of capabilities? **[LO 19.1]**
☐ Does economic growth always lead to economic development? **[LO 19.2]**
☐ Why may improving the education and health of the poorest help those who are more well off? **[LO 19.2]**

The Basics of Development Economics

Knowing there's a difference between economic growth and economic development, let's return with a fresh perspective to some ideas covered in earlier chapters. As we look at how countries can promote health, education, and good governance—all questions central to development economics—remember that we can think of these policies in two ways:

- We can see them as putting in place the conditions for economic growth.
- We also can see them as translating the fruits of economic growth into greater capabilities for people in society.

Human capital

Countries all over the world have witnessed dramatic improvements in health and education. This is especially true in Asia, and even countries in Africa that once lagged in health and education progress are now coming close to having all children in primary school. This is good news for both development and growth. Still, though, each year millions of kids die from diseases that could be prevented. These are improvements that could happen quickly and cheaply, but don't.

LO 19.3 Describe how improvements to health and education can develop human capital.

Health Why do these improvements fail to happen? Part of the problem is that health care facilities don't exist in many parts of the world. In rural areas, especially, getting to a modern clinic may involve trekking on foot for miles. Another part of the problem is that even where clinics do exist, many people don't use them. Many choose instead to resort to home remedies and traditional village "doctors" who have little or no training in medicine but charge lower fees than those charged by modern hospitals and often are more attentive.

Recognizing this, countries around the world, ranging from Thailand to Ghana, have started national health insurance programs. For a nominal fee, usually a couple of dollars per year, families can visit any national clinic or hospital to receive basic services. Still, often these national health care programs are not as effective as they could be. One study showed that in India, local health care workers were absent about 40 percent of the time on average. Even when the workers do show up, clinics sometimes run out of important drugs.

Improving health care in developing countries involves providing affordable clinics, encouraging their use, and incentivizing high-quality care from physicians who work in them.
©2p2play/Shutterstock

One study of health care clinics in Delhi, by Jishnu Das of the World Bank and Jeffrey Hammer of Princeton, found there were plenty of clinics available to poor households, but they provided much worse care than did private clinics in wealthier areas. It's not because the doctors were badly trained. Rather, Das and Hammer found that doctors serving poor patients often operated below their "knowledge frontiers"—the doctors provided care below the standard of their medical training. One study, for example, showed doctors in public clinics failing to ask even the most basic diagnostic questions when patients appeared to be having heart attacks. Why? Partly because doctors in private clinics receive a fee for their services, while in public clinics they receive a fixed salary. Doctors have a much higher incentive to get the treatment right when their income depends on customer satisfaction.[4] One of the challenges for development economists working in health care is to figure out a way to give doctors the right incentives when their own intrinsic motivation isn't enough.

Fixing these health care challenges can contribute greatly to economic growth as well as development. Well-nourished, healthy kids do better in school, making them more productive workers as adults. Epidemics that afflict young adults can have a profound impact on GDP. The AIDS epidemic alone has been found to lower growth rates by up to 1.5 percent per year throughout sub-Saharan Africa.

Is it first necessary to achieve economic growth to be able to fix health care challenges? Figure 19-1 shows the relationship between income measured in GDP per capita and life expectancy. As you would expect, people who live in countries with higher average incomes generally live longer lives. Still, the correlation is not exact. Compare Vietnam and Nigeria, for example. Nigeria has a slightly higher average income than Vietnam, but a baby born in Vietnam is expected to live about 22 years longer on average than a baby born in Nigeria. Clearly, it must be possible to improve health outcomes dramatically even without achieving strong growth in average incomes.

FIGURE 19-1

Income and life expectancy Overall, the higher the income within a country, the higher the life expectancy of the citizens within the country. At lower levels of income, this relationship isn't perfect, however. Some countries have made strides in income without making much progress in development in life expectancy, while others have high levels of life expectancy despite low incomes.

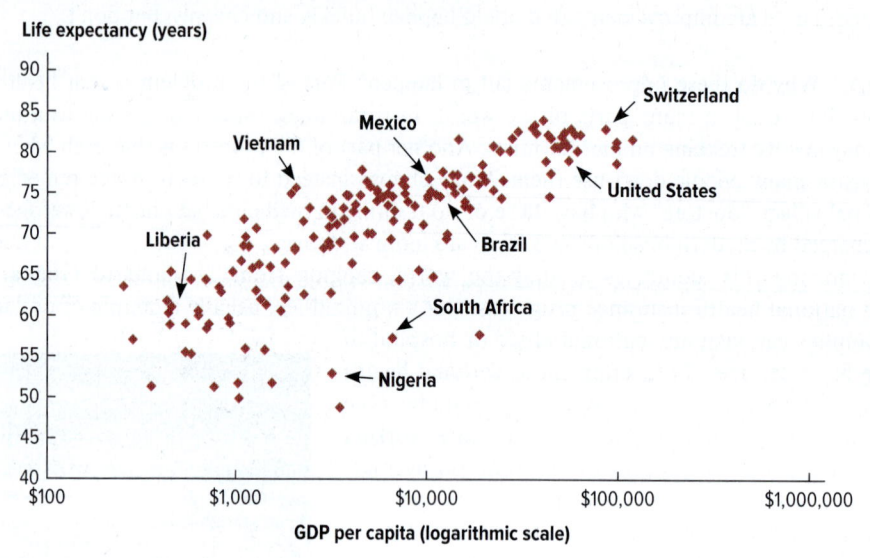

Source: The World Bank, *World Development Indicators* 2015 Data Set, http://databank.worldbank.org/data/reports.aspx?Code=SP.DYN.LE00.IN&id=af3ce82b&report_name=Popular_indicators&populartype=series&ispopular=y

Education As with health, the reasons for investing in teachers, schools, and books are related to both growth and capabilities:

- In terms of economic growth, educated workers are generally more productive: Each additional year of schooling is worth about 10 percent more in overall earnings over the course of a lifetime.
- In terms of capabilities, education can be seen as worthwhile in itself, as well as contributing to other capabilities. For example, more-educated women tend to make better decisions about family planning. Considerable data also indicate that more education tends to make a society more democratic and reduce its levels of inequality.

In 1997, 117 million children around the world were not attending school; 20 years later, in 2017, that number had fallen by nearly half to 64 million. Even countries without strong economic growth had made strong progress in school attendance. The abolishment of school fees is a major reason why more children are in school in a number of poorer countries. Even though the fees were usually small—about $30 a year—families living on just a few dollars per day simply could not afford them. Not surprisingly, when the fees were abolished, more kids went to school. In Kenya, for example, when school fees were eliminated in 2003, schools had to rush to find places for the one million more kids who enrolled around the country.

However, a sudden increase in students poses a new problem—crowded classrooms and overburdened teachers. In some countries, there is only one teacher for 100 students. Development economists have recently started to pay more attention to the challenge of improving the *quality* of education. Even in middle-income countries such as Mexico, where all kids go to primary school, 91 percent of kids do not learn math well enough to be competitive on the international stage. The situation is worse for lower-income countries. One study in Ghana found that sixth-graders on average performed at the same level on a basic literacy test as one could achieve simply by guessing.

There are many ideas for how to improve schools. Recent research by development economists has made great strides in testing which approaches are more effective and which are not. To work with children lagging behind on basic math and reading skills, Innovations for Poverty Action tested a remedial education program in India, Kenya, and Ghana and found the program to be particularly successful. The approach included training women in the community to offer supplemental lessons to the students who were furthest behind in their learning. Other approaches, such as distributing textbooks, helped only the best students in the class. Providing parents with information about the quality of the children's schools had no effect at all.[5]

Institutions and good governance

When we studied the determinants of economic growth, we discussed the importance of "good governance." Not surprisingly, good governance is also crucially important in economic development. Many basic capabilities rely on having a competent, well-intentioned government and good *institutions*.

Economist Douglass North of Washington University in St. Louis (and co-winner of the 1993 Nobel Prize for his contributions to economic history) defines **institutions** as the humanly devised constraints that shape human interactions.[6] This definition includes *laws* enforced by the government as well as *cultural norms*, such as whether people see it as unacceptable to avoid responsibility at work, embezzle funds from your employer, cheat on your taxes, and so on. Stated informally, institutions are the "rules of the game" in a society.

The term *institutions* is also commonly used to refer to government bodies (such as senates and ministries of education), development agencies (such as the World Bank), and international groups (such as the United Nations). According to North, to avoid confusion, in development economics we should instead think of these as examples of "organizations."

What exactly constitutes "good governance"? At first it seems like a highly normative question. Some think the best government is the smallest government, staying out of people's lives as much as possible. Others think that government should have its hand in many different sectors of the economy, all in the name of promoting stability, growth, and development. Most development economists agree that the most basic and important task of any government is to create a stable political system—one that ensures the important institutions of enforceable property rights and the rule of law.

LO 19.4 Explain the importance of institutions and good governance in development economics.

institutions
the humanly devised constraints that shape human interactions

Property rights and the rule of law   Say you'd like to sell a bucketful of apples. This will probably work just fine without your having to prove you actually own the apples. You set up shop at a market, someone gives you the cash, and you give them the apples.

What if you want to sell a house or a field? Would you ever buy land if you didn't have clear proof that the person selling it is the owner? No, you would want to see the *title* to the land, a document that certifies ownership of property. In many countries, the system of *titling* (providing legal documents proving ownership of assets) is weak.

Now imagine you own land and you want to use it as collateral for a loan—say, to buy a tractor so you can farm the land more effectively. Do you think the bank is going to lend you the money unless you can prove you own the land?

Hernando de Soto, a Peruvian economist and president of the Institute for Liberty and Democracy, says that that the weak titling system in Latin America results in "dead capital." Millions of people may have land or other assets, but without proper titles they are effectively unable to tap the financial power of those assets. Titles would allow owners to take out billions of dollars in loans that could be used productively to invest in starting new businesses or improving their farms. If only they had titles, De Soto argues, their capital could be put to better use—it could become "alive." The evidence supporting his claim is mixed, suggesting that titling may be important only if other conditions are in place too.

One of those conditions is the *rule of law*. The rule of law helps to create stability and provides a set of clear guides to govern transactions. There's no point in being able to prove you own something if the police and courts are corrupt or incompetent and won't help you if thieves take it away. Where crime is rampant and government unhelpful—or, worse, when a country falls into outright conflict—it's hard to sustain either economic growth or economic development.[7]

Is democracy necessary? Studies indicate a link between economic growth and political stability. The correlation between economic growth and democracy is less clear. Many of the stories of sustained growth in formerly poor countries occurred under governments that were far from democratic. Just think of China or Singapore.

The tiny, landlocked East African country of Rwanda is another illustration: Over the last decade and a half, growth has averaged about 7.5 percent per year, and residents are provided with basic and almost universal health insurance. Despite this growth, journalists critical of the government are routinely jailed; political opponents are routinely harassed and barred from participating in elections. The current president, Paul Kagame, won the last election with 93 percent of the vote, achieved by keeping any serious opponents from getting on the ballot.

Rwanda shows that even a relatively autocratic government can promote economic development as well as economic growth. Despite its democratic shortcomings, the government often makes good policy. Anti-corruption laws are some of the strongest in Africa and are enforced. Also, women are encouraged to participate in the political process—so much so that the Rwandan parliament is one of the only three in the world in which women outnumber men. (Cuba and Bolivia are the others.)

So if good policy and fair institutions do not require democratic elections, should we care about democracy? Amartya Sen's capabilities framework suggests that we should view democracy in its own right as an essential ingredient in improving lives and sustaining basic freedoms.[8]

Investment

LO 19.5 Evaluate the role of industrial policy and clusters in development.

We saw in Chapter 10, "Economic Growth," that investment is a key concern in promoting growth. Foreign direct investment is an important source of funds in many countries with low savings rates. Like many other facets of development, investment can promote or hinder economic development. To manage this challenge, governments turn to *industrial policy* in an attempt to favor some industries over others.

Industrial policy South Korea's GDP per capita in 1960 was about twice the size of Brazil's. By 2015, it was more than 2.5 times the size.[9] What accounts for these different rates of growth?

One important difference is that South Korea successfully pursued an industrial policy. **Industrial policy** is an effort by a government to favor some industries over others. The hope of such a policy is that coordinated investments in a chosen industry will help the overall economy develop and will spur growth in the long run. The tools at governments' disposal in pursuing industrial policy include trade barriers, tax breaks, subsidies, incentives for foreign direct investment, and investment in research. Traditionally, these tools have been used as part of two opposite philosophies of industrial policy: import substitution and export-led growth.

Import substitution is the practice of using trade policy to protect domestic industries until they are efficient enough to compete on the world market. Imagine you want to nurture a successful electronics industry in your country. But new electronics firms can't get off the ground because they have to compete with cheap imports from countries with well-established electronics industries. Why not impose temporary trade barriers to stop the cheap imports, allowing time for the domestic infant industry in electronics to grow big and strong enough to compete?

industrial policy effort by a government to favor some industries over others

Unfortunately, import substitution has failed to work well in the real world. A couple of problems related to import substitution can contribute to such failure:

- Without the spur of foreign competition to drive down costs, an infant industry might never grow up. For years, the Brazilian government protected domestic computer makers, but Brazilian-made machines still cost double the price of an American or Japanese machine.
- Decisions about which industries to protect are frequently made on the basis of *political* connections rather than real *economic* considerations. Naturally, companies would like to have their industry protected from foreign competition. That desire encourages large amounts of "rent-seeking" behavior—firms attempting to influence politicians in the name of profits. Protective policies have often persisted long after they were expected to lapse, at great cost to the taxpayer.

South Korea is achieving export-led growth by favoring companies, such as Hyundai, that are succeeding in the world market.
©Jean Chung/Bloomberg/Getty Images

Instead of using import substitution, some Asian countries have gone another route: *export-led growth*. This involves investing heavily in an industry through tax breaks and export subsidies (government monetary support for exporters) with the aim of selling goods around the world.

Rather than walling off domestic markets from international trade, export-led growth selects industries to push into the world market. Success depends on picking winners. The South Korean government, for example, has managed to do just that, supporting companies such as Samsung and Hyundai. As a result, South Korea made the jump from poor to rich over the course of five decades. Japan, Singapore, and Taiwan used similar strategies to create the so-called Asian miracle.

Unfortunately, export-led growth is getting harder for emerging economies. The unexpected and unprecedented success of these Asian countries led to many imitators, but not all are succeeding. China has become a massive exporter, creating competition for others wanting to follow its path. Meanwhile, the richer economies, like the United States, Japan, and European economies, can't buy everything that the rest of the world produces. International markets are fickle and competition can be fierce. While the benefits of picking winners can be huge, so can the costs if you end up picking losers.

Clusters As governments consider how to develop their industrial sectors, they often choose to focus on promoting not just one industry but *clusters*. **Clusters** are networks of interdependent firms, universities, and businesses that focus on the production of a specific type of good. Each part of the network is far less productive operating in isolation, so if governments can push each element of the cluster in unison, they should realize huge gains in productivity.

A successful example is Bangladesh's textile industry. Starting in the 1970s, the government made a concerted effort to develop a cluster around textiles. It ensured that complementary firms—such as those making fabrics and those sewing the fabric into clothes—were located in close proximity to minimize transportation costs. The government provided incentives for these firms to work together. Ready-made garments are now a multibillion-dollar industry in Bangladesh, accounting for about 80 percent of the country's export revenues.

clusters
networks of interdependent firms, universities, and businesses that focus on the production of a specific type of good

Trade

In earlier chapters, we studied the benefits of international trade: When one country can produce a good more efficiently than another country, both can specialize in the industry in which they have comparative advantage and experience mutual gains. As we saw, there are always winners and losers in trade. Some factories, for example, may get hit hard by competition when economies open to trade, so countries need to manage the process. But by opening up to foreign markets, countries can gain access to a wide array of new products, save money through access to cheaper goods, and find new customers for their products. It's not surprising, then, that trade plays a major role in development economics.

In the last few decades, there has been great growth in free trade worldwide. Tariffs (taxes on imports) in low-income countries have fallen by more than 20 percent. Part of this change has been due to the efforts of the **World Trade Organization (WTO)**, designed to monitor and enforce trade agreements while also promoting free trade. But about two-thirds of the reduction in tariffs in the past 20 years comes from reforms by national governments changing their own policies or making agreements with each other.

World Trade Organization (WTO) an international organization designed to monitor and enforce trade agreements, while also promoting free trade

Wealthy countries increasingly feel that trade can sometimes be a more powerful lever than aid to help poorer countries develop. In 2000, for example, the U.S. government initiated the African Growth and Opportunity Act, which gave preferential treatment to about 1,800 goods coming from Africa—especially goods like apparel and textiles, exempting them from duties and quotas. In 2005, aid donors began to offer "aid for trade" programs to fund initiatives in low-income countries that minimize barriers to trade and provide the infrastructure critical for imports and exports. While trade policy is often politically contentious, trade-related aid now accounts for over a quarter of official development assistance.

Migration

LO 19.6 Evaluate how migration and remittances promote development.

The prospect of a better life drives millions of people to move away from home to other cities, provinces, or countries thousands of miles away in search of opportunity. Research by economists Michael Clemens, Claudio Montenegro, and Lant Pritchett indicates that skilled workers in the United States earn about 15 times more than workers with exactly the same skills in Nigeria.[10] It's hardly surprising, then, that according to one Gallup World Values Survey, 40 percent of those living in the poorest quartile of countries would like to emigrate (move out of their home country).

However, it's difficult to legally move to a high-income country. Every year, the U.S. Diversity Visa lottery randomly gives more than 50,000 people and their dependents the chance to permanently immigrate to the United States. (There are other programs for people with special skills and asylum seekers; the diversity lottery is the main source of green cards for people from low-income countries.) In 2018, more than 23 million people applied, and only about 116,000 were selected.[11] That's a 0.5 percent chance of admission—much lower than admission rates to the most competitive U.S. colleges. Some of those who are unsuccessful are so desperate that they set off on perilous journeys—crossing the desert through Mexico or taking a rickety boat from Africa to Europe—to try to enter a high-income country illegally.

As we saw in Chapter 9, "Unemployment and the Labor Market," in host countries such as the United States, the influx of immigrants can be a highly controversial issue. But when we look at migration from the perspective of countries of origin, it presents a variety of opportunities to promote development.

One important consequence of migration is *remittances* (money sent home by migrants). As shown in Figure 19-2, remittances are a major financial flow in some countries. The largest overall recipients of remittances are China and India, which each gets more than $60 billion per year. Overall, remittances have become a powerful force in the world economy, growing impressively even after accounting for inflation. In 1990, less than $50 billion in inflation-adjusted dollars was transferred. In 2018, this figure was around $613 billion.[12]

In addition to the benefits from remittances, migrants often return home after a few years working overseas, bringing with them new ideas and skills that benefit their local economy. For Michael Clemens, an economist at the Center for Global Development, and Lant Pritchett, author of the book *Let Their People Come*, the world has much to gain by loosening migration restrictions so that workers can more freely seek jobs in other places.[13] See the From Another Angle box "Is immigration the answer?" for more.

FIGURE 19-2

Remittances around the world The top 10 countries in terms of remittances received are a diverse group. India and China are large countries, with many migrants abroad. The Philippines and Mexico are countries that have traditionally been associated with remittances. As the data for France and Germany show, remittances aren't strictly a flow from rich to poor countries.

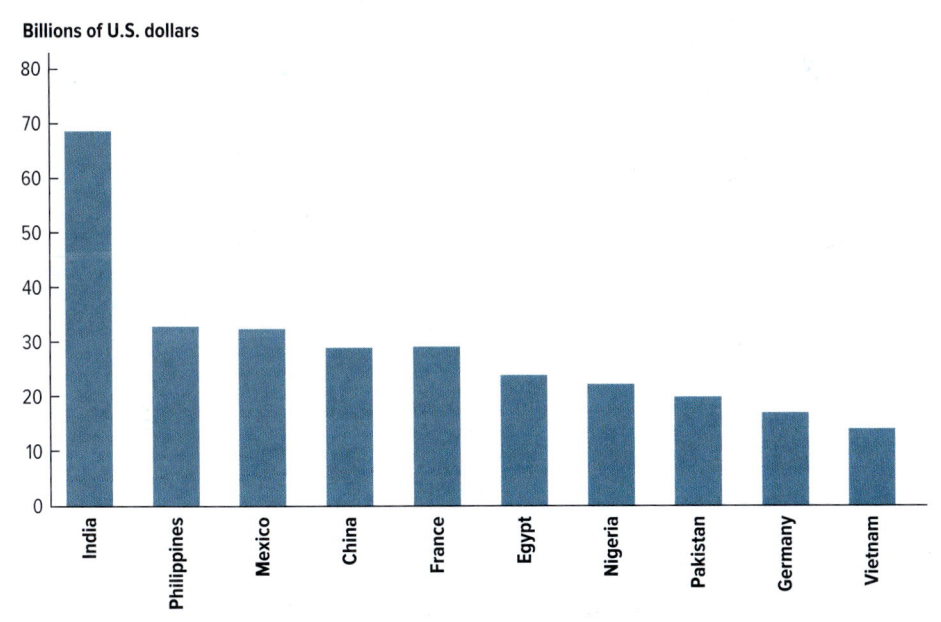

Billions of U.S. dollars

Country	Remittances (Billions USD)
India	~69
Philippines	~33
Mexico	~32
China	~29
France	~29
Egypt	~24
Nigeria	~22
Pakistan	~20
Germany	~17
Vietnam	~14

Source: The World Bank, 2017 data, https://data.worldbank.org/indicator/BX.TRF.PWKR.CD.DT?locations=IN-CN-DE-PK-BD.

Is immigration the answer?

From Another Angle

In 2011, Alabama enacted HB56, a law punishing employers that hire illegal immigrants. After the law passed, tomato farmer Chad Smith found himself needing to hire Americans to pick his 85 acres of tomatoes. But picking tomatoes turned out to be hard, sweaty, poorly paid work, and most of his U.S. workers quit after just a couple of days—even though he offered a higher than minimum wage. Without immigrant labor, Smith argued, his farm couldn't operate competitively.

This story shows that migration doesn't always fit the narrative you may hear in the news. After all, immigrants weren't taking away jobs from native workers—native workers didn't want to pick tomatoes at an entry-level wage. The result was rotting crops, higher food prices, and a missed opportunity for migrants to earn more money.

According to some economists, increased migration might be the best way to make a difference in the world. To see why, let's look at the economic costs and benefits. (We recognize that there are real normative issues to deal with, but that's something we are not able to tackle here.) To start, people who would migrate clearly benefit from the opportunity. Economists Michael Clemens, Claudio Montenegro, and Lant Pritchett found that when comparing outcomes of workers in 42 countries, those who left their home country earned 2.6 times what a same-skilled worker earned at home.

(continued)

But what about the effect on the countries that migrants move from? Common wisdom says that the workers who leave a country for better job opportunities naturally tend to be the most skilled. Their migration thus leaves the home country with limited-skilled workers to drive the growth of the economy. This phenomenon is often called "brain drain."

However, in a 2011 paper, John Gibson and David McKenzie concluded that lowering barriers to migration might actually *increase* the number of skilled workers in poorer countries. It makes sense, when you think about it: If workers in a low-income country know that it's possible to migrate, they may be more motivated to obtain crucial skills that would qualify them for jobs abroad. In the end, not everyone decides to move away—so the domestic economy also ends up with more highly skilled workers as a result. This opens up the possibility of "brain gain" instead of "brain drain."

The evidence also suggests that the shrinking labor supply in the countries sending immigrants abroad pushes wages up as the supply of labor falls. One study estimated the effect of emigration from Mexico to be worth about an 8 percent raise for low-income workers who stay in Mexico.

These benefits adds up. Assuming that migrants do not compete with native workers in the labor market (admittedly, a debated assumption), migrant workers earn higher wages without reducing wages. In the home country, wages for skilled workers rise, and many workers build human capital, a vital ingredient for economic growth.

Economists estimate that, on net, removing just 5 percent of barriers to the movement of workers between countries has the power to lift income around the world by trillions of dollars. Overall, this 5 percent reduction would have more of an effect than removing *all* existing tariffs, quotas, and barriers to capital movement around the world. The impact of making migration easier could dwarf anything foreign aid can hope to achieve.

Although the economic case for immigration is optimistic, the politics are much more difficult. Countries will be affected in ways that go well beyond economics, and like most big changes, there will be winners and losers. Whether states or countries will access the economic benefits will depend on how all the pieces—economic, social, political, and cultural—come together.

Sources: Dean Yang, "Migrant Remittances," *Journal of Economic Perspectives* 25, no. 3 (Summer 2011), pp. 129-152, http://pubs.aeaweb.org/doi/pdfplus/10.1257/jep.25.3.129; John Gibson and David McKenzie, "The Development Impact of a Best Practice Seasonal Worker Policy," Policy Research Working Paper, Impact Evaluation Series No. 48 (November 1, 2010), www.wds.worldbank.org/external/default/WDSContentServer/IW3P/IB/2010/11/30/000158349_20101130131212/Rendered/PDF/WPS5488.pdf; Michael Clemens, "Economics and Emigration: Trillion Dollar Bills on the Sidewalk," *Journal of Economic Perspectives* 25, no. 3 (Summer 2011), pp. 83-106, https://pubs.aeaweb.org/doi/pdf/10.1257/jep.25.3.83; Michael Clemens, Claudio Montenegro, and Lant Pritchett, "The Place Premium: Wage Differences for Identical Workers across the US Border," HKS Faculty Research Working Paper Series RWP09-004, John F. Kennedy School of Government, Harvard University (2009).

✓ TEST YOURSELF

☐ What do development economists mean by "institutions"? **[LO 19.4]**
☐ What are the three types of industrial policy named in this section? **[LO 19.5]**
☐ What are remittances and how do they promote development? **[LO 19.6]**

What Can Aid Do?

Foreign aid has long been seen as part of economic development, although a controversial part. Taxes in many countries go to provide aid to the poor around the world. Many citizens in these countries also give money to private charities such as Heifer International, CARE, Save the Children, and church-based organizations. In fact, private donations are larger than the entire budget for official foreign aid provided by the United States.

Why is foreign aid often the central focus of development efforts? It has direct intuitive appeal:

- If people are poor, then surely money would help make life a little easier.
- Are children not going to school? Why not give families money so that they don't have to choose between work and school?
- Are roads full of potholes, making it costly and difficult to get to markets and jobs? Why not help governments build and repair them?

These donations can be very important, whether in easing hunger in famine-ravaged areas or providing funding to would-be entrepreneurs.

The problem is how to make these funds go to the best uses. With many examples of misuse and waste, donating money often seems like a very unsure enterprise. Later in the chapter, we'll discuss how development economists are helping to discover what works—so that these donations can provide the most bang for their buck.

Children in Sudan look on as food and supplies are delivered by Save the Children, an international relief and development nonprofit organization.
©Mike Goldwater/Alamy

Perspectives on foreign aid

Foreign aid got its start following World War II. In an unprecedented show of generosity, the United States distributed, as part of the Marshall Plan, $12 billion to help 16 European countries rebuild after the devastation of the war. In today's money (accounting for inflation between 1948 and now), the sum is the equivalent of over $100 billion. Of course, this aid wasn't entirely altruistic on the part of the United States. There was a good deal of strategic self-interest involved: It was seen as imperative to have strong European allies on the western borders of the Soviet Union.

Aid then shifted to the world's poorer regions. The 1947 Truman Doctrine pledged $650 million to help "free peoples who are resisting attempted subjugation by armed minorities or by outside pressures." In other words, the United States was willing to put forth money to spread development—and to try to halt the spread of communism. Russia, too, got involved in the aid business, trying to woo unaligned countries to join the communist bloc. During the "Cold War," a period of competition between the United States and Russia, many dams and bridges built in developing countries were the product of such altruism combined with political strategy.

The Cold War has been over since 1991. Yet foreign aid continues and is still largely dedicated toward building public goods. Remember from Chapter 18, "Externalities," that public goods tend to be underprovided, considering the positive externalities they provide to the economy. This is especially true in countries that already lack means for collecting taxes and making capital investment. The result is a **financing gap**—the difference between the savings rate within an economy and the amount of investment needed to achieve sustainable growth.

To plug that gap, a large fraction of aid goes toward building schools, health care systems, and infrastructure networks. For much of the history of foreign aid, the financing gap has been a driving force in decisions about how much to give.

In 2002, at the Monterrey Conference on Financing for Development, the leaders of the world's most industrialized countries made a major pledge: They would devote 0.7 percent of their gross national income (GNI, a combination of GDP plus net capital flow from abroad) to foreign aid, formally called *official development assistance* (ODA). For the United States alone, this pledge would mean at least $90 billion per year. Hopes were high for what that money could accomplish.

However, actual foreign aid budgets have fallen well below that goal. Of the 22 richest countries that made the pledge, so far only six have followed through to the extent promised. As of 2017, the United States devotes only about 0.18 percent of GNI to ODA, far below the 0.7 percent target

LO 19.7 Describe the aims of foreign aid, the role of poverty traps, the main institutions delivering aid, and criticisms of foreign aid.

financing gap
the difference between the savings rate within an economy and the amount of investment needed to achieve sustainable growth

FIGURE 19-3

Official development assistance   In absolute terms, the amount of official development assistance (ODA) has steadily increased; over nearly 60 years, the net amount of aid money given by OECD countries has doubled. Despite the 0.7 percent of gross national income (GNI) target set in the 1970s, the amount of ODA as a percent of the GNI has fallen fall below this target.

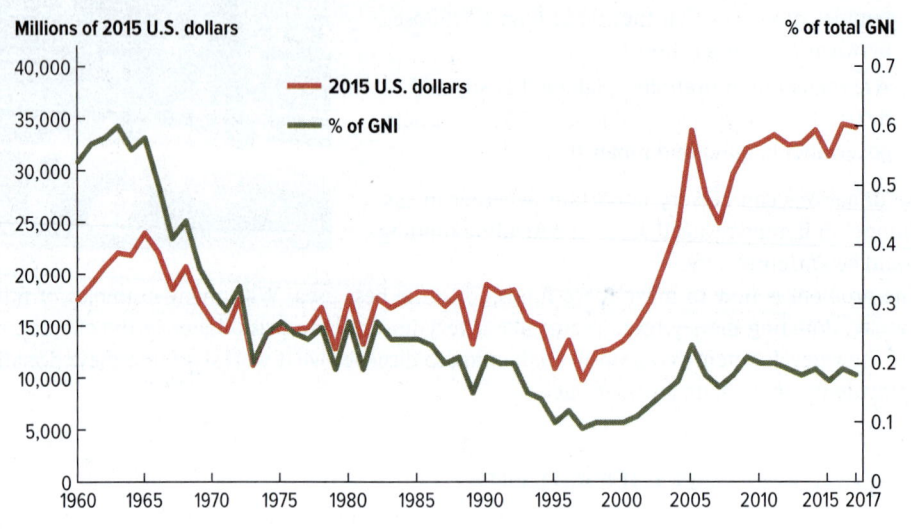

Source: Net flows by donor (ODA), https://data.oecd.org/oda/net-oda.htm.

and also below the average amount given by OECD countries. As you can see in Figure 19-3, the percentage has not increased much in recent decades.[14]

Over the past 55 years, the amount given in aid has increased in dollar terms, but has fallen and leveled off in terms of aid *as a share of GDP*. Should the United States meet its pledge to give 0.7 percent? See the What Do You Think? box "Should the United States give more in foreign aid?" for more on this debate.

Should the United States give more in foreign aid?
What Do You Think?

The United States is one of the wealthiest countries in the world, with an average income about 20 times higher than the world average. However, it spends a relatively small amount on foreign aid. In 2017, the U.S. government spent $34.1 billion on official development assistance, about 0.18 percent of the country's gross national income and less than 1 percent of the U.S. federal government's budget. This number is well below both what most Americans think the government spends on aid (25 percent of the budget) and how much they think is "appropriate" to spend (10 percent). Should the U.S. government do more?

On one hand, a small increase in foreign aid could make a big difference. The World Food Program, which provides badly needed food aid to areas of famine around the world, costs about $4 billion per year (which is a fairly modest cost given the size of aid budgets). Researchers estimate that a yearly investment of $7 billion would be enough to reduce the global prevalence of AIDS from 38 million cases to 1 million by 2050.

However, some believe that the United States should focus on problems at home first. Money spent on foreign aid could just as easily go toward addressing domestic problems, and many government programs are getting squeezed in future budgets. In March 2016, the U.S. government adopted a budget that cut spending by over $3 trillion during a 10-year period. This spending cut included removing $2.5 trillion in funding from health care programs for low- to moderate-income people. Other cuts included $125 billion from the SNAP program (formerly knows as food stamps) and about $300 billion from other entitlement programs.

Others note there is an important difference between providing food aid during a famine or providing assistance after a natural disaster and building health clinics or schools in a far-flung country. In this view, crisis assistance carries a larger moral imperative than infrastructure development and should be the focus of foreign aid spending.

WHAT DO YOU THINK?

1. At a time when U.S. government programs are facing cuts, does it make sense to help provide health insurance in Tanzania, roads in Afghanistan, hospitals in Iraq, and agricultural development in Mozambique?
2. How should the U.S. government weigh (a) providing humanitarian assistance after natural disasters abroad versus (b) investing in the long-term development of poorer countries?

Sources: www.worldpublicopinion.org/pipa/articles/brunitedstatescanadara/670.php?lb=btda&pnt=670&nid=&id; www.cbsnews.com/htdocs/pdf/poll_deficit_072909.pdf; www.washingtonpost.com/blogs/federal-eye/post/whats-getting-cut-in-the-fy-2011-budget/2011/04/11/AFMIynLD_blog.html; www.people-press.org/2013/02/22/as-sequester-deadline-looms-little-support-for-cutting-most-programs; www.cbpp.org/research/federal-budget/congressional-budget-plans-get-two-thirds-of-cuts-from-programs-for-people.

Poverty traps and the Sustainable Development Goals

Those who argue for ramping up foreign-aid budgets often assert that aid can help countries break out of poverty traps. A **poverty trap** is a self-reinforcing mechanism that causes the poor to stay poor. For instance, a poorly nourished and undereducated population is unlikely to have the energy or know-how to develop its economy. In the long run, it will struggle to earn enough to feed itself and educate its children. Foreign aid, the theory goes, can break this negative self-reinforcing mechanism and create a *virtuous cycle*, in which improvements build on improvements.

poverty trap
a self-reinforcing mechanism that causes the poor to stay poor

Some theories of economic development hold that escaping from poverty traps requires simultaneous investments in a wide variety of sectors as well as improvement of institutions. One variant of this idea, championed by Columbia University economist Jeffrey Sachs in his book *The End of Poverty*, is known as the "big push."[15]

The idea that concerted efforts in different sectors are necessary lay behind the United Nations' decision in 2000 to create eight *Millennium Development Goals*. These goals served as targets in all of the areas covered in Sachs's "big push." The goals include establishing universal primary education and halving the number of people living on one dollar per day.[16] They were supposed to be achieved by 2015. Some were, and some were not.

Of course, if a goal is not met, it doesn't mean the effort has been wasted. Even if universal primary education was not achieved by 2015, far more kids are going to school. As a result of this push, the number of children who were not in primary school fell from 100 million in 2000 to about 57 million in 2015.[17]

In 2015, the United Nations agreed on a set of 17 *Sustainable Development Goals* to meet by 2030. These goals shared some qualities with the Millennium Development Goals, including targets for poverty, education, and health. They also went further, setting targets for the environment, gender equality, and strong institutions. The number one goal is the complete elimination of extreme poverty.

However, not everyone is convinced that such "big push" ideas are the right way for foreign aid to go. Critics argue that there is no guarantee the idea could work if rolled out globally, and it would be extremely expensive to try. They suggest other, cheaper ways to kick-start economic development, such as a focus on setting up better institutions or improving the quality of credit or insurance markets.

The major distributors of aid

How do governments of wealthy countries give their foreign aid? Much of it is channeled through national development agencies or sectors of foreign-affairs ministries. The *United States Agency for International Development (USAID)* serves this purpose in the United States. About $11 billion of the $22.1 billion allocated by the United States toward official development assistance funds USAID, which works to improve economic growth, trade, and agriculture, among other things.[18]

Other resources are channeled through international institutions. About $2.3 billion per year comes from the **World Bank**, a multinational organization dedicated to providing financial and technical assistance to developing countries. Formed in 1948 at the same Bretton Woods conference that spawned the International Monetary Fund, the World Bank is actually two development organizations:

- Much like a bank, the International Bank for Reconstruction and Development (IBRD) makes loans that are used by middle-income and creditworthy poor countries to finance a wide variety of investment projects.
- The International Development Association (IDA), on the other hand, more closely resembles what we think of as a traditional aid agency. From 2000 to 2010, IDA funded immunizations for 310 million children and clean water for 113 million. This work has continued since, on large-scale budgets that include an average of $18 billion worth of commitments in the last three years.

Much development work is also conducted through a sprawling network of organizations under the **United Nations Development Program (UNDP)**—a global United Nations network that provides knowledge and resources to developing countries. In all, the UNDP is on the ground in 166 countries, operating a diverse set of projects, including everything from halting the spread of HIV/AIDS to developing democratic institutions. Within the UNDP, specialized organizations fund more targeted types of aid. The World Food Program, for example, spent around $6 billion in aid in 2017, 80 percent of which went toward fighting hunger in famine-ravaged areas, as part of its Emergency Preparedness and Response program.[19] Some government aid is also funneled through private, nonprofit organizations such as Heifer, CARE, and Save the Children.

World Bank
a multinational organization dedicated to providing financial and technical assistance to developing countries

United Nations Development Program (UNDP)
a global United Nations network that provides knowledge and resources to developing countries

Problems with foreign aid

With such a large system of aid, it's not surprising that not everyone is on board with the idea of doling out billions of dollars to poor countries around the world. It's not hard to find these critics—including some notable economists—who believe that aid can be inefficient and even counterproductive. Jean-Claude Duvalier, president of Haiti from 1971 to 1986, lived a fantastically lavish lifestyle while ordinary Haitians lived in intense poverty. Duvalier would regularly showcase Haiti's poor to international donors and then divert much of the resulting aid (one estimate is 80 percent) into his personal bank account. Foreign aid is now tracked more carefully than it was in Duvalier's day, and agencies and governments now require a greater degree of accountability. But problems still persist.

An intriguing insight was provided in 2011 when WikiLeaks, an organization that works to make classified documents public, released 250,000 classified cables from U.S. embassies. One of these cables revealed embezzlement and misplacement of funds from the UK Department for International Development (UK DfID) in projects around the world. In one example, almost $2 million given by the UK Ministry of Defense to "support peacekeeping" in Sierra Leone was instead embezzled by top generals in the Sierra Leone Ministry of Defense to buy plasma televisions and hunting rifles. In Kenya, the Ministry of Education admitted to losing $17.3 million worth of textbooks distributed through the "Free Education" program. In Uganda, officials managed to divert almost $27 million from an education fund. Disappearing money may be one reason why, despite the spending of half a trillion dollars in ODA from

1970 to 1994, productivity growth in developing countries was essentially zero and economic growth not much more.

Another big problem is that organizations such as the World Bank are not held accountable for what happens to funds once dispersed. Abhijit Banerjee notes the example of a World Bank computer kiosk program implemented in India, which the Bank trumpeted as a rousing success in its "Empowerment" sourcebook.[20] Many of these machines, however, were sitting uselessly in buildings that didn't have electricity or internet connections. William Easterly, an economist at NYU who spent years working at the World Bank, argues that aid agencies typically have nebulous goals—such as promoting empowerment or economic growth or governmental reform—rather than being charged with completing a task that is specific and measurable. Without measurable goals, it's not surprising that organizations have little incentive to be sure that what they are doing actually works.

There are even stronger critics of aid than Easterly. Dambisa Moyo, in her book *Dead Aid*, argues that aid actually hurts the countries that receive it.[21] In many countries, aid is a substantial part of the budget. In Kenya, for example, aid averaged 10 percent of GDP from 1970 to 2010. Such large flows can have serious effects throughout the economy, notably crowding out domestic investment. When foreign aid flows in, it also has to be traded for local currency; that currency trade bids up the price of the local currency and hurts the competitiveness of the local export sector.

Aid can be particularly counterproductive when it involves trucking in goods for free or at highly discounted prices. Such aid is known as *goods-in-kind donations*. One major source of goods-in-kind donations is TOMS™, which distributes shoes and eye care to kids as a part of their business model. The Econ and YOU box "Buy a shoe, give a shoe" outlines how TOMS started the program and how the company has refined the model to make it more effective.

Buy a shoe, give a shoe
Econ and YOU

You might own a pair of TOMS shoes, like their classic canvas slip-ons, or you may have seen them worn around campus. Or you might have heard about the company's unusual business model.

Blake Mycoskie, the founder of TOMS, built the company after traveling in poor parts of rural Argentina. His idea was to give away a pair of shoes to poor kids in Argentina and beyond for every pair he sold. The money to give away the shoes would come from selling TOMS shoes in the United States and other markets. Mycoskie recalls, "I'd been playing around with the phrase 'Shoes for a Better Tomorrow,' which eventually became 'Tomorrow's Shoes,' then TOMS."

After a decade, TOMS has given away nearly 90 million pairs and has become a model of "social entrepreneurship." By buying a pair of TOMS, you're contributing to their efforts to "shoe the world."

Mycoskie had good intentions, but good intentions are not always enough. You don't need to be an economist to start asking

TOMS, a model of "social entrepreneurship" that gave away nearly 90 million pairs of shoes in its first 10 years, has recently studied the impact of its giving and revised its strategy to be even more effective.
©Teresa Schaeffer/Shutterstock

(continued)

questions about the likely impacts: Are there really a lot of kids who don't have shoes? Might TOMS shoes simply replace older shoes—and thus not make a big difference in the kids' lives? Are there things, like better schools or healthy food, that would make a bigger difference than shoes? Worse, could giving away shoes in a poor community undermine local shoemakers? Maybe it's better to just give money so people can decide what they want and need?

The team at TOMS had some of the same questions. In 2010 they asked Bruce Wydick, an economist at the University of San Francisco, to evaluate the impact of giving away shoes. Wydick and his colleagues set up a study of 1,578 children in rural El Salvador. Some kids were randomly selected to receive free shoes; the others served as a control group (they didn't get shoes). Although the kids liked the shoes they were given, comparing the two groups showed only minor impacts on health and school attendance. It turned out that most kids already had a pair of shoes, so getting a better, newer pair made only a limited impact. The researchers also found a (very small) drop in demand for locally produced shoes.

TOMS listened and rethought some of its strategy. The company started giving away shoes that were more appropriate to local communities—like sports shoes for active kids and snow boots in cold regions. Another step has been to manufacture more shoes in poorer regions; TOMS now runs a shoe factory in Haiti.

The bottom line from the study is that giving away shoes isn't going to change the world. Other studies show that simply giving money is likely to be much more effective. (See the From Another Angle box "Cash, no strings attached," later in the chapter.) TOMS, though, should be commended for being willing to subject its strategy to an independent evaluation—and then adjusting the strategy to get a bit closer to helping make a "better tomorrow."

Sources: Bruce Wydick, Elizabeth Katz, Flor Colvo, Felipe Gutierrez, and Brendan Janet, "Shoeing the Children: The Impact of the TOMS Shoe Donation Program in Rural El Salvador," *The World Bank Economic Review*, 32, no. 3 (2018), pp. 727–751; www.acrosstwoworlds.net/?p=292; www.economist.com/finance-and-economics/2016/11/05/free-two-shoes; www.toms.com; www.entrepreneur.com/article/220350; www.vox.com/2015/7/23/9025975/toms-shoes-poverty-giving.

Do problems with foreign aid mean all aid should be stopped? Not necessarily. The lesson may be that more effort needs to go into improving the weak governments that embezzle aid or fail to use it productively. This idea was tested by economists Craig Burnside at Duke University and David Dollar, now at the U.S. Treasury Department. They found that in the decades of the 1980s and 1990s:

- Countries with sound fiscal, monetary, and trade policies and strong rule of law, combined with large amounts of aid, grew GDP at 1 percent.
- Countries with bad policy and high amounts of aid saw GDP shrink by 1 percent over the same time period.[22]

In fact, for countries with "bad" policy, aid was actually a detriment to growth. The example of Duvalier's Haiti at the beginning of this section suggests why: With aid flowing in to embezzle, Duvalier had little incentive to work to improve Haiti's economy because such improvements would reduce or eliminate aid.

The research behind the Dollar and Burnside study has been questioned (it turns out that more recent data do not show the same patterns). Nevertheless, their logic has spurred governments and aid organizations to think harder about links between aid and policy. In 2004, the United States created the Millennium Challenge Corporation to give cash to "worthy" governments. To qualify, these governments have to meet 17 requirements, including ruling justly, tamping down corruption, and maintaining a stable economy. By 2018, the Millennium Challenge Corporation had given out $12 billion in arrangements called "compacts" to 27 countries.[23]

Impact investing

Most thinking about foreign aid has little to do with business. But businesses, after all, are extremely good at generating new products, producing at the right scale, marketing, and creating efficient supply chains. Those are the exact qualities needed to solve some of the toughest social and economic problems.

Private investors and institutions are supporting this new breed of socially minded businesses through an idea called impact investing. **Impact investing** involves investing money in firms to generate both financial and social returns. In some ways, it's an alternative to foreign aid, though in fact the two ideas can work together. The firms that receive the impact-investing funds are called "social businesses." They are involved in all kinds of endeavors from building cheap but effective private schools in the slums of Nairobi, to hospitals that serve the poor for free in South India.

The guiding idea behind impact investing is simple: Markets can be powerful tools to promote human development, but not if investors are interested only in a quick financial return.[24] Impact investors, who may be foundations, wealth managers, private managers, or nonprofit organizations, are willing to be more patient and take greater risks. They sometimes accept lower financial returns as long as they're convinced that their money is being used to create social change.

One pioneering example of impact investing is the Acumen Fund, a "nonprofit global venture fund" that invests only in businesses that aim for social impact. Since its start in 2001, it has invested more than $110 million in health, housing, water, energy, education, and agriculture businesses across East Africa, West Africa, Latin America, India, and Pakistan. Among the firms supported by the Acumen Fund—to the tune of $1.5 million—is d.light design, which sells lanterns that produce light using solar energy. One out of four people in the world does not have electricity. The solar lanterns sold by d.light are a healthier solution than kerosene lanterns, which produce dangerous fumes.

Although the Acumen Fund's investments are a small fraction of the roughly $1.3 trillion in foreign direct investment that flows around the world each year, impact investing is growing quickly, particularly in Europe. Large banks are getting involved, as are universities: Colorado State University, for example, offers a Global Social and Sustainable Enterprise (GSSE) Master's in Business Administration. Stanford University's Entrepreneurial Design for Extreme Affordability class teaches students to design products to serve consumers at the lowest income level (and was the group that incubated the solar lantern behind d.light design).

LO 19.8 Understand how impact investing provides a new tool for creating social impact.

impact investing investing money in firms to generate both financial and social returns

Solar-powered lighting makes things we take for granted in the United States, like studying at night and charging a cell phone, much easier to do.
©Mark Boulton/Alamy

How do we know what works?

There is no shortage of ideas for how to promote economic development. These ideas include hydrological monitoring systems, footpaths, road maintenance, electric power grids, women's empowerment initiatives, and industrial parks. But because resources are limited, governments and aid agencies have to make some tough choices about which policies would be the best in reducing poverty. In short, *how do we know what works?*

For most of the twentieth century, development efforts proceeded on a trial-and-error basis. Certain strategies were tried. If they seemed to work, they were kept; if they looked like glaring failures, they were scrapped. The trouble is, many of the failures weren't glaring enough. Often, aid agencies simply couldn't be sure whether a particular strategy had helped or hurt.

In recent years, some development economists have started to argue against charging forward with ideas that might or might not work. Instead they promote a more informed approach by rigorously evaluating the impact of development programs and policies.

LO 19.9 Explain the need for impact evaluation, and analyze the role of randomized controlled trials in measuring impact.

Evaluations *Impact evaluation* entails answering one seemingly simple question: How did people's lives change after a program or policy, compared with how they would have changed without it? This question would be easy to answer if everything else were held constant except the program or policy—but that's not the case in the complexities of the real world.

Consider the challenge of enrolling kids in school and ensuring they learn while they are there. To achieve those goals, there are many options and promising programs. For example:

- Because schools in developing countries often have to make do with old, battered learning materials, one strategy is to provide students with better textbooks.
- Another strategy might be providing kids with school uniforms. Even when schooling itself is free, many schools require students to wear uniforms; when this is an expense that families cannot afford, their kids don't go to school.

At first glance, it seems as if it would be easy to evaluate efforts like these—just measure the test scores of kids in schools who receive the textbooks or the uniforms. If they're higher than before, great; if not, then back to the drawing board.

Unfortunately, that type of evaluation is far from foolproof. Beyond the question of whether the tests measure learning in a meaningful way, how do we know that the better test scores are not the result of something else? What if there's been an especially good harvest this year, so kids are learning better because they're no longer hungry while at school? In that case, we might be mistaken in thinking the textbooks are making the difference, and we'd keep pouring money into buying more textbooks when it could be put to better use elsewhere.

One way to avoid evaluation problems is by using **randomized controlled trials**, or **RCTs** for short. Randomized controlled trials randomly assign people into groups in order to focus on the impact of a particular intervention. Some of the stories told in this text, such as the one about giving out mosquito nets to protect from malaria (see the "Paying for bednets" box in Chapter 4, "Elasticity"), have been the result of such randomized controlled trials. In this chapter, the research cited in the Econ and YOU "Buy a shoe, give a shoe" box and the From Another Angle box "Cash, no strings attached" relied on RCTs.

How could we use the idea of RCTs to know the true impact of providing more textbooks on test scores? We could select 100 similar schools and divide them into two groups of 50 at random. The first group doesn't get the textbooks; the second group does. If it's the textbooks making the difference, then schools in the so-called *treatment group* (the one that receives the textbooks) will do better than those in the *control group*. The key to the process is dividing the schools at random: The two groups should be similar on average before the study, so any factor other than the treatment itself should affect them equally. The RCT doesn't completely control for other variables that could possibly affect schools' performance, but it's a start.

Evaluations using the RCT method can give surprising results. It turns out if you want to boost school attendance, there's something you can buy and give out that's sometimes more effective than either textbooks or uniforms—deworming pills. Worms are tiny, parasitic organisms that cause chronic sickness that keeps kids out of school. The parasites were once common in parts of the United States, and they are still common in other countries. One study in Kenya found that, overall, a deworming program led to a 7.5 percent gain in primary school participation. Deworming pills are also far cheaper than textbooks or uniforms, costing just 50 cents per child per year. In comparison, the state-run *Prospera* (previously called *Oportunidades* and, before that, *Progresa*) safety-net program in Mexico, which links cash benefits for families to activities such as getting kids vaccinated and sending them to school, costs many times this amount.[25] (Note that programs like *Prospera* also have other goals, not just increasing school attendance.)

Figure 19-4 shows the results from an RCT study of various programs intended to increase years of education. The figure shows that there is one intervention that is even more cost-effective than deworming. When researchers crunched the numbers of the program costs versus how effective

randomized controlled trial (RCT)
a method that randomly assigns subjects into control and treatment groups in order to assess the causal link from an intervention to specific outcomes

FIGURE 19-4

Impact of programs intended to increase years of education Evaluations allow researchers to compare the cost-effectiveness of various programs. Telling parents about the benefits of education ("Information on returns") was by far the most effective intervention, and resulted in 20 extra "child-years" of education for every $100 spent. Deworming is also very cost-effective. Although other programs were also effective at increasing schooling, they were not as cost-effective as the others.

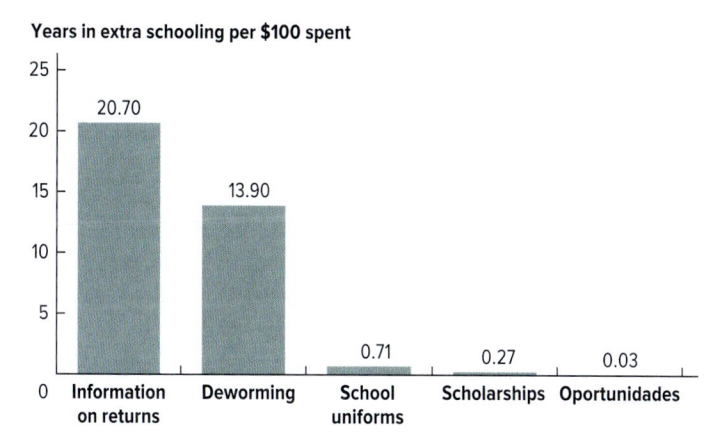

Years in extra schooling per $100 spent

Program	Years
Information on returns	20.70
Deworming	13.90
School uniforms	0.71
Scholarships	0.27
Oportunidades	0.03

Source: www.povertyactionlab.org/policy-lessons/education/improving-student-participation.

they were at increasing school enrollment, they found that a very simple program scored highest. That program involves simply informing parents of the potential benefits of giving their children an education. Many of these parents in parts of the developing world may never have attended school themselves. Explaining the benefits of education turned out to be by far the most effective intervention, resulting in 20 extra "child-years" of education for every $100 spent.

Thanks to randomized controlled trials, policy-makers and program managers can more confidently channel resources to approaches that work and are cost-effective.

Two organizations are dedicated to randomized controlled trials research. One is the Abdul Latif Jameel Poverty Action Lab (J-PAL), founded by economists at MIT and Harvard. The other is Innovations for Poverty Action (IPA), a nonprofit organization started by Dean Karlan (one of the authors of this text). Many other organizations and researchers have followed their lead in using RCTs to investigate sectors as varied as microfinance, education, health, agriculture, charitable giving, corruption, and social capital. Thanks to rigorous evaluations, the remedial education program we described earlier in this chapter, for example, is now being scaled up in Ghana, with the aim of reaching thousands of schools.

This is not to say that these organizations have found the solution to global poverty. Like so many other tools, RCTs have challenges and limitations. Some questions, like the effect on economic development of changing monetary policy, simply can't be evaluated with an RCT. Even for those programs that can be evaluated, it's possible that the observed effects will change if the intervention is repeated on another continent or even in different areas of a country. And often it's hard to tell from an RCT exactly why the intervention worked or failed.

Still, using economic theory to help design experiments, and replicating experiments at different times and in different places, can be critical in moving knowledge forward. Along with other kinds of analysis, RCTs are helping to build knowledge, piece by piece, which is already pointing to some seemingly small interventions that can make large differences.

For example, rather than trying to figure out what tool, program, or donation may best help the poor, RCTs have shown that it may be better to give people cash. The From Another Angle box "Cash, no strings attached" outlines GiveDirectly, an organization built around this model, and the evidence supporting the effectiveness of cash.

Cash, no strings attached
From Another Angle

Typically, charities and governments give out "things" to people—often donations of food, clothing (and, like TOMS, shoes), or a place to live. Or programs offer training on job skills, financial literacy, and similar ways to get ahead. These ideas make sense, but the donations may not in fact be what people most need or want to improve their lives.

The founders of GiveDirectly wondered whether there was a better way. That way was simply to give people cash—unconditionally—with no strings attached. (The idea has similarities to the "universal basic income" policies propounded by 2020 U.S. presidential candidate Andrew Yang, among others.)

GiveDirectly works in East Africa, where they identify poorer families and communities. Using donations collected from people around the world, GiveDirectly then transfers $1,000—about a year's worth of income—into recipients' accounts, which can be picked up from a local village agent or bank. The money can be spent on anything—such as school fees, capital to run a new business, or food.

Some critics worry, of course, that the cash will be spent on "frivolous" items (or worse)—cigarettes, alcohol, or drugs, for example. But an independent evaluation of the program showed that the transfers had no effect on the amount of money spent on those items. Instead, many people chose to improve their houses, like Grace, a recipient from Uganda:

> *My life has changed because I'm now sleeping well in [a] permanent house with enough fresh air. Before, I used to sleep in the kitchen and I could get [a] cough as a result of smoke. In addition, I have a phone for communicating with relatives and friends. In the past, I had no phone so I was not in-touch.*

Most recipients used the cash to improve their lives. The independent evaluation showed that transfers were largely spent on assets (such as a new motorbike, livestock, or business equipment) and nutrition. As a result, transfers were shown to increase mental health, reduce domestic violence, and improve food security in the short run. On average, earnings increased by $270 beyond the initial cash payment. Some of the results diminished over time, but a follow-up study showed that the impacts on asset-holdings remained robust three years later.

GiveDirectly is now experimenting with universal basic income (UBI) payments. In Kenya, the organization started the largest UBI program in the world, offering 26,000 people regular payments of $0.75 per day over 12 years (a meaningful sum for poor families). Researchers are collecting data to understand the impacts of basic income; they want to know whether UBI will encourage people to stop working and if receiving a steady flow of small payments is more effective than receiving larger lump-sum transfers.

GiveDirectly demonstrates the potential for simply giving cash to help people get ahead (at least in the places they work). It also raises an important question for programs based on donating things. The question is not just do the programs work well. Now the question is also, do they work better than simply giving cash?

Sources: Johannes Haushofer and Jeremy Shapiro, "The Short-Term Impact of Unconditional Cash Transfers to the Poor: Experimental Evidence from Kenya," *Quarterly Journal of Economics* 131, no. 4 (2016), pp. 1973–2042; www.givedirectly.org; www.givewell.org/charities/give-directly; https://blogs.worldbank.org/impactevaluations/givedirectly-three-year-impacts-explained.

✓ TEST YOURSELF

- ☐ How do financing gaps justify foreign aid? [LO 19.7]
- ☐ How many countries pledged to participate in official development assistance? How many of them actually gave the amount promised? [LO 19.7]
- ☐ What are the Sustainable Development Goals? [LO 19.7]
- ☐ Why might goods-in-kind donations cause problems for local producers? [LO 19.7]
- ☐ How does impact investing differ from foreign aid? [LO 19.8]
- ☐ What is a randomized controlled trial? [LO 19.9]

Conclusion

Although the work needed to put an end to global poverty may seem daunting, major strides have been made and continue to be made. Most obviously, decades of growth in the Chinese economy have lifted millions of people out of poverty. What worked for China was the product of a time and place that can't simply be bottled and shipped to other regions. Yet there are hopeful signs of improvements elsewhere, including Africa. Around the African continent, vigorously contested, democratic elections are taking place, and some countries are posting impressive growth figures. India's rapid economic progress has also been world-changing

Progress is being made through different mixes of good governance, aid, strengthened institutions, investment, and careful testing of what works and what does not among aid programs. While there is a long way to go, progress like this can promote the expansion of capabilities and help expand markets that truly work for the world's poor.

Key Terms

capability, p. 524
institutions, p. 529
industrial policy, p. 530
clusters, p. 531
World Trade Organization (WTO), p. 532
financing gap, p. 535
poverty trap, p. 537
World Bank, p. 538
United Nations Development Program (UNDP), p. 538
impact investing, p. 541
randomized controlled trial (RCT), p. 542

Summary

LO 19.1 Explain how the capabilities approach relates to economic development.

Development is a field of economics that studies the causes and nature of international poverty and human development. One way to think about development is known as the capabilities approach, developed by Amartya Sen. The goal of development is to increase human capabilities. There are many different types of capabilities, including very basic rights to health and education as well as other concepts like self-expression and reputation.

LO 19.2 Explain the relationship between economic growth and economic development.

The ideas of economic growth and development are similar but not identical. Economic growth can promote development. After all, when people have more money, you would expect them to spend more on improving their health and educating their children. There is general agreement, though, that the fundamentals of economic growth, including such elements as property rights, the rule of law, and human capital, will spark development.

LO 19.3 Describe how improvements to health and education can develop human capital.

By providing access to more and better schools and clinics, countries can develop human capital. Many countries are now mandating universal primary education and providing affordable health insurance to make great strides in basic human capital development. These efforts must be of high quality to be effective, though. Human capital is an important part of economic development, as it allows for more productive workers and greater economic growth. Improvements in human capital can also promote capacities development as people are able to lead more complete (better educated and healthier) lives.

LO 19.4 Explain the importance of institutions and good governance in development economics.

Development often takes root in places where there are strong institutions. Institutions are human-devised constraints that shape human interactions. In contrast, organizations are groups of people that act according to those constraints. Several institutions are important for development, including a strong system of property rights, the rule of law, and a government capable of implementing good policy.

LO 19.5 Evaluate the role of industrial policy and clusters in development.

Governments have turned to industrial policy in an attempt to favor some industries over others. Two popular types of industrial policy include import substitution and export-led industrialization. An alternative industrial policy is clustering, which promotes networks of interdependent firms, universities, and customers focusing on a specific type of good.

LO 19.6 Evaluate how migration and remittances promote development.

Every year, millions of people leave their home countries and villages to migrate in search of better-paying jobs. The money they send home to their families, called remittances, represents a large and growing financial flow around the world. As a result, governments and aid agencies work to make sure that these remittances best help the families back home escape poverty.

LO 19.7 Describe the aims of foreign aid, the role of poverty traps, the main institutions delivering aid, and criticisms of foreign aid.

Over the past 55 years, the amount given in foreign aid has increased in dollar terms but has fallen and leveled off as a share of GDP. Those who argue for ramping up foreign-aid budgets often assert that aid can help countries break out of *poverty traps*. Others suggest different ways to kick-start economic development, such as a focus on setting up better institutions or improving the quality of credit or insurance markets.

Much of the foreign aid governments do give is channeled through national development agencies like USAID, or through global organizations like the World Bank and the United Nations. Although foreign aid can provide money needed to finance developments in infrastructure, clinic and school construction, and other important measures that simply would not happen without outside assistance, critics point to cases in which foreign aid has been a destabilizing force that was wasted at best, and destructive at worst.

LO 19.8 Understand how impact investing provides a new tool for creating social impact.

Most thinking about foreign aid has little to do with business. But private investors and institutions are supporting socially minded businesses through *impact investing*, which involves investing money in firms to generate both financial and social returns. Markets can be powerful tools to promote human development, and impact investors sometimes accept lower financial returns as long as they're convinced their money is being used to create social change.

LO 19.9 Explain the need for impact evaluation, and analyze the role of randomized controlled trials in measuring impact.

Throughout history, ideas about how to spur development have mostly proceeded on a trial-and-error basis. Instead of wasting money on programs that may or may not work, economists have begun to evaluate the impact of various development programs. Impact evaluation tries to answer the question of how a particular program or policy changed people's lives. A *randomized controlled trial (RCT)* is one way to answer that question; it compares a treatment group with a control group to show the effect of a program.

Review Questions

1. Are capabilities and utility the same thing? If so, why do economists use two different terms for the same concept? If not, explain the difference, in terms of both their definitions and when each is best used in economic analysis. **[LO 19.1]**
2. Determine whether each of the following is true or false. **[LO 19.1]**
    a. The chance to see a musical is an example of a capability.
    b. The freedom to practice religion is not a capability because it is not directly related to economic development.
    c. Economists will make the same conclusions and recommendations using the utility-maximization approach as they will using the capabilities approach.
    d. The capabilities approach works better for analyzing what's best for society, while the utility-maximization approach works better for analyzing what's best for an individual.

3. Are economic growth and economic development the same? Why or why not? **[LO 19.2]**

4. Does economic growth lead to development? Or does the causation run the other way, with economic development leading to growth? Explain. **[LO 19.2]**

5. How can health and education work together to spur economic development? What does this imply about the best way to spend aid funds with the goal of increasing educational attainment in a developing nation? **[LO 19.3]**

6. Explain how better health care in a developing nation, such as increasing the number of immunized children, can have economic effects beyond fewer sick kids. **[LO 19.3]**

7. "I'm thinking about writing a paper for class on development economics," your friend tells you over lunch. "I'm going to focus on important institutions like government bodies and economic agencies." Is your friend using the term *institutions* correctly? Why or why not? **[LO 19.4]**

8. How can capital be considered "dead," and what do we mean by making this capital "alive"? **[LO 19.4]**

9. International trade is associated with economic growth and development—open economies tend to grow faster than closed economies, all else equal. Given this information, should a nation seeking to grow and develop faster use the method of import substitution or export-led growth? How would each of these two methods affect GDP through its net exports component? **[LO 19.5]**

10. Determine whether each of the following is an example of import substitution, export-led growth, or clustering. **[LO 19.5]**
    a. The government gives a $50 million grant to a leading university to work with car manufacturers and to research new ways to produce more fuel-efficient vehicles.
    b. The government gives $50 million to a domestic car company to subsidize its shipping costs to other countries.
    c. The government enacts a tariff on all cars imported from abroad.

11. How can emigration help the home economy in terms of income? Are the benefits of migration on income limited to those who actually migrate? Why or why not? **[LO 19.6]**

12. How does emigration affect wages and income in the migrant's country of origin? In the country the migrant immigrates to? **[LO 19.6]**

13. Say that the United States is considering giving direct aid to a nation run by a dictator known for his lavish lifestyle while the nation's citizens suffer through a terrible famine. What might be a problem with giving aid to this nation? Name at least one way to fix the problem. **[LO 19.7]**

14. What are goods-in-kind donations, and how can they hurt the economies they're meant to help? **[LO 19.7]**

15. How does impact investment differ from traditional foreign aid and traditional financial investment? **[LO 19.8]**

16. Explain briefly how you could set up an RCT to evaluate whether providing free breakfasts to elementary-school students helps them learn. **[LO 19.9]**

17. List three shortcomings of using an RCT to evaluate the success of a given economic program. **[LO 19.9]**

Problems and Applications

1. In a small town in the midwestern United States lives a drug dealer and manufacturer who supplies the illegal, addictive drug crystal meth. The drug dealer insists that making and selling the drug is what gives him the most satisfaction among any possible use of his time and resources. Using the utility-maximization approach, should he be allowed to continue supplying the drug? What about with the capabilities approach? Explain your answer. **[LO 19.1]**

2. Professor Bucks and Professor Liber are having a debate about the role of economic growth in contributing to economic development. Professor Bucks contends that economic growth is the only thing to consider in development, as people's utility is directly related to their income. Professor Liber agrees that income is directly related to development but says that there are other things to consider. Given what we've learned in this chapter, pick the option that is most correct according to the capabilities approach. **[LO 19.1]**
    a. Professor Bucks is correct because increases in income are the only way to measure economic development.
    b. Professor Bucks is correct because capabilities always increase when income does.
    c. Professor Liber is correct because income is unrelated to capabilities, which are the most important factor in development.
    d. Professor Liber is correct because income is related to development, but it is not the only contributor to capabilities.

3. Table 19P-1 shows the levels and annual growth rates of economic indicators for two countries, Nationavia and Countrystan. Assume these growth rates will remain constant for the foreseeable future. Use these data to

determine whether each of the following statements is true, false, or indeterminable. [LO 19.2]

TABLE 19P-1

Indicator	Level	Growth rate (%)
GDP per capita—Nationavia	$50,000	3.1
GDP per capita—Countrystan	$30,000	3.0
Average years of education per capita—Nationavia	15 years	2.0
Average years of education per capita—Countrystan	5 years	8.0
Life expectancy—Nationavia	72 years	0.5
Life expectancy—Countrystan	56 years	1.8

   a. The theory of income convergence (that national incomes in poor countries will "catch up" to those in wealthier countries) holds for Nationavia and Countrystan.
   b. Countrystan has higher levels of human capital than Nationavia.
   c. Inequality is greater in Nationavia.
   d. In 10 years, it's likely that Countrystan will have higher levels of human capital than Nationavia.

4. In Nation A, GDP per capita is $21,000 and is growing annually at a rate of 1.4 percent. The average citizen in Nation A lives for 51 years, and this figure is growing at 6 percent per year. Additionally, the average person in Nation A has 9 years of education, growing annually at 5.1 percent, and 60 percent of Nation A's population is currently literate, growing at a rate of 2 percent.

   In Nation B, GDP per capita is $40,000 and is growing annually at a rate of 0.8 percent. The average citizen in Nation B lives for 68 years, and this value is growing at 2 percent per year. The average person in Nation B has 10.5 years of education, increasing 2 percent annually, while 78 percent of its population is literate, a figure growing at 0.5 percent annually.

   Which nation is experiencing more economic growth? Which is wealthier? Which currently has more capabilities for its citizens? And which is experiencing more economic development? [LO 19.2]

5. Imagine that you are the leader of a low-income nation. You have identified lack of access to health care as a major contributor to your nation's low income, and the United States has offered to help by providing funds to build more health clinics. Will this solve the problem? Why or why not? If it won't, what's one alternative to using these foreign aid dollars to build clinics? [LO 19.3]

6. While listening to the radio on the way to school, you hear a politician from a small, low-income nation say the following: "Over the last five years, there has been a 10 percent increase in the number of children attending school full time. We can expect to see these children grow up to be more productive workers because their human capital has increased." Is the politician's statement true, false, or somewhere in between? Explain your answer. [LO 19.3]

7. Classify each of the following as an institution or organization. [LO 19.4]
   a. The United States Agency for International Development, a U.S. government agency that channels aid abroad.
   b. The United Nations Development Program.
   c. The UN Declaration of Human Rights, an agreement among members of the United Nations regarding the rights of individuals.
   d. The United Nations.
   e. The Sarbanes-Oxley Act (SOX), which established rules for how publicly traded firms must report information in their financial documents.

8. A given nation has a good titling system, but theft of productive equipment is rampant, with few consequences for those who steal. What is the term development economists use for what's lacking in this economy? What effect will this lack likely have on economic growth and economic development? Give one way to improve the situation. [LO 19.4]

9. The small, landlocked nation of Wheatleyton is just starting to develop an agricultural sector. Firms in this sector appeal to the government to temporarily limit imports of agricultural goods from other nations with more experience and larger scale, resulting in import prices so low domestic firms can't compete. What is this desired policy called? What problems are associated with it, and how can we reduce them? [LO 19.5]

10. The small nation of Movieheim wants to develop a film industry. It is considering two options for doing so:

    Option A: Reimburse relocation expenses for firms and give tax breaks to acting schools, film studios, digital artists, etc., to encourage them to work together and share ideas.

Option B: Make the purchase and exhibition of foreign films illegal for the next 10 years.

What would development economists call each of these options? Which is more likely to encourage long-term economic development, and why? **[LO 19.5]**

11. Consider separately each of the following hypothetical scenarios about South Africa and answer the included questions. Assume in each case that medical school has an 80 percent success rate—in other words, 80 percent of people who attend medical school graduate and become doctors. **[LO 19.6]**

    a. No doctors are allowed to emigrate, and the number of people going to medical school is given by D = 100,000 × I, where I is an index relating the income of doctors to those in other professions. If I = 4, how many students will go to medical school? How many more doctors will there be in South Africa?

    b. The United States decides to offer visas for any doctors from South Africa. Additionally, I in the above equation changes to 10. Assume that 30 percent of doctors educated in South Africa immigrate to the United States. How many students will go to medical school? How many will become doctors? How many of those doctors will practice in South Africa, and how many will practice in the United States?

    c. The United States decides to limit the number of doctors from South Africa who can obtain visas to no more than 10 percent of those graduating from medical school. Assume that I remains at 10. How many students will go to medical school? How many will become doctors? How many of those doctors will practice in South Africa, and how many will practice in the United States?

12. Table 19P-2 shows the size of hypothetical various flows to developing countries in 2017 and 2018 in billions of dollars. **[LO 19.7]**

TABLE 19P-2

Financial flow	Amount in 2017 (billions of $)	Amount in 2018 (billions of $)
Official development assistance	128	119
Foreign direct investment	510	573
Remittances	307	324

a. Rank each of the flows in 2018 as a percentage of ODA (official development assistance) in 2017, from highest to lowest.

b. Rank each of the flows in terms of their growth rates from 2017 to 2018, from highest to lowest.

13. The following equation provides an alternative calculation to determine a developing country's financing gap:

$$FG = (A \times g) - I_D$$

In this equation, FG is the financing gap; A is a variable that captures the country's starting income together with its ability to turn investment into growth (expressed in dollars); g is the targeted growth rate; and I_D is the amount of domestic investment currently in the economy. Assume that A = $50,000,000,000, g = 0.08, and I_D = $500,000,000, and answer the questions that follow. **[LO 19.7]**

a. What is the size of the financing gap?

b. Assume that the population of the United States is 300 million. How much would each U.S. citizen have to pay to fill the financing gap?

c. What percentage of GDP per capita in the United States does your answer from (b) represent if GDP per capita is currently $45,000?

Now assume that the United States decides to donate the amount of the financing gap to the developing country as aid. Assume also that there are administrative and competitive costs associated with receiving aid. Specifically, 23 cents of every dollar spent on aid will go to administrative costs. Also, for every dollar received from abroad intended to be used for investment, 50 cents will be used for noninvestment purposes.

d. Calculate the real increase in investment dollars the aid from the United States will provide in the recipient country.

e. Calculate the new financing gap by subtracting the above from the financing gap you calculated in part (a).

14. The president of an organization specializing in foreign investment says the following at a shareholder meeting: "Our one-year program was a failure. We were hoping for a 6 percent return on our investment, but we got only 3 percent." Use the idea of impact investing to provide an alternative argument that the program was not a failure. **[LO 19.8]**

15. Table 19P-3 displays the results of a study on how to improve vaccination rates in a developing nation. The baseline numbers represent the rates of vaccination at the beginning of the study, while the endline numbers represent the rates of vaccination at the study's conclusion. Answer the following questions. **[LO 19.9]**

TABLE 19P-3

Campaign	Vaccination rates (%)			
	Baseline, control	Baseline, treatment	Endline, control	Endline, treatment
Lectures	5	6	8	5
Free provision	5	4	8	8
Subsidy	5	5	8	10
Newspaper announcements	5	7	8	7

a. Which campaign(s) had a positive effect on vaccination rates in comparison to the control group?
b. Which campaign had the largest positive effect on vaccination rates in comparison to the control group?
c. Which campaign(s) had a negative effect on vaccination rates in comparison to the control group?
d. Which campaign(s) had no effect on vaccination rates in comparison to the control group?

16. Table 19P-4 displays the results of a study on how to improve vaccination rates in a developing nation. The baseline numbers represent the rates of vaccination at the beginning of the study, and the endline numbers represent the rates of vaccination at the study's conclusion. Rank the campaigns in order from most effective to least effective. Then refer to Table 19P-5, which shows the cost per person of each campaign. Combining information from the two tables, rank the campaigns that resulted in an increase in vaccinations from high to low in terms of cost-effectiveness (based on treatment effect alone). **[LO 19.9]**

TABLE 19P-4

Campaign	Vaccination rates (%)			
	Baseline, control	Baseline, treatment	Endline, control	Endline, treatment
Lectures	4	6	6	9
Free provision	4	7	6	8
Subsidy	4	5	6	9
Newspaper announcements	4	3	6	2

TABLE 19P-5

Campaign	Cost per person ($)
Lectures	10
Free provision	20
Subsidy	15
Newspaper announcements	5

Endnotes

1. Data are from 2015 (accessed April 2019): http://poverty-data.worldbank.org/poverty/home/. See also:http://www.worldbank.org/en/news/press-release/2015/10/04/world-bank-forecasts-global-poverty-to-fall-below-10-for-first-time-major-hurdles-remain-in-goal-to-end-poverty-by-2030.
2. www.stlouisfed.org/on-the-economy/2018/january/income-living-standards-china
3. http://blogs.ei.columbia.edu/2011/03/24/india-is-booming-so-why-are-nearly-half-of-its-children-malnourished-part-1/.
4. Jishnu Das and Jeffrey Hammer, "Strained Mercy: The Quality of Medical Care in Delhi," World Bank Policy Research Working Paper Series No. 3228 (2004).
5. Unpublished data from Innovations for Poverty Action.
6. Douglass C. North, "Institutions," *Journal of Economic Perspectives* 5, no. 1 (Winter 1991), pp. 97–112.
7. http://internationalpropertyrightsindex.org/introduction.
8. For evidence on the link between democracy and economic growth, see http://as.nyu.edu/docs/IO/2591/Development.pdf.
9. https://knoema.com/sijweyg/gdp-per-capita-ranking-2015-data-and-charts.
10. Michael Clemens, Claudio E. Montenegro, and Lant Pritchett, "The Place Premium: Wage Differences for Identical Workers across the U.S. Border," Center for Global Development Working Paper no. 148 (July 2008).
11. http://travel.state.gov/content/dam/visas/Diversity-Visa/DVStatistics/DV%20AES%20statistics%20by%20FSC%202016-2018.pdf.
12. www.forbes.com/sites/tobyshapshak/2018/05/21/global-remittances-reach-613bn-says-world-bank/#6e2743d45ddc.
13. Michael Clemens, "Economics and Emigration: Trillion Dollar Bills on the Sidewalk," Center for Global Development Working Paper no. 264 (August 2011); Lant Pritchett, *Let Their People Come* (Washington, DC: Center for Global Development, 2006).
14. The data in Figure 19-3 report *net ODA*. Because the United States receives loan repayments from countries (due on loans made in previous years), the net outflow is smaller than total (gross) ODA. Subtracting any loan repayments received from gross ODA yields *net ODA*.
15. Jeffrey Sachs, *The End of Poverty* (New York: Penguin Press, 2006).
16. www.unicef.org/publications/files/Children_and_the_MDGs.pdf.
17. www.undp.org/content/undp/en/home/librarypage/mdg/the-millennium-development-goals-report-2015.html.
18. www.usaid.gov/news-information/fact-sheets/fy-2017-development-and-humanitarian-assistance-budget.
19. www1.wfp.org/overview www.wfpusa.org/explore/wfps-work/ongoing-emergencies/#
20. Abhijit Banerjee, *Making Aid Work* (Cambridge, MA: MIT Press, 2007).
21. Dambisa Moyo, *Dead Aid: Why Aid Is Not Working and How There Is a Better Way for Africa* (New York: Farrar, Straus and Giroux, 2009).
22. Craig Burnside and David Dollar, "Aid, Policies and Growth: Revisiting the Evidence," WB Policy Research Paper no. O-2834 (Washington, DC: World Bank, 2004).
23. www.fas.org/sgp/crs/row/RL32427.pdf.
24. Jonathan Morduch, "Not So Fast: The Realities of Impact Investing," *America's Quarterly*, Fall 2011, www.americasquarterly.org/not-so-fast-the-realities-of-impact-investing.
25. www.povertyactionlab.org/policy-lessons/education/improving-student-participation.

Guide to Data Sources

Throughout this text . . . we've used data from a wide variety of sources to present theories on phenomena ranging from international aid to financial crises. Without accurate and timely data, we couldn't reliably say nearly as much about these issues.

Before recent advances in information technology, gathering data was much more cumbersome—and data sources were far less prevalent. Today, we have the opposite problem. The amount of data already collected is astounding. With so much data available, finding the right sources can seem like a challenge.

To help you dive into the real world of economics, we provide this guide to some of the most useful and widely used data sources for the economy. Since the quality of your data will have a big impact on the quality of any investigation in economics, you'll want to be sure you have the best data out there—and, more importantly, the correct data. Going to the right source can help you ensure that your data are from a trusted organization and up to date. (In the United States, the government is often the most reliable source.)

This short guide will introduce you to the sources that many economists use to answer thousands of different questions. In the sections that follow, we provide an overview of each source, including the organization's purpose and the data it hosts, and then we look at an example of how those data have been used. To gain experience using these sources, you'll need to explore each source on your own and learn how to manipulate the data as they appear on the site. To that end, we ask you to answer a few questions using the data you find.

National (United States) Data

Bureau of Economic Analysis (BEA)

http://bea.gov

Interactive database can be found at www.bea.gov/itable/index.cfm

The Bureau of Economic Analysis (BEA) is an agency within the U.S. Department of Commerce. Its mission is to promote "a better understanding of the U.S. economy by providing the most timely, relevant, and accurate economic accounts data in an objective and cost effective manner."

The BEA is one of the most widely cited sources for current economic news. Partly that's because it's responsible for publishing the granddaddy of all economic indicators, GDP. GDP is part of the National Income and Product Accounts, which give a broad overview of economic activity in the United States. The BEA publishes this information quarterly and houses historical data dating back to 1929.

A sample of the indicators you can find . . .

- GDP and its components
- Personal income and outlays
- Consumer spending
- Balance of payments
- Corporate profits
- Foreign direct investment

Note: When looking for information from the BEA (and other sources), be sure to look at the databases and not just the news releases. Only the databases will provide comprehensive information about the indicator over time.

TRY IT YOURSELF

✓ APPLICATIONS

Suppose you're an economic advisor to the president and are trying to gauge how well the economy is performing now in comparison to the last few years.

1. Find the historical database for seasonally adjusted real GDP and report the seasonally adjusted real GDP for the latest quarter available.
2. Use this same database to retrieve the quarterly data for GDP for the three most recent years in the database. Which quarter had the highest rate of GDP growth? Which quarter had the lowest? Graph these data over time.

✓ PROBLEMS

1. Does consumer spending in the United States tend to stay at the same levels throughout the year, or are there certain months in which it's higher than others?
2. Which countries have the most foreign direct investment in the United States? Where does the United States have the most foreign direct investment?

Federal Reserve Economic Data (FRED), Federal Reserve Bank of St. Louis

http://fred.stlouisfed.org

The Federal Reserve Bank of St. Louis hosts FRED, a database of more than 570,000 U.S. and international economic indicators (time series) from 87 sources. It's the most inclusive, "one-stop shop" data source available for the U.S. economy.

The FRED website allows you to download, graph, track, and compare vast amounts of data covering a wide array of categories. Those include banking, business/fiscal, employment and population, exchange rates, financial data, foreign exchange intervention, GDP, interest rates, international data, monetary aggregates, prices, reserves and monetary base, U.S. regional data, and U.S. Trade and International Transaction data.

In addition, the Atlanta Federal Reserve bank publishes a real-time estimate of GDP growth at www.frbatlanta.org/cqer/research/gdpnow.aspx.

A sample of the indicators you can find . . .

- The federal funds rate
- Yield on Treasury bills
- Money supply
- GDP data

TRY IT YOURSELF

✓ APPLICATIONS

Suppose you're an economist trying to examine how the Federal Reserve responds to various GDP growth rates in the economy.

1. Find the series for the monthly effective federal funds rate. (*Tip:* Use the search bar on the FRED home page.) What is the latest value for the effective federal funds rate? What was the value for the effective federal funds rate two years ago?
2. Now find the series for GDP growth. What is the average growth rate of annual GDP in the last two years?
3. Based on your answers to questions 1 and 2 (and lessons you learned from the macroeconomic chapters), do you think there's a relationship between the federal funds rate and GDP growth? If so, how would you describe that relationship?

✓ PROBLEMS

1. What was the average personal savings rate in 1950? What is it today?
2. How much money is in circulation in the United States today, using M2?

U.S. Bureau of Labor Statistics (BLS)

www.bls.gov

The U.S. Bureau of Labor Statistics (BLS) is a government agency that is the primary source of statistics on employment and prices. Each month, it publishes an "Employment Situation Summary," which, among other statistics, gives an account of the number of unemployed people and the unemployment rate.

Labor statistics are of interest to a diverse crowd: from labor economists trying to understand the relationship between minimum wage and employment, to college graduates attempting to predict their employment prospects.

A sample of the indicators you can find . . .

- Unemployment rate
- Consumer Price Index (CPI)
- Consumer spending
- Wages
- Worker productivity, workplace injuries, illnesses, and fatalities

TRY IT YOURSELF

✓ APPLICATION

Imagine you're advising a presidential candidate running against the incumbent. The candidate wants you to tell her about the employment situation, including specific information about whether certain parts of the population face higher unemployment rates than others do.

1. Find the latest Employment Situation Summary. When was it issued?
2. What was the unemployment rate for the last month? How did it compare to the unemployment rate for the month before that? Was it higher or lower?
3. Finally, look at the site's Table A-4, "Employment status of the civilian population 25 years and over by educational attainment." For the latest month available, what is the difference in the unemployment rate between those with a bachelor's degree and those without a high school diploma?

✓ PROBLEMS

1. What is the highest rate of unemployment the United States has experienced in the past 20 years?
2. In the past 20 years, when did the Consumer Price Index have the fastest rate of annual increase?

Congressional Budget Office (CBO)

www.cbo.gov

The Congressional Budget Office (CBO) is a federal agency responsible for providing objective, nonpartisan analysis to assist Congress with budgetary decisions. Whenever you hear politicians argue over whose plan to improve the economy will cost more, it's a good bet that they'll mention a projection from the CBO. The CBO is responsible for projecting the costs of government programs at the request of Congress. The CBO also provides regular reports to Congress on fiscal policy through the *Budget and Economic Outlook* and cost estimates of the president's budget through its *Analysis of the President's Budget.*

A sample of the indicators you can find . . .

- The federal deficit
- Federal spending
- Federal revenue

TRY IT YOURSELF

✓ APPLICATIONS

Imagine your professor has announced that the subject for a class debate is "Should the United States balance the budget?" You want to find the statistics that will back up your position.

1. Find the latest version of the *Budget and Economic Outlook* and navigate to the full document. Find the table titled "CBO's Baseline Budget Projections." What is the total deficit projected for this year in billions of dollars? What percentage of GDP does that represent?
2. According to the CBO's economic outlook, will the budget deficit increase, decrease, or remain the same over the next five years?

✓ PROBLEMS

1. What is the projected shortfall in Social Security in 2050?
2. What is the projected budget deficit/surplus in 2025 as a percentage of GDP?

U.S. Census Bureau

www.census.gov

Interactive database can be found at http://factfinder2.census.gov/faces/nav/jsf/pages/index.xhtml

The U.S. Census Bureau is an agency within the Department of Commerce. The Bureau is responsible for conducting the United States Census, which attempts to collect very detailed information about all households in the United States every 10 years. These data provide a very clear picture of the changes and trends happening throughout America. In addition to the Census, the Bureau collects data every year through the American Community Survey and other sources.

A sample of the indicators you can find . . .

- Population
- Demographic information about households (age, sex, ethnicity)
- School enrollment
- Poverty
- Health insurance
- The number of businesses in a region
- The number of houses in a region

TRY IT YOURSELF

✓ APPLICATIONS

Suppose you're a governor trying to determine whether your state's tax base will increase or decrease. As part of that effort, you want to know about population trends.

1. Find the two most recent population numbers for your state. How much did the population increase or decrease in the last decade?
2. Compare your state's population growth rate to the rate of population growth in the entire United States. Is the United States gaining population faster or slower than your state?

PROBLEMS

1. What is the state with the highest percentage of people living in poverty? With the lowest?
2. How many businesses are operating in your county?

International Data

The World Bank

http://databank.worldbank.org/data/home.aspx

The World Bank is an international financial institution that seeks to reduce poverty. As part of its efforts, it collects and analyzes statistics about economies around the world. Its World Development Indicators (WDI) are a widely cited source of statistics about development; its Global Development Finance indicators provide external debt and financial flows statistics for several countries. The bank publishes these two sources in an online database called the "World DataBank." The World DataBank catalogs indicators about a wide array of topics including income, education, health, gender, and the environment.

A sample of the indicators you can find . . .

- Government expenditure per student
- Urban population growth
- Real interest rate
- Net migration

- Gini coefficients
- Official development assistance

TRY IT YOURSELF

✓ APPLICATIONS

Imagine you're an entrepreneur trying to start a global company and are looking for the best country in which to start it.

1. Navigate to the "Doing Business" database and select it. Under the "Economy" section, click to "Select all." Under the "Series" drop-down, scroll down to the data series called "Ease of doing business index." Select that series, and click on the small icon at the left to see metadata about the series, including a "Long definition" of the series. In your *own* words, what does the ease of doing business index represent?
2. Close the metadata window and open the "Time" drop-down, then choose "Select all." You should now have selected variables for Country, Series, and Time. Click on "Table" (at the top of the screen) to see your choices in table view. On the left-hand side of the page, switch to the "Layout" tab and set the options that will format your table with Country in rows, Series on the page, and Time in columns. Based on the latest available year in the table, what country has the highest ease of doing business? What country has the lowest?
3. What country made the most progress in the index from the earliest year available to the latest year available?

✓ PROBLEMS

1. What country has the lowest literacy rate? What is that rate?
2. Which region in the world has the highest GDP per capita? The lowest?

CIA World Factbook

https://www.cia.gov/library/publications/the-world-factbook

Despite the sound of its title, the CIA's World Factbook is not a book for spies, filled with hidden facts about the inner workings of foreign governments. Rather, the World Factbook provides information on the history, people, government, economy, geography, communications, transportation, military, and transnational issues for 267 world entities. (Of course, spies could use it if they wanted to know any of that information.) If you're looking for the population of Armenia, or the percentage of people working in the agricultural sector in Vietnam, the World Factbook is the place to go.

The main advantage of the World Factbook is its ease of navigation. Whereas finding statistics on other sites is an exercise in sleuthing and patience, the World Factbook divides statistics by country and navigates like any other website—no databases to query here.

A sample of the indicators you can find . . .

- Maps of the major world regions
- Trade statistics
- Miles of paved roads

TRY IT YOURSELF

✓ APPLICATIONS

Suppose your boss is looking at a few countries to invest in and wants you to put together a general country brief for each. Find and state the information detailed below for four countries: Bulgaria, Moldova, Romania, and Poland.

1. People and society
   a. Age structure
   b. Life expectancy at birth
2. Economy
   a. Labor force—by occupation
   b. GDP (purchasing power parity)
   c. GDP—per capita
   d. GDP—real growth rate
   e. GDP—composition, by sector of origin
   f. Exports ($ value)
   g. Exports—partners
   h. Imports ($ value)
   i. Imports—partners

✓ PROBLEMS

1. What is the size, in square miles, of Eritrea? Of Ethiopia?
2. How many miles of paved roads are in Poland?

The United Nations Statistics Division

http://data.un.org

Human Development Index can be found at http://hdr.undp.org/en/data/trends

UNdata is an initiative by the United Nations Statistics Division (UNSD) that brings together several data sources hosted by the United Nations. The United Nations collects statistics from its member states on a wide variety of topics. These include crime, education, energy, environment, population, and health, among others. Among its most popular indicators is the Human Development Index, a measure of general well-being calculated across countries. The Human Development Report Office within the United Nations Development Program hosts a site devoted specifically to this indicator. In addition to providing data on HDI, the site allows users to graph the data in simple and compelling ways, distilling complex data into concise graphs.

A sample of the indicators you can find . . .

- Quantity traded of commodity goods
- Gender inequality
- CO_2 emissions
- Foreign direct investment
- Prevalence of HIV

TRY IT YOURSELF

✓ APPLICATIONS

Suppose you're the head of a foundation with the mission to support governments and organizations trying to improve primary-school enrollment around the world. You want to know where to start your efforts.

1. Go to data.un.org, navigate to "The State of the World's Children" database, and view the data for "Net attendance ratio in primary education (NAR)." Over what years are the observations given? What are the subgroups for the observations?
2. What country has the lowest attendance rate for males? What is it?
3. What country has the highest attendance rate for females? What is it?

PROBLEMS

1. What is the most populous country?
2. What country receives the most development assistance?

Other Directories of Data

Google's Public Data

www.google.com/publicdata/directory

Google's Public Data site publishes several publicly available datasets in an easy-to-use way. The site continues to add sources; current sources include the U.S. Bureau of Economic Analysis, World Bank, World Economic Forum, International Monetary Fund, and the U.S. Bureau of Labor Statistics, among others.

The U.S. Government

www.data.gov

The U.S. government has combined several government data sources into one site. This can be a good place to start if you know what category of data you need but aren't sure where to look for it.

Williams College Economics Department

http://econ.williams.edu/students/online-resources

The Economics Department at Williams College has provided links to many different data sources on one web page to help students like you conduct research in several areas.

glossary

A

absolute advantage the ability to produce more of a good or service than others can with a given amount of resources

absolute poverty line a measure that defines poverty as income below a certain amount, fixed at a given point in time

accounting profit total revenue minus explicit costs

administrative burden the logistical costs associated with implementing a tax

adverse selection a state that occurs when buyers and sellers have different information about the quality of a good or the riskiness of a situation, and this asymmetric information results in failure to complete transactions that would have been possible if both sides had the same information

agent a person who carries out a task on someone else's behalf

aggregate demand curve a curve that shows the relationship between the overall price level in the economy and total demand

aggregate expenditure (Y) the level of aggregate expenditure that consists of consumption, government spending, net exports, and actual investment by firms

aggregate price level a measure of the average price level for GDP; in practice, the CPI or GDP price deflator

aggregate supply curve a curve that shows the relationship between the overall price level in the economy and total production by firms

altruism a motive for action in which a person's utility increases simply because someone else's utility increases

anchoring estimating unknown quantities by starting from a known "anchor" point

arbitrage the process of taking advantage of market inefficiencies to earn profits

Arrow's impossibility theorem a theorem showing that no voting system can aggregate the preferences of voters over three or more options while satisfying the criteria of an ideal voting system

artificially scarce good a good that is excludable but not rival

autarky an economy that is self-contained and does not engage in trade with outsiders

automatic stabilizers taxes and government spending that affect fiscal policy without specific action from policy-makers

autonomous expenditure spending that is not directly influenced by income; it is instead independent of the current level of aggregate income in the economy

average fixed cost (AFC) fixed cost divided by the quantity of output

average revenue revenue generated per product, calculated as total revenue divided by the quantity sold

average total cost (ATC) total cost divided by the quantity of output

average variable cost (AVC) variable cost divided by the quantity of output

B

backward induction the process of analyzing a problem in reverse, starting with the last choice, then the second-to-last choice, and so on, to determine the optimal strategy

balance of trade the value of exports minus the value of imports

balance-of-payments identity an equation that shows that the value of net exports equals net capital outflow

barter directly offering a good or service in exchange for some good or service you want

behaving strategically acting to achieve a goal by anticipating the interplay between your own and others' decisions

behavioral economics a field of economics that draws on insights from psychology to expand models of individual decision making

bond a form of debt that represents a promise by the bond issuer to repay the face value of the loan, at a specified maturity date, and to pay periodic interest at a specific percentage rate

bubble trade in an asset whose price has risen unsustainably far above historically justified levels

budget constraint a line that is composed of all of the possible combinations of goods and services that a consumer can buy with her or his income

budget deficit an amount of money a government spends beyond the revenue it brings in

budget surplus an amount of revenue a government brings in beyond what it spends

bundle a unique combination of goods and services that a person could choose to consume

business cycle fluctuations of output around the level of potential output in the economy

C

capability something a person is able to be or do, such as to engage fully in life, including having economic and political freedoms

capital manufactured goods that are used to produce new goods

capital gains tax a tax on income earned by buying investments and selling them at a higher price

cartel a number of firms that collude to make collective production decisions about quantities or prices

causation a relationship between two events in which one brings about the other

GL-1

central bank the institution ultimately responsible for managing the nation's money supply and coordinating the banking system to ensure a sound economy

choice architecture the organization of the context and process in which people make decisions

circular flow model a simplified representation of how the economy's transactions work together

closed economy an economy that does not interact with other countries' economies

clusters networks of interdependent firms, universities, and businesses that focus on the production of a specific type of good

Coase theorem the idea that even in the presence of an externality, individuals can reach an efficient equilibrium through private trades, assuming zero transaction costs

collective-action problem a situation in which a group of people stands to gain from an action that it is not rational for any of the members to undertake individually

collusion the act of working together to make decisions about price and quantity

commitment device a mechanism that allows people to voluntarily restrict their choices in order to make it easier to stick to plans

commitment strategy an agreement to submit to a penalty in the future for defecting from a given strategy

commodity-backed money any form of money that can be legally exchanged into a fixed amount of an underlying commodity

common resource a good that is not excludable but is rival

comparative advantage the ability to produce a good or service at a lower opportunity cost than others

competitive market a market in which fully informed, price-taking buyers and sellers easily trade a standardized good or service

complements goods that are consumed together, so that purchasing one will make consumers more likely to purchase the other

complete information state of being fully informed about the choices that relevant economic actors face

compounding the process of accumulation that results from the additional interest paid on previously earned interest

conditional cash transfer a program in which financial support is given only to people who engage in certain actions

Condorcet paradox a situation in which the preferences of each individual member of a group are transitive, but the collective preferences of the group are not

constant returns to scale returns that occur when average total cost does not depend on the quantity of output

Consumer Price Index (CPI) a measure that tracks changes in the cost of a basket of goods and services purchased by a typical U.S. household

consumer surplus the net benefit that a consumer receives from purchasing a good or service, measured by the difference between willingness to pay and the actual price

consumption (C) spending on goods and services by private individuals and households

consumption externality an externality that occurs when a good or service is being consumed

contractionary fiscal policy decisions about government spending and taxation intended to decrease aggregate demand

contractionary monetary policy actions that reduce the money supply in order to decrease aggregate demand

convergence theory the theory that countries that start out poor will initially grow faster than rich ones but will eventually converge to the same growth rate

core inflation measure of inflation that measures price changes minus food and energy costs, which are traditionally volatile

correlation a consistently observed relationship between two variables

credit constraint inability to get a loan even though a person expects to be able to repay the loan plus interest

cross-price elasticity of demand a measure of how the demand for one good changes when the price of a different good changes

crowding out the reduction in private borrowing caused by an increase in government borrowing

cyclical unemployment unemployment caused by short-term economic fluctuations

D

deadweight loss a loss of total surplus that occurs because the quantity of a good that is bought and sold is below the market equilibrium quantity

debt service the amount that consumers have to spend to pay their debts, often expressed as a percentage of disposable income

default the failure of a borrower to pay back a loan according to the agreed-upon terms

default rule a rule defining what will automatically occur if a chooser fails to make an active decision otherwise

deflation an overall fall in prices in the economy

demand curve a graph that shows the quantities of a particular good or service that consumers will demand at various prices

demand deposits funds held in bank accounts that can be withdrawn ("demanded") by depositors at any time without advance notice

demand schedule a table that shows the quantities of a particular good or service that consumers are willing and able to purchase (demand) at various prices

depression a particularly severe or extended recession

derivative an asset whose value is based on the value of another asset

diminishing marginal product a principle stating that the marginal product of an input decreases as the quantity of the input increases

diminishing marginal utility the principle that the additional utility gained from consuming successive units of a good or service tends to be smaller than the utility gained from the previous unit

discount rate the interest rate charged by the Fed for loans of reserves through the discount window

discount window the lending facility run by the Fed that allows any bank to borrow reserves

discouraged workers people who have looked for work in the past year but have given up looking because of the condition of the labor market

discretionary spending public expenditures that have to be approved each year

discrimination making choices by using generalizations based on people's observable characteristics like race, gender, and age

diseconomies of scale returns that occur when an increase in the quantity of output increases average total cost

disinflation a period in which inflation rates are falling, but still positive

diversification the process by which risks are shared across many different assets or people, reducing the impact of any particular risk on any one individual

dividend a payment made periodically, typically annually or quarterly, to all shareholders of a company

domestic savings savings for capital investment that come from within a country; equal to domestic income minus consumption spending

dominant strategy a strategy that is the best one for a player to follow no matter what strategy other players choose

dual mandate the twin responsibilities of the Federal Reserve, to use monetary policy to ensure price stability and to maintain full employment

E

economic profit total revenue minus all opportunity costs, explicit and implicit

economic rent the gains that workers and owners of capital receive from supplying their labor or machinery in factor markets

economics the study of how people, individually and collectively, manage resources

economies of scale returns that occur when an increase in the quantity of output decreases average total cost

efficiency use of resources to ensure that people get what they most want and need given the available resources

efficiency wage a wage that is deliberately set above the market rate to increase worker productivity

efficient market an arrangement such that no exchange can make anyone better off without someone becoming worse off

efficient points combinations of production possibilities that squeeze the most output possible from all available resources

efficient scale the quantity of output at which average total cost is minimized

efficient-market hypothesis (EMH) the idea that market prices always incorporate all available information and therefore represent true value as correctly as is possible

elastic demand that has an absolute value of elasticity greater than 1

elasticity a measure of how much consumers and producers will respond to a change in market conditions

embargo a restriction or prohibition of trade in order to put political pressure on a country

endowment effect the tendency of people to place more value on something simply because they own it

equilibrium the situation in a market when the quantity supplied equals the quantity demanded; graphically, this convergence happens where the demand curve intersects the supply curve

equilibrium aggregate expenditure the level of aggregate expenditure where unplanned investment is equal to zero, or, equivalently, where planned aggregate expenditure is equal to actual aggregate expenditure

equilibrium price the price at which the quantity supplied equals the quantity demanded

equilibrium quantity the quantity that is supplied and demanded at the equilibrium price

excess reserves any additional amount, beyond the required reserves, that a bank chooses to keep in reserve

exchange rate the value of one currency expressed in terms of another currency

exchange-rate appreciation an increase in the value of a currency relative to the value of another currency

exchange-rate depreciation a decrease in the value of a currency relative to other currencies

excise tax a sales tax on a specific good or service

excludable a characteristic of a good or service that allows owners to prevent its use by people who have not paid for it

expansionary fiscal policy decisions about government spending and taxation intended to increase aggregate demand

expansionary monetary policy actions that increase the money supply in order to increase aggregate demand

expected value the average of each possible outcome of a future event, weighted by its probability of occurring

expenditure multiplier the factor by which output increases in response to an initial change in aggregate expenditure

explicit costs costs that require a firm to spend money

exports goods and services that are produced domestically and consumed in other countries

external benefits benefits that accrue without compensation to someone other than the person who caused it

external costs costs imposed without compensation on someone other than the person who caused them

externality a cost or benefit imposed without compensation on someone other than the person who caused it

F

factors of production the ingredients that go into making a good or service

federal funds rate the interest rate at which banks choose to lend reserves held at the Fed to one another

Federal Reserve ("the Fed") the system consisting of a seven-member Board of Governors and 12 regional banks that act as the central bank of the United States

fiat money money created by rule, without any commodity to back it

financial intermediaries institutions that channel funds from people who have them to people who want them

financial market a market in which people trade future claims on funds or goods

financial system the group of institutions that bring together savers, borrowers, investors, and insurers in a set of interconnected markets where people trade financial products

financing gap the difference between the savings rate within an economy and the amount of investment needed to achieve sustainable growth

first-mover advantage benefit enjoyed by the player who chooses first and, as a result, gets a higher payoff than those who follow

fiscal policy government decisions about the level of taxation and public spending

fixed costs costs that do not depend on the quantity of output produced

fixed exchange rate an exchange rate that is set by the government, instead of determined by the market

floating exchange rate an exchange rate whose value is determined by the market

foreign direct investment (FDI) investment that occurs when a firm runs part of its operation abroad or owns all or part of another company abroad

foreign portfolio investment investment in domestic financial assets, funded by foreign sources

fractional-reserve banking a banking system in which banks keep on reserve less than 100 percent of their deposits

free-rider problem a problem that occurs when the nonexcludability of a public good leads to undersupply

frictional unemployment unemployment caused by workers who are changing location, job, or career

fungible easily exchangeable or substitutable

G

gains from trade the improvement in outcomes that occurs when producers specialize and exchange goods and services

game a situation involving at least two people that requires those involved to think strategically

game theory the study of how people behave strategically under different circumstances

GDP deflator a measure of the overall change in prices in an economy, using the ratio between real and nominal GDP

GDP per capita a country's GDP divided by its population

Gini coefficient a single-number measure of income inequality; ranges from 0 to 1, with higher numbers meaning greater inequality

government purchases (G) spending on goods and services by all levels of government

Green GDP an alternative measure of GDP that subtracts the environmental costs of production from the positive outputs normally counted in GDP

gross domestic product (GDP) the sum of the market values of all final goods and services produced within a country in a given period of time

gross national product (GNP) the sum of the market values of all final goods and services produced by citizens of a country within a given period of time

H

headline inflation measure of inflation that measures price changes for all of the goods in the market basket of the average urban consumer

heuristic a mental shortcut for making decisions (sometimes in good ways, but sometimes not)

human capital the set of skills, knowledge, experience, and talent that determine the productivity of workers

hyperinflation extremely long-lasting and painful increases in the price level

I

idiosyncratic risk any risk that is unique to a particular company or asset

impact investing investing money in firms to generate both financial and social returns

implicit costs costs that represent forgone opportunities

import quota a limit on the amount of a particular good that can be imported

imports goods and services that are produced in other countries and consumed domestically

in-kind transfer a program that provides specific goods or services, rather than cash, directly to needy recipients

incentive something that causes people to behave in a certain way by changing the trade-offs they face

incidence a description of who bears the burden of a tax

income effect the change in consumption that results from a change in effective wealth due to higher or lower prices

income elasticity of demand a measure of how much the demand for a good changes in response to a change in consumers' incomes

income mobility the ability to improve one's economic circumstances over time

income tax a tax charged on the earnings of individuals and corporations

indexing the practice of automatically increasing payments in proportion to the cost of living

indifference curve a curve showing all the different consumption bundles that provide a consumer with equal levels of utility

industrial policy effort by a government to favor some industries over others

inelastic demand that has an absolute value of elasticity less than 1

inferior goods goods for which demand decreases as income increases

inflation an overall rise in prices in the economy

inflation rate the size of the change in the overall price level; the percent change in a price index such as the CPI from year to year

inflationary output gap an output gap that occurs when equilibrium aggregate expenditure is above the level needed for full employment

information asymmetry a condition in which one participant in a transaction knows more than another participant

institutions the humanly devised constraints that shape human interactions

interest rate the "price of money," typically expressed as a percentage per dollar per unit of time; for savers, it is the price received for letting a bank use money for a specified period of time; for borrowers, it is the price of using money for a specified period of time

inventory the stock of goods that a company produces now but does not sell immediately

investment (I) spending on productive inputs, such as factories, machinery, and inventories

investment trade-off a reduction in current consumption to pay for investment in capital intended to increase future production

K

Keynesian equilibrium a situation in which planned aggregate expenditure is equal to actual aggregate expenditure

L

labor demand curve a graph showing the relationship between the total quantity of labor demanded by all the firms in the economy and the wage rate

labor force people who are in the working-age population and are either employed or unemployed; people who are currently working or who are actively trying to find a job

labor supply curve a graph showing the relationship between the total labor supplied in the economy and the wage rate

labor unions groups of employees who join together to bargain with their employer(s) over salaries and work conditions

labor-force participation rate the number of people in the labor force divided by the working-age population

law of demand a fundamental characteristic of demand that states that, all else equal, quantity demanded rises as price falls

law of supply a fundamental characteristic of supply that states that, all else equal, quantity supplied rises as price rises

leverage the practice of using borrowed money to pay for investments

leverage ratio the ratio of a company's assets to its equity, where equity is defined as the firm's assets minus its liabilities

liquidity a measure of how easily a particular asset can be converted quickly to cash without much loss of value

liquidity-preference model idea that the quantity of money people want to hold is a function of the interest rate

loan an agreement in which a lender gives money to a borrower in exchange for a promise to repay the amount loaned plus an agreed-upon amount of interest

long-run aggregate supply (LRAS) curve a curve that shows the relationship between the overall price level in the economy and total production by firms in the long run

Lorenz curve a graphic representation of income distribution that maps percentage of the population against cumulative percentage of income earned by those people

loss aversion the tendency for people to put more effort into avoiding losses than achieving gains

lump-sum tax (head tax) a tax that charges the same amount to each taxpayer, regardless of their economic behavior or circumstances

M

M1 definition of money that includes cash plus checking account balances

M2 definition of money that includes everything in M1 plus savings accounts and other financial instruments where money is locked away for a specified amount of time; less liquid than M1

macroeconomics the study of the economy as a whole, and how policymakers manage the growth and behavior of the overall economy

mandatory spending public expenditure that "entitles" people to benefits by virtue of age, income, or some other factor

marginal cost (MC) the additional cost incurred by a firm when it produces one additional unit of output

marginal decision making comparison of additional benefits of a choice against the additional costs it would bring, without considering related benefits and costs of past choices

marginal product the increase in output that is generated by an additional unit of input

marginal propensity to consume (MPC) the amount that consumption increases when after-tax income increases by $1

marginal rate of substitution (MRS) the rate at which a consumer is willing to trade or substitute between two goods

marginal revenue the revenue generated by selling an additional unit of a good

marginal tax rate the tax rate charged on the last dollar a taxpayer earns

marginal utility the change in total utility that comes from consuming one additional unit of a good or service

market buyers and sellers who trade a particular good or service

market basket a list of specific goods and services in fixed quantities

market economy an economy in which private individuals, rather than a centralized planning authority, make the decisions

market failures situations in which the assumption of efficient, competitive markets fails to hold

market for loanable funds a market in which savers supply funds to those who want to borrow

market power the ability to noticeably affect market prices

market (systemic) risk any risk that is broadly shared by the entire market or economy; also called systemic risk

means-tested the characteristic of a program that defines eligibility for benefits based on recipients' income

median-voter theorem a model stating that under certain conditions, politicians maximize their votes by taking the policy position preferred by the median voter

medium of exchange the ability to use money to purchase goods and services

menu costs the costs (measured in money, time, and opportunity) of changing prices to keep pace with inflation

microeconomics the study of how individuals and firms manage resources

mid-point method method that measures percentage change in quantity demanded (or quantity supplied) relative to a point midway between two points on a curve; used to estimate elasticity

model a simplified representation of the important parts of a complicated situation

monetary base the sum of currency in circulation and reserves held by banks at the Federal Reserve

monetary policy actions by the central bank to manage the money supply, in pursuit of certain macroeconomic goals

money the set of all assets that are regularly used to directly purchase goods and services

money multiplier the ratio of money created by the lending activities of the banking system to the money created by the government's central bank

money supply the amount of money available in the economy

monopolistic competition a market with many firms that sell goods and services that are similar, but slightly different

monopoly a firm that is the only producer of a good or service with no close substitutes

monopsony a market in which there is only one buyer but many sellers

moral hazard the tendency for people to behave in a riskier way or to renege on contracts when they do not face the full consequences of their actions

multiplier effect the increase in consumer spending that occurs when spending by one person causes others to spend more too, increasing the impact on the economy of the initial spending

mutual fund a portfolio of stocks, bonds, and other assets managed by a professional who makes decisions on behalf of clients

N

Nash equilibrium an equilibrium reached when all players choose the best strategy they can, given the choices of all other players. It is a situation wherein, given the consequences, the player has no regrets about his or her decision

national savings the sum of the private savings of individuals and corporations plus the public savings of the government

natural monopoly a market in which a single firm can produce, at a lower cost than multiple firms, the entire quantity of output demanded

natural rate of unemployment the normal level of unemployment that persists in an economy in the long run

net capital flow the net flow of funds invested outside of a country; specifically, the difference between capital inflows (investment financed by savings from another country) and capital outflows (domestic savings invested abroad)

net exports (NX) exports minus imports; the value of goods and services produced domestically and consumed abroad minus the value of goods and services produced abroad and consumed domestically

net present value (NPV) a measure of the current value of a stream of cash flows expected in the future

network externality the effect that an additional user of a good or participant in an activity has on the value of that good or activity for others

neutrality of money the idea that, in the long run, changes in the money supply affect nominal variables, such as prices and wages, but do not affect real outcomes in the economy

nominal exchange rate the stated rate at which one country's currency can be traded for another country's currency

nominal GDP GDP calculation in which goods and services are valued at current prices

nominal interest rate the reported interest rate, not adjusted for the effects of inflation

non-accelerating inflation rate of unemployment (NAIRU) the lowest possible unemployment rate that will not cause the inflation rate to increase

normal goods goods for which demand increases as income increases

normative statement a claim about how the world should be

nudge an implementation of choice architecture that alters people's behavior in a deliberate and predictable way without changing economic incentives much

O

oligopoly a market with only a few firms, which sell a similar good or service

open economy an economy that interacts with other countries' economies

open-market operations sales or purchases of government bonds by the Fed, to or from banks, on the open market

opportunity cost the value to you of what you have to give up in order to get something; the value you could have gained by choosing the next-best alternative

output gap the difference between actual and potential output in an economy

P

payroll tax a tax on the wages paid to an employee

pension fund a professionally managed portfolio of assets intended to provide income to retirees

perfectly elastic demand demand for which any increase in price will cause quantity demanded to drop to zero; represented by a perfectly horizontal line

perfectly inelastic demand demand for which quantity demanded remains the same regardless of price; represented by a perfectly vertical line

Phillips curve a model that shows the connection between inflation and unemployment in the short run

physical capital the stock of equipment and structures that allow for production of goods and services

Pigovian tax a tax meant to counterbalance a negative externality

planned aggregate expenditure (PAE) the amount of spending and production that businesses, households, and others are planning to make, consisting of planned consumption, investment, government spending, and net exports

planned aggregate expenditure curve planned aggregate expenditure as a function of actual aggregate expenditure, holding all other factors constant

positive statement a factual claim about how the world actually works

potential output the total amount of output a country could produce if all of its resources were fully engaged

poverty rate the percentage of the population that falls below the absolute poverty line

poverty trap a self-reinforcing mechanism that causes the poor to stay poor

PPP-adjustment recalculating economic statistics to account for differences in price levels across countries

present value how much a certain amount of money that will be obtained in the future is worth today

price ceiling a maximum legal price at which a good can be sold

price control a regulation that sets a maximum or minimum legal price for a particular good

price discrimination the practice of charging customers different prices for the same good

price elasticity of demand the size of the change in the quantity demanded of a good or service when its price changes

price elasticity of supply the size of the change in the quantity supplied of a good or service when its price changes

price floor a minimum legal price at which a good can be sold

price index a measure showing how much the cost of a market basket has risen or fallen relative to the cost in a base time period or location

price taker a buyer or seller who cannot affect the market price. In a perfectly competitive market, firms are price takers as a consequence of many sellers selling standardized goods.

principal a person who entrusts someone with a task

prisoners' dilemma a game of strategy in which two people make rational choices that lead to a less-than-ideal result for both

private benefits benefits that accrue directly to the decision maker

private costs costs that fall directly on an economic decision maker

private goods goods that are both excludable and rival

private savings the savings of individuals or corporations within a country

producer surplus the net benefit that a producer receives from the sale of a good or service, measured by the difference between the producer's willingness to sell and the actual price

product differentiation the creation of products that are similar to competitors' products but more attractive in some ways

production externality an externality that occurs when a good or service is being produced

production function the relationship between quantity of inputs and the resulting quantity of outputs

production possibilities frontier (PPF) a line or curve that shows all the possible combinations of two outputs that can be produced using all available resources

productivity output produced per worker

profit the difference between total revenue and total cost

progressive tax a tax that charges low-income people a smaller percentage of their income than high-income people

property tax a tax on the estimated value of a home or other property

proportional/flat tax a tax that takes the same percentage of income from all taxpayers

protectionism a preference for policies that limit trade

public debt the total amount of money that a government owes at a point in time; the cumulative sum of all deficits and surpluses

public good a good that is neither excludable nor rival

public savings the difference between government tax revenue and government spending

purchase price the price paid to gain permanent ownership of a factor of production

purchasing power parity (PPP) the theory that purchasing power in different countries should be the same when stated in a common currency

purchasing power parity (PPP) index index that describes the overall difference in prices of goods between countries

Q

quantitative easing policies that are designed to directly increase the money supply by a certain amount

quantity demanded the amount of a particular good that buyers will purchase at a given price during a specified period

quantity equation the equation $M \times V = P \times Y$, which relates the money supply and velocity of money to the price value of real output

quantity supplied the amount of a particular good or service that producers will offer for sale at a given price during a specified period

quantity theory of money theory that the value of money (and thus the aggregate price level) is determined by the overall quantity of money in existence (the money supply); it states that changes in the price level (inflation or deflation) are primarily the result of changes in the quantity of money

quota rents profits earned by foreign firms or governments under a quota

R

randomized controlled trial (RCT) a method that randomly assigns subjects into control and treatment groups in order to assess the causal link from an intervention to specific outcomes

rational behavior making choices to achieve goals in the most effective way possible

rational ignorance choosing to remain ignorant when the opportunity costs of gathering information outweigh the benefits

real exchange rate the value of goods in one country expressed in terms of the same goods in another country

real GDP GDP calculation in which goods and services are valued at constant prices

real interest rate the interest rate adjusted for the effects of inflation

real-wage or classical unemployment unemployment that results from wages being higher than the market-clearing level

recession a period of significant economic decline

recessionary output gap an output gap that occurs when equilibrium aggregate expenditure is below the level needed for full employment

reciprocity responding to another's action with a similar action

regressive tax a tax that charges low-income people a larger percentage of their income than it charges high-income people

relative poverty line a measure that defines poverty in terms of the income of the rest of the population

rent-seeking the act of pursuing privileges that increase the surplus of a person or group without increasing total surplus

rental price the price paid to use a factor of production for a certain period or task

repeated game a game that is played more than once

required reserves the minimum fraction of deposits that banks are legally required (by the Federal Reserve) to keep on hand

reserve ratio the fraction of deposits a bank must hold as reserves; calculated as the amount of cash kept as reserves divided by the total amount of demand deposits

reserve requirement the regulation that sets the minimum fraction of deposits banks must hold in reserve

reserves the money that a bank keeps on hand, either in cash or in deposits at the Federal Reserve

revealed preference the idea that people's preferences can be determined by observing their choices and behavior

rise vertical distance; calculated as the change in y

risk exists when the costs or benefits of an event or choice are uncertain

risk pooling organizing people into a group to collectively absorb the risk faced by each individual

risk-averse having a low willingness to take on situations with risk; when faced with two options with equal expected value, the one with lower risk is preferred

risk-free rate the interest rate at which one would lend if there were no risk of default; usually approximated by interest rates on U.S. government debt

risk-seeking having a high willingness to take on situations with risk; when faced with two options with equal expected value, the one with higher risk is preferred

rival in consumption (rival) the characteristic of a good for which one person's consumption prevents or decreases others' ability to consume it

run horizontal distance; calculated as the change in x

S

sales tax a tax that is charged on the value of a good or service being purchased

savings the portion of income that is not immediately spent on consumption of goods and services

scarcity the condition of wanting more than we can get with available resources

screening taking action to reveal private information about someone else

securitization the practice of packaging individual debts into a single uniform asset

shoe-leather costs the costs (measured in time, money, and effort) of managing cash in the face of inflation

short-run aggregate supply (SRAS) curve a curve that shows the relationship between the overall price level in the economy and total production by firms in the short run

shortage (excess demand) a situation in which the quantity of a good that is demanded is higher than the quantity supplied

signaling taking action to reveal one's own private information

slope the ratio of vertical distance (change in y) to horizontal distance (change in x)

social benefit the entire benefits of a decision, including both private benefits and external benefits

social cost the entire cost of a decision, including both private costs and any external costs

social insurance government programs under which people pay into a common pool and are eligible to draw on benefits under certain circumstances

specialization spending all of your time producing a particular good

standard deviation a measurement of the amount of variation in a set of numbers

standardized good a good for which any two units have the same features and are interchangeable

statistical discrimination distinguishing between choices by generalizing based on observable characteristics in order to fill in missing information

status-quo bias the tendency to stick with the current situation over other options, even when it is cheap to switch

stock a financial asset that represents partial ownership of a company

store of value a certain amount of purchasing power that money retains over time

structural unemployment unemployment that results from a mismatch between the skills workers can offer and the skills in demand

subsidy a requirement that the government pay an extra amount to producers or consumers of a good

substitutes goods that serve a similar-enough purpose that a consumer might purchase one in place of the other

substitution effect the change in consumption that results from a change in the relative price of goods

sunk cost a cost that has already been incurred and cannot be recovered or refunded

supply curve a graph that shows the quantities of a particular good or service that producers will supply at various prices

supply schedule a table that shows the quantities of a particular good or service that producers will supply at various prices

supply shocks significant events that directly affect production and the aggregate supply curve in the short run

surplus (excess supply) a situation in which the quantity of a good that is supplied is higher than the quantity demanded

surplus a way of measuring who benefits from transactions and by how much

T

tariff a tax on imported goods

tax incidence the relative tax burden borne by buyers and sellers

tax wedge the difference between the price paid by buyers and the price received by sellers in the presence of a tax

time inconsistency a situation in which we change our minds about what we want simply because of the timing of the decision

tit-for-tat a strategy in which a player in a repeated game takes the same action that his or her opponent did in the preceding round

"too big to fail" so large in terms of assets or customers or so historically important that banking regulators allow the bank to keep operating despite insolvency

total cost the amount that a firm pays for all of the inputs that go into producing goods and services

total revenue the amount that a firm receives from the sale of goods and services; calculated as the quantity sold multiplied by the price paid for each unit

total surplus a measure of the combined benefits that everyone receives from participating in an exchange of goods or services

tradable allowance a production or consumption quota that can be bought and sold

trade deficit a negative balance of trade; a greater amount of imports than exports

trade liberalization policies and actions that reduce trade restrictions

trade surplus a positive balance of trade; a greater amount of exports than imports

tragedy of the commons the depletion of a common resource due to individually rational but collectively inefficient overconsumption

transaction costs the costs incurred by buyer and seller in agreeing to and executing a sale of goods or services

Treasury securities debt-financing arrangements made by the U.S. government

U

underemployed workers who are either working less than they would like to or are working in jobs below their skill level

unemployment situation in which someone wants to work but cannot find a job in the current market

unemployment insurance money paid by the government to people who are unemployed

unemployment rate the number of unemployed people divided by the number of people in the labor force

unit of account a standard unit of comparison

unit-elastic demand that has an absolute value of elasticity exactly equal to 1

United Nations Development Program (UNDP) a global United Nations network that provides knowledge and resources to developing countries

utility a measure of the amount of satisfaction a person derives from something

utility function a formula for calculating the total utility that a particular person derives from consuming a combination of goods and services

V

value of the marginal product the increase in revenue generated by the last unit of an input; calculated as the output generated by an input (marginal product) times the unit price of the output

variable costs costs that depend on the quantity of output produced

velocity of money the number of times the entire money supply turns over in a given period

W

willingness to pay (reservation price) the maximum price that a buyer would be willing to pay for a good or service

willingness to sell the minimum price that a seller is willing to accept in exchange for a good or service

World Bank a multinational organization dedicated to providing financial and technical assistance to developing countries

World Trade Organization (WTO) an international organization designed to monitor and enforce trade agreements, while also promoting free trade

Z

zero lower bound the natural lower limit on interest rates

zero-sum game a situation in which whenever one person gains, another loses an equal amount, such that the net value of any transaction is zero

index

Note: **Boldface** entries indicate key terms and the page numbers where they are defined.

A

Abdul Latif Jameel Poverty Action Lab (J-PAL), 543
Absolute advantage, 33–35
Absolute change in quantity, 83
Absolute value, defined, 83
Account-form balance sheets, 403
Accounting equation, 403
Acumen Fund, 541
AD/AS. *See* Aggregate demand/aggregate supply model
Adjustment time, 84–85, 94
Adverse selection, 361–362
Africa. *See also specific regions and countries*
    agriculture in, 260
    economic growth in, 260, 261
    HIV/AIDS in, 527
African Americans, unemployment rate among, 229
African Growth and Opportunity Act of 2000 (AGOA), 532
Age
    life expectancy and income, 528
    unemployment rates by, 229
    working-age population, 227, 228, 230
Aggregate consumption, 277–279, 304, 306
Aggregate demand, 301–308. *See also* Aggregate demand/aggregate supply model
    in classical theory of inflation, 431
    consumer spending and, 308
    contractionary monetary policy and, 413
    decreases in, 318–319
    defined, 301
    deflation and, 439–441
    expansionary monetary policy and, 413
    fiscal policy and, 334–336
    government expenditures and, 305–307
    increases in, 316–318
    multiplier effect and, 306–307
    shifts in, 316–319
Aggregate demand/aggregate supply (AD/AS) model, 299–327
    aggregate demand in, 301–308, 316–319
    aggregate supply in, 309–316, 319–321
    in classical theory of inflation, 431
    demand and supply shocks in, 316-7201
    economic fluctuations in, 316–324
    effect of policy in financial crisis of 2008, 475
    Kobe earthquake and, 324
    overview, 300
    Phillips curve and, 447, 448
    public policy and, 321–322, 324–327
    self-correcting economy in, 336

Aggregate demand curve, 301–306
    consumer spending and, 308
    defined, **301**
    downward-sloping, 301–303
    financial crisis and, 471, 472, 475
    government expenditures and, 325, 335
    government policies and, 305, 306
    housing price collapse and, 335
    price changes and, 302–303
    price level and, 301–303
    shifts in, 303–306, 317, 318
    tax policy and, 335
Aggregate expenditure (Y), 275–294
    actual vs. planned, 283–286
    autonomous, 286
    components of, 276–283, 301–302
    defined, **276**
    equilibrium, 287–289, 291, 298A–298C
    Keynesian equilibrium and, 286–289
    multiplier, 298B–298C
    multiplier effect and, 290–293
    output gaps and, 289–290
    planned, 284–286, 303, 304
    terminology considerations, 285
Aggregate price level, 430
Aggregate supply, 309–316. *See also* Aggregate demand/aggregate supply model
    in classical theory of inflation, 431
    defined, 309
    long run, 310–312
    shifts in, 319–321
    short run, 309–310
Aggregate supply curve, 309–316
    defined, **309**
    financial crisis and, 471, 472, 475
    long run (*See* Long-run aggregate supply curve)
    market supply curve vs., 309
    from oil embargo, 449
    short run (*See* Short-run aggregate supply curve)
    upward-sloping, 309, 310
AGOA (African Growth and Opportunity Act of 2000), 532
Agricultural Act (1949), 136
Agriculture
    fertilizer use in, 260
    Green Revolution in, 257, 259–260
    price floors in, 136–139
    technology for, 257, 259
AIDS/HIV, 527, 536, 538
AIG, 459, 473, 474
Airbnb, 119
Airline prices, 97
Aizenman, Joshua, 440

Alabama, illegal immigration law on, 533
Alessi, S. M., 87
Alexander, Rick, 225, 226, 228, 231
Algieri, Bernardina, 379
Alternative minimum tax (AMT), 437
Amazon, 154, 209
American Recovery and Reinvestment Act of 2009, 333
Andreyeva, T., 87
Anti-corruption laws, 530
Appelbaum, Binyamim, 40
Apple Inc., 461, 463, 485
Arbitrage, 382, 499
Area under linear curve, 128A–128B
Argentina
    debt crisis in, 513, 514
    hyperinflation in, 427–428
    immigrants in, 427
    public debt in, 348
Asia. *See also specific regions and countries*
    economic growth in, 253, 260
    export-led growth in, 531
    financial crisis in, 514, 515
    Green Revolution in, 257, 259–260
Asian Americans, unemployment rate among, 229
Asian financial crisis (1997–1998), 514, 515
Asian miracle, 253, 266, 531
Assembly lines, 37
Asset-price bubbles, 299, 337
Assets
    financial, 373–375
    illiquid, 372, 374, 376
    liquid, 372, 374, 414–415
Asset valuation, 379–384
    bubbles in, 383–384
    efficient-market hypothesis and, 382–383
    fundamental analysis in, 381
    net present value approach to, 381
    predicting returns in, 381–383
    risk-reward trade-off in, 379–381
    technical analysis in, 381
Assumptions, in models, 16
Astor, John Jacob, 209
Asymmetric information, 361–362
AuctionWeb, 103
Australia
    Big Mac Index and, 214
    hand-to-mouth living in, 278
Automatic stabilizers, 334, 341–342
Automobile industry, 37, 46B, 46C
Autonomous expenditure, 286, 303
Autor, David, 40
Axes, in Cartesian coordinate system, 46C–46D

IN-1

Index

B

Babcock, Linda, 108–109
Bacha, Edmar, 442
Bailouts, 473–474, 476–477
Balance-of-payments identity, 491–493
Balance of trade, 486–488
Balance sheet channel, 419
Balance sheets, 403, 473
Banerjee, Abhijit, 525–526, 539
Bangladesh
    Grameen Bank in, 3–4, 9, 10, 12, 104, 120
    lack of access to loans in, 5–6
    microloans in, 3–4, 8–10, 12, 120
    textile industry in, 531
Banking holidays, 406
Banknotes, 399, 401, 402, 404
Bank of America, 376, 471
Bank of England, 473
Bank runs, 376, 405–406, 408
Banks. *See also* Federal Reserve
    bailout of, 473–474, 476–477
    cell phone banking, 399–400
    central, 408–409, 443–444, 472
    commercial, 376, 465
    credit tightening by, 299
    demand deposits, 402
    in financial crisis of 2008, 472–475
    as financial intermediaries, 363, 372, 376
    fractional-reserve banking, 401, 404–406
    full-reserve banking, 404
    functions of, 362–364
    Glass-Steagall Act and, 376, 406, 465
    interbank borrowing of reserves, 413
    investment, 376, 465, 466, 468, 474
    lending long and borrowing short, 376
    leveraging of funds by, 463
    liability of, 402
    liquidity provided by, 363, 376
    loans by, 402–404
    in money-creation process, 401–407
    reserves, 402–406, 411–413
    risk diversification and, 363
    securitization of mortgages, 466, 468
    subprime mortgage loans, 299, 466, 467, 470
    "too big to fail," 473–474
    tranches and, 466
    unwillingness to lend, 471
Bar charts, 46A–46B
Barnhart, C., 87
Barro, Robert, 292
Barter, 397
Baseball, 34–35
Base year, 177, 201–202
Basic accounting equation, 403
Basket approach. *See* Market basket
Bear Sterns, 471
BEA (U.S. Bureau of Economic Analysis), 188
Behavioral economics. *See also* Consumer behavior
    psychological inertia of hyperinflation, 443
    rational behavior, 4, 6, 8
Behavioral finance, 382–383
Belobaba, P., 87

Belt and Road Initiative (China), 500
Benedict XVI (pope), 378
Bernanke, Ben, 387, 411, 459, 477
Berry, Dan, 66
Bertrand, Marianne, 108
Bezos, Jeff, 209
Big Mac Index, 213–214
Bimetallism, 441
Biofuel subsidies, 148–149
Bitcoin, 409
Black market, 187
Blacks, unemployment rate among, 229
Black Thursday (1929), 464
Blanchard, Olivier, 444
BLS. *See* U.S. Bureau of Labor Statistics
Blyth, Mark, 500
Board of Governors (Federal Reserve), 410, 411, 420
Bondholders, 374, 375
Bonds, 374–375, 412–413
Booker, Cory, 240
Booming economy, 312, 337, 342, 419, 434
Borrowing short, 376
Bowles, Hannah Riley, 108–109
Bracket creep, 437
Brain drain, 534
Brazil
    Big Mac Index and, 214
    GDP (2018), 180
    GDP vs. well-being in, 184
    as holder of U.S. debt, 349
    hyperinflation in, 442–443
    income and life expectancy in, 528
    industrial policy in, 531
    savings rate in, 262
    units of real value in, 442–443
Brexit, 500
Brownell, K. D., 87
Brown-Philpot, Stacy, 39
Bryan, William Jennings, 441
Bubbles. *See also* Housing bubble of 2007
    asset-price, 299, 337
    in asset valuation, 383–384
    defined, **460**
    investor-inflated, 460–461
    South Seas Company, 463–464
    tulip mania (1634–1637), 383, 460
Budget deficit
    causative factors, 345–346, 385
    changes in, 369
    defined, **344**
    impact on savings, 496
    as percentage of GDP, 344–345
    public debt vs., 347–348
    in U.S. (1940–2018), 345
Budget surplus, 344, 385
Bulgaria, GDP vs. well-being in, 184
Burnside, Craig, 540
Bush, George W., 343, 346
Business cycle
    cyclical unemployment in, 236–237
    defined, **312**
    potential output and, 312–313
    in United States, 312

Business firms
    in circular flow model, 15–16
    corporations, 374–375
    efficiency in, 11–12
    in financial system, 378
    foreign direct investment by, 263, 489–490
    impact investing, 541
    leveraging of funds by, 463
    total revenue for, 88–91
Buyers
    consumer surplus, 110–112
    demand and number of, 57
    as demand determinant, 57
    in financial markets, 361
    in financial system, 372
    market equilibrium and, 65
    missing markets and, 119–120
    subsidies to, 150
    taxes on, 143–144, 150
    willingness to buy, 53, 80
    willingness to pay, 105–106, 110

C

California
    ban on trans fats in, 140–141
    minimum wage in, 239
Canada
    Big Mac Index and, 214
    GDP (2018), 180
    hand-to-mouth living in, 278
    in NAFTA, 487
    trade with U.S., 487, 488
Capabilities, 524–526, 528
Capital
    dead, 529
    flight of, 513, 515
    flows of (*See* International capital flows)
    foreign investment of, 263, 489–491
    human (*See* Human capital)
    physical, 255, 262
    as shift factor for long-run aggregate supply curve, 315
Capital flows. *See* International capital flows
Capital goods, 171
Capital inflows, 386, 491
Capital outflows, 386, 491–493, 513
Cardoso, Fernando Henrique, 442, 443
CARE, 534, 538
Careers in economics, 97
Carnegie, Andrew, 209
Cars. *See* Automobile industry
Carter, Jimmy, 441
Cartesian coordinate system, 46C–46F
Cash transfer programs, 544
Catch-up effect, 260–261
Causation, 13–16
Cayman Islands, as holder of U.S. debt, 349
CBO (Congressional Budget Office), 345, 346
Cell phones
    banking with, 399–400
    market for, 49–72
    use by Indian fishermen, 71–72, 120

Central banks. *See also* Federal Reserve
  defined, **408**
  inflation targeting by, 443-444
  liquidity problems for, 472
  role of, 408-409
Ceteris paribus concept, 52
Chain-weighted index, 179
Chairman of Federal Reserve, 410
Cheap borrowing, 387
Chetty, Raj, 152-153
China
  Belt and Road Initiative, 500
  Big Mac Index and, 214
  economic growth in, 165, 526
  environmental degradation in, 188
  GDP (2018), 180
  GDP vs. well-being in, 184
  growth accounting in, 259
  growth planning in, 264
  as holder of U.S. debt, 349
  iPhone manufacturing in, 485
  new middle class in, 249-250
  pollution in, 267
  portfolio investments and, 489
  poverty in, 165
  productivity in, 257
  rate of change in, 257
  remittances sent to, 532, 533
  reserve ratio adjustments in, 412
  savings rate in, 262, 367, 496-497
  trade surplus, 486
  trade with U.S., 485, 487-488, 510-511
  U.S. trade deficit with, 485, 510-511
  yuan undervaluation, 510-511
Choices, effect of prices on, 197, 199
Chrysler Corporation, 473
Cigarettes
  as money, 395-396, 399
  no-smoking laws, 197
  taxes on, 131
Circular flow model, 15-16, 169
Citigroup, 471, 473
Clark, David A., 526
Classical (real-wage) unemployment, 236
Classical theory of inflation, 430-432
Clean technologies, 267
Clemens, Michael, 239, 532-534
Clement, Douglas, 500
Climate change, 267, 321
Clinton, Bill, 345
Closed economies, 170, **386,** 492
Close substitutes, 55
Clusters, 531
Coefficient of *x*, 78A
Cohen, Jessica, 87-88
Coincidence, 13-14
COLAs (cost-of-living adjustments), 209-211
Cold War, 535
Collateral, 10, 371
College education, 17-19
Colorado State University, 541
Columbus, Christopher, 486
Colvo, Flor, 540
Commercial banks, 376, 465

Commodity-backed money, 400-401
Comparative advantage
  in baseball, 35
  defined, **33**
  over time, 40-41
  in production, 33-34
Competitive markets. *See also* Perfectly competitive markets
  characteristics of, 50-52
  defined, **50**
  failure of, 131
  price in, 71-72, 79-80
Complements, 55-56
Compounding, 252-253
Condé Nast, 244
Congressional Budget Office (CBO), 345, 346
Constraints
  on borrowing, 367, 369
  in production possibilities frontier, 27
  on wants, 5-6
  in willingness to pay or sell, 105
Consumer behavior
  credit crisis and, 469
  innovation and, 204
  price elasticity of demand and, 81-91
  stimulus spending and, 340-341, 343
  substitution effect and, 204
  urban consumers, 203, 204, 206
Consumer confidence, 303-304, 316, 317
Consumer expectations. *See* Expectations
Consumer preferences, 54-55
Consumer Price Index (CPI)
  annual changes (2001-2019), 429
  base year for, 201-202
  calculation of, 202
  challenges associated with, 202-205
  cost-of-living adjustments, 209-211
  defined, **201**
  deflating nominal variables and, 207-209
  indexing for inflation, 209-211
  inflation rate and, 205-207
  innovation and, 204
  market basket for, 201-204
  for measurement of inflation and deflation, 428-429
  substitution effect and, 204
  in U.S. (1913-2018), 203
Consumer surplus
  calculation of, 110-111, 128A, 128B
  deadweight loss and, 118-119
  defined, **110**
  price ceilings and, 133-134
  price changes and, 110-112
  price floors and, 137-138
  subsidies and, 148-150
  total, 113-115
Consumption
  aggregate, 277-279, 304, 306
  defined, **170**
  deflation and, 439
  determinants of, 277-279
  disposable income and, 335
  in expenditure approach to GDP, 170-171, 277-279

  marginal propensity to consume, 277, 278
  policies to encourage or discourage, 131, 140-141, 143-144, 146
  price level and, 302
  savings vs., 366
  tax policy and, 335
Consumption-type government purchases, 172
Contagion of financial crises, 514
Continental Illinois Bank, 474
Contractionary fiscal policy, 335-338
Contractionary monetary policy, 413, 419-420, 446
Contrarian investing, 383
Control group, 542
Convergence theory, 260-261
Core inflation, 206, 429
Corporations, 374-375. *See also* Business firms; Stock
Correlation, 13-15
Corruption
  anti-corruption laws, 530
  embezzlement of foreign aid, 538, 540
  rule of law vs., 530
Cortelyou, George, 408
Cost-benefit analysis, 349-350, 366
Cost of living, 197-217
  adjusting for inflation, 209-211
  Big Mac Index and, 213-214
  challenges in measurement of, 202-205
  geographic differences in, 198-199, 212-216
  measurement of prices and, 198-205
  PPP-adjustment for, 214-215
  price changes over time, 197, 199-205
  price indexes and, 201-211
  purchasing power parity and, 212-216, 512
Cost-of-living adjustments (COLAs), 209-211
Cost-push inflation, 434
Costs
  college education, 18
  of inflation, 436-437
  of inputs, 314
  of living (*See* Cost of living)
  marginal, 8
  menu, 436-437
  opportunity (*See* Opportunity cost)
  production, 62, 313, 314
  of public debt, 350
  relative to income, 84
  resource, 401
  shoe-leather, 437
  sunk, 8
  transaction, 51, 212, 372
Coupon payments, 374
CPI. *See* Consumer Price Index
Credit cards, 387, 398
Credit crisis, 299-300, 469
Credit ratings, 350, 468
Credit risk, 371
Credit spread, 371
Credit tightening, 299
Cross-border capital flows, 386, 387
Cross-price elasticity of demand, 81, **94**-96
Crowding out, 335, 338, 350, **369**-370
Cryptocurrencies, 409

Cultural differences. *See* Race and ethnicity
Cultural norms, 529
Current-account deficit, 387
Current income, as determinant of aggregate consumption, 277, 279
Current Population Survey, 232
Current prices, 176
Cyclical unemployment, 236–237

D

Dalai Lama, 3
Darity, William, 240
Das, Jishnu, 527
Dead Aid (Moyo), 539
Dead capital, 529
Deadweight loss
 calculation of, 118
 defined, **118, 133**
 government intervention and, 118
 price ceilings and, 133
 price changes and, 118–119
 price floors and, 137, 138
 subsidies and, 147–148
 taxes and, 142, 144
Deaton, Angus, 185, 216
Debit cards, 398
Debt and debt market. *See also* Loans; Mortgages
 bonds, 374–375
 historical trends in U.S., 469–470
 securitization of, 466, 468
 tranches in, 466
Debt crises, 513, 514
Debt service, 469
Decision making, marginal, 8–9
Default
 defined, **371**
 on loans, 371
 on mortgages, 467, 470
 on public debt, 350, 513
Defined-benefit plans, 377
Defined-contribution plans, 377
Deflating nominal variables, 207–209
Deflation
 aggregate demand and, 439–441
 challenges presented by, 327
 defined, **428**
 gold standard and, 441
 in Great Depression, 439
 inflation as buffer against, 443
 real output vs., 434
Deflationary spiral, 439
Deflator, 178–179, 206–207, 430
Demand, 52–59
 aggregate (*See* Aggregate demand)
 cross-price elasticity of, 81, 94–96
 defined, 52
 determinants of, 53–59
 elastic, 85–86, 88–90, 151–152
 for ethanol, 139
 in foreign-exchange market, 502
 income elasticity of, 81, 95–96
 inelastic, 85–86, 88–90, 151–152

 for labor, 444
 law of, 52–53
 for loanable funds, 494
 market demand, 52
 for money, 414–415
 nonprice determinants of, 53–59
 perfectly elastic, 85
 perfectly inelastic, 85
 price elasticity of, 79–92, 96
 price influences on, 52–53
 quantity (*See* Quantity demanded)
 supply and (*See* Supply and demand)
 taxes and, 140
 trade-offs and, 59
 unit-elastic, 86, 91
Demand curve
 aggregate (*See* Aggregate demand curve)
 defined, **53**
 elasticity along, 88, 90–91
 elasticity of, 145
 example of, 54
 for labor, 232–234
 for loanable funds, 365–367, 369, 370
 market equilibrium and, 64
 movement along, 58, 141
 number of buyers and, 57
 shifts in, 57–59, 66–71, 141
 slope of, 46I
 subsidies and, 146, 150
 taxes and, 141, 143–144
 willingness to buy and, 53
 willingness to pay and, 105–106
Demand deposits, 402
Demand-pull inflation, 434
Demand schedule, 53, 54
Demand shocks
 effects of, 316–319
 equilibrium and, 316
 government expenditures to counter, 325–326
 in long run, 322
 in short run, 322
 supply shocks vs., 321–324
Democracy, 530
Demographics of unemployment, 228, 229
Dependent variables, 46D
Depression, 181–182. *See also* Great Depression
Derivatives, 375
De Soto, Hernando, 529
Devaluation, 508, 511
Developing countries. *See also* Economic development
 cell phones in, 55, 71–72
 foreign aid for, 535
 human capital investment in, 256
 impact evaluations in, 542–543
 regional growth rates (1980-2018), 261
Development as Freedom (Sen), 525
Diehl, M. A., 87
Direct costs of public debt, 350
Direction of slope, 46H–46I
Discount rate, 412
Discount window, 412

Discouraged workers, 231
Discretionary fiscal policy, 341–342
Disincentives, 9
Disinflation, 441
Disneyland, 94
Disposable income, 335
Diversification, 363, 373, 380–381
Diversity. *See* Race and ethnicity
Diversity Visa lottery, 532
Dividends, 374
Dollar, David, 540
Dollarization, 506–507
Dollars. *See also* Money
 in circular flow model, 16
 as fiat money, 401
 international use of, 499–500
 lack of intrinsic value, 399
 nominal vs. real value of, 207–208
Domestic income, 281, 282
Domestic investment, 494
Domestic markets, 494
Domestic savings, 262
Dorn, David, 40
Double-counting, 166, 168, 170, 171
Dow Jones Industrial Average, 374
Drayer, J., 87
Drought Tolerance Maize for Africa project, 260
Dual mandate, 411, 444–446, 449–451
Duflo, Esther, 260, 525–526
Dunkin' Donuts, 51, 79, 94–95
Dupas, Pascaline, 87–88
Dupriez, Olivier, 216
Durst, Seymour, 347
Duvalier, Jean-Claude, 538, 540

E

Earned Income Tax Credit (EITC), 211, 240
Earnings. *See* Income; Wages
East Africa, cash transfer programs in, 544
East Asia
 economic growth in, 253, 260–261
 growth planning in, 264–265
Easterly, William, 539
East India Company, 463
eBay, 103–108, 110–119, 132, 171, 176
Economic analysis, 12–19
 correlation and causation in, 13–15
 models for, 15–17
 overview, 12
 positive and normative, 17–19, 132
Economic conditions, 366–367, 369
The Economic Consequences of the Peace (Keynes), 442
Economic development, 523–545
 basics of, 526–534
 capabilities approach to, 524–526
 democracy and, 530
 economic growth vs., 524, 526
 foreign aid and, 534–544
 human capital for, 527–529
 immigration and, 532–534
 impact evaluations, 542–543

Index IN-5

impact investing for, 541
industrial policy for, 530–531
institutions for, 529–530
international trade and, 531–532
investment for, 530–531
Millennium Development Goals on, 537
poverty traps and, 537
property rights and, 529–530
rule of law and, 530
Sustainable Development Goals on, 537
Economic fluctuations, 316–327
   aggregate demand shifts, 316–319
   aggregate supply shifts, 319–321
   demand and supply shocks, 316–324
   limits of fiscal policy in, 343
   public policy and, 324–327, 335–338
Economic growth, 249–268
   accounting for, 258–259
   annual rates of, 252
   in China, 165, 526
   compounding and, 252–253
   convergence theory of, 260–261
   economic development vs., 524, 526
   education and health policy for, 263–264
   environmental issues related to, 266–267
   foreign direct investment and, 263, 489–490
   GDP growth rates, 181–183, 251
   good governance and, 265–266, 529–530
   history of, 250–251
   industrial policy for, 264–265, 530–531
   investment and savings for, 262–263
   planning for, 264–265
   poverty and, 249–250
   productivity as driver of, 254–261
   property rights and, 265
   public policies for, 263–267
   rates vs. levels of, 257–258
   regional growth rates (1980–2018), 260–261
   rule of 70 and, 252–254
   significance of, 249–250
   slowed by public debt, 350
   in South Korea vs. Ghana, 253–254
   standard of living and, 165
   Sustainable Development Goals for, 263
   technological development and, 265
   transformation in 1800s, 251
   worldwide (2017), 182, 183
   worldwide (1000 BC–2000 AD), 251
Economic health assessment, 179–183
Economic incidence, 146
Economics
   analysis in (*See* Economic analysis)
   basic insights of, 4–12
   behavioral (*See* Behavioral economics)
   careers in, 97
   defined, **4**
   development (*See* Economic development)
   macroeconomics, 4, 166–167, 316, 317, 509–511
   microeconomics, 4, 166, 167
   questions for problem solving in, 5
Economic Stimulus Act (2008), 343
The Economist
   Big Mac Index, 213–214

on food prices, 129
housing bubble predictions from, 461
Economy
   booming, 312, 337, 342, 419, 434
   circular flow model of, 15–16
   closed, 170, 386, 492
   contraction of, 181
   effect of foreign investment on, 494–496
   efficiency of, 11
   equilibrium in, 316
   fluctuations in, 316–327
   GDP for comparison of, 176–183
   interest rates and, 416, 418–420
   labor-force participation rate, 228, 230
   measuring size of, 165
   national income accounting for, 166, 285
   natural rate of unemployment in, 235–236
   open, 386, 492, 494–496, 505
   open-market operations impacting, 412–413
   output gap in, 289–290, 445–446
   potential output in, 311–313, 432, 444
   recession in (*See* Recession)
   self-correcting, 336
   shifts in aggregate demand curve, 303–306
   underground, 187–188
   valuing, 166–169
   as zero-sum game, 115
Ecuador, dollarization in, 506–507
Education
   college, 17–19
   economic development and, 528–529
   economic growth and, 256, 263–264
   impact evaluation of programs for, 542–543
   public policy on, 263–264
   quality of, 528
   remedial, 529
   as shift factor for long-run aggregate supply curve, 315
   unemployment rates by level of, 229
EEOC (U.S. Equal Employment Opportunity Commission), 244
Efficiency, 103–121. *See also* Surplus (efficiency)
   defined, **10**
   government intervention and, 11
   innovation and, 11
   market failures and, 11
   as maximization of total surplus, 104
   practical implications of, 11–12
   in production possibilities frontier, 30–31
   profit and, 12
Efficiency wage, 242
Efficient-market hypothesis (EMH), 382–383
Efficient markets, 117
Efficient points, 30–31
E-float accounts, 400
Egypt
   Big Mac Index and, 214
   public debt in, 348
   remittances sent to, 533
Einstein, Albert, 277
EITC (Earned Income Tax Credit), 211, 240
Elastic demand
   cross-price elasticity of demand, 81, 94–96
   defined, **86**

income elasticity of demand, 81, 95–96
perfectly elastic, 85
price changes and, 90
price elasticity of demand, 79–92, 96
taxes and, 145, 151–152
total revenue and, 88–89
Elasticity, 79–98. *See also* Price elasticity of demand; Price elasticity of supply
   airline prices and, 97
   calculation of, 102E
   defined, **80**
   measures of, 80–81, 96
   slope and, 102B–102E
   of supply and demand curves, 145
   variations along demand curve, 88, 90–91
Elastic supply, 93, 151–152
Embezzlement of foreign aid, 538, 540
EMH (efficient-market hypothesis), 382–383
Employees, 227, 228, 230, 239. *See also* Labor
Employment. *See also* Labor market; Unemployment
   careers in economics, 97
   guaranteed, 240–241
   internships, 243–244
   labor-force participation rate, 228, 230
   skills-job mismatch, 235
   underemployment, 231
   in U.S. (2006–2018), 228, 230
The End of Poverty (Sachs), 537
Entrepreneurs, 378
Entry-level workers, 239
Environmental issues. *See also* Pollution
   biofuels and, 149
   climate change, 267, 321
   economic growth and, 266–267
   externalities and, 188–189
   green GDP, 188–189
   Industrial Revolution and, 266–267
Epidemics, 527
Equations. *See also* Linear equations
   accounting, 403
   aggregate expenditure, 276
   area of triangle, 128A
   Consumer Price Index, 202
   cross-price elasticity of demand, 95
   equilibrium aggregate expenditure, 298B
   expenditure approach to GDP, 173
   GDP deflator, 178
   GDP growth rate, 181, 253
   government subsidy expenditure, 147
   government tax revenue, 142
   graphs turned into, 78B, 78C
   growth accounting, 258
   horizontal distance, 46G
   income, 384–386
   income approach to GDP, 173–175
   income elasticity of demand, 95
   inflation rate, 179, 205
   investment, 386
   labor force, 227
   labor-force participation rate, 228
   line, 78A
   money multiplier, 405
   national savings, 385

Equations—*Cont.*
  percentage change, 102A–102B, 200
  planned aggregate expenditure, 286
  PPP-adjusted GDP, 215
  price elasticity of demand, 81–82
  price elasticity of supply, 92–93
  private savings, 386
  public savings, 385
  quantity equation, 432
  real exchange rate, 511–512
  real GDP per capita growth rate, 251
  real interest rate, 438
  real value, 207
  rule of 70, 253
  savings-investment identity, 385
  slope, 46G
  tax wedge, 142
  turning graphs into, 78B–78D
  unemployment rate, 227
  velocity of money, 432
  vertical distance, 46G
  with *x* and *y* reversed, 78D–78E
Equatorial Guinea, GDP vs. well-being in, 184
Equilibrium
  in AD/AS model, 300
  in classical theory of inflation, 431
  defined, **63**
  Keynesian, 286–289
  in labor market, 232–234
  linear equations to solve for, 78H–78I
  long run, 316–319, 447
  market (*See* Market equilibrium)
  in market for loanable funds, 364–365, 367
  in national economy, 316
  shocks impacting, 316
  short run, 316, 317, 319, 320
Equilibrium aggregate expenditure, 287–289, 291, 298A–298C
Equilibrium exchange rate, 502–503
Equilibrium price
  defined, **63**
  demand shifts and, 66–71
  subsidies and, 146–147, 151
  supply shifts and, 67–71
  taxes and, 140–144, 146, 151–152
Equilibrium quantity
  defined, **63**
  subsidies and, 146–147, 150, 151
  taxes and, 140–144, 146, 151–152
Equilibrium rate of unemployment, 235–236
Equilibrium wage, 233, 239
Equities. *See* Stock
Ethanol, 139, 148–149
Ethnicity. *See* Race and ethnicity
Euro, 499–500, 505–507
Europe, foreign aid for, 535. *See also specific countries*
European Central Bank, 411, 473
Excess demand. *See* Shortage
Excess reserves, 402
Excess supply. *See* Surplus (excess supply)
Exchange rate, 498–512. *See also* Foreign-exchange market
  appreciation and depreciation, 500–501
  crises involving, 513–515
  in decimal form, 498
  defined, **498**
  equilibrium, 502–503
  exchange-rate regimes, 505–509
  expression of, 498
  fixed, 507–510, 513
  floating, 507–510
  macroeconomic policy and, 509–511
  as net export determinant, 281, 282
  net exports and, 501
  nominal, 511
  price level and, 302
  real, 281, 511–512
  U.S. trade deficit and, 501
Exchange-rate appreciation, 500–501
Exchange-rate depreciation, 501
Exchange-rate effect, 302
Exchange-rate regimes, 505–509
Expansionary fiscal policy, 335–337, 345
Expansionary monetary policy
  in classical theory of inflation, 431
  defined, **412–413**
  interest rates and, 418–419
  output gap and, 446
  for recession, 418–419, 446
Expectations
  as demand determinant, 57
  of future economic conditions, 367, 369
  future income, 279
  of future prices, 57, 62, 315–316
  irrational, 460–462
  of profitability, 280, 369
  as supply determinant, 62
Expected future income, 279
Expedia, 236
Expenditure approach to GDP, 169–174. *See also* Aggregate expenditure
  consumption in, 170–171, 277–279
  equation for, 173
  government spending in, 170, 172, 280–281
  illustration of, 174
  inventory in, 172
  investment in, 171–172, 279–280
  net exports in, 170, 172, 281–282
  overview, 169, 170
Expenditure multiplier, 291–292
Expenditures
  aggregate (*See* Aggregate expenditure)
  autonomous, 286, 303
  government (*See* Government expenditures)
  research and development, 265
  of urban consumers, 203, 204
Export-led growth, 531
Exports, 172, 486–489. *See also* International trade; Net exports
Externalities, 188–189, 265

F

Facebook, 46B, 409
Face value, 374
Factors of production
  capital (*See* Capital)
  in circular flow model, 15–16
  market for, 16
  as shift factors for long-run aggregate supply curve, 314, 315
Fajgelbaum, Pablo D., 40
Farming. *See* Agriculture
FDI (foreign direct investment), 263, 489–490
Fears, Darryl, 92
Federal Deposit Insurance Corporation (FDIC), 406, 465
Federal funds rate, 413, 441, 476
Federal Open Market Committee (FOMC), 411, 420
Federal Reserve Act (1913), 408
Federal Reserve ("the Fed"), 408–413
  balance sheet (2008-2009), 473
  Board of Governors, 410, 411, 420
  central bank role of, 408–409
  chairman of, 410
  classification of money by, 406–407
  contractionary monetary policy of, 413, 419–420, 446
  creation of, 408
  cuts in federal funds rate, 476
  defined, **410**
  dual mandate of, 411, 444–446, 449–451
  expansionary monetary policy of, 412–413, 418–419, 431, 446
  independence of, 411
  inflation and, 441
  interest rates and, 415, 416, 418–419, 443
  as lender of last resort, 409, 412, 472
  member banks of, 410
  on methods of payment, 398
  monetary policy of, 408–413
  in money-creation process, 401–407
  money supply set by, 415–416
  on mutual fund assets, 376
  organization of, 410–411
  policy tools for, 411–413
  quantitative easing and, 476–477
  regional banks of, 410
  required reserves, 402–404
  response to financial crisis of 2008, 472–477
  TARP and, 473–474
  Treasury Department vs., 408
Female labor-force participation, 186
Ferguson, Roger, 307–308
Ferri, Richard A., 377
Fertilizer use, 260
Fiat money, 401
Fight for $15 Movement, 154–155
Final goods and services, 167–168, 170, 309, 310
Financial assets, 373–375
  debt, 374–375
  derivatives, 375
  equities, 373–374
Financial crises, 459–478. *See also* Bubbles; Financial crisis of 2008; Great Depression; Great Recession
  Asian financial crisis (1997–1998), 514, 515
  contagion of, 514
  global, 512–515

from irrational expectations, 460-462
leverage and, 462-463
onset of, 459
origins of, 460-464
panic of 1907, 408
South Seas bubble, 463-464
stock market crash (1929), 275, 464
tulip mania (1634-1637), 383, 460
Financial crisis of 2008
aggregate demand and supply during, 471, 472, 475
buying on credit in, 469
housing bubble and, 299, 384, 465-472
Lehman Brothers bankruptcy and, 359
onset of, 299-300
policy responses to, 472-477
stimulus spending during, 476-477
subprime lending and, 299, 465-467, 470
Financial intermediaries, 363, **372,** 376
Financial investments, exclusion from GDP, 171
Financial markets, 359-387
arbitrage in, 382
complexity of, 362
defined, **361**
failures in (2008), 459
herd instinct and, 460
information asymmetry and, 361-362
investor-inflated bubbles in, 460-461
irrational expectations of, 460-461
for loanable funds, 364-371
nature of, 360
organizations dependent on, 360
real-world, 364
recency effect and, 461
role of, 360-364
SEC and, 465
traditional markets vs. 360
Financial system, 371-387. *See also* Banks; Financial markets
asset valuation, 379-384
in closed vs. open economies, 386
debt market, 374-375, 465-472
defined, **372**
derivatives market, 375
diversification of risk in, 363, 373
entrepreneurs and businesses in, 378
equity market, 373-374
functions of, 372-373
index funds, 376, 377, 381
intermediaries in, 363, 372, 376
life insurance policies, 377
liquidity provision in, 372-373
major financial assets, 373-375
market makers in, 373
mutual funds, 376, 377, 383
national accounts approach to, 384-387
national savings, 385-386
nature of, 360
net capital flow in, 386
participants in, 375-379
pension funds, 377
private savings, 384-386
public savings, 385-386, 496
speculators in, 378-379

Financing gap, 535-536
Firms. *See* Business firms
Fiscal policy, 333-351
aggregate demand and, 334-336
contractionary, 335-338
defined, **334**
discretionary, 341-342
expansionary, 335-337, 345
formulation lag for, 339-340
government budget and, 344-346
government expenditures and, 335
immediate response to crisis of 2008, 472-475
implementation lag for, 340, 341
information lag for, 339
Keynesian, 337
limits of, 342-343
monetary policy vs., 419-420
public debt and, 346-350
short-run fluctuations and, 335-338
stimulus spending and, 340-341
tax policy and, 335
time lags for, 339-340
Treasury Department role in, 408
Fisher, Irving, 275, 464
Fixed exchange rate, 507-510, 513
Fixed-income securities, 374-375
Floating exchange rate, 507-510
Folbre, Nancy, 187
FOMC (Federal Open Market Committee), 411, 420
Food prices, 129-130, 429
Food stamps, 129
Football, 13-14
Footman, Alex, 243-244
Ford, Henry, 242
Foreclosure, 470
Foreign aid, 534-544
during Cold War, 535
distributors of, 538
financing gap and, 535-536
impact evaluations, 542-543
impact investing, 541
Marshall Plan and, 535
poverty traps and, 537
problems with, 538-540
as share of GDP, 536
Truman Doctrine and, 535
Foreign direct investment (FDI), 263, 489-490
Foreign-exchange market
arbitrage in, 499
demand in, 502
examples, 503-505
exchange-rate appreciation and, 500-501
exchange-rate depreciation and, 501
exchange-rate regimes, 505-509
interest rates in, 502, 504-505
model of, 502-505
monetary policy and, 504-505
net exports and, 501-505
speculators in, 500, 508, 515
supply in, 502
Foreign income, 281, 282
Foreign investment, 263, 489-491, 494-497

Foreign portfolio investment, 489
Formulation lag, 339-340
Foulkes, Imogene, 244
401(k) plans, 377
Fox, Justin, 189
Fox Searchlight Pictures, 243-244
Fractional-reserve banking, 401, 404-406
France
GDP (2018), 180
hand-to-mouth living in, 278
public debt in, 348
remittances sent to, 533
trade with U.S., 488
Franco, Itamar, 442
Free-rider problem, 265
Frictional unemployment, 235
Frontier Airlines, 97
Full employment, 411, 444, 448-451
Fuller, Ida May, 210
Full information, 51
Full-reserve banking, 404
Fundamental analysis, 381
Futures contracts, 375
Future value, 381

G

Gains, relative, 17
Gains from trade, 26, **37-**40, 487
Gallup World Values Survey, 532
Garment industry, 25-39, 531
Gates, Bill, 209
GDP. *See* Gross domestic product
GDP deflator, 178-179, 206-207, 430
GDP per capita, 180-181, 184, 254-256, 528
Gender
income differences and, 108
labor-force participation of women, 186
unemployment rates by, 229
wage negotiations and, 108-109
General Motors, 171, 465, 473
Germany
GDP (2018), 180
hand-to-mouth living in, 278
hyperinflation in, 442
labor-force participation in, 186
remittances sent to, 533
reparations payments, 442
savings rate in, 262
trade surplus, 486
trade with U.S., 488
Gertner, Jon, 189
Ghana
education in, 528, 529
GDP per capita in, 254
Ghosh, Jayati, 241
Gibson, John, 534
Gillibrand, Kristen, 240
GiveDirectly, 544
Glass-Steagall Act (1933), 376, 406, 465
Glatt, Eric, 243-244
Global financial crises, 512-515
Global GDP per capita, 181
Global savings glut, 386-387, 497

Global warming. *See* Climate change
GNP (gross national product), 168
Gold, as money, 399
Goldin, Claudia, 17
Goldman Sachs, 376
Gold standard, 434, 441
Good governance, 265–266, 529–530
Goodman, Peter S., 500
Goods and services
    in AD/AS model, 301
    capital, 171
    in circular flow model, 15–16
    in Consumer Price Index, 202–204
    final, 167–168, 170, 309, 310
    home production of, 185–187
    inferior, 56
    intermediate, 168
    international flow of, 486–489
    market for, 16
    non-tradables, 212
    normal, 56
    in Producer Price Index, 206
    production of (*See* Production)
    quantity demanded (*See* Quantity demanded)
    quantity supplied (*See* Quantity supplied)
    rationing, 134
    real value of, 198
    related, 55–56, 61
    specialization in, 36–37
    standardized, 51
    subsidies to encourage consumption of, 131
    substitutes (*See* Substitutes)
    tastes for foreign goods, 282
Goods-in-kind donations, 539–540
Gopinath, Gita, 499
Government
    expenditures (*See* Government expenditures)
    health and education policy, 263–264
    infrastructure and industrial policy, 264–265
    intervention by (*See* Government intervention)
    investment in physical capital, 262
    process of going into public debt, 348–349
    purchase of excess supply by, 138
    regulation by (*See* Public policy)
    revenue, 344
    subsidy costs for, 150
    "too big to fail" dilemma, 473–474
    trusted to maintain reliable system of money, 401
Government bonds, 374–375, 412–413
Government budget, 344–346
Government expenditures
    aggregate, 280–281, 305–307
    aggregate demand curve and, 325, 335
    as automatic stabilizer, 342
    to counter demand and supply shocks, 325–327
    crowding-out effect and, 335, 338, 350, 369–370
    multiplier effect and, 335
    stimulus spending, 306–307, 333–334, 340–343, 476–477
    U.S. total (2018), 344

Government intervention, 129–156
    deadweight loss and, 118
    efficiency and, 11
    evaluation of, 150–155
    food prices and, 129–130
    in labor market, 131
    long-run vs. short-run impact of, 153–154
    normative analysis of, 132
    positive analysis of, 132
    price ceilings and, 132–136
    price floors and, 136–139
    public expectations of, 336
    real-world examples, 131–132
    reasons for, 130–131
    subsidies, 131, 146–151
    summary of, 151
Government policy. *See* Public policy
Government purchases, 170, **172**
Government revenue, 344
Grameen Bank, 3–4, 9, 10, 12, 104, 120
Graphs
    bar charts, 46A–46B
    Cartesian coordinate system, 46C–46F
    creating, 46A–46F
    equations turned into, 78B–78D
    line, 46B, 46C
    of one variable, 46A–46C
    pie charts, 46B, 46C
    time-series, 46B, 46C
    turning into equations, 78B, 78C
    of two variables, 46C–46F
Gray market, 187
Great Britain. *See* United Kingdom
Great Depression
    banking holiday during, 406
    causes of, 283
    comparison with Great Recession, 275
    deflation during, 439
    onset of, 275, 464
    policy responses to, 406, 465
Great Moderation, 465
Great Recession (2007–2009), 465–477
    comparison with Great Depression, 275
    credit crisis and, 300, 469
    home production during, 186–187
    housing bubble and, 299, 384, 465–472
    impact on government finances, 346
    labor-force participation rate and, 230
    multiplier effect and, 292–293
    onset of, 182
    stimulus spending during, 307, 333–334, 340–343, 476–477
    Treasury securities during, 349
    unemployment during, 225, 232, 333
Greece
    financial crisis in, 500, 513
    public debt in, 348
Green Climate Fund (UN), 267
Greenfield, Rebecca, 244
Green GDP, 188–189
Greenhouse gases, 267
Green New Deal, 240
Green Revolution, 257, 259–260

Gross domestic product (GDP), 167–189
    avoidance of double-counting and, 168, 170, 171
    budget deficit as percentage of, 344–345
    circular flow model in relation to, 169
    to compare economies, 176–183
    compounding and, 252–253
    data challenges, 185–189
    decline during credit crisis, 300
    defined, **167**
    in economic health assessment, 179–183
    environmental externalities and, 188–189
    expenditure approach to, 169–174, 276–283
    final goods and services in, 167–168, 170
    financial investments excluded from, 171
    GDP deflator, 178–179, 206–207, 430
    GDP per capita, 180–181, 184, 254–256, 528
    green GDP, 188–189
    gross national product vs., 168
    growth rates, 181–183, 252–253
    history of (1000 BC–2000 AD), 251
    home production excluded from, 185–187
    housing price collapse and, 335
    imports and exports as percentage of, 486
    income approach to, 169, 170, 173–175
    international comparisons, 179–183
    international trade and, 170, 172
    limitations of, 183–189
    location of production and, 168
    market values and, 167
    measurement of, 169–176
    of Mexico, 46B, 46C
    nominal GDP, 176–179, 251
    percentage of savings in China, 496
    PPP-adjusted, 214–215
    public debt as percentage of, 347–348
    quarterly calculation of, 168
    real GDP, 176–178, 181–183, 251–253, 415
    in recession and depression, 181–182
    seasonally adjusted estimates of, 168–169
    stimulus plan percentage of, 333
    time period for, 168–169
    underground economy and, 187–188
    unemployment and, 236–237
    value-added approach to, 170, 175–176
    well-being vs., 184–185
    worldwide growth (2017), 182, 183
Gross national product (GNP), 168
Group responsibility, 10
Growth. *See* Economic growth
Growth accounting, 258–259
Guaranteed employment, 240–241
Guardian Trust Company of Detroit, 406
Gutierrez, Felipe, 540

H

Haiti
    foreign aid in, 538, 540
    GDP per capita in, 180
Hamilton, Alexander, 347
Hamilton, Darrick, 240
Hammer, Jeffrey, 527
Hand-to-mouth living, 278

Hanson, Gordon, 40
Hanyecz, Laszlo, 409
Happiness, 184-185
Harris, Kamala, 240
Haushofer, Johannes, 544
Headline inflation, 206, 429
Health and health care
    for economic development, 527-528
    for economic growth, 263
    epidemics, 527
    insurance for, 527
    life expectancy, 528
    malaria prevention, 87-88
    public policy on, 263-264
Health insurance, 527
Hearst, 244
Hedonic quality adjustment, 205
Heifer International, 534, 538
Helbling, T., 87
Herding, 383
Herd instinct, 460
Hershbein, Brad, 17
Hill, Jason D., 149
Hispanic Americans, unemployment rate among, 229
HIV/AIDS, 527, 536, 538
Home production, 185-187
Hong Kong
    economic growth in, 253
    GDP per capita in, 180
Horwich, George, 324
Households
    in circular flow model, 15-16, 169
    debt as percent of income (1980-2018), 470
    savings rate for, 262, 367-369
Housing. *See also* Mortgages
    foreclosure, 470
    newly built, 171
Housing bubble of 2007
    consumer confidence and, 303-304, 316
    creation of, 466-468
    credit crisis and, 299-300, 469
    demand and supply shocks in, 316-318, 322
    effects of collapse, 469-472
    in global economy, 472
    global savings glut and, 387
    government response to, 325
    homeowners impacted by, 335
    policy responses to, 476-477
    predictions regarding, 461-462
    role in financial crisis, 299, 384-385, 465-472
    speculators in, 379
    subprime lending and, 299, 465-467, 470
    timeline of collapse, 468
Housing starts, 467
Huffman, E.S., 66
Huggins, Miller, 34-35
Human capital
    defined, **256**
    for economic development, 527-529
    education and, 263, 528-529
    health and, 263, 527-528
    productivity and, 256

Hungary, hyperinflation in, 442
Hurricane Katrina (2005), 349
Hyde, David, 243
Hyperinflation, 427-428, 440, **441**-443
Hyundai Motor Company, 253, 531

I

IBRD (International Bank for Reconstruction and Development), 538
ICP (International Comparison Program), 213, 215
IDA (International Development Association), 538
Idiosyncratic risk, 380-381, 466
Illegal immigrants, 533
Illegal transactions, 187-188
Illiquid assets, 372, 374, 376
Imbalance of trade, 497
IMF (International Monetary Fund), 444, 512-513, 538
Immigration
    to Argentina, 427
    brain drain issue and, 534
    economic development and, 532-534
    illegal, 533
    labor market and, 238-239
    remittances and, 532-533
Impact evaluations, 542-543
Impact investing, 541
Implementation lag, 340, 341
Imports, 486-489. *See also* International trade
Import substitution, 530-531
Incentives, 9-10, 242, 468
Incidence, tax, 144-146
Income. *See also* Wages
    as aggregate consumption determinant, 277, 279
    college education and, 17
    cost relative to, 84
    current, 277, 279
    as demand determinant, 56
    disposable, 335
    domestic, 281, 282
    expected future value of, 279
    foreign, 281, 282
    gender differences in, 108
    happiness and, 184, 185
    household debt as percent of, 470
    level vs. rate of increase for, 257-258
    life expectancy and, 528
    in New York City vs. Iowa City, 199
    universal basic income, 544
Income approach to GDP, 169, 170, 173-175
Income elasticity of demand, 81, **95**-96
Independent variables, 46D
Index funds, 376, 377, 381
Indexing, 209-211, **210**
India
    agriculture in, 259
    cell phone use by fishermen in, 71-72, 120
    economic growth without development in, 526
    education in, 256, 529

    environmental degradation in, 188
    GDP (2018), 180
    Green Revolution in, 259
    guaranteed employment in, 241
    health care in, 527
    new middle class in, 249-250
    remittances sent to, 532, 533
    savings rate in, 262
    trade with U.S., 488
Indirect costs of public debt, 350
Industrial policy, 264-265, **530**-531
Industrial Revolution, 40, 266-267, 314
Industry clusters, 531
Inefficiency, market failures and, 11
Inelastic demand, 85-**86**, 88-90, 151-152
Inelastic supply, 93, 151-152
Infant industries, 531
Inferior goods, 56
Inflation, 427-452. *See also* Inflation rate
    as buffer against deflation, 443
    classical theory of, 430-432
    core inflation, 206, 429
    cost-push, 435
    costs of, 436-437
    defined, **428**
    demand-pull, 434
    disinflation, 441
    Fed control of, 441
    GDP deflator and, 178-179
    headline inflation, 206, 429
    hyperinflation, 427-428, 440, 441-443
    indexing for, 209-211
    measurement of, 428-429
    monetary policy and, 419, 444-451
    neutrality of money and, 430-432
    to pay off public debt, 439-440
    Phillips curve and, 446-451
    predictable, 436-437, 439
    quantity theory of money and, 432-434
    during recession, 444, 445
    redistributive effects of, 439
    unemployment and, 446-451
    unpredictable, 437-439
    velocity of money and, 432-434
Inflationary output gaps, 289, 290
Inflation rate
    alternative measures of, 206-207
    calculation of (2008-2018), 206
    defined, **205**
    equation for, 179
    price indexes and, 205-207
    shock therapy for, 441, 450
    in United States (1970s), 441, 450
    in U.S. (1960-2018), 207
    worldwide (1980-2017), 436
Inflation targeting, 443-444
Information, full, 51
Information asymmetry, 361-362
Information lag, 339
Ingraham, Christopher, 155
Initial public offerings (IPOs), 171
Innovation
    Consumer Price Index and, 204
    efficiency and, 11

Innovation—*Cont.*
   free-rider problem and, 265
   positive externalities and, 265
Innovations for Poverty Action (IPA), 529, 543
Inputs
   availability of, 94
   in circular flow model, 16
   cost of, 314
   price elasticity of supply and availability of, 94
   prices of, 62, 309–310
Instant-noodle sales, 56–57
Institutions, 529–530, 541
Insurance
   health, 527
   life, 377
   premiums, 377
   unemployment, 243
Interest-rate effect, 302
Interest rates
   as aggregate consumption determinant, 279
   on bonds, 374
   caps on payday loans, 135
   compounding, 252
   default likelihood and, 371
   defined, **279,** 365
   demand for money and, 414–415
   discount rate, 412
   domestic investment and, 494
   economy and, 416, 418–420
   factors driving differences in, 370–371
   federal funds rate and, 413
   Fed management of, 415, 416, 418–419, 443
   in foreign-exchange market, 502, 504–505
   impact on savings, 496
   as investment determinant, 280, 494
   liquidity-preference model and, 414–416
   on loanable funds, 365–366, 369–371
   money supply and, 415–420
   nominal, 415, 438–439
   price ceiling on, 135
   price level and, 302
   on public debt, 350
   real, 438
   realistic view of, 370–371
   risk-free rate, 371
   riskiness of transactions and, 371
   supply and demand effects, 418–420
   teaser, 467
   time factor in, 371
   zero lower bound, 413, 476–477
Interest rate targeting, 413
Intermediaries, 363, 372, 376
Intermediate goods and services, 168
International Bank for Reconstruction and Development (IBRD), 538
International capital flows
   balance of payments and, 491–493
   cross-border, 386, 387
   determinants of, 493–494
   effects of, 494–496
   foreign direct investment, 263, 489–491
   foreign-exchange market, 498–501
   foreign portfolio investment, 489
   net capital flow, 386, 491–494

International Comparison Program (ICP), 213, 215
International Development Association (IDA), 538
International investment, 494
International market for loanable funds, 494–496
International Monetary Fund (IMF), 444, 512–513, 538
International Rice Research Institute, 259
International trade. *See also* Exchange rate; Foreign-exchange market
   absolute advantage in, 33, 34
   balance of trade, 486–488
   comparative advantage in, 33–34, 40–41
   components of U.S. trade, 487–489
   correcting imbalances in, 497
   economic development and, 531–532
   exports, 172, 486–489
   foreign direct investment and, 263, 489–490
   gains from trade, 26, 37–40, 487
   GDP and, 170, 172
   global financial crises and, 512–515
   history of, 486
   imports, 486–489
   import substitution and, 530–531
   major U.S. trading partners, 487, 488
   openness to, 266
   specialization and, 35–37
   winners and losers in, 39–40
   World Trade Organization in, 532
Internet, 110, 314, 315
Internships, 243–244
Intervention. *See* Government intervention
Intrinsic value, 399
Inventory, 172
Investment
   aggregate demand shifts and, 304–306
   in capital goods, 171
   cost-benefit analysis and, 366
   crowding-out effect and, 369–370
   defined, **171,** 364
   deflation and, 439
   determinants of, 279–280, 369–370, 494
   domestic, 494
   for economic development, 530–531
   expectations of future profitability and, 369
   in expenditure approach to GDP, 171–172, 279–280
   financial, 171
   foreign direct investment, 263, 489–490
   foreign portfolio investment, 489
   herd instinct and, 460
   impact investing, 541
   industrial, 264–265, 531
   international, 494
   in inventory, 172
   leverage and, 462–463
   in market for loanable funds, 364–366, 369–370
   net capital outflow, 491
   in newly built houses, 171
   in physical capital, 255, 262

   price level and, 302
   rate of return on, 366
   recency effect and, 461
   savings as source of, 255, 262
   as shift factor for long-run aggregate supply curve, 314
   trade-offs in poor countries, 266
   uncertainty and, 369
Investment banks, 376, 465, 466, 468, 474
Investment goods, 384
Investment trade-off, 262, 266
Investment-type government purchases, 172
Invisible hand, 26, 42, 50
Iowa City, cost of living in, 198, 199
IPA (Innovations for Poverty Action), 529, 543
IPOs (initial public offerings), 171
Ireland, as holder of U.S. debt, 349
Irrational expectations, 460–462
Israel, public debt in, 348
Italy
   GDP (2018), 180
   hand-to-mouth living in, 278
   public debt in, 348
   trade with U.S., 488

J

Jack, William, 400
Janet, Brendan, 540
Japan
   Big Mac Index and, 214
   GDP (2018), 180
   as holder of U.S. debt, 349
   Kobe earthquake (1995), 324
   lost decade of deflation, 439
   monetary policy in, 476–477
   public debt in, 348
   savings rate in, 262
   trade surplus, 486
   trade with U.S., 488
Jensen, Robert, 71–72
JetBlue, 97
Jobs. *See* Employment
Johnson, David, 343
J.P. Morgan & Co., 408
J-PAL (Abdul Latif Jameel Poverty Action Lab), 543
JP Morgan Chase, 376
JP Morgan Undiscovered Managers Behavioral Value Fund, 383

K

Kagame, Paul, 530
Kalkuhl, Matthias, 379
Kaplan, Greg, 278
Karlan, Dean, 543
Katrina, Hurricane (2005), 349
Katz, Elizabeth, 540
Katz, Lawrence, 17
Kayak, 236
Kearney, Melissa, 17
Kelton, Stephanie, 240
Kenya
   cell phone banking in, 399–400
   education in, 528, 529

Index   IN-11

foreign aid in, 538, 539
universal basic income in, 544
Kessler, Glenn, 211
Keynes, John Maynard, 276, 283, 286, 336, 337, 414, 442
Keynesian cross, 287, 288
Keynesian equilibrium, 286–289
Keynesian fiscal policy, 337
Khandelwal, Amit K., 40
Kia Motors, 253
King, Martin Luther, Jr., 3, 240
Kline, B., 87
Kobe earthquake (1995), 324
Kremer, Michael, 260
Krieg, Gregory, 241
Kroft, Kory, 152–153
Krugman, P., 87
Kuwait, income level vs. rate of growth in, 257
Kuznets, Simon, 166

L

Labor. *See also* Employees; Income; Wages
demand for, 444
market for (*See* Labor market)
as shift factor for long-run aggregate supply curve, 315
supply of (*See* Labor supply)
Labor demand, 444
Labor demand curve, **232–234**
Labor force, 227
Labor-force participation rate, 228, 230
Labor market. *See also* Employment; Unemployment
demand, 444
efficiency wage in, 242
equilibrium in, 232–234
female participation in, 186
government intervention in, 131
immigration and, 238–239
minimum wage in, 131
supply (*See* Labor supply)
surplus in, 233
unions and, 242
unpaid internships and, 243–244
Labor supply
immigration, 238–239
inflation targeting and, 444
wage rates and, 232–234
Labor supply curve, 232–234, **233**
Labor unions
contracts and sticky wages in, 310
defined, **241**
membership trends, 241
wages and, 242
Lagging indicators, 237
Lai, Lei, 108–109
Lanthrop, Yannet, 155
Latinos/Latinas, unemployment rate among, 229
Law of demand, 52–53
Law of supply, 59, 60
Leapfrog technology, 55
Lehman, Henry, 359

Lehman Brothers
bankruptcy of, 359, 459, 474
collapse of, 340, 362, 471
founding of, 359
as investment bank, 376
leverage ratio for, 463
stock price for, 471
Leibbrandt, Andres, 109
Lenders of last resort, 409, 412, 472, 512
Lending long, 376
Let Their People Come (Clemens & Pritchett), 532–533
Level of income, 257–258
Leverage, 462–463, **466–467**
Leverage ratio, 463
Levin, L., 87
Lewis, M. S., 87
LG, 253
Liability of banks, 402
Liberia, income and life expectancy in, 528
Libra, 409
Life, opportunity cost of, 7–8
Life expectancy, 528
Life insurance policies, 377
Life satisfaction, 184, 185
Life Satisfaction Index, 184
Linear curve, area under, 128A–128B
Linear equations
examples of, 78B
graphs turned into, 78B, 78C
to interpret equation of a line, 78A–78E
shifts and pivots, 78E–78H
solving for equilibrium, 78H–78I
turning graphs into, 78B–78D
with x and y reversed, 78D–78E
Line graphs, 46B, 46C
Lines, slope of, 46F
Liquid assets, 372, 374, 414–415
Liquidity
of assets, 372, 374
banks as providers of, 363, 376
classification of money by, 406–407
defined, **372**
from discount window, 412
in financial crisis of 2008, 472
of stock, 374
Liquidity-preference model, 414–416, 415
Liquidity providers, 373
Liquidity trap, 444
List, John, 109
Living hand-to-mouth, 278
Living standards. *See* Standard of living
Loanable funds
defined, 364
demand curve for, 365–367, 369, 370
interest rates on, 365–366, 369–371
market for, 364–371, 494–496
prices of, 365
sources of demand for, 494
supply and demand changes, 366–370
supply curve for, 365–369
Loans. *See also* Market for loanable funds
by banks, 402–404
borrowing constraints, 367, 369

cheap borrowing, 387
collateral for, 10, 371
credit risk of, 371
default on, 371
defined, **374**
group responsibility for, 10
by IMF, 512–513
lack of access to, 5–6
leverage, 462–463
microloans, 3–4, 8–10, 12, 120
payday, 135
risk premium and, 371
securitization of, 375
student loans, 18–19
subprime lending, 299, 465–467, 470
with unpredictable inflation, 438–439
Location of production, 168
Lohr, Steve, 14
Long, M. W., 87
Long run
aggregate supply in, 310–312, 319–321
defined, 310
demand and supply shocks in, 322
monetary policy in, 414
shifts in demand, 317–319
Long-run aggregate supply, 310–312
Long-run aggregate supply curve (LRAS)
in classical theory of inflation, 431
defined, **309**
demand shocks and, 317–319
factors of production and, 314, 315
fiscal policy and, 336
government expenditures and, 325
investment changes and, 314
potential output and, 311–312
as production function, 311, 313
shifts in, 313–316
short-run aggregate supply curve vs., 309–312
supply shocks and, 319, 320
technology and, 314, 315
Long-run equilibrium, 316–319, 447
Long-run Phillips curve, 448–450
Looney, Adam, 152–153
Lowell, Francis Cabot, 32
LRAS. *See* Long-run aggregate supply curve
Luxembourg, as holder of U.S. debt, 349
Lyft, 119

M

M1, 406–407, 433
M2, 407
Macroeconomics
defined, **4, 166**
exchange rate policy, 509–511
microeconomics vs., 167
model of macroeconomy, 316, 317
Mahatma Ghandi National Rural Employment Guarantee Act (India), 241
Major League Baseball (MLB), 34–35
Malaria prevention, 87–88
Malawi, education level in, 256
Malaysia, Big Mac Index and, 214

Mali, GDP vs. well-being in, 184
Mama Noodles Index, 56
Margin accounts, 462, 463
Marginal cost (MC), 8
Marginal decision making, 8-9
Marginal propensity to consume (MPC), 277, 278
Margin calls, 463
Marion, Nancy, 440
Market basket
   for Consumer Price Index, 201-204
   core inflation and, 206, 429
   decisions regarding contents of, 202-204
   defined, **200**
   headline inflation and, 206, 429
   innovation and, 204
   price changes and, 200-201, 204
   purchasing power indexes and, 213
   substitution effect and, 204
   updates to, 204
Market-clearing price, 64
Market-clearing wage level, 242
Market demand, 52
Market economy, 50
Market equilibrium
   changes in, 65-71
   convergence of supply and demand at, 63-64
   demand shifts and, 66-71
   in labor market, 232-234
   in perfectly competitive markets, 117
   prices below, 118-119
   reaching, 64-65
   subsidies and, 146-147, 151
   supply shifts and, 67-71
   surplus (efficiency) and, 115-117
   taxes and, 140-144, 151-152
   technology and, 72
Market failures, 11, **131,** 139
Market for factors of production, 16
Market for goods and services, 16
Market for loanable funds, 364-371
   default in, 371
   defined, **364**
   demand curve in, 365-367, 369, 370
   domestic, 494
   equilibrium in, 364-365, 367
   interest rates and, 365-366, 369-371
   international, 494-496
   prices in, 365
   savings and investment, 364-369
   supply and demand changes, 366-370
   supply curve in, 365-369
Market makers, 373
Markets, 49-72
   for cell phones, 49-72
   competitive (*See* Competitive markets)
   creating or improving, 119-120
   defined, **50**
   demand and (*See* Demand)
   domestic, 494
   efficient, 117
   equilibrium (*See* Market equilibrium)
   financial (*See* Financial markets)
   foreign exchange (*See* Foreign-exchange market)

   labor (*See* Labor market)
   for loanable funds, 364-371
   missing, 119-120
   for organ transplants, 120
   scope of, 85
   supply and (*See* Supply)
Market share, 46B, 46C
Market supply, 59
Market supply curve, 309
Market (systemic) risk, 380, 381
Market value, 167, 301
Marshall, Julian D., 149
Marshall Plan, 535
Maturity date for bonds, 374
Maxcy, J. G., 87
McClelland, Robert, 343
McDonald's, 37, 79, 213-214
McKenzie, David M., 534
McKinley, William, 441
MC (marginal cost), 8
Medicaid, 211, 342
Medical insurance, 527
Medium of exchange, 397
Mellon, Andrew, 464
Member banks (Federal Reserve), 410
Men. *See* Gender
Menu costs, 436-437
Merrill Lynch, 459, 465
Mexico
   Big Mac Index and, 213, 214
   education in, 528
   foreign direct investment in, 263
   GDP growth in, 46B, 46C
   impact evaluations in, 542
   income and life expectancy in, 528
   in NAFTA, 487
   price ceilings in, 132-134, 136
   remittances sent to, 533
   standard of living in, 215
   subsidies in, 146-150
   trade with U.S., 487, 488
Microeconomics, 5, 166, 167
Microloans, 3-4, 8-10, 12, 120
Microsoft Corporation, 209
Middle class, 249-250
Mid-point method, 81-82, 93
Migration. *See* Immigration
Milk Price Support Program, 136-139
Millennium Challenge Corporation, 540
Millennium Development Goals (UN), 537
Minimum wage
   defined, 239
   Fight for $15 Movement, 154-155
   government intervention and, 131
   indexing for inflation, 210
   nonbinding, 239
   poverty line and, 210-211
   real value (1938-2018), 211
   state and local levels, 239
   unemployment debate and, 239-240
Minorities. *See* Race and ethnicity
"Miracle rice," 259-260
Miron, Jeffrey, 211
MLB (Major League Baseball), 34-35

Models. *See also* Aggregate demand/aggregate supply model
   assumptions clearly stated by, 16
   circular flow, 15-16, 169
   defined, **15**
   economic analysis, 15-17
   economic growth, 260-261
   foreign-exchange market, 502-505
   prediction of cause and effect by, 16
   production possibilities frontier, 27-32
   real world descriptions in, 17
M1, 406-407, 433
Monetarists, 414
Monetary base, 406, 407
Monetary policy, 408-420
   aggregate demand and, 413
   challenges and advantages of, 419-420
   contractionary, 413, 419-420, 446
   defined, **408**
   discount rate and, 412
   discount window and, 412
   dollarization, 506-507
   economic effects of, 414-420
   expansionary, 412-413, 418-419, 431, 446
   federal funds rate and, 413, 476
   fiscal policy vs., 419-420
   foreign-exchange market and, 504-505
   for full employment, 411, 444
   immediate response to crisis of 2008, 472-475
   inflation and, 418-419, 444-451
   interest rates and, 414-420
   in Japan, 476-477
   liquidity-preference model, 414-416
   monetarist view of, 414
   open-market operations in, 411-413
   for price stability, 411, 444
   reserve requirements and, 402-404, 411-412
   role of Federal Reserve in, 408-413
   tools of, 411-413
   unemployment and, 446-451
Money, 395-420. *See also* Exchange rate; Foreign-exchange market; Monetary policy; Money supply
   banknotes, 399, 401, 402, 404
   bimetallism, 441
   bitcoin, 409
   cigarettes as, 395-396, 399
   classification by liquidity, 406-407
   commodity-backed, 400-401
   convenience of, 399
   creation process, 401-407
   defined, **396**
   demand for, 414-415
   fiat, 401
   functions of, 396-397
   future value of, 381
   gold standard, 434, 441
   happiness and, 185
   measurement of, 406-407
   as medium of exchange, 397
   neutrality of, 430-432
   present value of, 381
   quantity theory of, 432-434

stability of value, 399
as store of value, 397
as unit of account, 397
velocity of, 432-435
Money-creation process, 401-407
Money multiplier, 404-405
Money supply. *See also* Monetary policy
additions to economy (2008-2009), 473
central bank role in, 415-416
in classical theory of inflation, 430-432
decreasing, 412, 416
defined, **406**
federal funds rate and, 413, 476
increasing, 412, 416
interest rates and, 415-420
in liquidity-preference model, 415-416
M1, 406-407, 433
M2, 407
management of, 408-413
monetary base for, 406, 407
real output and, 432-434
role of central bank in, 408-413
in U.S. (1984-2019), 407
velocity of money and, 432-434
Monga, Celestin, 265
Montenegro, Claudio E., 532-534
Monterrey Conference on Financing for Development (2002), 535
Moore's law, 258
Moral hazard, 362
Morgan, John Pierpont, 408, 409, 472
Mortgage-backed securities, 466, 468, 470, 473
Mortgages
default on, 467, 470
as leverage, 466-467
refinancing, 467, 469
securitization of, 466, 468
subprime, 299, 465-467, 470
underwater, 467, 470
Mother Teresa, 3
Motor vehicles. *See* Automobile industry
Movement along demand curve, 58, 141
Movement along supply curve, 62-63, 141
Moyo, Dambisa, 539
MPC (marginal propensity to consume), 277, 278
M-Pesa, 399-400
M2, 407
Mugabe, Robert, 440
Multiculturalism. *See* Race and ethnicity
Multiplier effect
aggregate demand and, 306-307
aggregate expenditure and, 290-293, 298B-298C
defined, **290**
government expenditures and, 335
money multiplier, 404-405
Mutual funds, **376**, 377, 383
Mycoskie, Blake, 539-540

N

NAFTA (North American Free Trade Agreement), 487
NAIRU (non-accelerating inflation rate of unemployment), 448-451

Nakamoto, Satoshi (pseudonym), 409
Nasdaq, 374
National Academy of Sciences, 188
National accounts approach to finance, 384-387
capital flows in, 386
in closed vs. open economies, 386
private savings in, 384-386
public savings in, 385-386
savings-investment identity, 384-385
National Bureau of Economic Research (NBER), 182, 339
National Employment Law Project, 155
National Football League (NFL), 13-14
National income accounting, 166, 285
National Park Service, 91-92
National Rural Employment Guarantee Act (India), 241
National savings, 385-386
Natural rate of unemployment, 235-236
Natural resources. *See also* Environmental issues
productivity and, 256
as shift factor for long-run aggregate supply curve, 315
NBCUniversal, 244
NBER (National Bureau of Economic Research), 182, 339
Necessity, price elasticity of demand and, 84
Negative correlation, 13
Negative externalities, 188-189
Negative incentives, 9
Negative output gap, 445
Negative slope, 46I, 102B
Negotiation for wages, 108-109
Net capital flow, 386, 491-494
Net exports
aggregate demand shift and, 306
defined, **172**
determinants of, 281-282
equal to net capital outflow, 491-492
exchange rate and, 281, 282, 501
in expenditure approach to GDP, 170, 172, 281-282
foreign-exchange market and, 501-505
price level and, 302
trade policies and, 282
Net present value (NPV), 381
Neutrality of money, 430-432
Newton, Isaac, 464
New York City
cost of living in, 198, 199
public debt digital counter in, 346-347
New York Stock Exchange, 171, 408
New York Yankees, 34-35
NFL (National Football League), 13-14
Nigeria
income and life expectancy in, 528
remittances sent to, 533
Nike, Inc., 490
Nominal exchange rate, 511
Nominal GDP, 176-179, 251
Nominal interest rate, 415, 438-439
Nominal price changes, 198
Nominal value, 207-211, 430

Nominal variables, deflating, 207-209
Non-accelerating inflation rate of unemployment (NAIRU), 448-451
Nonbinding minimum wage, 239
Nonbinding price ceilings, 136
Nonbinding price floors, 139
Nonprice determinants of demand
consumer preferences, 54-55
defined, 53
expectations, 57
income, 56
number of buyers, 57
prices of related goods, 55-56
shifts in demand curve and, 57-59
Nonprice determinants of supply
defined, 60
expectations, 62
number of sellers, 62
prices of inputs, 62
prices of related goods, 61
shifts in supply curve and, 62-63
technology, 61
Nonrenewable resources, 256
Non-tradables, 212
Normal goods, 56
Normative analysis, 17-19, 132
Normative statements, 18
Norms, cultural, 529
North, Douglass C., 529
North American Free Trade Agreement (NAFTA), 487
Northern Rock Bank failure (2007), 405, 406
Norway, GDP vs. well-being in, 184
No-smoking laws, 197
NPV (net present value), 381
Numbeo, 199
Number of buyers, demand and, 57
Number of sellers, supply and, 62

O

Obama, Barack, 300, 307, 333, 340, 346, 476
Ocasio-Cortez, Alexandria, 240
Odoni, A., 87
O'Donnell, Rosie, 66
OECD (Organisation for Economic Co-operation and Development), 536
Official development assistance (ODA), 535-536, 538-539
Official unemployment rate, 231
Oil embargo, 441, 450
Oil prices, 313, 314, 321, 435
Olmstead, S. M., 87
Olmstead, T. A., 87
Omidyar, Pierre, 103
Omitted variables, 14
OPEC (Organization of Petroleum Exporting Countries), 435, 441, 449
Open economies, 386, 492, 494-496, 505
Open-market operations, 411-413, **412**
Opportunity cost. *See also* Trade-offs
defined, **6**
gains from trade and, 38-39
interest rates and, 371

Opportunity—*Cont.*
   of life, 7–8
   marginal cost and, 8
   of production, 61
   in production possibilities frontier, 29–30
   of related goods, 55
   trade-offs and, 6–7, 53, 59
   in willingness to pay, 106
   in willingness to sell, 108
Organisation for Economic Co-operation and Development (OECD), 536
Organization of Petroleum Exporting Countries (OPEC), 435, 441, 450
Organizations vs. institutions, 529
Organ transplants, 120
Origin, 46D
Output gap, 289–290, **445**–446
Outputs, 16, 27. *See also* Production

P

Pacula, R. L., 87
Paddison, Laura, 241
PAE (planned aggregate expenditure), 284–286, 303, 304
Pakistan, remittances sent to, 533
Panic of 1907, 408
Pao, Ellen, 109
Paper money, 399, 400
Parker, Jonathan, 343
Paul, Mark, 240
Paulson, Hank, 459
Payday loans, 135
Pension funds, 377
Per capita GDP. *See* GDP per capita
Percentage change
   calculation of, 102A–102B, 200
   mid-point method for, 81–82, 93
   price elasticity of demand and, 81–83
   price elasticity of supply and, 93
   in quantity, 83
   unemployment rate and, 230
Percentage point changes, 230
Peretti, Jonah, 490
Perfectly competitive markets
   characteristics of, 50–52
   equilibrium in, 117
   full information in, 51
   rarity of, 51
   standardized goods and services in, 51
   transaction costs and, 51
Perfectly elastic demand, 85
Perfectly elastic supply, 93
Perfectly inelastic demand, 85
Perfectly inelastic supply, 93
Permanent supply shocks, 320–321
Petry, N. M., 87
Philippines, remittances sent to, 533
Phillips, A. W., 446
Phillips curve, 446–451
   in AD/AS model, 447, 448
   defined, **447**
   long run, 448–450
   NAIRU and, 448–451

   origins of, 446
   short run, 447, 448
Physical capital, 255–256, 262
Pie charts, 46B, 46C
Pivots, 78E–78H
Planned aggregate expenditure curve, 286
Planned aggregate expenditure (PAE), 284–286, 303, 304
Policy-making. *See* Public policy
Polio, 14
Pollution
   biofuels and, 149
   green GDP and, 188–189
   Industrial Revolution and, 266–267
   taxes for, 146
Pollution taxes, 146
Poor Economics (Banerjee & Duflo), 525–526
Population
   GDP and size of, 179
   working-age, 227, 228, 230
   world population growth, 251
Portfolios, 380–381
Positive analysis, 17–19, 132
Positive correlation, 13
Positive externalities, 265
Positive incentives, 9
Positive output gap, 445
Positive slope, 46I, 102B
Positive statements, 18
Potential output
   business cycle and, 312–313
   in classical theory of inflation, 432
   defined, **444**
   long-run aggregate supply curve and, 311–312
Poverty
   decline of (2005–2015), 249–250
   economic growth and, 249–250
   extreme, 523
   Sustainable Development Goals on, 263, 537
Poverty line, 210–211
Poverty traps, 266, **537**
Poverty-weighted purchasing power parity indexes (PPPP), 216
Powell, Jerome, 411
PPF. *See* Production possibilities frontier
PPI (Producer Price Index), 206, 207
PPP-adjustment, 214–215
PPPP (poverty-weighted purchasing power parity indexes), 216
PPP (purchasing power parity), 212–216, 512
Predatory lending, 135
Predictable inflation, 436–437, 439
Preferences, 54–55
Premiums (insurance), 377
Present value, 381
Price ceilings, 132–136
   consumer surplus and, 133–134
   deadweight loss and, 133
   defined, **132**
   nonbinding, 136
   on payday loans, 135
   producer surplus and, 133–134
   shortages caused by, 132, 134
   welfare effects of, 133, 134

Price changes. *See also* Cost of living; Deflation; Inflation
   aggregate demand curve and, 302–303
   challenges in measurement of, 202–205
   consumer surplus and, 110–112
   deadweight loss and, 118–119
   expectations regarding, 57, 62, 315–316
   GDP deflator and, 178–179
   innovation and, 204
   market basket and, 200–201, 204
   menu costs, 436–437
   nominal, 198
   over time, 197, 199–205
   producer surplus and, 112–113
   quantity demanded and, 52–53, 81–84
   quantity supplied and, 59
   substitution effect and, 204
   total revenue and, 88–89
   total surplus and, 114
   uncertainty and, 432
Price controls, 132–139
   defined, **132**
   long- vs. short-run impact, 153–154
   price ceilings, 132–136
   price floors, 136–139, 153–154
   quantity supplied/demanded and, 132, 150
Priced in, 382
Price effect, total revenue and, 88–89
Price elasticity of demand, 79–92
   calculation of, 81–83
   cross-price elasticity of demand, 81, 94–95
   defined, **81**
   determinants of, 84–85
   estimated, 87
   extremes of, 85–86
   for gourmet coffee, 79–82, 94–96
   malaria prevention and, 87–88
   mid-point method and, 81–82
   national park entrance fees and, 91–92
   nature of, 80
   summary of, 96
   tax increases and, 151–152
   utilization of, 85–92
Price elasticity of supply
   calculation of, 92–93
   defined, **92**
   determinants of, 93–94
   mid-point method and, 93
   nature of, 80
   summary of, 96
   tax increases and, 151–152
Price floors, 136–139
   in agriculture, 136–139
   consumer surplus and, 137–138
   deadweight loss and, 137, 138
   defined, **136**
   long- vs. short-run impact, 153–154
   nonbinding, 139
   producer surplus and, 137–138
   welfare effects of, 138
Price frictions, 276
Price indexes. *See also* Consumer Price Index
   defined, **201**
   deflating nominal variables and, 207–209

indexing for inflation, 209-211
inflation rate and, 205-207
Producer Price Index, 206, 207
Price level. *See also* Deflation; Inflation
 aggregate, 430
 aggregate demand curve and, 301-303
 in Consumer Price Index, 428-429
 consumption effects and, 302
 cost of production vs., 314
 exchange-rate effect and, 302
 of final goods, 309, 310
 geographic differences in, 212-216
 importance of changes in, 436-444
 of inputs, 309-310
 interest-rate effect and, 302
 investment effects and, 302
 net exports effects and, 302
 neutrality of money and, 430-432
 quantity theory of money and, 432-434
 real-balances effect and, 302
 real vs., nominal values, 430
 velocity of money and, 432-434
Priceline, 236
Prices
 in AD/AS model, 301-303
 adjustment process for, 309-310
 below market equilibrium, 118-119
 in Big Mac Index, 213-214
 changes in (*See* Price changes)
 in competitive markets, 71-72, 79-80
 current price, 176
 demand curve shifts and, 57-59
 demand schedule and, 53, 54
 equilibrium (*See* Equilibrium price)
 food prices, 129-130, 429
 of inputs, 62
 of loanable funds, 365
 in macroeconomic model, 317
 market-clearing price, 64
 market value and, 167
 measurement of, 198-205
 money supply and, 430-432
 oil prices, 313, 314, 321, 435
 in permanent supply shocks, 320-321
 PPP-adjustment for, 214-215
 purchasing power indexes and, 213-214
 purchasing power parity and, 212-216
 real exchange rate and, 511
 real vs. nominal GDP and, 176
 of related goods, 55-56, 61
 stability of, 411, 444
 sticky prices, 276, 309, 320, 431
 supply curve shifts and, 62-63
 supply schedule and, 60
 tax wedge and, 142
 in temporary supply shocks, 319-320
 willingness to pay and, 105-106
 willingness to sale and, 105, 107-108
Prices of related goods, 55-56, 61
Price stability, 411, 444
Price takers, 51
Pricing analysts, 97
Pricing decisions, 79-80
Prime borrowers, 465

Principal, 374
Pritchett, Lant, 532-534
Private savings, 384-386
Producer Price Index (PPI), 206, 207
Producer surplus
 calculation of, 112, 128A-128B
 deadweight loss and, 118-119
 defined, **112**
 price ceilings and, 133-134
 price changes and, 112-113
 price floors and, 137-138
 subsidies and, 148-150
 total, 113-115
Production
 absolute advantage in, 33, 34
 assembly lines in, 37
 comparative advantage in, 33-34, 40-41
 coordination in, 26
 costs of, 62, 313, 314
 decisions in, 309, 311-312
 demand shocks and, 317-319
 expenditure and income in, 169
 factors of (*See* Factors of production)
 flexibility in, 94
 home, 185-187
 location of, 168
 long-run determination of, 311-312
 in macroeconomic model, 317
 measurement of, 430
 money supply and, 432-434
 opportunity cost of, 61
 in permanent supply shocks, 320-321
 policies to encourage or discourage, 131, 140-143, 146
 possibilities for, 27-32
 potential output, 311-313, 432, 444
 real output, 432-434
 real vs. nominal GDP and, 176
 specialization in, 26, 35-36
 stages of, 166
 in sweatshops, 490
 in temporary supply shocks, 319-320
 of T-shirts, 25-39
Production costs, 62, 313, 314
Production decisions, 309, 311-312
Production functions, 258, 311, 313
Production possibilities frontier (PPF)
 constraints in, 27
 defined, **27**
 efficient points in, 30-31
 gains from trade and, 38
 opportunity cost in, 29-30
 shifting, 31-32
 technology and, 32
 trade-offs in, 29
 wants in, 27
 wheat vs. T-shirt production example, 27-32
Productivity, 254-261
 accounting for growth, 258-259
 components of, 255-257
 convergence theory and, 260-261
 defined, **255**
 as driver of economic growth, 254-255
 human capital and, 256

natural resources and, 256
 physical capital and, 255-256
 rates vs. levels of, 257-258
 technology and, 256-258
Profit, 12, 280
Property rights
 economic development and, 529-530
 economic growth and, 265
 titling and, 529
Protectionism, 212-213, 531
Proxy, 376
Psychological inertia of hyperinflation, 443
Public companies, 374
Public debt, 346-350
 budget deficit vs., 347-348
 cost-benefit analysis of, 349-350
 default on, 350, 513
 defined, **346**
 digital counter in New York City, 346-347
 inflating away, 439-440
 international comparisons, 348
 as percentage of GDP, 347-348
 process of going into debt, 348-349
 size of, 347-348
 stimulus spending and increase in, 334
 of United States since 1940, 347
Public goods, 535
Public policy
 AD/AS model and, 321-322, 324-327
 aggregate demand shifts and, 305
 automatic stabilizers, 341-342
 to counter demand and supply shocks, 325-327
 economic fluctuations and, 324-327, 335-338
 for economic growth, 263-267
 on education and health, 263-264
 in financial crisis of 2008, 472-475
 during Great Depression, 406, 465
 industrial, 264-265, 530-531
 on infrastructure, 264
 multiplier effect and, 306-307
 savings rate and, 367
 unemployment and, 225, 238-244
Public savings, 385-386, 496
Purchasing power indexes, 213-214, 216
Purchasing power parity (PPP), 212-216, 512

Q

Quadrants, 46D-46F
Quality
 of education, 528
 hedonic adjustment, 205
 of life, 184, 524
Quantitative easing, 476-477
Quantity
 absolute vs. percentage change in, 83
 in AD/AS model, 301
Quantity demanded
 cross-price elasticity of demand and, 95
 defined, **52**
 determinants of, 53-57

Quantity demanded—*Cont.*
  income elasticity of demand and, 95-96
  linear equations and, 78H-78I
  perfectly elastic demand and, 85
  perfectly inelastic demand and, 85
  price changes and, 52-53, 81-84
  price controls and, 132, 150
  price elasticity and, 151-152
  shifts in demand curve and, 57-59
  shortage and, 65
  surplus and, 64-65
  tax increases and, 151
Quantity effect, total revenue and, 88-89
Quantity equation, 432
Quantity supplied
  defined, **59**
  determinants of, 60-62
  linear equations and, 78H-78I
  price changes and, 59
  price controls and, 132, 150
  shortage and, 65
  surplus and, 64-65
Quantity theory of money, 432-434

R

Race and ethnicity
  savings behavior and, 367
  unemployment rates by, 229
Radford, R. A., 396
R&D (research and development), 265
Randomized controlled trials (RCTs), 542-543
Random walk, 382
Rate of change, 257-258
Rate of increase in income, 257-258
Rate of return, 366
Rational behavior, 4, 6, 8
Rationing of goods, 134
RCTs (randomized controlled trials), 542-543
Reagan, Ronald W., 182, 345
Real-balances effect, 302
Real exchange rate, 281, 511-512
Real GDP
  calculation of, 176-178
  defined, **176**
  demand for money and, 415
  GDP deflator and, 178
  growth rates, 181-183, 251-253
  history of (1000 BC-2000 AD), 251
  in U.S. (1947-2018), 252
  in U.S. (1960-2018), 182
Real interest rate, 438
Real output, 432-434
Real value, 198, 207-211, 302, 430
Real-wage (classical) unemployment, 236
Real wages, inflation targeting and, 444
Real world descriptions, in models, 17
Real-world financial markets, 364
Recency effect, 461
Recession. *See also* Financial crisis (2008); Great Recession
  budget deficit and, 345, 346
  defined, **181**
  discretionary fiscal policy for, 341-342
  expansionary monetary policy and, 418-419, 446
  frequency of, 182
  inflation during, 444, 445
  labor-force participation rate and, 228, 230
  prediction of, 56
Recessionary output gaps, 289, 290
Reciprocal of fraction ratio, 498
Red Cross, 395-396, 399
Redistributive effects of inflation, 439
Refinancing, 467, 469
Regional unemployment, 225
Related goods, 55-56, 61
Relative gain, 17
Remedial education, 529
Remittances, 532-533
Renewable resources, 256
Renminbi (yuan), 500, 510-511
Rent, in New York City vs. Iowa City, 199
Rent-seeking, 134, 531
Required reserves, 402-404, **411**-412
Research and development (R&D), 265
Reservation price. *See* Willingness to pay
Reserve ratio, 403-405, 412
Reserve requirements, 402-404, **411**-412
Reserves, 402-406, 411-413
Residuals, in growth accounting, 259
Resource cost, 401
Resources
  allocation of, 11
  defined, 11
  intangible, 4
  natural, 256, 315
  nonrenewable, 256
  renewable, 256
Retirement benefits, 210, 377
Returns
  on portfolios, 380
  predicting, 381-383
Revaluation, 508
Revenue, 88-91, 344
Reverse causation, 14-15
Ricardian equivalence theory, 342-343
Rise, 46G
Risk
  assessment of, 468
  credit, 371
  diversifying, 363, 373, 380-381
  in foreign-exchange market, 502
  idiosyncratic, 380-381, 466
  market (systemic), 380, 381
  measurement of, 381
  pooling, 466
Risk-free rate, 371
Risk pooling, 466
Risk premium, 371
Risk-reward trade-off, 375, 379-381
Roaring Twenties, 464
Rockefeller, John D., 209, 408
Rockefeller Foundation, 259
Rogoff, Kenneth, 387
Romer, Christina, 292
Romer, Paul, 257
Roosevelt, Franklin D., 210, 240, 406
Ros, A. J., 87
Rossen, Jake, 66
Rule of law, 530
Rule of 70, 252-254
Run, 46G
Rungfapaisarn, Kwanchai, 57
Russia
  Big Mac Index and, 214
  financial crisis in, 513
  foreign aid from, 535
  growth planning in, 264-265
Ruth, Babe, 34-35
Rwanda, economic development in, 530

S

Sachs, Jeffrey, 490, 537
Sahm, Claudia R., 340-341
Salary. *See* Income; Wages
Sales tax, 152-153
Salk, Jonas, 14
Samsung, 253, 531
Sanders, Bernie, 240
Save the Children, 534, 538
Savings
  borrowing constraints and, 367
  consumption vs., 366
  cultural differences and, 367
  current economic conditions and, 366-367
  defined, **364**
  deflation and, 439
  determinants of, 366-369
  domestic, 262
  global savings glut, 386-387, 497
  by households, 262, 367-369
  international comparisons, 262
  life insurance policies, 377
  in market for loanable funds, 364-369
  in mutual funds, 376, 377
  national, 385-386
  private, 384-386
  by proxy, 376
  public, 385-386, 496
  social welfare policies and, 367
  as source of investment, 255, 262
  trade-offs and, 366
  uncertainty and, 367
  with unpredictable inflation, 438-439
  wealth in relation to, 366
Savings-investment identity, 384-385
Scarcity, 6-7
Schenk, Catherine, 500
Schlosser, Eric, 37
School. *See* Education
Scope of market, 85
Seasonally adjusted estimates at an annual rate, 168-169
Seasonally adjusted unemployment rate, 232
Securities and Exchange Act (1932), 465
Securitization, 375, 466, 468
SEC (U.S. Securities and Exchange Commission), 465
Sellers
  in financial markets, 361

in financial system, 372
market equilibrium and, 64
missing markets and, 119-120
number of, 62
producer surplus, 112-113
subsidies to, 146-147, 150
taxes on, 140-143, 150
willingness to sell, 60, 105, 107-108
Sen, Amartya, 524, 525, 530
Services. *See* Goods and services
Shapiro, Jeremy, 544
Shapiro, Matthew D., 340-341
Shareholders, 373
Shifts, 78E-78H
Shifts in demand curve
equilibrium changes and, 66-71
nonprice determinants of demand and, 57-59
taxes and, 141
Shifts in supply curve
equilibrium change and, 67-71
nonprice determinants of supply and, 62-63
taxes and, 141
Shi Jiangtao, 189
Shiller, Robert, 384
Shocks. *See* Demand shocks; Supply shocks
Shoe-leather costs, 437
Shortage (excess demand), 65-66, 132, 134
Short run
aggregate supply in, 309-310, 319-321
defined, 309
demand and supply shocks in, 322
monetary policy in, 414
shifts in demand, 317-319
Short-run aggregate supply, 309-310
Short-run aggregate supply curve (SRAS)
in classical theory of inflation, 431
defined, **309**
demand shocks and, 317-319
in financial crisis of 2008, 475
fiscal policy and, 336
government expenditures and, 325
long-run aggregate supply curve vs., 309-312
shifts in, 313-316
sticky wages effects and, 309
supply shocks and, 313, 319-321
Short-run economic fluctuations, 335-338
Short-run equilibrium, 316, 317, 319, 320
Short-run Phillips curve, 447, 448
Sierra Leone, foreign aid in, 538
Silk Road, 486
Sinatra, Frank, 199
Singapore, economic growth in, 253
Singer, Peter, 7, 8
Single-variable graphs, 46A-46C
Skills-job mismatch, 235
Slemrod, Joel, 340-341
Slope
calculation of, 46G-46H, 102E
defined, **46G**
of demand curve, 46I
direction of, 46H-46I
elasticity and, 102B-102E
of lines, 46F

negative, 46I, 102B
positive, 46I, 102B
of production possibilities frontier, 29-30
rise, 46G
run, 46G
steepness of, 46I-46J, 102C
of supply curve, 46I
Slope intercept form, 78A
Small loans. *See* Microloans
Smith, Adam, 26, 42
Smith, Chad, 533
Smoking. *See* Cigarettes
SNAP (Supplemental Nutrition Assistance Program), 240, 537
Social businesses, 541
Social media platforms, monthly average users of, 46A-46B
Social Security, 210
Social Security Act (1935), 210
Solar-powered lighting, 541
Solvency problem in financial crisis, 473
Sonn, Paul K., 155
Souleles, Nicholas, 343
South Africa
Big Mac Index and, 214
income and life expectancy in, 528
South Korea
Big Mac Index and, 214
economic growth in, 253-254
export-led growth in, 531
industrial policy in, 530, 531
trade with U.S., 488
South Seas bubble, 463-464
Southwest, 97
Spahn, Paul Bernd, 515
Spain, hand-to-mouth living in, 278
Specialization
defined, **36**
gains from trade and, 37-40
in goods and services, 36-37
international trade and, 35-37
in production, 26, 35-36
Specialized funds, 376
Speculative attacks, 508-509, 514
Speculators, 378-379, 500, 508, 515
Spending. *See* Government expenditures
Spice Route, 486
Spirit Airlines, 97
SRAS. *See* Short-run aggregate supply curve
Stability of value, 399
Stagflation, 320, 326, 450
Stalin, Joseph, 264, 265
Standard & Poor's 500, 374, 376, 377
Standard & Poor's credit rating, 350
Standard deviation, 381
Standardized goods and services, 51
Standard of living, 165, 204, 215, 239
Stanford University Entrepreneurial Design for Extreme Affordability class, 541
Starbucks, 79-81, 94-96
Statutory incidence, 146
Stavins, R. N., 87
Steepness of slope, 46I-46J, 102C
Stein, Jeff, 241

Steinbeck, John, 275
Sticky prices, 276, 309, 320, 431
Sticky wages, 237, 309-310, 320
Stiglitz, Joseph E., 265
Stimulus spending
consumer behavior and, 340-341, 343
disbursement options, 340
as discretionary fiscal policy, 341, 342
in Great Recession, 307, 333-334, 340-343
in Japan, 476-477
multiplier effect and, 306-307
at zero lower bound, 476-477
Stock. *See also* Stock market
bonds vs., 375
defined, **373**
foreign portfolio investment, 489
in index funds, 376
initial public offerings of, 171
liquidity of, 374
of major banks during financial crisis, 471
predicting returns, 382
reasons for issuing, 373-374
of South Seas Company, 463-464
undervalued, 383
valuation of, 382-383
Stockholders, 373, 374
Stock market
crash (1929), 275, 464
in England (17th century), 463
Super Bowl and, 13-14
Stone, Richard, 166
Store of value, 397
Strikes, 241
Structural unemployment, 235-236
Student loans, 18-19
Subprime lending, 299, 465-467, 470
Sub-Saharan Africa
economic growth in, 260, 261
HIV/AIDS in, 527
regional growth rates (1980-2018), 261
Subsidies, 146-151
for biofuels, 148-149
buyer response to, 150
deadweight loss and, 147-148
defined, **146**
effects of, 151
to encourage consumption, 131
seller response to, 146-147, 150
Substitutes
availability of, 84
close substitutes, 55
defined, **55**
import substitution, 530-531
price changes and, 204
price elasticity of demand and, 84
Substitution effect, 204
Sunk cost, 8
Super Bowl, 13-14
Supplemental Nutrition Assistance Program (SNAP), 240, 537
Supply, 59-63
aggregate (*See* Aggregate supply)
defined, 59
demand and (*See* Supply and demand)

Supply—*Cont.*
 determinants of, 60-63
 elastic, 93, 151-152
 in foreign-exchange market, 502
 inelastic, 93, 151-152
 of labor (*See* Labor supply)
 law of, 59, 60
 market supply, 59
 nonprice determinants of, 60-63
 perfectly elastic, 93
 perfectly inelastic, 93
 price elasticity of, 80, 92-94, 96
 quantity (*See* Quantity supplied)
 taxes and, 140, 141
 trade-offs and, 59
 unit-elastic, 93
Supply and demand. *See also* Aggregate demand/aggregate supply model
 cell phones, 49-72
 convergence at equilibrium, 63-64
 in foreign-exchange market, 502
 interaction in markets, 63
 interest rates and, 418-420
 for loanable funds, 366-370
 shifts in, 68-71
Supply curve
 aggregate (*See* Aggregate supply curve)
 defined, **60**
 elasticity of, 145
 for labor, 232-234
 for loanable funds, 365-369
 market, 309
 market equilibrium and, 64
 movement along, 62-63, 141
 shifts in, 62-63, 67-71, 141
 slope of, 46I
 subsidies and, 146, 150
 taxes and, 141, 143
 willingness to sell and, 60, 107-108
Supply schedule, 60
Supply shocks
 defined, **313**
 demand shocks vs., 321-324
 effects of, 319-321
 equilibrium and, 316
 government expenditures to counter, 326-327
 in long run, 322
 oil embargo, 441, 450
 permanent, 320-321
 in short run, 322
 temporary, 319-320
Suri, Tavneet, 400
Surplus (budget), 344, 385
Surplus (efficiency), 109-120
 changing distribution of, 130-131
 consumer (*See* Consumer surplus)
 deadweight loss and, 118-119
 defined, **109**
 government intervention and, 130-131
 market equilibrium and, 115-117
 measurement of, 109-115
 missing markets and, 119-120
 producer (*See* Producer surplus)
 reassignment of, 117-118
 total (*See* Total surplus)
 uses for, 104, 115-120
Surplus (excess supply)
 as area under linear curve, 128A-128B
 defined, **64**
 government purchase of, 138
 in labor market, 233
 price ceilings and, 133-134
 price floors and, 137-138, 153-154
 redistribution by taxes, 142-143
 subsidies and, 148-150
Surplus (trade), 486
Sustainable Development Goals (UN), 263, 537
Sweatshops, 490
Sweden, Big Mac Index and, 214
Switzerland
 Big Mac Index and, 214
 GDP per capita in, 180
 as holder of U.S. debt, 349
 income and life expectancy in, 528
 rate of growth in, 257
Systemic (market) risk, 380, 381

T

Tadesse, Getaw, 379
Taiwan, economic growth in, 253
TANF (Temporary Assistance to Needy Families), 240
TARP (Troubled Asset Relief Program), 473-474
TaskRabbit, 39
Tastes for foreign goods, 282
Tax cuts, 306, 307, 333, 342, 345, 346
Tax Cuts and Jobs Act (2017), 334
Tax distortion, 437
Taxes and taxation
 aggregate demand shifts and, 305, 335
 alternative minimum tax, 437
 as automatic stabilizers, 341-342
 bearing burden of, 144-146
 bracket creep, 437
 on buyers, 143-144, 150
 consumption impacted by, 335
 deadweight loss and, 142, 144
 to discourage production and consumption, 131, 140-146
 effects of, 151-152
 increases in, 151-152, 341
 as investment determinant, 280
 overall impact of, 144
 pollution tax, 146
 Ricardian equivalence theory on, 342-343
 sales tax, 152-153
 on sellers, 140-143, 150
 Tobin tax, 515
 unemployment and, 243
Tax incidence, 144-146
Tax revenue, 344
Tax wedge, 142, 144
T-bills (Treasury bills), 348-349
Teaser interest rates, 467
Technical analysis, 381
Technology. *See also* Cell phones
 agricultural, 257, 259
 clean, 267
 economic growth and, 265
 in growth accounting, 258-259
 Internet, 110, 314, 315
 leapfrog, 55
 market equilibrium and, 72
 Moore's law and, 258
 productive capacity and, 32
 productivity and, 256-258
 as shift factor for long-run aggregate supply curve, 314, 315
 as supply determinant, 61
Temporary Assistance to Needy Families (TANF), 240
Temporary supply shocks, 319-320
Tessuma, Christopher W., 149
Textile industry, 25-39, 531
Thailand
 Mama Noodles Index in, 56
 speculative attack on baht, 508-509
Thaler, Richard, 383
Thomas, Derek, 244
"Tickle Me Elmo" shortage, 66
Time
 adjustment time, 84-85, 94
 comparative advantage over, 40-41
 cost of living changes over, 197
 in GDP calculation, 168-169
 interest rates and, 371
 price changes over, 197, 199-205
 value over, 252-253
Time lags for fiscal policy, 339-340
Time-series graphs, 46B, 46C
Titling, 529
Tobacco use. *See* Cigarettes
Tobin, James, 515
Tobin tax, 515
TOMS shoes, 539-540
"Too big to fail," 473-474
Torres, Ritchie, 398
Total revenue, 88-91
Total surplus
 calculation of, 114-115, 128B
 changing distribution of, 117-118
 creation of new markets and, 119-120
 deadweight loss of, 118-119
 defined, **114**
 efficiency and, 104
 maximization of, 104
 price ceilings and, 133
 price changes and, 114
Toyota Motor Corporation, 94, 263
Toyota Prius, 503-504
Trade, international. *See* International trade
Trade agreements
 African Growth and Opportunity Act, 532
 North American Free Trade Agreement, 487
Trade deficit, 485, **486,** 501, 510-511
Trade gap, 485
Trade imbalances, 497
Trade-offs

assumptions regarding, 9-10
demand curve and, 53
economic growth vs. environment, 266-267
incentives and, 9-10
investment-consumption, 262, 266
in law of demand, 53
in law of supply, 59
in marginal decision making, 8
microloans and, 8-9
opportunity cost and, 6-7, 53, 59
in production possibilities frontier, 29
profit-borrowing costs, 369
risk-reward, 375, 379-381
in savings decisions, 366
unemployment-inflation, 446-451
in willingness to pay, 106
in willingness to sell, 108
Trade restrictions. *See* Protectionism
Trade surplus, 486
Trade unions. *See* Labor unions
Trailing indicators, 237
Tranches, 466
Transaction costs
defined, **51**
in financial system, 372
perfectly competitive markets and, 51
purchasing power parity and, 212
Transfer payments, 281, 344
Travelocity, 236
Treasury bills (T-bills), 348-349
Treasury bonds, 349
Treasury notes, 349
Treasury securities, 348-349
Treatment group, 542
Troubled Asset Relief Program (TARP), 473-474
Truman Doctrine, 535
Truman, Harry, 182
T-shirt production, 25-39
tulip mania (1634-1637), 383, 460
Tung, Irene, 155
Turkewitz, Julie, 92
Turkey, financial crisis in, 513
Tyco, 66

U

Uber, 119
UBI (universal basic income), 544
Uncertainty
in inflation, 437-439
investment and, 369
price changes and, 432
savings rate and, 367
Uncorrelated variables, 13
Underbanked persons, 398
Underemployment, 231
Underground economy, 187-188
Underwater mortgages, 467, 470
Underwriting, 376
Undiscovered Managers Behavioral Value Fund, 383

UNDP (United Nations Development Program), 538
Unemployment, 225-245. *See also* Labor market
categories of, 235-237
consequences of, 226
criteria for, 227
cyclical, 236-237
data sources on, 232
definitions of, **226-227**
discouraged workers, 231
frictional, 235
in Great Recession, 225, 232, 333
inflation and, 446-451
labor demand curve and, 232-234
labor supply curve and, 232-234
as lagging indicator, 237
measurement of, 227-232
minimum wage as potential cause of, 239-240
NAIRU, 448-451
natural rate of, 235-236
public policy influences, 225, 238-244
real-wage (classical), 236
reasons for, 226
regional, 225
structural, 235-236
taxation and, 243
in temporary supply-side shocks, 320
underemployment, 231
unions and, 242
in U.S. (2006-2018), 229
Unemployment insurance, 243
Unemployment rate
by age (2006-2018), 229
calculation of, 227-228
defined, **227**
demographic variations, 228, 229
discouraged workers and, 231
by educational level (2006-2018), 229
by gender (2006-2018), 229
in Great Recession, 225
natural rate of unemployment, 235-236
official, 231
percentage changes vs. percentage point changes, 230
by race and ethnicity (2006-2018), 229
seasonally adjusted, 232
underemployment and, 231
Unions. *See* Labor unions
United Kingdom
Brexit vote in, 500
Department for International Development, 538
GDP (2018), 180
hand-to-mouth living in, 278
as holder of U.S. debt, 349
Industrial Revolution in, 40
Northern Rock Bank failure in, 405, 406
trade with U.S., 488
United Nations
foreign aid from, 538
Green Climate Fund, 267
Millennium Development Goals, 537
Sustainable Development Goals, 263, 537

United Nations Development Program (UNDP), 538
United States
agricultural policies in, 136-139
balance of trade (1960-2018), 487
Big Mac Index and, 213, 214
biofuel subsidies in, 148-149
business cycle in, 312
categories of trade, 487-489
college completion rates in, 17
comparative advantage in, 41
Consumer Price Index (1913-2018), 203
cyclical unemployment in (1980-2018), 237
Diversity Visa lottery in, 532
domestic and imported vehicle types in, 46B, 46C
employment statistics (2006-2018), 228, 230
foreign aid from, 535-537
GDP (2018), 180
GDP breakdown for, 174
GDP per capita in, 180
GDP vs. well-being in, 184
Great Depression in, 275-276, 283, 406, 439, 464-465
hand-to-mouth living in, 278
historical debt trends in, 469-470
housing price collapse in, 461-462, 470
imports from China, 487
income and life expectancy in, 528
inflation rate (1960-2018), 207
inflation rate (1970s), 441, 450
labor-force participation in, 186
labor unions in, 241
major trading partners, 487, 488
Marshall Plan, 535
minimum wage in, 239
net capital flows (1980-2018), 493
output gap in (1980-2018), 445
postwar debt-to-GDP ratio, 440
public debt in, 346-348
real GDP (1947-2018), 252
real GDP (1960-2018), 182
research and development spending in, 265
savings rate in, 262, 367-369
trade deficit, 485, 486, 501
Truman Doctrine, 535
unemployment insurance in, 243
velocity of money in (1960-2018), 433
visa program in, 532
wealthiest Americans, 209
Unit-elastic demand, 86, 91
Unit-elastic supply, 93
Unit of account, 397
Units of real value (URVs), 442-443
Universal basic income (UBI), 544
Unpaid internships, 243-244
Unpredictable inflation, 437-439
Urban consumers, 203, 204, 206
URVs (units of real value), 442-443
U.S. Agency for International Development (USAID), 538
U.S. Bureau of Economic Analysis (BEA), 188
U.S. Bureau of Engraving and Printing, 408

U.S. Bureau of Labor Statistics (BLS)
  Consumer Price Index and, 201–205, 428–429
  Current Population Survey, 232
  on discouraged workers, 231
  measures of unemployment collected by, 231–232
  unemployment as defined by, 227
U.S. Department of Agriculture (USDA), 138
U.S. Department of Labor, 244
U.S. Department of the Treasury, 374, 408, 473
U.S. Equal Employment Opportunity Commission (EEOC), 244
U.S. Securities and Exchange Commission (SEC), 465
Utility and utility maximization, 525–526

V

Value
  absolute, 83
  of home production, 186–187
  intrinsic, 399
  market, 167, 301
  money as store of, 397
  nominal, 207–211, 430
  real, 198, 207–211, 302, 430
  resources in creation of, 11
  stability of, 399
Value-added approach to GDP, 170, 175–176
Value over time, 252–253
Valuing an economy, 166–169, 285
Vanderbilt, Cornelius, 209
Vanguard Index Fund, 377
Variables
  correlation of, 13–14
  dependent, 46D
  independent, 46D
  linear relationship of, 78A, 78B
  nominal, 207–209
  omitted, 14
  one variable graphs, 46A–46C
  two variable graphs, 46C–46F
Vehicles. *See* Automobile industry
Velocity of money, 432–435
Versailles Peace Conference (1919), 442
Vietnam
  income and life expectancy in, 528
  remittances sent to, 533
Violante, Giovanni L., 278
Virtuous cycle, 537

Visa program for U.S. immigration, 532
Volcker, Paul, 441, 450, 451
Voluntary transactions, 103–104, 115, 120
Von Braun, Joachim, 379

W

Wages. *See also* Income; Minimum wage
  changes over time, 197
  efficiency, 242
  equilibrium, 233, 239
  factors preventing fall in, 239–242
  Fight for $15 Movement, 154–155
  inflation and, 210–211, 444
  labor supply and wage rates, 232–234
  labor unions and, 242
  market-clearing wage level, 242
  negotiation for, 108–109
  price level and, 302
  sticky wages, 237, 309–310, 320
Wants
  constraints on, 5–6
  in production possibilities frontier, 27
  in willingness to pay or sell, 105
Warner, Tracy, 39, 40
Warner Music Group, 244
Warren, Elizabeth, 210, 211, 240
Washington Mutual, 459
Wealth
  as aggregate consumption determinant, 277–279
  living hand-to-mouth and, 278
  savings in relation to, 366
  wealthiest Americans, 209
Wealth effect, 302
WeChat, 46B
Weidner, Justin, 278
Weigel, David, 241
Welfare effects
  of price ceilings, 133, 134
  of price floors, 138
Welfare programs, 240, 342
Well-being vs. GDP, 184–185
WhatsApp, 46B
Where's George? (website), 435
WikiLeaks, 538
Willingness to buy, 53, 80
Willingness to pay (reservation price), 105–106, 110
Willingness to sell, 60, 105, 107–108
Wilson, Woodrow, 408

Wolak, F. A., 87
Women. *See* Gender
Work. *See* Employment; Labor market
Workers. *See* Employees; Labor
Working-age population, 227, 228, 230
World Bank
  defined, **538**
  foreign aid from, 538, 539
  on industrial policy, 265
  International Comparison Program, 213, 215
  poverty measures from, 215, 523
  on South Korea growth plan, 253
World Food Program, 536, 538
World Trade Organization (WTO), 532
World War I (1914–1918), 204, 442, 464
World War II (1939–1945)
  budget deficit during, 344
  cigarettes as money during, 395–396, 399
  food rationing during, 134
  hyperinflation following, 442
  postwar debt-to-GDP ratio, 440
Writers' Guild, 241
Wyatt, Edward, 377
Wydick, Bruce, 540

X

X-axis, 46C–46D
X-coordinates, 46D

Y

Yang, Andrew, 544
Yang, Dean, 534
Y-axis, 46C–46D
Y-coordinates, 46D
Yellen, Janet, 411
Yifu, Justin, 265
Y-intercept, 78A
YouTube, 46B
Yuan (renminbi), 500, 510–511
Yunus, Muhammad, 3–5, 9, 10, 12

Z

Zero lower bound, 413, 443, 476–477
Zero-sum game, 115
Zimbabwe, hyperinflation in, 440, 442
Zinke, Ryan, 91
Zombie banks, 476–477